Marketing

To Nancy, Michael, and Allen Pride

To Linda Ferrell

Sponsoring Editor: Kathleen Hunter
Senior Associate Editor: Susan M. Kahn
Senior Project Editor: Maria Morelli
Editorial Assistant: Lauren M. Gagliardi
Senior Production/Design Coordinator: Jill Haber
Senior Manufacturing Coordinator: Priscilla Bailey
Marketing Manager: Melissa Russell
Senior Designer: Henry Rachlin

Cover Design and Image: Rebecca Fagan

USATODAY.com Snapshots downloaded from *USA Today* are Copyright © 1999 *USA Today*, a division of Gannett Co., Inc.

Credits for advertisements and photographs:
Chapter 1 Vignette: Reproduced with permission of Mercedes-Benz. Fig 1.2 (left): © 1999 Advertisement provided courtesy of CNN. Cnnfn Financial Network is a trademark of Cable News Network. A Time Warner Company. All rights reserved. Fig. 1.2 (right): From Newsweek, © 1999 Newsweek, Inc. All rights reserved. Reprinted by permission. Fig. 1.3: District American Advertising Agency. Reproduced with permission of Peter James Design, Plantation, FL. Creative Director: Jim Spangler; Art Director: Keith Campbell; Copywriters: Jim Spangler, Wes Jones; Photographer: Ron Chapple; Project Supervisor: Bill Gregory. Fig. 1.5: Courtesy of Texaco, Inc. Reproduced with permission of BBDO, NY. Photography by Stephen Wilkes. Fig. 1.7: Urban Youth Bike Project/New York Cyclist/Reprinted with permission of DDB Needham Worldwide. Fig. 1.8 (left): Courtesy of Smithkline Beecham. Fig. p 1.5 (right): © 1999 The Coca-Cola Company. "Minute Maid®" is a registered trademark of The Coca-Cola Company. Fig. 1.9 (left): Courtesy of IBM. Fig. 1.9 (right): Manpower, Inc. Fig 1.10: Courtesy of The Minneapolis Animal Shelter Box: Image Copyright © 1999 PhotoDisk, Inc.
(Credits continue at the back of the book.)

Printed in the U.S.A.

Library of Congress Catalog Card Number: 99-071914

Student Edition IBSN: 0-395-97483-6
Library Edition ISBN: 0-395-97484-4

123456789-VH-03 02 01 00 99

Marketing
Concepts and Strategies

2000e

William M. Pride
Texas A & M University

O. C. Ferrell
Colorado State University

Houghton Mifflin Company   Boston   New York

Brief Contents

Contents

Behavior and Target Market Selection   135

Part Three   Product Decisions   247

Part Four   Distribution Decisions   347

Part Five   Promotion Decisions   429

Part Seven   Implementation and Electronic Marketing 563

Preface

As we enter the new millenium, Marketing 2000e *has been designed to meet your needs as well as those of your students.*

The way we teach the principles of marketing has to move and change just as marketing practices evolve in the real world. As it has in previous editions, *Marketing 2000e* keeps pace with the changes, providing new marketing knowledge, an integrated approach to using Internet resources, and vivid real-world examples.

A marketing textbook has to stay up-to-date—and even anticipate future change. We have completely revised this edition of *Marketing: Concepts and Strategies* to reflect the latest developments about the changes reshaping the development and implementation of marketing strategies. To put students in touch with the best marketing practices being used today, we have used a comprehensive framework that reflects the realities of marketing and links them to the changes in marketing knowledge.

But in this digital age in which new technologies seem to become obsolescent overnight, how does a textbook stay relevant? By exploiting the best of all the resources available to us to express the exciting challenge of marketing in the twenty-first century, and doing it in an engaging, readable way that connects to students.

Along with the challenges the Internet has brought for marketers, it has also allowed us to expand the discussion and learning opportunities beyond the traditional textbook. In today's time-pressured classroom, combining the text with a tightly integrated virtual extension of the teaching and learning material on the Internet is the best way to communicate and connect with the student. It is also an invaluable combination for helping students prepare to compete in a world where most businesses will have a virtual component. The online Pride/Ferrell Learning Center provides all the resources instructors and students need to maximize learning.

We have also been careful to retain the strengths that have made this the most successful introductory marketing text in the United States and throughout the world. Primary among those strengths is a dedication to customer value and customer relationships—two crucial aspects of today's competitive environment. We continue to listen closely to the feedback of both students and instructors, in order to keep providing exceptional student value and the most complete, usable, and relevant teaching package available today.

New in 2000e

To stay on top of the fast-paced changes in the practice of marketing—and new developments in teaching and learning about it—we have added a number of new features to *Marketing 2000e:*

- *A new text chapter, "Marketing on the Internet," focusing on what students need to understand about the Internet and its applications.* This new chapter delivers a cutting-edge perspective on the virtual marketing revolution, showing students how marketers are using the Internet right now in their strategies, their relationships with customers, and their day-to-day work. We focus on the strategic aspects of using the Internet to target markets and develop marketing mixes, including the basic characteristics of electronic marketing, e-marketing strategy, and the legal and ethical issues unique to e-commerce. Throughout the discussion, we have been careful to avoid the use of complex, technical terminology. Building on the resounding success of the tenth edition's groundbreaking virtual chapter, the web site again includes a virtual chapter. The chapter provides the latest statistics and practices marketers are using in Internet marketing. It is completely revised and it will evolve along with new developments in this dynamic area.

- *Critical coverage of marketing orientation, value-driven marketing, and relationship marketing.* Customer value and customer relationships have never been more important, and they have become crucial aspects of today's market-driven competitive environment. This edition provides increased coverage of these concepts starting with a strong foundation in Chapter 1 and then integrated throughout the text.

- *Strategic planning moved up front.* Newly revised, the strategic planning chapter has been moved to Chapter 2 to provide early and integrated coverage of the strategic planning process in marketing. Appendix C provides students with a sample marketing plan, and the online Pride/Ferrell Learning Center offers students downloadable marketing plan worksheets.

e

- *Greater emphasis on technology.* We have made extensive changes throughout the text to reflect the new uses of technology in marketing. Besides the Internet and online marketing, we also focus on the use of new technologies in marketing research—including database research, marketing decision support systems, single-source data, online information services, and e-mail surveys. Coverage of this important topic is highlighted by the marginal icon shown next to this paragraph.

- *Marketing citizenship as a part of strategic planning.* Marketing citizenship, defined as economic, legal, ethical, and philanthropic concerns in planning marketing strategies, has been integrated throughout the text in new Marketing Citizenship boxed features. Chapter 4, "Social Responsibility and Ethics in Marketing" has been reorganized using this framework, and many other chapters deal with specific legal or ethical issues.

- *Supply chain management as a framework for distribution.* We have integrated supply chain management into Part Four to provide a framework for distribution decisions. Wholesaling and physical distribution have been incorporated into one chapter to provide a seamless integration of these important parts of supply chain management. We have also linked retailing and marketing channels to supply chain management.

- *More logical organization within the product decisions chapters.* By significantly reorganizing the first two chapters in Part Three, we now cover the product life cycle and associated strategic issues in one chapter, and discuss product differentiation through product quality, design, and support services in the product development and management chapter.

- *Greater emphasis on integrated marketing communications.* A new section at the beginning of Chapter 17 focuses on integrated marketing communications. This section recognizes the importance of communicating efficiently within and outside the organization so that customers receive a consistent message.

- *More coverage of pricing strategies.* The Selection of a Pricing Strategy section in Chapter 21 now includes expanded coverage of differential pricing, negotiated pricing, secondary-market pricing, periodic discounting, random discounting, captive pricing, reference pricing, bundle pricing, everyday low prices (EDLP), and comparison discounting. The impact of new pricing practices on the Internet also receives new coverage.

- *Sequence change for target markets and customer behavior chapters.* Coverage of target markets and market segmentation has been moved so that these topics are covered before the buyer behavior chapters. While we believe that students can better grasp customer behavior after they have an understanding of market analysis and segmentation, these chapters can be covered in a different sequence.

Building on Established Strengths

Features of the Book

As with previous editions, we are providing a comprehensive and practical introduction to marketing that is both easy to teach and to learn. The entire text is structured to excite students about the subject and to help them learn completely and efficiently.

- An *organizational model* at the beginning of each part provides a "roadmap" of the text and a visual tool for understanding the connection between concepts.
- *Learning objectives* at the start of each chapter give students concrete expectations about what they are to learn as they read the chapter.
- An *opening vignette* about a particular organization or current market trend introduces the topic for each chapter. Vignettes in this edition include interesting anecdotes about the marketing issues surrounding a variety of products from diverse organizations such as Starbucks, Yahoo!, Barnes & Noble, Buy.com, Volkswagen, and McDonald's. Through these vignettes, students are exposed to contemporary marketing realities and are better prepared to understand and apply the concepts they will explore in the text.
- *Key term definitions* appear in the margin to help students build their marketing vocabulary.
- Numerous *figures, tables, photographs, advertisements,* and new *Snapshot* features increase comprehension and stimulate interest.
- Four types of *boxed features* reinforce students' awareness of the particular issues affecting marketing and the types of choices and decisions marketers must make.

  - The Tech*know boxes include discussions about the impact of technological advances on products and how they are marketed. Examples of topics are targeting tech buyers, clicking coupons instead of clipping them, differential pricing at online auctions, and data mining.
  - The Marking Citizenship boxes raise students' awareness of social responsibility and ethical issues and the types of ethical choices that marketers face every day. Some of the organizations on which we focus are Subway, eBay, and Sunbeam.
  - The Globalmarketing boxed features examine the challenges of marketing in widely diverse cultures for companies such as Avon, Columbia Sportswear, and Timberland.
  - The Building Customer Relationships boxes look at how organizations try to build long-term relationships with their customers. Examples include Great Harvest Bread Company, Radio Shack, and *More* magazine.

- A complete *chapter summary* reviews the major topics discussed, and the list of *important terms* provides another end-of-chapter study aid to reinforce students' marketing vocabulary.
- *Discussion and review questions* at the end of each chapter encourage further study and exploration of chapter content, and *application questions* enhance students' comprehension of important topics.
- An *Internet exercise* at the end of each chapter asks students to examine a web site and assess one or more strategic issues associated with the site. The *E-Center Resources* section points students to the various learning tools that are available on the text's web site, the Marketing Learning Center.
- Two in-depth *cases* at the end of each chapter help students understand the application of chapter concepts. One of the end-of-chapter cases is related to a video segment. Some examples of companies highlighted in video cases are Gulfstream, K'NEX Toys, Gillette, and Churchs Chicken.
- A *strategic case* at the end of each part helps students integrate the diverse concepts that have been discussed within the related chapters.
- *Appendixes* discuss marketing career opportunities, explore financial analysis in marketing, and present a comprehensive example of a marketing plan.
- A comprehensive *glossary* defines more than 625 important marketing terms.
- A *name index* and a *subject index* enable students to find topics of interest quickly.

Text Organization

We have organized the seven parts of *Marketing 2000e* to give students a theoretical and practical understanding of marketing decision making. Part 1 presents an overview of marketing and examines strategic market planning, marketing environment forces, social responsibility and ethics, and international marketing. Part 2 considers information systems and marketing research, target market analysis, and consumer and organizational buying behavior. Part 3 focuses on the conceptualization, development, management, and branding and packaging of goods and services. Part 4 deals with marketing channels and supply chain management, wholesaling and physical distribution, and retailing. Part 5 covers integrated marketing communications and promotion methods including advertising, personal selling, sales promotion, and public relations. Part 6 is devoted to pricing decisions. Part 7 discusses implementation and control, e-commerce, and marketing and the Internet.

A Comprehensive Instructional Resource Package

For instructors, this edition of *Marketing 2000e* includes an exceptionally comprehensive package of teaching materials.

- *Instructor's Resource Manual.* Written by the text's authors, the *Instructor's Resource Manual* includes a complete set of teaching tools. For each chapter of the text, there is (1) a teaching resources quick reference guide, (2) a purpose and perspective statement, (3) a guide for using the transparencies, (4) a comprehensive lecture outline, (5) special class exercises, (6) a debate issue, (7) a chapter quiz, (8) answers to discussion and review questions, (9) comments on the end-of-chapter cases, and (10) video information. In addition, the *Instructor's Resource Manual* includes comments on the end-of-part strategic cases and answers to the questions posed at the end of Appendix B, "Financial Analysis in Marketing."

- *Instructor's Web Site.* This continually updated, password-protected site includes valuable tools to help instructors design and teach the course. Contents include sample syllabi, downloadable text files from the *Instructor's Resource Manual* and PowerPoint® slides, and suggested answers to questions posed on the student web site.

- *Power Presentation Manager CD-ROM.* This new software package provides all the tools instructors need to create customized multimedia lecture presentations for display on computer-based projection systems. The software makes available lecture outlines from the *Instructor's Resource Manual,* figures and tables from the text and transparencies, the PowerPoint slides, and a link to the web. Instructors can quickly and easily select from and integrate all of these components, create and add their own images, and prepare a seamless customized classroom presentation.

- *PowerPoint® Slide Presentations.* For each chapter, over twenty-five slides related to the learning objectives have been specially developed for this edition. The slides, created by Milton Pressley of the University of New Orleans, are original representations of the concepts in the book, providing a complete lecture for each chapter. In addition, embedded within the slides are lecture notes that instructors can use or adapt as they wish. These slides, along with a PowerPoint® reader, are available on the web site.

- *Test Bank.* Written and class-tested by the text's authors, the *Test Bank* provides more than three thousand test items including true/false, multiple-choice, and essay questions. Each objective test item is accompanied by the correct answer, a main text page reference, and a key to whether the question tests knowledge, comprehension, or application. The *Test Bank* also provides difficulty and discrimination ratings derived from actual class testing for some of the multiple-choice questions. Lists of author-selected questions that facilitate quick construction of tests or quizzes appear in an appendix. These selected multiple-choice questions are representative of chapter content.

- *Computerized Test Bank.* This computerized version of the *Test Bank* allows instructors to select, edit, and add questions, or generate randomly selected questions to produce a test master for easy duplication. An Online Testing System and Gradebook function allows instructors to administer tests via a network system, modem, or personal computer, and sets up a new class, records grades from tests or assignments, analyzes grades, and produces class and individual statistics. This program is available for use on IBM, IBM-compatible, and Macintosh computers.

- *Call-in Test Service.* This service lets instructors select items from the *Test Bank* and call our toll-free number to order printed tests.

- *Color Transparencies.* A set of 250 color transparencies offers the instructor visual teaching assistance. About half of these are illustrations from the text; the rest are figures, tables, and diagrams that can be used as additional instructional aids.

- *Marketing Videos.* This series contains the videos for use with the end-of-chapter video cases. The *Instructor's Resource Manual* provides specific information about each video segment.

A Complete Package of Student Supplements

The complete package available with *Marketing: Concepts and Strategies* includes numerous support materials that facilitate student learning.

- *Pride/Ferrell Marketing Learning Center.* Our student web site at http://www.prideferrell.com contains the following:

  - *Chapter 24, "Electronic Marketing on the World Wide Web"* This chapter follows up on the new text chapter by exploring the world of online marketing and will be updated as needed to incorporate the latest developments.

  - *Internet exercises.* Including both the text exercises, updated as necessary, and additional exercises, these reinforce chapter concepts by guiding students through specific web sites and asking them to assess the online information from a marketing perspective.

  - *ACE online self-tests.* Written by the text authors, these questions allow students to practice taking tests and get immediate scoring results. For those students who wish to take computerized self-tests but do not have convenient access to the web, *PCStudy* can be downloaded and used on a PC.

  - *E-Center Resources.* This comprehensive list, which will be continually updated, provides links to numerous authoritative marketing information resources, categorized in a way that makes them accessible and helpful to both students and instructors.

  - *Company links.* Hot links to companies featured in the text are provided so that students can further their research and understanding of the marketing practices of these companies.

  - *Online glossary* and *chapter summary.* These sections help students review key concepts and definitions.

  - *Marketing Plan worksheets.* These worksheets take students step by step through the process of creating their own marketing plans. Along with the text discussion and sample marketing plan, this project helps students apply their knowledge of marketing theories.

  - *Career Center.* Downloadable Personal Career Plan Worksheets and links to various marketing careers web sites will help students explore their options and plan their job searches.

• *Study Guide.* Written by the text's authors, this printed supplement helps students to review and integrate key marketing concepts. The *Study Guide* contains questions different from those in the online study aids and includes chapter outlines as well as matching, true/false, multiple-choice, and minicase sample test items with answers.

Additional Supplements for Marketing Courses

For those instructors who like to supplement their courses with additional readings or activities, we have these offerings:

• *Marketer: A Simulation* (3d. ed.), by Jerry Smith and Peggy Golden, Florida Atlantic University. This business game lets teams of students experience simulated real-world experience in decision making, enabling them to see the relevance of the principles being taught in the course. The game is simple enough to learn in about an hour and yet includes all of the variables a student needs to know to understand the major concepts of the marketing process. The decisions each team must make relate to the price of the product, marketing budgets, ordering levels, quality and product development budgets, and market research. A unique feature of *Marketer: A Simulation* is the inclusion of optional minicase "incidents." Student decisions are recorded on Decision Forms and can be quickly analyzed and evaluated on a personal computer by the instructor. The instructor needs no heavy-duty computer knowledge to administer the game.

• *Perspectives: Marketing Tactics,* edited by David Snepenger, Montana State University. The contemporary articles presented in this collection help enliven class discussion and serve as concrete examples of real-world business practices. The topics covered are the same ones found in *Marketing: Concepts and Strategies,* making it easy to integrate these readings into your course.

• *Perspectives: Marketing on the Internet,* edited by A. Cemal Ekin, Providence College. The more than forty articles included in this reader focus on this burgeoning field. A Passport to the courselinks web site provides students an opportunity to explore additional learning resources that relate to web marketing.

Your Comments and Suggestions Are Valued

Through the years, professors and students have sent us many helpful suggestions for improving the text and ancillary components. We invite your comments, questions, and criticisms. We want to do our best to provide materials that enhance the teaching and learning of marketing concepts and strategies. Your suggestions will be sincerely appreciated. Please write us, or e-mail us at w_pride@tamu.edu or oferrell@lamar. colostate.edu, or call 409-845-5857 (Pride) or 970-491-4398 (Ferrell). You can also send a feedback message through the web site at http://www.prideferrell.com.

Acknowledgments

Like most textbooks, this one reflects the ideas of many academicians and practitioners who have contributed to the development of the marketing discipline. We appreciate the opportunity to present their ideas in this book.

A special faculty advisory board assisted us in making decisions both large and small throughout the entire development process of the text and the instructional package. For being "on call" and available to answer questions and make valuable suggestions, we are grateful to those who participated:

Bob Berl
University of Memphis

James Cagley
University of Tulsa

William J. Carner
University of Texas—Austin

Sylvia Keyes
Bridgewater State College

Martin Meyers
University of Wisconsin/Stevens Point

James R. Ogden
Kutztown University of Pennsylvania

Robert S. Owen
State University of New York—Oswego

Linda Pettijohn
Southwest Missouri State University

Roberta Slater
Cedar Crest College

Carmen Sunda
University of New Orleans

Steven A. Taylor
Illinois State University

Dale Varble
Indiana State University

Kirk L. Wakefield
University of Mississippi

A number of individuals have made helpful comments and recommendations in their reviews of this and earlier editions. We appreciate the generous help of these reviewers:

Zafar U. Ahmed
Minot State University

Thomas Ainscough
University of Massachusetts—Dartmouth

Joe F. Alexander
University of Northern Colorado

Mark I. Alpert
University of Texas at Austin

Linda K. Anglin
Mankato State University

George Avellano
Central State University

Emin Babakus
University of Memphis

Julie Baker
University of Texas—Arlington

Siva Balasabramanian
Southern Illinois University

Joseph Ballenger
Stephen F. Austin State University

Guy Banville
Creighton University

Joseph Barr
Framingham State College

Thomas E. Barry
Southern Methodist University

Charles A. Bearchell
California State University—Northridge

Richard C. Becherer
University of Tennessee—Chattanooga

Russell Belk
University of Utah

W. R. Berdine
California State Polytechnic Institute

Stewart W. Bither
Pennsylvania State University

Roger Blackwell
Ohio State University

Peter Bloch
University of Missouri—Columbia

Wanda Blockhus
San Jose State University

Paul N. Bloom
University of North Carolina

James P. Boespflug
Arapahoe Community College

Joseph G. Bonnice
Manhattan College

John Boos
Ohio Wesleyan University

James Brock
Montana State University

John R. Brooks, Jr.
Houston Baptist University

Jackie Brown
University of San Diego

William G. Browne
Oregon State University

John Buckley
Orange County Community College

Karen Berger
Pace University

Gul T. Butaney
Bentley College

Pat J. Calabro
University of Texas—Arlington

Linda Calderone
State University of New York College of Technology at Farmingdale

Joseph Cangelosi
University of Central Arkansas

James C. Carroll
University of Central Arkansas

Terry M. Chambers
Westminster College

Lawrence Chase
Tompkins Cortland Community College

Larry Chonko
Baylor University

Barbara Coe
University of North Texas

Ernest F. Cooke
Loyola College—Baltimore

Robert Copley
University of Louisville

John I. Coppett
University of Houston—Clear Lake

Robert Corey
West Virginia University

Deborah L. Cowles
Virginia Commonwealth University

Melvin R. Crask
University of Georgia

William L. Cron
Southern Methodist University

Gary Cutler
Dyersburg State Community College

Bernice N. Dandridge
Diablo Valley College

Norman E. Daniel
Arizona State University

Lloyd M. DeBoer
George Mason University

Sally Dibb
University of Warwick

Ralph DiPietro
Montclair State University

Paul Dishman
Idaho State University

Suresh Divakar
State University of New York—Buffalo

Casey L. Donoho
Northern Arizona University

Peter T. Doukas
Westchester Community College

Lee R. Duffus
Florida Gulf Coast University

Robert F. Dwyer
University of Cincinnati

Roland Eyears
Central Ohio Technical College

Thomas Falcone
Indiana University of Pennsylvania

James Finch
University of Wisconsin—La Crosse

Letty C. Fisher
SUNY/Westchester Community College

Gwen Fontenot
University of Northern Colorado

Charles W. Ford
Arkansas State University

John Fraedrich
Southern Illinois University, Carbondale

David J. Fritzsche
University of Washington

Donald A. Fuller
University of Central Florida

Terry Gable
California State University—Northridge

Ralph Gaedeke
California State University, Sacramento

Cathy Goodwin
University of Manitoba

Geoffrey L. Gordon
Northern Illinois University

Robert Grafton-Small
University of Strathclyde

Harrison Grathwohl
California State University—Chico

Alan A. Greco
North Carolina A&T State University

Blaine S. Greenfield
Bucks County Community College

Thomas V. Greer
University of Maryland

Sharon F. Gregg
Middle Tennessee University

Jim L. Grimm
Illinois State University

Charles Gross
University of New Hampshire

Roy R. Grundy
College of DuPage

Joseph Guiltinan
University of Notre Dame

Robert R. Harmon
Portland State University

Mary C. Harrison
Amber University

Lorraine Hartley
Franklin University

Michael Hartline
Samford University

Timothy Hartman
Ohio University

Salah S. Hassan
George Washington University

Del I. Hawkins
University of Oregon

Dean Headley
Wichita State University

Esther Headley
Wichita State University

Debbora Heflin-Bullock
*California State Polytechnic University—
    Pomona*

Merlin Henry
Rancho Santiago College

Neil Herndon
Stephen F. Austin State University

Lois Herr
Elizabethtown College

Charles L. Hilton
Eastern Kentucky University

Elizabeth C. Hirschman
Rutgers, State University of New Jersey

Robert D. Hisrich
University of Tulsa

George C. Hozier
University of New Mexico

John R. Huser
Illinois Central College

Ron Johnson
Colorado Mountain College

Theodore F. Jula
Stonehill College

Peter F. Kaminski
Northern Illinois University

Yvonne Karsten
Mankato State University

Jerome Katrichis
Temple University

James Kellaris
University of Cincinnati

Alvin Kelly
Florida A&M University

Philip Kemp
DePaul University

Sylvia Keyes
Bridgewater State College

William M. Kincaid, Jr.
Oklahoma State University

Roy Klages
State University of New York at Albany

Douglas Kornemann
Milwaukee Area Technical College

Priscilla LaBarbera
New York University

Patricia Laidler
Massasoit Community College

Bernard LaLonde
Ohio State University

Richard A. Lancioni
Temple University

David M. Landrum
University of Central Oklahoma

Irene Lange
California State University—Fullerton

Geoffrey P. Lantos
Stonehill College

Charles L. Lapp
University of Texas—Dallas

Virginia Larson
San Jose State University

John Lavin
Waukesha County Technical Institute

Hugh E. Law
East Tennessee University

Debbie Thorne LeClair
Mississippi State University

Ron Lennon
Barry University

Richard C. Leventhal
Metropolitan State College

Jay D. Lindquist
Western Michigan University

Terry Loe
Baylor University

Mary Logan
Southwestern Assemblies of God College

Paul Londrigan
Mott Community College

Anthony Lucas
Community College of Allegheny County

George Lucas
U.S. Learning, Inc.

William Lundstrom
Cleveland State University

Rhonda Mack
College of Charleston

Stan Madden
Baylor University

Patricia M. Manninen
North Shore Community College

Gerald L. Manning
Des Moines Area Community College

Allen S. Marber
University of Bridgeport

Gayle J. Marco
Robert Morris College

James McAlexander
Oregon State University

Donald McCartney
University of Wisconsin—Green Bay

Jack McNiff
*State University of New York College of
   Technology at Farmingdale*

Lee Meadow
Eastern Illinois University

Carla Meeske
University of Oregon

Jeffrey A. Meier
Fox Valley Technical College

James Meszaros
County College of Morris

Brian Meyer
Mankato State University

Martin Meyers
University of Wisconsin/Stevens Point

Stephen J. Miller
Oklahoma State University

William Moller
University of Michigan

Kent B. Monroe
University of Illinois

Carlos W. Moore
Baylor University

Carol Morris-Calder
Loyola Marymount University

David Murphy
Madisonville Community College

Keith Murray
Bryant College

Sue Ellen Neeley
University of Houston—Clear Lake

Francis L. Notturno, Sr.
Owens Community College

Terrence V. O'Brien
Northern Illinois University

Mike O'Neill
California State University—Chico

Allan Palmer
University of North Carolina at Charlotte

Teresa Pavia
University of Utah

John Perrachione
Truman State University

Michael Peters
Boston College

Lana Podolak
Community College of Beaver County

Raymond E. Polchow
Muskingum Area Technical College

Thomas Ponzurick
West Virginia University

William Presutti
Duquesne University

Kathy Pullins
Columbus State Community College

Victor Quinones
University of Puerto Rico

Daniel Rajaratnam
Baylor University

James D. Reed
Louisiana State University—Shreveport

William Rhey
University of Tampa

Glen Riecken
East Tennessee State University

Winston Ring
University of Wisconsin—Milwaukee

Ed Riordan
Wayne State University

Robert A. Robicheaux
University of Alabama

Robert H. Ross
Wichita State University

Michael L. Rothschild
University of Wisconsin—Madison

Bert Rosenbloom
Drexel University

Kenneth L. Rowe
Arizona State University

Elise Sautter
New Mexico State University

Ronald Schill
Brigham Young University

Bodo Schlegelmilch
*American Graduate School of
   International Management*

Edward Schmitt
Villanova University

Donald Sciglimpaglia
San Diego State University

Stanley Scott
University of Alaska—Anchorage

Harold S. Sekiguchi
University of Nevada—Reno

Gilbert Seligman
Dutchess Community College

Richard J. Semenik
University of Utah

Beheruz N. Sethna
Lamar University

Terence A. Shimp
University of South Carolina

Carolyn F. Siegel
Eastern Kentucky University

Dean C. Siewers
Rochester Institute of Technology

Lyndon Simkin
University of Warwick

Paul J. Solomon
University of South Florida

Robert Solomon
Stephen F. Austin State University

Sheldon Somerstein
City University of New York

Rosann L. Spiro
Indiana University

William Staples
University of Houston—Clear Lake

Bruce Stern
Portland State University

Claire F. Sullivan
Metropolitan State University

Robert Swerdlow
Lamar University

Hal Teer
James Madison University

Ira Teich
Long Island University—C. W. Post

Dillard Tinsley
Stephen F. Austin State University

Sharynn Tomlin
Angelo State University

Hale Tongren
George Mason University

James Underwood
University of Southwest Louisiana

Barbara Unger
Western Washington University

Tinus Van Drunen
Universiteit Twente (Netherlands)

Dale Varble
Indiana State University

R. Vish Viswanathan
University of Northern Colorado

Charles Vitaska
Metropolitan State College

Kirk Wakefield
University of Mississippi

Harlan Wallingford
Pace University

Jacquelyn Warwick
Andrews University

James F. Wenthe
Georgia College

Sumner M. White
Massachusetts Bay Community College

Alan R. Wiman
Rider College

Ken Wright
*West Australia College of Advanced
    Education—Churchland Campus*

George Wynn
James Madison University

We deeply appreciate the assistance of Barbara Gilmer, Pam Swartz, and Marian Wood for providing editorial suggestions, technical assistance, and support. Gwyneth M. Vaughn assisted in research, editing, and content development for the text, supplements, and the Pride/Ferrell Marketing Learning Center. For assistance in completing numerous tasks associated with the text and supplements, we express appreciation to Carol A. Rustad-LaCasse, Adele Lewis, Kay Colley, Tonia Goddard, Mike Cummings, Nina DeRouen, Kathryn O'Connor, and Clarissa Sims.

We especially want to thank Linda Ferrell, University of Northern Colorado, who participated in all aspects of content and supplement development. Daniel Sherrell, University of Memphis, developed the framework used in Chapter 23. We especially appreciate his work in developing the six major characteristics of marketing on the Internet. Michael Hartline, Samford University, helped in the development of the marketing plan outline and the sample marketing plan in Appendix C as well as the career worksheets on the web site. Debbie Thorne LeClair, Mississippi State University, provided assistance with marketing citizenship content and boxes.

We appreciate Milton Pressley, the University of New Orleans, for developing the PowerPoint slide presentations. We also wish to thank Kirk Wakefield, University of Mississippi, for developing the class exercises included in the *Instructor's Resource Manual*. We especially thank Jim L. Grimm, Illinois State University, for drafting the financial analysis appendix.

We express appreciation for the support and encouragement given to us by our colleagues at Texas A&M University and Colorado State University. We are also grateful for the comments and suggestions we receive from our own students, student focus groups, and student correspondents who provide ongoing feedback through the web site.

William M. Pride
O. C. Ferrell

Marketing

Part One

Marketing and Its Environment

Part 1 introduces the field of marketing and offers a broad perspective from which to explore and analyze various components of the marketing discipline. In Chapter 1, we define marketing and explore some key concepts, including customers and target markets, the marketing mix, relationship marketing, the marketing concept, and value. Chapter 2 provides an overview of strategic marketing issues, such as the effect of organizational resources and opportunities on the planning process; the role of the mission statement; corporate, business-unit, and marketing strategies; and the creation of the marketing plan. These issues are profoundly affected by competitive, economic, political, legal and regulatory, technological, and sociocultural forces in the marketing environment, the focus of Chapter 3. Chapter 4 deals with the role of social responsibility and ethics in marketing decisions. In Chapter 5, we discuss the nature, opportunities, and challenges of marketing in a global economy.

Economic forces · Political forces · Competitive forces · Legal and regulatory forces · Sociocultural forces · Technological forces · Product · Price · Customer · Distribution · Promotion

1

1

An Overview of Strategic Marketing

OBJECTIVES

- To be able to define *marketing* as focused on customers

- To begin to identify some important marketing terms, including *target market, marketing mix, marketing exchanges,* and *marketing environment*

- To become aware of the marketing concept and marketing orientation

- To understand the importance of value-driven marketing

- To learn about the process of marketing management

- To recognize the role of marketing in our society

Mercedes,
On the Road to New Success

Long revered by wealthy customers as a marketer of innovative, finely engineered luxury cars, Mercedes, marketed by DaimlerChrysler, is experiencing record sales in the United States, where it has a broader customer base than ever before. Just a few years ago, however, American buyers of luxury cars were showing more interest in Japanese brands like Lexus and Acura. With the Japanese promoting their luxury vehicles as less expensive but of "German quality," even many who could afford a $50,000 Mercedes were choosing to spend $35,000 for a comparable Lexus. In 1991, from its headquarters in Stuttgart, Germany, Mercedes watched its sales in the United States decline to 58,869 cars, just 5 percent of the U.S. luxury auto market.

To stage its turnaround, Mercedes launched an aggressive marketing strategy that included listening to customers, slashing prices on existing models, improving manufacturing efficiency to keep costs (and therefore prices) down, and pressuring dealers to match Japanese standards for sales and service. Mercedes redesigned its E-class sedans and wagons and launched several new models, including two C-class midsize sedans, the SLK two-seat roadster, and the CLK luxury coupe. It introduced its first sport utility vehicle (SUV), the M-class, which is built in Alabama. Several of these models are aimed at new customers for Mercedes, which has traditionally focused on wealthy buyers of sedans and station wagons. Advertising for Mercedes now promotes the cars' hipper, sportier image and conveys a sense of fun, especially for the sport utility. One ad for the M-class SUV, for example, features dancing executives and engineers singing, "I love my Benz now" to a 1950s rock beat. The company's turnaround also got some unexpected help from its Japanese rivals: When the Japanese hiked prices on their vehicles to boost profits, Mercedes held the line on prices.

Mercedes' turnaround strategy has been quite successful, with sales up 83 percent during a period when overall sales of luxury cars grew just 6 percent. The company is second only to BMW, another German company, for growth in sales in the U.S. market. The new SUV has been a hit; with over 43,000 vehicles sold in its first year, it is now Mercedes' second most popular model, the E-class luxury sedan being the most popular. The company's sales are even catching up to those of General Motors' Cadillac division and Ford's Lincoln. Mercedes' rivals aren't standing still, however. Lincoln has introduced its own midsize luxury cars, the LS6 and LS8, and Cadillac has launched an SUV, the Escalade. BMW has plans to introduce a hybrid "sports activity vehicle," and its Z3 roadster is selling well. Moreover, Mercedes' parent company, DaimlerChrysler, is working to blend its operations with the U.S.-based Chrysler Corporation with which it recently merged. Only time will tell how these factors will affect Mercedes' recaptured status as one of the world's successful and most prestigious car makers.[1]

Like all organizations, Mercedes must develop products that customers want, communicate useful information about them to excite interest, price them appropriately, and make them available when and where customers may want to buy them. Even if Mercedes does these things well, competition from rival car makers, economic conditions, and other factors may affect the company's success. Such factors influence the decisions that all organizations must make in strategic marketing.

This chapter introduces the strategic marketing concepts and decisions covered throughout the text. In this chapter, we first develop a definition of marketing and explore each element of the definition in detail. Next, we introduce the marketing concept and consider several issues associated with implementing it. We also take a brief look at the concept of value, which customers are demanding now more than ever before. We then explore the process of marketing management, which includes planning, organizing, implementing, and controlling marketing activities to encourage marketing exchanges. Finally, we examine the importance of marketing in our global society.

Defining Marketing

marketing The process of creating, distributing, promoting, and pricing goods, services, and ideas to facilitate satisfying exchange relationships with customers in a dynamic environment

If you ask several people what *marketing* is, you are likely to hear a variety of descriptions. Marketing encompasses many more activities than most people realize, however. In this book, we define **marketing** as the process of creating, distributing, promoting, and pricing goods, services, and ideas to facilitate satisfying exchange relationships with customers in a dynamic environment. Let's take a closer look at selected parts of this definition.

Marketing Focuses on Customers

customers The purchasers of organizations' products; the focal point of all marketing activities

As the purchasers of the products that organizations develop, promote, distribute, and price, **customers** are the focal point of all marketing activities (see Figure 1.1). Organizations have to define products not as what they make or produce but as what they do to satisfy customers. The Walt Disney Company is not in the business of establishing theme parks; it is in the business of making people happy. At Disney World,

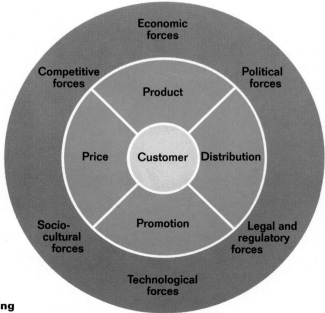

Figure 1.1
Components of
Strategic Marketing

Figure 1.2
Appealing to Target Market Needs
CNNfn and *Newsweek* adjust their products to serve a new target market—people who want access to news about current events over the Web.

customers are guests, the crowd is an audience, and employees are cast members. Customer satisfaction and enjoyment can come from anything received when buying and using a product. Procter & Gamble's Olestra, for example, permits customers to enjoy potato chips without the fat. Its Tide detergent helps keep clothes looking new, while Folger's aroma-roasted naturally decaffeinated coffee provides great coffee taste without the side effects of caffeine.

The essence of marketing is to develop satisfying exchanges from which both customers and marketers benefit. The customer expects to gain a reward or benefit in excess of the costs incurred in a marketing transaction. The marketer expects to gain something of value in return, generally the price charged for the product. Through buyer-seller interaction, a customer develops expectations about the seller's future behavior. To fulfill these expectations, the marketer must deliver on promises made. Over time, this interaction results in interdependencies between the two parties. Fast-food restaurants such as Wendy's and Burger King depend on repeat purchases from satisfied customers—many often live or work a few miles from these restaurants—while customer expectations revolve around good food, value, and dependable service.

target market   A specific group of customers on whom an organization focuses its marketing efforts

Organizations generally focus their marketing efforts on a specific group of customers, or **target market.** The marketer of Kix cereal, for example, targets its brand at mothers with children under twelve. Marketing managers may define a target market as a vast number of people or a relatively small group. Rolls-Royce, for example, targets its automobiles at a small, very exclusive market: wealthy people who want the ultimate in prestige in an automobile. Other companies target multiple markets, with different products, promotion, prices, and distribution systems for each one. Nike uses this strategy, marketing different types of shoes to meet specific needs of cross-trainers, rock climbers, basketball players, aerobics enthusiasts, and athletic shoe buyers. As Figure 1.2 indicates, both CNN's financial network and *Newsweek* are adapting their television and magazine products to target markets that access the Web for the latest information. We explore the concept of target markets in more detail in Chapter 7.

Marketing Deals with Products, Distribution, Promotion, and Price

Marketing is more than simply advertising or selling a product; it involves developing and managing a product that will satisfy customer needs. It focuses on making the product available in the right place and at a price acceptable to buyers. It also requires communicating information that helps customers determine if the product will satisfy their needs. These activities are planned, organized, implemented, and controlled to meet the needs of customers within the target market. Marketers refer to these activities—product, distribution, promotion, and pricing—as the **marketing mix** because they decide what type of each element to use and in what amounts. A primary goal of a marketing manager is to create and maintain the right mix of these elements to satisfy customers' needs for a general product type. Note in Figure 1.1 that the marketing mix is built around the customer.

> **marketing mix** Four marketing activities—product, distribution, promotion, and pricing—that a firm can control to meet the needs of customers within its target market

Marketing managers strive to develop a marketing mix that matches the needs of customers in the target market. The marketing mix for Ralph Lauren's Polo brand of clothing, for example, combines a specific level of product design and quality with coordinated distribution, promotion, and price appropriate for the target market. Before marketers can develop a marketing mix, they must collect in-depth, up-to-date information about customer needs. Such information might include data about the age, income, ethnicity, gender, and educational level of people in the target market; their preferences for product features; their attitudes toward competitors' products; and the frequency with which they use the product. Such research helped convince Apple Computer of the need for a low-cost, easy-to-connect, Internet-ready computer, and it responded by developing the iMac. Early demand for the iMac computer exceeded supply, suggesting that Apple's research was on target. In Chapter 6, we explore how organizations gather marketing research data. Armed with such data, marketing managers are better able to develop a marketing mix that satisfies a specific target market.

Let's look more closely at the decisions and activities related to each marketing mix variable.

The Product Variable.   Successful marketing efforts result in products that become a part of everyday life. Consider the satisfaction customers have had over the years from Coca-Cola, Xerox photocopiers, Visa credit cards, Bayer aspirin, and 3M Post-it notepads. The product variable of the marketing mix deals with researching customers' needs and wants and designing a product that satisfies them. A **product** can be a good, a service, or an idea. A *good* is a physical entity you can touch. A Honda Accord, a Garth Brooks compact disc, a Duracell battery, and a kitten in a pet store are examples of goods. A *service* is the application of human and mechanical efforts to people or objects to provide intangible benefits to customers. Air travel, dry cleaning, hair cuts, banking, medical care, and day care are examples of services. *Ideas* include concepts, philosophies, images, and issues. For instance, a marriage counselor, for a fee, gives spouses ideas to help improve their relationship. Other marketers of ideas include political parties, churches, and schools. Figure 1.3 illustrates a public service message promoting diversity and mutual respect as important ideas to society. Note, however, that the actual production of tangible goods is not a marketing activity.

> **product** A good, a service, or an idea

The product variable also involves creating or modifying brand names and packaging, and may include decisions regarding warranty and repair services. Even the world's greatest basketball player is a global brand name. In the last year he played for the Chicago Bulls, Michael Jordan had a $10 billion impact on the U.S. economy through increased NBA attendance and television and cable revenue. Jordan's persona and product line have been worth more than $5 billion to sports shoe and apparel manufacturer Nike. Jordan's name is associated with other sports products, as well as food products and movies.[2]

Product variable decisions and related activities are important because they are directly involved with creating products that meet customers' needs and wants. To maintain an assortment of products that helps an organization achieve its goals, marketers must develop new products, modify existing ones, and eliminate those that no

Figure 1.3
Marketing Ideas
Diversity is an idea that can be promoted through marketing.

longer satisfy enough buyers or that yield unacceptable profits. Ford Motor Company, for example, redesigned its classic Mustang with a "retro" look that appeals to customers' nostalgia for the original model, popular from the mid-1960s. We consider such product issues and many more in Chapters 10 through 13.

The Distribution Variable.   To satisfy customers, products must be available at the right time and in convenient locations. In dealing with the distribution variable, a marketing manager makes products available in the quantities desired to as many target market customers as possible, keeping total inventory, transportation, and storage costs as low as possible. With these objectives in mind, McDonald's expanded distribution by opening restaurants in Wal-Mart stores and in Amoco and Chevron service stations. This practice permits the fast-food giant to share costs with its partners and to reach more customers when and where hunger strikes.[3] A marketing manager may also select and motivate intermediaries (wholesalers and retailers), establish and maintain inventory control procedures, and develop and manage transportation and storage systems. The advent of the Internet and electronic commerce has also dramatically influenced the distribution variable. Companies can now make their products available throughout the world without having facilities in each country. The Great Southern Sauce Company, a small firm in Little Rock, Arkansas, for example, sells salsa, barbecue sauce, and other sauces through its Web site to buyers all over the United States and as far away as London and Saudi Arabia.[4] We examine distribution issues in Chapters 14 to 16.

SNAPSHOT

Where we do our Internet shopping
The top reason adults give for shopping via computer is convenience (71%) and the average purchase is $142.

83%
At home

16% At work

Copyright © 1999 *USA Today,* a division of Gannett Co., Inc.

The Promotion Variable.   The promotion variable relates to activities used to inform individuals or groups about an organization and its products. Promotion can be aimed at increasing public awareness of an organization and of new or existing products. Office Depot, for example, is using the cartoon character Dilbert, along with the slogan "Business is crazy. Office Depot makes sense" to help customers distinguish the chain from its competitors Office Max and Staples.[5] Promotional activities can also educate customers about product features or urge people to take a particular stance on a political or social issue, such as smoking or drug abuse. Promotion can help sustain interest in established products that have been available for decades, such as Arm & Hammer baking soda or Ivory soap. Many companies are using the Internet and the World Wide Web to communicate information about themselves and their products. Ragu's Web site, for example, offers Italian phrases, recipes, and a sweepstakes, while Southwest Airlines' Web site enables customers to make flight reservations. In Chapters 17 to 19, we take a detailed look at promotion activities.

The Price Variable.   The price variable relates to decisions and actions associated with establishing pricing objectives and policies and determining product prices. Price is a critical component of the marketing mix because customers are concerned about the value obtained in an exchange. Price is often used as a competitive tool. Intense price competition sometimes leads to price wars, but high prices can also be used competitively to establish a product's image. Gillette priced its revolutionary MACH3 brand three-blade razor cartridges 35 percent higher than its best-selling SensorExcel brand because it believed customers would pay more for a high-tech product that promises a smoother shave.[6] We explore pricing decisions in Chapters 20 and 21.

The marketing mix variables are often viewed as controllable because they can be modified. However, there are limits to how much marketing managers can alter them. Economic conditions, competitive structure, or government regulations may prevent a manager from adjusting prices frequently or significantly. Making changes in the size, shape, and design of most tangible goods is expensive; therefore, such product features cannot be altered very often. In addition, promotional campaigns and methods used to distribute products ordinarily cannot be rewritten or revamped overnight.

Marketing Builds Satisfying Exchange Relationships

exchanges The provision or transfer of goods, services, or ideas in return for something of value

Individuals and organizations engage in marketing to facilitate **exchanges**—that is, the provision or transfer of goods, services, or ideas in return for something of value. Any product (good, service, or even idea) may be involved in a marketing exchange. We assume only that individuals and organizations expect to gain a reward in excess of the costs incurred.

For an exchange to take place, four conditions must exist. First, two or more individuals, groups, or organizations must participate, and each must possess something of value that the other party desires. Second, the exchange should provide a benefit or satisfaction to both parties involved in the transaction. Third, each party must have confidence in the promise of the "something of value" held by the other. If you go to a Celine Dion concert, for example, you go with the expectation of a great performance. Finally, to build trust, the parties to the exchange must meet expectations.

Figure 1.4 depicts the exchange process. The arrows indicate that the parties communicate that each has something of value available to exchange. An exchange will

Figure 1.4
Exchange between Buyer and Seller

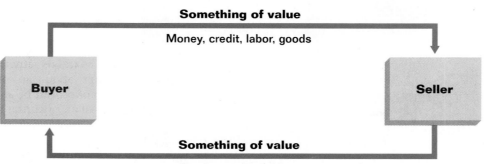

not necessarily take place just because these conditions exist; marketing activities can occur even without an actual transaction or sale. You may see an ad for a Viking refrigerator, for instance, but you might never buy the product. When an exchange occurs, products are traded for other products or for financial resources.

Marketing activities should attempt to create and maintain satisfying exchange relationships. To maintain an exchange relationship, buyers must be satisfied with the obtained good, service, or idea, and sellers must be satisfied with the financial reward or something else of value received. A dissatisfied customer who lacks trust in the relationship often searches instead for alternative organizations or products.

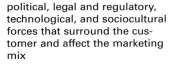

relationship marketing
Establishing long-term, mutually satisfying buyer-seller relationships

Maintaining positive relationships with customers is an important goal for marketers. The term **relationship marketing** refers to "long-term, mutually beneficial arrangements in which both the buyer and seller focus on value enhancement through the creation of more satisfying exchanges."[7] Relationship marketing continually deepens the buyer's reliance on the company, and as the customer's confidence grows, this in turn increases the firm's understanding of the customer's needs. Successful marketers respond to customer needs and strive to increase value to buyers over time. Eventually, this interaction becomes a solid relationship that allows for cooperation and mutual dependency. For example, customers depend on the Coca-Cola Company to provide a standardized, reliable, satisfying soft drink anyplace in the world. The company's success in satisfying customers has resulted in its gaining 50 percent of the global soft drink market. Due to its efforts to expand distribution to every possible location, Coca-Cola has the highest brand awareness of all foreign soft drinks sold in China. The company continues to expand distribution and to maintain a high-quality product.[8] Coca-Cola is also a good "corporate citizen," donating millions of dollars to education and health and human services each year.

Marketing Occurs in a Dynamic Environment

marketing environment
The competitive, economic, political, legal and regulatory, technological, and sociocultural forces that surround the customer and affect the marketing mix

Marketing activities do not take place in a vacuum. The **marketing environment,** which includes competitive, economic, political, legal and regulatory, technological, and sociocultural forces, surrounds the customer and affects the marketing mix (see Figure 1.1). The effects of these forces on buyers and sellers can be dramatic and difficult to predict. They can create threats to marketers and also generate opportunities for new products and new methods of reaching customers.

The forces of the marketing environment affect a marketer's ability to facilitate exchanges in three general ways. First, they influence customers by affecting their lifestyles, standards of living, and preferences and needs for products. Because a marketing manager tries to develop and adjust the marketing mix to satisfy customers, effects of environmental forces on customers also have an indirect impact on marketing mix components. The merging of telecommunications and computer technologies, for example, allows FedEx Corporation to interact with customers via the World Wide Web. FedEx customers can track packages from their home or office computers and send E-mail feedback to FedEx about its services. This technology thus enables FedEx to gather marketing research information directly from customers. Second, marketing environment forces help determine whether and how a marketing manager can perform certain marketing activities. Third, environmental forces may affect a marketing manager's decisions and actions by influencing buyers' reactions to the firm's marketing mix.

Marketing environment forces can fluctuate quickly and dramatically, which is one reason marketing is so interesting and challenging. Because these forces are closely interrelated, changes in one may cause changes in others. For example, after Star-Kist Foods received letters objecting to the killing of dolphins during tuna fishing, it faced an organized boycott of its canned tuna. The company turned the situation to its advantage by announcing that it would stop buying tuna from fishing vessels that net dolphins. Star-Kist's advantage was short-lived, however, as other tuna companies quickly adopted their own dolphin-safe policies to please customers.

Even though changes in the marketing environment produce uncertainty for marketers and at times hurt marketing efforts, they also create opportunities.

Marketers who are alert to changes in environmental forces can not only adjust to these changes and influence them, but also capitalize on the opportunities such changes provide. Most airlines offer frequent flyer miles as rewards to loyal customers who make a commitment to fly their airline. AirTran Airlines took the concept a step further by developing a frequent flier program that offers free trips on *other* airlines. The discount air carrier launched the program after recognizing that competitors were matching its low fares and that its frequent flyer program did not give it a competitive edge. Now, it offers customers who fly twelve coach or six business-class round trips on AirTran by the end of the calendar year a free ticket on another carrier. AirTran's creative response to competitive forces in the marketing environment helped give the company a competitive advantage by increasing customer loyalty.[9]

Marketing mix elements—product, distribution, promotion, price—are factors over which an organization has control; the forces of the environment, however, are subject to far less control. But even though marketers know they cannot predict changes in the marketing environment with certainty, they must nevertheless plan for them. Because these environmental forces have such a profound effect on marketing activities, we explore each of them in considerable depth in Chapter 3.

Understanding the Marketing Concept

Some firms have sought success by buying land, building a factory, equipping it with people and machines, and then making a product they believe buyers need. However, these firms frequently fail to attract customers with what they have to offer because they defined their business as "making a product" rather than as "helping potential customers satisfy their needs and wants." For example, when compact discs became more popular than vinyl records, turntable manufacturers had an opportunity to develop new products to satisfy customers' needs for home entertainment. Companies that did not pursue this opportunity, such as Dual and Empire, are no longer in business. Such organizations have failed to implement the marketing concept.

marketing concept A philosophy that an organization should try to satisfy customers' needs through a coordinated set of activities that also allows the organization to achieve its goals

According to the **marketing concept,** an organization should try to provide products that satisfy customers' needs through a coordinated set of activities that also allows the organization to achieve its goals. Customer satisfaction is the major focus of the marketing concept. To implement the marketing concept, an organization strives to determine what buyers want and uses this information to develop satisfying products. It focuses on customer analysis, competitor analysis, and integration of the firm's resources to provide customer value and satisfaction, as well as long-term profits.[10] The firm must also continue to alter, adapt, and develop products to keep pace with customers' changing desires and preferences. Ben & Jerry's, for example, constantly assesses customer demand for ice cream and sorbet. On its Web site, it maintains a "flavor graveyard" that lists combinations that have been tried and ultimately failed. It also notes its top ten flavors each month. Pharmaceutical companies such as Merck and Pfizer continually strive to develop new products to fight infectious diseases, viruses, cancer, and other medical problems. Drugs that lower cholesterol, control diabetes, eliminate depression, or improve the quality of life in other ways also provide huge profits for the drug companies. When new products—like Rogaine, a hair growth product—are developed, the companies must develop marketing activities to reach customers and communicate the products' benefits and side effects. Thus, the marketing concept emphasizes that marketing begins and ends with customers.

The marketing concept is not a second definition of marketing. It is a management philosophy guiding an organization's overall activities. This philosophy affects all organizational activities, not just marketing. Production, finance, accounting, human resources, and marketing departments must work together.

The marketing concept is also not a philanthropic philosophy aimed at helping customers at the expense of the organization. A firm that adopts the marketing concept must satisfy not only its customers' objectives, but also its own, or it will not stay

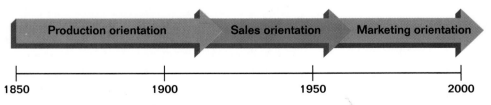

Figure 1.5
The Marketing Concept
Texaco continually researches new ways to deliver power to consumers. To address consumers' desire to travel longer distances without having to worry about coolant refills or changes, Texaco developed an innovative new coolant.

in business long. The overall objectives of a business might relate to increasing profits, market share, sales, or a combination of all three. The marketing concept stresses that an organization can best achieve these objectives by being customer-oriented. Thus, implementing the marketing concept should benefit the organization as well as its customers. As Figure 1.5 illustrates, Texaco addresses consumers' desire to travel longer distances without having to change the coolant in their cars.

It is important for marketers to consider not only their current buyers' needs, but also the long-term needs of society. Striving to satisfy customers' desires by sacrificing society's long-term welfare is unacceptable. For example, while many parents want disposable diapers that are comfortable, absorbent, and safe for their babies, society in general does not want nonbiodegradable disposable diapers that create tremendous landfill problems now and for the future. Marketers are expected to act in a socially responsible manner, an idea we discuss in more detail in Chapter 4.

Evolution of the Marketing Concept

The marketing concept may seem like an obvious approach to running a business. However, businesspeople have not always believed that the best way to make sales and profits is to satisfy customers. (See Figure 1.6.)

The Production Orientation.   During the second half of the nineteenth century, the Industrial Revolution was in full swing in the United States. Electricity, rail transportation, division of labor, assembly lines, and mass production made it possible to produce goods more efficiently. With new technology and new ways of using labor, products poured into the marketplace, where demand for manufactured goods was strong.

The Sales Orientation.   In the 1920s, strong demand for products subsided, and businesses realized they would have to "sell" products to buyers. From the mid-1920s to the early 1950s, businesses viewed sales as the major means of increasing profits, and this period came to have a sales orientation. Businesspeople believed that the most important marketing activities were personal selling, advertising, and distribution. Today, some people incorrectly equate marketing with a sales orientation.

The Marketing Orientation.   By the early 1950s, some businesspeople began to recognize that efficient production and extensive promotion did not guarantee that customers would buy products. These businesses, and many others since, found that they must first determine what customers want and then produce it, rather than making the products first and then trying to persuade customers that they need them. As

Production orientation	Sales orientation	Marketing orientation
1850	1900	1950	2000

Figure 1.6
The Evolution of the Marketing Concept

Figure 1.7
Developing a Market Orientation
The New York Cyclist responds to consumer needs by promoting its products and services for bicycle owners whose bikes have been stolen or damaged.

more organizations realized the importance of satisfying customers' needs, U.S. businesses entered the marketing era, one of marketing orientation.

A **marketing orientation** requires the "organizationwide generation of market intelligence pertaining to current and future customer needs, dissemination of the intelligence across departments, and organizationwide responsiveness to it."[11] In Figure 1.7 the New York Cyclist demonstrates a strong marketing orientation through the promotion of its products and services. Top management, marketing managers, nonmarketing managers (those in production, finance, human resources, and so on), and customers are all important in developing and carrying out a marketing orientation. Unless marketing managers provide continuous customer-focused leadership with minimal interdepartmental conflict, achieving a marketing orientation will be difficult. Nonmarketing managers must communicate with marketing managers to share information important to understanding the customer. Finally, a marketing orientation involves being responsive to ever-changing customer needs and wants. To accomplish this, Amazon.com, the online provider of books and compact discs, follows buyers' online purchases and recommends related topics.[12] Trying to assess what customers want, difficult to begin with, is further complicated by the speed with which fashions and tastes can change. Today, businesses want to satisfy customers and build meaningful long-term buyer-seller relationships.

marketing orientation
An organizationwide commitment to researching and responding to customer needs

Implementing the Marketing Concept

A philosophy may sound reasonable and look good on paper, but that does not mean it can be put into practice easily. To implement the marketing concept, a marketing-oriented organization must accept some general conditions and recognize and deal with several problems. Consequently, the marketing concept has yet to be fully accepted by all American businesses.

Management must first establish an information system to discover customers' real needs and then use the information to create satisfying products. When M&M/Mars asked customers to choose a new M&M color to replace tan, 10.2 million people voted by mail, phone, fax, and E-mail. Blue received 54 percent of the vote, with purple, pink, and "no change" losing.[13] Within months, blue joined red, green, yellow, orange, and dark brown in the M&M lineup. Similarly, Parker Brothers encouraged customers to vote online for a new Monopoly piece (a biplane, bag of money, or piggy bank). These examples illustrate one technique marketers can use to obtain information about customers' desires and to respond in a way that forges a positive marketing relationship. An information system is usually expensive; management must commit money and time for its development and maintenance. But without an adequate information system, an organization cannot be marketing-oriented.

To satisfy customers' objectives as well as its own, a company must also coordinate all its activities. This may require restructuring the internal operations and overall objectives of one or more departments. If the head of the marketing unit is not a member of the organization's top-level management, he or she should be. Some departments may have to be abolished and new ones created. Implementing the marketing concept demands the support not only of top management, but also of managers and staff at all levels.

Achieving the full profit potential of each customer relationship should be the fundamental goal of every marketing strategy. Marketing relationships with customers are the lifeblood of all businesses. At the most basic level, profits can be obtained through relationships in the following ways: (1) by acquiring new customers, (2) by enhancing the profitability of existing customers, and (3) by extending the duration of customer relationships. Implementing the marketing concept means optimizing the exchange relationship, which is the relationship between a company's financial investment in customer relationships and the return generated by customers responding to that investment.[14]

Value-Driven Marketing

value   A customer's subjective assessment of benefits relative to costs in determining the worth of a product

To implement the marketing concept and satisfy customers' needs, organizations must develop marketing mixes that create value for customers. We view **value** as a customer's subjective assessment of benefits relative to costs in determining the worth of a product (customer value = customer benefits − customer costs). The ads in Figure 1.8 illustrate that Tums and Minute Maid both offer extra value because they contain calcium.

Figure 1.8
Value-Driven Marketing
Tums and Minute Maid offer extra value by adding calcium to the existing benefits of the products.

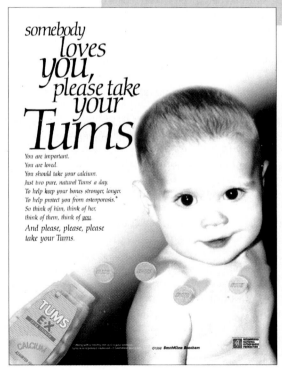

Customer benefits include anything a buyer receives in an exchange. Hotels and motels, for example, basically provide a room with a bed and bathroom, but each firm provides a different level of service, amenities, and atmosphere to satisfy its guests. Hampton Inns offers the minimum services necessary to maintain a quality, efficient, low-price overnight accommodation. In contrast, the Ritz Carlton provides every imaginable service a guest might desire and strives to ensure that all service is of the highest quality. Customers judge which type of accommodation offers the best value according to the benefits they desire and their willingness and ability to pay for the costs associated with the benefits.

Customer costs include anything a buyer must give up to obtain the benefits provided by the product. The most obvious cost is the monetary price of the product, but nonmonetary costs, though less obvious, can be equally important in a customer's determination of value. Two nonmonetary costs are the time and effort customers expend to find and purchase desired products. To reduce time and effort, a company can increase product availability, thereby making it more convenient for buyers to purchase the firm's products. Another nonmonetary cost is risk, which can be reduced by offering good basic warranties or extended warranties for an additional charge.[15] Another risk-reduction strategy is the offer of a 100 percent satisfaction guarantee. This strategy is increasingly popular in today's catalog/telephone/Internet shopping environment. L.L. Bean, for example, uses such a guarantee to reduce the risk of ordering merchandise from its catalogs.

The process people use to determine the value of a product is not highly scientific. All of us tend to get a feel for the worth of products based on our own expectations and previous experience. We can, for example, compare the value of tires, batteries,

BUILDING
customer relationships

Duracell Launches Long-Life Battery

In today's high-tech society, an increasing number of the products we depend on are battery-operated. These range from simple clocks and smoke alarms to digital cameras, handheld computers, video games, and even cell phones. Some of the more complicated gadgets quickly drain the life out of ordinary disposable batteries. The leading battery marketers, Energizer and Duracell, have long used clever advertising with animated toys to convince battery buyers that their products last longer. Despite the popularity of the Energizer bunny ads, most buyers don't perceive a significant difference among battery brands. Duracell International hopes to change this view with the Duracell Ultra, which gives some extra oomph to today's battery-draining high-tech toys and tools.

The Duracell Ultra is a line of AA and AAA alkaline batteries designed specifically for power-hungry digital cameras, camcorders, CD players, and other high-tech items. Duracell claims these batteries last up to 50 percent longer than regular alkaline batteries. With Duracell Ultra batteries, the company says, flash cameras take a hundred more photos, minidisk players perform an extra hour of music, and cell phones get an extra hour of talk time.

Duracell spent four years developing the Ultra, which has a reduced electrical resistance and reformu-lated chemistry to improve performance. The new batteries cost about 20 percent more than Duracell's ordinary alkaline batteries, but the company hopes the value of the Ultra will be obvious enough to buyers to increase Duracell's share of battery sales in the United States and Europe to 51 percent.

Duracell is also taking steps to ensure that more users of rechargeable batteries switch to the Ultra for the convenience. Just 8 percent of cell phones currently available can use alkaline batteries, but Duracell has persuaded several manufacturers, including Philips Electronics and Alcatel Alsthom, to offer cell phones that can run on the disposable Ultras. It is also working with manufacturers of a variety of products to create additional uses for the new batteries.

Will the advantages offered by Duracell's Ultra last long enough to give the company an edge in the battery wars? Competitors are already introducing similar long-lasting batteries for battery-draining devices. Energizer now has its own high-tech battery line, and Eastman Kodak has launched its Photolife AA batteries for digital cameras. Regardless of which company prevails in this round of the battle for buyers' dollars, the winner will be the customer who benefits from better performing products.

and computers directly with the value of competing products. We evaluate movies, sporting events, and performances by entertainers on the more subjective basis of personal preferences and emotions. For most purchases, we do not consciously try to calculate the associated benefits and costs. It becomes an instinctive feeling that Kellogg's Corn Flakes are a good value or that McDonald's is a good place to take children for a quick lunch. The purchase of an automobile or a mountain bike may have emotional components, but more conscious decision making may also figure in the process of determining value.

 In developing marketing activities, it is important to recognize that customers receive benefits based on their experiences. For example, many computer buyers consider services such as fast delivery, ease of installation, technical advice, and training assistance to be important elements of the product. Customers also derive benefits from the act of shopping and selecting products. These benefits can be affected by the atmosphere or environment of a store, such as Red Lobster's nautical/seafood theme. Even the ease of navigating a Web site can have a tremendous impact on perceived value. For this reason, General Motors has developed a user-friendly way to navigate its Web site for researching and pricing vehicles. Using the Internet to compare a Saturn with a Mercedes could result in different automobiles being viewed as an excellent value by different customers. The Saturn has been highly rated by owners as providing low-cost, reliable transportation and having dealers who provide outstanding service. A Mercedes may cost twice as much but has the advantage of being rated as a better-engineered automobile that also has a higher social status than the Saturn. Different customers may view each car as being an exceptional value for their own personal satisfaction.

The marketing mix can be used to enhance perceptions of value. A product that demonstrates value usually has a feature or an enhancement that provides benefits. Building Customer Relationships provides an example of a new product that the manufacturer claims lasts 50 percent longer than competing products, which may help customers see the product as having greater value. Promotional activities can also help create an image and prestige characteristics that customers consider in their assessment of a product's value. In some cases, value may simply be perceived as the lowest price. Many customers may not care about the quality of the paper towels they buy; they simply want the cheapest ones for use in cleaning up spills because they plan to throw them in the trash anyway. On the other hand, more people are looking for the fastest, most convenient way to achieve a goal and therefore become insensitive to pricing. Many busy customers are buying more prepared meals in supermarkets to take home and serve quickly even though these meals cost considerably more than meals prepared from scratch. In such cases, the products with the greatest convenience may be perceived as having the greatest value. The availability or distribution of products can also enhance their value. Taco Bell wants to have its Mexican fast-food products available at any time and any place people are thinking about consuming food. It has therefore introduced Taco Bell products into supermarkets, vending machines, college campuses, and other convenient locations. Thus, the development of an effective marketing strategy requires understanding the needs and desires of customers and designing a marketing mix to satisfy them and provide the value they want.

Marketing Management

marketing management
The process of planning, organizing, implementing, and controlling marketing activities to facilitate exchanges effectively and efficiently

Marketing management is the process of planning, organizing, implementing, and controlling marketing activities to facilitate exchanges effectively and efficiently. Effectiveness and efficiency are important dimensions of this definition. *Effectiveness* is the degree to which an exchange helps achieve an organization's objectives. *Efficiency* refers to minimizing the resources an organization must spend to achieve a specific level of desired exchanges. Thus, the overall goal of marketing management is to facilitate highly desirable exchanges and to minimize the costs of doing so.

Planning is a systematic process of assessing opportunities and resources, determining marketing objectives, and developing a marketing strategy and plans for implementation and control. Planning determines when and how marketing activities are performed and who performs them. It forces marketing managers to think ahead, to establish objectives, and to consider future marketing activities and their impact on society. Effective planning also reduces or eliminates daily crises. We take a closer look at marketing strategies and plans in the next chapter.

Organizing marketing activities involves developing the internal structure of the marketing unit. The structure is the key to directing marketing activities. The marketing unit can be organized by functions, products, regions, types of customers, or a combination of all four.

Proper implementation of marketing plans hinges on coordination of marketing activities, motivation of marketing personnel, and effective communication within the unit. Marketing managers must motivate marketing personnel, coordinate their activities, and integrate their activities both with those in other areas of the company and with the marketing efforts of personnel in external organizations, such as advertising agencies and research firms. If McDonald's runs a promotion advertising Big Macs for 99 cents, proper implementation of this plan requires that each of the company's restaurants have enough staff and product on hand to handle the increased demand. An organization's communication system must allow the marketing manager to stay in contact with high-level management, with managers of other functional areas within the firm, and with personnel involved in marketing activities both inside and outside the organization.

The marketing control process consists of establishing performance standards, comparing actual performance with established standards, and reducing the difference between desired and actual performance. An effective control process has four requirements. It should ensure a rate of information flow that allows the marketing manager to detect quickly any differences between actual and planned levels of performance. It must accurately monitor various activities and be flexible enough to accommodate changes. The costs of the control process must be low relative to costs that would arise without controls. Finally, the control process should be designed so that both managers and subordinates can understand it. In Chapter 22, we examine the organizing, implementing, and controlling of marketing strategies in greater detail.

The Importance of Marketing in Our Global Economy

Our definition of marketing and discussion of marketing activities reveal some of the obvious reasons why the study of marketing is relevant in today's world. In this section, we look at how marketing affects us as individuals and at its role in our increasingly global society.

Marketing Costs Consume a Sizable Portion of Buyers' Dollars

Studying marketing will make you aware that many marketing activities are necessary to provide satisfying goods and services. Obviously, these activities cost money. About one-half of a buyer's dollar goes for marketing costs. If you spend $15.00 on a new compact disc, about $7.50 goes toward activities related to distribution and the retailer's expenses and profit margins. The production (pressing) of the CD represents about 90 cents, or 6 percent of its price. A family with a monthly income of $3,000 that allocates $600 to taxes and savings spends about $2,400 for goods and services. Of this amount, $1,200 goes for marketing activities. If marketing expenses consume that much of your dollar, you should know how this money is used.

Marketing Is Used in All Organizations

From 25 to 33 percent of all civilian workers in the United States perform marketing activities. The marketing field offers a variety of interesting and challenging career opportunities throughout the world, such as personal selling, advertising, packaging, transportation, storage, marketing research, product development, wholesaling, and retailing. In addition, many individuals working for nonbusiness organizations engage in marketing activities to promote political, educational, cultural, church, civic, and charitable activities. Building Customer Relationships, for example, profiles one marketer's efforts to improve the satisfaction and value offered by a nonprofit museum. Whether a person earns a living through marketing activities or performs them voluntarily for a nonprofit group, marketing knowledge and skills are valuable personal and professional assets.

BUILDING
customer relationships

Florida International Museum

The Florida International Museum opened in St. Petersburg, Florida, in 1995 as a major international cultural center. Located in a 300,000-square-foot former department store, the nonprofit museum is connected by trolley to other museums and galleries in St. Petersburg's cultural arts district, the QuARTer. Despite its excellent location, the museum failed to break even after two world-class exhibitions, "Splendors of Ancient Egypt" and "Alexander the Great." Facing local criticism and huge debt, the museum's future was in doubt. The museum's board brought in Wayne Atherholt from the city's renowned Salvador Dali Museum to craft a new strategy.

Atherholt had to act quickly to ready the museum for its next exhibit, which included artifacts from the *Titanic* shipwreck and coincided with the release of the movie *Titanic.* He hired a completely new staff and created a logo for the museum, which it uses on stationery, brochures, and in the museum's interior to give it a distinctive identity. He then revamped the museum to create a more positive, relaxing atmosphere for visitors, allowing them to wander through the "Titanic" exhibit at their own pace while listening to a ninety-minute audio by actor Malcolm McDowell. Atherholt also computerized a mailing list of museum visitors. When analysis of this database suggested that many of the museum's visitors were book lovers, Atherholt had bookmarks imprinted with exhibit times, dates, prices, and other information and made these available to local bookstores to give away to

their customers. The museum also established a Web site to enhance its exposure worldwide.

To counter local criticism of the museum, Atherholt worked to improve relations between the museum and the community. He focused in particular on hotels and restaurants, the community's chief hospitality providers. He began by eliminating the museum's cafeteria, which competed with nearby restaurants. During the "Titanic" exhibit, Atherholt encouraged restaurants to re-create portions of the ocean liner's menu in exchange for discounts and free advertising by the museum. A downtown coffee shop served *Titanic*-style desserts, and several hotels offered variations of the last meal served aboard the *Titanic.* Atherholt also sent scratch pads, pens, and postcards to local hotels, restaurants, and transportation services. During inclement weather, he faxed every hotel in the city to remind the concierges that the museum offers a satisfying experience for their guests.

Atherholt's efforts to revitalize the Florida International Museum appear to have worked. On opening day, 3,300 visitors saw the sixteen-gallery "Titanic" exhibit, and it went on to experience record attendance levels for a Florida museum. The museum continues to work to enhance the experience it offers visitors. For its next exhibit, the "Empires of Mystery," the museum created a haunted-house atmosphere in which visitors search for "gold" while wandering through galleries devoted to Inca culture and its interaction with Spanish conquistadors.

Marketing Is Important to Business and the Economy

Businesses must sell products to survive and grow, and marketing activities help sell their products. Financial resources generated from sales can be used to develop innovative products. New products allow a firm to better satisfy customers' changing needs, which in turn enables the firm to generate more profits. Even nonprofit businesses need to "sell" to survive. Habitat for Humanity, for example, must market its philosophy of low-income housing to the public in order to raise funds and donations of supplies to build or renovate housing for low-income families, who contribute "sweat equity" to the construction of their own homes.

Marketing activities help produce the profits that are essential not only to the survival of individual businesses, but also to the health and ultimate survival of the global economy. Profits drive economic growth because without them businesses find it difficult, if not impossible, to buy more raw materials, hire more employees, attract more capital, and create additional products that in turn make more profits. Without profits, marketers cannot continue to provide jobs and contribute to social causes.

Marketing Fuels Our Global Economy

Figure 1.9
Technology, Marketing, and the Global Economy
IBM facilitates Motorola in selling cellular technology through IBM Web technology. Manpower promotes its Web site as a tool for global employment services.

Profits from marketing products contribute to the development of new products and technologies. Advances in technology, along with falling political and economic barriers and the universal desire for a higher standard of living, have made marketing across national borders commonplace while stimulating global economic growth. As a result of worldwide communications and increased international travel, many American brands have achieved widespread acceptance around the world. Figure 1.9

Ever since we've had her, she's been wagging her tail like crazy. Unfortunately her owner couldn't keep her any longer, and now, neither can we. Can you? *Adopt. Fast. 348-4250.* MINNEAPOLIS ANIMAL SHELTER

**Figure 1.10
Enhancing Consumer
Awareness**
Marketing can help
improve the well-being
of society and even help
dogs find good homes.

illustrates how Manpower, Motorola, and IBM have contributed to technology that facilitates global exchanges. At the same time, customers in the United States have greater choices among the products they buy, as foreign brands such as Toyota (Japan), Bayer (Germany), and British Petroleum now sell alongside American brands such as General Motors, Tylenol, and Chevron. People around the world watch CNN and MTV on Toshiba and Sony televisions they purchased at Wal-Mart. Electronic commerce via the Internet now enables businesses of all sizes to reach buyers around the world. We explore the international markets and opportunities for global marketing in Chapter 5.

Marketing Knowledge Enhances Consumer Awareness

Besides contributing to the well-being of our economy, marketing activities help improve the quality of our lives. Figure 1.10 spotlights a concern about animals and raises awareness about the opportunity to save a dog by finding him a home. Studying marketing allows us to assess a product's value and flaws more effectively. We can determine which marketing efforts need improvement and how to attain that goal. For example, an unsatisfactory experience with a warranty may make you wish for stricter law enforcement so that sellers would fulfill their promises. You may have also wished that you had more accurate information about a product before you purchased it. Understanding marketing enables us to evaluate corrective measures (such as laws, regulations, and industry guidelines) that could stop unfair, damaging, or unethical marketing practices. Thus, understanding how marketing activities work can help you be a better consumer.

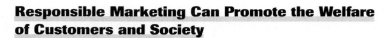

Responsible Marketing Can Promote the Welfare of Customers and Society

The success of our economic system depends on marketers whose values promote trust and cooperative relationships in which customers are treated with respect. The public is increasingly insistent that social responsibility and ethical concerns be considered in planning and implementing marketing activities. While some marketers' irresponsible or unethical activities end up on the front pages of *USA Today* or *The Wall Street Journal,* more firms are working to develop a responsible approach to developing long-term relationships with customers *and* society. By managing concern about the impact of marketing on society, a firm can protect the interests of the general public and the natural environment. We examine these issues and many others as we develop a framework for understanding more about marketing in the remainder of this book.

Summary

Marketing is the process of creating, distributing, promoting, and pricing goods, services, and ideas to facilitate satisfying exchange relationships with customers in a dynamic environment. As the purchasers of the products that organizations develop, promote, distribute, and price, customers are the focal point of all marketing activities. The essence of marketing is to develop satisfying exchanges from which both customers and marketers benefit. Organizations generally focus their marketing efforts on a specific group of customers, or target market.

Marketing involves developing and managing a product that will satisfy customer needs, making the product available in the right place and at a price acceptable to customers, and communicating information that helps customers determine if the product will satisfy their needs. These activities—product, distribution, promotion, and pricing—are known as the marketing mix because marketing managers decide what type of each element to use and in what amounts. Marketing managers strive to develop a marketing mix that matches the needs of customers in the target market. Before marketers can develop a marketing mix, they must collect in-depth, up-to-date information about customer needs. The product variable of the marketing mix deals with researching customers' needs and wants and designing a product that satisfies them. A product can be a good, a service, or an idea. In dealing with the distribution variable, a marketing manager tries to make products available in the quantities desired to as many customers as possible. The promotion variable relates to activities used to inform individuals or groups about an organization and its products. The price variable relates to decisions and actions associated with establishing pricing policies and determining product prices. These marketing mix variables are often viewed as controllable because they can be changed, but there are limits to how much they can be altered.

Individuals and organizations engage in marketing to facilitate exchanges—that is, the provision or transfer of goods, services, and ideas in return for something of value. Four conditions must exist for an exchange to occur: (1) two or more individuals, groups, or organizations must participate, and each must possess something of value that the other party desires; (2) the exchange should provide a benefit or satisfaction to both parties involved in the transaction; (3) each party must have confidence in the promise of the "something of value" held by the other; and (4) to build trust, the parties to the exchange must meet expectations. In an exchange, products are traded either for other products or for financial resources, such as cash or credit. Marketing activities should attempt to create and maintain satisfying exchange relationships. Relationship marketing involves establishing long-term, mutually satisfying buyer-seller relationships.

The marketing environment, which includes competitive, economic, political, legal and regulatory, technological, and sociocultural forces, surrounds the customer and the marketing mix. These forces can create threats to marketers, but they also generate opportunities for new products and new methods of reaching customers. These forces can fluctuate quickly and dramatically.

According to the marketing concept, an organization should try to provide products that satisfy customers' needs through a coordinated set of activities that also allows the organization to achieve its goals. Customer satisfaction is the marketing concept's major objective. The philosophy of the marketing concept emerged in the United States during the 1950s after the production and sales eras. Organizations that develop activities consistent with the marketing concept become marketing-oriented organizations. To implement the marketing concept, a marketing-oriented organization must establish an information system to discover customers' needs and use the information to create satisfying products. It must also coordinate all its activities and develop marketing mixes that create value for customers in order to satisfy their needs.

Value is a customer's subjective assessment of benefits relative to costs in determining the worth of a product. Benefits include anything a buyer receives in an exchange, while costs include anything a buyer must give up to obtain the benefits provided by the product. The marketing mix can be used to enhance perceptions of value.

Marketing management is the process of planning, organizing, implementing, and controlling marketing activities to facilitate effective and efficient exchanges. Planning is a systematic process of assessing opportunities and resources, determining marketing objectives, developing a marketing strategy, and preparing for implementation and control. Organizing marketing activities involves developing the marketing unit's internal structure. Proper implementation of marketing plans depends on coordinating marketing activities, motivating marketing personnel, and communicating effectively within the unit. The marketing control process consists of establishing performance standards, comparing actual performance with established standards, and reducing the difference between desired and actual performance.

Marketing is important in our society in many ways. Marketing costs absorb about half of each buyer's dollar. Marketing activities are performed in both business and nonbusiness organizations. Marketing activities help business organizations generate profits, and they help fuel the increasingly global economy. A knowledge of marketing enhances consumer awareness. Finally, responsible marketing can promote the welfare of customers and society.

Important Terms

Marketing	Marketing mix	Relationship marketing	Marketing orientation
Customers	Product	Marketing environment	Value
Target market	Exchanges	Marketing concept	Marketing management

Discussion and Review Questions

1. What is marketing? How did you define the term before you read this chapter?

2. What is the focus of all marketing activities? Why?

3. What are the four variables of the marketing mix? Why are these elements known as variables?

4. What conditions must exist before a marketing exchange can occur? Describe a recent exchange in which you participated.

5. What are the forces in the marketing environment? How much control does a marketing manager have over these forces?

6. Discuss the basic elements of the marketing concept. Which businesses in your area use this philosophy? Explain why.

7. Identify several businesses in your area that have not adopted the marketing concept. What characteristics of these organizations indicate nonacceptance of the marketing concept?

8. How can an organization implement the marketing concept?

9. What is value? How can marketers use the marketing mix to enhance the perception of value?

10. What types of activities are involved in the marketing management process?

11. Why is marketing important in our society? Why should *you* study marketing?

Application Questions

1. Felicia owns an automobile dealership in her hometown. Her typical day begins with breakfast at a local coffee shop where she usually "bumps into" her customers. After breakfast today, she contracted to redecorate and redesign the dealership showroom. Later, she met with advertising agency personnel to discuss next month's advertising for the dealership. Which of Felicia's actions would be considered marketing? Why?

2. Identify possible target markets for the following products:
   a. Kellogg's Corn Flakes
   b. Wilson tennis rackets
   c. Disney World
   d. Diet Pepsi

3. Discuss the variables of the marketing mix (product, price, promotion, and distribution) as they might relate to each of the following:
   a. a trucking company
   b. a men's clothing store
   c. a skating rink
   d. a campus bookstore

Internet Exercise & Resources

Online with the American Marketing Association

The American Marketing Association (AMA) is the marketing discipline's primary professional organization. In addition to sponsoring academic research, publishing marketing literature, and organizing meetings of local business people with student members, it helps individual members find employment in member firms. To see what the AMA has to offer you, visit the AMA Web site at

www.ama.org

1. What type of information is available on the AMA Web site to assist students in planning their careers and finding jobs?
2. If you joined a student chapter of the AMA, what benefits would you receive?
3. What marketing mix variable does the AMA's Internet marketing efforts exemplify?

E-Center Resources

Visit http://www.prideferrell.com to find several resources to help you succeed in mastering the material in this chapter, plus additional materials that will help you expand your marketing knowledge. The Web site includes

 Internet exercise updates plus additional exercises

 ACE self-tests

 Chapter summary with hotlinked glossary

 Hotlinks to companies featured in this chapter

 Resource Center

 Career Center

 Marketing plan worksheets

VIDEO CASE 1.1

"A Different Kind of Company, a Different Kind of Car"

In 1982, after years of losing sales to Japanese firms, General Motors decided to start a new company as a "laboratory" to find better ways to manufacture and market cars. From the beginning, GM wanted Saturn Corporation to be "a different kind of company, a different kind of car." To achieve this goal, GM made Saturn an independent, wholly owned subsidiary rather than a division like Chevrolet or Buick. To remove Saturn from the traditional auto-building mentality in Detroit, GM located Saturn's manufacturing facilities in Spring Hill, Tennessee. The latest and most efficient manufacturing technology was built into the Spring Hill plant to ensure that Saturn would produce high-quality cars. The company forged an unparalleled relationship with the United Auto Workers (UAW) union by signing a separate contract that established Saturn workers as partners with management and that involved them in all decision-making aspects of the organization. GM even involved Saturn's advertising agency, San Francisco-based Hal Riney & Partners, in key marketing decisions from the very beginning. Thus, GM viewed strategic partnerships—between labor and management, between company and supplier, and between company and advertising agency— as a key element of Saturn's future, with everyone sharing the risks and rewards.

During the 1980s, General Motors executives had been dismayed to learn from a survey by J.D. Power & Associates that 42 percent of new-car shoppers did not even look at a GM car, often buying Hondas and Toyotas instead. One of Saturn's greatest tasks, then, was to sell 80 percent of its cars to drivers who would not otherwise have bought a GM car. Saturn's strategy focused on college-educated men and women, aged 25 to 49, who preferred Japanese automobiles because of their perceived higher quality and value.

When Saturn rolled the first cars off the assembly line in Spring Hill on July 30, 1990, it offered just four products: the SC1 and SC2 coupes and SL1 and SL2 sedans. In 1993, the company introduced two station wagons (the SW1 and SW2) and an entry-level coupe (SC). These were followed in 1996 by the EV1 (a limited-production electric car), and in 1999 by the LS (mid-size car) and LW (mid-size wagon). The company plans to launch a small sport utility vehicle in 2002. The cars' simple appellations are the result of a decision made by a panel of ad agency representatives, employees, and dealers, who felt more descriptive names (such as "Chevrolet Camaro") would weaken the Saturn concept. Even the color descriptions are simple, with names like "red" rather than "raspberry red."

In keeping with its "different" philosophy, Saturn planned its distribution system very carefully. Saturn dealers are given large territories so that each competes with rival brands rather than each other. There is generally just one Saturn dealership in a metropolitan area. The company set up the first dealerships in areas where sales of imported cars are high; most were located on the East and West Coasts. Saturn was particularly careful to select dealers who know how to appeal to imported-car buyers. Dealers work to provide a relaxed, inviting showroom environment. Salespersons generally avoid high-pressure sales tactics, offering advice only when customers seek it.

The Saturn concept also included an innovative pricing strategy. Base prices are competitive with prices of imported cars; they range from $10,595 for the SL to $15,005 for the SC2, but optional features can raise prices to $20,000. With few exceptions, there are no rebates or promotions, no dealing or haggling. A price tag of $10,595 means that a customer pays $10,595, period. Because of legal considerations, Saturn cannot set prices or insist that dealers adhere to its fixed-price policy. However, because of tight profit margins and the high-integrity sales approach that is part of Saturn's marketing strategy, dealers have been very supportive of the pricing policy. Potential buyers can obtain pricing information at the company's online Interactive Pricing Center (www.saturn.com/car/ipc), where they can configure their own Saturn, starting with a base car and adding options. The Web site also allows customers to estimate monthly payments, choose financing options, and even explore the option of leasing rather than purchasing a Saturn.

The role of promotion is particularly integral to the Saturn concept. Along with the low-pressure sales approach used by dealers, advertising plays a key role in creating a tightly focused image for Saturn. The advertising agency adopted a straight-talk, people-oriented philosophy, stressing Saturn, the company, rather than Saturn, the car. To create awareness of the Saturn concept, initial ads concentrated on the Spring Hill heartland, Saturn employees, and how Saturn's management and the UAW had set aside their long-standing differences to cooperate in building the best car they could. After the first cars rolled off the assembly line, print ads and television commercials featured stories about Saturn customers and highlighted themes that Baby Boomers hold dear, such as safety, utility, and value. One commercial showed a Saturn representative traveling to Alaska to fix a Saturn owned by Robin Millage, an actual customer who had ordered her car sight unseen from a dealer in the continental United States.

Saturn's methods have revolutionized the way cars are produced and sold in the United States. First-day sales were tremendous, and the cars have continued to sell well. Although sales declined somewhat in the late 1990s, the company's new mid-size models and planned sport utility vehicle should help it compete strongly against comparable imports and regain sales momentum. GM's support for Saturn has occasionally wavered, but it continues to cite Saturn as a model for what the rest of the giant corporation could be. The company has plans to expand capacity in its Spring Hill plant, take over another facility in Wilmington, Delaware, add new dealerships, and upgrade existing models and develop new ones to satisfy customers. By any yardstick, GM's experiment to develop "a different kind of company, a different kind of car" appears to be a success.[16]

Questions for Discussion

1. Describe the target market for Saturn cars.
2. Describe the marketing mix—product, distribution, promotion, and price—for Saturn Corporation.
3. Does Saturn appear to be implementing the marketing concept? Explain your answer.

CASE 1.2

AutoZone: Where the Customer Is Boss

Founded by grocery wholesaler Malone & Hyde, Memphis-based Auto Shack opened its first auto parts retail stores in 1979. By focusing primarily on customer service and expanding into small markets where there was little competition, Auto Shack experienced tremendous growth. Following a lawsuit brought against it by home electronics giant Radio Shack, the company changed its name to AutoZone in 1988. That same year, the company posted sales of nearly $440 million, having by then established itself as a force to be reckoned with in the highly competitive do-it-yourself (DIY) auto parts industry.

The 1990s witnessed continued growth at AutoZone. In 1992, with 678 stores at year's end, the company had sales of over $1 billion for the first time in its relatively short history. The following year, *Forbes* magazine recognized AutoZone for having the second-highest average annual growth in earnings over the previous five years. In 1998, the company's tenth straight year of growth in net income,

AutoZone's 2,657 stores operating in thirty-eight states amassed sales of over $3.2 billion, up a full 20 percent from the previous year. By this time, the company was, on average, opening a new store every other day.

The DIY market is expanding as a result of several factors. First, as the price of the average automobile has steadily increased in recent years, so has the age of the typical vehicle on American roads. In fact, approximately one-third of all cars and light trucks in the United States are over ten years old, well beyond the coverage of automobile warranties. Second, with the average hourly rate of professional mechanics and other auto repair labor hovering around $50, more and more people are choosing to work on their cars themselves. Additionally, there are more cars on the road, and people are driving more miles every year. AutoZone believes it has but scratched the surface of its vast growth potential.

AutoZone targets the DIY customer with an extensive selection of automotive replacement parts, maintenance items, and accessories. Everything from lug nuts and antifreeze to floor mats, water pumps, and even complete engines can be found in the company's spacious retail outlets. However, these products can be purchased from many competitors. AutoZone differentiates itself from the competition in a number of ways. Although most of its competitors can claim that they too offer customers high-quality parts and accessories at low prices, AutoZone goes much further in the effort to give customers exactly what they want.

AutoZone stores are conspicuously clean and attractive, dispelling the common perception of auto parts stores as dirty, greasy establishments where only the most knowledgeable mechanics dare tread. More important, AutoZone differentiates itself by providing a premium level of customer service. The company has achieved its phenomenal success by adhering to one simple central premise: put the customer first. At Auto-Zone, the customer is the boss. Unlike many organizations, AutoZone regards "customer service" as more than a mere catch phrase. For the experienced mechanic, AutoZone offers not only a complete range of parts and accessories at low prices, but also the assistance and support of service personnel knowledgeable about the most technical aspects of automotive repair. The wide selection and low prices appeal to novices, too. But what matters most is that employees are there to listen and help customers find exactly what they want.

Every store manager's name tag says, "Manager of Customer Satisfaction," and every employee ("AutoZoner") goes the extra mile for the customer, whether a well-trained mechanic or a thrifty driver who wants to change her own oil. AutoZone's absolute commitment to customer service is even embodied in its own unique terminology. "Drop/Stop—30/30" means that AutoZoners drop whatever they are doing to wait on customers before they've been in the store for thirty seconds or stepped thirty feet from the front door. "GOTCHA" is the company's practice of going out to customers' cars to help install items or resolve problems.

To further enhance customer service, AutoZone developed its own information technology system. The system, which includes a nationwide satellite link, a centralized call center, and a computerized store management system, is called "WITT-JR"—Whatever It Takes To Do the Job Right. The satellite routes calls to the central calling center instead of putting customers on hold. There, "Phone Pros" answer questions, look up prices, and check availability in the ten stores closest to the caller's location. All parts warranties are registered on computer, reducing the hassles for customers who misplace their receipts. In-store electronic parts catalogs let customers quickly and accurately look up the exact parts and accessories they need and even identify where in the store the items are shelved. AutoZone's system also monitors and evaluates product sales and availability at each retail outlet.

AutoZone's commitment to customer service is evidenced in its pricing and product policies as well. Its outlets stock a wide range of automotive parts and accessories based on what customers tell the company they want. AutoZone has developed "flexograms," which tailor the parts inventory at each retail outlet to match the needs of that store's customers based on knowledge of the types of automobiles they drive. AutoZone's everyday low prices on these goods often beat the sale prices of competitors. Thus, AutoZone offers the customer savings all the time, a matter of particular importance given the nature of the auto parts industry. For example, when an alternator or water pump fails, it must be replaced immediately; the customer cannot wait for a sale. When it comes to more costly parts under a car's hood, AutoZone's own private brand line can save customers even more money.

In considering strategic alternatives for the future, AutoZone executives are seeking innovative ways to increase the company's share of the thriving DIY auto parts market. So far, AutoZone's aggressive growth strategy of continually adding new stores has been highly successful. In 1998, the chain opened 275 new stores. To continue to add value, the company is considering installing DIY repair bays where customers could install parts and accessories themselves with assistance from expert AutoZone service personnel when needed. Another option for AutoZone might be to employ mechanics, adding expert parts installation to the range of services it already offers. No matter how the company chooses to pursue future growth, one thing is certain: the customer will always be the ultimate boss at AutoZone.[17]

Questions for Discussion

1. What types of customers make up AutoZone's target market? Speculate as to why the firm has chosen to concentrate on this one segment of customers.
2. How does AutoZone implement the marketing concept?
3. Is AutoZone a marketing-oriented organization? Explain.

2

Strategic Planning

OBJECTIVES

- To be able to describe the strategic planning process
- To be able to explain how organizational resources and opportunities affect the planning process
- To understand the role of the mission statement in strategic planning
- To examine corporate, business-unit, and marketing strategies
- To learn about the process of creating the marketing plan

Surf's Up . . . Yahoo!

Yahoo!, an ad-supported directory of World Wide Web pages, was founded in 1994 by two Stanford University graduate students, David Filo and Jerry Yang, as a way of keeping track of their personal interests on the Internet. Originally known as Jerry's Guide to the World Wide Web, the directory quickly became popular among Internet surfers looking to make sense of the ever-expanding Web. Filo and Yang organized the guide into a customized database, developed software to help them locate and identify Web pages, and eventually renamed the guide Yahoo! (acronym for Yet Another Hierarchical Officious Oracle). With Yahoo!'s growing success, the two eventually abandoned their postgraduate educations to take their place in the history of the Internet. Yahoo! has evolved into a "portal," a multiservice gateway to the Internet, with guides targeted for demographic audiences (e.g., Yahooligans! for children), geographic audiences (e.g., Yahoo! Local), special-interest audiences (e.g., Yahoo! Finance, and Yahoo! News), and community services (e.g., Yahoo! Chat). Based in Santa Clara, California, the firm today operates guides in nine languages in fourteen countries, including Australia, China, Germany, and Japan. Yahoo! is one of the most frequently accessed Web sites on the Internet, with 40 million people logging on to the site every month—10 million more than those who watch the top-rated TV show *ER*.

As the first Internet firm to market a detailed search service, the first to go public, the first to turn a profit, and the first to go mainstream by advertising on television, Yahoo! is eager to maintain its prominent position in the fast-paced world of the Internet and, more impor-tantly, in consumers' minds. The company has therefore put its name on everything from T-shirts, shoes, kazoos, yo-yos, and computer bags to skateboards, surfboards, parachutes, and sailboats. Its name has also appeared on the hit TV shows *ER* and *Ally McBeal,* as well as the Ron Howard movie *Ed TV.* The firm is working on plans that will allow users to access Yahoo! via telephones, televisions, pagers, and hand-held organizers. It also has plans to provide users with a "Yahoo! wallet," which would allow them to register their credit card numbers and shipping addresses with the company. Users could then take their virtual wallet with them to make purchases instant-ly anywhere on the Web. Yahoo! would track their purchases and present them with a monthly online bill. Thanks to strong advertising revenues, the company is sitting on a pile of cash, which it will likely use to make strategic acquisitions to enhance its services.

For now, Yahoo!'s strategies seem to be working. Some 44 percent of Internet users know the name Yahoo!, more than recognize the names of rivals Excite, Alta Vista, Infoseek, and Lycos. However, the competition among Internet portals and search services is heating up as the Internet continues to grow and marketing-savvy media companies enter the fray. Disney, for example, has obtained a 43 percent interest in Infoseek, and Excite is looking at other media companies, including Time Warner, for a partner of its own. Netscape and America Online have joined forces, and software giant Microsoft has launched its own portal, msn.com. With industry analysts predicting that just a few of these portals will survive in the dynamic environment of the Internet, Yahoo! must plan carefully for the future.[1]

YAHOO!®
www.yahoo.com

With competition increasing, Yahoo! and many other companies are spending more time and resources on strategic planning—that is, on determining how to use their resources and abilities to achieve their objectives. Although most of this book deals with specific marketing decisions and strategies, this chapter focuses on "the big picture," on all the functional areas and activities—finance, production, human resources, research and development, as well as marketing—that must be coordinated to reach organizational goals. Effectively implementing the marketing concept of satisfying customers and achieving organizational goals requires that all organizations engage in strategic planning.

We begin this chapter with an overview of the strategic planning process. Next, we examine how organizational resources and opportunities affect strategic planning and the role played by the organization's mission statement. After discussing the development of both corporate and business-unit strategy, we explore the nature of marketing strategy and the creation of the marketing plan. These elements provide a framework for the development and implementation of marketing strategies, as we shall see throughout the remainder of this book.

Understanding the Strategic Planning Process

strategic planning
The process of establishing an organizational mission and goals, corporate strategy, marketing objectives, marketing strategy, and marketing plan

Through the process of **strategic planning,** a firm establishes an organizational mission and goals, corporate strategy, marketing objectives, marketing strategy, and, finally, a marketing plan.[2] A marketing orientation should guide the process of strategic planning to ensure that a concern for customer satisfaction is an integral part of the process. Figure 2.1 shows the components of strategic planning.

The process begins with a detailed analysis of the organization's strengths and weaknesses and identification of opportunities and threats within the marketing environment. Based on this analysis, the firm can establish or revise its mission and goals, and then develop corporate strategies to achieve these goals. Next, each functional

Figure 2.1
Components of Strategic Planning
Source: Figure adapted from *Marketing Strategy* by O.C. Ferrell, Michael Hartline, George Lucas, and David J. Luck. Copyright © 1999 by Harcourt Brace & Company, reproduced by permission of the publisher.

area of the organization (marketing, production, finance, human resources, etc.) establishes its own objectives and develops strategies to achieve them.[3] The objectives and strategies of each functional area must support the organization's overall goals and mission. Consider the efforts of Gateway Computers, which has grown from a two-person shop in a barn to a company with $6 billion in sales through a strategy of low-cost assembly and direct sales (via telephone and Internet) of customized personal computers. To reach a new corporate goal of $25 billion in sales by 2001, executives decided to move the firm's headquarters from North Sioux City, South Dakota, to San Diego, California, to attract more engineers and managers who can help the company develop new products to appeal to more customers. Gateway's strategy also includes plans to open more retail stores to reach the 75 percent of home and small business customers who are not buying computers over the telephone or through the Internet.[4]

Because our focus is marketing, we are, of course, most interested in the development of marketing objectives and strategies. Marketing objectives should be designed so that their achievement will contribute to the corporate strategy and so that they can be accomplished through efficient use of the firm's resources. To achieve its marketing objectives, an organization must develop a **marketing strategy,** which includes identifying and analyzing a target market and developing a marketing mix to satisfy individuals in that market. Thus, a marketing strategy includes a plan of action for developing, distributing, promoting, and pricing products that meets the needs of the target market. Marketing strategy is best formulated when it reflects the overall direction of the organization and is coordinated with all the firm's functional areas. When properly implemented and controlled, a marketing strategy will contribute to the achievement not only of marketing objectives but also of an organization's overall goals. General Motors' Saturn division, for example, represents an innovative effort by a U.S. automaker to define and serve a target market by offering value, quality, reliability, and service, as well as an image of being "a different kind of company." Saturn's strategy includes innovation in all marketing mix elements, particularly pricing and promotion.[5] These efforts helped create a community of loyal Saturn owners, which in turn helped Saturn fulfill its goals and objectives as part of General Motors' overall corporate strategy.

The strategic planning process ultimately yields a marketing strategy that is the framework for a **marketing plan,** which is a written document that specifies the activities to be performed to implement and control an organization's marketing activities. In the remainder of this chapter, we discuss the major components of the strategic planning process: organizational opportunities and resources, organizational mission and goals, corporate and business-unit strategy, marketing strategy, and the role of the marketing plan.

marketing strategy A strategy for identifying and analyzing a target market and developing a marketing mix to meet the needs of that market

marketing plan A written document that specifies the activities to be performed to implement and control an organization's marketing activities

Assessing Organizational Resources and Opportunities

The strategic planning process begins with an analysis of the marketing environment, by which it is very much affected. Economic, competitive, political, legal and regulatory, sociocultural, and technological forces can constrain an organization and influence its overall goals; they also affect the amount and type of resources a firm can acquire. However, these environmental forces can create favorable opportunities as well—opportunities that can be translated into overall organizational goals and marketing objectives. We examine these forces and their impact on the strategic planning process in detail in Chapter 3.

Any strategic planning effort must assess an organization's available financial and human resources and capabilities, as well as how the level of these is likely to change in the future. Additional resources may be needed to achieve the organization's goals and mission.[6] Resources can also include goodwill, reputation, and brand names. The reputations and well-known brand names of Rolex watch and Cross pen, for example, are resources that provide these firms with an advantage over their competitors.

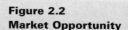

Figure 2.2
Market Opportunity
The plastics industry uses print advertising to communicate the less-known environmental benefits of plastic packaging.

It's true: In the last 20 years, empty milk jugs have lost a lot of weight. In fact, plastics are helping lots of products and packaging slim

product with less packaging • Even the plastic grocery bag uses 70 percent less plastic than it did in 1976. Big deal? You bet. Now it would

Would You Believe The Jug On The Right Is 45% Lighter?

down. That means using less energy and fewer raw materials to make them. Best of all, the milk jug on the right still holds the same amount of milk, delivering such benefits as shatter-resistance, a tamper-evident seal, a resealable cap and a convenient handle. • Soft drink bottles are slimmer too. That allows trucks to deliver more

take five trucks to deliver as many paper sacks as one truckload of plastic bags. Which also saves fuel. • To learn more, call the American Plastics Council at 1.800.777.9500 for a free booklet. • You'll find that, for a lightweight, the benefits of plastics are still pretty heavy.

American Plastics Council®

PLASTICS MAKE IT POSSIBLE.™
Visit us at http://www.plasticsresource.com

Such strengths also include **core competencies,** things a firm does extremely well—sometimes so well that they give the company an advantage over its competition.

Analysis of the marketing environment involves not only an assessment of resources, but also identification of opportunities in the marketplace. When the right combination of circumstances and timing permits an organization to take action to reach a particular target market, a **market opportunity** exists. As another example, environmental performance is important to businesses and consumers. Figure 2.2 illustrates how the American Plastics Council uses its advertising to teach how lighter plastic bottles reduce the consumption of natural resources in the manufacture and transportation of the packaging without compromising its strength. Advances in computer technology and the growth of the Internet have made it possible for real estate firms to provide prospective home buyers with databases of homes for sale all over the country. At www.realtor.com, the Internet site of the National Association of Realtors, buyers have access to a wealth of online information about homes for sale, including photos, floor plans, and details about neighborhoods, schools, and shopping. The World Wide Web represents a great market opportunity for real estate firms because its visual nature is perfectly suited to the task of shopping for a home.[7] Opportunities like these are often called **strategic windows,** meaning temporary periods of optimum fit between the key requirements of a market and the particular capabilities of a firm competing in that market.[8]

Marketers need to be able to recognize and analyze market opportunities and strategic windows. An organization's very survival depends on developing products that satisfy its target market(s). Few organizations can assume that products popular today will interest buyers in five years, or even next year. In fact, research indicates that U.S. corporations lose half their customers every five years.[9] To remain competitive, a company can modify existing products (as Oscar Mayer and Frito-Lay did when they reduced the fat content of some products to address increasing health concerns among consumers), introduce new products (such as Iomega's Zip and Jazz drives for computers), or eliminate those that customers no longer want (such as the Nissan 300ZX or Oldsmobile 88).

When a company matches a core competency to opportunities it has discovered in the marketplace, it is said to have a **competitive advantage.** In some cases, a company may possess manufacturing, technical, or marketing skills that it can match to market opportunities to create a competitive advantage. Microsoft, for example, used its marketing and technical skills to create the Windows operating system to make computers easier to use. Although most personal computers are now sold with Windows already installed, Microsoft strives to maintain its competitive advantage by improving Windows and introducing Windows-compatible software, such as its Web browser, Internet Explorer.

core competencies
Things a firm does extremely well, which sometimes give it an advantage over its competition

market opportunity
A combination of circumstances and timing that permits an organization to take action to reach a target market

strategic windows
Temporary periods of optimum fit between the key requirements of a market and a firm's capabilities

competitive advantage
The result of a company's matching a core competency to opportunities in the marketplace

Figure 2.3
Mission Statement
Ben & Jerry's communicates its mission.

Establishing an Organizational Mission and Goals

mission statement
A long-term view of what an organization wants to become

Once an organization has assessed its resources and opportunities, it can begin to establish goals and strategies to take advantage of those opportunities. The goals of any organization should be derived from its **mission statement,** which is a long-term view, or vision, of what the organization wants to become. Intel, for example, says that its mission is to "do a great job for our customers, employees, and stockholders by being the preeminent building block supplier to the computing industry worldwide."[10] Figure 2.3 provides an illustration of Ben & Jerry's commitment to a mission statement.

When an organization decides on its mission, it really answers two questions: Who are our customers? and What is our core competency? Although these questions seem very simple, they are two of the most important questions any firm can answer. Defining these customers' needs and wants gives direction to what the company must do to satisfy them.

Creating or revising a mission statement is quite challenging because of the many complex variables that must be considered. Nonetheless, having a mission statement can benefit an organization in many ways. As demonstrated by Figure 2.3, Ben & Jerry's mission statement gives the organization a clear purpose and direction, distinguishes it from competitors, provides direction for strategic planning, and fosters a marketing orientation. A mission statement provides anyone associated with the organization, anywhere in the world, with an understanding of what the organization is about.

An organization's goals, derived from its mission statement, guide the remainder of its planning efforts. Goals focus on the end results sought by the organization. Ben & Jerry's mission statement, for example, incorporates the company's goals of striving for a high-quality product, a sound financial position, and community responsibility.

Organizations can have both short-term and long-term goals. Companies experiencing a crisis or a situation involving negative publicity may be forced to focus solely on the short-term decisions necessary to stay in business, such as increasing cash flow by lowering prices or selling off parts of the business. After a federal investigation accused Columbia/HCA of overcharging the government for health care services, the company was forced to take a short-term focus. It sold off much of its home health care division to generate funds to pay fines, thus ridding itself of a service related to the overbilling charges while attempting to avoid future problems.[11] Other organizations have more optimistic, long-term goals. McDonald's, for example, is focusing on repositioning the company in the highly competitive fast-food business through new and improved products. In many cases, companies that pursue long-term goals have to sacrifice short-term results to achieve them. Best Buy, the giant electronics retailer, sacrificed profits for a number of years so that it could expand and build larger stores than its competition to boost sales and gain a greater share of consumer spending on electronics. This strategy paid off as Best Buy became more profitable.

Developing Corporate and Business-Unit Strategies

In any organization, strategic planning begins at the corporate level and proceeds from there to the business-unit and marketing levels. Corporate strategy is the broadest of these three levels and should be developed with the organization's overall mission in mind. Business-unit strategy should be consistent with the corporate strategy, and marketing strategy should be consistent with both the business-unit and corporate strategies. The relationships between these planning levels are shown in Figure 2.4. Before we examine marketing strategy, we must first discuss the broader topics of corporate and business-unit strategy.

Corporate Strategy

corporate strategy
A strategy that determines the means for utilizing resources in the various functional areas to reach an organization's goals

Corporate strategy determines the means for utilizing resources in the functional areas of marketing, production, finance, research and development, and human resources to reach the organization's goals. A corporate strategy determines not only the scope of the business, but also its resource deployment, competitive advantages, and overall coordination of functional areas. It addresses the two questions posed in the organization's mission statement: Who are our customers? and What is our core

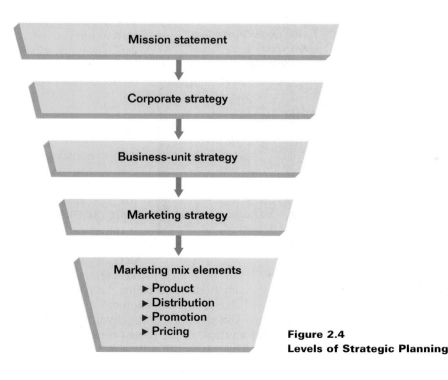

Figure 2.4
Levels of Strategic Planning

Figure 2.5
Corporate Strategy
Apple Computer has differentiated itself by providing unique products and creating a different corporate culture and image from its competitors.

competency? Figure 2.5 indicates that Apple Computer wants to "think different" and provide unique products in the computer industry. The term *corporate* in this context does not apply solely to corporations; corporate strategy is used by all organizations, from the smallest sole proprietorship to the largest multinational corporation.

Corporate strategy planners are concerned with broad issues such as corporate culture, competition, differentiation, diversification, interrelationships between business units, and environmental and social issues. They attempt to match the resources of the organization with the opportunities and threats in the environment. Corporate strategy planners are also concerned with defining the scope and role of the firm's business units so that they are coordinated to reach the ends desired. BMW, for example, purchased the Rolls-Royce brand name for $60 million because of its perceived value to auto buyers. In turn, BMW licensed Volkswagen to manufacture and sell Rolls-Royce cars.[12] The two companies' corporate planners are working together to take advantage of perceived broad market opportunities.

SNAPSHOT

What makes CEOs worry

Chief executives of some of the fastest-growing private companies say they can't afford to sit back and relax.

Competitors' strategies 18%

Managing people 17%

Keeping up with technology 13%

Copyright © 1999 *USA Today*, a division of Gannet Co., Inc.

strategic business unit (SBU) A division, product line, or other profit center within a parent company

Business-Unit Strategy

After analyzing corporate operations and performance, the next step in strategic planning is to determine future business directions and develop strategies for individual business units. A **strategic business unit (SBU)** is a division, product line, or other profit center within the parent company. Borden's strategic business units, for example, consist of dairy products, snacks, pasta, niche grocery products like ReaLemon juice and Cremora coffee creamer, and other units such as glue and paints. Each of these units sells a distinct set of products to an identifiable group of customers, and each competes with a well-defined set of competitors. The revenues, costs, investment, and strategic plans of each SBU can be separated from those of the parent company and evaluated. SBUs operate in a variety of markets, which have differing growth rates, opportunities, degrees of competition, and profit-making potential. From the perspective of corporate strategy, an SBU needs to be developed according to how well the company's skills and expertise fit with that unit's needs and success. In other words, can the corporate strategy contribute to the critical success factors of that unit?[13]

Portfolio Analysis. Strategic planners should recognize the different performance capabilities of each SBU and carefully allocate scarce resources among these divisions. Several tools allow a firm's portfolio of strategic business units, or even individual products, to be classified and visually displayed according to the attractiveness of various markets and the business's relative market share within those markets. A **market** is a group of individuals and/or organizations that have needs for products in a product class and have the ability, willingness, and authority to purchase these products. The percentage of a market that actually buys a specific product from a specific company is referred to as that product's (or business unit's) **market share.** Coca-Cola, for example, holds about 44 percent of the U.S. market for soft drinks, while its rival, PepsiCo, owns about 31 percent.[14]

One of the most helpful tools is the **market-growth/market-share matrix,** the Boston Consulting Group (BCG) approach, which is based on the philosophy that a product's market growth rate and its market share are important considerations in determining its marketing strategy. All the firm's SBUs and products should be integrated into a single, overall matrix and evaluated to determine appropriate strategies for individual products and overall portfolio strategies. Managers can use this model to determine and classify each product's expected future cash contributions and future cash requirements. Generally, managers who use this model should examine the competitive position of a product (or SBU) and the opportunities for improving that product's contribution to profitability and cash flow.[15] The BCG analytical approach is more of a diagnostic tool than a guide for making strategy prescriptions.

Figure 2.6, which is based on work by the BCG, enables the strategic planner to classify a firm's products into four basic types: stars, cash cows, dogs, and question marks.[16] *Stars* are products with a dominant share of the market and good prospects for growth. However, they use more cash than they generate to finance growth, add capacity, and increase market share. An example of a star might be Apple's recently introduced, Internet-friendly iMac computer. *Cash cows* have a dominant share of the market but low prospects for growth; typically, they generate more cash than is required to maintain market share. Oreos, the best-selling cookies in the United States, represent a cash cow for Nabisco. *Dogs* have a subordinate share of the market and low prospects for growth; these products are often found in established markets. Checkers, a fast-food chain that features twin drive-thru lanes is experiencing declining profits and market share and may be considered a dog relative to other fast-food chains with different formats. *Question marks,* sometimes called "problem children," have a small

---

market A group of individuals and/or organizations that have needs for products in a product class and have the ability, willingness, and authority to purchase these products

market share The percentage of a market that actually buys a specific product from a specific company

market-growth/market-share matrix A strategic planning tool based on the philosophy that a product's market growth rate and market share are important in determining marketing strategy

---

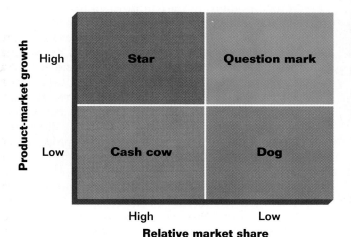

Figure 2.6
Growth-Share Matrix Developed by the Boston Consulting Group

Source: *Perspectives,* No. 66, "The Product Portfolio."
Reprinted by permission from The Boston Consulting Group, Inc., Boston, MA. Copyright © 1970.

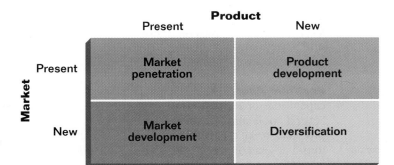

**Figure 2.7
Competitive Growth
Strategies**

Source: H.I. Ansoff, *New Corporate
Strategy* (New York: Wiley, 1988),
p. 109.

share of a growing market and generally require a large amount of cash to build market share. Mercedes mountain bikes, for example, are a question mark in comparison with Mercedes' automobile products.

The long-term health of an organization depends on having some products that generate cash (and provide acceptable profits) and others that use cash to support growth. Among the indicators of overall health are the size and vulnerability of the cash cows, the prospects for the stars, if any, and the number of question marks and dogs. Particular attention should be paid to those products with large cash appetites. Unless the company has an abundant cash flow, it cannot afford to sponsor many such products at one time. If resources, including debt capacity, are spread too thin, the company will end up with too many marginal products and will be unable to finance promising new product entries or acquisitions in the future.

Growth Strategies for Business Units.   Based on the analyses of each product or business unit, a firm may choose one or more competitive strategies, including intensive growth or diversified growth. Figure 2.7 shows these competitive strategies on a product-market matrix. This matrix can help in determining growth that can be implemented through marketing strategies.

intensive growth Growth occurring when current products and current markets have the potential for increasing sales

   Intensive growth can occur when current products and current markets have the potential for increasing sales. There are three main strategies for intensive growth: market penetration, market development, and product development. *Market penetration* is a strategy of increasing sales in current markets with current products. America Online (AOL), for example, increased its customer base from less than 1 million to 14 million by offering free service for limited time periods. *Market development* is a strategy of increasing sales of current products in new markets. Arm & Hammer, for instance, successfully introduced its baking soda, the firm's basic product, into new markets for use as a carpet deodorizer, as a freshener for litter boxes, and as a toothpaste. Market development also occurs whenever a company introduces its products into international markets for the first time. Although General Motors had to make minor modifications to the Saturn when it introduced the brand in Japan, the basic strategy was market development. Finally, *product development* is a strategy of increasing sales by improving present products or developing new products for current markets. Gillette, for example, developed a razor, the Mach3, which features three blades and other innovations to provide comfort and a smooth shave.[17] Perhaps the most common example of product development occurs in the automobile industry, in which car manufacturers regularly introduce redesigned or completely new models to their current markets. The 1999 Jeep Grand Cherokee was redesigned with a number of new performance features that significantly differentiated it from the 1998 model.

diversified growth
Growth occurring when new products are developed to be sold in new markets

   Diversified growth occurs when new products are developed to be sold in new markets. Firms have become increasingly diversified since the 1960s. J. C. Penney, for example, although best known for its chain of department stores and catalogs, has diversified into other retail markets with ownership of the Eckerd's drug store chain.[18] Diversification offers some advantages over single-business firms because it allows firms to spread their risk across a number of markets. Philip Morris has spread risk by diversifying with SBUs that include beer and food products, as well as cigarettes. More importantly, diversification allows firms to make better and wider use of their managerial, technical, and financial resources. Marketing expertise can be applied across businesses, which may also share advertising themes, distribution channels, warehouse facilities, and even sales forces.[19] Kimberly-Clark, which markets Kleenex tissues and Huggies diapers, was able to take advantage of this when it acquired Scott Paper Company, which also markets paper and tissue products.[20]

Developing a Marketing Strategy

The next phase in strategic planning is the development of sound strategies for each functional area of the organization. Within the marketing area, a strategy is typically designed around two components: (1) the selection of a target market and (2) the creation of a marketing mix that will satisfy the needs of the chosen target market. A marketing strategy articulates the best use of the firm's resources and tactics to achieve its marketing objectives. When properly implemented, a good marketing strategy also enables a company to achieve its business-unit and corporate objectives. While corporate, business-unit, and marketing strategies all overlap to some extent, the marketing strategy is the most detailed and specific of the three.

Target Market Selection

Selecting an appropriate target market may be the most important decision a company has to make in the planning process. This is so because the target market has to be chosen before the organization can adapt its marketing mix to meet this market's needs and preferences. As Figure 2.8 illustrates, Kellogg's has targeted children as an important market. Defining the target market and developing an appropriate marketing mix are the keys to strategic success. Alamo Rent-A-Car, for example, grew from a very small regional company to the nation's fourth-largest daily car rental company by defining its market as leisure travelers, while its major competitors focused on business travelers. Alamo introduced unlimited mileage and developed strong ties to travel agents and tour operators to dominate the leisure traveler market.[21] Should a company select the wrong target market, all other marketing decisions will be a waste of time. Checkers's strategy of having a twin drive-thru format and no inside dining area may have targeted a market too small to foster growth.

An organization should also examine whether it possesses the necessary resources and skills to create a marketing mix that will satisfy the needs of its target market. Organizations that do not possess the resources or skills to meet the needs of a particular target market are usually better off finding a different market to serve. Gateway Computers, for example, found that it did not have the resources to compete effectively with Dell Computer in the large corporate computer market, so it is focusing its resources on home and small business computer buyers.[22]

Accurate target market selection is crucial to productive marketing efforts. Products and even companies sometimes fail because marketers do not identify appropriate customer groups at whom to aim their efforts. Organizations that try to be all things to all people rarely satisfy the needs of any customer group very well. An organization's management should therefore designate which customer groups the firm is trying to serve and gather adequate information about

Figure 2.8
Selecting a Target Market
Kellogg's focuses on growing children as an important target market for its products.

Millions of growing

kids get nutrients they

need from a tiger.

Help yourself.
Kellogg's

these customers. AT&T, for example, developed for price-sensitive customers the OneRate calling card plan with a flat monthly access fee of $1.00 and a low per minute rate when competitors such as MCI and Sprint were charging access fees of up to 99 cents per call. This lowered the cost of using a calling card, giving AT&T a competitive advantage at that time. Identification and analysis of a target market provide a foundation on which a marketing mix can be developed.

Organizations should also choose their target markets carefully because of changes taking place in the U.S. population. Companies that have targeted baby boomers are finding that their market is aging. As they age, baby boomers are buying fewer products like homes and home furnishings and more products like financial services (for retirement) and health-related products. Building Customer Relationships describes how one firm is providing alternative programming to public radio stations to appeal to baby boomers. The population group just behind the baby boomers—aged 24 to 34 and usually referred to as Generation X—also creates many challenges and opportunities for marketers. Generation X represents a market of more than 47 million consumers and is more ethnically diverse than any previous generation. MCI has considered that in promoting its 1-800-COLLECT service, which is targeted directly at the Generation X market, for MCI's research has shown that 72 percent of all collect calls are made by people under the age of 34. In its advertising, MCI shows a diverse group of young people, along with the 1-800-COLLECT logo on everything from airborne blimps to graffiti on an inner-city wall. This type of advertising is intended to appeal to the ethnic diversity of this target market.[23]

When exploring possible target markets, marketing managers try to evaluate how entering them would affect the company's sales, costs, and profits. They assess whether the company has the resources to develop the right mix of product, price, promotion, and distribution to meet the needs of a particular target market. They also

BUILDING
customer relationships

World Radio Targets High-Income Listeners with New Programs

In an era of declining federal funding, rising programming costs, and increasing competition, public radio stations are searching for ways to distinguish themselves from their competitors and to provide greater customer satisfaction. World Radio, a national public radio network broadcasting from WRVG-FM in Georgetown, Kentucky, is attempting to accomplish these goals by offering programs that feature contemporary folk and acoustic music and up-to-the-minute news. The satellite-based network targets high-income professionals aged 25 to 54, especially baby boomer men. However, the station must satisfy not only its desired target market, but also affiliate stations that buy its programming and businesses that underwrite the cost of providing it.

To satisfy its target market, World Radio offers a hundred hours of live programming a week, including in-depth news coverage and a unique blend of music and dialogue. Its "Early World" program, for example, mixes blues, jazz, folk, funk, rock, and roots music with reviews, special features on artists, and interviews. Other programs include "Blues Party," "Society of Underground Poets," "Grateful Dead Hour," and "Culture Shock."

World Radio provides affiliates with affordable, original programming underwritten by corporate and foundation sponsors. Public radio stations that subscribe to the World Radio network pay just $375 for the first year and get as many programs as they want. The payment system is designed to help minimize the financial burden public radio stations face. Other public radio networks, including National Public Radio (NPR) and Public Radio International (PRI), assess an annual fee and also impose charges that vary by program and individual market.

World Radio provides underwriters with an affordable vehicle to reach a somewhat younger segment of the traditional public radio audience. In exchange for their donations, underwriters are mentioned on-air as supporters. These announcements, which cost $200 on World Radio, could cost a firm $2,000 on NPR's popular "Morning Edition" news show. Additionally, the network, through its Web site, offers links to underwriters and affiliate station sites.

Executives from World Radio believe they have found a way to "boldly reinvent" public radio to satisfy the changing needs of public radio stations, their listeners, and underwriters. As one radio station manager says, "So much of public radio is predictable and cut from the same cloth, it would be nice to have anybody experiment in a way that would create new models for us."

Table 2.1   Matching the Marketing Mix to Intensive Growth Strategies

Business-Unit Strategy	Marketing Strategy	Marketing Mix			
		Product	Pricing	Distribution	Promotion
Market Penetration	Increase sales of brand X	Increase quality	Lower prices	Make available at more outlets	Offer coupons; advertise new prices
	Increase sales in the 18–29 age group	Add features desired by this segment	Lower prices	Make available in outlets visited by this segment	Target advertising to this group via media selection
Market Development	Find new uses for the product; seek out new markets; move into global markets	Conduct research to discover new uses; add features desired by new markets	Changes will depend on new uses and new markets	Seek distribution outlets in new markets; find global distribution partners	Educate consumers on new uses via advertising; create new advertising appeals for new markets
Product Development	Improve existing products or develop new products	Invest in consumer research and product development	Increase prices on improved products	New products will require shelf space; gain the cooperation of retailers	Educate consumers on improvements; use advertising sales promotion to introduce new products

determine if satisfying those needs is consistent with the firm's overall objectives and mission. When Amazon.com, the number-one Internet bookseller, began selling music CDs on its Web site, it made the decision that efforts to target music buyers would increase profits and be consistent with its objectives in the book market.[24] The size and number of competitors already marketing products in possible target markets are of concern as well.

Creating the Marketing Mix

The selection of a target market serves as the basis for creating a marketing mix to satisfy the needs of that market. The decisions made in creating a marketing mix are only as good as the organization's understanding of the target market. This understanding typically comes from careful, in-depth research into the characteristics of the target market. Thus, while demographic information is important, the organization should also analyze customer needs, preferences, and behavior with respect to product design, pricing, distribution, and promotion. After research indicated that 60 to 75 percent of all customer transactions at mutual fund companies no longer involve a sales representative, companies like Fidelity and Vanguard developed easy-to-navigate Web sites that provide customers with information and allow them to conduct transactions online.[25] This not only lowers the prices charged for transactions and the cost of promotion, but also makes product information more available and services more accessible.

Marketing mix decisions should also have two other characteristics: consistency and flexibility. All marketing mix decisions should be consistent with the business-unit and corporate strategies. This consistency allows the organization to achieve its objectives on all three levels of planning. Flexibility, on the other hand, permits the organization to alter the marketing mix in response to changes in market conditions, competition, and customer needs. Gucci Group, a marketer of high-fashion products, achieved a company turnaround through improved consistency and flexibility. The company ensured that its brand had the same image and proper display around the world, and to be more competitive, it lowered prices for items like handbags.[26]

Table 2.1 offers some examples of how the marketing mix can be altered to match business-unit and marketing strategies for intensive growth. In market penetration, the goal of all marketing efforts is to increase sales of a particular brand or to increase sales within a specific target market segment. Figure 2.9 illustrates that makers of kitchen and laundry appliances focus on product features to increase sales. Some of the most common marketing mix decisions aimed at increasing sales volume include making the product more desirable, lowering prices, expanding the product's distribution, and engaging in promotion activities. For example, General Mills added X's to Cheerios, its O-shaped cereal, for a short time to help increase sales of the brand. The company also placed a detachable game board on the back of the cereal box so that consumers could use the X and O shapes to play games. This change in product design was the first for Cheerios since it was introduced in 1941.[27]

Different elements of the marketing mix can be adapted to accommodate different marketing strategies. The strategy of market development, for example, often involves moving into global markets in an effort to expand market share. One of the most important marketing decisions in global markets is the choice of distribution channels. In some cases, U.S. companies create partnerships with foreign companies to gain access to distribution networks. This is precisely what Anheuser-Busch did when it formed a joint venture with the Kirin Brewery, Japan's number-one beer maker, which has an extensive distribution network already in place. By forging an alliance with Kirin, Anheuser-Busch can move into foreign distribution more quickly and efficiently. Anheuser-Busch has plans to become the first foreign brewer to establish its own distribution network in Japan.[28] Tech*know describes one firm's efforts to modify its marketing mix by using a product development strategy.

Organizations should always strive to create very strong marketing mixes. The success of the marketing mix depends on the combination of all four elements. Each of the marketing mix elements must work together with the others. Pricing efforts, for example, should complement the overall marketing strategy by sending a message that reinforces the company's desired product image. Automobile companies have used large rebates or coupons for $1,000 off the sticker price of a new car to boost sales. The impact of such discounts on long-term customer relationships and coordination with other elements of the marketing unit is a major consideration in marketing strategy.[29] A company needs to assess its customers to discover how they value its product in order to make sound pricing, promotion, and distribution decisions.[30] When Hewlett-Packard introduced the PhotoSmart C20 digital camera, it entered a new market for digital photography. The product's marketing mix had to communi-

Figure 2.9
Using Product Features to Increase Sales
Makers of kitchen and laundry appliances focus on product features to increase sales.

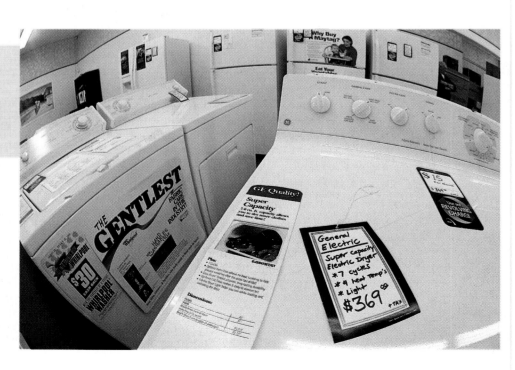

cate how this new system, which costs $700, provides digital snapshots that are easy to transfer to computers and to E-mail to friends. If one marketing mix element is improperly matched to the others or to the target market, the product is likely to fail.

Creating the Marketing Plan

marketing planning The process of assessing opportunities and resources, determining objectives, defining strategies, and establishing guidelines for implementation and control of the marketing program

A major concern in the strategic planning process is **marketing planning,** the systematic process of assessing marketing opportunities and resources, determining marketing objectives, defining marketing strategies, and establishing guidelines for implementation and control of the marketing program. The outcome of marketing planning is the development of a marketing plan. As noted earlier, a marketing plan is a written document that outlines and explains all the activities necessary to implement marketing strategies. It describes the firm's current position or situation, establishes marketing objectives for the product or product group, and specifies how the organization will attempt to achieve these objectives.

Marketing plans vary with respect to the time period they cover. Generally, short-range plans are for one year or less. Moderate-range plans cover periods of more than one year but less than five years. Both types of plans are usually quite detailed. Long-range plans cover periods of more than five years, perhaps up to fifteen years, and are

Tech*know

Gibson Greetings Embraces Technology with New Products

Gibson Greetings was founded in 1850 as a printer of labels and postage stamps. It soon branched out into greeting cards and was responsible for the famous "Gibson Girls" cards of the 1890s. Today, the Cincinnati-based firm markets everyday, special occasion, alternative market, and seasonal greeting cards, as well as gift wraps, party goods, candles, and related specialty products. However, the firm lags behind Hallmark and American Greetings in the U.S. greeting card market. With industry sales flat in recent years, all three firms have looked for ways to extend their product lines to appeal to a broader variety of buyers. Gibson is pursuing a strategy of fostering relationships by developing new products with entertainment value.

One of the company's most significant developments is the E-greetings Network, a Web site (www.egreetings.com) from which customers can send electronic Gibson greeting cards via E-mail for free. E-greetings are illustrated or animated postcards that customers can use to enliven their online communications. Some cards even have sound. Internet users can choose a card from a large selection and then personalize them with individual messages. Because of licensing arrangements, many of the cards feature characters from popular cartoons, tele-vision shows, and movies, including *King of the Hill, Austin Powers,* and the *Star Trek* films.

Another new product line offered by Gibson is Silly Slammers, colorful hand-sized "beanbags with an attitude." When dropped or thrown against a hard surface, they say humorous things. For example, the Boss Slammer, from the Office Group, says things like "You're fired!" and "Blah blah blah!" Other Silly Slammers relate to sports and characters that spout off hip phrases today's children can relate to. The $7 toys are distributed through such retail outlets as Toys "R" Us, Target, Wal-Mart, and 7-Eleven.

E-greetings and Silly Slammers represent a change in strategy that began with the arrival of new chairman, president, and CEO Fran O'Connell in 1996. O'Connell has helped shift Gibson Greetings from a traditional greeting card firm into an entertainment company. The Slammers, in particular, have been a success; Gibson sold more than 13 million in one year, to adults as well as children. With products like E-greetings and Silly Slammers, Gibson hopes to continue expanding beyond the boundaries of a traditional greeting card company to market products relevant to today's consumers.

usually not as specific. Marketing managers may have short-, medium-, and long-range plans all at the same time. Long-range plans are relatively rare. However, as the marketing environment continues to change and business decisions become more complex, profitability and survival will depend more and more on the development of long-range plans.[31]

The extent to which marketing managers develop and use plans also varies. A firm should have a plan for each marketing strategy it develops. Because such plans must be modified as forces in the firm and in the environment change, marketing planning is a continuous process. Figure 2.10 illustrates the marketing planning cycle, which is a circular process. As the feedback lines in the figure indicate, planning is not unidirectional. Feedback is used to coordinate and synchronize all stages of the planning cycle.

Developing a clear, well-written marketing plan, though time-consuming, is important. The plan is the basis for internal communication among employees. It covers the assignment of responsibilities and tasks, as well as schedules for implementation. It presents objectives and specifies how resources are to be allocated to achieve these objectives. Finally, it helps marketing managers monitor and evaluate the performance of a marketing strategy.

Although planning provides numerous benefits, some managers do not use formal marketing plans because they spend almost all their time focusing on daily problems, many of which would be eliminated by adequate planning. However, planning is becoming more important to marketing managers, who realize that planning is necessary to develop, coordinate, and control marketing activities effectively and efficiently. When formulating a marketing plan, a new enterprise or a firm with a new product does not have current performance to evaluate or an existing plan to revise. Therefore, its marketing planning centers on analyzing available resources and options to assess opportunities. Managers can then develop marketing objectives and a strategy for achieving them. In addition, many firms recognize the need to include

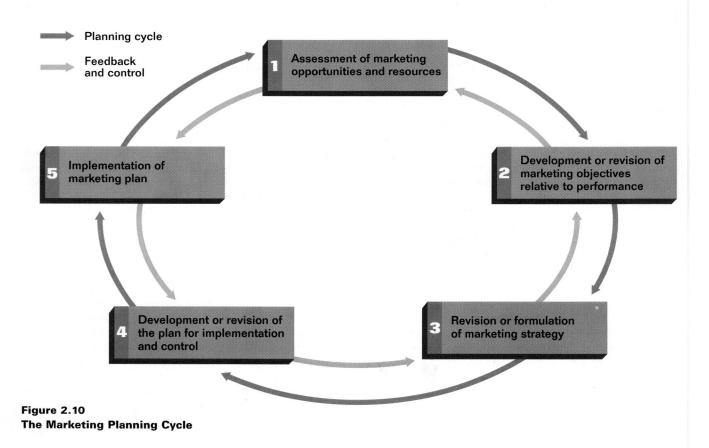

Figure 2.10
The Marketing Planning Cycle

Table 2.2	**Components of the Marketing Plan**
I. Executive Summary	V. Marketing Strategies
	A. Target market
II. Environmental Analysis	B. Marketing mix
A. The marketing environment	
B. Target market(s)	VI. Marketing Implementation
C. Current marketing objectives and performance	A. Marketing organization
	B. Activities and responsibilities
	C. Implementation timetable
III. SWOT Analysis	
A. Strengths and weaknesses	VII. Evaluation and Control
B. Opportunities and threats	A. Performance standards
	B. Financial controls
IV. Marketing Objectives	C. Monitoring procedures (audits)

 information systems in their plans so that they can have continuous feedback and keep their marketing activities oriented toward objectives. When Barnes & Noble developed a Web site for selling books online, its information system had to provide adequate feedback on opportunities, the resources needed for entering the online market, and the impact of online sales on store sales. (Information systems are discussed in Chapter 6.)

Components of the Marketing Plan

Organizations use many different formats when devising marketing plans. Plans may be written for strategic business units, product lines, individual products or brands, or specific markets. Most plans share some common ground, however, by including many of the same components (see Table 2.2). In the following sections, we consider the major parts of a typical marketing plan, as well as the purpose that each part serves.

Executive Summary.   The executive summary is a synopsis (often just one or two pages) of the entire marketing plan. It includes an introduction, an explanation of the major aspects of the plan, and a statement about the costs of implementing the plan. The executive summary does not provide detailed information but rather gives an overview of the plan so that readers can identify key issues pertaining to their roles in the planning and implementation process.[32]

The executive summary is one of the most important parts of the marketing plan because it is often furnished to people outside the organization. It may, for example, be useful to the organization's financial institution when it becomes involved in the financial aspects of the marketing plan. Suppliers or investors who play a pivotal role in implementing the plan may also be given access to the executive summary.

Environmental Analysis.   The environmental analysis supplies information about the company's current situation with respect to the marketing environment, the target market, and the firm's current objectives and performance. The first section of the environmental analysis is an assessment of all the external environmental factors—competitive, economic, political, legal and regulatory, technological, and sociocultural—that can affect marketing activities. (We examine the complexities and interactions of these factors in Chapter 3.) In addition, this section should include information about such internal environmental matters as the firm's current culture, the availability and deployment of human resources, the age and capacity of equipment or technology, and the availability of financial resources.

In the second section of the environmental analysis, the organization should examine the current status of its target markets. This section assesses the current needs of each target market, anticipated changes in these needs, and how well the organization's

Science is helping us
all live longer.
What a great time
to develop a
customer loyalty
program.

It's every marketer's dream to keep customers for life.
How convenient that science and Direct Mail are both
working to make your dream a long lasting reality.

Direct Mail is an effective way of building and nurturing
relationships. It lets you speak to people as individuals, and
provide them with relevant and timely information. In fact,
Direct Mail has been acknowledged as one of the best
ways to educate a consumer about complex issues.
And it lets you update and adapt your message, as
the wants and needs of your customers change.

It also gives you the space to tell your whole story.
Even if it's quite a long story. Because, thanks to science,
your customers probably aren't going anywhere, anytime soon.

For a free kit filled with information, examples and ideas
on how adding Direct Mail to your media mix can help build
your business, call 1-800-THE-USPS, ext DMXXXX.

Fly Like an Eagle.™

UNITED STATES POSTAL SERVICE®
www.usps.com

Figure 2.11
Environmental Analysis:
Assessing the Target
Market's Needs
The United States Postal
Service promotes its
services for direct mail
to a target market—
businesses who want to
reach their customers.

products are meeting these needs. In Figure 2.11 the United States Postal Service targets business customers who need to reach their own target markets. In assessing its target markets, the firm should try to understand all relevant customer behavior variables and product usage statistics. Knowing, for example, that about 90 percent of children's product requests to a parent are by brand name helps marketers to better understand the potential influence of children on their parents' spending.[33] Marketing-oriented organizations should know their customers well enough to have access to this type of information. Organizations that do not have this information may have to conduct marketing research to fully understand their current target markets.

The final aspect of environmental analysis is a critical evaluation of the firm's current marketing objectives and performance. All organizations should periodically examine their marketing objectives to ensure these objectives remain consistent with the changing marketing environment. This analysis yields important input for later stages of the marketing plan. The organization should also evaluate its current performance with respect to changes in the environment and the target markets. Poor or declining performance may be the result of holding on to marketing objectives that do not consider the current realities of the marketing environment. Apple Computer, for example, experienced a major decline in its market share for personal computers when it established objectives that were not realistic in the dynamic environment of the computer industry. Consumer acceptance of Microsoft's Windows operating system advanced rapidly, and this competitive force made Apple's objective of increasing the market for its own operating system impossible to fulfill. Apple's objectives for the iMac computer may prove more realistic.

The information needed for environmental analysis is obtained from both the internal and external environments, usually through the firm's marketing information system. However, if the required information is not available, it may have to be collected through marketing research. The environmental analysis phase is one of the most difficult parts of the marketing plan and often illustrates the need for an ongoing effort at collecting and organizing environmental data. Having this sort of information readily available makes the other parts of the marketing plan easier to develop.

SWOT analysis
Assessment of an organization's strengths, weaknesses, opportunities, and threats

strengths   Competitive advantages or core competencies that give a firm an advantage in meeting the needs of its target markets

weaknesses   Any limitations a company might face in developing or implementing a marketing strategy

opportunities   Favorable conditions in the environment that could produce rewards for an organization if acted upon properly

threats   Conditions or barriers that may prevent a firm from reaching its objectives

SWOT Analysis.   The **SWOT analysis** assesses an organization's strengths, weaknesses, opportunities, and threats (SWOT). These factors are derived from the environmental analysis in the preceding portion of the marketing plan.

The analysis of strengths and weaknesses focuses on internal factors that give an organization certain advantages and disadvantages in meeting the needs of its target markets. **Strengths** refer to competitive advantages or core competencies that give the firm an advantage in meeting the needs of its target markets. Any analysis of company strengths should be customer-focused because strengths are meaningful only when they assist the firm in meeting customer needs. For instance, a company may possess a highly trained and capable sales force, which would be considered a major strength in many industries. However, if product quality is poor relative to competitors', a good sales force may do little to help satisfy customer needs. Strengths are usually related to core competencies that provide a competitive advantage. John Deere, for example, promotes its service, experience, and reputation in the farm equipment business to emphasize the craftsmanship it uses in its lawn tractors and mowers for city dwellers.

Weaknesses refer to any limitations a company might face in developing or implementing a marketing strategy. PepsiCo, with fewer resources than the Coca-Cola Company, has found it difficult to expand in the fountain market, which includes restaurants, theaters, and sports arenas, where Coca-Cola holds two-thirds of the market.[34] Weaknesses should also be examined from a customer perspective because customers often perceive weaknesses that a company cannot see. Apple Computer's operating system became a weakness when the computer industry went to a Windows standard, but the strong loyalty of its customers remains a key strength.

Taking a customer-oriented approach toward the analysis of strengths and weaknesses does not mean that strengths and weaknesses that are not customer-oriented should be forgotten. Rather, it suggests that all firms should tie their strengths and weaknesses to customer requirements. Only those strengths that relate to satisfying customers should be considered true competitive advantages. Likewise, weaknesses that directly affect customer satisfaction should be considered competitive disadvantages.

The second section of the SWOT analysis examines the opportunities and threats that exist in the environment. Both opportunities and threats exist independently of the firm. They can, however, greatly affect its operations. The way to differentiate a strength or weakness from an opportunity or threat is to ask, Would this issue exist if the company did not exist? If the answer is yes, then the issue should be considered external to the firm.[35] Because opportunities and threats are external to the firm, they represent issues to be considered by all organizations, even those that do not compete with the firm.

Opportunities refer to favorable conditions in the environment that could produce rewards for the organization if acted upon properly. That is, opportunities are situations that exist but must be acted upon if the firm is to benefit from them. Amazon.com, for example, acted quickly when new technology made it possible to sell books on the Internet. **Threats,** on the other hand, refer to conditions or barriers that may prevent the firm from reaching its objectives. For instance, Barnes & Noble's launching of a Web site to sell books represented a threat to Amazon.com. Like opportunities, threats must be acted upon to prevent them from limiting the capabilities of the organization.

Opportunities and threats can stem from many sources within the environment. When a competitor's introduction of a new product threatens a firm, a defensive strategy may be required. If the firm can develop and launch a new product that meets or exceeds the competition's offering, it can transform the threat into an opportunity.[36] Because of competition from low-cost carriers such as Southwest Airlines, Delta Airlines has dramatically cut costs and is even launching a no-frills service to compete directly with its discount competitors. In fact, discount airlines are advancing steadily in 60 percent of Delta's markets. Although some Delta customers complain that service and on-time performance are declining, the competitive threat of discounters requires that Delta move quickly to maintain its markets.[37]

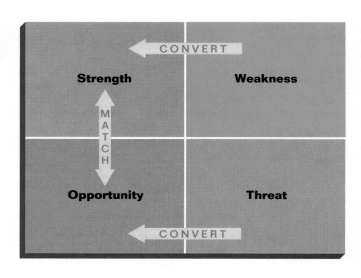

Figure 2.12
The Four-Cell SWOT Matrix
Source: Adapted from Nigel F. Piercy,
Market-Led Strategic Change,
Copyright © 1992 Butterworth-
Heinemann Ltd., p. 371. Used with
permission.

Figure 2.12 depicts a four-cell SWOT matrix that can help managers in the planning process. When an organization matches internal strengths to external opportunities, it creates competitive advantages in meeting the needs of its customers. In addition, an organization should act to convert internal weaknesses into strengths and external threats into opportunities. Toyota and Nissan converted the threats posed by luxury automobiles into opportunities when they introduced the Lexus and Infiniti, respectively. A firm that lacks adequate marketing skills can hire outside consultants to help convert a weakness into a strength.

The SWOT analysis framework has gained widespread acceptance because it is both a simple and powerful tool for marketing strategy development. However, like any planning tool, SWOT is only as good as the information it contains. Thorough marketing research and accurate information systems are essential if the SWOT analysis is to identify key issues in the environment.

marketing objective
A statement of what is to be accomplished through marketing activities

Marketing Objectives.   This section of the marketing plan delineates the marketing objectives that underlie the plan. A **marketing objective** states what is to be accomplished through marketing activities. A marketing objective of Ritz Carlton Hotels, for example, is to have 92 percent of its customers indicate they had a memorable experience at the hotel.[38] Marketing objectives should be based on a careful study of the SWOT analysis and should relate to matching strengths to opportunities and/or the conversion of weaknesses or threats. These objectives can be stated in terms of product introduction, product improvement or innovation, sales volume, profitability, market share, pricing, distribution, advertising, or employee training activities.

Marketing objectives should possess certain characteristics. First, a marketing objective should be expressed in clear, simple terms so that all marketing personnel understand exactly what they are trying to achieve. Second, an objective should be written so that it can be measured accurately. This allows the organization to determine if and when the objective has been achieved. If a company has an objective of increasing market share by 10 percent, the firm should be able to measure market share changes accurately. Third, a marketing objective should specify a time frame for its accomplishment. A firm that sets an objective of introducing a new product should state the time period in which this is to be done. Finally, a marketing objective should be consistent with both business-unit and corporate strategy. This ensures that the firm's mission is carried out at all levels of the organization. General Motors, for example, may have an overall marketing objective of maintaining a 31 percent share of the U.S. auto market. To achieve this objective, some GM divisions may have to increase market share while the shares of other divisions decline.

Marketing Strategies.   This section of the marketing plan outlines how the firm will achieve its marketing objectives. As already noted, marketing strategy consists of target market selection and the development of a marketing mix. In a broader sense, however, marketing strategy refers to how the firm will manage its relationships with customers so that it gains an advantage over the competition.

Can you bring that smile to Mom's face, too? You bet you can, with DigitalDNA™ technology. Seats and engine controls that know it's her. A GPS system that helps her steer away from traffic jams. Even that amazing innovation your engineers are working on right this minute. Make her happy with a car that's loaded with features that are smarter, more convenient, and easier to use.

Find out what consumers want and how DigitalDNA can boost your brand. Visit us online at www.digitaldna.motorola.com for the "S.M.A.R.T. Story: What Consumers Want."

Digital DNA
from Motorola
IT'S HERE.

Figure 2.13
Marketing Strategies:
The First Step
Motorola and The Big Mountain focus on specific target markets. Automobile makers would use DigitalDNA embedded solutions to enhance driving experience. Thrill-seeking skiers would be attracted to The Big Mountain.

You may only catch air for a few seconds, but your soul could take weeks to land.

booketh your reservations: 1-800-858-4152 www.bigmtn.com

THE BIG MOUNTAIN
Whitefish, Montana

sustainable competitive advantage An advantage that cannot be copied by the competition

Target market selection is the first stage of this process. The marketing plan should clearly define target markets in terms of demographics, geography, psychological profiles, product usage, and so on. This step is crucial because to develop a marketing mix that can satisfy customer needs, a marketer must understand those needs. In developing a marketing mix, the firm should determine how the elements of the mix—product, distribution, promotion, and price—will work together to satisfy the needs of the target market. Figure 2.13 illustrates two companies who have identified completely different target markets.

It is at the marketing mix level that a firm details how it will achieve a competitive advantage. To gain an advantage, the firm must do something better than its competition. In other words, its products must be of higher quality, its prices must be consistent with the level of quality (value), its distribution methods must be efficient and cost as little as possible, and its promotion must be more effective than the competition's. It is also important that the firm attempt to make these advantages sustainable. A **sustainable competitive advantage** is one that cannot be copied by the competition. Wal-Mart, for example, maintains a sustainable competitive advantage over Kmart because of its very efficient and low-cost distribution system. This advantage allows Wal-Mart to offer lower prices. However, Kmart has a sustainable advantage over Wal-Mart in terms of store locations. Since Kmart stores were in most urban areas before Wal-Mart began moving from rural areas, Kmart stores are typically in better and more convenient locations. In fact, location is often referred to as the most sustainable competitive advantage because it is almost impossible for competitors to change or copy it.[39]

Marketing Implementation.   This section of the marketing plan outlines how the marketing strategies will be implemented by answering many of the questions about the marketing activities outlined in the preceding section. What specific actions will be taken? How will these activities be performed? When will these activities be performed? Who is responsible for the completion of these activities? And how much will these activities cost? Without a workable plan for implementation, the success of the marketing strategy is in jeopardy. For this reason, the implementation phase of the marketing plan is just as important as any previous phase.

Because implementation is so important, we devote all of Chapter 22 to a discussion of issues in marketing implementation. In that discussion, we examine how the organization of the marketing function affects the implementation of marketing strategy. We also consider the importance of employees to marketing implementation. When discussing implementation, it is important to remember this fact: organizations do not implement strategies; people do. Thus, Chapter 22 addresses employee motivation, communication, and training as key factors in the implementation of marketing strategy.

Evaluation and Control.   The final section of the marketing plan details how the results of the plan will be measured and evaluated. The control phase of this section includes the actions that can be taken to reduce the differences between planned and actual performance. First, standards for assessing the actual performance need to be established. These standards can be based on increases in sales volume, profitability, or market share. They can even be advertising standards, such as brand name recognition or recall. The second part of the control process deals with the financial data that can be used to evaluate whether the marketing plan is working. If the marketing plan is not living up to expectations, the firm can use a number of monitoring procedures to pinpoint potential causes for the discrepancies. One such procedure is the marketing audit, which can help isolate weaknesses in the marketing plan and recommend actions to help improve performance. Because evaluation and control procedures are directly related to marketing implementation, they are discussed in detail in Chapter 22.

Using the Marketing Plan

The creation and implementation of a complete marketing plan will allow the organization to achieve not only its marketing objectives, but its business-unit and corporate goals as well. It is important to understand, however, that a marketing plan is only as good as the information it contains and the effort and creativity that went into its development. Thus, the importance of having a good marketing information system cannot be overstated. Equally important is the role of managerial judgment throughout the strategic planning process. Managers should always weigh any information against its accuracy and their own intuition when making marketing decisions. For example, Jill E. Barad, chairman and chief executive of Mattel Inc., is acutely tuned to planning efforts and her own insights about style, packaging, and consumer tastes related to products like Barbie and Hot Wheels.[40]

We should also note that the marketing plan outline in Table 2.2 should serve as a structure for the written document rather than as a series of sequential planning steps. In actual practice, many of the elements in the outline are decided on simultaneously. For example, the actual development of marketing strategies should take into account how those strategies will be implemented. This is one of the realities of marketing planning discussed in Chapter 22. It is also important to realize that most organizations have their own unique format and terminology to describe the marketing plan. For that reason, the outline in Table 2.2 should not be regarded as the only correct format for the creation of a marketing plan. Every marketing plan is and should be unique to the organization for which it was created.

While the creation of a marketing plan is an important milestone in strategic planning, it is by no means the final step. Some of the information used to create the plan may turn out to be inaccurate. Many of the managerial assumptions or projections used in the analysis often turn out differently when the plan is put into practice. These realities underscore the need to make the marketing plan flexible enough so that it can be adjusted on a daily basis. They also highlight the need for good environmental analysis, to which we turn our attention in the next chapter.

Summary

Through the process of strategic planning, a firm establishes an organizational mission and goals, corporate strategy, marketing objectives, marketing strategy, and, finally, a marketing plan. To achieve its marketing objectives, an organization must develop a marketing strategy, which includes identifying and analyzing a target market and developing a marketing mix that meets the needs of customers in that target market. The strategic planning process ultimately yields the framework for a marketing plan, which is a written document that specifies the activities to be performed to implement and control an organization's marketing activities.

The strategic planning process begins with an analysis of the marketing environment, including economic, competitive, political, legal and regulatory, sociocultural, and technological forces. These environmental forces affect the resources a firm can acquire. They can also create favorable opportunities. Resources include core competencies, things a firm does extremely well, sometimes so well that it gives the company an advantage over its competition. When the right combination of circumstances and timing permits an organization to take action to reach a particular target market, a market opportunity exists. Strategic windows are temporary periods of optimum fit between the key requirements of a market and the particular capabilities of a firm competing in that market. When a company matches a core competency to opportunities it has discovered in the marketplace, it is said to have a competitive advantage.

The goals of any organization should be derived from its mission statement, which is a long-term view, or vision, of what the organization wants to become. The mission statement answers two questions: Who are our customers? and What is our core competency? A well-formulated mission statement gives an organization a clear purpose and direction, distinguishes it from competitors, provides direction for strategic planning, and fosters an organizationwide focus on customers. An organization's short- and long-term goals, which focus on the end results sought, guide the remainder of its planning efforts.

Corporate strategy determines the means for utilizing resources in the functional areas of production, finance, research and development, human resources, and marketing to reach the organization's goals. Corporate strategy planners are concerned with broad issues such as corporate culture, competition, differentiation, diversification, interrelationships between business units, and environmental and social issues. They attempt to match the resources of the organization with the opportunities and threats in the environment.

After developing a corporate strategy, the next step in strategic planning involves a consideration of individual business units. A strategic business unit (SBU) is a division, product line, or other profit center within the parent company. A market is a group of individuals and/or organizations that have needs for products in a product class and have the ability, willingness, and authority to purchase these products. The percentage of a market that actually buys a specific product from a specific company is referred to as that product's market share. The Boston Consulting Group's market-growth/market-share matrix is a strategic planning tool based on the philosophy that a product's market growth rate and its market share are key factors influencing marketing strategy. It integrates a firm's products or SBUs into a single, overall matrix and evaluates them to determine appropriate strategies for individual products and overall portfolio strategies. Organizations can pursue a number of business-unit strategies to aid in the marketing of each SBU or product within its target markets. Strategies for intensive growth, which occurs when current products and current markets have the potential for increasing sales, include market penetration, market development, and product development. Diversified growth occurs when new products are developed to be sold in new markets.

While corporate, business-unit, and marketing strategies all overlap to some extent, the marketing strategy is the most detailed and specific of the three. Marketing strategy is typically composed of two elements: the selection of a target market and the creation of a marketing mix that will satisfy the needs of the chosen target market. Selecting an appropriate target market may be the most important decision a company has to make in the planning process because it serves as the basis for creating a marketing mix to satisfy the needs of that market. When exploring possible target markets, marketing managers try to evaluate how entering them would affect the company's sales, costs, and profits. Marketing mix decisions should be consistent with business-unit and corporate strategies; they should also be flexible enough to respond to changes in market conditions, competition, and customer needs. Different elements of the marketing mix can be changed to accommodate different marketing strategies.

Marketing planning is the systematic process of assessing marketing opportunities and resources, determining marketing objectives, defining marketing strategies, and establishing guidelines for implementation and control of the marketing program. The outcome of marketing planning is the development of a marketing plan, which outlines and explains all the activities necessary to implement marketing strategies. Short-range marketing plans cover one year or less; medium-range plans, one to five years; and long-range plans, more than five years. A firm should have a plan for each marketing strategy it develops. The marketing plan fosters internal communication among employees, assigns responsibilities and schedules, presents objectives, specifies how resources are to be allocated to achieve objectives, and helps marketing managers monitor and evaluate the performance of a marketing strategy.

Most marketing plans include many of the same components. The executive summary is a synopsis of the entire plan. The environmental analysis supplies information about the company's current situation with respect to the marketing environment, the target market, and the firm's current objectives and performance. The SWOT analysis assesses an organization's strengths, weaknesses, opportunities, and threats. The marketing objectives section states what is to be accomplished through marketing activities. The section on marketing strategies outlines how the firm will achieve its marketing objectives and achieve a competitive advantage, preferably a sustainable one that cannot be copied by the competition. The implementation section specifies how marketing strategies will be implemented by answering many of the questions about the marketing activities outlined in the marketing strategies section. Most marketing plans also detail how the results of the plan will be measured and evaluated.

A marketing plan is only as good as the information it contains and the effort and creativity that went into its development. Therefore, good marketing information systems and managerial judgment are important factors in creating a complete and workable marketing plan. Every marketing plan should be unique to the organization for which it is created. It should also be flexible enough to be adjusted on a daily basis.

Important Terms

Strategic planning	Mission statement	Market-growth/market-share matrix	Strengths
Marketing strategy	Corporate strategy		Weaknesses
Marketing plan	Strategic business unit (SBU)	Intensive growth	Opportunities
Core competencies		Diversified growth	Threats
Market opportunity	Market	Market planning	Marketing objective
Strategic windows	Market share	SWOT analysis	Sustainable competitive advantage
Competitive advantage			

Discussion and Review Questions

1. Identify the major components of strategic planning, and explain how they are interrelated.

2. What are the two major parts of a marketing strategy?

3. What are some of the issues that should be considered in analyzing a firm's resources and opportunities? How do these issues affect marketing objectives and marketing strategy?

4. Describe the benefits of a good mission statement. What role does the mission statement play in strategic planning?

5. Explain how an organization can create a competitive advantage at the corporate, business-unit, and marketing strategy levels.

6. Give examples of intensive and diversified growth strategies that are being used by today's firms. Which strategy appears to be the most effective in today's environment? Why?

7. Describe the role of the marketing plan in developing marketing strategy. How important is the SWOT analysis to the marketing planning process?

8. How should organizations set marketing objectives?

9. Refer to question 5. How can an organization make its competitive advantages sustainable over time? How difficult is it to create sustainable competitive advantages?

10. What benefits do marketing managers gain from planning? Is planning necessary for long-run survival? Why or why not?

Application Questions

1. Organizational goals are necessary for a firm to achieve success in a dynamic marketing environment. Contact three companies or organizations that appear to be successful. Talk with one of the managers or executives in the company, and ask if he or she would share with you the company's mission statement or organizational goals. Obtain as much information as possible about the statement and the organizational goals. Discuss how the statement matches the criteria outlined in the text.

2. Short-term goals help a firm reach its long-term goals. Assume that you own a new family-style restaurant that will open for business in the next year. Formulate a long-term goal for the company, and then develop short-term goals that will assist you in achieving the long-term goal.

3. The QVC home shopping network identified an opportunity to capitalize on a desire of many consumers to shop at home. This strategic window gave the network a very competitive position in a new

market. Consider the opportunities that may be present in your city, region, or the United States as a whole. Identify a strategic window, and discuss how a company could take advantage of this opportunity. What kind of core competencies are necessary?

4. The selection of a target market may be one of the most important decisions a marketer makes. McDonald's has been very successful in identifying and satisfying the needs of its target market. Identify the target market of each of the following companies:

a. American Express
b. Nike
c. Walt Disney
d. CompuServe

Internet Exercise & Resources

Sony: The Internet and Corporate Strategy

Internet analysts have praised Sony's Web site as one of the best organized and most informative on the Internet. See why by accessing

www.sony.com

1. Based on the information provided at the Web site, describe Sony's strategic business units.

2. Based on your existing knowledge of Sony as an innovative leader in the consumer electronics industry, describe the company's primary competitive advantage. How does Sony's online home page support this competitive advantage?

3. Assess the quality and effectiveness of Sony's home page. Specifically, perform a preliminary SWOT analysis comparing Sony's home page with other high-quality Web pages you have visited.

E-Center Resources

Visit http://www.prideferrell.com to find several resources to help you succeed in mastering the material in this chapter, plus additional materials that will help you expand your marketing knowledge. The Web site includes

 Internet exercise updates plus additional exercises

 ACE self-tests

 abc Chapter summary with hotlinked glossary

 Hotlinks to companies featured in this chapter

 Resource Center

 Career Center

 Marketing plan worksheets

VIDEO CASE 2.1

PETsMART: Looking to Be Man's Second-Best Friend

More than 50 percent of U.S. households have at least one pet, and more than twice as many households have a pet as have a child under the age of 18. The growth of pet ownership is being stoked by aging baby boomers and an increase in the elderly population. According to the Pet Industry Joint Advisory Council, pet owners spend about $27 billion a year on their furry friends, $10 billion of which goes toward pet health care. These trends in pet ownership have caught the attention of several retailers and fed the growth of a new form of retail outlet—the pet superstore.

During the early 1980s, 95 percent of pet owners shopped for pet food and other supplies at a supermarket. Although many pet owners still go to a supermarket to buy pet food, the number who do so has declined. When Fluffy, Fido, or Tweety run low on chow, pet owners today are likely to head to the nearest pet superstore. There, in a 25,000-square-foot, warehouselike facility, they can choose from a huge variety of pet foods, as well as from over 10,000 different pet toys and other nonfood items. Onsite services include grooming, obedience classes, and even good-health clinics, discounted versions of the annual check-ups provided by veterinarians.

In the years since pet superstores first began to appear, more than 1,150 such megamarts have opened across the United States. They have taken a bite out of supermarket pet food sales, reducing supermarket share to 55 percent of total pet food sales. One pet superstore estimates that nearly half its food sales are for items not available in supermarkets or other mass merchandise outlets. The superstores' nonfood supplies, such as leashes, shampoos, carriers, toys, and the like, also have not traditionally been stocked by grocery stores.

Phoenix-based PETsMART, Inc., one of the leaders of this retailing revolution, wants to be to pet lovers what Home Depot is to homeowners. PETsMART superstores offer more than 12,000 different products, including pet foods and a line of pet colognes, shampoos, conditioners, and health-maintenance items, such as eardrops and eyedrops. Like many of its competitors, PETsMART invites its human customers to bring their furred, feathered, and scaled companions into the stores to browse the aisles with them. With 520 superstores throughout the United States, Canada, and the United Kingdom, PETsMART dominates the pet superstore industry. Its sales climbed from $29.3 million in 1990 to nearly $2 billion in 1998.

PETsMART was founded by Jim and Janice Dougherty as the Pet Food Warehouse in 1987, with two stores in Arizona. After growing to seven stores in just two years, the firm began to lose money. In 1990, controlling investors ousted the Doughertys and brought in Sam Parker, a former executive of the Jewel supermarket chain, as chairman. Under Parker's guidance, the chain spruced up its stores, widening the aisles, brightening the lighting, and adding more product variety. By the end of 1993, when the company went public, the chain had 106 stores. Since 1994, the company has not only opened hundreds of new superstores, but also acquired related firms to enhance its operations, including Petzazz (with thirty superstores throughout the Midwest), Petstuff (fifty-two superstores in the eastern United States and four in Ontario, Canada), Sporting Dog Specialties (a pet-supply catalog retailer), Pet Food Giant (ten superstores in New Jersey, Long Island, and Philadelphia), and Pet City Holdings PLC (fifty superstores in Great Britain and Northern Ireland).

To achieve its corporate objective of being the dominant retailer of pet foods and supplies in the United States, PETsMART has adopted a step-by-step approach. During its first year of operation, its strategy was simply to introduce itself and create an awareness of PETsMART in consumers' minds. Advertising focused on PETsMART's wide selection of products and low prices, hoping to encourage consumers to visit the stores. The chain also capitalized on the strong emotional bond that exists between people and their pets with commercials featuring owner testimonials and such comments as, "I'd do anything to keep her happy, anything." Advertising slogans like "More than low prices, a whole lot more" and "PETsMART has thousands of things to keep your pet happy—for less" reinforced the emotional link.

In its second year of operation, PETsMART began to focus on creating brand loyalty. Its ads emphasized its trademark and encouraged repeat customer visits. In terms of customers' recall of ads, research found PETsMART commercials in the top 5 percent of all filmed advertisements tested. It also indicated that 27 percent of occasional shoppers could be motivated to increase their number of visits. PETsMART continued to focus on the bond between owners and their pets with such advertising taglines as "When is a pet more than a pet? When it's a friend" and "PETsMART—where pets are family."

PETsMART has a policy of not selling puppies or kittens because of the overpopulation of these animals in the United States. Instead, it has instituted an Adopt-a-Pet program. Each week, its stores feature several dogs and cats from local animal shelters in the hope of attracting adoptive families. Television commercials touting the program tell viewers, "We don't sell pets, but we help save thousands of them each year." This policy appeals to the social responsibility many animal lovers feel.

The estimated 53 million companion pets in this country have been associated with increasing the health and well-being of their owners, especially by lowering blood pressure and relieving stress. This has prompted PETsMART to target a very special segment of the market, senior citizens, with commercials featuring older pet owners. Advertising slogans strengthen this tie with the tagline, "There's no greater gift than love that's shared."

PETsMART has stated that its number one goal is to be the best in its class—the industry leader. To achieve this goal, the company offers a wider variety of products at lower prices than grocery stores do. But to ensure that it satisfies its customers, it further differentiates itself from other pet stores and mass merchandisers by focusing on emotional, nonprice issues as well.[41]

Questions for Discussion

1. Describe PETsMART's target market and marketing mix.
2. What strategy did PETsMART use during its first year of operation? Its second year? What strategy might it employ next?
3. Does PETsMART's advertising seem to be consistent with its overall strategies and objectives? Explain.

CASE 2.2

Reinventing Success at IBM

International Business Machines (IBM), also called "Big Blue," is perhaps best known for its pioneering role in developing the personal computer. Today, it is the world's leading marketer of computer hardware and the number-two provider of software, after Microsoft. It markets a broad range of computers, including PCs, mainframes, and network servers, as well as peripherals, software, and services. A number of IBM products—including the System/360 mainframe and the IBM XT and AT personal computers—have set industry standards. The multinational company has 269,465 employees and annual sales of nearly $78 billion—nearly 60 percent of them to foreign customers. The company's future looks promising, thanks to several strategic acquisitions and a focused strategy that exploits the increasing importance of information technology in our society.

IBM traces its origins to the late 1880s, a time when waves of immigrants were causing a rapid expansion of the nation's population. Realizing that its traditional techniques would be hopelessly slow in tabulating the results of the 1890 census, the U.S. Census Bureau sponsored a contest in which entrants submitted methods of speeding the count. The winner was Herman Hollerith, a German immigrant who worked as a Census Bureau statistician. Using an electric current, Hollerith's tabulating machine sensed holes in punched cards and kept a running total of data, and with it, the Census Bureau finished counting the 1890 census data in record time. To capitalize on his machine's success, Hollerith formed the Tabulating Machine Company in 1896. In 1911, this company merged with two others to become the Computing-Tabulating-Recording (C-T-R) Company. C-T-R manufactured a variety of machinery, including tabulators and punched card machines, industrial time recorders, commercial scales, and even meat and cheese slicers. In 1914, Thomas J. Watson, Sr., became IBM's general manager and, within a year, its president—a position he held until 1952, when his son took over the post. Watson focused the company on providing large-scale, custom-built tabulating solutions for businesses. He also expanded the company's operations to Europe, South America, Asia, and Australia, and in 1924, the company accordingly changed its name to International Business Machines.

Throughout its long history, IBM has been a leader in many areas. It was among the first corporations to provide employees with life insurance and paid vacations. It won the first contract to maintain employment records for the federal government after the passage of the Social Security Act of 1935. During World War II, it sponsored the development of the Mark I, the first electro-mechanical device that could automatically perform long mathematical calculations. The Mark I was followed in 1952 by the IBM 701, a fully electronic computer that ran on vacuum tubes, and later by one

of the first transistor-based mainframes, the IBM 7090, which could perform 229,000 computations per second. Under the leadership of Tom Watson, Jr., IBM in 1964 introduced the System/360, the first large "family" of computers to use interchangeable software and peripheral equipment. The launch of IBM's highly successful personal computer introduced computers into homes, schools, and small businesses and helped spark today's information revolution.

Despite nearly a century of successes and its leadership position in the computer industry, the 1980s and early 1990s were a very dark time for Big Blue. During this period, its share of the world computer market fell from 36 percent to 23 percent, and its share of the PC market plummeted from 43 percent to 14 percent under the onslaught of less expensive PC "clones." Customer dissatisfaction and declining sales, profits, and market share led the company to reorganize three times in five years. The lackluster performance continued despite these changes, so in 1993, the board of directors brought in Louis Gerstner, Jr., as chairman and CEO. Formerly head of RJR Nabisco, Gerstner was the first person from outside IBM's ranks ever to head the company.

Gerstner brought to IBM a strong customer orientation and strategic focus. He again reorganized the company, this time into five units: hardware, services, software, maintenance, and rentals and financing. He continued to reduce IBM's work force, decreased costs significantly, and revamped its product line. One of Gerstner's most significant contributions was to focus the company on providing *integrated solutions* for its customers by offering one-stop shopping for computer products. IBM's services unit plays a pivotal role in this strategy. The services unit advises clients on technology strategy and helps them prepare for disasters, train employees, and get on the Internet. For example, IBM has a contract with Monsanto, manufacturer of pharmaceutical and agricultural products, to run that firm's mainframe computer system, install and maintain its 20,000 personal computers, operate the network that links its facilities, write new application programs, and even share discoveries from IBM's computer labs that might help Monsanto map the gene structure of seeds and human cells. IBM provides accounting, inventory-management, and other computer-intensive services to many companies, large and small.

To help it achieve its focus of providing integrated solutions for customers, IBM acquired several companies, including Lotus Development Corporation in 1995 and Tivoli Systems in 1996. Lotus, in particular, was vital to IBM's strategy because of its Notes product, which allows multiple users to share information across networks and the Internet. However, the two companies had vastly different cultures. IBM was seen as an old-school bureaucracy with dark-suited employees, while Lotus was viewed as hip, irreverent, and cutting-edge, with a blue jeans and T-shirt mentality. Although IBM executives tried to reassure Lotus employees that their company's culture and values would not be affected by the takeover, many talented Lotus employees, including CEO Jim Manzi, left soon after. IBM remained true to its promise not to tamper with Lotus's culture, however, even promoting Lotus employees to run the unit after Manzi's departure. Although the two disparate cultures have sometimes clashed, IBM has allowed Lotus to operate relatively autonomously, and Lotus has rewarded its parent company with strong sales and new products that mesh well with IBM's strategy.

IBM says it has two missions: "to lead in the creation, development and manufacture of the most advanced information technologies" and "to translate advanced technologies into value for our customers." With the company's focus on providing "solutions for a small planet," IBM seems to have returned to roots established by long-time executive Thomas J. Watson, Sr. Although this focused vision should help guide the company's strategies into the twenty-first century, inevitable changes in the dynamic computer industry may someday result in Big Blue reinventing itself again.[42]

Questions for Discussion
1. Identify any core competencies or competitive advantages possessed by IBM.
2. Describe what appears to be IBM's corporate strategy for growth.
3. Does IBM's corporate strategy appear to be consistent with its two missions?

The Marketing Environment

OBJECTIVES

- To recognize the importance of environmental scanning and analysis

- To become familiar with how competitive and economic factors affect organizations' ability to compete and customers' ability and willingness to buy products

- To identify the types of political forces in the marketing environment

- To understand how laws, government regulations, and self-regulatory agencies affect marketing activities

- To explore the effects of new technology on society and on marketing activities

- To be able to analyze sociocultural issues that marketers must deal with as they make decisions

New Cures for What Ails You

In recent years, Americans have increasingly turned to herbs, nutritionally enhanced foods, vitamins, and other dietary supplements to improve their well-being. In fact, the *Nutrition Business Journal* estimates that consumers are spending $76 billion a year on "nutriceuticals," food products that may provide medical or health benefits. The growing use of nutriceuticals seems to be part of a larger trend toward healthier diets that contain less fat and red meat. According to the Food Marketing Institute, 93 percent of adults say they are making changes in their diets; of these, 78 percent indicate they are eating more fruits and vegetables, and 35 percent claim they are cutting back on fats and oils. The trend may also be related to the rising cost of health care and the prevalence of Health Maintenance Organizations (HMOs), which has left many consumers missing the close relationships they once had with their physicians. Getting a timely doctor's appointment for minor ailments, such as cold and flu, can be difficult, not to mention increasingly expensive. Regardless of the reasons, more consumers are using herbs and dietary supplements as preventive measures or to treat minor ailments themselves. One-third of adults, for example, say they regularly choose foods for specific medical purposes, such as cranberry juice for a urinary-tract infection or chicken soup for a cold.

One company particularly well-positioned to take advantage of this trend is Celestial Seasonings, which has marketed herbal teas like Sleepytime and Red Zinger for more than three decades. Based in Boulder, Colorado, the company now sells 1.2 billion cups of tea per year and is the largest marketer of herbal teas in North America. It initially marketed only herbal teas and specialty black teas, often through health-food stores, as flavorful, healthy beverages. In recent years, as American consumers have become more interested in herbs and teas, the company has extended its product line to include Wellness teas, Organic teas, green teas, throat lozenges, and herbal supplements, many with ingredients long touted for their medical benefits, such as echinacea and ginseng.

Celestial Seasonings is not the only firm to respond to the demand for nutritionally enhanced food products. When Starbucks realized that some customers were consuming its Frappucino product as a meal replacement, the coffee retailer decided to test the potential of Power Frappucino, a vitamin-enhanced drink that contains protein and complex carbohydrates. Kellogg, the cereal company, has allotted $65 million to the establishment of a new division for developing functional foods, although it has not yet introduced any new products.[1]

Companies like Celestial Seasonings and Starbucks are modifying marketing strategies in response to customers' changing desires. Recognizing and addressing such changes in the marketing environment are crucial to marketing success, so we will focus on the forces that contribute to these changes in some detail.

This chapter explores the competitive, economic, political, legal and regulatory, technological, and sociocultural forces that constitute the marketing environment. First, we define the marketing environment and consider why it is critical to scan and analyze it. Next, we discuss the effects of competitive forces and explore the effect of general economic conditions: prosperity, recession, depression, and recovery. We also examine buying power and forces that influence consumers' willingness to spend. We then discuss the political forces that generate government actions affecting marketing activities and examine the effect of laws and regulatory agencies on these activities. After analyzing the major dimensions of the technological forces in the environment, we consider the impact of sociocultural forces on marketing efforts.

Examining and Responding to the Marketing Environment

The marketing environment consists of external forces that directly or indirectly influence an organization's acquisition of inputs (human, financial, and natural resources and raw materials, and information) and creation of outputs (goods, services, or ideas). As indicated in Chapter 1, the marketing environment includes six such forces: competitive, economic, political, legal and regulatory, technological, and sociocultural.

Whether fluctuating rapidly or slowly, environmental forces are always dynamic. Changes in the marketing environment create uncertainty, threats, and opportunities for marketers. Although the future is not very predictable, marketers try to predict what may happen. We can say with certainty that marketers continue to modify their marketing strategies and plans in response to dynamic environmental forces. Consider, for example, how technological changes have affected the products offered by computer companies and how the public's growing emphasis on health and fitness has influenced the products of shoe, clothing, food, and health care companies. Marketing managers who fail to recognize changes in environmental forces leave their firms unprepared to capitalize on marketing opportunities or to cope with threats created by changes in the environment. Monitoring the environment is crucial to an organization's survival and to the long-term achievement of its goals.

Environmental Scanning and Analysis

environmental scanning
The process of collecting information about forces in the marketing environment

To monitor changes in the marketing environment effectively, marketers engage in environmental scanning and analysis. **Environmental scanning** is the process of collecting information about forces in the marketing environment. Scanning involves observation, secondary sources such as business, trade, government, and general-interest publications, and marketing research. The Internet has become a popular scanning tool, since it makes data more accessible and allows companies to gather needed information quickly. Environmental scanning gives companies an edge over competitors in taking advantage of current trends. However, simply gathering information about competitors and customers is not enough: companies must know how to use that information in the strategic planning process. Managers must be careful not to gather so much information that sheer volume makes analysis impossible.

environmental analysis
The process of assessing and interpreting the information gathered through environmental scanning

Environmental analysis is the process of assessing and interpreting the information gathered through environmental scanning. A manager evaluates the information for accuracy, tries to resolve inconsistencies in the data, and, if it is warranted, assigns significance to the findings. By evaluating this information, managers should be able to identify potential threats and opportunities linked to environmental changes. Understanding the current state of the marketing environment and recognizing threats and opportunities arising from changes within it help companies with strategic planning. In particular, it can help marketing managers assess the performance of current marketing efforts and develop future marketing strategies.

Nabisco, for example, took the opportunity presented by health-conscious customers in the mid-1990s to introduce its Snackwell's line of fat-free cookies and crackers, which achieved nearly $500 million in sales. However, after sales slumped and customers complained about taste, the company reintroduced the Snackwell's brand with improved taste, including some fat. Thus, Cracked Pepper crackers now have 1.5 grams of fat per serving, up from no fat, but still less than 50 percent of the fat of regular cracker products.[2] Customers' demands for no-fat food provided an opportunity for companies like Nabisco to develop successful new products, but concerns about the taste of no-fat products created a threat that harmed sales. Nabisco responded to changes in the market by modifying the product.

Responding to Environmental Forces

Marketing managers take two general approaches to environmental forces: accepting them as uncontrollable, or attempting to influence and shape them.[3] An organization that views environmental forces as uncontrollable remains passive and reactive toward the environment. Instead of trying to influence forces in the environment, its marketing managers adjust current marketing strategies to environmental changes. They approach with caution market opportunities discovered through environmental scanning and analysis. On the other hand, marketing managers who believe that environmental forces can be shaped adopt a more proactive approach. For example, if a market is blocked by traditional environmental constraints, proactive marketing managers may apply economic, psychological, political, and promotional skills to gain access and operate within it. Once they identify what is blocking a market opportunity, they assess the power of the various parties involved and develop strategies to overcome the obstructing environmental forces. Microsoft and Intel, for example, have responded to political, legal, and regulatory concerns about their power in the computer industry by communicating the value of their competitive approaches to various publics. The computer giants contend that their competitive success results in superior products for their customers.

A proactive approach can be constructive and bring desired results. Figure 3.1 illustrates how Ford is being proactive about environmental concerns in the produc-

Figure 3.1
Responding to Environmental Forces
Responding proactively to sociocultural environmental forces, Ford is making 75% of every one of its vehicles recyclable.

Open for Anything.

Ford Ranger 4-Door SuperCab

Consumers Digest's "Best Buy" for 1999.   America's   best-selling compact pickup for 12 straight years.

Figure 3.2
Brand Competitors
Ford, General Motors, Toyota, and Nissan are brand competitors for compact pickup trucks. While they all may have similar features and benefits, Ford promotes its compact truck as best-selling.

tion of cars. To exert influence on environmental forces, marketing management seeks to identify market opportunities or to extract greater benefits relative to costs from existing market opportunities. For example, a firm losing sales to competitors with lower-priced products may develop a technology that makes its production processes more efficient; greater efficiency allows it to lower prices of its own products. Political action is another way to affect environmental forces. The tobacco industry, for example, has been very effective in lobbying for fewer restrictions on tobacco marketing. However, managers must recognize that there are limits on how much environmental forces can be shaped. Although an organization may be able to influence legislation through lobbying, it is unlikely that a single organization can significantly increase the national birthrate or move the economy from recession to prosperity.

We cannot say whether a reactive or a proactive approach to environmental forces is best. For some organizations, the passive, reactive approach is most appropriate, but for other firms, the aggressive approach leads to better performance. Selection of a particular approach depends on an organization's managerial philosophies, objectives, financial resources, customers, and human skills, as well as on the environment within which the organization operates. Microsoft, for example, can take a proactive approach because of its financial resources and the highly visible image of its president, Bill Gates.

The remainder of this chapter explores in greater detail each of the six environmental forces—competitive, economic, political, legal and regulatory, technological, and sociocultural—that interact to create opportunities and threats that must be considered in strategic planning.

Competitive Forces

Few firms, if any, operate free of competition. In fact, for most goods and services, customers have many alternatives from which to choose. Thus, when marketing managers define the target market(s) their firm will serve, they simultaneously establish a set of competitors.[4] Additionally, marketing managers must consider the type of competitive structure in which the firm operates. In this section, we examine types of competition and competitive structures, as well as the importance of monitoring competitors' actions.

competition Other organizations that market products similar to or that can be substituted for a marketer's products in the same geographic area

brand competitors Firms that market products with similar features and benefits to the same customers at similar prices

Types of Competition

Broadly speaking, all firms compete with each other for customers' dollars. More practically, however, a marketer generally defines **competition** as other firms that market products similar to or that can be substituted for its products in the same geographic area. These competitors can be classified into one of four types. **Brand competitors** market products with similar features and benefits to the same customers at similar prices. For example, Ford Ranger's depiction as the best-selling compact pickup truck in Figure 3.2 challenges competitors whose trucks offer similar benefits and features. A

product competitors
Firms that compete in the same product class, but whose products have different features, benefits, and prices

generic competitors
Firms that provide very different products that solve the same problem or satisfy the same basic customer need

total budget competitors
Firms that compete for the limited financial resources of the same customers

thirsty, calorie-conscious customer may choose a diet soda, such as Diet Coke, Diet Pepsi, or Diet RC, from the soda machine. However, these sodas face competition from other types of beverages. **Product competitors** compete in the same product class, but their products have different features, benefits, and prices. The thirsty dieter, for instance, might purchase iced tea, juice, or coffee instead of a soda. **Generic competitors** provide very different products that solve the same problem or satisfy the same basic customer need. Our customer, for example, might simply have a glass of water from the kitchen tap to satisfy her thirst. **Total budget competitors** compete for the limited financial resources of the same customers.[5] Total budget competitors for Diet Coke, for example, might include gum, a candy bar, or a newspaper. Although all four types of competition can affect a firm's marketing performance, brand competitors are the most significant because buyers typically see the different products of these firms as direct substitutes for each other. Consequently, marketers tend to concentrate environmental analyses on brand competitors.

Types of Competitive Structures

The number of firms that supply a product may affect the strength of competitors. When just one or a few firms control supply, competitive factors exert a different sort of influence on marketing activities than when there are many competitors. Table 3.1 presents four general types of competitive structures: monopoly, oligopoly, monopolistic competition, and pure competition.

A **monopoly** exists when a firm offers a product that has no close substitutes, making the organization the sole source of supply. Because the organization has no competitors, it controls supply of the product completely and, as a single seller, can erect barriers to potential competitors. In actuality, most monopolies surviving today are local utilities, which are heavily regulated by local, state, or federal agencies. These monopolies are tolerated because of the tremendous financial resources needed to develop and operate them. For example, few organizations can obtain the financial or political resources to mount any competition against a local water supplier. On the other hand, competition is increasing in the electric and cable television industries.

An **oligopoly** exists when a few sellers control the supply of a large proportion of a product. In this case, each seller considers the reactions of other sellers to changes in marketing activities. Products facing oligopolistic competition may be homogeneous, such as aluminum, or differentiated, such as cereal and automobiles. Usually, barriers of some sort make it difficult to enter the market and compete with oligopolies. For example, because of the enormous financial outlay required, few companies or individuals could afford to enter oil-refining or steel-producing industries. Moreover, some industries demand special technical or marketing skills, a qualification that deters the entry of many potential competitors.

monopoly   A competitive structure in which an organization offers a product that has no close substitutes, making the organization the sole source of supply

oligopoly   A competitive structure in which a few sellers control the supply of a large proportion of a product

Table 3.1	Selected Characteristics of Competitive Structures			
Type of Structure	Number of Competitors	Ease of Entry into Market	Product	Example
Monopoly	One	Many barriers	Almost no substitutes	Fort Collins (Colorado) Water Utilities
Oligopoly	Few	Some barriers	Homogeneous or differentiated (with real or perceived differences)	General Mills (cereal)
Monopolistic competition	Many	Few barriers	Product differentiation, with many substitutes	Levi Strauss (jeans)
Pure competition	Unlimited	No barriers	Homogeneous products	Vegetable farm (sweet corn)

monopolistic competition   A competitive structure in which a firm has many potential competitors and, to establish its own market, tries to develop a differential marketing strategy

pure competition
A market structure characterized by an extremely large number of sellers, none strong enough to influence price or supply significantly

Monopolistic competition exists when a firm with many potential competitors attempts to develop a marketing strategy to differentiate its product. For example, Levi Strauss has established an advantage for its blue jeans through a well-known trademark, design, advertising, and a reputation for quality. Although many competing brands of blue jeans are available, this firm has carved out a market niche by emphasizing differences in its products.

Pure competition, if it existed at all, would entail a large number of sellers, not one of which could significantly influence price or supply. Products would be homogeneous, and there would be easy entry into the market. The closest thing to an example of pure competition is an unregulated farmers' market, where local growers gather to sell their produce.

Pure competition is an ideal at one end of the continuum. Monopoly is at the other end. Most marketers function in a competitive environment somewhere between these two extremes.

Monitoring Competition

Marketers need to monitor the actions of major competitors to determine what specific strategies competitors are using and how those strategies affect their own. Price is one of the marketing strategy variables that most competitors monitor. When AirTran or Southwest Airlines lowers the fare on a route, most major airlines attempt to match the price. Globalmarketing profiles one firm's response to a competitive threat related to price. Monitoring guides marketers in developing competitive advantages and aids them in adjusting current marketing strategies and in planning new ones.

Globalmarketing

Diamonds, De Beers' Best Friend

Long a tangible symbol of rites of passage, such as marriage, the diamond epitomizes luxury and longevity to consumers the world over. The diamond trade is effectively controlled by South Africa's De Beers Consolidated Mines Ltd., which supplies more than half the world's gemstones and markets them through its London-based subsidiary, the Central Selling Organization (CSO). For decades, De Beers has kept a tight rein on supplies, and therefore diamond prices, by dominating other producers. However, its share of the global market for rough, or unpolished, diamonds has tumbled 10 percent over the last five years. The key reason for the decline is a glut of low-quality stones, primarily from Russia and Australia.

In the early 1990s, facing economic turmoil and in desperate need of hard currency, Russians began dumping low-quality, "near-gem" stones on the market, in violation of Russia's contract with the Central Selling Organization. The CSO responded by slashing the market price of this type of diamonds. Angered by the price cut, Australia's Argyle Diamond Mines, the world's largest producer of near-gem stones, ended its own contract with the CSO. Producers from Russia and Australia have since flooded the market with near-gem diamonds.

Consequently, it is possible to buy a diamond bracelet at Kmart or Wal-Mart for a mere $29.99.

With so many low-price, low-quality diamonds available, De Beers has given up trying to maintain control of the market for near-gem stones and has instead shifted its focus to larger, higher-quality diamonds. To boost prices of these larger stones, De Beers halved the number of diamonds it offers to "sightholders," which buy rough stones, cut and polish them, and resell them to retailers like Tiffany and Cartier. By reducing the available supply of large diamonds, De Beers has succeeded in raising the price buyers are willing to pay for better-quality gems. Moreover, this strategy has left De Beers sitting on a stockpile of diamonds worth an estimated $5.6 billion. Thanks to the glut of near-gem diamonds, the price of smaller stones continues to fall, but De Beers may yet regain control over the market for these as well. Russian producers recently signed a new contract with the CSO in which they agreed to stop flooding the market with lower-quality stones. In the meantime, De Beers continues its long-time promotional campaign, "Diamonds are Forever," in the hope that consumers shopping for engagement rings and other diamond jewelry won't be tempted by the cheap, mass-market diamonds.

In monitoring competition, it is not enough to analyze available information; the firm must develop a system for gathering ongoing information about competitors. Understanding the market and what customers want, as well as what the competition is providing, will assist in marketing orientation.[6] Information about competitors allows marketing managers to assess the performance of their own marketing efforts and to recognize the strengths and weaknesses in their own marketing strategies. Data about market shares, product movement, sales volume, and expenditure levels can be useful. However, accurate information on these matters is often difficult to obtain. We explore how marketers collect and organize such data in Chapter 6.

Economic Forces

Economic forces in the marketing environment influence both marketers' and customers' decisions and activities. In this section, we examine the effects of general economic conditions as well as buying power and the factors that affect people's willingness to spend.

Economic Conditions

The overall state of the economy fluctuates in all countries. Changes in general economic conditions affect (and are affected by) supply and demand, buying power, willingness to spend, consumer expenditure levels, and the intensity of competitive behavior. Therefore, current economic conditions and changes in the economy have a broad impact on the success of organizations' marketing strategies.

Fluctuations in the economy follow a general pattern, often referred to as the **business cycle.** In the traditional view, the business cycle consists of four stages: prosperity, recession, depression, and recovery. From a global perspective, different regions of the world may be in different stages of the business cycle during the same period. For much of the 1990s, for example, the United States experienced booming growth (prosperity), while Japan experienced recession. Economic variation in the global marketplace provides a planning challenge for firms that sell products in multiple markets around the world.

During **prosperity,** unemployment is low and total income is relatively high. Assuming a low inflation rate, this combination causes buying power to be high. If the economic outlook remains prosperous, consumers generally are willing to buy. In the prosperity stage, marketers often expand their product offerings to take advantage of increased buying power. They can sometimes capture a larger market share by intensifying distribution and promotion efforts.

Because unemployment rises during a **recession,** total buying power declines. Pessimism accompanying a recession often stifles both consumer and business spending. As buying power decreases, many customers may become more price- and value-conscious and look for basic, functional products. During a recession, some firms make the mistake of drastically reducing their marketing efforts, thus damaging their ability to survive. Obviously, however, marketers should consider some revision of their marketing activities during a recessionary period. Because consumers are more concerned about the functional value of products, a company should focus its marketing research on determining precisely what functions buyers want and should make sure that these functions become part of its products. Promotional efforts should emphasize value and utility.

A prolonged recession may become a **depression,** which is a period in which unemployment is extremely high, wages are very low, total disposable income is at a minimum, and consumers lack confidence in the economy. A depression usually lasts for an extended period of time, often years, and has been experienced by Russia, Mexico, and Brazil in the last decade.

Recovery is the stage of the business cycle in which the economy moves from depression or recession to prosperity. During this period, high unemployment begins

business cycle   A pattern of economic fluctuations that has four stages: prosperity, recession, depression, and recovery

prosperity   A stage of the business cycle characterized by low unemployment and relatively high total income, which together cause buying power to be high (provided the inflation rate stays low)

recession   A stage of the business cycle during which unemployment rises and total buying power declines, stifling both consumer and business spending

depression   A stage of the business cycle when unemployment is extremely high, wages are very low, total disposable income is at a minimum, and consumers lack confidence in the economy

recovery   A stage of the business cycle in which the economy moves from recession or depression toward prosperity

to decline, total disposable income increases, and the economic gloom that reduced consumers' willingness to buy subsides. Both the ability and willingness to buy rise. Marketers face some problems during recovery—for example, difficulty in ascertaining how quickly and to what level prosperity will return. In this stage, marketers should maintain as much flexibility in their marketing strategies as possible so that they can make the needed adjustments.

Buying Power

buying power   Resources such as money, goods, and services that can be traded in an exchange

income   For an individual, the amount of money received through wages, rents, investments, pensions, and subsidy payments for a given period

disposable income   After-tax income

The strength of a person's **buying power** depends on economic conditions and the size of the resources—money, goods, and services that can be traded in an exchange—that enable the individual to make purchases. The major financial sources of buying power are income, credit, and wealth. From an individual's viewpoint, **income** is the amount of money received through wages, rents, investments, pensions, and subsidy payments for a given period, such as a month or a year. Normally, this money is allocated among taxes, spending for goods and services, and savings. The median annual household income in the United States is approximately $37,005.[7] However, because of differences in people's educational levels, abilities, occupations, and wealth, income is not equally distributed in this country.

Marketers are most interested in the amount of money left after payment of taxes. After-tax income is called **disposable income** and is used for spending or saving. Because disposable income is a ready source of buying power, the total amount available in a nation is important to marketers. Several factors determine the size of total disposable income. One is the total amount of income, which is affected by wage levels, rate of unemployment, interest rates, and dividend rates. Because disposable income is income left after taxes are paid, the number and amount of taxes directly affect the size of total disposable income. When taxes rise, disposable income declines; when taxes fall, disposable income increases.

discretionary income   Disposable income available for spending and saving after an individual has purchased the basic necessities of food, clothing, and shelter

Disposable income that is available for spending and saving after an individual has purchased the basic necessities of food, clothing, and shelter is called **discretionary income.** People use discretionary income to purchase entertainment, vacations, automobiles, education, pets, furniture, appliances, and so on. Changes in total discretionary income affect sales of these products—especially automobiles, furniture, large appliances, and other costly durable goods.

Credit enables people to spend future income now or in the near future. However, credit increases current buying power at the expense of future buying power. Several factors determine whether people use or forgo credit. First, credit must be available. Interest rates, too, affect buyers' decisions to use credit, especially for expensive purchases such as homes, appliances, and automobiles. When interest rates are low, the total cost of automobiles and houses becomes more affordable. Low interest rates in the United States throughout the 1990s induced many buyers to take on the high level of debt necessary to own a home, fueling a tremendous boom in the construction of new homes and in the sale of older homes. When interest rates are high, consumers are more likely to delay buying expensive items. Use of credit is also affected by credit terms, such as size of the down payment and amount and number of monthly payments.

wealth   The accumulation of past income, natural resources, and financial resources

Wealth is the accumulation of past income, natural resources, and financial resources. It exists in many forms, including cash, securities, savings accounts, jewelry, and real estate. Like income, wealth is unevenly distributed. A person can have a high income and very little wealth. It is also possible, but not likely, for a person to have great wealth but not much income. The significance of wealth to marketers is that as people become wealthier they gain buying power in three ways: they can use their wealth to make current purchases, to generate income, and to acquire large amounts of credit.

Income, wealth, and credit equip consumers with buying power to purchase goods and services. Marketing managers need to be aware of current levels and expected changes in buying power in their own markets because buying power directly affects the types and quantities of goods and services that customers purchase.

Information about buying power is available from government sources, trade associations, and research agencies. One of the most current and comprehensive sources of buying power data is the *Sales & Marketing Management Survey of Buying Power*, published annually by *Sales & Marketing Management* magazine. Just because customers have buying power, however, does not mean that they will buy. They must also be willing to use their buying power.

Willingness to Spend

willingness to spend
An inclination to buy because of expected satisfaction from a product, influenced by the ability to buy and numerous psychological and social forces

People's **willingness to spend** (their inclination to buy because of expected satisfaction from a product) is, to some degree, related to their ability to buy. That is, people are sometimes more willing to buy if they have the buying power. However, a number of other elements also influence willingness to spend. Some elements affect specific products; others influence spending in general. A product's price and value influence almost all of us. Cross pens, for example, appeal to customers who are willing to spend more for fine writing instruments, even when lower-priced pens are readily available. The amount of satisfaction received from a product already owned may also influence customers' desire to buy other products. Satisfaction depends not only on the quality of the currently owned product, but also on numerous psychological and social forces.

Factors that affect customers' general willingness to spend are expectations about future employment, income levels, prices, family size, and general economic conditions. If people are unsure whether or how long they will be employed, willingness to buy ordinarily declines. Willingness to spend may increase if people are reasonably certain of higher incomes in the future. Expectations of rising prices in the near future may also increase willingness to spend in the present. For a given level of buying power, the larger the family, the greater the willingness to spend. One of the reasons for this relationship is that as the size of a family increases, more dollars must be spent to provide the basic necessities to sustain family members.

Political Forces

Political, legal, and regulatory forces of the marketing environment are closely interrelated. Legislation is enacted, legal decisions are interpreted by courts, and regulatory agencies are created and operated, for the most part, by elected or appointed officials. Legislation and regulations (or their lack) reflect the current political outlook. Consequently, the political forces of the marketing environment have the potential to influence marketing decisions and strategies.

Marketing organizations strive to maintain good relations with elected political officials for several reasons. Political officials well disposed toward particular firms or industries are less likely to create or enforce laws and regulations unfavorable to these companies. For example, political officials who believe that oil companies are making honest efforts to control pollution are unlikely to create and enforce highly restrictive pollution control laws. In addition, governments are big buyers, and political officials can influence how much a government agency purchases and from whom. Finally, political officials can play key roles in helping organizations secure foreign markets.

Many marketers view political forces as beyond their control and simply adjust to conditions arising from those forces. Some firms, however, seek to influence political forces. In some cases, organizations publicly protest the actions of legislative bodies. At times, organizations help elect to political offices individuals who regard them positively. Much of this help is in the form of campaign contributions. Although laws restrict direct corporate contributions to campaign funds, corporate influence may be channeled into campaigns through corporate executives' or stockholders' personal contributions. Such actions violate the spirit of corporate campaign contribution laws. A sizable contribution to a campaign fund may carry with it an implicit understand-

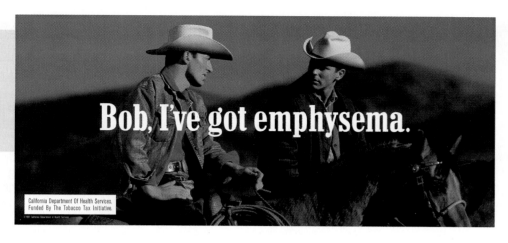

Figure 3.3
The Impact of Environmental Forces
Public service messages to communicate the negative effects of smoking are used to counter cigarette company advertising.

ing that the elected official will perform political favors for the executive's firm. Corporate executives may even contribute to the campaign funds of several candidates who seek the same office. Occasionally, some businesses find it so important to ensure favorable treatment that they make illegal corporate contributions to campaign funds.

While laws limit corporate contributions to campaign funds for specific candidates, it is legal for businesses and other organizations to contribute to political parties. Tobacco companies, including Philip Morris and RJR Nabisco, have contributed campaign funds to both the Democratic and Republican parties. Tobacco companies have long fought regulation of cigarette marketing through political support of elected officials, as well as by urging smokers to vote for the right to smoke, even in restricted environments. The heads of the world's largest cigarette companies once testified before a U.S. House subcommittee that they believed "nicotine is not addictive." Yet B.A.T. Industries, the world's second largest cigarette marketer, created Y-1, a high-nicotine tobacco for its Raleigh, Pall Mall, and Lucky Strike brands that exceeds Marlboro's nicotine level. When the public discovered that tobacco companies were acting to create addictive, high-nicotine products, political processes to regulate tobacco companies gained additional support.[8] Figure 3.3 is an ad designed to combat cigarette-company advertising.

Legal and Regulatory Forces

A number of federal laws influence marketing decisions and activities. Table 3.2 lists some of the most significant of these. In addition to discussing these laws, which deal with competition and consumer protection, this section examines the effects of regulatory agencies and self-regulatory forces on marketing efforts.

Procompetitive Legislation

Procompetitive laws are designed to preserve competition. Most of these were enacted to end various antitrade practices deemed unacceptable by society. The Sherman Act, for example, was passed in 1890 to prevent businesses from restraining trade and monopolizing markets. A request that a competitor agree to fix prices or divide markets would, if accepted, result in a violation of the Sherman Act.[9] Allegations of antitrade activities have brought Ticketmaster, the nation's largest distributor of sports and entertainment tickets, under investigation. Bands, fans, and competitors complain that Ticketmaster has a virtual monopoly over ticket sales, that it charges inflated service fees that make tickets outrageously expensive, especially for teenage fans,

Table 3.2   Major Federal Laws Affecting Marketing Decisions

Act	Purposes
Sherman Antitrust Act (1890)	Prohibits contracts, combinations, or conspiracies that restrain trade; establishes as a misdemeanor monopolizing or attempting to monopolize
Clayton Act (1914)	Prohibits specific practices such as price discrimination, exclusive dealer arrangements, and stock acquisitions in which the effect may notably lessen competition or tend to create a monopoly
Federal Trade Commission Act (1914)	Created the Federal Trade Commission; gives the FTC investigatory powers to be used in preventing unfair methods of competition
Robinson-Patman Act (1936)	Prohibits price discrimination that lessens competition among wholesalers or retailers; prohibits producers from giving disproportionate services or facilities to large buyers
Wheeler-Lea Act (1938)	Prohibits unfair and deceptive acts and practices regardless of whether competition is injured; places advertising of foods and drugs under the jurisdiction of the FTC
Lanham Act (1946)	Provides protection and regulation of brand names, brand marks, trade names, and trademarks
Celler-Kefauver Act (1950)	Prohibits any corporation engaged in commerce from acquiring the whole or any part of the stock or other share of the capital or assets of another corporation when the effect substantially lessens competition or tends to create a monopoly
Fair Packaging and Labeling Act (1966)	Outlaws unfair or deceptive packaging or labeling of consumer products
Magnuson-Moss Warranty (Federal Trade Commission) Act (1975)	Provides minimum disclosure standards for written consumer product warranties; defines minimum content standards for written warranties; allows the FTC to prescribe interpretive rules in policy statements regarding unfair or deceptive practices
Consumer Goods Pricing Act (1975)	Prohibits the use of price maintenance agreements among manufacturers and resellers in interstate commerce
Trademark Counterfeiting Act (1980)	Provides civil and criminal penalties against those who deal in counterfeit consumer goods or any counterfeit goods that can threaten health or safety
Trademark Law Revision Act (1988)	Amends the Lanham Act to allow brands not yet introduced to be protected through registration with the Patent and Trademark Office
Nutrition Labeling and Education Act (1990)	Prohibits exaggerated health claims and requires all processed foods to contain labels with nutritional information
Telephone Consumer Protection Act (1991)	Establishes procedures to avoid unwanted telephone solicitations; prohibits marketers from using an automatic telephone dialing system or an artificial or prerecorded voice to certain telephone lines
Children's Online Privacy Act (1998)	Requires FTC to formulate rules for collecting online information from children under age 13 (Enforcement of this act has been delayed while the courts determine its constitutionality.)

and that it has too much control over access to arenas. These accusations have led several consumers to file lawsuits charging the company with price gouging and antitrust violations, and prompted the U.S. Justice Department and several states' attorney general offices to investigate whether Ticketmaster is in fact engaging in monopolistic, antitrust behavior.[10]

Consumer Protection Legislation

Consumer protection legislation is not a recent development. During the mid-1800s, lawmakers in many states passed laws to prohibit adulteration of food and drugs. However, consumer protection laws at the federal level mushroomed in the mid-1960s and early 1970s. A number of them deal with consumer safety—such as the food and drug acts, designed to protect people from actual and potential physical harm caused

the Toyota Sienna did better in
Insurance Institute crash tests than any other vehicle, ever.
yes, you read that correctly.

TOYOTA | everyday

Based on 40-mph frontal offset crash tests done by the Insurance Institute for Highway Safety. 1-800-GO-TOYOTA (www.toyota.com)
©1998 Toyota Motor Sales, U.S.A., Inc. Buckle Up! Do it for those who love you.

Figure 3.4
Regulatory Forces
The government requires
that all automobiles, such
as Toyota's Sienna, pass
rigorous crash testing.

by adulteration or mislabeling. Other laws prohibit the sale of various hazardous products, such as flammable fabrics and toys that may injure children. Others concern automobile safety (see Figure 3.4). Congress has also passed several laws concerning information disclosure. Some require that information about specific products—such as textiles, furs, cigarettes, and automobiles—be provided on labels. Other laws focus on particular marketing activities—product development and testing, packaging, labeling, advertising, and consumer financing. For example, the 1990 Nutrition Labeling and Education Act attempts to prevent exaggerated health claims on food packages. Products affected by this law include cereals claiming to reduce heart disease and peanut butter touted as cholesterol free (as a vegetable product, peanut butter by nature does not contain cholesterol).

Encouraging Compliance with Laws and Regulations

Marketing activities are often at the forefront of organizational misconduct, with fraud and antitrust violations the most frequently sentenced organizational crimes. Legal violations usually begin when marketers develop programs that unknowingly or unwittingly overstep the legal bounds. Many marketers lack experience in dealing with complex legal actions and decisions. Some test the limits of certain laws by operating in a legally questionable way to see how far they can get with certain practices before being prosecuted. Other marketers, however, interpret regulations and statutes conservatively and strictly to avoid violating a vague law. When marketers interpret laws in relation to specific marketing practices, they often analyze recent court decisions, both to better understand what the law is intended to do and to predict future court interpretations.

To ensure that marketers comply with the law, the federal government is moving toward greater organizational accountability for misconduct. The U.S. Sentencing Commission (USSC) introduced a detailed set of guidelines to regulate the sentencing of companies convicted of breaking the law. The basic philosophy of the Federal Sentencing Guidelines for Organizations is that companies are responsible for crimes committed by their employees. These guidelines were designed not only to hold companies as well as employees accountable for illegal actions, but also to streamline the sentencing and fine structures for offenses. (Previously, laws punished only those employees directly responsible for an offense, not the company.) The underlying assumption is that "good citizen corporations" maintain compliance systems and internal controls to prevent misconduct and to educate employees about questionable activities. Thus, the new guidelines focus on crime prevention and detection by mitigating penalties for firms that have chosen to develop such compliance programs should one of their employees be involved in misconduct.

The bottom line is that unless a marketer works in a company with an effective compliance program that meets the minimum requirements of the U.S. Sentencing Commission's recommendations, both the individual and the company face severe penalties if the marketer violates the law. Daiwa Bank, for example, was hit with a $340 million fine for misrepresenting financial information, while Archer Daniels Midland received a $100 million fine for price fixing. Further, the Federal Sentencing Guidelines for individuals often mandate substantial prison sentences even for first-time offenders convicted of a felony, such as antitrust, fraud, or import/export violations, or environmental crimes. The minimum requirements for an organizational compliance program are described in Chapter 4.

Regulatory Agencies

Federal regulatory agencies influence many marketing activities, including product development, pricing, packaging, advertising, personal selling, and distribution. Usually, these bodies have the power to enforce specific laws, as well as some discretion in establishing operating rules and regulations to guide certain types of industry practices. Because of this discretion and overlapping areas of responsibility, confusion or conflict regarding which agencies have jurisdiction over which marketing activities is common.

Federal Trade Commission (FTC) An agency that regulates a variety of business practices and curbs false advertising, misleading pricing, and deceptive packaging and labeling

Of all the federal regulatory units, the **Federal Trade Commission (FTC)** influences marketing activities most. Although the FTC regulates a variety of business practices, it allocates a large portion of resources to curbing false advertising, misleading pricing, and deceptive packaging and labeling. When it receives a complaint or otherwise has reason to believe that a firm is violating a law, the commission issues a complaint stating that the business is in violation. If the company continues the questionable practice, the FTC can issue a cease-and-desist order, demanding that the business stop doing whatever caused the complaint. The firm can appeal to the federal courts to have the order rescinded. However, the FTC can seek civil penalties in court, up to a maximum penalty of $10,000 a day for each infraction if a cease-and-desist order is violated. The commission can also require companies to run corrective advertising in response to previous ads considered misleading. This mandated corrective advertising is proving to be costly to many companies.[11]

The FTC also assists businesses in complying with laws, and it evaluates new marketing methods every year. For example, the agency has held hearings to help firms establish guidelines for avoiding charges of price fixing, deceptive advertising, and questionable telemarketing practices. It has also held conferences and hearings on electronic (Internet) commerce. When general sets of guidelines are needed to improve business practices in a particular industry, the FTC sometimes encourages firms within that industry to establish a set of trade practices voluntarily. The FTC may even sponsor a conference bringing together industry leaders and consumers for this purpose.

Unlike the FTC, other regulatory units are limited to dealing with specific products, services, or business activities. For example, the Food and Drug Administration (FDA) enforces regulations prohibiting the sale and distribution of adulterated, misbranded, or hazardous food and drug products. The FDA may also delay advertising for products until final approval. For example, Pfizer waited for weeks after launching its Viagra to get FDA approval to advertise the product.[12] Table 3.3 outlines the areas of responsibility of six federal regulatory agencies.

Table 3.3	Major Federal Regulatory Agencies
Agency	**Major Areas of Responsibility**
Federal Trade Commission (FTC)	Enforces laws and guidelines regarding business practices; takes action to stop false and deceptive advertising, pricing, packaging, and labeling
Food and Drug Administration (FDA)	Enforces laws and regulations to prevent distribution of adulterated or misbranded foods, drugs, medical devices, cosmetics, veterinary products, and potentially hazardous consumer products
Consumer Product Safety Commission (CPSC)	Ensures compliance with the Consumer Product Safety Act; protects the public from unreasonable risk of injury from any consumer product not covered by other regulatory agencies
Federal Communications Commission (FCC)	Regulates communication by wire, radio, and television in interstate and foreign commerce
Environmental Protection Agency (EPA)	Develops and enforces environmental protection standards and conducts research into the adverse effects of pollution
Federal Power Commission (FPC)	Regulates rates and sales of natural gas producers, thereby affecting the supply and price of gas available to consumers; also regulates wholesale rates for electricity and gas, pipeline construction, and U.S. imports and exports of natural gas and electricity

Additionally, all states—as well as many cities and towns—have regulatory agencies that enforce laws and regulations regarding marketing practices within their states or municipalities. State and local regulatory agencies try not to establish regulations that conflict with those of federal regulatory agencies. They generally enforce laws dealing with the production and sale of particular goods and services. Utility, insurance, financial, and liquor industries are commonly regulated by state agencies. Among these agencies' targets are misleading advertising and pricing. Recent legal actions suggest that states are taking a firmer stance against perceived deceptive pricing practices and are using basic consumer research to define deceptive pricing.

Self-Regulatory Forces

In an attempt to be good corporate citizens and to prevent government intervention, some businesses try to regulate themselves. A number of trade associations have developed self-regulatory programs. Even though these programs are not a direct outgrowth of laws, many were established to stop or stall the development of laws and governmental regulatory groups that would regulate the associations' marketing practices. Sometimes trade associations establish ethics codes by which their members must abide or risk censure or exclusion from the association. For example, the Water Quality Association has developed a comprehensive Code of Ethics to help companies that sell water purification equipment avoid illegal and unethical activities.

Self-regulatory programs have several advantages over governmental laws and regulatory agencies. Establishment and implementation are usually less expensive and guidelines are generally more realistic and operational. In addition, effective self-regulatory programs reduce the need to expand government bureaucracy. However, these programs have several limitations. When a trade association creates a set of industry guidelines for its members, nonmember firms do not have to abide by them. Furthermore, many self-regulatory programs lack the tools or authority to enforce guidelines. Finally, guidelines in self-regulatory programs are often less strict than those established by government agencies.

Better Business Bureau
A local, nongovernmental regulatory agency, supported by local businesses, that helps settle problems between customers and specific business firms

Perhaps the best-known nongovernmental regulatory group is the **Better Business Bureau,** a local regulatory agency supported by local businesses. More than 140 bureaus help settle problems between consumers and specific business firms. Each bureau also acts to preserve good business practices in a locality, although it usually does not have strong enforcement tools for dealing with firms that employ questionable practices. When a firm continues to violate what the Better Business Bureau believes to be good business practices, the bureau warns consumers through local newspapers or broadcast media. The BBB has also developed a "BBBOnLine" site to help consumers recognize Web sites that handle the collection of personal information in an ethical manner. BBB members that use the site agree to binding arbitration with regard to online privacy issues.

The Council of Better Business Bureaus is a national organization composed of all local Better Business Bureaus. The National Advertising Division (NAD) of the Council of Better Business Bureaus operates a self-regulatory program that investigates claims regarding alleged deceptive advertising. For example, after investigating complaints about Spalding's advertising of its Top-Flite/Club System T golf balls, the NAD asked the sporting goods firm to modify the advertising to avoid making unsubstantiated claims about the product's performance.[13]

National Advertising Review Board (NARB)
A self-regulatory unit that considers challenges to issues raised by the National Advertising Division (an arm of the Council of Better Business Bureaus) about an advertisement

Another self-regulatory entity, the **National Advertising Review Board (NARB),** considers cases in which an advertiser challenges issues raised by the National Advertising Division about an advertisement. Spalding, for example, has appealed to the NARB the NAD's decision that its advertising of Top-Flite/Club System T golf balls contains unsubstantiated performance claims.[14] Cases are reviewed by panels drawn from NARB members representing advertisers, agencies, and the public. The NARB, sponsored by the Council of Better Business Bureaus and three advertising trade organizations, has no official enforcement powers. However, if a firm refuses to comply with its decision, the NARB may publicize the questionable practice and file a complaint with the FTC.

Technological Forces

Copyright © Houghton Mifflin Company. All rights reserved.

The word *technology* brings to mind scientific advances such as personal computers, compact discs, cellular phones, antilock brakes, fax machines, robots, cancer- and AIDS-treatment drugs, lasers, space shuttles, the Internet, and more. Such developments make it possible for marketers to operate ever more efficiently and to provide an exciting array of products for consumers. However, even though these innovations are outgrowths of technology, none of them *is* technology. **Technology** is the application of knowledge and tools to solve problems and perform tasks more efficiently. Technology grows out of research performed by businesses, universities, government agencies, and nonprofit organizations. More than half of this research is paid for by the federal government, which supports research in such diverse areas as health, defense, agriculture, energy, and pollution.

technology   The application of knowledge and tools to solve problems and perform tasks more efficiently

The rapid technological growth of the last several decades is expected to accelerate into the twenty-first century. It has transformed the U.S. economy into the most productive in the world and provided Americans with an ever-higher standard of living and tremendous opportunities for sustained business expansion. For example, Figure 3.5 illustrates an innovative product that was made possible by advances in technology. Technology and technological advancements clearly influence buyers' and marketers' decisions, so let's take a closer look at the impact of technology and its use on the marketplace.

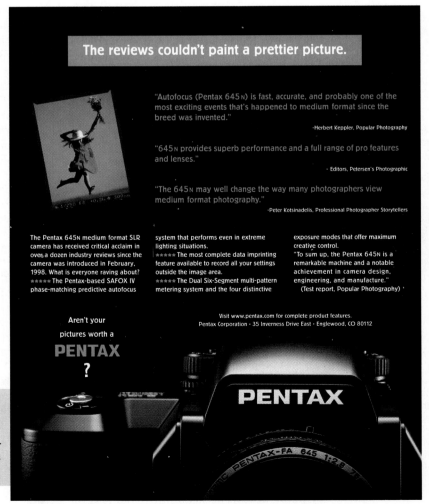

Figure 3.5
The Impact of Technology
Technological advances have made autofocus medium format cameras such as the Pentax 645N available.

Impact of Technology

Technology determines how we, as members of society, satisfy our physiological needs. In various ways and to varying degrees, eating and drinking habits, sleeping patterns, sexual activities, health care, and work performance are all influenced by both existing technology and changes in technology. Because of the technological revolution in communications, for example, marketers now can reach vast numbers of people more efficiently through a variety of media. E-mail, voice mail, cellular phones, pagers, and notebook computers help marketers stay in touch with clients, make appointments, and handle last-minute orders or cancellations. Telecommuting—using telecommunications technology to work from home or other nontraditional areas—is becoming an increasingly popular use of computer technology. About 11 million employees telecommute for at least part of their workweek, and marketing has become a significant telecommuting job.[15]

SNAPSHOT

Growth of cell-phone use

Use of cellular telephones is projected to more than double by 2002.

Cell-phone subscribers, in millions	1997	2002
United States	53.3	113.7
Japan	29.5	67.6
China	13.5	41.9
Italy	11.3	24.7
Germany	8.4	27.3
England	8.3	19.1
South Korea	6.7	15.6
Canada	4.3	10.1
Brazil	4.0	18.8
India	0.8	7.1

Newsweek-The Yankee Group. Copyright © 1998 Newsweek, Inc. All rights reserved. Reprinted by permission.

Personal computers are now in 40 percent of all U.S. consumers' homes, and millions of them include modems for phone line hookup. These consumers represent an opportunity for marketers to use online marketing communications, as well as to introduce new products to satisfy customers. More and more companies are using the World Wide Web to sell products. Club Med's page, for example, depicts its resorts, and Fidelity Investments has a Web page with descriptions of its funds, worksheets, and software samples available for downloading. Online stores sell everything from neckties and coffee to books and records, and whole cybermalls invite consumers to browse through catalogs and order merchandise.

Technology can help marketers become more productive. Many restaurants, for example, are using computers to track customers' eating habits, speed up order taking, and reduce waste and labor in food preparation. At the Stinking Rose in San Francisco, waiters record orders on hand-held computers, and Taco Bell is testing a computer system that would allow customers to place their own orders.[16] Computer technology also helps make warehouse storage and inventory control more efficient and therefore less expensive. Often these savings are passed on to consumers in the form of lower prices. Technological advances in transportation enable consumers to travel farther and more often to shop at a larger number of stores. They also improve producers' ability to deliver products to retailers and wholesalers. That manufacturers can ship relatively lightweight products to any of their dealers within twenty-four hours (via overnight carriers like UPS and FedEx) would astound their counterparts of fifty years ago.

Adoption and Use of Technology

Many companies do not stay market leaders because they fail to keep up with technological changes. It is important for firms to determine when a technology is changing the industry and to define the strategic influence of the new technology. Tech*know on page 70 describes one company's development of a new technology that helps improve communications.

The extent to which a firm can protect inventions stemming from research also influences its use of technology. How secure a product is from imitation depends on how easily it can be copied by others without violating its patent. If ground-breaking products and processes cannot be protected through patents, a company is less likely to market them and make the benefits of its research available to competitors.

Through a procedure known as *technology assessment,* managers try to foresee the effects of new products and processes on their firm's operation, on other business organizations, and on society in general. With information obtained through a technology assessment, management tries to estimate whether benefits of adopting a specific technology outweigh costs to the firm and to society at large. The degree to which a business is technologically based also influences its management's response to technology.

Sociocultural Forces

sociocultural forces
The influences in a society and its culture(s) that change people's attitudes, beliefs, norms, customs, and lifestyles

Sociocultural forces are the influences in a society and its culture(s) that bring about changes in attitudes, beliefs, norms, customs, and lifestyles. Profoundly affecting how people live, these forces help determine what, where, how, and when people buy products. Like the other environmental forces, sociocultural forces present marketers with both challenges and opportunities. For a closer look at sociocultural forces, we examine three major issues: demographic and diversity characteristics, cultural values, and consumerism. We further explore the effects of culture and subcultures on buying behavior in Chapter 8.

Tech*know

Andrea Electronics Quiets Technology

Although you may not recognize the name, Andrea Electronics has had a distinguished history in the annals of American technology. Its founder, Frank A.D. Andrea, once worked for Guglielmo Marconi, the radio pioneer, and later for Lee de Forest, who invented the vacuum tube. In the 1920s, Andrea went on to become one of the top five U.S. manufacturers of radios. In 1934, he founded another firm, then called Andrea Radio Corporation, to market radios in the United States and abroad, and in 1938, this firm began manufacturing televisions as well. The company thrived until the 1970s, when Japanese firms like Sony and Matsushita began to dominate global markets for consumer electronics. Like many U.S. consumer electronics firms, Andrea's sales plummeted, and by the late 1980s, the company was just barely surviving by selling radios and intercoms to the military.

Things began to change after the founder's grandsons, Douglas and John, joined their father, Frank, Jr., at the company. As the Andreas listened to their military customers, they noted that many pilots complained that the noise of wind and airplane engines kept them from hearing clearly through their headsets. Douglas Andrea, who had earlier had a career as a designer of industrial medical equipment, went to work with the company's engineers to address the pilots' problem. The noise-cancellation technology they developed relies on a set of two microphones. One mike faces the speaker and receives both speech and background noise, while the other faces away and picks up only background noise.

The signal from the second microphone is inverted so that it largely cancels out the background noise received by the first microphone, thereby reducing the volume of noise by as much as 20 decibels and enhancing communication.

The military proved a reluctant customer at first, so the company expanded its customer base to include telephone companies, which incorporated the technology for use in pay phones, on securities trading floors, and in other noisy environments. In recent years, Andrea has adapted the technology for use in the fast-growing areas of network communications and speech recognition. Its noise-cancellation technology is now used to amplify the performance of speech recognition, desktop dictation, audio-visual conferencing, Internet telephony, multiplayer online games, and home automation systems. The technology is particularly important in voice-recognition software, especially for computers used in noisy areas like airport waiting areas and factories.

The company now wants to provide the noise-cancellation technology used inside every cellular phone, personal computer, and personal digital assistant (PDA) made. To this end, it has licensed its technology to manufacturers. Although it may be ironic that a firm that began marketing products for generating sound now profits from a technology for reducing or even eliminating noise, the technology has boosted Andrea's sales, profits, and stock price considerably over the last ten years. Perhaps that's something the company won't want to keep quiet.

Demographic and Diversity Characteristics

Changes in a population's demographic characteristics—age, gender, race, ethnicity, marital and parental status, income, and education—have a significant bearing on relationships and individual behavior. These shifts lead to changes in how people live and ultimately in their consumption of such products as food, clothing, housing, transportation, communication, recreation, education, and health services. In this section, we take a look at a few of the changes in demographics and diversity that are affecting marketing activities.

One demographic change affecting the marketplace is the increasing proportion of older consumers. According to the U.S. Bureau of the Census, the number of people aged sixty-five and older is expected to more than double by the year 2050, reaching 80 million.[17] Consequently, marketers can expect significant increases in the demand for health-care services, recreation, tourism, retirement housing, and selected skin-care products. Del Webb Development Company is one firm taking advantage of this opportunity by creating several "Sun City" retirement communities for mature adults. In addition to providing housing, facilities, and activities designed for older residents, Del Webb's newest Sun City is located to take advantage of the scenic beauty and moderate climate of the Texas Hill Country, as well as close proximity to cultural events in nearby Austin. To reach older customers effectively, of course, marketers must understand the diversity within the mature market with respect to geographic location, income, marital status, and mobility and self-care limitations.

The number of singles is also on the rise. Nearly 40 percent of U.S. adults are single, and many plan to remain that way. Moreover, single men living alone comprise 10 percent of all households (up from 3.5 percent in 1970), and single women living alone make up nearly 15 percent (up from 7.3 percent in 1970).[18] Single people have quite different spending patterns from couples and families with children. They are less likely to own homes and so buy less furniture and fewer appliances. They spend more heavily on convenience foods, restaurants, travel, entertainment, and recreation. In addition, they tend to prefer smaller packages, whereas families often buy bulk goods and products packaged in multiple servings.

The United States is entering another baby boom, with 76 million Americans aged 18 or younger. The new baby boom represents 29 percent of the total population; the original baby boomers, now aged 35 to 54, account for 28.5 percent.[19] The children of the original baby boomers differ from one another radically in terms of race, living arrangements, and socioeconomic class. Thus, the newest baby boom is much more diverse than previous generations.

Another noteworthy population trend is the increasing multicultural nature of U.S. society. The number of immigrants into the United States has steadily risen during the last thirty years. In the 1960s, 3.2 million people immigrated to the United States; in the 1970s, 4.2 million came; and in the 1980s, the U.S. received over 6 million legal immigrants. In contrast to earlier immigrants, very few recent ones are of European origin. Another reason for the increasing cultural diversification of the United States is that most recent immigrants are relatively young, whereas U.S. citizens of European origin are growing older. These younger immigrants tend to have more children than their older counterparts, further shifting the population balance. By the end of the 1990s, the U.S. population will have shifted from one dominated by whites to one consisting largely of three racial and ethnic groups: whites, blacks, and Hispanics. By the year 2025, the U.S. government estimates nearly 59 million blacks, 43.5 million Hispanics, 21 million Asians, and 3 million Native Americans will call the United States home.[20] Table 3.4 illustrates this demographic mix.

Table 3.4	Projected U.S. Population by Age and Race for the Year 2025			
Age	**White**	**Black**	**Hispanic**	**Other**
0 to 17	12.7%	3.8%	5.7%	1.9%
18 to 34	12.5	3.1	4.6	1.8
35 to 54	15.0	3.0	3.9	1.8
55+	22.3	3.0	3.4	1.6
All ages	62.5%	13.0%	17.6%	7.1%
TOTAL PROJECTED POPULATION = 335,050,000				

Source: Bureau of the Census, *Statistical Abstract of the United States 1997* (Washington, D.C.: Government Printing Office, 1997), pp. 25–26.

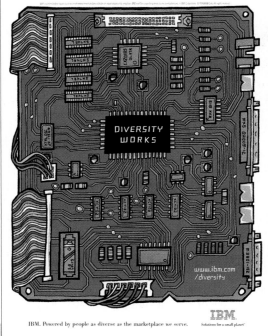

Figure 3.6
Sociocultural Forces
IBM and Fleet both recognize the importance of diversity and promote that understanding.

Marketers recognize that these profound changes in the U.S. population bring unique problems and opportunities. Ethnic minorities, for example, generate nearly $600 billion in annual buying power.[21] But a diverse population means a more diverse customer base, and marketing practices must be modified—and diversified—to meet its changing needs. Figure 3.6 shows that IBM and Fleet take this trend very seriously.

One way marketers modify their marketing mixes to reach ethnically diverse customers is by advertising in foreign-language newspapers and on foreign-language television. Many advertisers reach Spanish-speaking customers through Univision, a cable network that reaches 92 percent of Spanish-speaking households wired for cable TV. Additionally, some local television stations broadcast in-language programming to reach ethnically diverse audiences. For example, KMEX in Los Angeles broadcasts in Spanish, and KTSF in San Francisco, in Cantonese, Mandarin, Korean, Japanese, and Vietnamese. These stations tend to focus on news and programming of particular interest to their Hispanic- and Asian-American audiences, which can make them ideal vehicles for marketers looking to reach these markets. Among KTSF's major advertisers are Oxford Health Plans, Colgate-Palmolive, and McDonald's, as well as local businesses.[22]

Cultural Values

Changes in values have dramatically influenced people's needs and desires for products. Although cultural values do not shift overnight, they do change at varying speeds. Marketers try to monitor these changes knowing that this information can equip them to predict changes in consumers' needs for products at least in the near future.

For instance, cultural values seem to have veered away from formal business dress and toward a more casual work environment. This change affects not only the types of products customers desire, but also how these products are branded, priced, promoted, and distributed. As a result of the relaxed dress codes, the market for khaki pants that cost $20 to $100 has doubled in the last five years. Companies like Levi Strauss (Dockers) and the Gap have been able to take advantage of this market opportunity, and, in fact, these firms have promoted casual dress as fostering a more productive work environment.[23]

Starting in the late 1980s, issues of health, nutrition, and exercise grew in importance. People today are more concerned about the foods they eat and thus are choosing more low-fat, nonfat, and no-cholesterol products. Compared with Americans in the previous two decades, Americans today are more likely to favor smoke-free environments and reduced consumption of alcohol. They have also altered their sexual behavior to reduce the risk of contracting sexually transmitted diseases. Marketers have responded with a proliferation of foods, beverages, and exercise products that fit this new lifestyle, as well as with programs to help people quit smoking and contraceptives that are safer and more effective. Americans are also becoming increasingly open to alternative medicines and nutritionally improved foods. As a result, sales of herbs and herbal remedies, vitamins, and dietary supplements have escalated. More marketers are investing in research into traditional herbal medicines and fortified foods to take advantage of this market opportunity. Celestial Seasonings, for example, has developed herbal teas like Mama Bear's Cold Care with echinacea and mint, and Medical Foods has created such specialty products as the Nite Bite Time Release Glucose Bar for diabetics.[24]

The 500,000 men and women of America's Electric Utility Companies take great pride in protecting our environment. We're generating electricity more cleanly and efficiently than ever before. And we lead all U.S. industries in taking voluntary actions to mitigate greenhouse gases. To learn more about our environmental programs, and new ways you can use electricity wisely, visit our website (www.eei.org/enviro/). All living creatures deserve a cleaner planet. Together, we can help give it to them.

AMERICA'S ELECTRIC UTILITY COMPANIES

©1998, by the Edison Electric Institute. All rights reserved.

THANKS TO PHILLIPS, WEARY TRAVELERS WILL ALWAYS HAVE A PLACE TO STOP AND REFUEL.

By donating a former plant site to the Cactus Playa Lake Project, Phillips helped expand and protect the habitat of hundreds of thousands of migratory birds. The project resulted from the cooperative effort of Phillips, wildlife and conservation agencies and the community of Cactus, Texas. Now bald eagles, waterfowl and dozens of other bird species have a better place to rest along the Central Flyway. It's yet another example of what it means to be The Performance Company.

PHILLIPS PETROLEUM COMPANY 66

For a copy of our annual report, call 918-661-3700, write to Phillips Annual Report, B-41, Adams Bldg., Bartlesville, OK 74004 or visit us at www.phillips66.com

The major source of cultural values is the family. For years, when asked about the most important aspects of their lives, adults specified family issues and a happy marriage. These days, however, only one out of three marriages will last. Studies suggest that values about the permanence of marriage are changing. Because a happy marriage is prized so much, more people are willing to give up an unhappy one and seek a different marriage partner or opt to remain single.[25] Children remain important, however. Marketers have responded with safer, upscale baby gear and supplies, children's electronics, and family entertainment products. Marketers are also aiming more marketing efforts directly at children because children often play pivotal roles in purchasing decisions.

Children and family values are also a factor in the trend toward more eat-out and take-out meals. Busy families in which both parents work are usually eager to spend less time in the kitchen and more time together enjoying themselves. Beneficiaries of this trend have primarily been fast-food and casual restaurants like McDonald's, Taco Bell, Boston Market, and Applebee's, but 75 percent of grocery stores have added more ready-to-cook or ready-to-serve meal components to serve the needs of busy customers. For example, a Virginia firm, Ukrop's Super Markets, offers healthy, ready-to-serve meals at its deli counters.[26]

Today's consumers are more and more concerned about the natural environment. One of society's environmental hurdles is proper disposal of waste, especially of nondegradable materials, such as disposable diapers and polystyrene packaging. Companies have responded by developing more environmentally sensitive products and packaging. Procter & Gamble, for example, uses recycled materials in some of its packaging and sells environment-friendly refills. Raytheon has developed a new Amana refrigerator that does not use chlorofluorocarbons (CFCs), which harm the earth's ozone layer. A number of marketers sponsor recycling programs and encourage their customers to take part in them. Many organizations, including America's Electric Utility Companies and Phillips Petroleum, take pride in their efforts to protect the environment (see Figure 3.7).

Figure 3.7
Responding to Cultural Values
America's Electric Utility Companies and Phillips Petroleum Company recognize and share consumers' concerns about the natural environment and have developed programs to protect it.

Consumerism

Consumerism is a varied array of individuals, groups, and organizations seeking to protect consumers' rights. The movement's major forces are individual consumer advocates, consumer organizations and other interest groups, consumer education, and consumer laws.

To achieve their objectives, consumers and their advocates write letters to companies, lobby government agencies, broadcast public service announcements, and boycott companies whose activities they deem irresponsible. For example, several organizations evaluate children's products for safety, often announcing dangerous products at Christmastime so parents can avoid them. Consumer protests about child-proof medicine containers that seem to be adult-proof as well (especially for older adults with arthritis) led the U.S. Consumer Product Safety Commission to introduce new packaging standards. Under the revised rules, manufacturers must make it possible for adults to open containers designated as child-resistant within five minutes, while children must remain unable to open them.[27] Other actions by the consumer movement have resulted in seat belts and air bags in automobiles, dolphin-safe tuna, the banning of unsafe three-wheel motorized vehicles, and numerous laws regulating product safety and information.

Summary

The marketing environment consists of external forces that directly or indirectly influence an organization's acquisition of inputs (personnel, financial resources, raw materials, information) and generation of outputs (goods, services, ideas). The marketing environment includes competitive, economic, political, legal and regulatory, technological, and sociocultural forces.

To monitor changes in these forces, marketers practice environmental scanning and analysis. Environmental scanning is the process of collecting information about forces in the marketing environment; environmental analysis is the process of assessing and interpreting information obtained in scanning. This information helps marketing managers predict opportunities and threats associated with environmental fluctuation. Marketing management may assume either a passive, reactive approach or a proactive, aggressive approach in responding to these environmental fluctuations. The choice depends on an organization's structures and needs and on the composition of environmental forces that affect it.

All businesses compete for customers' dollars. A marketer, however, generally defines competition as other firms that market products similar to or that can be substituted for its products in the same geographic area. These competitors can be classified into one of four types: (1) brand competitors market products with similar features and benefits to the same customers at similar prices; (2) product competitors compete in the same product class, but their products have different features, benefits, and prices; (3) generic competitors provide very different products that solve the same problem or satisfy the same basic customer need; (4) total budget competitors compete for the limited financial resources of the same customers. The number of firms controlling the supply of a product may affect the strength of competitors. The four general types of competitive structures are

monopoly, oligopoly, monopolistic competition, and pure competition. Marketers monitor what competitors are currently doing and assess changes occurring in the competitive environment.

The economic factors that can strongly influence marketing decisions and activities are general economic conditions, buying power, and willingness to spend. The overall state of the economy fluctuates in a general pattern known as the business cycle. The stages of the business cycle are prosperity, recession, depression, and recovery. Consumers' goods, services, and financial holdings make up their buying power, or ability to purchase. Financial sources of buying power are income, credit, and wealth. After-tax income used for spending or saving is disposable income. Disposable income left after an individual purchases the basic necessities of food, clothes, and shelter is discretionary income. Factors affecting buyers' willingness to spend include product price, level of satisfaction obtained from currently used products, family size, and expectations about future employment, income, prices, and general economic conditions.

The political, legal, and regulatory forces of the marketing environment are closely interrelated. Current political outlook is reflected in legislation and regulations or the lack of them. The political environment may determine what laws and regulations affecting specific marketers are enacted and how much the government purchases and from which suppliers; it can also be important in helping organizations secure foreign markets.

Federal legislation affecting marketing activities can be divided into procompetitive legislation—laws designed to preserve and encourage competition—and consumer protection laws. Consumer protection laws generally relate to product safety and information disclosure. Actual effects of legislation are determined by how marketers and courts interpret the laws. Federal guidelines for sentencing violations of these laws represent an attempt to force marketers to comply with the law.

Federal regulatory agencies influence most marketing activities. Federal, state, and local regulatory units usually have power to enforce specific laws and some discretion in establishing operating rules and drawing up regulations to guide certain types of industry practices. Industry self-regulation represents another regulatory force; marketers view this type of regulation more favorably than government action because they have more opportunity to take part in creating guidelines. Self-regulation may be less expensive than government regulation, and its guidelines are generally more realistic. However, such regulation generally cannot ensure compliance as effectively as government agencies.

Technology is the application of knowledge and tools to solve problems and perform tasks more efficiently. Consumer demand, product development, packaging, promotion, prices, and distribution systems are all influenced directly by technology.

Sociocultural forces are the influences in a society and its culture that result in changes in attitudes, beliefs, norms, customs, and lifestyles. Major sociocultural issues directly affecting marketers include demographic and diversity characteristics, cultural values, and consumerism. Changes in a population's demographic characteristics, such as age, income, race, and ethnicity, can lead to changes in that population's consumption of products. With blacks and Hispanics representing a growing percentage of the population, the United States is becoming a diverse, multicultural society. Changes in cultural values, such as those relating to health, nutrition, family, and the natural environment, have had striking effects on people's needs for products and therefore are closely monitored by marketers. Consumerism refers to the efforts of individuals, groups, and organizations trying to protect consumers' rights. Consumer rights organizations inform and organize other consumers, raise issues, help businesses develop consumer-oriented programs, and pressure lawmakers to enact consumer protection laws.

Important Terms

Environmental scanning	Total budget competitors	Prosperity	Disposable income	Better Business Bureau
Environmental analysis	Monopoly	Recession	Discretionary income	National Advertising
Competition	Oligopoly	Depression	Wealth	Review Board (NARB)
Brand competitors	Monopolistic competition	Recovery	Willingness to spend	Technology
Product competitors	Pure competition	Buying power	Federal Trade	Sociocultural forces
Generic competitors	Business cycle	Income	Commission (FTC)	Consumerism

Discussion and Review Questions

1. Why are environmental scanning and analysis so important?

2. What are the four types of competition? Which is most important to marketers?

3. In what ways can each of the business cycle stages affect consumers' reactions to marketing strategies?

4. What business cycle stage are we experiencing currently? How is this stage affecting business firms in your area?

5. Define income, disposable income, and discretionary income. How does each type of income affect consumer buying power?

6. How is consumer buying power affected by wealth and consumer credit?

7. What factors influence a buyer's willingness to spend?

8. Describe marketers' attempts to influence political forces.

9. What types of problems do marketers experience as they interpret legislation?

10. What are the goals of the Federal Trade Commission? List the ways in which the FTC affects marketing activities. Do you think a single regulatory agency should have such broad jurisdiction over so many marketing practices? Why or why not?

11. Name several nongovernmental regulatory forces. Do you believe that self-regulation is more or less effective than governmental regulatory agencies? Why?

12. What does the term *technology* mean to you?

13. How does technology affect you as a member of society? Do the benefits of technology outweigh its costs and dangers? Defend your answer.

14. Discuss the impact of technology on marketing activities.

15. What factors determine whether a business organization adopts and uses technology?

16. What is the evidence that cultural diversity is increasing in the United States?

17. In what ways are cultural values changing? How are marketers responding to these changes?

18. Describe consumerism. Analyze some active consumer forces in your area.

Application Questions

1. Assume you are opening *one* of these retail stores. Identify publications at the library or online that provide information about the environmental forces likely to affect the store. Briefly summarize the information each provides.

   a. convenience store
   b. women's clothing store
   c. grocery store
   d. fast-food restaurant
   e. furniture store

2. For each of the following products, identify brand competitors, product competitors, generic competitors, and total budget competitors:

   a. a Dodge Caravan minivan   b. Levi's jeans
   c. *Star Wars: Episode I—The Phantom Menace*

3. Technological advances and sociocultural forces have a great impact on marketers. Identify at least one technological advancement and one sociocultural change that has affected you as a consumer. Explain the impact of each on your needs as a customer.

Internet Exercise & Resources

The Federal Trade Commission Online

Learn more about the FTC and its functions, look at the FTC's Web site at **www.ftc.gov**

1. Based on information on the Web site, describe the FTC's impact on marketing.
2. Examine the sections entitled "News Releases, Publications & Speeches" and "Formal Actions, Opinions & Activities." Describe three recent incidents of illegal or inappropriate marketing activities and the FTC's response to those actions.
3. How could the FTC's Web site assist a company in avoiding misconduct?

E-Center Resources

Visit http://www.prideferrell.com to find several resources to help you succeed in mastering the material in this chapter, plus additional materials that will help you expand your marketing knowledge. The Web site includes

 Internet exercise updates plus additional exercises

 ACE self-tests

abc Chapter summary with hotlinked glossary

 Hotlinks to companies featured in this chapter

 Resource Center

 Career Center

Marketing plan worksheets

VIDEO CASE 3.1

RadioLAN: *Un*wired for Success

Telecommunications technology is a major force in today's global economy. Cellular phones, E-mail, and computer networks have profoundly changed the way we do business, allowing us to communicate and operate more efficiently and productively. Among the companies that developed products to satisfy the demand for rapid and efficient telecommunications are Microsoft, IBM, Cisco, Motorola, and RadioLAN.

Many companies use local area networks (LANs) to improve interorganizational communication. A LAN, which links multiple computers together to form one system, allows users to share data and computer programs. Different computers on the network may store different programs or types of data, giving users access to more information and applications than they could store on one personal computer. Most LANs are "hardwired": cables physically link the computers. The cables are installed in walls and floors and sometimes laid in trenches dug between buildings. The hardwiring makes LANs expensive to install and inflexible: to be connected to the network, a computer must remain in a fixed location.

Recognizing that organizations need flexible networks that allow computers to be moved and that accommodate portable computers, RadioLAN introduced wireless LAN technology. Although other firms have tried to develop wireless networks, most gave up when they found that their systems could not compete with the speed of hardwired LANs and were more costly.

After its founding in 1993, RadioLAN conducted extensive environmental scanning and analyses to determine the telecommunications products customers would want in the future. The company's efforts paid off with its RadioLAN/10 system—wireless protocol software that is compatible with hardwired networks and that matches them in terms of speed and cost while offering the flexible access to information that today's competitive business environment demands.

RadioLAN's first target market consisted primarily of small offices and branch offices. In these settings, the wireless LAN typically links a mix of office PCs and laptop computers used by executives and salespeople who telecommute or travel frequently. When users bring their laptops into their office, they need to connect to the network at the fastest speed possible. RadioLAN's system offers both a speed and cost comparable to that of wired networks. The company's early products supported work groups of up to 128 stations, with an operating range of approximately 120 feet in an office environment and up to 300 feet in unobstructed areas. In 1997, after the Federal Communications Commission allocated three frequency bands—the Unlicensed National Information Infrastructure (U-NII)—in the 5-GHz range for high-speed wireless networking, RadioLAN introduced the first system approved for use in the U-NII. The new frequencies expand the range of operations so that the system can be used in large buildings and factories.

Scanning the environment for new opportunities, RadioLAN determined that schools could also benefit from wireless LANs. RadioLAN's CampusLink unit is designed to connect any two buildings on a "line-of-sight" path of up to 1,000 feet. Thanks to the company's software, the CampusLink unit can have networks up and running almost instantly. Hospitals, too are benefiting. With a wireless LAN, doctors and technicians can move between their offices or examination rooms and even between buildings and still have instant access to patients' records with a portable computer.

As of late 1998, RadioLAN was the only firm marketing a high-speed wireless LAN system, which positioned it nicely for a market expected to top $1 billion by 2001. The company continues to enhance its leading-edge technology, with plans to develop wireless LANs that can operate at faster speeds and handle multimedia and video network applications. RadioLAN is truly riding "the front waves of a new technology."[28]

Questions for Discussion

1. How has RadioLAN contributed to technological forces that can affect customers' marketing strategy?
2. How could RadioLAN's products influence a firm's technology assessment in strategic marketing planning?
3. Assess the market opportunity for RadioLAN's products.

CASE 3.2

Legal Issues at Archer Daniels Midland

The Archer Daniels Midland Company (ADM) reaches into so many of the products that consumers around the globe eat and drink that it call itself the "supermarket to the world." The nearly century-old firm mills flour and processes linseed oil, soybeans, corn, soybean-based vegetable protein, sugar, peanuts, citric acid, and a variety of vitamin products and additives for human and animal consumption. As the largest agricultural commodities processor in the United States, ADM employs nearly 15,000 to operate 200 plants processing 150,000 tons of grain, seed, and vegetable products each day. In 1995, ADM generated profits of $786 million on sales of $12.7 billion.

Although profitable, 1995 was a tumultuous year for ADM. Allegations surfaced that ADM and some of its rivals in the flour-milling industry had become too powerful, perhaps at the expense of consumer choice. There were charges that ADM's board of directors was overgrown, overpaid, and under the thumb of company insiders. While these issues alone raised serious ethical, legal, and peformance questions for ADM, the firm's major source of trouble involved accusations of price fixing, or conspiring with competitors to set artificially high prices for a product called lysine.

In 1989, ADM formed a new biochemical products division and hired Dr. Mark Whitacre to head it. Whitacre's first objective was to get into the production of lysine, an amino acid derived from corn used in swine and poultry feed to promote growth of lean muscle. ADM invested $150 million in lysine production and marketing and formally entered the market in early 1991. Adopting an aggressive price-cutting strategy, ADM gained market share quickly. A price war soon developed, and the per-pound price of lysine dropped from $1.30 to around $.60. Although ADM grabbed 30 percent of the global lysine market, it was losing millions of dollars a month on lysine operations.

Whitacre was asked to begin working with Terry Wilson, the president of ADM's corn-processing division, a fact that Whitacre says made him nervous, as he had heard rumors of Wilson's alleged involvement in price-fixing activities in several of the firm's other divisions. Wilson apparently asked Whitacre to set up a meeting with ADM's chief competitors, the two

Japanese companies that dominated the lysine industry, Kyowa Hakko and Ajinomoto. Wilson and Whitacre flew to Tokyo in April 1992. According to Whitacre, Wilson suggested that the firms form a cooperative association to promote and expand lysine sales, and Kyowa Hakko and Ajinomoto were receptive to this. Additional meetings in Hawaii and Mexico City followed.

ADM continued to lose money on its lysine operations. Production costs were running at roughly twice the market price as a result of contamination problems long since overcome by the Japanese producers, both of whom had sent engineers to inspect ADM facilities in the summer of 1992. During one of many phone calls to technical personnnel at Ajinomoto, Whitacre, frustrated by the contamination problem, says he joked, "Hey, you guys don't have a guy out here sabotaging our plant, do you?" The lack of a response made Whitacre wonder if there was indeed a saboteur.

He contacted Michael Andreas, the chairman's son and himself a vice chairman, about the issue. Whitacre says Andreas suggested that he offer the Ajinomoto technician a finder's fee for information about the problem. When Whitacre made the offer—a perfectly legal practice—the vague, neutral response reinforced his suspicion that the Japanese competitor had a mole inside ADM's plant. Whitacre claims that Andreas then told him that he should worry less about finding a saboteur and instead learn whether the informant would be willing to divulge technological information that could end the contamination problem and even improve ADM's competitive position in other ways. Although Whitacre maintains that he was aware that ADM had gained technical information this way in the past, he also realizes that it was risky. Conversations with the technician took place, but no deal was struck.

When Dwayne Andreas learned about the possible sabotage, he called a friend at the FBI. However, according to Whitacre, the younger Andreas was not pleased with his father's action. Whitacre asserts he was then coached by Michael Andreas about what to say—and what not to say—to the FBI. Accompanied by ADM head of security Mark Cheviron, Whitacre met with FBI officials to talk about the sabotage issue. As instructed, an uneasy Whitacre lied about the attempted technology purchase. However, when FBI agent Brian Shepard arrived at Whitacre's home that evening to install phone taps, Whitacre told him the truth about everything, including his concerns about possible price fixing.

The FBI soon began listening in as Whitacre talked from a phone in his home to contacts at Kyowa and Ajinomoto about the proposed lysine association. The FBI also supplied Whitacre with a recorder to tape lysine and other product-type meetings. Over the next three years, Whitacre recorded meetings using a concealed device, while the FBI, tipped off by Whitacre, wired hotel rooms in which meetings would take place. Whitacre says, "It's amazing, some of the stuff that came up on the tapes. There were recordings where agreements on world volume were reached, as well as prices." Based on this information, the FBI raided ADM in search of further evidence. Whitacre was fired soon after.

ADM denies the price-fixing allegations. In fact, Chairman Dwayne Andreas argues that fixing the price of a commodity such as lysine would be nearly impossible because inflating price would cause customers to switch to alternative feed additives. Furthermore, ADM filed a lawsuit against Whitacre, contending that he should return his salary because he was working for the FBI during his employment. In addition, ADM claimed Whitacre breached his confidentiality agreement with the company and that he embezzled $9 million. Whitacre denies any wrongdoing and claims the $9 million was "off-the-books" compensation, a practice he says was common for top ADM officials.

Angry shareholders and other critics pointed fingers at ADM's board of directors. They asserted that the price-fixing allegations, along with other antitrust and compensation-related issues for which the firm is under investigation, were clear evidence of director oversight. These issues, they insisted, should have been detected and dealt with long before they became public. Some protested that the board's large size, high levels of member compensation, and the fact that ten of the seventeen directors were retired ADM executives or relatives of senior management contributed to the problem.

These issues were addressed at a tense 1995 annual meeting of ADM shareholders. ADM's board members were barely re-elected, a sign that the composition and nature of the board had to change. In 1996, ADM's board of directors agreed to implement a reform plan, including cutting the board down to as few as nine members, with the majority being outsiders; trimming management seats from five to three; requiring committees to be composed entirely of outsiders, except for the executive committee; and mandating that outside directors retire at age 70. Dwayne Andreas retired in 1997, and was replaced by G. Allen Andreas.

In 1998, Whitacre pleaded guilty to thirty-seven counts of wire fraud, money laundering, conspiracy to defraud the IRS, filing false income tax returns, and interstate transportation of stolen goods, for which he received a nine-year sentence, some of which will be spent in a psychiatric hospital. Prior to sentencing, the distraught Whitacre attempted suicide. ADM, after cooperating with Department of Justice investigations, pleaded guilty to two felony counts for its participation in the lysine and citric-acid price-fixing conspiracies. Michael Andreas, executive vice president, and Terrance Wilson, retired head of ADM's corn-processing unit, were convicted of federal price-fixing charges in 1998. Reinhard Richter, former president of ADM's Mexico operations, was also convicted and received a sentence of one-year probation and a $25,000 fine after pleading guilty to fraud charges and income tax evasion. ADM has paid out at least $100 million in fines and has settled a number of legal suits for $45 million. None of the companies involved have admitted to any wrongdoing.[29]

Questions for Discussion

1. What factors in the marketing environment affected ADM's actions?
2. What do marketing managers need to know about price fixing in developing marketing strategy?
3. How could a compliance program be used to avoid legal problems in the development and implementation of marketing strategy?

Social Responsibility and Ethics in Marketing

OBJECTIVES

- To understand the concept and dimensions of social responsibility

- To be able to define and describe the importance of marketing ethics

- To become familiar with ways to improve ethical decisions in marketing

- To learn the role of social responsibility and ethics in improving marketing performance

Starbucks— Treating Employees Like Partners

Starbucks is the number-one retailer of specialty coffee in the United States. The gourmet coffee bar chain also operates in cities outside the United States, including Tokyo and Singapore. Founded in 1971, the company has grown from a local business with six stores into an international retail enterprise with more than 1,400 stores and 25,000 employees. For the last six years, its sales and profits have grown by more than 50 percent a year. Starbucks has also won a number of ethics awards and been recognized as a role model of social responsibility.

The company's first priority is taking care of the employees in its retail stores who communicate with and serve customers. Starbucks executives believe that by taking care of these employees, the company can provide long-term value to shareholders. To encourage employees to support the company's commitment to quality, Starbucks provides a stock option program worth 12 percent of each employee's annual base pay. Probably no other company has attempted a stock option plan as widespread and ambitious. Additionally, the company provides health care benefits to *all* employees, even part-time ones. These employee-focused benefits have resulted in an employee turnover rate that is one-fourth that of the competition.

The company's commitment to people extends beyond its coffee bar counters. Building on its concern for quality

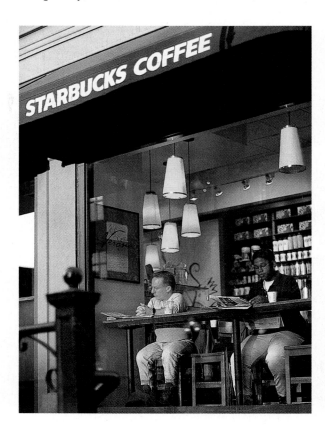

of life, Starbucks developed a framework for a code of conduct to improve working conditions in the countries from which it imports coffee; it was the first importer of an agricultural commodity to do so. By paying a premium (i.e., above-market) price for coffee, Starbucks hopes not just to increase the supply of high-quality coffee, but also to improve workers' lives. In addition, the company gives money to farms and mills in Guatemala and Costa Rica to help fund health care centers, farm schools, and scholarships for farmworkers' children.

Starbucks is the leading North American sponsor of CARE, an international relief and development organization. As well as making an annual corporate contribution to CARE, Starbucks gives CARE $2 for each of its coffee sampler products that the organization sells. In addition, Starbucks contributes to organizations that benefit AIDS research, child welfare, environmental awareness, and the arts. The company also empowers its employees to take an active role in helping their own neighbors.

A concern for social responsibility and ethics —respecting employees, protecting workers who supply the coffee beans, and educating consumers about the merits of high-quality coffee products—is basic to the Starbucks philosophy. As CEO Howard Schultz says, "we treat our employees like partners and our customers like stars."[1]

By taking a socially responsible, customer-focused approach to marketing, Starbucks has quickly grown into a successful marketing firm. The company's efforts to improve conditions for employees and coffee growers have met with public approval and helped position Starbucks as an ethical and responsible "good corporate citizen." Like Starbucks, most marketers operate responsibly and within the limits of the law. Some companies, however, choose to engage in activities that customers, other marketers, and society in general deem unacceptable. Such activities include questionable selling practices, bribery, price discrimination, deceptive advertising, misleading packaging, and the marketing of defective products. Practices of this kind raise questions about marketers' obligations to society. Inherent in these questions are the issues of social responsibility and marketing ethics.

Because social responsibility and ethics can have a profound impact on the success of marketing strategies, we devote this chapter to their role in marketing decision making. We begin by defining social responsibility and exploring its dimensions. We also discuss social responsibility issues, such as the natural environment and the marketer's role as member of the community. Next, we define and examine the role of ethics in marketing decisions. We consider ethical issues in marketing, the ethical decision-making process, and ways to improve ethical conduct in marketing. Finally, we incorporate social responsibility and ethics into strategic market planning.

The Nature of Social Responsibility

social responsibility
An organization's obligation to maximize its positive impact and minimize its negative impact on society

In marketing, **social responsibility** refers to an organization's obligation to maximize its positive impact and minimize its negative impact on society. Social responsibility thus deals with the total effect of all marketing decisions on society. There is ample evidence to demonstrate that ignoring society's demands for responsible marketing can destroy customers' trust and even prompt government regulations. Irresponsible actions that anger customers, employees, or competitors may not only jeopardize a marketer's financial standing, but have legal repercussions as well. For instance, many insurance companies, such as Prudential and MetLife, have been fined and experienced negative publicity for misrepresenting their products in sales presentations. In contrast, socially responsible activities can generate positive publicity and boost sales. The Breast Cancer Awareness Crusade sponsored by Avon Products, for example, has raised over $25 million to help fund community-based breast cancer education and early detection services. Within the first two years of the Awareness Crusade, more than 400 stories about Avon's efforts appeared in major media, which contributed to an increase in company sales. Avon, a marketer of women's cosmetics, is also known for employing a large number of women and promoting them to top management; the firm has more female top managers (86 percent) than any other Fortune 500 company.[2]

Socially responsible efforts like Avon's have a positive impact on local communities; at the same time, they indirectly help the sponsoring organization by attracting goodwill, publicity, and potential customers and employees. Thus, while social responsibility is certainly a positive concept in itself, most organizations embrace it in the expectation of indirect long-term benefits. Table 4.1 provides a sampling of some of the many socially responsible actions companies have taken in recent years.

The Dimensions of Social Responsibility

marketing citizenship
The incorporation of economic, legal, ethical, and philanthropic concerns into a firm's marketing strategies

Socially responsible organizations strive for **marketing citizenship** by incorporating economic, legal, ethical, and philanthropic concerns into their marketing strategies. As shown in Figure 4.1, these dimensions can be viewed as a pyramid.[3] The economic and legal aspects have long been acknowledged, but philanthropic and ethical issues have gained recognition more recently.

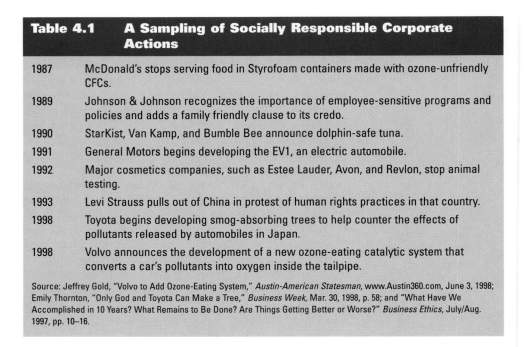

Table 4.1	A Sampling of Socially Responsible Corporate Actions
1987	McDonald's stops serving food in Styrofoam containers made with ozone-unfriendly CFCs.
1989	Johnson & Johnson recognizes the importance of employee-sensitive programs and policies and adds a family friendly clause to its credo.
1990	StarKist, Van Kamp, and Bumble Bee announce dolphin-safe tuna.
1991	General Motors begins developing the EV1, an electric automobile.
1992	Major cosmetics companies, such as Estee Lauder, Avon, and Revlon, stop animal testing.
1993	Levi Strauss pulls out of China in protest of human rights practices in that country.
1998	Toyota begins developing smog-absorbing trees to help counter the effects of pollutants released by automobiles in Japan.
1998	Volvo announces the development of a new ozone-eating catalytic system that converts a car's pollutants into oxygen inside the tailpipe.

Source: Jeffrey Gold, "Volvo to Add Ozone-Eating System," *Austin-American Statesman*, www.Austin360.com, June 3, 1998; Emily Thornton, "Only God and Toyota Can Make a Tree," *Business Week*, Mar. 30, 1998, p. 58; and "What Have We Accomplished in 10 Years? What Remains to Be Done? Are Things Getting Better or Worse?" *Business Ethics*, July/Aug. 1997, pp. 10–16.

At the most basic level, all companies have an economic responsibility to be profitable so they can provide a return on investment to their stockholders, create jobs for the community, and contribute goods and services to the economy. How organizations relate to stockholders, employees, competitors, customers, the community, and the natural environment affects the economy. Marketing Citizenship describes how one company's efforts to improve its performance affected its relationship with stockholders and employees. An organization's sense of economic responsibility is especially significant for employees, raising such issues as equal job opportunities, workplace diversity, job safety, health, and employee privacy. In Germany, BMW is reducing workers' hours from thirty-seven to thirty-one per week while keeping their pay at the original levels. BMW's goal is to introduce a shift system that will keep the

Figure 4.1
The Pyramid of Corporate Social Responsibility
Source: Archie B. Carroll, "The Pyramid of Corporate Social Responsibility: Toward the Moral Management of Organizational Stakeholders," adaptation of Figure 3, p. 42. Reprinted from *Business Horizons*, July/Aug. 1991. Copyright © 1991 by the Foundation for the School of Business at Indiana University. Used with permission.

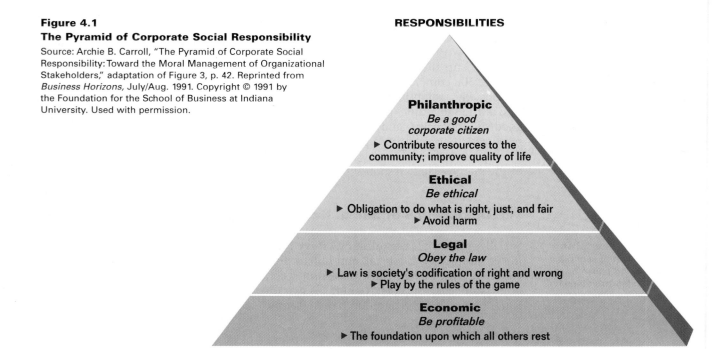

RESPONSIBILITIES

Philanthropic
Be a good corporate citizen
▶ Contribute resources to the community; improve quality of life

Ethical
Be ethical
▶ Obligation to do what is right, just, and fair
▶ Avoid harm

Legal
Obey the law
▶ Law is society's codification of right and wrong
▶ Play by the rules of the game

Economic
Be profitable
▶ The foundation upon which all others rest

plant operating around the clock at double the current productivity level. Sharing the profits with employees assures a more successful transition, as well as employee support of BMW's goals for product quality.[4]

To be socially responsible in their management of employees, companies should address several key issues. They should consider employees' economic security by ensuring that the wage and total compensation package satisfies employees' basic needs. They should attempt to maximize safety in the workplace to minimize employee injuries on the job, which cost companies $10 billion per year. They should train their employees to improve their skills, motivation, and, potentially, productivity. To foster diversity, companies should consider options (flextime, job-sharing, parental leave, subsidized day care, etc.) that create a family-friendly workplace. Southwest Airlines, for example, offers employees training through its "University for People," and many employees have very flexible work arrangements that include flextime and

MARKETING CITIZENSHIP

Sunbeam's Turnaround: Profits and Problems

For over a hundred years, Sunbeam has successfully manufactured and marketed consumer products, including the well-known Mixmaster and Oster brands. By the mid-1990s, however, the company's sales and profits were falling precipitously, causing a major decline in its stock price. To turn the corporation around, Sunbeam's board of directors hired Albert Dunlap (sometimes called "Chainsaw Al" because of his reputation for ruthlessly eliminating jobs when restructuring troubled corporations) to take over as chairman and CEO. Dunlap quickly brought in a new management team and, true to his reputation, announced layoffs of *half* the firm's 12,000 employees at facilities around the world. He shuttered eighteen factories and forty-three warehouses and consolidated six headquarters into one office in Delray Beach, Florida. He redefined Sunbeam's core focus as electric appliances and appliance-related businesses and divested everything that didn't fit into these categories. He devised a new strategy that included differentiating Sunbeam's products, moving into new geographic areas, and introducing new products that matched emerging customer trends. Within just fifteen months, the refocused company's revenues were back on track and its stock price was climbing: Dunlap's turnaround of Sunbeam was complete.

Or was it? In addition to unhappy employees who feared they would be next to fall to Dunlap's chainsaw, rumors about how the the company managed to purchase Coleman (camping gear), Signature Brands (Mr. Coffee), and First Alert (smoke and gas alarms) surfaced. In fact, Sunbeam had taken to using a "bill and hold" strategy, which involves selling products to retailers at large discounts and holding them in third-party warehouses for

delivery at a later date. By booking sales months before their actual shipment or billing, Sunbeam was able to shift sales from future quarters to the current one, thereby inflating its quarterly earnings. The strategy helped boost Sunbeam's revenues by 18 percent during Dunlap's turnaround in 1997.

A "bill and hold" strategy is not illegal, but when stockholders learned of its use at Sunbeam, they felt the company had misled them into purchasing Sunbeam's artificially inflated stock. Many joined a class-action lawsuit against the firm and its chief executive, charging that Sunbeam had violated securities laws by misrepresenting material information about its business operations and sales. The suit further alleged that Dunlap's motivation was to inflate the price of Sunbeam's common stock so that the company could complete hundreds of millions of dollars of debt financing to carry out the purchases of Coleman, First Alert, and Signature Brands. Soon after, Sunbeam officially restated its earnings as significantly lower than previously estimated, which caused the stock price to plummet. Dissatisfied Sunbeam board members launched a review of Dunlap's tenure and practices at Sunbeam. Their findings led many members to lose confidence in Dunlap's ability to continue running the company. The next layoff from Sunbeam was "Chainsaw Al" himself.

Sunbeam now faces scrutiny from the Securities and Exchange Commission, and it has determined that it may have to restate earnings for quarters during Dunlap's reign. In the meantime, the company is again reorganizing operations and revamping its strategies to demonstrate to both shareholders and customers that it remains a strong company that can satisfy their needs.

Figure 4.2
The Nature of Social Responsibility
Micrografx contributes to the community by sponsoring the annual Chili for Children Cook-off. Soliciting donations from high-tech companies, Micrografx organizes this event, which provides funding for the National Center for Missing and Exploited Children.

marketing ethics
Principles and standards that define acceptable marketing conduct as determined by various stakeholders

special work/family programs. The company has never laid off an employee, and it was the first airline to implement a profit-sharing bonus (4 to 8 percent of base pay).[5]

Marketers also have an economic responsibility to compete fairly. Size frequently gives companies an advantage over others. Large firms can often generate economies of scale that allow them to put smaller firms out of business. Consequently, small companies and even whole communities may resist the efforts of firms like Wal-Mart, Home Depot, and Best Buy to open stores in their vicinity. These firms are able to operate at such low costs that small local firms cannot compete. While consumers appreciate lower prices, the failure of small businesses increases unemployment, which places a burden on communities.[6] Such issues create concerns about social responsibility for organizations, communities, and consumers.

Marketers are also expected, of course, to obey laws and regulations. The efforts of elected representatives and special interest groups to promote responsible corporate behavior have resulted in laws and regulations designed to keep U.S. companies' actions within the range of acceptable conduct. When customers, interest groups, or businesses become outraged over what they perceive as irresponsibility on the part of a marketing organization, they may urge their legislators to draft new legislation to regulate the behavior, or they may engage in litigation to force an organization to "play by the rules." For example, Teva, which markets a line of popular sport sandals, sued Wal-Mart, accusing the retailer of selling Teva knockoffs for 25 percent less than Teva's sandals. The knockoffs may have been a factor in the decline of Teva's sales by $69 million in two years. Teva won the lawsuit, and Wal-Mart was forced to stop selling the sandals.[7]

Economic and legal responsibilities are the most basic levels of social responsibility for a good reason: failure to consider them may mean that a marketer is not around long enough to engage in ethical or philanthropic activities. Beyond these dimensions is **marketing ethics,** which refers to principles and standards that define acceptable conduct in marketing as determined by various stakeholders, including the public, government regulators, private interest groups, consumers, industry, and the organization itself. The most basic of these principles have been codified as laws and regulations to encourage marketers to conform to society's expectations of conduct. For example, new laws prohibit organizations from collecting information from children 13 and younger on the Internet without specific parental permission.[8] Internet marketers need to be aware of this new law and to inform their employees of its implications. Even though the new law's constitutionality has been questioned, a socially responsible marketer would want to implement its requirements. However, it is important to realize that marketing ethics goes beyond legal issues. Ethical marketing decisions foster trust, which helps to build long-term marketing relationships. We take a more detailed look at the ethical dimension of social responsibility later in this chapter.

At the top of the pyramid are philanthropic responsibilities. These responsibilities, which go beyond marketing ethics, are not required of a company, but they promote human welfare or goodwill, as do the economic, legal, and ethical dimensions of social responsibility. That many companies have demonstrated philanthropic responsibility is evidenced by over $6 billion in annual donations and contributions to environmental and social causes.[9] Ben & Jerry's, for example, has aggressively supported social causes (children and families, disenfranchised groups, and the environment) with 7.5 percent of its pretax profits. The Body Shop has been involved in "Trade Not Aid" and supports numerous other social causes while championing environmentally friendly refillable packaging. SmithKline Beecham has formed a partnership with the World Health Organization to develop and donate drugs to eradicate Lymphatic Filariasis, a disease affecting 120 million people worldwide.[10] Micrografx is another example of a socially responsible company, as illustrated in Figure 4.2. Even small companies participate in philanthropy through donations and volunteer support of local causes and national charities, such as the Red Cross and the United Way.

Many firms link their products to a particular social cause on an ongoing or short-term basis. One of the first companies to apply this practice, known as **cause-related marketing,** was American Express, which donated to the Statue of Liberty restoration fund every time customers used their American Express card. The promotion was extraordinarily successful, generating new customers and increasing the use of charge cards dramatically. Customers tend to like such cause-related programs because they provide an additional reason to "feel good" about a particular purchase. Marketers like the programs because well-designed ones increase sales and create positive feelings of respect and admiration for the companies involved. Stonehenge Ltd. has capitalized on this halo effect with its "Cocktail Collection" of men's ties. Sales of the ties, the second best-selling ones in the United States, have generated $500,000 for Mothers Against Drunk Driving. The ties depict the molecular structure of popular alcoholic drinks, while hangtags provide information about the impact of drunk driving on society, such as that each year 17,000 are killed and 1.2 million are injured. The company's slogan is "This is the only way to tie one on before driving."[11]

cause-related marketing
The practice of linking products to a particular social cause on an ongoing or short-term basis

Social Responsibility Issues

Although social responsibility may seem to be an abstract ideal, managers make decisions related to social responsibility every day. To be successful, a business must determine what customers, government regulators, and competitors, as well as society in general, want or expect in terms of social responsibility. Table 4.2 summarizes four major categories of social responsibility issues: the natural environment, consumerism, diversity, and community relations.

Table 4.2   Social Responsibility Issues

Issue	Description	Major Societal Concerns
Natural Environment	Consumers insisting not only on the quality of life, but also on a healthful environment so they can maintain a high standard of living during their lifetimes	Conservation Water pollution Air pollution Land pollution
Consumerism	Activities undertaken by independent individuals, groups, and organizations to protect their rights as consumers	The right to safety The right to be informed The right to choose The right to be heard
Diversity	Employees and consumers pressing for greater awareness and acknowledgment of demographic and lifestyle diversity issues, which are increasing in importance for organizations as diversity in the work force and general population grows	Equal opportunity in employment Integration Appreciation of how differences can contribute to success
Community Relations	Society anxious to have marketers contribute to its well-being, wishing to know what marketers do to help solve social problems	Equality issues Disadvantaged members of society Safety and health Education and general welfare

The Natural Environment.   One of the more common ways marketers demonstrate social responsibility is through programs designed to protect and preserve the natural environment. Many companies are making contributions to environmental protection organizations, sponsoring and participating in clean-up events, promoting recycling, retooling manufacturing processes to minimize waste and pollution, and generally reevaluating the effects of their products on the natural environment. Wal-Mart, for example, provides onsite recycling for customers and encourages its suppliers to reduce wasteful packaging. S. C. Johnson reformulated Raid, its roach-killing product, to make it less harmful to the environment. Sonoco Products, a packaging manufacturer, uses recycled materials for more than two-thirds of its raw-material needs and created a new package for Lipton Ice Tea that is 70 percent recyclable.[12] Such efforts generate positive publicity and often increase sales for the companies involved.

green marketing The specific development, pricing, promotion, and distribution of products that do not harm the natural environment

    Green marketing refers to the specific development, pricing, promotion, and distribution of products that do not harm the natural environment. Figure 4.3 illustrates the Forest Stewardship Council label, certifying the highest standards for environmentally and socially responsible forestry. Home Depot is one firm with a strong commitment to green marketing. It employs an outside firm to validate all environmental claims made for each product it sells. If a product or manufacturer does not live up to its claims, Home Depot will no longer carry the product. Developing a green marketing program is not easy, however. Despite its strong commitment to environmental responsibility, Home Depot faces a boycott from some consumer groups that say the retailer sells products harvested from environmentally significant "old-growth" forests.[13]

    Although demand for economic, legal, and ethical solutions to environmental problems is widespread, the environmental movement in marketing includes many different groups, whose values and goals often conflict. Some environmentalists and

Figure 4.3
Green Marketing
Socially responsible forestry is promoted to protect wood products for future generations. Consumers concerned with this issue can look for wood that has been certified by the Forest Stewardship Council.

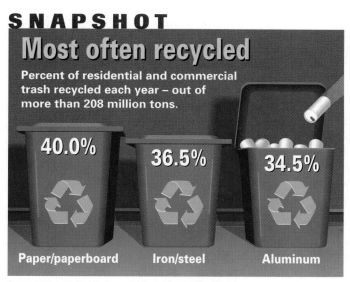

SNAPSHOT
Most often recycled
Percent of residential and commercial trash recycled each year – out of more than 208 million tons.

40.0% Paper/paperboard

36.5% Iron/steel

34.5% Aluminum

Copyright © 1999 *USA Today*, a division of Gannett Co., Inc.

marketers believe that companies should work to protect and preserve the natural environment by implementing the following goals:

1. *Eliminate the concept of waste.* Recognizing that pollution and waste usually stem from inefficiency, the question is not what to do with waste but how to make things without waste.

2. *Reinvent the concept of a product.* Products should be reduced to only three types and eventually just two. The first type is consumables, which are eaten or, when placed in the ground, turn into soil with few harmful side effects. The second type is durable goods—such as cars, televisions, computers, and refrigerators—which should be made, used, and returned to the manufacturer within a closed loop system. Such products should be designed for disassembly and recycling. The third category is unsalables and includes such products as radioactive material, heavy metals, and toxins.

These products should always belong to the original makers, who should be responsible for them and their full life-cycle effects. Reclassifying products in this way encourages manufacturers to design products more efficiently.

3. *Make prices reflect the cost.* Every product should reflect or at least approximate its actual cost—not only the direct cost of production, but also the cost of air, water, and soil. For example, the cost of a gallon of gasoline, according to the World Resources Institute in Washington, D.C., is approximately $4.50 when pollution, waste disposal, health effects, and defense expenditures like those of the Persian Gulf War are factored in.

4. *Make environmentalism profitable.* Consumers are beginning to recognize that competition in the marketplace should not be between companies harming the environment and those trying to save it.[14]

A program developed by Xerox Corporation illustrates these principles. Many photocopiers and ink cartridges end up in landfills after outliving their usefulness. To reduce this waste, Xerox's Asset Recycle Management program encourages customers to return used ink cartridges by providing a prepaid mailing envelope, and 60 percent of customers do so. The company then recycles parts of the used cartridges into new ones. The company has also designed its copiers to last longer and has reduced the number of chemicals involved from five hundred to fifty. These efforts have been good for both Xerox and the environment: the company saves more than $200 million a year.[15]

Consumerism.   Another significant issue in socially responsible marketing is consumerism, which we defined in Chapter 3 as the efforts of independent individuals, groups, and organizations to protect the rights of consumers. A number of interest groups and individuals have taken action against companies they consider irresponsible by lobbying government officials and agencies, engaging in letter-writing campaigns and boycotts, and making public service announcements. The consumer movement has been helped by news-format television programs, such as "Dateline," "60 Minutes," and "Prime Time Live," as well as by twenty-four-hour news coverage from CNN and MSNBC. The Internet, too, has changed the way consumers obtain information about companies' goods, services, and activities.

Ralph Nader, one of the best-known consumer activists, continues to crusade for consumer rights. Consumer activism by Nader and others has resulted in legislation requiring many features that make cars safer: seat belts, air bags, padded dashboards, stronger door latches, head restraints, shatter-proof windshields, and collapsible steering columns. Activists' efforts have also helped facilitate the passage of several consumer protection laws, including the Wholesome Meat Act of 1967, the Radiation

Control for Health and Safety Act of 1968, the Clean Water Act of 1972, and the Toxic Substance Act of 1976.

Also of great importance to the consumer movement are four basic rights spelled out in a consumer "bill of rights" drafted by President John F. Kennedy. These rights include the right to safety, the right to be informed, the right to choose, and the right to be heard.

Ensuring consumers' *right to safety* means that marketers have an obligation not to market a product that they know could harm consumers. This right can be extended to imply that all products must be safe for their intended use, must include thorough and explicit instructions for proper and safe use, and must have been tested to ensure reliability and quality.

Consumers' *right to be informed* means that consumers should have access to and the opportunity to review all relevant information about a product before buying it. Many laws require specific labeling on product packaging to satisfy this right. In addition, labels on alcoholic and tobacco products inform consumers that these products may cause illness and other problems.

The *right to choose* means that consumers should have access to a variety of products and services at competitive prices; they should also be assured of satisfactory quality and service at a fair price. Activities that reduce competition among businesses in an industry might jeopardize this right.

The *right to be heard* ensures that consumers' interests will receive full and sympathetic consideration in the formulation of government policy. The right to be heard also promises consumers fair treatment when they complain to marketers about their products. This right benefits marketers, too, because when consumers complain about a product, manufacturers can use this information to modify the product and make it more satisfying.

Diversity Issues.   Diversity in the work environment, as we discussed in Chapter 3, is the integration and utilization of an increasingly diverse work force. Companies that successfully utilize the work force are experiencing increases in creativity and motivation and reductions in turnover. From a marketing perspective, the more closely the work force matches the population, the better it understands consumer needs and wants. Consequently, many firms have instituted programs to hire more women and minorities to better reflect their customer base. Sara Lee, for example, began a program in the early 1990s to hire a significant number of female MBAs (40 percent in 1996). Today, women at Sara Lee hold one in four management positions.[16] As Figure 4.4 indicates, companies such as UPS support diversity by providing the opportunity for women and minorities to advance to all levels of operations and management.

Community Relations.   Social responsibility also extends to marketers' roles as community members. Individual communities expect marketers to make philanthropic contributions to civic projects and institutions and to be "good corporate citizens." While most charitable donations come from individuals, corporate philanthropy is on the rise. Home Depot, for example, had a philanthropic budget of $12.5 million for 1998, which it gave to the communities it serves through direct contributions and an employee gift-matching program. It also established Team Depot, an organized volunteer force, to promote volunteer activities within local communities. The company concentrates its charitable initiatives on at-risk youth, the environment, and affordable housing.[17] Home Depot has developed a particularly close relationship with Habitat for Humanity by providing building materials for Habitat home-building projects in low-income neighborhoods. Given that Home Depot's core business is home improvement and maintenance, its charitable contribution to Habitat for Humanity is logical. This type of giving is sometimes referred to as *strategic philanthropy* because it recognizes the close relationship between philanthropy and the overall business goals of the organization and seeks to make the philanthropic effort support these overall goals.

Many marketers view social responsibility as including contributions of resources (money, products, time) to community causes, such as the natural environment, arts

With her most recent promotion,
Patrice nabbed the best
window office in the company.

Patrice Clarke Washington, UPS DC-8 Captain

**Figure 4.4
Diversity issues**
UPS made history by promoting the first African-American woman to Captain at a major airline. By supporting diversity, UPS makes sure it has the best-qualified employees.

and recreation, disadvantaged members of the community, and education. Concern about the quality of education in the United States grew after many firms recognized that the current pool of prospective employees lacks the basic reading, writing, and spelling skills necessary to work. Acknowledging that today's students are tomorrow's customers and employees, many firms, including Kroger, Campbell Soup, Kodak, American Express, Coca-Cola Enterprises, and Microsoft, have donated money, equipment, and employee time to help improve local schools. IBM, Hewlett-Packard, and Apple all donate computer equipment to schools to support education, as well as in the hope of building long-term customer loyalty. McDonald's provides scholarship money for college students who work part-time in its restaurants. Although some members of the public are wary of marketers' involvement in education and other social areas, business participation is necessary in helping to educate the employees and customers of the future.

Recently, some companies have been criticized for their exploitation of employees and subcontractors, especially outside the borders of the United States. Abuses have included use of child labor, long shifts without breaks, low wages, and inhumane working conditions. Several companies have been accused of using low-cost labor (in some cases, running "sweatshops") overseas to make their products. One group has accused J. C. Penney of selling Arizona jeans for $14.99 a pair, while the workers manufacturing them earn only 11 cents a pair. These critics also say that for every $12 garment sewn for Victoria's Secret, the worker earns 3 cents.[18] However, many companies do try to do "the right thing" for their employees and the community at large. For example, a consortium of hotels in San Francisco is donating 15 cents per employee hour ($1.5 million per year) to assist lower-income employees with both child and elder care. Hotel employees can receive $125 per month for newborn care and $60 to $100 per month for child care.[19] Another hotel firm, Marriott International, puts welfare recipients through its Pathways to Independence program, which trains them in self-confidence, budgeting, and checking-account management, as well as specific job skills. The hotel chain then hires graduates of the program. According to J. W. Marriott, the company's chairman, "We're getting good employees for the long term, but we're also helping these communities. If we don't step up in these inner cities and provide work, they'll never pull out of it."[20] Marketers need to be aware of the trade-offs involved in contracting low-cost labor, which results in negative publicity that can damage the company's products and long-term reputation, versus the positive publicity that can accrue from socially responsible behavior.

The Nature of Ethics

As noted earlier, marketing ethics is a dimension of social responsibility involving principles and standards that define acceptable conduct in marketing. Acceptable standards of conduct in making individual and group decisions in marketing is determined by various stakeholders and by an organization's ethical climate.

Marketers should be aware of ethical standards for acceptable conduct from several viewpoints—company, industry, government, customers, special interest groups, and society at large. When marketing activities deviate from accepted standards, the exchange process can break down, resulting in customer dissatisfaction, lack of trust, and lawsuits. In fact, 78 percent of consumers say they avoid certain businesses or products because of negative perceptions about them.[21] One such business may be Columbia/HCA, a hospital chain that is under investigation because of allegations that it fraudulently billed for Medicare and home health care. Other unethical practices of which Columbia/HCA is accused include having a conflict of interest stemming from its relationships with doctors, setting profit goals that may have sacrificed the quality of patient care, and creating unfair competition through its purchase of nonprofit hospitals.[22] When managers engage in activities that deviate from accepted principles to further their own interests, continued marketing exchanges become difficult, if not impossible. The best time to deal with such problems is during the strategic planning process, not after major problems materialize.

As we have already noted, marketing ethics goes beyond legal issues. Marketing decisions based on ethical considerations foster mutual trust in marketing relationships. Although we often try to draw a boundary between legal and ethical issues, the distinction between the two is often blurred in decision making. Marketers operate in an environment in which overlapping legal and ethical issues color many decisions.

MARKETING CITIZENSHIP

Subway Sells Millions of Sandwiches and Has Hundreds of Ethical Dilemmas

Subway Sandwich Shops, the entrepreneurial dream of founder Frederick DeLuca, has over thirteen thousand franchises in sixty-four countries, second only to McDonald's in number of outlets. The franchiser has grown rapidly, making its founder a billionaire. However, the fast growth has brought Subway a host of problems, including unhappy franchisees, conflicts with landlords, and major problems with regulators. While most companies have some problems, Subway has had more than any of its competitors and has distinguished itself as a business that must deal with conflict and rebellion.

Disputes disclosed in an annual report required by the Federal Trade Commission total 160—more than the combined total listed by Subway's seven largest competitors (McDonald's, Burger King, KFC, Pizza Hut, Wendy's, Taco Bell, and Hardee's). Some complaints come from Subway's own salespeople—who arrange franchise relationships with first-time entrepreneurs—who say the company has broken its contracts with them. Many franchisees claim Subway has harmed them by opening too many new franchises in their neighborhoods. After the U.S. House Committee on Small Business studied the franchise industry for six years, staff economist Dean Sagar concluded: "Subway is the biggest problem in franchising and emerges as one of the key examples of every abuse you can think of."

One consultant estimates that about 25 percent of franchisees are unhappy and suffering, while about 40 percent are just getting by and making a few dollars. It has been reported that with Subway's knowledge, the company's food vendors overcharged franchisees and then returned money to the company for local advertising. When franchisees learned of the system, they formed a purchasing co-op that has already saved them some $55 million annually. In addition, an Illinois appeals court found "overwhelming proof that Subway had committed far-reaching fraud" in a real estate case in which the company had a deceptive policy of using shell (or hidden ownership) leasing companies to avoid rental obligations.

Subway says it is tired of all the fighting and litigation and wants to resolve everything as soon as possible. The company has announced social responsibility projects, such as making small loans to disadvantaged people so that they can launch businesses. Finally, Frederick DeLuca has put his accomplishments on tape and starred in educational videos that will be distributed to more than five hundred colleges. The founder's accomplishments are being broadcast over the Young Entrepreneur's Network and present DeLuca as a role model for students.

To separate legal and ethical decisions, one must assume that marketing managers can instinctively differentiate legal and ethical issues.[23] However, while the legal ramifications of some issues and problems may be obvious, others are not. Questionable decisions and actions often result in disputes that must be resolved through litigation. The legal system therefore provides a formal venue for marketers to resolve ethical disputes as well as legal ones. For example, Honda Motor Company settled a class-action lawsuit, brought by its dealers, for $316 million. The dealers charged that executives in Honda's U.S. division demanded cash, cars, and other gifts in exchange for providing them with larger inventories of the popular Accord and Acura models. More than 1,800 U.S. car dealers received a portion of the cash settlement, as well as auto parts and signs.[24] Subway, discussed in Marketing Citizenship, is another company that has been brought to court to settle ethical and legal disputes. In fact, many of the examples we cite in this chapter had to be resolved through the courts.

Before we proceed with our discussion of ethics in marketing, it is important to state that it is not our purpose to question anyone's ethical beliefs or personal convictions. Nor is it our purpose to examine the conduct of consumers, although they, too, may be unethical (engaging, for instance, in coupon fraud, shoplifting, returning clothing after they have been worn, and other abuses). Instead, our goal here is to underscore the importance of resolving ethical issues in marketing and to help you learn about marketing ethics.

Ethical Issues in Marketing

ethical issue An identifiable problem, situation, or opportunity requiring a choice among several actions that must be evaluated as right or wrong

An **ethical issue** is an identifiable problem, situation, or opportunity requiring an individual or organization to choose from among several actions that must be evaluated as right or wrong, ethical or unethical. Anytime an activity causes marketing managers or customers in their target market to feel manipulated or cheated, a marketing ethical issue exists, regardless of the legality of that activity. For example, organizational objectives that call for increased profits or market share may pressure marketers to knowingly bring an unsafe product to market. Such pressures represent ethical issues. Regardless of the reasons behind specific ethical issues, marketers must be able to identify these issues and decide how to resolve them. To do so requires familiarity with the many kinds of ethical issues that may arise in marketing. Some examples of ethical issues related to product, promotion, price, and distribution (the marketing mix) appear in Table 4.3.

Table 4.3 Typical Ethical Issues Related to the Marketing Mix	
Product Issue	
Product trademark	The prospective appearance of a new Muppet in the movie *Muppet Treasure Island* resulted in a lawsuit. Jim Henson Productions, Inc., named the new Muppet, an exotic wild boar, "Spa'am." Hormel Foods Corporation, which manufactures Spam, feared that the use of the Spa'am character would harm sales of Spam and sued Henson. A U.S. district court judge ruled that the Spa'am Muppet would be unlikely to harm Hormel's Spam trademark.
Promotion Issue	
Advertising	Many local auto dealers advertise deals that are too good to be true. One dealer advertised a $30,000 Mercedes C-class for $18,036. The down payment and other conditions were vague.
Pricing Issue	
Price fixing	Archer Daniels Midland, a Decatur, Illinois, company, was accused of fixing prices on key agricultural commodities—high fructose corn syrup, citric acid, and lysine.
Distribution Issue	
Distributing counterfeit products	Some record stores offer counterfeit recordings as authentic; in fact, one in four record albums is counterfeit. China and Bulgaria distribute $1 billion in pirated CDs each year. Some direct marketing companies have been set up to sell counterfeit products.

Sources: *Hormel Foods Corporation v Jim Henson Productions, Inc.*, 95 civ. 5473 (KMW); Earle Eldridge, "Some Offers Too Good To Be True," *USA Today*, Nov. 27, 1995, p. 3B; and Robyn Nerdith, "Archer Daniels' Investors Launch Revolt: Price Fixing Investigation Secrecy Causes Stir," *USA Today*, Oct. 20, 1995, p. 1B.

Product-related ethical issues generally arise when marketers fail to disclose risks associated with a product or information regarding the function, value, or use of a product. Pressures can build to substitute inferior materials or product components to reduce costs. Chrysler, for example, has experienced negative publicity and lawsuits associated with the tailgate latch on some of its minivan models. The latch has allegedly failed in certain rear-impact collisions, resulting in death and injury to minivan occupants. Ethical issues also arise when marketers fail to inform customers about existing conditions or changes in product quality; this failure is a form of dishonesty about the nature of the product. Consider the introduction of a new size of candy bar, labeled with a banner touting its "new larger size." However, when placed in vending machines alongside older candy bars of the same brand, it was apparent that the product was actually slightly smaller than the candy bar it replaced. Although this could have been a mistake, the firm still has to defend and deal with the consequences of its actions.

Promotion can create ethical issues in a variety of ways, among them false or misleading advertising and manipulative or deceptive sales promotions, tactics, and publicity. The Federal Trade Commission, for example, has accused Chrysler of using deceptive advertising by omitting critical cost information from ads or providing it in such small print that it could not be read. In addition, some Chrysler print ads displayed a luxury vehicle next to lease terms for other, less expensive automobiles.[25] A major ethical issue in promotion pertains to minorities and children. In this regard, two African-American health groups have filed a lawsuit against twelve tobacco companies, alleging that the firms specifically target menthol cigarettes to African-American consumers and thus violate their civil rights. The suit also charges that menthol cigarettes are more dangerous than regular cigarettes.[26] Some critics believe that the familiar Joe Camel advertising character used by R. J. Reynolds may attract children, even those in elementary schools; this illustrates the ongoing legal and ethical concerns about the promotion and distribution of tobacco products. Similarly, a number of companies that market video games have been accused of promoting violence and weapons to children. Many other ethical issues are linked to promotion, including the use of bribery in personal selling situations. Even when a bribe is offered to benefit the organization, it is usually considered unethical. Because it jeopardizes trust and fairness, it hurts the organization in the long run.

In pricing, common ethical issues are price fixing, predatory pricing, and failure to disclose the full price of a purchase. The emotional and subjective nature of price creates many situations in which misunderstandings between the seller and buyer cause ethical problems. Marketers have the right to price their products so they earn a reasonable profit, but ethical issues may crop up when a company seeks to earn high profits at the expense of its customers. Some pharmaceutical companies, for example, have been accused of pricing products at exorbitant levels and taking advantage of customers who must purchase the medicine to survive or to maintain their quality of life.

Ethical issues in distribution involve relationships among producers and marketing middlemen. Marketing middlemen, or intermediaries (wholesalers and retailers), facilitate the flow of products from the producer to the ultimate customer. Each intermediary performs a different role and agrees to certain rights, responsibilities, and rewards associated with that role. For example, producers expect wholesalers and retailers to honor agreements and to keep them informed of inventory needs. Ingram Entertainment, the largest wholesaler of recorded videocassettes, plans to sell videos and books over the Internet. If it does engage in direct selling, Ingram will become a direct competitor of its retail customers, who trust Ingram to be a partner, not a competitor.[27] Such a decision represents an ethical issue but may have legal concerns as well. Other serious ethical issues with regard to distribution include manipulating a product's availability for purposes of exploitation and using coercion to force intermediaries to behave in a specific manner.

The Ethical Decision-Making Process

To grasp the significance of ethics in marketing decision making, it is helpful to examine the factors that influence the ethical decision-making process. As shown in Figure

Figure 4.5
Factors That Influence the
Ethical Decision-Making
Process in Marketing

4.5, individual factors, organizational relationships, and opportunity interact to determine ethical decisions in marketing.

Individual Factors.   When people need to resolve ethical conflicts in their daily lives, they often base their decisions on their own values and principles of right or wrong. In a survey of high school students, almost all indicated that they feel it is important to be a person of "good character"; nonetheless, 47 percent admitted to cheating on an exam and 92 percent confessed to lying to their parents.[28] People learn values and principles through socialization by family members, social groups, religion, and formal education. In the workplace, however, research has established that an organization's values often have more influence on marketing decisions than a person's own values.[29]

organizational (corporate) culture   A set of values, beliefs, goals, norms, and rituals that members of an organization share

Organizational Factors.   Although people can and do make ethical choices pertaining to marketing decisions, no one operates in a vacuum.[30] Ethical choices in marketing are most often made jointly, in work groups and committees or in conversations and discussions with coworkers. Marketers resolve ethical issues not only on the basis of what they learned from their backgrounds, but also on the basis of what they learn from others in the organization. The outcome of this learning process depends on the strength of each individual's personal values, opportunity for unethical behavior, and exposure to others who behave ethically or unethically. Superiors, peers, and subordinates in the organization influence the ethical decision-making process. Although people outside the organization, such as family members and friends, also influence decision makers, organizational culture and structure operate through organizational relationships to influence ethical decisions.

   Organizational, or **corporate, culture** can be defined as a set of values, beliefs, goals, norms, and rituals that members of an organization share. A firm's culture may be expressed formally through codes of conduct, memos, manuals, dress codes, and ceremonies (Figure 4.6), but it is also expressed informally through

Figure 4.6
Formal Organizational Factors in the
Ethical Decision-Making Process
Sears provides a formal ethics program with training materials to promote ethical conduct throughout the organization.

IT'S ONE OF THE MAGICAL THINGS ABOUT BUSINESS.

START TREATING YOUR PEOPLE AS YOUR GREATEST ASSET AND SUDDENLY THAT'S WHAT THEY BECOME.

Hidden within your company lies the resource that can provide you with the ultimate competitive advantage. They're called people. Often overlooked in the era of reengineering, reorganizing, TQM and other "sure-fire" ways to increase shareholder value, your human capital – not physical or financial capital – holds the key to providing true, sustainable, long-term growth. Within them lie untold fountains of innovation and effort. Unleash their potential, harness their energy, align them with your business strategy, and watch your company take off. To learn how people can become your greatest asset, call your local Watson Wyatt office or 1-800-851-4346, or visit our web site at www.watsonwyatt.com.

Watson Wyatt Worldwide
Making Strategy Work®

Figure 4.7
Informal Organizational Factors in the Ethical Decision-Making Process
Watson Wyatt—a global consulting firm—advocates an organizational culture that treats employees as the firm's greatest asset because employee satisfaction has been linked to an ethical organizational climate.

work habits, extracurricular activities, and anecdotes (Figure 4.7). An organization's culture gives its members meaning and suggests rules for how to behave and deal with problems within the organization.

With regard to organizational structure, most experts agree that the chief executive officer or vice president of marketing sets the ethical tone for the entire organization. Lower-level managers obtain their cues from top managers, but they, too, impose some of their personal values on the company. This interaction between corporate culture and executive leadership helps determine the ethical value system of the firm.

Coworkers' influence on ethical choices depends on a person's exposure to unethical behavior. Especially in gray areas, the more a person is exposed to unethical activity by others in the organizational environment, the more likely it is that he or she will behave unethically. Most marketers take their cues from coworkers in learning how to solve problems—including ethical problems.[31]

Organizational pressure plays a key role in creating ethical issues. For example, because of pressure to meet a schedule, a salesperson may be asked by a superior to lie to a customer over the phone about a late product shipment. Similarly, pressure to meet a sales quota may result in overly aggressive sales tactics. In one survey of workers, 50 percent said they had felt pressure to act unethically, and 48 percent admitted they had committed unethical acts as a result of the pressure of coworkers.[32] In a survey of human resource professionals, 50 percent indicated they had witnessed conduct in violation of the law or company policies.[33] Nearly all marketers face difficult issues whose solutions are not obvious or that present conflicts between organizational objectives and personal ethics.

Opportunity. Another factor that may shape ethical decisions in marketing is opportunity—that is, conditions that limit barriers or provide rewards. If a marketer takes advantage of an opportunity to act unethically and is rewarded or suffers no penalty, he or she may repeat such acts as other opportunities arise. For example, a salesperson who receives a raise after using a deceptive sales presentation to increase sales is being rewarded and so will probably continue the behavior. Indeed, opportunity to engage in unethical conduct is often a better predictor of unethical activities

Colombia is one of the best places in the hemisphere to do business.

Pablo Escobar
Medellin Cartel

Jose Santacruz Landono
Cali Cartel

Jose Gonzalo Rodriguez Gacha
Medellin Cartel

Unless, of course, you're in the wrong business.

Colombia is proving to be tremendously inhospitable to one industry. Drugs. We've taken dramatic steps that have severely curtailed the ability of narco-traffickers to operate in our country.

On the other hand, we have also taken steps to assure an ideal climate for the growth of legitimate businesses, domestic and otherwise. We have made huge investments in infrastructure and security. We allow foreign investors to invest on equal terms with local investors in almost any sector. And our tax rates and bases are very competitive with other Latin American countries.

It is worth noting, too, that Colombia has enjoyed positive GNP growth over a fifty year period and a Moody's Baa3 rating on its bonds.

We are a hemispheric leader in so many different industries, ranging from metals and precious stones to agribusinesses such as coffee and flowers.

We have a booming oil industry as well. Recent petroleum explorations in eastern Colombia have proved enormously fruitful. Indeed, we now hold the third largest reserves in the hemisphere, capable of extending our self-sufficiency and the production of exportable surpluses well beyond the year 2010.

Hundreds of multi-nationals now have a significant presence here, recognizing our country's long commitment to democratic principles, a stable economy, tremendous natural resources and an educated work force.

U.S. investment alone now exceeds 6 billion dollars, and Colombia is the number 3 buyer in Latin America of American products.

Undeniably, Colombia has had its share of problems. The plague of drugs has taken a toll on so many good people in our country and elsewhere, but we are well on our way to winning that war and regaining our status as one of the most progressive and admirable countries in the Americas.

The 37 million people of Colombia.
37 million based on the 1998 census revision.

Working to change the way you think about our country.

This advertisement is brought to you by The Fund For The Promotion of Colombian Exports, ProExport-Colombia. 1001 South Bayshore Drive Suite 1904 Miami, Florida 33131

Figure 4.8
Assessing Opportunity for Unethical Behavior
To improve its image, Colombia promotes a desire for only responsible and ethical companies to do business there.

than personal values.[34] Beyond rewards and the absence of punishment, other elements in the business environment may create opportunities. Professional codes of conduct and ethics-related corporate policy also influence opportunity by prescribing what behaviors are acceptable, as we shall see later. The larger the rewards and the milder the punishment for unethical conduct, the greater is the likelihood that unethical behavior will occur.

However, just as the majority of people who go into retail stores do not try to shoplift at each opportunity, most marketers do not try to take advantage of every opportunity for unethical behavior in their organizations. Individual factors as well as organizational culture may influence whether an individual becomes opportunistic and tries to take advantage of situations unethically.

Whistle blowers, those who report unethical or illegal organizational conduct, often do so because of a strong personal conviction about doing the right thing regardless of what the organization condones. Blowing the whistle on corporate wrongdoing can be risky, however. Hercules, Inc., a manufacturer of nuclear rockets, eventually agreed to pay $36 million to an employee it fired after the employee questioned the firm's quality-control inspections for rocket motors. The company admitted no wrongdoing and says it settled to end costly litigation in the matter.[35] Figure 4.8 illustrates that there is concern about business ethics even at the national level. The Republic of Colombia is attempting to change the way people think about opportunities for unethical conduct in that country.

Improving Ethical Conduct in Marketing

It is possible to improve ethical conduct in an organization by hiring ethical employees and eliminating unethical ones, and by improving the organization's ethical standards. One way to approach improvement of an organization's ethical standards is to use a "bad apple–bad barrel" analogy. Some people always do things in their own self-interest, regardless of organizational goals or accepted moral standards; they are sometimes called "bad apples." To eliminate unethical conduct, an organization must rid itself of bad apples through screening techniques and enforcement of the firm's ethical standards. However, organizations sometimes become "bad barrels," not because the individuals within them are bad, but because the pressures to survive and succeed create conditions (opportunities) that reward unethical behavior. A way of resolving the problem of the bad barrel is to redesign the organization's image and culture so that it conforms to industry and societal norms of ethical conduct.[36]

If top management develops and enforces ethics and legal compliance programs to encourage ethical decision making, then it becomes a force to help individuals make better decisions. When marketers understand the policies and requirements for ethical conduct, they can more easily resolve ethical conflicts. However, marketers can never fully abdicate their personal ethical responsibility in making decisions. Claiming to be an agent of the business ("the company told me to do it") is not accepted as a legal excuse and is even less defensible from an ethical perspective.[37]

In Chapter 3, we briefly discussed the Federal Sentencing Guidelines for Organizations established by the U.S. Sentencing Commission to deter corporate misconduct. The guidelines urge organizations to develop ethics and legal compliance programs *before* infractions occur. If individuals within an organization act illegally, the firm must show that it had implemented reasonable programs for deterring and preventing misconduct to avoid penalties under the new sentencing guidelines. The

Table 4.4   Seven Steps to Ethical Compliance
1. Establish codes of conduct.
2. Appoint or hire high-level compliance manager (ethics officer).
3. Take care in delegating authority.
4. Institute a training program and communication system (ethics training).
5. Monitor and audit for misconduct.
6. Enforce and discipline.
7. Revise program as needed.
Source: U.S. Sentencing Commission, Federal Sentencing Guidelines for Organizations, 1991.

seven minimum requirements for a compliance program, listed in Table 4.4, are not "a superficial checklist requiring little analysis or thought."[38] Rather, a firm's compliance and ethics program must be capable of reducing the opportunity that employees have to engage in misconduct.

codes of conduct
Formalized rules and standards that describe what the company expects of its employees

Codes of Conduct. Without compliance programs and uniform standards and policies regarding conduct, it is hard for employees to determine what conduct is acceptable within a company. In the absence of such programs and standards, employees will generally make decisions based on their observations of how their peers and superiors behave. To improve ethics, many organizations have developed **codes of conduct** (also called *codes of ethics*), which consist of formalized rules and standards that describe what the company expects of its employees. Most large corporations have formal codes of conduct. Codes of conduct promote ethical behavior by reducing opportunities for unethical behavior; employees know both what is expected of them and what kind of punishment they face if they violate the rules. Codes help marketers deal with ethical issues or dilemmas that develop in daily operations by prescribing or limiting specific activities. Codes of conduct have also made companies that subcontract manufacturing operations abroad more aware of the ethical issues associated with supporting facilities that underpay and even abuse their work force. New industry codes of conduct have been established to help companies identify and deal with these ethical issues.[39]

Codes of conduct do not have to be so detailed that they take into account every situation, but they should provide guidelines that enable employees to achieve organizational objectives in an ethical, acceptable manner. The American Marketing Association Code of Ethics, reprinted in Table 4.5, does not cover every possible ethical issue, but it *does* provide a useful overview of what marketers believe are sound principles for guiding marketing activities. This code serves as a helpful model for structuring an organization's code of conduct.

Ethics Officers. A marketing compliance program must have oversight by a high-ranking person in the organization who is known to abide by legal and common ethical standards. This person is referred to as an ethics officer. In 1997, 45 percent of U.S. companies had ethics offices, up from just 11 percent in 1987.[40] Ethics officers are usually responsible for

- Meeting with the board of directors, top managers, and employees to discuss or provide advice about ethical issues and to identify potential ethical risks to the organization

- Drafting, disseminating, and updating a code of conduct

- Training employees to deal with potential ethical issues

- Creating and maintaining a confidential system to answer questions about ethical issues (online, ethics hotlines, etc.)

- Taking action on possible violations of the code of conduct

- Working with people in other organizations and associations to gain greater understanding of how to manage ethics and compliance programs effectively

Table 4.5　Code of Ethics of the American Marketing Association

Members of the American Marketing Association (AMA) are committed to ethical professional conduct. They have joined together in subscribing to this Code of Ethics embracing the following topics:

Responsibilities of the Marketer

Marketers must accept responsibility for the consequences of their activities and make every effort to ensure that their decisions, recommendations, and actions function to identify, serve, and satisfy all relevant publics: consumers, organizations and society. Marketers' professional conduct must be guided by:

1. The basic rule of professional ethics: not knowingly to do harm;
2. The adherence to all applicable laws and regulations;
3. The accurate representation of their education, training and experience; and
4. The active support, practice and promotion of this Code of Ethics.

Honesty and Fairness

Marketers shall uphold and advance the integrity, honor, and dignity of the marketing profession by:

1. Being honest in serving consumers, clients, employees, suppliers, distributors and the public;
2. Not knowingly participating in conflict of interest without prior notice to all parties involved; and
3. Establishing equitable fee schedules including the payment or receipt of usual, customary and/or legal compensation for marketing exchanges

Rights and Duties of Parties in the Marketing Exchange Process

Participants in the marketing exchange process should be able to expect that:

1. Products and services offered are safe and fit for their intended uses;
2. Communications about offered products and services are not deceptive;
3. All parties intend to discharge their obligations, financial and otherwise, in good faith; and
4. Appropriate internal methods exist for equitable adjustment and/or redress of grievances concerning purchases.

It is understood that the above would include, but is not limited to, the following responsibilities of the marketer:

In the area of product development management:
- Disclosure of all substantial risks associated with product or service usage
- Identification of product component substitution that might materially change the product or affect the buyer's purchase decision
- Identification of extra-cost added features

In the area of promotions:
- Avoidance of false and misleading advertising
- Rejection of high pressure manipulations, or misleading sales tactics
- Avoidance of sales promotions that use deception or manipulation

In the area of distribution:
- Not manipulating the availability of a product for purpose of exploitation
- Not using coercion in the marketing channel
- Not exerting undue influence over the resellers' choice to handle a product

In the area of pricing:
- Not engaging in price fixing
- Not practicing predatory pricing
- Disclosing the full price associated with any purchase

In the area of marketing research:
- Prohibiting selling or fund raising under the guise of conducting research
- Maintaining research integrity by avoiding misrepresentation and omission of pertinent research data
- Treating outside clients and suppliers fairly

Organizational Relationships

Marketers should be aware of how their behavior may influence or impact on the behavior of others in organizational relationships. They should not demand, encourage or apply coercion to obtain unethical behavior in their relationships with others, such as employees, suppliers or customers.

1. Apply confidentiality and anonymity in professional relationships with regard to privileged information;
2. Meet their obligations and responsibilities in contracts and mutual agreements in a timely manner;
3. Avoid taking the work of others, in whole, or in part, and representing this work as their own or directly benefit from it without compensation or consent of the originator or owner; and
4. Avoid manipulation to take advantage of situations to maximize personal welfare in a way that unfairly deprives or damages the organization or others.

Any AMA members found to be in violation of any provision of this Code of Ethics may have his or her Association membership suspended or revoked.

Source: Reprinted by permission of the American Marketing Association.

In addition to selecting a high-level compliance officer, companies must take care in delegating authority to ensure that individuals prone to misconduct are not given management positions.

Implementing Ethics and Legal Compliance Programs.   To nurture ethical conduct in marketing, open communication and coaching on ethical issues are essential. This requires providing employees with ethics training, clear channels of communication, and follow-up support throughout the organization. Some firms set up ethics hotlines to handle employee questions on ethical issues. About 5 percent of Northrop's 32,000 employees have used its "Open Line" hotline.[41] However, when a Prudential Insurance employee reported repeated ethics violations (everything from churning policies to misrepresenting policies) on the company hotline, he was fired. The employee has sued for wrongful termination, and the matter is being privately arbitrated.[42]

It is important that companies consistently enforce standards and impose penalties or punishment on those who violate codes of conduct. In addition, the company must take reasonable steps in response to violations of standards and, as appropriate, revise the compliance program to diminish the likelihood of future misconduct. If a compliance program is to succeed, it must be viewed as a part of the overall marketing strategy implementation. If ethics officers and other executives are not committed to the principles and initiatives of marketing ethics and social responsibility, then the program's effectiveness will be in question. On the other hand, ethics officers still must focus most of their attention on the development of the organization's culture. While the Federal Sentencing Guidelines for Organizations may have been the chief motivating factor in the creation of ethics offices, a survey of ethics officers reported that 76 percent feel the purpose of their ethics office is to "insure commitment to corporate values," and 68 percent said they were motivated by the need to establish a better corporate culture. Today, the purpose of most compliance programs is not to check off boxes corresponding to the Federal Sentencing Guidelines' seven requirements for a compliance program, but to create a values-based corporate culture.[43]

Although the virtues of honesty, fairness, and openness are often assumed to be self-evident and universally accepted, marketing strategy decisions involve complex and detailed matters in which correctness may not be so clear-cut. A high level of personal morality may not be sufficient to prevent an individual from violating the law in an organizational context in which even experienced lawyers debate the exact meaning of the law. Because it is impossible to train all the members of an organization as lawyers, the identification of ethical issues and implementation of compliance programs and codes of conduct that incorporate both legal and ethical concerns constitute the best approach to preventing violations and avoiding litigation. Codifying ethical standards into meaningful policies that spell out what is and is not acceptable gives marketers an opportunity to reduce the probability of behavior that could create legal problems. Without proper ethical training and guidance, it is impossible for the average marketing manager to understand the exact boundaries of illegality in the areas of price fixing, copyright violations, fraud, export/import violations, and so on. A corporate focus on ethics helps create a buffer zone on issues that could potentially trigger serious legal complications for the company.

Incorporating Social Responsibility and Ethics into Strategic Planning

Although the concepts of marketing ethics and social responsibility are often used interchangeably, it is important to distinguish between the two concepts. Ethics relates to individual and group decisions—judgments about what is right or wrong in a particular decision-making situation—whereas social responsibility deals with the total effect of marketing decisions on society. The two concepts are interrelated because a company that supports socially responsible decisions and adheres to a code of conduct is likely to have a positive effect on society. Because ethics and social

Table 4.6	**Considerations in Implementing a Social Responsibility Program**

- Decide which social responsibility practices will support both marketing goals and social goals.
- Ensure that key stakeholders understand your mission and goals.
- Involve all levels in the organization in developing and implementing the program.
- Build early support by choosing simple programs with immediate results (e.g., a vacation bank to reward employees for volunteer work).
- Ensure that the program is economically feasible so the organization can provide support from beginning to end.
- Develop a contingency plan to address problems or shortcomings.
- Solicit feedback on the program and adapt accordingly.

Source: Table "Considerations in Implementing a Social Responsibility Program," from Betsy Zeidman, "Corporate Social Responsibility: Beyond Traditional Ethics Programs," *Ethics Today 3,* (Winter 1998): 11. Reprinted by permission.

responsibility programs can be profitable as well, an increasing number of companies are incorporating them into their overall strategic market planning. Table 4.6 summarizes some considerations in implementing a social responsibility program.

As we have emphasized throughout this chapter, ethics is one dimension of social responsibility. Being socially responsible relates to doing what is economically sound, legal, ethical, and socially conscious. One way to evaluate whether a specific activity is ethical and socially responsible is to ask other persons in an organization if they approve of it. Contact with concerned consumer groups and industry or government regulatory groups may be helpful. A check to see whether there is a specific company policy about an activity may help resolve ethical questions. If other persons in the organization approve of the activity and it is legal and customary within the industry, chances are that the activity is acceptable from both an ethical and a social responsibility perspective. Table 4.7 provides an audit of mechanisms to help control ethics and social responsibility in marketing.

Table 4.7	**Organizational Audit of Social Responsibility and Ethics Control Mechanisms**

Answer True or False for each statement.

T	F	1. No mechanism exists for top management to detect social responsibility and ethical issues relating to employees, customers, the community, and society.
T	F	2. There is no formal or informal communication within the organization about procedures and activities that are considered acceptable behavior.
T	F	3. The organization fails to communicate its ethical standards to suppliers, customers, and groups that have a relationship with the organization.
T	F	4. There is an environment of deception, repression, and cover-ups concerning events that could be embarrassing to the company.
T	F	5. Compensation systems are totally dependent on economic performance.
T	F	6. The only concerns about environmental impact are those that are legally required.
T	F	7. Concern for the ethical value systems of the community with regard to the firm's activities is absent.
T	F	8. Products are described in a misleading manner, with no information on negative impact or limitations communicated to customers.

True answers indicate a lack of control mechanisms, which, if implemented, could improve ethics and social responsibility.

A rule of thumb for resolving ethical and social responsibility issues is that if they can withstand open discussion that results in agreement or limited debate, then an acceptable solution may exist. Nevertheless, even after a final decision is reached, different viewpoints on the issue may remain. Openness is not the end-all solution to the ethics problem. However, it does create trust and facilitates learning relationships.[44]

Being Socially Responsible and Ethical Is Not Easy

To promote socially responsible and ethical behavior while achieving organizational goals, marketers must monitor changes and trends in society's values. For example, companies around the world are developing and marketing more nutritional, healthier products in response to increasing public concern about cancer and heart disease. When Frito-Lay introduced WOW potato chips with 50 percent less fat than regular chips, it was hard for retailers to maintain enough inventory to meet demand. Furthermore, marketers must develop control procedures to ensure that daily decisions do not damage their company's relations with the public. An organization's top management must assume some responsibility for employees' conduct by establishing and enforcing policies.

After determining what society wants, marketers must then attempt to predict the long-term effects of decisions pertaining to those wants. Specialists outside the company, such as doctors, lawyers, and scientists, are often consulted, but there is sometimes a lack of agreement within a discipline as to what is an acceptable marketing decision. Forty years ago, for example, tobacco marketers promoted cigarettes as being good for one's health. Now, years after the discovery that cigarette smoking is linked to cancer and other medical problems, society's attitude toward smoking has changed, and marketers are confronted with new social responsibilities, such as providing a smoke-free atmosphere for customers. Most major hotel chains allocate at least some of their rooms to nonsmokers, many rental car companies provide smoke-free cars, and most other businesses within the food, travel, and entertainment industries provide smoke-free environments or sections.

There are costs associated with many of society's demands. For example, society wants a cleaner environment and the preservation of wildlife and their habitats, but it also wants low-priced products. Consider the plight of the gas station owner who asked his customers if they would be willing to spend an additional 1 cent per gallon if he instituted an air filtration system to eliminate harmful fumes. The majority indicated they supported his plan. However, when the system was installed and the price increased, many of his customers went to a competitor across the street for the cost savings. Thus, companies must carefully balance the costs of providing low-priced products against the costs of manufacturing, packaging, and distributing their products in an environmentally responsible manner.

In trying to satisfy the desires of one group, marketers may dissatisfy others. In the smoking debate, for example, marketers must balance nonsmokers' desires for a smoke-free environment against smokers' desires, or need, to continue to smoke. Some anti-tobacco crusaders call for the complete elimination of tobacco products to ensure a smoke-free world. However, this attitude fails to consider the difficulty smokers have in quitting (now that tobacco marketers have admitted their product is addictive) and the impact on U.S. communities and states that depend on tobacco crops for their economic survival. Thus, this, like most ethical and social responsibility issues, cannot be viewed in black and white.

Balancing society's demands to satisfy all members of society is difficult, if not impossible. Marketers must evaluate the extent to which members of society are willing to pay for what they want. For instance, customers may want more information about a product yet be unwilling to pay the costs the firm incurs in providing the data. Marketers who want to make socially responsible decisions may find the task a challenge because, ultimately, economic survival must be ensured.

Social Responsibility and Ethics Improve Marketing Performance

Do not think, however, that the challenge is not worth the effort. On the contrary, there is increasing evidence that being socially responsible and ethical pays. Research suggests that a relationship exists between a marketing orientation and an organizational climate that supports marketing ethics and social responsibility. This relationship implies that being ethically and socially concerned is consistent with meeting the demands of customers and other stakeholders. By encouraging their employees to understand their markets, companies can help them respond to stakeholders' demands.[45]

A survey of marketing managers found a direct association between corporate social responsibility and profits.[46] For example, Figure 4.9 illustrates that the drive to support socially responsible business involvement can be linked to activities that yield profits. In a survey of consumers, nearly 90 percent indicated that when quality, service, and price are equal among competitors, they would be more likely to buy from the company with the best reputation for social responsibility. In addition, 54 percent would pay more for a product that supported a cause they care about, 66 percent would switch brands to support such a cause, and 62 percent would switch retailers.[47]

Thus, recognition is growing that the long-term value of conducting business in a socially responsible manner far outweighs short-term costs.[48] Companies that do not develop strategies and programs to incorporate ethics and social responsibility into their organizational culture may pay the price with poor marketing performance and the potential costs of legal violations, civil litigation, and damaging publicity when questionable activities are made public. Consider, for example, the issue of silicon breast implants, which may have contributed to health problems in thousands of women. Faced with a protracted class-action lawsuit and negative publicity, several marketers of silicone-gel implants have tentatively agreed to a $4.2 billion global settlement to compensate women who claim they have been harmed by the implants.

On the other hand, organizations that do incorporate ethics and social responsibility into their strategic plans are likely to experience improved marketing performance as a result of a more positive reputation among consumers, which may lead to increased sales. In some cases, such efforts can also save a company money. Nortel, which phased out CFCs (chlorofluorocarbons) in three years, estimated that every $1 million invested in equipment related to the phaseout saved the company $4 million in waste disposal and CFC purchasing costs.[49] Likewise, 3M's Pollution Prevention Pays program eliminated 1.5 billion pounds of air, land, and water pollution and saved the company $790 million. Sometimes the results are even more dramatic. DuPont rose from being the seventh largest herbicide marketer to the second largest after its agricultural division developed a line of biodegradable herbicides that are applied by the thimbleful rather than the barrel. Moreover, use of these less toxic products reduced the annual amount of herbicides applied worldwide by 8 percent.[50] Thus, responsible actions by marketers can help not only society, but also a company's bottom line.

Because marketing ethics and social responsibility are not always viewed as organizational performance issues, many managers do not believe they need to be considered in the strategic planning process. Individuals also have different ideas as to what is ethical or unethical, leading them to confuse the need for workplace ethics and the right to maintain their own personal values and ethics. While it is true that the concepts are controversial, it is possible—and desirable—to incorporate ethics and social responsibility into the planning process.[51]

Figure 4.9
Social Responsibility Improves Marketing Performance
BMW links the support of a socially responsible cause—finding a cure for breast cancer—with the opportunity to increase sales of new cars by donating $1 for every mile customers test drive.

The Ultimate Drive™ for the Susan G. Komen Breast Cancer Foundation

Do you have The Drive...
to help find The Cure?

BMW invites you to a very special driving event – where Your Drive can make a difference. For each mile you test drive, BMW will donate $1 to the Susan G. Komen Breast Cancer Foundation. Call toll-free 1-877-4-A-DRIVE today to reserve the car of your choice.

The Ultimate Driving Machine®

Summary

Social responsibility refers to an organization's obligation to maximize its positive impact and minimize its negative impact on society. It deals with the total effect of all marketing decisions on society. Although social responsibility is a positive concept, most organizations embrace it in the expectation of indirect long-term benefits.

Marketing citizenship involves incorporating economic, legal, ethical, and philanthropic dimensions into a firm's marketing strategies. At the most basic level, companies have an economic responsibility to be profitable so they can provide a return on investment to their stockholders, create jobs for the community, and contribute goods and services to the economy. Marketers are also expected to obey laws and regulations. Marketing ethics refers to principles and standards that define acceptable conduct in marketing as determined by various stakeholders, including the public, government regulators, private interest groups, industry, and the organization itself. Philanthropic responsibilities go beyond marketing ethics; they are not required of a company, but they promote human welfare or goodwill. Many firms use cause-related marketing, the practice of linking products to a social cause on an ongoing or short-term basis.

Four major categories of social responsibility issues are the natural environment, consumerism, diversity, and community relations. One of the more common ways marketers demonstrate social responsibility is through programs designed to protect and preserve the natural environment. Green marketing refers to the specific development, pricing, promotion, and distribution of products that do not harm the environment. Consumerism consists of the efforts of independent individuals, groups, and organizations to protect the rights of consumers. Consumers expect to have the right to safety, the right to be informed, the right to choose, and the right to be heard. Fostering diversity in the workplace requires the integration and utilization of a work force that reflects the general population. Many marketers view social responsibility as including contributions of resources (money, products, time) to community causes, such as the natural environment, arts and recreation, disadvantaged members of the community, and education.

Whereas social responsibility is achieved by balancing the interests of all stakeholders in an organization, ethics relates to acceptable standards of conduct in making individual and group decisions. Marketing ethics goes beyond legal issues. Ethical marketing decisions foster mutual trust in marketing relationships.

An ethical issue is an identifiable problem, situation, or opportunity requiring an individual or organization to choose from among several actions that must be evaluated as right or wrong, ethical or unethical. A number of ethical issues relate to the marketing mix (product, promotion, price, and distribution).

Individual factors, organizational relationships, and opportunity interact to determine ethical decisions in marketing. Individuals often base their decisions on their own values and principles of right or wrong. However, ethical choices in marketing are most often made jointly, in work groups and committees or in conversations and discussions with coworkers. Organizational culture and structure operate through organizational relationships (with superiors, peers, and subordinates) to influence ethical decisions. Organizational, or corporate, culture can be defined as a set of values, beliefs, goals, norms, and rituals that members of an organization share. The more a person is exposed to unethical activity by others in the organizational environment, the more likely it is that he or she will behave unethically. Organizational pressure plays a key role in creating ethical issues, as does opportunity—that is, conditions that limit barriers or provide rewards.

It is possible to improve ethical behavior in an organization by hiring ethical employees and eliminating unethical ones, and by improving the organization's ethical standards. If top management develops and enforces ethics and legal compliance programs to encourage ethical decision making, then it becomes a force to help individuals make better decisions. To improve company ethics, many organizations have developed codes of conduct, formalized rules and standards that describe what the company expects of its employees. A marketing compliance program must have oversight by a high-ranking person in the organization known to abide by legal and common ethical standards; this person is usually called an ethics officer. To nurture ethical conduct in marketing, open communication and coaching on ethical issues are essential. This requires providing employees with ethics training, clear channels of communication, and follow-up support throughout the organization. Companies must consistently enforce standards and impose penalties or punishment on those who violate codes of conduct.

An increasing number of companies are incorporating ethics and social responsibility programs into their overall strategic market planning. To promote socially responsible and ethical behavior while achieving organizational goals, marketers must monitor changes and trends in society's values. They must determine what society wants and attempt to predict the long-term effects of decisions of those wants. Costs are associated with many of society's demands, and balancing these demands to satisfy all of society is difficult. However, there is more evidence that being socially responsible and ethical provides good benefits: an enhanced public reputation, which can increase market share, costs savings, and profits.

Important Terms

Social responsibility
Marketing citizenship
Marketing ethics

Cause-related marketing
Green marketing
Ethical issue

Organizational (corporate) culture
Codes of conduct

Discussion and Review Questions

1. What is social responsibility, and why is it important?

2. What are four dimensions of social responsibility? What impact do they have on marketing decisions?

3. What are some major social responsibility issues? Give an example of each.

4. What is the difference between ethics and social responsibility?

5. Why is ethics an important consideration in marketing decisions?

6. How do the factors that influence ethical or unethical decisions interact?

7. What ethical conflicts could exist if business employees fly on certain airlines just to receive benefits for their personal "frequent flyer" program?

8. Give an example of how each of the components of the marketing mix can be affected by ethical issues.

9. How can the ethical decisions involved in marketing be improved?

10. How can people with different personal values work together to make ethical decisions in organizations?

11. What tradeoffs might a company have to make to be socially responsible and responsive to society's demands?

12. What evidence is there that being socially responsible and ethical is worthwhile?

Application Questions

1. Some organizations promote their social responsibility. These companies often claim that being ethical is good business and that it pays to be a good citizen of the community. Identify a company or organization in your community that has a reputation for being ethical and socially responsible. What activities account for this image? Is the company successful? Why?

2. If you had to conduct a social audit of your organization's ethics and social responsibility, what information would you be most concerned with obtaining? What key stakeholders would you want to communicate with? How could such an audit, conducted by a company, assist it in improving its ethics and social responsibility?

3. Suppose that in your job you face situations that require you to make decisions about what is right or wrong, and then you have to act on these decisions. Describe such a situation. Without disclosing your actual decision, explain what you based it on. What and whom did you think of when you were considering what to do? Why did you consider these things or people?

4. Consumers interact with many businesses daily and weekly. Not only do companies in an industry acquire a reputation for being ethical or unethical; entire industries also become known as ethical or unethical. Identify two types of businesses with which you or your friends have had the most conflict involving ethical issues. Describe these ethical issues.

Internet Exercise & Resources

DePaul University's Institute for Business and Professional Ethics

The Web site for the Institute for Business and Professional Ethics at DePaul University offers much information on marketing ethics. You can access recent articles from newspapers like the *Chicago Sun-Times* plus an "Online Journal of Ethics," and other useful hotlinks. Visit this site at

http://condor.depaul.edu/ethics

1. Identify three articles from the *Chicago Sun-Times* that you believe deal with ethical issues in marketing.

2. For each article, tell how ethical issues relate to a concept covered in Chapter 4.

3. Identify one article in the "Online Journal of Ethics" that deals with an ethical issue that someone might encounter early in his or her marketing career.

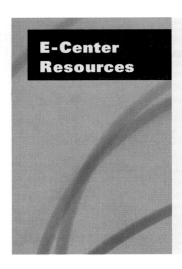

E-Center Resources

Visit http://www.prideferrell.com to find several resources to help you succeed in mastering the material in this chapter, plus additional materials that will help you expand your marketing knowledge. The Web site includes

- Internet exercise updates plus additional exercises
- ✔ ACE self-tests
- abc Chapter summary with hotlinked glossary
- ↻ Hotlinks to companies featured in this chapter
- ✪ Resource Center
- ▢ Career Center
- ▤ Marketing plan worksheets

VIDEO CASE 4.1

Social Responsibility at Home Depot

Home Depot, the home-improvement superstore chain, does everything on a grand scale, including putting its corporate muscle behind a tightly focused social responsibility agenda. Founded in 1978, Home Depot quickly became a major force in home-improvement retailing. Today, the company employs 155,000 people and operates 742 stores in the United States, Canada, Puerto Rico, and Chile. It rings up more than $24 billion in annual sales and controls 14 percent of the $140 billion U.S. market for home-improvement retailing. The company has remained well ahead of its nearest rivals, Lowes Companies (the number-two company) and Hechinger (number three).

Do-it-yourselfers can find just about anything they need in a Home Depot superstore. Browsing through one of the 100,000-square-foot buildings attached to a 22,000-square-foot outdoor garden center, homeowners and contractors alike can buy 50,000 products for the home and yard, from kitchen and bathroom fixtures to carpeting, lumber, and tools. Want to know how to tile a bathroom or wallpaper the dining room? The company offers free home-improvement clinics every week to teach consumers how to tackle a wide variety of everyday projects. And if you really don't want to do it yourself, most stores offer installation services. Knowledgeable employees are always on hand to help customers find just the right item or to demonstrate the proper use of a particular tool.

Just because Home Depot is a big corporation doesn't mean it is an uncaring and impersonal one. In fact, cofounders Bernard Marcus and Arthur Blank (chairman and president, respectively) have nurtured a corporate culture that emphasizes meaningful social responsibility. The company has an annual philanthropic budget of $12.5 million, which it directs back

to the communities it serves and to the interests of its employees through its Matching Gift Program. Rather than scatter its philanthropic resources, the company has chosen to concentrate on three areas: affordable housing, at-risk youth, and the natural environment.

The company posts a "Social Responsibility Report" on its Web site that specifies how it distributes its annual charitable contributions. In one recent year, Home Depot sponsored more than 100 Habitat for Humanity construction projects and provided support to dozens of local housing groups, including the Clearwater Neighborhood Housing Services and the New Orleans Neighborhood Development Foundation. The company also contributed to more than 120 youth programs, including Big Brothers/Big Sisters, the National Center for Missing and Exploited Children, and the Youth Job Center of Evanston. It donated to a long list of environmental causes, including Keep America Beautiful, the Tampa Audubon Society, and the World Wildlife Fund Canada. The company has also established a set of "environmental principles" that include selling responsibly marketed products, eliminating unnecessary packaging, recycling and encouraging the use of products with recycled content, and conserving natural resources by using them wisely. Home Depot's environmental programs earned the company an A on the Corporate Report Card of the Council on Economic Priorities.

On a more personal level, Home Depot encourages its employees to get involved in the community through volunteer and civic activities. On any given day, a small army of Home Depot volunteers may be found wielding paintbrushes to fix up a family shelter, planting trees to spruce up an inner-city park, or framing a Habitat for Humanity house for a deserving family. Such contributions allow employees to make a real difference in their communities while enhancing the company's reputation.

Home Depot also strives to apply social responsibility to its employment practices, with the goal of assembling a truly diverse work force that reflects the population of the markets it serves. Despite these efforts, the company recently settled a class action lawsuit brought by women employees who charged they were paid less than men, awarded fewer pay raises, and promoted less often. The $87.5 million settlement was one of the largest settlements of a gender discrimination lawsuit in U.S. history. As part of the settlement, Home Depot was required to establish a formal system to ensure that employees can notify management of their interest in advancing to a management or sales position. In announcing the settlement, the company stressed that it was not admitting to wrongdoing. In fact, it defended its position, saying it "provides opportunities for all of its associates to develop successful professional careers and is proud of its strong track record of having successful women involved in all areas of the company."

Knowing that customers feel good about buying from a company that actively commits resources to social and environmental issues, company executives believe that social responsibility can and should be an integral part of Home Depot's business operations. Home Depot remains committed to its focused strategy of philanthropy and volunteerism. This commitment extends throughout the company, fueled by top-level support from the cofounders and reinforcement from a corporate culture that places great value on being part of the solution, not part of the problem.[52]

Questions for Discussion

1. In addition to contributing to groups that address affordable housing, youth at risk, and the environment, what other social issues might Home Depot choose to support that fit well with its strategic plans?
2. As a publicly traded company, how can Home Depot justify budgeting more than $10 million annually for philanthropic causes?
3. As part of its settlement of the gender discrimination lawsuit brought against it, Home Depot agreed to establish a formal system whereby employees can inform management of their interest in advancement. What other actions might Home Depot take to strengthen the rights of its employees to equal treatment in the workplace?

CASE 4.2

Columbia/HCA Creates a New Culture of Ethics

In 1987, hoping to take advantage of the growing trend toward managed health care, entrepreneur Richard L. Scott and Texas billionaire Richard Rainwater founded Columbia Hospital Corporation. Their plan was to establish a profitable, low-cost, high-volume health care provider in as many cities as possible. To implement this strategy, CEO Scott went on a hospital-buying binge, acquiring many for-profit and nonprofit hospitals and hospital chains, including Galen Health Care and HealthTrust. In 1994, Columbia merged with Hospital Corporation of America (HCA), and by 1997, with 343 hospitals, Columbia/HCA was the nation's largest hospital chain. The corporation also operated 136 outpatient surgery centers and 550 home health locations, and it provided extensive outpatient and ancillary services in thirty-seven states, as well as overseas. With revenues of nearly $20 billion, Columbia/HCA was the seventh largest U.S. employer. To achieve the kind of competitive advantage it enjoyed, the corporation had rigorously followed its initial strategy of controlling internal costs and acquiring a high volume of business.

Many critics, however, maintained that health care services and staffing often took a back seat to Columbia's focus on profits. For example, Columbia's training periods were often shorter than those at competing hospitals. One former administrator observed that training that typically takes six months was sometimes done in as little as two weeks in a Columbia/HCA hospital. The corporation was also accused of "patient dumping," the practice of discharging emergency room patients or transferring them to other hospitals before they are in a stable condition. In 1997, officials at the Department of Health and Human Services indicated that they were considering fining Columbia/HCA for an unspecified number of patient dumping cases.

But these were not the only problems to surface at Columbia/HCA that year. In July 1997, Fawcett Memorial Hospital, a Columbia/HCA facility in Port Charlotte, Florida, became the focal point of the largest case of health care fraud in the history of the industry. A federal investigation resulted in the indictment of three mid-level Columbia/HCA executives on charges of filing false reports for Fawcett that cost Medicare, Medicaid, and other federal health programs more than $4.4 million. The government alleged that Columbia/HCA not only overcharged and billed for nonreimbursable expenses, but also shifted Medicare costs to its home health care business in order to obtain higher reimbursements.

The investigation ultimately led to charges that Columbia/HCA's corporate officers and managers had engaged in a "systematic corporate scheme" to defraud government health care programs. Federal investigators quoted confidential witnesses as saying that CEO Scott and President David Vandewater were routinely briefed on issues relating to Medicare reimbursement claims—claims that the government maintains were fraudulent; that Samuel Greco, Columbia's chief of operations, knew of the alleged fraud at Fawcett Memorial Hospital; that Columbia attempted to conceal from federal regulators internal documents that could have exposed the alleged fraud; and that a top executive instructed employees to soften the language used in internal financial audits that were critical of Columbia's practices. In addition to the federal investigation, attorneys general in several states launched their own investigations of Columbia's practices.

As the magnitude of the scandal became public, consumers, doctors, and the general public lost confidence in Columbia/HCA, and its stock price plummeted more than 50 percent. Meanwhile, new management focused on resolving the corporation's problems and developing an ethical compliance program. At a conference in Phoenix, twenty Columbia managers were asked to raise their hands if they had escaped taunts from friends about being a crook. Not one hand went up, and the discussion focused not on surgery or profit margins, but on the importance of values and the corporate image.

In the aftermath of the scandal, Columbia sold some hospitals, clinics, and part of its home health business. CEO and chairman Richard Scott was replaced by Dr. Thomas Frist, Jr., who had been founder and president of Hospital Corporation of America before its merger with Columbia. Frist vowed to cooperate fully with the government on the investigation and, within a hundred days, to develop a plan to change the company's culture. "We have to take the company in a new direction," Dr. Frist said. "The days when Columbia/HCA was seen as an adversarial or in your face, a behind-closed-doors kind of place, is a thing of the past."

One hundred days later, Frist outlined the changes that would reshape Columbia/HCA. His reforms included a new mission statement, which emphasizes a commitment to quality medical care and honesty in business practices, but makes no mention of financial performance. He also hired Alan Yuspeh, a specialist in corporate ethics, to serve as Senior Vice President of Ethics, Compliance, and Corporate Responsibility. Yuspeh was given a staff of twelve at the corporate headquarters and assigned to work with group, division, and facility presidents to create a corporate culture in which "Columbia workers feel compelled to do what is right." Yuspeh indicated that he would begin his tenure by refining monitoring techniques, boosting workers' ethics and compliance training, developing a code of conduct for employees, and creating an internal mechanism for workers to report any wrongdoing.

Yuspeh sent a fifteen-minute videotape to managers throughout Columbia/HCA announcing the launch of a compliance training program and the unveiling of a code of conduct that emphasizes compliance, integrity, and social responsibility. The company also designated employees to serve as Ethics and Compliance Officers (ECOs) at each of its facilities. The ECOs, who will implement the compliance training program locally, will be the key links in ensuring that the company continues to develop a culture of ethical conduct and corporate responsibility. Other actions taken to date include production of a forty-minute videotaped program that introduces employees to the code of conduct and the overall ethics and compliance program; creation of numerous policies to support the code of conduct; establishment of a compliance committee within the board of directors, as well as an internal compliance committee; and development of an ethics hotline for employees to report ethics and compliance issues. The videotaped program includes presentations from senior management and small group discussions in which participants discuss applications of the new code of conduct in three ethics-related scenarios; it was shown to all 285,000 employees in 1998.

Alan Yuspeh does not believe that employees will have to change personal values. Although Columbia/HCA wants individuals to bring their highest sense of personal values to work each day, the purpose of the compliance training program is to help employees understand how the corporation defines ethical behavior. Columbia/HCA's ethical guidelines tackle basic issues, such as whether nurses can accept $100 tips—they can't—and complicated topics, such as what constitutes Medicare fraud. The hotline deals with employees' billing questions, as do random audits and continuing education on ethics topics. The company has also developed certification tests for employees who determine billing codes to ensure that no laws are violated.

The effort to change Columbia's corporate culture quickly is a real challenge for Columbia/HCA. This health care provider learned the hard way that maintaining an ethical organizational climate is the responsibility of top management. Alan Yuspeh hopes Columbia's new ethics and compliance program will become a model for the health care industry. He has the full support of CEO Frist, who says, "We are making a substantial investment in our ethics and compliance program in order to ensure its success." Frist adds that "instituting a values-based culture throughout this company is something our employees have told us is critical to forming our future." It appears that Columbia/HCA has recognized the importance of ethical conduct and quality service to its customers and payment providers.[53]

Questions for Discussion

1. What ethical issues existed at Columbia/HCA in 1997?
2. What role did organizational culture play in the events at Columbia/HCA in 1997?
3. Evaluate the new ethical compliance program developed by Columbia/HCA. Does it meet the seven criteria listed in Table 4.4?

Global Markets and International Marketing

OBJECTIVES

- To understand the nature of global markets and international marketing

- To analyze the environmental forces affecting international marketing efforts

- To be able to identify several important regional trade alliances, markets, and agreements

- To learn about methods of involvement in international marketing activities

- To recognize that international marketing strategies fall along a continuum from customization to globalization

Japan, A Bumpy Road for American Cars

U.S. companies—automakers in particular—have long considered Japan a tough market to crack because of formidable trade barriers. American automakers have spent tens of millions of dollars reengineering cars for the Japanese market (e.g., moving the steering wheels to the right-hand side) and developing their own dealer networks there. Despite these efforts, Japanese consumers remain largely indifferent to American cars, preferring instead to buy models made by familiar Japanese firms like Toyota and Honda. U.S. automakers, especially General Motors, haven't given up, however.

GM's Saturn division is working very hard to push its brand into Japan. Unlike many other foreign companies that have promoted their models as upscale novelties in Japan, Saturn is positioning its cars as everyday vehicles. In addition to right-hand steering, the company installs folding side mirrors, a virtual necessity on Japan's narrow streets. Saturn has established its own network of dealers to set itself apart from other imports. It prices the cars at about $14,000, less than what most imports cost and about the same as Japanese models. The company also employs the same fixed-price, no-haggle policy in Japan that has proven so successful in the United States. Advertising portrays the company as user-friendly, with warm scenes of Saturn's headquarters in Tennessee along with images of young Japanese parents lauding their new Saturns. To appeal to families, Saturn's Japanese showrooms

include playrooms and toys. Japanese salespeople echo Saturn's friendly, relaxed image in their apparel, wearing polo shirts and white knit sweaters instead of the usual suit. The result of all these efforts? Just 1,400 vehicles sold in sixteen months. Chrysler and Ford have experienced the same lukewarm reception with the vehicles they've introduced in Japan.

Some experts suggest these companies aren't using the right strategy to reach Japanese buyers. They say that when the Japanese buy a foreign vehicle, they typically want one that stands out from the crowd. This may be a factor in the relative success in Japan of distinctively "American" models like Chrysler's Jeep Cherokee and GM's Cadillac Seville and Chevrolet Astra. In fact, even with the steering wheel on the left side and very little promotion by the company, 14,000 Astra vans were sold in Japan in a recent year. However, most Astras are sold not by Chevrolet, but through Japan's "gray market," a network of independent organizations that import the cars for resale, often at a discounted price. Astras are especially popular among young Japanese families, who often customize them with fancy paint jobs, luxurious interiors, and fog lights and use them for camping.

The inadvertent success of the Chevrolet Astra suggests that American automakers should indeed rethink their marketing strategies for Japanese markets. Saturn remains committed to Japan and may yet learn to satisfy Japanese tastes.[1]

Before picking up an Egg McMuffin at McDonald's, a young woman in Hong Kong this morning may have brightened her smile with Colgate toothpaste and highlighted her eyes with Avon eye shadow. Her brother, while on business that same day in Frankfurt, can cash a check in a local Citicorp branch bank. Elsewhere that day, a Polish office worker can enjoy a pizza from Pizza Hut, fried chicken from KFC, or a taco from Taco Bell for lunch. An Australian mother shopping for a birthday present in Melbourne can drop in at Daimaru, a Japanese department store, while a New Yorker in Syracuse may shop for a train set for his two-year-old son at the Lost Forest, an Australian toy boutique. As we enter the twenty-first century, the earth is populated by nearly 7 billion people whose lives are intertwined in one tremendous global marketplace. In fact, experts forecast that global exports of goods and services will reach $11.4 trillion by 2005, up from about $6.5 trillion in 1998.[2]

Because of the increasingly global nature of marketing, we devote this chapter to the unique features of global markets and international marketing. We begin by exploring the environmental forces that create opportunities and threats for international marketers. Next, we consider several regional trade alliances, markets, and agreements. Finally, we examine the levels of commitment U.S. firms have to international marketing and their degree of involvement in it. These represent significant factors that must be considered in any marketing plan that includes an international component.

The Nature of International Marketing

international marketing
Developing and performing marketing activities across national boundaries

Technological advances and rapidly changing political and economic conditions are making it easier for more companies to market their products overseas as well as at home. **International marketing** involves developing and performing marketing activities across national boundaries. Wal-Mart, for example, serves more than 90 million customers weekly in the United States, Canada, China, Mexico, Indonesia, Brazil, and Argentina, while the Coca-Cola Company sells more than one billion servings of Coca-Cola per day around the world.[3] Some products originally developed for sale in foreign markets have become quite successful in U.S. markets. Haagen-Dazs, for example, originally developed its "dulce de leche" caramel-flavored ice cream for Argentina, but in U.S. markets where it has been introduced, it is second in sales to vanilla. Similarly, soccer boots that Nike designed for Brazil are selling well in the United States, where the sport is gaining in popularity.[4]

Many U.S. firms are finding that international markets provide tremendous opportunities for growth. For example, Figure 5.1 indicates that Apple Computer now sells its products in Germany as well as many other countries. The consulting firm Deloitte and Touche estimates that about 95 percent of the world's population and two-thirds of its total purchasing power are outside the United

Figure 5.1
Global Markets Provide Opportunity for Growth
Apple has expanded its market for its PowerBook by going international, as shown in this advertisement made for Germany. (Headline translation: "Faster than any of its natural enemies")

States.[5] Accessing these markets can promote innovation, while intensifying global competition spurs companies to market better, less expensive products.[6] Most automobile marketers, for instance, are developing products for use by customers worldwide. In the future, just ten auto brands may be recognized globally. Some of these are likely to be from General Motors, whose many globally recognized brands include Saab, Opel, Chevrolet, and Cadillac. The Cadillac Seville is sold in forty countries, and approximately 20 percent of the vehicles have right-hand drive to satisfy different driving conditions. Saturn, another GM brand, has established a network of dealers in Japan, reflecting GM's strong commitment to establishing a global market.[7]

Environmental Forces in International Markets

Firms that enter foreign markets often find that they must make significant adjustments in their marketing strategies. The environmental forces that affect foreign markets may differ dramatically from those that affect domestic markets. Thus, a successful international marketing strategy requires a careful environmental analysis. Conducting research to understand the needs and desires of foreign customers is crucial to international marketing success. Many firms have demonstrated that such efforts can generate tremendous financial rewards, increase market share, and heighten customer awareness of their products around the world. In this section, we explore how differences in the sociocultural, economic, political, legal, and technological forces of the marketing environment in other countries can profoundly affect marketing activities.

Cultural, Social, and Ethical Forces

Cultural, social, and ethical differences among nations can have significant effects on marketing activities. Because marketing activities are primarily social in purpose, they are influenced by beliefs and values regarding family, religion, education, health, and recreation. For example, in Greece, where sunbathing is a common form of recreation, American products such as Johnson & Johnson Baby Sunblock have a large target market. By identifying major sociocultural deviations among countries, marketers lay groundwork for an effective adaptation of marketing strategy. For instance, because India's Hindu population considers eating beef to be taboo, McDonald's markets beefless burgers there, serving chicken, fish, and vegetable patties instead. Although football is a popular sport in the United States and a major opportunity for many television advertisers, soccer is the most popular televised sport in Europe.

Beliefs about family roles influence marketing activities in various ways. Many countries ban the use of children in advertising, for example. In some countries, advertising that features people in nontraditional roles may be unsuccessful. Procter & Gamble has been very careful in experimenting with advertisements in India that depict men doing housework. In India, as in the United States, more men are helping out with the housework as more wives work, but ads that show men doing the housework may be unappealing to Asian women. Nonetheless, Korea's LG Electronics and Kuala Lumpur's National Panasonic have successfully used advertising showing men cleaning house and parenting.[8]

Cultural differences may also affect marketing negotiations and decision-making behavior. In Japan, showing the bottoms of one's feet is considered insulting, so a person doing business in Japan should take care not to cross his legs. Similarly, it is deemed rude to cross your arms when facing someone in Turkey.[9] Figure 5.2 shows the varied cultural backgrounds of an international work force. Marketing negotiations thus proceed differently in various cultures. Research has shown that when marketers use a problem-solving approach—that is, gain information about a particular client's needs and tailor goods or services to meet those needs—it leads to increased customer satisfaction in marketing negotiations in France, Germany, the United Kingdom, and

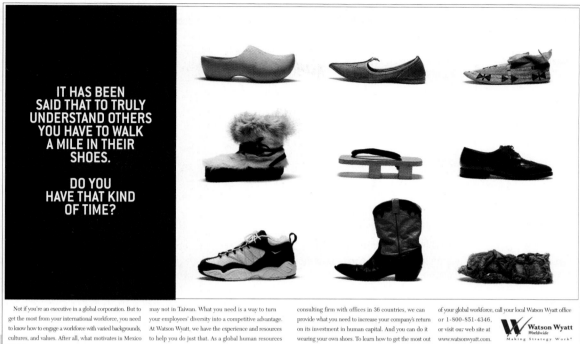

Not if you're an executive in a global corporation. But to get the most from your international workforce, you need to know how to engage a workforce with varied backgrounds, cultures, and values. After all, what motivates in Mexico may not in Taiwan. What you need is a way to turn your employees' diversity into a competitive advantage. At Watson Wyatt, we have the experience and resources to help you do just that. As a global human resources consulting firm with offices in 36 countries, we can provide what you need to increase your company's return on its investment in human capital. And you can do it wearing your own shoes. To learn how to get the most out of your global workforce, call your local Watson Wyatt office or 1-800-851-4346, or visit our web site at www.watsonwyatt.com.

Figure 5.2
Cultural Forces in International Markets
The global consulting firm Watson Wyatt helps companies understand the cultural diversity issues involved in employing an international workforce.

the United States. However, the attractiveness of the salesperson and his or her similarity to the customer increase satisfaction only for Americans; the role and status of the seller are more important in both the United Kingdom and France.[10] Cultural differences in the emphasis placed on personal relationships, status, decision-making styles, and approaches to bidding have been known to complicate business dealings between Americans and Japanese.[11] In the Far East, a gift may be considered a necessary introduction before negotiation, but in the United States or Canada, a gift may be misconstrued as an illegal bribe.

Buyers' perceptions of other countries can influence product adoption and use. When people are unfamiliar with products from another country, their perceptions of the country itself may affect their attitude toward the product and help determine whether they will buy it. If a country has a reputation for producing quality products and therefore has a positive image in consumers' minds, marketers of products from that country will want to make the country of origin well known. For example, a generally favorable image of Western computer technology has fueled sales of American personal computers and Microsoft software in Japan. On the other hand, marketers may want to dissociate themselves from a particular country. Because Mexico has not always been viewed by the world as producing quality products, Volkswagen may not want to advertise that some of the models it sells in the United States, including the Beetle, are made in Mexico.

When products are introduced from one nation into another, acceptance is far more likely if there are similarities between the two cultures. A new global sensitivity about food has resulted in middle-class U.S. families eating more like their counterparts in Japan, France, and Canada. For international marketers, cultural differences have implications for product development, advertising, packaging, and pricing. Schlotzsky's, for example, experienced slower-than-expected sales when it opened a new restaurant in Beijing. Although the Texas-based sandwich chain has experienced great success in the United States, the Chinese are less accustomed to eating foods with their hands, and they often like to share their meals with companions, which is difficult to do with a sandwich. The company hopes that training staff and placing pictures on restaurant tables to demonstrate how to hold and eat the sandwiches will

Table 5.1	Cross-Cultural Similarities in Eating Trends	
Country	**Past Dietary Trends**	**Current Dietary Trends**
Japan	• Home-cooked fish and rice, as well as gourmet foods • Generally low-fat (contributing to a longer life span) • Small fish and vegetable dishes served with rice and miso soup	• Frozen, take-out, and precooked foods • Fast-food outlets such as McDonald's and KFC more popular than in the U.S. • Microwavable entrees growing in popularity
France	• Fat-filled dishes prepared with fresh ingredients from the market • Homemade pastries and desserts • Warm chicken gizzards, sliced baguettes (bread), pâté, green salad	• Take-out pizzas, hamburgers, Tex-Mex, and convenience foods • Leaner cuts of meat and fewer traditional dishes rich in butter and cream
Canada	• Red meat, poultry, whole milk, potatoes, eggs • Traditional meat and potatoes	• Fresh vegetables, cereals, frozen foods, ethnic foods, snack foods
United States	• Steak, pork chops, boiled potatoes, french fries, bacon, whole milk, eggs • Traditional meat and potatoes	• Pizza, tacos and burritos, bagels, pasta, frozen entrees, rice, instant potatoes, diet soft drinks, bottled water, frozen yogurt, microwave popcorn

Sources: Tullio Caputo and Neil Poutanen, "What Canadians Are Eating," *Canadian Social Trends,* Statistics Canada, Winter 1990; Kathleen Deveny, "America's Heartland Acquires Global Taste, *Wall Street Journal,* Oct. 11, 1995, pp. B1, B6; "Hot Stuff!" *Canadian Grocer,* June 1996, pp. 9–13; "Out of the Deep Freeze," *Canadian Grocer,* Oct. 1996, pp. 22–23; Norihiko Shirouzu, "Home-Cooked Fish, Rice Lose Importance in Japan," *Wall Street Journal,* Oct. 11, 1995, p. B1; "Snack Solutions for Guiltless Grazing," *Canadian Grocer,* Sept. 1996, pp. 9–19; and Gabriella Stern, "French Add Convenience to Customary Cuisine," *Wall Street Journal,* Oct. 11, 1995, pp. B1, B6.

help Chinese customers appreciate the large sandwiches and thus will increase sales.[12] Cross-cultural similarities in eating trends are shown in Table 5.1.

Differences in ethical standards can also affect marketing efforts. China and Vietnam, for example, do not have the same standards regarding intellectual property as the United States. This creates an issue for marketers of computer software, music CDs, and books. Because of differences in cultural and ethical standards, many companies are working both individually and collectively to establish ethics programs and standards for international business conduct.[13] Levi Strauss's code of ethics, for example, bars the firm from manufacturing in countries where workers are known to be abused. Starbucks's global code of ethics strives to protect the agricultural workers who harvest coffee. Many companies choose to standardize their ethical behavior across national boundaries to maintain a consistent and well-integrated corporate culture.

Economic Forces

Global marketers need to understand the international trade system, particularly the economic stability of individual nations as well as trade barriers that may stifle marketing efforts. Economic differences among nations—differences in standards of living, credit, buying power, income distribution, national resources, exchange rates, and the like—dictate many of the adjustments that must be made in marketing abroad.

The United States and Western Europe are more stable economically than many other regions of the world. In recent years, a number of countries, including Russia, Japan, Korea, Thailand, and Singapore, have experienced such economic problems as depression, high unemployment, corporate bankruptcies, instability in currency markets, trade imbalances, and financial systems that need major reforms. Even more stable developing countries, such as Mexico and Brazil, tend to have greater fluctuations in their business cycles than the United States does. Economic instability can disrupt the markets for U.S. products in places that otherwise would seem to be great marketing opportunities.

Beyond assessing the stability of a nation's economy, marketers should also consider whether the nation imposes trade restrictions, such as tariffs. An **import tariff**

import tariff   A duty levied by a nation on goods bought outside its borders and brought in

is any duty levied by a nation on goods bought outside its borders and brought in. Because they raise the price of foreign goods, tariffs impede free trade between nations. Tariffs are usually designed either to raise revenue for a country or to protect domestic products.

quota A limit on the amount of goods an importing country will accept for certain product categories in a specific time period

Nontariff trade barriers include quotas and embargoes. A **quota** is a limit on the amount of goods an importing country will accept for certain product categories in a specific time period. An **embargo** is a government's suspension of trade in a particular product or with a given country. Embargoes are generally directed at specific goods or countries and are established for political, health, or religious reasons. The United States forbids the importation of cigars from Cuba for political reasons. However, demand for Cuban cigars is so strong that many enter the U.S. market illegally, and corporate pressure to end sanctions against Cuba is increasing.[14] Laws regarding pricing policies may also serve as trade barriers. Great Britain, for example, has weaker antitrust laws than the United States and is generally more accepting of price collusion. Consequently, many products cost much more in Britain than in the United States. A Ford Escort, for instance, costs $10,000 in New York and $20,000 in London.[15] Because customers may not be able to afford the higher prices of imported products, such policies effectively create barriers to foreign trade.

embargo A government's suspension of trade in a particular product or with a given country

exchange controls Government restrictions on the amount of a particular currency that can be bought or sold

Exchange controls, government restrictions on the amount of a particular currency that can be bought or sold, may also limit international trade. They can force businesspeople to buy and sell foreign products through a central agency, such as a central bank. On the other hand, to promote international trade, some countries have joined together to form free trade zones—multinational economic communities that eliminate tariffs and other trade barriers. Such regional trade alliances are discussed later in the chapter. Foreign currency exchange rates also affect the prices marketers can charge in foreign markets. Fluctuations in the international monetary market can change the prices charged across national boundaries on a daily basis. Consequently, these fluctuations must be considered in any international marketing strategy.

balance of trade The difference in value between a nation's exports and imports

Countries may limit imports to maintain a favorable balance of trade. The **balance of trade** is the difference in value between a nation's exports and imports. When a nation exports more products than it imports, a favorable balance of trade exists because money is flowing into the country. The United States has a negative balance of trade for goods and services of $115 billion, the largest deficit since 1988. The major contributors to this gap are automobiles and consumer goods.[16] A negative balance of trade is considered harmful because it means that U.S. dollars are supporting foreign economies at the expense of U.S. companies and workers.[17]

gross domestic product (GDP) The market value of a nation's total output of goods and services for a given period; an overall measure of economic standing

In terms of the value of all products produced by a nation, the United States has the largest gross domestic product in the world, nearly $7 trillion. **Gross domestic product (GDP)** is an overall measure of a nation's economic standing; it is the market value of a nation's total output of goods and services for a given period. However, it does not take into account the concept of GDP in relation to population (GDP per capita). The United States has a GDP per capita of $26,438. Switzerland is roughly 230 times smaller than the United States—a little larger than the state of Maryland—but its population density is six times greater than that of the United States. Although Switzerland's GDP is about one-fourth the size of the U.S. GDP, its GDP per capita is about the same. Even Canada, which is comparable in size to the United States, has a lower GDP and GDP per capita.[18] Table 5.2 provides a comparative economic analysis of Switzerland, Canada, and the United States. Knowledge about per capita income, credit, and the distribution of income provides general insights into market potential.

Table 5.2	A Comparative Economic Analysis of Canada, Switzerland, and the United States		
	Canada	**Switzerland**	**United States**
Land area (sq. mi.)	3,560,219	15,355	3,539,227
Population (millions)	29.12	7.25	267.96
Population density (persons per sq. mi.)	8	472	76
GDP, 1995 ($ billions)	$623	$176	$6,955
GDP per capita	$21,031	$24,809	$26,438

Source: Bureau of the Census, *Statistical Abstract of the United States* (Washington, D.C.: Government Printing Office, 1997), pp. 829–831, 839, 845.

Opportunities for international trade are not limited to countries with the highest incomes. Some nations are progressing at a much faster rate than they were a few years ago, and these countries—especially in Latin America, Africa, Eastern Europe, and the Middle East—have great market potential. However, marketers must understand the political and legal environment before they can convert buying power of customers in these countries into actual demand for specific products.

Political and Legal Forces

A nation's political system, laws, regulatory bodies, special interest groups, and courts all have great impact on international marketing. A government's policies toward public and private enterprise, consumers, and foreign firms influence marketing across national boundaries. Some countries have established import barriers. Many nontariff barriers, such as quotas and minimum price levels set on imports, port-of-entry taxes, and stringent health and safety requirements, still make it difficult for American companies to export their products.[19] Just a few years ago, companies exporting electronic equipment to Japan had to wait for the Japanese government to inspect each item. A government's attitude toward importers has a direct impact on the economic feasibility of exporting to that country. Globalmarketing describes how Mexico's legal and regulatory climate affected the success of two U.S. firms attempting to market long-distance telephone services there.

Globalmarketing

Trouble with Tapping Into Mexico's Phones

When AT&T and MCI Communications each decided to establish joint ventures to market long-distance telephone services in Mexico, they thought they would ring up huge profits. After all, before it was privatized in 1991, Telefonos de Mexico SA, or Telmex as the former state-owned telephone monopoly is known, was regarded as the worst-run utility in Latin America. Since privatization, however, Telmex has spent billions of dollars to upgrade its antiquated systems with new technology. It has priced its services aggressively, used savvy promotional tactics, and exploited Mexico's weak regulatory and legal systems to dominate the market for long-distance service. Thus, despite a total of $2 billion in investments, AT&T's Alestra SA and MCI's Avantel SA have between them managed to capture just 25 percent of the $3.5 billion long-distance market in Mexico, and both firms have experienced huge losses.

AT&T and MCI blame their Mexican ventures' losses on regulations they say are stacked in favor of Telmex. Telmex was allowed to negotiate the cost of completing calls in Mexico, and AT&T and MCI claim that the rates Telmex set are more than five times its actual costs. To complete calls on local lines, Telmex charges an interconnection fee of about 6 cents a minute—one of the highest such fees in the world. It also receives a huge subsidy for handling inbound calls to Mexico, most of them from the United States. AT&T and MCI further contend that Telmex is allowed to subsidize its sharply dis-

counted long-distance rates from huge profits on its local telephone services—profits they believe derive in part from the stiff fees they must pay to route calls through Telmex's local lines. They also charge that regulators allowed Telmex to restrict competition to a limited number of cities.

In an effort to "level the playing field," Alestra and Avantel have filed several lawsuits against Telmex in Mexico, charging that its actions are anticompetitive. The two ventures have also appealed to Mexican regulators for relief, arguing that no new carriers will succeed as long as Telmex has an unfair advantage. Mexico's Federal Telecommunications Commission, however, appears reluctant to take up the charges against Telmex, Mexico's largest public corporation and one of its largest employers. In its defense, Telmex points to its rivals' success in capturing a quarter of the long-distance business in just a year as proof that the market is competitive.

The conflict between the companies moved to a new front in 1998 when Telmex, in a joint venture with Sprint Communications, became the first foreign firm to obtain the permission of the Federal Communications Commission to market long-distance services in the United States. Telmex-Sprint Communications LLC has since launched a specialized long-distance service targeting the 18 million U.S. residents of Mexican descent, which in turn may give Telmex an even greater advantage on its home turf.

Figure 5.3
Technological Forces in International Markets
Recognizing the opportunity created by businesses that want to capture a share in the global marketplace, SPSSmr provides technological solutions to support global marketing research.

Differences in national standards of ethics are illustrated by what the Mexicans call *la mordida,* "the bite." The use of payoffs and bribes is deeply entrenched in many governments. Because U.S. trade and corporate policy, as well as U.S. law, prohibits direct involvement in payoffs and bribes, American companies may have a hard time competing with foreign firms that do engage in these practices. Some U.S. businesses that refuse to make payoffs are forced to hire local consultants, public relations firms, or advertising agencies—which results in indirect payoffs. The ultimate decision about whether to give small tips or gifts where they are customary must be based on a company's code of ethics. However, under the Foreign Corrupt Practices Act of 1977, it is illegal for U.S. firms to attempt to make large payments or bribes to influence policy decisions of foreign governments. However, facilitating payments, or small payments to support the performance of standard tasks, are often acceptable. The act also subjects all publicly held U.S. corporations to rigorous internal controls and record-keeping requirements for their overseas operations.

Technological Forces

Advances in technology have made international marketing much easier. E-mail, voice mail, fax, cellular phones, and the Internet make international marketing activities more affordable and convenient. WorldCell, an international cellular service provider, offers a pocket phone with a single number that works in over seventy countries. Finland's cellular phone industry, fueled by global giant Nokia, has grown to $9.8 billion in sales, and Finland, with one of the strongest technological infrastructures in the world, is quickly emerging as an "electronic society."[20] Blockbuster Video, recognizing the global demand for its products, has a Web site, as well as stores in twenty-six countries. With its borderless nature, the Internet is making it possible for businesses of all sizes to market their wares globally. Figure 5.3 indicates that SPSSmr provides information technologies for global marketing research. We take a closer look at the use of the Internet in global marketing in Chapter 23.

In many developing countries that lack the level of technological infrastructure found in the United States and Finland, marketers are beginning to capitalize on opportunities to "leapfrog" existing technology. For example, cellular and wireless phone technology is reaching many countries at less expense than traditional hard-wired telephone systems. In China, few households have private phone lines, partly because they cost as much as $440 to install and require a wait of several months. Many

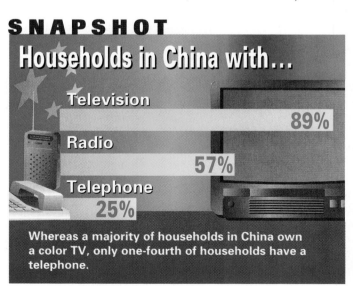

SNAPSHOT
Households in China with...
Television 89%
Radio 57%
Telephone 25%
Whereas a majority of households in China own a color TV, only one-fourth of households have a telephone.

Copyright © 1999 *USA Today,* a division of Gannett Co., Inc.

customers have bypassed these expensive private lines in favor of wireless communications, doubling the mobile phone market to 13 million units. With the market expected to rise to 50 million units by the year 2000, many firms, including Motorola, Nokia, and Ericsson, have started marketing wireless communications to the Chinese.[21]

Regional Trade Alliances, Markets, and Agreements

Although many more firms are beginning to view the world as one huge marketplace, various regional trade alliances and specific markets affect companies engaging in international marketing; some create opportunities, others impose constraints. This section examines several regional trade alliances, markets, and changing conditions affecting markets, including the North American Free Trade Agreement between the United States, Canada, and Mexico; the unification of Europe; the Pacific Rim markets; the General Agreement on Tariffs and Trade (GATT); and the World Trade Organization. (See Figure 5.4.)

The North American Free Trade Agreement (NAFTA)

North American Free Trade Agreement (NAFTA) An alliance that merges Canada, Mexico, and the United States into a single market

The **North American Free Trade Agreement (NAFTA),** which went into effect in 1994, effectively merged Canada, Mexico, and the United States into one market of about 374 million consumers. NAFTA will eliminate virtually all tariffs on goods produced and traded between Canada, Mexico, and the United States to create a free trade area by 2009. The estimated annual output for this trade alliance is $7 trillion. As Figure 5.5 indicates, airlines have more opportunity with business travel because of NAFTA.

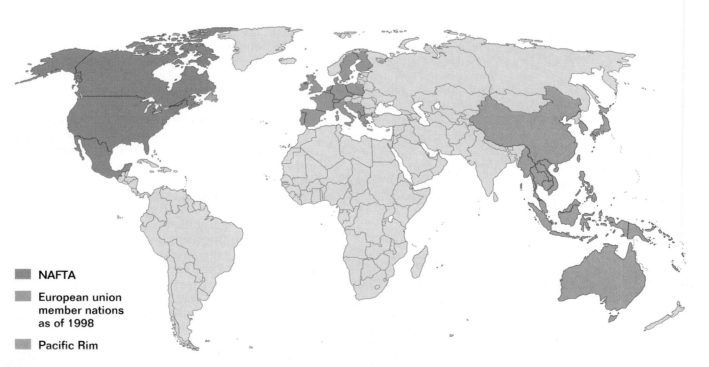

- ■ NAFTA
- ■ European union member nations as of 1998
- ■ Pacific Rim

Figure 5.4
Regional Trade Alliances: NAFTA, the European Union, and the Pacific Rim

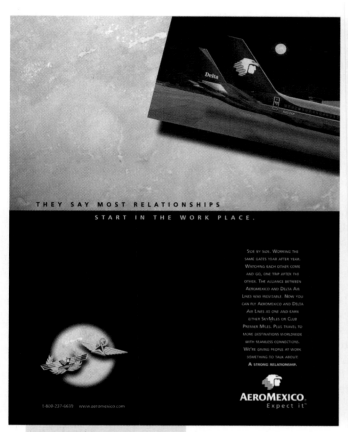

Figure 5.5
NAFTA
Regional trade alliances such as NAFTA provide new opportunities for business. Airlines such as Continental Airlines, AeroMexico, and Delta Air benefit from the increase in business travel between member countries.

NAFTA makes it easier for U.S. businesses to invest in Mexico and Canada, provides protection for intellectual property (of special interest to high-technology and entertainment industries), expands trade by requiring equal treatment of U.S. firms in both countries, and simplifies country-of-origin rules, hindering Japan's use of Mexico as a staging ground for further penetration into U.S. markets. Although most tariffs on products coming to the United States will be lifted, duties on more sensitive products such as household glassware, footware, and some fruits and vegetables will be phased out over a fifteen-year period.

Canada's 29 million consumers are relatively affluent, with a per capita GDP of $21,031.[22] Trade between the United States and Canada totals about $300 billion, up more than 50 percent from 1988 when the two nations signed the free trade agreement that laid the groundwork for NAFTA. Currently, exports to Canada support approximately 1.5 million U.S. jobs. Canadian investments in U.S. companies are also increasing, and various markets, including air travel, are opening as regulatory barriers dissolve.[23]

With a per capita GDP of $7,383, Mexico's 98 million consumers are less affluent than Canadian consumers. However, they bought $71.4 billion worth of U.S. products last year. In fact, Mexico has become the United States' second-largest trading market, after Canada.[24] Many U.S. companies, including Hewlett-Packard, IBM, and General Motors, have taken advantage of Mexico's low labor costs and close proximity to the United States to set up production facilities, sometimes called *maquiladoras.*[25] Mexico currently exports $19.2 billion in autos and related parts, up from $7.2 billion just five years ago, and that figure likely will continue to rise as U.S. tariffs on autos produced in Mexico are eliminated after 2004.[26] Although Mexico has experienced financial instability throughout the 1990s, privatization of some government-owned firms and other measures instituted by the Mexican government and businesses, along with a booming U.S. economy, have helped the country's economy. Moreover, increasing trade between the United States and Canada constitutes a strong base of support for the ultimate success of NAFTA. Mexico's membership in NAFTA also links the United States with other Latin American countries, providing additional opportunities for integrating trade among all the nations in the Western Hemisphere. Chile, for example, is expected to become the fourth member of NAFTA, but politics may delay its entry into the agreement for several years.

Although NAFTA has been controversial, it has become a positive factor for U.S. firms wishing to engage in international marketing. Because licensing requirements have been relaxed under the pact, smaller businesses that previously could not afford to invest in Mexico and Canada will be able to do business in those markets without having to locate there. NAFTA's long phase-in period provides ample time for adjustment by those firms affected by reduced tariffs on imports. Furthermore, increased competition should lead to a more efficient market, and the long-term prospects of including most of the countries in the Western Hemisphere in the alliance promise additional opportunities for U.S. marketers.

The European Union

The European Union (EU), also called the European Community or Common Market, was established in 1958 to promote trade among its members, which initially included Belgium, France, Italy, West Germany, Luxembourg, and the Netherlands. In 1991, East and West Germany united, and by 1995, the United Kingdom, Spain, Denmark, Greece, Portugal, Ireland, Austria, Finland, and Sweden had joined as well. (Cyprus, Poland, Hungary, the Czech Republic, Slovenia, and Estonia have begun formal negotiations to join the EU; Latvia, Lithuania, Slovakia, Romania, and Bulgaria have requested membership as well.[27]) Until 1993, each nation functioned as a separate market, but at that time, the members officially unified into one of the largest single world markets, which today includes 370 million consumers. Figure 5.6 exemplifies Austria's support of a global market.

To facilitate free trade among members, the EU is working toward the standardization of business regulations and requirements, import duties, and value-added taxes; the elimination of customs checks; and the creation of a standardized currency for use by all members. Many European nations (Austria, Belgium, Finland, France, Germany, Ireland, Italy, Luxembourg, the Netherlands, Portugal, and Spain) have already begun linking their exchange rates together in preparation for a common currency, the *euro,* which began circulating in 1999. The common currency may require many marketers to modify their pricing strategies and will subject them to increased competition. However, the use of a single currency will free companies that sell goods among European

Austria. Your Springboard into Eastern Europe.

*) 9th Annual World Convention of Investment Promotion Agencies.

A B A EUROPEAN INVESTMENT PROMOTION AGENCY OF THE YEAR*

Austria not only lies at the crossroads of East and West, it also offers the necessary infrastructure and contacts to ensure business certainty in turbulent markets. More than 15,000 joint ventures with Eastern Europe – and an estimated 1,000 international companies with Central European headquarters in Austria – speak for themselves: Austria is the EU's Eastern specialist. For more facts about Austria, contact the **AUSTRIAN BUSINESS AGENCY Official Consultants for Foreign Investment: Opernring 3, A-1010 Vienna, Austria, Fax +43-1-586 86 59,** e-mail: austrian.business@telecom.at, Internet:http://www.aba.gv.at

AUSTRIA EUROpportunity

Figure 5.6
The European Market
Austria promotes itself as a home base for U.S. companies that want to manage their European operations.

countries from the nuisance of dealing with complex exchange rates.[28] The long-term goals are to eliminate all trade barriers within the EU, to improve the economic efficiency of the EU nations, to stimulate economic growth, and thus to make the union economy more competitive in global markets, particularly against Japan and other Pacific Rim nations, and North America. However, several disputes and debates still divide the member nations, and many barriers to completely free trade remain. Consequently, it may take many years before the EU is truly one deregulated market.

As the EU nations attempt to function as one large market, consumers in the EU may become more homogeneous in their needs and wants. Marketers should be aware, however, that cultural differences among the fifteen nations may require modifications in the marketing mix for customers in each nation. Differences in taste and preferences in these diverse markets are significant for international marketers. The British, for example, prefer front-loading washing machines, whereas the French prefer top-loaders. Consumers in Spain eat far more poultry products than Germans do.[29] Such differences may exist even within the same country, depending on the geographic region. Gathering information about these distinct tastes and preferences is likely to remain a very important factor in developing marketing mixes that satisfy the needs of European customers.

Pacific Rim Nations

Despite economic turmoil and a recession in Asia in recent years, companies of the Pacific Rim nations—Japan, China, South Korea, Taiwan, Thailand, Singapore, Hong Kong, Malaysia, and Vietnam as well as other countries shown in Figure 5.1—have become increasingly competitive and sophisticated in global business in the last three decades. Moreover, the markets of the Pacific Rim offer tremendous opportunities to marketers who understand them.

The Japanese in particular have made tremendous inroads on world markets for automobiles, motorcycles, watches, cameras, and audio and video equipment. Products from Sony, Sanyo, Toyota, Mitsubishi, Canon, Suzuki, and Toshiba are sold all over the world and have set standards of quality by which other products are often judged. Despite the high volume of trade between the United States and Japan, the two economies are less integrated than the U.S. economy is with Canada's and Western Europe's. Economists estimate that if Japan imported goods at the same rate as other major nations, the United States would sell $50 billion more each year to Japan.[30] Few U.S. firms have large investments in Japan, and Japanese investment in the U.S. is concentrated in the auto and technology industries. The United States and Japan continually struggle with cultural and political differences and are, in general, at odds over how to do business with each other.[31] Among the Japanese markets opening up for the United States are telecommunications products, such as cellular phones and personal computers. Personal computer purchases in Japan have doubled in recent years, and America's Intel makes the chips that run most of the machines Japan now buys.[32] Compaq, Apple, IBM, and other U.S. marketers have gained 30 percent of Japan's $9 billion PC market, partly by pricing their products 20 to 30 percent below those of rival Japanese companies, which have traditionally dominated this market. These PC purchases, along with Japan's importation of Japanese autos manufactured in U.S. facilities and an increase in the number of U.S. retailers (such as the Gap) that operate stores in Japan, have helped the United States reduce its trade deficit with Japan.[33]

The People's Republic of China, a country of 1.2 billion people, has launched a program of economic reform to stimulate its economy by privatizing many industries, restructuring its banking system, and increasing public spending on infrastructure (including railways and telecommunications).[34] Although per capita annual income is less than $500, a Chinese middle class is slowly developing. The potential of China's consumer market is so vast that it is almost impossible to measure, but doing business in China also entails many risks. Political and economic instability, especially inflation, corruption, and erratic policy shifts, have undercut marketers' efforts to stake a claim in what could become the world's largest market. Moreover, piracy is a major issue, and protecting a brand name in China is difficult. Because China denies foreign access to many of its markets, the country is flooded with counterfeit videos, movies, compact discs, and computer software. This piracy costs U.S. companies more than $1 billion a year.[35] China's trade surplus with the United States reached nearly $50 billion last year.[36] If current trends continue, China's trade surplus will surpass Japan's U.S. trade surplus before the year 2000.[37] Nike and Adidas shoes have shifted most of their production to China, and more recently, China has become a major producer of compact disc players, cellular phones, portable stereos, and personal computers. It is apparent that the Chinese intend to use American and European investments to accelerate their export of automobiles, automobile parts, semiconductors, and telecommunications products.

Despite an economic crisis in the late 1990s, South Korea has been quite successful in global markets. Even before Korean brand names such as Samsung, Daewoo, and Hyundai became household words, these products prospered under U.S. company labels, including GE, GTE, RCA, and J. C. Penney. Korean companies are now grabbing market share from Japanese companies in global markets for videocassette recorders, color televisions, and computers, even though the Korean market for these products is limited. With entry blocked to some European and Japanese markets, Korean firms have decided to go head-to-head with Japanese and American domestic firms for a piece of the U.S. market.

Less visible and sometimes less stable Pacific Rim regions, such as Thailand, Singapore, Taiwan, and Hong Kong, have become major manufacturing and financial centers. Singapore boasts huge global markets for rubber goods and pharmaceuticals. Hong Kong's future, however, became less certain after it reverted from British to Chinese control in 1997. Vietnam is becoming one of Asia's fastest growing markets for U.S. businesses, but Taiwan may have the most promising future of all the Pacific Rim nations, as a strong local economy and low import barriers draw increasing imports. Firms from Thailand and Malaysia are also blossoming, carving out niches in the world markets for a variety of products, from toys to automobile parts.[38]

General Agreement on Tariffs and Trade (GATT)

General Agreement on Tariffs and Trade (GATT)
An agreement among nations to reduce worldwide tariffs and increase international trade

Like NAFTA and the European Union, the **General Agreement on Tariffs and Trade (GATT)** is based on negotiations between member countries to reduce worldwide tariffs and increase international trade. Originally signed by 23 nations in 1947, GATT provides a forum for tariff negotiations and a place where international trade problems can be discussed and resolved. GATT negotiations currently involve some 124 nations and have had far-reaching ramifications for the international marketing strategies of U.S. firms.

GATT sponsors rounds of negotiations aimed at reducing trade restrictions. Seven rounds of GATT negotiations have reduced the average worldwide tariffs on manufactured goods from 45 percent to 5 percent, and negotiators have been able to eliminate or ease nontariff trade restrictions, such as import quotas, red tape in customs procedures, and "buy national" agreements.

dumping Selling products at unfairly low prices

The most recent round, the Uruguay Round (1988–1994), further reduced trade barriers for most products and provided new rules to prevent **dumping,** the selling of products at unfairly low prices. In the United States, apparel retailers and marketers of large equipment, toys, paper, scientific instruments, aluminum, furniture, steel, liquor, and medical equipment will benefit from these tariff reductions. Japan, however, may experience an adverse effect, at least in the short run, because the elimination of some trade barriers that have long protected such Japanese industries as steel, agricultural, processed food, and dairy products will open these markets to outside competition. Some U.S. industries are dissatisfied with the Uruguay Round because they face continued barriers. The motion picture industry, for example, had hoped to gain greater access to European markets, and pharmaceutical companies are concerned about the additional ten years during which developing countries can pirate drugs without penalty.

World Trade Organization (WTO)
An entity that promotes free trade among member nations

Another important outcome of the Uruguay Round of GATT negotiations was the creation of the **World Trade Organization (WTO)** to promote free trade among member nations. Fulfilling this purpose requires eliminating trade barriers; educating individuals, companies, and governments about trade rules around the world; and assuring global markets that there will be no sudden changes of policy. The WTO also serves as a forum for trade negotiations and dispute resolution. At the heart of the WTO are agreements that provide legal ground rules for international commerce and trade policy.[39]

International Involvement

Marketers engage in international marketing activities at several levels of involvement that cover a wide spectrum, as Figure 5.7 shows. Domestic marketing involves marketing strategies aimed at markets within the home country; at the other extreme, global marketing means developing marketing strategies for major regions or for the entire world. Many firms with an international presence start out as small companies serving local and regional markets and expand to national markets before considering opportunities in foreign markets. Limited exporting may occur even though a firm makes little or no effort to obtain foreign sales. Foreign buyers may seek out the company and/or its products, or a distributor may discover the firm's products and export them. The level of commitment to international marketing is a major variable in international marketing strategies. In this section, we examine importing and exporting, trading companies, licensing and franchising, contract manufacturing, joint ventures, direct ownership, and other approaches to international involvement.

Importing and Exporting

importing The purchase of products from a foreign source

exporting The sale of products to foreign markets

Importing and exporting require the least amount of effort and commitment of resources. **Importing** is the purchase of products from a foreign source. **Exporting**—the sale of products to foreign markets—enables businesses of all sizes to participate in global business. In fact, according to the Department of Commerce, 60 percent of U.S. firms engaged in exporting have fewer than 100 employees.[40] A firm

Domestic marketing
All marketing strategies focus
on the market in the country of origin.

Limited exporting
The firm develops no international marketing strategies,
but international distributors or foreign firms
purchase some of its products.

International marketing
International markets are a consideration in the marketing strategy.

Globalized marketing
Marketing strategies are developed for major regions or
the entire world so firms can compete globally.

Figure 5.7
Levels of Involvement in Global Marketing

Over 50 Years of
Exporting Excellence.

- Export packing, crating & containerization
- Over 170 overseas agents & offices
- On-location packing crews
- Full service shipping, forwarding & logistics
- Heavy machinery & electronics packing
- Hazardous material packing
- 55,000 sq. ft. facility with crane
- Military specification packaging
- **ISO 9002 CERTIFIED**
- **I.A.T.A. LICENSED**
- **F.M.C. BONDED - N.V.O.C.C.**

H HORN
      INTERNATIONAL
      PACKAGING, INC.

44 Dunham Road, Billerica, Ma 01821
Ph 978.667.8797 Fax 978.667.5058
www.horninternational.com
e-mail:horn@horninternational.com

Figure 5.8
Importing and Exporting
Although importing
and exporting require
less effort than other
forms of international
involvement, they still
present companies with
challenges. Horn Inter-
national Packaging, Inc.,
assists firms in exporting
by providing a variety of
services.

trading company
A company that links buyers and
sellers in different countries

licensing An alternative to
direct investment requiring a
licensee to pay commissions or
royalties on sales or supplies
used in manufacturing

may find an exporting intermediary to take over most marketing functions associated with selling to other countries. This approach entails minimal effort and cost. Modifications in packaging, labeling, style, or color may be the major expenses in adapting a product for the foreign market. Figure 5.8 features an export firm that assists in packaging and shipping products.

Export agents bring together buyers and sellers from different countries; they collect a commission for arranging sales. Export houses and export merchants purchase products from different companies and then sell them abroad. They are specialists at understanding foreign customers' needs. There is limited risk in using exporting intermediaries because no direct investment in the foreign country is required.

Buyers from foreign companies and governments provide a direct method of exporting and eliminate the need for an intermediary. These buyers encourage international exchange by contacting overseas firms about their needs and the opportunities available in exporting to them. A study of minority firms' participation in international marketing indicated that only 10 percent reported previous exporting experience, but 70 percent expressed an interest in exporting. These firms identify limited experience and lack of knowledge as the major barriers to getting involved in exporting.[41] Domestic firms that want to export with a minimum of effort and investment should seek out export intermediaries.

Trading Companies

Marketers sometimes employ a **trading company,** which links buyers and sellers in different countries but is not involved in manufacturing and does not own assets related to manufacturing. Trading companies buy goods in one country at the lowest price consistent with quality and sell them to buyers in another country. The best-known U.S. trading company is Sears World Trade, which specializes in consumer goods, light industrial items, and processed foods. A trading company acts like a wholesaler, taking on much of the responsibility of finding markets while facilitating all marketing aspects of a transaction. An important function of trading companies is taking title to products and performing all the activities necessary to move the products from the domestic country to a foreign country. For example, large grain-trading companies operating out of home offices in both the United States and overseas control a major portion of the world's trade in basic food commodities. These trading companies sell homogeneous agricultural commodities that can be stored and moved rapidly in response to market conditions.

Trading companies reduce risk for firms interested in getting involved in international marketing. A trading company provides producers with information about products that meet quality and price expectations in domestic and international markets. Additional services a trading company may provide include consulting, marketing research, advertising, insurance, product research and design, legal assistance, warehousing, and foreign exchange.

Licensing and Franchising

When potential markets are found across national boundaries—and when production, technical assistance, or marketing know-how is required—**licensing** is an alternative to direct investment. The licensee (the owner of the foreign operation) pays commissions or royalties on sales or supplies used in manufacturing. The licensee may also

Over 320 hotels in 34 countries.

You've changed time zones, continents, even centuries. But that doesn't mean you have to change the way you work. Our hotels in 34 countries have VOICEMAIL, BUSINESS SERVICES like faxing, even easy-to-reach DATAPORTS. Call your travel agent or 800-228-9290, or visit www.marriott.com. We believe:

When you're comfortable you can do anything.®   **Marriott**
HOTELS · RESORTS · SUITES

Figure 5.9
Franchising
Hotels like Marriott expand through franchising on a worldwide basis. Marriott now operates and franchises over 320 hotels in 34 countries.

franchising A form of licensing in which a franchiser, in exchange for a financial commitment, grants a franchisee the right to market its product in accordance with the franchiser's standards

contract manufacturing The practice of hiring a foreign firm to produce a designated volume of product to specification

joint venture A partnership between a domestic firm and a foreign firm or government

pay an initial down payment or fee when the licensing agreement is signed. Exchanges of management techniques or technical assistance are primary reasons for licensing agreements. Yoplait is a French yogurt that is licensed for production in the United States; the Yoplait brand tries to maintain a French image.

Licensing is an attractive alternative to direct investment when the political stability of a foreign country is in doubt or when resources are unavailable for direct investment. Licensing is especially advantageous for small manufacturers wanting to launch a well-known brand internationally. For example, the Questor Corporation owns the Spalding name but produces not a single golf club or tennis ball itself; all Spalding sporting products are licensed worldwide. Lowenbrau has used licensing agreements, including one with Miller in the United States, to increase sales worldwide without committing capital to building breweries.

Franchising is a form of licensing in which a company (the franchiser) grants a franchisee the right to market its product, using its name, logo, methods of operation, advertising, products, and other elements associated with the franchiser's business, in return for a financial commitment and an agreement to conduct business in accordance with the franchiser's standard of operations. This arrangement allows franchisers to minimize the risks of international marketing in four ways: (1) the franchiser does not have to put up a large capital investment; (2) the franchiser's revenue stream is fairly consistent because franchisees pay a fixed fee and royalties; (3) the franchiser retains control of its name and increases global penetration of its product; and (4) franchise agreements ensure a certain standard of behavior from franchisees, which protects the franchise name.[42] Kentucky Fried Chicken, Wendy's, McDonald's, Holiday Inn, and Marriott (see Figure 5.9) are well-known franchisers with international visibility.

Contract Manufacturing

Contract manufacturing occurs when a company hires a foreign firm to produce a designated volume of the firm's product to specification, and the final product carries the domestic firm's name. The Gap, for example, relies on contract manufacturing for some of its apparel; Reebok uses Korean contract manufacturers to manufacture many of its athletic shoes. Marketing may be handled by the contract manufacturer or by the contracting company.

Joint Ventures

In international marketing, a **joint venture** is a partnership between a domestic firm and a foreign firm or government. Joint ventures are especially popular in industries that call for large investments, such as natural resources extraction or automobile manufacturing. Control of the joint venture may be split equally, or one party may control decision making. Joint ventures are often a political necessity because of nationalism and government restrictions on foreign ownership. They also provide legitimacy in the eyes of the host country's citizens. Local partners have firsthand knowledge of the economic and sociopolitical environment and of distribution networks, and they may have privileged access to local resources (raw material, labor management, and so on). Entrepreneurs in many less-developed countries actively seek associations with a foreign partner as a ready means of implementing their own corporate strategy.[43]

Joint ventures are assuming greater global importance because of cost advantages and the number of inexperienced firms entering foreign markets. They may be the result of a tradeoff between a firm's desire for completely unambiguous control of an enterprise and its quest for additional resources. They may occur when acquisition or internal development is not feasible or when the risks and constraints leave no other alternative. As project sizes increase in the face of global competition and firms attempt to spread the huge costs of technological innovation, there is a stronger impetus to form joint ventures.[44]

strategic alliances
Partnerships formed to create competitive advantage on a worldwide basis

Strategic alliances, the newest form of international business structure, are partnerships formed to create competitive advantage on a worldwide basis. They are very similar to joint ventures. What distinguishes international strategic alliances from other business structures is that partners in the alliance may have been traditional rivals competing for market share in the same product class.[45] An example of such an alliance is New United Motor Manufacturing, Inc. (NUMMI), formed by Toyota and General Motors to make automobiles for both firms. This alliance united the quality engineering of Japanese cars with the marketing expertise and market access of General Motors. Partners in international strategic alliances often retain their distinct identities, and each brings a core competency to the union.

International alliances have a success rate of 30 to 40 percent. The success rate could be higher if there were a better fit between the companies. A strategic alliance

Globalmarketing

Flying High on Partnerships

With political barriers falling and international markets opening up, marketers are traveling ever farther afield to conduct business. To meet the rising demand for more seamless flying experiences and to extend its reach, Delta, like many other airlines, has joined a strategic global alliance. Its partners in the Atlantic Excellence Alliance are Austrian Airlines, Sabena Belgian World Airlines, and Swissair. Thanks to the direct links created by the alliance, travelers can now take one of Delta's daily flights from its Atlanta hub to Zurich, where they can make connections to the Middle East, Africa, and other parts of Europe. Other such global partnerships include the Star Alliance (United, Air Canada, Lufthansa, SAS, Varig, and Thai Airways) and "oneworld" (American Airlines, British Airways, Canadian Airlines, Cathay Pacific Airways, and Qantas Airways). As Susan Snider, Delta's director of international alliances, says, "Alliances are not an option anymore. . . . The only way you can fill in the voids is through global partnerships."

To establish prices and schedules jointly, partners in global airline alliances must obtain permission from antitrust authorities in the partners' countries. Some alliances take the form of "code-sharing" arrangements, in which partners agree to books seats and issue tickets for each other's flights. Delta, for example, has code-sharing deals with Aer Lingus, Aeromexico, Air Jamaica, Finnair, Korean Air, Malev, TAP Air Portugal, and Transbrasil, and is negotiating for such arrangements with Air France, All Nippon Airways, and China Southern.

The new alliances are not without problems. For one thing, they are subject to close scrutiny from government regulators in the partners' countries, and deals are not always approved. In addition, they are not popular among all employees and labor unions. Pilots, in particular, fear that alliances may limit their companies' growth and therefore their future earning potential. Business travelers are concerned that the alliances' ability to control capacity and fares will far outweigh the potential advantages. There are also some worries about the safety records of some foreign partners.

Generally, however, the airlines contend that their partnerships will improve the services they can provide customers. Among the benefits they cite are enhanced frequent-flyer programs and smoother transfers for passengers traveling across partners' global networks. Consider that just a few years ago, a trip from Birmingham, Alabama, to Cairo, Egypt, required a traveler to fly from Birmingham to Washington, then to New York, and finally onto Cairo. The trip took 24 hours, 55 minutes. Through the Atlantic Excellence Alliance, the same traveler can now fly Delta to Atlanta and on to Zurich and then switch to a Swissair flight to Cairo, in just 17 hours, 35 minutes, all on one ticket.

should focus on a joint market opportunity from which all partners can benefit.[46] In the automobile, computer, and airline industries, strategic alliances are becoming the predominant means of competing. International competition is so fierce and the costs of competing on a global basis so high that few firms have all the resources needed to do it alone. Firms that lack the internal resources essential for international success may seek to collaborate with other companies.[47] One such collaboration is "oneworld," a partnership of American Airlines, British Airways, Canadian Airlines, Cathay Pacific Airways, and Qantas Airways, designed to improve customer service among the five companies.[48] Globalmarketing further explores strategic alliances in the airline industry.

Direct Ownership

direct ownership
A situation in which a company owns subsidiaries or other facilities overseas

multinational enterprise
A firm that has operations or subsidiaries in many countries

Once a company makes a long-term commitment to marketing in a foreign nation that has a promising political and economic environment, **direct ownership** of a foreign subsidiary or division is a possibility. Korea's Daewoo Motor Company, for example, plans to open fifteen company-owned (not franchised) dealerships in California, Florida, and the northeastern United States and to expand to forty within a year.[49] Most foreign investment covers only manufacturing equipment or personnel because the expenses of developing a separate foreign distribution system can be tremendous. The opening of retail stores in Europe, Canada, or Mexico can require a staggering financial investment in facilities, research, and management.

The term **multinational enterprise** refers to firms that have operations or subsidiaries in many countries. Often the parent company is based in one country and carries on production, management, and marketing activities in other countries. The firm's subsidiaries may be quite autonomous so they can respond to the needs of individual international markets. Firms such as General Motors, Citicorp, ITT, and Ford are multinational companies with worldwide operations. Table 5.3 lists the fifteen largest global corporations.

Table 5.3   The Fifteen Largest Global Public Corporations*

Company	Country	Business	Revenue ($ millions)
General Electric	United States	Electrical equipment	90,840
HSBC Group	United Kingdom	Banking	48,404
Royal Dutch/Shell Group	Netherlands	Energy	128,108
Ford	United States	Autos & trucks	145,348
General Motors	United States	Autos & trucks	178,174
Exxon	United States	International oil	120,279
Toyota	Japan	Automobiles	95,181
IBM	United States	Computer systems	78,508
Travelers Group	United States	Insurance	37,609
Citicorp	United States	Multinational banks	34,697
Nippon Tel & Tel	Japan	Telecommunications	77,019
Chase Manhattan	United States	Multinational bank	30,381
ING Group	Netherlands	Financial services	38,724
AT&T	United States	Telecom-carriers	51,319
Philip Morris	United States	Tobacco	56,114

Source: "The World Super Fifty," *Forbes*, July 27, 1998, p. 118.
* Composite ranking based on revenues, assets, profits, and market value.

A wholly owned foreign subsidiary may be allowed to operate independently of the parent company so that its management can have more freedom to adjust to the local environment. Cooperative arrangements are developed to assist in marketing efforts, production, and management. A wholly owned foreign subsidiary may export products to the home country. Some U.S. automobile manufacturers, for example, import cars built by their foreign subsidiaries. A foreign subsidiary offers important tax, tariff, and other operating advantages. One of the greatest advantages is the cross-cultural approach. A subsidiary usually operates under foreign management, so that it can develop a local identity. The greatest danger in such an arrangement comes from political uncertainty: a firm may lose its foreign investment.

Customization versus Globalization of International Marketing Strategies

Like domestic marketers, international marketers develop marketing strategies to serve specific target markets. Traditionally, international marketing strategies have customized marketing mixes according to cultural, regional, and national differences. Many soap and detergent manufacturers, for example, adapt their products to local water conditions, equipment, and washing habits. Colgate-Palmolive even devised an inexpensive, plastic, hand-powered washing machine for use in households that have no electricity in less-developed countries. Ford Motor Company has customized its F-series truck to accommodate global differences in roads, product use, and economic conditions. The strategy has been quite successful, with more than 26 million Ford trucks sold around the world in thirty years.[50]

globalization The development of marketing strategies that treat the entire world (or its major regions) as a single entity

At the other end of the spectrum, **globalization** of marketing involves developing marketing strategies as though the entire world (or its major regions) were a single entity; a globalized firm markets standardized products in the same way everywhere.[51] Nike and Adidas shoes, for example, are standardized worldwide. Other examples of globalized products include electronic communications equipment, Western American clothing, movies, soft drinks, rock and alternative music CDs, cosmetics, and toothpaste. Sony televisions, Levi jeans, and American cigarette brands post year-to-year gains in the world market. Figure 5.10 illustrates that Dunkin' Donuts can globalize its coffee and doughnut chain worldwide.

For many years, organizations have attempted to globalize their marketing mixes as much as possible by employing standardized products, promotion campaigns, prices, and distribution channels for all markets. The economic and competitive payoffs for globalized

Figure 5.10
Customization versus Globalization
Dunkin' Donuts has globalized its coffee and doughnuts chain. This store in Korea is just one of the over 3,700 stores the company currently operates in the U.S. and 21 other countries around the world.

marketing strategies are certainly great. Brand name, product characteristics, packaging, and labeling are among the easiest marketing mix variables to standardize; media allocation, retail outlets, and price may be more difficult. In the end, the degree of similarity between the various environmental and market conditions determines the feasibility and degree of globalization. Honda, for example, is working to overhaul its top-selling Accord automobile into the first truly "world car" despite strong differences among its target markets in the United States, Europe, and Japan. By creating a unique flexible platform, Honda can market a family-sized Accord that competes head-on with the Ford Taurus in the United States, a stylish, sportier compact Accord for the Japanese, and a smaller Accord for Europe's narrower roads.[52] Even take-out food lends itself to globalization: McDonald's, KFC, and Taco Bell restaurants seem to satisfy hungry customers in every hemisphere, although menus may be customized to some degree to satisfy local tastes.

International marketing demands some strategic planning if a firm is to incorporate foreign sales into its overall marketing strategy. International marketing activities often require customized marketing mixes to achieve the firm's goals. Globalization requires a total commitment to the world, regions, or multinational areas as an integral part of the firm's markets; world or regional markets become as important as domestic ones. Regardless of to what extent a firm chooses to globalize its marketing strategy, extensive environmental analysis and marketing research are necessary to understand the needs and desires of the target market(s) and to successfully implement the chosen marketing strategy. We take a closer look at marketing research in the next chapter.

Summary

International marketing involves developing and performing marketing activities across national boundaries. International markets can provide tremendous opportunities for growth.

A detailed analysis of the environment is essential before a company enters a foreign market. Environmental aspects of special importance include cultural, social, ethical, economic, political, legal, and technological forces. Because marketing activities are primarily social in purpose, they are influenced by beliefs and values regarding family, religion, education, health, and recreation. Cultural differences may affect marketing negotiations, decision-making behavior, and product adoption and use. A nation's economic stability and trade barriers can affect marketing efforts. Significant trade barriers include import tariffs, quotas, embargoes, and exchange controls. Gross domestic product (GDP) and GDP per capita are common measures of a nation's economic standing. Political and legal forces include a nation's political system, laws, regulatory bodies, special interest groups, and courts. Advances in technology have made international marketing much easier.

Various regional trade alliances and specific markets create both opportunities and constraints for companies engaged in international marketing. These include the North American Free Trade Agreement (NAFTA) between the United States, Canada, and Mexico; the European Union; the Pacific Rim nations; the General Agreement on Tariffs and Trade (GATT); and the World Trade Organization.

There are several ways of getting involved in international marketing. Importing (the purchase of products from a foreign source) and exporting (the sale of products to foreign markets) are the easiest and most flexible methods. Marketers may employ a trading company, which links buyers and sellers in different countries but is not involved in manufacturing and does not own assets related to manufacturing. Licensing and franchising are arrangements whereby one firm pays fees to another for the use of its name, expertise, and supplies. Contract manufacturing occurs when a company hires a foreign firm to produce a designated volume of the firm's product to specification, and the final product carries the domestic firm's name. Joint ventures are partnerships between a domestic firm and a foreign firm or a government, while strategic alliances are partnerships formed to create competitive advantage on a worldwide basis. Finally, a firm can build its own marketing or production facilities overseas. When companies have direct ownership of facilities in many countries, they may be considered multinational enterprises.

Although most firms adjust their marketing mixes for differences in target markets, some firms standardize their marketing efforts worldwide. Traditional full-scale international marketing involvement is based on products customized according to cultural, regional, and national differences. Globalization, however, involves developing marketing strategies as if the entire world (or regions of it) were a single entity; a globalized firm markets standardized products in the same way everywhere. International marketing demands some strategic planning if a firm is to incorporate foreign sales into its overall marketing strategy.

Important Terms

International marketing
Import tariff
Quota
Embargo
Exchange controls
Balance of trade
Gross domestic product
    (GDP)

North American Free
    Trade Agreement (NAFTA)
General Agreement on Tariffs
    and Trade (GATT)
Dumping
World Trade Organization
    (WTO)

Importing
Exporting
Trading company
Licensing
Franchising
Contract manufacturing
Joint venture

Strategic alliances
Direct ownership
Multinational enterprise
Globalization

Discussion and Review Questions

1. How does international marketing differ from domestic marketing?

2. What factors must marketers consider as they decide whether to become involved in international marketing?

3. Why are the largest industrial corporations in the United States so committed to international marketing?

4. Why was so much of this chapter devoted to an analysis of the international marketing environment?

5. A manufacturer recently exported peanut butter with a green label to a nation in the Far East. The product failed because it was associated with jungle sickness. How could this mistake have been avoided?

6. If you were asked to provide a small tip (or bribe) to have a document approved in a foreign nation where this practice is customary, what would you do?

7. How will NAFTA affect marketing opportunities for U.S. products in North America (U.S., Mexico, and Canada)?

8. In marketing dog food to Latin America, what aspects of the marketing mix would a U.S. firm need to alter?

9. What should marketers consider as they decide whether to license or to enter into a joint venture in a foreign nation?

10. Discuss the impact of strategic alliances on marketing strategies.

11. Contrast globalization with customization of marketing strategies. Is one practice better than the other?

Application Questions

1. Understanding the complexities of the marketing environment is necessary if a marketer is to implement marketing strategies in the international marketplace successfully. Which environmental forces (sociocultural, economic, political/legal, and technological) might a marketer need to consider when marketing the following products in the international marketplace, and why?
   a. Barbie doll
   b. beer
   c. financial services
   d. television sets

2. Many firms, including Procter & Gamble, FedEx, and Occidental Petroleum, wish to do business in Eastern Europe and in the countries that were once part of the Soviet Union. What events could occur that would make marketing in these countries more difficult? What events might make it easier?

3. Various organizational approaches to international marketing are discussed in the chapter. Which would be the best arrangements for international marketing of the following products, and why?
   a. construction equipment manufacturing
   b. cosmetics
   c. automobiles

4. Procter & Gamble has made a substantial commitment to foreign markets, especially in Latin America. Its actions may be described as a "globalization of marketing." Describe how a shoe manufacturer would go from domestic marketing, to limited exporting, to international marketing, and finally to a globalization of marketing. Give examples of some of the activities that might be involved in this process.

Internet Exercise & Resources

FTD Online

Founded in 1910 as "Florists' Telegraph Delivery," FTD was the first company to offer a "flowers-by-wire" service. FTD does not itself deliver flowers, but depends on local florists to provide this service. In 1994, FTD expanded its toll-free telephone-ordering service by establishing a Web site. Visit the site at

www.ftd.com

1. Click on International. Select a country to which you would like to send flowers. Summarize the delivery information and pricing information that would apply to that country.
2. Determine the cost of sending fresh-cut seasonal flowers to Germany.
3. What are the benefits of this global distribution system for sending flowers worldwide? What other consumer products could be distributed globally through the Internet?

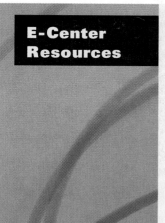

E-Center Resources

Visit http://www.prideferrell.com to find several resources to help you succeed in mastering the material in this chapter, plus additional materials that will help you expand your marketing knowledge. The Web site includes

 Internet exercise updates plus additional exercises

 ACE self-tests

abc Chapter summary with hotlinked glossary

 Hotlinks to companies featured in this chapter

 Resource Center

Career Center

Marketing plan worksheets

VIDEO CASE 5.1

Dat'l Do-It Cooks Up Hot Exports

Christopher Way started cooking up hot, spicy datil pepper sauces for his Barnacle Bill's Seafood House restaurant in St. Augustine, Florida, in the early 1980s. The sauces proved so popular that the jars he put on the restaurants' tables kept disappearing. Way reasoned that if his customers liked the sauce well enough to steal it, they would pay for it if given the opportunity. So, in 1983, Way founded Dat'l Do-It to create and market hot sauces and relishes. Little did he know that in just a few years, his little company would have a global presence.

The timing of Dat'l Do-It's launch was fortuitous as consumer interest in spicy foods was increasing. Way's sauces were uniquely positioned to capitalize on this trend since they employ datil peppers—one of the hottest peppers in the world, just slightly less blister-

ing than the habanero pepper—as a primary ingredient. The potent peppers, grown only in the St. Augustine area, flavor Way's products in a range of heat intensities, from Dat'l Do-It Pepper Jelly on the mild end of the scale to Devil Drops at the volcanic end.

Way initially cooked up the sauces in the kitchen of Barnacle Bill's, but he soon had a food chemist adapt the recipes for mass production. The adapted formulas were designed both to taste good and to have a longer shelf life. Way then contracted with a commercial food-manufacturing plant to produce the sauces on a large scale. He also hired local farmers to grow hundreds of bushels of peppers a season to supply enough datils to cook up truckloads of sauce. Within a few years, Way established his own "Dat'l Do-It farm," which has the capacity to produce up to 20,000 pounds of peppers a season. The Dat'l Do-It farm grows the peppers outside on platforms, where they are drip-watered and naturally pest-controlled by a legion of lady bugs.

Way soon developed a whole line of datil-based products, including Hot Sauce, Hot Vinegar, Salsa, Wing Sauce, Pepper Jelly, Hellish Relish, Minorcan Mustard, Devil Drops, and GargOil. With a full line of products ready for market, Way needed to find a way to get them to customers, a task that proved both time-consuming and costly for a start-up firm. Even though a vice president of the giant Winn-Dixie supermarket chain loved Dat'l Do-It's sauces and wanted to carry the line, Way was able to get his products onto the shelves of just a few of the Winn-Dixie stores. "The 'gourmet' or specialized food arena is still a really difficult market to get into," Way says.

Despite these challenges, Dat'l Do-It's sales continued to grow. By 1993, the company was breaking even with sales just below $500,000. Way decided it was time to set up a Dat'l Do-It Hot Shop to sell his sauces in St. Augustine, and he made plans to franchise similar shops throughout the South. He also opened small kiosks in high-traffic shopping malls during the Christmas shopping season and started a mail-order operation to reach customers all over the United States.

Soon after, Kodo Matsumoto, an exporter based in St. Petersburg, Florida, encouraged Way to export Dat'l Do-It products to Japan. Matsumoto pointed out that studies indicate that Japanese people enjoy spicy foods and that he himself had successfully marketed a variety of products to the Japanese market. However, Way couldn't simply put his products into boxes and ship them to Japan. He first had to modify the ingredients and labels to comply with stringent Japanese regulations. He had to rely on Matsumoto for guidance in navigating the complex customs and practices of the Japanese distribution system, which has traditionally been geared toward protecting locally made products.

Thanks to Matsumoto's expert knowledge of the Japanese market, Way has been able to continue expanding his export business year after year. In fact, Way is so excited about prospects for international sales that he recently changed the sign at the Dat'l Do-It farm to read, "World Headquarters." No doubt Dat'l Do-It will continue to expand globally as Way cooks up new plans for his company in the coming years.[53]

Questions for Discussion

1. Trade restrictions required Christopher Way to make changes to his products in order to export them to Japan. What other changes might be required as Dat'l Do-It expands into other foreign countries?

2. What economic forces might affect the cost of Dat'l Do-It products in Japan, thereby influencing demand?

3. As Dat'l Do-It grows and expands its global distribution, the company may want to consider a higher level of involvement in international marketing. What level of involvement would be most appropriate? Defend your answer.

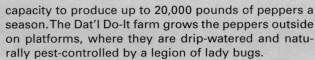

CASE 5.2

Value Club Misses Its Mark and Pays the Price

Wal-Mart and C. P. Pokphand dissolved Ek Chor Distribution System, their joint venture to build retail stores in Hong Kong and mainland China, after just eighteen months of operation. Wal-Mart, one of the world's largest discount retailers, had brought to the venture its expertise in operating warehouse-style discount stores. Pokphand, a Thai agricultural, industrial, and retailing conglomerate with many previous joint ventures in China, had brought expertise in dealing with the complex Chinese cultural and legal environment. The key reason cited for the venture's failure was Wal-Mart's unwillingness to give Pokphand greater say in location merchandising decisions for Wal-Mart stores being built in mainland China. Another significant factor contributing to the demise of the venture, however, was that Ek Chor's Value Club stores in Hong Kong failed to attract customers.

Occupying about 20,000 square feet each, the three Value Club stores Ek Chor opened in Hong Kong were essentially miniature Sam's Clubs—the members-only, warehouse-style stores Wal-Mart operates in the United States. Although one-fifth their size, the Value Clubs were modeled after these facilities, which offer popular consumer brands, usually in bulk packaging, in a "no-frills" environment. By keeping costs low and turning over merchandise frequently, warehouse clubs can offer low prices to their members. But whereas members of U.S. warehouse clubs are small businesses and individuals from lower- and middle-income groups, Value Club's limited clientele included more upscale customers with monthly incomes over HK $20,000 (US $2,580), twice the Hong Kong average monthly income of about HK $10,000 (US $1,290).

Value Club's low-price strategy should have appealed to the majority of Hong Kong shoppers, who are very price-sensitive. However, they also place a high value on shopping convenience, largely because of the difficulty of transporting purchases home. There are few private automobiles in Hong Kong, and most people travel by subway, bus, or taxi. Those without

cars must transport large or bulky purchases by taxi, the most expensive of their three options. To keep costs and prices low, Value Club, like most warehouse clubs, did not offer home delivery services. Adding to the inconvenience, the Value Club stores were located in low-rent areas away from the public transportation backbone, which required shoppers to spend extra time in taxis or buses.

The inconvenient location of Value Club stores was even more of a drawback because most Hong Kong residents are in the habit of shopping every day. They do so not only to bring home the freshest food for their families, but also because most live in small apartments in which storage space is limited; three adults commonly share a space no larger than 300 square feet. With small refrigerators and limited storage space, daily shopping is a necessity; a gallon of orange juice may not fit in the refrigerator, and the only place to store a gallon of cooking oil may be on the floor.

Lack of storage space thus also makes buying in bulk, even at bargain prices, inconvenient for most Hong Kong consumers. In addition, one Hong Kong housewife told researchers that it is difficult for petite Asian women to pour a small amount out of a large bottle of cooking oil or soy sauce. She said she had to buy a smaller container that was easier for her to handle, pour some of the oil from the large bottle into it, then store both containers somewhere in her tiny kitchen. She pointed out that it's easier just to buy a smaller size in the first place. To avoid the problems of transporting and storing bulky items bought at warehouse stores, most Hong Kong consumers are willing to spend a few extra dollars shopping at convenient stores on their way home from work or in their apartment complexes.

Another factor in the failure of the three Value Club stores may have been their product mix of about a thousand different items: 70 percent U.S. merchandise and 30 percent local products. Many of the American products Value Club stocked were unfamiliar to Hong Kong consumers, and many of the local products were not the most popular brands in Hong Kong or ones that households there commonly use, especially in bulk sizes or multipacks. If Value Club had offered products in smaller sizes, shoppers might have been willing to try them, but they did not want to risk wasting money and losing face by throwing out a large amount of a new product they did not like.

Finally, the Value Club stores attracted very few small business customers, the large-volume purchasers that account for the majority of Sam's Club sales in the United States. The problems of transportation and storage that affect Hong Kong consumers shopping for personal or household products affect owners of small businesses as well. Because the cost of retail space is very high, a retail store may serve as the owner's living room, dining room, and bedroom at night, further reducing the space needed to store goods even though they could be obtained at a reduced price.

Value Club is not the only warehouse-style chain to stumble in Hong Kong. Consumers have also bypassed two U-Save Warehouses in favor of grocery stores with more familiar products in more convenient sizes. GrandMart, however, has generated considerably higher traffic than Value Club by offering bulk packages of familiar products that are often consumed quickly, such as snack foods a family might consume in an evening while watching television or playing mahjong with friends. Located close to large public housing complexes, GrandMart's seven outlets also appear to be better suited for daily shopping.

Although Wal-Mart has had tremendous success with Sam's Clubs in the United States, the company's domestic experiences did not translate well to the unique marketing environment of Hong Kong. Moreover, Wal-Mart failed to take advantage of its partner's expertise in dealing with Chinese culture. Although the fundamental nature of warehouse-style clubs may simply be incompatible with consumers' desire for convenience as well as low prices in the crowded urban environment of Hong Kong, GrandMart's relative success there suggests otherwise. The failure of Value Club highlights how important a clear understanding of the marketing environment is in the success, or failure, of international marketing efforts.[54]

Questions for Discussion

1. What factors limited the success of Value Club stores in Hong Kong?
2. How could Ek Chor's managers have addressed the factors identified in question 1?
3. What could Wal-Mart have done to increase the likelihood of success of its joint venture?

STRATEGIC CASE 1

Kentucky Fried Chicken Expands Globally

During the 1960s and 1970s, Kentucky Fried Chicken Corporation (KFC) pursued an aggressive strategy of restaurant expansion, quickly establishing itself as one of the largest fast-food chains in the United States. KFC was also one of the first U.S. fast-food chains to expand overseas. By 1990, restaurants located outside the United States were generating over 50 percent of KFC's total profits. Today, KFC is one of the largest fast-food operations operating outside the United States with almost 10,000 outlets in more than 79 countries serving 2.5 billion meals worldwide.

Japan, Australia, and the United Kingdom accounted for the greatest share of KFC's international expansion during the 1970s and 1980s. During the 1990s, other markets became attractive. China, with a population of over 1 billion, as well as Europe and Latin America, offered expansion opportunities. By 1998, KFC had established 157 company-owned restaurants and franchises in Mexico. In addition to Mexico, KFC was operating 281 restaurants in the Caribbean, and Central and South America.

Company History

Fast-food franchising was still in its infancy in 1954 when Harland Sanders began his cross-country travels to market "Colonel Sanders' Recipe Kentucky Fried Chicken." By 1963, the number of KFC franchises numbered over 300. Tiring of running the daily operations of his business, Colonel Sanders sold his company in 1964 at the age of 74 to two Louisville businessmen—Jack Massey and John Young Brown, Jr.—for $2 million. Brown, who later became governor of Kentucky, was named president, and Massey was named chairman; "the Colonel" stayed on in a public relations capacity.

In 1966, Massey and Brown took KFC public, and the company was listed on the New York Stock Exchange. During the late 1960s, Massey and Brown turned their attention to international markets and signed a joint venture with Mitsuoishi Shoji Kaisha Ltd. in Japan. Subsidiaries were also established in Great Britain, Hong Kong, South Africa, Australia, New Zealand, and Mexico. In the late 1970s, Brown's desire to seek a political career led him to seek a buyer for KFC. Soon after, KFC merged with Heublein, Inc., a producer of alcoholic beverages with little restaurant experience. Conflicts quickly arose between Heublein management and Colonel Sanders, who was concerned about quality control issues and restaurant cleanliness. In 1977, Heublein sent in a new management team to redirect KFC's strategy. New unit construction was discontinued until existing restaurants could be upgraded and operating problems eliminated. The overhaul emphasized cleanliness, service, profitability, and product consistency. By 1982, KFC was once again aggressively building new restaurant units.

In October 1986, Kentucky Fried Chicken was sold to PepsiCo. First incorporated in Delaware in 1919, Pepsi-Cola Co. acquired Frito-Lay in 1965, creating one of the largest consumer companies in the United States. PepsiCo first entered the restaurant business in 1977 when it acquired Pizza Hut's 3,200 units. In 1978, Taco Bell was added. The Kentucky Fried Chicken acquisition gave PepsiCo the leading market share in three of the four largest and fastest-growing segments in the U.S. quick-service industry. Marketing fast food complemented PepsiCo's consumer product orientation and followed much the same pattern as marketing soft drinks and snack foods. Pepsi soft drinks and fast-food products could be marketed together in the same restaurants and through coordinated national advertising, providing higher returns for each advertising dollar.

In 1997, however, PepsiCo decided to reposition itself as a packaged goods company and therefore spun off its restaurant operation—including KFC, Pizza Hut, and Taco Bell—into a new corporation called Tricon Global Restaurants, Inc. The new company, with 350,000 employees, is based in KFC's headquarters in Louisville, Kentucky. With 29,700 outlets in more than 100 countries, Tricon's triumvirate of restaurant chains makes it the largest fast-food restaurant company, but it lags behind McDonald's in terms of global sales, with 1997 sales of $9.7 billion.

The Fast Food Industry

Six major business segments make up the fast-food market of the food service industry. Sandwich chains comprise the largest segment. Many have recently expanded menu offerings to include fried chicken (Hardee's and McDonald's), fried clams and shrimp (Burger King), pita sandwiches (Wendy's), and "wraps" (Taco Bell). In addition to new products, sandwich chains reduced prices, improved customer service, and established restaurants in nontraditional locations (McDonald's, for example, has installed hundreds of restaurants in Wal-Mart stores across the country) to boost sales. Co-branding is also a potential source of expansion for many food chains. PepsiCo is implementing plans to add Taco Bell signs and menus to approximately 800 existing KFC restaurants over the next few years, increasing Taco Bell's 4,500 unit system by almost 18 percent.

The third largest fast-food segment is pizza, long dominated by Pizza Hut. Little Caesar's, Domino's, and Papa John's are the other primary players in this market. The success of home delivery has driven competitors to look for new methods of increasing their customer base by, for example, diversifying into nonpizza items, nontraditional units (airport kiosks and university campus stores), and special promotions.

In the chicken segment, KFC continues to dominate, with sales in 1997 of $3.9 billion. KFC's closest competitors are Boston Market and Popeye's Famous Fried Chicken. Despite KFC's long supremacy in the chicken segment, it has lost market share over the last two years to new restaurant chains that emphasize roasted chicken over traditional fried chicken. In order to expand distribution to new customers, many chains have begun to offer home delivery and home-replacement take-out meals (KFC's $14.99 megameal, for example).

Intense marketing by the leading chain will no doubt continue to stimulate demand for fast food. However, a number of demographic and societal changes are likely to affect the future demand for fast food in different directions. On the one hand, demand should be stimulated by the rise in number of dual-income families and by increased disposable income given the increase in single-person households (approximately 25 percent of U.S. households). Americans are expected to spend 55 percent of their food dollars at restaurants, up from 34 percent in 1970. On the other hand, the proliferation of microwaves into approximately 70 percent of all U.S. homes has resulted in a shift in the types of products sold for home preparation and consumption. In addition, the aging American population may increase the frequency with which people patronize more upscale restaurants.

Although the number of fast-food outlets is near saturation in the United States, fast-food chains are relatively scarce internationally. The United States represents the largest consumer market in the world, accounting for over one-fifth of the world's gross domestic product. Many other cultures have strong culinary traditions that have not been easy to penetrate. KFC previously failed in the German market because Germans were not accustomed to take-out food or to ordering food over a counter. KFC has been more successful in the Asian markets, where chicken is a staple dish. Aside from cultural factors, international business carries risks not present in the U.S. market. Long distances between headquarters and foreign franchises often make it difficult to control the quality of individual franchises. Long distances also cause transportation, servicing, and support problems.

Marketing Strategy

As KFC entered the mid-1990s, it grappled with a number of important issues. During the 1980s, consumers began to demand healthier foods, and KFC's limited menu, consisting mainly of fried foods, was a distinct liability. In order to soften its fried chicken chain image, the company changed its name and logo from Kentucky Fried Chicken to KFC in 1991. In addition, it responded to consumer demands for greater variety by introducing several new products. Consumers have also become more mobile, demanding fast food in a variety of nontraditional locations such as grocery stores, restaurants, airports, and outdoor events. This has forced fast-food restaurant chains in general to investigate nontraditional distribution channels and restaurant designs. Additionally, families continue to seek greater value in the food they buy, further increasing the pressure on fast-food chains to reduce operating costs and prices.

Many of KFC's problems during the late 1980s surrounded its limited menu and its inability to bring new products to market quickly. The popularity of its Original Recipe fried chicken allowed KFC to expand through the 1980s without significant competition from other chicken competitors. As a result, new-product introductions were never an important part of KFC's overall strategy. However, the introduction of chicken sandwiches and fried chicken by hamburger chains has changed the make-up of KFC's competitors. Most important, McDonald's introduced its McChicken sandwich to the U.S. market in 1989, while KFC was still testing its version. By beating KFC to the counter, McDonald's was able to develop a strong consumer awareness for its sandwich. This setback significantly complicated KFC's task of developing consumer awareness for its chicken sandwich, which was introduced several months later.

The growing popularity of healthier foods and consumers' increasing demand for greater variety have led to a number of changes in KFC's menu. It introduced Oriental Wings, Popcorn Chicken, Honey BBQ Chicken, the Chunky Chicken Pot Pie, the Colonel's Crispy Strips, and Hot Wings as alternatives to its Original Recipe fried chicken. In 1993, KFC launched "Rotisserie Gold," a line of roasted whole chickens, to compete with Boston Market. However, the "Rotisserie Gold" product was withdrawn a few years later when research indicated that most customers preferred to buy chicken by the piece. "Rotisserie Gold" was replaced in 1996 with a new roasted chicken product called "Tender Roast," which is sold by the piece and can even be mixed with KFC's Original Recipe and Extra Crispy Chicken. KFC also introduced a dessert menu that included a variety of pies and cookies. In 1993, KFC began to promote its lunch and dinner buffet. The buffet, which includes thirty items, had been introduced into almost 1,600 KFC restaurants in twenty-seven states by the end of 1993.

One aggressive strategy employed by KFC was its "Neighborhood Program." By mid-1993, almost 500 company-owned restaurants in New York, Chicago, Philadelphia, Washington, D.C., St. Louis, Los Angeles, Houston, and Dallas had been outfitted with special menu offerings to appeal to the African-American community. Menus were beefed up with side dishes such as greens, macaroni and cheese, sweet-potato pie, and red beans and rice. In addition, restaurant employees have been outfitted with African-inspired uniforms. The introduction of the Neighborhood Program has increased sales by 5–30 percent in restaurants catering directly to the African-American community. KFC is currently testing Hispanic-oriented restaurants in the Miami area, which offer such side dishes as fried plantains, flan, and *très leches*.

As the growth in sales of traditional, freestanding fast-food restaurants has slowed during the last decade, consumers have demanded quick meals in more and more nontraditional locations. As a result, distribution has taken on increasing importance. KFC is relying on nontraditional units to spur much of its future growth. The chicken giant is currently testing such unusual distribution channels as mall stores, cafeteria snack shops, kiosks in airports, amusement parks, supermarkets, and office buildings; and mobile units that can be transported to outdoor concerts and fairs. The company also introduced a home-delivery program in 1994. In 1996 the company embarked on a strategy of "dual branding" with sister chain Taco Bell to expand its daytime business. KFC derives about two-thirds of its sales at dinnertime, but Taco Bell's main business is lunch. Corporate parent Tricon believed that combining the two concepts in the same unit would significantly boost sales at individual restaurants, so the company began adding the Taco Bell menu to existing KFC restaurants. By 1997, 349 KFC restaurants had added the Taco Bell menu and displayed both the KFC and Taco Bell logos.

Although marketing and operating strategies can improve sales and profitability in existing outlets, an important part of success in the quick-service industry is investment growth. KFC is now the third-largest quick-service, and largest chicken restaurant system in the world. In the future, KFC's international operations will be called on to provide an increasing percentage of KFC's overall sales and profit growth as the U.S. market continues to mature.

Mexico and Latin America

KFC was operating 207 company-owned restaurants and 231 franchises in Mexico, the Caribbean, and Latin America at the end of 1997. Before 1990, KFC had concentrated its company operations in Mexico and Puerto Rico, and its franchisee operations in the Caribbean and Central America. By 1994, KFC had altered its Latin American strategy to begin franchising in Mexico, expand its company-owned restaurants in the Caribbean, and reestablish a subsidiary in Venezuela.

Franchising, though popular in the United States, was virtually unknown in Mexico until 1990, when a new law governing franchising resulted in an explosion of fast-food restaurants, services, hotels, and retail outlets. Mexico is a potentially profitable location for U.S. direct investment and trade. With a population of over 91 million, Mexico is approximately one-third the size of the United States. Its geographical proximity makes transportation costs minimal, increasing the competitiveness of U.S. goods over those from Asia or Europe. The United States is Mexico's largest trading partner, accounting for over 65 percent of its imports. Mexico in turn, exports about 69 percent of its goods to the United States. Despite the importance of the U.S. market to Mexico, it still represents a small percentage of overall U.S. trade and investment, largely because of Mexico's history of restrictions on trade and foreign direct investment.

Prior to 1989, Mexico levied high tariffs on most imported goods, and many others were subjected to quotas, licensing requirements, and other nontariff trade barriers. The 1994 North American Free Trade Agreement (NAFTA) created a trading block with a larger population and gross domestic product than the European Union. Mexico should benefit from the lower cost of imported goods and increased employment from higher investment from Canada and the United States. Canada and the United States should benefit from lower labor and transportation costs related to investments in Mexico.

In 1994, Ernesto Zedillo was elected as Mexico's new president. Zedillo's objective was to maintain stability in prices, wages, and exchange rates. However, Salinas had achieved stability largely on the basis of price, wage, and foreign exchange controls. Giving the appearance of stability, an overvalued peso continued to encourage imports, which exacerbated Mexico's balance of trade deficit. Anticipating a devaluation of the peso, investors began to move capital into U.S. dollar investments at the end of 1994. The continued devaluation of the peso in early 1995 resulted in higher import prices, runaway inflation, destabilization of the stock market, and exorbitant interest rates. The peso crisis led to a recession in Mexico and left KFC managers uncertain about Mexico's economic and political future.

KFC's approach to investment in Mexico has been to remain conservative, at least until greater economic and political stability is achieved. Although resources could be redirected toward other investment areas with less risk, such as Japan, Australia, China, and Europe, KFC still views Mexico as its most important foreign growth market. Significant opportunities also exist for KFC to expand its franchise base through the Caribbean and South America. Tricon's commitments to these markets are unlikely to be affected by its investment decisions in Mexico. The danger in taking a conservative approach in Mexico is the potential loss of market share in a country where KFC enjoys enormous popularity.[55]

Questions for Discussion

1. What are KFC's greatest marketing challenges in the domestic fast-food market?
2. What is the role of globalization of marketing in KFC's plans to expand sales? Can KFC use the same marketing strategies worldwide?
3. Why are environmental forces so important to KFC's sales success in Latin America and Mexico?

Part Two

Buyer Behavior and Target Market Selection

Part 2 focuses on the buyer. The development of a marketing strategy begins with the buyer. Chapter 6 provides a foundation for analyzing buyers through a discussion of marketing information systems and the basic steps in the marketing research process. Understanding elements that affect buying decisions enables marketers to better analyze customers' needs and evaluate how specific marketing strategies can satisfy those needs. Chapter 7 focuses on one of the major steps in the development of a marketing strategy: selecting and analyzing target markets. In Chapter 8 we examine consumer buying decision processes and factors that influence buying decisions. Then, in Chapter 9, we stress organizational markets, organizational buyers, the buying center, and the organizational buying decision process.

6

Marketing Research and Information Systems

OBJECTIVES

- To learn the basic steps for conducting marketing research

- To become familiar with the fundamental methods of gathering data for marketing research

- To describe the nature and role of information systems in marketing decision making

- To explore how such tools as databases, decision support systems, and the Internet facilitate marketing research

- To understand key ethical and international considerations in marketing research

Conoco Satisfies "Convenience Connoisseurs"

Conoco is a major, integrated company based in Houston, Texas, and active in forty countries. Because the market for gas stations has become saturated and less profitable while customer buying habits have changed, the company has been looking for new ways to attract and retain customers. After conducting extensive research on every aspect of the convenience store, Conoco recently launched a new concept, called "breakplace."

Conoco's telephone research in thirty-eight states identified its most profitable target market as "convenience connoisseurs"—people who have average incomes, visit the same convenience store an average of fourteen times a month, and want the convenience of in-and-out shopping. Additional research indicated that these customers like modern amenities, such as credit-card readers on gas pumps and ATMs, but they want service delivered "the way it used to be." The company also learned that customers of convenience stores value courtesy, efficiency, spaciousness, safety, cleanliness, convenient parking, and logical organization. Research even suggested that the perfect name to appeal

to these demanding customers would be "breakplace."

Conoco's research guided its design team to craft the breakplace concept as a distinctive, high-quality convenience store. The stores, which resemble trendy restaurants, have red brick exteriors, vaulted entryways, and green awnings. "Retro" pictures on the walls and corrugated metal on the coolers give the interiors a contemporary, yet nostalgic feeling. A cafe-style area inside the store features a deli counter (called "freshbreak"), a cold-drink area ("thirstbreak"), and a coffee bar with fourteen selections ("coffeebreak"). A grocery area stocks bulk merchandise. The checkout counter, an island at the front of the store, is designed to minimize the separation between employees and customers. A first-of-its-kind curved-glass safety partition, which provides extra security for cashiers on the night shift, is retracted into the wall during the day to allow more customer contact.

To ensure that breakplace stores offer the high-quality experience its "convenience connoisseurs" demand, Conoco strives for the best possible customer service. "Breakplace" stores brew fresh coffee every half-hour, and any coffee left in the pot at the end of that time is dumped out. Unlike most convenience stores, which offer prewrapped, prepackaged foods, breakplace stores bake their own deli breads on premises and make sandwiches fresh to order.

By designing a store to satisfy its demanding "convenience connoisseurs," Conoco hopes to appeal to other customers whose needs overlap those of its target market. So far, the results have been excellent: 98 percent of surveyed customers who tried the new stores indicated they would make breakplace their regular convenience store.[1]

The marketing research conducted by Conoco illustrates that to implement the marketing concept, marketers require information about the characteristics, needs, and desires of target market customers. Such information, when used effectively, facilitates relationship marketing by helping marketers focus their efforts on meeting and even anticipating the needs of their customers. Marketing research and information systems that can provide practical and objective information to help firms develop and implement marketing strategies are therefore essential to effective marketing.

In this chapter, we focus on how marketers gather information needed to make marketing decisions. We first define marketing research and examine the individual steps of the marketing research process, including various methods of collecting data. Next, we look at how technology aids in collecting, organizing, and interpreting marketing research data. Finally, we consider ethical and international issues in marketing research.

The Importance of Marketing Research

marketing research The systematic design, collection, interpretation, and reporting of information to help marketers solve specific marketing problems or take advantage of market opportunities

Marketing research is the systematic design, collection, interpretation, and reporting of information to help marketers solve specific marketing problems or take advantage of marketing opportunities. As the word *research* implies, it is a process for gathering information not currently available to decision makers. The purpose of market research is to inform an organization about customers' needs and desires, marketing opportunities for particular goods and services, and changing attitudes and purchase patterns of customers. Detecting shifts in buyers' behaviors and attitudes helps companies stay in touch with the ever-changing marketplace. Marketers of pet supplies, for example, would be very interested in knowing that sales of cat-related products have edged out dog-related products, 32 percent to 31 percent, and that the market for cat supplies is growing quickly, up 7 percent in one year, representing nearly $4 billion in sales.[2] Strategic planning requires marketing research to facilitate the process of assessing such opportunities or threats. (Figure 6.1 illustrates one service provider that facilitates marketing research.)

Marketing research can help a firm better understand market opportunities, ascertain the potential for success for new products, and determine the feasibility of a particular marketing strategy. Consider the failure of SpringClean, a spring-action toothbrush introduced by Carewell Industries. The small Florida firm did not have the financial resources to support extensive marketing research. Although SpringClean was a genuinely innovative product in the overcrowded and heavily advertised toothbrush market, toothbrush buyers did not know what SpringClean was or were not able to see that it was a "better" product.[3] Marketing research might have indicated that small companies are not likely to succeed in the competitive toothbrush market without adequate financial

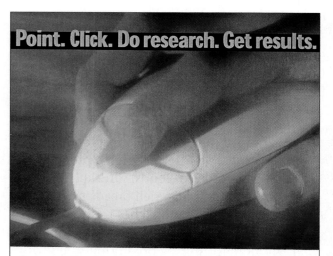

Announcing Harris Interactive. Using the Internet to fulfill all your market research objectives.

Harris Black International (HBI), an established research leader for over 40 years, is proud to announce the formation of a new division, Harris Interactive. Now, in less than a year, HBI has pioneered the use of the Internet for marketing research. And Harris Interactive, based in New York City, reaffirms HBI's commitment to developing Internet research methods and providing leading edge Internet solutions for our clients.

Internet milestones include:
• 1.5 million household cooperative panel, increasing daily
• Harris Poll Online with parallel Internet and telephone survey validation

• First Internet poll predicting 1998 gubernatorial and senatorial election results
• Proven Internet advantages of less time, larger samples and improved research quality

The Harris Interactive client list is growing, as more companies learn the benefits of Internet research. Could your business benefit? You're just a click away from finding out.

For more information, email michelles@harrisblackintl.com or see our website at www.harrisblackintl.com Or call 1-888-557-7492.

Harris Black International

Louis Harris & Associates • Harris Interactive • Harris Black International Consulting • Gordon S. Black Corporation • Data Collection Services • Harris Black International Network

Figure 6.1
Gathering Information
Marketing research is critical in helping companies succeed. However, it requires skills and resources that may not exist within a firm. Specializing in marketing research, Harris Black International has pioneered the use of the Internet to provide information for its clients.

resources or, perhaps, a partnership with a larger firm such as Colgate, which spent more than $100 million to launch its Total toothpaste.

Marketing research is used by all sorts of organizations to help develop marketing mixes to match the needs of customers. Supermarkets, for example, have learned from marketing research that roughly half of all Americans prefer to have their dinners ready in fifteen to thirty minutes. Such information highlights a tremendous opportunity for supermarkets to offer high-quality "heat and eat" meals to satisfy this growing segment of the food market, which represents $44 billion in sales.[4] Political candidates also depend on marketing research to understand the scope of issues that their constituents view as important.

The real value of marketing research is measured by improvements in a marketer's ability to make decisions. Marketers should treat information in the same manner as other resources utilized by the firm, and they must weigh the costs of obtaining information against the benefits derived. Information should be judged worthwhile if it results in marketing activities that better satisfy the firm's target customers, that lead to increased sales and profits, or that help the firm achieve some other goal.

The Marketing Research Process

To maintain the control needed to obtain accurate information, marketers approach marketing research as a process with logical steps: (1) locating and defining problems or issues, (2) designing the research project, (3) collecting data, (4) interpreting research findings, and (5) reporting research findings (Figure 6.2). These steps should be viewed as an overall approach to conducting research rather than as a rigid set of rules to be followed in each project. In planning research projects, marketers must consider each of the steps carefully and determine how they can best be adapted to resolve the particular issues at hand.

Locating and Defining Problems or Research Issues

The first step toward launching a research study is problem or issue definition, which focuses on uncovering the nature and boundaries of a situation or question related to marketing strategy or implementation. The first sign of a problem is typically a departure from some normal function, such as conflicts between or failures in attaining objectives. If a corporation's objective is a 12 percent sales increase and the current marketing strategy resulted in a 6 percent increase, this discrepancy should be analyzed to help guide future marketing strategies. It is a symptom that something inside or outside the organization blocked the attainment of the desired goal or that the goal was unrealistic. Declining sales, increasing expenses, and decreasing profits also signal problems. Conversely, when an organization experiences a dramatic rise in sales or some other positive event, it may conduct marketing research to discover the reasons and maximize the opportunities stemming from them.

Marketing research is often focused on identifying and defining market opportunities or changes in the environment. When a firm discovers a market opportunity, it may need to conduct research to understand the situation more precisely so that it can craft an appropriate marketing strategy. For example, global sales of hot drinks

Figure 6.2
The Five Steps of the Marketing Research Process

| 1 Locating and defining issues or problems | 2 Designing the research project | 3 Collecting data | 4 Interpreting research findings | 5 Reporting research findings |

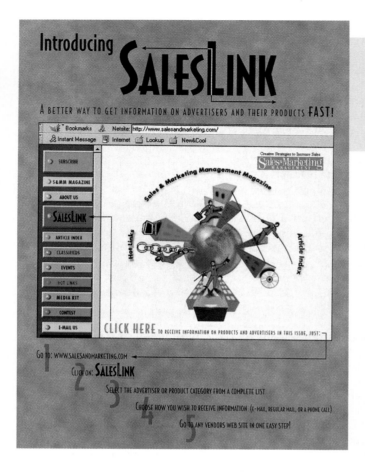

Figure 6.3
Defining Research Issues
Marketing decision makers will find that companies such as *Sales & Marketing Management* provide information and online services such as Connect and SalesLink that are useful in locating and refining marketing issues for research.

increased by 23 percent in a recent year, to $53 billion.[5] Marketers of hot beverages would do well to determine what regions of the world are experiencing increases and whether the increase represents an emerging trend or a temporary fluctuation based on weather or some other factor.

To pin down the specific boundaries of a problem or an issue through research, marketers must define the nature and scope of the situation in a way that requires probing beneath the superficial symptoms. The interaction between the marketing manager and the marketing researcher should yield a clear definition of the research need. Researchers and decision makers should remain in the problem or issue definition stage until they have determined precisely what they want from marketing research and how they will use it. Figure 6.3 illustrates that *Sales & Marketing Management* provides marketing information that can be useful in defining research problems. Deciding how to refine a broad, indefinite problem or issue into a precise, researchable statement is a prerequisite for the next step in the research process.

Designing the Research Project

research design   An overall plan for obtaining the information needed to address a research problem or issue

Once the problem or issue has been defined, the next step is **research design,** an overall plan for obtaining the information needed to address it. This step requires formulating a hypothesis and determining what type of research is most appropriate for testing the hypothesis so that the results are reliable and valid.

hypothesis   An informed guess or assumption about a certain problem or set of circumstances

Developing a Hypothesis   The objective statement of a marketing research project should include hypotheses based on both previous research and expected research findings. A **hypothesis** is an informed guess or assumption about a certain problem or set of circumstances. It is based on all the insight and knowledge available about the problem or circumstances from previous research studies and other sources. As information is gathered, a researcher can test the hypothesis. For example, a food marketer like H. J. Heinz might propose the hypothesis that children today have considerable influence on their families' buying decisions regarding ketchup and other grocery products. A marketing researcher would then gather data, perhaps through surveys of children and their parents, and draw conclusions as to whether the hypothesis is correct. Supermarkets concerned about shoplifting would be interested in the findings of a recent research study in which 40 percent of the supermarket managers who were surveyed reported cigarettes and alcoholic beverages as their most frequently shoplifted items.[6] If a supermarket manager had hypothesized that smaller packaged goods, such as candy, were more susceptible to shoplifting than liquor and cigarettes, this research would lead him to reject that hypothesis. Sometimes several hypotheses are developed during an actual research project; the hypotheses that are accepted or rejected become the study's chief conclusions.

Types of Research   The hypothesis being tested determines whether an exploratory, descriptive, or causal approach will be used for gathering data. When marketers need more information about a problem or want to make a tentative hypothesis more specific, they may conduct **exploratory research.** For instance, they may review the information in the firm's own records or examine publicly available data. Questioning knowledgeable people inside and outside the organization may yield new insights into the problem. Information available on the Internet about industry trends and competitive firms may also be an excellent source for exploratory research. Compaq, for example, can quickly obtain price and product information about competitors like Dell and Gateway by accessing their Web sites. An advantage of the exploratory approach is that it permits marketers to conduct ministudies with a very restricted database.

exploratory research
Research conducted to gather more information about a problem or to make a tentative hypothesis more specific

If marketers need to understand the characteristics of certain phenomena to solve a particular problem, **descriptive research** can aid them. Such studies may range from general surveys of customers' education, occupation, or age to specifics on how often families eat pasta or how often teenagers eat at fast-food restaurants after school. Fast-food restaurants such as McDonald's, Wendy's, and Taco Bell would be particularly interested in a research study of teenagers' eating habits, which shows that 15 percent of after-school snacking occurs at fast-food restaurants. The average check for these snacks is $5.72. In fact, teens spend $12.7 billion per year at fast-food restaurants.[7] Such descriptive research can be used to develop specific marketing strategies for the after-school snack market. Descriptive studies generally demand much prior knowledge and assume that the problem or issue is clearly defined. Some descriptive studies require statistical analysis and predictive tools. The marketers' major task is to choose adequate methods for collecting and measuring data.

descriptive research
Research conducted to clarify the characteristics of certain phenomena to solve a particular problem

Hypotheses about causal relationships call for a more complex approach than a descriptive study. In **causal research,** it is assumed that a particular variable X causes a variable Y. Marketers must plan the research so that the data collected prove or disprove that X causes Y. To do so, marketers must try to hold constant all variables except X and Y. For example, to determine whether new carpeting, pet-friendly policies, or outside storage increase the number of rentals in an apartment complex, researchers need to keep all variables constant except one of these variables in a specific time period.

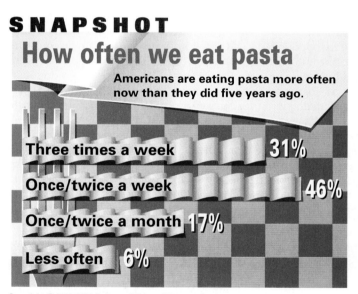

S N A P S H O T

How often we eat pasta

Americans are eating pasta more often now than they did five years ago.

Three times a week — 31%

Once/twice a week — 46%

Once/twice a month — 17%

Less often — 6%

Copyright © 1999 *USA Today*, a division of Gannett Co., Inc.

causal research   Research in which it is assumed that a particular variable X causes a variable Y

Research Reliability and Validity   In designing research, marketing researchers must ensure that research techniques are both reliable and valid. A research technique has **reliability** if it produces almost identical results in repeated trials. But a reliable technique is not necessarily valid. To have **validity,** the method must measure what it is supposed to measure, not something else. In a survey of the wealthiest 1 percent of Americans, for example, 76 percent indicated that gains from stock market investments would cause them to "be more charitably inclined."[8] Such information might motivate charitable organizations to pursue donors more aggressively. However, if respondents were stating what they thought they should say, rather than indicating their true attitudes, then the study would not be valid, nor would it be useful to nonprofit organizations. A study to measure the effect of advertising on sales would be valid if advertising could be isolated from other factors or variables that affect sales. The study would be reliable if replications of it produced the same results.

reliability   A condition existing when a research technique produces almost identical results in repeated trials

validity   A condition existing when a research method measures what it is supposed to measure

Collecting Data

The next step in the marketing research process is collecting data to help prove (or disprove) the research hypothesis. The research design must specify what types of data to collect and how they will be collected.

primary data Data observed and recorded or collected directly from subjects

secondary data Data compiled both inside and outside the organization for some purpose other than the current investigation

Types of Data   Marketing researchers have two types of data at their disposal. **Primary data** are observed and recorded or collected directly from subjects. This type of data must be gathered by observing phenomena or surveying people of interest. **Secondary data** are compiled both inside and outside the organization for some purpose other than the current investigation. Secondary data include general reports supplied to an enterprise by various data services and internal and online databases. Such reports might concern market share, retail inventory levels, and customers' buying behavior. Commonly, secondary data are already available in private or public reports or have been collected and stored by the organization itself. The opportunity to obtain data via the Internet has resulted in more than half of all marketing research coming from secondary sources.

Sources of Secondary Data   Marketers often begin the data collection phase of the marketing research process by gathering secondary data. They may use available reports and other information from both internal and external sources to study a marketing problem.

Internal sources of secondary data can contribute tremendously to research. An organization's own database may contain information about past marketing activities, such as sales records and research reports, which can be used to test hypotheses and pinpoint problems. Accounting records are also an excellent source of data but, strangely enough, are often overlooked. The large volume of data an accounting department collects does not automatically flow to other departments. As a result, detailed information about costs, sales, customer accounts, or profits by product category may not be easily accessible to the marketing area. This condition develops particularly in organizations that do not store marketing information on a systematic basis.

External sources of secondary data include periodicals, government publications, unpublished sources, and online databases. Periodicals such as *Business Week, The Wall Street Journal, Sales & Marketing Management, American Demographics, Marketing Research,* and *Industrial Marketing* publish general information that can help marketers define problems and develop hypotheses. *Survey of Buying Power,* an annual supplement to *Sales & Marketing Management,* contains sales data for major industries on a

Table 6.1	Guide to External Sources of Secondary Data
Databases	Many databases are collections of information arranged for easy access and retrieval through online information services or the Internet. Users select key words (such as the name of a subject) to search a database and generate references.
Government	The federal government, through its various departments and agencies, collects, analyzes, and publishes statistics on practically everything. Many government agencies have data available online.
Periodical Indexes	The reference section of most libraries contains indexes on virtually every discipline. *The Business Periodicals Index,* for example, indexes each article in all major business publications.
Trade Journals	Virtually every industry or type of business is covered by a trade journal. These journals give a feel for the industry—its size, degree of competition, range of companies involved, and problems. To find trade journals in the field of interest, check *Ulrich's,* a reference book that lists U.S. and foreign periodicals by subject.
Trade Associations	Almost every industry, product category, and profession has organized its own association. These often conduct research, publish journals, provide training sessions, and hold conventions. To find out which associations serve which industries, check the *Encyclopedia of Associations.*
Web Sites	Many companies have established Web sites on the Internet to disseminate information about their products and activities.

Table 6.2	Top Ten Markets for NFL Merchandise
1. Green Bay, Wisconsin	6. Dallas, Texas
2. Jacksonville, Florida	7. Denver, Colorado
3. Kansas City, Missouri	8. Oakland, California
4. Buffalo, New York	9. San Francisco, California
5. Pittsburgh, Pennsylvania	10. Charlotte, North Carolina

Source: From "Marketing Brief," *Marketing News*, September 28, 1998, p. 2. Reprinted by permission of the American Marketing Association.

county-by-county basis. Many marketers also consult federal government publications such as the *Statistical Abstract of the United States,* the *Census of Business,* the *Census of Agriculture,* and the *Census of Population;* some of these government publications are available through online information services or the Internet. Table 6.1 summarizes the major external sources of secondary data, excluding syndicated services. Table 6.2 provides an example of secondary data that would be of interest to sports-oriented stores and manufacturers. Cities with a history of strong purchases of National Football League merchandise represent excellent locales to test new product extensions and market NFL clothing in general.

Methods of Collecting Primary Data   The collection of primary data is a more lengthy, expensive, and complex process than the collection of secondary data. To gather primary data, researchers use sampling procedures, survey methods, observation, and experimentation. These efforts can be handled in-house by a firm's own research department or contracted to a private research firm, such as Maritz Marketing Research, A. C. Nielsen, Information Resources, Inc., and IMS International. Figure 6.4 illustrates that Quality Controlled Services provides primary data collection assistance to marketing researchers.

Figure 6.4
Primary Data Collection
Private data research firms often assist companies with their marketing research. Quality Controlled Services provides most data collection services, including focus groups and telephone interviewing.

population All the elements, units, or individuals of interest to researchers for a specific study

sample A limited number of units chosen to represent the characteristics of a total population

sampling The process of selecting representative units from a total population

probability sampling A sampling technique in which every element in the population being studied has a known chance of being selected for study

random sampling A type of probability sampling in which all units in a population have an equal chance of appearing in the sample

stratified sampling A type of probability sampling that divides the population into groups according to a common attribute, and then a random sample is chosen within each group

nonprobability sampling A sampling technique in which there is no way to calculate the likelihood that a specific element of the population being studied will be chosen

quota sampling A nonprobability sampling technique in which researchers divide the population into groups and then arbitrarily choose subjects from each group

Sampling   Because the time and resources available for research are limited, it is almost impossible to investigate all the members of a target market or other population. A **population,** or "universe," includes all the elements, units, or individuals of interest to researchers for a specific study. For a Gallup poll designed to predict the results of a presidential election, all registered voters in the United States would constitute the population. By systematically choosing a limited number of units—a **sample**—to represent the characteristics of a total population, researchers can project the reactions of a total market or market segment. (In the case of the presidential poll, a representative national sample of several thousand registered voters would be selected and surveyed to project the probable voting outcome.) **Sampling** in marketing research, therefore, is the process of selecting representative units from a total population. Sampling techniques allow marketers to predict buying behavior fairly accurately on the basis of the responses from a representative portion of the population of interest. Most types of marketing research employ sampling techniques.

There are two basic types of sampling: probability sampling and nonprobability sampling. With **probability sampling,** every element in the population being studied has a known chance of being selected for study. Random sampling is a kind of probability sampling. When marketers employ **random sampling,** all the units in a population have an equal chance of appearing in the sample. The various events that can occur have an equal or known chance of taking place. For example, a specific card in a regulation deck should have a 1/52 probability of being drawn at any one time. Similarly, if each student at a university or college has a unique identification number and these numbers are mixed up in a large basket, each student's number would have a known probability of being selected. Sample units are ordinarily chosen by selecting from a table of random numbers statistically generated so that each digit, zero through nine, will have an equal probability of occurring in each position in the sequence. The sequentially numbered elements of a population are sampled randomly by selecting the units whose numbers appear in the table of random numbers.

Another kind of probability sampling is **stratified sampling,** which divides the population of interest into groups according to a common attribute, and then a random sample is chosen within each group. The stratified sample may reduce some of the error that could occur in a simple random sample. By ensuring that each major group or segment of the population receives its proportionate share of sample units, investigators avoid including too many or too few sample units from each group. Samples are usually stratified when researchers believe there may be variations among different types of subjects. For example, many political opinion surveys are stratified by gender, race, age, and/or geographic location.

The second type of sampling, **nonprobability sampling,** is more subjective than probability sampling because there is no way to calculate the likelihood that a specific element of the population being studied will be chosen. Quota sampling, for example, is highly judgmental because the final choice of subjects is left to the researchers. In **quota sampling,** researchers divide the population into groups and then arbitrarily choose subjects from each group. A study of people who wear eyeglasses, for example, may be conducted by interviewing equal numbers of men and women who wear eyeglasses. In quota sampling, there are some controls—usually limited to two or three variables, such as age, gender, or race—over the selection of subjects. The controls attempt to ensure that representative categories of subjects are interviewed. Because quota samples are not probability samples, not everyone has an equal chance of being selected, and sampling error therefore cannot be measured statistically. Quota samples are used most often in exploratory studies, when hypotheses are being developed. Often, a small quota sample will not be projected to the total population, although the findings may provide valuable insights into a problem. Quota samples are useful when people with some common characteristic are found and questioned about the topic of interest. A probability sample used to study people allergic to cats would be highly inefficient.

Survey Methods   Marketing researchers often employ sampling to collect primary data through mail, telephone, online, or personal interview surveys. The results of such surveys are used to describe and analyze buying behavior. Selection of a survey method depends on the nature of the problem or issue, the data needed to test the hypothesis, and the resources, such as funding and personnel, available to the researcher. Table 6.3 summarizes and compares the advantages of the various survey methods.

Gathering information through surveys is becoming increasingly difficult because fewer people are willing to participate. Many people feel that responding to surveys takes up too much scarce personal time, especially as surveys become longer and more detailed. Others have concerns about how much information marketers are gathering and whether their privacy is being invaded. Moreover, fear of crime sometimes makes respondents unwilling to trust personal interviewers. The unethical use of selling techniques disguised as marketing surveys has also contributed to decreased cooperation. These factors contribute to nonresponse rates for any type of survey.

mail survey   A research method in which respondents answer a questionnaire sent through the mail

In a **mail survey,** questionnaires are sent to respondents, who are encouraged to complete and return them. Mail surveys are used most often when the individuals in the sample are spread over a wide area and funds for the survey are limited. A mail survey is the least expensive survey method as long as the response rate is high enough to produce reliable results. The main disadvantages of this method are the possibility of a low response rate or of misleading results if respondents are significantly different from the population being sampled.

Premiums or incentives that encourage respondents to return questionnaires have been effective in developing panels of respondents who are interviewed regularly by mail. Such mail panels, selected to represent a target market or market segment, are especially useful in evaluating new products and providing general information about customers, as well as records of their purchases (in the form of purchase diaries). Mail panels and purchase diaries are much more widely used than custom mail surveys, but both panels and purchase diaries have shortcomings. Research indicates that the people who take the time to fill out a diary have higher income and are more educated than the general population. But if researchers include less-educated consumers in the panel, they risk poorer response rates.[9]

Table 6.3	Comparison of the Three Basic Survey Methods		
	Mail and Online Surveys	**Telephone Surveys**	**Personal Interview Surveys**
Economy	Potentially the lowest cost per interview if there is an adequate response rate.	Avoids interviewers' travel expenses; less expensive than in-home interviews.	In-home interviewing is the most expensive interviewing method; shopping mall, or focus-group interviewing have lower costs.
Flexibility	Inflexible; questionnaire must be short, easy for respondents to complete.	Flexible because interviewers can ask probing questions, but observations are impossible.	Most flexible method; respondents can react to visual materials; demographic data are more accurate; in-depth probes are possible.
Interviewer Bias	Interviewer bias eliminated; questionnaires can be returned anonymously.	Some anonymity; may be hard to develop trust in respondents.	Interviewers' personal characteristics or inability to maintain objectivity may result in bias.
Sampling and Respondents' Cooperation	Obtaining a complete mailing list is difficult; nonresponse is a major disadvantage; E-mail surveys require computer and online access.	Sample must be limited to respondents with telephones; devices that screen calls, busy signals, and refusals are problems.	Not-at-homes are a problem which focus-group and shopping mall interviewing may overcome.

telephone survey
A research method in which respondents' answers to a questionnaire are recorded by interviewers on the phone

In a **telephone survey,** an interviewer records respondents' answers to a questionnaire over a phone line. A telephone survey has some advantages over a mail survey. The rate of response is higher because it takes less effort to answer the telephone and talk than to fill out a questionnaire and return it. If there are enough interviewers, a telephone survey can be conducted very quickly. Thus, political candidates or organizations seeking an immediate reaction to an event may choose this method. In addition, a telephone survey permits interviewers to gain rapport with respondents and ask probing questions.

However, only a small proportion of the population likes to participate in telephone surveys. Over three-fourths of Americans feel indifferent toward telephone surveys or don't like them at all.[10] This poor image can significantly limit participation and distort representation in a telephone survey. Moreover, telephone surveys are limited to oral communication; visual aids or observation cannot be included. Interpreters of results must make adjustments for subjects who are not at home or who do not have telephones. Many households are excluded from telephone directories by choice (unlisted numbers) or because the residents moved after the directory was published. Potential respondents often use telephone answering machines, voice mail, or Caller ID to screen or block calls. These issues have serious implications for the use of telephone samples in conducting surveys. Some adjustment must be made for groups of subjects that may be undersampled because of a smaller-than-average incidence of telephone listings. Nondirectory telephone samples can overcome such bias. Various methods are available, including random-digit dialing (adding random numbers to the telephone prefix) and plus-one telephone sampling (increasing the last digit of a directory number by one). These methods make it feasible to dial any working number, whether or not it is listed in a directory.

online survey A research method in which respondents answer a questionnaire via E-mail or on a Web site

Online surveys are evolving as an alternative to telephone surveys. In an **online survey**, questionnaires can be transmitted to respondents who have agreed to be contacted and have provided their E-mail addresses. Because E-mail is semi-interactive, recipients can ask for clarification of specific questions or pose questions of their own. The potential advantages of E-mail surveys are quick response and lower cost than traditional mail and telephone surveys, but these advantages have not yet been realized because of limited access to subjects and unreliable response rates.[11] Additionally, more firms are using their Web sites to conduct surveys. Evolving technology and the interactive nature of the Internet allow for considerable flexibility in designing online questionnaires.

Given the growing number of households that have computers with Internet access, marketing research is likely to rely heavily on online surveys in the future. And, as negative attitudes toward telephone surveys render that technique less representative and more expensive, the integration of E-mail, fax, and voice mail functions into one computer-based system provides a promising alternative for survey research. E-mail surveys have especially strong potential within organizations whose employees are networked and for associations that publish members' E-mail addresses. However, there are some ethical issues to consider when using E-mail for marketing research, such as unsolicited E-mail and privacy.

personal interview survey A research method in which subjects respond to survey questions face to face

In a **personal interview survey,** subjects respond to questions face to face. Various audiovisual aids—pictures, products, diagrams, or prerecorded advertising copy—can be incorporated in a personal interview. Rapport gained through direct interaction usually permits more in-depth interviewing, including probes, follow-up questions, or psychological tests. In addition, because personal interviews can be longer, they may yield more information. Finally, respondents can be selected more carefully, and reasons for nonresponse can be explored. In one study, it was found that respondents in personal interviews had the most favorable attitudes toward survey research in general. They liked seeing the person who was asking the questions and having the personal contact that is part of the interview.[12]

in-home (door-to-door) interview A personal interview that takes place in the respondent's home

One such research technique is the **in-home (door-to-door) interview.** The in-home interview offers a clear advantage when thoroughness of self-disclosure and the elimination of group influence are important. In an in-depth interview of forty-five to ninety minutes, respondents can be probed to reveal their real motivations, feelings, behaviors, and aspirations.

focus-group interview
A research method involving observation of group interaction when members are exposed to an idea or concept

The object of a **focus-group interview** is to observe group interaction when members are exposed to an idea or concept. Often these interviews are conducted informally, without a structured questionnaire, in small groups of eight to twelve people. They allow customer attitudes, behavior, lifestyles, needs, and desires to be explored in a flexible and creative manner. Questions are open-ended and stimulate respondents to answer in their own words. Researchers can ask probing questions to clarify something they do not fully understand or something unexpected and interesting that may help explain buying behavior. For example, Mercedes may use focus groups to determine whether to change its advertising to emphasize a vehicle's safety features rather than its style and performance. Building Customer Relationships describes why and how researchers are using focus groups and other techniques to better understand teenagers.

shopping mall intercept interviews   A research method that involves interviewing a percentage of persons passing by "intercept" points in a mall

The nature of personal interviews has changed. In the past, most personal interviews, which were based on random sampling or prearranged appointments, were conducted in the subject's home. Today, most personal interviews are conducted in shopping malls. **Shopping mall intercept interviews** involve interviewing a

BUILDING
customer relationships

Tapping into the Teen Market

After focusing for years on the huge market of 77 million baby boomers born between 1946 and 1964, marketers have lately noticed that the teen market is growing rapidly and has more money to spend than ever before. In fact, demographers project that the population of 12- to 19-year-olds will surge to 35 million by 2010, up from 31 million now. Thanks to hefty allowances and part-time jobs, these teens are spending an average of $94 a week. With few bills to worry about, teenagers have truly disposable income to spend on things they really want, such as clothes, games, music, movies, and eating out. Moreover, in today's busy families, teens often have a large say in family decisions. Marketers who want to tap into teens' increasing clout are turning to marketing research for a better understanding of today's teenagers so they can customize marketing mixes to satisfy this desirable target market.

Because teenagers tend to act up or clam up in focus groups, marketing researchers have had to devise innovative techniques to gain insight into their buying behavior. One firm, Teenage Research, has learned to divine trends in clothing by asking teen research subjects to pretend to be costume designers for popular TV shows, such as "Dawson's Creek," and to describe how they would dress their favorite characters. To determine how teens feel about fast-food restaurants, another technique asks subjects to match a list of restaurants with celebrities they think are likely to eat there. Teenage Research has also put together a mail panel representing the nation's 13- to 17-year-olds; it pays panelists about $60 to fill out surveys every couple of months. In one survey, the company sent disposable cameras to thirty-six teens on the panel and asked them to record their favorite places, possessions, and people. From this research, the firm discovered that teenagers, especially girls, are more into sports than ever, a trend that marketers like PepsiCo and Levi Strauss are beginning to exploit in promoting their products to this market.

Researchers have also learned that teens watch 11.16 hours of television per week and talk on the phone 6.18 hours a week, nearly twice the time they spend on their studies. One of the most significant research findings is that teenagers are quite sophisticated about the marketing and retailing of consumer products. When one company asked teenagers for feedback about a new backpack, they quickly pointed out that none of the pockets were large enough to carry a Walkman. Their favorite stores are currently J.C. Penney and Old Navy, and they love to shop. This is particularly good news for retailers because shopping seems to be on the decline among other age groups. Just 55 percent of Americans aged 21 to 62 indicate they like shopping, but 88 percent of girls aged 13 to 17 say they love shopping. In fact, teens make 40 percent more trips to a mall than shoppers from other age groups. Understanding what these teenagers want to spend their money on at a shopping mall will help marketers better satisfy these savvy young consumers, who will be their primary customers in just a few short years.

percentage of persons passing by certain "intercept" points in a mall. Like any face-to-face interviewing method, mall intercept interviewing has many advantages. The interviewer is in a position to recognize and react to respondents' nonverbal indications of confusion. Respondents can be shown product prototypes, videotapes of commercials, and the like, and asked for their reactions. The mall environment lets the researcher deal with complex situations. For example, in taste tests, researchers know that all the respondents are reacting to the same product, which can be prepared and monitored from the mall test kitchen. In addition to the ability to conduct tests requiring bulky equipment, lower cost and greater control make shopping mall intercept interviews popular.

on-site computer interview   A variation of the shopping mall intercept interview in which respondents complete a self-administered questionnaire displayed on a computer monitor

An **on-site computer interview** is a variation of the mall intercept interview, in which respondents complete a self-administered questionnaire displayed on a computer monitor. A computer software package can be used to conduct such interviews in shopping malls. After a brief lesson on how to operate the software, respondents can proceed through the survey at their own pace. Questionnaires can be adapted so that the respondent sees only those items (usually a subset of an entire scale) that may provide useful information about the respondent's attitude.[13]

Questionnaire Construction   A carefully constructed questionnaire is essential to the success of any survey. Questions must be clear, easy to understand, and directed toward a specific objective—that is, they must be designed to elicit information that meets the study's data requirements. Researchers need to define the objective before trying to develop a questionnaire because the objective determines the substance of the questions and the amount of detail. A common mistake in constructing questionnaires is to ask questions that interest the researchers but do not yield information useful in deciding whether to accept or reject a hypothesis. Finally, the most important rule in composing questions is to maintain impartiality.

The questions are usually of three kinds: open-ended, dichotomous, and multiple-choice.

Open-Ended Question

What is your general opinion of the American Express Optima Card?

_____

_____

_____

Dichotomous Question

Do you presently have an American Express Optima Card?

Yes _____   No _____

Multiple-Choice Question

What age group are you in?

Under 20 _____

20–29 _____

30–39 _____

40–49 _____

50–59 _____

60 and over _____

Researchers must be very careful about questions that a respondent might consider too personal or that might require an admission of activities that other people are likely to condemn. Questions of this type should be worded in such a way as to make them less offensive.

Observation Methods   In using observation methods, researchers record subjects' overt behavior, taking note of physical conditions and events. Direct contact with subjects is avoided; instead, their actions are examined and noted systematically. For instance, researchers might use observation methods to answer the question "How long does the average McDonald's restaurant customer have to wait in line before being served?"

Observation may also be combined with interviews. For example, during a personal interview, the condition of a respondent's home or other possessions may be observed and recorded. The interviewer can also directly observe and confirm such demographic information as race, approximate age, and sex.

Data gathered through observation can sometimes be biased if the subject is aware of the observation process. However, an observer can be placed in a natural market environment, such as a grocery store, without biasing or influencing shoppers' actions. If the presence of a human observer is likely to bias the outcome or if human sensory abilities are inadequate, mechanical means may be used to record behavior. Mechanical observation devices include cameras, recorders, counting machines, scanners, and equipment that records physiological changes. A special camera can be used to record the eye movements of people as they look at an advertisement; the camera detects the sequence of reading and the parts of the advertisement that receive greatest attention. The electronic scanners used in supermarkets are very useful in marketing research. They provide accurate data on sales and customers' purchase patterns, and marketing researchers may buy such data from the supermarkets.

Observation is straightforward and avoids a central problem of survey methods: motivating respondents to state their true feelings or opinions. However, observation tends to be descriptive. When it is the only method of data collection, it may not provide insights into causal relationships. Another drawback is that analyses based on observation are subject to the biases of the observer or the limitations of the mechanical device.

Experimentation   Another method for gathering primary data is experimentation. In an **experiment,** marketing researchers attempt to maintain certain variables while measuring the effects of experimental variables. Experimentation requires that an independent variable (one not influenced by or dependent on other variables) be manipulated and the resulting changes in a dependent variable (one contingent on, or restricted to, one value or set of values assumed by the independent variable) be measured. For example, when Houghton Mifflin introduces a new edition of its *American Heritage Dictionary,* it may want to estimate the number of dictionaries that could be sold at various levels of advertising expenditure and price. The dependent variable would be sales, and the independent variable would be advertising expenditure and price. Researchers would design the experiment so that other independent variables that might influence sales—such as distribution and variations of the product—would be controlled. Experimentation is used in marketing research to improve hypothesis testing.

experiment   A research method that attempts to maintain certain variables while measuring the effects of experimental variables

Interpreting Research Findings

After collecting data to test their hypotheses, marketers need to interpret the research findings. Interpretation of the data is easier if marketers carefully plan their data analysis methods early in the research process. They should also allow for continual evaluation of the data during the entire collection period. They can then gain valuable insight into areas that ought to be probed during the formal interpretation.

The first step in drawing conclusions from most research is displaying the data in table format. If marketers intend to apply the results to individual categories of the things or people being studied, cross tabulation may be quite useful, especially in tabulating joint occurrences. For example, using the two variables, gender and purchase rates of automobile tires, a cross tabulation could show how men and women differ in purchasing automobile tires.

statistical interpretation
Analysis of what is typical or
what deviates from the average

After the data are tabulated, they must be analyzed. **Statistical interpretation** focuses on what is typical or what deviates from the average. It indicates how widely responses vary and how they are distributed in relation to the variable being measured. When marketers interpret statistics, they must take into account estimates of expected error or deviation from the true values of the population. The analysis of data may lead researchers to accept or reject the hypothesis being studied.

Data require careful interpretation by the marketer. If the results of a study are valid, the decision maker should take action; if it is discovered that a question has been incorrectly worded, the results should be ignored. For example, if a study by an electric utility company reveals that 50 percent of its customers believe that meter readers are "friendly," is that finding good, bad, or indifferent? Two important benchmarks help interpret the result: how the 50 percent figure compares with that for other electric utility companies and how it compares with a previous time period. Managers must understand the research results and relate the results to a context that permits effective decision making.[14]

Reporting Research Findings

The final step in the marketing research process is reporting the research findings. Before preparing the report, the marketer must take a clear, objective look at the findings to see how well the gathered facts answer the research question or support or negate the initial hypotheses. In most cases, it is extremely doubtful that the study can provide everything needed to answer the research question. Thus, the researcher must point out the deficiencies, and the reasons for them, in the report.

The report of research results is usually a formal, written document. Researchers must allow time for the writing task when they plan and schedule the project. Because the report is a means of communicating with the decision makers who will use the research findings, researchers need to determine beforehand how much detail and supporting data to include. They should keep in mind that corporate executives prefer reports that are short, clear, and simply expressed. Researchers often give their summary and recommendations first, especially if decision makers do not have time to study how the results were obtained. A technical report allows its users to analyze data and interpret recommendations because it describes the research methods and procedures and the most important data gathered. Thus, researchers must recognize the needs and expectations of the report user and adapt to them.

Bias and distortion can be a major problem if the researcher is intent upon obtaining favorable results. Consider the following examples: (1) Levi Strauss purportedly asked students which clothes would be most popular this year; 90 percent said Levis 501 jeans, but Levi's were apparently the only jeans on the list for students to select. (2) A Gallup poll sponsored by the disposable diaper industry posed the following: "It is estimated that disposable diapers account for less than 2 percent of the trash in today's landfills. In contrast, beverage containers, third-class mail, and yard waste are estimated to account for about 21 percent of the trash in landfills. Given this, in your opinion, would it be fair to ban disposable diapers?" Of those interviewed, 84 percent said no.[15] The findings of both these surveys would be positive in the view of the research sponsors, but of what value?

These examples illustrate research conducted for public consumption and to further the interests of the parties conducting the research. Most research for internal decision making is conducted objectively. Marketing researchers want to know about behavior and opinions, and they want accurate data to help in making decisions. Careful wording of questions is very important because a biased or emotional word can change the results tremendously. Marketing research and marketing information systems can provide an organization with accurate and reliable customer feedback, which a marketer must have to understand the dynamics of the marketplace. As managers recognize the benefits of marketing research, they assign it a much larger role in decision making.

Using Technology to Improve Marketing Information Gathering and Analysis

Technology is making information for marketing decisions increasingly accessible. The ability of marketers to track customer buying behavior and to better discern what buyers want is changing the nature of marketing. For example, the airlines have discovered that many of their most desirable customers have computers and can communicate with them online. Frequent flyers—people who fly ten or more times a year—account for just 8 percent of all airline customers but book 44 percent of all trips. Northwest Airlines invited customers to take part in survey research conducted via fax, telephone, and the Internet. From this research, Northwest learned that its affluent frequent flyers travel at Christmas, like beach vacations, and, most of all, want flights to be on time.[16] With this information, the airline attempted to fine-tune its marketing mix to satisfy these customers.

The integration of telecommunications and computer technologies is allowing marketers to access a growing array of valuable information sources related to industry forecasts, business trends, and customer buying behavior. Electronic communication tools can be effectively utilized to gain accurate information with minimal customer interaction. Most marketing researchers have E-mail, voice mail, teleconferencing, and fax machines at their disposal. In fact, many firms use marketing information systems to network all these technologies and organize all the marketing data available to the firm. In this section, we look at marketing information systems and specific technologies that are helping marketing researchers obtain and manage marketing research data.

Marketing Information Systems

marketing information system (MIS)   A framework for the management and structuring of information gathered regularly from sources inside and outside an organization

A **marketing information system (MIS)** is a framework for the day-to-day management and structuring of information gathered regularly from sources both inside and outside an organization. As such, an MIS provides a continuous flow of information about prices, advertising expenditures, sales, competition, and distribution expenses. Kraft General Foods, for example, operates one of the largest marketing information systems in the food industry, maintaining, using, and sharing information with others to increase the value of what the company offers customers. Kraft seeks to develop a dialogue with customers by providing toll-free numbers. It receives hundreds of thousands of calls annually from customers who ask questions and express concerns about products.

The main focus of the marketing information system is on data storage and retrieval, as well as on computer capabilities and management's information requirements. Regular reports of sales by product or market categories, data on inventory levels, and records of salespersons' activities are examples of information that is useful in making decisions. In the MIS, the means of *gathering* data receive less attention than do the procedures for expediting the *flow* of information.

 An effective marketing information system starts by determining the objective of the information—that is, by identifying decision needs that require certain information. The firm can then specify an information system for continuous monitoring to provide regular, pertinent information on both the external and internal environment. FedEx, for example, has developed interactive marketing systems to provide instantaneous communication between the company and its customers. Through the telephone and Internet, customers can track their packages and receive immediate feedback concerning delivery. The company's Web site provides valuable information about customer usage, and it allows customers to express directly what they think about company services. The evolving development of telecommunications and computer technology is allowing marketing information systems to cultivate one-to-one relationships with customers.

Databases

database   A collection of information arranged for easy access and retrieval

Most marketing information systems include internal databases. A **database** is a collection of information arranged for easy access and retrieval. Databases allow marketers to tap into an abundance of information useful in making marketing decisions: internal sales reports, newspaper articles, company news releases, government economic reports, bibliographies, and more, often accessed through a computer system. Wal-Mart, for example, maintains one of the largest corporate databases in the United States, with data about sales, profits, and inventory levels, as well as data mined from customer receipts from all its stores. These data help Wal-Mart pinpoint purchasing patterns, such as what products customers typically buy together (e.g., bananas and cereal, tissues and nonprescription cold medicine). Such information helps the firm determine the most effective product placement—for example, stocking tissues both on the paper-goods aisle and next to over-the-counter cold medicines. Wal-Mart's database also helps it manage inventory levels to keep costs down while ensuring that customers can still find the products they want. Thus, the retailer's database helps the company control costs, boost sales, and, most importantly, improve shoppers' satisfaction.[17] Wal-Mart's database may be more accurately described as a data warehouse, which is discussed further in Tech*know.

Companies can also sell their databases to other firms. *Reader's Digest,* for example, markets a database that covers 100 million households. One of the best databases available to assess potential markets for consumer products, it lets *Reader's Digest*

Tech*know

Making the Most of Data

Thanks to advances in information technology, especially data storage and processing, marketers have available an ever-growing quantity of data about customer buying behavior. To extract from this mound of data useful information to guide marketing decisions, marketers have been developing methods of "mining" the data. *Data mining* refers to the discovery of patterns hidden in databases that can contribute to marketers' understanding of their customers and their needs. Data mining employs computer technology to capture data from internal and external sources; to translate and format the data; to analyze, substantiate, and attach meaning to the data; to organize databases; and to build and implement decision support systems to make the results of data mining accessible to decision makers. Effective data mining can help firms acquire new customers, retain profitable customers, identify customers who aren't profitable, and identify potential relationships among product purchases in point-of-sale transactions.

Many firms are beginning to build data warehouses and data marts to facilitate data mining. A *data warehouse* is an organizationwide data collection and storage system that draws data from all of a firm's critical operation systems and from selected external sources. Data warehouses require a substantial investment ($10 million or more and one to three years to develop) and therefore demand significant planning and commitment to ensure useful results. In contrast, a *data mart* is a subject-area or division-based data repository that collects data from a department or division's critical systems and from selected external sources. Because of the reduced scale of involvement, data marts can often be developed and implemented for $10,000 to $1 million within six months. Regardless of scale, both systems combine data storage, data analysis, and computer processing technology to help marketers make sense of the vast quantity of data that were collected by their marketing information systems.

Building a data warehouse is no guarantee that a firm will gain significant insights into its customers. Many companies have established expensive systems that generate overwhelming amounts of data but little information useful for decision making. However, a number of firms, including Empire Blue Cross and Blue Shield, Safeway Stores PLC, Wal-Mart, and Burlington Coat Factories, have built data warehouses or marts that have produced amazing results and greatly enhanced decision making. Burlington Coat Factories, for example, created a data warehouse to track sales and to guide the buying of the coats and outwear it sells in its retail outlets. During a recent unseasonably warm winter, Burlington's data warehouse enabled it to monitor the effects of the weather on individual store sales and to conservatively stock, and selectively restock, each store as appropriate. Thus, a well-planned data-mining system can improve marketing decisions and strategies and contribute to the bottom line.

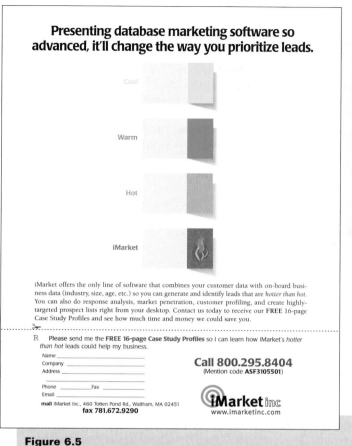

Figure 6.5
Using Databases to Improve Information Gathering and Analysis
Database software can be used to analyze customer data. Companies such as iMarket inc
and Acxiom Corporation provide tools to help firms better manage and use their data.

management know the likes and dislikes of many of its readers. It also permits a
linkup to test products, assess retailers, examine media alternatives, and evaluate the
effectiveness of promotions. In fact, the *Reader's Digest* database is possibly as valuable
to the company as the magazine itself.[18]

Marketing researchers can also use commercial databases developed by information research firms, such as LEXIS-NEXIS, to obtain useful information for marketing
decisions. Many of these commercial databases are accessible online for a fee. They
can also be obtained in printed form or on computer compact discs (CD-ROMs). In
most commercial databases, the user typically does a computer search by key word,
topic, or company, and the database service generates abstracts, articles, or reports that
can then be printed out. Accessing multiple reports or a complete article may cost
extra. iMarket inc provides software to facilitate database marketing. Acxiom provides
a database via the Internet (see Figure 6.5).

Information provided by a single firm on household demographics, purchases,
television viewing behavior, and responses to promotions such as coupons and free
samples is called **single-source data.**[19] For example, Behavior Scan, offered by
Information Resources, Inc., screens about 60,000 households in twenty-six U.S. markets. This single-source information service monitors consumer household televisions
and records the programs and commercials watched. When buyers from these households shop in stores equipped with scanning registers, they present Hotline cards
(similar to credit cards) to cashiers. This enables each customer's identification to be
electronically coded so that the firm can track each product they purchase and store
the information in a database.

single-source data
Information provided by a
single marketing research firm

Marketing Decision Support Systems

A **marketing decision support system (MDSS)** is customized computer software that aids marketing managers in decision making by helping them anticipate the effect of certain decisions. Some decision support systems have a broader range and offer greater computational and modeling capabilities than spreadsheets; they let managers explore a greater number of alternatives. For example, a decision support system can determine how sales and profits might be affected by higher or lower interest rates, or how sales forecasts, advertising expenditures, production levels, and the like might affect overall profits. For this reason, decision support system software is often a major component of a company's marketing information system. Some decision support systems incorporate artificial intelligence and other advanced computer technologies.

The Internet and Online Information Services

The Internet has evolved as a most powerful communication medium, linking customers and companies around the world via computer networks with E-mail, forums, Web pages, and more. Growth of the Internet, and especially the World Wide Web, has launched an entire industry that is working to make marketing information easily accessible to both marketing firms and customers.

Table 6.4 lists a number of Web sites that may serve as valuable resources for marketing research. The Bureau of the Census, for example, uses the World Wide Web to disseminate information that may be useful to marketing researchers, particularly through the *Statistical Abstract of the United States* and data from the most recent census. The Census Lookup option allows marketing researchers to create their own customized information. With this online tool, researchers can select tables by clicking boxes to select a state and then, within the state, the county, place, and urbanized area or metropolitan statistical area to be examined. Figure 6.6 illustrates another resource. Etak is a database supplier of maps with geographic details that provide important marketing information. Another tool, Map Stats, enables users to view profiles of states and counties in both tabular and graphic form. Researchers can select which state to display simply by clicking on a map.

Companies can also mine their own Web sites for useful information. Amazon.com, for example, has built a relationship with its customers by tracking the type of books and music that they purchase. Each time a customer logs onto the Web

Table 6.4	Resources for Marketing Information
Government Sources	
U.S. Bureau of the Census	**www.census.gov**
U.S. Department of State	**www.state.gov**
FedWorld	**www.fedworld.gov**
Chamber of Commerce	**chamber-of-commerce.com**
Commercial Sources	
A. C. Nielsen	**www.acnielsen.com**
Information Resources, Inc.	**www.infores.com**
Gallup	**www.gallup.com**
Arbitron	**www.arbitron.com**
Periodicals and Books	
American Demographics	**www.americandemographics.com**
Advertising Age	**www.adage.com**
Sales & Marketing Management	**www.salesandmarketing.com**
Fortune	**www.pathfinder.com/fortune**
Inc.	**www.inc.com**
Business Week	**www.businessweek.com**
Bloomberg Report	**www.bloomberg.com**

site, the company can offer recommendations based on the customer's previous purchases. Such a marketing system helps the company track the changing desires and buying habits of its most valued customers.

Marketing researchers can also subscribe to online services, such as CompuServe, Delphi, Prodigy, DIALOG, and NEXIS. These services typically offer their subscribers such specialized services as databases, news services, and forums, as well as access to the Internet itself. Marketers can subscribe to "mailing lists" that periodically deliver electronic newsletters to their computer screens, and they can participate in on-screen discussions with thousands of network users. This enhanced communication with a firm's customers, suppliers, and employees provides a high-speed link that boosts the capabilities of a firm's marketing information system.

While most Web pages are open to anyone with Internet access, big companies like US West also maintain internal Web pages, called "intranets," that allow employees to access such internal data as customer profiles and product inventory—information once hidden in databases only technicians could unlock. Such sensitive corporate information can be protected from outside users of the World Wide Web by special security software called "firewalls." Turner Broadcasting System uses intranets to test products during the development phase. Marketing department employees view animated clips and listen to sound bites from popular cartoon talk shows. They then express their opinions by E-mailing the animators directly. The animators use this feedback to revise the cartoon before it appears on the firm's public cartoon site on America Online. Most marketers who get in the habit of accessing their companies' internal Web pages often move on to seek information externally via the rest of the World Wide Web as well.[20]

Figure 6.6
Online Information Services
With the Internet, marketers can now find information at their fingertips. Etak provides positionally accurate digital maps useful in marketing decision making. Survey of Buying Power Online is an easy-to-use research tool that helps analyze markets.

Most people don't know this, but between his winter residence in the Canary Islands and his summer home, 3,268 miles away in Maine, Frank Puffin calls Etak for geocoding services and positionally accurate digital maps.

Stay on track with Etak.

With its freshly updated database of streets, directions and addresses, Etak offers positionally accurate digital maps with superb geographic detail and compatibility with formats from ESRI and MapInfo. And if you need real-time geocoding via the Internet, or batch geocoding for high-volume requirements—Etak is the answer. Get your applications, customers and projects on track with Etak. **For complete map information and access to 100 Free Geocodes,** call 800-765-0555 or visit our Web site at www.etak.com/frank8.

www.etak.com/frank8   **etak.**

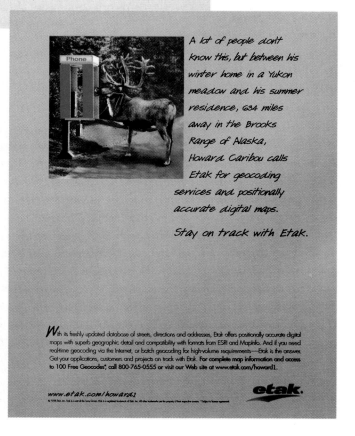

A lot of people don't know this, but between his winter home in a Yukon meadow and his summer residence, 634 miles away in the Brooks Range of Alaska, Howard Caribou calls Etak for geocoding services and positionally accurate digital maps.

Stay on track with Etak.

With its freshly updated database of streets, directions and addresses, Etak offers positionally accurate digital maps with superb geographic detail and compatibility with formats from ESRI and MapInfo. And if you need real-time geocoding via the Internet, or batch geocoding for high-volume requirements—Etak is the answer. Get your applications, customers and projects on track with Etak. **For complete map information and access to 100 Free Geocodes,** call 800-765-0555 or visit our Web site at www.etak.com/howard1.

www.etak.com/howard1   **etak.**

Issues in Marketing Research

The Importance of Ethical Marketing Research

Marketing managers and other professionals are relying more and more on marketing research, marketing information systems, and new technologies to make better decisions. It is therefore essential that professional standards be established by which such research may be judged reliable. Such standards are necessary because of the ethical and legal issues that develop in gathering marketing research data. In addition, the relationships between research suppliers, such as marketing research agencies, and the marketing managers who make strategy decisions require ethical behavior. Organizations like the Marketing Research Association have developed codes of conduct and guidelines to promote ethical marketing research. For such guidelines to be effective, they must instruct those who participate in marketing research how to avoid misconduct. Table 6.5, for example, recommends the explicit steps interviewers should follow when introducing a questionnaire.

The ethical and legal considerations of new technologies for marketing research are taking shape slowly. Many people have concerns about how much information marketers can gather with these technologies as well as how the data are used. An example of this concern is the use of membership cards by some grocery store chains. The Safeway Club card, for example, allows customers to receive discounts and specials while it enables the company to track customers' purchases and detect purchasing patterns. Some shoppers are reluctant to use these cards for fear that the information gathered will violate their privacy; however, the stores say they use the data only on an aggregate basis to improve their marketing mixes. On the Internet, there are increasing concerns about "cookies"—strings of text a Web site can store in a file on a user's computer. Cookies are often employed to enable users to customize their use of a particular Web site. Some people, however, fear that cookies can be used to violate their privacy. E-mail surveys and Web cookies create privacy issues that both professional marketing research associations and marketing research companies will have to address in the future.

Because so many parties are involved in the marketing research process, developing shared ethical concern is difficult. The relationships among respondents who cooperate and share information, interviewing companies, marketing research agencies that manage projects, and organizations that use the data are interdependent and complex. Trust and the perceived quality of interaction between information users

Table 6.5	Guidelines for Questionnaire Introduction

Questionnaire introduction should:

- Allow interviewers to introduce themselves by name.
- State the name of the research company.
- Indicate this is a marketing research project.
- Explain there will be no sales involved.
- Note the general topic of discussion (if this is a problem in a "blind" study, a statement such as "consumer opinion" is acceptable).
- State the likely duration of the interview.
- Assure the anonymity of the respondent and confidentiality of all answers.
- State the honorarium if applicable (for many business-to-business and medical studies this is done up front for both qualitative and quantitative studies).
- Reassure the respondent with a statement such as, "There are no right or wrong answers, so please give thoughtful and honest answers to each question" (recommended by many clients).

Source: Reprinted with permission of The Marketing Research Association, P.O. Box 230, Rocky Hill, CT 06067-0230, (860)257-4008.

and information providers have been found to contribute significantly to research utilization.[21] Uncertainty and ethical conflict may stem from lack of agreement among these different parties.[22] Ethical conflict typically occurs because the parties involved in the marketing research process often have different objectives. For example, the organization that uses data tends to be result-oriented, and success is often based on performance rather than a set of standards. On the other hand, a data-gathering subcontractor is evaluated based on the ability to follow a specific set of standards or rules. The relationships among all participants in marketing research must be understood so that decision making becomes ethical. Without clear understanding and agreement, including mutual adoption of standards, ethical conflict will lead to mistrust and questionable research results.[23]

International Issues in Marketing Research

As we indicated in Chapter 5, sociocultural, economic, political, legal, and technological forces vary in different regions of the world. These variations create challenges for organizations attempting to understand foreign customers through marketing research. The marketing research process we described in this chapter is used globally, but to ensure that the research is valid and reliable, data-gathering methods may have to be modified to allow for regional differences. In Russia, for example, the last brand purchased is more often an indication of availability than of a customer's true brand preference. In fact, brand names have little meaning to the average Russian consumer, although country of origin does have significance.[24] A firm desiring to do business in Russia would probably want to conduct primary marketing research to gather information about specific brand preferences to ensure validity.

Experts recommend a two-pronged approach to international marketing research. The first phase involves a detailed search for and analysis of secondary data to gain greater understanding of a particular marketing environment and to pinpoint issues that must be taken into account in gathering primary research data. Secondary data can be particularly helpful in building a general understanding of the market, including economic, legal, cultural, and demographic issues, as well as in assessing the risks of doing business in that market and in forecasting demand.[25] Marketing researchers often begin by studying country trade reports from the U.S. Department of Commerce as well as country-specific information from local sources, such as a country's Web site, and trade and general business publications such as *The Wall Street Journal*. These sources can offer insight into the marketing environment in a particular country and can even indicate untapped market opportunities abroad (see Figure 6.7).

Figure 6.7
International Issues in Marketing Research
Learning about new markets outside of one's home country can be a challenge. Hispanic & Asian Marketing Communication Research, Inc., provides a range of services to reach multicultural markets. This company gives marketers the opportunity to examine international target markets.

The second phase involves field research using many of the methods we described earlier, including focus groups and telephone surveys, to refine a firm's understanding of specific customer needs and preferences. Specific differences among countries can have a profound influence on data gathering. For example, in-home (door-to-door) interviews are illegal in some countries. In China, few people have regular telephone lines, making telephone surveys both impractical and nonrepresentative of the total population. Primary data gathering may have a greater chance of success if the firm employs local researchers who better understand how to approach potential respondents and can do so in their own language.[26] Regardless of the specific methods used to gather primary data, whether in the United States or abroad, the goal is to better understand the needs of specific target markets in order to craft the best marketing strategy to satisfy the needs of customers in each market, as we shall see in the next chapter.

Summary

To implement the marketing concept, marketers need information about the characteristics, needs, and wants of target market customers. Marketing research and information systems that furnish practical, unbiased information help firms avoid assumptions and misunderstandings that could lead to poor marketing performance.

Marketing research is the systematic design, collection, interpretation, and reporting of information to help marketers solve specific marketing problems or take advantage of marketing opportunities. It is a process for gathering information not currently available to decision makers. The value of marketing research is measured by improvements in a marketer's ability to make decisions.

To maintain the control needed to obtain accurate information, marketers approach marketing research as a process with logical steps: (1) locating and defining problems or issues, (2) designing the research project, (3) collecting data, (4) interpreting research findings, and (5) reporting research findings.

The first step toward launching a research study is problem or issue definition, which focuses on uncovering the nature and boundaries of a situation or question related to marketing strategy or implementation. After defining the problem or issue, marketing researchers must design a research project to obtain the information needed to address it. This step requires formulating a hypothesis and determining what type of research to employ to test the hypothesis so that the results are reliable and valid. A hypothesis is an informed guess or assumption about a problem or set of circumstances. The type of hypothesis being tested dictates whether an exploratory, descriptive, or causal approach will be used for gathering data. Research is considered reliable if it produces almost identical results in repeated trials; it is valid if it measures what it is supposed to measure.

For the third step of the research process, collecting data, two types of data are available. Primary data are observed and recorded or collected directly from subjects; secondary data are compiled inside or outside the organization for some purpose other than the current investigation. Sources of secondary data include an organization's own database and other internal sources, periodicals, government publications, unpublished sources, and online databases. Methods of collecting primary data include sampling, surveys, observation, and experimentation. Sampling involves selecting representative units from a total population. In probability sampling, every element in the population being studied has a known chance of being selected for study. Nonprobability sampling is more subjective than probability sampling because there is no way to calculate the likelihood that a specific element of the population being studied will be chosen. Marketing researchers employ sampling to collect primary data through mail, telephone, online, or personal interview surveys. A carefully constructed questionnaire is essential to the success of any survey. In using observation methods, researchers record respondents' overt behavior and take note of physical conditions and events. In an experiment, marketing researchers attempt to maintain certain variables while measuring the effects of experimental variables.

To apply research data to decision making, marketers must interpret and report their findings properly—the final two steps in the research process. Statistical interpretation focuses on what is typical or what deviates from the average. After interpreting the research findings, the researchers must prepare a report on the findings that the decision makers can understand and use. Researchers must also take care to avoid bias and distortion.

Many firms use computer technology to create a marketing information system (MIS), which is a framework for the management and structuring of information gathered regularly from sources both inside and outside an organization. A database is a collection of information arranged for easy access and retrieval. A marketing decision support system (MDSS) is customized computer software that aids marketing managers in decision making by helping them anticipate the effect of certain decisions. Online information services and the Internet also enable marketers to communicate with customers and obtain information.

Eliminating unethical marketing research practices and establishing generally acceptable procedures for conducting research are important goals of marketing research. Both domestic marketing and international marketing use the same marketing research process, but for international marketing, data gathering methods may require modification to address regional differences.

Important Terms

Marketing research
Research design
Hypothesis
Exploratory research
Descriptive research
Causal research
Reliability
Validity
Primary data

Secondary data
Population
Sample
Sampling
Probability sampling
Random sampling
Stratified sampling
Nonprobability
   sampling

Quota sampling
Mail survey
Telephone survey
Online survey
Personal interview
   survey
In-home (door-
   to-door) interview

Focus-group interview
Shopping mall
   intercept interview
On-site computer
   interview
Experiment
Statistical
   interpretation

Marketing information
   system (MIS)
Database
Single-source data
Marketing decision
   support system
   (MDSS)

Discussion and Review Questions

1. What is marketing research? Why is it important?

2. List the five steps in the marketing research process.

3. What is the difference between defining a research problem and developing a hypothesis?

4. Describe the different types of approaches to marketing research and indicate when each should be used.

5. Where are data for marketing research obtained? Give examples of internal and external data.

6. What is the difference between probability sampling and nonprobability sampling? In what situation would it be best to use random sampling? Stratified sampling? Quota sampling?

7. Suggest some ways of encouraging respondents to cooperate in mail surveys.

8. If a survey of all homes with listed telephone numbers is conducted, what sampling design should be used?

9. Describe some marketing problems that could be solved through information gained from observation.

10. What is a marketing information system and what should it provide?

11. Define a database. What is its purpose, and what does it include?

12. How can marketers use online services and the Internet to obtain information for decision making?

13. What role does ethics play in marketing research? Why is it important for marketing researchers to be ethical?

14. How does marketing research in other countries differ from marketing research in the United States?

Application Questions

1. After observing customers' traffic patterns, Bashas' Markets repositioned the greeting card section in its stores, and card sales increased substantially. To increase sales for the following types of companies, what information might marketing researchers want to gather from customers?
   a. furniture stores
   b. gasoline outlets/service stations
   c. investment companies
   d. medical clinics

2. When a company wants to conduct research, it must first identify a problem or possible opportunity to market its goods or services. Choose a company in your city that you think might benefit from a research project. Develop a research question and outline a method to approach this question. Explain why you think the research question is relevant to the organization and why the particular methodology is suited to the question and the company.

3. Input for marketing information systems can come from internal or external sources. Nielsen Marketing Research is the largest provider of single-source marketing research in the world. Indicate two firms or companies in your city that might benefit from internal sources and two that would benefit from external sources, and explain why they would benefit. Suggest the type of information each should gather.

4. Suppose you were opening a health insurance brokerage firm and wanted to market your services to small businesses with under fifty employees. Determine which database for marketing information you would use in your marketing efforts, and explain why you would use it.

Internet Exercise & Resources

American Demographics' Marketing Tools Directory

American Demographics makes a directory of marketing research tools available to the marketing information industry. Known as the Marketing Tools Directory, it includes numerous resources that are searchable by topic. Visit the site at

www.marketingtools.com

1. What information in the directory could assist in a marketing research project?
2. What resources listed in the directory would be helpful in maintaining an internal marketing information system?
3. What research tools are available through the directory?

E-Center Resources

Visit http://www.prideferrell.com to find several resources to help you succeed in mastering the material in this chapter, plus additional materials that will help you expand your marketing knowledge. The Web site includes

 Internet exercise updates plus additional exercises

 ACE self-tests

 abc Chapter summary with hotlinked glossary

 Hotlinks to companies featured in this chapter

 Resource Center

 Career Center

 Marketing plan worksheets

VIDEO CASE 6.1

Marketing Research for Advertising V-8 Vegetable Juice, Maidenform, and AT&T 800 Service Advertising

Marketing research is the systematic design, collection, interpretation, and reporting of information to help marketers solve specific problems or take advantage of market opportunities. The development of an advertising campaign involves a series of steps, starting with the identification of the right target market. Advertisers research and analyze various audiences or markets to determine such factors as buying behavior; geographic distribution of the target group; demographic factors, such as age, income, sex, and education; and consumer attitudes toward purchase and use of both the advertiser's products and competing products. The exact kind of information an organization finds useful depends on the type of product being advertised, the characteristics of the target market, and the type and amount of competition. Generally, the more an advertiser knows about the target market, the more likely the firm is to develop an effective advertising campaign. When the advertising target is not precisely identified and properly analyzed, the campaign may not succeed. The following case examples show how marketing research improved advertising for three products.

Case One: Campbell's V-8 Vegetable Juice

Marketing research was undertaken to develop a new advertising campaign to reverse the trend of decreasing sales. Research indicated that consumers needed to be reminded to purchase V-8 because of competition and the many choices available to beverage purchasers. In-depth consumer interviews probed consumers' childhood memories to try to understand their thinking about V-8. Consumers were asked to express their thoughts and feelings about the V-8 brand. The technique was to ask the same question over and over again: "What do you really want in a V-8?" Four factors came out of the research: the overall healthfulness of V-8; its healthfulness relative to other types of foods; its beta carotene (disease preventive) content; and its vegetable goodness. A test TV commercial was produced using the research results.

Marketing research on test TV commercials indicated that the four-factor strategy in an actual advertising situation was confusing to consumers. Therefore, a new creative concept was developed. Additional research recast the message. Advertising needed to focus on the product as healthful, while conveying a simpler, clearer message about V-8. When the message was simplified to stress taste and health benefits, the advertising campaign resulted in double-digit increases in sales as long as it ran. The key to success in this case was marketing research to help refine a message so that it was simple, easy to understand, and had a call for action to purchase the product.

Case Two: Maidenform

Historically, Maidenform felt certain that it stood for women's self-esteem. Nevertheless, the company needed to know more about the Maidenform consumer and her purchasing habits. Maidenform wanted to do a broad-based check on who buys lingerie and why. The company began with mall intercepts. Interviewers went into shopping malls and spoke to over 3,000 women between 18 and 65 years of age who had purchased two or more bras recently. Each interview lasted forty-five minutes, long enough for a thorough discussion of lingerie purchasing behavior.

The results were surprising. There turned out to be far more lapsed purchasers of Maidenform than current purchasers. Many women had heard of Maidenform but had never bought a Maidenform bra and had little perception of the product. This finding amazed Maidenform product managers. Startling numbers of women were not aware of Maidenform at all or associated the name more with their mothers than with contemporary lifestyles. The company had wrongly assumed that Maidenform was a highly regarded brand name with fabulous, obvious attributes. Maidenform was so overwhelmed by the findings that the researchers conducted a second study.

After analyzing the results of the second study, the company decided on a new creative strategy to promote its products. Research indicated that the most important objective was to convince customers to try the products. Confidence and self-esteem were considered the best positioning message for advertising.

Case Three: AT&T 800 Numbers

Before 1993, 800 numbers were assigned by long-distance carrier, but since then, 800 numbers have been portable; that is, users can take their numbers with them when they change carriers. The 800-number business is worth several billion dollars to AT&T, Sprint,

and MCI. Therefore, a market-share loss of even a few percentage points could mean millions of dollars of loss to AT&T. Following the change in regulations, AT&T decided to do research to determine what might cause its customers to change companies or to stay with AT&T. If AT&T could anticipate what its competitors might do, then it could better defend and protect its market share. Marketing research was needed to identify messages that would retain customers.

A strategic understanding of the 800-number concept was developed from personal interviews with business users of AT&T's 800 service. The goal was to gain insights into how AT&T should respond to the competition's expected tactics. The researchers went to Boston, where they interviewed executives of large, medium, and small companies to get a sense of what message would be most effective in retaining AT&T's customers. Without an effective marketing research effort to determine how to preempt competitors' moves, AT&T could not hope to develop a strong advertising campaign.

The research found that reliability was very important; therefore, promotional messages were developed showing what AT&T does to maintain reliability and depicting the cost to a company of a breakdown in reliability. AT&T produced twenty-two TV commercials, which were tested, along with competitors' ads, among 800-service customers. By doing in-depth interviews with executives and showing them potential commercial messages, the researchers were able to confirm that reliability was the key factor triggering business use of AT&T's 800 service. Acting on this research, AT&T achieved a major victory. It retained most of its users and made millions of dollars. The whole mindset of the study was an attempt to hold on to existing customers, but the research actually helped AT&T gain new customers.[27]

Questions for Discussion

1. How did marketing research help increase the sales of V-8?
2. What discovery did research reveal to Maidenform? Why had managers overlooked this information?
3. Of what value were the personal interviews conducted with business executives in formulating the AT&T advertising message?

CASE 6.2

Eagle Hardware Keeps a Keen Eye on Its Environment

Eagle Hardware & Garden operates more than thirty home-improvement retail stores in Alaska, California, Colorado, Hawaii, Idaho, Montana, Oregon, Utah, and Washington. The company was founded in 1989 after careful study of successful home-improvement chains, such as Home Depot and Orchard Hardware Supply. Eagle has succeeded against more established competitors by offering a large product selection, convenient locations, competitive prices, exceptional service, and customer-friendly store environments. Through a customer-focused strategy, the company has grown to sales of $971.5 million.

Eagle offers one-stop shopping for customers' home-improvement needs at competitive prices. The company's "More of Everything" merchandising philosophy fosters a product selection broad enough to allow a customer to purchase virtually every item needed to build a house. Each store stocks more than 65,000 products—over 30 percent more items than most competing stores. Eagle maintains competitive, everyday low prices on products carried by other home centers and does not engage in promotional "sale" pricing. At the same time, the company benefits from higher margins on hard-to-find merchandise and products its competitors do not carry.

The company's hybrid "retail/warehouse home centers" average 128,000 square feet and have clean, well-lighted aisles, attractive displays, and clearly marked signs. Each store features a "design idea center," where customers can work with design coordinators to plan virtually any home-improvement project. The design center is surrounded by a "race track" aisle, which provides convenient access to well-defined departments around the central core of the store. Each store has sixteen to twenty-three cashier stations; a large, convenient return and exchange counter; and a separate checkout and loading area for lumber and other bulky purchases. These store elements are designed to appeal to a broad range of customers, many of whom are not attracted to traditional, warehouse-style home centers like Home Depot. Consequently, Eagle has built strong loyalty among its customers, especially women, who account for about 50 percent of its sales. Women typically account for only 25 to 50 percent of sales in warehouse-style home-improvement stores. The company believes its hybrid stores effectively integrate the selection and value found in large, traditional home centers with the customer-friendly attributes and expertise of small, service-oriented specialty retailers.

Eagle's commitment to quality customer service and convenience requires more than having just adequate sales personnel on the floor. To attract more experienced personnel, Eagle pays what it believes are the most competitive wages in the areas in which it operates. It also invests millions of dollars in employee training annually. Each store has its own training director, and employees receive an average of sixty hours of formal training each year. The "Eagle Expert" program honors employees who successfully complete a study course and test. "Experts" receive a salary increase and other recognition. Through the "Expert" program and formal training sessions, sales associates gain the confidence they need to offer customers practical solutions to do-it-yourself questions. Incentives also play an important role in providing outstanding customer service. Store employees are paid bonuses based on customer service reports, and after two years of service, all employees are eligible for the Employee Stock Ownership Plan (ESOP). Eagle consistently promotes from within to develop employees who excel at the company's service-oriented approach —people who can deliver the "Eagle Experience."

Eagle operates in a highly competitive environment that includes traditional hardware, plumbing, electrical, and other home-supply retailers; wholesale clubs; discount retail stores; and catalog companies.

Eagle Hardware's competitors include Home Depot, HomeBase, HQ (previously known as Builder's Square), and Payless Cashways. Approximately two-thirds of Eagle stores compete locally with Home Depot outlets. A favorable influence on Eagle's growth was the closing of Ernst Home Center, a major competitor, in 1996. Ernst had operated eighty-six mid-sized home-improvement stores in the western United States, and more than half of these had competed directly with Eagle stores.

Fisher Broadcasting, Inc., which operates a television network affiliate in the Seattle area, assessed the impact of Ernst's withdrawal from the Puget Sound market. As part of an independent survey, 403 people (79 percent of them former Ernst customers) were asked where they planned to shop for home-improvement products after the Ernst stores closed. Over 36 percent of the Ernst's shoppers surveyed named Eagle, twice as many as named Home Depot, the nation's largest home-improvement retailer. HomeBase, the eighth largest retailer in the industry, was selected by 11 percent of those surveyed. Considering that more than 75 percent of Eagle stores competed with at least one Ernst store, Eagle executives were quite encouraged by the results of this survey. At the time the survey was taken, Eagle operated ten stores, Home Depot had nine, and HomeBase had seven in the Puget Sound area.

After Ernst went out of business and Eagle began to see significant increases in sales, management had to decide whether to maintain or increase the number of sales associates in Eagle's outlets. Management opted to forgo the immediate benefit of "leveraging" payroll dollars and added additional sales staff to provide existing and new customers with a high level of customer service. The wisdom of that decision has since been validated by the independent customer service surveys that are taken in each store every month. The stores scored higher than ever before on these surveys.

In 1998, Eagle Hardware was acquired by Lowe's, the number-two home-improvement chain in the United States. Lowe's, which operates nearly five hundred stores in twenty-six states and has annual sales in excess of $10 billion, viewed Eagle as a perfect vehicle for establishing a presence in the Pacific Northwest. The two companies share similar values and a strong customer focus. Lowe's targets the same do-it-yourself and commercial customers, and its employee stock ownership plan, one of the first of its kind, is among the largest in the nation. Employees own nearly 21 percent of Lowe's stock. The acquired outlets will carry both the Eagle and Lowe's names.[28]

Questions for Discussion

1. How did Eagle Hardware use marketing research to capitalize on the closing of Ernst Home Center?
2. What other types of marketing research data could benefit Eagle Hardware in the face of such intense competition?
3. How can Lowe's use marketing research and information systems to integrate Eagle into its operations without alienating Eagle's customers?

Target Markets: Segmentation and Evaluation

OBJECTIVES

- To learn what a market is

- To understand the differences among general targeting strategies

- To be familiar with the major segmentation variables

- To know what segment profiles are and how they are used

- To understand how to evaluate market segments

- To be aware of the factors that influence the selection of specific market segments for use as target markets

- To become familiar with sales forecasting methods

Save Time
with Streamline Online

A busy two-career couple wants to spend more time with their two children and less time going to the grocery store, the dry cleaners, and the photo developer. To save about five hours a week, would they pay someone else to do these and other routine chores? Streamline, Inc., an Internet-based home shopping and delivery service, hopes this couple and thousands like them will pay a flat fee of $30 a month for the convenience of such a service.

Founded in 1993, the Boston-based firm creates a personal shopping list (PSL) for each customer, posts this list on its password-protected Web site where customers can access their private accounts, provides a specially designed "Streamline Box" to hold products delivered to a customer's basement or garage, and installs a keypad system that allows Streamline personnel to access the box to deliver products without the customer's needing to be home. By shopping online, clients can order any time up until the night before their scheduled delivery day. Every time they log on, they can modify their PSL by shopping in the Marketplace. In addition to ordering from over 10,000 brand name and specialty products—from prepared meals and sliced-to-order deli to diapers and cold remedies—virtual shoppers can arrange to have their dry cleaning picked up and delivered, their photos processed by Kodak Premium Processing, and their packages shipped by UPS. Streamline will also deliver videos from Blockbuster, coffee from Starbucks, and bagels from Finagle A Bagel. Customers simply leave items to be processed in their Streamline Box for pick-up.

Who are these people willing to pay someone else to do their chores? Streamline identifies its target market as busy suburban families: time-starved couples aged 25 to 45 with at least one child and household incomes upwards of $60,000 a year. Because the company requires that its customers have a basement or garage that can be accessed for delivery, Streamline targets suburbanites only. In the words of the company's founder and CEO, "We're focusing our business to be successful to one specific market."

Streamline is convinced that its Web site (www.streamline.com) is one of its most significant marketing tools. Initially containing only plain text, Streamline recently improved its site to be information-packed and visually rich. Shoppers see bright animated graphis and product packaging, plus they can read nutrition, ingredient, and size information. Although Streamline's customers can place orders via phone or fax, the majority of the orders are placed through the Web site. Streamline expects this number to grow, because its target market is increasingly comfortable with and adept at purchasing a variety of products and services online.[1]

To compete effectively, Streamline has singled out a specific customer group toward which it will direct its marketing efforts. Any organization that wants to succeed must identify its customer group and develop and maintain marketing mixes that satisfy the needs of its customer group.

In this chapter we explore markets and market segmentation. Initially, we define the term *market* and discuss the major requirements of a market. Then we examine the steps in the target market selection process, including identifying the appropriate targeting strategy; determining which variables to use for segmenting consumer and organizational markets; developing market segment profiles; evaluating relevant market segments; and selecting target markets. Finally, we discuss various methods for developing sales forecasts.

What Are Markets?

The word *market* has a number of meanings. People sometimes use it to refer to a specific location where products are bought and sold—for example, a flea market. A large geographic area may also be called a market. Sometimes the word refers to the relationship between supply and demand of a specific product, as in the question "How is the market for disposable cameras?" *Market* may also be used as a verb, meaning to sell something.

A market is a group of people who, as individuals or as organizations, have needs for products in a product class and have the ability, willingness, and authority to purchase such products. In general use, the term *market* sometimes refers to the total population—or mass market—that buys products. However, our definition is more specific; it refers to persons seeking products in a specific product category. For example, students are part of the market for textbooks, as well as the markets for software, pens, paper, food, music, and other products. Obviously, there are many different markets in our complex economy.

Requirements of a Market

As stated in our definition, to be a market, the people in the aggregate must meet the following four requirements:

1. They must need or desire a particular product. If they do not, then that aggregate is not a market.
2. They must have the ability to purchase the product. Ability to purchase is a function of their buying power, which consists of resources such as money, goods, and services that can be traded in an exchange situation.
3. They must be willing to use their buying power.
4. They must have the authority to buy the specific products.

Individuals can have the desire, the buying power, and the willingness to purchase certain products but may not be authorized to do so. For example, teenagers may have the desire, the money, and the willingness to buy liquor, but a liquor producer does not consider them a market because teenagers are prohibited by law from buying alcoholic beverages. An aggregate of people that lacks any one of the four requirements thus does not constitute a market.

Types of Markets

Markets fall into one of two categories: consumer markets and organizational or business-to-business markets. These categories are based on the characteristics of the individuals and groups that make up a specific market and the purposes for which

Figure 7.1
Consumer and Organizational Markets
Neutrogena Rainbath products are aimed at consumer markets whereas 3M audio-visual equipment is marketed to organizational markets.

consumer market
Purchasers and household members who intend to consume or benefit from the purchased products and who do not buy products to make profits

organizational or business-to-business market
Individuals or groups that purchase a specific kind of product for resale, direct use in producing other products, or use in general daily operations

they buy products. A **consumer market** consists of purchasers and individuals in their households who intend to consume or benefit from the purchased products and who do not buy products for the main purpose of making a profit. Each of us belongs to numerous consumer markets. The millions of individuals with the ability, willingness, and authority to buy make up a multitude of consumer markets for such products as housing, food, clothing, vehicles, personal services, appliances, furniture, and recreational equipment. The Neutrogena Rainbath products in Figure 7.1 (left) are usually marketed to customers in consumer markets.

An **organizational or business-to-business market** consists of individuals or groups who purchase a specific kind of product for one of three purposes: resale, direct use in producing other products, or use in general daily operations. For example, a lamp producer who buys electrical wire to use in the production of lamps is a part of an organizational market for electrical wire. This same firm purchases dust mops to clean its office areas. Although the mops are not used in the direct production of lamps, they are used in the operations of the firm; thus, this manufacturer is part of an organizational market for dust mops. The four categories of organizational markets are producer, reseller, government, and institutional. The dataconferencing system in Figure 7.1 (right) is ordinarily sold to customers in organizational markets.

Target Market Selection Process

In Chapter 1 we indicate that the first of two major components for developing a marketing strategy is to select a target market. Although marketers may employ several methods for target market selection, generally they use a five-step process. This process is shown in Figure 7.2, and we discuss it in the rest of this section.

Figure 7.2
Target Market Selection Process

| 1 Identify the appropriate targeting strategy | 2 Determine which segmentation variables to use | 3 Develop market segment profiles | 4 Evaluate relevant market segments | 5 Select specific target markets |

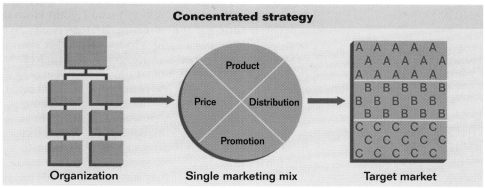

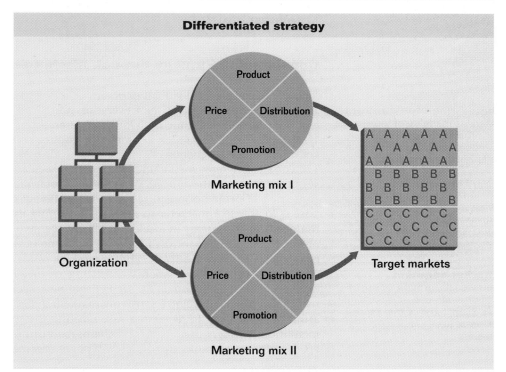

Figure 7.3
Targeting Strategies
The letters in each target market represent potential customers. Customers with the same letters have similar characteristics and similar product needs.

Step 1: Identify the Appropriate Targeting Strategy

As you may recall from Chapter 1, a target market is a group of persons or organizations for which a business creates and maintains a marketing mix that is specifically designed to satisfy the needs of group members. The strategy used to select a target market is affected by target market characteristics, product attributes, and the organization's objectives and resources. Figure 7.3 illustrates the three basic targeting strategies: undifferentiated, concentrated, and differentiated.

Undifferentiated Strategy

undifferentiated targeting strategy   A strategy in which an organization defines an entire market for a particular product as its target market, designs a single marketing mix, and directs it at that market

An organization sometimes defines an entire market for a particular product as its target market. When a company designs a single marketing mix and directs it at the entire market for a particular product, it is using an **undifferentiated targeting strategy.** As Figure 7.3 shows, the strategy assumes that all customers in the target market for a specific kind of product have similar needs, and so the organization can satisfy most customers with a single marketing mix. This mix consists of one type of product with little or no variation, one price, one promotional program aimed at everybody, and one distribution system to reach most customers in the total market. Products marketed successfully through the undifferentiated strategy include staple food items, such as sugar and salt, and certain kinds of farm produce.

homogeneous market
A market in which a large proportion of customers have similar needs for a product

The undifferentiated targeting strategy is effective under two conditions. First, a large proportion of customers in a total market must have similar needs for the product—a situation termed a **homogeneous market.** A marketer using a single marketing mix for a total market of customers with a variety of needs would find that the marketing mix satisfies very few people. A "universal car" meant to satisfy everyone would satisfy very few customers' needs for cars because it would not provide the specific attributes that a specific person wants. Second, the organization must be able to develop and maintain a single marketing mix that satisfies customers' needs. The company must be able to identify a set of needs common to most customers in a total market and have the resources and managerial skills to reach a sizable portion of that market.

Although customers may have similar needs for a few products, for most products their needs decidedly differ. In such instances, a company should use a concentrated or a differentiated strategy.

Concentrated Strategy through Market Segmentation

heterogeneous markets
Markets made up of individuals or organizations with diverse product needs for products in a specific product class

market segmentation
The process of dividing a total market into groups with relatively similar product needs in order to design a marketing mix that matches those needs

market segment
Individuals, groups, or organizations with one or more similar characteristics that cause them to have similar product needs

Markets made up of individuals or organizations with diverse product needs are called **heterogeneous markets.** Not everyone wants the same type of car, furniture, or clothes. For example, some individuals want an economical car, others desire a status symbol, and still others seek a roomy and comfortable vehicle. The automobile market, then, is heterogeneous.

For such heterogeneous markets, market segmentation is appropriate. **Market segmentation** is the process of dividing a total market into groups, or segments, consisting of people or organizations with relatively similar product needs. The purpose is to enable a marketer to design a marketing mix that more precisely matches the needs of consumers in a selected market segment. A **market segment** consists of individuals, groups, or organizations with one or more similar characteristics that cause them to have relatively similar product needs. For instance, the cola market could be divided into segments consisting of diet cola drinkers and regular cola drinkers. The main rationale for segmenting heterogeneous markets is that a company is better able to develop a satisfying marketing mix for a relatively small portion of a total market than to develop a mix meeting the needs of all people. Market segmentation is widely used. Fast-food chains, soft drink companies, magazine publishers, hospitals, and banks are just a few types of organizations that employ market segmentation.

For market segmentation to succeed, five conditions must exist. First, customers' needs for the product must be heterogeneous; otherwise there is little reason to segment a market. Second, segments must be identifiable and divisible. The company must find a characteristic or variable for effectively separating individuals in a total market into groups containing people with relatively uniform needs for the product. Third, the total market should be divided so that segments can be compared with respect to estimated sales potential, costs, and profits. Fourth, at least one segment must have enough profit potential to justify developing and maintaining a special marketing mix for that segment. Finally, the company must be able to reach the chosen segment with a particular marketing mix. Some market segments may be difficult or impossible to reach because of legal, social, or distribution constraints. For instance, marketers of Cuban rum and cigars cannot sell to U.S. consumers because of political and trade restrictions.

When an organization directs its marketing efforts toward a single market segment using one marketing mix, it is employing a **concentrated targeting strategy.** Porsche focuses on the luxury sports car segment and directs all its marketing efforts toward high-income individuals who want to own high-performance sports cars. Cross Pen Company aims its products at the upscale gift segment of the pen market and does not compete with Bic or Papermate, which focus on less expensive pen segments. Notice in Figure 7.3 that the organization using the concentrated strategy is aiming its marketing mix only at "B" customers. The chief advantage of the concentrated strategy is that it allows a firm to specialize. The firm analyzes characteristics and needs of a distinct customer group and then focuses all its energies on satisfying that group's needs. A firm may generate a large sales volume by reaching a single segment. Also, concentrating on a single segment permits a firm with limited resources to compete with larger organizations, which may have overlooked smaller segments.

Specialization, however, means that a company puts all its eggs in one basket, which can be hazardous. If a company's sales depend on a single segment and the segment's demand for the product declines, the company's financial strength also declines. Moreover, when a firm penetrates one segment and becomes well entrenched, its popularity may keep it from moving into other segments. For example, it is very unlikely that Cross could or would want to compete with Bic in the low-end, disposable pen market segment.

concentrated targeting strategy   A strategy in which an organization targets a single market segment using one marketing mix

Differentiated Strategy through Market Segmentation

differentiated targeting strategy   A strategy in which an organization targets two or more segments by developing a marketing mix for each

With a **differentiated targeting strategy,** an organization directs its marketing efforts at two or more segments by developing a marketing mix for each (see Figure 7.3). After a firm uses a concentrated strategy successfully in one market segment, it sometimes expands its efforts to include additional segments. For example, Fruit of the Loom underwear has traditionally been aimed at one segment: men. However, the company now markets underwear for women and children as well. Marketing mixes for a differentiated strategy may vary as to product features, distribution methods, promotion methods, and prices. Figure 7.4 illustrates that Volkswagen aims multiple marketing mixes at multiple target markets, thus employing a differentiated targeting strategy.

Let's break it down. **Sports.** As in biking, kayaking, windsurfing or let's say carting a trio of junior soccer players around. **Car.** As in a German-engineered, autobahn-eating road machine. A little shake, a little bake, and voilà. The 1999 Passat wagon. For around $21,750; it's the sports car, redefined.

The Passat Wagon. **Drivers wanted.**

Figure 7.4
Differentiated Targeting Strategy
Using marketing mixes aimed at multiple target markets, Volkswagen employs a differentiated targeting strategy based on variation in product features, promotional methods, and prices.

A firm may increase sales in the aggregate market through a differentiated strategy because its marketing mixes are aimed at more people. For example, the Gap, which established its retail clothes reputation by targeting people under 25, now targets several age groups, from infants to people over 60. A company with excess production capacity may find a differentiated strategy advantageous because the sale of products to additional segments may absorb excess capacity. On the other hand, a differentiated strategy often demands more production processes, materials, and people. Thus, production and costs may be higher than with a concentrated strategy.

Step 2: Determine Which Segmentation Variables to Use

segmentation variables
Characteristics of individuals, groups, or organizations used to divide a market into segments

Segmentation variables are the characteristics of individuals, groups, or organizations used to divide a market into segments. For example, location, age, gender, or rate of product usage can all be bases for segmenting markets.

To select a segmentation variable, several factors are considered. The segmentation variable should relate to customers' needs for, uses of, or behavior toward the product. Stereo marketers might segment the stereo market based on income and age—but not on religion, because people's stereo needs do not differ due to religion. Furthermore, if individuals or organizations in a total market are to be classified accurately, the segmentation variable must be measurable. Age, location, and gender are measurable because such information can be obtained through observation or questioning. But segmenting a market on the basis of intelligence is extremely difficult because this attribute is harder to measure accurately.

A company's resources and capabilities affect the number and size of segment variables used. The type of product and degree of variation in customers' needs also dictate the number and size of segments a particular firm targets. In short, there is no best way to segment markets.

Choosing a segmentation variable or variables is a critical step in targeting a market. Selecting an inappropriate variable limits the chances of developing a successful marketing strategy. To help you better understand possible segmentation variables, we examine the major types of variables used to segment consumer markets and the types used to segment organizational markets.

Variables for Segmenting Consumer Markets

A marketer using segmentation to reach a consumer market can choose one or several variables from an assortment of possibilities. As shown in Figure 7.5, segmentation variables can be grouped into four categories: (1) demographic, (2) geographic, (3) psychographic, and (4) behavioristic.

Demographic Variables Demographers study aggregate population characteristics, such as the distribution of age and gender, fertility rates, migration patterns, and mortality rates. Demographic characteristics that marketers commonly use in segmenting markets include age, gender, race, ethnicity, income, education, occupation, family size, family life cycle, religion, and social class. Marketers rely on these demographic characteristics because they are often closely linked to customers' needs and purchasing behavior and can be readily measured. Like demographers, a few marketers even use mortality rates. Service Corporation International (SCI), the largest U.S. funeral services company, attempts to locate its facilities in higher-income suburban areas with high

SNAPSHOT

Targeting teens and twenty somethings

Share of movie ticket sales vs. share of population by age

Age	Tickets	Population
12–15	9%	7%
16–20	17%	8%
21–24	11%	6%
25–29	12%	9%
30–39	19%	20%
40–49	15%	18%
50–up	18%	32%

Note: May exceed 100% due to rounding

Copyright © 1999 *USA Today*, a division of Gannett Co., Inc.

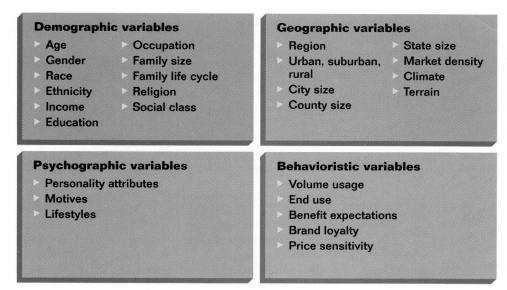

Figure 7.5
Segmentation Variables for Consumer Markets

mortality rates. SCI operates over 3,700 funeral service locations, cemeteries, and crematoriums.[2]

Because age is a commonly used variable for segmentation purposes, marketers need to be aware of age distribution and how that distribution is changing. All age groups under 55 are expected to decrease by the year 2025, and all age categories 55 and older are expected to increase. In 1970, the average age of a U.S. citizen was 27.9; currently, it is about 35.7. According to projections, the average age in the year 2025 will be 38.[3] As shown in Figure 7.6, Americans 65–74 years old outspend not only customers in the 25–34 age group, but also the average U.S. customer for numerous product categories.

Most marketers recognize the purchase influence of children and are targeting more marketing efforts at them. Teenagers spend $33.5 billion on family grocery shopping. In households with only one parent or where both parents work, children take on additional responsibilities such as cooking, cleaning, and grocery shopping. Moreover, the 54 million children under age 13 have about $20 billion to spend on their own. Children are believed to influence household purchases in excess of $200 billion annually. Numerous products are aimed at children—toys, clothing, food,

Figure 7.6
Spending Levels of Two Age Groups for Selected Product Categories
Index of 100 equals the spending of the average U.S. consumer.

Source: Reprinted from *American Demographics Magazine,* with permission. © 1997 PRIMEDIA Intertec, Stanford, CT.

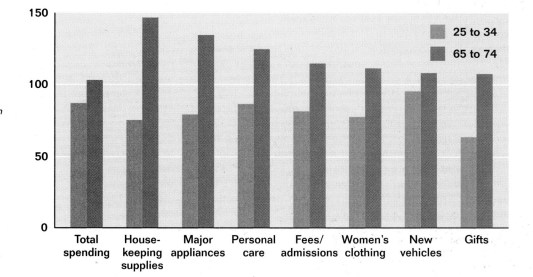

drinks, and entertainment, such as Nickelodeon, the most-watched cable network in the country since 1995.[4]

Gender is another demographic variable commonly used to segment markets, including the markets for clothing, soft drinks, nonprescription medications, toiletries, magazines, and even cigarettes. The Bureau of the Census reports that girls and women account for 51.1 percent and boys and men for 48.9 percent of the total U.S. population.[5] Some deodorant marketers utilize gender segmentation: Secret deodorant is marketed specifically to women, whereas Old Spice deodorant is directed toward men. A number of Web sites are aimed at females. These include Cybergirl, Girl Tech, Moms Online, Women's Wire, and Online Women's Business Center. Effective targeting of women online relies heavily on personalization, sense of community, and trust.[6] As discussed in Building Customer Relationships, *More* magazine is striving to target effectively women in the 40–64 age group.

Marketers also choose race and ethnicity as means of segmenting markets for such goods as food, music, clothing, and cosmetics and for services like banking and insurance. The U.S. Hispanic population illustrates the importance of ethnicity as a segmentation variable. Made up of people of Mexican, Cuban, Puerto Rican, and Central and South American heritage, this ethnic group is growing five times faster than the

BUILDING
customer relationships

More Targets Less Sought-After Customers

Magazines today are targeted at teenage girls, golfers, gardeners, do-it-yourselfers, rock music lovers, and dozens of other market segments. In fact, if there is an interest, there is probably a magazine designed to attract readers with that interest. Fly fishermen alone have 140 different magazines targeted specifically at them. However, until the launch of *More* magazine in April 1997, very few magazines were designed for women aged 40 to 64. *More* is a bi-monthly publication with features and columns targeted specifically at women in this age group. Asserts the magazine's editor, *"More* is a magazine for women who don't have a magazine."

According to the U.S. Bureau of the Census, women aged 40 to 64 will make up 24 percent of the population by the year 2015. At present, women in this age group spend more than $26 billion a year on clothes and beauty products. Recognizing the potential of this market, Meredith Corporation, publisher of *Ladies Home Journal,* created *More.* The magazine's basic premise is that the interests and attitudes of post-child-bearing, pre-retirement women are different not only from those of younger women, but also from those of middle-aged women a generation ago. The magazine believes these women feel differently about aging than their mothers did and that they are generally vibrant, active, healthier, wealthier, "younger" older women. *More*, which touts itself as "smart talk for smart women," has positioned itself to reach this group.

More's publishers believe women in their 40s and 50s don't want to be reminded that they are no longer in their 20s and 30s. Thus, all the models who appear in the magazine are over 40, including 50-year-old Cheryl Tiegs and 48-year-old Cybil Shepherd. Many of the magazine's writers are women in this age group, and the magazine's articles about relationships, careers, health, beauty, fashion, celebrities, and finance are written with the interests and needs of older women in mind. The articles in *More's* first issue, for example, included "In Bed with Viagra," "Rating TV Finance Shows," "The Hormone Chronicles," and an interview with Tipper Gore. One of the magazine's regular features is an advice column called "Ask Mrs. Robinson." Women have written to it for advice on such issues as why it bothers them that men no longer whistle at them even though they look good, how to discuss contraception with an adult daughter, and the complications involved when both marriage partners are having affairs.

Since the publication of *More,* older women have had available a magazine targeted directly at them— one whose editors and writers are determined to stay focused on what women in the 40–60-year age group want to know. Although other magazines targeted at older women have failed, industry analysts, such as Media Industry Newsletter, believe *More* magazine will succeed.

**Figure 7.7
Segmentation Based on Income**
Gramophone targets its sound systems, ranging from $5,000 to $120,000, at high-income customers.

general population. Consequently, Campbell Soup, Procter & Gamble, and other companies target Hispanic consumers, viewing this segment as attractive because of its size and growth potential. However, targeting Hispanic customers is not an easy task. For example, although marketers have long believed that Hispanic consumers are exceptionally brand-loyal and prefer Spanish-language broadcast media, research does not support these assumptions. Not only do advertisers disagree about the merits of using Spanish-language media, they also realize that they cannot effectively advertise to Mexicans, Puerto Ricans, and Cubans using a common Spanish language.[7]

Because it strongly influences people's product needs, income often provides a way of dividing markets. It affects ability to buy and aspirations to certain lifestyles. Product markets segmented by income include sporting goods, housing, furniture, cosmetics, clothing, jewelry, home appliances, automobiles, and electronics. As depicted in Figure 7.7, Gramophone targets its sound systems, ranging from $5000 to $120,000, at high-income customers.

Among the factors influencing household income and product needs are marital status and the presence and age of children. These characteristics, often combined and called the *family life cycle,* affect needs for housing, appliances, food, automobiles, recreational equipment, and many other products. Oscar Mayer, for example, employs family life cycle segmentation for its Lunchable products, which are aimed at families with school-age children.

Family life cycle can be broken down in various ways. Figure 7.8 shows a breakdown into nine categories. The composition of the American household in relation to family life cycle has changed. The "typical" American family of a single-earner married couple with children dropped from 21 percent of all households in 1970 to just 8 percent

**Figure 7.8
Family Life Cycle Stages as a Percentage of All Households**
Source: Bureau of the Census, *Current Population Survey.*

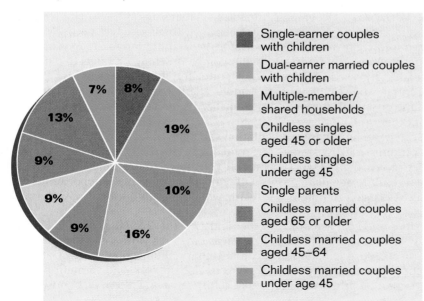

- Single-earner couples with children
- Dual-earner married couples with children
- Multiple-member/shared households
- Childless singles aged 45 or older
- Childless singles under age 45
- Single parents
- Childless married couples aged 65 or older
- Childless married couples aged 45–64
- Childless married couples under age 45

Audi TT Coupé 1.8 5V Turbo 180 Hk kr 400.500. Audi TT Coupé 1.8 5V Turbo 180 Hk quattro kr 427.500. Audi TT Coupé 1.8 5V Turbo 225 Hk quattro kr 520.500.   Prisene er veiledende levert importør Harald A. Møller AS, inklusive registreringsomkostninger. Frakt kommer i tillegg. www.audi.no

Figure 7.9
Family Life Cycle
Segmentation
The Audi TT Coupé is
aimed at single people.

in 1990, and the number of households in which one person lives alone or with unrelated people increased from 23 percent to 35 percent. Childless singles under age 45 headed just 3 percent of the households in 1970, but their share increased to 9 percent by 1990.[8] Persons in a particular life cycle stage may have very specific needs that can be satisfied by precisely designed marketing mixes. For example, as shown in Figure 7.9, Audi targets its Audi TT Coupé at singles.

Marketers also use many other demographic variables. For instance, dictionary publishing companies segment markets by education level. Some insurance companies segment markets using occupation, targeting health insurance at college students and at younger workers whose employers are small and do not provide health coverage.

Geographic Variables   Geographic variables—climate, terrain, city size, population density, and urban/rural areas—also influence customer product needs. Markets may be divided into regions because one or more geographic variables can cause customers to differ from one region to another. A company selling products to a national market might divide the United States into the following regions: Pacific, Southwest, Central, Midwest, Southeast, Middle Atlantic, and New England. A firm operating in one or several states might regionalize its market by counties, cities, zip code areas, or other units.

City size can be an important segmentation variable. Some marketers focus efforts on cities of a certain size. For example, one franchised restaurant organization will not locate in cities of less than 200,000 people. It concluded that a smaller population base would not result in adequate profits. Other firms, however, seek opportunities in smaller towns. A classic example is Wal-Mart, which initially located only in small towns.

Because cities often cut across political boundaries, the U.S. Bureau of the Census developed a system to classify metropolitan areas (any area with a city or urbanized area of at least 50,000 population and a total metropolitan population of at least 100,000). Metropolitan areas are categorized as one of the following: a metropolitan statistical area (MSA), a primary metropolitan statistical area (PMSA), or a consolidated metropolitan statistical area (CMSA). An MSA is an urbanized area encircled by nonmetropolitan counties and is neither socially nor economically dependent on any other metropolitan area. A metropolitan area within a complex of at least 1 million inhabitants can elect to be named a PMSA. A CMSA is a metropolitan area of at least 1 million consisting of two or more PMSAs. Of the twenty CMSAs, the five largest—New York, Los Angeles, Chicago, San Francisco, and Philadelphia—account for 20 percent of the U.S. population. The federal government provides a considerable amount of socioeconomic information about MSAs, PMSAs, and CMSAs that can aid market analysis and segmentation.

market density   The number of potential customers within a unit of land area

Market density refers to the number of potential customers within a unit of land area, such as a square mile. Although market density relates generally to population density, the correlation is not exact. For example, in two different geographic markets of approximately equal size and population, market density for office supplies would be much higher in one area if it contained a much greater proportion of business customers than the other area. Market density may be a useful segmentation variable because low-density markets often require different sales, advertising, and distribution activities than do high-density markets.

geodemographic segmentation   Marketing segmentation that clusters people in ZIP code areas and smaller neighborhood units based on lifestyle and demographic information

A number of marketers have begun using what is called geodemographic segmentation. **Geodemographic segmentation** clusters people in ZIP code areas and even smaller neighborhood units based on lifestyle information and especially demographic data, such as income, education, occupation, type of housing, ethnicity, family life cycle, and level of urbanization. These small, precisely described population clusters help marketers isolate demographic units as small as neighborhoods where the demand for specific products is strongest. Information companies such as Donnelley Marketing Information Services, Claritas, and C.A.C.I., Inc., provide geodemographic data services called ClusterPlus, PRIZM, and Acorn, respectively. PRIZM is based on a classification of the over 500,000 U.S. neighborhoods into one of forty cluster types, such as "shotguns and pickups," "money and brains," and "gray power." As shown in Figure 7.10, Geoscape provides software to help marketers perform geodemographic analysis.

**Figure 7.10
Geodemographic Segmentation**
Several organizations such as Geoscape provide software and services to assist marketers in segmenting marketing based geodemographics.

micromarketing An approach to market segment-ation in which organizations focus precise marketing efforts on very small geographic markets

Geodemographic segmentation allows marketers to engage in micromarketing. **Micromarketing** is the focusing of precise marketing efforts on very small geographic markets, such as community and even neighborhood markets. Providers of financial and health care services, retailers, and consumer products companies use micromarketing. Special advertising campaigns, promotions, retail-site location analyses, special pricing, and unique retail product offerings are a few examples of micromarketing facilitated through geodemographic segmentation. Target Stores relies on micromarketing, especially for determining the specific mix of products for each store. The products sold at Target's Scottsdale store are different from those offered in its east-side Phoenix store, which is only fifteen minutes away. For example, the Scottsdale store carries a large stock of in-line skates for its affluent shoppers, whereas the Phoenix store stocks only a few pairs. The Phoenix store's customers have an average household income 42 percent below that of the Scottsdale store customers. The Phoenix store stocks a large inventory of religious candles to serve its many Hispanic Catholic customers. Only a few religious candles are carried at the Scottsdale store.[9]

Climate is commonly used as a geographic segmentation variable because of its broad impact on people's behavior and product needs. Product markets affected by climate include air-conditioning and heating equipment, clothing, gardening equipment, recreational products, and building materials.

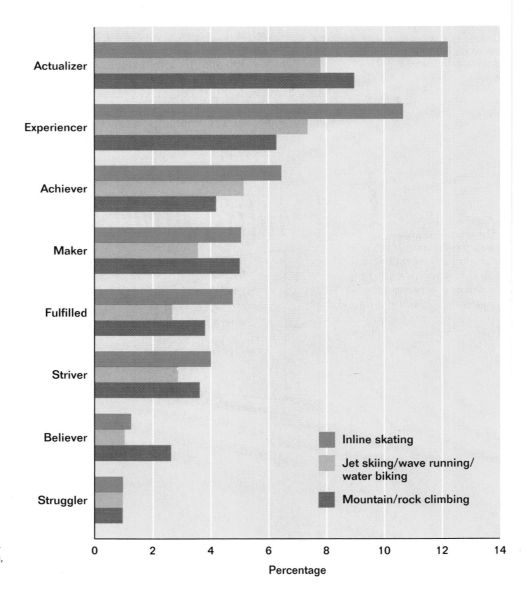

Figure 7.11
Percentage of U.S. Adults, Classified by VALS 2 Type, Who Participated in Selected Sports in 1996

Source: Reprinted from *American Demographics Magazine,* with permission. © 1997 PRIMEDIA Intertec, Stanford, CT.

Psychographic Variables   Marketers sometimes use psychographic variables, such as personality characteristics, motives, and lifestyles, to segment markets. A psychographic dimension can be used by itself to segment a market or combined with other types of segmentation variables.

Personality characteristics can be useful for segmentation when a product resembles many competing products and consumers' needs are not greatly affected by other segmentation variables. However, segmenting a market according to personality traits can be risky. Although marketing practitioners have long believed that consumer choice and product use vary with personality, until recently marketing research had indicated only weak relationships. It is hard to measure personality traits accurately—especially since most personality tests were developed for clinical use, not for segmentation purposes.

Before aiming at people with active lifestyles, wouldn't you like to know who's playing?

BehaviorBank. Tightly targeting your promotions to the right audience delivers the best response. Today, many marketers turn to Experian's BehaviorBank to do just that. A self-reported database with key demographic information on more than 30 million U.S. households, BehaviorBank is segmented into more than 300 categories according to interests, activities and lifestyle...characteristics that influence buying behavior. More than 800,000 new names are added each month, making BehaviorBank a fresh and accurate source of prospects. And to meet lead generation and marketing research objectives, we offer custom Question Sponsorship on our nationally distributed BehaviorBank surveys, product registration cards and consumer web site. So whether you're a pharmaceutical or packaged goods marketer looking for new consumers, a fundraiser seeking new donors, or a financial services firm targeting new investors, BehaviorBank can sharpen your aim.

Want to know what influences buying behavior?
Call 1-888-446-3611 x 8001.
www.experian.com

BehaviorBank®

experian

For more information, circle No. 52

Figure 7.12
Lifestyle Segmentation
Experían's BehaviorBank is a database of self-reported consumer information that helps marketers segment markets based on lifestyles. BehaviorBank contained categories based on customers' interests and activities.

When appealing to a personality characteristic, marketers almost always select one that many people view positively. Individuals with this characteristic, as well as those who would like to have it, may be influenced to buy that marketer's brand. Marketers taking this approach do not worry about measuring how many people have the positively valued characteristic; they assume that a sizable proportion of people in the target market either have or want to have it.

When motives are used to segment a market, the market is divided according to consumers' reasons for making a purchase. Personal appearance, affiliation, safety, and status are examples of motives affecting the types of products purchased and the choice of stores in which they are bought. For example, two possible motives for purchasing dieting-related products are appearance and health.

Lifestyle segmentation groups individuals according to how they spend their time, importance of things in their surroundings (homes or jobs, for example), beliefs about themselves and broad issues, and some demographic characteristics, such as income and education.[10] Lifestyle analysis provides a broad view of buyers because it encompasses numerous characteristics related to people's activities (work, hobbies, entertainment, sports), interests (family, home, fashion, food, technology), and opinions (politics, social issues, education, future).

One of the more popular programs that studies lifestyles is conducted by the Stanford Research Institute's Value and Lifestyle Program (VALS). This program surveys American consumers to select groups with identifiable values and lifestyles. Initially it identified three broad consumer groups: Outer-Directed, Inner-Directed, and Need-Driven consumers. A VALS 2 classification categorizes consumers into five basic lifestyle groups: Strugglers, Action-Oriented, Status-Oriented, Principle-Oriented, and Actualizers. An expanded set of VALS 2 lifestyle groups appears in Figure 7.11, which shows the proportion of each group that participated in selected sports recently. Marketers of products related to inline skating, jet skiing, wave running, water biking, and mountain and rock climbing would most likely focus on the "actualizer" and "experiencer" lifestyle segments.[11] The VALS studies have been used to create products, as well as to segment markets. While VALS studies are widely used for segmenting consumers by lifestyle, many other lifestyle classification systems exist. Several companies, such as Experían's BehaviorBank, have lifestyle data on millions of consumers (see Figure 7.12).

Behavioristic Variables   Firms can divide a market according to some feature of consumer behavior toward a product, commonly involving some aspect of product use. For example, a market may be separated into users, classified as heavy, moderate, or light, and nonusers. To satisfy a specific group, such as heavy users, marketers may create a distinctive product, set special prices, or initiate special promotion and distribution activities. Per capita consumption data help identify different levels of usage. For example, economic census data show that per capita spending on building supplies at building-material stores varies widely across the United States, ranging from $537 per resident in New Hampshire to $29 per resident in Wyoming. This information helps companies like Home Depot plan expansion and resource allocation, as pointed out in Tech*know.

How customers use or apply products may also determine segmentation. To satisfy customers who use a product in a certain way, some feature—say, packaging, size, texture, or color—may be designed precisely to make the product easier to use, safer, or more convenient. For instance, a number of products are designed for customers with disabilities. Cannondale makes a racing wheelchair, Lionel makes a special model-train controller for disabled customers, and adaptAbility markets lightweight glasses that double the size of TV images.[12]

benefit segmentation
The division of a market according to benefits that customers want from the product

Benefit segmentation is the division of a market according to benefits that consumers want from the product. Although most types of market segmentation assume a relationship between the variable and customers' needs, benefit segmentation is dif-

Tech*know

Targeting Technology Customers

What is the difference between a "techno-striver" and a "neo-hearthminder"? According to Forrester Research, if marketers of high-tech products don't know, they had better find out. Forrester is a leading research firm that helps its clients assess the effect of technology on their businesses. The firm believes traditional targeting methods work for soap and soft drinks but not for high-tech products. For a better reflection of the diversity among consumers of technology, Forrester invented Technographics, which segments customers according to their attitudes toward, and motivation to buy, technology.

Forrester helps clients like Gateway 2000, Delta Airlines, Sprint, Ford, and Bank of America target customers more effectively by separating people into distinct categories based on their motivations, buying habits, and financial ability to buy the products of new technology. "Fast Forwards" spend the most and adopt new technology for all uses. "Techno-Strivers" use high-tech products like cell phones, pagers, and online services primarily for career purposes. "Hand-Shakers" are older consumers who tend to shun new technology. "Neo-Hearthminders," who make up the largest American segment, spend a lot on technology for home use, such as a family PC. Although "Digital Hopefuls" have limited budgets, they are interested in technology and are good customers for less expensive products, such as computers that cost under $1,000. Although "Traditionalists" use technology, they tend not to spend

money on upgrades and add-ons. "Mouse-Potatoes" like using technology for entertainment and are willing to spend money for the latest products in this line, such as video games and software. Although "Gadget-Grabbers" like online entertainment, they won't spend much to get it. Finding little entertainment to attract them online, "Media Junkies" prefer to be entertained by more traditional technology, such as television.

When a company wants to know how to target a new product, Technographics can help it segment its customers. For example, Delta Airlines wanted to know which customers in its database were most likely to purchase tickets online. Using Technographics, Delta determined that time-strapped Fast Forwards and Neo-Hearthminders were most likely to take advantage of this service, and it therefore aimed its promotional campaign at customers in those two groups.

Technological products include everything from computer hardware and Internet services to cellular phones and satellite TV dishes. Some of these products are tremendous marketplace successes, while others fail. WebTV, for example, has failed to attract the predicted number of subscribers. Forrester asserts that if marketers of WebTV (and other high-tech products) would target customers by using Technographics rather than demographics, geographics, or psychographics, their chances of launching successful products would increase tremendously.

ferent in that the benefits customers seek *are* their product needs. For example, a customer who purchases over-the-counter medication may be specifically interested in two benefits—stopping a runny nose and relieving chest congestion. Thus, individuals are segmented directly according to their needs. By determining the desired benefits, marketers may be able to divide people into groups seeking certain sets of benefits. The effectiveness of such segmentation depends on three conditions: the benefits sought must be identifiable; using these benefits, marketers must be able to divide people into recognizable segments; and one or more of the resulting segments must be accessible to the firm's marketing efforts. Both Timberland and Avia, for example, segment the foot apparel market based on benefits sought.

As this discussion shows, consumer markets can be divided according to numerous characteristics. Some of these variables, however, are not particularly helpful for segmenting organizational markets.

Variables for Segmenting Organizational Markets

Like consumer markets, organizational markets are frequently segmented. Marketers segment organizational markets according to geographic location, type of organization, customer size, and product use.

Geographic Location   We noted that the demand for some consumer products can vary considerably among geographic areas because of differences in climate, terrain, customer preferences, and similar factors. Demand for organizational products also varies according to geographic location. For example, producers of certain types of lumber divide their markets geographically because their customers' needs vary from region to region. Geographic segmentation may be especially appropriate for reaching industries concentrated in certain locations. Furniture and textile producers, for example, are concentrated in the Southeast.

Type of Organization   A company sometimes segments a market by types of organizations within that market. Different types of organizations often require different product features, distribution systems, price structures, and selling strategies. Given these variations, a firm may either concentrate on a single segment with one marketing mix (concentration strategy) or focus on several groups with multiple mixes (a differentiated targeting strategy). A carpet producer could segment potential customers into several groups, such as automobile makers, commercial carpet contractors (firms that carpet large commercial buildings), apartment complex developers, carpet wholesalers, and large retail carpet outlets.

Customer Size   An organization's size may affect its purchasing procedures and the types and quantities of products it wants. Size can thus be an effective variable for segmenting an organizational market. To reach a segment of a particular size, marketers may have to adjust one or more marketing mix components. For example, customers who buy in extremely large quantities are sometimes offered discounts. In addition, marketers must often expand personal selling efforts to serve large organizational buyers properly. Because the needs of large and small buyers tend to be quite distinct, marketers frequently use different marketing practices to reach various customer groups.

Product Use   Certain products, especially basic raw materials like steel, petroleum, plastics, and lumber, are used in numerous ways. How a company uses products affects the types and amounts of products purchased, as well as the purchasing method. For example, computers are used for engineering purposes, basic scientific research, and business operations, such as word processing, accounting, and telecommunications. A computer maker may segment the computer market by types of use because organizations' needs for computer hardware and software depend on the purpose for which products are purchased.

Table 7.1   Market Segment Profiles of Golfers

Golfer Segment	% of Golfers	Gender	Average Age	Average Household Income	Golf Spending per Year	Rounds per Year
Swinging Seniors (57% of rounds on private course, almost 50% belong to private clubs)	6.1	Female	56.8	$31,144	$1,625	42.3
Country Club Traditionals (86% of their rounds on private courses)	9.2	Male	52.6	$77,323	$4,413	68.9
Public Pundits (zealous golfers, 88% of rounds on public courses)	13.1	Male	44.5	$50,629	$1,999	44.5
Junior Leaguers (less enthusiastic than income would allow)	13.2	Female	42.6	$57,832	$1,604	42.6
Pull-Carts (60% retired or unemployed)	15.3	Male	51.7	$32,212	$1,367	51.7
Tank Tops 'n' Tennis Shoes (very casual golfers, most golfing while on vacation)	16.6	Male	34.8	$36,716	$565	12.9
Dilettante Duffers (weekend-athlete approach to golf, only 8% belong to a golf club, spend larger than average portion of annual vacation golfing)	26.5	Male	40.6	$64,180	$1,149	15.6

Sources: Deborah Bosanko, "Seven Ways to Swing a Club," *American Demographics*, July 1995, pp. 16–18; and Don Jozwiak, "All about Golf: Who Are Your Customers?" *PGA Magazine*, Nov. 1994.

Step 3: Develop Market Segment Profiles

A market segment profile describes the similarities among potential customers within a segment and explains the differences among people and organizations in different segments. A profile may cover such aspects as demographic characteristics, geographic factors, product benefits sought, lifestyles, brand preferences, and usage rates. Individuals and organizations within segments should be quite similar with respect to several characteristics and product needs and differ considerably from individuals or organizations within other market segments. Table 7.1 illustrates market segment profiles resulting from a Professional Golfers' Association study of golfers' lifestyles. Marketers use market segment profiles to assess the degree to which the organization's possible products can match or fit potential customers' product needs. Market segment profiles provide marketers with an understanding of how an organization can use its capabilities to serve potential customer groups.

Marketers benefit in several ways through the use of market segment profiles. Such profiles help a marketer determine which segment or segments are most attractive to the organization relative to the firm's strengths, weaknesses, objectives, and resources. While marketers may initially believe that certain segments are quite attractive, development of market segment profiles may yield information that indicates the opposite. For the market segment or segments chosen by the organization, the information included in market segment profiles can be highly useful in making marketing decisions.

Step 4: Evaluate Relevant Market Segments

After analyzing the market segment profiles, a marketer is likely to identify several relevant market segments for which further analysis is required and to eliminate certain segments from consideration. To further assess relevant market segments, several important factors, including sales estimates, competition, and estimated costs associated with each segment, should be determined and analyzed.

Sales Estimates

Potential sales for a segment can be measured along several dimensions, including product level, geographic area, time, and level of competition.[13] With respect to product level, potential sales can be estimated for a specific product item (for example, Diet Coke) or an entire product line (for example, Coca-Cola Classic, Caffeine-Free Coke, Diet Coke, Caffeine-Free Diet Coke, Cherry Coca-Cola, and Diet Cherry Coca-Cola comprise one product line). A manager must also determine the geographic area to be included in the estimate. In relation to time, sales estimates can be short-range (one year or less), medium-range (one to five years), or long-range (longer than five years). The competitive level specifies whether sales are being estimated for a single firm or for an entire industry.

market potential The total amount of a product that customers will purchase within a specified period at a specific level of industrywide marketing activity

Market potential is the total amount of a product, for all firms in an industry, that customers will purchase within a specified period at a specific level of industrywide marketing activity. Market potential can be stated in terms of dollars or units. A segment's market potential is affected by economic, sociocultural, and other environmental forces. Marketers must assume a certain general level of marketing effort in the industry when they estimate market potential. The specific level of marketing effort varies from one firm to another, but the sum of all firms' marketing activities equals industrywide marketing efforts. A marketing manager must also consider whether and to what extent industry marketing efforts will change.

company sales potential The maximum percentage of market potential that an individual firm can expect to obtain for a specific product

Company sales potential is the maximum percentage of market potential that an individual firm within an industry can expect to obtain for a specific product. Several factors influence company sales potential for a market segment. First, the market potential places absolute limits on the size of the company's sales potential. Second, the magnitude of industrywide marketing activities has an indirect but definite impact on the company's sales potential. Those activities have a direct bearing on the size of the market potential. When Domino's Pizza advertises home-delivered pizza, for example, it indirectly promotes pizza in general; its commercials may indirectly help sell Pizza Hut's and other competitors' home-delivered pizza. Third, the intensity and effectiveness of a company's marketing activities relative to those of its competitors affect the size of the company's sales potential. If a company spends twice as much as any of its competitors on marketing efforts and if each dollar spent is more effective in generating sales, the firm's sales potential will be quite high compared with that of its competitors.

breakdown approach Measuring company sales potential based on a general economic forecast for a specific period and the market potential derived from it

There are two general approaches to measuring company sales potential: breakdown and buildup. In the **breakdown approach,** the marketing manager first

buildup approach
Measuring company sales potential by estimating how much of a product a potential buyer in a specific geographic area will purchase in a given period, multiplying the estimate by the number of potential buyers, and adding the totals of all the geographic areas considered

develops a general economic forecast for a specific time period. Next, market potential is estimated on the basis of this economic forecast. The company's sales potential is then derived from the general economic forecast and estimate of market potential. In the **buildup approach,** an analyst begins by estimating how much of a product a potential buyer in a specific geographic area, such as a sales territory, will purchase in a given period. The analyst then multiplies that amount by the total number of potential buyers in that area. The analyst performs the same calculation for each geographic area in which the firm sells products and then adds the totals for each area to calculate market potential. To determine company sales potential, the analyst must estimate, based on planned levels of company marketing activities, the proportion of the total market potential the company can obtain.

Competitive Assessment

Besides obtaining sales estimates, it is crucial to assess competitors already operating in the segments being considered. Unless they are tempered with competitive information, sales estimates may be misleading. A market segment that seems attractive based on sales estimates may prove to be much less so when a competitive assessment is made. In such an assessment, several questions must be asked about competitors. How many of them are there? What are their strengths and weaknesses? Do several competitors have major market shares and together dominate the segment? Can our company create a marketing mix to compete effectively against competitors' marketing mixes? Is it likely that new competitors will enter this segment? If so, how will they affect our firm's ability to compete successfully? Answers to such questions are important for proper assessment of the competition in potential market segments.

The actions of a national food company that considered entering the dog food market illustrate the importance of competitive assessment. Through a segmentation study, the food company determined that dog owners can be divided into three segments according to how they view their dogs and dog foods. One group saw their dogs as performing a definite utilitarian function, such as protecting family members, playing with children, guarding the property, or herding farm animals. These people wanted a low-priced, nutritional dog food and were not interested in a wide variety of flavors. The second segment of dog owners treated their dogs as companions and family members. These individuals were willing to pay relatively high prices for dog foods and wanted a variety of types and flavors so that their dogs would not get bored. Dog owners in the third segment had negative feelings and, in fact, were found to hate their dogs. These people wanted the cheapest dog food they could buy and were not concerned with nutrition, flavor, or variety. The food company examined the extent to which competitive brands were serving all these dog owners. It found that in each segment there were at least three well-entrenched competing brands, which together dominated the segment. The food company's management decided not to enter the dog food market because of the strength of the competing brands.

Cost Estimates

To fulfill the needs of a target segment, an organization must develop and maintain a marketing mix that precisely meets the wants and needs of individuals and organizations in that segment. Developing and maintaining such a mix can be expensive. Distinctive product features, attractive package design, generous product warranties, extensive advertising, attractive promotional offers, competitive prices, and high-quality personal service consume considerable organizational resources. Indeed, to reach certain segments, the costs may be so high that a marketer may see the segment as inaccessible. Another cost consideration is whether an organization can effectively reach a segment at costs equal to or below competitors' costs. If the firm's costs are likely to be higher, it will not be able to compete in that segment in the long run.

Step 5: Select Specific Target Markets

An important initial issue to consider in selecting a target market is whether there are enough differences in customers' needs to warrant the use of market segmentation. If segmentation analysis shows customer needs to be fairly homogeneous, a firm's management may decide to use the undifferentiated approach, discussed earlier. However, if customer needs are heterogeneous, which is much more likely, then one or more target markets must be selected. On the other hand, marketers may decide not to enter and compete in any of the segments.

Assuming that one or more of the segments offer significant opportunities for the organization to achieve its objectives, marketers must decide in which segments to participate. Ordinarily, information gathered in the previous step—about sales estimates, competitors, and cost estimates—requires critical consideration in this final step to determine long-term profit opportunities. Also, the firm's management must investigate whether the organization has the financial resources, managerial skills, labor expertise, and facilities to enter and compete effectively in selected segments. Furthermore, the requirements of some market segments might be at odds with the firm's overall objectives, and the possibility of legal problems, conflicts with interest groups, and technological advancements could make certain segments unattractive. In addition, when prospects for long-term growth are taken into account, some segments might appear very attractive and others less desirable.

Selecting appropriate target markets is important to an organization's adoption and use of the marketing concept philosophy. In Figure 7.13, SIMMS carefully selected the target market for its chest-high waders. Identifying the right target market is the key to implementing a successful marketing strategy, whereas failure to do so can

Figure 7.13
Selecting Specific Target Markets
SIMMS Fishing Products designed their waders for fishing enthusiasts.

lead to low sales, high costs, and severe financial losses. A careful target market analysis places an organization in a better position both to serve customers' needs and to achieve its objectives.

Developing Sales Forecasts

sales forecast
The amount of a product a company expects to sell during a specific period at a specified level of marketing activities

A **sales forecast** is the amount of a product the company actually expects to sell during a specific period at a specified level of marketing activities. The sales forecast differs from the company sales potential. It concentrates on what the actual sales will be at a certain level of company marketing effort, whereas the company sales potential assesses what sales are possible at various levels of marketing activities, assuming that certain environmental conditions will exist. Businesses use the sales forecast for planning, organizing, implementing, and controlling their activities. The success of numerous activities depends on this forecast's accuracy. Common problems in companies that fail are improper planning and lack of realistic sales forecasts. Overly ambitious sales forecasts lead to overbuying, overinvestment, and higher costs.

To forecast sales, a marketer can choose from a number of forecasting methods, some arbitrary, and others more scientific, complex, and time-consuming. A firm's choice of method or methods depends on the costs involved, type of product, market characteristics, time span of the forecast, purposes of the forecast, stability of the historical sales data, availability of required information, managerial preferences, and forecasters' expertise and experience.[14] Common forecasting techniques fall into five categories: executive judgment, surveys, time series analysis, regression analysis, and market tests.

Executive Judgment

executive judgment
Sales forecasting based on the intuition of one or more executives

At times, a company forecasts sales chiefly on the basis of **executive judgment,** the intuition of one or more executives. This approach is unscientific but expedient and inexpensive. Executive judgment may work reasonably well when product demand is relatively stable and the forecaster has years of market-related experience. However, because intuition is swayed most heavily by recent experience, the forecast may be overly optimistic or overly pessimistic. Another drawback to intuition is that the forecaster has only past experience as a guide for deciding where to go in the future.

Surveys

Another way to forecast sales is to question customers, sales personnel, or experts regarding their expectations about future purchases.

customer forecasting survey A survey of customers regarding the quantities of products they intend to buy during a specific period

In a **customer forecasting survey,** marketers ask customers what types and quantities of products they intend to buy during a specific period (see Figure 7.14). This approach may be useful to a business with relatively few customers. For example, Intel, which markets to a limited number of companies (primarily computer manufacturers), could conduct customer forecasting surveys. PepsiCo, though, has millions of customers and could not feasibly use a customer survey to forecast future sales.

Customer surveys have several drawbacks. Customers must be able and willing to make accurate estimates of future product requirements. Although some organizational buyers can estimate their anticipated purchases accurately from historical buying data and their own sales forecasts, many cannot make such estimates. In addition, customers may not want to take part in a survey. Occasionally, a few respondents give answers they know are incorrect, making survey results inaccurate. Moreover, customer surveys reflect buying intentions, not actual purchases. Customers' intentions may not be well formulated, and even when potential purchasers have definite buy-

Figure 7.14
Customer Forecasting Surveys
Software such as Apian's Survey Pro can help marketers with customer forecasting surveys by streamlining the collection and analysis of survey data.

ing intentions, they do not necessarily follow through on them. Finally, customer surveys consume much time and money.

sales-force forecasting survey A survey of members of a firm's sales force regarding anticipated sales in their territories for a specified period

In a **sales-force forecasting survey,** members of the firm's sales force estimate anticipated sales in their territories for a specified period. The forecaster combines these territorial estimates to arrive at a tentative forecast. A marketer may survey the sales staff for several reasons. The most important is that the sales staff is closer to customers on a daily basis than other company personnel and should therefore know more about customers' future product needs. Moreover, when sales representatives assist in developing the forecast, they are more likely to work toward its achievement. Another advantage of this method is that forecasts can be prepared for single territories, divisions consisting of several territories, regions made up of multiple divisions, and the total geographic market. Thus, the method provides sales forecasts from the smallest geographic sales unit to the largest.

Despite these benefits, a sales-force survey has certain limitations. Salespeople can be too optimistic or pessimistic because of recent experiences. In addition, salespeople tend to underestimate sales potential in their territories when they believe their sales goals will be determined by their forecasts. They also dislike paperwork because it takes up the time that could be spent selling. If preparation of a territorial sales forecast is time-consuming, the sales staff may not do the job adequately.

Nonetheless, sales-force surveys can be effective under certain conditions. First of all, the salespeople as a group must be accurate—or at least consistent—estimators. If the aggregate forecast is consistently over or under actual sales, then the marketer who develops the final forecast can make the necessary adjustments. Assuming that the survey is well administered, the sales force can have the satisfaction of helping to establish reasonable sales goals and the assurance that its forecasts are not being used to set sales quotas.

expert forecasting survey Sales forecasts prepared by experts such as economists, management consultants, advertising executives, college professors, or other persons outside the firm

When a company wants an **expert forecasting survey,** it hires professionals to help prepare the sales forecast. These experts are usually economists, management consultants, advertising executives, college professors, or other persons outside the firm with solid experience in a specific market. Drawing on this experience and their analyses of available information about the company and the market, experts prepare and present forecasts or answer questions regarding a forecast. Using experts is expedient and relatively inexpensive. However, because they work outside the firm, these forecasters may not be as motivated as company personnel to do an effective job.

delphi technique A procedure in which experts create initial forecasts, submit them to the company for averaging, and then refine the forecasts

A more complex form of the expert forecasting survey is to incorporate the Delphi technique. The **Delphi technique** is a procedure in which experts create initial forecasts, submit them to the company for averaging, and have the results returned to them so that they can make individual refined forecasts. The premise is that the experts will use the averaged results when making refined forecasts and that these forecasts will be in a narrower range. The procedure may be repeated several times until the experts—each working separately—reach a consensus on the forecasts. The ultimate goal in using the Delphi technique is to develop a highly accurate sales forecast.

Time Series Analysis

time series analysis
A forecasting method that uses historical sales data to discover patterns in the firm's sales over time and generally involves trend, cycle, seasonal, and random factor analyses

With **time series analysis,** the forecaster uses the firm's historical sales data to discover a pattern or patterns in the firm's sales over time. If a pattern is found, it can be used to forecast sales. This forecasting method assumes that past sales patterns will continue in the future. The accuracy, and thus usefulness, of time series analysis hinges on the validity of this assumption.

In a time series analysis, a forecaster usually performs four types of analyses: trend, cycle, seasonal, and random factor. **Trend analysis** focuses on aggregate sales data, such as a company's annual sales figures, from a period of many years to determine whether annual sales are generally rising, falling, or staying about the same. Through **cycle analysis,** a forecaster analyzes sales figures (often monthly sales data) from a period of three to five years to ascertain whether sales fluctuate in a consistent, periodic manner. When performing **seasonal analysis,** the analyst studies daily, weekly, or monthly sales figures to evaluate the degree to which seasonal factors, such as climate and holiday activities, influence sales. **Random factor analysis** is an attempt to attribute erratic sales variations to random, nonrecurrent events, such as a regional power failure, a natural disaster, or political unrest in a foreign market. After performing each of these analyses, the forecaster combines the results to develop the sales forecast. Time series analysis is an effective forecasting method for products with reasonably stable demand but not for products with highly erratic demand.

trend analysis   An analysis that focuses on aggregate sales data over a period of many years to determine general trends in annual sales

cycle analysis   An analysis of sales figures for a period of three to five years to ascertain whether sales fluctuate in a consistent, periodic manner

seasonal analysis   An analysis of daily, weekly, or monthly sales figures to evaluate the degree to which seasonal factors influence sales

Regression Analysis

random factor analysis
An analysis attempting to attribute erratic sales variation to random, nonrecurrent events

Like time series analysis, regression analysis requires the use of historical sales data. In **regression analysis,** the forecaster seeks to find a relationship between past sales (the dependent variable) and one or more independent variables, such as population, per capita income, or gross domestic product. Simple regression analysis uses one independent variable while multiple regression analysis includes two or more independent variables. The objective of regression analysis is to develop a mathematical formula that accurately describes a relationship between the firm's sales and one or more variables; however, the formula indicates only an association, not a causal relationship. Once an accurate formula is established, the analyst plugs the necessary information into the formula to derive the sales forecast.

Regression analysis is useful when a precise association can be established. However, a forecaster seldom finds a perfect one. Furthermore, this method can be used only when available historical sales data are extensive. Thus, regression analysis is futile for forecasting sales of new products.

regression analysis
A method of predicting sales based on finding a relationship between past sales and one or more variables, such as population or income

Market Tests

market test   Making a product available to buyers in one or more test areas and measuring purchases and consumer responses

Conducting a **market test** involves making a product available to buyers in one or more test areas and measuring purchases and consumer responses to distribution, promotion, and price. Test areas are often cities with populations of 200,000 to 500,000, but can be larger metropolitan areas or towns with populations of 50,000 to 200,000. A market test provides information about consumers' actual, rather than intended, purchases. In addition, purchase volume can be evaluated in relation to the intensity of other marketing activities—advertising, in-store promotions, pricing, packaging, and distribution. Forecasters base their sales estimate for larger geographic units on customer response in test areas.

Because it does not require historical sales data, a market test is effective for forecasting sales of new products or sales of existing products in new geographic areas. A market test also gives a marketer an opportunity to test various elements of the marketing mix. But these tests are often time-consuming and expensive. In addition, a marketer cannot be certain that consumer response during a market test represents the total market response or that such a response will continue in the future.

Using Multiple Forecasting Methods

Although some businesses depend on a single sales forecasting method, most firms use several techniques. A company is sometimes forced to use several methods when marketing diverse product lines, but even for a single product line, several forecasts may be needed, especially when the product is sold to different market segments. Thus, a producer of automobile tires may rely on one technique to forecast tire sales for new cars and on another to forecast sales of replacement tires. Variation in the length of needed forecasts may call for several forecasting methods. A firm that employs one method for a short-range forecast may find it inappropriate for long-range forecasting. Sometimes a marketer verifies results of one method by using one or several other methods and comparing outcomes.

Summary

A market is an aggregate of people who, as individuals or as organizations, have needs for products in a product class and who have the ability, willingness, and authority to purchase such products.

In general, marketers employ a five-step process when selecting a target market. Step 1 is to identify the appropriate targeting strategy. When a company designs a single marketing mix and directs it at the entire market for a particular product, it is using an undifferentiated targeting strategy. The undifferentiated strategy is effective in a homogeneous market, whereas a heterogeneous market needs to be segmented through a concentrated targeting strategy or a differentiated targeting strategy. Both these strategies divide markets into segments consisting of individuals, groups, or organizations that have one or more similar characteristics and so can be linked to similar product needs. When using a concentrated strategy, an organization directs marketing efforts toward a single market segment through one marketing mix. With a differentiated targeting strategy, an organization directs customized marketing efforts at two or more segments.

Certain conditions must exist for effective market segmentation. First, customers' needs for the product should be heterogeneous. Second, the segments of the market should be identifiable and divisible. Third, the total market should be divided so that segments can be compared with respect to estimated sales, costs, and profits. Fourth, at least one segment must have enough profit potential to justify developing and maintaining a special marketing mix for that segment. Fifth, the firm must be able to reach the chosen segment with a particular marketing mix.

Step 2 is determining which segmentation variables to use. Segmentation variables are the characteristics of individuals, groups, or organizations used to divide a total market into segments. The segmentation variable should relate to customers' needs for, uses of, or behavior toward the product. Segmentation variables for consumer markets can be grouped into four categories: demographic (e.g., age, gender, income, ethnicity, family life cycle), geographic (population, market density, climate), psychographic (personality traits, motives, lifestyles), and behavioristic (volume usage, end use, expected benefits, brand loyalty, price sensitivity). Variables for segmenting organizational markets include geographic location, type of organization, customer size, and product use.

Step 3 in the target market selection process is to develop market segment profiles. Profiles describe the similarities among potential customers within a segment and explain the differences among people and organizations in different market segments. Step 4 is evaluating relevant market segments, which requires that several important factors—including sales estimates, competition, and estimated costs associated with each segment—be determined and analyzed. Step 5 involves the final selection of specific target markets. In this final step, companies consider whether enough differences in customers' needs exist to warrant segmentation and which segments to focus on.

A sales forecast is the amount of a product the company actually expects to sell during a specific period at a specified level of marketing activities. To forecast sales, marketers can choose from a number of methods. The choice depends on various factors, including the costs involved, type of product, market characteristics, and time span and purposes of the forecast. There are five categories of forecasting techniques: executive judgment, surveys, time series analysis, regression analysis, and market tests. Executive judgment is based on the intuition of one or more executives. Surveys include customer forecasting surveys and sales-force forecasting surveys and expert forecasting surveys. Time series analysis uses the firm's historical sales data to discover patterns in the firm's sales over time and employs four major types of analyses: trend, cycle, seasonal, and random factor. With regression analysis, forecasters attempt to find a relationship between past sales and one or more independent variables. Market testing involves making a product available to buyers in one or more test areas and measuring purchases and consumer responses to distribution, promotion, and price. Many companies employ multiple forecasting methods.

Important Terms

Consumer market
Organizational or business-to-business market
Undifferentiated targeting strategy
Homogeneous market
Heterogeneous market
Market segmentation
Market segment

Concentrated targeting strategy
Differentiated targeting strategy
Segmentation variables
Market density
Geodemographic segmentation
Micromarketing
Benefit segmentation

Market potential
Company sales potential
Breakdown approach
Buildup approach
Sales forecast
Executive judgment
Customer forecasting survey
Sales-force forecasting survey

Expert forecasting survey
Delphi technique
Time series analysis
Trend analysis
Cycle analysis
Seasonal analysis
Random factor analysis
Regression analysis
Market test

Discussion and Review Questions

1. What is a market? What are the requirements for a market?

2. In your local area, can you identify a group of people with unsatisfied product needs who represent a market? Could this market be reached by a business organization? Why or why not?

3. Outline the five major steps in the target market selection process.

4. What is an undifferentiated strategy? Under what conditions is it most useful? Describe a present market situation in which a company is using an undifferentiated strategy. Is the business successful? Why or why not?

5. What is market segmentation? Describe the basic conditions required for effective segmentation. Identify several firms that use market segmentation.

6. List the differences between concentrated and differentiated strategies, and describe the advantages and disadvantages of each.

7. Identify and describe four major categories of variables that can be used to segment consumer markets. Give examples of product markets that are segmented by variables in each category.

8. What dimensions are used to segment organizational markets?

9. Define geodemographic segmentation. Name several types of firms that might employ this type of market segmentation, and explain why.

10. What is a market segment profile? Why is it an important step in the target market selection process?

11. Describe the important factors that marketers should analyze in order to evaluate market segments.

12. Why is a marketer concerned about sales potential when trying to find a target market?

13. Why is selecting appropriate target markets important to an organization that wants to adopt the marketing concept philosophy?

14. What is a sales forecast? Why is it important?

15. What are the two primary types of surveys a company might use to forecast sales? Why would a company use an outside expert forecasting survey?

16. Under what conditions are market tests useful for sales forecasting? Discuss the advantages and disadvantages of market tests.

17. Discuss the benefits of using multiple forecasting methods.

Application Questions

1. MTV Latino targets the growing Hispanic market in the United States. Identify another product marketed to a distinct target market. Identify the target market, and describe how the marketing mix appeals specifically to that group.

2. Generally, marketers use one of three basic targeting strategies to focus on a target market: (1) undifferentiated, (2) concentrated, or (3) differentiated. Locate an article that describes the targeting strategy of a particular company or organization. Describe the tar-

get market, and explain the strategy being used to reach that market.

3. The stereo market may be segmented according to income and age. Name two ways the market for each of the following products might be segmented.
   a. candy bars
   b. travel agency services
   c. bicycles
   d. hair spray

4. If you were using a time series analysis to forecast sales for your company for the next year, how would you use the following sets of sales figures?

   a.
1990	$145,000	1995	$149,000
1991	$144,000	1996	$148,000
1992	$147,000	1997	$180,000
1993	$145,000	1998	$191,000
1994	$148,000	1999	$227,000

   b.
	1997	1998	1999
Jan.	$12,000	$14,000	$16,000
Feb.	$13,000	$14,000	$15,500
Mar.	$12,000	$14,000	$17,000
Apr.	$13,000	$15,000	$17,000
May	$15,000	$17,000	$20,000
June	$18,000	$18,000	$21,000
July	$18,500	$18,000	$21,500
Aug.	$18,500	$19,000	$22,000
Sep.	$17,000	$18,000	$21,000
Oct.	$16,000	$15,000	$19,000
Nov.	$13,000	$14,000	$19,000
Dec.	$14,000	$15,000	$18,000

   c. 1997 sales increased 21.2% (opened additional store in 1997)
   1999 sales increased 18.8% (opened another store in 1999)

Internet Exercise & Resources

American Express Company

American Express Company is well known for its credit card, which is accepted for purchases around the world. American Express markets many other products as well. Learn more about its goods, services, and ideas through its Web site at

www.americanexpress.com

1. Based on the information given at the Web site, describe American Express's basic products.

2. What market segments does American Express appear to be targeting with its Web site? What segmentation variables are being used to segment these markets?

3. How does American Express appeal to college students through its Web site? Why?

E-Center Resources

Visit http://www.prideferrell.com to find several resources to help you succeed in mastering the material in this chapter, plus additional materials that will help you expand your marketing knowledge. The Web site includes

 Internet exercise updates plus additional exercises

 ACE self-tests

 Chapter summary with hotlinked glossary

 Hotlinks to companies featured in this chapter

 Resource Center

 Career Center

 Marketing plan worksheets

Ryka Athletic Shoes: For Women Only

Ryka, Inc., manufactures and markets athletic foot-wear—shoes for walking, aerobics, cross-training, hiking, and running—exclusively for women. Founded in 1987 by Sheri Poe, Ryka has battled for every small success. In the beginning, Ryka had diffi-culty with product quality, many retailers wouldn't carry the brand because it wasn't nationally recog-nized, and in 1995, a planned merger with L.A. Gear fell through. When Ryka merged with KPR Sports, the company's CEO saw an opportunity to expand the business. Through all these difficulties and changes, Ryka has never strayed from its commitment to pro-vide a brand of athletic shoe designed solely for women.

The idea for Ryka athletic shoes began when Sheri Poe and several of her aerobics classmates real-ized they were experiencing back pain because their shoes didn't fit correctly. Poe surveyed department stores and athletic footwear shops, asking customers and salespeople what kinds of shoes they wanted. She discovered that no one was paying attention to the women's market. The majority of women's shoes were designed simply as scaled-down versions of men's shoes. To get a proper and painless fit, women need athletic shoes with higher arches and thinner heels, but such shoes didn't seem to exist. Poe decid-ed there was a future for a company that made athlet-ic shoes shaped just for women's feet and biome-chanical needs.

Rather than cater to the whims of fashion, Ryka concentrates on manufacturing only high-perform-ance athletic shoes that conform to the anatomy of a woman's foot. The company's patented Nitrogen E/S system provides cushioning and shock absorption for the heel and ball of the foot. Ryka's Ultra-Lite aerobics shoes and training shoes weigh only 7.7 ounces, about one-third the weight of regular aerobic shoes. Its Sport-Walker has more cushion in the heel and more arch support than most other walking shoes. *Consumer Reports* recently gave Ryka's 10K Stability shoe its top rating in women's running shoes.

When Ryka was founded, it was committed not only to its unique product line, but also to being a socially responsible company. As a young college stu-dent, Sheri Poe was assaulted and raped. In launching Ryka, she was determined that her company find ways to help women who, like her, had been victims of violent crimes. Seven percent of Ryka Shoes' pre-tax profits went to the ROSE Fund, ROSE being an acronym for "restoring one's self-esteem." When women bought a pair of Rykas, they knew that some of their money supported battered women's shelters, violence-prevention programs, and nonprofit treat-ment centers. A card attached to shoelaces outlined physical safety tips for women. In 1997, Ryka discon-tinued its support of the ROSE Fund.

Recently, Ryka launched an advertising campaign in women's health and fitness magazines. Presenting a feminist interpretation of the Cinderella story in which the glass slipper is replaced with one of three Ryka athletic shoes, the ads bear the tag line "The shoe fits. Wear it." According to the company's mar-keting director, the launch of a new campaign reflects Ryka's confidence that the women's athletic footwear category is growing. Evidence of this growth lies in increasing health club memberships, the popularity of walking, and the growing number of young women who engage in sports.

In its efforts to serve its target market better, Ryka recently introduced a line of women's athletic apparel with design and sizing features focusing on cus-tomers' individual body types. Women can find their sizes by matching height with weight, in much the same way they choose a size of pantyhose. Designed for body types more realistic than those of fashion models, Ryka's clothing includes running, walking, workout, and cover-up pieces. The line's launch includ-ed intense public relations efforts and an advertising campaign with the tag line, "Women come in shapes, not sizes."

To enhance its image as a company that creates products to fit women, Ryka is funding a study to determine how women's feet change as they age. The company's goal is to improve the fit of their shoes for women of all ages. Although the results of this study are not yet available, Ryka has already begun offering a greater number of widths.

Ryka's president believes that women want a brand designed exclusively for them, a belief support-ed by surveys showing that women will support an authentic women's product if it is available. Ryka's goal is to make that product available. Asserts the company's president, "Our real strategy is to make our products more relevant, to make the technology more relevant to women and to make a strong emo-tional connection to women."[15]

Questions for Discussion

1. What type of general targeting strategy is Ryka using? Explain.
2. Which segmentation variable is Ryka using?
3. Evaluate Ryka management's decision to end its support of the ROSE Fund.
4. What recommendations do you have for Ryka man-agement regarding the company's current targeting strategy or future targeting strategies?

CASE 7.2

LifeSource Targets Seniors with a Taste for Nutrition

Once upon a time, seniors with diabetes or heart disease had no choice but to settle for bland, boring meals. How times change. Now people with chronic health conditions can order tasty and nutritionally balanced frozen meals—spiced with sound dietary advice—for delivery direct to their doorsteps.

Who's in the kitchen cooking up these special meals? Not Campbell Soup, which recently folded its Intelligent Quisine line of healthy meals sold through a network of doctors. In this case, the culinary mastermind is LifeSource Nutrition Solutions, a California-based company with strong financial backing from life sciences giant Monsanto. At LifeSource, chefs, physicians, gerontologists, and nutritionists collaborate on mouth-watering prepared foods to tempt the palate of seniors who have diabetes, congestive heart failure, and heart disease. These ready-to-heat meals not only taste good; they also pack a huge nutritional punch, far beyond the requirements set by the American Heart Association, National Institutes of Health, and the American Diabetes Association.

Like an upscale version of Meals on Wheels, LifeSource delivers such elegant entrees as Grilled Chicken Broccoli Alfredo, Roast Turkey with Cranberry Wild Rice Pilaf, and Salmon Ravioli with Artichokes, Spinach, and Tomatoes—all in microwavable containers. To start the meal, LifeSource offers hearty soups, such as Tortellini Minestrone and Creamy Chicken Soup with Spring Vegetables. To end the meal, it offers "smoothies" (choices include fruit flavors and chocolate) that are both healthy and satisfying. By design, LifeSource foods minimize fat, sodium, and calories while maximizing flavor and nutritional value.

LifeSource's segmentation strategy is to divide the market by using a blend of demographic, geographic, psychographic, and behavioristic variables. The key demographic variables are age (people over 50) and income (affluent seniors able to afford a $5.50 meal). According to the company's research, some 56 million U.S. seniors have heart disease, while 14 million have diabetes. By 2005, the U.S. senior population will grow to 85 million, with more than three-quarters of those over 65 suffering from serious chronic illnesses. This fast-growing senior segment is also relatively well-off, collectively holding about 70 percent of the net worth of the country's households, or almost $9 trillion. Moreover, seniors' spending on health care tops $525 billion, mostly for chronic health conditions like heart disease, which hints at the enormous potential for sales of health-related products, such as vitamin-rich prepared foods.

The key geographic variable in LifeSource's recipe is location. To ensure that its meals arrive without the defrosting and refreezing problems that can damage food quality, LifeSource has uniformed drivers in refrigerated trucks delivering orders to each customer's home or office. For this reason, the company is targeting only customers who live in San Francisco, the original market, or in one of the geographic markets targeted for later expansion, including Seattle, Phoenix, and Salt Lake City.

LifeSource's key psychographic variable is lifestyle, which is directly connected to the health of its customers. Seniors with heart conditions or diabetes often have less active lifestyles. Those who lack "the energy or the means to get to a conventional grocery store," notes John Hale, LifeSource's chief operating officer, appreciate home delivery of meals.

In addition, the company is segmenting the senior market using the behavioristic variable of benefit expectations. This segmentation strategy allows LifeSource to target seniors who want what COO Hale calls "diet freedom," a compelling benefit for those who have medical conditions that dictate certain dietary restrictions. "We're offering convenient, healthy foods with great taste to provide [seniors] with diet freedom," he says. "There's a customization of diets to reach individuals' health goals, and if they want to substitute 15, 20, or 50 percent of their diet, it's up to them."

LifeSource uses a value-added approach in that it delivers more than meals; it also delivers easy access to free information and advice about nutrition. When customers call the firm's toll-free number to order meals, they have the option of speaking with a registered dietician about menu planning, dietary needs, and other concerns. LifeSource's information systems track each customer's ordering patterns, thus speeding reorders. Even the product's packaging has been specially designed for this market segment, with larger type on the heating instructions and a microwave container that stays cool as the contents heat up.

To gauge interest in its products and to develop accurate sales forecasts, LifeSource started test-marketing its meals in the San Francisco area. To do so, the company engaged in public relations events, such as tasting parties in retirement communities, as well as in direct-response marketing aimed at stimulating demand and encouraging trial usage. LifeSource's initial goal was to capture 1.75 percent of the Bay area's 500,000 seniors as customers. At this point, Hale is pleased with the level of reorders his company's meals are enjoying in San Francisco. He plans to introduce LifeSource nationwide over the coming years and to expand its market segment to include seniors with other health problems, such as osteoporosis and cancer.[16]

Questions for Discussion

1. What kind of targeting strategy is LifeSource using?
2. How can LifeSource use micromarketing to focus on specific geographic markets?
3. If LifeSource expects to do business with 1.75 percent of Bay area seniors, does this sales estimate refer to market potential or company sales potential?

8

Consumer Buying Behavior

eatZi's Goal Is to Make Customers Say "Wow!"

In 1879, Heinz heralded its ready-made ketchup as "blessed relief of mother and other women in the household." In 1953, the newly invented TV dinner promised to help "mothers burdened with baby boom offspring." In the years since the introduction of convenience foods, fast-food restaurants and "take-out" dinners have become an American way of life. Americans spend over $21 billion a year on take-out meals from restaurants and supermarkets, making the "home-meal replacement" category the fastest growing in the food service industry. Despite the category's growth, a problem persists. Restaurants that specialize in home-meal replacement don't have as broad an assortment of foods as grocery stores, but grocery stores don't have a reputation for serving quality foods. Enter eatZi's, a market that combines supermarket variety with restaurant quality.

At eatZi's, "take-out" does not mean hamburgers, fries, and a drink passed through a window in a paper bag, or salads with iceberg lettuce picked over by customers from behind sneeze guards. It means over 400 food items, including 100 entrees, 75 cheeses, 50 kinds of bread baked fresh daily, deli items, Italian specialties, racks of newly made pizzas, salads made to order from a choice of nine varieties of lettuce and two dozen other ingredients, soups, pastries, sandwiches, sushi, 125 different desserts, and more, all "to go." Although many meals are on display and ready to serve, others are individually made as customers wait. While waiting, they hear the strains of classical music, smell the aroma of freshly baked apple walnut raisin bread or rosemary garlic baguettes, and see chefs in white hats and jackets cooking and serving entrees like rainbow trout in white wine with mango glaze or migas frittata with apple-smoked bacon.

EatZi's attracts busy executives, working couples, new parents, and others who want to eat dinner at home, but don't have the time or inclination to cook it. The market does have tables where customers can sit down to eat. However, in keeping with the company's slogan, "Food for the Taking," only 10 percent of the food prepared there is eaten on the premises. Asserts one industry analyst, eatZi's is "the ultimate expression of convenience for a busy family."[1]

Marketers at successful organizations, like eatZi's, go to great efforts to understand their customers' needs and to gain a better grasp of their customers' buying behavior. A firm's ability to establish and maintain satisfying customer relationships requires an understanding of buying behavior. **Buying behavior** is the decision processes and acts of people involved in buying and using products. **Consumer buying behavior** refers to the buying behavior of ultimate consumers, those persons who purchase products for personal or household use, not for business purposes. Marketers attempt to understand buying behavior for several reasons. First, buyers' reactions to a firm's marketing strategy have a great impact on the firm's success. Second, as indicated in Chapter 1, the marketing concept stresses that a firm should create a marketing mix that satisfies customers. To find out what satisfies buyers, marketers must examine the main influences on what, where, when, and how consumers buy. Third, by gaining a better understanding of the factors that affect buying behavior, marketers are in a better position to predict how consumers will respond to marketing strategies.

In this chapter, we first examine how the customer's level of involvement affects the type of problem solving employed and discuss the types of consumer problem-solving processes. We then analyze the major stages of the consumer buying decision process, beginning with problem recognition, information search, and evaluation of alternatives and proceeding through purchase and postpurchase evaluation. Next, we examine situational influences—surroundings, time, purchase reason, and buyer's mood and condition—that affect purchasing decisions. We go on to consider psychological influences on purchasing decisions: perception, motives, learning, attitudes, personality and self-concept, and lifestyles. We conclude with a discussion of social influences that affect buying behavior. These include roles, family, reference groups and opinion leaders, social classes, and culture and subcultures.

buying behavior   The decision processes and acts of people involved in buying and using products

consumer buying behavior   Buying behavior of persons who purchase products for personal or household use, not for business purposes

Level of Involvement and Consumer Problem-Solving Processes

level of involvement
An individual's intensity of interest in a product and the importance of the product for that person

A consumer generally tries to acquire and maintain an assortment of products that satisfy his or her current and future needs. To do so, a consumer engages in problem solving. For example, to solve problems, people purchase such products as food, clothing, shelter, medical care, education, recreation, or transportation. When making these purchases, they engage in different types of problem-solving processes. The amount of effort, both mental and physical, that buyers expend in solving problems varies considerably. A major determinant of the type of problem-solving process employed depends on the customer's **level of involvement**—the individual's degree of interest in a product and the importance he or she places on this product. High-involvement products tend to be those visible to others (such as clothing, furniture, or automobiles) and products that are expensive. Expensive bicycles, for example, are usually high-involvement products. High importance issues such as health care (see Figure 8.1) are associated with high levels of involvement. Low-involvement products tend to be those that are less expensive and have less social risk associated with them, such as many grocery items; see Figure 8.1. When a person's interest in a product category is ongoing and long-term, it is referred to as *enduring involvement*. In contrast, *situational involvement* is temporary and dynamic and results from a particular set of circumstances. Involvement level, as well as other factors, affects a consumer's selection of one of three types of consumer problem solving: routinized response behavior, limited problem solving, or extended problem solving.

routinized response behavior   A type of consumer problem-solving process used when buying frequently purchased, low-cost items that require very little search-and-decision effort

A consumer uses **routinized response behavior** when buying frequently purchased, low-cost items needing very little search-and-decision effort. When buying such items, a consumer may prefer a particular brand but is familiar with several brands in the product class and views more than one as being acceptable. Typically, low-involvement products are bought through routinized response behavior almost automatically. Most buyers, for example, do not spend much time or effort selecting

196

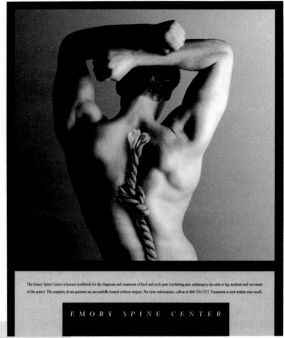

Figure 8.1
Levels of Involvement
Decisions about health care are associated with high levels of involvement, whereas purchase decisions in regard to many grocery products are associated with low levels of involvement.

limited problem solving
A type of consumer problem-solving process that buyers use when they purchase products occasionally or need information about an unfamiliar brand in a familiar product category

extended problem solving
A type of consumer problem-solving process employed when unfamiliar, expensive, or infrequently bought products are purchased

impulse buying An unplanned buying behavior involving a powerful urge to buy something immediately

consumer buying decision process A five-stage purchase decision process that includes problem recognition, information search, evaluation of alternatives, purchase, and postpurchase evaluation

a soft drink or a brand of cereal. If the nearest soft drink machine does not offer Sprite, they will likely choose 7Up instead.

Buyers engage in **limited problem solving** when buying products occasionally or when they need to obtain information about an unfamiliar brand in a familiar product category. This type of problem solving requires a moderate amount of time for information gathering and deliberation. For example, if Procter & Gamble introduces an improved Tide laundry detergent, buyers will seek additional information about the new product, perhaps by asking a friend who has used the product or watching a commercial, before making a trial purchase.

The most complex type of problem solving, **extended problem solving,** occurs when unfamiliar, expensive, or infrequently bought products are purchased—for instance, cars, homes, or a college education. The buyer uses many criteria to evaluate alternative brands or choices and spends much time seeking information and deciding on the purchase. Extended problem solving is frequently used for purchasing high-involvement products.

Purchase of a particular product does not always elicit the same type of problem-solving process. In some instances, we engage in extended problem solving the first time we buy a certain product but find that limited problem solving suffices when we buy it again. If a routinely purchased, formerly satisfying brand no longer satisfies us, we may use limited or extended problem solving to switch to a new brand. Thus, if we notice that the brand of pain reliever we normally buy is not working, we may seek out a different brand through limited problem solving. Most consumers occasionally make purchases solely on impulse, and not on the basis of any of these three problem-solving processes. **Impulse buying** involves no conscious planning but results from a powerful urge to buy something immediately.

Consumer Buying Decision Process

The **consumer buying decision process,** shown in Figure 8.2, includes five stages: problem recognition, information search, evaluation of alternatives, purchase, and postpurchase evaluation. Before we examine each stage, consider these important points. First, the actual act of purchasing is only one stage in a process, and usually not the first stage. Second, even though we indicate that a purchase occurs, not all decision processes lead to a purchase; individuals may end the process at any stage.

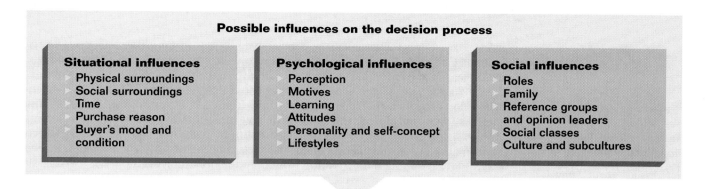

Possible influences on the decision process

Situational influences
- Physical surroundings
- Social surroundings
- Time
- Purchase reason
- Buyer's mood and condition

Psychological influences
- Perception
- Motives
- Learning
- Attitudes
- Personality and self-concept
- Lifestyles

Social influences
- Roles
- Family
- Reference groups and opinion leaders
- Social classes
- Culture and subcultures

Consumer buying decision process

Problem recognition → Information search → Evaluation of alternatives → Purchase → Postpurchase evaluation

Figure 8.2
Consumer Buying Decision Process and Possible Influences on the Process

Finally, all consumer decisions do not always include all five stages. Persons engaged in extended problem solving usually go through all stages of this decision process, whereas those engaged in limited problem solving and routinized response behavior may omit some stages.

Problem Recognition

Problem recognition occurs when a buyer becomes aware of a difference between a desired state and an actual condition. Consider a student who owns a nonprogrammable calculator and learns that she needs a programmable one for her math course. She recognizes that a difference exists between the desired state—having a programmable calculator—and her actual condition. She therefore decides to buy a new calculator.

The speed of consumer problem recognition can be quite rapid or rather slow. Sometimes a person has a problem or need but is unaware of it. Marketers use sales personnel, advertising, and packaging to help trigger recognition of such needs or problems. For example, a university bookstore may advertise programmable calculators in the university newspaper at the beginning of the term. Students who see the advertisement may recognize that they need these calculators for their course work. The ad in Figure 8.3 helps sore-throat sufferers recognize their problem and recommends Vicks Chloraseptic Throat Spray as a solution.

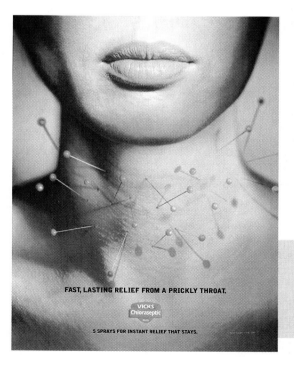

FAST, LASTING RELIEF FROM A PRICKLY THROAT.

VICKS
Chloraseptic

5 SPRAYS FOR INSTANT RELIEF THAT STAYS.

Figure 8.3
Problem Recognition
The maker of Vicks Chloraseptic Throat Spray uses this advertisement to trigger problem recognition that a sore throat can become painful and Vicks Chloraseptic Throat Spray can relieve the pain.

Information Search

After recognizing the problem or need, buyers (if continuing the decision process) search for product information that helps resolve the problem or satisfy the need. For example, the above-mentioned student, after recognizing the need for a programmable calculator, may search for information about different types and brands of calculators. She acquires information over time from her surroundings. However, the information's impact depends on how the consumer interprets it.

An information search has two aspects. In an **internal search,** buyers search their memories for information about products that might solve the problem. If they cannot retrieve enough information from their memory for a decision, they seek additional information in an **external search.** The external search may focus on communication with friends or relatives, comparison of available brands and prices, marketer-dominated sources, and/or public sources. An individual's personal contacts—friends, relatives, associates—often are influential sources of information because the consumer trusts and respects them. A consumer study has shown that word-of-mouth communication has a stronger impact on consumer judgments about products than printed communication, unless the buyer has a well-defined prior impression of a product or unless printed information about a product is extremely negative.[2] Utilizing marketer-dominated sources of information—such as salespersons, advertising, package labeling, and in-store demonstrations and displays—typically does not require much effort on the consumer's part. Buyers also obtain information from public sources—for instance, government reports, news presentations, publications such as *Consumer Reports,* and reports from product-testing organizations. Consumers frequently view information from public sources as highly credible because of its factual and unbiased nature.

Repetition, a technique well known to advertisers, increases consumers' learning of information. When seeing or hearing an advertising message for the first time, recipients may not grasp all its important details but learn more details as the message is repeated. Nevertheless, even when commercials are initially effective, repetition eventually may cause wearout, meaning that consumers pay less attention to the commercial and respond to it less favorably than they did at first.

Information can be presented verbally, numerically, or visually. Many consumers remember pictures better than words, and the combination of pictures and words further enhances learning.[3] Consequently, marketers pay great attention to the visual components of their advertising materials.

internal search An information search in which buyers search their memories for information about products that might solve their problem

external search An information search in which buyers seek information from outside sources

Evaluation of Alternatives

A successful information search yields a group of brands that a buyer views as possible alternatives. This group of brands is sometimes called a **consideration set** (also called *evoked set*). For example, a consideration set of calculators might include those made by Texas Instruments, Hewlett-Packard, Sharp, and Casio.

To assess the products in a consideration set, the buyer uses **evaluative criteria,** which are objective (such as an EPA mileage rating) and subjective (such as style) characteristics that are important to a buyer. For example, one calculator buyer may want a rechargeable unit with a large display and large buttons, whereas another may have no size preferences but happens to dislike rechargeable calculators. The buyer also assigns a certain level of importance to each criterion; some features and characteristics carry more weight than others. Using the criteria, a buyer rates and eventually ranks brands in the consideration set. The evaluation stage may yield no brand the buyer is willing to purchase. In that case, a further information search may be necessary.

Marketers may influence consumers' evaluations by *framing* the alternatives—that is, by describing the alternatives and their attributes in a certain manner. Framing can make a characteristic seem more important to a consumer and facilitate its recall from memory. For example, by stressing a car's superior comfort and safety features over those of a competitor's, a car maker can direct consumers' attention toward these points of superiority as Chrysler does with its Dodge Caravan ad in Figure 8.4.

consideration set A group of brands that a buyer views as alternatives for possible purchase

evaluative criteria Objective and subjective characteristics that are important to a buyer

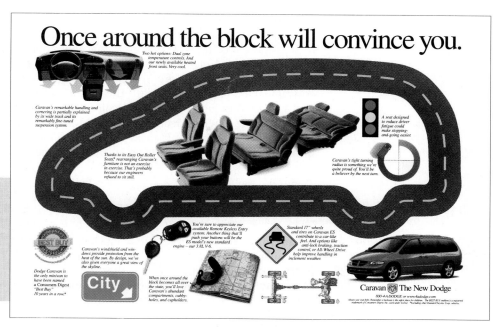

Figure 8.4
Framing Product Attributes
This advertisement helps to frame product attributes by highlighting the superior comfort and safety features of the Dodge Caravan.

Framing probably influences the decision processes of inexperienced buyers more than those of experienced ones. If the evaluation of alternatives yields one or more brands that the consumer is willing to buy, the consumer is ready to move on to the next stage of the decision process—the purchase.

Purchase

In the purchase stage, the consumer chooses the product or brand to be bought. Selection is based on the outcome of the evaluation stage and on other dimensions. Product availability may influence which brand is purchased. For example, if the brand ranked highest in evaluation is unavailable, the buyer may purchase the brand ranked second. If a consumer wants a black pair of Nikes and cannot find them in her size, she might buy a black pair of Reeboks.

During this stage, buyers also pick the seller from whom they will buy the product. The choice of seller may affect final product selection—and so may the terms of sale, which, if negotiable, are determined at this stage. Other issues, such as price, delivery, warranties, maintenance agreements, installation, and credit arrangements, are also settled. Finally, the actual purchase takes place during this stage, unless the consumer decides to terminate the buying decision process.

Postpurchase Evaluation

After the purchase, buyers begin evaluating the product to ascertain if its actual performance meets expected levels. Many criteria used in evaluating alternatives are applied again during postpurchase evaluation. The outcome of this stage is either satisfaction or dissatisfaction, which influences whether consumers complain, communicate with other possible buyers, and repurchase the brand or product. Building Customer Relationships on page 200 provides details about handling customer complaints.

cognitive dissonance
A buyer's doubts shortly after a purchase about whether it was the right decision

Shortly after purchase of an expensive product, evaluation may result in **cognitive dissonance**—doubts in the buyer's mind about whether the right decision was made in purchasing the product. For example, after buying a pair of $169 inline skates, a person may feel guilty about the purchase or wonder whether she purchased the right brand and quality. Cognitive dissonance is most likely to arise when a person has recently bought an expensive, high-involvement product that does not have some of the desirable features of competing brands. A buyer experiencing cognitive dissonance may attempt to return the product or to seek positive information about it to justify choosing it. Marketers sometimes attempt to reduce cognitive dissonance by having salespeople telephone recent purchasers to make sure they are satisfied with their new purchases. At times, recent buyers are sent results of studies showing that consumers are very satisfied with the brand.

As shown in Figure 8.2, three major categories of influences are believed to affect the consumer buying decision process: situational, psychological, and social. The remainder of this chapter focuses on these influences. Although we discuss each major influence separately, their effects on the consumer decision process are interrelated.

Situational Influences on the Buying Decision Process

situational influences
Influences resulting from circumstances, time, and location that affect the consumer buying decision process

Situational influences result from circumstances, time, and location that affect the consumer buying decision process. For example, buying an automobile tire after noticing while washing your car that the tire is badly worn is a different experience from buying a tire right after a blowout on the highway derails your vacation. Situational factors can influence the buyer during any stage of the consumer buying

BUILDING
customer relationships

When Customers Complain

Customers complain about product quality, service, safety, color, size, the way they've been treated, shipping errors, broken promises, employee attitudes, and misleading ads, among a number of other things. Regardless of the type of business they are in, all companies receive such complaints, whether justified or not. Some companies treat them as dreaded events or necessary evils. They characterize complainers as "difficult customers" or "jerks" who "gripe" and "bellyache." Companies that treat complaints as opportunities, however, can improve service, increase sales, and enhance their reputations.

When customers complain, they are usually looking for help, not trouble. Research indicates that most unhappy customers don't complain; they simply buy another product, frequent another store, or choose another company. If, however, their problems are satisfactorily addressed in a timely manner, customers remain loyal. Studies show that 96 percent of customers who experience a problem that a firm deals with satisfactorily are likely to purchase from that firm again, but only 26 percent are likely to make another purchase if the firm does not handle a complaint well.

Companies benefit from customer complaints only if they are handled well, and, unfortunately, many companies do not handle them well. Experts offer the following suggestions for effective complaint handling: Approach complaints as strategic opportunities. Educate employees at all levels about the value of complaints and the need to respond. Make it easy for customers to complain. Work hard to respond to every complaint promptly. Do not be defensive or angry. Do not deny responsibility or give phony excuses. And never raise expectations that cannot be met.

Paying attention to customer complaints helps companies launch successful new products. Kimberly-Clark's three-ply Cold Care Tissues are the result of complaints that two-ply tissues tear. Gillette's Clear Stick Deodorant is targeted at customers who complained about residue left on skin. Lancôme's transfer-resistant Rouge Idole cosmetic line is a response to complaints about lipstick left on coffee mugs, collars, and cheeks.

Soliciting complaints can translate into savings. Consider Wonderwood Corporation, a $12 million wood products manufacturer. Each year, the company spent about $50,000 answering customers' complaints. When Wonderwood began asking complainers, "How would you like us to handle the situation?" they received solutions that not only satisfied their customers, but saved the company money as well. For example, after Wonderwood spent $2,000 replacing an entire picket fence twice, the customer was still unhappy. When Wonderwood finally asked him how he'd like the situation handled, he came up with a $100 solution. Today, the company spends under $2,000 a year addressing customer complaints.

decision process and may cause the individual to shorten, lengthen, or terminate the process.

Situational factors can be classified into five categories: physical surroundings, social surroundings, time perspective, purchase reason, and the buyer's momentary mood and condition.[4] Physical surroundings refer to location, store atmosphere, aromas, sounds, lighting, weather, and other factors in the physical environment in which the decision process occurs. Marketers at some banks, department stores, and specialty stores go to considerable trouble and expense to create physical settings conducive to making purchase decisions. Numerous restaurant chains, such as Olive Garden and Chili's, invest heavily in facilities, often building from the ground up, to provide special surroundings that enhance customers' dining experiences.

Clearly, in some settings, there are dimensions, such as weather, traffic sounds, and odors, that marketers cannot control; instead they must try to make customers more comfortable. General climatic conditions, for example, may influence a customer's decision to buy a specific type of vehicle (such as an SUV) and certain accessories (such as four-wheel drive).[4] Current weather conditions, depending on whether they are favorable or unfavorable, may either encourage or discourage consumers to go shopping and to seek out specific products.

Social surroundings include characteristics and interactions of others who are present when a purchase decision is being made—friends, relatives, salespeople, and other customers. Buyers may feel pressured to behave in a certain way because they are in places such as restaurants, stores, or sports arenas. Thoughts about who will be around when the product is used or consumed is also a dimension of the social setting. An overcrowded store or an argument between a customer and a salesperson may cause consumers to stop shopping and to leave the store.

The time dimension, too, influences the buying decision process in several ways, such as the amount of time required to become knowledgeable about a product, to search for it, and to buy it. Time plays a major role in that the buyer considers the possible frequency of product use, the length of time required for the product to be used, and the length of the overall life of the product. Other time dimensions that influence purchases include time of day, day of the week or month, seasons, and holidays. The amount of time pressure that a consumer is under affects how much time is devoted to purchase decisions. A customer under severe time constraints is likely either to make quick purchase decisions or to delay them.

The purchase reason raises the questions of what exactly the product purchase should accomplish and for whom. Generally, consumers purchase an item for their own use, for household use, or as a gift. For example, people buying a gift might buy a different product if they were purchasing it for themselves. If you own a Cross pen, it is unlikely that you bought it for yourself.

The buyer's momentary moods (such as anger, anxiety, contentment) or momentary conditions (fatigue, illness, being flush with cash) may have a bearing on the consumer buying decision process. These moods or conditions immediately precede the current situation and are not chronic. Any of these moods or conditions can affect a person's ability and desire to search for information, to receive information, or to seek and evaluate alternatives. They can also significantly influence a consumer's postpurchase evaluation.

Psychological Influences on the Buying Decision Process

psychological influences
Factors that in part determine people's general behavior, thus influencing their behavior as consumers

Psychological influences partly determine people's general behavior and thus influence their behavior as consumers. Primary psychological influences on consumer behavior are perception, motives, learning, attitudes, personality and self-concept, and lifestyles. Even though these psychological factors operate internally, they are very much affected by social forces outside the individual.

**Figure 8.5
Fish or Birds?**

Perception

perception   The process of selecting, organizing, and interpreting information inputs to produce meaning

information inputs
Sensations received through the sense organs

selective exposure
The process of selecting inputs to be exposed to our awareness while ignoring others

selective distortion   An individual's changing or twisting of information when it is inconsistent with personal feelings or beliefs

selective retention
Remembering information inputs that support personal feelings and beliefs and forgetting inputs that do not

Different people perceive the same thing at the same time in different ways. When you first look at Figure 8.5, do you see the fish changing into birds or the birds changing into fish? Similarly, an individual at different times may perceive the same item in a number of ways. **Perception** is the process of selecting, organizing, and interpreting information inputs to produce meaning. **Information inputs** are sensations received through sight, taste, hearing, smell, and touch. When we hear an advertisement, see a friend, smell polluted air or water, or touch a product, we receive information inputs.

As the definition indicates, perception is a three-step process. Although we receive numerous pieces of information at once, only a few reach awareness. We select some inputs and ignore others because we do not have the ability to be conscious of all inputs at one time. This phenomenon is sometimes called **selective exposure** because an individual selects which inputs will reach awareness. If you are concentrating on this paragraph, you probably are not aware that cars are outside making noise, that the light is on, or that you are touching this page. Even though you receive these inputs, they do not reach your awareness until they are mentioned.

An individual's current set of needs affects selective exposure. Information inputs that relate to one's strongest needs at a given time are more likely to be selected to reach awareness. It is not by random chance that many fast-food commercials are aired near meal times. Customers are more likely to tune in to these advertisements at these times.

The selective nature of perception may result not only in selective exposure, but also in two other conditions: selective distortion and selective retention. **Selective distortion** is changing or twisting currently received information; it occurs when a person receives information inconsistent with personal feelings or beliefs. For example, on seeing an advertisement promoting a disliked brand, a viewer may distort the information to make it more consistent with prior views. This distortion substantially lessens the effect of the advertisement on the individual. In the case of **selective retention,** a person remembers information inputs that support personal feelings and beliefs and forgets inputs that do not. After hearing a sales presentation and leaving a store, a customer may forget many selling points if they contradict personal beliefs.

The second step in the process of perception is perceptual organization. Information inputs that do reach awareness are not received in an organized form. To produce meaning, an individual must mentally organize and integrate new information with what is already stored in memory. People use several methods to organize. One method, called *closure,* occurs when a person mentally fills in missing elements in a pattern or statement. An advertiser, in an attempt to draw attention to its brand, will capitalize on closure by using incomplete images, sounds, or statements in its advertisements.

Interpretation—the third step in the perceptual process—is the assignment of meaning to what has been organized. A person bases interpretation on what he or she expects or what is familiar. For this reason, a manufacturer that changes a product or its package faces a major problem. When people are looking for the old familiar product or package, they may not recognize the new one. For instance, when Smucker's redesigned its packaging, marketers told designers that although they wanted a more contemporary package design, they also wanted a classic look so that customers would perceive their products to be the familiar ones they had been buying for years. Unless a product or package change is accompanied by a promotional program that makes people aware of the change, an organization may suffer a sales decline.

Although marketers cannot control buyers' perceptions, they often try to influence them through information. Several problems may arise from such attempts, however. First, a consumer's perceptual process may operate so that a seller's information never reaches that person. For example, a buyer may block out a salesperson's presentation. Second, a buyer may receive a seller's information but perceive it differently than was intended. For example, when a toothpaste producer advertises that "35 percent of the people who use this toothpaste have fewer cavities," a customer could infer that 65 percent of those using the product have more cavities. Third, a buyer who perceives information inputs to be inconsistent with prior beliefs is likely to forget the information quickly.

Motives

motive   An internal energizing force that directs a person's behavior toward satisfying needs or achieving goals

A **motive** is an internal energizing force that orients a person's activities toward satisfying needs or achieving goals. Buyers' actions are affected by a set of motives rather than by just one motive. At a single point in time, some of a person's motives are stronger than others. For example, a person's motives for having a cup of coffee are much stronger right after waking up than just before going to bed. Motives also affect the direction and intensity of behavior. Some motives may help an individual achieve his or her goals, whereas others create barriers to goal achievement.

Maslow's hierarchy of needs   The five levels of needs that humans seek to satisfy, from most to least important

Abraham Maslow, an American psychologist, conceived a theory of motivation based on a hierarchy of needs. According to Maslow, humans seek to satisfy five levels of needs, from most important to least important, as shown in Figure 8.6. This sequence is known as **Maslow's hierarchy of needs.** Once needs at one level are met, humans seek to fulfill needs at the next level up in the hierarchy.

Figure 8.6
Maslow's Hierarchy of Needs Maslow believed that people seek to fulfill five categories of needs.

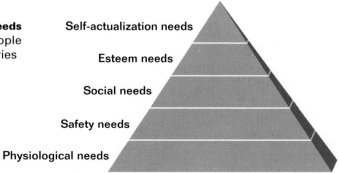

Self-actualization needs

Esteem needs

Social needs

Safety needs

Physiological needs

At the most basic level are *physiological needs,* requirements for survival such as food, water, sex, clothing, and shelter, which people try to satisfy first. Food and beverage marketers often appeal to physiological needs. Marketers of whitening toothpastes, such as Ultrabrite, sometimes promote their brands based on sex appeal.

At the next level are *safety needs,* which include security and freedom from physical and emotional pain and suffering. Life insurance, automobile air bags, carbon monoxide detectors, vitamins, and decay-fighting toothpastes are products that consumers purchase to meet safety needs.

Next are *social needs,* the human requirements for love and affection and a sense of belonging. Advertisements frequently appeal to social needs. Ads for cosmetics and other beauty products, jewelry, and even cars often suggest that purchasing these products will bring love. Certain types of trendy clothing, such as Gap khakis, Nike athletic shoes, or T-shirts imprinted with logos or slogans, appeal to the customers' need to belong.

At the level of *esteem needs,* people require respect and recognition from others as well as self-esteem, a sense of their own worth. Owning a Lexus automobile, having a beauty makeover, or flying first class can satisfy esteem needs.

At the top of the hierarchy are *self-actualization needs.* These refer to people's need to grow and to develop and to become all they are capable of becoming. Some of the products that satisfy these needs include fitness center memberships, education, self-improvement workshops, and skiing lessons. In its recruiting advertisements, the U.S. Army tells potential enlistees to "be all that you can be in the Army." These messages imply that people can reach their full potential in the U.S. Army.

patronage motives
Motives that influence where a person purchases products on a regular basis

Motives that influence where a person purchases products on a regular basis are called **patronage motives.** A buyer may shop at a specific store because of such patronage motives as price, service, location, product variety, or friendliness of salespeople. To capitalize on patronage motives, marketers try to determine why regular customers patronize a store and to emphasize these characteristics in the store's marketing mix.

Learning

learning   Changes in an individual's thought processes and behavior caused by information and experience

Learning refers to changes in a person's thought processes and behavior caused by information and experience. Consequences of behavior strongly influence the learning process. Behaviors that result in satisfying consequences tend to be repeated. For example, a consumer who buys a Snickers candy bar and enjoys the taste is more likely to buy a Snickers again. In fact, the individual will probably continue to purchase that brand until it no longer provides satisfaction. When effects of the behavior are no longer satisfying, the person may switch brands or stop eating candy bars altogether.

When making purchasing decisions, buyers process information. Individuals have differing abilities in this regard. The type of information inexperienced buyers use may differ from the type used by experienced shoppers familiar with the product and purchase situation. Inexperienced buyers use price as an indicator of quality more frequently than do buyers with some knowledge of a particular product category.[5] Thus, two potential purchasers of an antique desk may use different types of information in making their purchase decisions. The inexperienced buyer may judge the desk's value by price, whereas the more experienced buyer may seek information about the manufacturer, period, and place of origin to judge the desk's quality and value. Consumers lacking experience may seek information from others when making a purchase and even take along an informed "purchase pal." More experienced buyers have greater self-confidence and more knowledge about the product and can recognize which product features are reliable cues to product quality.

Marketers help customers learn about their products by letting them gain experience with them. Free samples, sometimes coupled with coupons, can successfully encourage trial and reduce purchase risk. For example, because some consumers may be wary of exotic menu items, restaurants sometimes offer free samples. In-store demonstrations foster knowledge of product uses. A software producer may use point-of-sale product demonstrations to introduce a new product. Test drives give potential new car purchasers some experience with an automobile's features.

Consumers also learn by experiencing products indirectly, through information from salespersons, advertisements, friends, and relatives. Through sales personnel and advertisements, marketers offer information before (and sometimes after) purchases to influence what consumers learn and to create more favorable attitudes toward the products. Yet their efforts are seldom fully successful. Marketers encounter problems in attracting and holding consumers' attention, in providing consumers with important information for making purchase decisions, and in convincing them to try the product.

Attitudes

attitude   An individual's enduring evaluation, feelings, and behavioral tendencies toward an object or idea

An **attitude** is an individual's enduring evaluation, feelings, and behavioral tendencies toward an object or idea. The objects toward which we have attitudes may be tangible or intangible, living or nonliving. For example, we have attitudes toward sex, religion, politics, and music, just as we do toward cars, football, and what we eat for breakfast. Over the last twenty-five years, Americans have increased their per capita consumption of corn cereals by 97 percent and oat cereals by 93 percent, and cut their per capita consumption of milk by 18 percent, coffee by 22 percent, and eggs by 24 percent.[6] Although attitudes do change, an individual's attitudes remain generally stable and do not vary from moment to moment. However, all of a person's attitudes do not have equal impact at any one time; some are stronger than others. Individuals acquire attitudes through experience and interaction with other people.

An attitude consists of three major components: cognitive, affective, and behavioral. The cognitive component is a person's knowledge and information about the object or idea, whereas the affective component comprises feelings and emotions toward the object or idea. The behavioral component manifests itself in a person's actions regarding the object or idea. Changes in one of these components may or may not alter the other components. Thus, a consumer may become more knowledgeable about a specific brand without changing the affective or behavioral components of his or her attitude toward that brand.

Consumer attitudes toward a company and its products greatly influence success or failure of the firm's marketing strategy. When consumers have strong negative attitudes toward one or more aspects of a firm's marketing practices, they may not only stop using its products, but also urge relatives and friends to do likewise.

Because attitudes play such an important part in determining consumer behavior, marketers should measure consumer attitudes toward prices, package designs, brand names, advertisements, salespeople, repair services, store locations, features of existing or proposed products, and social responsibility efforts. Several methods help marketers gauge these attitudes. One of the simplest ways is to question people directly. An attitude researcher for a computer keyboard manufacturer, for example, might ask respondents what they think about the style and design of its newest keyboard.

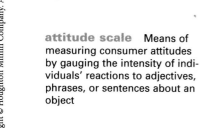

attitude scale   Means of measuring consumer attitudes by gauging the intensity of individuals' reactions to adjectives, phrases, or sentences about an object

Marketers also evaluate attitudes through attitude scales. An **attitude scale** usually consists of a series of adjectives, phrases, or sentences about an object. Respondents indicate the intensity of their feelings toward the object by reacting to the adjectives, phrases, or sentences in a certain way. For example, a marketer measuring people's attitudes toward shopping might ask respondents to indicate the degree to which they agree or disagree with a number of statements, such as "Shopping is more fun than watching television." By using an attitude scale, a marketing research company was able to identify and classify six major types of clothing purchasers. The scale was based on such attributes as demographics, media use, and purchase behavior.

When marketers determine that a significant number of consumers have negative attitudes toward an aspect of a marketing mix, they may try to change those attitudes to make them more favorable. This task is generally long, expensive, and difficult and may require extensive promotional efforts. For example, the California Prune

Growers, an organization of prune producers, has tried to use advertising to change consumers' attitudes toward prunes by presenting them as a nutritious snack high in potassium and fiber.[7] To alter consumers' responses so that more of them buy a given brand, a firm might launch an information-focused campaign to change the cognitive component of a consumer's attitude, or a persuasive (emotional) campaign to influence the affective component. Distributing free samples might help change the behavioral component. Both business and nonbusiness organizations try to change people's attitudes about many things, from health and safety to prices and product features.

Personality and Self-Concept

Personality is a set of internal traits and distinct behavioral tendencies that result in consistent patterns of behavior in certain situations. An individual's personality arises from hereditary characteristics and personal experiences that make the individual unique. Personalities typically are described as having one or more characteristics, such as compulsiveness, ambition, gregariousness, dogmatism, authoritarianism, introversion, extroversion, and competitiveness. Marketing researchers look for relationships between such characteristics and buying behavior. Even though a few links between several personality traits and buyer behavior have been determined, results of many studies have been inconclusive. The weak association between personality and buying behavior may be the result of unreliable measures rather than a lack of a relationship. A number of marketers are convinced that consumers' personalities do influence types and brands of products purchased. For example, the type of clothing, jewelry, or automobile a person buys may reflect one or more personality characteristics.

At times, marketers aim advertising at certain types of personalities. For example, ads for certain cigarette brands are directed toward specific types of personalities. Marketers focus on positively valued personality characteristics, such as security

Figure 8.7
Self-Concept
Hi-Tec boots uses this advertisement to appeal to individuals whose self-concepts include being adventuresome.

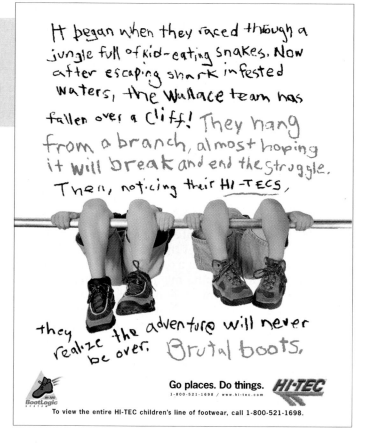

Figure 8.8
Lifestyle Influences
The Globe Corner Bookstore appeals to people who enjoy travel.

consciousness, gregariousness, independence, or competitiveness, not negatively valued ones like insensitivity or timidity.

self-concept Perception or view of oneself

A person's self-concept is closely linked to personality. **Self-concept** (sometimes called self-image) is a person's view or perception of himself or herself. Individuals develop and alter their self-concept based on an interaction of psychological and social dimensions. Research shows that a buyer purchases products that reflect and enhance the self-concept and that purchase decisions are important to the development and maintenance of a stable self-concept. Consumers' self-concept may influence whether they buy a product in a specific product category and may have an impact on brand selection as well. For example, if a person's self-concept includes being adventuresome, the ad for Hi-Tec boots in Figure 8.7 might be of interest.

Lifestyles

lifestyle An individual's pattern of living expressed through activities, interests, and opinions

A **lifestyle** is an individual's pattern of living expressed through activities, interests, and opinions. Lifestyle patterns include the ways people spend time, the extent of their interaction with others, and their general outlook on life and living. People partially determine their own lifestyles, but the pattern is also affected by personality, as well as by demographic factors such as age, education, income, and social class. Lifestyles are measured through a lengthy series of questions.

Lifestyles have a strong impact on many aspects of the consumer buying decision process—from problem recognition to postpurchase evaluation. Lifestyles influence consumers' product needs, brand preferences, types of media used, and how and where they shop. The Globe Corner Bookstore (Figure 8.8) focuses on people who enjoy travel.

Social Influences on the Buying Decision Process

social influences The forces that other people exert on one's buying behavior

Forces that other people exert on buying behavior are called **social influences.** As shown in Figure 8.2, they are grouped into five major areas: roles, family, reference groups and opinion leaders, social classes, and culture and subcultures.

He leads a double life.

At work, he's tough. At home, he's nurturing. But when it comes

to protecting his family and their financial future, he leans

on one source.   His New England representative.

Everyone leads multiple lives. It's part of living in these tricky times. It's nice to know that so many successful people have been coming to The New England for exceptional insurance and financial advice. We have the ability to handle all facets of their lives, both personal and professional. We've been doing it for over 160 years. Our financial strength is reassuring. But it's our commitment to serving everyone on an individual basis that really makes the difference when handling as many aspects of your life as possible.

Planning for your success.

For your complimentary personalized financial needs analysis, please call 1-800-955-1079.

E-mail us at: asktne@tne.com or visit our Web site: http://www.tne.com

NE The New England®
Insurance and Investment

A MetLife Affiliate

New England Life Insurance Co., Boston, MA. Securities products offered through New England Securities Corp., Boston, MA.

Figure 8.9
Role Influences
As The New England puts it, "He leads a double life." The influences of double roles affect the purchase decision process for many products, including insurance and other financial services.

role Actions and activities that a person in a particular position is supposed to perform, based on expectations of the individual and surrounding persons

consumer socialization
The process through which a person acquires the knowledge and skills to function as a consumer

Roles

All of us occupy positions within groups, organizations, and institutions. Associated with each position is a **role**—a set of actions and activities a person in a particular position is supposed to perform, based on expectations of both the individual and surrounding persons. Because people occupy numerous positions, they have many roles. For example, a man may perform the roles of son, husband, father, employee or employer, church member, civic organization member, and student in an evening college class. The New England ad in Figure 8.9 focuses on multiple roles. Thus, multiple sets of expectations are placed on each person's behavior.

An individual's roles influence both general behavior and buying behavior. The demands of a person's many roles may be diverse and even inconsistent. Consider, for example, the various types of clothes that you buy and wear depending on whether you are going to class, going to work, going to a sorority party, going to church, or going to your aerobics class. You and the people in these organizations have expectations about what is acceptable clothing for these events. Thus, the expectations of those around us affect the purchases of clothing and many other products.

Family Influences

Family influences have a very direct impact on the consumer buying decision process. Parents teach children how to cope with a variety of problems, including those dealing with purchase decisions. **Consumer socialization** is the process through which a person acquires the knowledge and skills to function as a consumer. Often, children gain this knowledge and set of skills by observing parents and older siblings in purchase situations, as well as through their own purchase experiences. Children observe brand preferences and buying practices in their families and, as adults, use some of these brand preferences and buying practices as they establish and raise their own families. Buying decisions made by a family are a combination of group decision making and individual decision making.

Although female roles continue to change, women still make buying decisions related to many household items, including health care products, laundry supplies, paper products, and foods. Spouses participate jointly in the purchase of a variety of products, especially durable goods. Due to changes in men's roles, a significant proportion of men are major grocery shoppers. Children make many purchase decisions and influence numerous household purchase decisions.

The extent to which either one or both of the two adult family members take part in family decision making varies among families and product categories. Traditionally, family decision-making processes have been grouped into four categories: autonomic, husband-dominant, wife-dominant, and syncratic. Autonomic decision making means that an equal number of decisions are made by each adult household member. In husband-dominant or wife-dominant decision making, the husband or the wife makes most of the family decisions. Syncratic decision making means that most decisions concerning purchases are made jointly by both partners. The type of family decision making employed depends on the values and attitudes of family members.

When two or more family members participate in a purchase, their roles may dictate that each is responsible for performing certain purchase-related tasks, such as initiating the idea, gathering information, determining if the product is affordable, deciding whether to buy the product, or selecting the specific brand. The specific purchase tasks performed depend on the types of products being considered, the kind of family purchase decision process typically employed, and the amount of influence that children have in the decision process. Thus, different family members may play different roles in the family buying process. To develop a marketing mix that precisely meets the needs of target market members, marketers must know not only who does the actual buying, but also which other family members perform purchase-related tasks.

The family life cycle stage affects individual and joint needs of family members. (Family life cycle stages were discussed in Chapter 7.) For example, consider how the car needs of recently married "twenty-somethings" differ from those of the same couple when they are "forty-somethings" with a 13-year-old daughter and a 17-year-old son. Family life cycle changes can affect which family members are involved in purchase decisions and the types of products purchased.

Reference Groups and Opinion Leaders

reference group   Any group that positively or negatively affects a person's values, attitudes, or behavior

A **reference group** is any group that positively or negatively affects a person's values, attitudes, or behavior. Reference groups can be large or small. Most people have several reference groups, such as families, work-related groups, fraternities, sororities, civic clubs, professional organizations, or church-related groups.

In general, there are three major types of reference groups: membership, aspirational, and disassociative. A membership reference group is one to which an individual actually belongs; the individual identifies with group members strongly enough to take on the values, attitudes, and behaviors of people in that group. An aspirational reference group is a group to which one aspires to belong; one desires to be like those group members. A group that a person does not wish to be associated with is a disassociative reference group; the individual does not want to take on the values, attitudes, and behavior of group members.

A reference group may serve as an individual's point of comparison and source of information. A customer's behavior may change to be more in line with actions and beliefs of group members. For example, a person might stop buying one brand of shirts and switch to another based on reference-group members' advice. An individual may also seek information from the reference group about other factors regarding a prospective purchase, such as where to buy a certain product.

The extent to which a reference group affects a purchase decision depends on the product's conspicuousness and on an individual's susceptibility to reference-group influence. Generally, the more conspicuous a product, the more likely that the purchase decision will be influenced by reference groups. The degree of a product's conspicuousness is determined by whether it can be seen by others and whether it can attract attention. Reference groups can affect whether you do or do not buy a product at all, buy a type of product within a product category, or buy a specific brand.

A marketer sometimes tries to use reference-group influence in advertisements by suggesting that people in a specific group buy a product and are highly satisfied with it. In this type of appeal, the advertiser hopes that many will accept the suggested group as a reference group and buy (or react more favorably to) the product. Whether this kind of advertising succeeds depends on three factors: how effectively the advertisement communicates the message, the type of product, and the individual's susceptibility to reference-group influence.

opinion leader   A reference-group member who provides information about a specific sphere that interests reference-group participants

In most reference groups, one or more members stand out as opinion leaders. An **opinion leader** provides information about a specific sphere that interests reference-group participants who seek information. Opinion leaders are viewed by other group members as being well informed about a particular area and as easily accessible. An opinion leader is not the foremost authority on all issues. However, because such individuals know that they are opinion leaders, they feel a responsibility to remain informed about their sphere of interest and thus seek out advertisements, manufacturers' brochures, salespeople, and other sources of information.

An opinion leader is likely to be most influential when consumers have high product involvement but low product knowledge, when they share the opinion leader's values and attitudes, and when the product details are numerous or complicated.

Social Classes

social class An open group of individuals with similar social rank

In all societies, people rank others into higher or lower positions of respect. This ranking results in social classes. A **social class** is an open group of individuals with similar social rank. A class is referred to as "open" because people can move into and out of it. Criteria for grouping people into classes vary from one society to another. In the United States, we take into account many factors, including occupation, education, income, wealth, race, ethnic group, and possessions. A person who is ranking someone does not necessarily apply all of a society's criteria. Sometimes, too, the role of income in social class determination tends to be overemphasized. Although income does help determine social class, the other factors mentioned also figure in social class assessment. Within social classes, both incomes and spending habits differ significantly among members.

Table 8.1   Social Class Behavioral Traits and Purchasing Characteristics

Class (% of Population)	Behavioral Traits	Buying Characteristics
Upper (14%); includes upper-upper, lower-upper, upper-middle	Income varies among the groups, but goals are the same Various lifestyles: preppy, conventional, intellectual, etc. Neighborhood and prestigious schooling important	Prize quality merchandise Favor prestigious brands Products purchased must reflect good taste Invest in art Spend money on travel, theater, books, tennis, golf, and swimming clubs
Middle (32%)	Often in management Considered white collar Prize good schools Desire an attractive home in a nice, well-maintained neighborhood Often emulate the upper class Enjoy travel and physical activity Often very involved in children's school and sports activities	Like fashionable items Consult experts via books, articles, etc., before purchasing Spend for experiences they consider worthwhile for their children (e.g., ski trips, college education) Tour packages, weekend trips Attractive home furnishings
Working (38%)	Emphasis on family, especially for economic and emotional supports (e.g., job opportunity tips, help in times of trouble) Blue collar Earn good incomes Enjoy mechanical items and recreational activities Enjoy leisure time after working hard	Buy vehicles and equipment related to recreation, camping, and selected sports Strong sense of value Shop for best bargains at off-price and discount stores Purchase automotive equipment for making repairs Enjoy local travel, recreational parks
Lower (16%)	Often down and out through no fault of their own (e.g., layoffs, company takeovers) Can include individuals on welfare and the homeless Often have strong religious beliefs May be forced to live in less desirable neighborhoods In spite of their problems, often good-hearted toward others Enjoy everyday activities when possible	Most products purchased are for survival Ability to convert good discards into usable items

Source: Adapted with permission from Richard P. Coleman, "The Continuing Significance of Social Class to Marketing," *Journal of Consumer Research*, Dec. 1983, pp. 265–280, with data from J. Paul Peter and Jerry C. Olson, *Consumer Behavior: Marketing Strategy Perspective* (Homewood, Ill.: Irwin, 1987), p. 433.

We deliver.

Pittsburgh Water Cooler Service, Inc. 682-2147

Figure 8.10
Social Class Influences
In this advertisement, Pittsburgh Water Cooler appeals to consumers in the upper classes.

Analyses of social class in the United States commonly divide people into three to seven categories. Social scientist Richard P. Coleman suggests that for purposes of consumer analysis the population be divided into the four major status groups shown in Table 8.1, but he cautions marketers that considerable diversity exists in people's life situations within each status group.

To some degree, persons within social classes develop and assume common behavioral patterns. They may have similar attitudes, values, language patterns, and possessions. Social class influences many aspects of our lives. For example, it affects our chances of having children and their chances of surviving infancy. It influences our childhood training, choice of religion, selection of occupation, and leisure time activities. Because social class has a bearing on so many aspects of a person's life, it also affects buying decisions.

Social class influences people's spending, saving, and credit practices. It determines to some extent the type, quality, and quantity of products that a person buys and uses. For example, it affects our purchases of clothing, foods, financial and health care services, travel, recreation, entertainment, and home furnishings. Social class also affects an individual's shopping patterns and types of stores patronized. In some instances, marketers attempt to focus on certain social classes through store location and interior design, product design and features, pricing strategies, personal sales efforts, and advertising. For example, in Figure 8.10, Pittsburgh Water Cooler focuses on upper social classes.

Culture and Subcultures

culture The values, knowledge, beliefs, customs, objects, and concepts of a society

Culture is the accumulation of values, knowledge, beliefs, customs, objects, and concepts that a society uses to cope with its environment and passes on to future generations. Examples of the objects are foods, furniture, buildings, clothing, and tools. Concepts include education, welfare, and laws. Culture also includes core values and the degree of acceptability of a wide range of behaviors in a specific society. For example, in our culture not only are businesspeople expected to behave ethically, but customers are expected to meet ethical standards as well.

Culture influences buying behavior because it permeates our daily lives. Our culture determines what we wear and eat and where we reside and travel. Society's interest in the healthfulness of food affects food companies' approaches to developing and promoting their products. Culture also influences how we buy and use products and our satisfaction from them. In the U.S. culture, makers of furniture, cars, and clothing strive to understand how people's color preferences are changing. Currently, preferences for dramatic dark hues and lighter, brighter, softer colors are growing.[8]

SNAPSHOT

Multicultural affluence and buying power
The U.S. Census Bureau reports that these are the three largest and fastest growing segments of the U.S. population.

African-American   Hispanic   Asian

Households with annual income over $100,000
- 259,000
- 193,000
- 111,000

Buying power (in billions)
- $400
- $270
- $220

FOR SALE
UNDER CONTRACT

Because culture to some degree determines product purchases and uses, cultural changes affect product development, promotion, distribution, and pricing. Food marketers, for example, have made a multitude of changes in their marketing efforts. Thirty years ago, most families in our culture ate at least two meals a day together, and the mother spent four to six hours a day preparing those meals. Now, more than 75 percent of women between the ages of 25 and 54 work outside the home, and average family incomes have risen considerably. These shifts, along with the problem of time scarcity, have resulted in dramatic changes in the national per capita consumption of certain foods: take-out foods, frozen dinners, and shelf-stable foods.

When U.S. marketers sell products in other countries, they realize the tremendous impact that culture has on product purchases and use. Global marketers find that people in other regions of the world have different attitudes, values, and needs, which call for different methods of doing business, as well as different types of marketing mixes. (See Global Marketing for a discussion on how Avon applies its knowledge of consumer buying behavior around the World.) Some international marketers fail because they do not or cannot adjust to cultural differences.

A culture consists of various subcultures. **Subcultures** are groups of individuals whose characteristic values and behavior patterns are similar and differ from those of the surrounding culture. Subcultural boundaries are usually based on geographic designations and demographic characteristics, such as age, religion, race, and ethnicity. Our culture is marked by a number of different subcultures, among them, West Coast, teenage, Asian-American, and college students. Within subcultures, greater similarities exist in people's attitudes, values, and actions than within the broader culture. Relative to other subcultures, individuals in one subculture may have stronger preferences for specific types of clothing, furniture, or foods. For example, a significant proportion of college students (about one-half of the women and one-third of the men) support the concept of vegetarianism, although their diets are not strictly meatless. Among similar-aged persons not attending college, the percentage of people eating primarily vegetarian diets is considerably less.[9] It is important to understand that a person can be a member of more than one subculture and that the behavioral patterns and values attributed to specific subcultures do not necessarily apply to all group members.

In the twenty-first century, the percentage of the American population comprising ethnic and racial subcultures will grow. By 2050, about one-half of the people of the United States will be members of racial and ethnic minorities. The Bureau of the Census reports that the three largest and fastest growing ethnic U.S. subcultures are African-Americans, Hispanics, and Asians. The population growth of these subcultures interests marketers. To target these groups more precisely, marketers are striving to become increasingly sensitive to and knowledgeable about their differences. Businesses recognize that to succeed, their marketing strategies will have to take into account the values, needs, interests, shopping patterns, and buying habits of various subcultures.

African-American Subculture
In the United States, the largest racial or ethnic subculture is African-American. Since 1990, African-American consumer spending has increased 54 percent nationwide.[10] Research reveals that African-American consumers possess distinct buying patterns. For example, African-American consumers shop as often as four times a week and spend more on boys' clothing, athletic footwear, personal care services, and automobile rentals than do white consumers. In 1996,

subcultures Groups of individuals whose characteristic values and behavior patterns are similar and differ from those of the surrounding culture

African-Americans spent twice as much per person as white consumers for online services.[11] Compared with white consumers, African-Americans use coupons less often. In addition, research reveals that African-Americans respond positively to advertising and products that reflect their heritage and prefer promotional messages appearing in media that target them specifically. They most commonly learn about products from television advertisements, salespeople, and information provided by calling manufacturers' toll-free numbers.

Increasingly, organizations are directing marketing efforts toward African-American consumers. More African-Americans are featured in advertisements for a wide array of products, including automobiles, athletic shoes, clothing, cosmetics, fast foods, soft drinks, and telecommunication services. In 1987, Hallmark Cards launched its Afrocentric brand, Mahogany, with sixteen cards. Today, Mahogany's selection includes eight hundred different cards. Sears created its Mosaic clothing line specifically for African-American women. The retailer plans to spend about $15 million a year to market this line to African-Americans.[12]

Hispanic Subculture In the next ten years, Hispanics will become the largest ethnic group in the United States. Industry experts estimate that the purchasing power of Hispanics will almost double in less than four years.[13] Because of its growth and purchasing power, understanding the Hispanic subculture is critical to marketers. In general, Hispanics have strong family values, a need for respect, concern for product quality, and strong brand loyalty. Studies reveal that the majority of Hispanic consumers not only are brand-loyal, but also will pay more for a well-known brand. They tend to spend more time shopping in grocery stores than other consumers but use far fewer coupons. Promotions using Hispanic celebrities are effective in getting marketing messages across to Hispanic audiences. Incorporating prominent members of the Hispanic

Globalmarketing

Avon: A Fresh Face in Global Markets

Understanding customer behavior means money—big money—for Avon Products and most other companies. Now in its second century of direct sales, Avon is among the ten best-selling cosmetics brands in the world. But Avon has faced difficult challenges in recent years. In the United States, where the company is struggling with a dowdy image and drooping profits, it is mounting a "makeover" by opening a stylish Manhattan spa, expanding its product line, and airing hip new ads.

Avon's main strength is outside the United States, where double-digit annual sales growth has pushed non-U.S. revenues past $3 billion. More than two million representatives in 135 countries, from Argentina to Vietnam, sell Avon products. Despite financial and political upheavals in South America and Asia, the company continues to build customer relationships there by using its knowledge of consumer buying behavior.

Many beauty brands appeal to the customer's self-concept and need for esteem by hinting at luxury and status. Avon takes a different approach in global markets, positioning its cosmetics as affordable glamour, Western-style. Knowing that brand names influence customer attitudes, the company has unified numerous product lines under a few simple but evocative global brand names like Color Trend cosmetics, sold in forty countries, and Far Away fragrances, sold in sixty-two countries.

Before Avon opens for business in any country, it thoroughly investigates the culture and the key social influences. For example, as more women enter the work force in other countries, they have less time to shop. Avon has found these customers highly receptive to representatives who visit them at home or at work to demonstrate new products and offer beauty tips. The company has also expanded its sponsorship of running events into global markets to send the message that women's health is as important as their looks.

Customers are clearly responding to Avon's approach. Sales in Russia skyrocketed to $56 million in just four years, and the company has enjoyed similar sales growth in China. Looking ahead, Avon sees Kazakhstan and other developing nations as the next beauty frontier.

community, such as athletes and performers, in promotions is often successful. For many adult Hispanics, the language of choice is Spanish. Recently, *People* magazine launched *People en Espanol* and initially expects to reach 300,000 Hispanics per issue.[14] Studies reveal that Hispanics respond strongly to ads on Spanish television and radio. Shopping is more likely to be a family event in Hispanic households. When considering the buying behavior of Hispanics, marketers must keep in mind that this subculture is really composed of nearly two dozen nationalities, including Cuban, Mexican, Puerto Rican, Caribbean, Spanish, and Dominican. Each has its own history and unique culture that affect consumer preferences and buying behavior.

To attract this powerful subculture, marketers are taking Hispanic values and preferences into account when developing products and creating advertising and promotions. Recognizing that Hispanics are family-oriented and fond of eating out, McDonald's, Denny's, and Churchs Chicken actively market to Hispanics. Recently, Burger King launched campaigns directed at this subculture. Dallas-based Carnival Food Stores works hard to understand their Hispanic customers. Carnival has bilingual employees; provides signs, brochures, and all promotional materials in Spanish; and runs a Spanish infomercial and special Hispanic "customer appreciation" promotions.[15] Procter & Gamble's recent launch of a shelf-stable version of its orange-flavored drink, Sunny Delight, and its efforts to move the drink into convenience stores were driven by the desire to reach Hispanic consumers. Sunny Delight's flavor appeals to this subculture's preference for sweet drinks. Procter & Gamble has also developed Spanish-language television spots for Sunny Delight.[16]

Asian-American Subculture   Asian-Americans are the fastest growing, most affluent, and perhaps the most diverse American subculture. The term "Asian-American" includes people from more than fifteen ethnic groups, including Filipinos, Chinese, Japanese, Indians, Koreans, and Vietnamese. The individual language, religion, and value system of each group influences its members' purchasing decisions. Some traits of this subculture, however, carry across ethnic divisions, including an emphasis on hard work, strong family ties, and a high value placed on education. Asian-Americans prefer to communicate and to read and listen to media in their native languages. With respect to buying behavior, marketers recognize that Asians are generally willing to pay more for distinct, well-known brands.

Retailers with a large population of Chinese shoppers have begun to capitalize on this group's celebration of the Chinese Lunar New Year. For example, during this time in the Los Angeles area, supermarkets stock traditional Chinese holiday foods and items used in the celebration, such as candles, greeting cards, and party goods.[17] According to SRI/Gallup, 63 percent of Asian-Americans purchased new cars in 1996, compared with only 43 percent of car buyers in general. With this statistic in mind, Toyota dealers in the Los Angeles area began to advertise in Chinese media. Since the launch of this targeted advertising, ownership of Toyotas among Asian-Americans has increased from 25 percent in 1989 to 44 percent today.[18]

Summary

Buying behavior is the decision processes and acts of people involved in buying and using products. Consumer buying behavior refers to the buying behavior of ultimate consumers.

An individual's level of involvement—the importance and intensity of interest in a product in a particular situation—affects the type of problem-solving process used. Enduring involvement is an ongoing interest in a product class because of personal relevance, whereas situational involvement is a temporary interest stemming from the particular circumstance or environment in which buyers find themselves. There are three kinds of consumer problem solving: routinized response behavior, limited problem solving, and extended problem solving.

Consumers rely on routinized response behavior when buying frequently purchased, low-cost items requiring little search-and-decision effort. Limited problem solving is used for products purchased occasionally or when buyers need to acquire information about an unfamiliar brand in a familiar product category. Consumers engage in extended problem solving when purchasing an unfamiliar, expensive, or infrequently bought product. Purchase of a certain product does not always elicit the same type of decision making. Impulse buying is not a consciously planned buying behavior but involves a powerful urge to buy something immediately.

The consumer buying decision process includes five stages: problem recognition, information search, evaluation of alternatives, purchase, and postpurchase evaluation. Not all decision processes culminate in a purchase, nor do all consumer decisions always include all five stages. Problem recognition occurs when buyers become aware of a difference between a desired state and an actual condition. After recognizing the problem or need, buyers search for information about products to help resolve the problem or satisfy the need. In the internal search, buyers search their memories for information about products that might solve the problem. If they cannot retrieve from memory enough information for a decision, they seek additional information through an external search. A successful search yields a group of brands, called a consideration set, that a buyer views as possible alternatives. To evaluate the products in the consideration set, a buyer establishes certain criteria by which to compare, rate, and rank different products. Marketers can influence consumers' evaluation by framing alternatives.

In the purchase stage, consumers select products or brands on the basis of results from the evaluation stage and on other dimensions. Buyers also choose the seller from whom they will buy the product. After the purchase, buyers evaluate the product to determine if its actual performance meets expected levels. Shortly after the purchase of an expensive product, for example, the postpurchase evaluation may result in cognitive dissonance, which is dissatisfaction brought on by the consumer's doubts as to whether he or she should have bought the product in the first place or would have been better off buying another desirable brand.

Three major categories of influences affect the consumer buying decision process: situational, psychological, and social. Situational influences are external circumstances or conditions existing when a consumer makes a purchase decision. Situational influences include surroundings, time, purchase reason, and buyer's mood and condition.

Psychological influences partly determine people's general behavior, thus influencing their behavior as consumers. The primary psychological influences on consumer behavior are perception, motives, learning, attitudes, personality and self-concept, and lifestyles. Perception is the process of selecting, organizing, and interpreting information inputs (sensations received through sight, taste, hearing, smell, and touch) to produce meaning. The three steps in the perceptual process are selection, organization, and interpretation. Individuals have numerous perceptions of packages, products, brands, and organizations, which affect their buying decision processes. A motive is an internal energizing force that orients a person's activities toward satisfying needs or achieving goals. Learning refers to changes in a person's thought processes and behavior caused by information and experience. Marketers try to influence what consumers learn in order to influence what they buy. An attitude is an individual's enduring evaluation, feelings, and behavioral tendencies toward an object or idea. An attitude refers to positive or negative feelings about an object or idea and consists of three major components: cognitive, affective, and behavioral. Personality is the set of traits and behaviors that make a person unique. Self-concept is closely linked to personality. Self-concept is a person's view or perception of himself or herself. Research indicates that buyers purchase products that reflect and enhance their self-concept. Lifestyle is an individual's pattern of living expressed through activities, interests, and opinions. Lifestyles influence consumers' needs, brand preferences, and how and where they shop.

Forces that other people exert on buying behavior are called social influences. Social influences include roles, family, reference groups and opinion leaders, social class, and culture and subcultures. Everyone occupies positions within groups, organizations, and institutions, and each position has a role—a set of actions and activities that a person in a particular position is supposed to perform, based on expectations of both the individual and surrounding persons. In a family, children learn from parents and siblings how to make decisions, such as purchase decisions. Consumer socialization is the process through which a person acquires the knowledge and skills to function as a consumer. The consumer socialization process is partially accomplished through family influences. A reference group is any group that positively or negatively affects a person's values, attitudes, or behavior. The three major types of reference groups are membership, aspirational, and disassociative. In most reference groups, one or more members stand out as opinion leaders by furnishing requested information to reference-group participants. A social class is an open group of individuals with similar social rank. Social class influences people's spending, saving, and credit practices. Culture is the accumulation of values, knowledge, beliefs, customs, objects, and concepts that a society uses to cope with its environment and passes on to future generations. A culture is made up of subcultures. A subculture is a group of individuals whose characteristic values and behavior patterns are similar and differ from those of the surrounding culture. Marketers focus on three major ethnic subcultures: African-American, Hispanic, and Asian-American.

Important Terms

Buying behavior
Consumer buying
  behavior
Level of involvement
Routinized response
  behavior
Limited problem solving
Extended problem solving
Impulse buying
Consumer buying decision
  process

Internal search
External search
Consideration set
Evaluative criteria
Cognitive dissonance
Situational influences
Psychological influences
Perception
Information inputs
Selective exposure

Selective distortion
Selective retention
Motive
Maslow's hierarchy
  of needs
Patronage motives
Learning
Attitude
Attitude scale
Personality

Self-concept
Lifestyle
Social influences
Role
Consumer socialization
Reference group
Opinion leader
Social class
Culture
Subcultures

Discussion and Review Questions

1. How does a consumer's level of involvement affect his or her choice of a problem-solving process?

2. Name the types of consumer problem-solving processes. List some products that you have bought using each type. Have you ever bought a product on impulse? Describe the circumstances.

3. What are the major stages in the consumer buying decision process? Are all these stages used in all consumer purchase decisions? Why or why not?

4. What are the categories of situational factors that influence consumer buying behavior? Explain how each of these factors influences buyers' decisions.

5. What is selective exposure? Why do people engage in it?

6. How do marketers attempt to shape consumers' learning?

7. Why are marketers concerned about consumer attitudes?

8. In what ways do lifestyles affect the consumer buying decision process?

9. How do roles affect a person's buying behavior? Provide examples.

10. What are family influences and how do they affect buying behavior?

11. Describe reference groups. How do they influence buying behavior? Name some of your own reference groups.

12. How does an opinion leader influence the buying decision process of reference-group members?

13. In what ways does social class affect a person's purchase decisions?

14. What is culture? How does it affect a person's buying behavior?

15. Describe the subcultures to which you belong. Identify buying behavior that is unique to one of your subcultures.

Application Questions

1. Consumers use one of three problem-solving processes when purchasing goods or services: routinized response behavior, limited problem solving, or extended problem solving. Describe three buying experiences you have had (one for each type of problem solving), and identify which problem-solving type you used. Discuss why that particular process was appropriate.

2. The consumer buying process consists of five stages: problem recognition, information search, evaluation of alternatives, purchase, and post purchase evaluation. Not every consumer goes through all five stages, and the process does not necessarily conclude in a purchase. Interview a fellow student about the last purchase he or she made. Report the stages used and skipped.

3. Attitudes toward products or companies often affect consumer behavior. The three components of an attitude are cognitive, affective, and behavioral. Briefly describe how a beer company might alter the cognitive and affective components of consumer attitudes toward beer products and the company.

4. An individual's roles influence that person's buying behavior. Identify two of your roles and give an example of how they have influenced your buying decisions.

5. Select five brands of toothpaste and explain how the appeals used in advertising these brands relate to Maslow's hierarchy of needs.

Internet Exercise & Resources

Security First Network Bank and the Internet

One of the first banking firms to establish a Web site, Security First Network Bank (SFNB) has established itself as a leading Internet marketer by effectively appealing to consumers' motivations and addressing their concerns about security, privacy, and other issues associated with electronic funds transfer. Access the SFNB Web site at

www.sfnb.com

1. What might motivate consumers to use the Security First Network Bank?
2. Is the consumer's level of involvement with the service SFNB promotes likely to be high or low? How do the firm's Internet marketing efforts address this issue?
3. Discuss the consumer buying decision process as it relates to a decision to utilize the SFNB.

E-Center Resources

Visit http://www.prideferrell.com to find several resources to help you succeed in mastering the material in this chapter, plus additional materials that will help you expand your marketing knowledge. The Web site includes

 Internet exercise updates plus additional exercises

 ACE self-tests

 abc Chapter summary with hotlinked glossary

 Hotlinks to companies featured in this chapter

 Resource Center

 Career Center

 Marketing plan worksheets

VIDEO CASE 8.1

IRI's High-Tech Window on Consumer Buying Behavior

What are consumers really buying? When are they buying? And what price are they paying? These deceptively simple questions used to stump manufacturers and retailers. They could easily see how many products were selling overall but critical details like timing and selling prices were much fuzzier. Just as bad, marketers could not determine whether consumers bought more or less when a new ad campaign began, a competitor launched a new product, a product's price was changed, or a product was moved to a new shelf position.

Now, thanks to Information Resources Inc. (IRI), manufacturers like Lever Brothers, PepsiCo, and Nestlé, as well as retailers like Kroger, Walgreen, and Target, have a high-tech window on consumer purchasing patterns. Chicago-based IRI has developed a system for collecting checkout scanner data from more than 20,000 supermarkets, drug stores, and mass merchandisers across the United States. Knowing that consumers may visit any number of retail outlets during a shopping expedition, IRI also has portable scanners in 55,000 U.S. households to gather data about purchases made in warehouse clubs, convenience stores, specialty outlets, and other shops. In addition, 60,000 households participate in IRI's special study of grocery shopping. Members provide personal data for IRI's files and then present a scannable ID card every time they buy groceries, letting IRI track their product preferences, brand and store loyalty, and other details about buying behavior.

By deciphering the UPC codes recorded by these scanners, IRI can distinguish the brand, size, and selling price of many millions of items purchased every day. These details come flooding into IRI's computers, where they are put together with consumer data and then sorted according to product category, manufacturer, store, consumer demographics, and any other criteria specified by participating manufacturers and retailers. IRI then analyzes the results and produces customized reports to help marketers analyze shoppers' reactions to their latest marketing moves.

When IRI identifies meaningful patterns in this mountain of data, it can alert marketers to significant shifts in consumer behavior. Consider the trend toward "home meal replacement"—industry jargon for fast foods, ready-to-eat complete meals, and snacks that substitute for home-cooked meals. IRI recently noticed an upswing in purchases of entrees and packaged dinners, particularly frozen meals. Consumers were not only buying more meal replacements; they were not balking at higher-than-average prices for newly introduced frozen meals, an important piece of information for food manufacturers cooking up new products. In addition, IRI executives saw potential for supermarkets to cash in on this trend by expanding their selection of "take-out" foods and grouping frozen, refrigerated, and shelf-stable foods to create whole-meal sections inside their stores.

Consumers are changing their breakfast habits, as well, an important insight for marketers of breakfast foods. IRI's scanner data reveal that consumers have been buying more bagels and breakfast bars. Cereal sales, on the other hand, are experiencing a downward slide, with manufacturers like Kellogg suffering steep drops in sales. As a result, Quaker Oats and other cereal makers are putting more money into marketing as they fight to retain their share of this shrinking market.

IRI also helps marketers take advantage of timely sales opportunities by determining when, where, and why consumers buy. The Fourth of July is a good example. Although this holiday may not seem like a major sales bonanza, IRI has shown many marketers of picnic and barbecue products how to grab a heftier share of consumer spending for start-of-summer meals, snacks, and tableware. According to IRI's research, sales of charcoal, baked beans, relish, frankfurters, and disposable plates explode during the weeks leading up to the Fourth of July holiday—especially in particular store locations. "The challenge for us is to help [marketers] prepare for the holiday by identifying the products likely to be most in demand, thereby avoiding missed sales opportunities," explains an IRI senior vice president. "In fact, with our store-by-store census data, some of our clients may take advantage of the power of this information and treat certain stores as higher opportunity targets, like those near beaches, parks, and other places where people might gather to celebrate the holiday."

By analyzing scanner data, IRI is able to determine exactly how much money consumers spend on specific types of products during peak periods—and to pinpoint where sales are heaviest. For example, in the month before Halloween, consumers splurge on more than $650 million worth of chocolates, candies, and caramel apples. On a dollar basis, chocolate candy sales are highest in Portland, Oregon, followed by Salt Lake City, Utah, and Boise, Idaho. This information helps manufacturers select sales hot spots for special consumer and trade promotions; it also helps manufacturers, wholesalers, and retailers map out suitable shipping strategies.

Such seemingly small details as the way products are arranged on the shelves can make a big difference in consumer behavior, as IRI scanner-data analyses have shown. How shelf space is utilized is important in any store, particularly with the number of new products introduced every year. One of IRI's high-tech products helps retailers evaluate sales performance for each product and category in their stores and then set up profit-driven plans for arranging products on shelves. The IRI system also helps retailers determine how to rearrange items when they add new products or delete slow movers.

Many companies use IRI information to address critical questions about the marketing mix when launching new products. How will consumers respond to a higher price? Is the ad campaign helping sales? Is the product selling better in a particular city, retail chain, or individual outlet? What are competitors doing in response to the new product? What kinds of consumers are buying the new product? What is the level of repeat purchasing? These are just some of the questions that IRI can help companies answer as they get ready to launch a product into national markets.[19]

Questions for Discussion
1. Why would a marketer need IRI's scanner data if it is already conducting surveys to obtain purchasing data directly from its customers?
2. Which situational influences on consumer buying are illuminated by IRI data? Explain.
3. How can IRI data help marketers increase sales by increasing their understanding of the psychological influences on consumer buying?

CASE 8.2

Marketing to Women: A Lucrative New Direction for Automakers

Automakers have finally noticed that women are in the driver's seat when it comes to vehicle purchases. Surveys show that eight out of ten car or truck purchases in the United States are made or influenced by women. In financial terms, this means that American women are spending an estimated $83 billion on cars and trucks every year. Sales of sport utility vehicles (SUVs), minivans, and light trucks now make up more than half of all new vehicle purchases—a national craze fueled, in large part, by the huge purchasing power of women. It's small wonder, then, that car manufacturers are tuning up their knowledge of consumer buying behavior to compete more aggressively for a larger share of this lucrative and influential market.

A "tremendous buying force" is the way one top official of DaimlerChrysler characterizes women's influence on vehicle purchases, especially of vehicles other than cars. He notes that most women "don't want to return to a car after driving a light truck such as a minivan" because they like the higher vantage point, a sharp contrast to the seats in today's low-slung car bodies.

Clearly, lifestyles and life stages are powerful influences on women's buying decisions. Women with families find minivans, SUVs, and light trucks roomier and more convenient than cars for ferrying children, pets, and possessions, which is why almost 20 percent of all women own such vehicles. Upscale SUVs, such as the Lexus RX 300, are increasingly popular among women, who are attracted by the more luxurious styling, higher seating, and all-terrain handling. Says the head of one market research firm, "The RX 300 is a vehicle that really appeals to female buyers. It comes off much softer" than its major competitor, the Mercedes line of SUVs.

Cindy Hess, vice president of small-car platform engineering at DaimlerChrysler, had women's lifestyles in mind when designing the PT Cruiser, a small SUV that handles like a passenger car. "One of the things we find is that people get to the point where they want to carry a lot of stuff or friends," says Hess. "They're saying, 'I don't want the minivan, I don't want the look,' but they need space and a little cargo room. And they see that this is stylish."

Another dimension of women's car buying behavior is catching the eye of automakers. U.S. women tend to be highly brand-loyal, with nearly three-quarters choosing American car brands. The story is very different for U.S. men, who increasingly steer toward the purchase of imported vehicles. "Viva la difference," say automakers as they step up their targeting of women with special marketing programs, such as educational events, sports sponsorships, and cause-related marketing.

DaimlerChrysler, for example, has begun offering special events during Women's Day at the prestigious North America International Auto Show, a gigantic annual event at which manufacturers show off futuristic car concepts and unveil new models. At the first Women's Day in 1999, DaimlerChrysler invited women to meet with members of its Women's Advisory Committee, who were standing next to the vehicles they drive (DaimlerChrysler models, of course). The company also presented four safety seminars for women during the day.

Acura puts women in the marketing spotlight through its sponsorship of the Acura Women's Cycle Team, while its corporate parent, Toyota, has cosponsored the Dinah Shore LPGA golf tournament for over fifteen years. Subaru is working with a partner, Specialized Bicycles, on a series of mountain biking clinics to introduce American women to this fast-growing sport.

Ford has appointed Linda Lee manager of women's marketing to coordinate the company's strategies for this important target market. One of Ford's special events combines sports sponsorship with cause-related marketing. Known as the Race for the Cure, this event, a series of 5K races, raises money for breast cancer education and treatment. General Motors is also merging sports sponsorship with cause-related marketing through its support of the Women's National Basketball Association and the National Alliance of Breast Cancer Organizations. GM donates 50 cents for each ticket sold during the regular WNBA season to the National Alliance; in the first year alone, GM donated $575,000 through this program.

In addition, GM has teamed up with the Council of Fashion Designers of America to start Concept:Cure. This long-term program raises money for breast cancer research by giving away GM vehicles designed by such famous fashion designers as Tommy Hilfiger. Consumers can enter the national sweepstakes to win one of these vehicles by calling a toll-free number and pledging a contribution to breast cancer research. The sweepstakes brings in some $700,000 for Concept:Cure every year.

Why so much emphasis on cause-related marketing for women? "It's not just about putting your name next to a cause, it's being a catalyst for the cure," explains a GM vice president. "Concept:Cure is building relationships that make a measurable difference by raising awareness and money for issues that are important to women."

Even as automakers in the United States are putting new emphasis on women's buying behavior, their European counterparts are moving more cautiously. For example, a top executive of Peugeot's

European ad agency stresses that corporate fleet buyers and men are the most important targets for many Peugeot models. "We are not going to target a Peugeot 406 directly at women, because the vast majority who buy these cars are men, and are going to be alienated," he says.

Many car commercials in the United Kingdom show women in practical, small cars rather than in larger or more glamorous ones, a custom that annoys half of all women aged 18 to 44, research shows—not a good foundation on which to build customer relationships. Still, women are definitely part of the European marketing plans made by multinational automakers like Ford. "We always ensure women's views are taken on board and made to count because they are an important audience," confirms the brand manager for Mondeo, a Ford model sold in Europe. "Whoever is within the buying audience of a car, we will target, and women are counted within every category now."[20]

Questions for Discussion

1. Which of the needs in Maslow's hierarchy do women seem to be satisfying when they buy a car or light truck?
2. How do women's lifestyles influence their decisions about buying vehicles?
3. When planning marketing activities, why should automakers take into account the role women play in the family?

9

Organizational Markets and Buying Behavior

OBJECTIVES

- To become familiar with the various types of organizational markets

- To identify the major characteristics of organizational buyers and transactions

- To understand several attributes of organizational demand

- To become familiar with the major components of a buying center

- To understand the stages of the organizational buying decision process and the factors that affect this process

- To become aware of industrial classification systems and explain how they can be used to identify and analyze organizational markets

At Roberts Express, Customer Service Is Not a Trendy Buzzword

When Oprah Winfrey decided at the last minute to do her talk show live from Texas, Roberts Express, a charter air service, was hired to deliver special lighting apparatus to the location. When James Cameron was filming *Titanic*, Roberts Express to delivered equipment to the set in Nova Scotia. When a nuclear power plant in the Amazon rain forest needed to replace a malfunctioning gauge to avert a potentially dangerous situation, Roberts Express was able to deliver it to Brazil in less than thirty-six hours. Roberts Express is the largest "expedited" freight carrier in North America. Seven days a week, twenty-four hours a day, Roberts delivers nonstop door-to-door.

Although it was formed in 1948 through the merger of two trucking companies, Roberts Express didn't begin expedited shipping until 1981. Before then, when businesses needed to ship things in a hurry, they had to pay extremely high rates for air freight or be willing to wait several days for a truck to make the delivery. Shipments that meet the requirements of Roberts Express's regular service, weighing under five hundred pounds and traveling less than eight hundred miles, usually can be delivered in less time and for about one-third the cost of air freight. Roberts can pick up a shipment within ninety minutes of receiving a customer's order, and about 96 percent of the time, deliver it within 15 minutes of the time-specific promise.

To provide a maximum level of customer service, Roberts employs satellite tracking and onboard computers that let the company know where shipments are at all times. To build long-term customer relationships, Roberts employs Customer Assistance Teams (CATs), groups of seven to nine people trained to organize the movement of a load from beginning to end. Assigned to a specific geographic area, each CAT makes it a priority to know and understand its customers' needs. Reports one customer, "When I call Roberts and give them my name and company, they know everything about me."

At Roberts, customer service is more than a trendy buzzword. Every month, Roberts pays an outside consulting firm to survey 150 of its most recent customers regarding the quality of service they have received. Bonuses are based on whether CATs lag behind, meet, or exceed their service objectives. On-time delivery and quality of phone service are the most emphasized dimensions.[1]

An understanding of organizational markets and the buying decision process is required to effectively serve those markets. Roberts Express marketers' understanding of their customers allows them to provide more effective service and to develop and maintain long-term customer relationships. Like consumer marketers, organizational marketers are concerned about satisfying their customers.

In this chapter, we look at organizational markets and organizational buying decision processes. We first discuss various kinds of organizational markets and types of buyers making up these markets. Next, we explore several dimensions of organizational buying, such as characteristics of transactions, attributes and concerns of buyers, methods of buying, and distinctive features of demand for products sold to organizational purchasers. We then examine how organizational buying decisions are made and who makes the purchases. Finally, we consider how organizational markets are analyzed.

Organizational Markets

organizational markets
Individuals or groups that purchase a specific kind of product for resale, direct use in producing other products, or use in general daily operations

business-to-business markets Producer and reseller markets

producer markets
Individuals and business organizations that purchase products to make profits by using them to produce other products or by using them in their operations

An **organizational market** consists of individuals or groups that purchase a specific kind of product for one of three purposes: resale, direct use in producing other products, or use in general daily operations. The four categories of organizational markets are producer, reseller, government, and institutional. In the remainder of this section, we discuss each of these types of organizational markets. The term **business-to-business markets** refers to both producer and reseller markets.

Producer Markets

Individuals and business organizations that purchase products for the purpose of making a profit by using them to produce other products or by using them in their operations are classified as **producer markets.** Producer markets include buyers of raw materials, as well as purchasers of semifinished and finished items used to produce other products. For example, manufacturers buy raw materials and component parts for direct use in product production. Grocery stores and supermarkets are part of producer markets for numerous support products, such as paper and plastic bags, counters, and scanners. Farmers are part of producer markets for farm machinery, fertilizer, seed, and livestock. Producer markets include a broad array of industries, ranging from agriculture, forestry, fisheries, and mining to construction (see Figure 9.1), transportation, communications, and utilities. As Table 9.1 indicates, the number of business establishments in national producer markets is enormous.

Manufacturers are geographically concentrated. More than half are located in only seven states: New York, California, Pennsylvania, Illinois, Ohio, New Jersey, and Michigan. This concentration sometimes enables industrial marketers to serve

Table 9.1	Number of Establishments in Industry Groups
Industry	**Number of Establishments**
Agriculture, forestry, fishing	104,000
Mining	28,000
Construction	621,000
Manufacturing	387,000
Transportation, public utilities	276,000
Finance, insurance, real estate	617,000
Services	2,342,000

Source: Bureau of the Census, *Statistical Abstract of the United States* (Washington, D.C.: Government Printing Office, 1997), p. 544.

Quality you can rely on

YOU MIGHT RETIRE
BEFORE *IT* DOES

For long-lasting productivity and reliability, Komatsu equipment will never let you down. Strengthened components, sophisticated electronic monitoring systems and easy maintenance designs all help make Komatsu some of the most durable equipment you can buy — not to mention the most advanced and comfortable. Year after year, you can count on Komatsu to help you reach your goals. Even if one of them is to not have to worry about goals anymore. To learn more, contact your local Komatsu distributor or dial 1-800-KOMATSU.

© 1998 Komatsu America International Company   Web Site: http://www.KomatsuAmerica.com

KOMATSU

Figure 9.1
Aiming at Producer Markets
Komatsu promotes its construction equipment to producer markets.

customers more efficiently. Within certain states, production in just a few industries may account for a sizable proportion of total industrial output.

Reseller Markets

Reseller markets consist of intermediaries, such as wholesalers and retailers, who buy finished goods and resell them for profit. Aside from making minor alterations, resellers do not change the physical characteristics of the products they handle. Except for items that producers sell directly to consumers, all products sold to consumer markets are first sold to reseller markets.

Wholesalers purchase products for resale to retailers, to other wholesalers, and to producers, governments, and institutions. Of the 512,000 wholesalers in the United States, a large percentage are located in New York, California, Illinois, Texas, Ohio, Pennsylvania, and New Jersey.[2] Although some technical products are sold directly to end users, many manufacturers sell their products to wholesalers, who, in turn, sell the products to other firms in the distribution system. Thus, wholesalers are very important in helping producers get a product to customers. Professional buyers and buying committees make wholesalers' initial purchase decisions. Reordering is often automated.

reseller markets
Intermediaries who buy finished goods and resell them for profit

Retailers purchase products and resell them to final customers. There are approximately 1.6 million retailers in the United States. They employ almost 20 million people and generate over $2.3 trillion in annual sales.[3] Some retailers carry a large number of items. Supermarkets may handle as many as 30,000 different products. In small, individually owned retail stores, owners or managers make purchasing decisions. In chain stores, a central office buyer or buying committee frequently decides whether a product will be made available for selection by store managers. For most products, however, local management makes the actual buying decisions for a particular store.

When making purchase decisions, resellers consider several factors. They evaluate the level of demand for a product to determine in what quantity and at what prices the product can be resold. Retailers assess the amount of space required to handle a product relative to its potential profit. In fact, they sometimes evaluate products on the basis of sales per square foot of selling area. Because customers often depend on resellers to have products available when needed, resellers typically appraise a supplier's ability to provide adequate quantities when and where wanted. Resellers also take into account the ease of placing orders and the availability of technical assistance and training programs from the producer. When resellers consider buying a product not previously carried, they try to determine whether the product competes with or complements products the firm currently handles. These types of concerns distinguish reseller markets from other markets.

Table 9.2	Annual Expenditures by Government Units for Selected Years (in billions of dollars)		
Year	Total Government Expenditures	Federal Government Expenditures	State and Local Expenditures
1970	$ 333	$ 185	$ 148
1975	560	292	268
1980	959	526	432
1985	1,581	1,032	658
1990	2,369	1,393	976
1994	2,894	1,630	1,264

Source: Bureau of the Census, *Statistical Abstract of the United States* (Washington, D.C.: Government Printing Office, 1997), p. 299.

Government Markets

government markets
Federal, state, county, and local governments that buy goods and services to support their internal operations and to provide products to their constituencies

Federal, state, county, and local governments make up **government markets.** They spend billions of dollars annually for a variety of goods and services to support their internal operations and to provide citizens with such products as highways, education, water, energy, and national defense. The federal government spends about $266 billion annually on national defense alone.[4] Government expenditures annually account for about 21 percent of the U.S. gross domestic product.

Besides the federal government, there are 50 state governments, 3,043 county governments, and 81,912 local governments.[5] The amount spent by federal, state, and local units during the last thirty years has increased rapidly because the total number of government units and the services they provide have both increased. Costs of providing these services have also increased. As noted in Table 9.2, the federal government spends over half the total amount spent by all governments.

The types and quantities of products bought by government markets reflect societal demands on various government agencies. As citizens' needs for government services change, so does demand for products by government markets. Not all government expenditures are for big-ticket, high-tech products. For instance, Maple Donuts, Inc., one of the largest donut producers in Pennsylvania, was awarded a contract to supply fortified donuts to all schools in the Chicago school system for one-half cent per donut.[6]

Because government agencies spend public funds to buy the products needed to provide services, they are accountable to the public. This accountability explains their relatively complex set of buying procedures. Some firms do not even try to sell to government buyers because they want to avoid the tangle of red tape. However, many marketers have learned to deal efficiently with government procedures and do not find them a stumbling block. For certain products, such as defense-related items, the government may be the only customer. The U.S. Government Printing Office publishes and distributes several documents explaining buying procedures and describing the types of products various federal agencies purchase.

Governments make purchases through bids or negotiated contracts. Although companies may be reluctant to approach government markets because of the complicated bidding process, once they understand the rules of this process, some firms routinely penetrate government markets. To make a sale under the bid system, firms must apply for and be approved to be placed on a list of qualified bidders. When a government unit wants to buy, it sends out a detailed description of the products to qualified bidders. Businesses wishing to sell such products submit bids. The government unit is usually required to accept the lowest bid.

When buying nonstandard or highly complex products, a government unit often uses a negotiated contract. Under this procedure, the government unit selects only a

Figure 9.2
Targeting Government Markets
Both MasterCard and Maximus promote their services to government markets.

few firms and then negotiates specifications and terms; it eventually awards the contract to one of the negotiating firms. Most large defense-related contracts, once held by such companies as McDonnell Douglas and General Dynamics, were negotiated in this fashion. However, as the number and size of such contracts has declined, these companies have had to strengthen their marketing efforts and look to other markets. Although government markets can impose intimidating requirements, they can also be very lucrative. Examples of organizations that are marketing to governments are shown in Figure 9.2.

Institutional Markets

institutional markets
Organizations with charitable, educational, community, or other nonbusiness goals

Organizations with charitable, educational, community, or other nonbusiness goals constitute **institutional markets.** Members of institutional markets include churches, some hospitals, fraternities and sororities, charitable organizations, and private colleges. Institutions purchase millions of dollars' worth of products annually to provide goods, services, and ideas to congregations, students, patients, and others. Because institutions often have different goals and fewer resources than other types of organizations, marketers may use special marketing efforts to serve them. Sam's Club, a division of Wal-Mart, targets institutional and other organizational markets. The giant warehouse outlet permits institutional and other qualified members to purchase supplies on a self-service basis at prices lower than those charged by high-service wholesalers.

Dimensions of Organizational Buying

Having considered different types of organizational customers, we turn to the dimensions of organizational buying. We examine several characteristics of organizational transactions and then discuss attributes of organizational buyers, as well as some of their primary concerns when making purchase decisions. Next, we consider organizational buying methods and major types of purchases. We conclude this section with a discussion of the characteristics of demand for industrial products.

Characteristics of Organizational Transactions

Organizational transactions differ from consumer sales in several ways. Orders by organizational buyers tend to be much larger than individual consumer sales. Suppliers often must sell products in large quantities to make profits; consequently, they prefer not to sell to customers who place small orders. For example, Airborne Express competes successfully against FedEx and UPS by providing low-cost overnight delivery services primarily to businesses that buy such services in high volume.

e   Some organizational purchases involve expensive items, such as computers. Other products, such as raw materials and component items, are used continuously in production, and the supply may need frequent replenishing. However, the contract regarding terms of sale of these items is likely to be a long-term agreement.

Discussions and negotiations associated with organizational purchases can require considerable marketing time and selling effort. Purchasing decisions are often made by committee; orders are frequently large and expensive; and products may be custom-built. Several people or departments in the purchasing organization will probably be involved. One department might express a need for a product; a second department might develop the specifications; a third might stipulate maximum expenditures; and a fourth might place the order.

reciprocity An arrangement unique to organizational marketing in which two organizations agree to buy from each other

One practice unique to organizational markets is **reciprocity,** an arrangement in which two organizations agree to buy from each other. Although such cooperation brings risks, companies that develop long-term relationships based on reciprocity and trust find cooperation to be an effective competitive tool.[7] Reciprocal agreements that threaten competition are illegal. The Federal Trade Commission and the Justice Department take actions to stop anticompetitive reciprocal practices. Nonetheless, a certain amount of reciprocal activity occurs among small businesses and, to a lesser extent, among larger companies. Because reciprocity influences purchasing agents to deal only with certain suppliers, it can lower morale among agents and lead to less-than-optimal purchases.

Working together to reach the top: that's what a relationship with F&D is all about.

At F&D, we've always understood the value of teamwork and long term relationships. That's one reason why we get to know our customers and their requirements so well.

So it isn't surprising that F&D has maintained a century-long relationship with the construction industry, through good times and bad. Or that so many of our clients are old friends who keep coming back year after year.

Next time, see how good a surety relationship can be.

Add F&D to your team, and let us help you reach the top.

F&D Surety

The Fidelity & Deposit Companies
since 1890
A member of the ❷ ZURICH Group

Contract Bonds / Builders Risk Insurance /
License, Permit and Miscellaneous Bonds /
Judicial Bonds / Public Official Bonds

 Reader Service Card No. 219

Attributes of Organizational Buyers

Organizational buyers differ from consumer buyers in their purchasing behavior in that they are better informed about the products they purchase. They demand detailed information about products' functional features and technical specifications to ensure that the products meet the organization's needs. Personal goals, however, may also influence organizational buyers' behavior. Most organizational purchasing agents seek the psychological satisfaction that comes with organizational advancement and financial rewards. Agents who consistently exhibit rational organizational buying behavior are likely to attain these personal goals because they help their firms achieve organizational objectives. Today many suppliers and their customers build and maintain mutually beneficial relationships, sometimes called partnerships. The ad in Figure 9.3 focuses on F & D Surety's desire to develop long-term, teamwork-focused relationships with customers.

Figure 9.3
Building Long-Term Relationships with Organizational Customers
Many companies, like F & D Surety, strive to build long-term relationships with customers.

Primary Concerns of Organizational Buyers

When making purchasing decisions, organizational customers take into account a variety of factors. Among their chief considerations are price, product quality, and service. Price matters greatly to organizational customers because it influences operating costs and costs of goods sold, and these costs affect selling price, profit margin, and ultimately, the ability to compete. When purchasing major equipment, an industrial buyer views price as the amount of investment necessary to obtain a certain level of return or savings. An organizational purchaser is likely to compare the price of a product with the value of the benefits that the product will yield.

Most organizational customers try to achieve and maintain a specific level of quality in the products they offer. (See Building Customer Relationships for an example of a bank that understands the importance of service to organizational customers.) To achieve this goal, most firms establish standards (usually stated as a percentage of defects allowed) for these products and buy them on the basis of a set of expressed characteristics, commonly called *specifications*. An organizational buyer evaluates the quality of the products being considered to determine whether they meet specifications. If a product fails to meet specifications or malfunctions for the ultimate consumer, the organizational customer may drop that product's supplier and switch to a different one. On the other hand, organizational customers are ordinarily cautious about buying products that exceed specifications because such products often cost more, thus increasing an organization's overall costs. Specifications are designed to meet a customer's wants, and anything that does not contribute to meeting those wants is considered wasteful.

Organizational buyers value service. Services offered by suppliers directly and indirectly influence organizational customers' costs, sales, and profits. In some instances, the mix of customer services is the major way marketers gain a competitive

BUILDING
customer relationships

Victory State Bank Builds Strong Relationships with Commercial Customers

Victory State Bank in Staten Island, New York, trains employees to welcome every customer with a friendly personal greeting and never to use the word *policy*. In operation since 1997, Victory State is primarily a commercial institution serving small business owners and focusing on nurturing long-term relationships by offering personal attention and superior customer service. Asserts its CEO, "The personal attention we deliver to customers is our greatest strength."

Victory State Bank is the brainchild of a few Staten Island business professionals. Gathering over coffee, they decided their community needed a commercial bank that would be responsive to the needs of local businesses. They felt the big Manhattan branch banks were not in touch with the needs of the home builders and retailers that constitute the majority of the Staten Island business community. They wanted a commercial bank that would be responsive to these needs and that would also deliver superior customer service. With these ideas in mind, they founded Victory State Bank, a "friendly, local alternative."

Although it is uncommon for bank executives to go out "knocking on doors," Victory's executives go out in the community to make personal contact with potential customers. For example, in one day, one of the bank's owners called on an appliance store, a tool-and-dye maker, a nonprofit organization selling T-shirts, and an automotive detailing shop, and the bank's vice president chased a local contractor on the street to tell him about Victory State Bank. Although only one of these businesses wanted a loan, Victory knows that this kind of hands-on treatment wins friends and engenders loyalty in a close-knit community of small business owners. So does the trust implied by instant credit on deposited checks, which the bank offers. While large banks can take up to two weeks to make loan decisions, Victory State personnel are authorized to make loans of a certain size while applicants wait.

To attract customers, Victory is relying on positive word-of-mouth communication about its superior service, as well as on the excellent reputation its officials enjoy with local businesses. To date, its plan seems to be working very well. In the first five months of operations, deposits at Victory State Bank exceeded $13 million, almost twice the $7.5 million its founders predicted.

SNAPSHOT
Who's making purchasing decisions?

A study of 1,100 decision makers indicated shifts since 1993 in who does the purchasing for companies

- 1993
- Today

Technical staff/managers	Purchasing agents	Line managers
11% / 44%	58% / 35%	31% / 21%

advantage. Typical services desired by customers are market information, inventory maintenance, on-time delivery, and repair services. Organizational buyers are likely to need technical product information, data regarding demand, information about general economic conditions, or supply and delivery information. Maintaining adequate inventory is critical because it helps make products accessible when an organizational buyer needs them and reduces the buyer's inventory requirements and costs. Since organizational buyers are usually responsible for ensuring that products are on hand and ready for use when needed, on-time delivery is crucial. Furthermore, reliable, on-time delivery saves organizational customers money because it enables them to carry less inventory. Purchasers of machinery are especially concerned about obtaining repair services and replacement parts quickly because inoperable equipment is costly. Caterpillar Inc., manufacturer of earth-moving, construction, and materials-handling machinery, has built an international reputation, as well as a competitive advantage, by providing prompt service and replacement parts for its products around the world.

Quality of service has become a critical issue because customer expectations about service have broadened. Using traditional service quality standards based only on traditional manufacturing and accounting systems is not enough. Communication channels that allow customers to ask questions, complain, submit orders, and trace shipments are indispensable components of service. Marketers should strive for uniformity of service, simplicity, truthfulness, and accuracy. They should also develop customer service objectives and monitor customer service programs. Firms can monitor service by formally surveying customers or informally calling on customers and asking questions about the service they receive. Taking the time and making the effort to ensure that customers are happy can greatly benefit marketers by increasing customer retention. One study found that boosting customer retention by 5 percent could double a small firm's profitability in about ten years and could double the average Fortune 500 company's revenue growth rate almost immediately.[8] Proper complaint handling helps to retain a customer and significantly reduces the likelihood that he or she will tell eleven or twelve other customers about a negative experience (which *does* occur when a customer is very dissatisfied).[9]

Methods of Organizational Buying

Although no two organizational buyers do their jobs the same way, most use one or more of the following purchase methods: *description, inspection, sampling,* and *negotiation.* When products are standardized according to certain characteristics (such as size, shape, weight, and color) and graded using such standards, an organizational buyer may be able to purchase simply by describing or specifying quantity, grade, and other attributes. Agricultural products often fall into this category. Sometimes buyers specify a particular brand or its equivalent when describing the desired product. Purchases on the basis of description are especially common between a buyer and seller with an ongoing relationship built on trust.

Certain products, such as industrial equipment, used vehicles, and buildings, have unique characteristics and may vary with regard to condition. For example, a particular used truck might have a bad transmission. Consequently, organizational buyers of such products must base purchase decisions on inspection.

Sampling entails taking a specimen of the product from the lot and evaluating it on the assumption that its characteristics represent the entire lot. This method is appropriate when the product is homogeneous—for instance, grain—and examining the entire lot is not physically or economically feasible.

**Figure 9.4
Purchases Through
Negotiated Contracts**
One way commercial
vehicles are purchased
is through negotiated
contracts.

Some industrial purchasing is based on negotiated contracts. In certain instances, buyers describe exactly what is needed and ask sellers to submit bids. They then negotiate with the suppliers who submit the most attractive bids. When acquiring commercial vehicles like those in Figure 9.4, this approach can be used. In other cases, the buyer may not be able to identify specifically what is to be purchased but can provide only a general description—as might be the case for a special piece of custom-made equipment. A buyer and seller might negotiate a contract that specifies a base price and provides for the payment of additional costs and fees. These contracts are most commonly used for one-time projects, such as buildings, capital equipment, and special projects.

Types of Organizational Purchases

new-task purchase
An initial purchase by an organization of an item to be used to perform a new job or to solve a new problem

straight rebuy purchase
A routine purchase of the same products by an organizational buyer

modified rebuy purchase
A new-task purchase that is changed on subsequent orders or when the requirements of a straight rebuy purchase are modified

Most organizational purchases are one of three types: new-task purchase, straight rebuy purchase, and modified rebuy purchase. In a **new-task purchase,** an organization makes an initial purchase of an item to be used to perform a new job or to solve a new problem. A new-task purchase may require development of product specifications, vendor specifications, and procedures for future purchases of that product. To make the initial purchase, the organizational buyer usually needs much information. New-task purchases are important to suppliers, for if organizational buyers are satisfied with the products, suppliers may be able to sell buyers large quantities of them for many years.

A **straight rebuy purchase** occurs when buyers purchase the same products routinely under approximately the same terms of sale. Buyers require little information for these routine purchase decisions and tend to use familiar suppliers that have provided satisfactory service and products in the past. These suppliers try to set up automatic reordering systems to make reordering easy and convenient for organizational buyers. A supplier may even monitor the organizational buyer's inventories and indicate to the buyer what should be ordered and when.

In a **modified rebuy purchase,** a new-task purchase is changed the second or third time it is ordered or requirements associated with a straight rebuy purchase are modified. An organizational buyer might seek faster delivery, lower prices, or a different quality level of product specifications. A modified rebuy situation may cause regular suppliers to become more competitive to keep the account, since other suppliers could obtain the business. For example, when a firm buys a slightly different set of communication services (see Figure 9.5), the organization has made a modified purchase.

Figure 9.5
Modified Re-buy Purchase
A purchase of a slightly different set of communication services is likely to be a modified re-buy purchase for many organizations.

Demand for Industrial Products

Products sold to organizational customers are called industrial products; consequently, demand for these products is called industrial demand. Unlike consumer demand, industrial demand can be described as (1) derived, (2) inelastic, (3) joint, and (4) fluctuating.

Derived Demand Because organizational customers, especially producers, buy products for direct or indirect use in the production of goods and services to satisfy consumers' needs, the demand for industrial products derives from the demand for consumer products; it is therefore called **derived demand.** In the long run, no industrial demand is totally unrelated to the demand for consumer goods. The derived nature of industrial demand is usually multilevel. Industrial sellers at different levels are affected by a change in consumer demand for a particular product. For instance, consumers today are more concerned with health and good nutrition than ever before and as a result are purchasing more products with less fat, cholesterol, and salt. When consumers reduced their purchases of high-fat foods, it caused a change in the demand for products marketed by food processors, equipment manufacturers, suppliers of raw materials, and even fast-food restaurants. When consumer demand for a product changes, a wave is set in motion that affects demand for all firms involved in the production of that consumer product.

Inelastic Demand **Inelastic demand** means that a price increase or decrease will not significantly alter demand for an industrial product. Because many industrial products contain a number of parts, price increases affecting only one or two parts of the product may yield only a slightly higher per-unit production cost. When a sizeable price increase for a component represents a large proportion of the product's cost, then demand may become more elastic because the price increase in the component causes the price at the consumer level to rise sharply. For example, if aircraft engine manufacturers substantially increase the price of engines, forcing Boeing to raise the prices of the aircraft it manufactures, the demand for airliners may become more elastic as airlines reconsider whether they can afford to buy new aircraft. An increase in the price of windshields, however, is unlikely to greatly affect the price of airliners or the demand for them.

Inelasticity applies only to industry demand for industrial products, not to the demand curve faced by an individual firm. Suppose that a spark plug producer increases the price of spark plugs sold to manufacturers of small engines, but its competitors continue to maintain lower prices. The spark plug company would probably experience reduced unit sales because most small-engine producers would switch to lower-priced brands. A specific firm is vulnerable to elastic demand, even though industry demand for a particular product is inelastic.

Joint Demand Demand for certain industrial products, especially raw materials and components, is subject to joint demand. **Joint demand** occurs when two or more items are used in combination to produce a product. For example, a firm that manufactures axes needs the same number of ax handles as it does ax blades; these two

derived demand Demand for industrial products that stems from demand for consumer products

inelastic demand Demand that is not significantly altered by a price increase or decrease

joint demand Demand involving the use of two or more items in combination to produce a product

products are demanded jointly. If a shortage of ax handles exists, then the producer buys fewer ax blades. Understanding the effects of joint demand is particularly important for a marketer selling multiple jointly demanded items. Such a marketer realizes that when a customer begins purchasing one of the jointly demanded items, a good opportunity exists for selling related products.

Demand Fluctuation   Because it is derived from consumer demand, the demand for industrial products may fluctuate enormously. In general, when particular consumer products are in high demand, their producers buy large quantities of raw materials and components to ensure meeting long-run production requirements. In addition, these producers may expand production capacity, which entails acquiring new equipment and machinery, more workers, and more raw materials and component parts. Conversely, a decline in demand for certain consumer goods significantly reduces demand for industrial products used to produce those goods.

Marketers of industrial products may notice changes in demand when customers change inventory policies, perhaps because of expectations about future demand. For example, if several dishwasher manufacturers who buy timers from one producer increase their inventory of timers from a two-week to a one-month supply, the timer producer will have a significant immediate increase in demand.

Sometimes price changes lead to surprising temporary changes in demand. A price increase for an industrial item may initially cause organizational customers to buy more of the item because they expect the price to rise further. Similarly, demand for an industrial product may be significantly lower following a price cut because buyers are waiting for further price reductions. Fluctuations in demand can be significant in industries in which prices change frequently.

Organizational Buying Decisions

organizational buying behavior   The purchase behavior of producers, government units, institutions, and resellers

Organizational buying behavior refers to the purchase behavior of producers, resellers, government units, and institutions. Although several of the factors affecting consumer buying behavior (discussed in the previous chapter) also influence organizational buying behavior, a number of factors are unique to the latter. We first analyze the buying center to learn who participates in organizational purchase decisions. We then focus on the stages of the buying decision process and the factors affecting it.

The Buying Center

buying center   The people within an organization, including users, influencers, buyers, deciders, and gatekeepers, who make organizational purchase decisions

Relatively few organizational purchase decisions are made by just one person; mostly, they are made through a buying center. The **buying center** is the group of people within an organization who make organizational purchase decisions. They include users, influencers, buyers, deciders, and gatekeepers.[10] One person may perform several roles. These participants share some goals and risks associated with their decisions.

Users are the organization members who actually use the product being acquired. They frequently initiate the purchase process and/or generate purchase specifications. After the purchase, they evaluate product performance relative to the specifications. Influencers are often technical personnel, such as engineers, who help develop the specifications and evaluate alternative products. Technical personnel are especially important influencers when products being considered involve new, advanced technology.

Buyers select suppliers and negotiate terms of purchase. They may also become involved in developing specifications. Buyers are sometimes called purchasing agents or purchasing managers. Their choices of vendors and products, especially for new-task purchases, are heavily influenced by persons occupying other roles in the buying center. For straight rebuy purchases, the buyer plays a major role in vendor selection and negotiations. Deciders actually choose the products. Although buyers may be deciders, it is not unusual for different people to occupy these roles. For routinely purchased items, buyers are commonly deciders. However, a buyer may not be authorized to make purchases exceeding a certain dollar limit, in which case higher-level management personnel are deciders. Gatekeepers, such as secretaries and technical personnel, control the flow of information to and among persons who occupy other roles in the buying center. Buyers who deal directly with vendors also may be gatekeepers because they can control information flows. The flow of information from a supplier's sales representatives to users and influencers is often controlled by personnel in the purchasing department.

The number and structure of an organization's buying centers are affected by the organization's size and market position, the volume and types of products being purchased, and the firm's overall managerial philosophy regarding exactly who should be involved in purchase decisions. The size of a buying center is influenced by the stage of the buying decision process and the type of purchase (new-task, straight rebuy, or modified rebuy).[11] Varying goals among members of a buying center can have both positive and negative effects on the purchasing process.

A marketer attempting to sell to an organizational customer should determine who is in the buying center, the types of decisions each individual makes, and which individuals are most influential in the decision process. Because in some instances many people make up the buying center, marketers cannot contact all participants; instead, they must be certain to contact a few of the most influential.

Stages of the Organizational Buying Decision Process

Like consumers, organizations follow a buying decision process; this process is summarized in the lower portion of Figure 9.6. In the first stage, one or more individuals recognize that a problem or need exists. Problem recognition may arise under a variety of circumstances—for instance, when machines malfunction or a firm modifies an

Figure 9.6
Organizational Buying Decision Process and Factors That May Influence It

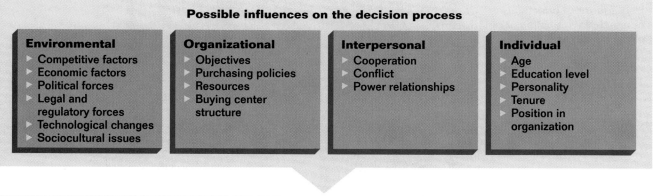

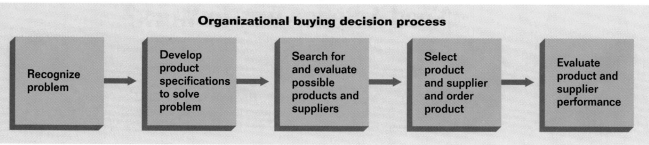

existing product or introduces a new one. Individuals in the buying center—such as users, influencers, or buyers—may be involved in problem recognition, but it may be stimulated by external sources, such as sales representatives or advertisements like the one in Figure 9.7.

The second stage of the process, development of product specifications, requires that buying center participants assess the problem or need and determine what is necessary to resolve or satisfy it. During this stage, users and influencers, such as engineers, often provide information and advice for developing product specifications. By assessing and describing needs, the organization should be able to establish product specifications.

Searching for and evaluating possible products and suppliers is the third stage in the decision process. Search activities may involve looking in company files and trade directories, contacting suppliers for information, soliciting proposals from known vendors, and examining Web sites, catalogs, and trade publications. To facilitate vendor search, some organizations such as Wal-Mart (see Figure 9.8) advertise their desire to build partnerships with specific types of vendors such as those owned by women or by minorities. During this stage some organizations engage in **value analysis**, an evaluation of each component of a potential purchase. Value analysis examines quality, designs, materials, and possibly item reduction or deletion in order to acquire the product in the most cost-effective way. The American Plastics Council encourages automakers, under considerable pressure to build lighter cars, to consider plastic parts and components when doing value analysis.[12] Some vendors may not be deemed acceptable because they are not large enough to supply needed quantities; others may

value analysis An evaluation of each component of a potential purchase

**Figure 9.7
Stimulating Problem
Recognition**
Aimed at organizations, this HotOffice advertisement is used to trigger problem recognition by claiming that there is a better way to stay organized and more effectively connected with colleagues, clients, and vendors.

Figure 9.8
Vendor Search
To enhance its vendor search, Wal-Mart promotes its willingness to establish partnerships with vendors owned by women and minorities.

vendor analysis   A formal, systematic evaluation of current and potential vendors

multiple sourcing   An organization's decision to use several suppliers

sole sourcing   An organization's decision to use only one supplier

be excluded because of poor delivery and service records. Sometimes the product is not available from any existing vendor and the buyer must find an innovative company, like 3M, to design and make the product. Products are evaluated to make sure that they meet or exceed product specifications developed in the second stage. Usually, suppliers are judged according to multiple criteria. A number of firms employ **vendor analysis.** Vendor analysis is a formal, systematic evaluation of current and potential vendors, focusing on such characteristics as price, product quality, delivery service, product availability, and overall reliability.

Results of deliberations and assessments in the third stage are used during the fourth stage to select the product to be purchased and the supplier from which to buy it. In some cases, the buyer selects and uses several suppliers, which is known as **multiple sourcing.** In others, only one supplier is selected—a situation known as **sole sourcing.** Sole sourcing has traditionally been discouraged except when a product is available from only one company. Firms with federal government contracts are required to have several sources for an item. Sole sourcing is considerably more common today, partly because such an arrangement means better communications between buyer and supplier, stability and higher profits for suppliers, and often lower prices for buyers. However, many organizations still prefer multiple sourcing because this approach lessens the possibility of disruption caused by strikes, shortages, or bankruptcies. The actual product is ordered in this fourth stage, and specific details regarding terms, credit arrangements, delivery dates and methods, and technical assistance are finalized.

During the fifth stage, the product's performance is evaluated by comparing it with specifications. Sometimes, even though the product meets the specifications, its performance does not adequately solve the problem or satisfy the need recognized in the first stage. In that case, product specifications must be adjusted. The supplier's performance is also evaluated during this stage. If supplier performance is inadequate, the organizational purchaser seeks corrective action from the supplier or searches for a new one. Results of the evaluation become feedback for the other stages in future organizational purchase decisions.

This organizational buying decision process is used in its entirety primarily for new-task purchases. Several stages, but not necessarily all, are used for modified rebuy and straight rebuy situations. See Tech*know for a discussion on how Cisco invites business customers and prospects to use its web site throughout the buying decision process.

Influences on Organizational Buying

Figure 9.6 also lists four major categories of factors that influence organizational buying decisions: environmental, organizational, interpersonal, and individual.

 Environmental factors include competitive and economic factors, political forces, legal and regulatory forces, technological changes, and sociocultural issues. These factors generate considerable uncertainty for an organization, and uncertainty can make individuals in the buying center apprehensive about certain types of purchases. Changes in one or more environmental forces can create new purchasing opportunities and threats. For example, changes in competition and technology can make buying decisions difficult in the case of products like software, computers, and telecommunications equipment.

Tech*know

Cisco Systems: Wired for Success to Serve Organizational Markets

Cisco Systems, a $9.6 billion company, practices what it preaches. Its brand is on 85 percent of the networking equipment used on the Internet—so naturally, Cisco markets to business customers directly from its Web site (www.cisco.com). At any hour of the day or night, organizational buyers around the world can log on to the Networking Products MarketPlace section of Cisco's site as they work through the stages in the buying decision process, from developing product specifications to ordering products and beyond.

Buyers start by registering at the Cisco site, filling out a profile form about their company, and obtaining a password for entry. Before they can buy, they are required to submit a signed copy of Cisco's Internet Commerce Agreement, in which they agree that their electronic orders are as legally binding as printed purchase orders. They can then click around the site whenever they are considering any of Cisco's high-tech products.

In the early stages of the buying decision process, customers may log on in search of products, specifications, prices, and lead times. They can even try out different product configurations online to see how changes affect pricing before they make any final decisions. When they are ready to order, they select the products and the proper configurations from the Web site and then submit electronic purchase orders.

After ordering, buyers can use Cisco's Web site to check on the status of their purchases, to download data about their orders, and to see invoices, credits, and debits posted to their accounts. They also have access to extensive after-sale service and support via the Internet, including the ability to order services, parts, and product upgrades; to locate qualified service firms; and to arrange to return items for credit.

With computer networks and telecommunications converging, Cisco is staying ahead of the curve by expanding into products that can send both data and voice traffic over telephone lines. Watch for Cisco to enlarge its Internet presence as it offers its convenient, user-friendly marketing and support to new customers in the telephone business.

Organizational factors influencing the buying decision process include the company's objectives, purchasing policies, and resources, as well as the size and composition of its buying center. An organization may have certain buying policies to which buying center participants must conform. For instance, a firm's policies may mandate long-term contracts, perhaps longer than most sellers desire. An organization's financial resources may require special credit arrangements. Any of these conditions could affect purchase decisions.

Interpersonal factors are the relationships among people in the buying center. Use of power and level of conflict among buying center participants influence organizational buying decisions. Certain persons in the buying center may be better communicators than others and may be more persuasive. Often, these interpersonal dynamics are hidden, making them difficult for marketers to assess.

Individual factors are personal characteristics of individuals in the buying center, such as age, education, personality and tenure, and position in the organization. For example, a fifty-five-year-old manager who has been in the organization for twenty-five years may affect decisions made by the buying center differently than a thirty-year-old person employed only two years. How influential these factors are depends on the buying situation, the type of product being purchased, and whether the purchase is new-task, modified rebuy, or straight rebuy. Negotiating styles of people vary within an organization and from one organization to another. To be effective, marketers must know customers well enough to be aware of these individual factors and the effects they may have on purchase decisions.

Using Industrial Classification Systems

Marketers have access to a considerable amount of information about potential organizational customers for much of this information is available through government and industry publications and Web sites. Marketers use this information to identify potential organizational customers and to estimate their purchase potential.

Identifying Potential Organizational Customers

Standard Industrial Classification (SIC) system The federal government system for classifying selected economic characteristics of industrial, commercial, financial, and service organizations

North American Industry Classification System (NAICS) An industry classification system that will generate comparable statistics among the United States, Canada, and Mexico

Much information about organizational customers is based on industrial classification systems. In the United States, marketers traditionally have relied on the **Standard Industrial Classification (SIC) system,** which the federal government developed to classify selected economic characteristics of industrial, commercial, financial, and service organizations. However, the SIC system is being replaced by a new industry classification system called the **North American Industry Classification System (NAICS).** NAICS is a single industry classification system that all three NAFTA partners (United States, Canada, and Mexico) will use to generate comparable statistics among all three countries. NAICS is similar to the International Standard Industrial Classification (ISIC) system used in Europe and many other parts of the world. Whereas the SIC system divides industrial activity into ten divisions, NAICS divides industrial activity into twenty sectors. NAICS contains 1,172 industry classifications, compared with 1,004 in the SIC system. NAICS is more comprehensive and will be more up to date; all three countries have agreed to update it every five years. In addition, NAICS will provide considerably more information about service industries and high-tech products. A comparison of the SIC system and NAICS appears in Table 9.3.[13] Over the next few years, all three NAFTA countries will be converting from previously used industrial classification systems to NAICS.

Industrial classification systems are ready-made tools that allow marketers to divide organizations into groups based mainly on the types of goods and services provided. Although an industrial classification system is a vehicle for segmentation, it is most appropriately used in conjunction with other types of data to determine exactly how many and which customers a marketer can reach.

Table 9.3	Comparison of the SIC System and NAICS for Manufacturers of Magnetic and Optical Media		
SIC Hierarchy		**NAICS Hierarchy**	
Division D	Manufacturing	Sector 31-33	Manufacturing
Major Group 36	Manufacturers of electronic and other electrical equipment, except computer equipment	Subsector 334	Computer and electronic manufacturing
Industry Subgroup 369	Manufacturers of miscellaneous electrical machinery, equipment, and supplies	Industry Group 3346	Manufacturing and reproduction of magnetic and optical media
Detailed Industry 3695	Manufacturers of magnetic and optical recording media	Industry 33461	Manufacturing and reproduction of magnetic and optical media
		U.S. Industry 334611	U.S. specific— reproduction of software

Source: Robert W. Haas and Thomas R. Wotruba, "From SIC to NAICS—What Does It Mean for Business Marketers?" *Agency Sales Magazine,* Jan. 1998, p. 31. Copyright © 1998, Manufacturers' Agents National Association 23016 Mill Creek Road, P. O. Box 3467, Laguna Hills, CA 9265403467. Phone (949) 859-4040; fax (949) 855-2973. All rights reserved. Reproduction without permission is strictly prohibited.

input-output data
Information that tells what types of industries purchase the products of a particular industry

Input-output analysis works well in conjunction with an industrial classification system. This type of analysis is based on the assumption that the output or sales of one industry are the input or purchases of other industries. **Input-output data** tell what types of industries purchase products of a particular industry. A major source of national input-output data is the *Survey of Current Business,* published by the Office of Business Economics, U.S. Department of Commerce. After learning which industries purchase the major portion of an industry's output, the next step is finding the industrial classification numbers for those industries. Because firms are grouped differently in input-output tables and industrial classification systems, ascertaining industrial classification numbers can be difficult. However, the Office of Business Economics provides some limited conversion tables with input-output data. These tables can help marketers assign classification numbers to industry categories used in input-output analysis.

Having determined the classification numbers of industries that buy the firm's output, a marketer is in a position to ascertain the number of organizations that are potential buyers. Government sources, such as the *Census of Business,* the *Census of Manufacturers,* and *County Business Patterns,* report the number of establishments, the value of industry shipments, the number of employees, percentage of imports and exports, and industry growth rates within classifications. Commercial sources also provide information about organizations categorized by industrial classifications.

A marketer can take several approaches to determine the identities and locations of organizations in specific groups. One approach is to use state directories or commercial industrial directories, such as *Standard & Poor's Register* and Dun & Bradstreet's *Million Dollar Directory.* These sources contain such information about a firm as its name, industrial classification, address, phone number, and annual sales. By referring to one or more of these sources, marketers isolate organizational customers with industrial classification numbers, determine their locations, and develop lists of potential customers by desired geographic area. A more expedient, although more expensive, approach is to use a commercial data service. Dun & Bradstreet, for example, can provide a list of organizations that fall into a particular industrial classification group. For each company on the list, Dun & Bradstreet gives the name, location, sales volume, number of employees, type of products handled, names of chief executives, and other pertinent information. Either method can effectively identify and locate a group of potential customers. However, a marketer probably cannot pursue all organizations on the list. Because some companies have greater purchasing potential than others, marketers must determine which customer or customer group to pursue.

Estimating Purchase Potential

To estimate the purchase potential of organizational customers or groups of customers, a marketer must find a relationship between the size of potential customers' purchases and a variable available in industrial classification data, such as the number of employees. For example, a paint manufacturer might attempt to determine the average number of gallons purchased by a specific type of potential customer relative to the number of persons employed. A marketer with no previous experience in this market segment will probably have to survey a random sample of potential customers to establish a relationship between purchase sizes and numbers of persons employed. Once this relationship is established, it can be applied to potential customer groups to estimate their purchases. After deriving these estimates, a marketer is in a position to select the customer groups with the most sales and profit potential.

Despite their usefulness, industrial classification data pose several problems. First, a few industries do not have specific designations. Second, because a transfer of products from one establishment to another is counted as a part of total shipments, double counting may occur when products are shipped between two establishments within the same firm. Third, because the Bureau of the Census is prohibited from providing data that identify specific business organizations, some data—such as value of total shipments—may be understated. Finally, because government agencies provide industrial classification data, a significant lag usually exists between data collection time and the time that the information is released.

Summary

Organizational markets consist of individuals and groups that purchase a specific kind of product for resale, direct use in producing other products, or use in day-to-day operations. Producer markets include those individuals and business organizations purchasing products for the purpose of making a profit by using them to produce other products or by using them in their operations. Intermediaries that buy finished products and resell them to make a profit are classified as reseller markets. Government markets consist of federal, state, county, and local governments, which spend billions of dollars annually for goods and services to support internal operations and to provide citizens with needed services. Organizations with charitable, educational, community, or other not-for-profit goals constitute institutional markets.

Organizational transactions differ from consumer transactions in several ways. Organizational transactions tend to be larger, and negotiations occur less frequently, though they are often lengthy. Organizational transactions often involve more than one person or department in the purchasing organization. They may also involve reciprocity, an arrangement in which two organizations agree to buy from each other. Organizational customers are usually better informed than ultimate consumers and more likely to seek information about a product's features and technical specifications.

When purchasing products, organizational customers are particularly concerned about quality, service, and price. Quality is important because it directly affects the quality of products the buyer's firm produces. To achieve an exact level of quality, organizations often buy products on the basis of a set of expressed characteristics, called specifications. Because services have such a direct influence on a firm's costs, sales, and profits, such matters as market information, on-time delivery, and availability of parts are crucial to an organizational buyer.

Although organizational customers do not depend solely on price to decide which products to buy, price is of prime concern because it directly influences profitability.

Organizational buyers use several purchasing methods, including description, inspection, sampling, and negotiation. Most organizational purchases are new-task, straight rebuy, or modified rebuy. In new-task purchases, organizations make an initial purchase of items to be used to perform new jobs or to solve new problems. In a modified rebuy purchase, a new-task purchase is changed the second or third time it is ordered or requirements associated with a straight rebuy purchase are modified. A straight rebuy purchase occurs when buyers purchase the same products routinely under approximately the same terms of sale.

Industrial demand differs from consumer demand along several dimensions. Industrial demand derives from demand for consumer products. At the industry level, industrial demand is inelastic. If an industrial item's price changes, product demand will not change as much proportionally. Some industrial products are subject to joint demand, which occurs when two or more items are used in combination to make a product. Finally, because organizational demand derives from consumer demand, the demand for organizational products can fluctuate widely.

Organizational buying behavior refers to the purchase behavior of producers, resellers, government units, and institutions. Organizational purchase decisions are made through a buying center—the group of people involved in making organizational purchase decisions. Users are those in the organization who actually use the product. Influencers help develop specifications and evaluate alternative products for possible use. Buyers select suppliers and negotiate purchase terms. Deciders choose the products. Gatekeepers control flow of information to and among persons occupying other roles in the buying center.

The stages of the organizational buying decision process are problem recognition, development of product specifications to solve problems, search for and evaluation of products and suppliers, selection and ordering of the most appropriate product, and evaluation of the product's and supplier's performance.

Four categories of factors influence organizational buying decisions: environmental, organizational, interpersonal, and individual. Environmental factors include politics, laws and regulations, sociocultural factors, economic conditions, competitive forces, and technological changes. Organizational factors include the company's objectives, purchasing policies, and resources, as well as the size and composition of its buying center. Interpersonal factors are the relationships among people in the buying center. Individual factors are personal characteristics of individuals in the buying center, such as age, education, personality, tenure, and position in the organization.

Organizational marketers have a considerable amount of information available for use in planning marketing strategies. Much of this information is based on an industrial classification system, which categorizes businesses into major industry groups, industry subgroups, and detailed industry categories. An industrial classification system provides marketers with information needed to identify organizational customer groups. Currently, the United States is converting from the traditional SIC system to NAICS. It can best be used for this purpose in conjunction with other information, such as input-output data. After identifying target industries, a marketer can obtain the names and locations of potential customers by using government and commercial data sources. Marketers then must estimate potential purchases of organizational customers by finding a relationship between a potential customer's purchases and a variable available in industrial classification data.

Important Terms

Organizational markets	Reciprocity	Organizational buying	Standard Industrial
Business-to-business	New-task purchase	behavior	Classification (SIC)
markets	Straight rebuy purchase	Buying center	system
Producer markets	Modified rebuy purchase	Value analysis	North American Industry
Reseller markets	Derived demand	Vendor analysis	Classification System
Government markets	Inelastic demand	Multiple sourcing	(NAICS)
Institutional markets	Joint demand	Sole sourcing	Input-output data

Discussion and Review Questions

1. Identify, describe, and give examples of the four major types of organizational markets.

2. Regarding purchasing behavior, why might organizational buyers generally be considered to be more rational than ultimate consumers?

3. What are the primary concerns of organizational buyers?

4. List several characteristics that differentiate organizational transactions from consumer ones.

5. What are the commonly used methods of organizational buying?

6. Why do buyers involved in a straight rebuy purchase require less information than those making a new-task purchase?

7. How does industrial demand differ from consumer demand?

8. What are the major components of an organization's buying center?

9. Identify the stages of the organizational buying decision process. How is this decision process used when making straight rebuys?

10. How do environmental, organizational, interpersonal, and individual factors affect organizational purchases?

11. What function does an industrial classification system help marketers perform?

12. List some sources that an organizational marketer can use to determine the names and addresses of potential organizational customers.

Application Questions

1. Identify organizations in your area that fit each organizational market category (producer, reseller, government, institutional). Explain your classifications.

2. Indicate the method of buying (description, inspection, sampling, negotiation) an organization would be most likely to use when purchasing each of the following items. Defend your selection.
   a. a building for the home office of a light bulb manufacturer
   b. wool for a clothing manufacturer
   c. an Alaskan cruise for a company retreat, assuming that a regular travel agency is used
   d. one-inch nails for a building contractor

3. Purchases by organizations may be described as new-task, modified rebuy, or straight rebuy. Categorize the following purchase decisions and explain your choice.
   a. Bob has purchased toothpicks from Smith Restaurant Supply for twenty-five years and recently placed an order for yellow toothpicks rather than the usual white ones.

   b. Jill's investment company has been purchasing envelopes from AAA Office Supply for a year and now needs to purchase boxes to mail year-end portfolio summaries to clients. Jill calls AAA to purchase these boxes.
   c. Reliance Insurance has been supplying its salespeople with small personal computers to assist in their sales efforts. The company recently agreed to begin supplying them with faster, more sophisticated computers.

4. Identifying qualified customers is important to the survival of any organization. NAICS provides helpful information about many different organizations. Find the NAICS manual at the library and identify the NAICS code for the following items:
   a. chocolate candy bars
   b. automobile tires
   c. men's athletic running shoes

Internet Exercise & Resources

Boeing Company

Boeing manufactures jets, helicopters, and other aircraft, as well as missiles. The company is also building some components of the International Space Station. Visit Boeing's Web site at

www.boeing.com

1. At what type of organizational markets are Boeing's products targeted?
2. How does Boeing's Web site address some of the concerns of organizational buyers?
3. What environmental factors do you think affect demand for Boeing's products?

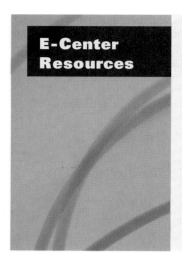

VIDEO CASE 9.1

Gulfstream Serves Organizational Customers

Ordering an airplane with a multimillion dollar price tag is hardly an everyday occurrence, even for a global corporation. Yet more than a thousand times in the past forty years, businesses and government agencies have plunked down as much as $37 million to buy a new Gulfstream jet. Alfred Lerner, chairman of MBNA Corporation, racks up 250,000 miles every year as he flies across the United States in his Gulfstream. Top executives of Montreal-based Seagram travel comfortably on the company's ultra-long-distance Gulfstream. And Gulfstreams are in regular use by top military officials of several nations, including the United States and Japan.

The corporate market for large-cabin private jets consists of about eight-thousand U.S. companies and thousands of international ones that fly their own aircraft. With $2 billion in annual sales and a 60 percent market share, Savannah-based Gulfstream is in a dogfight with Montreal's Bombardier—owner of such well-known brands as Learjet and de Havilland—for control of this lucrative market. Having weathered heavy financial turbulence during the early 1990s, Gulfstream is flying high these days, despite its intense competition with Bombardier. Its huge backlog of jet orders, worth $3 billion, is sure to keep employees busy well into the next decade.

Economic factors heavily influence the decision process and the timing of jet purchases. In bad economic times, when corporate profits nosedive and layoffs climb, many companies do not want to flaunt the big-ticket purchase of a private jet. Instead, they hold the line on costs by postponing or canceling aircraft purchases, which is why Gulfstream experienced low demand during the recession of 1990. Even companies that already own their own aircraft feel pressure during recessions to lower expenses by jettisoning their jets. Clearly, organizational customers are more apt to open their doors to Gulfstream's sales force when the economy is booming.

Financial and human resources also influence the purchase of corporate jets. Companies with international operations often justify such purchases by pointing to the savings in time and money when executives must visit far-flung factories and client sites, especially on short notice. In many cases, sending a management team via private jet is less expensive than buying a block of tickets on a commercial flight—and much more convenient, since airline schedules are not set according to the company's requirements. From a financial standpoint, few companies want high-salaried CEOs wasting their time waiting in airports.

Like other organizational customers, Gulfstream's customers value service. Gulfstream's support services are available all day, every day, by phone and online, to help customers locate a part, handle repairs, or obtain information. Quality is also a primary concern for Gulfstream's customers, who want their jets to be not only safe, but also stylish and comfortable. Gulfstream experts put in about 25,000 hours custom-crafting each jet's interior decor and furnishings (as much time as it takes to construct the shell and systems) to meet customer specifications.

In fact, the plane's interior is such an important element of the purchase that the head of the business or government agency generally plays an active role in its design. "I'd say the principal signs off on 95 percent of all the stuff we do," notes Gulfstream's vice president for completion services. In the course of planning the interior, some top executives consult their spouses or a professional designer. As construction progresses, Gulfstream works through a comprehensive checklist to ensure that each customer's choices and preferences have been clarified and confirmed. At a cost of roughly $12,000 per square foot, these organizational customers expect—and receive—lavish appointments, such as state-of-the-art stereo and video systems. And for $400,000 more, customers have the option of adding a satellite communications system capable of handling inflight E-mail, fax, and telephone transmissions.

Price is another key consideration for organizational buyers of aircraft. In this market, demand is inelastic, so raising the price will not significantly alter demand. Yet because customers are often aggressively courted by rival Bombardier, Gulfstream cannot afford to charge sky-high prices if it wants to retain its market share. For the past decade, the company has concentrated on slashing costs to keep prices as low as possible. It has also set up outsourcing arrangements as a way of containing costs.

At times, however, customers cannot justify the outright purchase of a new jet. Gulfstream has two programs to meet these customers' needs. First, Gulfstream allows businesses to buy a fraction of a new jet for a fixed monthly fee; in this way, customers can avoid an initial outlay of many millions of dollars and yet still have access to a private plane when needed. Second, customers can buy used aircraft that were traded in as part of the purchase price of new Gulfstream jets. These aircraft are completely refur-

bished and come with a warranty, making them an attractive alternative for customers who are concerned about cost. At the same time, selling used jets is a good way to introduce new customers to Gulfstream's quality products and its attentive service—two key reasons for the company's success.

Marketing is everybody's job at Gulfstream. The chairman flies around the world wooing prospects, and members of the board of directors also get involved. Board members, among them retired General Colin L. Powell and former Secretary of State George P. Schultz, receive a copy of Gulfstream's prospect list every month. By making phone calls or visiting prospects, board members demonstrate high-level interest and a personal touch that can tip the scale in favor of Gulfstream and clinch a sale.

Questions for Discussion

1. What type of organizational markets is Gulfstream most likely to serve?
2. Can a company's purchase of a new Gulfstream jet be classified as a new-task, modified rebuy, or straight rebuy purchase? Explain.
3. What role within the buying center is typically played by the CEO of an organization that is buying a jet from Gulfstream?
4. Gulfstream says its jets are largely designed by its customers. What does this imply about the stage at which Gulfstream becomes involved in the buying decision process?

CASE 9.2

Resellers Sweet on Jo's Candies

The customer list of Jo's Candies reads like a who's who of upscale retailing. Neiman Marcus, Starbucks, Norm Thompson, Williams-Sonoma, and Borders are just some of the top-drawer chains that are sweet on the confectioner's hand-dipped, chocolate-covered graham crackers. Jo's Candies, which began as a small chocolate shop in Southern California, has expanded over the past decade. It now sells 500,000 graham treats every month in more than three thousand gourmet shops, specialty stores, and coffee bars on four continents. While moving the company toward its goal of $15 million in annual sales by 2005, CEO Tom King has learned some important lessons about the tricky but profitable business of marketing to resellers.

The first lesson was that buyers for large chains want something unique. No retail giant wants to place an order if the same product—in identical packaging—is available in competing stores. For this reason, Jo's Candies happily customizes its packaging and its prod-

ucts to each chain's specifications. For example, the company puts its chocolate grahams in three-packs with Borders labeling for the book chain. No matter what the request, Jo's Candies stands ready to go along. When the Starbucks buyer requested a special product for the coffee chain's mail-order catalog and the Williams-Sonoma buyer wanted a different product for its gourmet kitchen catalog, CEO King said yes—then got busy behind the scenes making sure the orders were filled and the buyers were satisfied.

The company has also found that personal attention is important for building trust and strengthening relationships with resellers. "I always try to communicate with major customers once a week—by fax, phone, or E-mail—and try to meet with my largest accounts face-to-face every four to six weeks," explains CEO King. Even small gestures are important. Retail buyers hear from Jo's Candies when birthdays and anniversaries roll around. But they also know that

King is willing to hop on a jet and meet with them when problems arise. And Jo's Candies guarantees every sale, offering to buy back its chocolate grahams if resellers are unhappy after three months of selling them. The only time the company had to make good on this guarantee was when a customer asked to return a case of cookies that he had inadvertently left in the sun.

The third lesson about doing business with resellers was a painful and expensive one for King. The Nordstrom chain, the largest of Jo's Candies retail accounts, was buying more than $200,000 worth of Jo's Candies every year. Then, one by one, various Nordstrom stores decided it was cheaper to cook up their own chocolate grahams than to keep buying from an outside source. Soon, all but six Nordstrom stores stopped selling Jo's Candies, a loss that hit the company quite hard. This episode taught the CEO the necessity of constantly expanding the customer base so that the company will not become overly dependent on any one reseller. In fact, Jo's Candies now has a strict rule whereby no single customer is allowed to account for more than 60 percent of overall sales.

Still, every order from a retail chain represents a major profit opportunity for a small manufacturer like Jo's Candies, which is why the company continues targeting larger resellers in particular. In the reseller market, size matters. National chains have many shelves to fill, so they buy tremendous quantities, which makes them an attractive target for many suppliers. On the other hand, these big buyers are often tough negotiators who look closely at the terms of every sale, especially price. In addition, they sometimes request a period of exclusivity, asking Jo's Candies not to sell the same product to a competitor for several months or more. King has on occasion accepted this condition, but sometimes he will agree only if the reseller says it will guarantee a certain volume of purchases for that period. "Usually, they can't make the guarantee, so they back down," says the CEO.

While the large resellers never lose sight of the enormous buying power they wield, they also know they need suppliers who can provide them with good merchandise for their stores. Product quality, service, and timing are important concerns for these chains. So, as Jo's Candies continues to grow, it paves the way for more and bigger orders by following the pattern of establishing a relationship with a reseller and then proving it can deliver as promised. "You're selling a product," observes the CEO, "but you're also selling your reputation."

The success of Jo's Candies—as well as awards and rave reviews in *Food & Wine* and other magazines—has attracted imitators. With six or more rivals bringing out their own versions of chocolate-covered grahams, King has had to don his apron and go back into the kitchen to experiment with chocolate and other ingredients. In his words, the challenge is "to create new combinations to be one jump ahead." The CEO says he already has "at least three proven winners [which] I will roll out in the next three years." Many of the company's new products are being marketed first through Jo's Candies' mail-order business in gift baskets, and then sold to resellers in large volume.

The final lesson King has learned in nearly a decade of selling to resellers is to respect their time. Before meeting with a reseller, the CEO does his homework, reviewing information about the account and writing a short agenda to guide the discussion. Some small suppliers may quake at the thought of pitching a product to the buyer for a well-known chain, but not King, who says: "I am never, ever intimidated, because I go in there prepared."

Questions for Discussion

1. If you were a buyer for a large reseller, what information would you request from Jo's Candies before you decide whether to order for the first time?

2. If you were Tom King, what information would you research about a large reseller in advance of your first sales call?

3. How should Tom King respond if a reseller mentions a preference for multiple sourcing?

STRATEGIC CASE 2

PalmPilot: Computing Power in the Palm of Your Hand

A computer in the palm of your hand? Apple Computer tried it with the Newton—which the company dubbed a PDA ("personal digital assistant")—and failed miserably, spending an estimated $500 million in the process. In 1994, just two months after Newton's debut, Palm Computing, founded by Jeff Hawkins, introduced Zoomer PDA for the Radio Shack chain. Zoomer was also a flop. But Hawkins and his technoteam learned enough from these two flawed products to create the PalmPilot, a pocket-sized device that lets users track appointments, access an address book, write memos, and even surf the Net and send messages via wireless communications. The PalmPilot quickly and unexpectedly became the fastest-selling computer product in history; well over 2 million have been sold throughout the United States.

Who Was Buying the Zoomer—and Why?

In 1994, although humbled by the failure of the Zoomer PDA, Hawkins and his colleagues were not ready to give up. Instead, they used in-depth surveys to find out exactly who had bought the Zoomer and—just as important—why. The results completely contradicted their assumptions about who would want a PDA and what it would be used for. Palm Computing had been targeting the consumer market, but it turned out that businesses were the biggest buyers. The company had envisioned the PDA as competition for a personal computer, but users saw it as complementary, more like a substitute for paper and pencil with which they could take notes and juggle appointments on the fly. Armed with these findings, Hawkins took some time to rethink the PDA concept and emerged with two critical conclusions.

A New Approach for PalmPilot

First, Hawkins concluded that trying to make a device that can decipher anyone's handwriting was asking too much from a device as small as a PDA. That had been the main problem for Apple's Newton. Hawkins envisioned an entirely new approach. Rather than have the PDA learn the user's handwriting, the user would learn the PDA's writing system. "People like learning," he explains. "People can learn to work with tools. Computers are tools. People like to learn how to use things that work." On the basis of this insight, Palm Computing developed Graffiti, a system of simplified pen strokes representing letters. Once users mastered the Graffiti system, the PDA would be able to decode their handwritten messages every time.

Hawkin's second conclusion was that size matters. To be convenient, the PDA had to be able to fit in a shirt pocket, no small feat for a multifunctional computer product. Once again, the Palm Computing team rose to the challenge, crafting a six-ounce pocket-sized computer powered by AAA batteries and designed to sell for under $300. Even more amazing, the entire new-product development effort involved just twenty-eight employees and cost a relatively modest $3 million, a small price tag in the high-spending computer world.

A New Parent for PalmPilot

Needing deeper pockets to fund production of its new product, Palm Computing approached U.S. Robotics and ultimately agreed to be acquired for $44 million in stock (U.S. Robotics was later acquired by 3Com). With the parent company providing production funding, distribution connections, manufacturing savvy, and an international reputation that opened many doors, Palm Computing was off and running, launching its first two products in April 1996. The PalmPilot 1000 was a basic PDA model; the PalmPilot 5000 was a memory-enhanced one. Computer magazines raved and people gawked over the new gadgets. In short order, PalmPilots were seen tucked in shirt pockets at business meetings all over the United States.

New Uses for PalmPilot

"By midsummer, we couldn't build enough of them," remembers Palm Computing's marketing manager." Customers were stamping their feet. And we weren't just selling to geeks in Silicon Valley. We were selling all over the place." As the research had indicated, businesses were the prime purchasers, pushing sales to heady levels as they found many everyday uses for PalmPilots. Some examples of the PalmPilot in action:

- At Harley-Davidson in York, Pennsylvania, engineers and technicians use PalmPilots to collect quality control data and statistical information about motorcycle products on the assembly line.
- At Bankers Trust in New York City, employees use PalmPilots to manage their schedules, to-do lists, and contacts.
- At Outreach Health Services in Austin, Texas, home health care workers use PalmPilots to report on changes in patients' conditions and to structure their daily activities.
- At Massachusetts General Hospital in Boston, physicians serving their residencies carry PalmPilots so they can have phone numbers and patient notes at their fingertips as they rotate between two hospital buildings.

New Competition for PalmPilot

Palm Computing's success has resulted in competition for the handheld computer market. Philips, Everex, Casio, and other manufacturers recently introduced palm-sized PCs based on a Microsoft operating system; this is a significant competitive threat because Microsoft wields so much power in the marketplace. PalmPilots do not use Microsoft systems, but they have enjoyed such domination of the market from the start that 12,000 other software developers have committed to creating new programs specifically for PalmPilots. The competitive landscape may change, however, when Microsoft releases an upgraded operating system for palm-sized PCs and the joint venture of Nokia, Motorola, Ericsson, and Psion starts selling a new handheld computer that will compete directly with the PalmPilot.

Palm Computing continues to build on its success by making the PalmPilot increasingly convenient. It has added two-way wireless communication capabilities, improved the viewing screen, and reduced the size of the device—all of this while keeping the price at a reasonable level for its business customers.

New Company, New Targets

These days, Palm Computing is moving ahead without its founder. Jeff Hawkins and fellow executive Donna Dubinsky left Palm in 1998 to form Handspring, a start-up company that will specialize in handheld computers for the consumer market. Handspring's products will use a licensed version of the PalmPilot operating system rather than the Microsoft system.

This time around, Hawkins is targeting young segments of the consumer market, especially teenagers and college students. "You can imagine everyone in high school having one of these on their desks," he says. Dubinsky, who is Handspring's CEO, notes, "Kids have very complex schedules. You'd be surprised how many people they could put in an address book." Looking ahead, she confidently predicts that "every college kid will be carrying one of these things within five years." Just as the PalmPilot touched off a buying frenzy in the business market, the new Handspring devices may spark a similar frenzy in the consumer market.

Questions for Discussion

1. What type of targeting strategy is being used for the PalmPilot? What segmentation variables did Palm Computing use for the PalmPilot? Explain your answers.

2. If a company is considering the purchase of PalmPilots for its sales force, what issues are likely to be the most important?

3. What marketing research do you think Handspring should conduct to support its development and introduction of a new handheld computer for the consumer market?

4. How is Handspring applying its knowledge of consumer lifestyles in the creation of its new product?

Product Decisions

We are now prepared to analyze the decisions and activities associated with developing and maintaining effective marketing mixes. In Parts 3 through 6, we focus on the major components of the marketing mix: product, distribution, promotion, and price. Part 3 explores the product ingredient of the marketing mix. In Chapter 10, we introduce basic concepts and relationships that must be understood if one is to make effective product decisions. In Chapter 11, we analyze a variety of dimensions regarding product management, including line extensions and product modification, new product development, and product deletions. Branding, packaging, and labeling are discussed in Chapter 12. The nature, importance, and characteristics of services are explored in Chapter 13.

Economic forces

Competitive forces

Product

Political forces

Price

Customer

Distribution

Socio-cultural forces

Promotion

Legal and regulatory forces

Technological forces

10

Product Concepts

OBJECTIVES

- To understand the concept of a product

- To understand how to classify products

- To become familiar with the concepts of product item, product line, and product mix and understand how they are connected

- To understand the concept of product life cycle and its impact on marketing strategies

- To become familiar with the product adoption process

- To understand why some products fail and some succeed

Going Batty
for the New Beetle

In 1998, Beetlemania broke out across North America. Nearly two decades after Volkswagen stopped selling the original Bug, the nostalgic design and efficient performance of its New Beetle drove buyers back into VW dealerships throughout the United States and Canada. Baby boomers and Generation X buyers alike put their names on waiting lists, hoping for the chance to buy the colorful little car with the curvy fenders and the bug-eye headlights.

The saga of the New Beetle stretches back to 1994, when a financially troubled VW displayed a prototype—whose styling echoed the rounded lines of the original Bug—at the North American International Auto Show in Detroit. Reaction was so positive that VW immediately pushed the prototype into full production at its Mexican factory. Although the New Beetle's styling was reminiscent of the original Bug, the rest of the car was strictly state-of-the-art, with front and side air bags, air conditioning, and a peppy engine located up front (not in the rear, where the orig-

inal Bug's engine was). What's more, the price was right, with the basic model carrying a price tag well under $20,000.

VW launched the New Beetle early in 1998, backed by witty advertising that reflected the car's decidedly unconventional personality. "If you sold your soul in the '80s, here's your chance to buy it back," proclaimed one ad. Consumers smiled, got the message, and raced down to the nearest VW showroom to test-drive a New Beetle. The initial supply of cars sold out quickly, leading to waiting lists at most dealerships.

VW had projected first-year sales of 50,000 for the new car, but demand was so strong that in the first ten months, the company sold 55,000 in the United States alone and another 9,500 in Canada. Building on this spectacular success, VW introduced a New Super Beetle at the 1999 Auto Show. It has a more powerful engine, but its price tag is still shy of $20,000. In win-win fashion, the New Beetle is helping VW make a financial U-turn while making a lot of car buyers very happy.[1]

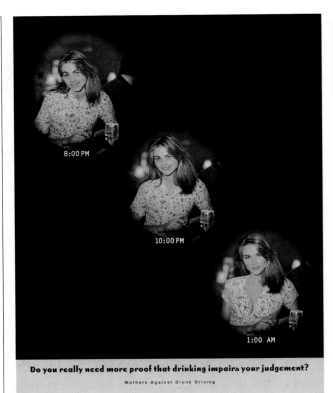

Do you really need more proof that drinking impairs your judgement?

Mothers Against Drunk Driving

Figure 10.1
Examples of a Marketer of Services and a Marketer of Ideas
Kim's Martial Arts is a marketer of services, whereas MADD is primarily a marketer of ideas.

The product is an important variable in the marketing mix. Products such as Volkswagen's New Beetle can be a firm's most important asset and visible contact with buyers. If a company's products do not meet its customers' desires and needs, the company will fail unless it makes adjustments. Developing successful products like the New Beetle requires knowledge of fundamental marketing and product concepts.

In this chapter, we first define a product and discuss how buyers view products. Next, we examine the concepts of product line and product mix. We then explore the stages of the product life cycle and the effect of each life cycle stage on marketing strategies. Next, we outline the product adoption process. Finally, we discuss the factors that contribute to a product's failure or success.

What Is a Product?

product Anything, tangible or intangible, received in an exchange

good A tangible physical entity

service An intangible result of the application of human and mechanical efforts to people or objects

ideas Concepts, philosophies, images, or issues

A **product** is anything you receive in an exchange. It can be either tangible or intangible and includes functional, social, and psychological utilities or benefits. A product can be an idea, a service, a good, or any combination of these three. This definition also covers supporting services that go with goods, such as installation, guarantees, product information, and promises of repair or maintenance. A **good** is a tangible physical entity, such as a Black & Decker drill or a Big Mac. A **service,** by contrast, is intangible; it is the result of the application of human and mechanical efforts to people or objects. Examples of services include a game at Madison Square Garden between the New York Knicks and the Boston Celtics, medical examinations, child day care, real estate services, and martial arts lessons (see Figure 10.1). (Chapter 13 provides a detailed discussion of services.) **Ideas** are concepts, philosophies, images, or issues. They provide the psychological stimulation that aids in solving problems or adjusting to the environment. For example, MADD (Mothers Against Drunk Driving) promotes safe consumption of alcohol and stricter enforcement of laws against drunk driving (see Figure 10.1).

When buyers purchase a product, they are really buying the benefits and satisfaction they think the product will provide. A Rolex watch, for example, is purchased to make a statement of success, not just for telling time. Services, in particular, are pur-

250

chased on the basis of promises of satisfaction. Promises, suggested by images and symbols, help consumers make judgments about tangible and intangible products.[2] Often, symbols and cues are used to make intangible products more tangible or real to the consumer. Allstate Insurance Company, for example, uses giant hands to symbolize security, strength, and friendliness.

Classifying Products

consumer products
Products purchased to satisfy personal and family needs

business products
Products bought to use in an organization's operations, to resell, or to make other products

convenience products
Relatively inexpensive, frequently purchased items for which buyers exert minimal purchasing effort

Products fall into one of two general categories. Products purchased to satisfy personal and family needs are **consumer products.** Those bought to use in a firm's operations, to resell, or to make other products are **business products.** Consumers buy products to satisfy their personal wants, whereas business buyers seek to satisfy the goals of their organizations.

The same item can be both a consumer product and a business product. For example, when consumers buy a computer disk for their home computer, it is classified as a consumer product. However, when an organization purchases computer disks for office use, they are considered business products because they are used in daily operations. Thus, the buyer's intent—or the ultimate use of the product—determines whether an item is classified as a consumer or a business product.

Why do we need to know about product classifications? The main reason is that classes of products are aimed at particular target markets, and this affects distribution, promotion, and pricing decisions. Furthermore, the types of marketing efforts needed differ among the classes of consumer and business products. In short, the entire marketing mix can be affected by how a product is classified. In this section, we examine the characteristics of consumer and business products and explore the marketing activities associated with some of them.

Consumer Products

**Figure 10.2
Advertisement for
Convenience Products**
The burden for promoting convenience products, like Tic Tac® Mints, falls primarily on the manufacturer.

The most widely accepted approach to classifying consumer products is based on characteristics of consumer purchasing behavior. It divides products into four categories: convenience, shopping, specialty, and unsought products. However, not all buyers behave in the same way when purchasing a specific type of product. Thus, a single product can fit into several categories. To minimize this problem, marketers think in terms of how buyers *generally* behave when purchasing a specific item. In addition, they recognize that the "correct" classification can be determined only by considering a particular firm's intended target market. With these thoughts in mind, let us examine the four traditional categories of consumer products.

Convenience Products **Convenience products** are relatively inexpensive, frequently purchased items for which buyers exert only minimal purchasing effort. They range from bread, soft drinks, and chewing gum to gasoline and newspapers. The buyer spends little time planning the purchase or comparing available brands or sellers. Even a buyer who prefers a specific brand will readily choose a substitute if the preferred brand is not conveniently available.

Classifying a product as a convenience product has several implications for a firm's marketing strategy. A convenience product is normally marketed through many retail outlets. Because sellers experience high inventory turnover, per-unit gross margins can be relatively low. Producers of convenience products, such as Tic Tac® Mints (see Figure 10.2), expect little promotional effort at the retail level and thus must provide it themselves with advertising and sales promotion. Packaging is also an important element of the marketing mix for convenience products. The package may have to sell the product because many convenience items are available only on a self-service basis at the retail level.

shopping products Items for which buyers are willing to expend considerable effort in planning and making purchases

Shopping Products   **Shopping products** are items for which buyers are willing to expend considerable effort in planning and making the purchase. Buyers spend much time comparing stores and brands with respect to prices, product features, qualities, services, and perhaps warranties. Appliances, bicycles, furniture, stereos, cameras, and shoes (see Figure 10.3) exemplify shopping products. These products are expected to last a fairly long time and thus are purchased less frequently than convenience items. Even though shopping products are more expensive than convenience products, few buyers of shopping products are particularly brand-loyal. If they were, they would be unwilling to shop and compare among brands.

To market a shopping product effectively, a marketer considers several key issues. Shopping products require fewer retail outlets than convenience products. Because shopping products are purchased less frequently, inventory turnover is lower, and middlemen expect to receive higher gross margins. Although large sums of money may be required to advertise shopping products, an even larger percentage of resources is likely to be used for personal selling. Usually, the producer and the middlemen expect some cooperation from one another with respect to providing parts and repair services and performing promotional activities.

specialty products Items with unique characteristics that buyers are willing to expend considerable effort to obtain

Specialty Products   **Specialty products** possess one or more unique characteristics, and generally buyers are willing to expend considerable effort to obtain them. Buyers actually plan the purchase of a specialty product; they know exactly what they want and will not accept a substitute. Examples of specialty products include a Mont Blanc pen and a one-of-a-kind piece of baseball memorabilia, such as a ball signed by

Figure 10.3
Examples of Shopping Products
Shoes and cameras generally are viewed as shopping products because of their characteristics and the manner in which consumers behave in the purchase of these products.

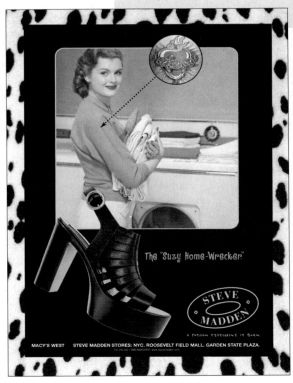

Babe Ruth. When searching for specialty products, buyers do not compare alternatives; they are concerned primarily with finding an outlet that has the preselected product available.

The fact that an item is a specialty product can affect a firm's marketing efforts in several ways. Specialty products are often distributed through a limited number of retail outlets. Like shopping products, they are purchased infrequently, causing lower inventory turnover and thus requiring relatively high gross margins.

unsought products
Products purchased to solve a sudden problem, products of which customers are unaware, and products that people do not necessarily think about buying

Unsought Products   **Unsought products** are products purchased when a sudden problem must be solved, products of which customers are unaware, and products that people do not necessarily think of purchasing. Emergency automobile repairs and some types of auto accessories, such as snow chains, are examples of products needed quickly to solve a problem. Life insurance is a product that individuals may not necessarily think about buying.

Business Products

Business products are usually purchased on the basis of an organization's goals and objectives. Generally, the functional aspects of the product are more important than the psychological rewards sometimes associated with consumer products. Business products can be classified into seven categories according to their characteristics and intended uses: installations, accessory equipment, raw materials, component parts, process materials, MRO supplies, and business services.

installations   Facilities and nonportable major equipment

Installations   **Installations** include facilities, such as office buildings, factories, and warehouses, and major equipment that is nonportable, such as production lines and very large machines. Major equipment usually is used for production purposes. Some major equipment is custom-made to perform specific functions for a particular organization, but other items are standardized and perform similar tasks for many types of firms. Normally, installations are expensive and intended to be used for a considerable length of time. Because they are so expensive and normally a long-term investment of capital, purchase decisions are often made by high-level management. Marketers of installations frequently must provide a variety of services, including training, repairs, maintenance assistance, and even aid in financing such purchases.

accessory equipment
Equipment used in production or office activities

Accessory Equipment   **Accessory equipment** does not become a part of the final physical product but is used in production or office activities. Examples include file cabinets, fractional-horsepower motors, calculators, and tools. Compared with major equipment, accessory items are usually much cheaper; purchased routinely, with less negotiation; and treated as expense items rather than capital items because they are not expected to last as long. Accessory products are standardized items that can be used in several aspects of a firm's operations. More outlets are required for distributing accessory equipment than for installations, but sellers do not have to provide the multitude of services expected of installations marketers.

raw materials   Basic natural materials that become part of a physical product

Raw Materials   **Raw materials** are the basic natural materials that actually become part of a physical product. They include minerals, chemicals, agricultural products, and materials from forests and oceans. They are usually bought and sold according to grades and specifications, and in relatively large quantities. For example, consider the use of rose oil and jasmine in making perfume, as discussed in Globalmarketing.

component parts   Items that become part of the physical product and are either finished items ready for assembly or ones that need little processing before assembly

Component Parts   **Component parts** become a part of the physical product and are either finished items ready for assembly or products that need little processing before assembly. Although they become part of a larger product, component parts can often be easily identified and distinguished. Spark plugs, tires, clocks, and switches are all component parts of the automobile. Buyers purchase such items according to their own specifications or industry standards. They expect the parts to be of specified quality and delivered on time so that production is not slowed or stopped. Producers that are primarily assemblers, such as most lawn mower or computer manufacturers, depend heavily on the suppliers of component parts.

process materials
Materials used directly in the production of other products but that are not readily identifiable

Process Materials **Process materials** are used directly in the production of other products. Unlike component parts, however, process materials are not readily identifiable. For example, a salad dressing manufacturer includes vinegar in its salad dressing. The vinegar is a process material because it is included in the salad dressing but is not identifiable. As with component parts, process materials are purchased according to industry standards or the purchaser's specifications.

MRO supplies
Maintenance, repair, and operating items that facilitate production and operations but do not become part of the finished product

MRO Supplies **MRO supplies** are maintenance, repair, and operating items that facilitate production and operations but do not become part of the finished product. Paper, pencils, oils, cleaning agents, and paints are in this category. MRO supplies are commonly sold through numerous outlets and are purchased routinely. To ensure that supplies are available when needed, buyers often deal with more than one seller.

business services
The intangible products that many organizations use in their operations

Business Services **Business services** are the intangible products that many organizations use in their operations. They include financial, legal, marketing research, information technology, and janitorial services. American Express Corporate Purchasing credit cards and Arthur Andersen, both shown in Figure 10.4, are providers of business services. Firms must decide whether to provide their own services internally or obtain them from outside the organization. This decision depends on the costs associated with each alternative and how frequently the services are needed.

Globalmarketing

The Sweet Smell of Global Perfume Markets

With over a thousand brands on the market and a hundred new brands launched last year in the United States alone, perfume is a growing business. Often sold in stylish retail establishments full of glass, polished granite, and chrome, such as Sephora in Paris, perfumes have names like "Joy," "Beautiful," and "La Dolce Vita." Most upscale fashion designers and jewelers have a perfume bearing their brand name. Before they reach this level of glamor, however, fragrances have to be created, and suppliers like Givaudan Roure, International Flavors & Fragrances, Firmenich, and Quest International compete to do just that.

When a company like Christian Dior or Calvin Klein decides to market a new fragrance, it prepares a brief —an outline of the perfume's concept and target customer—which it then gives to suppliers. Suppliers, known as perfumers, may spend as much as $250,000 to create a fragrance in the laboratory with no guarantee of winning a contract to supply the scent.

Traditional perfume-making requires the blending of four or five hundred ingredients, including essential oils from roses, jasmine, lavender, and other plants. At one time, all perfume ingredients were grown and hand-picked in France. Because labor costs in France are high, a pound of French rose oil concentrate, which requires eight hundred pounds of roses, costs almost $4,000. Jasmine oil produced near the town of Grasse in southern France costs about $12,000 a pound. In recent years, perfumers have been able to lower their costs by purchasing essential oils from developing countries, such as Bulgaria, India, Turkey, and Morocco, where labor costs are much lower. Moroccan rose oil, for example, costs $600 a pound.

In addition to seeking out global suppliers, perfumers are hoping to appeal to global customers. U.S. perfumers insist that although France may be the center of the fragrance universe in the minds of French consumers, the words *made in France* don't mean as much to consumers in the United States and other countries. In fact, because fragrance sales in Europe and the United States are flat, perfumers are creating scents that they hope will appeal to customers in Eastern Europe, China, South America, and the Middle East. Perfumers are particularly interested in Saudi Arabia, where women are reported to splash on more gallons of perfume each year per capita than anywhere else in the world. What was once an elite French enterprise is becoming a truly global one. Rather than creating fragrances designed to appeal to a select few, perfumers are looking for fragrance concepts that will be globally accepted.

Figure 10.4
Providers of Business Services
Both American Express and Arthur Andersen provide a large number of services to businesses.

Product Line and Product Mix

product item   A specific version of a product

product line   A group of closely related product items viewed as a unit because of marketing, technical, or end-use considerations

product mix   The total group of products that an organization makes available to customers

width of product mix
The number of product lines a company offers

depth of product mix
The average number of different products offered in each product line

Marketers must understand the relationships among all the products of their organization if they are to coordinate the marketing of the total group of products. The following concepts help describe the relationships among an organization's products. A **product item** is a specific version of a product that can be designated as a distinct offering among an organization's products. An L.L. Bean flannel shirt represents a product item. A **product line** is a group of closely related product items that are considered to be a unit because of marketing, technical, or end-use considerations. For example, L.L. Bean's product line of children's clothing differs from its product line of outdoor clothing for adults. The exact boundaries of a product line (although sometimes confusing) are usually indicated by using descriptive terms such as "frozen dessert" product line or "shampoo" product line. To come up with the optimum product line, marketers must understand buyers' goals. Specific product items in a product line usually reflect the desires of different target markets or the different needs of consumers.

A **product mix** is the composite, or total, group of products that an organization makes available to customers. For example, all the health care, beauty care, laundry and cleaning, food and beverage, paper, cosmetic, and fragrance products that Procter & Gamble manufactures constitute its product mix. The **width of product mix** is measured by the number of product lines a company offers. The **depth of product mix** is the average number of different products offered in each product

Laundry detergents	Toothpastes	Bar soaps	Deodorants	Shampoos	Tissue/Towel
Oxydol 1914	Gleem 1952	Ivory 1879	Old Spice 1948	Prell 1946	Charmin 1928
Ivory Snow 1930	Crest 1955	Camay 1926	Secret 1956	Pantene 1947	Puffs 1960
Dreft 1933		Zest 1952	Sure 1972	Head & Shoulders 1961	Bounty 1965
Tide 1946		Safeguard 1963		Vidal Sassoon 1974	Royale 1996
Cheer 1950		Coast 1974		Pert Plus 1979	
Bold 1965		Oil of Olay 1993		Ivory 1983	
Gain 1966					
Era 1972					

Depth

Width

Figure 10.5
The Concepts of Product Mix Width and Depth Applied to Selected Procter & Gamble Products

Source: Reprinted by permission of Procter & Gamble.

line. Figure 10.5 shows the width and depth of a part of Procter & Gamble's product mix. Procter & Gamble is known for using distinctive branding, packaging, and consumer advertising to promote individual items in its detergent product line. Tide, Bold, Gain, Cheer, and Era—all Procter & Gamble detergents—share the same distribution channels and similar manufacturing facilities. Yet each is promoted as a distinctive product adding depth to the product line.

Product Life Cycles and Marketing Strategies

product life cycle
The progression of a product through four stages: introduction, growth, maturity, and decline

Just as biological cycles progress from birth through growth and decline, so do product life cycles. As Figure 10.6 shows, a **product life cycle** has four major stages: introduction, growth, maturity, and decline. As a product moves through its cycle, the strategies relating to competition, promotion, distribution, pricing, and market information must be periodically evaluated and possibly changed. Astute marketing managers use the life cycle concept to make sure that the introduction, alteration, and termination of a product are timed and executed properly. By understanding the typical life cycle pattern, marketers are better able to maintain profitable products and drop unprofitable ones.

Figure 10.6
The Four Stages of the Product Life Cycle

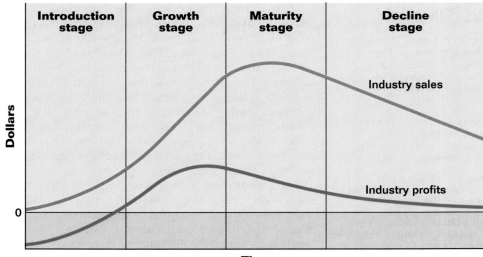

Introduction

introduction stage   The initial stage of a product's life cycle—its first appearance in the marketplace—when sales start at zero and profits are negative

The **introduction stage** of the life cycle begins at a product's first appearance in the marketplace, when sales start at zero and profits are negative. Profits are below zero because initial revenues are low, and the company generally must cover large expenses for promotion and distribution. Notice in Figure 10.6 how sales should move upward from zero, and profits should also move upward from a position in which profits are negative because of high expenses.

Developing and introducing a new product can mean an outlay of $20 million or more. The risk of new product failure is quite high, depending on the industry and how product failure is defined. Because of high risks and costs, few product introductions represent revolutionary inventions. More typically, product introductions involve a new packaged convenience food, a new model of automobile, or a new fashion in clothing, rather than a major product innovation.

Potential buyers must be made aware of the new product's features, uses, and advantages. Two difficulties may arise at this point. First, sellers may not have the resources, technological knowledge, and marketing know-how to launch the product successfully. And, second, the initial product price may have to be high to recoup expensive marketing research or development costs. Given these difficulties, it is not surprising that many products never get beyond the introduction stage.

Most new products start off slowly and seldom generate enough sales to bring immediate profits. As buyers learn about the new product, marketers should be alert for product weaknesses and make corrections quickly to prevent the product's early demise. Marketing strategy should be designed to attract the segment that is most interested and has the fewest objections. As the sales curve moves upward and the breakeven point is reached, the growth stage begins.

Growth

growth stage   The stage of a product's life cycle when sales rise rapidly and profits reach a peak and then start to decline

During the **growth stage**, sales rise rapidly, and profits reach a peak and then start to decline (see Figure 10.6). The growth stage is critical to a product's survival because competitive reactions to the product's success during this period will affect the product's life expectancy. For example, the maker of Tabasco successfully marketed the first hot pepper sauce but today competes against numerous other brands. Profits begin to decline late in the growth stage as more competitors enter the market, driving prices down and creating the need for heavy promotional expenses. At this point, a typical marketing strategy encourages strong brand loyalty and competes with aggressive emulators of the product. During the growth stage, an organization tries to strengthen its market share and develop a competitive niche by emphasizing the product's benefits. Aggressive pricing, including price cuts, is also typical during this stage. For example, the pore strip (see Figure 10.7) is in its growth stage.

As sales increase, management must support the momentum by adjusting the marketing strategy. The goal is to establish and fortify the product's market position by encouraging brand loyalty. To achieve greater market penetration, segmentation

Figure 10.7
Growth Stage
The pore strip category is in the growth stage.

may have to be used more intensely. That would require developing product variations to satisfy the needs of people in several different market segments. Marketers should also analyze the competing brands' product position relative to their own brands and take corrective actions.

Gaps in geographic market coverage should be filled during the growth period. As a product gains market acceptance, new distribution outlets usually become easier to obtain. Marketers sometimes move from an exclusive or selective exposure to a more intensive network of dealers to achieve greater market penetration. Marketers must also make sure that the physical distribution system is running efficiently so that customers' orders are processed accurately and delivered on time.

Promotion expenditures may be slightly lower than during the introductory stage but are still quite substantial. As sales increase, promotion costs should drop as a percentage of total sales. A falling ratio between promotion expenditures and sales should contribute significantly to increased profits. The advertising messages should stress brand benefits. Coupons and samples may be used to increase market share.

After recovering development costs, a business may be able to lower prices. As sales volume increases, efficiencies in production can result in lower costs. These savings may be passed on to buyers. If demand remains strong and there are few competitive threats, prices tend to remain stable. If price cuts are feasible, they can help a brand gain market share and discourage new competitors from entering the market.

Maturity

maturity stage The stage of a product's life cycle when the sales curve peaks and starts to decline and profits continue to decline

During the **maturity stage,** the sales curve peaks and starts to decline, and profits continue to decline (see Figure 10.6). This stage is characterized by intense competition, as many brands are in the market. Competitors emphasize improvements and differences in their versions of the product. As a result, during the maturity stage, weaker competitors are squeezed out or lose interest in the product. For example, some brands of VCRs have perished as the VCR experiences the maturity stage.

During the maturity phase, the producers who remain in the market are likely to change their promotional and distribution efforts. Advertising and dealer-oriented promotions are typical during this stage of the product life cycle. Marketers must also take into account that as the product reaches maturity, buyers' knowledge of it attains a high level. Consumers of the product are no longer inexperienced generalists but instead are experienced specialists. Marketers of mature products sometimes expand distribution into global markets. Often, the products have to be adapted to more precisely fit differing needs of global customers.

Because many products are in the maturity stage of their life cycles, marketers must know how to deal with these products and be prepared to adjust their marketing strategies. There are many approaches to altering marketing strategies during the maturity stage. Some of these are shown in Table 10.1. As noted there, to increase the sales of mature products, marketers may suggest new uses of their products. Arm & Hammer has boosted demand for its baking soda by this method. Kraft General Foods continues to stimulate sales of Jell-O by promoting new uses. As customers become more experienced and knowledgeable about products during the maturity stage (particularly about business products), the benefits they seek may change as well, necessitating product modifications.

During the maturity stage, marketers actively encourage dealers to support the product. Dealers may be offered promotional assistance in lowering their inventory costs. In general, marketers go to great lengths to serve dealers and to provide incentives for selling their brands.

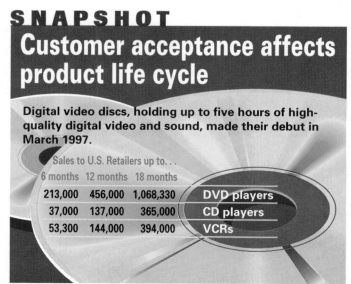

SNAPSHOT

Customer acceptance affects product life cycle

Digital video discs, holding up to five hours of high-quality digital video and sound, made their debut in March 1997.

Sales to U.S. Retailers up to...

	6 months	12 months	18 months	
	213,000	456,000	1,068,330	DVD players
	37,000	137,000	365,000	CD players
	53,300	144,000	394,000	VCRs

Table 10.1	Selected Approaches for Managing Products in the Maturity Stage
Approaches	**Examples**
Develop new product uses	Knox gelatin used as a plant food Arm & Hammer baking soda marketed as a refrigerator deodorant Cheez Whiz promoted as a microwavable cheese sauce
Increase product usage among current users	Multiple packaging used for products in which a larger supply at the point of consumption actually increases consumption (such as for soft drinks or beer)
Increase the number of users	Global markets or small niches in domestic markets pursued
Add product features	CD-ROM built into computers Dual air bags used in automobiles
Change package sizes	Single-serving sizes introduced Travel-size packages of personal care products introduced
Increase product quality	Life of light bulbs increased Reliability and durability of U.S.-made automobiles increased
Change nonproduct marketing mix variables—promotion, price, distribution	Focus of Dr Pepper advertisements shifted from teenagers to people 18–54 years of age A package of dishwasher detergent containing one-third more product offered for the same price Computer hardware marketed through mail-order outlets

To maintain market share during the maturity stage requires moderate, and sometimes large, promotion expenditures. Advertising messages focus on differentiating a brand from the field of competitors, and sales promotion efforts are aimed at both consumers and resellers.

A greater mixture of pricing strategies is used during the maturity stage. Strong price competition is likely and may ignite price wars. Firms also compete in other ways than price, such as through product quality or service. In addition, marketers also develop price flexibility to differentiate offerings in product lines. Markdowns and price incentives are common. Prices may have to be increased, however, if distribution and production costs increase.

Decline

decline stage The stage of a product's life cycle when sales fall rapidly

During the **decline stage,** sales fall rapidly (see Figure 10.6). When this happens, the marketer considers pruning items from the product line to eliminate those not earning a profit. At this time, too, the marketer may cut promotion efforts, eliminate marginal distributors, and, finally, plan to phase out the product.

An organization can justify maintaining a product as long as it contributes to profits or enhances the overall effectiveness of a product mix. In this stage, marketers must determine whether to eliminate the product or to try to reposition it to extend its life. Usually, a declining product has lost its distinctiveness because similar competing products have been introduced. Competition engenders increased substitution and brand switching as buyers become insensitive to minor product differences. For these reasons, marketers do little to change a product's style, design, or other attributes during its decline. New technology or social trends, product substitutes, or environmental considerations may also indicate that the time has come to delete a product.

During a product's decline, outlets with strong sales volumes are maintained, and unprofitable outlets are weeded out. An entire marketing channel may be eliminated if it does not contribute adequately to profits. An outlet not previously used, such as a factory outlet, will sometimes be used to liquidate remaining inventory of an obsolete product. As sales decline, the product becomes more obscure, but loyal buyers seek out dealers who carry it.

Spending on promotion efforts usually is considerably reduced. Advertising of special offers may slow the rate of decline. Sales promotions, such as coupons and premiums, may temporarily regain buyers' attention. As the product continues to decline, the sales staff shifts its emphasis to more profitable products.

To have a product return a profit may be more important to a firm than maintaining a certain market share through repricing. To squeeze out all possible remaining profits, marketers may maintain the price despite declining sales and competitive pressures. Prices may even be increased as costs rise if a loyal core market still wants the product. In other situations, the price may be cut to reduce existing inventory so that the product can be deleted. Severe price reductions may be required if a new product is making an existing product obsolete.

Because most businesses have a product mix consisting of multiple products, a firm's destiny is rarely tied to one product. A composite of life cycle patterns is formed when various products in the mix are at different cycle stages. As one product is declining, other products are in the introduction, growth, or maturity stage. Marketers must deal with the dual problem of prolonging the life of existing products and introducing new products to meet organizational sales goals.

Product Adoption Process

The acceptance of new products—especially new-to-the-world products—usually doesn't happen overnight. In fact, it can take a very long time. People are sometimes cautious or even skeptical about adopting new products, as indicated by some of the remarks quoted in Table 10.2. Customers who eventually accept a new product do so through an adoption process. The stages of the **product adoption process** buyers go through in accepting a product are as follows:

product adoption process   The stages buyers go through in accepting a product

1. *Awareness.* The buyer becomes aware of the product.
2. *Interest.* The buyer seeks information and is receptive to learning about the product.
3. *Evaluation.* The buyer considers the product's benefits and decides whether to try it.

Table 10.2   Most New Ideas Have Their Skeptics
"I think there is a world market for maybe five computers." —Thomas Watson, Chairman of IBM, 1943
"This 'telephone' has too many shortcomings to be seriously considered as a means of communication. The device is inherently of no value to us." —Western Union internal memo, 1876
"The wireless music box has no imaginable commercial value. Who would pay for a message sent to nobody in particular?" —David Sarnoff's associates in response to his urgings for investment in the radio in the 1920s
"The concept is interesting and well-formed, but in order to earn better than a 'C,' the idea must be feasible." —A Yale University management professor in response to Fred Smith's paper proposing reliable overnight delivery service (Smith went on to found Federal Express Corp.)
"Who the hell wants to hear actors talk?" —H. M. Warner, Warner Brothers, 1927
"A cookie store is a bad idea. Besides, the market research reports say America likes crispy cookies, not soft and chewy cookies like you make." —Banker's response to Debbie Fields's idea of starting Mrs. Fields' Cookies
"We don't like their sound, and guitar music is on the way out." —Decca Recording Co. rejecting the Beatles, 1962

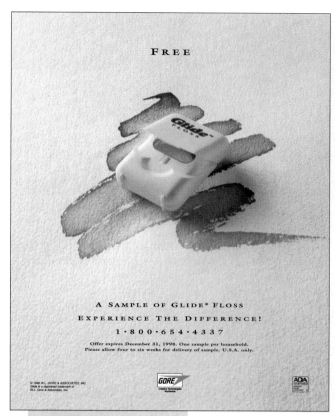

Figure 10.8
Encouraging Product Trial
Organizations, especially those in highly competitive markets, employ free samples to encourage customers to try the product.

4. *Trial.* The buyer examines, tests, or tries the product to determine if it meets his or her needs.

5. *Adoption.* The buyer purchases the product and can be expected to use it again whenever the need for this general type of product arises.[3]

In the first stage, when individuals become aware that the product exists, they have little information about it and are not concerned about obtaining more. For example, one might be aware that Polaroid offers a talking camera that has built-in recorded comic messages to evoke smiles, but have no plans to gather more information about it. Consumers enter the interest stage when they are motivated to get information about the product's features, uses, advantages, disadvantages, price, or location. During the evaluation stage, individuals consider whether the product will satisfy certain criteria that are crucial to meeting their specific needs. In the trial stage, they use or experience the product for the first time, possibly by purchasing a small quantity, by taking advantage of free samples (see Figure 10.8), or by borrowing the product from someone. Supermarkets, for instance, frequently offer special promotions to encourage consumers to taste products. During this stage, potential adopters determine the usefulness of the product under the specific conditions for which they need it.

Individuals move into the adoption stage by choosing the specific product when they need a product of that general type. However, because a person enters the adoption process does not mean that she or he will eventually adopt the new product. Rejection may occur at any stage, including the adoption stage. Both product adoption and product rejection can be temporary or permanent.

This adoption model has several implications when a new product is being launched. First, the company must promote the product to create widespread awareness of its existence and its benefits. Samples or simulated trials should be arranged to help buyers make initial purchase decisions. At the same time, marketers should

Figure 10.9
Distribution of Product Adopter Categories

Source: Reprinted with permission of The Free Press, a Division of Simon & Schuster, Inc., from *Diffusion of Innovations,* Fourth Edition by Everett M. Rogers. Copyright © 1995 by Everett M. Rogers. Copyright © 1962, 1971, 1983 by The Free Press.

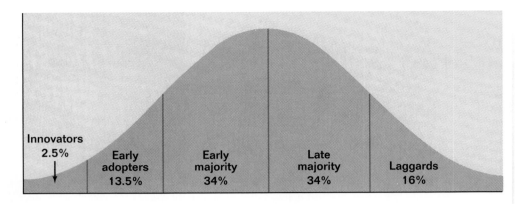

Innovators
2.5%

Early adopters
13.5%

Early majority
34%

Late majority
34%

Laggards
16%

emphasize quality control and provide solid guarantees to reinforce buyer opinion during the evaluation stage. Finally, production and physical distribution must be linked to patterns of adoption and repeat purchases.

When an organization introduces a new product, people do not begin the adoption process at the same time, nor do they move through the process at the same speed. Of those who eventually adopt the product, some enter the adoption process rather quickly, whereas others start considerably later. For most products, too, there is a group of nonadopters who never begin the process.

Depending on the length of time it takes them to adopt a new product, people can be divided into five major adopter categories: innovators, early adopters, early majority, late majority, and laggards.[4] Figure 10.9 illustrates each adopter category and the percentage of total adopters that it typically represents. **Innovators** are the first to adopt a new product; they enjoy trying new products and tend to be venturesome. **Early adopters** choose new products carefully and are viewed as "the people to check with" by persons in the remaining adopter categories. Persons in the **early majority** adopt just prior to the average person; they are deliberate and cautious in

innovators   First adopters of new products

early adopters   Careful choosers of new products

early majority   Those adopting new products just before the average person

Tech∗know

DVD: Moving Beyond Early Adopters

DVD is such a new technology that most consumers think the letters stand for "digital video disc." Actually, they stand for "digital versatile disc." DVD players installed in home entertainment electronics or personal computers deliver a sharp screen image, crisp sound, and the versatility to store three movie-viewing formats on a single disc (standard television size, widescreen letterbox format, and a larger television format). Because DVDs are digital, users can quickly locate a particular movie scene or select a different camera angle. Another plus is the enormous storage capacity of DVDs. The DVD's capacity, measured in gigabytes, is much larger than that of CDs or videotapes.

Despite their many advantages, DVD players will not become standard fixtures in U.S. homes overnight. Still, their sales are accelerating much faster than sales of VCRs and CD players did at the same stage of the product life cycle. In 1998, 1 million DVD players were shipped to U.S. stores, nearly triple the 350,000 players that were shipped in 1997. Sales of VCRs did not reach the

1 million mark until they had been on the market for six years, and CD players did not reach this milestone until three years after their introduction.

These days, almost 90 percent of all U.S. households have a VCR, indicating widespread acceptance—even among laggards. By contrast, DVD players are in fewer than 1 percent of all U.S. households, indicating that they have been purchased only by innovators and early adopters. Industry experts see higher sales growth ahead as prices drop from the initial level of nearly $1,000 to below $400. Being able to rent a wide range of DVD movies is another factor expected to increase sales. More than 2,000 movies are already available in DVD format, with thousands more on the way from Paramount and other top studios. Now that Wal-Mart, Target, and other mass-market retail chains are selling DVD players, it is only a matter of time before people in the "early majority" category begin adding these products to their home entertainment centers.

late majority   Skeptics who adopt new products when they feel it is necessary

laggards   The last adopters, who distrust new products

trying new products. **Late majority** people, who are quite skeptical of new products, eventually adopt new products because of economic necessity or social pressure. **Laggards,** the last to adopt a new product, are oriented toward the past. They are suspicious of new products, and when they finally adopt the innovation, it may already have been replaced by a new product. Tech*know discusses the product adoption process for DVD players.

Why Some Products Fail and Others Succeed

Thousands of new products are introduced annually, and many of them fail. Statistical bureaus, consulting firms, and trade publications estimate the number of new products that fail each year, and although some suggest that one in three new products fail, others report an annual new-product failure rate as high as 80 to 90 percent. The annual cost of product failures to American firms can reach $100 billion. Failure and success rates vary from organization to organization, but, in general, consumer products fail more often than business products. Table 10.3 shows examples of recent product successes and failures.

When examining the problem of product failure, it is important to distinguish the degree of failure. Absolute failure occurs when an organization loses money on a new product because it is unable to recover development, production, and marketing costs. This product usually is deleted from the product mix. Relative product failure occurs when a product returns a profit but does not meet a company's profit or market share objectives. If a company repositions or improves a relative product failure, that product might become a successful member of the product line.

Products fail for many reasons. One of the most common reasons is the company's failure to match product offerings to customer needs. When products do not offer value and do not have the features customers want, they fail in the marketplace. New products sometimes fail because of poor timing. If a company delays its launch of a new product, customers may already be loyal to a competing product that became available earlier. In some cases, market conditions may have already reduced the value of the product to customers. For example, when Miller Brewing Company launched Miller Clear Beer, it was hoping to take advantage of the clear-products fad. By the time it launched the beer, however, the fad was already waning, and customers were no longer clamoring for clear-drink products.[5] Being a product pioneer (i.e., being one of the first brands launched in a product category) is no guarantee of success. One study found that in fifty product categories, only half of the product pioneers survived.[6]

Table 10.3 **Product Successes and Failures**	
Product Successes	**Product Failures**
SmithKline Beecham's Nicoderm CQ	McDonald's Arch Deluxe
Hellmann's One-Step Dressings	Miller Clear Beer
Gatorade Frost	Saratoga Sweets Chocolate Salsa
3M Active Strips flexible bandages	Ben-Gay aspirin
French Toast Crunch Cereal	New Coke
Folger's Coffee House	Varaflame adjustable flame butane candles
Kellogg Co.'s Honey Crunch Corn Flakes	Nestlé Tea-Whiz
Nabisco Reduced Fat Oreos	R.J. Reynolds Premier smokeless cigarettes
Nestlé Butterfinger BBs	IBM PC jr.
Coca-Cola Co.'s Surge	Eastman Kodak disc camera

Sources: Judann Pollack, "New Products Top Ads in Helping Brands Grow," *Advertising Age,* May 11, 1998, p. 28; Paul Lukas, "The Ghastliest Product Launches," *Fortune,* Mar. 16, 1998, p. 4; David Raymond, "Famous Flops," *Forbes,* June 2, 1997, pp. 101–103; and "Famous Flops," *IW,* Dec. 16, 1998, p. 46.

Ineffective or inconsistent branding has also been blamed for product failures. Examples of products that failed because their brands failed to convey the right message include Frito-Lay lemonade (customers associate Frito-Lay with thirst-creating salty snacks, not thirst-quenching beverages) and Nestlé's yellowish carbonated beverage called Tea-Whiz.[7] Other reasons cited for new-product failure include technical or design problems, overestimation of market size, poor promotion, and insufficient distribution.

Despite this gloomy picture of new-product failure, some new products are successful. Perhaps the most important ingredient for success is the product's ability to provide a significant and perceivable benefit to a sizable number of customers. New products with an observable advantage over similar available products, such as more features, ease of operation, or improved technology, have a greater chance to succeed. For example, Nokia recently introduced the 9000 Communicator, which is a combination of a cellular phone and personal digital assistant that provides wireless Web surfing capabilities. Critical to launching a product that will achieve market success is effective planning and management. Companies that follow a systematic, customer-focused plan for new product development, such as Procter & Gamble, Gillette, and 3M, are well positioned to launch successful products.

Summary

A product is anything you receive in an exchange. It can be either tangible or intangible and includes functional, social, and psychological utilities or benefits. A product can be an idea, a service, a good, or any combination of these three. When consumers purchase a product, they are buying the benefits and satisfaction they think the product will provide.

Products can be classified on the basis of the buyer's intentions. Consumer products are those purchased to satisfy personal and family needs. Business products, on the other hand, are purchased for use in a firm's operations, to resell, or to make other products. Consumer products can be subdivided into convenience, shopping, specialty, and unsought products. Business products can be classified as installations, accessory equipment, raw materials, component parts, process materials, MRO supplies, and business services.

A product item is a specific version of a product that can be designated as a distinct offering among an organization's products. A product line is a group of closely related product items that are considered a unit because of marketing, technical, or end-use considerations. The composite, or total, group of products that an organization makes available to customers is called the product mix. The width of the product mix is measured by the number of product lines a company offers. The depth of a product mix is the average number of different products offered in each product line.

The product life cycle describes how product items in an industry move through four stages: introduction, growth, maturity, and decline. The life cycle concept is used to make sure that the introduction, alteration, and termination of a product are timed and executed properly. The sales curve is at zero at introduction, rises at an increasing rate during growth, peaks at maturity, and

then declines. Profits peak toward the end of the growth stage of the product life cycle. The life expectancy of a product is based on buyers' wants, the availability of competing products, and other environmental conditions. Most businesses have a composite of life cycle patterns for various products. It is important to manage existing products and develop new ones to keep the overall sales performance at a desired level.

When customers accept a new product, they usually do so through an adoption process that has five stages. The first stage is awareness, when buyers become aware that a product exists. Interest, the second stage, occurs when buyers seek information and are receptive to learning about the product. The third stage is evaluation; buyers consider the product's benefits and decide whether to try it. The fourth stage is trial. During this stage, buyers examine, test, or try the product to determine if it meets their needs. The last stage is adoption, when buyers actually purchase the product and use it whenever a need for this general type of product arises.

Of the thousands of new products introduced every year, many fail. Absolute failure occurs when an organization loses money on a new product. Absolute failures are usually removed from the product mix. Relative failure occurs when a product returns a profit but fails to meet a company's objectives. Some of the reasons for product failure include failure to match product offerings to customer needs, poor timing, and ineffective or inconsistent branding. Some new products do succeed, especially those that provide significant and observable benefits to customers. Products that have perceivable advantages over similar products also have a better chance to succeed. Effective market planning and product management are important factors in a new product's chances of success.

Important Terms

Product	Unsought products	Product line	Decline stage
Good	Installations	Product mix	Product adoption
Service	Accessory equipment	Width of product mix	process
Ideas	Raw materials	Depth of product mix	Innovators
Consumer products	Component parts	Product life cycle	Early adopters
Business products	Process materials	Introduction stage	Early majority
Convenience products	MRO supplies	Growth stage	Late majority
Shopping products	Business services	Maturity stage	Laggards
Specialty products	Product item		

Discussion and Review Questions

1. List the tangible and intangible attributes of a pair of Nike athletic shoes. Compare the benefits of the Nike shoes with those of an intangible product, such as a hairstyling in a salon.

2. A product has been referred to as a "psychological bundle of satisfaction." Is this a good definition of a product? Why or why not?

3. Is a personal computer sold at a retail store a consumer product or a business product? Defend your answer.

4. How do convenience products and shopping products differ? What are the distinguishing characteristics of each type of product?

5. In the category of business products, how do component parts differ from process materials?

6. How does an organization's product mix relate to its development of a product line? When should an enterprise add depth to its product lines rather than width to its product mix?

7. How do industry profits change as a product moves through the four stages of its life cycle?

8. What is the relationship between the concepts of product mix and product life cycle?

9. What are the stages in the product adoption process, and how do they affect the commercialization phase?

10. What are the five major adopter categories that describe the length of time required for a consumer to adopt a new product, and what are the characteristics of each?

11. In what ways does the marketing strategy for a mature product differ from the marketing strategy for a growth product?

12. What are the major reasons for new-product failure?

Application Questions

1. Name a product that could be described as both a consumer and a business product, and discuss why. Describe its uses and product perceptions by customers in both markets.

2. Choose a familiar clothing store. Describe its product mix, including its depth and width. Evaluate the mix and make suggestions to the owner.

3. Tabasco is a product that has entered the maturity stage of the product life cycle. Name products that would fit into each of the four stages (introduction, growth, maturity, and decline). Describe them and explain why they fit in that stage.

4. Generally, buyers go through a product adoption process before becoming loyal customers. Describe your experience in adopting a product you now use consistently. Did you go through all the stages?

5. Identify and describe a friend or family member who fits into each of the following adopter categories. How would you use this information if you were product manager for a fashion-oriented, medium-priced clothing retailer, such as J. Crew or J. C. Penney?
   a. innovator
   b. early adopter
   c. early majority
   d. late majority
   e. laggard

Internet Exercise & Resources

Goodyear Tire & Rubber Company

In addition to providing information about the company's products, Goodyear's Web site helps consumers find the exact products they want and will even direct them to the nearest Goodyear retailer. Visit the Goodyear site at

www.goodyear.com

1. How does Goodyear use its Web site to communicate information about the quality of its tires?
2. How does Goodyear's Web site demonstrate product design and features?
3. Based on what you learned at the Web site, describe what Goodyear has done to position its tires.

E-Center Resources

Visit http://www.prideferrell.com to find several resources to help you succeed in mastering the material in this chapter, plus additional materials that will help you expand your marketing knowledge. The Web site includes

 Internet exercise updates plus additional exercises

 ACE self-tests

 Chapter summary with hotlinked glossary

 Hotlinks to companies featured in this chapter

 Resource Center

 Career Center

 Marketing plan worksheets

VIDEO CASE 10.1

K'NEX Connects Through Effective Product Decisions

Walk into the lobby of the Pennsylvania headquarters of K'NEX Industries, Inc., and you will see a full-size motorcycle and a model of the Empire State Building, both made from colorful plastic parts. All the people you see building ferris wheels, space ships, and roller coasters with rods, connectors, pulleys, and tires are really researchers and engineers at work. K'NEX is the maker of innovative plastic construction toys for children five and older. In the highly competitive toy industry, where everyone dreams of launching the next Barbie and where today's Tickle Me Elmo is tomorrow's dust collector, K'NEX has found a niche. With annual sales of over $100 million in twenty-five countries, K'NEX is number two in the world's $550 million construction-toy market. According to founder and CEO Joel Glickman, focusing on customers is his company's strategy for success.

In 1988, Glickman was sitting at a table at a wedding reception bending colored plastic drinking straws and connecting them to make geometric shapes. Relying on his background in the plastics industry, Glickman eventually perfected his designs, creating sturdy, brightly colored plastic components. Although Glickman and his associates first tried to sell their idea to established toy marketers like Mattel and Hasbro, they received only rejections and so decided to get into the toy business themselves. In less than two years, what began as a way to avoid dancing at a wedding turned into K'NEX. Instead of showing drawings or prototypes to toy retailers, K'NEX created and packaged actual products. Toys "R" Us, Kmart, and Target all signed up to test market K'NEX in Philadelphia and Detroit.

Starting with one set of twenty-two multifunctional pieces, K'NEX now markets dozens of products. With names such as "Rip 'n' Go Racers," "K-Force Defense Station," and "Knexcavators," K'NEX toys range in price from $1.99 to over $100. Knowing that moving construction toys are more exciting than immobile ones, K'NEX always builds motion into its designs. The earliest sets were powered by rubber bands, cranks, and gears. In 1994, K'NEX added plug-in electric motors. Two years later came battery power, and, in 1997, K'NEX launched solar-powered building sets. In 1998, the toy maker created Power Controllers, which give builders remote control of motor-driven models.

K'NEX recognizes that it must continually modify its toys to keep them engaging. By monitoring its competitors and identifying what its customers like, the toy maker learns what to change and what to add. K'NEX always knows what competitors, such as Lego and Mattel's Construx, are doing—where they are advertising, what new products they are launching, what tie-ins they have—and then adjusts its own products and strategies. For example, K'NEX asked itself what Lego, the world's number-one maker of construction toys, had that K'NEX didn't. The answer was themed sets and human figures. K'NEX recently introduced "Hyperspace," new sets based on space adventure that include "good guy" and "bad guy" figures, and "Lost Mines of K'nexor" with Indiana Jones–like themes and figures.

K'NEX customers are children aged five to twelve and the parents, grandparents, and friends who give the construction toys as gifts. To learn what these customers want, K'NEX conducts focus groups, each comprising five to ten children who experiment with pieces and finished toys. A moderator guides participants through professionally developed questionnaires, and the resulting information helps K'NEX revise and enhance its toys. Focus groups assess building instructions for age-appropriateness, readability, and errors. The company also uses focus groups to test packaging and advertising effectiveness. From these focus groups come such product ideas as smaller, more modestly priced kits; toys for children older than ten; more detailed and color-coded instructions; and new items, such as snap-in building panels and flexible rods. CEO Glickman asserts that he cannot overestimate the vital role that focus groups play at K'NEX.

Glickman tells people that inventing K'NEX was the easy part of starting his toy business and building a company around it was the hardest part. Glickman is doing very well with the hardest part. K'NEX has won numerous awards, such as *Family Fun* magazine's 1997 Toy of the Year Award; it is also on *Playthings* magazine's 1998 list of specialty toy retailers' top ten best-selling toys. Glickman acknowledges that K'NEX's new television ads and sales promotion efforts, as well as intensive public relations efforts, are contributing to his company's success. It is K'NEX's commitment to bringing a child's perspective to the marketing process, however, that is making construction-toy king Lego move over and make room on the shelf for K'NEX.[8]

Questions for Discussion

1. Describe the major dimensions of K'NEX's product mix.
2. How might K'NEX's product life cycle stage affect the company's marketing strategies?
3. Considering that many new products fail, why have K'NEX products been successful?

CASE 10.2

Schwinn: Reviving a Classic American Brand

For decades, American children yearned for Schwinn bicycles. Kids who rode Schwinn Excelsiors, Phantoms, and Sting-Rays were the envy of their neighborhoods. In the United States, *Schwinn* meant *bicycle.* Today, however, if you ask people under 30 to name a popular brand of bicycle, they would probably come up with Trek or Cannondale, but not Schwinn. When consumer tastes changed from sturdy low-cost bikes to trendy high-priced ones, the company's sales plummeted. Unwilling to let Schwinns disappear along with Underwood typewriters and Zenith televisions, the venerable bicycle maker launched an all-out effort to bring back the best-known brand name on two wheels.

Over one hundred years ago, Iganz Schwinn founded his bicycle company and built it into the most prestigious in the industry. For years, Schwinn ruled as the number-one U.S. bicycle brand. In the late 1970s and early 1980s, however, cyclists got serious. To pedal off sidewalks and roads and into mountains and woods, they wanted upright handlebars, fat tires, and additional climbing gears. They also wanted the state-of-the-art technology provided by Cannondale, Giant, Waterloo, and market-leading Trek. Through most of the 1980s, however, Schwinn wasn't paying attention. By 1993, two-thirds of bikes sold were mountain bikes, and the once-mighty Schwinn was filing for bankruptcy. Believing in Schwinn's name and reputation, Sam Zell bought the company, moved its headquarters to Boulder, Colorado, and formulated a strategy for driving Schwinn to the top of a crowded bicycle market.

Zell's goal was to get the Schwinn name on everything from $100 children's bicycles to $2,500 mountain bikes. The first step toward that goal was to upgrade the entire product line. To make its bicycles stronger and lighter, for example, Schwinn turned to EMF Industries, a company whose new electromagnetic process turns out aluminum that makes bicycle frames much stronger. Schwinn also restyled all forty-eight of its models to make them attractive to today's customers. Zell's strategy was successful. Between 1993 and 1997, Schwinn rose from ninth to second in the market, selling more than 350,000 bicycles and fitness products a year. Stated the owner of a bicycle shop in Boulder, "Two years ago we said, 'There is no way we would ever sell a Schwinn mountain bike.' Now they're responsible for about one-third of our annual sales. "

It wasn't easy for Schwinn to transform its image from stodgy to stylish. The company launched a $10 million advertising campaign and several creative promotional efforts. Print ads featured enthusiasts mountain biking and racing on Schwinn bicycles, and Schwinn's professional mountain bike team raced every weekend between April and September. To generate positive word of mouth about its products, Schwinn developed "Project Underground." Through this program, the company began selling its elite models before their general release at lower-than-cost prices to employees of Schwinn dealers. When a customer comes into the shop looking for a new bicycle, those employees can rave about Schwinn bikes based on personal experience.

By 1997, Schwinn's new products and intense promotions had revived the company. The bicycle maker had not, however, achieved its goal of becoming the number-one bicycle company in the world. Toward that end, Zell recently sold Schwinn to Questor's Partners L.P., an organization with the finances and vision to complete the rebirth begun in 1993. The company's well-known, well-respected name will stay the same, but some of its strategies will change. The company will focus on building international sales, increasing sales of parts and accessories, and capitalizing on the growing popularity of its retro-style 1950s models.

One of Schwinn's hottest new products is a retro-style model: the Cruiser Deluxe, a one-speed model with a wide seat, chrome fenders, authentic 1950s pedals, and balloon tires, which sells for about $480. For those nostalgic cyclists who don't mind spending a bit more, there is the Black Phantom. Built from the 1949 blueprints, this model has faux-wood grain trim and exact replicas of the original fenders, horn, tires, and chrome, and, of course, coaster breaks. In fact, the only difference between the original and the reproduction is the price. In the old days, it cost about $80. Today, the price is about $3,000.[9]

Questions for Discussion

1. How would Schwinn mountain bicycles be classified as a product?
2. In what stage of the product life cycle is the bicycle industry? Explain.
3. Evaluate Schwinn management's decision to launch the Black Phantom.

Developing and Managing Products

OBJECTIVES

- To become aware of how companies manage existing products through line extensions and product modifications

- To gain insight into how businesses develop a product idea into a commercial product

- To understand the importance of product differentiation and the elements that differentiate one product from another

- To become aware of how products are positioned and repositioned in the customer's mind

- To understand how product deletion is used to improve product mixes

- To gain insight into organizational structures used for managing products

In Flight and Doing It Right, Midwest Express

What do business travelers want from an airline? What does it take to satisfy their needs? Midwest Express, a Milwaukee-based airline, asks these questions week in and week out, month after month. Acting on the answers has taken the fast-growing carrier to new heights in customer satisfaction. As a result, its highly profitable, full-price product draws passengers even during periods of economic turbulence.

Founded as a subsidiary of Kimberly-Clark, Midwest Express has always catered to the business market. When it became a scheduled carrier in 1984, it faced not only strong competition from low-fare start-ups, but also a tough economic environment. These pressures left other carriers with empty seats, but Midwest Express steadily increased revenues and profits by delivering what its customers value the most: comfort, service, and on-time performance.

The pampering starts the minute passengers come on board. On Midwest Express jets, nobody gets stuck in a middle seat, because there are none. The planes have just two extra-roomy leather seats on each side of the aisle, with lots of legroom, so every seat feels like first class. Even the meals are first class, accompanied by complimentary wine or champagne and, on luncheon flights, cookies baked fresh during the flight. And meal service comes complete with china plates and linen napkins. Best of all, Midwest Express flights almost always arrive on time, with few cancellations or delays. No wonder revenues have soared to $389 million.

Thanks to ongoing research, the airline knows exactly who the majority of its customers are: affluent male baby boomers. And it knows exactly how to translate this knowledge into a very attractive product, as well as how to position the product.

Professor Leonard Berry, a well-known services marketing expert, notes that on Midwest Express, "the passengers' experience is fundamentally and perceptually different than it is on other airlines." Customers definitely recognize the difference, which is why Midwest Express often comes out on top when magazines rank the best U.S. airlines.[1]

MIDWEST EXPRESS AIRLINES
The best care in the air.®

To compete effectively and achieve their goals, organizations like Midwest Express must be able to adjust their product mixes in response to changes in customers and customers' needs. A firm often has to introduce new products, modify existing products, or delete products that were successful perhaps only a few years ago. To provide products that satisfy target markets and that achieve the organization's objectives, a marketer must develop, alter, and maintain an effective product mix. An organization's product mix may need several types of adjustments. Because customers' attitudes and product preferences change over time, their desire for certain products may wane.

In some cases, a company needs to alter its product mix for competitive reasons. A marketer may have to delete a product from the mix because a competitor dominates the market for that product. Similarly, a firm may have to introduce a new product or modify an existing one to compete more effectively. A marketer may expand a firm's product mix to take advantage of excess marketing and production capacity.

This chapter examines several ways to improve an organization's product mix, including management of existing products, development of new products, product differentiation, positioning and repositioning of products, and elimination of weak products from the product mix. First, we discuss managing existing products through effective line extension and product modification. Next, we examine the stages of new product development. We go on to discuss the ways in which companies differentiate their products in the marketplace and follow with an explanation of product positioning and repositioning. The importance of deleting weak products and the methods companies use to eliminate them is examined next. Finally, we look at the organizational structures used to manage products.

Managing Existing Products

line extension
Development of a product closely related to existing products in the line but that meets different customer needs

An organization can benefit by capitalizing on its existing products. By assessing the composition of the current product mix, a marketer can identify weaknesses and gaps. This analysis can then lead to improvement of a product mix through line extension and through product modification.

Line Extensions

A **line extension** is the development of a product closely related to one or more products in the existing product line but designed specifically to meet somewhat different needs of customers. For example, Nabisco has extended its cookie line to include Reduced Fat Oreos and Double Stuffed Oreos. As shown in Figure 11.1, Clorox has extended its line to include Ultra Clorox 2. Many of the so-called new products introduced each year are in fact line extensions. Line extensions are more common than new products because they are a less expensive, lower-risk alternative for increasing sales. A line extension may focus on a different market segment or may be an attempt to increase sales within the same market

To get whites this white, you have to be powerful.

Well, you don't get colors this clean and bright by being a shrinking violet.

What Clorox® Bleach does for whites, Clorox 2® does for colors. In a fresh, floral scent.

Figure 11.1
Line Extensions
A number of organizations, like the makers of Clorox, use line extensions to appeal to more customers.

segment by more precisely satisfying the needs of people in that segment. Line extensions also are used to take market share from competitors. For example, MCI introduced a line extension, called 10-10-321, to take market share from AT&T. Using an access code, a customer can purchase low-cost long distance service on a call-by-call basis without the hassle of changing long-distance carriers. While 10-10-321 has cannibalized some MCI long distance sales, it has helped MCI increase its market share, partially at the expense of AT&T.[2]

Product Modifications

product modification
Change in one or more characteristics of a product

Product modification means changing one or more characteristics of a product. A product modification differs from a line extension in that the original product does not remain in the line. For example, U.S. automakers use product modifications annually when they create new models of the same brand. Once the new models are introduced, the manufacturers stop producing last year's model. Like line extensions, product modifications entail less risk than developing new products.

Product modification can indeed improve a firm's product mix, but only under certain conditions. First, the product must be modifiable. Second, customers must be able to perceive that a modification has been made. Third, the modification should make the product more consistent with customers' desires so that it provides greater satisfaction. There are three major ways to modify products: quality modifications, functional modifications, and aesthetic modifications.

quality modifications
Changes relating to a product's dependability and durability

Quality Modifications   **Quality modifications** are changes that relate to a product's dependability and durability. The changes usually are executed by altering the materials or the production process. For example, as indicated in Figure 11.2, Energizer has increased its product's durability by using better materials—a larger cathode and anode interface.

functional modifications
Changes affecting a product's versatility, effectiveness, convenience, or safety

Reducing a product's quality may allow an organization to lower its price and to direct the item at a different target market. In contrast, increasing the quality of a product may give a firm an advantage over competing brands. In fact, over the last twenty years, increased global competition, rapid technological changes, and more demanding customers have forced marketers to improve product integrity to remain competitive.[3] Higher quality may enable a company to charge a higher price by creating customer loyalty and by lowering customer sensitivity to price. However, higher quality may require the use of more expensive components and processes, thus forcing the organization to cut costs in other areas. Some firms, such as Caterpillar, are finding ways to increase quality while reducing costs.

Functional Modifications   Changes that affect a product's versatility, effectiveness, convenience, or safety are called **functional modifications;** they usually require that the product be redesigned. Product categories that have undergone considerable functional

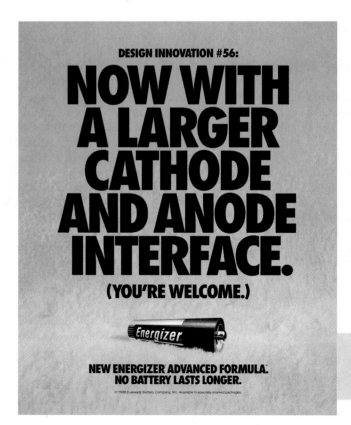

DESIGN INNOVATION #56:

NOW WITH A LARGER CATHODE AND ANODE INTERFACE.

(YOU'RE WELCOME.)

Energizer

**NEW ENERGIZER ADVANCED FORMULA.
NO BATTERY LASTS LONGER.**

**Figure 11.2
Product Modifications**
Energizer is using quality modification.

modification include office and farm equipment, appliances, and cleaning products. Procter & Gamble, for example, modified Tide by adding bleach, which improved the detergent's effectiveness. Functional modifications can make a product useful to more people and thus enlarge its market. They can place a product in a favorable competitive position by providing benefits that competing brands do not offer. They can also help an organization achieve and maintain a progressive image. Functional modifications are sometimes made to reduce the possibility of product liability lawsuits.

aesthetic modifications
Changes to the sensory appeal of a product

Aesthetic Modifications   **Aesthetic modifications** change the sensory appeal of a product by altering its taste, texture, sound, smell, or appearance. A buyer making a purchase decision is swayed by how a product looks, smells, tastes, feels, or sounds. Thus, an aesthetic modification may strongly affect purchases. For years, automobile makers have relied on aesthetic modifications.

Through aesthetic modifications, a firm can differentiate its product from competing brands and thus gain a sizable market share. The major drawback in using aesthetic modifications is that their value is determined subjectively. Although a firm may strive to improve the product's sensory appeal, customers may actually find the modified product less attractive.

Developing New Products

Figure 11.3
One Type of New Product
Crayola School Glue can be viewed as a new product because it is new for the Crayola organization.

A firm develops new products as a means of enhancing its product mix and adding depth to a product line. Developing and introducing new products is frequently expensive and risky. For example, Maxwell House introduced Maxwell House Brewed Coffee in a 48-ounce package resembling a milk carton with a handy screw-on plug. This ready-to-microwave, instantly recognizable product located in supermarket refrigerated sections failed because customers did not value the benefits it provided.[4] New-product failures are not uncommon, as discussed in the previous chapter. They can create major financial problems for organizations, sometimes even causing them to go out of business.

Although new-product development is risky, so is failure to introduce new products. For example, the makers of Timex watches gained a large share of the U.S. watch market through effective marketing strategies during the 1960s and early 1970s. By 1983, Timex's market share had slipped considerably, in part because Timex had failed to introduce new products. In recent times, however, Timex has introduced technologically advanced new products and has regained market share.

The term *new product* can have more than one meaning. A genuinely new product offers innovative benefits. But products that are different and distinctly better are often viewed as new. The following items (listed in no particular order) are product innovations of the last thirty years: Post-it notes, fax machines, birth-control pills, personal computers, felt-tip pens, disposable razors, quartz watches, and VCRs. Thus, a new product can be an innovative product that has never been sold by any organization, such as the digital camera when it was introduced for the first time. It can also be a product that a given firm has not marketed previously, although similar products may have been available from other companies (see the Crayola School Glue example in Figure 11.3). Eddie Bauer, best known for its rugged outdoor wear, extended this image with the introduction of a new line of men's cologne. It was considered a new product because Eddie Bauer had not previously marketed cologne or cosmetics. Finally, a product can be viewed

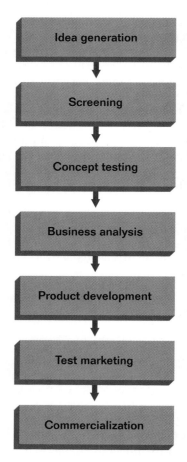

Figure 11.4
Phases of New-Product Development

as new when it is brought to one or more markets from another. For example, making the Dodge minivan available in Japan is viewed as a new-product introduction in Japan.

Before a product is introduced, it goes through the seven phases of the **new-product development process** shown in Figure 11.4: (1) idea generation, (2) screening, (3) concept testing, (4) business analysis, (5) product development, (6) test marketing, and (7) commercialization. A product may be dropped, and many are, at any stage of development. In this section, we look at the process through which products are developed, from idea inception to fully commercialized product.

Idea Generation

Businesses and other organizations seek product ideas that will help them achieve their objectives. This activity is **idea generation.** That only a few ideas are good enough to be commercially successful underscores the difficulty of the task. Although some organizations get their ideas almost by chance, firms that try to manage their product mixes effectively usually develop systematic approaches for generating new-product ideas. At the heart of innovation is a purposeful, focused effort to identify new ways to serve a market. Unexpected occurrences, incongruities, new needs, industry and market changes, and demographic shifts all may indicate new opportunities.[5]

New-product ideas can come from several sources. They may come from internal sources—marketing managers, researchers, sales personnel, engineers, or other organizational personnel. Brainstorming and incentives or rewards for good ideas are typical intrafirm devices for stimulating the development of ideas. For example, the idea for 3M Post-it adhesive-backed notes came from an employee. As a church choir member, he used slips of paper to mark songs in his hymnal. Because the pieces of paper fell out, he suggested developing an adhesive-backed note. New product ideas may also arise from sources outside the firm—customers, competitors, advertising agencies, management consultants, and private research organizations. In a single year, companies pay marketing research firms more than $6 billion for research services.[6] A significant portion of this money is used to assess customers' needs. Asking customers what they want from products and organizations has helped many firms to become successful and to remain competitive (see Building Customer Relationships on page 276).

Screening

new-product development process   A seven-phase process for introducing products

idea generation   Seeking product ideas to achieve objectives

In the process of **screening,** the ideas with the greatest potential are selected for further review. During screening, product ideas are analyzed to determine whether they match the organization's objectives and resources. If a product idea results in a product similar to the firm's existing products, marketers must assess the degree to which the new product could cannibalize the sales of current products. The company's overall abilities to produce and market the product are also analyzed. Other aspects of an idea that should be weighed are the nature and wants of buyers and possible environmental changes. At times, a checklist of new-product requirements is used when making screening decisions. It encourages evaluators to be systematic and so reduces the chances of their overlooking some pertinent fact. Compared with other phases, the largest number of new-product ideas are rejected during the screening phase.

screening   Choosing the most promising ideas for further review

Concept Testing

concept testing   Seeking potential buyers' responses to a product idea

To evaluate ideas properly, it may be necessary to test product concepts. **Concept testing** is a phase in which a small sample of potential buyers is presented with a product idea through a written or oral description (and perhaps a few drawings) to determine their attitudes and initial buying intentions regarding the product. For a single product idea, an organization can test one or several concepts of the same product.

Product description

An insecticide company is considering the development and introduction of a new tick and flea control product for pets. This product would consist of insecticide and a liquid dispensing brush for applying the insecticide to dogs and cats. The insecticide is in a cartridge that is installed in the handle of the brush. The insecticide is dispensed through the tips of the bristles when they touch the pet's skin (which is where most ticks and fleas are found). The actual dispensing works very much like a felt-tip pen. Only a small amount of insecticide actually is dispensed on the pet because of this unique dispensing feature. Thus the amount of insecticide that is placed on your pet is minimal compared to conventional methods of applying a tick and flea control product. One application of insecticide will keep your pet free from ticks and fleas for fourteen days.

Please answer the following questions:

1. In general, how do you feel about using this type of product on your pet?

2. What are the major advantages of this product compared with the existing product that you are currently using to control ticks and fleas on your pet?

3. What characteristics of this product do you especially like?

4. What suggestions do you have for improving this product?

5. If it is available at an appropriate price, how likely are you to buy this product?

        Very likely   Semi-likely   Not likely

6. Assuming that a single purchase would provide 30 applications for an average-size dog or 48 applications for an average-size cat, approximately how much would you pay for this product?

Figure 11.5
Concept Test for a Tick and Flea Control Product

Concept testing is a low-cost procedure that lets an organization determine customers' initial reactions to a product idea before it invests considerable resources in research and development. The results of concept testing can help product development personnel better understand which product attributes and benefits are most important to potential customers.

Figure 11.5 shows a concept test for a proposed tick and flea control product. Notice that the concept is briefly described; then a series of questions is presented. The questions asked vary considerably depending on the type of product being tested. The typical questions are these: In general, do you find this proposed product attractive? Which benefits are especially attractive to you? Which features are of little or no interest to you? Do you feel that this proposed product would work better for you than the product you currently use? Compared with your current product, what are the primary advantages of the proposed product? If this product were available at an appropriate price, would you buy it? How often would you buy this product? How could this proposed product be improved?

Business Analysis

business analysis
Assessing the potential of a product idea for the firm's sales, costs, and profits

During the **business analysis** stage, the product idea is evaluated to determine its potential contribution to the firm's sales, costs, and profits. In the course of a business analysis, evaluators ask a variety of questions: Does the product fit in with the organization's existing product mix? Is demand strong enough to justify entering the market, and will the demand endure? What types of environmental and competitive changes can be expected, and how will these changes affect the product's future sales, costs, and profits? Are the organization's research, development, engineering, and production capabilities adequate to develop the product? If new facilities must be constructed, how quickly can they be built, and how much will they cost? Is the necessary financing for development and commercialization on hand or obtainable at terms consistent with a favorable return on investment?

In the business analysis stage, firms seek market information. The results of consumer polls, along with secondary data, supply the specifics needed for estimating potential sales, costs, and profits.

For many products in this stage (when they are still just product ideas), forecasting sales accurately is difficult. This is especially true for innovative and completely new products. Organizations sometimes employ breakeven analysis to determine how many units they would have to sell to begin to make a profit. At times, an organization also uses payback analysis, in which marketers compute the time period required to recover the funds that would be invested in developing the new product. Because breakeven and payback analyses are based on estimates, they are usually viewed as useful but not particularly precise during this stage.

BUILDING
customer relationships

How Are Customer-Satisfying Products Developed? By Talking to Customers

A design engineer from Bose Corporation, the world's largest manufacturer of quality sound system components, tells a story about his visit to a new customer's home. Noticing that the customer repeatedly got up from his chair and crossed the room to change the volume, tone, and balance, the engineer asked why he didn't simply use the remote control. The customer's reply, "I can't figure the thing out," was the catalyst for development of Bose's redesigned, easier-to-use remote device. Bose, like many other companies, has learned that the best way to generate successful new products is to involve customers in product design.

Through focus groups, surveys, and open-ended interviews that encourage user-comments, companies gain valuable insights into the products, features, and services that customers really want and that ultimately have the most likelihood of satisfying them. Some firms protest that they can't afford the time or money to conduct this kind of research, and design engineers at technology-driven organizations are often skeptical about customers' knowing what they want. However, many companies, including 3M, GTE Laboratories, automotive supplier Dana Corporation, and toy manufacturer Ohio Arts, are listening to the voices of their customers and thereby increasing their chances of developing successful new products.

When Amtrak decided to begin premium high-speed rail service between Boston, New York, and Washington, D.C., the company sought the opinions of over 20,000 customers to find out what features would persuade commuters to choose riding the train over flying. Through focus groups and phone surveys, Amtrak received input that helped it design everything from car interiors to platforms to the train's name. Asserts one Amtrak executive, "You need to know what your customers are thinking. You have to know what they want and keep on following their changing needs."

Traditionally, photography giant Kodak had permitted technological developments to drive new-product introductions. In 1993, however, the company instituted Voice of the Consumer, a dramatic reversal in its approach to new-product development. Voice of the Consumer allows new-product ideas to come from customer needs rather than from research and development. For example, when customers told Kodak they wanted comfortable, attractive, and easy-to-use cameras, the company devised the very successful Fun Saver Pocket Camera.

Experts offer some general advice for organizations that are considering involving customers more intrinsically in the product development process. First, companies should not publicly commit themselves to a program of customer involvement unless they are willing to follow through. Second, support from management is essential. Third, dealers and distributors also can offer valuable input. Fourth, management needs to intervene if designers and engineers try to ignore customer feedback. Finally, it is impossible to satisfy each and every customer's needs and desires each and every time.

Product Development

product development
Determining if producing a product is feasible and cost-effective

Product development is the phase in which the organization determines if it is technically feasible to produce the product and if it can be produced at costs low enough to make the final price reasonable. To test its acceptability, the idea or concept is converted into a prototype, or working model. The prototype should reveal tangible and intangible attributes associated with the product in consumers' minds. The product's design, mechanical features, and intangible aspects must be linked to wants in the marketplace. Through marketing research and concept testing, product attributes important to buyers are identified. These characteristics must be communicated to customers through the design of the product.

After a company has developed a prototype, its overall functioning must be tested. This means that its performance, safety, convenience, and other functional qualities are tested both in a laboratory and in the field. Functional testing should be rigorous and long enough to test the product thoroughly.

A crucial question that arises during product development is how much quality to build into the product. For example, a major dimension of quality is durability. Keds, well known for its canvas shoes, decided to enhance product durability by developing a highly durable, washable leather. Higher quality often calls for better materials and more expensive processing, which increase production costs and, ultimately, the product's price. In determining the specific level of quality, a marketer must ascertain approximately what price the target market views as acceptable. In addition, a marketer usually tries to set a quality level consistent with that of the firm's other products. Obviously, the quality of competing brands is also a consideration.

The development phase of a new product is frequently lengthy and expensive; thus, a relatively small number of product ideas are put into development. If the product appears sufficiently successful during this stage to merit test marketing, then during the latter part of the development stage marketers begin to make decisions regarding branding, packaging, labeling, pricing, and promotion for use in the test marketing stage.

SNAPSHOT
New products pay off

The Best — 61% Line extensions Improvements Cost reductions Repositionings / 39% New products

The Rest — 77% Line extensions Improvements Cost reductions Repositionings / 23% New products

% of revenues

Test Marketing

test marketing
Introducing a product on a limited basis to measure the extent to which potential customers will actually buy the product

A limited introduction of a product in geographic areas chosen to represent the intended market is called **test marketing.** Its aim is to determine the extent to which potential customers will buy the product. For example, Arm & Hammer test-marketed its plaque-fighting Baking Soda Gum in cities in California, Iowa, Texas, and Massachusetts.[7] Test marketing is not an extension of the development stage; it is a sample launching of the entire marketing mix. Test marketing should be conducted only after the product has gone through development and initial plans regarding the other marketing mix variables have been made. Numerous pizza and breakfast food companies have test-marketed breakfast varieties of pizza with limited success.

Companies use test marketing to lessen the risk of product failure. The dangers of introducing an untested product include undercutting already profitable products and, should the new product fail, loss of credibility with distributors and customers.

Test marketing provides several benefits. It lets marketers expose a product in a natural marketing environment to measure its sales performance. While the product is being marketed in a limited area, the company can strive to identify weaknesses in the product or in other parts of the marketing mix. A product weakness discovered after a

Table 11.1   Popular Test Markets in the United States

Tulsa, OK	Wichita, KS	Longview, TX	Pittsfield, MA
Charleston, WV	Bloomington, IL	Lafayette, LA	Jacksonville, FL
Midland, TX	Oklahoma City, OK	Omaha, NE	Edmond, OK
Springfield, IL	Indianapolis, IN	Phoenix, AZ	High Point, NC
Lexington-Fayette, KY	Rockford, IL	Gastonia, NC	Salt Lake City, UT
Eau Claire, WI	Grand Junction, CO	Rome, GA	Marion, IN
Cedar Rapids, IA	Visalia, CA		

Source: Strategic Mapping, Inc., Santa Clara, Calif., and Betsy Spethmann, "Test Market USA," *Brandweek*, May 8, 1995, p. 42.

nationwide introduction can be expensive to correct. Moreover, if consumers' early reactions are negative, marketers may not be able to persuade consumers to try the product again. Thus, making adjustments after test marketing can be crucial to the success of a new product. On the other hand, testing results may be positive enough to cause a company to accelerate the introduction of a new product. Test marketing also allows marketers to experiment with variations in advertising, pricing, and packaging in different test areas and to measure the extent of brand awareness, brand switching, and repeat purchases that result from these alterations in the marketing mix.

Selection of appropriate test areas is very important because the validity of test market results depends heavily on selecting test sites that provide accurate representation of the intended target market. Table 11.1 lists some of the most popular test market cities. The criteria used for choosing test cities depend on the product's characteristics, the target market's characteristics, and the firm's objectives and resources.

Test marketing is not without risks. It is expensive, and a firm's competitors may try to interfere. A competitor may attempt to "jam" the test program by increasing advertising or promotions, lowering prices, and offering special incentives—all to combat the recognition and purchase of a new brand. Any such tactics can invalidate test results. Sometimes, too, competitors copy the product in the testing stage and rush to introduce a similar product. It is therefore desirable to move to the commercialization phase as soon as possible after successful testing.

Because of these risks, many companies use alternative methods to measure customer preferences. One such method is simulated test marketing. Typically, consumers at shopping centers are asked to view an advertisement for a new product and are given a free sample to take home. These consumers are subsequently interviewed over the phone and asked to rate the product. The major advantages of simulated test marketing are greater speed, lower costs, and tighter security, which reduces the flow of information to competitors and reduces jamming. Gillette's Personal Care Division spends less than $200,000 for a simulated test that lasts three to five months. A live test market costs Gillette $2 million, counting promotion and distribution, and takes one to two years to complete. Several marketing research firms, such as A. C. Nielsen Company, offer test marketing services to help provide independent assessment of proposed products.

Clearly, not all products that are test-marketed are launched. At times, problems discovered during test marketing cannot be resolved. For example, Procter & Gamble test-marketed a "laundry sheet," a fabric softener with detergent and bleach. The sheet releases soap and bleach in the washer and travels with the wet laundry into the dryer. The product had too many technical problems that were discovered during test marketing.[8]

Commercialization

commercialization
Deciding on full-scale manufacturing and marketing plans and preparing budgets

During the **commercialization** phase, plans for full-scale manufacturing and marketing must be refined and settled, and budgets for the project must be prepared. Early in the commercialization phase, marketing management analyzes the results of test marketing to find out what changes in the marketing mix are needed before the

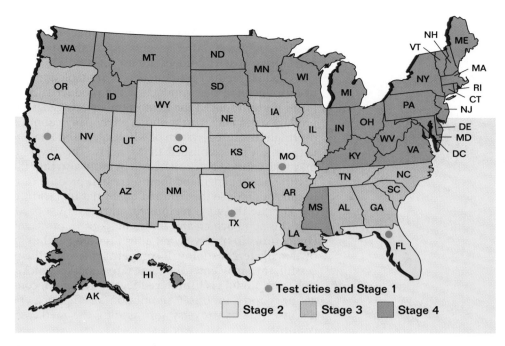

Figure 11.6
Stages of Expansion into a National Market during Commercialization
Source: Adapted from Herbert G. Hicks, William M. Pride, and James D. Powell, *Business: An Involvement Approach.* Copyright © 1975. Reproduced with permission of The McGraw-Hill Companies.

product is introduced. The results of test marketing may tell the marketers to change one or more of the product's physical attributes, modify the distribution plans to include more retail outlets, alter promotional efforts, or change the product's price. However, as more and more changes are made based on test marketing findings, the test marketing projections may become less valid.

During the early part of this stage, marketers must not only gear up for larger-scale production, but also make decisions about warranties, repairs, and replacement parts. The type of warranty a firm provides can be a critical issue for buyers, especially when expensive, technically complex goods like appliances are involved. Maytag, for example, provides a money-back guarantee on its refrigerators. Establishing an effective system for providing repair services and replacement parts is necessary to maintain favorable customer relationships. Although the producer may furnish these services directly to buyers, it is more common for the producer to provide such services through regional service centers. Regardless of how services are provided, it is important to customers that they be performed quickly and correctly.

The product enters the market during the commercialization phase. When introducing a product, a firm may spend enormous sums of money for advertising, personal selling, and other types of promotion, as well as for plant and equipment. Such expenditures may not be recovered for several years. Smaller organizations may find the commercializing of a product especially difficult.

Products are not usually launched nationwide overnight but are introduced through a process called a *roll-out*. Through a roll-out, a product is introduced in stages, starting in one set of geographic areas and gradually expanding into adjacent areas. It may take several years to market the product nationally. Sometimes the test cities are used as initial marketing areas, and the introduction of the product becomes a natural extension of test marketing. A product test-marketed in Sacramento, Fort Collins, Abilene, Springfield, and Jacksonville, as the map in Figure 11.6 shows, could be introduced first in those cities. After the stage 1 introduction is complete, stage 2 could include market coverage of the states in which the test cities are located. In stage

3, marketing efforts could be extended into adjacent states. All remaining states would then be covered in stage 4. Gradual product introductions do not always occur state by state; however, other geographic combinations, such as groups of counties that overlap across state borders, are used as well.

Gradual product introduction is desirable for several reasons. It reduces the risks of introducing a new product. If the product fails, the firm will experience smaller losses if it introduced the item in only a few geographic areas than if it marketed the product nationally. Furthermore, a company cannot introduce a product nationwide overnight because a system of wholesalers and retailers, necessary to distribute a product, cannot be established that quickly. The development of a distribution network may take considerable time. Keep in mind also that the number of units needed to satisfy the national demand for a successful product can be enormous, and a firm usually cannot produce the required quantities in a short time.

Despite the good reasons for introducing a product gradually, marketers realize that this approach creates some competitive problems. A gradual introduction allows competitors to observe what a firm is doing and to monitor results, just as the firm's own marketers are doing. If competitors see that the newly introduced product is successful, they may enter the same target market quickly with similar products. In addition, as a product is introduced region by region, competitors may expand their marketing efforts to offset promotion of the new product. Marketing Citizenship discusses the controversy surrounding the marketing of tobacco products in other countries.

MARKETING CITIZENSHIP

Is Global Tobacco Marketing Ethical?

Is it ethical to market tobacco products around the world? As the U.S. market for cigarettes becomes more regulated and less profitable, many tobacco companies see international markets as promising sources of sales growth. The Marlboro brand has been galloping into global markets for years, spearheading Philip Morris's international search for profits. Backed by strong marketing, Philip Morris has captured 17 percent of the global cigarette market. Right behind, with a 16 percent share, is British American Tobacco (BAT), maker of Lucky Strike, Kent, and other brands. Another major player is R.J. Reynolds (RJR), which has taken its well-known Camel, Winston, and Salem brands global and created new products for regional markets.

Cigarette makers are putting particular emphasis on developing countries, where Western brands are especially coveted. Although cigarettes are entirely legal in these countries, critics charge that the companies' advertising campaigns, by glamorizing smoking, are increasing demand for an unhealthy product. Regulations differ from country to country, so using television commercials and other mass media to advertise cigarettes may be acceptable in some places (although not in the United States). For their part, the tobacco firms say they are lawfully meeting a need by offering more choices to local consumers, and rather than trying to entice youngsters and nonsmokers to take up smoking, they are merely trying to induce smokers to switch brands.

In recent years, Russia has become a marketing battleground for tobacco companies seeking global growth. Philip Morris, RJR, and BAT have all spent millions of dollars building factories in Russia and Eastern Europe to support regional product roll-outs. RJR holds 20 percent of the Russian market, and its St. Petersburg facilities are gearing up to turn out 37 billion cigarettes yearly under a variety of brands. In areas where price is an obstacle, the tobacco companies obligingly offer cheaper roll-your-own products. As competition intensifies, consumers are likely to be exposed to more and more marketing messages, bringing attention back to the ethical question: Should tobacco manufacturers be allowed to market globally?

Product Differentiation through Quality, Design, and Support Services

product differentiation
Creating and designing products so that customers perceive them as different from competing products

Some of the most important characteristics of products are the elements that distinguish them from one another. **Product differentiation** is the process of creating and designing products so that customers perceive them as different from competing products. The issue of customer perception is critically important in differentiating products. Perceived differences might include quality, features, styling, price, or image. A crucial element used to differentiate one product from another is the brand, which is discussed in the next chapter. In this section, we examine three aspects of product differentiation that companies must consider when creating and offering products for sale: product quality, product design and features, and product support services. These aspects involve the company's attempt to create real differences between products. Later in this chapter, we discuss how companies position their products in the marketplace based on these three aspects.

Product Quality

quality The overall characteristics of a product that allow it to perform as expected in satisfying customer needs

Quality refers to the overall characteristics of a product that allow it to perform as expected in satisfying customer needs. The words *as expected* are very important to this definition because quality usually means different things to different customers. For some, durability signifies quality. Among the most durable products on the market today is the Craftsman line of tools at Sears. Indeed, Sears provides a lifetime guarantee on the durability of these tools. For other consumers, a product's ease of use may indicate quality.

The concept of quality also varies between consumer and organizational markets. According to one study, American consumers consider high-quality products to have these characteristics (in order): reliability, durability, ease of maintenance, ease of use, a known and trusted brand name, and reasonable price.[9] For organizational markets, technical suitability, ease of repair, and company reputation are important characteristics. Unlike consumers, most organizations place far less emphasis on price than on product quality.

level of quality The amount of quality a product possesses

One important dimension of quality is **level of quality**, which is the amount of quality a product possesses. The concept is a relative one. That is, the quality level of one product is difficult to describe unless it is compared with that of other products. For example, most consumers would consider the quality level of Timex watches to be good, but when they compare Timex with Rolex, most consumers would say that a Rolex's level of quality is higher. How high should the level of quality be? It depends on the product. A 99.9 percent accuracy rate would mean that 1,314 phone calls would be misplaced every minute, 500 incorrect surgical procedures would be performed daily, and 22,000 checks would be deducted from the wrong accounts each hour. Is 99.9 percent accuracy good enough?[10]

consistency of quality
The degree to which a product is the same over time

A second important dimension is consistency. **Consistency of quality** refers to the degree to which a product has the same level of quality over time. Consistency means giving consumers the quality they expect every time they purchase the product. Like the level of quality, consistency is a relative concept; however, it implies a quality comparison within the same brand over time. The quality level of McDonald's French fries is generally consistent from one location to another. If FedEx delivers more than 99 percent of overnight packages on time, then its service has consistent quality.

The consistency of product quality can also be compared across competing products. It is at this stage that consistency becomes critically important for a company's success. Companies that can provide quality on a consistent basis have a major competitive advantage over their rivals. FedEx is viewed as more consistent in delivery schedules than the U.S. Postal Service. In simple terms, no company has ever succeeded by creating and marketing low-quality products. Many companies have taken major steps, such as implementing total quality management (TQM), to improve the quality of their products. (TQM is discussed further in Chapter 22.)

By and large, higher product quality means that marketers will charge a higher price for the product. This fact forces marketers to consider quality carefully in their product-planning efforts. Not all customers want or can afford the highest-quality products available. Thus, many companies offer a range of products that vary widely in quality.

Product Design and Features

product design   How a product is conceived, planned, and produced

Product design refers to how a product is conceived, planned, and produced. Design is a very complex topic because it involves the total sum of all the product's physical characteristics. Many companies are known for the outstanding designs of their products: Sony for personal electronics, Hewlett-Packard for laser printers, Levi Strauss for clothing, and JanSport for backpacks. Good design is one of the best competitive advantages any brand can possess.

styling   The physical appearance of a product

One component of design is **styling,** or the physical appearance of the product. The style of a product is one design feature that can cause certain products to sell very rapidly. Good design, however, means more than just appearance; it also involves a product's functioning and usefulness. For example, a pair of jeans may look great, but if they fall apart after three washes, clearly the design was poor. Most consumers seek out products that look good and also function well.

product features   Specific design characteristics that allow a product to perform certain tasks

Product features are specific design characteristics that allow a product to perform certain tasks. By adding or subtracting features, a company can differentiate its products from those of the competition. Chrysler promotes its line of minivans as having more features related to passenger safety—dual air bags, steel-reinforced doors, and integrated child safety seats—than any other auto company. As shown in Figure 11.7, Andersen Tilt–Wash Windows have multiple product design features to differentiate them from competing products. Product features can also be used to differentiate products within the same company. For example, Nike offers both a walking shoe and a run-walk shoe for specific consumer needs. In these cases, the company's products are sold with a wide range of features, from low-priced "base" or "stripped-down" versions to high-priced and prestigious "feature-packed" ones. The automotive industry regularly sells products with a wide range of features. In general, the more features

Figure 11.7
Product Differentiation Through Product Design
Andersen Windows uses product design to differentiate its products from those of competitors.

Warranty: Standard.
Guarantee: Standard.
Worry: Not an option.

The AutoNation USA bumper-to-bumper warranty and money-back guarantee make buying a pre-owned car worry free.

People have been conditioned to expect that worry and doubt come standard with every pre-owned car they buy. That will never be the case at AutoNation USA. Each of our Reconditioned-To-Perform-Like-New™ vehicles is backed by a 99 day bumper-to-bumper limited warranty (it covers everything), a 7 day money-back

guarantee and 24-hour roadside assistance for a full year: features you'd never expect to find with pre-owned vehicles. So now instead of driving away in a permanent state of worry, you can take off in a terrific pre-owned car. Come see for yourself why buying a car at AutoNation USA is as enjoyable as driving one.

The Better Way To Buy A Car™

4401 West Sample Road at Coconut Creek · Exit I-95 at Sample Road. Go West 3.5 miles. · 954 - 984-3500
Showroom Hours: Monday-Thursday, 9am to 9pm; Friday & Saturday, 9am to 10pm; Sunday, 10am to 7pm
Automotive Service Center Hours: Monday-Saturday, 7am to 7pm; Sunday, 10am to 6pm

**Figure 11.8
Differentiation Through
Product Support
Services**
AutoNation USA offers multiple product support services such as warranties and guarantees to differentiate their product from competing products.

customer services
Human or mechanical efforts or activities that add value to a product

a product has, the higher its price and, often, the higher the perceived quality.

For a brand to have a sustainable competitive advantage, marketers must determine the product designs and features that customers desire. Information from marketing research efforts and from databases can help in assessing customers' product design and feature preferences. Samsonite Corporation, the Denver-based luggage manufacturer, uses three databases to determine what customers do and don't like about their own brands and competing brands. Samsonite shares this information with its dealers so they can better serve customers.[11] Being able to meet customers' desires for product design and features at prices they can afford is crucial to a product's long-term success.

Product Support Services

Many companies differentiate their product offerings by providing support services. These services are usually referred to as **customer services** and include any human or mechanical efforts or activities a company provides that add value to a product.[12] Examples of customer services include delivery and installation, financing arrangements, customer training, warranties and guarantees, repairs, layaway plans, convenient hours of operation, adequate parking, and information through toll-free numbers. For example, Nike's 800 number provides callers with product information and prerecorded messages from well-known athletes. Nike uses this support service to build customer databases.[13] AutoNation provides a ninety-nine-day warranty and a money-back guarantee, as shown in Figure 11.8.

Whether as a major or a minor part of the total product offering, all marketers of goods sell customer services. Providing good customer service may be the only way a company can differentiate its products when all products in a market have essentially the same quality, design, and features. This is especially true in the computer industry. When consumers buy a personal computer, they shop more for fast delivery, technical support, warranties, and price than for product quality and design. Through research, a company can discover the types of services customers want and need. For example, some customers are more interested in financing, whereas others may be more concerned with installation and training. When Black & Decker introduced its DeWalt line of high-priced professional power tools to compete with Makita, the market leader at the time, it did customer research to determine which support services were needed. The support services that Black & Decker provides include rapid order processing, efficient inquiry and complaint handling, protected distribution for resellers, and job-site product demonstrations. Today, Black & Decker's DeWalt line is the market leader.[14] Companies like Black & Decker must design their customer support services with as much care as they design their products.

Product Positioning and Repositioning

product positioning
Creating and maintaining a certain concept of a product in customers' minds

Product positioning refers to the decisions and activities intended to create and maintain a certain concept of the firm's product (relative to competitive brands) in customers' minds. When marketers introduce a product, they try to position it so that it seems to possess the characteristics the target market most desires. This projected image is crucial. Crest is positioned as a fluoride toothpaste that fights cavities, and

**Figure 11.9
Product Positioning**
Northland positions its
juices as being 100% juice.

Close-Up is positioned as a whitening toothpaste that enhances the user's sex appeal. As shown in Figure 11.9, Northland positions its juices as 100% juice.

Product position is the result of customers' perceptions of a product's attributes relative to those of competitive brands. Buyers make numerous purchase decisions on a regular basis. To avoid a continuous reevaluation of numerous products, buyers tend to group, or "position," products in their minds to simplify buying decisions. Rather than allowing customers to position products independently, marketers often try to influence and shape consumers' concepts or perceptions of products through advertising. Marketers sometimes analyze product positions by developing perceptual maps, as shown in Figure 11.10. Perceptual maps are created by questioning a sample of consumers about their perceptions of products, brands, and organizations with respect to two or more dimensions. To develop a perceptual map like the one in Figure 11.10, respondents would be asked how they perceive selected pain relievers in regard to price and type of pain for which they are used. Also, respondents would be asked about their preferences for product features to establish "ideal points" or "ideal clusters," which represent a consensus about what a specific group of customers desires in terms of product features. Then, a marketer can compare how his or her brand is perceived compared with the ideal points.

Product positioning is part of a natural progression when market segmentation is used. Segmentation lets the firm aim a given brand at a portion of the total market. Effective product positioning helps serve a specific market segment by creating an appropriate concept in the minds of customers in that market segment. A firm can position a product to compete head-on with another brand, as PepsiCo has done

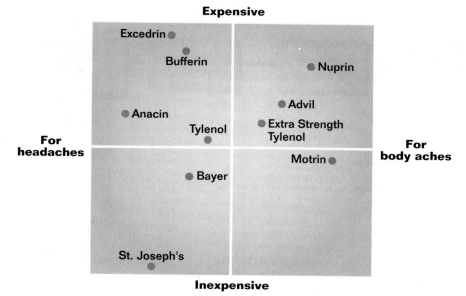

Figure 11.10
Hypothetical Perceptual Map for Pain Relievers

against Coca-Cola, or to avoid competition, as 7Up has done relative to other soft drink producers. Head-to-head competition may be a marketer's positioning objective if the product's performance characteristics are at least equal to those of competitive brands and if the product is priced lower. Head-to-head positioning may be appropriate even when the price is higher if the product's performance characteristics are superior. Conversely, positioning to avoid competition may be best when the product's performance characteristics do not differ significantly from competing brands. Moreover, positioning a brand to avoid competition may be appropriate when that brand has unique characteristics that are important to some buyers. Volvo, for example, has for years positioned itself away from competitors by focusing on the safety characteristics of its cars. While some auto companies mention safety issues in their advertisements, many are more likely to focus on style, fuel efficiency, performance, or terms of sale. Avoiding competition is critical when a firm introduces a brand into a market in which it already has one or more brands. Marketers usually want to avoid cannibalizing sales of their existing brands, unless the new brand generates substantially larger profits.

If a product has been planned properly, its features and brand image will give it the distinct appeal needed. Style, shape, construction, quality of work, and color help create the image and the appeal. If the benefits can be easily identified, then buyers are, of course, more likely to purchase the product. When the new product does not offer certain preferred attributes, there is room for another new product.

Positioning decisions are not just for new products. Evaluating the positions of existing products is important because a brand's market share and profitability may be strengthened by product repositioning. For example, several years ago Kraft was on the verge of discontinuing Cheez Whiz because its sales had declined considerably. Kraft marketers repositioned Cheez Whiz as a fast, convenient microwavable cheese sauce, causing its sales to rebound to new heights. When introducing a new product into a product line, one or more existing brands may have to be repositioned to minimize cannibalization of established brands and to assure a favorable position for the new brand.

Repositioning can be accomplished by physically changing the product, its price, or its distribution. Rather than making any of these changes, marketers sometimes reposition a product by changing its image through promotional efforts. For example,

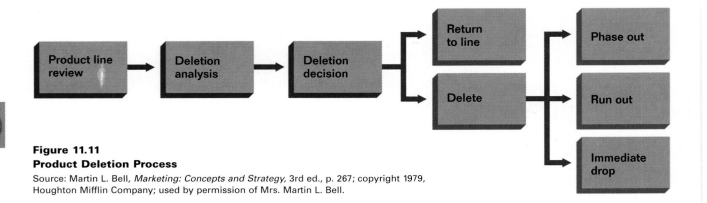

Figure 11.11
Product Deletion Process
Source: Martin L. Bell, *Marketing: Concepts and Strategy,* 3rd ed., p. 267; copyright 1979, Houghton Mifflin Company; used by permission of Mrs. Martin L. Bell.

to compete more effectively with Visa and MasterCard, American Express, through promotion, is shifting its elite credit card image to a broader, more accessible image. This image repositioning has been facilitated by forging acceptance deals at retailers where customers frequently shop, including supermarkets, gas stations, and even Wal-Mart.[15]

Product Deletion

product deletion
Eliminating a product from the product mix

Generally, a product cannot satisfy target market customers and contribute to the achievement of an organization's overall goals indefinitely. **Product deletion** is the process of eliminating a product from the product mix, usually because it no longer satisfies a sufficient number of customers. A declining product reduces an organization's profitability and drains resources that could instead be used to modify other products or to develop new ones. A marginal product may require shorter production runs, which can increase per-unit production costs. Finally, when a dying product completely loses favor with customers, the negative feelings may transfer to some of the company's other products.

Most organizations find it difficult to delete a product. A decision to drop a product may be opposed by management and other employees who feel the product is necessary in the product mix. Salespeople who still have some loyal customers are especially upset when a product is dropped. Considerable resources and effort are sometimes spent trying to change a slipping product's marketing mix to improve its sales and thus to avoid having to eliminate it.

Some organizations delete products only after they have become heavy financial burdens. A better approach is some form of systematic review in which each product is evaluated periodically to determine its impact on the overall effectiveness of the firm's product mix. Such a review should analyze a product's contribution to the firm's sales for a given period, as well as estimate future sales, costs, and profits associated with the product. It should also gauge the value of making changes in the marketing strategy to improve the product's performance. A systematic review allows an organization to improve product performance and to ascertain when to delete products. Although many companies do systematically review their product mixes, relatively few have formal, written policies for deleting products.

Basically, there are three ways to delete a product: phase it out, run it out, or drop it immediately (see Figure 11.11). A *phase out* allows the product to decline without a change in the marketing strategy. No attempt is made to give the product new life. A *run out* exploits any strengths left in the product. Intensifying marketing efforts in core markets or eliminating some marketing expenditures, such as advertising, may cause a sudden jump in profits. This approach is commonly taken for technologically obsolete products, such as older models of computers and calculators. Often the price is reduced to get a sales spurt. The third alternative, an *immediate drop* of an unprofitable product, is the best strategy when losses are too great to prolong the product's life.

Organizing to Develop and Manage Products

After reviewing the concepts of product line and mix, life cycles, positioning, and repositioning, it should be obvious that managing products is a complex task. Often, the traditional functional form of organization—in which managers specialize in such business functions as advertising, sales, and distribution—does not fit a company's needs. In this case, management must find an organizational approach that accomplishes the tasks necessary to develop and manage products. Alternatives to functional organization include the product or brand manager approach, the market manager approach, and the venture team approach.

product manager   The person within an organization responsible for a product, a product line, or several distinct products that make up a group

A **product manager** is responsible for a product, a product line, or several distinct products that make up an interrelated group within a multiproduct organization. A **brand manager,** on the other hand, is responsible for a single brand. General Foods, for example, has one brand manager for Maxim coffee and one for Maxwell House coffee. A product or brand manager operates cross-functionally to coordinate the activities, information, and strategies involved in marketing an assigned product. Product managers and brand managers plan marketing activities to achieve objectives by coordinating a mix of distribution, promotion (especially sales promotion and advertising), and price. They must consider packaging and branding decisions and work closely with personnel in research and development, engineering, and production. Marketing research helps product managers understand consumers and find target markets. The product or brand manager approach to organization is used by many large, multiple-product companies in the consumer packaged-goods business.

brand manager   The person responsible for a single brand

market manager   The person responsible for managing the marketing activities that serve a particular group of customers

A **market manager** is responsible for managing the marketing activities that serve a particular group of customers. This organizational approach is particularly effective when a firm engages in different types of marketing activities to provide products to diverse customer groups. A company might have one market manager for business markets and another for consumer markets. These broad market categories might be broken down into more limited market responsibilities.

venture team   A cross-functional group that creates entirely new products that may be aimed at new markets

A **venture team**'s purpose is to create entirely new products that may be aimed at new markets. Some firms require a certain percentage of annual revenue to be generated by new products introduced within specific time periods. For example, 3M Company now requires 30 percent of annual revenue to be accounted for by products introduced within the last four years. Such a goal may be impossible to reach without unique organizational structures focused on developing new products. A venture team is such a structure.

Unlike a product or market manager, a venture team is responsible for all aspects of a product's development: research and development, production and engineering, finance and accounting, and marketing. Venture teams work outside established divisions to create inventive approaches to new products and markets. This flexibility enables them to develop new products that can take advantage of opportunities in highly segmented markets.

The members of a venture team come from different functional areas of an organization. When the commercial potential of a new product has been demonstrated, the members may return to their functional areas, or they may join a new or existing division to manage the product. The new product may be turned over to an existing division or to a market manager or product manager. Venture teams can be especially useful for well-established firms operating primarily in mature markets. These companies must take a dual approach to marketing organization, accommodating the management of mature products while encouraging the development of new ones.

Summary

Organizations must be able to adjust their product mixes to compete effectively and achieve their goals. A product mix can be improved through line extension and through product modification. A line extension is the development of a product closely related to one or more products in the existing line but designed specifically to meet different customer needs.

Product modification is the changing of one or more characteristics of a product. This approach to altering a product mix can be effective when the product is modifiable, when customers can perceive the change, and when customers want the modification. Quality modifications are changes that relate to a product's dependability and durability. Changes that affect a product's versatility, effectiveness, convenience, or safety are called functional modifications. Aesthetic modifications change the sensory appeal of a product.

Developing new products is a way of enhancing a firm's product mix and adding depth to the product line. A new product may be an innovation that has never been sold by any organization; a product that a given firm has not marketed previously, although similar products may have been available from other organizations; or a product brought from one market to another.

Before a product is introduced, it goes through the seven phases of the new-product development process. In the idea generation phase, new-product ideas may come from internal or external sources. In the process of screening, ideas are evaluated to determine whether they are consistent with the firm's overall objectives and resources.

Concept testing, the third phase, involves having a small sample of potential customers review a brief description of the product idea to determine their initial perceptions of the proposed product and their early buying intentions. During the business analysis stage, the product idea is evaluated to determine its potential contribution to the firm's sales, costs, and profits. Product development is the stage in which the organization determines if it is technically feasible to produce the product and if it can be produced at a cost low enough to make the final price reasonable. Test marketing is a limited introduction of a product in areas chosen to represent the intended market. The decision to enter the commercialization phase means that full-scale production of the product begins and a complete marketing strategy is developed.

Product differentiation is the process of creating and designing products so that customers perceive them as different from competing products. Product quality, product design and features, and product support services are three aspects of product differentiation that companies consider when creating and marketing products. Product quality includes the overall characteristics of a product that allow it to perform as expected in satisfying customer needs. The level of quality is the amount of quality a product possesses. Consistency of quality is the degree to which a product has the same level of quality over time. Product design refers to how a product is conceived, planned, and produced. Components of product design include styling (the physical appearance of the product) and product features (the specific design characteristics that allow a product to perform certain tasks). Companies often differentiate their products by providing support services, usually called customer services. Customer services are human or mechanical efforts or activities that add value to a product.

Product positioning refers to the decisions and activities that create and maintain a certain concept of the firm's product in the customer's mind. Product position is the result of customers' perceptions of a product's attributes relative to competitive brands. Product positioning plays a role in market segmentation. Organizations can position a product to compete head-to-head with another brand if a product's performance is at least equal to the competitive brand's and if the product is priced lower. When a brand possesses unique characteristics that are important to some buyers, positioning a brand to avoid competition is appropriate. It is important for a company to avoid positioning a product so that it competes with sales of the company's existing products. Positioning is not just important for new products. Companies can increase an existing brand's market share and profitability through product repositioning. Repositioning can be accomplished by making physical changes in the product, by changing its price or distribution, or by changing its image.

Product deletion is the process of eliminating a product that no longer satisfies a sufficient number of customers. Although a firm's personnel may oppose product deletion, weak products are unprofitable, consume too much time and effort, may require shorter production runs, and can create an unfavorable impression of the firm's other products. A product mix should be systematically reviewed to determine when to delete products. Products to be deleted can be phased out, run out, or dropped immediately.

Often, the traditional functional form of organization does not lend itself to the complex task of developing and managing products. Alternative organizational forms include the product or brand manager approach, the market manager approach, and the venture team approach. A product manager is responsible for a product, a product line, or several distinct products that make up an interrelated group within a multiproduct organization. A brand manager is a product manager who is responsible for a single brand. Market managers are responsible for managing the marketing activities that serve a particular group or class of customers. A venture team is sometimes used to create entirely new products that may be aimed at new markets.

Important Terms

Line extension	Idea generation	Product differentiation	Customer services
Product modification	Screening	Quality	Product positioning
Quality modifications	Concept testing	Level of quality	Product deletion
Functional modifications	Business analysis	Consistency of quality	Product manager
Aesthetic modifications	Product development	Product design	Brand manager
New-product development	Test marketing	Styling	Market manager
process	Commercialization	Product features	Venture team

Discussion and Review Questions

1. What is a line extension and how is it different from a product modification?

2. Compare and contrast the three major ways of modifying a product.

3. Identify and briefly explain the seven major phases of the new-product development process.

4. Do small companies that manufacture just a few products need to be concerned about developing and managing products? Why or why not?

5. Why is product development a cross-functional activity within an organization? That is, why must finance, engineering, manufacturing, and other functional areas be involved?

6. What is the major purpose of concept testing, and how is it accomplished?

7. What are the benefits and disadvantages of test marketing?

8. Why can the process of commercialization take a considerable amount of time?

9. What is product differentiation, and how can it be achieved?

10. Explain how the term *quality* has been used to differentiate products in the automobile industry in recent years. What are some of the makes and models of automobiles that come to mind when you hear the terms *high quality* and *poor quality*?

11. What is product positioning? Under what conditions would head-to-head product positioning be appropriate? When should head-to-head positioning be avoided?

12. What types of problems are caused by a weak product in a product mix? Describe the most effective approach for avoiding such problems.

13. What type of organization might use a venture team to develop new products? What are the advantages and disadvantages of such a team?

Application Questions

1. When developing a new product, a company often test-markets the proposed product in a specific area or location. Coca-Cola did this with Surge. Suppose you wish to test-market your new revolutionary SuperWax car wax, which requires only one application for a lifetime finish. Where and how would you test-market your new product?

2. Product positioning aims to create a certain concept of a product in the mind of the consumer relative to its competition. Pepsi positions itself in direct competition with Coca-Cola, whereas Volvo has traditionally positioned itself away from its competitors by emphasizing its safety features. Below are several distinct positions in which an organization may place its product. Identify a product that would fit into each of them.
   a. high-price/high-quality
   b. low-price
   c. convenience
   d. uniqueness

3. Select an organization that you think should reposition itself in the eye of the consumer. Identify where it is currently positioned, and make recommendations for repositioning. Explain and defend your suggestions.

4. A product manager may make quality, functional, or aesthetic modifications when modifying a product. Identify a familiar product that recently has been modified, categorize the modification (quality, functional, or aesthetic), and describe how you would have modified it differently.

5. Phasing out a product from the product mix often is difficult for an organization. Visit a retail store in your area. Ask the manager what products he or she has had to discontinue in the recent past. Find out what factors influenced the decision to delete the product and who was involved in the decision. Ask the manager to identify any products that should be but have not been deleted, and try to ascertain the reason.

Internet Exercise & Resources

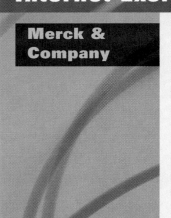

Merck & Company

Merck, a leading global pharmaceutical company, develops, manufactures, and markets a broad range of products to improve human health. In addition, the firm's Merck-Medco Managed Care Division manages pharmacy benefits for more than 40 million Americans. The company has established a Web site to serve as an educational and informational resource for Internet users around the world. To learn more about the company and its research, visit its award-winning site at

www.merck.com

1. What products has Merck developed and introduced recently?

2. What role does research play in Merck's success? How does research facilitate new-product development at Merck?

3. Find Merck's mission statement. Is Merck's focus on research consistent with the firm's mission and values?

E-Center Resources

Visit http://www.prideferrell.com to find several resources to help you succeed in mastering the material in this chapter, plus additional materials that will help you expand your marketing knowledge. The Web site includes

 Internet exercise updates plus additional exercises

 ACE self-tests

 Chapter summary with hotlinked glossary

 Hotlinks to companies featured in this chapter

 Resource Center

 Career Center

 Marketing plan worksheets

VIDEO CASE 11.1

Gillette Succeeds Through Product Development

Humorist Dave Barry predicts that some day soon, Gillette will announce a new razor so advanced it can travel forward in time and shave beards that don't yet exist. That would be good news to men, who shave about twenty-seven feet of hair off their faces in a lifetime. Although Gillette hasn't yet developed products suitable for science fiction, the $10 billion company does generate enough cutting-edge products every year to make it a Wall Street superstar. For the last five years, 49 percent of the company's sales have come from new products. Selling everything from Right Guard deodorants and shaving systems to Braun hair dryers and Duracell flashlight batteries, Gillette bases its strategy for success on aggressively rolling out new products.

The company traces its origins to 1895, when King C. Gillette came up with the idea of disposable razor blades. After six years of searching for interested investors and toolmakers to back him, he found machinist William Nickerson. In 1903, they perfected the safety razor and formed the American Safety Razor Company. In its first year of operation, the company sold just 51 safety razors. The next year, it sold over 90,000, and a little more than a decade later, during World War I, it sold 3.5 million shaving kits to the U.S. government.

In 1948, the American Safety Razor Company began to diversify, and during the 1950s, after buying Paper Mate Pens, it changed its name to Gillette. During the 1960s and 1970s, the company developed and expanded its product lines to include Right Guard deodorants, Eraser Mate erasable pens, Braun electric shavers, Liquid Paper, and Oral B dental products. Continuing the pattern it began at the end of World War

II, Gillette has never stopped developing and launching new products. This flow of innovation has evolved from a steady stream into a torrent. In 1997, the company introduced over twenty products, including Gillette Series Body Wash for men and two deodorants based on proprietary technologies. In 1998, the pace of product development continued with a series of major new-product introductions, including the revolutionary MACH3 razor for men.

Gillette will not even put a prototype into production until a model for the product's next generation is ready to test. This is an unusual approach, since many consumer product companies typically develop new products in response to competition or consumer demand. Gillette releases new products only if they represent significant improvements. Just one out of three product ideas makes it to the development stage, and many prototypes are not further developed into commercialized products. CEO Alfred Zein rejects the idea of making superficial changes to existing products and labeling them innovations. An annual research and development budget of 2.2 percent of sales, twice as much as that of the average consumer products company, facilitates the kind of technological breakthroughs that make Gillette's new products truly new. Gillette spent $275 million to develop and launch its Sensor Razor, for example, a product with twenty-nine patented features, including a skin guard comprising "microfins," a "Flexgrip" handle, water-activated moisturizers, and a flow-through cartridge.

To develop and launch its most recent shaving innovation, the triple-bladed MACH3, Gillette invested $750 million over a period of ten years. In addition to its three blades, MACH3 features six other innovations, such as a new method of loading cartridges and a blade edge three times stronger, yet thinner, than stainless steel. Each stroke of the triple-blade removes 40 percent more stubble than Gillette's SensorExcel. The MACH3 is covered by thirty-five patents, an astonishing number for a razor.

Zein believes that great products come from a combination of research and development and effective market research. So while Gillette's research and development staff work in the labs, its marketing research staff is out in the field talking to potential customers. When the company was developing its line of men's toiletries, researchers spoke to 70,000 men about what they like in shaving creams, aftershaves, and deodorants. On a typical day at Gillette, over three hundred employees come to work unshaven and test shaving products in the company's on-site "Shaving Test Lab." During the development stage of the MACH3 alone, Gillette conducted thousands of shaving tests.

As aggressive as Gillette is about launching new products, the company is equally determined to get rid of them if they don't perform well. Over the last fifteen years, the company has deleted twenty-two product lines. While many firms stick with weak products, hoping for a turnaround, Gillette will not waste time, money, and talent on products that have no chance of becoming market leaders.

What innovations are currently in the Gillette product pipeline? Female shavers will soon get their own version of the MACH3. And even now, a team of Gillette scientists is employing the latest technology to dig deeper into the mysteries of shaving. The next breakthrough is expected in the year 2006.[16]

Questions for Discussion

1. When Gillette introduces the MACH3 for women, will that be a line extension or a modified product? Explain.
2. While Gillette differentiates its razors from competitors on several dimensions, which dimension does it emphasize most?
3. Gillette does not put a prototype into production until a model for the product's next generation is ready for testing. Evaluate this practice.
4. Gillette appears to have an aggressive program of product deletion. What benefits does such a program provide to Gillette?

CASE 11.2

Can Pepsi Make Pepsi One the One?

In 1992, with much hype and hoopla, PepsiCo introduced what it thought was going to be the newest soft drink sensation, Crystal Pepsi. The product was a dismal failure. Now, Pepsi is preparing to do it again, this time with Pepsi One, the first domestic soft drink made with the artificial sweetener acesulfame potassium (ace K). Pepsi One has one calorie and, according to its marketers, tastes exactly like regular Pepsi. Why is Pepsi chancing another product flop? To compete, the company believes it must continually innovate, move

fast, and introduce new products. Its hope, of course, is that it will create the soft drink of the century—one that will steal market share from archrival Coca-Cola, the number-one soft drink maker.

On the day that the Federal Drug Administration (FDA) approved ace K for use in soft drinks, Pepsi announced plans for launching Pepsi One, a blend of aspartame and Sunett, the ace K brand. Within hours of FDA approval, Pepsi made sure that its bottlers were trying samples of the new drink. Industry experts and the media noted the lightning speed with which the soft drink maker acted. But for over ten years, while waiting for FDA approval of ace K, Pepsi's researchers had spent much of their time and resources searching for a better-tasting diet cola, one that would taste "more like regular cola." The vice president of Pepsi research believes that Pepsi One is it, stating, "It's the most regular tasting diet product on the market."

Although Pepsi acted quickly to announce its plans for launching Pepsi One, it did not actually launch the product until testing indicated that consumers liked its taste as much as its creators did. What were the test results? As described by one Pepsi executive, they were "extraordinary" and "the best we've seen in twenty years." In extensive home-use tests, almost 70 percent of those who tried Pepsi One reported they would purchase the product again. Those results were good enough for Pepsi, which had a $100 million marketing plan in place.

To differentiate Pepsi One from a horde of diet soft drinks, its marketers focus on its taste, which is almost indistinguishable from the taste of sugared soft drinks. Understating the diet aspect of Pepsi One helps attract a market segment that is unusual for any diet drink: cola-loving males in their 20s and 30s. Pepsi's executives insist that Pepsi One will not compete head-to-head with Diet Pepsi, citing steps the organization has taken to differentiate Pepsi One from the older brand. The new soft drink doesn't have the word *diet* in its name, and even the word *Pepsi* is secondary to the thick, black lettering of the word *One.* Remarked one of Pepsi's marketing directors, "We'd be thrilled if consumers just call it 'One.'"

Pepsi One's launch, backed by radio, print, outdoor, and in-store advertising, as well as massive sampling, ranks as the most expensive ever for the number-two cola company. Ads with the tagline "Only ONE has it all" and featuring Cuba Gooding, Jr., aired almost around the clock on virtually every television network in the United States. To lure impulse buyers, Pepsi created over 11,000 supermarket end-of-aisle displays. At shopping malls all over the country, the company set up "lounges" with inflatable couches where shoppers could sit down for a taste of Pepsi One. Customers ordering home-delivered pizza from Pizza Hut received free cans of Pepsi One, and sandwich buyers at 7-Eleven stores got free samples. Even greeters at Wal-Mart handed out little cups of Pepsi One with each "hello."

During the 1980s and early 1990s, Pepsi acquired a reputation for being a well-run company. Industry experts extolled its ability and willingness to launch new products. Customers thought its ads that emphasized taste were fun and creative. According to analysts, however, by the mid-1990s, the company seemed to have lost its focus. Pepsi hopes that its intensive product development efforts and careful product management will make Pepsi One the product that proves Pepsi is back.[17]

Questions for Discussion

1. Is Pepsi One a new product, a modified product, or a line extension? Explain.
2. In what way is Pepsi One positioned?
3. Over the years Pepsi has had a number of product failures. Evaluate Pepsi management's decision to introduce Pepsi One.

Branding and Packaging

OBJECTIVES

- To become aware of the value of branding
- To understand brand loyalty
- To analyze the major components of brand equity
- To recognize the types of brands and their benefits
- To understand how to select and protect brands
- To examine three types of branding policies
- To understand co-branding and brand licensing
- To become aware of the major packaging functions and design considerations and how packaging is used in marketing strategies
- To examine the functions of labeling and its legal issues

293

Dean's Foods Turns Milk Into a Cash Cow

With everyone from Vanna White to Bill Clinton sporting milk mustaches in magazine ads and on billboards and television, it seems as if more Americans than ever would be drinking milk. Not so. Although the campaign conducted by the National Fluid Milk Processors' Education Program has been enormously successful in raising awareness of milk as a healthy drink, per capita milk consumption in the United States continues to fall. Why? Some industry analysts believe it is because milk containers do not fit today's mobile lifestyle; they are not easily portable, they are difficult to open, and they are not resealable. To turn milk into a cash cow, milk producers are introducing innovative, convenient, consumer-oriented milk packaging.

Several Michigan dairies have introduced plastic pint bottles. "MiniSips," single-serve milk pouches for schools, and "Squish Packs," squeezable eight-ounce bottles, have both been extremely successful in test markets. Golden Guernsey Dairy introduced portable plastic milk containers whose bottle caps read, "Grip it. Sip it." Perhaps the most comprehensive and successful launch of new milk packaging, however, is the Milk Chug, a product of Dean's Foods, America's largest dairy processor.

Dean's introduced single-serve Chugs to compete with carbonated beverages, juices, and bottled waters. Shaped like a classic milk bottle, Chugs have resealable screw-off caps and fit in coolers, lunch sacks, car cupholders, and even in hip pockets. Milk drinkers can gulp down skim, whole, or 2 percent white milk, as well as whole or low fat chocolate milk, packaged in pints, quarts, or eight-ounce servings from a multipack. To launch its new milk container, Dean's allocated $40 million to retrofit its plants, conducted about 150 hours of focus groups and two years of market testing, and budgeted $12 million for market support. Its research revealed that consumers are pleased with the container's versatility, resealable cap, and easy-to-hold tapered shape. In test markets in Illinois, Florida, and Wisconsin, pint sales of Dean's milk rose over 70 percent, and some test cities reported sales increases of up to 500 percent.

Encouraged by the success of Milk Chugs, Dean's has plans to offer new flavors, such as "Strawberry Moo," and to introduce a blue-ice freezer pack with six-packs of milk. Dean's is convinced that containers deserve much of the credit for transforming water, the most commonplace drink in the world, into a trendy beverage, and if water can do it, why not milk?[1]

Brands and packages (such as the new milk packages) are part of a product's tangible features, the verbal and physical cues that help customers identify the products they want and that influence their choices when they are unsure. As such, branding and packaging play an important role in marketing strategy. A good brand is distinct and memorable; without one, firms could not differentiate their products, and shoppers' choices would essentially be arbitrary. A good package design is cost-effective, safe, environmentally responsible, and valuable as a promotional tool.

In this chapter, we discuss branding, including its value to customers and marketers, brand loyalty, and brand equity. Next, we examine the various types of brands. We then consider how companies choose and protect brands, the various branding policies employed, co-branding, and brand licensing. We look at packaging's critical role as part of the product and how it is marketed. The functions of packaging, issues to consider in packaging design, how the package can be a major element in marketing strategy, and packaging criticisms are also explored. We conclude with a discussion of labeling.

Branding

brand   An identifying name, term, design, or symbol

brand name   The part of a brand that can be spoken

brand mark   The part of a brand not made up of words

Marketers must make many decisions about products, including choices about brands, brand names, brand marks, trademarks, and trade names. A **brand** is a name, term, design, symbol, or any other feature that identifies one seller's good or service as distinct from those of other sellers. A brand may identify one item, a family of items, or all items of that seller.[2] A **brand name** is the part of a brand that can be spoken—including letters, words, and numbers—such as 7Up. A brand name is often a product's only distinguishing characteristic. Without the brand name, a firm could not identify its products. To consumers, brand names are as fundamental as the product itself. Indeed, many brand names have become synonymous with the product, such as Scotch Tape and Xerox copiers. Through promotional activities, the owners of these brand names try to protect them from being used as generic names for tape and photocopiers. Table 12.1 lists the world's top twenty-five brands in terms of dominance over competitors, successful extension into other markets, breadth of types of customers (age, nationality), and depth of customer loyalty. The challenges of developing a global brand are discussed in Globalmarketing.

The element of a brand that is not made up of words, but is often a symbol or design, is called a **brand mark.** One example is the Golden Arches, which identify McDonald's restaurants and can be seen on patches worn by athletic teams—from U.S.

Table 12.1	The World's Top Twenty-Five Brands		
Rank	**Brand**	**Rank**	**Brand**
1	McDonald's	14	Visa
2	Coca-Cola	15	Nescafé
3	Disney	16	Kellogg's
4	Kodak	17	Pepsi Cola
5	Sony	18	Apple Computer
6	Gillette	19	BMW
7	Mercedes-Benz	20	American Express
8	Levi's	21	Tampax
9	Microsoft	22	Nintendo
10	Marlboro	23	Lego
11	IBM	24	Ikea
12	Nike	25	Sega
13	Johnson & Johnson		

Source: "The World's Greatest Brands," Interbrand, 1998.

trademark   A legal designation of exclusive use of a brand

Olympic teams to little league softball teams—sponsored by McDonald's. In Figure 12.1, the Swiss Army shield and the encircled Quaker in the lower right corners of the ads are brand marks. A **trademark** is a legal designation indicating that the owner has exclusive use of a brand or a part of a brand and that others are prohibited by law from using it. To protect a brand name or brand mark in the United States, an organization must register it as a trademark with the U.S. Patent and Trademark Office. As of 1997, the Patent and Trademark Office had 839,071 active trademark registrations.[3] Finally, a **trade name** is the full and legal name of an organization, such as Ford Motor Company, rather than the name of a specific product.

trade name   Full legal name of an organization

Value of Branding

Both buyers and sellers benefit from branding. Brands help buyers identify specific products that they do and do not like, which in turn facilitates the purchase of items that satisfy their needs and reduces the time required to purchase the product. Without brands, product selection would be quite random because buyers could have no assurance that they were purchasing what they preferred. The purchase of certain brands can be a form of self-expression. For example, clothing brand names can be

Globalmarketing

Challenges of Developing Global Brands

Cadbury Schweppes has a problem. Customers around the world have different perceptions of its brand. For example, the British think of Schweppes as tonic water, but Germans consider it to be bitter lemon. To create a global brand identity, Schweppes has initiated a study to determine exactly how the Schweppes brand is viewed in various countries. As business becomes increasingly global, companies like Schweppes are eager to create brands that will be universally recognized and that will also reflect the same values to all customers. What many companies would like is the kind of global brand recognition achieved by Nike, McDonald's, and Coca-Cola. Customers in almost every corner of the world recognize Nike's swoosh, McDonald's golden arches, and a can of Coke.

In today's marketplace, assert industry experts, truly global brands are those conceived as global from the start, rather than being developed domestically and then expanded globally later on. The process, however, presents a challenge. A name must be legally available and understandable in dozens of countries and languages. Words and symbols must have no negative associations in specific cultures. In addition to creating a name that can overcome cultural, legal, and regulatory hurdles, a firm must also

create a universally recognizable logo and other graphics that convey a consistent brand image.

Examples of organizations attempting to develop global brands are easy to find. Pharmaceutical maker Glaxo Wellcome is striving for one brand that will use a standard logo and graphics worldwide. Compaq Computer recently launched its first worldwide brand advertising campaign featuring a new logo that highlights the Q in its name. Dell Computers, now employing simple images and the tag line "Be Direct," is launching its first global image campaign in Europe, Japan, and Asia. In an attempt to have a truly global brand name, office supply marketer Staples is changing the names of its German and Canadian subsidiaries from Maxi-Papier and Business Depot, respectively, to Staples.

Not all marketing experts agree that global branding is the best direction for organizations to take. No brand, they assert, is universally applicable, because every culture has its own unique values and associations. In addition, in some countries, such as China, a substantial number of customers will purchase only local brands. In the long run, marketers may determine that for certain product categories, global brands work well, while for others, global brands are unworkable.

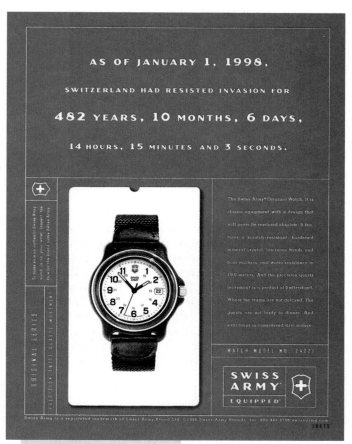

Figure 12.1
Brand Marks
The Swiss Army shield and the encircled Quaker man in these advertisements are examples of brand marks.

important to teenage boys. Names such as Tommy Hilfiger, Polo, Champion, Guess, and Nike give manufacturers an advantage in the marketplace. A brand also helps buyers evaluate the quality of products, especially when they are unable to judge a product's characteristics. That is, a brand may symbolize a certain quality level to a customer, and in turn the person lets that perception of quality represent the quality of the item. A brand helps reduce a buyer's perceived risk of purchase. In addition, a psychological reward may come from owning a brand that symbolizes status. The Mercedes-Benz brand is an example.

Sellers benefit from branding because each company's brands identify its products, which makes repeat purchasing easier for customers. Branding helps a firm introduce a new product that carries the name of one or more of its existing products because buyers are already familiar with the firm's existing brands. Branding also facilitates promotional efforts because the promotion of each branded product indirectly promotes all other similarly branded products. Coca-Cola's brand extensions—additional products marketed under the Coca-Cola brand—improved its market share from 36 percent in the early 1980s to 42 percent in the 1990s. Branding also helps sellers by fostering brand loyalty. To the extent that buyers become loyal to a specific brand, the company's market share for that product achieves a certain level of stability, allowing the firm to use its resources more efficiently. Once a firm develops some degree of customer loyalty for a brand, it can maintain a fairly consistent price rather than continually cutting the price to attract customers. A brand is just as much of an asset as the company's building or machinery. When marketers increase their brand's value, they also are raising the total asset value of the organization. (We discuss brand value in more detail later in this chapter.) At times marketers must decide whether to change a brand name. This is a difficult decision because the value in the existing brand name must be given up to gain the potential for building a higher value in a new brand name.

Brand Loyalty

brand loyalty A customer's favorable attitude toward a specific brand

As we just noted, creating and maintaining customer loyalty toward a brand is a major benefit of branding. **Brand loyalty** is a customer's favorable attitude toward a specific brand. If brand loyalty is strong enough, customers may consistently purchase this brand when they need a product in this product category. Although brand loyalty may not result in a customer's purchasing a specific brand all the time, the brand is at least considered as a potentially viable brand in the set of brands being considered for purchase. Development of brand loyalty by a customer reduces his or her risks and shortens the time spent buying the product. However, the degree of brand loyalty for products varies from one product category to another. For example, it is challenging to develop brand loyalty for produce (see Figure 12.2) because most customers can judge its quality and do not need to refer to a brand as an indicator of quality. It also varies by country. Customers in France, Germany, and the United Kingdom tend to be less brand-loyal than U.S. customers.

brand recognition A customer's awareness that a brand exists and is an alternative purchase

There are three degrees of brand loyalty: recognition, preference, and insistence. **Brand recognition** exists when a customer is aware that the brand exists and views it as an alternative purchase if the preferred brand is unavailable or if the other available brands are unfamiliar. This is the mildest form of brand loyalty. The term *loyalty* clearly is being used very loosely here. One of the initial objectives of a marketer introducing a new brand is to create widespread awareness of the brand in order to generate brand recognition.

brand preference
The degree of brand loyalty in which a customer prefers one brand over competitive offerings

Brand preference is a stronger degree of brand loyalty in which a customer definitely prefers one brand over competitive offerings and will purchase this brand if available. However, if the brand is not available, the customer will accept a substitute brand rather than expending additional effort finding and purchasing the preferred brand. A marketer is likely to be able to compete effectively in a market when a number of customers have developed brand preference for its specific brand.

brand insistence The degree of brand loyalty in which a customer strongly prefers a specific brand and will accept no substitute

Brand insistence is the degree of brand loyalty in which a customer strongly prefers a specific brand, will accept no substitute, and is willing to spend a great deal of time and effort to acquire that brand. If a brand-insistent customer goes to a store and finds the brand unavailable, rather than purchasing a substitute brand, the customer will seek the brand elsewhere. Brand insistence is the strongest degree of brand loyalty. It is a brander's dream. However, it is the least common type of brand loyalty. Customers vary considerably regarding the product categories for which they may be brand-insistent. Can you think of products for which you are brand-insistent? Perhaps a brand of deodorant, soft drink, jeans (see Figure 12.3), or even pet food, if your pet is brand-insistent.

Brand loyalty, in general, seems to be declining, partly because of marketers' increased reliance on sales, coupons, and other short-term promotions, and partly because of the sometimes overwhelming array of similar new products from which customers can

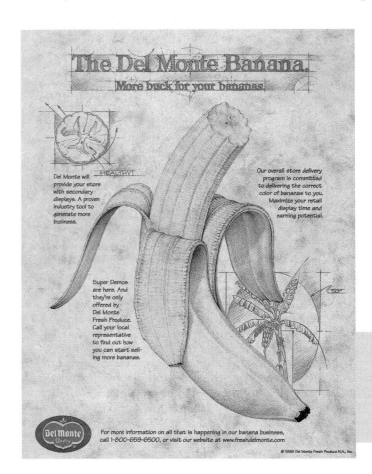

Figure 12.2
Branding Challenge
Developing brand loyalty for products such as produce that customers can judge for quality for themselves is challenging. Del Monte uses its well-respected brand name to convince customers that its produce is high-quality.

choose. However, a study of brands as an influence on supermarket purchase decisions showed an increase from 6.1 in 1993 to 6.4 in 1996 based on a 10 point scale.[4]

Building brand loyalty is a major challenge for many marketers. It is an extremely important issue. The creation of brand loyalty significantly contributes to an organization's ability to achieve a sustainable competitive advantage.

Brand Equity

A well-managed brand is an asset to an organization. The value of this asset is often referred to as brand equity. **Brand equity** is the marketing and financial value associated with a brand's strength in a market. Besides the actual proprietary brand assets, such as patents and trademarks, four major elements underlie brand equity. These components are brand name awareness, brand loyalty, perceived brand quality, and brand associations, as shown in Figure 12.4.[5]

Being aware of a brand leads to brand familiarity, which in turn results in a level of comfort with the brand. A familiar brand is more likely to be selected than an unfamiliar brand because the familiar brand often is viewed as reliable and of acceptable quality compared with the unknown brand. The familiar brand is likely to be in a customer's consideration set, whereas the unfamiliar brand is not.

Brand loyalty is a valued component of brand equity because it reduces a brand's vulnerability to competitors' actions. Brand loyalty allows an organization to keep its existing customers and to avoid spending an enormous amount of resources gaining new customers. Loyal customers provide brand visibility and reassurance to potential new customers. And because customers expect their brand to be available when and where they shop, retailers strive to carry the brands known for their strong customer following.

Customers associate a certain level of perceived overall quality with a brand. A brand name itself actually stands for a certain level of quality in a customer's mind and is used as a substitute for actual judgment of quality. In many cases, customers can't actually judge the quality of the product for themselves and instead must rely on the brand as a quality indicator. Perceived high brand quality helps support a premium price, allowing a marketer to avoid severe price competition. Also, favorable perceived brand quality can ease the introduction of brand extensions, as the high regard for the brand will likely translate into high regard for the related products.

Figure 12.3
Brand Insistence
Some customers are brand-insistent regarding the brand of jeans that they wear.

brand equity   The marketing and financial value associated with a brand's strength in a market

Figure 12.4
Major Elements of Brand Equity

Source: Adapted with the permission of The Free Press, a division of Simon & Schuster, Inc., from *Managing Brand Equity: Capitalizing on the Value of a Brand Name* by David A. Aaker. Copyright © 1991 by David A. Aaker.

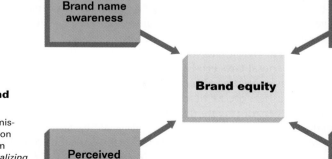

The set of associations linked to a brand is another key component of brand equity. At times, a marketer works to connect a lifestyle, or in some instances a certain personality type, with a particular brand. For example, customers associate Michelin tires with protecting family members, a De Beers diamond with a loving, long-lasting relationship (a diamond is forever), and Dr Pepper with a unique taste. These types of brand associations contribute significantly to the brand's equity. Brand associations are sometimes facilitated by using trade characters, such as the Pillsbury Dough Boy, Charlie the Tuna, and the Kool-Aid pitcher man. Placing these trade characters in advertisements and on packages helps consumers link the ads and packages to the brands.[6]

Although difficult to measure, brand equity represents the value of a brand to an organization. An organization may buy a brand from another company at a premium price because outright brand purchase may be less expensive and less risky than creating and developing a brand from scratch. Brand equity helps give a brand the power to capture and maintain a consistent market share, which provides stability to an organization's sales volume. The ten brands with the highest economic value are shown in Table 12.2. The values in Table 12.2 were determined by multiplying a brand's net profits by the brand's strength index.[7] Any company that owns a brand listed in Table 12.2 would agree that the economic value of that brand is likely to be the greatest single asset in the organization's possession. A brand's overall economic value rises and falls with the brand's profitability, brand awareness, brand loyalty, perceived brand quality, and the strength of positive brand associations.

Table 12.2 The World's Most Valuable Brands	
Brand	**Brand Value (in millions)**
Coca-Cola	$47,978
Marlboro	47,635
IBM	23,701
McDonald's	19,939
Disney	17,069
Sony	14,464
Kodak	14,442
Intel	13,274
Gillette	11,992
Budweiser	11,985

Source: Kurt Bradenhausen, "Most Valuable Brands," *Financial World*, Sep./Oct. 1997, p. 62.

Types of Brands

manufacturer brands
Brands initiated by producers

private distributor brands Brands initiated and owned by resellers

There are three categories of brands: manufacturer brands, private distributor brands, and generic brands. **Manufacturer brands** are initiated by producers and ensure that producers are identified with their products at the point of purchase—for example, Green Giant, Compaq Computer, and Levi's jeans (see Figure 12.5). A manufacturer brand usually requires a producer to become involved in distribution, promotion, and, to some extent, pricing decisions. Brand loyalty is encouraged by promotion, quality control, and guarantees; it is a valuable asset to a manufacturer. The producer tries to stimulate demand for the product, which tends to encourage sellers and resellers to make the product available.

Private distributor brands (also called *private brands, store brands,* or *dealer brands*) are initiated and owned by resellers—wholesalers or retailers (see Figure 12.5). The major characteristic of private brands is that the manufacturers are not identified on the products. Retailers and wholesalers use private distributor brands to develop more efficient promotion, to generate higher gross margins, and to improve store image. Private distributor brands give retailers or wholesalers freedom to purchase products of a specified quality at the lowest cost without disclosing the identity of the manufacturer. Wholesaler brands include IGA (Independent Grocers' Alliance) and Topmost (General Grocer). Familiar retailer brand names include Sears's Kenmore and J. C. Penney's Arizona. Many successful private brands are distributed nationally. Kenmore washers are as well known as most manufacturer brands. Sometimes retailers with successful private distributor brands start manufacturing their own products to gain more control over product costs, quality, and design with the hope of increasing profits. Private brands account for over 16 percent of dollar volume sales and over 20 percent of unit volume sales in supermarkets.[8] Supermarket private brands are popular globally, too. In the United Kingdom, private brand products generate over 30

Figure 12.5
Types of Brands
Shown here are examples of store brands, generic brands, and manufacturer's brands.

percent of supermarket revenues; in France, 25 percent; Belgium and Germany, over 22 percent; Holland, 18 percent; and Spain, 10 percent.

Competition between manufacturer brands and private distributor brands (sometimes called "the battle of the brands") is intensifying in several major product categories. Figure 12.6 shows the percentage of private brand expenditures for the top ten packaged-goods items by frequent, occasional, and infrequent private brand buyers. Note that milk and bread are the most heavily purchased private brand products. For manufacturers, developing multiple manufacturer brands and distribution systems has been an effective means of combating the increased competition from private brands. By developing a new brand name, a producer can adjust various elements of a marketing mix to appeal to a different target market. The growth of private brands has been steady, but the rate of growth is slowing because some manufacturer brand makers have stopped price increases or even cut their prices, which has narrowed the price gap, the major advantage of buying a private brand. Traditionally, private brands have appeared in packaging that directly imitates the packaging of competing manufacturers' brands, without significant legal ramifications. While this practice continues, the legal risks of using look-alike packaging are increasing for private branders.[9]

Figure 12.6
Top Ten Private Brand Product Groups
Percentage of private label dollars spent for the top ten packaged-goods items, by frequent, occasional, and infrequent private label shoppers.
Source: A. C. Nielsen, Nielsen Consumer Information Services, reported in Marcia Mogelonsky, "When Stores Become Brands," *American Demographics,* Feb. 1995, p. 34. Copyright © 1995. Reprinted with permission.

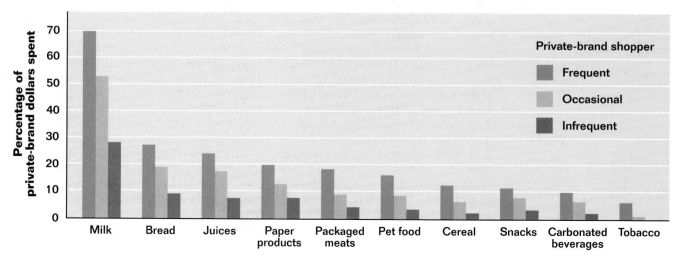

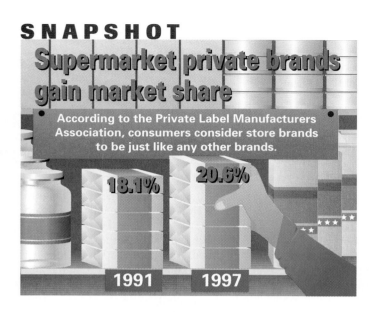

SNAPSHOT

Supermarket private brands gain market share

According to the Private Label Manufacturers Association, consumers consider store brands to be just like any other brands.

18.1%　　20.6%

1991　　1997

generic brands Brands indicating only the product category

Some private distributor brands are produced by companies that specialize in making only private distributor brands, while other private brands are made by producers of manufacturer brands. Producers of both types of brands at times find it difficult to ignore the opportunities that come from producing private distributor brands. If a producer decides not to produce a private brand for a reseller, a competitor probably will. Moreover, the production of private distributor brands allows the producer to use excess capacity during periods when its own brands are at nonpeak production. The ultimate decision whether to produce a private or a manufacturer brand depends on a company's resources, production capabilities, and goals.

Some marketers of traditionally branded products have embarked on a policy of not branding, often called *generic branding*. **Generic brands** indicate only the product category (such as aluminum foil) and do not include the company name or other identifying terms (see Figure 12.5). Generic brands are usually sold at lower prices than comparable branded items. Although at one time generic brands may have represented as much as 10 percent of all retail grocery sales, today they account for less than 1/10 of 1 percent.[10]

Selecting a Brand Name

Marketers consider a number of factors in selecting a brand name. The name should be easy for customers (including foreign buyers, if the firm intends to market its products in other countries) to say, spell, and recall. Short, one-syllable names, such as Cheer, often satisfy this requirement. The brand name should indicate the product's major benefits and, if possible, should suggest in a positive way the product's uses and special characteristics; negative or offensive references should be avoided. For example, the brand names of such household cleaning products as Ajax dishwashing liquid, Vanish toilet bowl cleaner, Formula 409 multipurpose cleaner, Cascade dishwasher detergent, and Wisk laundry detergent connote strength and effectiveness. The brand in Figure 12.7 relates directly to product benefits. To set it apart from competing brands, the brand should be distinctive. If a marketer intends to use a brand for a product line, it must be compatible with all products in the line. Finally, a brand should be designed so that it can be used and recognized in all types of media. Finding the right brand name has become a challenging task because many obvious product names have already been used. In 1997, the U.S. Patent and Trademark Office issued 97,294 new trademarks.[11]

How are brand names devised? Brand names can be created from single or multiple words—for example, Bic or Dodge Grand Caravan. Letters and numbers are used to create such brands as IBM PC or Z71. Words, numbers, and letters are combined to yield brand names like Mazda RX7 or Mitsubishi 3000GT. To avoid terms that have negative connotations, marketers sometimes use fabricated words that have absolutely no meaning when they are created—for example, Kodak and Exxon. Occasionally, a brand is simply brought out of storage and used as is or modified. Firms often maintain banks of registered brands, some of which may have been used in the past. Cadillac, for example, has a bank of approximately 360 registered trademarks. The LaSalle brand, used in the 1920s and 1930s, could be called up for a new Cadillac model in the future. Possible brand names sometimes are tested in focus groups or in other settings to assess customers' reactions.

Who actually creates brand names? Brand names can be created internally by the organization. Sometimes a name is suggested by individuals who are close to the

Figure 12.7
Brand Names That Highlight Product Uses
Friskies Dental Diet is a brand name that indicates the product's uses and benefits.

development of the product. Some organizations have committees that participate in brand name creation and approval. Large companies that introduce numerous new products annually are likely to have a department that develops brand names. At times, outside consultants and companies that specialize in brand name development are used. When Triarc named a new Snapple beverage, its brand team sought ideas from most traditional sources of brand names, including all of Snapple's promotional agencies, all individuals who worked on the Snapple brand, and their friends and relatives. The company ran a contest offering prizes to employees for the best brand suggestions. In addition, three agencies that specialize in brand naming were used. In total, about 1,000 names were generated. Eventually, "Whipper Snapple" was selected.[12]

Even though most of the important branding considerations apply to both goods and services, branding a service has some additional dimensions. The service brand is usually the same as the company name. Financial companies, such as Fidelity Investments and Charles Schwab Discount Brokerage, have established strong brand recognition. These companies have used their names to create an image of value and friendly, timely, responsible, accurate, and knowledgeable customer assistance. Service providers (such as United Air Lines) are perceived by customers as having one brand name, even though they offer multiple products (first class, business class, and coach). Because the service brand name and company name are so closely interrelated, a service brand name must be flexible enough to encompass a variety of current services, as well as new ones that the company might offer in the future. Geographical references like *western* and descriptive terms like *trucking* limit the scope of associations that can be made with the brand name. Because Southwest Airlines now flies to many parts of the country, its name has become too limited in its scope of associations. *Humana,* with its connotations of kindness and compassion, is flexible enough to encompass all services that a hospital, insurance plan, or health care facility offers. Frequently, a service marketer will employ a symbol along with its brand name to make the brand distinctive and to communicate a certain image. For example, the Wausau Insurance Company's advertising of its distinctive name and brand logo (a train station) has increased both its response rates to direct mail and general consumer acceptance of the company.[13]

Protecting a Brand

A marketer should also design a brand so that it can be protected easily through registration. A series of court decisions has created a broad hierarchy of protection based on brand type. From most protectable to least protectable, these brand types are fanciful (Exxon), arbitrary (Dr Pepper), suggestive (Spray 'n Wash), descriptive (Minute Rice), and generic (aluminum foil). Generic brands are not protectable. Surnames and descriptive geographic or functional names are difficult to protect.[14] Because of their designs, some brands can be legally infringed upon more easily than others. Although registration protects trademarks domestically for ten years and can be renewed indefinitely, a firm should develop a system for ensuring that its trademarks will be renewed as needed.

To protect its exclusive rights to a brand, a company must make certain that the brand is not likely to be considered an infringement on any brand already registered with the U.S. Patent and Trademark Office. This task may be complex because infringement is determined by the courts, which base their decisions on whether a brand causes consumers to be confused, mistaken, or deceived about the source of the product. McDonald's is one company that aggressively protects its trademarks against infringement; it has brought charges against a number of companies with "Mc" names because it fears that the use of the prefix will give consumers the impression that these companies are associated with or owned by McDonald's. Auto Shack changed its name to AutoZone when faced with legal action from the Tandy Corporation, owner of Radio Shack. Tandy maintained that it owned the name *Shack*. After research showed that virtually every auto supply store in the country used *auto* in its name, *zone* was deemed the best word to pair with *auto*.

If possible, a marketer should guard against allowing a brand name to become a generic term used to refer to a general product category. Generic terms cannot be protected as exclusive brand names. For example, *aspirin, escalator,* and *shredded wheat*—all brand names at one time—eventually were declared generic terms that refer to product classes; thus, they no longer could be protected. To keep a brand name from becoming a generic term, the firm should spell the name with a capital letter and use it as an adjective to modify the name of the general product class, as in Kool-Aid Brand Soft Drink Mix.[15] Including the word *brand* just after the brand name is also helpful. An organization can deal with this problem directly by advertising that its brand is a trademark and should not be used generically. The firm can also indicate that the brand is a registered trademark by using the symbol ®.

In the interest of strengthening trademark protection, Congress enacted the 1988 Trademark Law Revision Act, the only major federal trademark legislation since the Lanham Act of 1946. The purpose of this more recent legislation is to increase the value of the federal registration system for U.S. firms relative to foreign competitors and to better protect the public from counterfeiting, confusion, and deception.[16]

A U.S. firm that tries to protect a brand in a foreign country frequently encounters problems. In many countries, brand registration is not possible; the first firm to use a brand in such a country has the rights to it. In some instances, U.S. companies actually have had to buy their own brand rights from a firm in a foreign country because the foreign firm was the first user in that country.

Marketers trying to protect their brands must also contend with brand counterfeiting. In the United States, for instance, one can purchase counterfeit General Motors parts, Cartier watches, Louis Vuitton handbags, Walt Disney character dolls, Warner Brothers clothing, Mont Blanc pens, and a host of other products illegally marketed by manufacturers that do not own the brands. Annual losses caused by counterfeit products are estimated to be between $250 billion and $350 billion annually. Many counterfeit products are manufactured overseas—in Turkey, China, Thailand, Italy, and Columbia, for example—but some are counterfeited in the United States. Counterfeit products are often hard to distinguish from the real brands. Products most likely to be counterfeited are well-known brands that appeal to a mass market and products for which the physical materials are inexpensive compared with the products' prices. Microsoft estimates that its revenues would double if counterfeiting of its brand name products were eliminated. Some $40 billion a year is lost in the computer software business because of counterfeit and pirated products. Brand fraud not only results in lost revenue for the brand's owner; it also means that customers get a low-quality product, it distorts competition, it affects investment levels, it reduces tax revenues and legitimate employment, it creates safety risks, and it affects international relations.[17]

Branding Policies

Before establishing branding policies, a firm must first decide whether to brand its products at all. If a company's product is homogeneous and similar to competitors' products, it may be difficult to brand. Raw materials—such as coal, sand, and farm produce—are hard to brand because of the homogeneity of such products and their physical characteristics.

If a firm chooses to brand its products, it may opt for one or more of the following branding policies: individual, family, and brand-extension branding. **Individual branding** is a policy of naming each product differently. Lever Brothers relies on an

individual branding A policy of naming each product differently

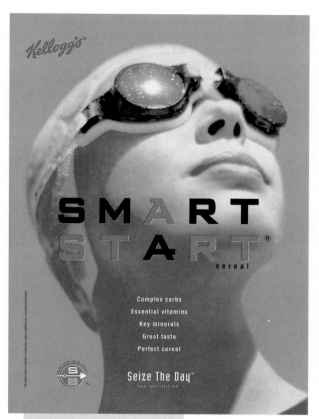

Figure 12.8
Family Branding
Kellogg's uses family branding. For each of its branded cereals, the name Kellogg's appears as part of the brand name.

family branding   Branding all of a firm's products with the same name

brand-extension branding   Using an existing brand name for an improved or new product

co-branding   Using two or more brands on one product

individual branding policy for its line of detergents, which includes Wisk, Surf, and All. A major advantage of individual branding is that if an organization introduces a poor product, the negative images associated with it do not contaminate the company's other products. An individual branding policy may also facilitate market segmentation when a firm wishes to enter many segments of the same market. Separate, unrelated names can be used, and each brand can be aimed at a specific segment. Sara Lee utilizes individual branding among its many divisions. Sara Lee markets Coach luggage, Hanes underwear, L'eggs pantyhose, Champion sportswear, and other vastly different brands.

In **family branding,** all of a firm's products are branded with the same name or at least part of the name, such as Kellogg's Frosted Flakes, Kellogg's Rice Krispies, and Kellogg's Corn Flakes (see Figure 12.8). In some cases, a company's name is combined with other words to brand items. Arm & Hammer uses its name on all its products, along with a generic description of the item, such as Arm & Hammer Heavy Duty Detergent, Arm & Hammer Pure Baking Soda, and Arm & Hammer Carpet Deodorizer. Unlike individual branding, family branding means that the promotion of one item with the family brand promotes the firm's other products. Family branding has been practiced by such major companies as Mitsubishi, Kodak, and Fisher-Price.

Brand-extension branding occurs when a firm uses one of its existing brand names as part of a brand for an improved or new product, which is often in the same product category as the existing brand. McNeil Consumer Products, the makers of Tylenol and Extra Strength Tylenol, also introduced Extra Strength Tylenol P.M., thus extending the Tylenol brand. Marketers share a common concern that if a brand is extended too many times or extended too far away from its original product category, the brand can be significantly weakened. For example, Miller Brewing Company has extended its brand to Miller Lite, Genuine Draft, Draft Lite, Ice, Ice Lite, Milwaukee's Best, Ice House, and Red Dog. So many extensions may confuse customers and encourage them to do considerable brand switching. The Nabisco Snackwell brand initially appeared only on crackers, cookies, and snack bars, all of which fall into the baked snack category. However, extending the brand to yogurts and gelatin mixes goes further afield. Healthy Choice has extended its brand, initially limited to frozen meals, to ice cream, breakfast cereals, and over 160 other products. This volume of extension, as well as extensions into other product categories, may threaten the Healthy Choice brand.[18]

An organization is not limited to a single branding policy. A company that primarily uses individual branding for many of its products may also use brand extensions. Branding policy is influenced by the number of products and product lines the company produces, the characteristics of its target markets, the number and types of competing products available, and the size of its resources.

Co-Branding

Co-branding is the use of two or more brands on one product. Marketers employ co-branding to capitalize on the brand equity of multiple brands. Co-branding is popular in a number of processed food categories and in the credit card industry. The brands used for co-branding can be owned by the same company. For example, Kraft's Lunchables product teams the Kraft cheese brand with Oscar Mayer lunch meats, another Kraft-owned brand. The brands may also be owned by different companies. Both Visa and MasterCard, for instance, team up with the brands of numerous other

Unlike other so-called "highly mobile" notebooks, the Compaq Armada 3500 doesn't swap performance for portability. Designed for the savvy traveler, its topflight specs include a Mobile Pentium II processor soaring to 366 MHz—in a sleek package as light as 4.4 pounds. With built-in 6.4 GB hard drive, full-size keyboard, extended-life battery option and extra-durable magnesium alloy display casing, the Armada 3500 has everything you need for maximum flexibility—and unlimited mileage. To learn more, call 1-800-AT-COMPAQ. Or visit www.compaq.com/soar.

All notebooks travel. Is there one that soars?

COMPAQ. Better answers.

Figure 12.9
Co-Branding
This ad highlighting a Compaq computer with an Intel Pentium II processor is an example of co-branding by two different companies.

companies, including General Motors, AT&T, and MCI. An example of co-branding appears in Figure 12.9.

Effective co-branding capitalizes on the trust and confidence customers have in the brands involved. The brands should not lose their identities, and it should be clear to customers which brand is the main brand. For example, it is fairly obvious that Kellogg owns the brand and is the main brander of Kellogg's Healthy Choice Cereal. It is important for marketers to understand that when a co-branded product is unsuccessful, both brands are implicated in the product failure. To gain customer acceptance, the brands involved must represent a complementary fit in the minds of buyers. Trying to link a brand like Harley-Davidson to a brand like Healthy Choice will not achieve co-branding objectives because customers are not likely to perceive these brands as compatible.

Co-branding can help an organization differentiate its products from those of its competitors. By using the product development skills of a co-branding partner, an organization can create a distinctive product. For example, Hiram Walker partnered with Sara Lee to produce a Kahlua White Russian Brownie; a Hiram Walker gift package includes an eight-ounce serving of these special brownies along with a bottle of Kahlua. Co-branding also can take advantage of the distribution capabilities of co-branding partners. Fannie May, which traditionally distributed its candies through its own retail stores and department stores, has developed a co-branding program with Hallmark; packages of Fannie May Celebrated Selection chocolates bearing Hallmark's Gold Crown logo will be featured in over 1,000 Hallmark stores.[19]

While co-branding has been used for a number of years, it began to grow in popularity in the 1980s when Monsanto aggressively promoted its NutraSweet product as an ingredient in such well-known brands as Diet Coke. The company also used this approach with lesser-known brands to instill trust and confidence in buyers' minds. Intel, too, has capitalized on ingredient co-branding through its "Intel Inside" program. The effectiveness of ingredient co-branding relies heavily on continued promotional efforts by the ingredient's producer.

Brand Licensing

brand licensing An agreement whereby a company permits another organization to use its brand on other products for a licensing fee

A trend in branding strategies involves **brand licensing.** By means of a licensing agreement, a company permits an organization to use its brand on other products for a licensing fee. Royalties may be as low as 2 percent of wholesale revenues or higher than 10 percent. The licensee is responsible for all manufacturing, selling, and advertising functions and bears the costs if the licensed product fails. Not long ago, only a few firms licensed their corporate trademarks, but today licensing is a multi-billion dollar business. The retail value of licensed products was over $73 billion in 1997.[20] Fashion designers engage heavily in brand licensing. Designer brands, such as Calvin Klein, Ralph Lauren, Bill Blass, Anne Klein, Pierre Cardin, and Tommy Hilfiger, appear on numerous products in a variety of product categories through licensing agreements.[21]

The advantages of licensing range from extra revenues and low cost or free publicity to new images and trademark protection. For example, Coca-Cola has licensed its trademark for use on glassware, radios, trucks, and clothing in the hope of protecting its trademark. However, brand licensing is not without drawbacks. The major disadvantages are a lack of manufacturing control, which could hurt the company's name, and bombarding consumers with too many unrelated products bearing the same name. Licensing arrangements can also fail because of poor timing, inappropriate distribution channels, or mismatching of product and name.

Packaging

Packaging involves the development of a container and a graphic design for a product. A package can be a vital part of a product, making it more versatile, safer, and easier to use. Like a brand name, a package can influence customers' attitudes toward a product and so affect their purchase decisions. For example, several producers of jellies, sauces, and ketchups have packaged their products in squeezable containers to make use and storage more convenient. Package characteristics help shape buyers' impressions of a product at the time of purchase or during use. In this section, we examine the main functions of packaging and consider several major packaging decisions. We also analyze the role of the package in a marketing strategy.

Packaging Functions

Effective packaging means more than simply putting products in containers and covering them with wrappers. First of all, packaging materials serve the basic purpose of protecting the product and maintaining its functional form. The ads in Figure 12.10 promote the protective qualities of plastics and paperboard when used as packaging materials. Fluids like milk, orange juice, and hair spray need packages that preserve and protect them; the packaging should prevent damage that could affect the product's usefulness and thus lead to higher costs. Since product tampering has become a problem for marketers of many types of goods, several packaging techniques have been developed to counter this danger. Some packages are also designed to deter shoplifting.

Figure 12.10
Product Protection
These organizations promote the protective qualities of their packaging materials.

The Etch A Sketch® product name and the configuration of the Etch A Sketch® product are registered trademarks owned by The Ohio Art Company.

Another function of packaging is to offer convenience to consumers. For example, small aseptic packages—individual-sized boxes or plastic bags that contain liquids and do not require refrigeration—strongly appeal to children and young adults with active lifestyles. The size or shape of a package may relate to the product's storage, convenience of use, or replacement rate. Small, single-serving cans of vegetables, for instance, may prevent waste and make storage easier. A third function of packaging is to promote a product by communicating its features, uses, benefits, and image. At times, a reusable package is developed to make the product more desirable. For example, the CoolWhip package doubles as a food-storage container.

Major Packaging Considerations

As they develop packages, marketers must take many factors into account. Obviously, one major consideration is cost. Although a variety of packaging materials, processes, and designs are available, costs vary greatly. In recent years, buyers have shown a willingness to pay more for improved packaging, but there are limits. Marketers should try to determine, through research, just how much customers are willing to pay for effective and efficient package designs.

As already mentioned, developing tamper-resistant packaging is very important for certain products. Although no package is tamper-proof, marketers can develop packages that are difficult to tamper with. At a minimum, all packaging must comply with the Food and Drug Administration's packaging regulations. However, packaging should also make any product tampering evident to resellers and consumers. Although effective tamper-resistant packaging may be expensive to develop, when balanced against the costs of lost sales, loss of consumer confidence and company reputation, and potentially expensive product liability lawsuits, the costs of ensuring consumer safety are minimal.

Marketers should also consider how much consistency is desirable among an organization's package designs. No consistency may be the best policy, especially if a firm's products are unrelated or aimed at vastly different target markets. To promote an overall company image, a firm may decide that all packages should be similar or include one major element of the design. This approach is called **family packaging.** Sometimes it is used only for lines of products, as with Campbell's soups, Weight Watcher's foods, and Planter's nuts.

A package's promotional role is an important consideration. Through verbal and nonverbal symbols, the package can inform potential buyers about the product's content, features, uses, advantages, and hazards. A firm can create desirable images and associations by its choice of color, design, shape, and texture. Many cosmetics manufacturers, for example, design their packages to create impressions of richness, luxury, and exclusiveness. A package performs a promotional function when it is designed to be safer or more convenient to use, if such characteristics help stimulate demand.

To develop a package that has a definite promotional value, a designer must consider size, shape, texture, color, and graphics. Beyond the obvious limitation that the package must be large enough to hold the product, a package can be designed to appear taller or shorter. Lighter-colored packaging may make a package appear larger, while darker colors may minimize the perceived size.

Colors on packages are often chosen to attract attention. People associate specific colors with certain feelings and experiences. Red, for example, is linked with fire, blood, danger, and anger; yellow suggests sunlight, caution, warmth, and vitality; blue can imply coldness, sky, water, and sadness.[22] A trend toward colorless packages stems from the New Age mentality. Clear products and packaging give consumers the impression of a pure, natural product. When opting for color on packaging, marketers must judge whether a particular color will evoke positive or negative feelings when it is linked to a specific product. Rarely, for example, do processors package meat or bread in green materials because customers may associate green with mold. Marketers must also determine whether a specific target market will respond favorably or unfavorably to a particular color. Cosmetics for women are more likely to be sold in pastel

family packaging Using similar packaging for all of a firm's products or packaging that has one common design element

packaging than are personal-care products for men. Packages designed to appeal to children often use primary colors and bold designs.

Packaging must also meet the needs of resellers. Wholesalers and retailers consider whether a package facilitates transportation, storage, and handling. Resellers may refuse to carry certain products if their packages are cumbersome. Concentrated versions of laundry detergents and fabric softeners aid retailers in offering more product diversity within the existing shelf space.

A final consideration is whether to develop packages that are environmentally responsible. Nearly one-half of all garbage consists of discarded plastic packaging, such as polystyrene containers, plastic soft drink bottles, and carryout bags. Plastic packaging material does not biodegrade, and paper requires the destruction of valuable forests. Consequently, a number of companies have changed to environmentally sensitive packaging; they are also recycling more materials. Procter & Gamble markets several cleaning products in a concentrated form, which requires less packaging than the ready-to-use version; H. J. Heinz is looking for alternatives to its plastic ketchup squeeze bottles. Other companies are also searching for alternatives to environmentally harmful packaging. In some instances, customers have objected to such switches because the new environmentally responsible packaging may be less effective or more inconvenient. Thus, marketers must carefully balance society's desires to preserve the environment against customers' desires for convenience.

Packaging and Marketing Strategy

Packaging can be a major component of a marketing strategy. A new cap or closure, a better box or wrapper, or a more convenient container may give a product a competitive advantage. For example, Kraft is introducing Post Snackabouts, in small, snack-size bags. By packaging the top eight Post cereals in individually sized pouches, Kraft believes that it will extend the product life cycle of these top Post brands.[23] The right type of package for a new product can help it gain market recognition very quickly. In the case of existing brands, marketers should reevaluate packages periodically. Especially for consumer convenience products, marketers should view packaging as a major strategic tool. For instance, in the food industry, jumbo and large package sizes for such products as hot dogs, pizzas, English muffins, frozen dinners, and biscuits have been very successful. When considering the strategic uses of packaging, marketers must also analyze the cost of packaging and package changes. The biggest packaging spenders are listed in Table 12.3. In this section, we examine several ways in which packaging can be used strategically.

Table 12.3	Companies That Spend The Most on Packaging	
Rank	**Company**	**Expenditures (in millions)**
1	Coca-Cola	$856.25
2	PepsiCo	754.25
3	Procter & Gamble	682.72
4	Anheuser-Busch	484.25
5	Kraft USA	412.50
6	Campbell Soup	400.31
7	Coca-Cola Foods	358.00
8	Kraft General Foods	331.50
9	General Mills	312.26
10	Miller Brewing	282.50

Source: *Packaging Magazine*, Jan. 1994.

Altering the Package.   At times, a marketer changes a package because the existing design is no longer in style, especially when compared with the packaging of competitive products. Arm & Hammer now markets a refillable plastic shaker for its baking soda. Quaker Oats hired a package design company to redesign its Rice-A-Roni package to give the product the appearance of having evolved with the times while retaining its traditional taste appeal. Rice-A-Roni had been experiencing a lag in sales because of increased competition. An overhaul of the product packaging to a refreshing and more up-to-date look was credited with a 20 percent increase in sales compared with the previous year. Similarly, Del Monte introduced a contemporary look for its tomato products and experienced a double-digit gain in the first year. A package may also be redesigned because new product features need to be highlighted or because new packaging materials have become available. An organization may decide to change a product's packaging to make the product more convenient or safer to use or to reposition the product.

Secondary-Use Packaging.   A secondary-use package is one that can be reused for purposes other than its initial function. For example, a margarine container can be reused to store leftovers, and a jelly container can be used as a drinking glass. Secondary-use packages can be viewed by customers as adding value to products. If customers value this type of packaging, then its use should stimulate unit sales.

Category-Consistent Packaging.   Category-consistent packaging means that the product is packaged in line with the packaging practices associated with a particular product category. Some product categories—for example, mayonnaise, mustard, ketchup, and peanut butter—have traditional package shapes. Other product categories are characterized by recognizable color combinations—red and white for soup; red, white, and blue for Ritz-like crackers. When an organization introduces a brand in one of these product categories, marketers will often use traditional package shapes and color combinations to ensure that customers will recognize the new product as being in that specific product category. Marketing Citizenship discusses the controversy surrounding the use of copycat packaging by private brands.

Innovative Packaging.   Sometimes, a marketer will employ a unique cap, design, applicator, or other feature to make a product distinctive. Such packaging can be effective when the innovation makes the product safer or easier to use or when the unique package provides better protection for the product. In some instances, marketers use innovative or unique packages that are inconsistent with traditional packaging practices to make the brand stand out from its competitors. To distinguish their products, marketers in the beverage industry have used innovative shapes and packaging materials. Unusual packaging sometimes requires the expenditure of a considerable amount of resources, not only on package design, but also in making customers aware of the unique package and its benefit.

Multiple Packaging.   Rather than packaging a single unit of a product, marketers sometimes use twin packs, tri-packs, six-packs, or other forms of multiple packaging. For certain types of products, multiple packaging may increase demand because it increases the amount of the product available at the point of consumption (in one's house, for example). It may also increase consumer acceptance of the product by encouraging the buyer to try the product several times. However, multiple packaging does not work for all types of products. One would not use additional table salt simply because an extra box is in the pantry. Multiple packaging can make products easier to handle and store, as in the case of six-packs for soft drinks; it can also facilitate special price offers, such as two-for-one sales.

Handling-Improved Packaging.   Packaging of a product may be changed to make it easier to handle in the distribution channel—for example, by changing the outer carton or using special bundling, shrink-wrapping, or pallets. In some cases, the shape of the package is changed. An ice-cream producer, for instance, may change from a cylindrical package to a rectangular one to facilitate handling. In addition, at the retail level, the ice-cream producer may be able to get more shelf-facings with a rectangular package as opposed to a round one. Outer containers for products are sometimes changed so that they will proceed more easily through automated warehousing systems.

Criticisms of Packaging

The last several decades have brought a number of improvements in packaging. However, some packaging problems still need to be resolved.

Some packages suffer from functional problems in that they simply do not work well. The packaging for flour and sugar is, at best, poor. Both grocers and consumers are very much aware that these packages leak and are easily torn. Can anyone open and close a bag of flour without spilling at least a little bit? Certain packages, such as refrigerated biscuit cans, milk cartons with foldout spouts, and potato chip bags, are frequently difficult to open. The traditional shapes of packages for products like ketchup and salad dressing make the product inconvenient to use. Have you ever wondered when tapping on a ketchup bottle why the producer didn't put the ketchup in a mayonnaise jar?

Although many steps have been taken to make packaging safer, critics still focus on the safety issues. Containers with sharp edges and easily broken glass bottles are sometimes viewed as a threat to safety. Certain types of plastic packaging and aerosol containers represent possible health hazards.

At times, packaging is viewed as being deceptive. Package shape, graphic design, and certain colors may be used to make a product appear larger than it actually is. The inconsistent use of certain size designations—such as giant, economy, family, king, and super—can certainly lead to customer confusion. Although customers in this country traditionally have liked attractive, effective, convenient packaging, the cost of such packaging is high.

MARKETING CITIZENSHIP

The Controversy over Copycat Packaging

When does category-consistent packaging step over the line and become illegal copycat packaging? This issue is heating up as competition between manufacturer brands and private brands become more intense. *Trade dress*—the distinctive look of a product, including its packaging and labeling—can, like a brand, be legally protected. Consumers who recognize a product by its trade dress scan store shelves in search of the particular shape or color of that product's container. To protect such distinctive features from imitation, manufacturers have been known to take the owners of private brands to court.

But, even a striking similarity between the trade dress of a private brand and a manufacturer brand does not necessarily mean the private brand has crossed the line into illegal territory. The legal issue is whether consumers are likely to be confused by the similarity. Consider what happened when Venture Stores started selling its private brand of hand lotion in packaging similar to that of Vaseline Intensive Care hand lotion. Conopco, owner of the Vaseline Intensive Care brand,

quickly filed suit against Venture, charging trade dress infringement. However, the private brand was prominently marked with Venture's logo and invited consumers to "Compare to Vaseline Intensive Care." The court ruled against Conopco, saying that because the Venture lotion was clearly marked as a private label product and specifically encouraged comparison with the manufacturer brand, it would not confuse consumers.

A similar lawsuit filed by McNeil's Consumer Products charged Arbor Drugs' Arbor Ultra Lactase with infringing on the trade dress of Lactaid Ultra. In court, Arbor Drugs pointed to the prominently displayed private brand identification, the label wording that invited consumers to compare with the manufacturer brand, and a statement on the label noting that the product was not made by McNeil. McNeil won this case because the court found that its packaging was "inherently distinctive" and Arbor therefore could not legally copy it. There will undoubtedly be more such legal skirmishes in the future as manufacturer brands continue to square off against private brands in the war against copycat packaging.

Labeling

labeling Providing identifying, promotional, or other information on package labels

Labeling is very closely interrelated with packaging and is used for identification, promotion, and informational and legal purposes. Labels can be small or large relative to the size of the product and carry varying amounts of information. The sticker on a Chiquita banana, for example, is quite small and displays only the brand name of the fruit. A label can be part of the package itself or a separate feature attached to the package. The label on a can of Coke is actually part of the can, while the label on a two-liter bottle of Coke is separate and can be removed. Information presented on a label may include the brand name and mark, the registered trademark symbol, package size and content, product features, nutritional information, type and style of the product, number of servings, care instructions, directions for use and safety precautions, the name and address of the manufacturer, expiration dates, seals of approval, like the one in Figure 12.11, and other facts.

Universal Product Code (UPC) A series of electronically readable lines identifying a product and containing inventory and pricing information

For many products, the label includes a **universal product code (UPC),** a series of thick and thin electronically readable lines identifying the product and providing inventory and pricing information for producers and resellers. The UPC is electronically read at the retail checkout counter.

Labels can facilitate the identification of a product by displaying the brand name in combination with a unique graphic design. For example, Heinz ketchup is easy to identify on a supermarket shelf because the brand name is easy to read and the label has a distinctive crownlike shape. By drawing attention to products and their benefits, labels can strengthen an organization's promotional efforts. Labels may contain such promotional messages as the offer of a discount or a larger package size at the same price, or information about a new or improved product feature.

A number of federal laws and regulations specify information that must be included on the labels of certain products. Garments must be labeled with the name of the manufacturer, country of manufacture, fabric content, and cleaning instructions. Labels on nonedible items like shampoos and detergents must include both safety precautions and directions for use. In 1966, Congress passed the Fair Packaging and Labeling Act, one of the most comprehensive pieces of labeling and packaging legislation. This law focuses on mandatory labeling requirements, voluntary adoption of packaging standards by firms within industries, and the provision of power to the Federal Trade Commission and the Food and Drug Administration to establish and enforce packaging regulations.

The Nutrition Labeling Act of 1990 requires the FDA to review food labeling and packaging, focusing on nutrition content, label format, ingredient labeling, food descriptions, and health messages. This act regulates much of the labeling on over 250,000 products made by 17,000 U.S. companies. Any food product for which a nutritional claim is made must have nutrition labeling that follows a standard format. Food product labels must state the number of servings per container, serving size, number of calories per serving, number of calories derived from fat, number of carbohydrates, and amounts of specific nutrients, such as vitamins. Although consumers have responded favorably to this type of information on labels, evidence as to whether they actually use it has been mixed. At a recent Washington conference on food policy, some researchers argued that despite nutritional labeling that lists calories from fat and even breaks down the amounts of each variety of fat, obesity rates continue to rise in the United States.[24]

Despite legislation to make labels as accurate and informative as possible, questionable labeling practices persist. The Center for Science in the Public Interest questions the practice of naming a product "Strawberry Frozen Yogurt Bars" when it contains strawberry flavoring but no strawberries, or of calling a breakfast cereal "lightly sweetened" when sugar makes up 22 percent of its ingredients. Many labels on vegetable oils say "no cholesterol," but many of these oils contain saturated fats that can raise cholesterol levels. The Food and Drug Administration recently amended its regulations to forbid producers of vegetable oil from making "no cholesterol" claims on their labels. The administration also recently directed its attention to the

THE SEAL
IS LIKE A GOOD
AD CAMPAIGN:

LIMITED WARRANTY TO CONSUMERS
★
Good Housekeeping
Promises
REPLACEMENT OR REFUND IF DEFECTIVE

EVERYONE
KNOWS ABOUT IT.

Lori Neill
Grey Advertising
New York City

THE DIFFERENCE IS *Guaranteed*

©1998 Good Housekeeping, published by Hearst Communications, Inc.

Figure 12.11
Seal of Approval
Seals of approval generally are viewed as being part of a product's label.

word *fresh* on labels of Del Monte canned vegetables. The FDA is concerned that the labels say "Fresh Cut," implying that Del Monte's vegetables are fresher than other canned vegetables. A Del Monte spokesperson insists the label does not mislead consumers, that it only indicates vegetables go directly into cans rather than being frozen or reconstituted.[25]

Another area of concern is the issue of "green labeling." Consumers who are committed to making environmentally responsible purchasing decisions are sometimes fooled by labels. The U.S. Public Interest Research Group accused several manufacturers of "greenwashing" customers, using misleading claims to sell products by playing on customers' concern for the environment. For example, some manufacturers put a recycling symbol on labels for products made of polyvinyl chloride plastic, which cannot be recycled in the vast majority of American communities.

Of concern to many manufacturers are the Federal Trade Commission's guidelines regarding "Made in the U.S.A." labels, a growing problem due to the increasingly global nature of manufacturing. The FTC requires that "all or virtually all" of a product's components be made in the United States if the label says "Made in the U.S.A." Although the FTC recently considered changing its guidelines to read "substantially all," it rejected this idea and maintains the "virtually all" standard.[26] In light of this decision, the FTC ordered New Balance to stop making the claim on its athletic shoe labels because some components (rubber soles) are made in China. New Balance is challenging this decision, and, in a compromise effort, the FTC has proposed a new label, "Assembled in the U.S.A."[27] JanSport Europe recently filed a claim against competitor Eastpak. JanSport claims that its competitor's "Made in the U.S.A." label is misleading because Eastpak's work force and facilities are located in Puerto Rico.[28]

Summary

A brand is a name, term, design, symbol, or any other feature that identifies one seller's good or service and distinguishes it from those of other sellers. A brand name is the part of a brand that can be spoken; the element that cannot be spoken is called a brand mark. A trademark is a legal designation indicating that the owner has exclusive use of a brand or part of a brand and that others are prohibited by law from using it. A trade name is the legal name of an organization. Branding helps buyers identify and evaluate products, helps sellers facilitate repeat purchasing and product introduction, and fosters brand loyalty.

Brand loyalty is a customer's favorable attitude toward a specific brand. If brand loyalty is strong enough, customers may consistently purchase this brand when they need a product in this product category. The three degrees of brand loyalty are recognition, preference, and insistence. Brand recognition exists when a customer is aware that the brand exists and views it as an alternative purchase if the preferred brand is unavailable. Brand preference is the degree of brand loyalty in which a customer prefers one brand over competing brands and will purchase it if available. Brand insistence is the degree of brand loyalty in which a customer will accept no substitute.

Brand equity is the marketing and financial value associated with a brand's strength. It represents the value of a brand to an organization. The four major elements underlying brand equity include brand name awareness, brand loyalty, perceived brand quality, and brand associations.

A manufacturer brand, initiated by the producer, ensures that the firm is associated with its products at the point of purchase. A private distributor brand is initiated and owned by a reseller, sometimes taking on the name of the store or distributor. Manufacturers combat the growing competition from private distributor brands by developing multiple brands. A generic brand indicates only the product category and does not include the company name or other identifying terms.

When selecting a brand name, a marketer should choose one that is easy to say, spell, and recall and that alludes to the product's uses, benefits, or special characteristics. Brand names can be devised from words, letters, numbers, nonsense words, or a combination of these. Brand names are created inside an organization by individuals, committees, or branding departments, and by outside consultants. Services as well as products are branded, often with the company name and an accompanying symbol that makes the brand distinctive or that conveys a desired image.

Producers protect ownership of their brands through registration with the U.S. Patent and Trademark Office. A company must make certain that the brand name it selects does not infringe on an already registered brand by confusing or deceiving consumers about the source of the product. In most foreign countries, brand registration is on a first-come, first-served basis, making protection more difficult. Brand counterfeiting, increasingly common, can, among other things, undermine consumers' confidence in a brand. Companies brand their products in several ways. Individual branding designates a unique name for each of a company's products; family branding identifies all of a firm's products with a single name; and brand-extension branding applies an existing name to a new or improved product.

Co-branding is the use of two or more brands on one product. It is a popular branding method in a number of processed food categories and in the credit card industry. The brands may be owned by the same company or by different companies. Effective co-branding profits from the trust and confidence that customers have in the brands involved. To avoid confusion, marketers must ensure that customers understand which brand is the main brand. Co-brands must have a complementary fit in buyers' minds. Co-branding sometimes allows an organization to differentiate its products from those of competitors. It can also take advantage of the distribution capabilities of the co-branding partners.

Through a licensing agreement, and for a licensing fee, a firm may permit another organization to use its brand on other products. Brand licensing enables producers to earn extra revenue, receive low-cost or free publicity, and protect their trademarks.

Packaging involves development of a container and a graphic design for a product. Effective packaging offers protection, economy, safety, and convenience. It can influence a customer's purchase decision by promoting features, uses, benefits, and image. When developing a package, marketers must consider the value to the customer of efficient and effective packaging, offset by the cost that the customer is willing to pay. Other considerations include how to make the package tamper-resistant, whether to use multiple packaging and family packaging, how to design the package as an effective promotional tool, how best to accommodate resellers, and whether to develop environmentally responsible packaging. Firms choose particular colors, designs, shapes, and textures to create desirable images and associations. Packaging can be an important part of an overall marketing strategy and can be used as a way to target certain market segments, such as singles, children, or senior citizens. Modifications in packaging can revive a mature product and extend its product life cycle. Producers alter packages to convey new features or to make them safer or more convenient. If a package has a secondary use, the product's value to the consumer may be increased. Category-consistent packaging makes products more easily recognized by consumers, and innovative packaging enhances a product's distinctiveness. Consumers may criticize packaging that does not work well, poses health or safety problems, is deceptive in some way, or is not biodegradable or recyclable.

Labeling, being closely interrelated with packaging, is used for identification, promotion, and informational and legal purposes. The labels of many products include a universal product code, a series of electronically readable lines identifying a product and containing inventory and pricing information. Various federal laws and regulations require that certain products be labeled or marked with warnings, instructions, nutritional information, manufacturer's identification, and the like. Despite legislation, questionable labeling practices exist, including misleading information about fat content and cholesterol, freshness, and the ability to recycle packaging.

Important Terms

Brand	Brand recognition	Generic brands	Brand licensing
Brand name	Brand preference	Individual branding	Family packaging
Brand mark	Brand insistence	Family branding	Labeling
Trademark	Brand equity	Brand-extension branding	Universal product code
Trade name	Manufacturer brands	Co-branding	(UPC)
Brand loyalty	Private distributor brands		

Discussion and Review Questions

1. What is the difference between a brand and a brand name? Compare and contrast the terms *brand mark* and *trademark*.

2. How does branding benefit consumers and marketers?

3. What are the three major degrees of brand loyalty?

4. What is brand equity? Identify and explain the major elements that underlie brand equity.

5. Compare and contrast manufacturer brands, private distributor brands, and generic brands.

6. Identify the factors that a marketer should consider in selecting a brand name.

7. The brand name Xerox is sometimes used generically to refer to photocopying, and Kleenex is used to refer to tissues. How can the manufacturers protect their brand names, and why should they want to?

8. What is co-branding? What major issues should be considered when using co-branding?

9. What are the major advantages and disadvantages of brand licensing?

10. Describe the functions that a package can perform. Which function is most important? Why?

11. When developing a package, what are the main factors a marketer should consider?

12. In what ways can packaging be used as a strategic tool?

13. What are the major criticisms of packaging?

14. What are the major functions of labeling?

15. In what ways do regulations and legislation affect labeling?

Application Questions

1. Identify two brands for which you are brand-insistent. Why do you no longer use other brands? How did you begin using these brands?

2. General Motors introduced the subcompact Geo with a name that appeals to a world market. Invent a brand name for a line of luxury sports cars that also would appeal to an international market. Suggest a name that implies quality, luxury, and value.

3. When a firm decides to brand its products, it may choose one of several different strategies. Name one company that utilizes each of the following strategies. How does each strategy help the company?
   a. individual branding
   b. family branding
   c. brand-extension branding

4. For each of the following product categories, choose an existing brand. Then, for each selected brand, suggest a co-brand, and explain why the co-brand would be effective.
   a. cookies
   b. pizza
   c. long distance telephone service
   d. sports drink

5. Packaging provides product protection, customer convenience, and promotion of image, key features, and benefits. Identify a product that utilizes packaging in each of these ways, and evaluate the effectiveness of the package.

6. Identify a package that you believe to be inferior. Explain why the package is inferior, and discuss your recommendations for improving this package.

Internet Exercise & Resources

Frito-Lay

Like many other marketers of consumer products, Frito-Lay has set up a Web site to inform and entertain consumers. Frito-Lay's site is organized by brand, with full descriptions, product lists, packaging descriptions, and histories given for each brand. Learn about Frito-Lay's brands by visiting its Web site at

www.fritolay.com

1. What branding policy does Frito-Lay seem to be using with regard to the snack products it presents online?
2. How does Frito-Lay's Web site promote brand loyalty?
3. What degree of consistency exists in Frito-Lay's packaging of its snack chips?

E-Center Resources

Visit http://www.prideferrell.com to find several resources to help you succeed in mastering the material in this chapter, plus additional materials that will help you expand your marketing knowledge. The Web site includes

 Internet exercise updates plus additional exercises

 ACE self-tests

abc Chapter summary with hotlinked glossary

 Hotlinks to companies featured in this chapter

 Resource Center

 Career Center

 Marketing plan worksheets

VIDEO CASE 12.1

Beefing Up Meat Sales Through Packaging and Labeling

Consumers buying meat in the supermarket these days see rows and rows of plastic-wrapped foam trays. In the future, they may see branded, multi-ingredient meat products in colorful packages designed to promote and inform as well as protect. Various groups in the meat industry are using new packaging and labeling to compete more effectively for a larger share of consumers' food purchases.

The American Meat Institute (AMI), an industry association, reports that meat and poultry purchases and consumption are both on the rise in the United States. Total industry sales of beef, poultry, lamb, and other meats top $100 billion yearly. However, health-conscious consumers concerned about fat and cholesterol have been buying more chicken rather than other meats. As a result, beef's market share has plummeted 20 percent over the last fifteen years.

The industry is fighting back in a number of ways. Advertising campaigns (such as "Pork: the other white meat") are helping make consumers more aware of the nutrition and taste benefits of specific types of meat. Beef producers are also teaming up with makers of complementary products, such as A-1 Steak Sauce, to promote their products. But beef producers want to find other ways to educate consumers about meat and, just as important, to increase demand, especially for beef products made from chuck and round cuts.

Packages of beef and all fresh meats are legally required to carry the Nutrition Facts label developed by the Food and Drug Administration and the U.S. Department of Agriculture's Food Safety and Inspection Service. This label must show the meat's nutritional information, including calories, fat, and vitamin content. Beef marketers have to follow strict regulatory guidelines on the exact placement of this label, and they have no leeway on the specific wording, type size, and type style. In addition, the U.S. Department of Agriculture requires that all packages of raw meat carry warnings about safe handling procedures.

Congressional proposals may require producers to crowd raw meat packages with yet another mandated label. If the proposals become law, beef and lamb products will have to carry country-of-origin labeling showing whether the contents were produced in the United States, imported from other countries, or blended from U.S. and imported meats. One agricultural economist projects that this new label requirement would have the effect of restricting beef imports even as U.S. beef production is on the decline. If this happens, less beef will be available to American consumers, and beef consumption will drop considerably. Moreover, industry sources estimate that complying with this labeling requirement would cost producers and retailers millions of dollars every year.

Some experts say that meat producers can go further with marketing-oriented labeling. For example, they can do a better job of using labels to tout the taste of beef and describe meat's role as an integral ingredient in nutritious meals. This approach is already in the works, with point-of-purchase posters and labels under development for use by supermarkets and other meat retailers. Industry officials do, however, express concern about how to convey detailed information about nutrition to an extremely wide range of consumers, some of whom have difficulty reading.

Packaging is critical for fresh meat because it protects the product from spoilage and extends its shelf life in the store. Technological innovations have improved meat packaging, allowing red meats to remain fresh in the supermarket refrigerator case for up to twelve days. Now high-barrier packaging materials are about to come into more widespread use. This packaging relies on vacuum technology to remove air from the package so the meat inside stays red and fresh for even longer periods, up to twenty-one days. On the drawing board are packages containing biosensors to detect when meat products are decomposing, a feature that would enhance food safety.

Looking ahead, experts suggest that beef producers take a cue from makers of chicken, seafood, and processed meats by figuring out how to package meat with other ingredients. This would give consumers a complete entree or meal in one convenient package, along with detailed cooking instructions. Keep an eye on your local supermarket meat case to see what the American meat industry is cooking up.[29]

Questions for Discussion

1. How does category-consistent packaging affect the American meat industry's ability to change supermarket packaging of fresh beef products?
2. Most consumers buy fresh meat as needed instead of stocking up a freezer-full. What are the implications of this habit for changes in meat packaging?
3. What changes in packaging and labeling can you suggest to boost consumer purchases and consumption of beef products?

CASE 12.2

Hearts on Fire: Branding the Symbol of Commitment

People are often very particular about the brands of shampoo and deodorant they buy, and they sometimes insist on certain brands of jeans or shoes. When they shop for a diamond, however, they probably don't have a specific brand in mind. Although an engaged couple might have done some homework regarding the "Four Cs" of diamond value (carat weight, color, clarity, and cut), they are unlikely to walk into a jewelry store and ask for a diamond by name—unless they want a "Hearts on Fire" diamond from Di-Star Ltd. The Boston-based diamond wholesaler produces the "Hearts on Fire" diamond, which it calls the first "consumer-branded" diamond. Complete with a logo and marketing plan, the Hearts on Fire is cut in a way designed to give it the extra sparkle that inspired the brand's slogan, "The difference is perfection. It's a difference you can see."

Glenn Rothman, owner of Di-Star, went into the diamond wholesaling business in 1972, but it wasn't until 1994 that he decided to create a branded diamond backed by a full-fledged marketing campaign. On a business trip to Belgium, he saw the diamonds he wanted to brand, stones that had been perfected and sold in Japan for years under the name "Hearts and Arrows." With fewer than one in a million diamonds cut to their level of perfection, these stones looked more brilliant than other diamonds of comparable size. Rothman renamed them "Hearts on Fire," brought the diamond cut back to the United States, and began planning a marketing strategy. At the time, many industry experts voiced skepticism about marketing diamonds by cut, which they asserted was too subjective a measure, especially considering that there was no accepted international grading system for diamond cut. In 1996, however, the American Gem Society, which represents 1,500 jewelers, opened an independent laboratory to certify cut. Hearts on Fire received its highest cut grade. That same year, Di-Star test-marketed Hearts on Fire in twenty-six markets during the holiday season. Sales the first year were promising, and by the end of 1997, diamond shoppers were asking for and purchasing Hearts on Fire diamonds in two hundred stores in forty-two states and at Harrod's department store in London.

Branded diamonds are not a new concept. The "Keepsake Diamonds" brand was popular in the 1960s and 1970s, but it died out after the company was sold. Lazare Kaplan International has been promoting and selling its brand since 1986. Marketers at organizations that brand diamonds believe the brand enhances credibility, conveys an exclusive image, and differentiates their diamonds from those sold by high-volume discounters, such as Zales and Service Merchandise. "Ideal cut" brands, such as Lazare's stones and Hearts on Fire, project an upscale image and bring shoppers into high-end stores. According to Di-Star's CEO, however, branding diamonds does not guarantee success. Diamond companies also must be good marketers, using marketing tools to build the right brand associations and brand familiarity.

Toward that end, Di-Star has developed a comprehensive marketing program that includes public relations, promotional support, and sales training and incentives. The company's public relations strategy focuses on publicity that maintains the visibility of the Hearts on Fire brand name. Promotional support includes brochures, displays, prepared print ads, posters, counter cards, and special-event and seasonal promotions. Employing an advertising agency with a history of building high-end consumer brands, the company recently launched its first radio and television advertising campaign. The themes of the first two ads are "The Difference is Perfection" and "How to Tell Your Heart's on Fire." These ads, asserts the company's marketing director, educate consumers and make them more aware of the Hearts on Fire diamond. Di-Star provides free and comprehensive training for all its retailers and their employees to enhance their knowledge and improve their ability to sell the Hearts on Fire brand. Salespeople earn cash incentives and prizes, which range from hats and T-shirts to diamonds and trips to Asia or Europe.

To make sure customers remember that Hearts on Fire diamonds are different from any others they might have considered, Di-Star employs some untraditional marketing tools. The company laser-inscribes a unique identification number on an edge at the middle of each stone. Of course, customers can't see this mark with the naked eye, or the cut that make the stones sparkle so dramatically. To overcome that difficulty, Di-Star provides retailers with a "proportion scope" that magnifies stones while filtering out white light. When shoppers gaze at a Hearts on Fire diamond through this mechanism, they see eight perfect hearts and eight arrows, impressing them and assuring them they are purchasing the brand they want. When a buyer leaves the jewelry store with a Hearts on Fire diamond, the jewelry piece is wrapped in a Japanese silk box and comes with a guarantee in a velvet folder.

Asserts one jeweler, "Hearts on Fire is the best diamond program I have ever seen, one that is a role model for all lines of branded diamonds." The program appears to be working. Even though Hearts on Fire diamonds cost about 20 percent more than ordinary diamonds of similar size, Di-Star's sales rose 37 percent in one year to reach $11 million. The brand has even attracted the attention of the New York City Museum of Natural History, which recently chose Hearts on Fire diamonds to be a part of its new "Nature of Diamonds" exhibit because they "exemplify the perfecting of the modern day round brilliant cut."[30]

Questions for Discussion

1. Why would a customer have an interest in a branded diamond?
2. Evaluate the phrase "Hearts on Fire" as a brand name.
3. In what ways can Di-Star build brand equity for "Hearts on Fire" diamonds?

13

Services

OBJECTIVES

- To understand the nature and importance of services

- To become familiar with the characteristics of services that differentiate them from goods

- To gain an understanding of how the characteristics of services influence the development of marketing mixes for services

- To become aware of the importance of service quality and be able to explain how to deliver exceptional service quality

- To explore the nature of nonprofit marketing

319

USAA— "Customer-Care Superstars"

USAA is one of the largest home and automobile insurers in the United States. Based in San Antonio, Texas, the company serves about 3 million people worldwide, most of them present or former military personnel and their dependents. USAA also offers health insurance, annuities, mutual funds, and brokerage and banking services. Analysts agree that USAA's ability to provide the level of customer service that builds exceptional customer loyalty has propelled it to the forefront of the insurance and financial service industry.

To provide what has become the industry's standard of excellence service, USAA learns as much as it can about its customers. From sales and marketing offices in over twenty-eight states and in Europe, six thousand customer service representatives talk with customers each week. Nearly 95 percent of the company's business is conducted via toll-free telephone lines, direct mail, and the Internet. USAA's sophisticated computer system facilitates implementation of ECHO (Every Contact Has Opportunity), the company's approach to dealing with customers. When service representatives receive customer complaints, they assign them to "action agents," who respond to the complaints quickly. Until problems are resolved, "banner" messages remain in the computer system. USAA reports that 86 percent of the calls their agents receive are successfully handled on the first contact.

Experts agree that personal relationships with customers, not technology, are what builds customer loyalty, and USAA works hard to achieve such relationships. Every year, the company conducts about one hundred phone and mail surveys and focus groups asking thousands of customers to judge new services and to suggest others they'd like to see offered. USAA also periodically surveys its 3 million customers to update information, such as how many children they have, if they've moved, and when they are planning to retire. Based on these surveys, the company tailors its marketing to satisfy customers' changing needs. For example, if a client has college-aged children, USAA sends those children information on how to manage credit card debt. Reports one of the company's clients, "USAA's mailers seem to say 'We're here to serve you.' "

Despite the ongoing military cuts that have steadily shrunk USAA's customer base, its membership continues to grow by about 100,000 members a year. USAA's superior service has earned it unwavering customer loyalty and numerous industry awards. The company boasts an almost 98 percent rate of customer satisfaction and a 98 percent customer retention rate. In a recent Coopers & Lybrand study of customer service at sixty companies, USAA was judged to be one of six "customer-care superstars."[1]

The products offered by USAA and other insurance companies are services, not tangible goods. This chapter presents concepts that apply specifically to products that are services. The organizations that market service products include for-profit firms, such as those that offer financial, personal, and professional services, as well as nonprofit ones, such as educational institutions, churches, charities, and governments.

We begin this chapter with a focus on the growing importance of service industries in our economy. We then address the unique characteristics of services. In the next section, we deal with the challenges that these characteristics present to marketers managing and marketing mixes for services. We then discuss customers' judgment of service quality and the importance of delivering high-quality services. Finally, we define nonprofit marketing and examine the development of nonprofit marketing strategies.

The Nature and Importance of Services

service An intangible product involving a deed, performance, or effort that cannot be physically possessed

All products—goods, services, or ideas—are to some extent intangible. A **service** is an intangible product involving a deed, a performance, or an effort that cannot be physically possessed.[2] Services are usually provided through the application of human and/or mechanical efforts directed at people or objects. For example, a service like education involves the efforts of service providers (teachers) directed at people (students). In janitorial and interior decorating services, the efforts of service providers are directed at objects. Services can also involve the use of mechanical efforts directed at people (air transportation) or objects (freight transportation). A wide variety of services, such as health care or landscaping, involve both human and mechanical efforts. Although, many services entail the use of tangibles like tools and machinery, the primary difference between a service and a good is that a service is dominated by the intangible portion of the total product.

Services as products should not be confused with the related topic of customer services. Customer service involves any human or mechanical activity that adds value to the product.[3] Although customer service is typically associated with the marketing of goods, service marketers also provide customer services. For example, many service companies offer guarantees to their customers in an effort to increase value. Hampton Inns, a national chain of mid-price hotels, gives its guests a free night if they are not 100 percent satisfied with their stay (fewer than .5 percent of Hampton customers ask for a refund).[4] In some cases, a 100 percent satisfaction guarantee or similar service commitment may motivate employees to provide high-quality service, not because failure to do so leads to personal penalties but because they are proud to be part of an organization that provides such a strong service promise.

The increasing importance of services in the U.S. economy has led many people to call the United States the world's first service economy. Service industries account for over half of the country's gross domestic product (GDP) and about three-quarters of its nonfarm jobs. More than one-half of new businesses are service businesses, and service employment is expected to continue to grow. These industries have absorbed much of the influx of women and minorities into the work force.

One major catalyst in the growth of consumer services has been long-term economic growth in the United States, which has led to increased interest in financial services, travel, entertainment, and personal care. Lifestyle changes have similarly encouraged expansion of the service sector. In the past forty years, the number of women in the work force has more than doubled. With approximately 60 percent of women 16 years old and older now working, and contributing up to 40 percent of household income,[5] the need for child care, domestic services, and other time-saving services has increased. Consumers want to avoid such tasks as meal preparation, house cleaning, home maintenance, and tax preparation; consequently, franchise operations, such as Subway, Merry Maids, ChemLawn, and H&R Block, have experienced rapid growth. Also, Americans have become more fitness- and recreation-oriented, and so the demand for fitness and recreational facilities has escalated. In terms of demographics, the U.S. population is growing older, and this change has promoted tremendous expansion of health care services. Finally, the increasing number and complexity of high-tech goods have spurred demand for repair services.

Not only have consumer services grown in our economy, but business services have prospered as well. Business services include repairs and maintenance, consulting, installation, equipment leasing, marketing research, advertising, temporary office personnel, and janitorial services. Expenditures for business services have risen even faster than expenditures for consumer services. A contributing factor has been the recent trend in downsizing among many U.S. companies, which has dramatically raised the demand for temporary office personnel. The growth in business services has been attributed to the increasingly complex, specialized, and competitive business environment.

Characteristics of Services

The issues associated with marketing service products are not exactly the same as those associated with marketing goods. To understand these differences, it is first necessary to understand the distinguishing characteristics of services. Services have six basic characteristics: intangibility, inseparability of production and consumption, perishability, heterogeneity, client-based relationships, and customer contact.[6]

Intangibility

intangibility   A service is not physical and cannot be touched

As already noted, the major characteristic that distinguishes a service from a good is intangibility. **Intangibility** means that a service is not physical and cannot be touched. For example, it is impossible to touch the education that students derive from attending classes, but the intangible benefit is that of becoming more knowledgeable. In addition, services cannot be physically possessed. Students obviously cannot physically possess knowledge as they can a stereo or a car.

Figure 13.1 depicts a tangibility continuum from pure goods (tangible) to pure services (intangible). Pure goods, if they exist at all, are rare since practically all marketers of goods also provide customer services. For example, even a tangible product like sugar must be delivered to the store, priced, and placed on a shelf before a customer can purchase it. Intangible, service-dominant products like education or health

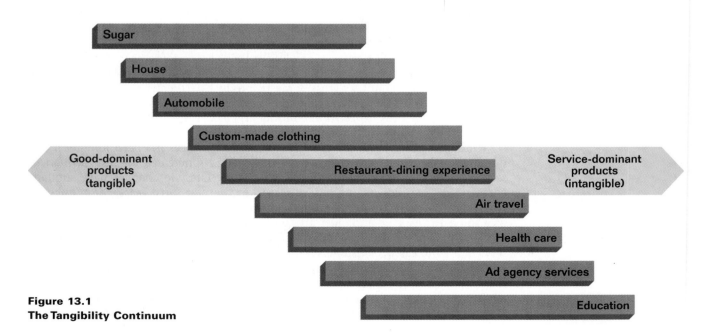

Figure 13.1
The Tangibility Continuum

Ahhhhhhhhhhh ENVOY CLASS

ENVOY CLASS TO EUROPE

Frankfurt, London, Madrid, Munich, Paris, Rome

U·S AIRWAYS

Figure 13.2
Inseparability of Production and Consumption
The production and consumption of air passenger service is inseparable. Both must occur simultaneously.

care are clearly service products. But what about products near the center of the continuum? Is a restaurant like Chili's a goods marketer or a service marketer? Services like airline flights have something tangible to offer, such as drinks and meals. Knowing where the product lies on the continuum is important in creating marketing strategies for service-dominant products.

Inseparability of Production and Consumption

inseparability Being produced and consumed at the same time

Another important characteristic of services that creates challenges for marketers is **inseparability,** which refers to the fact that the production of a service cannot be separated from its consumption by customers. For example, air passenger service (see Figure 13.2) is produced and consumed simultaneously. In other words, services are often produced, sold, and consumed simultaneously. In goods marketing, a customer can purchase a good, take it home, and store it until such time that the good is consumed; the manufacturer of the good may never see an actual customer. Customers, however, must often be present at the production of a service (such as investment consulting and surgery) and cannot take the service home. Because of inseparability, customers not only want a specific type of service, but expect it to be provided in a specific way by a specific individual. For example, the production and consumption of a medical exam occurs simultaneously, and the patient knows in advance who the physician is and generally understands how the exam will be done.

Perishability

perishability The impossibility of storing unused service capacity

Services are characterized by **perishability** because the unused service capacity of one time period cannot be stored for future use. For example, empty seats on an air flight today cannot be stored and sold to passengers at a later date. Other examples of service perishability include unsold basketball tickets, unscheduled dentists' appointment times, and empty hotel rooms. Although some goods, such as meat, milk, and produce, are perishable, goods generally are less perishable than services; if a pair of jeans have been sitting on a department store shelf for a week, someone can still buy them the next day. Goods marketers can handle the supply-demand problem through production scheduling and inventory techniques. Service marketers do not have the same advantage, and they face several hurdles in trying to balance supply and demand. They can, however, plan for demand that fluctuates according to day of the week, time of day, or season.

Heterogeneity

heterogeneity Variation in quality

Services delivered by people are susceptible to **heterogeneity,** or variation in quality. Quality of manufactured goods is easier to control with standardized procedures, and mistakes are easier to isolate and correct. Because of the nature of human behavior, however, it is very difficult for service providers to maintain a consistent quality of service delivery. This variation in quality can occur from one organization to another, from one service to another within the same organization, and from one outlet to another within the same organization. For example, one bank may provide more convenient hours and charge fewer fees than the one next door, or the retail clerks in one bookstore may be more knowledgeable and therefore more helpful than those in another bookstore owned by the same chain. In addition, the service that a single employee provides can vary from customer to customer, day to day, or even hour to hour. Although many service problems are one-time events that cannot be predicted or controlled ahead of time, training and establishment of standard procedures can help increase consistency and reliability.

Heterogeneity usually increases as the degree of labor-intensiveness increases. Many services, such as auto repair, education, and hair care, rely heavily on human labor. Other services, such as telecommunications, health clubs, and public transportation, are more equipment-intensive. People-based services are often prone to fluctuations in quality from one time period to the next. For example, the fact that a hairstylist gives a customer a good haircut today does not guarantee that customer a haircut of equal quality from the same hairstylist at a later date; a customer in the morning may receive a better haircut than another customer who comes to the same stylist at the end of the day. This happens because the hairstylist's performance can change from day to day or even from hour to hour. Equipment-based services do not suffer from this problem to the same degree as people-based services. For instance, automated teller machines have reduced inconsistency in the quality of teller services at banks, and bar code scanning has improved the accuracy of service at the checkout counters in grocery stores.

Denny's, a family restaurant chain, provides an example of the difficulties involved in the control of heterogeneity. This company introduced a new menu that offers more than 150 choices for breakfast, lunch, dinner, and late-night dining. With most outlets open twenty-four hours a day, Denny's usually serves thousands of customers daily. In performing their numerous duties, Denny's 47,000 employees can deliver quality service to restaurant customers, or they can fail to do so. With so many menu items, operating hours, and employees, the possibility of service mistakes is high. To cope with uncontrolled service heterogeneity, Denny's instituted changes throughout its 1,500 U.S. outlets. The company restructured restaurant management so that regional managers are accountable for the service in all restaurants, whether franchised or company-owned. Both individual restaurant managers and field managers earn bonuses for quality service. The restaurant manager training course has been lengthened from seven to thirteen weeks. To free restaurant managers from excessive administrative functions, automated systems order inventory and schedule labor. To improve service speed and meal consistency, Denny's is testing new kitchen technology including cooking by computer.[7]

Client-Based Relationships

client-based relationships Interactions that result in satisfied customers who repeatedly use a service over time

The success of many services depends on creating and maintaining **client-based relationships,** or interactions with customers that result in satisfied customers who repeatedly use a service over time.[8] In fact, some service providers, such as lawyers, accountants, and financial advisers, call their customers clients and often develop and maintain close, long-term relationships with them. For service providers like these, it is not enough to attract customers; they are successful only to the degree that they can maintain a group of clients who use their services on an ongoing basis. For example, a doctor may serve a family in his or her area for decades. If the members of this family like the quality of the doctor's services, they are likely to recommend the doctor to other families. If several different families repeat this positive word-of-mouth communication, it does not take long for the doctor to acquire a long list of satisfied clients. This process is the very essence of creating and maintaining client-based relationships. To ensure that the process actually occurs, the service provider must take steps to build trust, demonstrate customer commitment, and satisfy customers so well that they become very loyal to the provider and unlikely to switch to competitors.

Customer Contact

customer contact
Interaction between provider and customer needed to deliver the service

Not all services require a high degree of customer contact, but many do. **Customer contact** refers to the level of interaction between the service provider and customer that is necessary to deliver the service. High-contact services include health care, real estate, and legal and hair care services. Examples of low-contact services are tax preparation, auto repair, and dry cleaning. As Figure 13.3 shows, Deaconess Hospital is a high-contact service provider. Note that high-contact services generally involve actions directed toward people, who must be present during production. A hairstylist's customer, for example, must be present during the styling process. Because the customer must be present, the process of production may be just as important as its final outcome. Although it is sometimes possible for the service provider to go to the customer, high-contact services typically require that the customer go to the production facility. Thus, the physical appearance of the facility may be a major component of the customer's overall evaluation of the service. While low-contact services do not require the physical presence of the customer during delivery, he or she will likely need to be present to initiate and terminate the service. For example, customers of tax preparation services must bring in all necessary documents but often do not remain during the preparation process.

Service employees of high-contact service providers are a very important ingredient in creating satisfied customers. A fundamental precept of customer contact is that satisfied employees lead to satisfied customers. In fact, research indicates that employee satisfaction is the single most important factor in providing high service quality. Thus, to minimize the problems that can be created by customer contact, service organizations must take steps to understand and meet the needs of employees by training them, empowering them to make more decisions, and rewarding them for customer-oriented behavior.[9] To provide the quality of customer service that has made it the fastest growing coffee retailer in the United States, Starbucks provides extensive employee training. Employees receive about twenty-five hours of initial training, which includes memorizing recipes and learning the differences among a variety of coffees, proper coffee-making techniques, and many other skills that stress Starbuck's dedication to customer service.

Figure 13.3
Customer Contact
Services provided by Deaconess Hospital are high-contact services.

Table 13.1	Service Characteristics and Marketing Challenges
Service Characteristics	**Resulting Marketing Challenges**
Intangibility	Difficult for customer to evaluate Customer does not take physical possession Difficult to advertise and display Difficult to set and justify prices Service process usually not protectable by patents
Inseparability of production and consumption	Service provider cannot mass-produce services Customer must participate in production Other consumers affect service outcomes Services are difficult to distribute
Perishability	Services cannot be stored Very difficult to balance supply and demand Unused capacity is lost forever Demand may be very time-sensitive
Heterogeneity	Service quality is difficult to control Difficult to standardize service delivery
Client-based relationships	Success depends on satisfying and keeping customers over the long term Generating repeat business is challenging Relationship marketing becomes critical
Customer contact	Service providers are critical to delivery High levels of service employee training and motivation are required Changing a high-contact service into a low-contact service to achieve lower costs without reducing customer satisfaction

Sources: K. Douglas Hoffman and John E. G. Bateson, *Essentials of Services Marketing* (Ft. Worth: Dryden Press, 1997), pp 25–38; Valarie A. Zeithaml, A. Parasuraman, and Leonard L. Berry, *Delivering Quality Service: Balancing Customer Perceptions and Expectations* (New York: Free Press, 1990); and Leonard L. Berry and A. Parasuraman, *Marketing Services: Competing through Quality* (New York: Free Press, 1991), p. 5.

Developing and Managing Marketing Mixes for Services

The characteristics of services discussed in the previous section create a number of challenges for service marketers (see Table 13.1). These challenges are especially evident in the development and management of marketing mixes for services. Although such mixes contain the four major marketing mix variables—product, distribution, promotion, and price—the characteristics of services require that marketers consider additional issues and conditions.

Development of Services

A service offered by an organization generally is a package, or bundle, of services consisting of a core service and one or more supplementary services. A core service is the basic service experience or commodity that a customer expects to receive. A supplementary service is a supportive one related to the core service and is used to differentiate the service bundle from that of competitors. For example, Hampton Inns provides a room as a core service. Bundled with the room are such supplementary services as free local phone calls, cable television, and a complimentary continental breakfast.

As discussed earlier, heterogeneity results in variability in service quality and makes it difficult to standardize service delivery. However, heterogeneity provides one advantage to service marketers in that they can customize their services to match the specific needs of individual customers. Health care is an example of an extremely customized service; the services provided differ from one patient to the next. Such customized services can be expensive for both the provider and customer, and some service marketers therefore face a dilemma: how to provide service at an acceptable level of quality in an efficient and economic manner and still satisfy individual customer needs. To cope with this problem, some service marketers offer standardized packages. For example, a lawyer may offer a divorce package at a specified price for an uncontested divorce. When service bundles are standardized, the specific actions and activities of the service provider usually are highly specified. Automobile quick-lube providers frequently offer a service bundle for a single price; the specific actions to be taken are quite detailed about what will be done to a customer's car. Various other equipment-based services are also often standardized into packages. For instance, cable television providers frequently offer several packages, such as "Basic," "Standard," "Premier," and "Hollywood."

The characteristic of intangibility makes it difficult for customers to evaluate a service prior to purchase. When a customer is shopping for a pair of jeans, she can try them on before buying them, but how does she evaluate a haircut before the service is performed? Intangibility requires service marketers like hair stylists to market promises to customers. The customer is forced to place some degree of trust in the service provider to perform the service in a manner that meets or exceeds these promises. Service marketers must guard against making promises that raise customer expectations beyond what the marketer can provide.

To cope with the problem of intangibility, marketers employ tangible cues to help assure customers about the quality of the service. Tangible cues such as neat, clean, professional-appearing contact personnel and clean, attractive physical facilities help provide customers with some assurance of service quality. Life insurance companies sometimes try to make the quality of their policies more tangible by putting them on very high quality paper and enclosing them in leather sheaths. Since customers often rely on brand names as an indicator of product quality, service marketers at organizations whose names are the same as their service brand names should strive to build a strong national image for their companies. For example, American Express, McDonald's, American Life (see Figure 13.4), and America Online try to maintain strong, positive national company images because these names are the brand names of the services they provide.

Figure 13.4
Maintaining a Positive National Image
American Life, like a number of other major service providers, uses significant levels of advertising to maintain a strong, favorable national image for its brand.

You wore the same dress to the prom. You would always finish her sentences. And if it seemed as though you were equal parts of each other, it was probably because you were.

friends for life

Friends. It's about watching over someone close. It's about sharing a future. It's about dedication, and how we do business. Which could explain why so many friends recommend American Life to their friends. And why American Life and our policyholders are friends for life.

Annuities
401(k) Programs
Variable Universal Life
Individual Retirement Annuities

AMERICAN LIFE
A WHOLLY OWNED SUBSIDIARY OF MUTUAL OF AMERICA

320 Park Avenue, New York, NY 10022   1-800-957-5432
The American Life Insurance Company of New York is a wholly owned subsidiary of Mutual of America Life Insurance Company. Mutual of America Life Insurance Company is a registered Broker/Dealer and distributes the variable products of The American Life Insurance Company of New York.

The inseparability of production and consumption and the level of customer contact also influence the development and management of services. The fact that the customers take part in the production of a service means that other customers can affect the outcome of a service. For instance, if a nonsmoker dines in a restaurant without a no-smoking section, then the overall quality of service experienced by the nonsmoking customer declines. For this reason, many restaurants have no-smoking sections or have prohibited smoking in their establishments. Service marketers can reduce these problems by encouraging customers to cooperate in sharing the responsibility of maintaining an environment that allows all participants to receive the intended benefits of the service.

Distribution of Services

Marketers deliver services in a variety of ways. In some instances, customers go to a service provider's facility. For example, most health care, dry cleaning, hair care, and tanning services are delivered at service providers' facilities. Some services are provided at the customer's home or business; lawn care, air conditioning and heating repair, and carpet cleaning are examples. Some services are delivered primarily at "arm's length," meaning there is no face-to-face contact between the customer and the service provider. A number of equipment-based services are delivered at arm's length, including telephone, electric, online, and cable television services.

Marketing channels for services are usually short and direct, meaning that the producer delivers the service directly to the end user. For some services, however, intermediaries are employed. For example, travel agents facilitate the delivery of airline services, independent insurance agents participate in the marketing of a variety of insurance policies, and financial planners market investment services.

Service marketers are less concerned with warehousing and transportation than are goods marketers. They are, however, very concerned about inventory management, especially the problem of balancing supply and demand for services. The service characteristics of inseparability and level of customer contact contribute to the challenges of demand management. In some instances, service marketers use appointments and reservations as approaches for scheduling the delivery of services. Health care providers, attorneys, accountants, auto mechanics, and restaurants often use reservations or appointments to plan and pace the delivery of their services. To increase the supply of a service, marketers use multiple service sites and also increase the number of contact service providers at each site. National and regional eye care and hair care services are examples.

To make delivery more accessible to customers and to increase the supply of a service, as well as to reduce labor costs, some service providers have reduced the use of contact personnel and replaced them with equipment. In other words, they have changed a high-contact service into a low-contact one. The banking industry is an example. By installing ATMs, banks have increased production capacity and reduced customer contact. In addition, a number of automated banking services are now available by telephone twenty-four hours a day. Such services have helped lower costs by reducing the need for customer service representatives. Changing the delivery of services from human beings to equipment has created some problems, however. For example, some customers complain that these types of services are less personal. When designing service delivery, marketers must pay attention to the degree of personalization customers desire.

Promotion of Services

The intangibility of services results in several promotion-related challenges to service marketers. Since it may not be possible to depict the actual performance of a service in an advertisement or display it in a store, explaining a service to customers can be a difficult task. Promotion of services typically includes tangible cues that symbolize the service. For example, Trans America uses its pyramid-shaped building to symbolize strength, security, and reliability, which are important features associated with insurance and other financial services. Similarly, the hands Allstate uses in its ads symbolize personalized service and trustworthy, caring representatives. While these symbols have nothing to do with the actual service, they make it much easier for customers to understand the intangible attributes associated with insurance services. To make a service more tangible, advertisements for services often show pictures of facilities, equipment, and service personnel. Marketers may also promote their services as a tangible expression of consumers' lifestyles, as discussed in Marketing Citizenship.

Compared with goods marketers, service providers are more likely to promote price, guarantees, performance documentation, availability, and training and certification of contact personnel. When preparing advertisements, service marketers are careful to use concrete, specific language to help make services more tangible in the minds of customers. They are also careful not to promise too much regarding their services because customer expectations may be raised to unattainable levels.

Through their actions, service contact personnel can be directly or indirectly involved in the personal selling of services. Personal selling is often important because personal influence can be effective in helping the customer visualize the benefits of a given service.

As noted earlier, intangibility makes experiencing a service prior to purchase difficult, if not impossible. A car can be test-driven, a snack food can be sampled in a supermarket, a new brand of bar soap can be sent to customers in the mail as a free sample. While some services also can be offered on a trial basis at little or no risk to the customer, a number of services cannot be sampled before purchase. Promotional programs that encourage the trial use of insurance, health care, or auto repair are difficult to design because even after purchase of such services, a considerable length of time may be required to assess their quality. For example, an individual may purchase auto insurance from the same provider for ten years before filing a claim. Yet the quality of auto insurance coverage is based primarily on how the customer is treated and protected when a claim is made.

Because of heterogeneity and the intangibility of services, word-of-mouth communication is important in service promotion. What other people say about a service provider can have a tremendous impact on whether an individual decides to use that service provider. Some service marketers attempt to stimulate positive word-of-mouth communication by asking satisfied customers to tell their friends and associates about the service and may even provide incentives for doing so.

Pricing of Services

Prices for services can be established on several different bases. The prices of pest control services, dry cleaning, carpet cleaning, and a physician's consultation are usually based on the performance of specific tasks. Other service prices are based on time. For example, attorneys, consultants, counselors, piano teachers, and plumbers often charge by the hour or day.

MARKETING CITIZENSHIP

Encouraging More Debt or Providing a Service?

First USA wants to put its credit cards in the wallets of vegetarians, gamblers, humanitarians, and various other customer segments across the United States. A division of Bank One, First USA is one of the nation's largest credit card issuers, serving more than 60 million customers. The company teams up with such marketing partners as Save the Children, Dell Computer, the American Medical Association, and Yale University to create specialized credit card promotions for specific customer segments. But in appealing to these customers' interests, is First USA—or any credit card company—encouraging higher debt or simply offering a valuable service?

First USA's Las Vegas Visa Platinum credit card, for example, gives customers a rebate on everything they charge, as well as gift certificates redeemable at Las Vegas hotels and casinos. Customers who live in Las Vegas earn higher rebates when they use the card locally. The Save the Children MasterCard, imprinted with children's artwork, provides

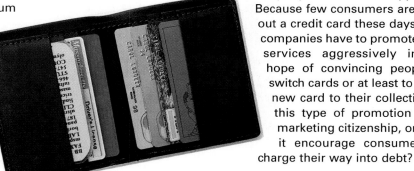

high credit lines—up to $100,000—and generates revenue to support the charity's programs in thirty-nine countries. The First Platinum MasterCard for Vegetarians, featuring pictures of fruits and vegetables, also provides high credit lines, a low introductory interest rate, and a free combination steamer-rice cooker. In addition, First USA offers credit cards to Internet enthusiasts, university alumni, computer buyers, golfers, doctors, and many other customer segments.

Promoting a service on the basis of the targeted segment's lifestyle or interests is not new, nor is First USA the first or only credit card company to take this approach. Because few consumers are without a credit card these days, card companies have to promote their services aggressively in the hope of convincing people to switch cards or at least to add a new card to their collection. Is this type of promotion good marketing citizenship, or does it encourage consumers to charge their way into debt?

Some services use demand-based pricing. When demand for a service is high, the price also is high; when demand for a service is low, so is the price. The perishability of services means that when demand is low, the unused capacity cannot be stored and is therefore lost forever. Every empty seat on an airline flight or in a movie theater represents lost revenue. Some services are very time-sensitive in that there is a particular time when a significant number of customers desire the service. This point in time is called peak demand. A provider of time-sensitive services brings in most of its revenue during peak demand. For an airline, peak demand is usually early and late in the day; for cruise lines, peak demand occurs in the winter for Caribbean cruises and in the summer for Alaskan cruises. Providers of time-sensitive services often use demand-based pricing to manage the problem of balancing supply and demand. They charge top prices during peak demand and lower their prices during times of off-peak demand to encourage more customers to use the service. This is why the price of a matinee movie is often half the price of the same movie shown at night. Major airlines maintain sophisticated databases to help them adjust ticket prices in an effort to fill as many seats as possible on every flight. On a single day, each airline makes thousands of fare changes to maximize the use of its seating capacity and thus maximize its revenues. To accomplish this objective, these airlines have to overbook flights and discount fares.

When services are offered to customers in a bundle, marketers must decide whether to offer the services at one price, to price them separately, or to use a combination of the two methods. For example, some hotels offer a package of services at one price, while others charge separately for the room, phone service, breakfast, and even in-room safes. Some service providers offer a one-price option for a specific bundle of services and make add-on bundles available at additional charges. For example, a number of cable television companies offer a standard package of channels for one price and offer add-on channel packages for additional charges. Telephone services such as call waiting and caller ID (see Figure 13.5) are frequently bundled and sold as a package for one price.

Figure 13.5
Pricing Services
Telephone services such as call waiting and caller ID are often sold as a package for a single price. Many services can also be purchased individually at a single although often higher overall price.

See if you can spot the home without The BASICS℠ Value Pak.

Six helpful services. One special price. That's The BASICS℠ Value Pak from Southwestern Bell. A new package of services that helps you keep pace with today's world. There's CallNotes' voice mail, Caller ID, Call Waiting, Call Return and Call Blocker. Plus your choice of a sixth service like Call Forwarding or Three-Way Calling. They'll give you the flexibility to manage your daily life. Without them, who knows how far you'll fall behind. Call 1-888-573-MOVE.

friendly. neighborhood. global. Southwestern Bell

Some restrictions may apply. Call for details. CallNotes service provided by Southwestern Bell Messaging Services. All other services provided by Southwestern Bell Telephone.

Because of the intangible nature of services, customers rely heavily at times on price as an indicator of quality. If customers perceive the available services in a service category as being similar in quality, and if the quality of such services is difficult to judge even after these services are purchased, customers may seek out the lowest-priced provider. For example, many customers seek auto insurance providers with the lowest rates. If the quality of different service providers is likely to vary, customers may rely heavily on the price-quality association. For example, if you have to have an appendectomy, will you choose the surgeon who charges an average price of $1,500 or the surgeon who will take your appendix out for $399?

For certain types of services, market conditions may limit how much can be charged for a specific service, especially if the services in this category are perceived as being generic in nature. For example, the prices charged by a self-serve laundromat are likely to be limited by the going price for laundromat services in a given community. Also, price flexibility may be reduced by state and local government regulations. The prices charged for auto insurance, utilities, television cable service, and even housing rentals may be significantly controlled by state or local government regulations.

Service Quality

service quality
Customers' perception of how well a service meets or exceeds their expectations

The delivery of high-quality services is one of the most important and most difficult tasks any service organization faces. Because of their characteristics, services are very difficult to evaluate. Hence, customers must look closely at service quality when comparing services. **Service quality** is defined as customers' perceptions of how well a service meets or exceeds their expectations.[10] Note that service quality is judged by customers, not the organization. This distinction is critical because it forces service marketers to examine quality from the customer's viewpoint. For example, a bank may view service quality as having friendly and knowledgeable employees. However, the customers of this bank may be more concerned with waiting time, ATM access, security, and statement accuracy. Thus, it is important for service organizations to determine what customers expect and then develop service products that meet or exceed those expectations.

Customer Evaluation of Service Quality

search qualities
Tangible attributes that can be judged before the purchase of a product

experience qualities
Attributes gaugeable only during purchase and consumption of a service

credence qualities
Attributes that customers may be unable to evaluate even after purchasing and consuming a service

The biggest obstacle for customers in evaluating service quality is the intangible nature of the service. How can customers evaluate something they cannot see, feel, taste, smell, or hear? The evaluation of a good is much easier because all goods possess **search qualities,** tangible attributes, such as color, style, size, feel, or fit, that can be evaluated prior to the purchase of a product. Trying on a new coat and taking a car for a test drive are examples of how customers evaluate search qualities. Services, on the other hand, have very few search qualities; instead, they abound in experience and credence qualities. **Experience qualities,** such as taste, satisfaction, or pleasure, are attributes that can be assessed only during the purchase and consumption of a service.[11] Restaurants and vacations are examples of services high in experience qualities. **Credence qualities** are attributes that customers may be unable to evaluate even after the purchase and consumption of the service. Examples of services high in credence qualities are surgical operations, automobile repairs, consulting, and legal representation. Most consumers lack the knowledge or skills to evaluate the quality of these types of services. Consequently, they must place a great deal of faith in the integrity and competence of the service provider.

Despite the difficulties in evaluating quality, service quality may be the only way customers can choose one service over another. For this reason, service marketers live or die by understanding how consumers judge service quality. Table 13.2 defines five dimensions that consumers use when evaluating service quality: tangibles, reliability, responsiveness, assurance, and empathy. Note that all of them have links to employee performance. Of the five, reliability is the most important in determining customer

Table 13.2   Dimensions of Service Quality

Dimension	Evaluation Criteria	Examples
Tangibles: Physical evidence of the service	Appearance of physical facilities Appearance of service personnel Tools or equipment used to provide the service	A clean and professional-looking doctor's office A clean and neatly attired repairman The quality of food in a restaurant The equipment used in a medical exam
Reliability: Consistency and dependability in performing the service	Accuracy of billing or record keeping Performing services when promised	An accurate bank statement A confirmed hotel reservation An airline flight departing and arriving on time
Responsiveness: Willingness or readiness of employees to provide the service	Returning customer phone calls Providing prompt service Handling urgent requests	A waiter refilling a customer's cup of tea without being asked An ambulance arriving within 3 minutes
Assurance: Knowledge/competence of employees and ability to convey trust and confidence	Knowledge and skills of employees Company name and reputation Personal characteristics of employees	A highly trained financial adviser A known and respected service provider A doctor's bedside manner
Empathy: Caring and individual attention provided by employees	Listening to customer needs Caring about the customer's interests Providing personalized attention	A store employee listening to and trying to understand a customer's complaint A nurse counseling a heart patient

Sources: Adapted from Leonard L. Berry and A. Parasuraman, *Marketing Services: Competing through Quality* (New York: Free Press, 1991); Valarie A. Zeithaml, A. Parasuraman, and Leonard L. Berry, *Delivering Quality Service: Balancing Customer Perceptions and Expectations* (New York: Free Press, 1990); and A. Parasuraman, Leonard L. Berry, and Valarie A. Zeithaml, "An Empirical Examination of Relationships in an Extended Service Quality Model," *Marketing Science Institute Working Paper Series,* Report no. 90-122 (Cambridge, Mass.: Marketing Science Institute, 1990), p. 29.

evaluations of service quality.[12] As shown in Figure 13.6, Pacific Bell promotes the reliability of its telecommunication services.

Service marketers pay a great deal of attention to the tangibles of service quality. Tangible elements, such as the appearance of facilities and employees, are often the only aspects of a service that can be viewed before purchase and consumption. Therefore, service marketers must ensure that these tangible elements are consistent with the overall image of the service product.

Figure 13.6
Service Reliability
Pacific Bell promotes the reliability of its telecommunication services.

Except for the tangibles dimension, the criteria that customers use to judge service quality are intangible. For instance, how does a customer judge reliability? Since dimensions like reliability cannot be examined with the senses, consumers must rely on other ways of judging service. One of the most important factors in customer judgments of service quality is service expectations. Service expectations are influenced by past experiences with the service, word-of-mouth communication from other customers, and the service company's own advertising. For example, customers are usually eager to try a new restaurant, especially when friends recommend it. These same customers may have also seen advertisements placed by the restaurant. As a result, they have an idea of what to expect when they visit the restaurant for the first time. When they finally dine at the restaurant, the quality they experience will change the expectations they have for their next visit. That is why providing consistently high service quality is important. If the quality of a restaurant, or of any service, begins to deteriorate, customers will alter their own expectations and change their word-of-mouth communication to others accordingly.

Delivering Exceptional Service Quality

Providing high-quality service on a consistent basis is very difficult. All consumers have experienced examples of poor service: late airline departures and arrivals, inattentive waiters in a restaurant, rude bank employees, and long lines (see Building Customer Relationships). Obviously, it is impossible for a service organization to

BUILDING customer relationships

Do You Always Choose the Wrong Line?

People spend several years of their lives waiting in lines at banks, supermarkets, movie theaters, fast-food restaurants, theme parks, and countless other places. Waiting in line for five minutes can seem like five hours, and having to do so often produces stress and provokes frustration and anger. At a Milwaukee supermarket, for example, a woman became so angry with the shopper ahead of her for having too many items in the express line that she followed her to the parking lot and attacked her with a pocket knife. Even if it doesn't cause such an extreme reaction, waiting in long lines does negatively affect customers' perceptions of service quality.

For many organizations, making the wait in line more palatable and pleasant is an integral part of improving customer service. Some restaurants provide vibrating beepers so customers can go to the bar or walk around outside while they wait for a table. The Kroger supermarket chain is testing "U-Scan Express," a checkout system that allows customers with few items to scan, bag, and pay for their purchases without help from clerks. In a pilot program initiated by restaurant owners and AMC studios, restaurant customers can buy movie tickets to a nearby theater while they are dining, pay for them with their meal, and avoid long lines at the theater.

For businesses that serve long lines of customers, delivering excellent customer service can hinge on whether to line up customers in multiple or single lines.

In places that have multiple lines for cash registers, like supermarkets and some fast-food restaurants, customers try to assess which line is shortest or moving fastest and then get in that line. Many times, they choose incorrectly and become irritated by the wait or angry with the service provider. With single lines, commonly used at banks and airline ticket counters, customers wait in one line, and as they reach the head of the line proceed to the first available counter. Because they know they are being served in the order they arrive, customers waiting in a single line often believe they are being treated fairly. This perceived fairness can translate into positive perceptions of the level of service. Over seventy McDonald's restaurants in California are testing the use of single lines, and after eighteen months, results are encouraging.

Customers who have to wait in line don't always believe they have received poor customer service. However, studies reveal that if they become angry or irritated while they wait, have to wait longer than they expected, see others who came after them being served first, or just feel as if they've waited a long time, customers will conclude that the level of customer service has been unsatisfactory. Experts advise businesses to be sensitive to the customers' costs of waiting, to provide appropriate explanations and apologies, and to be constantly on the lookout for ways to reduce waits.

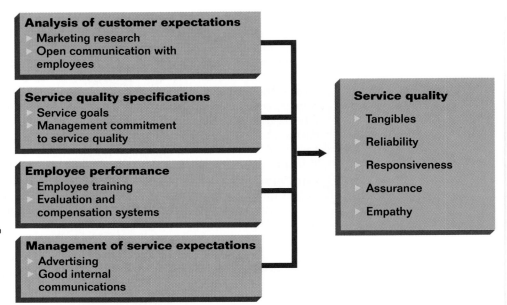

Figure 13.7
Service Quality Model

Source: "Service Quality Model," adapted from A. Parasuraman, Leonard L. Berry, and Valarie A. Zeithaml, "An Empirical Examination of Relationships in an Extended Service Quality Model," *Marketing Science Institute Working Paper Series,* no. 90-112 (Cambridge, Mass.: Marketing Science Institute, 1990). Used with permission.

ensure exceptional service quality 100 percent of the time. However, there are many steps an organization can take to increase the likelihood of providing high-quality service. First, though, the service company must understand the four factors that affect service quality. As shown in Figure 13.7 they are (1) analysis of customer needs, (2) service quality specifications, (3) employee performance, and (4) management of service expectations.[13]

Analysis of Customer Expectations   Providers need to understand customer expectations when designing a service to meet or exceed those expectations; only then can they deliver good service. Progressive Insurance, the fifth largest U.S. auto insurer, is able to exceed customers' expectations by writing checks for auto damage at the accident scene.[14] Customers usually have two levels of expectations—desired and acceptable. The desired level of expectations is what the customer really wants. If this level of expectations is provided, the customer would be very satisfied. The acceptable level is viewed as a reasonable level of performance that the customer views as being adequate. The difference between these two levels of expectations is called the customer's zone of tolerance.[15]

Service companies sometimes use marketing research, such as surveys and focus groups, as a means of discovering customer needs and expectations. Other service marketers, especially restaurants, use comment cards, on which customers can complain or provide suggestions. Still another approach is to ask employees. Because customer-contact employees interact daily with customers, they are in a good position to know what customers want from the company. Service managers should regularly interact with their employees by asking their opinions on the best way to serve customers.

Service Quality Specifications   Once an organization understands its customers' needs, it must establish goals to help ensure good service delivery. These goals, or service specifications, are typically set in terms of employee or machine performance. For example, a bank may require its employees to conform to a dress code. Likewise, the bank may require that all incoming phone calls be answered by the third ring. Specifications like these can be very important in providing quality service as long as they are tied to the needs expressed by customers.

Perhaps the most critical aspect of service quality specifications is managers' commitment to service quality. Service managers who are committed to quality become role models for all employees in the organization.[16] Such commitment motivates customer-contact employees to comply with service specifications. It is crucial that all managers within the organization embrace this commitment—especially front-line managers, who are much closer to customers than higher-level managers.

Employee Performance Once an organization sets service quality standards and managers are committed to them, the organization must find ways to ensure that customer-contact employees perform their jobs well. Contact employees in most service industries—bank tellers, flight attendants, waiters, sales clerks—are often the least-trained and lowest-paid members of the organization. What service organizations must realize is that contact employees are the most important link to the customer, and thus their performance is critical to customer perceptions of service quality.[17] The means to ensure that employees perform well is to train them well so that they understand how to do their jobs. Providing information about customers, service specifications, and the organization itself during the training promotes this understanding.[18]

The evaluation and compensation system used by the organization also plays a part in employee performance. Many service employees are evaluated and rewarded on the basis of output measures, such as sales volume (automobile salespeople) or a low error rate (bank tellers). But systems using output measures overlook other major aspects of job performance: friendliness, teamwork, effort, and customer satisfaction. These customer-oriented measures of performance may be a better basis of evaluation and reward. Customer satisfaction levels are Compaq Computer's basis for compensating its authorized solutions providers.[19] At Galletin Medical Foundation, doctors can receive a merit bonus of up to 30 percent of their annual compensation based on patient satisfaction levels.[20]

Management of Service Expectations Because expectations are so significant in customer evaluations of service quality, service companies recognize that they must set realistic expectations about the service they can provide. They can set these expectations through advertising and good internal communication. In their advertisements, service companies make promises about the kind of service they will deliver. For example, by promoting the promised benefits of their services, both Alamo Rent-A-Car and GM Goodwrench Service are building service expectations on the part of customers (see Figure 13.8). As already noted, a service company is forced to make

**Figure 13.8
Building Service
Expectations**
As Alamo Rent-A-Car and GM Goodwrench Service Plus promote the benefits of their services, they are building customers' service expectations.

promises since the intangibility of services prevents it from showing them in the advertisement. However, the advertiser should not promise more than it can deliver. Doing otherwise may mean disappointed customers.

SNAPSHOT

Do *you* tip for good service?

Percentage of adults who decide whether to tip based on quality of service

Waitstaff	54.5%
Hairstylists/barbers	50.9%
Bartenders	44.3%
Taxi/limo drivers	39.0%
Luggage handlers	37.3%
Parking valets	32.0%

To deliver on promises made, a company needs to have good internal communication among its departments—especially management, advertising, and store operations. Assume, for example, that a restaurant's radio advertisements guaranteed service within five minutes or the meal would be free. If top management or the advertising department failed to inform store operations about the five-minute guarantee, the restaurant very likely would not meet its customers' service expectations. Even though customers might appreciate a free meal, the restaurant would lose some credibility.

As mentioned earlier, word-of-mouth communication from other customers also shapes customer expectations. However, service companies cannot manage this "advertising" directly. The best way to ensure positive word-of-mouth communication is to provide exceptional service quality. It has been estimated that customers tell four times as many people about bad service as they do about good service.

Nonprofit Marketing

nonprofit marketing
Marketing conducted to achieve some goal other than ordinary business goals of profit, market share, or return on investment

Nonprofit marketing includes marketing activities conducted by individuals and organizations to achieve some goal other than ordinary business goals of profit, market share, or return on investment. Nonprofit marketing can be divided into two categories: nonprofit-organization marketing and social marketing. Nonprofit-organization marketing is the use of marketing concepts and techniques by organizations whose goals do not include making profits. Social marketing promotes social causes, such as AIDS research and recycling.

Most of the previously discussed concepts and approaches to service products also apply to nonprofit organizations. Indeed, many nonprofit organizations provide mainly service products. In this section, we examine the concept of nonprofit marketing to determine how it differs from marketing activities in for-profit business organizations. We also explore the marketing objectives of nonprofit organizations and the development of their product strategies.

Why Is Nonprofit Marketing Different?

Many nonprofit organizations strive for effective marketing activities. Charitable organizations and supporters of social causes are major nonprofit marketers in this country. Political parties, unions, religious sects, and fraternal organizations also perform marketing activities, yet they are not considered businesses. Whereas the chief beneficiary of a business enterprise is whoever owns or holds stock in it, in theory the only beneficiaries of a nonprofit organization are its clients, its members, or the public at large. The American Museum of Natural History, for example, is a nonprofit service organization. For example, the Negro Leagues Baseball Museum and Utah's Hogle Zoo, shown in Figure 13.9, are nonprofit organizations.

Nonprofit organizations have a greater opportunity for creativity than most for-profit business organizations, but trustees or board members of nonprofit organizations are likely to have trouble judging the performance of the trained professionals they oversee. It is harder for administrators to evaluate the performance of professors

Figure 13.9
Nonprofit Organizations That Provide Services
The Negro Leagues Baseball Museum and the Utah's Hogle Zoo are examples of nonprofit organizations.

or social workers than it is for sales managers to evaluate the performance of salespersons in a for-profit organization.

Another way in which nonprofit marketing differs from for-profit marketing is that nonprofit marketing is sometimes quite controversial. Nonprofit organizations like Greenpeace, the National Rifle Association, and the National Organization for Women spend lavishly on lobbying efforts to persuade Congress, the White House, and even the courts to support their interests, in part because not all of society agrees with their aims. However, marketing as a field of study does not attempt to state what an organization's goals should be or to debate the issue of nonprofit versus for-profit business goals. Marketing tries only to provide a body of knowledge and concepts to help further an organization's goals. Individuals must decide whether they approve or disapprove of a particular organization's goal orientation. Most marketers would agree that profit and consumer satisfaction are appropriate goals for business enterprises, but there would probably be considerable disagreement about the goals of a controversial nonprofit organization.

Nonprofit Marketing Objectives

The basic aim of nonprofit organizations is to obtain a desired response from a target market. The response could be a change in values, a financial contribution, the donation of services, or some other type of exchange. Nonprofit marketing objectives are shaped by the nature of the exchange and the goals of the organization. These objectives should state the rationale for an organization's existence. An organization that defines its marketing objective as providing a product can be left without a purpose if the product becomes obsolete. However, servicing and adapting to the perceived needs and wants of a target public, or market, enhances an organization's chance to survive and achieve its goals.

Developing Nonprofit Marketing Strategies

Nonprofit organizations develop marketing strategies by defining and analyzing a target market and creating and maintaining the total marketing mix that appeals to that market.

target public People interested in or concerned about an organization, product, or social cause

Target Markets   We must revise the concept of target markets slightly to apply it to nonprofit organizations. Whereas a business is supposed to have target groups that are potential purchasers of its product, a nonprofit organization may attempt to serve many diverse groups. For our purposes, a **target public** is broadly defined as a collective of individuals who have an interest in or concern about an organization, a product, or a social cause. The terms *target market* and *target public* are difficult to distinguish for many nonprofit organizations. The target public of the Partnership for a Drug Free America consists of parents, adults, and concerned teenagers. However, the target market for the organization's advertisements consists of potential and current drug users. When an organization is concerned about changing values or obtaining a response from the public, it views the public as a market.[21]

client publics Direct consumers of a product

general publics Indirect consumers of a product

In nonprofit marketing, direct consumers of the product are called **client publics** and indirect consumers are called **general publics**.[22] For example, the client public for a university is its student body, and its general public includes parents, alumni, and trustees. The client public usually receives most of the attention when an organization develops a marketing strategy.

Developing a Marketing Mix   A marketing mix strategy limits alternatives and directs marketing activities toward achieving organizational goals. The strategy should include a blueprint for making decisions about product, distribution, promotion, and price. These decision variables should be blended to serve the target market.

In developing the product, nonprofit organizations usually deal with ideas and services. Problems may evolve when an organization fails to define what is being provided. What product does the Peace Corps provide? Its services include vocational training, health services, nutritional assistance, and community development. It also markets the ideas of international cooperation and the implementation of U.S. foreign policy. The product of the Peace Corps is more difficult to define than the average business product. As indicated in the first part of this chapter, services are intangible and therefore need special marketing efforts. The marketing of ideas and concepts is likewise more abstract than the marketing of tangibles, and it requires much effort to present benefits.

Distribution decisions in nonprofit organizations relate to how ideas and services will be made available to clients. If the product is an idea, selecting the right media to communicate the idea will facilitate distribution. By nature, services consist of assistance, convenience, and availability. Availability is thus part of the total service. Making a product like health services available calls for knowledge of such retailing concepts as site location analysis.

Developing a channel of distribution to coordinate and facilitate the flow of nonprofit products to clients is a necessary task, but in a nonprofit setting, the traditional concept of the marketing channel may need to be revised. The independent whole-salers available to a business enterprise do not exist in most nonprofit situations. Instead, a very short channel—nonprofit organization to client—is prevalent because production and consumption of ideas and services are often simultaneous.

Making promotional decisions may be the first sign that nonprofit organizations are performing marketing activities. Nonprofit organizations use advertising and publicity to communicate with clients and the public. As shown in Figure 13.10, the National Multiple Sclerosis Society targets employers, and Bottomless Closet targets women who may have clothing to donate to unemployed women on assistance. Direct mail remains the primary means of fundraising for social services, such as those provided by the Red Cross and Special Olympics. Personal selling is also used by many nonprofit organizations, although it may be called something else. Churches and charities rely on personal selling when they send volunteers to recruit new members or request donations. The U.S. Army uses personal selling when its recruiting officers attempt to persuade men and women to enlist. Special events to obtain funds, communicate ideas, or provide services are also effective promotional activities. Amnesty International, for example, has held worldwide concert tours featuring well-known musical artists to raise funds and increase public awareness of political prisoners around the world.

Although product and promotional techniques might require only slight modification when applied to nonprofit organizations, pricing is generally quite different and the decision making is more complex. The different pricing concepts that the nonprofit organization faces include pricing in user and donor markets. There are two types of monetary pricing: *fixed* and *variable*. There may be a fixed fee for users, or the price may vary depending on the user's ability to pay. When a donation-seeking organization will accept a contribution of any size, variable pricing is being used.

The broadest definition of price (valuation) must be used to develop nonprofit marketing strategies. Financial price, an exact dollar value, may or may not be charged for a nonprofit product. Economists recognize the giving up of alternatives as a cost.

Figure 13.10
Promotion of Non-Profit organizations
The National Multiple Sclerosis Society's advertisements encourage employers to hire people with MS, and the Bottomless Closet, a provider of business clothing for women on assistance seeking employment, advertises on hangers distributed by dry cleaners to encourage clothing donations.

opportunity cost   Value
of the benefit given up by
choosing one alternative over
another

Opportunity cost is the value of the benefit that is given up by selecting one alternative rather than another. This traditional economic view of price means that if a nonprofit organization can persuade someone to donate time to a cause or to change his or her behavior, then the alternatives given up are a cost to (or a price paid by) the individual. Volunteers who answer phones for a university counseling service or suicide hotline, for example, give up the time they could have spent studying or doing other things and the income they might have earned from working at a for-profit business organization.

For other nonprofit organizations, financial price is an important part of the marketing mix. Nonprofit organizations today are raising money by increasing the prices of their services or are starting to charge for services if they have not done so before. They are using marketing research to determine what kinds of products people will pay for. Pricing strategies of nonprofit organizations often stress public and client welfare over equalization of costs and revenues. If additional funds are needed to cover costs, then donations, contributions, or grants may be solicited.

Summary

Services are intangible products involving deeds, performances, or efforts that cannot be physically possessed. They are the result of applying human or mechanical efforts to people or objects. Services are a growing part of the U.S. economy. They have six fundamental characteristics: intangibility, inseparability of production and consumption, perishability, heterogeneity, client-based relationships, and customer contact. Intangibility means that a service cannot be seen, touched, tasted, or smelled. Inseparability refers to the fact that the production of a service cannot be separated from its consumption by customers. Perishability means that unused service capacity of one time period cannot be stored for future use. Heterogeneity is variation in service quality. Client-based relationships are interactions with customers that lead to the repeated use of a service over time. Customer contact is the interaction between providers and customers needed to deliver a service.

Core services are the basic service experiences customers expect, and supplementary services are those that relate to and support core services. Because of the characteristics of services, service marketers face several challenges in developing and managing marketing mixes. To address the problem of intangibility, marketers use cues that help assure customers about the quality of services. The development and management of service products are also influenced by the service characteristics of inseparability and level of customer contact. Some services require that customers come to the service provider's facility, and others are delivered with no face-to-face contact. Marketing channels for services are usually short and direct, but some services do employ intermediaries. Service marketers are less concerned with warehousing and transportation than are goods marketers, but they are very concerned about inventory management and with balancing supply and demand for services. Intangibility of services poses several promotion-related challenges. Advertisements with tangible cues that symbolize the service and that picture facilities, equipment,

and personnel help address these challenges. Service providers are likely to promote price, guarantees, performance documentation, availability, and training and certification of contact personnel. Through their actions, service personnel can be involved directly or indirectly in the personal selling of services. Intangibility makes it difficult to experience a service before purchasing it. Heterogeneity and intangibility make word-of-mouth communication an important means of promotion. The prices of services are based on task performance, time required, or demand. Perishability creates difficulties in balancing supply and demand because unused capacity cannot be stored. The point in time when a significant number of customers desire a service is called peak demand. Demand-based pricing results in higher prices being charged for services during peak demand. When services are offered in a bundle, marketers must decide whether to offer them at one price, to price them separately, or to use a combination of the two methods. Because services are intangible, customers may rely on price as a sign of quality. For some services, market conditions may dictate the price; for others, state and local government regulations may limit price flexibility.

Service quality is the customers' perception of how well a service meets or exceeds their expectations. Service quality, although one of the most important aspects of service marketing, is very difficult for customers to evaluate. The reason for this difficulty is that services render benefits impossible to assess before actual purchase and consumption. These benefits include experience qualities, such as taste, satisfaction, or pleasure, and credence qualities, which customers may not be able to evaluate even after consumption. When competing services are very similar, service quality may be the only way for customers to distinguish between them. Service marketers can increase the quality of their services by following the four-step process of understanding customer needs, setting service specifications, ensuring good employee performance, and managing customers' service expectations.

Nonprofit marketing is marketing aimed at nonbusiness goals, including social causes. It uses most of the same concepts and approaches that apply to business situations. The chief beneficiary of a business enterprise is whoever owns or holds stock in it, but the beneficiary of a nonprofit enterprise should be its clients, its members, or its public at large. The goals of a nonprofit organization reflect its unique philosophy or mission. Some nonprofit organizations have very controversial goals, but many organizations exist to further generally accepted social causes.

The marketing objective of nonprofit organizations is to obtain a desired response from a target market.

Developing a nonprofit marketing strategy consists of defining and analyzing a target market and creating and maintaining a marketing mix. In nonprofit marketing, the product is usually an idea or a service. Distribution is aimed at the communication of ideas and the delivery of services. The result is a very short marketing channel. Promotion is very important to nonprofit marketing. Nonprofit organizations use advertising, publicity, and personal selling to communicate with clients and the public. Direct mail remains the primary means of fundraising for social services. Price is more difficult to define in nonprofit marketing because of opportunity costs and the difficulty of quantifying the values exchanged.

Important Terms

Service	Heterogeneity	Search qualities	Target public
Intangibility	Client-based relationships	Experience qualities	Client publics
Inseparability	Customer contact	Credence qualities	General publics
Perishability	Service quality	Nonprofit marketing	Opportunity cost

Discussion and Review Questions

1. How important are services in the U.S. economy?
2. Identify and discuss the major service characteristics.
3. For each marketing mix element, which service characteristics are most likely to have an impact?
4. What is service quality?
5. Why do customers experience difficulty in judging service quality?
6. Identify and discuss the five components of service quality. How do customers evaluate these components?
7. What is the significance of tangibles in service marketing?
8. How do search, experience, and credence qualities affect the way customers view and evaluate services?
9. What steps should a service company take to provide exceptional service quality?
10. How does nonprofit marketing differ from marketing in for-profit organizations?
11. What are the differences among clients, publics, and customers? What is the difference between a target public and a target market?
12. Discuss the development of a marketing strategy for a university. What marketing decisions must be made as the strategy is developed?

Application Questions

1. Imagine you are the owner of a new service business. What is your service? Be creative. What are some of the most important considerations in developing the service, training salespeople, and communicating to potential customers about your service?
2. As discussed in this chapter, the characteristics of services affect the development of marketing mixes for services. Choose a specific service and explain how each marketing mix element could be affected by these service characteristics.
3. In advertising services, a company often must use symbols to represent the offered product. Identify three service organizations you see in outdoor advertising. What symbols are used to represent their services? What message do the symbols convey to potential customers?
4. Delivering consistently high-quality service is difficult for service marketers. Describe an instance when you received high-quality service and an instance when you experienced low-quality service. What contributed to your perception of high quality? Of low quality?

Internet Exercise & Resources

Group Health Cooperative Goes Online

Health care providers have never had as many different forms of communication available for marketing their products as they do today. However, choosing among these options is increasingly difficult because of market uncertainty and the ongoing segmentation of health care consumers into specialized clinical groups. In this context, the Internet has emerged as a cost-effective and practical means of marketing health care services. One firm that has realized the benefits of Internet marketing is Group Health Cooperative (GHC), which provides managed health care services in Washington and Idaho. Visit the GHC Web site at

www.ghc.org

1. Classify GHC's products in terms of their position on the service continuum and category of service.

2. How does GHC enhance customer service and foster better client-based relationships through its Internet marketing efforts?

3. Discuss the degree to which experience and credence qualities exist in the services offered by GHC and other health care providers. How does GHC's Web site lessen or otherwise address potential problems arising from high levels of these qualities?

E-Center Resources

Visit http://www.prideferrell.com to find several resources to help you succeed in mastering the material in this chapter, plus additional materials that will help you expand your marketing knowledge. The Web site includes

 Internet exercise updates plus additional exercises

 ACE self-tests

 Chapter summary with hotlinked glossary

 Hotlinks to companies featured in this chapter

 Resource Center

 Career Center

 Marketing plan worksheets

VIDEO CASE 13.1

Fireworks by Grucci Entertains America

Accompanied by the sounds of Jerry Lee Lewis's "Great Balls of Fire," showers of red, blue, green, and white light fill the night sky. Golden comets crisscross the dark to the tune of Bruce Springsteen's "Born in the U.S.A." Crowds gasp in admiration as Fireworks by Grucci does business as usual. For almost 150 years, the Grucci family has been in the business of entertaining audiences with fireworks displays. At the Olympics and the Goodwill Games, five U.S. presidential inaugurations, and even at an Yves Saint Laurent champagne gala, Fireworks by Grucci was there. Grucci's vice president, Felix Grucci, Jr., states that his family members are entertainers whose shows will go on in rain, snow, sleet, wind, and cold—everything except fog. States Grucci, "It is gratifying when you can deliver smiles on faces."

In 1900, the family-owned, family-run firm moved to New York from Bari, Italy, where Angelo Lanzetta had established it in 1850. In 1929, Lanzetta's nephew, Felix Grucci, took over the organization, renaming it the New York Pyrotechnic Company. Over the next two decades, Grucci gained a reputation as a master of his art, inventing the stringless shell, which made fireworks less dangerous by eliminating burning fallout, and creating inventive and unique displays. Although many fireworks producers disappeared during the 1960s when demand for fireworks displays waned, Fireworks by Grucci survived.

In 1976, cities across America booked Grucci for U.S. bicentennial celebrations. In 1979, the company became the first American entry to win the gold medal in the Monte Carlo International Fireworks Championship, defeating competitors from Denmark, France, Italy, and Spain. Winning this competition earned Grucci the title "First Family of Fireworks." The Grucci family was struck by tragedy when two family members died in an explosion that destroyed the Grucci factory, but the company eventually recovered.

Today, Fireworks by Grucci employs thirty full-time and four hundred part-time workers and stages about three hundred shows a year. In the $75 million-a-year commercial fireworks market, the Gruccis compete with the Souza family's PyroSpectaculars and the Zambellis' International Fireworks. When economic conditions are adverse, the competition intensifies because many communities can't afford to pay for the kind of extravaganza these companies produce.

Fireworks by Grucci produces two basic types of programs, which it calls Traditional and State-of-the-Art. Traditional programs include an opening barrage, "grand illuminations," and a grand finale. Although these programs are considered spectacular, the company's State-of-the-Art program is uniquely Grucci.

Grucci's State-of-the-Art clients have come to expect dazzling pyrotechnics, precise synchronization between music and visual displays, and Monte Carlo–class grand finales. To meet these expectations, Grucci custom-designs every production. Each firework is handmade, and music is recorded and edited at a professional sound studio. Grucci specialties include split comets, ring shells, butterflies with crosses, swaying leaves and meteors, splendid white flowers, serpents, and happy gates (boxes that fire a hundred shells of various colors simultaneously). To set up a major fireworks production involving such unique creations, Grucci's pyrotechnicians require about seven miles of cable, twenty-five tons of sand, enough lumber to build a small home, as many as six thousand launching tubes, and about two hundred hours of labor.

Small programs that last two or three minutes cost about $3,000. City- and state-class events cost over $800 a minute. For a twenty-five minute display, this rate adds up to over $20,000. To stage world-class productions, such as a presidential inauguration, the Grucci meter ticks away at $3,000 per minute. Along with stunning and memorable spectacles, part of Grucci's service to its clients is to provide them with fireworks display liability insurance, as well as advice on promoting their events through press releases and radio and television commercials.

To promote the company's products, the Gruccis rely primarily on word-of-mouth communication and on brand awareness established by media coverage of their premier shows. They do not advertise. When the vice president for marketing meets with potential clients, whether they be communities or businesses, he uses a videotape of previous productions to help him explain the firm's services. This low-key approach has persuaded customers like Lever Brothers, PepsiCo, and Maxwell House Coffee to pay $20,000 to $50,000 for shows at sales meetings and other corporate events.[23]

Questions for Discussion

1. Discuss the six characteristics of services shown in Table 13.1 as they relate to the services provided by Fireworks by Grucci.
2. In what ways do customers evaluate the quality of Grucci's services?
3. Evaluate the methods that Fireworks by Grucci uses to promote its services.

CASE 13.2

Harrah's Casinos Gambles on Its Strategy

Americans who love to gamble have many legal ways to indulge, and 25 percent of American adults do. They can buy a lottery ticket at the local supermarket, cruise for an evening on a gambling riverboat, or fly to Las Vegas for a few days of casino games. To find a casino, bettors no longer even have to go to Las Vegas or Atlantic City. In fact, twenty-six states permit casino gambling in some form, and more Americans go to gambling casinos each year than attend major league baseball games or Broadway shows. Eighty-two percent of those responding to a recent survey agreed that going to a casino would be "a fun night out."

Harrah's Entertainment Company, America's largest casino enterprise, welcomes the growing appeal of casino gaming.

Gambling has been part of life in the United States since the country began. The funds to launch the *Mayflower,* raise the colonial army, and found Harvard, Yale, and Dartmouth came from lotteries. Until the early twentieth century, legal gaming flourished all over the United States. However, when Americans began associating gaming with corruption and violence, prohibitive laws were enacted. After Nevada legalized casino gambling in 1931, it maintained a monopoly on betting until 1976, when New Jersey became the second state to make the activity legal. Because of the growing number of gambling alternatives and intense industry competition, assert many experts, the days are over when companies can simply open a casino and be certain that people will come.

In operation since 1937, Harrah's today competes with such gaming giants as Circus Circus, Caesar's World, Mirage Resorts, Bally's, Hilton, and many others, including a growing number of casinos run by Native Americans. With competition increasing, casinos strive for ways to differentiate themselves. To make their hotels or resorts appeal to the largest audience, many casino companies are marketing themselves as family vacation destinations, complete with theme parks and children's activities. When the Luxor recently renovated its Las Vegas casino and hotel, it created a gaming-free reception area that allows customers to get to their rooms without passing through any gaming areas; stated one recent guest, "A casino? You'll have to hunt for it." To set themselves apart from the ever-increasing crowd of rivals, Caesar's World is putting a Planet Hollywood restaurant in each of its casinos, and Hilton and Viacom's Paramount Parks are teaming up to create a Star Trek Virtual Reality attraction in Las Vegas.

Some experts believe that with the changes these gambling establishments are making, older casinos, such as the Riviera and Tropicana, will be unable to compete because they have only gaming attractions. Harrah's, however, remains convinced that people don't go to casinos to zip down waterslides or play virtual reality video games; they go to interact with adults and enjoy themselves gambling. Harrah's executive vice president of marketing reports that his company doesn't urge Mom and Dad to "bring the kids." Instead, the company focuses on making gaming inside the casino an exciting entertainment experience for adults. Harrah's executives believe that gambling is not about getting rich but about having fun. At the front entrance to Harrah's Las Vegas casino, dealers "capture" passersby, encouraging them to come in. Inside, dealers in the Fun Pit joke with customers, ring bells, whack players on the head with rubber hammers, and joust with collapsible swords. "Celebration

stations" serve drinks and cake, and the "win committee" sprinkles "lucky dust" on winners and presents them with medals reading, "I won at Harrah's." When someone hits the jackpot at a slot machine, Harrah's employees bring over a cellular phone so that the winner can call anyone, anywhere.

Harrah's is also attempting to establish and maintain the highest standard of customer service. Its guest-satisfaction rating system tracks customer opinions, and it is the first casino to extend to customers an "unconditional guarantee of service excellence." During one recent six-month period, the company surveyed 13,000 patrons concerning their Harrah's experience; 78 percent of those who visited land-based casinos and 74 percent of those who played on the company's riverboats reported that their overall experience had been one of the best ever or better than their experiences at Harrah's competitors.

Not every Harrah's effort is quite as successful. Harrah's riverboat casinos are not flourishing, and its efforts to build the world's largest gambling casino, which was located in New Orleans, ended in bankruptcy. Despite these setbacks and falling earnings, Harrah's CEO is forging ahead, putting $985 million into casino and riverboat expansions. The company has introduced a "Gold Card," a frequent-user program offering gamblers incentives to visit Harrah's casinos all over the country. It is spending about $200 million on a thirty-five-story hotel and gaming area in Las Vegas and $405 million to expand its Atlantic City property. With all this development, however, Harrah's visitors will not be seeing artificial volcanoes or pirate ships. Harrah's is concentrating on building less flashy, more hospitable casinos that appeal to its core customers.[24]

Questions for Discussion

1. In what ways is Harrah's affected by perishability and by heterogeneity?
2. Describe Harrah's attitude toward service quality. What criteria are Harrah's customers most likely to use when evaluating service quality?
3. In what ways is Harrah's differentiating itself from competitors?

STRATEGIC CASE 3

Mattel Toys Sings, "Oh, You Beautiful Doll!"

By the time Barbie celebrated her 40th birthday in 1999, she had long ago claimed the coveted title of most successful brand name toy ever sold. In an industry where last year's hit is this year's loser, Mattel's Barbie sells on and on; to date, more than 1 billion have been sold in 140 countries. Initially dismissed as a passing fad, the glamorous doll has outlasted her critics, selling enough units to circle the earth more than three and a half times if laid head to pointed toe. What is Mattel's secret to success in this age of high-tech toys? By continually reinventing the product and introducing imaginative brand extensions, Mattel is keeping Barbie forever young—and forever contributing to the company's annual sales of $5 billion.

Barbie Is Born

Mattel, started making toys in 1945, operating out of a converted garage in California. The company's first product was toy furniture. Within seven years, Mattel had expanded into burp guns and musical toys, ringing up annual sales of over $5 million. Then, in 1959, Mattel changed forever the way little girls play with dolls by introducing the golden-haired Barbie, named after the owner's daughter. Along with her extensive and fashionable wardrobe and countless accessories, Barbie was an instant hit. Soon afterward, Mattel introduced her boyfriend Ken, named for the owner's son. More Barbies and friends followed as the foot-high doll with the improbably figure catapulted Mattel to the top of the toy industry.

A Barbie for Everyone

If Barbie suffers from something of an identity crisis, blame Mattel, which has turned out more than five hundred variations of the doll over the years. Barbie has dabbled in seventy-five careers, always stylishly outfitted, whether working as a television news reporter, a veterinarian, an astronaut, a doctor, a women's basketball star, a presidential candidate, or an air force lieutenant colonel. The doll has also hopped national borders. Barbies in the Dolls of the World collection represent forty-five nationalities, Jamaican, Japanese, Austrian, and Peruvian, among others. Still, the best-selling Barbie in history is Totally Hair Barbie, whose hair stretches from head to toes and turns pink when sprayed.

In her travels, Barbie has picked up a string of doll friends modeled after such celebrities as Rosie O'Donnell, Hammer, and Elvis. Barbie also has her own line of dollhouses, sports cars, grocery stores, and fast-food restaurants—even motor homes complete with camping equipment and glow-in-the-dark adhesive stars. Her owners can use Barbie Fashion Designer software to print patterns on fabric, cut them out, stitch the seams, and dress their favorite Barbies. With so many dolls and accessories available, F.A.O.

Schwarz and other toy stores have created separate Barbie Boutiques to display and sell Barbie products. Mattel showcases the brand in its own Barbie store in Beverly Hills, California.

Barbie Gets a Makeover, Over and Over

After conquering the hearts of preteen girls in the United States and Western Europe, Barbie went to Asia. Before introducing Barbie in Japan, Mattel made some changes in the all-American doll. Her face was too sophisticated and her makeup too heavy for Japanese tastes, so Barbie received a face-lift, acquiring a more wide-eyed, innocent look that appealed to Japanese consumers.

Mattel has now decided that Barbie needs more radical plastic surgery to keep up with the latest cultural trends. The biggest change is to Barbie's exaggerated hourglass figure, which is being resculpted into a more naturally proportioned bust, waist, and hip size. This move has been applauded by critics who worried that Barbie's original figure contributed to girls' self-image problems. The makeover is continuing above the neckline, where a closed mouth, less makeup, and softer hair are replacing the toothy smile, made-up look, and platinum tresses the doll has sported since her last major makeover in 1977. "In the '80s, Barbie's world was more blond, targeted to glamour and beauty and activities that were right then," says the head of Mattel's Barbie division. "Now she'll have a contemporary look that's more natural and today."

Collectible Barbie

The fastest-growing segment of the Barbie empire is the adult market for collectibles. Although fans have snapped up vintage Barbies and accessories for years through collector's networks, until recently Mattel did not make a point of targeting adults. Now, in a bid for a piece of the $9.1 billion collectibles market, Mattel has created a series of dolls for collectors, ranging from Nascar Barbie and Fashion Savvy Barbie to the Hollywood Legends Collection and the Grand Ole Opry Collection.

More upscale are the limited-edition Barbies, such as Fabergé Imperial Elegance Barbie, Presidential Porcelain Barbie, and the Barbie Couture Collection. Evidently, they are in great demand. When Bloomingdale's offered limited-edition Donna Karan designer Barbies, its stores sold 30,000 of them in just three weeks. Some of the limited-edition Barbies are even numbered, enhancing their value as collectibles.

Mattel adds several dolls to the Barbie collections every year, giving collectors more choices. Many of the collectibles sport porcelain heads with hand-painted faces and specially designed clothing and accessories. As adaptable as ever, collectible Barbie might be a singing star, sports lover, or motorcycle enthusiast. The Harley-Davidson Barbie, available only at Toys

"R" Us, has long red hair, a helmet, sporty sunglasses, and realistic leatherlike riding gear.

Barbie in the New Millennium

Just as Barbie keeps up with the latest fashions, she also keeps up with the latest technology. Barbie's Web site (www.barbie.com) invites girls to participate in interactive activities, such as voting for their favorite Barbie styles and attending special online birthday parties. Mattel also sells Barbie dolls and related software on the site. And for under $50, customers can order a customized My Design doll, selecting the hair, face, hair color, eye color, fashions, name, and personality they prefer. Barbie's Web site has 1 million visitors every week—and 16 percent of them are male.

As lucrative as the Barbie franchise has been, Mattel wants to reduce its dependence on traditional toy stores. To gain a toehold in catalog retailing, it recently acquired the Pleasant Company, which does most of the marketing for its highly successful American Girl line of dolls, books, and accessories by mail. The Pleasant Company will also help Mattel diversify into Barbie magazines, books, videos, and similar spinoffs. The Learning Company, another recent acquisition, will help Mattel branch out into software by sharing the expertise it has gained through marketing Carmen Sandiego, Myst, Riven, and other software hits.

After more than forty years, Barbie's appeal still spans generations. Mattel continues to sell two Barbie dolls every second of the day. According to research studies, 98 percent of American households recognize the Barbie name. A doting 200,000 collectors hold conventions, join clubs, publish Barbie magazines, and exchange ideas on the Internet. What accounts for Barbie's perennial appeal? "It's about fantasy and dreaming," says one Mattel official. Some things never change, not even for the new millennium.[25]

Questions for Discussion

1. What actions have Mattel's marketers taken to extend Barbie's life cycle and to maintain this product's success?
2. Describe how Mattel has positioned Barbie.
3. Evaluate Barbie's brand equity.
4. In terms of the four categories of consumer products, how would you classify ordinary Barbie dolls? My Design dolls? Collectible Barbie dolls? What implications do these categories have for marketing the dolls?

Distribution Decisions

Developing products that satisfy customers is important but not enough to guarantee successful marketing strategies. Products must also be available in adequate quantities in accessible locations at the times when customers desire them. The chapters in Part 4 deal with the distribution of products and the marketing channels and institutions that provide the structure for making products available. In Chapter 14, we discuss the structure and functions of marketing channels and present an overview of institutions that make up these channels. In Chapter 15, we analyze the types of wholesalers and their functions, as well as the decisions and activities associated with the physical distribution of products, such as order processing, materials handling, warehousing, inventory management, and transportation. In Chapter 16, we focus on retailing and retailers. Specifically, we examine types of retailers, nonstore retailing, franchising, and strategic retailing issues.

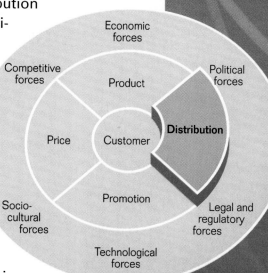

14

Marketing Channels and Supply Chain Management

OBJECTIVES

- To describe the nature and functions of marketing channels

- To explain how supply chain management can facilitate distribution for the benefit of all channel members, especially customers

- To identify the types of marketing channels

- To examine the major levels of marketing coverage

- To explore the concepts of leadership, cooperation, and conflict in channel relationships

- To specify how channel integration can improve channel efficiency

- To examine the legal issues affecting channel management

Barnes & Noble Distributes through Multiple Avenues

Barnes & Noble, the number-one bookseller in the United States, peddles one out of every eight books sold in the country. With more than 500 Barnes & Noble, Bookstop, and Bookstar "superstores" and about 500 B. Dalton, Doubleday, and Scribner's mall-based stores, the company sold $2.8 billion worth of books in 1998. It also sells books directly through a Web site (www.barnesandnoble.com), which includes indexes, online events, book forums, and book reviews to enhance customer satisfaction. Because Barnes & Noble sells books through so many marketing channels, managing the distribution variable is critical to its success.

Barnes & Noble deals with 20,000 publishers, segmented by a variety of topics and company size, and handles hundreds of thousands of different book titles, as well as related merchandise, including magazines, cards, and gifts. Efficient handling of all this merchandise requires an orderly distribution system that involves technology and cooperation among all members of the book supply chain. To supply its stores, Barnes & Noble maintains a distribution center in Jamesburg, N.J., which stocks 600,000 titles. When shipments of books arrive at stores, they are already presorted by major product class for efficient and effective handling. Each store replenishes inventory daily, and thanks to electronic ordering systems, employees scan each product once at the back door before putting it on the shelves. To satisfy orders from the company's Web site, Barnes & Noble operates a separate fulfillment center that provides customers with same-day shipping of 600,000 titles.

Satisfying customers' literary tastes requires that Barnes & Noble build cooperative, long-term relationships with book publishers. Sometimes, however, it is not cost-effective for the company to establish direct relationships with smaller publishers that supply only a few books a month. Barnes & Noble has therefore established an outreach program to help small- and medium-size presses find intermediaries to get their books into Barnes & Noble's stores and Web site. Through intermediaries, such as wholesalers, it is possible to develop both access and convenience for the small publisher to reach a national firm like Barnes & Noble.

When managed effectively, supply chains like that operated by Barnes & Noble serve customers and create competitive advantage. All members of the supply chain—publishers, trucking companies, and Barnes & Noble itself—are involved in providing service to customers and controlling costs. When supply chain members work together, the cooperative relationship results in continuous adjustments to meet customers' needs regarding delivery, scheduling, packaging, and other requirements to provide book buyers the products they desire.[1]

distribution   The activities that make products available to customers when and where they want to purchase them

Barnes & Noble has achieved success in a competitive industry by choosing to distribute its products through multiple avenues. Such decisions relate to the **distribution** component of the marketing mix, which focuses on the decisions and actions involved in making products available to customers when and where they want to purchase them. Choosing which channels of distribution to use is a major decision in the development of marketing strategies.

This chapter describes and analyzes marketing channels. After discussing the nature of marketing channels and the need for intermediaries, we analyze the primary functions they perform. Next, we outline the types of marketing channels and explore how marketers determine the appropriate intensity of market coverage for a product. We also consider supply chain management, including behavioral patterns within marketing channels and forms of channel integration. Finally, we look at several legal issues affecting channel management.

The Nature of Marketing Channels

marketing channel
A group of individuals and organizations directing products from producers to customers

marketing intermediary
A middleman linking producers to other middlemen or ultimate consumers through contractual arrangements or through the purchase and resale of products

A **marketing channel** (also called a channel of distribution or distribution channel) is a group of individuals and organizations that directs the flow of products from producers to customers. The major role of marketing channels is to make products available at the right time at the right place in the right quantities. Providing customer satisfaction should be the driving force behind marketing channel decisions. Buyers' needs and behavior are therefore important concerns of channel members.

Some marketing channels are direct—from producer straight to customer—but most channels of distribution have marketing intermediaries. A **marketing intermediary** (middleman) links producers to other middlemen or to ultimate consumers through contractual arrangements or through the purchase and reselling of products. Marketing intermediaries perform the activities described in Table 14.1. Wholesalers and retailers are examples of intermediaries. Wholesalers buy and resell products to other wholesalers, to retailers, and to industrial customers. Retailers purchase products and resell them to ultimate consumers. For example, your local supermarket probably purchased the Tylenol or Advil on its shelves from Bergen Brunswig or some other wholesaler, which purchased the product, along with other over-the-counter and prescription drugs, from manufacturers like McNeil Consumer Labs and Whitehall-

Table 14.1	**Marketing Channel Activities Performed by Intermediaries**
Category of Marketing Activities	**Possible Activities Required**
Marketing information	Analyze sales data and other information in databases and information systems Perform or commission marketing research
Marketing management	Establish strategic plans for developing customer relationships and organizational productivity
Facilitating exchanges	Choose product assortments that match the needs of customers Cooperate with channel members to develop partnerships
Promotion	Set promotional objectives Coordinate advertising, personal selling, sales promotion, publicity, and packaging
Price	Establish pricing policies and terms of sales
Physical distribution	Manage transportation, warehousing, materials handling, inventory control, and communication

Figure 14.1
Supply Chains Benefit Channel Members
PeopleSoft, a company that provides a variety of business management software solutions, assists retailers in planning and managing their inventories with supply chain management services.

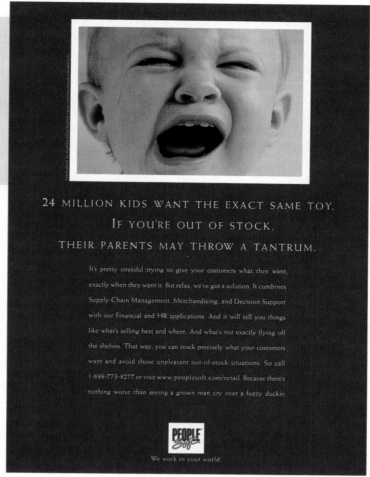

Robins. Chapters 15 and 16 discuss in greater detail the functions of wholesalers and retailers in marketing channels.

Marketing intermediaries, or channel members, share certain significant characteristics. Each member has different responsibilities within the overall structure of the channel. Mutual profit and success for channel members can be attained most readily when channel members cooperate to deliver satisfying products to customers.

Although distribution decisions need not precede other marketing decisions, they are a powerful influence on the rest of the marketing mix. Channel decisions are critical because they determine a product's market presence and buyers' accessibility to the product. For example, because small businesses are more likely to purchase computers from office supply stores like Office Depot or warehouse clubs like Sam's, computer companies may be at a disadvantage without distribution at these outlets. Channel decisions have additional strategic significance because they entail long-term commitments. Thus, it is usually easier to change prices or promotion than to change marketing channels.

Marketing channels serve many functions, including creating utility and facilitating exchange efficiencies. Although some of these functions may be performed by a single channel member, most functions are accomplished through both independent and joint efforts of channel members. When managed effectively, the relationships among channel members can also form supply chains that benefit all members of the channel, including the ultimate consumer. As shown in Figure 14.1, PeopleSoft promotes its supply chain management services to assist retailers in maintaining sufficient inventories to meet customers' demand.

Marketing Channels Create Utility

Marketing channels create three types of utility: time, place, and possession. *Time utility* is having products available when the customer wants them. *Place utility* is created by making products available in locations where customers wish to purchase them. *Possession utility* is created by the customer's having access to the product to use or to store for future use. Possession utility can occur through ownership or through arrangements that give the customer the right to use the product, such as lease or rental agreements. Channel members sometimes create form utility by assembling, preparing, or otherwise refining the product to suit individual customer needs.

Marketing Channels Facilitate Exchange Efficiencies

Marketing intermediaries can reduce the costs of exchanges by efficiently performing certain services or functions. Even if producers and buyers are located in the same city, there are costs associated with exchanges. As Figure 14.2 shows, when four buyers seek products from four producers, sixteen transactions are possible. If one intermediary serves both producers and buyers, the number of transactions can be reduced to eight. Intermediaries are specialists in facilitating exchanges. They provide valuable assistance because of their access to, and control over, important resources used in the proper functioning of marketing channels.

Nevertheless, the press, consumers, public officials, and other marketers freely criticize intermediaries, especially wholesalers. Critics accuse wholesalers of being inefficient and parasitic. Buyers often wish to make the distribution channel as short

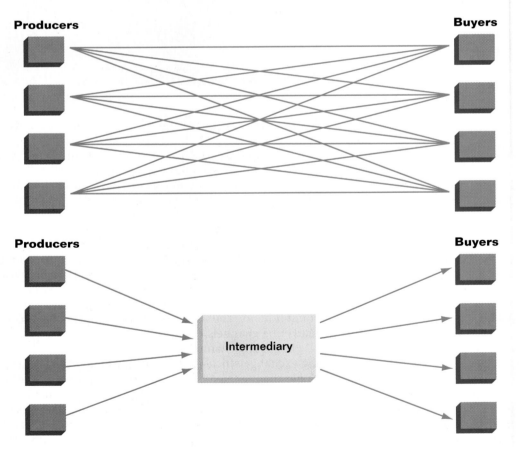

Figure 14.2
Efficiency in Exchanges Provided by an Intermediary

as possible, assuming that the fewer the intermediaries, the lower the price will be. Because suggestions to eliminate them come from both ends of the marketing channel, wholesalers must be careful to perform only those marketing activities that are truly desired. To survive, they must be more efficient and more customer-focused than other marketing institutions.

Critics who suggest that eliminating wholesalers would lower customer prices do not recognize that this would not eliminate the need for services that wholesalers provide. Although wholesalers can be eliminated, the functions they perform cannot. Other channel members would have to perform those functions, and customers would still have to fund them. In addition, all producers would have to deal directly with retailers or customers, meaning that every producer would have to keep voluminous records and hire enough personnel to deal with a multitude of customers. Customers might end up paying a great deal more for products because prices would reflect the costs of less efficient channel members.

To illustrate the efficiency of wholesalers' services, assume that all wholesalers have been eliminated. Because there are more than 1.5 million retail stores, a widely purchased consumer product—say, candy—would require an extraordinary number of sales contacts, possibly more than a million, to maintain the current level of product exposure. For example, Mars, Inc., would have to deliver candy, purchase and service thousands of vending machines, establish warehouses all over the country, and maintain fleets of trucks. Selling and distribution costs for candy would skyrocket. Instead of a few contacts with food brokers, large retail organizations, and merchant wholesalers, candy manufacturers would have to make thousands of expensive contacts with and shipments to smaller retailers. Such an operation would be highly inefficient, and costs would be passed on to consumers. Candy bars would cost more and be harder to find. Wholesalers are often more efficient and less expensive.

Marketing Channels Form a Supply Chain

An important function of the marketing channel is the joint effort of all channel members to create a supply chain, a total distribution system that serves customers and creates a competitive advantage. **Supply chain management** refers to long-term partnerships among marketing channel members working together to reduce inefficiencies, costs, and redundancies in the entire marketing channel, and to develop innovative approaches, in order to satisfy customers.[2]

Supply chain management involves manufacturing, research, sales, advertising, shipping, and, most of all, cooperation and understanding of tradeoffs throughout the whole channel to achieve the optimal level of efficiency and service. Table 14.2 outlines the key tasks involved in supply chain management. Whereas traditional marketing channels tend to focus on producers, wholesalers, retailers, and customers, the supply chain is a broader concept that includes facilitating agencies, such as component parts suppliers, shipping companies, communication companies, and other organizations that take part in marketing exchanges. Thus, the supply chain includes all entities that facilitate product distribution and that benefit from cooperative

supply chain management   Long-term partnerships among marketing channel members to reduce inefficiencies, costs, and redundancies, and to develop innovative approaches, in order to satisfy customers

Table 14.2	Key Tasks in Supply Chain Management
Planning	Organizational and systemwide coordination of marketing channel partnerships to meet customers' product needs
Sourcing	Purchasing of necessary resources, goods, and services from suppliers to support all supply chain members
Facilitating delivery	All activities designed to move the product through the marketing channel to the end user
Relationship building	All marketing activities related to selling, service, and the development of long-term customer relationships

efforts. Building Customer Relationships looks at supply chain management in the health care industry.

Supply chain management is helping more firms realize that optimizing the supply chain costs through partnerships will improve all members' profits. All parties should focus on cooperating to reduce the costs of all affected channel members. When the buyer, the seller, marketing intermediaries, and facilitating agencies work together, the cooperative relationship results in compromise and adjustments that meet customers' needs regarding delivery, scheduling, packaging, or other requirements. The National Association of Purchasing Management predicts that corporate strategy will be increasingly influenced by supply chain management.[3]

Supply chains start with the customer and require the cooperation of channel members to satisfy customer requirements. For example, The Home Depot, North America's largest home-improvement retailer, is reengineering itself to become more efficient in inventory control, security, and information systems. One of the company's goals is to help its suppliers improve their productivity and thereby supply The Home Depot with better-quality products at less cost for the benefit of its customers. In an effort that includes about twenty competitors, including Wal-Mart, Handy Andy, and other home centers, the company has suggested a cooperative partnership so that regional trucking companies making deliveries can provide better

BUILDING
customer relationships

Supply Chain Management in the Health Care Industry

Supply chain management involves long-term relationships among marketing channel members working together to reduce inefficiencies, costs, and redundancies in distribution channels and to develop innovative approaches to satisfy customers. More and more companies have adopted supply chain management techniques to optimize costs through partnerships that improve all members' profits. In health care, however, reducing inefficiencies and redundancies is a little more complicated in an industry where sufficient stocks of medicine and supplies can literally mean the difference between life and death.

Health care providers began to look at supply chain management when a study by a cross-industry consortium determined that supply chain inefficiencies are responsible for wasting $11 billion. When medicine was conducted on a fee-for-service basis—when private insurance companies could be counted on to pick up 80 percent of the tab—hospitals, clinics, and doctors faced few cost pressures. They typically maintained high levels of buffer stocks to ensure they could meet patients' needs. However, today's popular managed care systems, such as HMOs, often place caps on the rates that providers can charge, so reducing costs has become a high priority in recent years.

Many firms have pinpointed excess inventory as a good opportunity for reducing costs in the health care supply chain. Lifeplus, a home medical equipment dealer that serves northern New England, is one example of a company turning to supply chain management to slash the costs of owning the inventory. Because inventory ownership ties up capital, especially in equipment that can cost thousands of dollars, Lifeplus now rents about 65 percent of the equipment it supplies. When a doctor orders an expensive piece of equipment, Lifeplus rents the equipment from another supplier to fill the order, which reduces the company's own acquisition and storage costs.

Another firm that has benefitted from the shift to supply chain management practices is Picker Health Care Products, a specialized distributor of medical imaging supplies based in Cleveland. Picker has created value-added asset management programs to own and manage its customers' on-site inventories. However, Picker allows the health-care provider to dictate its own level of comfort with inventory levels. For a large hospital, an inventory reduction from two-months supply to ten days is not unreasonable.

An optimal healthcare supply chain needs to balance cost-saving just-in-time and bulk-buying strategies with adequate buffer supplies to meet patient care needs. Reducing the costs associated with owning and managing inventory can help health-care providers become more cost-efficient. In many cases, the cost savings can be passed along to the ultimate consumer to help counter the ever increasing costs of quality medical care.

Figure 14.3
Technology Aids Supply Chain Management
J. D. Edwards provides SCOREx, supply chain management software, to assist its customers in improving efficiency and coordination.

service, faster delivery, and greater efficiency in their operations. The Home Depot also made suggestions for standardizing packaging and delivery that saved its suppliers millions of dollars.[4]

Most companies do not set out to develop a supply chain, but like The Home Depot they see a need to rework the way they serve their customers. Often, there is a need to increase the quality of a good or service, which results in such goals as reducing the time from production to customer purchase, reducing transportation costs, or reducing information management or administrative costs. Achieving these goals for a more competitive position often requires that channel members cooperate and share information, as well as accommodate one another's needs.

Technology has dramatically improved the capability of supply chain management on a global basis. The information technology revolution, in particular, has created a virtually seamless distribution process for matching inventory needs to customers' requirements.[5] With integrated information sharing among channel members, costs can be reduced, service can be improved, and value provided to the customer can be enhanced. For example, one key to Wal-Mart's success is the use of bar-code and electronic data interchange (EDI) technology, extending from the firm's suppliers to the warehouse to the customer at the store checkout. Tools like electronic billing, purchase order verification, bar-code technology, and image processing integrate needed data into the supply chain and improve overall performance.[6] Even small businesses benefit from this technology. New technological applications allow small cattle ranchers to trace their product from "calf to cutlet." This gives ranchers unprecedented data to help them cut costs, improve efficiency, and increase the safety and quality of beef. Intensely competitive industries, such as the telecommunications, computer, apparel, and retail industries, operate the most sophisticated systems of supply chain management.[7] J. D. Edwards provides supply chain management software to assist customers in managing sales orders, procurement, warehousing, transportation, and customer service (see Figure 14.3).

Supply chain management should not be considered just a new buzzword. Reducing inventory and transportation costs, speeding order cycle times, cutting administrative and handling costs, and improving customer service—these improvements provide rewards for *all* channel members.[8] The rewards will come as companies determine their position in the supply chain, identify their partners and their roles, and establish partnerships that focus on customer relationships.

Types of Marketing Channels

Because marketing channels appropriate for one product may be less suitable for others, many different distribution paths have been developed. The various marketing channels can be classified generally as channels for consumer products and channels for business products.

Channels for Consumer Products

Figure 14.4 illustrates several channels used in the distribution of consumer products. Channel A depicts the direct movement of goods from producer to consumers. Producers that sell goods directly from their factories to end users are using direct-marketing channels, as are companies that sell their own products over the Internet, such as Dell Computer. In fact, with Internet purchases projected to reach $37.5 billion by 2002, direct channels via the Internet are likely to become significant components of many companies' distribution strategies.[9] Although direct-marketing channels are the simplest, they are not necessarily the most effective distribution method. Faced with the strategic choice of going directly to the customer or using intermediaries, a firm must evaluate the benefits to customers of going directly to the market versus the transaction costs involved in using intermediaries.[10]

Channel B, which moves goods from the producer to a retailer and then to customers, is a frequent choice of large retailers, for they can buy in quantity from manufacturers. Retailers like Kmart and Wal-Mart sell clothing, stereos, and many other items purchased directly from producers. New automobiles and new college textbooks are also sold through this type of marketing channel. Primarily nonstore retailers, such as L.L. Bean and J. Crew, also use this type of channel.

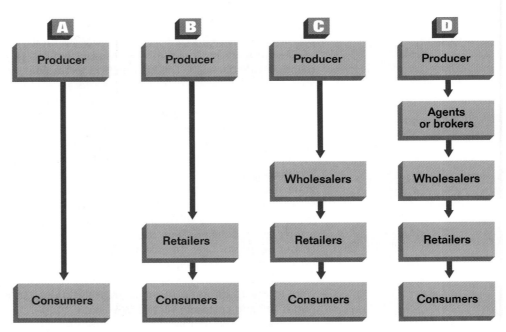

Figure 14.4
Typical Marketing Channels for Consumer Products

A long-standing distribution channel, especially for consumer products, Channel C takes goods from the producer to a wholesaler, then to a retailer, and finally to consumers. It is a practical option for producers that sell to hundreds of thousands of customers through thousands of retailers. A single producer finds it hard to do business directly with thousands of retailers. Consider the number of retailers marketing Wrigley's chewing gum. It would be extremely difficult, if not impossible, for Wrigley's to deal directly with each retailer that sells its brand of gum. Manufacturers of tobacco products, some home appliances, hardware, and many convenience goods sell their products to wholesalers, which then sell to retailers, which in turn do business with individual consumers.

Channel D—through which goods pass from producer to agents to wholesalers to retailers and then to consumers—is frequently used for products intended for mass distribution, such as processed foods. For example, to place its cracker line in specific retail outlets, a food processor may hire an agent (or a food broker) to sell the crackers to wholesalers. Wholesalers then sell the crackers to supermarkets, vending machine operators, and other retail outlets.

Contrary to popular opinion, then, for some consumer goods, a long channel may be the most efficient distribution channel. When several channel intermediaries perform specialized functions, costs may be lower than when one channel member tries to perform them all.

Channels for Business Products

Figure 14.5 shows four of the most common channels for business products. As with consumer products, manufacturers of business products sometimes work with more than one level of wholesalers.

Channel E illustrates the direct channel for business products. In contrast to consumer goods, more than half of all business products—especially expensive equipment—are sold through direct channels. Organizational buyers like to communicate directly with producers, especially when expensive or technically complex products are involved. For this reason, business buyers prefer to purchase expensive and highly complex mainframe computers directly from IBM, Cray, and other mainframe producers. Intel has established direct-marketing channels for selling its microprocessor chips to computer manufacturers.[11] In these circumstances, a customer wants the technical assistance and personal assurances that only a producer can provide. In

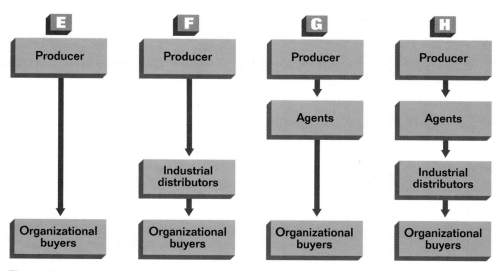

Figure 14.5
Typical Marketing Channels for Business Products

Figure 14.6 Ingersoll-Rand communicates directly with retailers about the benefits of its Dor-O-Matic doors.

industrial distributor
An independent business that takes title to business products and carries inventories

In the second organizational distribution channel (Channel F), an industrial distributor facilitates exchanges between the producer and customer. An **industrial distributor** is an independent business that takes title to products and carries inventories. Industrial distributors usually sell standardized items, such as maintenance supplies, production tools, and small operating equipment. Some industrial distributors carry a wide variety of product lines; others specialize in one or a small number of lines. Industrial distributors can be most effectively used when a product has broad market appeal, is easily stocked and serviced, is sold in small quantities, and is needed on demand to avoid high losses (as is a part for an assembly line machine).[12]

Industrial distributors offer sellers several advantages. They can perform the needed selling activities in local markets at relatively low cost to a manufacturer and reduce a producer's financial burden by providing customers with credit services. And because industrial distributors usually maintain close relationships with their customers, they are aware of local needs and can pass on market information to producers. By holding adequate inventories in their local markets, industrial distributors reduce the producers' capital requirements.

Using industrial distributors has several disadvantages, however. Industrial distributors may be difficult to control since they are independent firms. Because they often stock competing brands, a producer cannot depend on them to sell its brand aggressively. Furthermore, industrial distributors maintain inventories, for which they incur numerous expenses; consequently, they are less likely to handle bulky or slow-selling items or items that need specialized facilities or require extraordinary selling efforts. In some cases, industrial distributors lack the technical knowledge necessary to sell and service certain products.

The third organizational channel (Channel G) employs a manufacturers' agent, an independent businessperson who sells complementary products of several producers in assigned territories and is compensated through commissions. Unlike an industrial distributor, a manufacturers' agent does not acquire title to the products and usually does not take possession. Acting as a salesperson on behalf of the producers, a manufacturers' agent has little or no latitude in negotiating prices or sales terms.

Using manufacturers' agents can benefit an organizational marketer. These agents usually possess considerable technical and market information and have an established set of customers. For an organizational seller with highly seasonal demand, a manufacturers' agent can be an asset because the seller does not have to support a year-round sales force. That manufacturers' agents are paid on a commission basis may also be an economical alternative for a firm that has highly limited resources and cannot afford a full-time sales force.

Certainly, the use of manufacturers' agents is not problem-free. Even though straight commissions may be cheaper, the seller may have little control over manufacturers' agents. Because of the compensation method, manufacturers' agents generally want to concentrate on their larger accounts. They are often reluctant to spend time following up sales, to put forth special selling efforts, or to provide sellers with market information when such activities reduce the amount of productive selling time. Because they rarely maintain inventories, manufacturers' agents have a limited ability to provide customers with parts or repair services quickly.

Finally, Channel H includes both a manufacturers' agent and an industrial distributor. This channel may be appropriate when the producer wishes to cover a large geographic area but maintains no sales force because of highly seasonal demand or because the firm cannot afford a sales force. This type of channel can also be useful for an organizational marketer that wants to enter a new geographic market without expanding the firm's existing sales force.

Make sure they walk into your place. Not your doors.

Automatic doors should never be a pain. To you or your customers. Doors should work dependably day in day out so you never have to worry about them. That's the beauty of Dor-O-Matic doors for retail stores. They work right, they work safely, and they work a long time. And should there ever be a problem, we'll fix it fast and fix it right. If you want doors that help your customers rather than hinder them, call Dor-O-Matic.

INGERSOLL-RAND
ARCHITECTURAL HARDWARE

DOR-O-MATIC

Figure 14.6
Direct Industrial Channel
Ingersoll-Rand markets automatic sliding glass doors directly to retailers.

Figure 14.7
Using Multiple Marketing Channels
Coca-Cola distributes its products through fast-food restaurants, vending machines, supermarkets, and convenience stores.

Multiple Marketing Channels and Channel Alliances

To reach diverse target markets, manufacturers may use several marketing channels simultaneously, each channel involving a different group of intermediaries. For example, a manufacturer uses multiple channels when the same product is directed to both consumers and organizational customers. When Del Monte markets ketchup for household use, it is sold to supermarkets through grocery wholesalers or, in some cases, directly to retailers, whereas ketchup going to restaurants or institutions follows a different distribution channel. In some instances, a producer may prefer **dual distribution,** the use of two or more marketing channels for distributing the same products to the same target market. An example of dual distribution is a firm that sells products through retail outlets and its own mail-order catalog or Web site. Victoria's Secret, for instance, sells merchandise through both retail stores and catalogs. Gateway sells its computers through a toll-free number, a Web site, and company-owned retail outlets called Country Stores.[13] Coca-Cola (Figure 14.7) uses multiple channels—fountain sales, vending machines, supermarkets, and convenience stores—to distribute its soft drinks. Kellogg sells its cereals directly to large retail grocery chains and to food wholesalers that, in turn, sell them to retailers. Dual distribution can cause dissatisfaction among wholesalers and smaller retailers when they must compete with large retail grocery chains that make direct purchases from manufacturers like Kellogg. The practice of dual distribution recently has drawn considerable scrutiny from those who consider it anticompetitive.[14] The legal dimensions of dual distribution are discussed later in this chapter.

A **strategic channel alliance** exists when the products of one organization are distributed through the marketing channels of another organization. The products of the two firms are often similar with respect to target markets or uses, but they are not direct competitors. For example, a brand of bottled water might be distributed through a marketing channel for soft drinks, or a domestic cereal producer might form a strategic channel alliance with a European food processor. Alliances can provide benefits for both the organization that owns the marketing channel and the company whose brand is being distributed through the channel.

dual distribution   The use of two or more channels to distribute the same product to the same target market

strategic channel alliance   An agreement whereby the products of one organization are distributed through the marketing channels of another

Intensity of Market Coverage

In addition to deciding which marketing channels to use to distribute a product, marketers must determine the intensity of coverage a product should get—that is, the number and kinds of outlets in which it will be sold. This decision depends on the characteristics of the product and the target market. To achieve the desired intensity of market coverage, distribution must correspond to behavior patterns of buyers. Chapter 10 divided consumer products into three categories—convenience products, shopping products, and specialty products—according to how consumers make purchases. In considering products for purchase, consumers take into account replacement rate, product adjustment (services), duration of consumption, time required to find the product, and similar factors.[15] These variables directly affect the intensity of market coverage. Three major levels of market coverage are intensive, selective, and exclusive distribution.

Intensive Distribution

intensive distribution
Using all available outlets to distribute a product

In **intensive distribution,** all available outlets for distributing a product are used. Intensive distribution is appropriate for convenience products like bread, chewing gum, soft drinks, and newspapers. Convenience products have a high replacement rate and require almost no service. To meet these demands, intensive distribution is necessary, and multiple channels may be used to sell through all possible outlets. For example, soft drinks, snacks, laundry detergent, and aspirin are available at convenience stores, service stations, supermarkets, discount stores, and other types of retailers. To consumers, availability means that a store is located nearby and minimum time will be necessary to search for the product at the store. Sales may have a direct relationship to availability. The successful sale of such products as bread and milk at service stations or of gasoline at convenience grocery stores illustrates that availability of these products is more important than the nature of the outlet. Producers of consumer packaged items, such as Procter & Gamble, rely on intensive distribution for many of

BUILDING
customer relationships

Radio Shack Blankets the U.S.

More than one million Americans visit Radio Shack every day, and one of three households purchases products from Radio Shack each year. This may be due to the fact that 94 percent of all Americans live or work within a five-minute drive of one of the 6,800 company- or franchiser-owned Radio Shack stores across the U.S. Founded in 1921 as a mail-order company supplying ham radio operators and electronics enthusiasts, Radio Shack stores today offer about 3,500 products like electronic parts and accessories, telecommunications goods and services, direct-to-home satellite systems, and repair services for most major brands of consumer electronics. The company has built a reputation for being the place to go for advice on how to rewire a stereo or set up a satellite system, or to find an obscure battery for a TV remote.

With the objective to "demystify technology for all Americans," Radio Shack has adopted the promotion theme, "You've Got Questions. We've Got Answers." To fulfill this promise, Radio Shack offers a toll-free number to help customers locate Radio Shack stores and dealers and to access its Radio Shack Unlimited special order program that stocks more than 100,000 unique and hard-to-find personal electronics products, accessories, replacement parts, and components from many name-brand manufacturers. Radio Shack stores also sell and service Compaq computers, and they provide repair services for most major brands of consumer electronics and

computers, even if out of warranty. Although the repair services do not generate big profits for Radio Shack, they help build customer loyalty. The company has also helped local communities through its donation of 350,000 smoke detectors to Operation Firesafe, a community service project that collects smoke detectors for fire departments to install in the homes of low-income and elderly residents.

In recent years, Radio Shack has formed a number of joint marketing agreements with the likes of RCA and PRIMESTAR (to offer direct-to-home satellite TV solutions), ORCA Monitoring Services (to provide monitoring services for the wireless home security systems sold in Radio Shack stores), and Sprint. The agreement with Sprint puts a Sprint boutique that sells Sprint-branded telephones and Sprint wireless, Internet, and long-distance services in every Radio Shack store. The arrangement gives Sprint nationwide distribution, while Radio Shack gains revenue from Sprint and a strong national brand to supplement its own private label, Realistic.

Although Radio Shack already has intensive distribution across the United States, the company continues to look for ways to expand. It recently opened the first of 1,000 planned small displays in hardware, video, and office-supply stores in small towns across the country. These 500-square-foot displays will help Radio Shack extend its reach into nearly every community in the U.S. at relatively low cost.

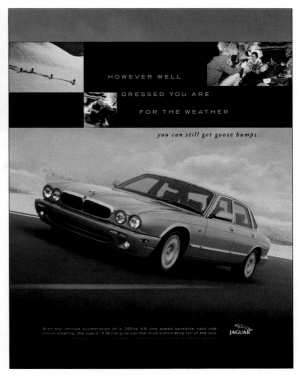

Figure 14.8
Intensive versus Exclusive Distribution
Crayola utilizes intensive distribution for its crayons (via supermarkets, drugstores, toy stores, and so on), in contrast with Jaguar, which utilizes exclusive distribution for its automobiles.

their products (for example, soaps, detergents, food and juice products, and personal care products) because consumers want availability provided quickly. Building Customer Relationships describes Radio Shack's intensive strategy for widely distributing electronics goods and services.

Selective Distribution

selective distribution
Using only some available outlets to distribute a product

In **selective distribution,** only some available outlets in an area are chosen to distribute a product. Selective distribution is appropriate for shopping products. Durable goods like television sets and stereos usually fall into this category. These products are more expensive than convenience goods, and consumers are willing to spend more time visiting several retail outlets to compare prices, designs, styles, and other features.

Selective distribution is desirable when a special effort—such as customer service from a channel member—is important. Shopping products require differentiation at the point of purchase. To motivate retailers to provide adequate presale service, selective distribution and company-owned stores are often used. Many business products are sold on a selective basis to maintain some control over the distribution process. For example, agricultural herbicides are distributed on a selective basis because dealers must offer services to buyers, such as instructions about how to apply herbicides safely or the option of having the dealer apply the herbicide. Evinrude outboard motors are also sold by dealers on a selective basis.

Exclusive Distribution

exclusive distribution
Using a single outlet in a fairly large geographic area to distribute a product

In **exclusive distribution,** only one outlet is used in a relatively large geographic area. Exclusive distribution is suitable for products purchased rather infrequently, consumed over a long period of time, or requiring service or information to fit them to buyers' needs. It is also used for expensive, high-quality products, such as Porsche automobiles. It is not appropriate for convenience products and many shopping products. Figure 14.8 contrasts an intensively distributed product, crayons, with an exclusively distributed product, Jaguar automobiles.

Exclusive distribution is often used as an incentive to sellers when only a limited market is available for products. For example, automobiles like the Bentley, made by

Rolls-Royce, are sold on an exclusive basis, and Patek Philippe watches, which may sell for $10,000 or more, are available in only a few select locations. Such exclusive distribution affords a company tighter image control because the types of distributors and retailers that distribute the product can be closely monitored.[16] A producer using exclusive distribution generally expects dealers to carry a complete inventory, send personnel for sales and service training, participate in promotional programs, and provide excellent customer service. Some products are appropriate for exclusive distribution when first introduced, but as competitors enter the market and the product moves through its life cycle, other types of market coverage and distribution channels often become necessary. A problem that can arise with exclusive distribution (and selective distribution) is that unauthorized resellers acquire and sell products, violating the agreement between a manufacturer and its exclusive authorized dealers. This has been a problem for Rolex, manufacturer of prestige watches.

Supply Chain Management

To fulfill the potential of effective supply chain management and to ensure customer satisfaction, marketing channels require leadership, cooperation, and management of channel conflict. They may also require consolidation of marketing channels through channel integration.

Channel Leadership, Cooperation, and Conflict

Each channel member performs a different role in the system and agrees (implicitly or explicitly) to accept certain rights, responsibilities, rewards, and sanctions for nonconformity. Moreover, each channel member holds certain expectations of other channel members. Retailers, for instance, expect wholesalers to maintain adequate inventories and to deliver goods on time. Wholesalers expect retailers to honor payment agreements and to keep them informed of inventory needs.

Channel partnerships facilitate effective supply chain management when partners agree on objectives, policies, and procedures for ordering and physical distribution of the supplier's products.[17] Such partnerships eliminate redundancies and reassign tasks for maximum systemwide efficiency. One of the best-known partnerships is the relationship between Wal-Mart and Procter & Gamble. Procter & Gamble locates some of its staff near Wal-Mart's purchasing department in Bentonville, Arkansas, to establish and maintain the supply chain. Sharing information through a cooperative computer system, Procter & Gamble monitors Wal-Mart's inventory and additional data to determine production and distribution plans for its products. The results are increased efficiency, decreased inventory costs, and greater satisfaction for the customers of both companies. Wal-Mart believes these efforts provide it with a significant competitive advantage.[18] At this point, most suppliers have not been willing or able to make this level of commitment. In this section, we discuss channel member behavior, including leadership, cooperation, and conflict, which marketers must understand in order to make effective channel decisions.

Channel Leadership   Many marketing channels are determined by consensus. Producers and intermediaries coordinate efforts for mutual benefit. Some marketing channels, however, are organized and controlled by a single leader, or **channel captain** (also called channel leader). The channel captain may be a producer, wholesaler, or retailer. Channel captains may establish channel policies and coordinate development of the marketing mix. Wal-Mart, for example, dominates the supply chain for its retail stores by virtue of the magnitude of its resources (especially information management) and strong, nationwide customer base. To become a captain, a channel member must want to influence overall channel performance. To attain desired objectives, the captain must possess **channel power,** the ability to influence another channel member's goal achievement. The member that becomes the channel

channel captain The dominant member of a marketing channel or supply chain

channel power The ability of one channel member to influence another member's goal achievement

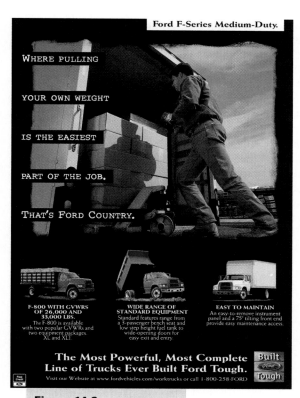

Figure 14.9
Channel Leadership
Ford provides channel leadership in the distribution of its medium-duty trucks

captain will accept the responsibilities and exercise the power associated with this role.[19] To strive for higher-quality products, for example, GM, in its role as channel captain, announced that it would select only suppliers that could provide the highest-quality parts at the lowest cost, including parts made by GM.[20] Ford maintains channel leadership with its line of medium-duty trucks (see Figure 14.9).

When a manufacturer's large-scale production efficiency demands increasing sales volume, the manufacturer may exercise power by giving channel members financing, business advice, ordering assistance, advertising, and support materials. After Rubbermaid increased product distribution from 60,000 to 100,000 outlets, it improved cooperative advertising plans and increased channel members' margins, both to motivate new channel members and to appease older channel members that now had to compete with more outlets carrying Rubbermaid products.[21]

As already noted, retailers may also function as channel captains and, with the rise of national chain stores and private brand merchandise, many, such as Wal-Mart, are doing so. Small retailers, too, may assume leadership roles when they gain strong customer loyalty in local or regional markets. These retailers control many brands and sometimes replace uncooperative producers. Increasingly, leading retailers are concentrating their buying power with fewer suppliers and, in the process, improving their market effectiveness and efficiency. Single-source supply relationships are often successful, whereas multiple-source supply relationships based on price competition are decreasing. Long-term commitments enable retailers to place smaller and more frequent orders as needed rather than waiting for large volume discounts or placing huge orders early in the season and assuming the risks associated with carrying an unsold inventory.[22]

Wholesalers assume channel leadership roles as well, although they were more powerful decades ago, when most manufacturers and retailers were small, underfinanced, and widely scattered. Today, wholesaler leaders may form voluntary chains with several retailers, which they supply with bulk buying or management services; these chains may also market their own brands. In return, the retailers shift most of their purchasing to the wholesaler leader. The Independent Grocers' Alliance (IGA) is one of the best-known wholesaler leaders in the United States. IGA's power is based on the expert advertising, pricing, and purchasing knowledge it makes available to independent business owners. Other wholesaler leaders help retailers with store layouts, accounting, and inventory control.

Channel Cooperation   Channel cooperation is vital if each member is to gain something from other members. By cooperating, retailers, wholesalers, and suppliers can speed up inventory replenishment, improve customer service, and cut the costs of bringing products to the consumer.[23] Without cooperation, neither overall channel goals nor member goals can be realized. All channel members must recognize and understand that the success of one firm in the channel depends, in part, on other firms in the channel. Thus, marketing channel members should take actions that provide a coordinated effort to satisfy market requirements. Channel cooperation leads to greater trust among channel members and improves the overall functioning of the channel.[24] It also leads to more satisfying relationships among channel members.[25]

There are several ways to improve channel cooperation. If a marketing channel is viewed as a unified supply chain competing with other systems, then individual members will be less likely to take actions that create disadvantages for other members. Similarly, channel members should agree to direct efforts toward common objectives so that channel roles can be structured for maximum marketing effectiveness, which in turn can help members achieve individual objectives. Heineken, for example, was having difficulty with its 450 distributors, with time between order and delivery reaching twelve weeks. A cooperative system of supply chain management, with

Internet-based communications, decreased the lead time from order to delivery to four weeks, and Heineken's sales increased 24 percent.[26] A critical component in cooperation is a precise definition of each channel member's tasks. This provides a basis for reviewing the intermediaries' performance and helps reduce conflicts because each channel member knows exactly what is expected of it.

Channel Conflict   Although all channel members work toward the same general goal—distributing products profitably and efficiently—members may sometimes disagree about the best methods for attaining this goal. However, if self-interest creates misunderstanding about role expectations, the end result is frustration and conflict for the whole channel. For individual organizations to function together, each channel member must clearly communicate and understand role expectations. Communication difficulties are a potential form of channel conflict because ineffective communication leads to frustration, misunderstandings, and ill-coordinated strategies, jeopardizing further coordination.

Channel conflicts also arise when intermediaries overemphasize competing products or diversify into product lines traditionally handled by other intermediaries. Sometimes conflict develops because producers strive to increase efficiency by circumventing intermediaries, as is happening in marketing channels for computer software. Many software-only stores are establishing direct relationships with software producers, bypassing wholesale distributors altogether. Some dishonest retailers pirate software or make unauthorized copies, thus cheating other channel members out of their due compensation. Produce companies sometimes promote directly to retailers, also bypassing wholesalers.

When a producer that traditionally used franchised dealers broadens its retailer base to include other types of retail outlets, considerable conflict can arise. Goodyear intensified its market coverage by allowing Sears and Discount Tire to market Goodyear tires. While this action significantly increased the company's sales revenues, it also greatly angered 2,500 independent Goodyear dealers.[27]

Although there is no single method for resolving conflict, partnerships can be reestablished if two conditions are met. First, the role of each channel member must be specified. To minimize misunderstanding, all members must be able to expect unambiguous, agreed-on performance levels from each other. Second, channel members must institute certain measures of channel coordination, which requires leadership and benevolent exercise of control.[28] To prevent channel conflict from arising, producers, or other channel members, may provide competing resellers with different brands, allocate markets among resellers, define policies for direct sales to avoid potential conflict over large accounts, negotiate territorial issues between regional distributors, and provide recognition to certain resellers for their importance in distributing to others. Hallmark, for example, distributes its Ambassador greeting-card line in discount stores and its name brand Hallmark line in upscale department stores and Hallmark stores, thus limiting the amount of competition between retailers that carry its products.[29]

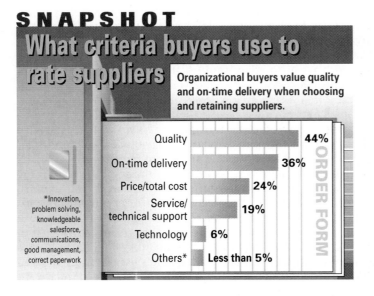

SNAPSHOT

What criteria buyers use to rate suppliers

Organizational buyers value quality and on-time delivery when choosing and retaining suppliers.

Quality	**44%**
On-time delivery	**36%**
Price/total cost	**24%**
Service/ technical support	**19%**
Technology	**6%**
Others*	**Less than 5%**

*Innovation, problem solving, knowledgeable salesforce, communications, good management, correct paperwork

ORDER FORM

Channel Integration

Channel functions may be transferred between intermediaries and to producers and even customers. Channel members can either combine and control most activities or pass them on to another channel member. However, the channel member cannot eliminate functions; unless buyers themselves perform the functions, they must pay for the labor and resources needed for the functions to be performed.

Various channel stages may be combined under the management of a channel captain either horizontally or vertically. Such integration may stabilize supply, reduce costs, and increase coordination of channel members.

vertical channel integration   Combining two or more stages of the marketing channel under one management

Vertical Channel Integration   **Vertical channel integration** combines two or more stages of the channel under one management. This may occur when one member of a marketing channel purchases the operations of another member or simply performs the functions of another member, eliminating the need for that intermediary, as a separate entity. For example, Warner Brothers, the television and movie production unit of Time Warner, Inc., sells such items as cookie jars, puzzles, photo albums, and stuffed animals featuring its popular cartoon characters directly through its own retail outlets. Warner has also created distribution systems to get its cartoon characters, like Pinky and the Brain and Sylvester and Tweety, directly to the public. Previously broadcasting many of its children's cartoon programs over the Fox network, Warner now runs these shows on its own WB network.[30]

Whereas members of conventional channel systems work independently, participants in vertical channel integration coordinate efforts to reach a desired target market. In this more progressive approach to distribution, channel members regard other members as extensions of their own operations. Vertically integrated channels are often more effective against competition because of increased bargaining power, the ability to inhibit competitors, and the sharing of information and responsibilities.[31] At one end of a vertically integrated channel, a manufacturer might provide advertising and training assistance, and the retailer at the other end would buy the manufacturer's products in large quantities and actively promote them.

vertical marketing systems (vmss)   Marketing channels managed by a single channel member

Integration has been successfully institutionalized in marketing channels called **vertical marketing systems (VMSs),** in which a single channel member coordinates or manages channel activities to achieve efficient, low-cost distribution aimed at satisfying target market customers. Vertical integration brings most or all stages of the marketing channel under common control or ownership. The Limited, a retail clothing chain, uses a wholly owned subsidiary, Mast Industries, as its primary supply source. Such marketing channel partnerships strive for some of the efficiencies of a VMS but without common ownership.[32] Radio Shack operates as a vertical marketing system, encompassing both wholesale and retail functions. Because efforts of individual channel members are combined in a VMS, marketing activities can be coordinated for maximum effectiveness and economy, without duplication of services. Vertical marketing systems are competitive, accounting for a share of retail sales in consumer goods.

Most vertical marketing systems take one of three forms: corporate, administered, or contractual. A *corporate VMS* combines all stages of the marketing channel, from producers to consumers, under a single owner. For example, The Limited established a corporate VMS that operates corporate-owned production facilities and retail stores. Supermarket chains that own food-processing plants, as well as large retailers that purchase wholesaling and production facilities, are other examples of corporate VMSs.

In an *administered VMS,* channel members are independent, but a high level of interorganizational management is achieved by informal coordination. Members of an administered VMS may, for example, adopt uniform accounting and ordering procedures and cooperate in promotional activities for the benefit of all partners. Although individual channel members maintain autonomy, as in conventional marketing channels, one channel member (such as a producer or large retailer) dominates the administered VMS, so that distribution decisions take into account the whole system. Because of its size and power, Intel exercises a strong influence over distributors and manufacturers in its marketing channels, as do Kellogg (cereal) and Magnavox (television and other electronic products).

Under a *contractual VMS,* the most popular type of vertical marketing system, channel members are linked by legal agreements spelling out each member's rights and obligations. Franchise organizations, such as McDonald's and KFC, are contractual VMSs. Other contractual VMSs include wholesaler-sponsored groups, such as IGA (Independent Grocers' Alliance) stores, in which independent retailers band together under the contractual leadership of a wholesaler. Retailer-sponsored cooperatives, which own and operate their own wholesalers, are a third type of contractual VMS.

**horizontal channel
integration** Combining
organizations at the same
level of operation under one
management

Horizontal Channel Integration   Combining organizations at the same level of operation under one management constitutes **horizontal channel integration.** An organization may integrate horizontally by merging with other organizations at the same level in a marketing channel. The owner of a dry cleaning firm might buy and combine several other existing dry cleaning establishments. Horizontal integration may enable a firm to generate sufficient sales revenue to integrate vertically as well.

Although horizontal integration permits efficiencies and economies of scale in purchasing, marketing research, advertising, and specialized personnel, it is not always the most effective method of improving distribution. Problems of size often follow, resulting in decreased flexibility, difficulties in coordination, and the need for additional marketing research and large-scale planning. Unless distribution functions for the various units can be performed more efficiently under unified management than under the previously separate managements, horizontal integration will neither reduce costs nor improve the competitive position of the integrating firm.

Legal Issues in Channel Management

The multitude of federal, state, and local laws governing channel management are based on the general principle that the public is best served by protecting competition and free trade. Under the authority of such federal legislation as the Sherman Antitrust Act and the Federal Trade Commission Act, courts and regulatory agencies determine under what circumstances channel management practices violate this underlying principle and must be restricted. Although channel managers are not expected to be legal experts, they should be aware that attempts to control distribution functions may have legal repercussions. The following practices are among those frequently subject to legal restraint.

Dual Distribution

Earlier, we said that some companies may use dual distribution by utilizing two or more marketing channels to distribute the same products to the same target market. Compaq, for example, sells computers directly to consumers through a toll-free telephone line and a Web site, as well as through electronics retailers, such as Best Buy. Courts do not consider this practice illegal when it promotes competition. A manufacturer can also legally open its own retail outlets. But the courts view as a threat to competition a manufacturer that uses company-owned outlets to dominate or drive out of business independent retailers or distributors that handle its products. In such cases, dual distribution violates the law. To avoid this interpretation, producers should use outlet prices that do not severely undercut independent retailers' prices.

Restricted Sales Territories

To tighten control over distribution of its products, a manufacturer may try to prohibit intermediaries from selling its products outside designated sales territories. Intermediaries themselves often favor this practice because it gives them exclusive territories, allowing them to avoid competition for the producer's brands within these territories. In recent years, the courts have adopted conflicting positions in regard to restricted sales territories. Although the courts have deemed restricted sales territories a restraint of trade among intermediaries handling the same brands (except for small or newly established companies), they have also held that exclusive territories can actually promote competition between dealers handling different brands. At present, the producer's intent in establishing restricted territories and the overall effect of doing so on the market must be evaluated for each case individually.

Tying Agreements

tying agreement An agreement requiring a channel member to buy other products from a supplier besides the one it wants

When a supplier (usually a manufacturer or franchiser) furnishes a product to a channel member with the stipulation that the channel member must purchase other products as well, a **tying agreement** exists.[33] Suppliers may institute tying arrangements to move weaker products along with more popular items, or a franchiser may tie purchase of equipment and supplies to the sale of franchises, justifying the policy as necessary for quality control and protection of the franchiser's reputation.

A related practice is *full-line forcing,* in which a supplier requires that channel members purchase the supplier's entire line to obtain any of the supplier's products. Manufacturers sometimes use full-line forcing to ensure that intermediaries accept new products and that a suitable range of products is available to customers.

The courts accept tying agreements when the supplier alone can provide products of a certain quality, when the intermediary is free to carry competing products as well, and when a company has just entered the market. Most other tying agreements are considered illegal.

Exclusive Dealing

exclusive dealing
Forbidding an intermediary to carry products of a competing manufacturer

When a manufacturer forbids an intermediary to carry products of competing manufacturers, the arrangement is called **exclusive dealing.** Manufacturers receive considerable market protection in an exclusive dealing arrangement and may cut off shipments to intermediaries who violate the agreement.

The legality of an exclusive dealing contract is generally determined by applying three tests. If the exclusive dealing blocks competitors from as much as 10 percent of the market, if the sales revenue involved is sizable, and if the manufacturer is much larger (and thus more intimidating) than the dealer, the arrangement is considered anticompetitive.[34] If dealers and customers in a given market have access to similar products or if the exclusive dealing contract strengthens an otherwise weak competitor, the arrangement is allowed.

Refusal to Deal

For over seventy years, courts have held that producers have the right to choose channel members with which they will do business (and the right to reject others). Within existing distribution channels, however, suppliers may not legally refuse to deal with wholesalers or dealers just because these wholesalers or dealers resist policies that are anticompetitive or in restraint of trade. Suppliers are further prohibited from organizing some channel members in refusal-to-deal actions against other members that choose not to comply with illegal policies.[35]

Summary

A marketing channel, or channel of distribution, is a group of individuals and organizations that directs the flow of products from producers to customers. The major role of marketing channels is to make products available at the right time at the right place in the right amounts. In most channels of distribution, producers and consumers are linked by marketing intermediaries, or middlemen. Of the two major types of intermediaries, retailers purchase products and resell them to ultimate consumers, and wholesalers buy and resell products to other wholesalers, retailers, and organizational customers.

Marketing channels serve many functions. They create time, place, and possession utility by making products available when and where customers want them and providing customers with access to product use through sale or rental. Marketing intermediaries facilitate exchange efficiencies, often reducing the costs of exchanges by performing certain services and functions. Although critics suggest eliminating wholesalers, their functions must be performed by someone in the marketing channel. Because intermediaries serve both producers and buyers, they reduce the total number of transactions that would otherwise be needed to move products from producer to ultimate users.

Marketing channels also form a supply chain, a total distribution system that serves customers and creates a competitive advantage. Supply chain management refers to long-term partnerships among channel members working together to reduce inefficiencies, costs, and redundancies, and to develop innovative approaches in order to satisfy customers. The supply chain includes all entities—shippers and other firms that facilitate distribution, as well as producers, wholesalers, and retailers—that distribute products and benefit from cooperative efforts. Supply chains start with the customer and require the cooperation of channel members to satisfy customer requirements.

Channels of distribution are broadly classified as channels for consumer products and channels for business products. Within these two broad categories, different marketing channels are used for different products. Although consumer goods can move directly from producer to consumers, consumer product channels that include wholesalers and retailers are usually more economical and efficient. Distribution of business products differs from that of consumer products in the types of channels used. A direct distribution channel is common in organizational marketing. Also used are channels containing industrial distributors, manufacturers' agents, and both agents and distributors. Most producers have multiple or dual channels so that the distribution system can be adjusted for various target markets.

A marketing channel is managed so that products receive appropriate market coverage. In choosing intensive distribution, producers strive to make a product available to all possible dealers. In selective distribution, only some outlets in an area are chosen to distribute a product. Exclusive distribution usually gives one dealer exclusive rights to sell a product in a large geographic area.

Each channel member performs a different role in the system and agrees to accept certain rights, responsibilities, rewards, and sanctions for nonconformance. Although many marketing channels are determined by consensus, some are organized and controlled by a single leader, or channel captain. A channel captain may be a producer, wholesaler, or retailer. Channels function most effectively when members cooperate, but when they deviate from their roles, channel conflict can arise.

Integration of marketing channels brings various activities under one channel member's management. Vertical integration combines two or more stages of the channel under one management. The vertical marketing system (VMS) is managed centrally for the mutual benefit of all channel members. Vertical marketing systems may be corporate, administered, or contractual. Horizontal integration combines institutions at the same level of channel operation under a single management.

Federal, state, and local laws regulate channel management to protect competition and free trade. Courts may prohibit or permit a practice depending on whether it violates this underlying principle. Various procompetitive legislation applies to distribution practices. Channel management practices frequently subject to legal restraint include dual distribution, restricted sales territories, tying agreements, exclusive dealing, and refusal to deal. When these practices strengthen weak competitors or increase competition among dealers, they may be permitted; in most other cases, when competition may be weakened considerably, they are deemed illegal.

Important Terms

Distribution	Dual distribution	Channel captain	Horizontal channel
Marketing channel	Strategic channel alliance	Channel power	integration
Marketing intermediary	Intensive distribution	Vertical channel integration	Tying agreement
Supply chain management	Selective distribution	Vertical marketing systems	Exclusive dealing
Industrial distributor	Exclusive distribution	(VMSs)	

Discussion and Review Questions

1. Describe the major functions of marketing channels. Why are these functions better accomplished through combined efforts of channel members?

2. Can one channel member perform all the channel functions?

3. "Shorter channels are usually a more direct means of distribution and therefore are more efficient." Comment on this statement.

4. Why do consumers often blame intermediaries for distribution inefficiencies? List several reasons.

5. Compare and contrast the four major types of marketing channels for consumer products. Through which type of channel is each of the following products most likely to be distributed?

   a. new automobiles
   b. saltine crackers
   c. cut-your-own Christmas trees
   d. new textbooks
   e. sofas
   f. soft drinks

6. Outline the four most common channels for business products. Describe the products or situations that lead marketers to choose each channel.

7. Describe an industrial distributor. What types of products are marketed through an industrial distributor?

8. Under what conditions is a producer most likely to use more than one marketing channel?

9. Explain the differences between intensive, selective, and exclusive methods of distribution.

10. "Channel cooperation requires that members support the overall channel goals to achieve individual goals." Comment on this statement.

11. Name and describe firms that use (a) vertical integration and (b) horizontal integration in their marketing channels.

12. Explain the major characteristics of each of the three types of vertical marketing systems (VMSs)—corporate, administered, and contractual.

13. Under what conditions are tying agreements, exclusive dealing, and dual distribution judged illegal?

Application Questions

1. Supply chain management refers to long-term partnerships among channel members working together to reduce inefficiencies, costs, and redundancies, and to develop innovative approaches, in order to satisfy customers. Select one of the following companies and explain how supply chain management could increase marketing productivity.
   a. Dell Computer
   b. Federal Express
   c. Nike
   d. Taco Bell

2. Organizations often form strategic channel alliances when they find it more profitable or convenient to distribute their products through the marketing channel of another organization. Find an article in a newspaper or library that describes such a strategic channel alliance. Briefly summarize the article and indicate the benefits each organization expects to gain.

3. There are three major levels of market coverage from which to select when determining the number and kinds of outlets in which a product will be sold: intensive, selective, and exclusive. Characteristics of the product and its target market determine the intensity of coverage a product should receive. Indicate the intensity level best suited for the following products and explain why it is appropriate.
   a. personal computer
   b. deodorant
   c. collector baseball autographed by Mark McGwire
   d. Windows 98 computer software

4. Describe the decision process you might go through if you were attempting to determine the most appropriate distribution channel for one of the following:
   a. shotguns for hunters
   b. women's lingerie
   c. telephone systems for small businesses
   d. toy trucks for 2-year-olds

Internet Exercise & Resources

Amazon.com

At Amazon.com's Web site, people around the world who want to buy books can spend hours viewing an electronic library of millions of titles, reading other customers' online reviews, and ordering. When you select a book, the site shows you related titles, and it will also E-mail you recommendations based on your interests and favorite authors. Peruse Amazon.com's shelves at

www.amazon.com

1. What type of marketing channel is Amazon.com using?

2. Evaluate the Web site's graphics and descriptions of books. How does this information compare to the information one could gather by visiting a bookstore or reviewing a mail-order catalog?

3. It takes Amazon.com a week to deliver a book that isn't a best seller. Assess how well this distribution strategy works for Amazon.com's target market.

E-Center Resources

Visit http://www.prideferrell.com to find several resources to help you succeed in mastering the material in this chapter, plus additional materials that will help you expand your marketing knowledge. The Web site includes

 Internet exercise updates plus additional exercises

✔ ACE self-tests

abc Chapter summary with hotlinked glossary

↻ Hotlinks to companies featured in this chapter

✱ Resource Center

▢ Career Center

▤ Marketing plan worksheets

VIDEO CASE 14.1

CUTCO Cutlery: Differentiation via Direct Sales

The fastest growing segment of the $240 million cutlery industry is in high-quality, relatively high-priced knives and accessories used primarily in cooking or kitchen applications. Typically, high-quality knives from manufacturers such as Henckels, Wusthof, Sabatier/Cuisine de France, and Chicago Cutlery can be purchased in fine department stores or in cutlery shops specializing in such goods. CUTCO Cutlery has used a different marketing channel to develop a successful marketing strategy. The Alcas Corporation, manufacturer of CUTCO knives, has succeeded in differentiating its products from others in the upscale end of the cutlery industry by employing a unique method of sales and distribution—direct selling—used most notably by encyclopedia marketers, vacuum cleaner manufacturers, and cosmetic firms such as Avon and Mary Kay, as well as by Amway, a marketer of household products.

The Alcas Corporation has manufactured and marketed CUTCO Cutlery since 1949. As a result of several corporate restructurings, Alcas now exists essentially as a holding company composed of two wholly owned operating subsidiaries: (1) the CUTCO Cutlery Corporation, manufacturer of CUTCO Cutlery, and (2) the Vector Marketing Corporation, a direct and exclusive sales agent for CUTCO products in North America. Alcas has experienced consistent growth over the last ten years, with annual sales expanding by an average of 22 percent since 1985. Sales in 1998 topped $80 million.

The CUTCO product line consists of a wide variety of kitchen (food preparation and table) cutlery, hunting, fishing, and utility pocket knives, as well as related accessories like wood chopping blocks. The CUTCO product line comprises over fifty individual items, most ranging in price from $30 to $80, which are often

sold in sets and gift packs priced from $160 to $680. Pricing is consistent with that of other high-quality cutlery products such as those made by Henckels and Wusthof. CUTCO Cutlery products are promoted as "CUTCO—The World's Finest Cutlery" and are sold on the basis of quality and performance tests against competitive products and a lifetime guarantee.

Unlike its competitors, who sell and distribute their cutlery through fine department stores and specialty shops, CUTCO, via its Vector Marketing sales subsidiary, engages in direct selling through one-to-one in-home demonstrations. The CUTCO sales force is made up primarily of college students recruited during summer vacation months. Vector Marketing recruits more than 35,000 salespeople, between 85 and 90 percent of them college students. The recruiting, training, and ongoing counseling of salespeople, all of whom work as independent contractors, is done in decentralized fashion, utilizing approximately 165 district sales and distribution managers located strategically in communities across the United States and Canada. During its peak summer months, Vector also opens up an additional 200 temporary "branch offices" staffed by college students with prior selling and management experience.

One reason for the effectiveness of CUTCO's direct sales and distribution approach is that the high price of its products necessitates that potential buyers see them in use before committing to purchase. CUTCO's competitors usually address this issue by using in-store sales specialists or interactive video demonstrations.

One-to-one in-home or workplace selling is the most popular form of direct selling. Between 1987 and 1997, the number of persons involved in direct selling increased from 3.6 million to over 9 million, with the total volume of sales made rising from $8.8 billion to over 22 billion. However, some experts have criticized direct sales and distribution as being limited in today's increasingly competitive and high-tech business environment. Specifically, they suggest that direct sellers expand the number of channels through which their products are offered. As evidence, they cite the problems faced by Encyclopedia Britannica Corporation. The 225-year-old company, analysts contend, lost market share and profits to competitors not only because it failed to offer its encyclopedias in a much less costly CD-ROM format, but also because it continued to market its products exclusively through its direct sales network. These analysts suggested that Encyclopedia Britannica would have been well advised to diversify its sales and distribution approach, as had competitors, by marketing its products through retail outlets, direct mail, telemarketing, and online computer marketing.

In the face of stagnant growth in the early 1990s CUTCO did indeed experience problems trying to expand its operations exclusively through direct selling. In 1993, Vector Marketing was cited by the Wisconsin State Department of Agriculture, Trade, and Consumer Protection for overly aggressive salesperson recruitment. As a result, Vector was ordered to disclose in more exacting detail to its young recruits the nature of positions offered. The dispute centered around three issues: (1) some recruits were led to believe that they would be working for Vector when in fact they were to work as independent sales contractors, (2) the company failed to tell potential recruits that they "would be strongly urged" to purchase a $200 sales kit, and (3) Vector did not inform recruits that they would not be paid until a minimum number of sales demonstrations had been made.

As a result of these problems, Vector might consider exploring other means of product sales and distribution to supplement its current direct approach.

One promising alternative is marketing its products directly to potential buyers online. Not only would such an approach allow the all-important demonstration of CUTCO products, but it would also facilitate customer convenience (as opposed to the sometimes intrusive in-home sales call), instant order transmission, and greater marketer efficiency (by reducing sales and commissions costs).

In 1990, Alcas established Vector Canada as a distinct international marketing entity utilizing the direct sales and distribution approach used in its domestic operations. Vector Canada has been a highly successful venture. The company expanded into Korea in 1992, and into Australia, Germany, and Costa Rica in 1996 and 1997. The decision to enter Korea was made partly on the basis of the availability of U.S.-trained, Korean-born managers. Alcas's direct sales and distribution approach proved not to be as effective in Korea as it was in Canada, with the company experiencing losses in 1992, 1993, 1994, and 1995 totaling $2.5 million. As a result, in February 1995, Vector Korea supplemented direct selling by hiring Korean housewives as the recruiting base for a "party plan" approach most notably used by marketers of Tupperware home products. This tactic has proven very successful; the party plan approach accounted for 65 percent of Korean sales in 1995. Vector Korea plans to move exclusively to the party plan sales and distribution approach in 1996.[36]

Questions for Discussion

1. Discuss the strengths and weaknesses associated with Alcas's direct selling approach to the sales and distribution of CUTCO Cutlery.
2. Is the marketing channel traditionally employed for CUTCO products vertically or horizontally integrated?
3. Discuss the level and nature of channel power now held by Alcas. What would be the impact on the firm's power of diversifying to include online marketing?

CASE 14.2

New Distribution Channels for Automobiles

If the idea of buying a used car makes you think of overbearing salespeople pitching dishonest praise about rundown jalopies, you are certainly not alone. In the opinion of one major auto industry executive, "If you look into all of the buying processes in this country, the used-car-buying process image ranks close to the bottom." However, sticker shock over prices of new cars has driven many consumers to used-car lots. Moreover, because of the popularity of short-term leases, more two- and three-year-old, low-mileage cars

and trucks are on the market than ever before. Americans are buying about 35 million used cars and trucks each year, compared with about 15 million new ones. Customer dissatisfaction with the car-shopping process has created a market opportunity for savvy firms to develop new channels for marketing cars.

Circuit City Stores, Inc., which operates electronics superstores throughout the nation, has applied its expertise in customer service, logistics, sales of high-dollar merchandise, and financing to the development of a chain called CarMax Auto Superstores. It has already opened twenty-five dealerships in seven states, primarily in the Mid-Atlantic and Southeast, and has plans to open ten stores in Los Angeles in 2000. At these superstores, customers can use touch-screen computer terminals to browse through an electronic car lot of hundreds of used cars and trucks. CarMax focuses on reconditioned cars under six years old that have less than 60,000 miles. They come with a five-day money-back guarantee and a thirty-day warranty; longer warranties are available at extra cost. CarMax tries to ease the stressful car-buying experience in several ways. Vehicle prices are fixed, so negotiating is eliminated. Salespeople earn salaries instead of commissions, so they provide assistance and advice rather than high-pressure sales tactics. Customer-friendly amenities like nanny-supervised child-care areas and coffee bars help alleviate shoppers' anxiety. Circuit City's ideas for selling used cars seem to be working well. CarMax sold $874 million worth of vehicles in 1998, up 71 percent from the year before.

Potential competitors have taken note. H. Wayne Huizenga, the entrepreneur who built Blockbuster Entertainment, created Republic Industries, Inc., to operate a chain of twenty-five used-car superstores, as well as new-car dealerships. Known as AutoNation, the chain offers one-price, no-haggle shopping, but with extensive warranty and return policies. Its salespersons are paid on commission, based on volume and customer satisfaction. In addition, several large U.S. franchise car dealers have joined forces to create Driver's Mart, a chain of one hundred used-car superstores that will be built across the nation over the next five years.

Auto industry executives have also taken note of CarMax's success. To compete, GM has responded by offering more extensive used-car warranties. Richard E. Colliver, senior vice president of American Honda Motor Company, believes CarMax and similar superstores will persuade traditional car dealers to focus more on serving used-car customers. Chrysler even gave CarMax a franchise in Norcross, Georgia, to sell new Chryslers and Jeeps. Chrysler sales vice president E. Thomas Pappert says, "It is our plan to observe the CarMax process to determine what application, if any, these policies might have in the new-car sales process."

The success of used-car superstores and the interest of automobile manufacturers' in their techniques have many new-car dealers worried, perhaps with good reason. J.D. Power & Associates, which annually ranks car-buyer satisfaction, believes that within ten years, auto manufacturers may begin to bypass the traditional franchise dealer system by opening factory outlets and creating other distribution channels through national retailers like Sears and Wal-Mart. Other industry observers foresee automotive supermarkets where shoppers will be able to compare new Hondas, Toyotas, Fords, and Chevrolets, much as they now compare televisions and stereos at Circuit City. United Auto, a franchise chain, already permits consumers to shop for twenty-two brands of new cars from 8:00 AM to midnight. It also offers its customers full-service cafeterias, playgrounds, and plush waiting rooms.

In recent years, the Internet has provided another channel for marketing cars. According to J.D. Powers & Associates, 16 percent of new-car buyers have used the Internet for comparison shopping, and 4 percent have tried an online car-buying service. In fact, experts estimate that 2 percent of 1998 new-car sales resulted from purchase requests through services like Autobytel.com. Autobytel, which runs a free referral service with a network of 2,700 dealers through the World Wide Web, is responsible for about $500 million worth of car sales a month. At its Web site, shoppers complete online request forms, which are then forwarded to one of Autobytel's affiliated dealerships; the company responds to the customer with a quote, usually within twenty-four hours. Autoweb.com and Microsoft's CarPoint offer similar services. Chrysler and GM are experimenting with Web sites that connect online shoppers to dealers in some regions; both have plans to take their programs nationwide. The automakers' online services allow car shoppers to specify a desired model, search for the nearest dealer that has a vehicle matching their specifications, request a quote, and even arrange a test drive and financing.

The success of these new channels of distribution carries a message to new-car dealers: change or die. Pushed by auto manufacturers, many dealers are experimenting with new selling approaches, such as computerized displays, no-haggle pricing, greater selection, and customer-friendly amenities. Several dealers have established their own presence on the Internet. Whether or not these experiments succeed, customers will be the big winners, with more choices in how they shop for both new and used vehicles.[37]

Questions for Discussion

1. Why does CarMax represent a "new" marketing channel for automobiles?
2. How does a new-car franchise dealer's marketing channel differ from the "new" marketing channels?
3. What would happen if auto manufacturers bypassed their traditional dealer system and used multiple channels (e.g., Sears, Wal-Mart, and the Internet) to distribute cars?

Wholesaling and Physical Distribution

OBJECTIVES

- To understand the nature of wholesaling in the marketing channel

- To learn about wholesalers' functions

- To understand how wholesalers are classified

- To be able to recognize how physical distribution activities are integrated into marketing channels and overall marketing strategies

- To examine the major physical distribution functions of order processing, inventory management, materials handling, warehousing, and transportation

- To discuss the strategic implications of physical distribution systems

FedEx, an Important Partner in Supply Chains

In 1973, Frederick W. Smith turned his idea for an overnight package delivery service into reality. That idea has grown into the world's largest express transportation company, FedEx, a subsidiary of FDX Corporation, based in Memphis, Tennessee. FedEx delivers about 3 million packages to 200 countries every working day, generating revenues of more than $13 billion for the global firm. To ensure that all those packages reach their destinations safely and on time, FedEx employs 145,000 people, operates a fleet of 524 aircraft and 42,4500 vehicles, and runs 1,400 service centers and 34,000 drop boxes around the world.

Few customers realize what their packages go through once they are left in a drop box or at a shipping center. Most packages are flown overnight from one of 366 airports worldwide to FedEx's primary distribution hub at the Memphis International Airport. Every night, millions of packages converge from all over the country and pass through a sorting corral, which can handle up to 175,000 packages an hour. Each package must be turned label-side up so that its label can be scanned electronically and routed onto the correct conveyer belt to be dispatched to an aircraft waiting to take it to its ultimate destination. FedEx's Memphis super hub maintains 12,000 employees; 400 more employees from the company's headquarters may pitch in to help during busy holiday seasons. FedEx also

operates hubs in Hong Kong, Toronto, Brussels, and Miami to process many packages destined for overseas.

Thanks to FedEx (known fondly in Memphis as "Big Bear") and other freight companies—including UPS, Emery, Airborne, and the U.S. Postal Service—the Memphis International Airport ranks number one in the world for cargo and mail handling. According to airport officials, the amount of cargo processed through the airport is equivalent to lifting and moving the Empire State Building five times a year. Geography, time zones, climate, and a convergence of transportation modes make Memphis a perfect site for freight and cargo handling hubs like that operated by FedEx. In addition to the barge traffic from the Mississippi River, Memphis is served by six long-haul railroads and 200 long-haul trucking companies that operate out of 163 terminals within a two-daysdrive of 45 states.

With its efficient and strategically located Super Hub in Memphis, FedEx has truly revolutionized the shipping industry. To satisfy today's ever more time-sensitive consumers and business customers, many companies have come to depend on the overnight package delivery service pioneered by FedEx as an important component of their distribution strategies. As such FedEx, has become an important partner in many supply chains, especially "when it absolutely positively has to be there overnight."[1]

Companies like FedEx facilitate the marketing channels that provide the structure for making products available to customers when and where they want them. Supply chain management provides the coordination and strategic direction to reduce inefficiencies in the marketing channel, optimizing customer service. Physical distribution is a crucial function in supply chain management because it includes those activities associated with handling and moving products through the marketing channel. Wholesalers often play a key role in supply chain management, although manufacturers and retailers can perform wholesaling activities, too.

This chapter explores the role of wholesaling and physical distribution in supply chain management. First, we examine the importance of wholesalers in marketing channels, including their functions and classifications. Next, we consider critical physical distribution concepts, including order processing, inventory management, materials handling, warehousing, and transportation.

The Nature of Wholesaling

wholesaling Transactions in which products are bought for resale, for making other products, or for general business operations

wholesaler An individual or organization that facilitates and expedites wholesale transactions

Wholesaling refers to all transactions in which products are bought for resale, for making other products, or for general business operations. It does not include exchanges with ultimate consumers. A **wholesaler** is an individual or organization that facilitates and expedites exchanges that are primarily wholesale transactions. In other words, wholesalers buy products and resell them to reseller, government, and institutional users. For example, SYSCO, the nation's number-one food-service distributor, supplies restaurants, hotels, schools, industrial caterers, and hospitals with everything from frozen and fresh food and paper products to medical and cleaning supplies. There are approximately 512,000 wholesaling establishments in the United States,[2] and more than half of all products sold in the country pass through these firms.

Table 15.1 lists the major activities wholesalers perform, but individual wholesalers may perform more or fewer functions than the table shows. Distribution of all

Table 15.1	Major Wholesaling Functions
Supply Chain Management	Creating long-term partnerships among channel members
Promotion	Providing a sales force, advertising, sales promotion, and publicity
Warehousing, Shipping, and Product Handling	Receiving, storing, and stockkeeping Packaging Shipping outgoing orders Materials handling Arranging and making local and long distance shipments
Inventory Control and Data Processing	Processing orders Controlling physical inventory Recording transactions Tracking sales data for financial analysis
Risk Taking	Assuming responsibility for theft, product obsolescence, and excess inventories
Financing and Budgeting	Extending credit Borrowing Making capital investments Forecasting cash flow
Marketing Research and Information Systems	Providing information about markets Conducting research studies Managing computer networks to facilitate exchanges and relationships

SNAPSHOT

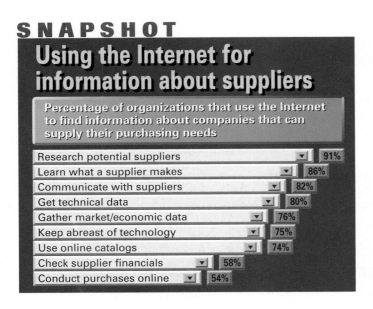

Using the Internet for information about suppliers

Percentage of organizations that use the Internet to find information about companies that can supply their purchasing needs

Research potential suppliers	91%
Learn what a supplier makes	86%
Communicate with suppliers	82%
Get technical data	80%
Gather market/economic data	76%
Keep abreast of technology	75%
Use online catalogs	74%
Check supplier financials	58%
Conduct purchases online	54%

goods requires wholesaling activities, whether a wholesaling firm is involved or not. Wholesaling activities are not limited to goods; service companies, such as financial institutions, also use active wholesale networks. For example, some banks buy loans in bulk from other financial institutions as well as making loans to their own retail customers.

Wholesalers perform services for other organizations in the marketing channel. They bear the primary responsibility for the physical distribution of products from manufacturers to retailers. In addition, they may establish information systems that help producers and retailers better manage the supply chain from producer to customer. For example, E3 Corporation (Figure 15.1) provides purchasing and inventory management services to wholesalers. Many wholesalers are using information technology and the Internet to allow their employees, customers, and suppliers to share information between intermediaries and facilitating agencies, such as trucking companies and warehouse firms. For example, FedEx, which serves as a facilitating agency in providing overnight or even same-day delivery of packages, provides online tracking of packages for the benefit of its customers. Other firms are making their databases and marketing information systems available to their supply chain partners to facilitate order processing, shipping, and product development, and to share information about changing market conditions and customer desires. This results in some wholesalers playing a key role in supply chain management decisions.

Services Provided by Wholesalers

Wholesalers provide essential services to both producers and retailers. By initiating sales contacts with a producer and by selling diverse products to retailers, wholesalers serve as an extension of the producer's sales force. Wholesalers also provide financial assistance. They often pay for transporting goods; they reduce a producer's warehousing expenses and inventory investment by holding goods in inventory; they extend credit and assume losses from buyers who turn out to be poor credit risks; and when they buy a producer's entire output and pay promptly or in cash, they are a source of working capital. Wholesalers also serve as conduits for information within the marketing channel, keeping producers up-to-date on market developments and passing along the manufacturers' promotional plans to other intermediaries. Using wholesalers therefore gives producers a distinct advantage because the specialized services performed by wholesalers allow producers to concentrate on developing and manufacturing products that match customers' needs and wants.

Many producers would prefer more direct interaction with retailers. Wholesalers, however, are more likely to have closer contact with retailers because of their strategic position in the marketing channel. Although a producer's own sales force is probably more effective at selling, the costs of maintaining a sales force and performing functions normally done by wholesalers are sometimes higher than the benefits received from an independent sales staff. Wholesalers can spread sales costs over many more products than most producers, resulting in lower costs per product unit. For these reasons, many producers shift informational, financing, and physical distribution activities, such as transportation and warehousing, to wholesalers. Thus, the wholesaler often becomes a major link in the supply chain, creating an optimal level of efficiency and customer service.

Wholesalers support retailers by assisting with marketing strategy, especially the distribution component. Wholesalers also help retailers select inventory. They are often specialists in understanding market conditions and experts at negotiating final

**Figure 15.1
Wholesalers Perform
Services**
E3 Corporation provides
inventory management
control systems to whole-
salers to improve efficiency
and cost effectiveness.

purchases. In industries in which obtaining supplies is important, skilled buying is indispensable. For example, Atlanta-based Genuine Parts Company (GPC), the nation's top automotive parts wholesaler, has more than sixty-five years of experience in the auto parts business; this experience helps it serve its customers effectively. GPC obtains more than 150,000 replacement parts from 150 different suppliers and resells them to retail stores and job shops (which in turn resell to garages) in the United States, Canada, and Mexico.[3] Effective wholesalers make an effort to understand the businesses of their customers. They can relieve a retailer's buyer of the responsibility of looking for and coordinating supply sources. If the wholesaler purchases for several different buyers, expenses can be shared by all customers. Another advantage is that a manufacturer's salesperson offers retailers only a few products at a time, but independent wholesalers always have a wide range of products available. Thus, through partnerships, wholesalers and retailers can forge successful relationships for the benefit of customers.

By buying in large quantities and delivering to customers in smaller lots, wholesalers are able to perform physical distribution activities efficiently. These activities (discussed later in this chapter) include transportation, materials handling, inventory planning, and warehousing. Wholesalers furnish greater service than might be feasible for a producer's or retailer's own physical distribution system. Furthermore, wholesalers offer quick and frequent delivery even when demand fluctuates. They can provide fast delivery at low cost, which lets the producer and the wholesalers' customers avoid risks associated with holding large inventories.

The distinction between services performed by wholesalers and those provided by other businesses has blurred in recent years. Changes in the competitive nature of business, especially the growth of strong retail chains like Wal-Mart, Home Depot, and Best Buy, are changing supply chain relationships. In many product categories, such as electronics, furniture, and even food products, retailers have discovered that they may be able to deal directly with producers, performing wholesaling activities them-

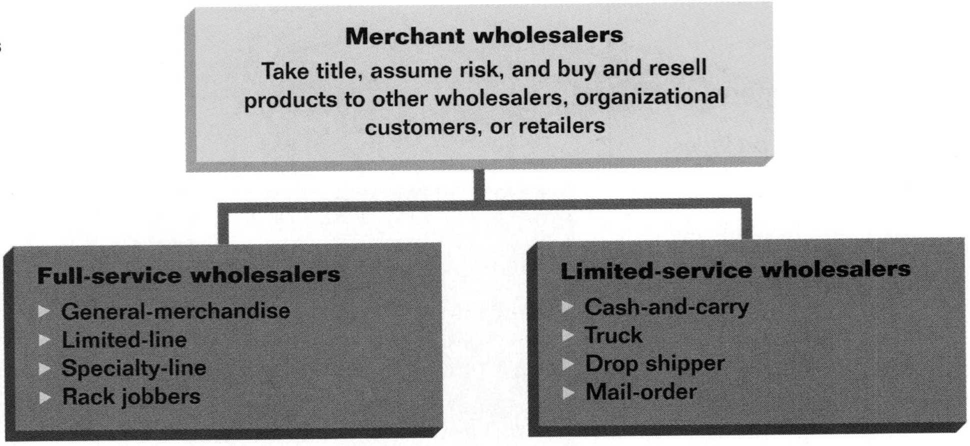

Figure 15.2
Types of Merchant Wholesalers

Merchant wholesalers
Take title, assume risk, and buy and resell products to other wholesalers, organizational customers, or retailers

Full-service wholesalers
▸ General-merchandise
▸ Limited-line
▸ Specialty-line
▸ Rack jobbers

Limited-service wholesalers
▸ Cash-and-carry
▸ Truck
▸ Drop shipper
▸ Mail-order

selves at a lower cost. An increasing number of retailers are relying on computer technology to expedite ordering, delivery, and handling of goods. Technology is thus allowing retailers to take over many wholesaling functions. Although the wholesaler as an identifiable institution may be eliminated from the marketing channel, the functions listed in Table 15.1 will still have to be performed by some member of the marketing channel—producer, retailer, or facilitating agency. These wholesaling activities are critical components of supply chain management.

Types of Wholesalers

Wholesalers are classified according to several criteria. Whether a wholesaler is independently owned or owned by a producer influences how it is classified. Wholesalers can also be grouped as to whether they take title to (own) the products they handle. The range of services provided is another criterion used for classification. Finally, wholesalers are classified according to the breadth and depth of their product lines. Using these criteria, we discuss three general types of wholesaling establishments: merchant wholesalers, agents and brokers, and manufacturers' sales branches and offices.

merchant wholesalers
Independently owned businesses that take title to goods, assume ownership risks, and buy and resell products to other wholesalers, organizational customers, or retailers

Merchant Wholesalers. **Merchant wholesalers** are independently owned businesses that take title to goods, assume risks associated with ownership, and generally buy and resell products to other wholesalers, organizational customers, or retailers. A producer is likely to rely on merchant wholesalers when selling directly to customers would be economically unfeasible. Merchant wholesalers are also useful for providing market coverage, making sales contacts, storing inventory, handling orders, collecting market information, and furnishing customer support.[4] Some merchant wholesalers are even involved in packaging and developing private brands to help retail customers be competitive. Merchant wholesalers go by various names, including wholesaler, jobber, distributor, assembler, exporter, and importer. They fall into one of two broad categories: full-service and limited-service (see Figure 15.2).

full-service wholesalers
Merchant wholesalers that perform the widest range of wholesaling functions

Full-service wholesalers perform the widest possible range of wholesaling functions. Customers rely on them for product availability, suitable assortments, breaking large quantities into smaller ones, financial assistance, and technical advice and service.[5] Universal Corporation, the world's largest buyer and processor of leaf tobacco, is an example of a full-service wholesaler. Based in Richmond, Virginia, the firm buys, ships, packs, processes, and resells tobacco, and provides financing for its customers, which include cigarette manufacturers like Philip Morris (which accounts for 41 percent of Universal's sales). Universal is also involved in sales of lumber, rubber, tea, nuts, dried fruit, and other products and has operations in thirty-three countries.[6] Full-service wholesalers handle either consumer or business products and provide numerous marketing services to interested customers. Many large grocery wholesalers help retailers with store design, site selection, personnel training, financing, merchandising, advertising, coupon redemption, and scanning. Although full-service wholesalers often earn higher gross margins than other wholesalers, their operating expenses are also higher because they perform a wider range of functions. Full-service wholesalers are categorized as general-merchandise, limited-line, and specialty-line wholesalers, and as rack jobbers.

General-merchandise wholesalers carry a wide product mix but offer limited depth within product lines. They deal in such products as drugs, nonperishable foods, cosmetics, detergents, and tobacco. **Limited-line wholesalers** carry only a few product lines—such as groceries, lighting fixtures, or oil-well drilling equipment—but offer an extensive assortment of products within those lines. Bergen Brunswig Corporation, for example, is a limited-line wholesaler of pharmaceuticals and health and beauty aids. Limited-line wholesalers provide a range of services similar to those of general-merchandise wholesalers. **Specialty-line wholesalers** offer the narrowest range of products, usually a single product line or a few items within a product line. Wholesalers that specialize in shellfish, fruit, or other food delicacies are specialty-line wholesalers. **Rack jobbers** are full-service, specialty-line wholesalers that own and maintain display racks in supermarkets, drugstores, and discount and variety stores. They set up displays, mark merchandise, stock shelves, and keep billing and inventory records; retailers need furnish only space. Rack jobbers specialize in nonfood items with high profit margins, such as health and beauty aids, books, magazines, hardware, and housewares.

Limited-service wholesalers provide fewer marketing services than full-service wholesalers, and specialize in just a few functions. Producers perform the remaining functions or pass them on to customers or to other middlemen. Limited-service wholesalers take title to merchandise but often do not deliver merchandise, grant credit, provide marketing information, store inventory, or plan ahead for customers' future needs. Because they offer restricted services, limited-service wholesalers are compensated with lower rates and have smaller profit margins than full-service wholesalers. The decision about whether to use a limited-service wholesaler or a full-service one depends on the structure of the marketing channel and the need to manage the supply chain to provide competitive advantage. Although certain types of limited-service wholesalers are few in number, they are important in the distribution of such products as specialty foods, perishable items, construction materials, and coal. Table 15.2 summarizes the services provided by four typical limited-service wholesalers: cash-and-carry wholesalers, truck wholesalers, drop shippers, and mail-order wholesalers.

Cash-and-carry wholesalers are intermediaries whose customers—usually small businesses—pay cash and furnish transportation. Cash-and-carry wholesalers usually handle a limited line of products with a high turnover rate, such as groceries, building materials, and electrical or office supplies. Many small retailers whose

general-merchandise wholesalers Full-service wholesalers with a wide product mix but limited depth within product lines

limited-line wholesalers Full-service wholesalers that carry only a few product lines but many products within those lines

specialty-line wholesalers Full-service wholesalers that carry only a single product line or a few items within a product line

rack jobbers Full-service, specialty-line wholesalers that own and maintain display racks in stores

limited-service wholesalers Merchant wholesalers that provide some services and specialize in a few functions

cash-and-carry wholesalers Limited-service wholesalers whose customers pay cash and furnish transportation

Table 15.2 Services That Limited-Service Wholesalers Provide				
	Cash-and-Carry	Truck	Drop Shipper	Mail-Order
Physical possession of merchandise	Yes	Yes	No	Yes
Personal sales calls on customers	No	Yes	No	No
Information about market conditions	No	Some	Yes	Yes
Advice to customers	No	Some	Yes	No
Stocking and maintenance of merchandise in customers' stores	No	No	No	No
Credit to customers	No	No	Yes	Some
Delivery of merchandise to customers	No	Yes	No	No

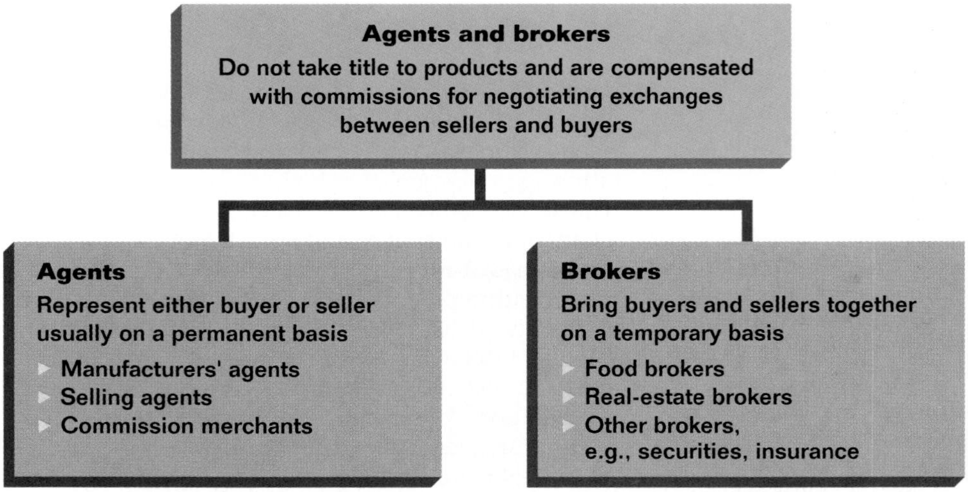

Figure 15.3
Types of Agents and Brokers

truck wholesalers
Limited-service wholesalers that transport products directly to customers for inspection and selection

drop shippers Limited-service wholesalers that take title to products and negotiate sales but never take actual possession of products

mail-order wholesalers
Limited-service wholesalers that sell products through catalogs

agents Middlemen that represent either buyers or sellers on a permanent basis

brokers Middlemen that bring buyers and sellers together temporarily

manufacturers' agents
Independent middlemen that represent more than one seller and offer complete product lines

accounts are refused by other wholesalers survive because of cash-and-carry wholesalers. **Truck wholesalers,** sometimes called truck jobbers, transport a limited line of products directly to customers for on-the-spot inspection and selection. They are often small operators who own and drive their own trucks. They usually have regular routes, calling on retailers and other institutions to determine their needs. **Drop shippers,** also known as desk jobbers, take title to goods and negotiate sales but never take actual possession of products. They forward orders from retailers, organizational buyers, or other wholesalers to manufacturers and arrange for carload shipments of items to be delivered directly from producers to these customers. They assume responsibility for products during the entire transaction, including the costs of any unsold goods. **Mail-order wholesalers** use catalogs instead of sales forces to sell products to retail and organizational buyers. Wholesale mail-order houses generally feature cosmetics, specialty foods, sporting goods, office supplies, and automotive parts. Mail-order wholesaling enables buyers to choose and order particular catalog items for delivery through United Parcel Service, the U.S. Postal Service, or other carriers. This is a convenient and effective method of selling small items to customers in remote areas that other wholesalers might find unprofitable to serve. The Internet has provided an opportunity for mail-order wholesalers to sell products over their own Web sites and have the products shipped by the manufacturer.

Agents and Brokers. Agents and brokers negotiate purchases and expedite sales but do not take title to products (see Figure 15.3). Sometimes called functional middlemen, they perform a limited number of services in exchange for a commission, which is generally based on the product's selling price. **Agents** represent either buyers or sellers on a permanent basis, whereas **brokers** are middlemen that buyers or sellers employ temporarily.

Although agents and brokers perform even fewer functions than limited-service wholesalers, they are usually specialists in particular products or types of customers and can provide valuable sales expertise. They know their markets well and often form long-lasting associations with customers. Agents and brokers enable manufacturers to expand sales when resources are limited, to benefit from the services of a trained sales force, and to hold down personal selling costs. Despite the advantages they offer, agents and brokers face increased competition from merchant wholesalers, manufacturers' sales branches and offices, and direct-sales efforts through manufacturer-owned Web sites. We look here at three types of agents—manufacturers' agents, selling agents, and commission merchants—as well as at the brokers' role in bringing about exchanges between buyers and sellers. Table 15.3 summarizes the services that agents and brokers provide.

Manufacturers' agents—accounting for over half of all agent wholesalers—are independent middlemen that represent two or more sellers and usually offer customers complete product lines. They sell and take orders year-round, much like a manufacturer's sales force. Restricted to a particular territory, a manufacturers' agent

Table 15.3   Services That Agents and Brokers Provide

	Manufacturers' Agents	Selling Agents	Commission Merchants	Brokers
Physical possession of merchandise	Some	Some	Yes	No
Long-term relationship with buyers or sellers	Yes	Yes	Yes	No
Representation of competing product lines	No	No	Yes	Yes
Limited geographic territory	Yes	No	No	No
Credit to customers	No	Yes	Some	No
Delivery of merchandise to customers	Some	Yes	Yes	No

handles noncompeting and complementary products. The relationship between the agent and manufacturer is governed by written contracts that outline territories, selling price, order handling, and terms of sale relating to delivery, service, and warranties. Manufacturers' agents have little or no control over producers' pricing and marketing policies. They do not extend credit and may not be able to provide technical advice. They do occasionally store and transport products, assist producers with planning and promotion, and help retailers advertise. Some maintain a service organization; the more services offered, the higher the agent's commission. Manufacturers' agents are commonly used in sales of apparel, machinery and equipment, steel, furniture, automotive products, electrical goods, and certain food items.

selling agents Middlemen that market a whole product line or a manufacturer's entire output

Selling agents market either all of a specified product line or a manufacturer's entire output. They perform every wholesaling activity except taking title to products. Selling agents usually assume the sales function for several producers simultaneously and are often used in place of marketing departments. In fact, selling agents are used most often by small producers or by manufacturers that have difficulty maintaining a marketing department because of seasonal production or other factors. In contrast to manufacturers' agents, selling agents generally have no territorial limits and have complete authority over prices, promotion, and distribution. To avoid conflicts of interest, selling agents represent noncompeting product lines. They play a key role in advertising, marketing research, and credit policies of the sellers they represent, at times even advising on product development and packaging.

commission merchants Agents that receive goods on consignment and negotiate sales in large central markets

Commission merchants receive goods on consignment from local sellers and negotiate sales in large central markets. Sometimes called factor merchants, these agents have broad powers regarding prices and terms of sales. They specialize in obtaining the best price possible under market conditions. Most often found in agricultural marketing, commission merchants take possession of truckloads of commodities, arrange for necessary grading or storage, and transport the commodities to auction or markets where they are sold. When sales are completed, the agents deduct commission, and the expense of making the sale, and then turn over profits to the producer. Commission merchants also offer planning assistance and sometimes extend credit but usually do not provide promotional support.

A broker's primary purpose is to bring buyers and sellers together. Thus, brokers perform fewer functions than other intermediaries. They are not involved in financing or physical possession, have no authority to set prices, and assume almost no risks. Instead, they offer customers specialized knowledge of a particular commodity and a network of established contacts. Brokers are especially useful to sellers of certain types of products, such as supermarket products and real estate. Food brokers, for example, sell food and general merchandise to retailer-owned and merchant wholesalers, grocery chains, food processors, and organizational buyers.

Manufacturers' Sales Branches and Offices.   Sometimes called manufacturers' wholesalers, manufacturers' sales branches and offices resemble merchant wholesalers' operations.

sales branches Manufacturer-owned middlemen that sell products and provide support services to the manufacturer's sales force

Sales branches are manufacturer-owned middlemen that sell products and provide support services to the manufacturer's sales force. Situated away from the manufacturing plant, they are usually located where large customers are concentrated and

We've taken the
Land O'Lakes Deli Division
to the power of three.

DELI CHEESE

Alpine Lace

Premium Quality **60** *Traditional Deli-Style*
years
NEW YORKER

**Three great brands. One order. One truck.
One bill. More profits all around.**

The biggest brands in deli—Land O'Lakes® Deli Cheese, Alpine Lace® and New Yorker®—join forces to create the Land O'Lakes Deli Division, so it's easier than ever to grow and manage your deli department more efficiently and profitably. Now you can place *one* order for all three brands with *one* sales contact, who'll send *one* delivery and *one* invoice. With streamlined ordering and billing, you'll have more time than ever to devote to your deli. And only the Land O'Lakes Deli Division delivers strong consumer pull programs year after year to consistently drive sales. Look to the deli experts, the Land O'Lakes Deli Division, for the brand power it takes to build deli sales.

THE BRANDS GREAT DELIS ARE BUILT ON
Visit our website at www.landolakes.com

©1998 Land O'Lakes, Inc.

Figure 15.4
Manufacturers' Sales Branch
Land O'Lakes Deli Division is an example of a manufacturers' sales branch. It sells its own three brands of cheese directly to retailers who have only to place one order and receive one delivery and one invoice for all three brands.

demand is high. They offer credit, deliver goods, give promotional assistance, and furnish other services. In many cases, they carry inventory (although this practice often duplicates functions of other channel members and is now declining). Customers include retailers, organizational buyers, and other wholesalers. Manufacturers of electrical supplies, such as Westinghouse Electric, and of plumbing supplies, such as American Standard, often have branch operations. They are also common in the lumber and automotive parts industries.

Sales offices are manufacturer-owned operations that provide services normally associated with agents. Like sales branches, they are located away from manufacturing plants, but unlike branches, they carry no inventory. A manufacturer's sales office (or branch) may sell products that enhance the manufacturer's own product line. Companies like Campbell Soup provide diverse services to their wholesale and retail customers. Hiram Walker, a liquor producer, imports wine from Spain to increase the number of products its sales offices can offer wholesalers.

sales offices
Manufacturer-owned operations that provide services normally associated with agents

Manufacturers may set up these branches or offices to reach their customers more effectively by performing wholesaling functions themselves. For example, Land O'Lakes Deli Division (Figure 15.4) sells its three lines of cheeses directly to retailers. A manufacturer may also set up such a facility when specialized wholesaling services are not available through existing middlemen. A manufacturers' performance of wholesaling and physical distribution activities through its sales branch or office may strengthen supply chain efficiency. In some situations, though, a manufacturer may bypass its sales office or branches entirely—for example, if the producer decides to serve large retailer customers directly. As noted in Chapter 14, Procter & Gamble maintains a direct partnership with Wal-Mart, exchanging data about inventory levels and product availability to create a partnership that maximizes opportunities for profits and competitive advantage for both firms.[7]

The Nature of Physical Distribution

physical distribution
Activities used to move products from producers to consumers and other end users

Physical distribution, also known as logistics, refers to the activities used to move products from producers to consumers and other end users. These activities include order processing, inventory management, materials handling, warehousing, and transportation. Planning an efficient physical distribution system is crucial to developing an effective marketing strategy because it can decrease costs and increase customer satisfaction. Speed of delivery, service, and dependability are often as important to customers as costs. Companies that have the right goods in the right place, at the right time, in the right quantity, and with the right support services are able to sell more than competitors that do not. A construction-equipment dealer with a low inventory of replacement parts requires fast, dependable service from component suppliers when it needs parts not in stock. Even when the demand for products is unpredictable, suppliers must be able to respond quickly to inventory needs.[8] In such cases, physical distribution costs may be a minor consideration when compared with service, dependability, and timeliness.

Physical distribution deals with the physical movement and storage of products and supplies both within and among marketing channel members. Physical distribution systems must meet the needs of both the supply chain and customers. Distribution activities are thus an important part of supply chain planning and require the cooperation of all partners. Often, one channel member manages physical distribution for all supply chain members. In fact, there is a trend toward centralizing, with one member's having the responsibility and authority for physical distribution for the entire chain.[9]

Within the marketing channel, physical distribution activities are often performed by a wholesaler, but they may be performed by the producer or retailer or outsourced. In the context of distribution, **outsourcing** is the contracting of physical distribution tasks to third parties who do not have managerial authority within the marketing channel. (Building Customer Relationships takes a close look at how some companies are managing relationships with their outsourcing partners.) Most physical distribution activities can be outsourced to third-party firms that have special expertise in such areas as warehousing, transportation, and information technology. Cooperative relationships with third-party organizations, such as trucking companies, warehouses, and data-service providers, can help reduce marketing channel costs and boost service and customer satisfaction for all supply chain partners. For example, Hewlett-Packard's Laser Jet Production Completion & Distribution Organization

outsourcing The contracting of physical distribution tasks to third parties who do not have managerial authority within the marketing channel

BUILDING
customer relationships

Outsourcing for Performance

More and more companies are looking to outsourcing to reduce costs and improve service and customer satisfaction. Outsourcing refers to the contracting of physical distribution tasks to third parties that do not have managerial authority within the marketing channel. According to consultant Mike Corbett of Michael F. Corbett and Associates, "Outsourcing is not abdicating responsibility. It's leveraging the specialized expertise of another company." Research by the Outsourcing Research Council indicates that firms that achieve the greatest benefit from outsourcing are those that focus on the structure of the relationship, the management structure, and the leadership skills required of the relationship's managers. Other key elements of structuring the outsourced relationship include managing expectations, developing clear measures of performance, and using a pricing structure that is tied to results. Thus, effective control of outsource relationship requires clear communication of expectations, performance standards, and results.

Thomson Consumer Electronics (TCE), a French firm that manufactures such brands as RCA and GE, operates in a highly competitive industry often marked by sharp price cuts. Containing costs and providing excellent service are therefore critical. One way TCE has corralled costs is by outsourcing nearly all of its distribution and warehousing activities. GATX Logistics operates a 950,000 square-foot distribution center for TCE in El Paso, Texas, as well as a 1.3 million square-foot facility in

Indianapolis, Indiana, and a 500,000 square-foot multipurpose facility in Los Angeles. To ensure the relationship works well for both firms, TCE and GATX maintain open, frank communications, and Thomson managers regularly tour the facilities and conduct onsite performance reviews to ensure they meet Thomson's goals. The two firms also collaborate in personnel, technology, and training.

The Scotts Company, the largest horticultural products marketer in the world, must provide fast, flexible service to both retail and professional customers in a highly seasonal business. To provide such service while keeping a lid on costs, Scotts maintains a network of warehouses run by eleven third-party providers. The company says the key to managing these relationships successfully is consistent, ongoing communications and recognition of provider performance. At its annual Logistics Conference, Scotts briefs its third-party providers about its plans and objectives for the coming year, and it recognizes outstanding performance by its third-party warehouse and transportation providers.

Thomson Electronics and the Scotts Company are just two companies that have recognized that successful outsourcing relationships are true partnerships that benefit all supply chain partners. For those companies that truly collaborate and communicate with their outsourcing partners, the ultimate benefit is increased satisfaction for everyone in the supply chain, from producer to final consumer.

outsources physical distribution activities, including shipping and warehousing, to build a supply chain of strategic partners to maximize customer service.[10] Such relationships are increasingly being integrated in the supply chain to achieve wholesaling and physical distribution objectives.

Physical Distribution Objectives

For most companies, the main objectives of physical distribution are to decrease costs and transit time while increasing customer service. However, few distribution systems achieve these goals in equal measure. The large inventories and rapid transportation necessary for good customer service drive up costs. Supply chain managers therefore strive for a reasonable balance among service, costs, and resources. They determine what level of customer service is acceptable and realistic and then develop a "system" outlook to minimize total distribution costs and cycle time.

Meeting Standards of Customer Service.   In physical distribution, availability, timeliness, and quality are important dimensions of customer service. To keep the nation's farmers, lawn-care firms, and other agricultural companies at work, John Deere sets rigorous distribution objectives. Deere expects its dealers to be able to fulfill 80 to 85 percent of orders from their own stock, 85 percent of orders from one of Deere's regional depots in the United States and Canada, and 95 percent from its parts distribution center in Milan, Illinois. Although Deere could reduce its distribution costs significantly by cutting these inventories, it would not then be able to meet its strict standards of customer service. When a part is not in a dealer's stock, Deere is committed to shipping the part from one of its regional distribution centers the same day it is ordered. Deere ships more than 99 percent of orders the same day, and most orders are received within one day.[11]

Customers seeking a high level of customer service may also want sizable inventories, efficient order processing, availability of emergency shipments, progress reports, postsale services, prompt replacement of defective items, and warranties. Customers' inventory requirements influence the expected level of physical distribution service. Organizational customers seeking to reduce their inventory storage and shipping costs may expect wholesalers or third-party firms to take responsibility for maintaining inventory in the marketing channel or to assume the cost of premium transportation. Because service needs vary from customer to customer, companies must analyze—and adapt to—customer preferences. Attention to customer needs and preferences is crucial to increasing sales and obtaining repeat orders. A company's failure to provide the desired level of service may mean loss of customers.

Companies must also examine the service levels competitors offer and match or exceed those standards when the costs of providing the services can be justified by the sales generated. Many companies guarantee service performance to win customers. Services are provided most effectively when service standards are developed and stated in measurable terms—for example, "98 percent of all orders filled within 48 hours." Standards should be communicated clearly to both customers and employees and diligently enforced. Many service standards outline delivery times and specify provisions for backordering, returning goods, and obtaining emergency shipments.

Reducing Total Distribution Costs.   Although physical distribution managers try to minimize the costs associated with order processing, inventory management, materials handling, warehousing, and transportation, decreasing the costs in one area often raises them in another. (Figure 15.5 shows the percentage of total costs that physical distribution functions represent.) A total-cost approach to physical distribution enables managers to view physical distribution as a system rather than a collection of unrelated activities. This approach shifts the emphasis from lowering the separate costs of individual activities to minimizing overall distribution costs.

The total-cost approach involves analyzing the costs of all distribution alternatives, even those considered too impractical or expensive. Total-cost analyses weigh

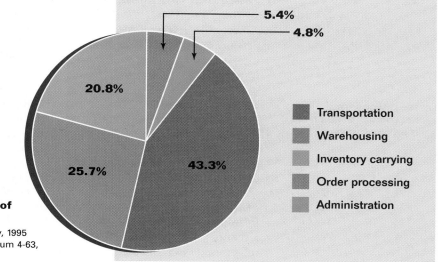

Figure 15.5
Proportional Cost of Each Physical Distribution Function as a Percentage of Total Distribution Costs

Source: Data from Herbert W. Davis and Company, 1995 Physical Distribution Cost and Service Memorandum 4-63, Mar. 19, 1996, p. 2.

- Transportation
- Warehousing
- Inventory carrying
- Order processing
- Administration

5.4%
4.8%
20.8%
25.7%
43.3%

inventory levels against warehousing expenses, materials costs against various modes of transportation, and all distribution costs against customer service standards. Costs of potential sales losses from lower performance levels must also be considered. In many cases, accounting procedures and statistical methods are used to figure total costs. When hundreds of combinations of distribution variables are possible, computer simulations are helpful. A distribution system's lowest total cost is never the result of using a combination of the cheapest functions; instead, it is the lowest overall cost compatible with the company's stated service objectives.

cycle time   The time it takes to complete a process

Supply chain managers must be sensitive to the issue of cost tradeoffs. Higher costs in one functional area of a distribution system may be necessary to achieve lower costs in another. Tradeoffs are strategic decisions to combine (and recombine) resources for greatest cost-effectiveness. When distribution managers regard the system as a network of integrated functions, tradeoffs become useful tools in implementing a unified, cost-effective distribution strategy.

Reducing Cycle Time.   Another important goal of physical distribution involves reducing **cycle time,** the time it takes to complete a process; doing so can reduce costs and/or increase customer service.[12] Many companies, particularly overnight delivery firms, major news media, and publishers of books of current interest, are using cycle-time reduction to gain a competitive advantage. FedEx believes so strongly in this concept that, in the interest of being the fastest provider of overnight delivery, it conducts research on reducing cycle time and identifying new management techniques and procedures for its 140,000 employees (see Figure 15.6).

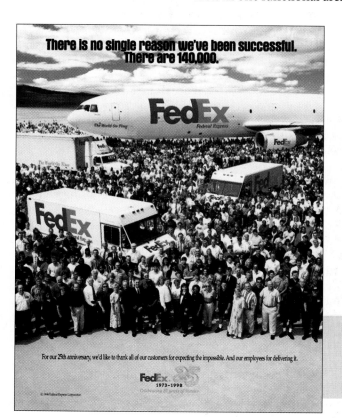

Figure 15.6
Reducing Cycle Time
FedEx helps its customers reduce cycle time by providing express overnight delivery service.

Functions of Physical Distribution

As we said earlier, physical distribution includes the activities necessary to get products from producers to customers. In this section, we take a closer look at these activities, which include order processing, inventory management, materials handling, warehousing, and transportation.

order processing The receipt and transmission of sales order information

Order Processing. **Order processing** is the receipt and transmission of sales order information. Although management sometimes overlooks the importance of these activities, efficient order processing facilitates product flow. Computerized order processing provides a database for all supply chain members to increase their productivity. When carried out quickly and accurately, order processing contributes to customer satisfaction, decreased costs and cycle time, and increased profits.

Order processing entails three main tasks: order entry, order handling, and order delivery. Order entry begins when customers or salespersons place purchase orders via telephone, mail, E-mail, or Web site. Electronic ordering is less time-consuming than a manual, paper-based ordering system and reduces costs. In some companies, sales representatives receive and enter orders personally, also handling complaints, preparing progress reports, and forwarding sales order information.

Order handling involves several tasks. Once an order is entered, it is transmitted to a warehouse, where product availability is verified, and to the credit department, where prices, terms, and the customer's credit rating are checked. If the credit department approves the purchase, warehouse personnel (sometimes assisted by automated equipment) pick and assemble the order. If the requested product is not in stock, a production order is sent to the factory or the customer is offered a substitute.

When the order has been assembled and packed for shipment, the warehouse schedules delivery with an appropriate carrier. If the customer pays for rush service, overnight delivery by FedEx, UPS, or an other overnight carrier is used. The customer is sent an invoice, inventory records are adjusted, and the order is delivered.

Whether to use a manual or an electronic order-processing system depends on which method provides the greatest speed and accuracy within cost limits. Manual processing suffices for small-volume orders and is more flexible in certain situations.

electronic data interchange (EDI) A computerized means of integrating order processing with production, inventory, accounting, and transportation

Most companies, however, use **electronic data interchange (EDI),** which uses computer technology to integrate order processing with production, inventory, accounting, and transportation. At Delta Beverage Group, for example, an EDI system utilizing handheld computers conveys orders directly to the bottling plant and allows drivers to print invoices on delivery. Delta's system is accurate, fast, easy for employees, and has reduced distribution costs and cycle time.[13] Within the supply chain, EDI functions as an information system that links marketing channel members and outsourcing firms together. It reduces paperwork for all members of the supply chain and allows them to share information on invoices, orders, payments, inquiries, and scheduling. Consequently, many companies have pushed their suppliers toward EDI to reduce distribution costs and cycle times. For example, AutoZone and Dobbs International, an airline food-service company, have all their merchandising vendors on EDI systems and request that all their other suppliers be EDI-capable. At FedEx, more than 70 percent of major business customers carry out transactions via EDI.[14]

inventory management Developing and maintaining adequate assortments of products to meet customers' needs

Inventory Management. **Inventory management** involves developing and maintaining adequate assortments of products to meet customers' needs. Because a firm's investment in inventory usually represents a significant portion of its total assets, inventory decisions have a major impact on physical distribution costs and the level of customer service provided. When too few products are carried in inventory, the result is *stockouts,* or shortages of products, which in turn result in brand switching, lower sales, and loss of customers. When too many products (or too many slow-moving products) are carried, costs increase, as do risks of product obsolescence, pilferage, and damage. The objective of inventory management is to minimize inventory costs while maintaining an adequate supply of goods to satisfy customers. To achieve this objective, marketers focus on two major issues: when to order and how much to order.

To determine when to order, a marketer calculates the *reorder point,* the inventory level that signals the need to place a new order. To calculate the reorder point, the marketer must know the order lead time, the usage rate, and the amount of safety stock required. The *order lead time* refers to the average time lapse between placing the order and receiving it. The *usage rate* is the rate at which a product's inventory is used or sold during a specific time period. *Safety stock* is the amount of extra inventory that a firm keeps to guard against stockouts resulting from above-average usage rates and/or longer than expected lead times. The reorder point can be calculated using the following formula:

Reorder Point = (Order Lead Time × Usage Rate) + Safety Stock

Thus, if order lead time is 10 days, usage rate is 3 units per day, and safety stock is 20 units, the reorder point is 50 units. As shown in Figure 15.7, Dannon provides a video for retailers to assist in avoiding stockouts,which are estimated to cost the supermarket industry 7 to 12 billion dollars a year in lost sales.

just-in-time (JIT)
An inventory management approach in which supplies arrive just when needed for production or resale

Efficient inventory management with accurate reorder points are crucial for firms that use a **just-in-time (JIT)** approach, in which supplies arrive just as they are needed for use in production or for resale. When using the JIT approach, companies maintain low inventory levels and purchase products and materials in small quantities whenever they are needed. Usually, there is no safety stock, and suppliers are expected to provide consistently, high-quality products. Just-in-time inventory management requires a high level of coordination between producers and suppliers, but it eliminates waste and reduces inventory costs significantly. This approach has been used successfully by many well-known firms, including Chrysler, Harley Davidson, and Dell Computer, to reduce costs and boost customer satisfaction. When a JIT approach is used in a supply chain, suppliers often move close to their customers. For example, Japanese auto parts suppliers that use the JIT approach often send engineers to work at their

Figure 15.7
Avoiding Stockouts
Dannon assists retailers in understanding how to avoid sales losses due to out-of-stock inventory.

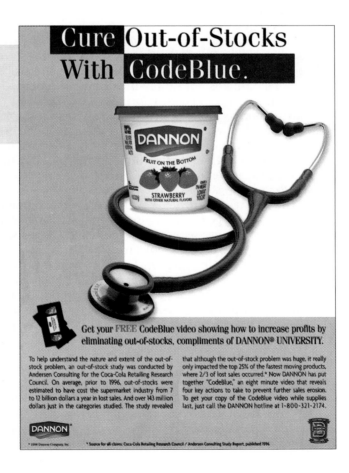

customers' sites or locate plants near their customers' facilities. This results in low transportation and inventory costs and improved product development coordination.[15]

materials handling
Physical handling of products

Materials Handling.   **Materials handling,** the physical handling of products, is an important factor in warehouse operations, as well as in transportation from points of production to points of consumption. Efficient procedures and techniques for materials handling minimize inventory management costs, reduce the number of times a good is handled, improve customer service, and increase customer satisfaction. Systems for packaging, labeling, loading, and movement must be coordinated to maximize cost reduction and customer satisfaction.

Product characteristics often determine handling. For example, the characteristics of bulk liquids and gases determine how they can be moved and stored. Internal packaging is also an important consideration in materials handling; goods must be packaged correctly to prevent damage or breakage during handling and transportation. Most companies employ packaging consultants to help them decide which packaging materials and methods will result in the most efficient handling.

Unit loading and containerization are two common methods used in materials handling. With *unit loading,* one or more boxes are placed on a pallet or skid; these units can then be efficiently loaded by mechanical means, such as forklifts, trucks, or conveyer systems. *Containerization* is the consolidation of many items into a single large container, which is sealed at its point of origin and opened at its destination. Containers are usually eight-feet wide, eight-feet high, and ten- to forty-feet long. They can be conveniently stacked and shipped via train, barge, or ship. Once containers reach their destinations, wheel assemblies can be added to make them suitable for ground transportation. Because individual items are not handled in transit, containerization greatly increases efficiency and security in shipping.

warehousing   The design and operation of facilities for storing and moving goods

Warehousing.   **Warehousing,** the design and operation of facilities for storing and moving goods, is another important physical distribution function. Warehousing provides time utility by enabling firms to compensate for dissimilar production and consumption rates. When mass production creates a greater stock of goods than can be sold immediately, companies may warehouse the surplus until customers are ready to buy. Warehousing also helps stabilize prices and availability of seasonal items.

Warehousing is not simply the storage of products. The basic distribution functions that warehouses perform include receiving, identifying, sorting, and dispatching goods to storage; holding goods in storage until needed; recalling and assembling stored goods for shipment; and dispatching shipments. When warehouses receive goods by carloads or truckloads, they break down the shipments into smaller quantities for individual customers (the operation is sometimes called "breaking bulk"). When goods arrive in small lots, warehouses sometimes consolidate them into bulk loads that can be shipped more economically.[16]

The choice of warehouse facilities is an important strategic consideration. By using the right type of warehouse, a company may reduce transportation and inventory costs or improve service to customers; the wrong warehouse may drain company resources. Beyond deciding how many facilities to operate and where to locate them, a company must determine which type of warehouse is most appropriate. Warehouses fall into two general categories, private and public. In many cases, a combination of private and public facilities provides the most flexible warehousing approach.

private warehouses
Company-operated facilities for storing and shipping products

Private warehouses are operated by companies for the purpose of shipping and storing their own products. A firm usually leases or purchases a private warehouse when its warehousing needs in a given geographic market are substantial and stable enough to make a long-term commitment to a fixed facility. Private warehouses are also appropriate for firms that require special handling and storage and that want control of warehouse design and operation. Retailers like Sears, Radio Shack, and Kmart find it economical to integrate private warehousing with purchasing and distribution for their retail outlets. When sales volumes are fairly stable, ownership and control of a private warehouse may provide benefits, such as property appreciation. Private warehouses, however, face fixed costs, such as insurance, taxes, maintenance, and debt expense. They also limit flexibility when firms wish to move inventories to more strategic locations. Before tying up capital in a private warehouse or entering into a long-term lease, a company should consider its resources, level of expertise in warehouse management, and the role of the warehouse in overall marketing strategy. Many private warehouses are being eliminated by direct links between producers and customers, reduced cycle times, and outsourcing to public warehouses.

public warehouses
Businesses that lease storage space and related physical distribution facilities to other firms

Public warehouses lease storage space and related physical distribution facilities as an outsource service to other companies. They sometimes provide such distribution services as receiving, unloading, inspecting, and reshipping products; filling orders; providing financing; displaying products; and coordinating shipments. They are especially useful to firms with seasonal production or low-volume storage needs, to firms with inventories that must be maintained in many locations, to those that are testing or entering new markets, and to those that own private warehouses but occasionally require additional storage space. Public warehouses also serve as collection points during product-recall programs. Whereas private warehouses have fixed costs, public warehouses offer variable (and often lower) costs because users rent space and purchase warehousing services only as needed.

Many public warehouses furnish security for products being used as collateral for loans, a service provided at either the warehouse or the site of the owner's inventory. *Field public warehouses* are established by public warehouses at the owner's inventory location. The warehouser becomes custodian of the products and issues a receipt that can be used as collateral for a loan. Public warehouses also provide *bonded storage,* a warehousing arrangement under which imported or taxable products are not released until the products' owners pay U.S. customs duties, taxes, or other fees. Bonded warehouses enable firms to defer tax payments on such items until they are delivered to customers.

distribution centers
Large, centralized warehouses that focus on moving goods rather than storing them

Distribution centers are large, centralized warehouses that receive goods from factories and suppliers, regroup them into orders, and ship them to customers quickly, the focus being on the movement of goods rather than storage.[17] Distribution centers are specially designed for rapid flow of products. They are usually one-story buildings (to eliminate elevators) with access to transportation networks, such as major highways or railway lines. Many distribution centers are highly automated, with computer-directed robots, forklifts, and hoists collecting and moving products to loading docks. Although some public warehouses offer such specialized services, most distribution centers are privately owned. They serve customers in regional markets and, in some cases, function as consolidation points for a company's branch warehouses. Distribution centers are typically located within 500 miles of half a company's market.[18]

Distribution centers offer several benefits, the foremost being improved customer service. Distribution centers ensure product availability by maintaining full product lines, and the speed of their operations cuts delivery time to a minimum. Distribution centers also reduce costs. Instead of making many smaller shipments to scattered warehouses and customers, factories ship large quantities of goods directly to distribution centers at bulk rates, thus lowering transportation costs. Furthermore, rapid inventory turnover lessens the need for warehouses and cuts storage costs. Whirlpool, for example, consolidated several facilities into one 650,000-square-foot distribution center for handling its appliances.[19] Some distribution centers facilitate production by receiving and consolidating raw materials and providing final assembly for certain products.

transportation   The movement of products from where they are made to where they are used

Transportation.   **Transportation,** the movement of products from where they are made to where they are used, is the most expensive physical distribution function. Because product availability and timely deliveries depend on transportation functions, transportation decisions directly affect customer service. A firm may even build its distribution and marketing strategy around a unique transportation system if that system can ensure on-time deliveries and thereby give the firm a competitive edge. Companies may build their own transportation fleets (private carriers) or outsource the transportation function to a common or contract carrier, such as Consolidated Freightways.

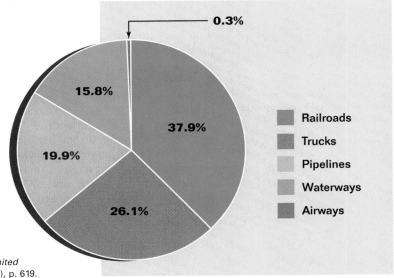

Figure 15.8
Proportion of Intercity Freight Carried by Various Transportation Modes
Source: Bureau of the Census, *Statistical Abstract of the United States* (Washington, D.C.: Government Printing Office, 1997), p. 619.

Transportation Modes   There are five basic transportation modes for moving physical goods: railroads, trucks, waterways, airways, and pipelines. Each mode offers distinct advantages. Many companies adopt physical handling procedures that facilitate the use of two or more modes in combination. Figure 15.8 indicates the percentage of intercity freight carried by each transportation mode; Table 15.4 shows typical transportation modes for various products.

Railroads like Union Pacific and Canadian National (see Figure 15.9) carry heavy, bulky freight that must be shipped long distances overland. Railroads commonly haul minerals, sand, lumber, chemicals, and farm products, as well as low-value manufactured goods and an increasing number of automobiles. They are especially efficient for transporting full carloads, which can be shipped at lower rates than smaller quantities because they require less handling. Many companies locate factories or warehouses near major rail lines or on spur lines for convenient loading and unloading.

Trucks provide the most flexible schedules and routes of all major transportation modes because they can go almost anywhere. Because trucks have a unique ability to move goods directly from factory or warehouse to customer, they are often used in conjunction with other forms of transport that cannot provide door-to-door deliveries. Although trucks usually travel much faster than trains, they are more expensive and somewhat more vulnerable to bad weather. They are also subject to size and weight restrictions on the products they carry. Trucks are sometimes criticized for high levels of loss and damage to freight and for delays caused by the rehandling of small shipments. In response, the trucking industry has turned to computerized tracking of shipments and the development of new equipment to speed up loading and unloading.

Table 15.4	Typical Transportation Modes for Various Products			
Railroads	**Trucks**	**Waterways**	**Airways**	**Pipelines**
Coal	Clothing	Petroleum	Flowers	Oil
Grain	Paper goods	Chemicals	Perishable food	Processed coal
Chemicals	Computers	Iron ore	Instruments	Natural gas
Lumber	Books	Bauxite	Emergency parts	Water
Automobiles	Livestock	Grain	Overnight mail	Chemicals
Steel				

YOU CAN NEVER BE TOO POWERFUL.

We are CN. Delivering more power. And more connections.

The power.

New locomotives give us power and payloads like never before. We're moving trains faster, more efficiently and more economically.

The connections.

CN is the only transcontinental railway in North America, and provides the best access to the Chicago hub there is. Simply put, CN's network spans the continent. From coast to coast. From the far north to the deep south.

You can never be too powerful. Or too well connected. At CN, we're dedicated to this proposition — and it's giving our customers every strategic advantage there is. For more information, call 1-888-MOVIN-CN.

OR TOO WELL CONNECTED.

CANADIAN NATIONAL
www.cn.ca

Figure 15.9
Railroads
Canadian National provides long-haul freight services for heavy cargo.

Waterways are the cheapest method of shipping heavy, low-value, nonperishable goods, such as ore, coal, grain, and petroleum products. Water carriers offer considerable capacity. Powered by tugboats and towboats, barges that travel along intercoastal canals, inland rivers, and navigation systems can haul at least ten times the weight of one rail car, and ocean-going vessels can haul thousands of containers. However, many markets are inaccessible by water transportation unless it is supplemented by rail or truck. Furthermore, water transport is extremely slow and sometimes comes to a standstill during freezing weather. Companies depending on waterways may ship their entire inventory during the summer and then store it for winter use. Droughts and floods also create difficulties for users of inland waterway transportation. Nevertheless, the extreme fuel efficiency of water transportation and the continuing globalization of marketing will likely increase its use in the future.

Air transportation is the fastest yet most expensive form of shipping. It is used most often for perishable goods; for high-value, low-bulk items; and for products requiring quick delivery over long distances, such as emergency shipments. Some air carriers transport combinations of passengers, freight, and mail. Despite its expense, air transit can reduce warehousing and packaging costs and losses from theft and damage, thus helping lower total costs (but truck transportation needed for pickup and final delivery adds to cost and transit time). Although air transport accounts for less than 1 percent of total ton-miles carried, its importance as a mode of transportation is growing. In fact, the success of many businesses is now based on the availability of overnight air delivery service provided by such organizations as UPS, Airborne, FedEx, DHL, RPS Air, and the U.S. Postal Service. Amazon.com, for example, ships many books ordered online within a day of order via UPS.

Pipelines, the most automated transportation mode, usually belong to the shipper and carry the shipper's products. Most pipelines carry petroleum products or chemicals. The Trans-Alaska Pipeline, owned and operated by a consortium of oil companies that includes Exxon, Mobil, and British Petroleum, transports crude oil from remote oil-drilling sites in central Alaska to shipping terminals on the coast. Slurry pipelines carry pulverized coal, grain, or wood chips suspended in water. Pipelines move products slowly but continuously and at relatively low cost. They are dependable and minimize the problems of product damage and theft. However, contents are subject to as much as 1 percent shrinkage, usually from evaporation. Pipelines have also been a concern to environmentalists, who fear that installation and leaks could harm plants and animals.

Choosing Transportation Modes Distribution managers select a transportation mode based on the combination of cost, speed, dependability, load flexibility, accessibility, and frequency that is most appropriate for their product and generates the desired level of customer service. Table 15.5 on page 392 shows relative ratings of each transportation mode by these selection criteria.

Marketers compare alternative transportation modes to determine whether benefits from a more expensive mode are worth higher costs. Air freight carriers—for instance, FedEx—promise many benefits, such as speed, and dependability, but at much higher costs than other transportation modes. When such benefits are less important, marketers prefer lower costs. Bicycles, for instance, are often shipped by

| | | | | Load | | |
Mode	Cost	Speed	Dependability	Flexibility	Accessibility	Frequency
Railroads	Moderate	Average	Average	High	High	Low
Trucks	High	Fast	High	Average	Very high	High
Waterways	Very low	Very slow	Average	Very high	Limited	Very low
Airways	Very high	Very fast	High	Low	Average	Average
Pipelines	Low	Slow	High	Very low	Very limited	Very high

Table 15.5   Relative Ratings of Transportation Modes by Selection Criteria

rail because an unassembled bicycle can be shipped more than a thousand miles on a train for as little as $3.60. Bicycle wholesalers plan purchases far enough in advance to capitalize on this cost advantage. Companies such as Schneider Logistics (see Figure 15.10) can assist marketers in analyzing a variety of transportation options.

Speed is measured by the total time a carrier has possession of goods, including the time required for pickup and delivery, handling, and movement between points of origin and destination. Speed obviously affects a marketer's ability to provide service, but there are some less obvious implications as well. Marketers take advantage of transit time to process orders for goods en route, a capability especially important to agricultural and raw materials shippers. Some railroads also let carloads in transit be redirected for maximum flexibility in selecting markets. A carload of peaches may be shipped to a closer destination if the fruit is in danger of ripening too quickly.

Dependability of a transportation mode is determined by the consistency of service provided. Marketers must be able to count on carriers to deliver goods on time and in an acceptable condition. Along with speed, dependability affects a marketer's inventory costs, including sales lost when merchandise is not available. Undependable transportation necessitates higher inventory levels to avoid stockouts,

**Figure 15.10
Choosing Transportation Modes**
Schneider Logistics helps companies evaluate shipping alternatives and consolidate shipments to improve logistics efficiency.

whereas reliable delivery service enables customers to carry smaller inventories at lower cost. Security problems vary considerably among transportation modes and are a major consideration in carrier selection. A firm does not incur costs directly when goods are lost or damaged because the carrier is usually held liable. Nevertheless, poor service and lack of security indirectly lead to increased costs and lower profits because damaged or lost goods are not available for immediate sale or use.

Load flexibility is the degree to which a transportation mode can provide appropriate equipment and conditions for moving specific kinds of goods and can be adapted for moving other products. Many products must be shipped under controlled temperature and humidity. Other products, such as liquids or gases, require special equipment or facilities for shipment. A marketer with unusual transport needs can consult the *Official Railway Equipment Register,* which lists the various types of cars and equipment each railroad owns. As Table 15.5 shows, waterways and railroads have the highest load flexibility, while pipelines have the lowest.

Accessibility refers to a carrier's ability to move goods over a specific route or network. For example, marketers evaluating transportation modes for reaching Great Falls, Montana, would consider rail lines, truck routes, and scheduled airline service but would eliminate water-borne carriers because Great Falls is inaccessible by water. Some carriers differentiate themselves by serving areas their competitors do not. After deregulation, many large railroad companies sold off or abandoned unprofitable routes, making rail service inaccessible to facilities located on spur lines. Some marketers were forced to buy or lease their own truck fleets to get their products to market. In recent years, small, short-line railroad companies have started buying up track and creating networks of low-cost feeder lines to reach underserved markets.

Frequency refers to how often a company can send shipments by a specific transportation mode. When using pipelines, shipments can be continuous. A marketer shipping by railroad or waterway is limited by the carriers' schedules.

Coordinating Transportation   To take advantage of the benefits offered by various transportation modes and to compensate for deficiencies, marketers often combine and coordinate two or more modes. In recent years, **intermodal transportation,** as this integrated approach is sometimes called, has become easier because of new developments within the transportation industry.

intermodal transportation   Two or more transportation modes used in combination

Several kinds of intermodal shipping are available. All combine the flexibility of trucking with the low cost or speed of other forms of transport. Containerization facilitates intermodal transportation by consolidating shipments into sealed containers for transport by *piggyback* (shipping that uses both truck trailers and railway flatcars), *fishyback* (truck trailers and water carriers), and *birdyback* (truck trailers and air carriers). As transportation costs have increased, intermodal shipping has gained in popularity.

freight forwarders   Organizations that consolidate shipments from several firms into efficient lot sizes

Specialized outsource agencies provide other forms of transport coordination. Known as **freight forwarders,** these firms combine shipments from several organizations into efficient lot sizes. Small loads (less than five hundred pounds) are much more expensive to ship than full carloads or truckloads, which frequently requires consolidation. Freight forwarders take small loads from various marketers, buy transport space from carriers, and arrange for goods to be delivered to buyers. Freight forwarders' profits come from the margin between the higher, less-than-carload rates they charge each marketer and the lower carload rates they themselves pay. Because large shipments require less handling, use of freight forwarders can speed delivery. Freight forwarders can also determine the most efficient carriers and routes and are useful for shipping goods to foreign markets. Some companies prefer to outsource their shipping to freight forwarders because they provide door-to-door service.

megacarriers   Freight transportation firms that provide several modes of shipment

Another transportation innovation is the development of **megacarriers,** freight transportation companies that offer several shipment methods, including rail, truck, and air service. CSX, for example, has trains, barges, container ships, trucks, and pipelines, thus offering a multitude of transportation services. In addition, air carriers have increased their ground transportation services. As they expand the range of transportation alternatives, carriers, too, put greater stress on customer service.

Strategic Issues in Physical Distribution

The physical distribution functions discussed in this chapter—order processing, inventory management, materials handling, warehousing, and transportation—account for about half of all marketing costs. Whether these functions are performed by a producer, wholesaler, or retailer, or outsourced to some other firm, they have a significant impact on customer service and satisfaction, which are of prime importance to all members of the supply chain.

The strategic importance of physical distribution is evident in all elements of the marketing mix. Product design and packaging must allow for efficient stacking, storage, transport, and tracking. Differentiating products by size, color, and style must take into account additional demands placed on warehousing and shipping facilities. Competitive pricing may depend on a firm's ability to provide reliable delivery or emergency shipments of replacement parts. Firms trying to lower inventory costs may offer quantity discounts to encourage large purchases. Promotional campaigns must be coordinated with distribution functions so that advertised products are available to buyers and order-processing departments can handle additional sales orders efficiently. Supply chain members must consider warehousing and transportation costs, which may influence a firm's policy on stockouts or its choice to centralize (or decentralize) inventory.

Improving physical distribution starts by closing the gap with customers. The entire supply chain must understand and meet customers' requirements. An effective way of improving physical distribution is to integrate processes across the boundaries of all members of the supply chain. The full scope of the physical distribution process includes suppliers, manufacturers, wholesalers, retailers, transportation firms, and

Globalmarketing

Timberland Overhauls Its Supply Chain

The Timberland Company produces and markets men's, women's, and children's shoes (including its famous yellow hiking boot), clothing, and accessories. Its product lines include apparel such as outerwear, sweaters, shirts, pants, shorts, skirts, and socks, and accessories such as sunglasses, watches, gloves, wallets, belts, and day packs. These products are sold through department stores, specialty shoe stores, and about 75 company-owned stores in more than 90 countries. Today roughly one-third of Timberland's $796.5 million in revenues comes from outside the U.S.

As Timberland expanded rapidly into Europe and Asia during the 1980s, it leased numerous small warehouses close to its markets and supply sources. Ultimately, it wound up with four distribution centers in the United States and four in Europe, as well as a dozen warehouses in Asian countries from which it obtains supplies to manufacture various products. Maintaining so many small facilities was becoming a financial burden. Timberland was also experiencing difficulties integrating the information required to maintain a flexible distribution system. As the company's overseas sales volume escalated in the 1990s, overhauling the supply chain to control the flow of supplies and products more efficiently and flexibly became a major priority.

The first part of Timberland's supply chain overhaul involved consolidating its physical distribution infrastructure. The company consolidated operations into three distribution centers, in California, Kentucky, and Enschede, The Netherlands. It also completely outsourced its distribution operations in Asia to ACS, a San-Francisco-based freight forwarder. Timberland's Asian suppliers now feed ACS's facilities, which in turn supply the U.S. and European distribution centers as needed.

The second part of the overhaul involved sophisticated improvements to the firm's logistics information system. The new system now links the entire supply chain and integrates internal shipping data with external data. It tracks more than 95 percent of shipments in-transit, allowing Timberland to quickly route and reroute products to where they are needed, thereby improving customer service. These efforts have helped Timberland to enhance flexibility and improve delivery times. Ultimately, these efforts should improve Timberland's inventory management and help it get closer to both its customers *and* suppliers.

warehouses. To work well, the process requires a formal, integrated plan to balance supply and demand within a defined time period. Physical distribution can also be improved by developing cooperative relationships with suppliers of component parts and services. These relationships should emphasize joint improvement rather than just transferring costs and inefficiencies from one party to another.[20] Cooperation can be enhanced through information technology that allows channel partners to work together to plan production and physical distribution activities, to improve the efficiency and safety of product handling and movement, and to reduce waste and costs for the benefit of all supply chain members, including the customer.

No single distribution system is ideal for all situations, and any system must be evaluated continually and adapted as necessary. Pressures to adjust service levels or to reduce costs may lead to a total restructuring of supply chain relationships. The ensuing changes in transportation, warehousing, materials handling, and inventory may affect speed of delivery, reliability, and economy of service. Globalmarketing explores how one firm has revamped its supply chain to move materials more efficiently and flexibly to and from overseas locations. Recognizing that changes in any major distribution function may affect all other functions, marketing strategists consider customers' changing needs and preferences. Customer-oriented marketers analyze the characteristics of their target markets and plan distribution systems to provide products in the right place, at the right time, and at acceptable cost.

Summary

Wholesaling refers to all transactions in which products are bought for resale, for making other products, or for general business operations. Wholesalers are individuals or organizations that facilitate and expedite exchanges that are primarily wholesale transactions. For producers, wholesalers are a source of financial assistance and information, and by performing specialized accumulation and allocation functions, they allow producers to concentrate on manufacturing products. Wholesalers provide retailers with buying expertise, wide product lines, efficient distribution, and warehousing and storage.

Merchant wholesalers are independently owned businesses that take title to goods and assume ownership risks. They are either full-service wholesalers, offering the widest possible range of wholesaling functions, or limited-service wholesalers, providing only some marketing services and specializing in a few functions. Full-service merchant wholesalers include general-merchandise wholesalers, which offer a wide but relatively shallow product mix; limited-line wholesalers, which offer extensive assortments within a few product lines; specialty-line wholesalers, which carry only a single product line or a few items within a line; and rack jobbers, which own and service display racks in supermarkets and other stores. Limited-service merchant wholesalers include cash-and-carry wholesalers, which sell to small businesses, require payment in cash, and do not deliver; truck wholesalers, which sell a limited line of products from their own trucks directly to customers; drop shippers, which own goods and negotiate sales but never take possession of products; and mail-order wholesalers, which sell to retail and organizational buyers through direct-mail catalogs.

Agents and brokers, sometimes called functional middlemen, negotiate purchases and expedite sales in exchange for a commission, but they do not take title to products. Usually specializing in certain products, they can provide valuable sales expertise. Whereas agents represent buyers or sellers on a permanent basis, brokers are middlemen that buyers and sellers employ on a temporary basis to negotiate exchanges. Manufacturers' agents offer customers the complete product lines of two or more sellers. Selling agents market a complete product line or a producer's entire output and perform every wholesaling function except taking title to products. Commission merchants are agents that receive goods on consignment from local sellers and negotiate sales in large central markets.

Manufacturers' sales branches and offices are owned by manufacturers. Sales branches sell products and provide support services for the manufacturer's sales force in a given location. Sales offices carry no inventory and function much as agents do.

Physical distribution, or logistics, refers to the activities used to move products from producers to customers and other end users. These activities include order processing, inventory management, materials handling, warehousing, and transportation. An efficient physical distribution system is an important component of an overall marketing strategy because it can decrease costs and increase customer satisfaction. Within the marketing channel, physical distribution activities are often performed by a wholesaler, but they may be performed by a producer or retailer or outsourced to a third party.

The main objectives of physical distribution are to decrease costs and transit time while increasing customer service. Physical distribution managers strive to balance service, distribution costs, and resources. Because customers' service needs vary, companies must adapt to them. They must also offer service comparable to or better than that of their competitors and develop and communicate desirable customer service policies. Costs of providing service are minimized most effectively through the total-cost approach, which evaluates costs of the distribution system as a whole rather than as a collection of separate activities. Reducing cycle time, the time it takes to complete a process, is also important.

Order processing is the receipt and transmission of sales order information. It consists of three main tasks. Order entry begins when customers or salespersons place purchase orders by mail, telephone, or computer. Order handling involves verifying product availability, checking customer credit, and preparing products for shipping. Order delivery is provided by the carrier most suitable for a desired level of customer service. Order processing can be done manually, but it is usually accomplished through electronic data interchange (EDI), a computerized system that integrates order processing with production, inventory, accounting, and transportation.

The objective of inventory management is to minimize inventory costs while maintaining a supply of goods adequate for customers' needs. To avoid stockouts without tying up too much capital in inventory, firms must have systematic methods for determining a reorder point, the inventory level that signals the need to place a new order. When firms use the just-in-time approach, products arrive just as they are needed for use in production or resale.

Materials handling, the physical handling of products, is an important factor in warehouse operations, as well as in transportation from points of production to points of consumption. Systems for packaging, labeling, loading, and movement must be coordinated to maximize cost reduction and customer satisfaction. Basic handling systems include unit loading, which entails placing boxes on pallets or skids and using mechanical devices to move them, and containerization.

Warehousing involves the design and operation of facilities for storing and moving goods. Private warehouses are operated by companies for the purpose of distributing their own products. Public warehouses are businesses that lease storage space and related physical distribution facilities to other firms. Distribution centers are large, centralized warehouses specially designed for rapid movement of goods to customers. In many cases, a combination of private and public facilities is the most flexible warehousing approach.

Transportation adds time and place utility to a product by moving it from where it is made to where it is purchased and used. The basic modes of transporting goods are railroads, trucks, waterways, airways, and pipelines. The criteria marketers use when selecting a transportation mode are cost, speed, dependability, load flexibility, accessibility, and frequency. Intermodal transportation allows marketers to combine advantages of two or more modes of transport. Freight forwarders coordinate transport by combining small shipments from several organizations into efficient lot sizes, while megacarriers offer several shipment methods.

Physical distribution functions account for about half of all marketing costs and have a significant impact on customer satisfaction. Effective marketers are therefore actively involved in the design and control of physical distribution systems. Physical distribution affects every element of the marketing mix: product, price, promotion, and distribution. To satisfy customers, marketers consider consumers' changing needs and shifts within major distribution functions. They then adapt existing physical distribution systems for greater effectiveness.

Important Terms

Wholesaling	Cash-and-carry wholesalers	Sales offices	Warehousing
Wholesaler	Truck wholesalers	Physical distribution	Private warehouses
Merchant wholesalers	Drop shippers	Outsourcing	Public warehouses
Full-service wholesalers	Mail-order wholesalers	Cycle time	Distribution centers
General-merchandise wholesalers	Agents	Order processing	Transportation
Limited-line wholesalers	Brokers	Electronic data interchange (EDI)	Intermodal transportation
Specialty-line wholesalers	Manufacturers' agents	Inventory management	Freight forwarders
Rack jobbers	Selling agents	Just-in-time (JIT)	Megacarriers
Limited-service wholesalers	Commission merchants	Materials handling	
	Sales branches		

Discussion and Review Questions

1. What is wholesaling?
2. What services do wholesalers provide to producers and retailers?
3. What is the difference between a full-service merchant wholesaler and a limited-service merchant wholesaler?

4. Drop shippers take title to products but do not accept physical possession of them, whereas commission merchants take physical possession of products but do not accept title. Defend the logic of classifying drop shippers as wholesale merchants and commission merchants as agents.

5. Why are manufacturers' sales offices and branches classified as wholesalers? Which independent wholesalers are replaced by manufacturers' sales branches? Which independent wholesalers are replaced by manufacturers' sales offices?

6. Discuss the cost and service tradeoffs involved in developing a physical distribution system.

7. What factors must physical distribution managers consider when developing a customer service mix?

8. What are the main tasks involved in order processing?

9. Discuss the advantages of using an electronic order-processing system. Which types of organizations are most likely to utilize electronic order processing?

10. Explain the tradeoffs inventory managers face when reordering products or supplies. How is the reorder point computed?

11. How does a product's package affect materials handling procedures and techniques?

12. What is containerization? Discuss its major benefits.

13. Explain the major differences between private and public warehouses. What is a field public warehouse?

14. The focus of distribution centers is on the movement of goods. Describe how distribution centers are designed for the rapid flow of products.

15. Compare and contrast the five major transportation modes in terms of cost, speed, dependability, load flexibility, accessibility, and frequency.

16. Discuss ways marketers can combine or coordinate two or more modes of transportation. What is the advantage of doing so?

Application Questions

1. Contact a local retailer with which you do business, and ask the manager to describe the relationship the store has with one of its wholesalers. Using Table 15.1 as a guide, identify the activities performed by the wholesaler. Are any of the functions shared by both the retailer and the wholesaler?

2. Assume you are responsible for the physical distribution of computers at a mail-order company. What would you do to ensure product availability, timely delivery, and quality service for your customers?

3. The type of warehouse facilities used has important strategic implications for a firm. What type of warehouse would be most appropriate for the following situations and why?

a. A propane gas company recently entered the market in the state of Washington. The company's customers need varied quantities of propane on a timely basis and, at times, on short notice.

b. A suntan lotion manufacturer has little expertise in managing warehouses and needs storage space in several locations in the Southeast.

c. A book publisher must have short cycle time to get its products to customers quickly and needs to send the products to many different retailers.

4. Marketers select a transportation mode based on cost, speed, dependability, load flexibility, accessibility, and frequency (see Table 15.5). Identify a product and then select a mode of transportation based on these criteria. Explain your choice.

Internet Exercise & Resources

Frieda's Finest Markets the Unusual

Frieda's, Inc., is unique in being the first wholesale produce company in the United States to be founded, owned, and operated by a woman, and remains a family-owned and operated business, with founder Frieda Caplan's daughter Karen currently serving as president and CEO. To learn more about Frieda's goods and services, visit its Web site at

www.friedas.com

1. Based on its Web site, what type of wholesaler is Frieda's?

2. What products does Frieda's market?

3. What services does Frieda's offer its retailer customers? What else can you find on Frieda's Web site?

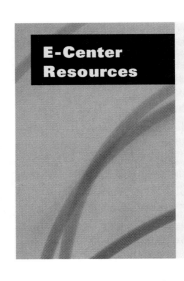

E-Center Resources

Visit http://www.prideferrell.com to find several resources to help you succeed in mastering the material in this chapter, plus additional materials that will help you expand your marketing knowledge. The Web site includes

- Internet exercise updates plus additional exercises
- ✔ ACE self-tests
- abc Chapter summary with hotlinked glossary
- ↻ Hotlinks to companies featured in this chapter
- ✪ Resource Center
- ▭ Career Center
- ▤ Marketing plan worksheets

VIDEO CASE 15.1

SYSCO Keeps Pace with America's Food Trends

Today's active families are spending less time preparing meals at home and more time eating at fast-food restaurants or bringing home takeout meals from restaurants, delis, or supermarkets, and SYSCO Corp. plays a major role in serving this expanding "food-prepared-away-from-home" market. SYSCO, the largest food-service distributor in the U.S., sells $15.3 billion worth of products to more than 300,000 restaurants, schools, hotels, restaurants, hospitals, industrial caterers, and other food service customers. The Houston-based wholesaler supplies 275,000 different products, ranging from fresh and frozen meat, fruits and vegetables, and canned and dry products, to paper products and tableware, chemical and janitorial items, and kitchen equipment and medical supplies.

Before 1969, small, independent regional operators were the primary distributors of food products to restaurants, hotels, and other nongrocers. At that time, John Baugh, a Houston-based wholesale foods distributor, recognized that Americans were increasingly dining outside the home. To exploit this opportunity to better serve food-service providers, Baugh convinced eight other U.S. wholesalers to combine and form SYSCO, a national distribution company. In its first year of operation, SYSCO recorded sales of $115 million. Since then, the wholesaler has grown to nearly 100 times its original size through increased sales efforts to existing customers, expanded product lines, and acquisitions of local distributors. Although 3,000 small companies still account for three-fourths of all food-service distribution sales volume, SYSCO has grown larger than its closest six competitors combined.

Throughout its history, a significant key to SYSCO's success and growth has been its guiding phi-

losophy to work in the best interests of its customers and to deliver excellent customer service. SYSCO offers numerous services to its retail and institutional customers, including assistance with marketing strategy, inventory selection and storage, and financial assistance. In addition to helping customers reduce their inventory and storage requirements, SYSCO provides quick and guaranteed order response. In fact, SYSCO boasts a 100 percent rate of order fulfillment and on-time delivery. When customers have last-minute emergency needs, SYSCO personnel go to the warehouse, put goods into their own cars, and deliver them immediately.

The company's services to manufacturers and suppliers extend beyond warehousing and product distribution. SYSCO is involved in every step from selection of products in the field, to developing product lines, to onsite inspection of the manufacturing process. To minimize customers' preparation time and personnel requirements, for example, SYSCO created "hand-turned vegetables," miniature potatoes, squash, carrots, and other hand-cut vegetables in vacuum-sealed pouches ready for overnight delivery. To facilitate customers' carry-out business, SYSCO developed leak-resistant, heat-tolerant carry-out containers. More than 180 quality-assurance professionals work directly on the manufacturing line to assist manufacturers in making sure that products meet SYSCO's quality and freshness standards.

SYSCO also helps customers increase sales by serving as a source of information about new developments in the industry. SYSCO solicits input from its food-service customers to help manufacturers and suppliers generate ideas for new products; it even helps create them. For example, when SYSCO's research indicated that a growing number of U.S. restaurants were including Italian items on their menus, SYSCO launched its Arrezzio line, a complete line of authentic Italian foods. Developed with both chefs and manufacturers, Arrezzio product sales have more than doubled each year. When "Fajita Wraps," flour tortillas wrapped around a variety of foods, became popular, SYSCO began to offer several flavors of tortillas and packages of precooked, frozen vegetables to fill them.

As a wholesaler, SYSCO has become a major link in the food product supply chain by offering optimal levels of efficiency and customer service for its restaurant, hotel, school, and hospital customers. By providing customers with quality products delivered on time in excellent condition at reasonable prices, SYSCO has lived up to its own slogan: "North America's Leading Marketer of Quality Assured Foodservice Products."[21]

Questions for Discussion

1. What type of wholesaler is SYSCO?
2. What services does SYSCO provide to manufacturers and to its retail and business customers?
3. What strategies have helped SYSCO become successful?

CASE 15.2

The Home Depot Initiates New Cooperation in Supply Chain Management

Atlanta-based The Home Depot is the leading chain of home-improvement stores in the United States with sales of $24 billion and profits of $731.5 million. With almost 750 stores in the United States, Canada, Puerto Rico, and Chile, The Home Depot ranks among the twenty largest U.S. retailers. It plans to double its number of stores by 2002, including new locations in Mexico and overseas. *Fortune* magazine named The Home Depot "America's most admired retailer" for five years running, and it consistently makes *Fortune's* list of "America's most admired corporations."

The Home Depot was founded in 1978 by Bernard Marcus, Arthur Blank, and Ronald Brill, all former Handy Dan Home Improvement Centers executives. Their first three stores opened in the Atlanta area in 1979, and they added a fourth in 1980. Over the years, the firm has acquired Bowater Home Centers (with stores in Texas, Louisiana, and Alabama), Modell's Shoppers World stores (Long Island), and Aikenhead, a Canadian home-improvement retailer. In 1987, the chain initiated its policy of "low day-in day-out pricing."

The typical Home Depot store stocks 40,000 to 50,000 home improvement materials, building supplies, and lawn and garden items in more than 100,000 square feet. To cater to both do-it-yourselfers and professional contractors, the stores follow a strategy of providing superior customer service, low prices, and a broad product assortment. They also offer product installation services, free professional consultation on home improvement projects, and how-to seminars on a variety of do-it-yourself projects.

The Home Depot has also opened several Expo Design Centers, which offer upscale interior design products and services, rather than building supplies. Also in 1995, the firm launched Right at Home, a line of coordinated home furnishings, including textiles, wall coverings, floor tiles, and lighting fixtures.

The Home Depot also operates the Maintenance Warehouse, a wholly owned subsidiary that supplies building repair and replacement products to owners and managers of multi-family housing, lodging, and commercial properties throughout the U.S. The Maintenance Warehouse stocks more than 11,000 different items, including hardware, electrical, plumbing, appliance, and heating and air-conditioning products. To supply items in the Maintenance Warehouse's 1,600 page catalog, the company operates 13 distribution centers that provide same-day shipping. As a leader in both its supply chain and its industry, The Home Depot is using re-engineering to become more efficient in physical distribution—particularly logistics, inventory control, security, and electronic data interchange systems—to help manufacturers improve their productivity and thereby supply The Home Depot with better quality products at less cost. After recognizing that it needed to implement a core carrier program (with 89 percent of its deliveries going direct from supplier to store, store-receiving docks were often overwhelmed with incoming trucks from multiple shipping companies), The Home Depot required its suppliers to switch to designated regional and national carriers. This stipulation was met with substantial resistance for several years until The Home Depot began listening to suppliers' concerns and implementing some of their suggestions. The Home Depot now offers two choices of carriers in each region.

Its success has led The Home Depot to form the Inbound Logistics Consortium, a cooperative partnership of retailers such as Wal-Mart, Handy Andy, Caldor, Rickels, Target, Venture, Lowes, HomeQuarters, and others, in which regional trucking companies making deliveries can provide better service, faster delivery, and greater efficiency in their operations. "We think Wal-Mart and The Home Depot can help each other," insists Rebecca Nash, director of traffic. The Home Depot has also made suggestions for standardizing packaging and delivery that saves its suppliers millions of dollars.

Another radical change was The Home Depot's insistence that its 5,000 suppliers switch from shipping products on wooden pallets to plastic slip-sheets. Slip-sheets cost about one-sixth as much as wooden pallets and, because they are thin, take up less room in storage and on trucks, allowing more goods to be transported at one time. According to Pete Cleveland, The Home Depot's vice president for traffic and distribution, "The slip-sheeting program will result in significant cost and manpower savings for our industry." If it had not switched to slip-sheeting, The Home Depot would have paid carriers more than $700,000 to haul away pallets in 1994 alone. To motivate suppliers to switch to slip-sheets, The Home Depot distributed a humorous promotional video to vendors and conducted seminars stressing the advantages of slip-sheeting. The company also has a toll-free answer line for vendors converting to slip-sheeting and is working with its core carriers to help vendors convert to the new system. It has also founded a Slip-sheet Retailer Coalition to share the benefits and expand the uses of slip-sheeting throughout the retail industry. Says Nash,

"We want to share our experience with other retailers. We went to the vendor community and said, 'We want to sell your stocks and reduce your lead time.' "

The Home Depot is also making greater use of Electronic Data Interchange (EDI), a paperless system that electronically processes orders from stores to manufacturers, alerts stores when merchandise is scheduled to arrive, and transmits invoice data. The system helps The Home Depot avoid stockouts and allows it to track shipments almost instantly, resulting in better customer service.

The Home Depot is also trying to persuade the retail industry to standardize other elements, such as UPC (bar code) symbols and security devices. Such standardization and reengineering will enable The Home Depot to become even more efficient in its role as supply chain leader while providing better value and service to its customers.[22]

Questions for Discussion

1. Explain why physical distribution is so important in The Home Depot's marketing strategy.
2. How has The Home Depot positioned itself as a leader of supply chain management in the home improvement industry?
3. Why do you think The Home Depot has formed a cooperative partnership with Wal-Mart and other competitors?

16

Retailing

OBJECTIVES

- To understand the purpose and function of retailers in the marketing channel

- To be able to identify the major types of retailers

- To recognize the various forms of nonstore retailing

- To examine major types of franchising and this method's benefits and weaknesses

- To explore strategic issues in retailing

West Edmonton Mall's Smart Retailing

What has 800 retail stores, including 5 department stores and 110 eating establishments, an ice-skating rink, an indoor amusement park, an indoor water park, *and* a 350-room hotel? It's the West Edmonton Mall, located in West Edmonton, Alberta, Canada. The world's largest shopping mall covers 238 acres and has 5.4 million square feet of retail space. But it's so much more than just a shopping center that it's no wonder that the mall generates more than 20 billion visits a year.

The seventeen-year-old mall is the vision of the local Ghermezian family, which also happens to own part of another huge mall, the Mall of America in Minneapolis. The West Edmonton Mall actually started out in 1981 as a typical regional shopping center, with 220 stores in 1.125 million square feet. Two years later, the owners doubled the mall's square footage, added 240 stores, and opened the skating rink and amusement park. A few short years after that, the mall added the water park, hotel, dolphin lagoon, aquarium, and submarine rides.

Dolphin lagoon? Submarines rides? Yes, in addition to the usual Gap, Banana Republic, and Benetton outlets found in most malls, the West Edmonton Mall features a Dolphin Lagoon, where four dolphins perform in three shows daily. In fact, the mall's marine theme extends to the five-acre World Waterpark, with bungee jumping and the world's largest indoor wave pool; the Sea Life Cavern, a huge indoor aquarium complete with waterfall and exotic species; Deep Sea Adventure, which includes four submarines (three more than the Canadian Navy) that visitors can ride; and a replica of Columbus' ship the Santa Maria. Additionally, the mall's Galaxyland indoor amusement park features twenty-five attractions, including the world's largest indoor triple-loop roller coaster. Shoppers may even catch a glimpse of the Edmonton Oilers, which occasionally practice on the mall's NHL regulation size indoor ice-skating rink. If that's too much excitement, visitors can always play a little miniature golf or check into the hotel. With so much to see and do (and maybe even buy) at the mall, the 350-room Fantasyland hotel encourages visitors stay for several days. The hotel, which caters to adults with or without children, includes 118 themed rooms like the Hollywood room, the Igloo room, and the Polynesian room. With a 94 percent occupancy, the hotel is usually booked three to four months in advance.

Although many patrons are Edmontonians, who visit an average of four times a year and often bring out-of-town guests, many visitors are tourists and shoppers who live more than thirty miles from the mall. They come to shop, eat, play, and just hang out. By offering so much, West Edmonton Mall definitely stands out from other shopping centers and provides its customers with educational and entertainment value beyond the usual shopping experience.[1]

402

Shopping malls like the West Edmonton Mall provide a convenient, and even enter-taining, venue for consumers to access multiple retailers. Retailers like J. C. Penney, the Gap, and Old Navy are the most visible and accessible channel members to consumers. They are an important link in the marketing channel because they are both marketers for and customers of producers and wholesalers. They perform many marketing functions, such as buying, selling, grading, risk taking, and developing and maintaining information databases about customers. Retailers are in a strategic position to develop relationships with consumers and partnerships with producers and intermediaries in the marketing channel.

In this chapter, we examine the nature of retailing and its importance in supplying consumers with goods and services. We discuss the major types of retail stores and describe several forms of nonstore retailing. We also look at franchising, a retailing form that continues to grow in popularity. Finally, we present several strategic issues in retailing: location, retail positioning, store image, scrambled merchandising, and the wheel of retailing.

The Nature of Retailing

retailing Transactions in which ultimate consumers are the buyers

retailer An organization that purchases products for the purpose of reselling them to ultimate consumers

Retailing includes all transactions in which the buyer intends to consume the product through personal, family, or household use. Buyers in retail transactions are therefore the ultimate consumers. A **retailer** is an organization that purchases products for the purpose of reselling them to ultimate consumers. Although most retailers' sales are directly to the consumer, nonretail transactions occasionally occur when retailers sell products to other businesses. Retailing often takes place in stores or service establishments, such as Crate & Barrel in Figure 16.1, but it also occurs through direct selling, direct marketing, and vending machines outside stores.

Retailing is important to the national economy. There are approximately 1.56 million retailers operating in the United States.[2] This number has remained relatively constant for the past twenty years, but sales volume has increased more than fourfold. Most personal income is spent in retail stores, and nearly one of every seven persons employed in the United States works in a retail store.

Retailers add value, provide services, and assist in making product selections. They can enhance the value of the product by making the shopping experience more convenient, as in home shopping. Through its location, a retailer can facilitate comparison shopping. For example, it is not unusual for car dealerships to cluster in the

Figure 16.1
Example of a Retailer
Crate & Barrel retails furniture and houseware items directly to the consumer.

same general vicinity. Product value is also enhanced when retailers offer services, such as technical advice, delivery, credit, and repair services. Finally, retail sales personnel can demonstrate to customers how a product can help address their needs or solve a problem.

The value added by retailers is significant for both producers and ultimate consumers. Retailers are the critical link between producers and ultimate consumers because they provide the environment in which exchanges with ultimate consumers occur. Ultimate consumers benefit through retailers' performance of marketing functions that result in the availability of broader arrays of products. As discussed in Chapter 14, retailers play a major role in creating time, place, and possession utility and, in some cases, form utility.

Leading retailers, such as Wal-Mart, Home Depot, Taco Bell, Macy's, and Toys "R" Us offer consumers a place to browse and compare merchandise to find just what they need. However, such traditional retailing is being challenged by direct marketing channels that provide home shopping through catalogs, television, and the Internet. Traditional retailers are responding to this change in the retail environment in various ways. Wal-Mart has joined forces with fast-food giants like McDonald's and KFC to attract consumers and offer them the added convenience of eating where they shop. In response to the phenomenal success of Amazon.com, Barnes & Noble has set up a Web site to sell books over the Internet.

New store formats and advances in information technology are making the retail environment highly dynamic and competitive. The key to success in retailing is to have a strong customer focus with a retail strategy that provides the level of service, product quality, and innovation that consumers desire. Partnerships among noncompeting retailers and other marketing channel members are providing new opportunities for retailers. For example, airports are leasing space to retailers like Sharper Image, McDonald's, Burger King, and The Body Shop.[3] Kroger and Nordstrom's have developed joint cobranded credit cards that offer rebates to customers at participating stores. The Kroger Mastercard provides a 1 percent rebate toward future Kroger grocery purchases.[4]

Retailers are also finding global opportunities. For example, The Gap is now opening more international stores than domestic ones, a trend that is likely to continue for the foreseeable future. Wal-Mart and Home Depot are rapidly opening stores in Canada, Mexico, and South America. McDonald's is growing faster outside the United States than domestically and even has stores in Russia and China.

Major Types of Retail Stores

There are many different types of retail stores. One way to classify them is by the breadth of products offered. Two general categories include general merchandise retailers and specialty retailers.

General Merchandise Retailers

general merchandise retailer A retail establishment that offers a variety of product lines, which are stocked in depth

A retail establishment that offers a variety of product lines, stocked in considerable depth, is referred to as a **general merchandise retailer.** The types of product offerings, mixes of customer services, and operating styles of retailers in this category vary considerably. The primary types of general merchandise retailers are department stores, discount stores, supermarkets, superstores, hypermarkets, warehouse clubs, and warehouse and catalog showrooms (Table 16.1).

department stores Large retail organizations characterized by wide product mixes and organized into separate departments to facilitate marketing efforts and internal management

Department Stores   **Department stores** are large retail organizations characterized by wide product mixes and employing at least twenty-five people. To facilitate marketing efforts and internal management in these stores, related product lines are organized into separate departments, such as cosmetics, housewares, apparel, home furnishings, and appliances. Often, each department functions as a self-contained business, and buyers for individual departments are fairly autonomous.

Table 16.1   General Merchandise Retailers

Type of Retailer	Description	Examples
Department store	Large organization offering wide product mix and organized into separate departments	Macy's, JC Penney, Sears
Discount store	Self-service, general merchandise store offering brand name and private brand products at low prices	Wal-Mart, Target, Kmart
Supermarket	Self-service store offering complete line of food products and some nonfood products	Kroger, Albertson's, Winn-Dixie
Superstore	Giant outlet offering all food and nonfood products found in supermarkets, as well as most routinely purchased products	Wal-Mart Supercenters
Hypermarket	Combination supermarket and discount store, larger than a superstore	Carrefours
Warehouse club	Large-scale, members-only establishments combining cash-and-carry wholesaling with discount retailing	Sam's Club, Costco
Warehouse showroom	Facility in a large, low-cost building with large on-premises inventories and minimum service	Ikea
Catalog showroom	Type of warehouse showroom where consumers shop from a catalog and products are stored out of buyers' reach and provided in manufacturer's carton	Service Merchandise

Department stores are distinctly service-oriented. Their total product includes credit, delivery, personal assistance, merchandise returns, and a pleasant atmosphere. Although some so-called department stores are actually large, departmentalized specialty stores, most department stores are shopping stores. Consumers can compare price, quality, and service at one store with those at competing stores. Along with large discount stores, department stores are often considered retailing leaders in a community and are found in most places with populations of more than fifty thousand.

Typical department stores—Macy's (see Figure 16.2), Sears, Marshall Field's, Dillard's, and Neiman Marcus—obtain a large proportion of sales from apparel, accessories, and cosmetics. Other products these stores carry include gift items, luggage, electronics, home accessories, and sports equipment. Some department stores offer such services as automobile insurance, hair care, income tax preparation, and travel and optical services. In some cases, space for these specialized services is leased out, with proprietors managing their own operations and paying rent to department stores.

Figure 16.2
Department Stores
A department store, such as Macy's, offers wide product mixes.

discount stores Self-service, general-merchandise stores offering brand name and private brand products at low prices

Discount Stores **Discount stores** are self-service, general merchandise outlets regularly offering brand name and private brand products at low prices. Discounters accept lower margins than conventional retailers in exchange for high sales volume. To keep turnover high, they carry a wide but carefully selected assortment of products, from appliances to housewares and clothing. Major discount establishments also offer food products, toys, automotive services, garden supplies, and sports equipment. Wal-Mart, Target, and Kmart are the three largest discount stores. Many discounters are regional organizations, such as Venture, Bradlees, and Meijer. Most operate in large (50,000 to 80,000 square feet), no-frills facilities. Discount stores usually offer everyday low prices rather than relying on sales events.

Discount retailing developed on a large scale in the early 1950s, when postwar production began catching up with consumer demand for appliances, home furnishings, and other hard goods. Discount stores were often cash-only operations in warehouse districts, offering goods at savings of 20 to 30 percent over conventional retailers. Facing increased competition from department stores and other discount stores, some discounters have improved store services, atmosphere, and location, raising prices and sometimes blurring the distinction between discount stores and department stores. Other discounters continue to focus on price alone.

supermarkets Large, self-service stores that carry a complete line of food products, along with some nonfood products

Supermarkets **Supermarkets** are large, self-service stores that carry a complete line of food products, as well as some nonfood products, such as cosmetics and nonprescription drugs. Supermarkets are arranged in departments for maximum efficiency in stocking and handling products but have central checkout facilities. They offer lower prices than smaller neighborhood grocery stores, usually provide free parking, and may also cash checks. Supermarkets must operate efficiently because net profits after taxes are usually less than 1 percent of sales. Supermarkets may be independently owned but are often part of a chain operation. Top U.S. supermarket chains include Kroger, Albertson's, Safeway, and A & P. Ralph's is an example of a regional supermarket chain (see Figure 16.3).

Today, consumers make more than three-quarters of all grocery purchases in supermarkets. Even so, supermarkets' total share of the food market is declining

Figure 16.3
Supermarkets
Ralph's is an example of a regional supermarket chain that carries a complete line of food products, as well as some nonfood items.

because consumers now have widely varying food preferences and buying habits, and in most communities, shoppers can choose from a number of convenience stores, discount stores, and specialty food stores, as well as a wide variety of restaurants.

superstores Giant retail outlets that carry food and nonfood products found in supermarkets, as well as most routinely purchased consumer products

Superstores Superstores—which originated in Europe—are giant retail outlets that carry not only food and nonfood products ordinarily found in supermarkets, but also routinely purchased consumer products. Besides a complete food line, superstores sell housewares, hardware, small appliances, clothing, personal-care products, garden products, and tires—about four times as many items as supermarkets. Services available at superstores include dry cleaning, automotive repair, check cashing, bill paying, and snack bars.

Superstores combine features of discount stores and supermarkets. Examples include Wal-Mart Supercenters, some Kroger stores, and Super Kmart Centers. To cut handling and inventory costs, they use sophisticated operating techniques and often have tall shelving that displays entire assortments of products. Superstores can have an area of as much as 200,000 square feet (compared with 20,000 square feet in supermarkets). Sales volume is two to three times that of supermarkets, partly because locations near good transportation networks help generate the in-store traffic needed for profitability.

hypermarkets Stores that combine supermarket and discount shopping in one location

Hypermarkets Hypermarkets combine supermarket and discount store shopping in one location. Larger than superstores, they range from 225,000 to 325,000 square feet and offer 45,000 to 60,000 different types of low-priced products. They commonly allocate 40 to 50 percent of their space to grocery products and the remainder to general merchandise, including athletic shoes, designer jeans, and other apparel; refrigerators, televisions, and other appliances; housewares; cameras; toys; jewelry; hardware; and automotive supplies. Many lease space to noncompeting businesses, such as banks, optical shops, and fast-food restaurants. All hypermarkets focus on low prices and vast selection. Although Kmart, Wal-Mart, and Carrefours (a French retailer) have operated hypermarkets in the United States, most of these stores have been unsuccessful and have closed. Such stores are too big for time-constrained U.S. shoppers. However, hypermarkets are quite successful in Europe and South America.[5]

warehouse clubs Large-scale, members-only establishments that combine features of cash-and-carry wholesaling with discount retailing

Warehouse Clubs Warehouse clubs, a rapidly growing form of mass merchandising, are large-scale, members-only selling operations combining cash-and-carry wholesaling with discount retailing. For a nominal annual fee (usually about $35), small retailers purchase products at wholesale prices for business use or for resale. Warehouse clubs also sell to ultimate consumers affiliated with government agencies, credit unions, schools, hospitals, and banks, but instead of paying a membership fee, individual consumers may pay about 5 percent more on each item than do business customers.

Sometimes called buying clubs, warehouse clubs offer the same types of products as discount stores but in a limited range of sizes and styles. Whereas most discount stores carry 40,000 items, a warehouse club handles only 3,500 to 5,000 products, usually acknowledged brand leaders.[6] Sam's Club stores, for example, stock about 4,000 items, with 1,400 available most of the time and the rest being one-time buys. Costco leads the $47 billion warehouse club industry with sales of $21.5 billion; Sam's Club is second with $20.7 billion in store sales. A third company, BJ's Wholesale Club, which operates in the Northeast and Florida, has a much smaller market.[7] All these establishments offer a broad product mix, including food, beverages, books, appliances, housewares, automotive parts, hardware, and furniture. Warehouse clubs appeal to many price-conscious consumers and small retailers unable to obtain wholesaling services from large distributors. The average warehouse club shopper has more education, higher income, and a larger household than the average supermarket shopper.[8]

To keep prices lower than those of supermarkets and discount stores, warehouse clubs provide few services. They generally do not advertise, except through direct mail. Their facilities, often located in industrial areas, have concrete floors and aisles wide enough for forklifts. Merchandise is stacked on pallets or displayed on pipe racks. All payments must be in cash, and customers must transport purchases themselves.

warehouse showrooms
Retail facilities in large, low-cost buildings with large on-premise inventories and minimum services

Warehouse and Catalog Showrooms   **Warehouse showrooms** are retail facilities with five basic characteristics: large, low-cost buildings, warehouse materials-handling technology, vertical merchandise displays, large on-premises inventories, and minimum services. IKEA, a Swedish company, sells furniture, household goods, and kitchen accessories in warehouse showrooms and through catalogs around the world, including China and Russia (see Figure 16.4).[9] Wickes Furniture and Levitz Furniture also operate warehouse showrooms. These high-volume, low-overhead operations stress fewer personnel and services. Lower costs are possible because some marketing functions have been shifted to consumers, who must transport, finance, and perhaps store merchandise. Most consumers carry away purchases in the manufacturer's carton, although stores will deliver for a fee.

catalog showrooms   A form of warehouse showroom, where consumers shop from a catalog and products are stored out of buyers' reach

In **catalog showrooms,** one item of each product is displayed, often in a locked case, with remaining inventory stored out of the buyer's reach. Using catalogs that have been mailed to their homes or are on store counters, customers order products by phone or in person. Clerks fill orders from the warehouse area, and products are presented in the manufacturer's carton. In contrast to traditional catalog retailers, which offer no discounts and require that customers wait for delivery, catalog showrooms regularly sell below list price and often provide goods immediately.

Catalog showrooms usually sell jewelry, luggage, photographic equipment, toys, small appliances and housewares, sporting goods, and power tools. They advertise extensively and carry established brands and models that are not likely to be discontinued. Because catalog showrooms have higher product turnover, fewer losses through shoplifting, and lower labor costs than department stores, they are able to feature lower prices. They offer minimal services, however. Customers may have to stand in line to examine items or place orders. Pressure is being applied to catalog showrooms by the rapid growth of discounters and warehouse clubs. Service Merchandise (the market leader), Best Products, and Consumer Distributing are examples of catalog showroom retailers.

IKEA Introduces Home Shopping.
Now you can shop for a new carpet, a floor lamp, or for that   1997 IKEA catalogue and a telephone. The catalogue is available matter a complete dining room suite from the comfort   for just five dollars (which, incidentally, is redeemable of your own home. All you need is a copy of our new   [IKEA]   on your first purchase) when you call 1-800-661-1907.
Make yourself at home.

Figure 16.4
Warehouse Showroom and Catalog Sales
IKEA promotes its catalog sales of furniture and household goods and also has several showroom retail stores.

traditional specialty retailers   Stores that carry a narrow product mix with deep product lines

Specialty Retailers

In contrast to general merchandise retailers with their broad product mixes, specialty retailers emphasize narrow and deep ones. Despite their name, specialty retailers do not sell specialty items (except when specialty goods complement the overall product mix). Instead, they offer substantial assortments in a few product lines. We examine three types of specialty retailers: traditional specialty retailers, off-price retailers, and category killers.

Traditional Specialty Retailers   **Traditional specialty retailers** are stores that carry a narrow product mix with deep product lines. Sometimes called *limited-line retailers,* they may be referred to as *single-line retailers* if they carry unusual depth in one main product category. Specialty retailers commonly sell such shopping products as apparel, jewelry, sporting goods, fabrics, computers, and pet supplies. The Limited, Radio Shack, Hickory Farms, the Gap, and Disney Store are examples of retailers offering limited product lines but great depth within those lines.

Although the number of chain specialty stores is increasing, most specialty stores are independently owned. They occupy about two-thirds of the space in most shopping centers and malls, accounting for 40 to 50 percent of all general merchandise sales.[10] Florists, bakery shops, and bookstores are among the small independent specialty retailers that appeal to local target markets, although these stores can be owned and managed by large corporations. Even if this kind of retailer adds a few supporting product lines, the store may still be classified as a specialty store.

Because they are usually small, specialty stores may have high costs in proportion to sales, and satisfying customers may require carrying some products with low turnover rates. However, these stores sometimes obtain lower prices from suppliers by purchasing limited lines of merchandise in large quantities. Successful specialty stores understand their customer types and know what products to carry, thus reducing the risk of unsold merchandise. For example, Restoration Hardware, a small chain of forty-one stores specializing in home furnishings, offers hard-to-find hardware items that customers need to renovate old homes, as well as reproduction furniture and accessories to furnish them.[11] Specialty stores usually offer better selections and more sales expertise than department stores, their main competitors. By capitalizing on fashion, service, personnel, atmosphere, and location, specialty retailers position themselves strategically to attract customers in specific market segments. They may even become exclusive dealers in their markets for certain products. Through specialty stores, small business owners provide unique services to match consumers' varied desires. For consumers dissatisfied with the impersonal nature of large retailers, the close, personal contact offered by a small specialty store can be a welcome change.

off-price retailers Stores that buy manufacturers' seconds, overruns, returns, and off-season merchandise for resale to consumers at deep discounts

Off-Price Retailers   **Off-price retailers** are stores that buy manufacturers' seconds, overruns, returns, and off-season production runs at below-wholesale prices for resale to consumers at deep discounts. Unlike true discount stores, which pay regular wholesale prices for goods and usually carry second-line brand names, off-price retailers offer limited lines of national-brand and designer merchandise, usually clothing, shoes, or housewares. The number of off-price retailers has grown since the mid-1980s and now includes such major chains as T.J. Maxx (see Figure 16.5), Stein Mart, Burlington Coat Factory, and Marshalls.

Off-price stores charge 20 to 50 percent less than do department stores for comparable merchandise but offer few customer services. They often feature community dressing rooms, central checkout counters, and no credit, returns, or exchanges. Off-price stores may or may not sell goods with original labels intact (Filene's Basement Stores do, Loehmann's outlets do not). They turn over their inventory nine to twelve times a year, three times as often as traditional specialty stores. They compete with department stores for the same customers: price-conscious members of suburban households who are knowledgeable about brand names. Another form of off-price retailer is the manufacturer's outlet mall, which makes available manufacturer overstocks and unsold merchandise from other retail outlets. Prices are low, and diverse manufacturers are represented in these malls.

To ensure a regular flow of merchandise into their stores, off-price retailers establish long-term relationships with suppliers that can provide large quantities of goods at reduced prices.

**Figure 16.5
Off-Price Retailers**
T. J. Maxx offers brand name clothing at reduced prices.

Manufacturers may approach retailers with samples, discontinued products, or items that have not sold well; or retailers may seek out manufacturers, offering to pay cash for goods produced during the manufacturers' off season. Although manufacturers benefit from such arrangements, they also risk alienating their specialty and department store customers. Department stores tolerate off-price stores as long as they do not advertise brand names, limit merchandise to lower-quality items, and are located away from the department stores. When off-price retailers obtain large stocks of in-season, top-quality merchandise, tension builds between department stores and manufacturers.

category killer A very large specialty store concentrating on a major product category and competing on the basis of low prices and product availability

Category Killers   Over the last decade, a new breed of specialty retailer, the category killer, has evolved. A **category killer** is a very large specialty store that concentrates on a major product category and competes on the basis of low prices and enormous product availability. These stores are referred to as category killers because they expand rapidly and gain sizable market shares, taking business away from smaller, high-cost retail outlets. Examples of category killers include Home Depot (building materials), Office Depot (office supplies and equipment), Toys "R" Us (toys), and Best Buy (electronics).

Nonstore Retailing

nonstore retailing The selling of products outside the confines of a retail facility

Nonstore retailing is the selling of products outside the confines of a retail facility. This form of retailing accounts for an increasing percentage of total sales. Three factors are spurring its growth. Consumers—especially women, because of their increased participation in the work force—have less time for shopping in retail stores; some retail store salespeople are poorly informed and therefore less able to assist shoppers; and the number of older consumers, who are less prone to shop in stores, is rising. Approximately 15 percent of all consumer purchases are made through nonstore retailing. The three major types of nonstore retailing are direct selling, direct marketing, and automatic vending.

Direct Selling

direct selling The marketing of products to ultimate consumers through face-to-face sales presentations at home or in the workplace

Direct selling is the marketing of products to ultimate consumers through face-to-face sales presentations at home or in the workplace. Traditionally called door-to-door selling, direct selling began in our country with the peddler over a century ago and has grown into a sizable industry of several hundred firms. Although direct sellers historically used a cold canvass, door-to-door approach for finding prospects, many companies today, such as World Book, Kirby, Amway, Mary Kay, and Avon, use other approaches. They initially identify customers through the mail, telephone, or shopping mall intercepts and set appointments. Probably less than 1 percent of direct selling purchases result from sales efforts without prearranged appointments.

The "party plan" is sometimes used in direct selling and can occur in homes or in the workplace. When a party plan is used, a consumer acts as a host and invites a number of friends and associates to view merchandise in a group setting, where a salesperson is available to demonstrate products. The congenial party atmosphere overcomes customers' suspicions and encourages them to buy. Direct selling through the party plan requires effective salespersons, who can identify hosts and provide encouragement and incentives for them to organize a gathering of friends and associates. Companies that commonly use the party plan include Tupperware, Stanley Home Products, and Sarah Coventry.

Direct selling has both benefits and limitations. It provides the marketer with an opportunity to demonstrate the product in an environment—customers' homes—

where it would most likely be used. The door-to-door seller can give the customer personal attention, and the product can be presented to the customer at a convenient time and location. Personal attention to the customer is the foundation on which some direct sellers, such as Mary Kay, have built their businesses. Because commissions for salespersons are so high, ranging from 30 to 50 percent of the sales price, and great effort is required to isolate promising prospects, overall costs of direct selling make it the most expensive form of retailing. Furthermore, some customers view direct selling negatively, owing to unscrupulous and fraudulent practices used by direct sellers in the past. Some communities even have local ordinances that control or, in some cases, prohibit direct selling.

Direct Marketing

direct marketing The use of the telephone and nonpersonal media to introduce products to consumers, who then can purchase them via mail, telephone, or the Internet

Direct marketing is the use of the telephone and nonpersonal media to communicate product and organizational information to customers, who then can purchase products via mail, telephone, or the Internet. Direct marketing can occur through catalog marketing, direct-response marketing, telemarketing, television home shopping, and online retailing.

catalog marketing A type of marketing in which an organization provides a catalog from which customers make selections and place orders by mail or telephone

Catalog Marketing   In **catalog marketing**, an organization provides a catalog from which customers make selections and place orders by mail or telephone. Catalog marketing began in 1872, when Montgomery Ward issued its first catalog to rural families. Today, there are over 7,000 catalog marketing companies in the United States, as well as a number of retail stores, such as J.C. Penney, that engage in catalog marketing. Some organizations, including Spiegel and J.C. Penney, offer a broad array of products spread over multiple product lines. Catalog companies like L.L. Bean, the Pottery Barn, and J. Crew offer considerable depth in one major line of products. Still other catalog companies specialize in only a few products within a single line.

The advantages of catalog retailing include efficiency and convenience for customers. The retailer can benefit by locating in remote, low-cost areas, saving on expensive store fixtures, and reducing both personal selling and store operating expenses. On the other hand, catalog retailing is inflexible, provides limited service, and is most effective for a selected set of products. Some catalog retailers—for instance, Crate and Barrel and Sharper Image—have opened stores in major metropolitan areas.

Consumer mail-order catalog sales are about $130 billion each year, the equivalent of every American's spending about $500 annually on catalog purchases.[12] Even though the cost of mailing catalogs continues to rise, catalog sales are growing at double the rate of over-the-counter retailing in the United States.[13] Williams-Sonoma, for example, sells kitchenware and home and garden products through five catalogs, including Pottery Barn and Gardeners' Eden. Catalog sales have been increasing due to the convenience of catalog shopping. Product quality is often high, and because consumers can call toll-free twenty-four hours a day, charge the purchase to a credit card, and have the merchandise delivered to their door in one to two days, such shopping is much easier than going to a store.[14]

direct-response marketing A type of marketing that occurs when a retailer advertises a product and makes it available through mail or telephone orders

Direct-Response Marketing   **Direct-response marketing** occurs when a retailer advertises a product and makes it available through mail or telephone orders. Generally, a purchaser may use a credit card, but other forms of payment are acceptable. Examples of direct-response marketing include a television commercial offering a recording artist's musical collection available through a toll-free number, a newspaper or magazine advertisement for a series of children's books available by filling out the form in the ad or calling a toll-free number, and even a billboard promoting floral services available by calling 1-800-FLOWERS. Direct-response marketing can also be achieved by sending letters, samples, brochures, or booklets to prospects on a mailing list and asking that they order the advertised products by mail or telephone. In general, products must be priced above $20 to justify the advertising and distribution costs associated with direct-response marketing.

telemarketing The performance of marketing-related activities by telephone

Telemarketing   A number of organizations, including Merrill Lynch, Allstate, Avis, Ford, Time, and American Express, use the telephone to strengthen the effectiveness of traditional marketing methods. **Telemarketing** is the performance of marketing-related activities by telephone. Some organizations use a prescreened list of prospective clients, whereas others rely primarily on a cold canvass approach using telephone directories. Telemarketing can help generate sales leads, improve customer service, speed up payment on past-due accounts, raise funds for nonprofit organizations, and gather marketing data. It is often combined with other marketing efforts, and both nonstore retailers and retailers with establishments use it.

television home shopping A form of selling in which products are presented to television viewers, who buy them by calling a toll-free number and paying with credit cards

Television Home Shopping   **Television home shopping** presents products to television viewers, urging them to order through toll-free numbers and pay with credit cards. Home Shopping Network in Florida originated and popularized this format. Today, there are numerous home shopping cable channels, several of which specialize in certain product categories. The most popular products sold through television home shopping are jewelry (40 percent of total sales), clothing, housewares, and electronics.

MARKETING CITIZENSHIP

eBay Fights Fraud

One of the most successful online retail venues to date is eBay, a sort of online flea market. eBay runs a million auctions a day through which members can buy and sell personal items such as antiques, dolls, coins, collectibles, computers, jewelry, memorabilia, stamps, and trading cards. Merchandise sellers pay a fee to have their items auctioned on eBay's Web site, on which potential buyers can browse and bid on available merchandise. After an auction ends, the winning bidder arranges payment and shipping with the seller, and eBay collects a small commission on each listing and sale.

To ensure that eBay transactions are legal and ethical, the company recently announced a set of initiatives to combat fraud, misrepresentation, and bidding irregularities. These measures include offering members the option of being certified as "accredited" users after having their identities verified independently by an outside party. eBay will also offer customers free insurance against fraud or mislabeled goods, with a $25 deductible and $200 of coverage, and make it easier for customers to use third-party escrow services, especially for large transactions. The company also decided to ban sellers from bidding on their own merchandise and to sanction winning bidders who fail to collect and pay for their merchandise.

eBay has long given members the opportunity to add complements or criticisms to trading partners' online profiles, and it computes a score for each member based on the positive and negative feedback received.

Members who earn ratings of +10 or higher are rewarded with a star any time their names appear in an auction; those who rack up scores of -4 or worse are evicted. This system, developed by eBay founder Pierre Omidyar, has become strained as a result of the firm's phenomenal growth and some less-than-honest members who tried to increase their scores by getting friends to submit positive feedback. To strengthen the rating system, eBay now counts only feedback related to actual transactions.

Ironically, just a week after eBay announced its fraud-combating measures, the New York City Department of Consumer Affairs announced that it had launched an investigation into complaints by consumers who say they were cheated by dealers in eBay auctions. In a press release, eBay responded that it averages just twenty-seven complaints of fraud per million auctions. Additionally, it pointed to the user agreement on its Web site, which states, "We have no control over the quality, safety or legality of the items advertised, the truth or accuracy of the listings, the ability of sellers to sell items or the ability of buyers to buy items."

Whether eBay's new initiatives will reduce fraud, and head off New York city's investigation, remains to be seen. As Eileen Harrington, director of marketing practices at the Federal Trade Commission, says, "There's always an element of risk when buyers and sellers don't know each other. The Internet makes that sort of anonymity much easier."

Home shopping channels have grown so rapidly in recent years that more than 60 percent of all U.S. households have access to home shopping programs. Home Shopping Network and QVC are two of the largest home shopping networks. Approximately 60 percent of home shopping sales revenues comes from repeat purchasers. When asked why they purchase through television home shopping, shoppers indicate that they perceive the prices to be lower, the service faster, and the sales personnel friendlier and better informed about the products than they are in stores.[15]

The television home shopping format offers several benefits. Products can be easily demonstrated, and an adequate amount of time can be spent showing the product so that viewers are well informed. The length of time a product is shown depends not only on the time required for doing demonstrations, but also on whether the product is selling. Once the calls peak and begin to decline, then a new product is shown. Another benefit is that customers can shop at their convenience from the comfort of their own homes.

online retailing Retailing that makes products available to buyers through computer connections

Online Retailing   **Online retailing** makes products available to buyers selling through computer connections. The phenomenal growth of the Internet's World Wide Web and of online information services like America Online has created new retailing opportunities. Many retailers have set up Web sites to disseminate information about their companies and their products. Although most retailers with Web sites are currently using them primarily to promote products, a number of companies, including Barnes & Noble, REI, Lands' End, and OfficeMax, sell goods online. Consumers can purchase hard-to-find items, like Pez candy dispensers and Elvis memorabilia, at eBay, an Internet flea market that, for a commission, brings buyers and sellers together.[16] Marketing Citizenship looks at how eBay is trying to reduce the potential for fraud in its online technology. Even banks and brokerage firms have established Web sites to give their customers direct access to manage their accounts and to enable them to trade online. With advances in computer technology continuing and consumers ever more pressed for time, online retailing will continue to escalate. In fact, online retail sales are projected to reach $37.5 billion by 2002.[17]

Although online retailing represents a major new retailing venue, security remains an issue. In a survey conducted by Forrester Research, 53 percent of online merchants cited security as the main reason consumers do not buy from their Web sites. However, most online retailers say that current encryption technology and the limited liability incurred by credit card users for stolen card numbers make it safe to conduct transactions online. For example, Amazon.com, the largest online bookseller, claims it has not experienced any fraud because of the steps it takes to protect customers' transactions. Online retailers can reduce consumers' security fears, and thereby increase sales, through use of current security technology and clear explanations of their guarantees and how they protect online transactions.[18]

Automatic Vending

automatic vending The use of machines to dispense products

Automatic vending is the use of machines to dispense products. It accounts for less than 2 percent of all retail sales. Video game machines provide an entertainment service, and many banks now offer automatic teller machines (ATMs), which dispense cash and perform other services.

Automatic vending is one of the most impersonal forms of retailing. Small, standardized, routinely purchased products (chewing gum, candy, newspapers, cigarettes, soft drinks, coffee) can be sold in machines because consumers usually buy them at the nearest available location. Machines in areas of heavy traffic provide efficient and continuous services to consumers. Such high-volume areas may have more diverse product availability—for example, hot and cold sandwiches, as well as soups. Since vending machines need only a small amount of space and no sales personnel, this retailing method has some advantages over stores. The advantages are partly offset, however, by the high costs of equipment and frequent servicing and repairs.

Franchising

Franchising is an arrangement whereby a supplier, or franchiser, grants a dealer, or franchisee, the right to sell products in exchange for some type of consideration. The franchiser may receive some percentage of total sales in exchange for furnishing equipment, buildings, management know-how, and marketing assistance to the franchisee. The franchisee supplies labor and capital, operates the franchised business, and agrees to abide by the provisions of the franchise agreement. Table 16.2 lists the top ten franchises.

Because of changes in the international marketplace, shifting employment options in the United States, the expanding U.S. service economy, and corporate interest in more joint venture activity, franchising is rapidly increasing. A new franchise opens somewhere in the United States every 6.5 minutes, every business day. Franchising accounts for $900 billion annually, or 40 percent of all U.S. retail sales, and revenues are expected to reach $1 trillion by the year 2000.[19] In this section, we look at major types of retail franchises and the advantages and disadvantages of franchising.

Table 16.2   Top Ten Franchises
1. Yogen Fruz Worldwide
2. McDonald's
3. Subway
4. Wendy's International Inc.
5. Jackson Hewitt Tax Service
6. KFC
7. Mail Boxes Etc.
8. TCBY Treats
9. Taco Bell
10. Jani-King

Source: "Franchise 500," *Entrepreneur*, www.entrepreneurmag.com/franchise500, Oct. 30, 1998. Reprinted with permission from *Entrepreneur Magazine*, January, 1999.

Major Types of Retail Franchises

Retail franchise arrangements fall into three general categories. In one type of arrangement, a manufacturer authorizes a number of retail stores to sell a certain brand name item. This franchise arrangement, one of the oldest, is common in the sales of cars and trucks, farm equipment, shoes, paint, earth-moving equipment, and petroleum. About 90 percent of all gasoline is sold through franchised independent service stations, and franchised dealers handle virtually all sales of new cars and trucks. In the second type of retail franchise, a producer licenses distributors to sell a given product to retailers. This arrangement is common in the soft drink industry. Most national manufacturers of soft drink syrups—Coca-Cola, Dr Pepper, PepsiCo—grant franchises to bottlers, which then serve retailers. In the third type of retail franchise, a franchiser supplies brand names, techniques, or other services, instead of complete products. The franchiser may provide certain production and distribution services, but its primary role in the arrangement is careful development and control of marketing strategies. This approach to franchising, very common today, is used by such organizations as Holiday Inn, AAMCO, McDonald's, Dairy Queen, KFC, and H&R Block.

Advantages and Disadvantages of Franchising

Franchising offers several advantages to both the franchisee and the franchiser. It enables a franchisee to start a business with limited capital and to benefit from the business experience of others. Moreover, nationally advertised franchises, such as ServiceMaster and Burger King, are often assured of customers as soon as they open. If business problems arise, the franchisee can obtain guidance and advice from the franchiser at little or no cost. Franchised outlets are generally more successful than independently owned businesses. Less than 10 percent of franchised retail businesses fail during the first two years of operation, whereas approximately half of independent retail businesses fail during that period. The franchisee also receives materials to use in local advertising and can benefit from national promotional campaigns sponsored by the franchiser. Taco Bell franchisees, for example, have profited from a national advertising campaign featuring a Chihuahua that demands, *Yo quiero Taco Bell* ("I want some Taco Bell"). The ads have helped boost same-store sales at Taco Bell by 3 percent in an otherwise flat industry. The talking dog has been especially popular among teenagers, who spend $12.7 billion per year at fast-food restaurants.[20]

Buying a Franchise

The average investment in a franchise, including fees and additional expenses is $143,260. The cost including fees, expenses, etc., is. . .

Less than $100,000 — **43%**

More than $100,000 — **41%**

Don't know/ no answer — **14%**

Copyright © 1999 *USA Today*, a division of Gannett Co., Inc.

The franchiser gains fast and selective product distribution through franchise arrangements without incurring the high cost of constructing and operating its own outlets. The franchiser therefore has more capital for expanding production and advertising. It can also ensure, through the franchise agreement, that outlets are maintained and operated according to its own standards. The franchiser benefits from the fact that the franchisee, being a sole proprietor in most cases, is likely to be very highly motivated to succeed. Success of the franchise means more sales, which translate into higher income for the franchiser.

Despite numerous advantages, franchise arrangements have several drawbacks. The franchiser can dictate many aspects of the business: decor, design of employees' uniforms, types of signs, and numerous details of business operations. In addition, franchisees must pay to use the franchiser's name, products, and assistance. Usually, there is a one-time franchise fee and continuing royalty and advertising fees, often collected as a percentage of sales. For example, Subway requires franchisees to come up with $40,000 to $80,000 in startup costs. Franchisees often must work very hard, putting in ten- to twelve-hour days, six days a week. In some cases, franchise agreements are not uniform; one franchisee may pay more than another for the same services. The franchiser also gives up a certain amount of control when entering into a franchise agreement. Consequently, individual establishments may not be operated exactly the way the franchiser would like.

Strategic Issues in Retailing

Consumers often have vague reasons for making retail purchases. Whereas most business purchases are based on economic planning and necessity, consumer purchases may result from social influences and psychological factors. Because consumers shop for a variety of reasons—to search for specific items, escape boredom, or learn about something new—retailers must do more than simply fill space with merchandise. They must make desired products available, create stimulating shopping environments, and develop marketing strategies that increase store patronage. In this section, we discuss how store location, retail positioning, store image, scrambled merchandising, and the wheel of retailing affect retailing objectives.

Location of Retail Stores

Location, the least flexible of the strategic retailing issues, is one of the most important because location dictates the limited geographic trading area from which a store draws its customers. Retailers consider a variety of factors when evaluating potential locations, including location of the firm's target market within the trading area, kinds of products being sold, availability of public transportation, customer characteristics, and competitors' locations.

In choosing a location, retailers evaluate the relative ease of movement to and from the site, including such factors as pedestrian and vehicular traffic, parking, and transportation. Most retailers prefer sites with high pedestrian traffic. Preliminary site investigations often include a pedestrian count to determine how many passersby are prospective customers. The nature of the area's vehicular traffic is also analyzed. The customers of certain retailers, such as service stations and many convenience stores, drive to these retail sites, and so overly congested locations should be avoided. Parking space must be adequate for projected demand, and transportation networks (major thoroughfares and public transit) must accommodate customers and delivery vehicles.

Retailers also evaluate the characteristics of the site itself: types of stores in the area; size, shape, and visibility of the lot or building under consideration; and rental, leasing, or ownership terms. Retailers look for compatibility with nearby retailers because stores that complement each other draw more customers for everyone. When making site location decisions, retailers select from among several general types of locations: free-standing structures, traditional business districts, traditional shopping centers, or nontraditional shopping centers.

Free-Standing Structures   Free-standing structures are buildings unconnected to other buildings. Organizations may build such structures or lease or buy them. A retailer, for example, may find that it is most successful when stores are in free-standing structures close to a shopping mall but not in the mall. Use of free-standing structures allows retailers to physically position themselves away from or close to competitors. It is not unusual for quick-service oil-change dealers and fast-food restaurants to use free-standing structures and locate close to each other. Toys "R" Us and Home Depot also tend to locate in free-standing structures.

Traditional Business Districts   A traditional business district—"the downtown shopping district"—consists of structures usually attached to one another and located in a central part of a town or city. Often, these structures are old. In some cities, traditional business districts are decaying and are not viewed as viable locations for retailers. However, many towns and cities are preserving or revitalizing traditional business districts, thus making them attractive locations for certain types of retailers. Some cities have enclosed walkways, shut off streets from traffic, and provided free parking and trolley systems to help traditional business districts compete with shopping malls more effectively.

Traditional Shopping Centers   Traditional shopping centers include neighborhood, community, and regional shopping centers. **Neighborhood shopping centers** usually consist of several small convenience and specialty stores, such as small grocery stores, gas stations, and fast-food restaurants. Many of these retailers consider their target markets to be consumers who live within two to three miles of their stores, or ten minutes' driving time. Because most purchases are based on convenience or personal contact, there is usually little coordination of selling efforts within a neighborhood shopping center. Generally, product mixes consist of essential products, and depth of the product lines is limited. Convenience stores are most successful when they are closer to consumers than, for example, supermarkets. A good strategy for neighborhood centers is to locate near hotels or interstate highways, or on the route to regional shopping centers.

Community shopping centers include one or two department stores and some specialty stores, as well as convenience stores. They draw consumers looking for shopping and specialty products not available in neighborhood shopping centers. Because they serve larger geographic areas, consumers drive longer distances to community shopping centers than to neighborhood shopping centers. Community shopping centers are planned and coordinated to attract shoppers. Special events, such as art exhibits, automobile shows, and sidewalk sales, stimulate traffic. Overall management of a community shopping center looks for tenants that complement the center's total assortment of products. Such centers have wide product mixes and deep product lines.

Regional shopping centers usually have the largest department stores, the widest product mixes, and the deepest product lines of all shopping centers (see Figure 16.6). Many shopping malls are regional shopping centers, although some are community shopping centers. Regional shopping centers carry most products found in a downtown shopping district. With 150,000 or more consumers in their target market, regional shopping centers must have well-coordinated management and marketing activities. Target markets may include consumers traveling from a distance to find products and prices not available in their hometowns.

neighborhood shopping centers Shopping centers usually consisting of several small convenience and specialty stores

community shopping centers Shopping centers with one or two department stores, some specialty stores, and convenience stores

regional shopping centers A type of shopping center with the largest department stores, the widest product mix, and the deepest product lines of all shopping centers

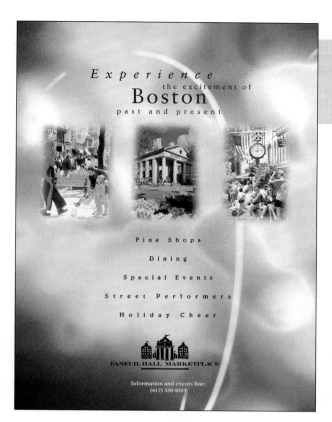

Experience
the excitement of
Boston
past and present

Fine Shops

Dining

Special Events

Street Performers

Holiday Cheer

FANEUIL HALL MARKETPLACE

Information and events line:
(617) 338-2323

Figure 16.6
Regional Shopping Centers
Regional shopping centers, such as Faneuil Hall Marketplace in Boston, provide many and varied product lines.

Because of the expense of leasing space in regional shopping centers, tenants are more likely to be national chains than small independent stores. Large centers usually advertise, have special events, furnish transportation to some consumer groups, maintain their own security forces, and carefully select the mix of stores. Mall of America, near Minneapolis, is one of the largest shopping malls in the world. It contains eight hundred stores, including Nordstrom's and Bloomingdale's, and one hundred restaurants and nightclubs. The shopping center features Camp Snoopy, a theme park based on Charlie Brown's famous dog, as well as hotels, miniature golf courses, and water slides.

Nontraditional Shopping Centers   Three new types of shopping centers have emerged that differ significantly from traditional shopping centers. Factory outlet malls feature discount and factory outlet stores carrying traditional manufacturer brands, such as Van Heusen, Levi Strauss, HealthTex, and Wrangler. Manufacturers own these stores and make a special effort to avoid conflict with traditional retailers of their products. Manufacturers claim that their stores are in noncompetitive locations, and indeed most factory outlet malls are located outside metropolitan areas. Not all factory outlets stock closeouts and irregulars, but most avoid comparison with discount houses. Factory outlet malls attract customers because of lower prices for quality and major brand names. They operate in much the same way as regional shopping centers but probably draw traffic from a larger shopping radius. Promotional activity is at the heart of these shopping centers. Craft and antique shows, contests, and special events attract a great deal of traffic.

Another nontraditional shopping center is the miniwarehouse mall. These loosely planned centers sell space to retailers, who operate what are essentially retail stores out of warehouse bays. Developers of the miniwarehouse mall may also sell space to wholesalers or to light manufacturers that maintain a retail facility in their warehouse bays. Some of these miniwarehouses are located in high-traffic areas and provide ample customer parking, as well as display windows that can be seen from the street. Home improvement materials, specialty foods, pet supplies, and garden and yard supplies are often sold in these malls. Unlike traditional shopping centers, miniwarehouse malls usually do not have coordinated promotional programs and store mixes. This type of nontraditional shopping center comes closest to neighborhood or community shopping centers.

A third type of emerging shopping center is one that does not include a traditional anchor department store. Most malls have one to three main anchor department stores to ensure a continuous stream of mall traffic. With traditional mall sales declining, this new type of shopping mall may be anchored by a store like the Gap. One such mall in Wheaton, Illinois, has a 17,000-square-foot Gap, which is surrounded by other specialty stores, such as Banana Republic and GapKids. Other likely stores for the new malls include Toys "R" Us, Circuit City, PETsMART and Home Depot. Shopping center developers are combining off-price stores with category killers in "power center" formats. Off-price centers are expanding rapidly, resulting in a variety of formats vying for the same retail dollar. To compete, regional malls will have to adapt by changing their store mix.[21]

Retail Positioning

retail positioning
Identifying an unserved or underserved market niche, or segment, and serving it through a strategy that distinguishes the retailer from others in the minds of persons in that segment

Emergence of new types of stores (warehouse clubs, combination stores, and category killers) and expansion of product offerings by traditional stores have intensified retailing competition. Retail position is therefore an important consideration. **Retail positioning** involves identifying an unserved or underserved market niche, or segment, and serving the segment through a strategy that distinguishes the retailer from others in the minds of persons in that segment.[22] Pacific Sunwear stores, for example, target teens by carrying trendy clothing with popular brand names, such as Quicksilver, Birdhouse, and Hook-ups.[23]

The ways in which retailers position themselves vary. A retailer may position itself as a seller of high-quality, premium-priced products and provide many services. Neiman Marcus, for example, specializes in expensive high-fashion clothing and jewelry, sophisticated electronics, and exclusive home furnishings, and provides wrapping and delivery, valet parking, and personal shopping consultants. Another type of retail organization may be positioned as a marketer of reasonable-quality products at everyday low prices. Pizza Hut, for example, has positioned itself as the value alternative by offering a variety of large pizzas at low prices in more than 7,000 locations. Its rival, Papa John's, has established its position with the slogan, "Better ingredients. Better pizza."[24] Building Customer Relationships looks at J. C. Penney's efforts to improve its position.

Store Image

To attract customers, a retail store must project an image—a functional and psychological picture in the consumer's mind—that is acceptable to its target market. Store environment, merchandise quality, and service quality are key determinants of store image.[25]

atmospherics The physical elements in a store's design that appeal to consumers' emotions and encourage buying

Atmospherics, the physical elements in a store's design that appeal to consumers' emotions and encourage buying, helps to create an image and position a retailer. For example, Nickelodeon, the television network, has designed its new stores to appeal to children. The stores have purple ceilings, giant lava-light totem poles, fitting-room benches with built-in whoopee cushions, and an area called the Compound Vat, where children can see how some of the company's toys are made. The 5,000- to 6,000-square-foot stores offer 2,000 products, many based on the network's television shows.[26]

Exterior atmospheric elements include the appearance of the storefront, display windows, store entrances, and degree of traffic congestion. Exterior atmospherics are particularly important to new customers, who tend to judge an unfamiliar store by its outside appearance and may not enter if they feel intimidated by the building or inconvenienced by the parking lot. Interior atmospheric elements include aesthetic considerations, such as lighting, wall and floor coverings, dressing facilities, and store fixtures. Interior sensory elements contribute significantly to atmosphere. Color can attract shoppers to a retail display. Many fast-food restaurants use bright colors, such as red and yellow, because these have been shown to make customers feel hungrier and eat faster, which increases turnover. Sound is another important sensory component of atmosphere and may consist of silence, soft music, or even noise. A store's layout—arrangement of departments, width of aisles, grouping of products, and location of checkout areas—is another determinant of atmosphere. Department stores, restaurants, hotels, service stations, and shops combine these elements in different ways to create specific atmospheres that may be perceived as warm, fresh, functional, or exciting.

Retailers must assess the atmosphere the target market seeks and then adjust atmospheric variables to encourage desired consumer awareness and action. High-fashion boutiques generally strive for an atmosphere of luxury and novelty. Ralph Lauren's Polo Shops offer limited merchandise in large open areas, with props like saddles or leather chairs adding to the exclusive look and image. On the other hand, discount department stores must *not* seem too exclusive and expensive. To appeal to multiple market segments, a retailer may create different atmospheres for different operations within the store; for example, the discount basement, the sports department, the housewares department, and the women's shoe department may each have a unique atmosphere.

Although heavily dependent on atmospherics, a store's image is also shaped by its reputation for integrity, number of services offered, location, merchandise assortments, pricing policies, promotional activities, and community involvement. Characteristics of the target market—social class, lifestyle, income level, and past buying behavior—help form store image as well. How consumers perceive the store can be a major determinant of store patronage. Consumers from lower socioeconomic groups tend to patronize small, high-margin, high-service food stores and prefer small, friendly loan companies over large, impersonal banks, even though the former charge high interest. Affluent consumers look for exclusive establishments offering high-quality products and prestigious labels. Retailers should be aware of the multiple factors contributing to store image and recognize that perceptions of image vary.

BUILDING
customer relationships

J. C. Penney Gets a Face-lift

J.C. Penney, the number-four retailer in the United States, operates more than 1,200 department stores selling apparel, accessories, and home furnishings across the U.S. and in Puerto Rico, Mexico, and Chile. The company, based in Plano, Texas, also sells merchandise through its J. C. Penney Catalog. The company operates 2,800 Eckerd drugstores, making it the number-four drugstore chain in the U.S., and it sells life, health, accident, and credit insurance, as well. In recent years, J. C. Penney's department stores have abandoned hard goods such as appliances and electronics in favor of fashion, especially its own brands, like the Original Arizona Jean Company and Worthington. However, the chain experienced weak sales and earnings during the mid 1990s, largely because it was slow to reduce costs, move inventory, attract popular designer labels, and, most importantly, get the latest fashions into its stores quickly.

To squeeze more profits out of the venerable department store chain, new CEO James E. Oesterreicher slashed costs, improved inventory management, and implemented a new buying strategy designed to get products into stores faster and more efficiently. Through voluntary early retirements and layoffs, Oesterreicher found savings of nearly $200 million annually. The chain's new buying policy consolidates purchasing functions for 50 to 60 percent of all store merchandise in Plano. Store managers still purchase 40 percent of their stores' offerings to cater to local demographics. The more centralized buying strategy is expected to shave four to five weeks off buying time, and earlier commitments from Penney buyers should help the firm negotiate lower prices on merchandise. The company has also upgraded its fashion offerings with more private and national brands, like Crazy Horse, a line of misses' sportswear designed by Liz Claiborne Inc.

All these changes are designed to help J. C. Penney reach its target market of middle and middle/upper income consumers. To satisfy these consumers, the company's strategy is "to fulfill the customer's expectations for value, selection, and convenience." The chain has also adapted its marketing strategy to accommodate changing demographics in its target market. The company established the Grandparent Club in 1998 to reward the growing number of Americans over age 55 who spend at least $150 at J. C. Penney with a 30 percent discount on future purchases. Additionally, the chain has hired fashion segment merchandisers to select products that will appeal to increasing numbers of African-, Hispanic-, and Asian-American shoppers. The company has added more older and minority models to its advertising. Penney executives hope these substantial changes will improve customer satisfaction and help boost the chain's margins to 8 percent from 6.7 percent now.

Figure 16.7
Scrambled Merchandising
Target continues to expand its product lines and services.

Scrambled Merchandising

scrambled merchandising The addition of unrelated products and product lines to an existing product mix, particularly fast-moving items that can be sold in volume

When retailers add unrelated products and product lines—particularly fast-moving items that can be sold in volume—to an existing product mix, they are practicing **scrambled merchandising.** Retailers adopting this strategy hope to accomplish one or more of the following: (1) convert stores into one-stop shopping centers, (2) generate more traffic, (3) realize higher profit margins, and (4) increase impulse purchases. For example, at its superstores, Wal-Mart has added grocery products to its marketing mix. The chain's 500 supercenters ring up an estimated $12 billion in sales of grocery products.[27] Similarly, Target has expanded its product lines in many locations (see Figure 16.7). In scrambling merchandising, retailers must deal with diverse marketing channels. In Wal-Mart's case, the retailer has used its efficient distribution system and supply chain leadership to stock its grocery shelves.[28] Scrambling merchandise can also blur a store's image in consumers' minds, making it more difficult for a retailer to succeed in today's highly competitive, saturated markets. Finally, scrambled merchandising intensifies competition among traditionally distinct types of stores and forces suppliers to adjust distribution systems to accommodate new channel members.

The Wheel of Retailing

wheel of retailing A hypothesis that holds that new types of retailers usually enter the market as low-status, low-margin, low-price operators but eventually evolve into high-cost, high-price merchants

As new types of retail businesses come into being, they strive to fill niches in a dynamic retailing environment. One hypothesis regarding the evolution and development of new types of retail stores is the **wheel of retailing.** According to this theory, new retailers enter the marketplace with low prices, margins, and status. Their low prices are usually the result of innovative cost-cutting procedures and soon attract imitators. Gradually, as these businesses attempt to broaden their customer base and increase sales, their operations and facilities become more elaborate and more expensive. They may move to more desirable locations, begin to carry higher-quality merchandise, or add services. Eventually, they emerge at the high end of the price, cost, and service scales, competing with newer discount retailers following the same evolutionary process.[29]

Supermarkets, for example, have undergone many changes since their introduction in 1921. Initially, they offered limited services and low food prices. However, over time they developed a variety of new services, including free coffee, gourmet food sections, and children's play areas. Now, supermarkets are challenged by superstores, which offer more product choices than the supermarkets and have undercut supermarket prices.

Consider the evolution of department stores, discount stores, warehouse clubs, category killers, and online retailers, shown in Figure 16.8. Department stores like Sears started out as high-volume, low-cost merchants competing with general stores and other small retailers. Discount stores developed later in response to rising expenses of services in department stores. Many discount outlets now appear to be following the wheel of retailing by offering more services, better locations, quality inventories, and therefore higher prices. Some discount stores are almost indistinguishable from department stores. In response have emerged category killers, such as PETsMART and Office Depot, which concentrate on a major product category and offer enormous product depth at, in many cases, lower prices than discount stores. Yet even these retailers seem to be following the wheel. Lowe's, a home-improvement retailer, has added big-ticket items and more upscale brands, such as Laura Ashley. Home Depot has gone a step further by launching Expo, a chain of stores that concentrates on big-ticket renovation projects and higher-priced hardware, accessories, and appliances, including designer ceramic tiles and upscale brands like Sub-Zero. Expo even designs and installs custom kitchens and bathrooms.[30] The new entry on the wheel of retailing is the online retailer, such as Amazon.com, which can pass on to consumers the savings associated with not having a real storefront.

The wheel of retailing, along with other changes in the marketing environment and buying behavior itself, requires that retailers adjust in order to survive and compete. Consumers have less time than ever to shop and seem less interested in the shopping experience. Shopping today centers on "needs fulfillment" and thus is more utilitarian and work-oriented, a fact that many major retailing executives have noticed. As one retail consultant says, "People don't want to be sold anything. All they want is help buying the products they already know they need."[31] Consequently, consumers desire less personal service and more "assisted self-service." These changes in retailing

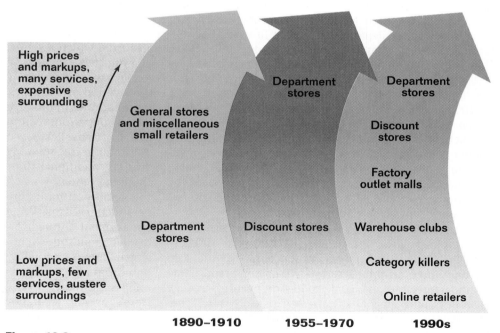

Figure 16.8

The Wheel of Retailing

If the "wheel" is considered to be turning slowly in the direction of the arrows, then the department stores around 1900 and the discounters that came later can be viewed as coming on the scene at the low end of the wheel. As it turns slowly, they move with it, becoming higher-price operations and leaving room for lower-price firms to gain entry at the low end of the wheel.

Source: Adapted from Robert F. Hartley, *Retailing: Challenge and Opportunity,* 3rd ed., p. 42. Copyright © 1984 by Houghton Mifflin Company. Used by permission.

and buying behavior mean retailers must change as well.[32] As consumers have less time to shop, more direct routes to manufacturers, and greater access to more sophisticated technology, retailing venues like catalog retailing, television home shopping, and online retailing will take on greater importance. New retailers will evolve to capitalize on these opportunities and respond to these challenges, while those retailers that cannot adapt will not survive.

Summary

Retailing includes all transactions in which buyers intend to consume products through personal, family, or household use. Retailers—organizations that sell products primarily to ultimate consumers—are important links in the marketing channel because they are both marketers for and customers of wholesalers and producers. Retailers add value, provide services, and assist in making product selections.

Retail stores can be classified according to the breadth of products offered. Two general categories are general merchandise retailers and specialty retailers. The primary types of general merchandise retailers include department stores, discount stores, supermarkets, superstores, hypermarkets, warehouse clubs, and warehouse and catalog showrooms. Department stores are large retail organizations employing at least twenty-five people and characterized by wide product mixes in considerable depth for most product lines. Their products are organized into separate departments, which function like self-contained businesses. Discount stores are self-service, low-price, general merchandise outlets. Supermarkets are large, self-service food stores that also carry some nonfood products. Superstores are giant retail outlets carrying all the products found in supermarkets and most consumer products purchased on a routine basis. Hypermarkets offer supermarket and discount store shopping at one location. Warehouse clubs are large-scale, members-only discount operations. Warehouse and catalog showrooms are low-cost operations characterized by warehouse methods of materials handling and display, large inventories, and minimum services.

Specialty retailers offer substantial assortments in a few product lines. They include traditional specialty retailers, which carry narrow product mixes with deep product lines; off-price retailers, which sell brand name manufacturers' seconds and production overruns at deep discounts; and category killers—large specialty stores that concentrate on a major product category and compete on the basis of low prices and enormous product availability.

Nonstore retailing is the selling of goods or services outside the confines of a retail facility. The three major types of nonstore retailing include direct selling, direct marketing, and automatic vending. Direct selling is the marketing of products to ultimate consumers through face-to-face sales presentations at home or in the workplace. Direct marketing is the use of telephone and nonpersonal media to communicate product and organizational information to consumers who then can purchase products by mail or telephone. Forms of direct marketing include catalog marketing, direct-response marketing, telemarketing, television home shopping, and online retailing. Automatic vending is the use of machines to dispense products.

Franchising is an arrangement whereby a supplier grants a dealer the right to sell products in exchange for some type of consideration. Retail franchises are of three general types. A manufacturer may authorize a number of retail stores to sell a certain brand name item; a producer may license distributors to sell a given product to retailers; or a franchiser may supply brand names, techniques, or other services instead of a complete product. Franchise arrangements have a number of advantages and disadvantages over traditional business forms, and their use is increasing.

To increase sales and store patronage, retailers must consider strategic issues. Location determines the trading area from which a store draws its customers and should be evaluated carefully. When evaluating potential sites, retailers take into account a variety of factors, including the location of the firm's target market within the trading area, kinds of products being sold, availability of public transportation, customer characteristics, and competitors' locations. Retailers can choose among several types of locations: free-standing structures, traditional business districts, traditional shopping centers, or nontraditional shopping centers.

Retail positioning involves identifying an unserved or underserved market niche, or segment, and serving the segment through a strategy that distinguishes the retailer from others in people's minds. Store image, which various customers perceive differently, derives not only from atmosphere, but also from location, products offered, customer services, prices, promotion, and the store's overall reputation. Atmospherics refers to the physical elements of a store's design that can be adjusted to appeal to consumers' emotions and thus induce consumers to buy. Scrambled merchandising adds unrelated product lines to an existing product mix and is being used by a growing number of stores to generate sales.

The wheel-of-retailing hypothesis holds that new retail institutions start as low-status, low-margin, and low-price operations. As they develop, they increase service and prices and eventually become vulnerable to newer institutions, which enter the market and repeat the cycle.

Important Terms

Retailing
Retailer
General merchandise
  retailer
Department stores
Discount stores
Supermarkets
Superstores
Hypermarkets
Warehouse clubs

Warehouse showrooms
Catalog showrooms
Traditional specialty
  retailers
Off-price retailers
Category killer
Nonstore retailing
Direct selling
Direct marketing

Catalog marketing
Direct-response marketing
Telemarketing
Television home shopping
Online retailing
Automatic vending
Franchising
Neighborhood shopping
  centers

Community shopping
  centers
Regional shopping centers
Retail positioning
Atmospherics
Scrambled merchandising
Wheel of retailing

Discussion and Review Questions

1. What value is added to the product by retailers? What value is added by retailers for producers and for ultimate consumers?

2. Differentiate between the two general categories of retail stores based on breadth of product offering.

3. What are the major differences between discount stores and department stores?

4. How does a superstore differ from a supermarket?

5. In what ways are traditional specialty stores and off-price retailers similar? How do they differ?

6. Describe the three major types of nonstore retailing. List some products you have purchased through nonstore retailing in the last six months. Why did you choose this method for making your purchases instead of going to a retail outlet?

7. Why is door-to-door selling a form of retailing? Some consumers feel that direct-response orders skip the retailer. Is this true?

8. Evaluate the following statement: "Telemarketing, television home shopping, and online retailing will eventually eliminate the need for traditional forms of retailing."

9. If you were to open a retail business, would you prefer to open an independent store or to own a store under a franchise arrangement? Explain your preference.

10. What major issues should be considered when determining a retail site location?

11. Describe the three major types of traditional shopping centers. Give an example of each type in your area.

12. Discuss the major factors that help determine a retail store's image.

13. How does atmosphere add value to products sold in a store? How important is atmospherics for convenience stores?

14. Is it possible for a single retail store to have an overall image that appeals to sophisticated shoppers, extravagant buyers, and bargain hunters? Why or why not?

15. In what ways does the use of scrambled merchandising affect a store's image?

Application Questions

1. Juanita wants to open a small retail store that specializes in high-quality, high-priced children's clothing. What concerns should Juanita have in the competitive retail environment? Specifically, with what competitors or types of competitors should she be concerned? Why?

2. Location of retail outlets is an issue in strategic planning. What initial steps would you recommend to Juanita (in question 1) when she considers a location for her store?

3. Godiva Chocolate stores offer a very narrow assortment of products but provide great depth. Different types of stores offer various breadth and depth of assortments. Visit a discount store, a specialty store, or a department store. Report the number of different product lines offered and the depth within each line. Identify the name and type of store you visited.

4. Atmospherics is an important tool used by retailers in their efforts to position stores. Visit a retail store you shop in regularly or one in which you would like to shop. Identify the store and describe the atmospherics. Be specific about both exterior and interior elements and indicate how the store is being positioned through its use of atmospherics.

Internet Exercise & Resources

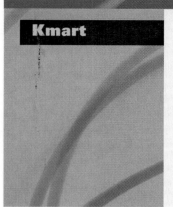

Kmart

Kmart provides a Web site where you can find the nearest Kmart store and even window shop with a click of your mouse. The Web site also lets browsers see what's currently on sale and view company information. Access Kmart's Web site at

> **www.kmart.com**

1. Review several recent press releases from Kmart and determine how this information attempts to position Kmart in a highly competitive retail market.
2. Compare the "atmospherics" of Kmart's Web site to the atmospherics of a traditional Kmart store. Are they consistent? Should they be?
3. Read the Kmart Story. Relate the firm's history to the wheel of retailing concept.

E-Center Resources

Visit http://www.prideferrell.com to find several resources to help you succeed in mastering the material in this chapter, plus additional materials that will help you expand your marketing knowledge. The Web site includes

  Internet exercise updates plus additional exercises

  ACE self-tests

abc Chapter summary with hotlinked glossary

  Hotlinks to companies featured in this chapter

  Resource Center

  Career Center

▤ Marketing plan worksheets

VIDEO CASE 16.1

Goldberg's Bagels: Benefits All Around

Constantly on-the-go Americans often skip what experts say is the most important meal of the day—breakfast. Taking time to prepare a healthy meal in the morning before rushing out the door to work or dropping the kids off at school just doesn't seem to fit into today's busy schedules. Sales of ready-to-eat cereal have declined by more than $800 million, and consumers are eating less toast and fewer eggs, too. Many consumers have instead turned to toaster pastries, breakfast bars, and bagels, which are easier to eat on the run. About 26 percent of consumers eat "deskfast" or breakfast at their desks after they get to work. To help busy consumers fuel up for the day, All American Food Group, Inc., based in South Plainfield, New Jersey, has franchised a fast, healthy, and cheap solution: old-fashioned bagels.

The All American Food Group was founded in 1993 to license and franchise contemporary food concepts.

In 1994 the company purchased a New Jersey bagel chain and began to franchise it nationwide as a retailer of authentic bagels under the name Goldberg's New York Bagels. A year later, the company purchased Sammy's New York Bagels, a certified kosher food producer, and renamed it Goldberg's New York Kosher Bagels. The company also purchased the Soup Man, Inc. in 1997, renaming it The SoupChef, to serve as the foundation of an international gourmet soup program. The SoupChef is perhaps best known from the Seinfeld TV series as the place where Jerry and his friends were abused by the "The Soup Nazi."

Goldberg's New York Bagels franchise outlets prepare bagels the old-fashioned way, using a secret recipe developed by Isadore Goldberg, a Polish immigrant, in 1937. The Goldberg family's recipe, along with its proprietary baking equipment and preparation methods, was acquired by the All American Food

Group in 1993. Unlike other bagel makers, which mass-produce the product in one step in steam ovens, Goldberg's bagels are first boiled in a kettle and then baked in a special oven. The boil-and-bake process results in a large bagel with a shiny crust and chewy texture. All Goldberg franchisees not only use the original recipe, equipment, and preparation methods, but also are required to use the same ingredients bought from the same suppliers. Additionally, all franchisees are trained at Goldberg University to ensure consistency of product and service.

Of course, breakfast is not the only time Goldberg's bagels can be eaten. Bagels are considered an alternative for a snack or meal because most are fat-free and thus appeal to more heath-conscious Americans looking for alternative healthy, yet fast, food. Whether a bagel is fat-free depends on what flavors are added to the bagel as well as what they are topped with. Goldberg's bagels can be flavored with blueberries, bananas, or even chocolate chips. They can be eaten with or without cream cheese, topped with egg and ham as a breakfast, or loaded with meats and vegetables as a lunch or dinner sandwich.

All American Food Group also operates Goldberg's New York Kosher Bagels, which serves both traditional and kosher products and strives to provide a venue where all customers—Jews and non-Jews, Orthodox and non-Orthodox—can feel comfortable. There is a difference in operations but not in the quality of the bagels. Goldberg's Kosher is believed to be the only franchised food chain subject to national kosher certification currently operating in the United States.

Goldberg's Bagel shops are conveniently located in neighborhoods with high traffic and easy accessibility. Bagel sandwiches can be made in the same amount of time as a burger, or any other fast food bought at chain restaurants. Half of Goldberg stores are under 1,000 square feet, which helps franchisees keep rent costs down and maintain the appearance of small neighborhood stores. Another convenience for

customers and a cost saver for Goldberg's was the decision to engage in co-branding, locating two businesses in one location. Co-branding allows customers to accomplish two things in one trip, while allowing separate businesses to share real estate costs. Thus, customers can order a Goldberg's bagel while pumping Mobil gas and then pick up their order inside the store or at a convenient drive-through window.

Various factors make obtaining a Goldberg's franchise an attractive opportunity. There are just 3,000 bagel shops in the United States, compared to the 11,000 nationwide outlets operated by the McDonald's hamburger chain. These numbers suggest that the market for bagel stores is far from saturated and, indeed, it is expanding rapidly. Goldberg's mostly fat-free product is positioned to appeal to people who are choosing healthier foods. Goldberg's trains franchisees in all aspects of operations, from how to produce the bagels to how to run a successful business. Its marketing programs, promotional concepts, and advertising are an additional benefit available at minimal cost. Franchisees contribute 1 percent of gross sales to the Advertising Fund.

Overall, Goldberg's Bagels seem to provide benefits for everyone involved. The consumer benefits from a fast, healthy alternative to traditional fast food hamburgers. All American franchisees earn profits from sales to health-conscious consumers, while the franchiser's shareholders reap the profits gained through the increasing value of All American Food Group's stock.[33]

Questions for Discussion

1. What type of retailer is Goldberg's Bagels?
2. What benefits does All American Food Group offer to Goldberg's Bagels franchisees? What disadvantages exist for franchisees?
3. Describe how Goldberg's Bagels is positioned to serve its selected target market. How do strategic issues such as location and store image affect this retail position?

CASE 16.2

Whole Foods Grows Up

In just two decades, Whole Foods Market, Inc., has grown into the nation's largest chain of natural-food supermarkets. Specializing in foods that contain no additives or preservatives and in produce organically grown without pesticides or other chemicals, its eighty-five stores ring up more than $1 billion a year in sales. The firm also operates a coffee company, a vitamin company, eight bakeries, and a seafood wharf. Whole Foods controls just 7 percent of a market dominated by independent stores. However, the natural-

foods segment of the U.S. grocery industry has expanded by more than 20 percent a year and now totals $14.8 billion in sales. Sales of organic foods have grown from $173 million in 1980 to $4.2 billion. Although small, independently owned stores and co-ops still reign over the market for these products, Whole Foods has taken the concept of marketing natural foods to a new level.

Whole Foods started out in 1978 as Safer Way, a tiny grocery store located in a Victorian house in

Austin, Texas. In a progressive city that already had two dozen health-food stores, Safer Way was just another market where hippies shopped for natural and organic foods. But Safer Way's owner, John Mackey, had a vision of a natural-foods supermarket that would stock everything customers might need, from brown rice and soy milk to toilet paper and toothpaste. With a $50,000 investment from his father and a customer, Mackey went to Mark Skiles and Craig Weller, who ran rival Clarksville Natural Grocery, and pointed out that neither of their enterprises would survive against the bigger grocery chains and health-food stores unless they joined forces. The "Tofu Triplets" closed their respective businesses and opened Whole Foods Market in 1980 in a former nightclub. The 11,000-square-foot store offered a much larger selection of products than traditional health-food stores, which tended to shun refined sugar, alcohol, red meat, and products containing caffeine. Whole Foods chose to stock those items and many more, along with the usual herbal teas, organic produce, and natural toothpaste. The clean, intimate, and friendly store was an instant success.

So successful was the venture that by 1985, Whole Foods had expanded to three stores in Austin and one in Houston. However, financial difficulties and differences in management styles caused friction among the three partners. Skiles eventually sold off his share of the venture, and Mackey emerged as the leader and chief executive of the growing enterprise. Soon there were stores in Dallas, and in 1988, the company acquired several stores in New Orleans by buying the Whole Food Company. By the early 1990s, the firm had a total of twelve stores located in Texas, California, North Carolina, and Louisiana. When Whole Foods went public in 1992, it raised $23 million, which funded a buying spree that resulted in the acquisition of Bread & Circus, a six-store chain in New England; Mrs. Gooch's Natural Food Markets, a Los Angeles chain; and Fresh Fields, a twenty-two-store chain in Maryland. It also opened new stores in new markets.

The first Whole Foods store, like many health-food stores in the 1970s and early 1980s, catered primarily to Birkenstock-shod college students and health-conscious customers looking for more natural products than those found in the grocery stores of giant corporations like Kroger and Albertson's. As they matured, many of these baby boomers moved into well-paying corporate jobs—or in Austin, into high-paying high-tech jobs—and became affluent, sport-utility-vehicle-driving Yuppies. Today, Whole Foods targets these health-conscious, college-educated city dwellers by opening big, inviting stores in affluent neighborhoods.

A typical Whole Foods Market occupies 24,000 square feet and has an earth-friendly, feel-good atmosphere. The company's Boulder store, for example, is "industrial chic" with track lighting on high ceilings; it also offers valet parking and a restaurant with a fireplace and a view of the Rocky Mountains. The line

between conventional supermarket and natural-food store is blurry in a Whole Foods Market. Alongside natural and organic products, vitamins, and bulk items, shoppers can find well-known brand names like Fritos and Cheerios, as well as Whole Foods' own "365" line of private label products, which range from pet food to olive oil. As Mackey says, "Whole Foods has never been Holy Foods. We didn't want to send people elsewhere to shop." Thus, customers can browse well-stocked shelves of fine wines, ales and stouts, fresh breads, free-range poultry, and filet mignon. If they want, they can get an in-store massage, a cup of cappuccino, and a meal. At the checkout stand, they can have their purchases sacked in beige and green canvas shopping bags that have become status symbols in some locales.

But Whole Foods is not the only company looking for a bigger piece of the grocery pie. Wild Oats Markets has become Whole Foods' archrival; its fifty-four stores around the country give it a 2 percent stake of the industry, making it the second largest natural-food supermarket chain. The two companies compete fiercely head-to-head in some markets, including Boulder, Chicago, Dallas, and Los Angeles. The success of Trader Joe's, a chain of 113 specialty stores on the East and West coasts that is popular for its low prices, is one of the reasons Whole Foods launched its "365" private brand. Of course, all these companies face significant competition from more conventional national grocery chains like Kroger, A&P, and Albertson's, as well as from growing regional chains like Randall's and H-E-B. H-E-B has proven to be a particularly savvy competitor in Texas, where it has augmented many of its stores' offerings with some of the organic, natural, and bulk products that attract Whole Foods' customers.

In the face of such strong competition, Whole Foods must plan carefully. Mackey believes the U.S. market can absorb 500 natural-foods supermarkets, and, of course, he'd like most of those to be Whole Foods Markets. By 2003, he plans to increase the chain's number of stores from 85 to 140, with some located in new markets like Seattle and Atlanta. The new stores may be as large as 33,000 square feet, almost as big as some conventional grocery stores. But Wild Oats, as always, is close behind, with plans to expand to 100 stores of its own by 2000.[34]

Questions for Discussion

1. What type of retail store is Whole Foods? Who are its target customers?
2. Using each of the strategic retailing issues discussed in the chapter, describe Whole Foods' strategy.
3. How can Whole Foods respond to the intense competition it faces? Would franchising be a good option? What other retailing alternatives might the company consider?

STRATEGIC CASE 4

Bass Pro Shops

Bass Pro Shops is a privately owned company that operates an extensive catalog operation, a large retail store called Outdoor World in Springfield, Missouri, and Tracker Marine, a fishing-boat manufacturer. The company caters to outdoor enthusiasts, with a strong emphasis on hunting and fishing.

Catalog Sales

Bass Pro's catalog operation keeps about five hundred employees busy around the clock, seven days a week, answering 170 toll-free phone lines. Although Bass Pro managers do not reveal sales or profit figures for the privately owned company, they say it distributes about 36 million catalogs a year and ships 400,000 packages a month to customers via United Parcel Service and the U.S. Postal Service. The company's 388-page, full-color Outdoor World master catalog lists more than 17,000 items. The company also issues specialty catalogs focusing on sportsmen's clothing, and hunting, fishing, and boating equipment. Customers pay $2 for the master catalog, but it comes with a coupon good for $3 off merchandise purchases. For many outdoor enthusiasts, the catalog is a convenient way to obtain items with minimal effort. In addition, many of the items that Bass Pro offers are not available in rural areas and small towns.

Outdoor World

In 1981, Bass Pro opened Outdoor World to showcase the thousands of items offered in its catalogs. Bass Pro's president, Johnny Morris, calls Outdoor World the "world's greatest sporting goods store." Four million people visit the store each year—more than visit the Gateway Arch in St. Louis, which makes Outdoor World the most visited tourist attraction in Missouri.

Occupying 280,000 square feet, Outdoor World is organized by departments, and because it offers both entertainment and a variety of services, it is rather like a mall. The store's departments feature a wide variety of merchandise with many choices within each line. While signs help customers find departments, merchandise lines, and clothing sizes, promotional elements attract attention to specific merchandise. These elements include flyers announcing special in-store sales and displays of stuffed animals and birds. Northern geese, for example, suspended in mid-air, appear to be preparing to land over the Tracker Marine boat area, while a raccoon raids a box of Cracker Jacks above a display of men's caps.

To help customers select the equipment best suited to their interests and needs, Outdoor World provides useful product information. Salespeople are trained not only to sell products—all of which have a 100 percent satisfaction guarantee—but also to demonstrate their proper use and maintenance. Free pamphlets explain how to select such items as baseball bats, bows, camp foods, canoes, golf clubs, rifle scopes, slalom water skies, sleeping bags, and water fowl decoys, while videos demonstrate equipment. Camping equipment, such as tents, is displayed just as it would be used. Outdoor World also provides indoor shooting ranges for testing rifles, handguns, and bows on a variety of stationary and moving targets. About two hundred types of bows are available, and seven display cases, each about six feet long, hold around fifteen handguns each. Golfers can test putters on an indoor putting green and other clubs at an indoor driving range. The store repairs fishing rods and reels and sharpens knives. Trophy animals can be mounted at Wildlife Creations, the store's award-winning taxidermy shop.

Customers can also visit a trout stream, a live-alligator pit, and six aquariums, one of which contains a 96-pound snapping turtle. At Uncle Buck's 250-seat auditorium on the lower level, they can watch scuba divers hand-feeding freshwater fish. The store has large displays of antique fishing lures and mounted trophy fish and animals, including a 3,247-pound great white shark and a lion poised to leap. For customers who want their pictures taken with the displays, a loaner camera is available.

Taking the stairs or one of two glass-enclosed elevators to the fourth floor, customers have a choice of two restaurants. The Gravel Bar offers cafeteria-style family dining. Hemingway's Blue Water Cafe, which contains a 29,000-gallon aquarium, is more exotic. Its decorations include antique fishing and hunting equipment, mounted animal trophies, and African ritual masks. Near the entrance to Hemingway's, a four-story waterfall cascades down into a 64,000-gallon reflecting pool stocked with native Missouri fish.

Also located on the fourth floor is the Tall Tales Barbershop, where customers can get a haircut while sitting in one of four real "fighting chairs"—the kind used on deep-sea fishing boats. They can also have strands of their freshly cut hair made into a fishing lure. The barbershop provides an excellent view of the Tracker Marine boat showroom below.

Special events are an important part of marketing at Outdoor World. The Bass Pro Shops World's Fishing Fair, held in the spring, draws about 50,000 people on each of the five days it runs. It features 150 fishing seminars (including fly-fishing demonstrations) and 200 displays. The Fall Hunting Classic attracts about 80,000 visitors over its four-day run. Bass Pro also uses sweepstakes as a sales promotion tool. More than half a million people nationwide submitted entries in the Skoal Sportsman's Sweepstakes sponsored by Bass Pro and the U.S. Tobacco Sales and Marketing Company. The winner received a $100,000 line of credit at Outdoor World.

Bass Pro tries to be a good corporate citizen, especially with regards to the local Ozark region. Outdoor

World employees collect coins tossed into the store's aquariums and fountains and donate them to the Ronald McDonald House, which benefits critically ill children and their families. The 400,000 items Bass Pro ships each month are packed with biodegradable material made from recycled paper rather than less environmentally safe foam "peanuts." When Berkley, a manufacturer of fishing equipment, promised to stock one fish for each postcard sent in by anglers purchasing its fishing line, Bass Pro Shops president Johnny Morris promised to match the number of fish stocked by Berkley; Fellows Lake near Springfield ultimately received 5,000 channel catfish from Berkley and 5,000 walleye from Bass Pro.

Tracker Marine

Bass Pro has always wanted to provide anglers with everything needed to go fishing, including boats. Bass Pro initially sold boats obtained from other companies, but in 1978, it established a subsidiary, Tracker Marine, to manufacture its boats. Today, Tracker Marine produces forty-one different models, including pontoon, aluminum, and fiberglass boats, as well as boat trailers, at five plants in Missouri and Florida.

Tracker Marine now sells its boats and trailers through a network of about 250 dealers across the United States, as well as 25 in Canada and 1 in Australia. Tracker plans to expand the number of dealerships in Canada and to enter the boat market in Europe and other parts of the world. Tracker Marine's executives believe expansion will help keep the company's prices competitive.

Outdoor World is Tracker Marine's largest customer, and Tracker Marine is the largest advertiser in the Outdoor World master catalog. Together, Bass Pro's two subsidiaries—retail store and boat manufacturer—employ about 4,000 people in the peak season (a minimum of about 1,800 in Outdoor World and 1,500 in Tracker Marine year round) and have an annual payroll of about $40 million. Although Bass Pro has acquired the Spectrum and Fisher boat lines from Brunswick Corporation, it has no plans to sell them through Outdoor World.

Competitive Threats

Bass Pro does not seem to have any direct competitors. Small tackle shops, marine dealers, and sources of other outdoor products generally cannot match its prices or selection. Although L.L. Bean sells outdoor products through its large catalog operation and its retail store in Freeport, Maine, its offerings and store location among outlets like Ralph Lauren and London Fog appear to be targeted at a more upscale market. Neither Bass Pro nor L.L. Bean sells firearms through their catalogs because of federal regulations. Outdoor World, however, offers a very large selection of rifles, shotguns, and handguns, while L.L. Bean's store offers a smaller selection of rifles and shotguns only. Nonetheless, Bass Pro executives, do keep an eye on L.L. Bean.

New Retailing Directions

Bass Pro executives say their key operating philosophy has not been to add more and more to their organization, but rather to stock items that seem important to the outdoor enthusiast in terms of providing a new experience or element of pleasure. The key idea seems to be adding value to products that meet the needs of customers, an idea at the very heart of the marketing concept.

Until 1995, Bass Pro Shops' retail activities were centered on the Springfield store. In that year, however, Bass Pro opened a second store, called Sportsman's Warehouse, in Atlanta. This store has an outdoor feel similar to that of Outdoor World and may serve as a concept test for a warehouse-style retailing operation. Bass Pro opened a third store in Islamorada, Florida; known as Worldwide Sportsman, it stocks goods mainly for saltwater fishermen.

The company is now opening four new stores carrying the Outdoor World name in Gurnee, Illinois; Grapevine, Texas; Nashville, Tennessee; and Fort Lauderdale, Florida. The 133,000-square-foot Grapevine store is expected to produce $100 million in gross sales annually. These stores will be quite similar to the parent Springfield store, with comparable decor, entertainment, and merchandise. A facade pioneered at the Gurnee store location is being added to the Springfield store and will likely become a signature of all Outdoor World stores.

Bass Pro Shops is locating Outdoor World stores close to family attractions. The Grapevine store, for example, is near a "megamall," and a wilderness-themed hotel and convention center are being built nearby. The Nashville facility is close to a "shopper-tainment," music-themed megamall on the site of the former Opryland Theme Park. The Fort Lauderdale store is next to the site of the International Game Fish Association Hall of Fame, which is being built on land donated by Bass Pro's president, Johnny Morris. Morris is also donating $10 million in cash, land, and exhibits for the creation of the $40 million American National Fish and Wildlife Living Museum and Aquarium, to be located next to the Outdoor World store in Springfield. Although the Missouri Conservation Commission views this venture as a positive effort to promote conservation and has even donated $2.5 million toward its completion, some critics envision the attraction as a big room full of stuffed animals created to boost business for Outdoor World.[35]

Questions for Discussion:

1. Describe the marketing channels that Bass Pro Shops is using to distribute outdoor products.
2. What role does physical distribution play in Bass Pro's success with its catalog and retail operations?
3. What type of retailer is Outdoor World? Describe its retailing strategy.
4. How can Bass Pro Shops use its internal strengths to respond to threats and opportunities in the marketing environment?

Promotion
Decisions

Part 5 focuses on communication with target market members and, at times, other groups. A specific marketing mix cannot satisfy people in a particular target market unless they are aware of the product and where to find it. Some promotion decisions relate to a specific marketing mix, whereas others, broader in scope, are geared to promoting the entire organization. Chapter 17 discusses integrated marketing communications. It describes the communication process and the major promotional methods that can be included in promotion mixes. In Chapter 18, we analyze the major steps required to develop an advertising campaign, and we explain what public relations is and how it can be used. Chapter 19 deals with the management of personal selling and the role it can play in a firm's promotional efforts. This chapter also explores the general characteristics of sales promotion and sales promotion techniques.

Economic forces

Competitive forces

Product

Political forces

Price

Customer

Distribution

Promotion

Socio-cultural forces

Legal and regulatory forces

Technological forces

17

Integrated Marketing Communications

OBJECTIVES

- To become aware of the nature of integrated marketing communications
- To understand the role of promotion in the marketing mix
- To examine the process of communication
- To understand the objectives of promotion
- To explore the elements of the promotion mix
- To acquire an overview of the major methods of promotion
- To explore factors that affect the choice of promotional methods
- To examine criticisms and defenses of promotion

St. Paul Saints—A Winning Combination of Sport and Promotion

As baseball fans line up outside Midway Stadium in St. Paul, Minnesota, to pay $4.00 for general admission tickets, bands play and a machine blows thousands of huge bubbles into the air. Inside, as the game is about to start, an enormous pig named Hamlet runs out of the dugout and delivers two saddlebags of baseballs to the home plate umpire. At the end of the game, fans stream out of the stadium to the strains of Louis Armstrong's rendition of "When the Saints Go Marching In." This is the world of St. Paul Saints' baseball.

The St. Paul Saints are a minor league team, part of the Northern League, but they are very "major league" in some important respects. Since 1994, they have set league attendance records and last year sold out forty-one of forty-three games. Although the Saints have been called "the hottest minor league commodity going," it is not stellar baseball or home run records that make the team so popular. One of the primary reasons for its success is its outstanding program of integrated marketing communications.

Through public relations tools, such as publicity and event sponsorship, and through sales promotions, such as contests and giveaways, the Saints' marketers have generated a level of fan excitement and loyalty that major league teams envy. When pigs deliver baseballs, when "Lady Dynamite" blows herself up behind second base, when the Minnesota orchestra shows up to play before a game, when one of the team's owners appears on the Conan O'Brien show, and when "60 Minutes" does a feature on the team, the Saints receive very favorable publicity. Team-sponsored community events, such as a reading program for fourth- and fifth-graders that awards prizes from the Saints and the club's annual charity golf tournament, also generate positive public relations.

Every Saints' home game has a special theme, such as "Jerry Garcia Night" and "Wizard of Oz Night," which increases attendance and generates enthusiasm for the team. Giveaways, such as the Opening Night Magnetic Schedule Giveaway and the Tombstone Pizza Baseball Glove Giveaway, do the same. Contests function not only as sales promotion efforts, but generate positive public relations as well. For example, the team held a "Name the Pig" contest for local school children, and it also sponsors the Saints' Scholarships, an essay contest for currently enrolled college students.

The Saints' owners insist that as long as they continue selling out games, they will not advertise. With the reputation the team's public relations and sales promotion programs maintain, it seems likely the Saints will continue packing the stadium. Experts assert that minor league baseball is a combination of sport and promotion. The Saints have created a winning combination.[1]

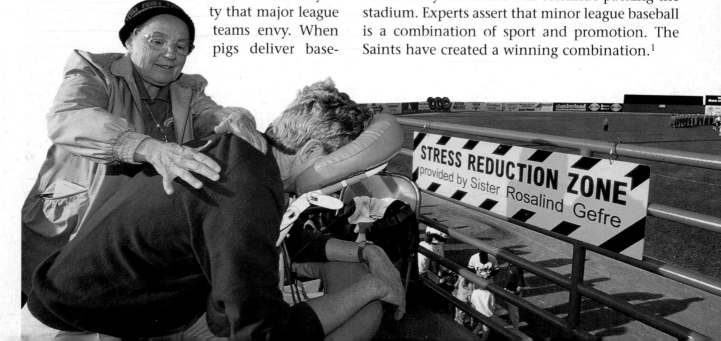

STRESS REDUCTION ZONE
provided by Sister Rosalind Gefre

Organizations like the St. Paul Saints employ a variety of promotional methods to communicate with their target markets. Providing information to customers is vital to initiating and developing long-term customer relationships.

This chapter looks at the general dimensions of promotion. First, we discuss the nature of integrated marketing communications. We then define and examine the role of promotion. Next, we analyze the meaning and process of communication and explore some of the reasons promotion is used. After that, we consider major promotional methods and the factors that influence marketers' decisions to use particular methods. Finally, we examine criticisms and defenses of promotion.

The Nature of Integrated Marketing Communications

integrated marketing communications
Coordination of promotion and other marketing efforts for maximum informational and persuasive impact

Integrated marketing communications is the coordination of promotion and other marketing efforts to ensure the maximum informational and persuasive impact on customers. Coordinating multiple marketing tools so they have this kind of synergistic effect requires a marketer to employ a broad perspective. A major goal of integrated marketing communications is to send a consistent message to customers. Because various units both inside and outside of a company have traditionally planned and implemented promotional efforts, the messages customers have received have not always been consistent. Integrated marketing communications provides an organization with a way to coordinate and manage its promotional efforts to ensure that customers do receive consistent messages. This approach fosters not only long-term customer relationships, but also the efficient use of promotional resources.

The concept of integrated marketing communications has been increasingly accepted for several reasons. Mass media advertising, a very popular promotional method in the past, is used less today because of its high cost and unpredictable audiences. Marketers can now take advantage of more precisely targeted promotional tools, such as cable TV, direct mail, CD ROMs, the Internet, special interest magazines, and videocassettes. Database marketing is also allowing marketers to be more precise in targeting individual customers. Until recently, suppliers of marketing communications were specialists. Advertising agencies provided advertising campaigns, sales promotion companies provided sales promotion activities and materials, and public relations organizations engaged in publicity efforts. Today, a number of promotion-related companies provide one-stop shopping to the client seeking advertising, sales promotion, and public relations, thus reducing coordination problems for the sponsoring company. Because the overall cost of marketing communications has risen significantly, upper management demands systematic evaluations of communication efforts and a reasonable return on investment. Managers of marketing communications are expected to demonstrate that promotional resources are being used efficiently.[2] While the fundamental role of promotion is not changing, the specific communication vehicles employed and the precision with which they are used are changing.

The Role of Promotion

promotion Communication to build and maintain relationships by informing and persuading one or more audiences

Promotion is communication that builds and maintains favorable relationships by informing and persuading one or more audiences to view an organization more positively and to accept its products. While a company may pursue a number of promotional objectives (discussed later in this chapter), the overall role of promotion is to stimulate product demand. Toward this end, many organizations spend considerable resources on promotion to build and enhance relationships with current and potential customers. Marketers also indirectly facilitate favorable relationships by focusing information about company activities and products on interest groups (such as environmental and consumer groups), current and potential investors, regulatory agencies, and society in general. For example, some producers promote responsible use of

Figure 17.1
Enhancing an Organization's Image by Encouraging Positive, Beneficial Behavior
Alachua General Hospital urges parents to encourage their children to wear bike helmets. This type of promotion also enhances the organization's image.

potentially harmful products like tobacco and alcohol. Some organizations, such as Alachua General Hospital, promote specific issues to encourage positive beneficial behavior and to enhance the organization's image (see Figure 17.1). Companies sometimes promote programs that help selected groups. McDonald's, for instance, promotes Ronald McDonald Houses, which aid families of children suffering from cancer. Some marketers use *cause-related marketing,* which links the purchase of their products to philanthropic efforts for one or more causes. By contributing to causes that its target markets support, cause-related marketing can help marketers boost sales and generate goodwill. Marketers also sponsor special events, often leading to news coverage and positive promotion of organizations and their brands.

For maximum benefit from promotional efforts, marketers strive for proper planning, implementation, coordination, and control of communications. Effective management of integrated marketing communications is based on information about customers and the marketing environment, often obtained from an organization's marketing information system (see Figure 17.2). How successfully marketers use promotion to maintain positive relationships depends largely on the quantity and quality of information an organization receives. Because promotion is communication, we now analyze what communication is and how the communication process works.

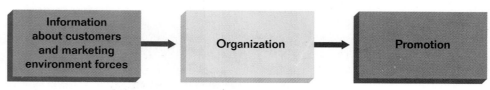

Figure 17.2
Information Flows into and out of an Organization

Promotion and the Communication Process

Communication can be viewed as the transmission of information. For communication to take place, both the sender and receiver of information must share some common ground. They must have a common understanding of the symbols, words, and pictures used to transmit information. An individual transmitting the following message may believe he or she is communicating with you:

在工廠吾人製造化粧品,在商店吾人銷售希望。

However, communication has not taken place if you don't understand the language in which the message is written.[3] Thus, we define **communication** as a sharing of meaning.[4] Implicit in this definition is the notion of transmission of information because sharing necessitates transmission.

communication
A sharing of meaning

source   A person, group, or organization with a meaning it wants and tries to share with an audience

As Figure 17.3 shows, communication begins with a source. A **source** is a person, group, or organization with a meaning it intends and attempts to share with an audience. A source could be a salesperson wishing to communicate a sales message or an organization wanting to send a message to thousands of customers through an advertisement. A **receiver** is the individual, group, or organization that decodes a coded message, and an audience is two or more receivers. The intended receivers or audience of an advertisement for Motorola cellular telephones, for example, might be businesspersons who frequently travel.

receiver   The individual, group, or organization that decodes a coded message

To transmit meaning, a source must convert the meaning into a series of signs or symbols representing ideas or concepts. This is called the **coding process** or *encoding*. When coding meaning into a message, a source must consider certain characteristics of the receiver or audience. To share meaning, the source should use signs or symbols familiar to the receiver or audience. Marketers who understand this realize how important it is to know their target market and to make sure that an advertisement, for example, uses language that the target market understands. Thus, when General Mills advertises Cheerios, it does not mention all the ingredients used to make the cereal because some of the ingredients would have little meaning to consumers. There have been some notable problems in translating English advertisements into other languages to communicate with customers in global markets. For example, Budweiser has been advertised in Spain as the "Queen of Beers," and the Chinese have been encouraged to "eat their fingers off" when receiving KFC's slogan "Finger-Lickin' Good."[5] Clearly, it is important that people understand the language used in promotion.

coding process
Converting meaning into a series of signs or symbols

When coding a meaning, a source needs to use signs or symbols that the receiver or audience uses for referring to the concepts the source intends to convey. Marketers try to avoid signs or symbols that may have several meanings for an audience. For example, *soda* as a general term for soft drinks might not work well in national advertisements. Although in some parts of the United States the word means "soft drink,"

Figure 17.3
The Communication Process

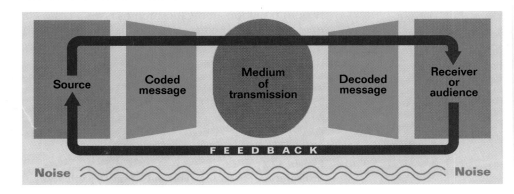

in other regions it may connote bicarbonate of soda, an ice cream drink, or something one mixes with Scotch whiskey.

To share a coded meaning with the receiver or audience, a source selects and uses a medium of transmission. A **medium of transmission** carries the coded message from the source to the receiver or audience. Transmission media include ink on paper, air wave vibrations produced by vocal cords, chalk marks on a chalkboard, and electronically produced vibrations of air waves—in radio and television signals, for example.

When a source chooses an inappropriate medium of transmission, several problems may arise. A coded message may reach some receivers, but not the right ones. Suppose a community theater spends most of its advertising dollars on radio advertisements. If theatergoers depend mainly on newspapers for information about local drama, then the theater will not reach its intended target audience. Coded messages may also reach intended receivers in incomplete form because the intensity of the transmission is weak. For example, radio signals are received effectively only over a limited range, which varies depending on climatic conditions. Members of the target audience living on the fringe of the broadcast area may receive a weak signal; others well within the broadcast area may also receive an incomplete message if they listen to radios while busy driving or studying.

In the **decoding process,** signs or symbols are converted into concepts and ideas. Seldom does a receiver decode exactly the same meaning that a source coded. When the result of decoding is different from what was coded, noise exists. **Noise** is anything that reduces the clarity and accuracy of the communication; it has many sources and may affect any or all parts of the communication process. Noise sometimes arises within the medium of transmission itself. Radio static, faulty printing processes, and laryngitis are sources of noise. Noise also occurs when a source uses signs or symbols that are unfamiliar to the receiver or that have a different meaning from the one intended. Noise also may originate in the receiver. A receiver may be unaware of a coded message when perceptual processes block it out.

The receiver's response to a message is **feedback** to the source. The source usually expects and normally receives feedback, although perhaps not immediately. During feedback, the receiver or audience is the source of a message directed toward the original source, which then becomes a receiver. Feedback is coded, sent through a medium of transmission, and decoded by the receiver, the source of the original communication. Thus, communication is a circular process.

During face-to-face communication, such as occurs in personal selling and product sampling, verbal and nonverbal feedback can be immediate. Instant feedback lets communicators adjust messages quickly to improve the effectiveness of their communication. For example, when a salesperson realizes through feedback that a customer does not understand a sales presentation, the salesperson adapts the presentation to make it more meaningful to the customer. In interpersonal communication, feedback occurs through talking, touching, smiling, nodding, eye movements, and other body movements and postures.

When mass communication like advertising is used, feedback is often slow and difficult to recognize. If Disney World increased advertising to attract more visitors, it might be six to eighteen months before the firm could notice the effects of expanded advertising. Although it is harder to discern, feedback does exist for mass communication. Advertisers obtain feedback in the form of changes in sales volume or in consumers' attitudes and awareness levels.

Each communication channel has a limit on the volume of information it can handle effectively. This limit, called **channel capacity,** is determined by the least efficient component of the communication process. Consider communications that depend on speech. An individual source can talk only so fast, and there is a limit to how much an individual receiver can take in aurally. Beyond that point, additional messages cannot be decoded; thus, meaning cannot be shared. Although a radio announcer can read several hundred words a minute, a one-minute advertising message should not exceed 150 words because most announcers cannot articulate words into understandable messages at a rate beyond 150 words per minute. Marketers should keep this limit in mind when developing radio commercials. At times, a firm creates a television advertisement containing several types of visual materials and

medium of transmission The means of carrying the coded message from the source to the receiver

decoding process Converting signs or symbols into concepts and ideas

noise Whatever reduces a communication's clarity and accuracy

feedback The receiver's response to a message

channel capacity The limit on the volume of information a communication channel can handle effectively

Table 17.1	Possible Objectives of Promotion
• Create awareness	• Retain loyal customers
• Stimulate demand	• Facilitate reseller support
• Encourage product trial	• Combat competitive promotional efforts
• Identify prospects	• Reduce sales fluctuations

several forms of audio messages, all transmitted to viewers at the same time. While the simultaneous use of multiple audio and video messages can be very effective, in some instances such communication may not be successful because receivers cannot decode all messages simultaneously.

Objectives of Promotion

Promotional objectives differ considerably from one organization to another and within organizations over time. Large organizations with multiple promotional programs operating simultaneously may have quite varied promotional objectives. For the purpose of analysis, we focus on the eight promotional objectives shown in Table 17.1. Although the list is not exhaustive, one or more of these objectives underlie many promotional programs.

Create Awareness

Figure 17.4
Creating Awareness
Tyson uses advertising to create awareness of its new Chicken Burger, a line extension.

A considerable amount of promotion is directed at creating awareness. For an organization introducing a new product or a line extension (see Figure 17.4), making customers aware of the product is crucial to initiating the product adoption process. A marketer that has invested heavily in product development strives to create product awareness quickly in order to generate revenues to offset the high costs of product

Figure 17.5
Stimulating Primary Demand
Both the Washington State Potato Commission and the Newspaper Association of America use advertising to stimulate primary demand.

development and introduction. Volkswagen, for instance, spent $45 million on an advertising campaign to introduce the new Beetle in the United States. This campaign included print ads in *Details, Vanity Fair,* and *GQ,* as well as a battery of six television ads on the most popular prime-time shows.[6]

Creating awareness is important for existing products, too. Promotional efforts may be aimed at increasing awareness of brands, product features, image-related issues (such as organizational size or socially responsive behavior), or operational characteristics (such as store hours, locations, and credit availability). Some organizations are unsuccessful because marketers fail to generate awareness of critical issues among a significant portion of target market members.

Stimulate Demand

primary demand Demand for a product category rather than for a specific brand

pioneer promotion Promotion that informs consumers about a new product

When an organization is the first to introduce an innovative product, it tries to stimulate **primary demand**—demand for a product category rather than for a specific brand of product—through pioneer promotion. **Pioneer promotion** informs potential customers about the product: what it is, what it does, how it can be used, and where it can be purchased. Because pioneer promotion is used in the introductory stage of the product life cycle, which means there are no competing brands, it neither emphasizes brand names nor compares brands. The first company to introduce the DVD player, for instance, initially attempted to stimulate primary demand by emphasizing the benefits of DVD players in general rather than the benefit of its specific brand.

Primary demand stimulation is not just for new products. At times an industry trade association, rather than a single firm, uses promotional efforts to stimulate primary demand. For example, the National Ski Area Association, an organization of 300 ski area operators in North America, launched a $20 million ad campaign to increase the number of skiers from 54 million to 60 million annually.[7] Similarly, as shown in Figure 17.5, the Newspaper Association of America and the Washington State Potato Commission use advertising to stimulate primary demand.

selective demand
Demand for a specific brand

To build **selective demand,** which is demand for a specific brand, a marketer employs promotional efforts that point out the strengths and benefits of a specific brand. Building selective demand also requires singling out attributes important to potential buyers. Selective demand can be stimulated by differentiating the product from competing brands in the minds of potential buyers. It can also be stimulated by increasing the number of product uses and promoting them through advertising campaigns, as well as through free samples, coupons, consumer contests and games, and sweepstakes. Promotions for large package sizes or multiple-product packages are directed at increasing consumption, which in turn can stimulate demand. In addition, selective demand can be stimulated by encouraging existing customers to use more of the product. For example, Sara Lee, through a television and print advertising campaign with the theme, "Add Some Delicious to Your Life," encouraged customers to use Sara Lee products often, and not just for special occasions.[8]

Encourage Product Trial

When attempting to move customers through the product adoption process, a marketer may be successful at creating awareness and interest, but customers may stall during the evaluation stage. In this case, certain types of promotion, such as free samples, coupons, test drives or limited free-use offers, contests, and games, are employed to encourage product trial. A magazine publisher, for example, might offer several free issues to entice potential readers to become new subscribers. Whether a marketer's product is the first of a new product category, a new brand in an existing category, or simply an existing brand seeking customers, trial-inducing promotional efforts aim at making product trial convenient and low risk for potential customers. As shown in Figure 17.6, for example, Elizabeth Arden uses a special promotion to encourage product trial.

Identify Prospects

Certain types of promotional efforts are directed at identifying customers who are interested in the firm's product and are most likely to buy it. A marketer may utilize a magazine advertisement with a direct-response information form, requesting the reader to complete and mail the form to receive additional information. Some advertisements have toll-free numbers to facilitate direct customer response. Customers who fill out information blanks or call the organization usually have higher interest in the product, which makes them likely sales prospects. The organization can respond with phone calls, follow-up letters, or personal contact by salespeople.

Retain Loyal Customers

Clearly, maintaining long-term customer relationships is a major goal of most marketers. Such relationships are quite valuable. For example, a major pizza chain recently determined that the lifetime receipts from one loyal customer amount to $8,000.[9] Promotional efforts directed at customer retention can help an organization control its costs because the costs of retaining customers are usually considerably lower than those of acquiring new ones. Frequent-user programs, such as those relied on by airlines, car rental agencies, and hotels, aim at rewarding loyal customers and encourag-

**Figure 17.6
Encouraging Product Trial**
The maker of Elizabeth Arden cosmetics encourages product trial through the use of buy-one-get-one-free promotions.

**Figure 17.7
Retaining Loyal
Customers**
Continental Airlines uses
a frequent-flyer program
and promotion to retain
loyal customers.

ing them to remain loyal. Some organizations employ special offers that can be used only by their existing customers. To retain loyal customers, marketers not only advertise loyalty programs, but also use reinforcement advertising, which assures current users they have made the right brand choice and tells them how to get the most satisfaction from the product. As shown in Figure 17.7, Continental Airlines encourages brand loyalty by promoting its award-winning frequent-flyer program.

Facilitate Reseller Support

Reseller support is a two-way street. Producers generally want to provide support to resellers to maintain sound working relationships, and, in turn, they expect resellers to support their products. When a manufacturer advertises a product to consumers, this promotion should be viewed by resellers as being strong manufacturer support. In some instances, a producer agrees to pay a certain proportion of retailers' advertising expenses for promoting its products. When a manufacturer is introducing a new consumer brand in a highly competitive product category, it may be difficult to persuade supermarket managers to carry this brand. If the manufacturer promotes the new brand with free sample and coupon distribution in the retailer's area, a supermarket manager views these actions as strong support and is much more likely to handle the product.

To encourage wholesalers and retailers to increase their inventories, a manufacturer may provide them with special offers and buying allowances. In certain industries, a producer's salesperson may provide support to a wholesaler by working with the wholesaler's customers (retailers) in the presentation and promotion of the products. Strong relationships with resellers are important to a firm's capability to maintain a sustainable competitive advantage. The use of various promotional methods can help an organization achieve this goal.

Combat Competitive Promotional Efforts

At times a marketer's objective in using promotion is to offset or lessen the effect of a competitor's promotional program. This type of promotional activity does not necessarily increase the organization's sales or market share, but it may prevent a sales or market share loss. A combative promotional objective is used most often by firms in extremely competitive consumer markets, such as the fast-food industry, or in local competitive markets. For example, a local supermarket may mail out store coupons to residents living within a two-mile radius of the store. Coupons might be redeemable only Tuesdays and Wednesdays for the purchase of common items, such as milk, bread, or eggs, at very low prices. To offset the effects of these coupons, a competing store could advertise in the newspaper that it will accept any store's coupons on any day of the week.

Reduce Sales Fluctuations

Demand for many products varies from one month to another because of such factors as climate, holidays, and seasons. A business, however, cannot operate at peak efficiency when sales fluctuate rapidly. Changes in sales volume translate into changes in production, inventory levels, personnel needs, and financial resources. When promotional techniques reduce fluctuations by generating sales during slow periods, a firm can use its resources more efficiently.

Promotional techniques are often designed to stimulate sales during sales slumps. For example, advertisements promoting price reduction of lawn-care equipment can increase sales during fall and winter months. During peak periods, a marketer may refrain from advertising to prevent stimulating sales to the point that the firm cannot handle all the demand. On occasion, an organization advertises that customers can be better served by coming in on certain days. A pizza outlet might distribute coupons that are valid only Monday through Thursday because on Friday through Sunday the restaurant is extremely busy.

To achieve the major objectives of promotion discussed here, companies must develop appropriate promotional programs. In the next section, we consider the basic components of such programs: the promotion mix elements.

The Promotion Mix

promotion mix   A combination of promotional methods used to promote a specific product

Several promotional methods can be used to communicate with individuals, groups, and organizations. When an organization combines specific methods to promote a particular product, that combination constitutes the promotion mix for that product. The four possible elements of a **promotion mix** are advertising, personal selling, public relations, and sales promotion (see Figure 17.8). For some products, firms use all four ingredients; for others, only two or three. As discussed in Globalmarketing, Columbia Sportswear uses multiple promotional methods to create a highly effective promotion mix.

Advertising

Advertising is a paid nonpersonal communication about an organization and its products transmitted to a target audience through mass media, including television, radio, the Internet, newspapers, magazines, direct mail, outdoor displays, and signs on mass transit vehicles. Individuals and organizations use advertising to promote goods, services, ideas, issues, and people. Being highly flexible, advertising can reach an extremely large target audience or focus on a small, precisely defined segment. For instance, Burger King's advertising focuses on a large audience of potential fast-food customers, ranging from children to adults, whereas advertising for corporate jets focuses on a much smaller and more specialized target market.

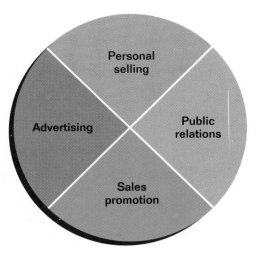

Figure 17.8
The Four Possible Elements of a Promotion Mix

Advertising offers several benefits. It is extremely cost-efficient when it reaches a vast number of people at a low cost per person. For example, the cost of a four-color, one-page advertisement in *Time* magazine is $176,000. Because the magazine reaches 4 million subscribers, the cost of reaching a thousand subscribers is only $44. Advertising also lets the user repeat the message several times. Levi Strauss, for example, advertises on television, in magazines, and in outdoor displays. Furthermore, advertising a product a certain way can add to its value, and the visibility an organization gains from advertising can enhance its image. At times, a firm tries to enhance the company's or product's image by including celebrity endorsers in its advertisements.

Advertising has disadvantages as well. Even though the cost per person reached may be low, the absolute dollar outlay can be extremely high, especially for commercials during popular television shows. High costs can limit, and sometimes prevent, use of advertising in a promotion mix. Moreover, advertising rarely provides rapid feedback. Measuring its effect on sales is difficult, and it is ordinarily less persuasive than personal selling. In most instances, the time available to communicate a message to customers is limited to seconds, since people look at a print advertisement for only a few seconds and most broadcast commercials are thirty seconds or less. Of course, the use of infomercials can increase exposure time for viewers.

Globalmarketing

Gert Boyle Promotes Columbia's Image

In 1974, Columbia Sportswear, the world's largest maker of active outdoor apparel and footwear, discovered that 30 percent of its "Gore-Tex" parkas were being sold in Japan. Owners Gert Boyle and son Tim knew it was time to take Columbia global. The company soon began offering its products in Europe and Canada, as well as in Japan and the United States. Established in 1938 as a family-owned hat distributor, the company today sells its rugged fashions in 10,000 retail establishments in over thirty countries. To outdoor enthusiasts around the world, "dressed for success" is likely to mean dressed in Columbia Sportswear. The company's Bugaboo parka is the best-selling ski parka in apparel history. Thanks in large part to its unconventional boss, Gert Boyle, and its extensive global promotional program, Columbia posted annual sales of about $353 million in 1997.

Gert Boyle has become an international celebrity, known from New York to New Zealand as an exceptional, dynamic, tough leader with the "born to nag" tattoo on her arm. Her slogan—"Early to bed, early to rise, work like hell, and advertise"—is borne out in the company's multimillion dollar global advertising campaign. Columbia consistently reaches millions around the world with its irreverently humorous and unforgettable ads.

They appear in international print and broadcast media, including *GQ, Rolling Stone,* and *Ski* magazines, the "Late Show with David Letterman," and cable networks ESPN and MTV. Although the language varies and messages are sometimes tailored to fit individual cultures, the humor remains distinctly American. One

Korean print ad, for example, features Gert Boyle's face with mountains in the background and reads, "When you're as old as the hills, you tend to know what to wear in them."

Public relations, sales promotion, and aggressive personal selling efforts also build customers' brand awareness of Columbia and increase the company's sales. High-profile sponsorships, such as being the official outerwear supplier to CBS Sports for a recent Winter Olympics and outfitting the first all-female America's Cup sailing team, create positive publicity. Chatting on television talk shows one day and mingling with bikers at advertising shoots the next, Gert Boyle comfortably navigates the globe to foster favorable public relations. In one month, for example, she went from Las Vegas to Atlanta and to Germany and France for trade shows. Wherever she goes, she pleases customers by shaking their hands and autographing posters.

In North America, Asia, Latin America, Australia, New Zealand, and some parts of Europe, Columbia works through its own sales office and with independent sales agencies and distributors to bring its products to retail outlets. Identifying Asia as its strongest international market, Columbia recently launched retail stores in Korea and Japan. Striving to reinforce the company's active outdoor image, sales personnel provide retailers with Columbia's "Merchandising Manual." It contains visual merchandising accessories and in-store promotions bearing Gert Boyle's imposing—but apparently irresistible—face.

Personal Selling

Personal selling is a paid personal communication that seeks to inform customers and to persuade them to purchase products in an exchange situation. The phrase *purchase products* is interpreted broadly to encompass acceptance of ideas and issues. Telemarketing, described in Chapter 16 as direct selling over the telephone, relies heavily on personal selling.

Personal selling has both advantages and limitations when compared with advertising. Advertising is general communication aimed at a relatively large target audience, whereas personal selling involves more specific communication aimed at one or several persons. Reaching one person through personal selling costs considerably more than through advertising, but personal selling efforts often have greater impact on customers. Personal selling also provides immediate feedback, allowing marketers to adjust their messages to improve communication. It helps them determine and respond to customers' information needs.

kinesic communication Communicating through the movement of head, eyes, arms, hands, legs, or torso

proxemic communication Communicating by varying the physical distance in face-to-face interactions

tactile communication Communicating through touching

When a salesperson and customer meet face to face, they use several types of interpersonal communication. The predominant communication form is language—both spoken and written. A salesperson and customer frequently use **kinesic communication,** which is communication through the movement of head, eyes, arms, hands, legs, or torso. Winking, head nodding, hand gestures, and arm motions are forms of kinesic communication. A good salesperson can often evaluate a prospect's interest in a product or presentation by noting eye contact and head nodding. **Proxemic communication,** a less obvious form of communication used in personal selling situations, occurs when either person varies the physical distance separating them. When a customer backs away from a salesperson, for example, that individual may be displaying a lack of interest in the product or expressing dislike for the salesperson. Touching, or **tactile communication,** is also a form of communication, although less popular in the United States than in many other countries. Handshaking is a common form of tactile communication both in the United States and elsewhere.

Public Relations

While many promotional activities are focused on a firm's customers, other groups or publics—suppliers, employees, stockholders, the media, educators, potential investors, government officials, and society in general—are important to an organization as well. To communicate with customers and these publics, a company employs public relations. Public relations is a broad set of communication efforts used to create and maintain favorable relationships between an organization and its publics. Maintaining a positive relationship with one or more publics can affect a firm's current sales and profits, as well as its long-term survival.

Public relations uses a variety of tools, including annual reports, brochures, event sponsorship, and sponsorship of socially responsible programs aimed at protecting the environment or helping disadvantaged individuals. Other tools arise from the use of publicity, which is a part of public relations. Publicity is nonpersonal communication in news story form about an organization or its products, or both, transmitted through a mass medium at no charge. A few examples of publicity-based public relations tools are news releases, press conferences, and feature articles. Ordinarily, public relations efforts are planned and implemented to be consistent with and to support other elements of the promotion mix. Public relations efforts may be the responsibility of an individual or a department within an organization, or an organization may hire an independent public relations agency. Unpleasant situations and negative events like product tampering may provoke unfavorable public relations for an organization. To minimize the damaging effects of unfavorable coverage, effective marketers have policies and procedures in place to help manage any public relations problems.

Public relations should not be viewed as a set of tools to be used only during crises. To get the most from public relations, an organization should have someone responsible for public relations either internally or externally and should have an ongoing public relations program.

Sales Promotion

Sales promotion is an activity or material that acts as a direct inducement, offering added value or incentive for the product, to resellers, salespersons, or consumers.[10] Examples include free samples, games, rebates, sweepstakes, contests, premiums, and coupons. (Coupons are increasingly being issued over the Internet, as discussed in Tech*know.) *Sales promotion* should not be confused with *promotion;* sales promotion is just one part of the comprehensive area of promotion. Currently, marketers spend about $3 on sales promotion for every $1 spent on advertising. Sales promotion appears to be a faster-growing area than advertising.

Tech*know

Clicking Coupons Instead of Clipping Them

Instead of picking up scissors and clipping coupons out of newspapers, magazines, and direct-mail pieces, many value-conscious shoppers are sitting down at their personal computers and logging onto the Internet. There, they can download coupons worth a dollar off on two 12-packs of Mountain Dew, 35 cents off on Ritz crackers, 50 cents off on Ben & Jerry's ice cream, 20 percent off anything at the new Barnes & Noble bookstore, and varying amounts off any number of other products offered by manufacturers and retailers. According to recent studies, the Internet is drawing an increasing number of shoppers in search of coupons, and retailers are discovering that this method of coupon distribution not only rewards loyal customers, but also attracts new ones.

A pioneer in the Internet-coupon field is Catalina Marketing Corporation, operator of ValuPage. At its Internet site, www.valupage.com, shoppers enter their zip codes and are shown a list of money-saving offers at supermarkets in their area. After printing the list from their computers, they present it at the supermarket, where cashiers scan the bar code at the top of the printed page, along with the items being purchased. For each purchased item that appears on the list, customers receive "Web Bucks," which they can apply to the purchase of any products on their next trip to the store. Customers can also receive coupons weekly by E-mail by signing up and answering a few demographic questions. About 7,000 supermarkets participate in ValuPage and ValuE-mail, together with over thirty-five manufacturers, including Lever Brothers, General Mills, Nabisco, and Kimberly-Clark.

ValuPage is not the only place on the Internet that issues coupons. Interactive Coupon Network (ICN) operates a Web site (www.coolsavings.com) that allows registered shoppers to print coupons for discounts on items ranging from clothing to office supplies to airline tickets. Participants include Royal Caribbean, Kinney Shoes,

PETsMART, LensCrafters, CBS Sportsline Superstore, Kmart, and Barnes & Noble. Money Mailer, which mails out packets of coupons for advertisers, now also issues coupons on its "Hot Coupons" Web site (www.hot-coupons.com). Companies that use Money Mailer's direct-mail services can add coupons to its Web site at no extra charge. Newspaper publishers, such as Scripps-Howard and Metro Publishing, Inc., also offer coupons on their Web pages.

Internet coupon providers are addressing concerns about potential fraud and privacy in several ways. Because instantly redeemable coupons can easily be duplicated, altered, or counterfeited, ValuPage does not issue them, but instead has customers present supermarket cashiers with the bar-coded page redeemable for Web Bucks. To date, this format is the only one that manufacturers of consumer packaged goods are willing to use on the Internet. To ensure that customers receive only one coupon for each offer, ICN's coupons disappear from the computer screen as soon as they are downloaded. To ensure privacy, Catalina Marketing and ICN never supply or sell customers' E-mail addresses or demographic information without explicit informed consent.

Current indications about the potential success of issuing coupons on the Internet are encouraging. For example, about 20 percent of the 100,000 people who have printed out the ValuPage lists have purchased the promoted products, in contrast to the 1 to 2 percent redemption rate for coupon inserts in newspapers.

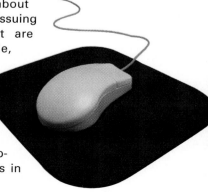

Generally, when companies employ advertising or personal selling, they depend on them continuously or cyclically. However, a marketer's use of sales promotion tends to be irregular. Many products are seasonal. A company like Toro may offer more sales promotions in August than in the peak selling season of April or May, when more people buy tractors, lawn mowers, and other gardening equipment. Marketers frequently rely on sales promotion to improve the effectiveness of other promotion mix ingredients, especially advertising and personal selling. For example, when Johnson and Johnson/Merck launched its antacid Mylanta Supreme with new flavors, it coupled sampling and coupons with a $19 million advertising campaign.[11]

An effective promotion mix requires the right combination of components. To see how such a mix is created, we examine the factors and conditions affecting the selection of promotional methods that an organization uses for a particular product.

Selecting Promotion Mix Elements

Marketers vary the composition of promotion mixes for many reasons. Although all four elements can be included in a promotion mix, frequently a marketer selects fewer than four. Many firms that market multiple product lines use several promotion mixes simultaneously.

When making decisions about the composition of promotion mixes, marketers must recognize that commercial messages, whether from advertising, personal selling, sales promotion, or public relations, are limited in the extent to which they can inform and persuade customers and move them closer to making purchases. Depending on the type of customers and the products involved, buyers to some extent rely on word-of-mouth communication from personal sources, such as family members and friends. Over 40 percent of Americans seek information from friends and family members when buying medical, legal, and auto repair services. Word-of-mouth communication is also very important when people are selecting restaurants, entertainment, banking, and personal services like hair care. Effective marketers who understand the importance of word-of-mouth communication attempt to identify advice-givers and to encourage them to try their products in the hope that they will spread favorable word about them. Chrysler did this when it introduced the Dodge Intrepid, Chrysler Concorde, and Eagle Vision. Chrysler dealers in a multistate region offered these models for a weekend to over 6,000 opinion leaders (advice-givers), resulting in over 32,000 exposures of these new models.[12] Marketers must not underestimate the importance of both word-of-mouth communication and personal influence, nor should they have unrealistic expectations about the performance of commercial messages.

Promotional Resources, Objectives, and Policies

The size of an organization's promotional budget affects the number and relative intensity of promotional methods included in a promotion mix. If a company's promotional budget is extremely limited, the firm is likely to rely on personal selling because it is easier to measure a salesperson's contribution to sales than to measure the sales effectiveness of advertising. Businesses must have sizable promotional budgets to use regional or national advertising. Organizations with extensive promotional resources generally include more elements in their promotion mixes, but having more promotional dollars to spend does not necessarily mean using more promotional methods.

An organization's promotional objectives and policies also influence the types of promotion selected. If a company's objective is to create mass awareness of a new convenience good, such as a breakfast cereal, its promotion mix probably leans heavily toward advertising, sales promotion, and possibly public relations. If a company hopes to educate consumers about the features of a durable good, such as a home appliance, its promotion mix may combine a moderate amount of advertising, possibly some sales promotion designed to attract customers to retail stores, and a great deal of personal selling because this method is an excellent way to inform customers about such products. If a firm's objective is to produce immediate sales of consumer nondurables, the promotion mix will probably stress advertising and sales promotion.

Characteristics of the Target Market

Size, geographic distribution, and demographic characteristics of an organization's target market help dictate the methods to be included in a product's promotion mix. To some degree, market size determines composition of the mix. If the size is quite limited, the promotion mix will probably emphasize personal selling, which can be quite effective for reaching small numbers of people. Organizations selling to industrial markets and firms marketing products through only a few wholesalers frequently make personal selling the major component of their promotion mixes. When a product's market consists of millions of customers, organizations rely on advertising and sales promotion because these methods reach masses of people at a low cost per person.

Geographic distribution of a firm's customers also affects the choice of promotional methods. Personal selling is more feasible if a company's customers are concentrated in a small area than if they are dispersed across a vast region. When the company's customers are numerous and dispersed, advertising may be more practical.

Distribution of a target market's demographic characteristics, such as age, income, or education, may affect the types of promotional techniques a marketer selects. For example, personal selling may be more successful than print advertisements for communicating with less-educated people.

Characteristics of the Product

Generally, promotion mixes for business products concentrate on personal selling, while advertising plays a major role in promoting consumer goods. This generalization should be treated cautiously, though. Marketers of business products use some advertising to promote products. Advertisements for computers, road-building equipment, and aircraft are not uncommon, and some sales promotion is also used occasionally to promote business products. Personal selling is used extensively for consumer durables, such as home appliances, automobiles, and houses, while consumer convenience items are promoted mainly through advertising and sales promotion. Public relations appears in promotion mixes for both business and consumer products.

Marketers of highly seasonal products often emphasize advertising, and sometimes sales promotion as well, because off-season sales generally will not support an extensive year-round sales force. Although most toy producers have sales forces to sell to resellers, many of these companies depend chiefly on advertising to promote their products.

A product's price also influences the composition of the promotion mix. High-priced products call for personal selling because consumers associate greater risk with the purchase of such products and usually want information from a salesperson. Few of us, for example, are willing to purchase a refrigerator from a self-service establishment. For low-priced convenience items, marketers use advertising rather than personal selling.

A further consideration in creating an effective promotion mix is the stage of the product life cycle. During the introduction stage, much advertising may be necessary for both business and consumer products to make potential users aware of them. For many products, personal selling and sales promotion are also helpful in this stage. In the growth and maturity stages, consumer nondurables require heavy emphasis on advertising, while business products often require a concentration of personal selling and some sales promotion. In the decline stage, marketers usually decrease promotional activities, especially advertising.

Intensity of market coverage is another factor affecting composition of the promotion mix. When products are marketed through intensive distribution, firms depend strongly on advertising and sales promotion. Many convenience products, such as lotions, cereals, and coffee, are promoted through samples, coupons, and money refunds. When marketers choose selective distribution, promotion mixes vary considerably. Items handled through exclusive distribution, such as expensive watches, furs, and high-quality furniture, typically require a significant amount of personal selling.

A product's use affects the combination of promotional methods, too. Manufacturers of highly personal products, such as laxatives, nonprescription contraceptives, feminine hygiene products, and hemorrhoid medications, depend on advertising because many customers do not want to talk with salespersons about these products.

Costs and Availability of Promotional Methods

Costs of promotional methods are major factors to analyze when developing a promotion mix. National advertising and sales promotion require large expenditures. However, if these efforts are effective in reaching extremely large audiences, the cost per individual reached may be quite small, possibly a few pennies per person. Not all

Figure 17.9
Media Availability
Both 24/7 Media and Yahoo promote media availability and capabilities.

forms of advertising are expensive. Many small, local businesses advertise products through local newspapers, magazines, radio and television stations, outdoor displays, and signs on mass transit vehicles.

Another consideration that marketers explore when formulating a promotion mix is availability of promotional techniques. Despite the tremendous number of media vehicles in the United States, a firm may find that no available advertising medium effectively reaches a certain target market. Some organizations, such as those represented in Figure 17.9, promote media availability as well as their capabilities for reaching specific audiences. The problem of media availability becomes more pronounced when marketers advertise in foreign countries. Some media, such as television, simply may not be available or it may not be legal to advertise on television. Available media may not be open to certain types of advertisements. In some countries, advertisers are forbidden to make brand comparisons on television. Other promotional methods also have limitations. A firm may wish to increase its sales force but be unable to find qualified personnel.

Push and Pull Channel Policies

push policy   Promoting a product only to the next institution down the marketing channel

pull policy   Promoting a product directly to consumers to develop strong consumer demand that pulls products through the marketing channel

Another element marketers consider when planning a promotion mix is whether to use a push policy or a pull policy. With a **push policy**, the producer promotes the product only to the next institution down the marketing channel. In a marketing channel with wholesalers and retailers, the producer promotes to the wholesaler because in this case the wholesaler is the channel member just below the producer (see Figure 17.10). Each channel member in turn promotes to the next channel member. A push policy normally stresses personal selling. Sometimes sales promotion and advertising are used in conjunction with personal selling to push the products down through the channel.

As Figure 17.10 shows, a firm using a **pull policy** promotes directly to consumers to develop a strong consumer demand for the products. It does so primarily through advertising and sales promotion. Because consumers are persuaded to seek the products in retail stores, retailers in turn go to wholesalers or the producer to buy the products. This policy is intended to pull the goods down through the channel by creating demand at the consumer level. For example, if marketers at Post Cereals were launching a new cereal such as Frosted Grape-Nuts, they would likely use a pull policy, aiming a large amount of advertising at consumers and encouraging them to look for Frosted Grape-Nuts at their favorite stores. Consumers are told that if the stores don't have it, ask them to get it. Stimulating demand at the consumer level for Frosted Grape-Nuts causes the product to be pulled through the channel. Push and pull policies are not mutually exclusive. At times an organization uses both simultaneously.

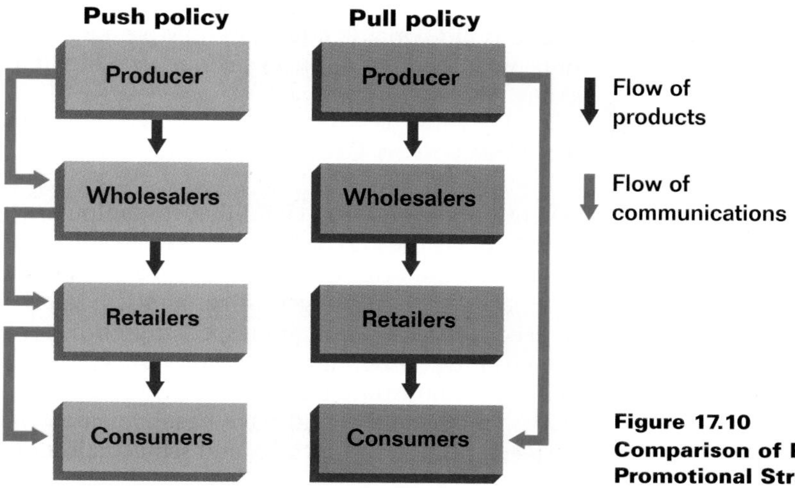

Push policy

Producer → Wholesalers → Retailers → Consumers

Pull policy

Producer → Wholesalers → Retailers → Consumers

Flow of products

Flow of communications

**Figure 17.10
Comparison of Push and Pull Promotional Strategies**

Criticisms and Defenses of Promotion

Even though promotional activities can help customers make informed purchasing decisions, social scientists, consumer groups, government agencies, and members of society in general have long criticized promotion. There are two main reasons for such criticism: promotion does have flaws, and it is a highly visible business activity that pervades our daily lives. Although people almost universally complain that there is simply too much promotional activity, a number of more specific criticisms have been lodged. In this section we discuss some of the criticisms and defenses of promotion.

Is Promotion Deceptive?

One common criticism of promotion is that it is deceptive and unethical. During the nineteenth and early twentieth centuries, much promotion was blatantly deceptive. Although no longer widespread, some deceptive promotion does still occur. Critics of some state lottery advertisements claim the ads are deceptive because they overemphasize the lottery as the solution to financial problems and downplay the odds against winning.[13] Metropolitan Life and other insurers have employed questionable selling techniques to disguise whole-life insurance policies.[14] American Family Publishers has been accused of using deceit and trickery to sell magazines through its $10 million sweepstakes.[15] Questionable weight loss claims are made about various exercise devices and diet programs. Some promotions are unintentionally deceiving; for instance, when advertising to children, it is easy to mislead them because they are more naive than adults and less able to separate fantasy from reality. A promotion may also mislead some receivers because words can have diverse meanings for different people. All promotion, however, should not be condemned because a small portion is flawed. Laws, government regulation, and industry self-regulation have caused a decrease in deceptive promotion.

Does Promotion Increase Prices?

Promotion is also castigated for raising prices, but often it tends to lower them. The ultimate purpose of promotion is to stimulate demand. If it does, then a business should be able to produce and market products in larger quantities and thus reduce per-unit production and marketing costs, which can result in lower prices. For example, as demand for personal computers and compact disc players has increased, their prices have dropped. When promotion fails to stimulate demand, then the price of the promoted product increases because promotion costs must be added to other costs. Promotion also helps keep prices lower by facilitating price competition. When firms advertise prices, their prices tend to remain lower than when prices are not promoted. Gasoline pricing illustrates how promotion fosters price competition. Service stations with the highest prices seldom have highly visible price signs.

Does Promotion Create Needs?

Some critics of promotion claim that it manipulates consumers by persuading them to buy products they do not need, hence creating needs. In his theory of motivation, A. H. Maslow indicates that an individual tries to satisfy five levels of needs: physiological needs, such as hunger, thirst, and sex; safety needs; needs for love and affection; needs for self-esteem and respect from others; and self-actualization needs (that is, the need to realize one's potential).[16] When needs are viewed in this context, it is difficult to demonstrate that promotion creates them. If there were no promotional activities, people still would have needs for food, water, sex, safety, love, affection, self-esteem, respect from others, and self-actualization.

Figure 17.11
Promoting Health-Related Issues
Several organizations, such as the California Department of Health Servies, provide information about the health hazards associated with tobacco use.

Even though promotion does not create needs, it does capitalize on them (which may be why some critics feel promotion creates needs). Many marketers base their appeals on these needs. For example, several mouthwash, toothpaste, and perfume advertisements associate these products with needs for love, affection, and respect. These advertisers rely on human needs in their messages, but they do not create the needs.

Does Promotion Encourage Materialism?

Another frequent criticism of promotion is that it leads to materialism. The purpose of promoting goods is to persuade people to buy them, and so if promotion works, consumers will want to buy more and more things. Marketers assert that values are instilled in the home and that promotion does not change people into materialistic consumers. However, the behavior of today's children and teenagers contradicts this view; they insist on high-priced, name-brand apparel, such as Girbeaud, Nike, and Ralph Lauren.

Does Promotion Help Customers without Costing Too Much?

Every year, firms spend billions of dollars for promotion. The question is whether promotion helps customers enough to be worth the cost. Consumers do benefit because promotion informs them about product uses, features, advantages, prices, and locations where the products can be bought. Consumers thus gain more knowledge about available products and can make more intelligent buying decisions. Promotion also informs consumers about services—for instance, health care, educational programs, and day care—as well as about important social, political, and health-related issues. For example, several organizations, such as the California Department of Health Services (see Figure 17.11), inform people about the health hazards associated with tobacco use.

Should Potentially Harmful Products Be Promoted?

Finally, some critics of promotion, including consumer groups and government officials, suggest that certain products should not be promoted at all. Primary targets are products associated with violence and other possibly unhealthy activities—products like handguns, alcohol, tobacco, and gambling. Cigarette advertisements, for example, promote smoking, a behavior proven to be harmful and even deadly. Tobacco companies, which spend over $6 billion annually on promotion, have countered criticism of their promotions by pointing out that promoters of butter and red meat are not censured even though their cholesterol-filled products might cause heart disease. Recently, a few publishers of newspapers and magazines have adopted guidelines stating that they will not publish tobacco-related advertisements with cartoonlike characters if they can be interpreted to be targeted at children or teenagers.[17] Those who defend such promotion assert that as long as it is legal to sell a product, promoting that product should be allowed.

Summary

Integrated marketing communications is the coordination of promotion and other marketing efforts to ensure the maximum informational and persuasive impact on customers.

Promotion is communication to build and maintain relationships by informing and persuading one or more audiences.

Communication is a sharing of meaning. The communication process involves several steps. First, the source translates meaning into code, a process known as coding or encoding. The source should employ signs or symbols familiar to the receiver or audience. The coded message is sent through a medium of transmission to the receiver or audience. The receiver or audience then decodes the message and usually supplies feedback to the source. When the decoded message differs from the encoded one, a condition called noise exists.

Although promotional objectives vary from one organization to another and within organizations over time, eight primary objectives underlie many promotional programs. Promotion aims to create awareness of a new product, new brand, or existing product; to stimulate primary and selective demand; to encourage product trial through the use of free samples, coupons, limited free-use offers, contests, and games; to identify prospects; to retain loyal customers; to facilitate reseller support; to combat competitive promotional efforts; and to reduce sales fluctuations.

The promotion mix for a product may include four major promotional methods: advertising, personal selling, public relations, and sales promotion. Advertising is a paid nonpersonal communication about an organization and its products transmitted to a target audience through a mass medium. Personal selling is paid personal communication that attempts to inform customers and to persuade them to purchase products in an exchange situation. Public relations is a broad set of communication efforts used to create and maintain favorable relationships between an organization and its public. Sales promotion is an activity or material that acts as a direct inducement, offering added value or incentive for the product, to resellers, salespersons, or consumers.

Major determinants of which promotional methods to include in a product's promotion mix are an organization's promotional resources, objectives, and policies; characteristics of the target market; characteristics of the product; and cost and availability of promotional methods. Marketers also consider whether to use a push policy or a pull policy. With a push policy, the producer promotes the product only to the next institution down the marketing channel. Normally, a push policy stresses personal selling. Firms that use a pull policy promote directly to consumers, with the intention of developing strong consumer demand for the products. Once consumers are persuaded to seek products in retail stores, retailers go to wholesalers or the producer to buy the products.

Promotional activities can help consumers make informed purchasing decisions, but they have also evoked many criticisms. Promotion has been accused of deception. Although some deceiving or misleading promotions do exist, laws, government regulation, and industry self-regulation minimize deceptive promotion. Promotion has been blamed for increasing prices, but it usually tends to lower them. When demand is high, production and marketing costs decrease, which can result in lower prices. Moreover, promotion helps keep prices lower by facilitating price competition. Other criticisms of promotional activity are that it manipulates consumers into buying products they do not need, that it leads to a more materialistic society, and that consumers do not benefit sufficiently from promotional activity to justify its high cost. Finally, some critics of promotion suggest that potentially harmful products, especially those associated with violence, sex, and unhealthy activities, should not be promoted at all.

Important Terms

Integrated marketing
  communications
Promotion
Communication
Source
Receiver

Coding process
Medium of transmission
Decoding process
Noise
Feedback

Channel capacity
Primary demand
Pioneer promotion
Selective demand
Promotion mix

Kinesic communication
Proxemic communication
Tactile communication
Push policy
Pull policy

Discussion and Review Questions

1. What does *integrated marketing communications* mean?

2. What is the major task of promotion? Do firms ever use promotion to accomplish this task and fail? If so, give several examples.

3. What is communication? Describe the communication process. Is it possible to communicate without using all the elements in the communication process? If so, which ones can be omitted?

4. Identify several causes of noise. How can a source reduce noise?

5. Describe the possible objectives of promotion and discuss the circumstances under which each of these objectives might be used.

6. Identify and briefly describe the four promotional methods an organization can use in its promotion mix.

7. What forms of interpersonal communication besides language can be used in personal selling?

8. How do target market characteristics determine which promotional methods to include in a promotion mix? Assume that a company is planning to promote a cereal to both adults and children. Along what major dimensions would these two promotional efforts have to be different?

9. How can a product's characteristics affect the composition of its promotion mix?

10. Evaluate the following statement: "Appropriate advertising media are always available if a company can afford them."

11. Explain the difference between a pull policy and a push policy. Under what conditions should each policy be used?

12. Which criticisms of promotion do you believe to be the most valid? Why?

13. Should organizations be allowed to promote offensive, violent, sexual, or unhealthy products that can be legally sold and purchased? Support your answer.

Application Questions

1. The overall objective of promotion is to stimulate demand for a product. Through television advertising, the American Dairy Association promotes the benefits of drinking milk, which is aimed at stimulating primary demand. Advertisements for a specific brand of milk are aimed at stimulating selective demand. Identify two television commercials, one aimed at stimulating primary demand and one aimed at stimulating selective demand. Describe each and discuss how they attempt to achieve these objectives.

2. Developing a promotion mix is contingent upon many factors. The type of product and the product's attributes influence the mix. Which of the promotional methods (advertising, personal selling, public relations, or sales promotion) would you emphasize if you were developing the promotion mix for the products listed below? Explain your answer.

   a. washing machine
   b. cereal
   c. Halloween candy
   d. compact disc

3. Suppose marketers at Falcon International Corporation have come to you for recommendations on how they should promote their products. They are interested in developing a comprehensive promotional campaign and have a generous budget with which to implement their plans. What questions would you ask them, and what would you suggest they consider before developing a promotional program?

4. Marketers must consider whether to use a push or a pull policy when deciding on a promotion mix (see Figure 17.10). Identify a product for which marketers should use each of these and a third product that might best be promoted using a mix of the two policies. Explain your answers.

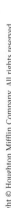

Internet Exercise & Resources

University of Iowa Alumni Association Hits the Net

As you will probably discover in a few years, university alumni associations are themselves marketing organizations. Thanks in large part to a popular course related to Internet marketing taught at the University of Iowa and to the Iowa City Chamber of Commerce and a local bank and bookstore, the University of Iowa Alumni Association is now online. Visit its Web site at

www.biz.uiowa.edu/Iowalum

1. Who are the target markets for the alumni association's Internet marketing efforts?

2. What is being promoted to these individuals?

3. What are the promotional objectives of the Web site?

E-Center Resources

Visit http://www.prideferrell.com to find several resources to help you succeed in mastering the material in this chapter, plus additional materials that will help you expand your marketing knowledge. The Web site includes

 Internet exercise updates plus additional exercises

 ACE self-tests

 abc Chapter summary with hotlinked glossary

 Hotlinks to companies featured in this chapter

 Resource Center

 Career Center

Marketing plan worksheets

VIDEO CASE 17.1

Churchs Chicken: "Gotta Love It"

Churchs Chicken wants its customers to laugh—and then buy a take-out bucket (or two) of Southern-style fried chicken. Humor plays a major role in the fast-food chain's integrated marketing communication (IMC) program. Using wacky television and radio commercials, newspaper ads, and point-of-purchase materials, as well as cause-related marketing and sales promotions, Atlanta-based Churchs is aiming to boost sales while broadening its appeal to a number of customer segments.

Founded in 1952, Churchs originally offered only traditional fried chicken. As the chain expanded, it began offering other chicken specialties, such as chicken sandwiches and spicy chicken wings, and side dishes like okra and mashed potatoes. Churchs now has over 1,360 stores in twenty-eight states and nine countries, including Canada, China, the Dominican Republic, Indonesia, Mexico, and Taiwan. Its market-leading rival KFC, however, has many more stores and higher sales. Churchs is striving to close the gap by

opening new stores and increasing sales at a healthy pace, supported by its IMC program.

Churchs' strategy of making humor the focal point of its promotion did not come about by accident. The company and its advertising agency first agreed on promotional goals and then conducted extensive marketing research to learn more about customers and their behavior. They studied not only customers' demographics, but also how often they buy fast-food meals, how much they spend on these meals, and what television shows they watch. The research revealed that Churchs' customers particularly enjoy television situation comedies—hence, the promotional emphasis on humor. At the time, KFC was putting most of its promotional muscle into suburban markets, so Churchs chose to concentrate first on urban areas.

Building on the research, Churchs' ad agency created a series of humorously irreverent television commercials featuring a former tough-talking sitcom star. Whether she was chasing Santa Claus out of her kitchen or trying to decide which Churchs Chicken meal to order, she ended every commercial with the slogan "Gotta love it!" And customers did. Franchise owners also loved it, reporting that sales soared whenever the commercials aired in their areas.

Recently, Churchs switched ad agencies but retained the humor and the popular slogan that helps unify its message across all media. "We have a tremendous equity in 'Gotta love it,' " commented Churchs' vice president of marketing. "It's positioned us as a brand and helped us get across the message that we have a great product at great prices." The company's next series of television commercials, based on the theme of "the crave," showed the outrageous things that can happen when people get irresistible cravings for Churchs chicken. A later round of humorous commercials, based on the theme of "How Churchs changed my life," was designed specifically for suburban markets, where 40 percent of the chain's stores are located.

Because research indicated that Hispanic consumers tend to patronize restaurants that advertise in their native language, Churchs hired a separate agency to create ads in Spanish for the Hispanic market in Texas. The agency developed four humorous commercials (two in English and Spanish and two in Spanish only) featuring Tejano music star Jay Perez. "We're interested in the Hispanic market as a whole, but in Texas, the Tejano music is something Hispanic people could relate to especially well," a Churchs' marketing executive explained. "As a result, we've got awfully strong sales down there."

To boost its appeal to the African-American market and fuel expansion into more urban neighborhoods, Churchs arranged for Grammy Award-winning gospel music singer Kirk Franklin to write, produce, and star in a series of television and radio ads. In exchange, Franklin was given fifteen new inner-city Churchs franchises, including ten in the Dallas area, as part of the chain's plan to bring in more urban franchisees.

Using a combination of media enables Churchs to communicate with all customer segments in all markets. For example, colorful newspaper inserts play up attractive price promotions and new products, while radio commercials reinforce the brand's positioning. To bring in more customers and encourage more frequent store visits, Churchs has run a variety of sales promotions, supported by advertising. A sweepstakes during one recent holiday season offered customers the chance to win electronic games. Churchs promoted the sweepstakes on television, on radio, through direct mail, and in its stores.

Cause-related marketing is an integral part of Churchs' promotion strategy. Among the causes the company supports are the United Negro College Fund and the Hispanic Association of Colleges and Universities. Habitat for Humanity International, based near the chain's Atlanta headquarters, is one of its favorite causes. Every September, Churchs sponsors a "Day of Dreams" fundraiser, giving Habitat a portion of all proceeds from that day's sale of chicken products. Although the company pledged to build 200 Habitat homes over a five-year period, it actually ended up building 204 homes. It donated or raised $7 million for materials and encouraged its employees to give more than 800,000 volunteer hours to the construction projects. Some of the chain's print and television ads mention the company's connection with Habitat, encouraging community support and giving customers yet another reason to feel good about buying from Churchs.

In a highly competitive industry where recognition of a brand name is a prerequisite, Churchs knows that special events are a good way to obtain wide exposure while demonstrating the company's commitment to the local community. For example, Churchs is the main sponsor of the Bob Hayes Invitational Track and Field Meet, which annually brings thousands of athletes from U.S. high schools to compete in Jacksonville, Florida. As one franchise owner explained, "We believe that each time we make a contribution to events such as this track meet, we strengthen individuals and communities."[18]

Questions for Discussion

1. What promotional objectives is Churchs pursuing?
2. What did Churchs' marketers learn through marketing research, and what impact did this information have on the original "Gotta Love It" advertising campaign?
3. What role does cause-related marketing play in Churchs' promotion mix?
4. What recommendations would you make to Churchs about including the Internet in its promotion mix?

CASE 17.2

Anheuser-Busch Tackles America's Alcohol-Related Problems

According to a study by the Harvard School of Public Health, 44 percent of college students consume more than five alcoholic drinks in a row in any given two-week period. The National Institute of Alcohol Abuse and Alcoholism estimates that alcohol disorder rates are highest among people 18 to 29 years old. Although educational efforts by alcoholic beverage companies have helped reduce drunk driving in the United States, these statistics reveal that there is much more work to be done. Today, producers of alcoholic beverages are addressing not only the problem of drunk driving, but also the issues of alcohol abuse, underage drinking, and other alcohol-related concerns.

As early as the turn of the century, Anheuser-Busch, the world's largest brewer, advocated moderation in drinking. Its 1982 launch of the "Know When to Say When" advertising campaign was an industry first. Today, using educational videos, community outreach programs, television ads, and public service announcements, the brewer leads the industry in promoting alcohol awareness and education.

To deliver its message about personal responsibility at home, at school, and wherever alcohol is served, Anheuser-Busch administers and supports more than a dozen community-based alcohol awareness and education programs. "Family Talk About Drinking" provides free guidebooks and videos to help parents talk with their children about family rules, respect for the law, and dealing with peer pressure. Since the program's introduction in 1990, over 2 million parents and other concerned adults have received its materials. To educate high school and college students about the consequences of underage drinking and drunk driving, the company produced the video "Make the Right Call." Barbara Babb, a critical-care flight nurse, presents the video to about 50,000 students a year and delivers a graphic and factual presentation based on her experiences.

Anheuser-Busch is a major supporter of alcohol education on American college campuses, creating such programs as "BACCHUS," a peer network designed to boost awareness of alcohol's effect on health, and sponsoring National Collegiate Alcohol Awareness Week. In addition, the company was the first brewer to develop its own code for college marketing and to distribute it to colleges across the United States. The code covers the company's policies on advertising, promotion, product sampling, and promotional materials on college campuses. For example, during spring break, Anheuser-Busch does not advertise beer or sponsor promotions at beaches or other outdoor locations where students typically gather.

Since 1989, Anheuser-Busch's "Alert Cab" program has taxied over 140,000 people home safely. Alert Cab brings together alcohol retailers and cab companies to provide free rides home to bar and restaurant patrons. Anheuser-Busch also works with tens of thousands of wholesalers to promote the use of designated drivers through its "I'm Driving" program. The brewer recently entered a partnership with 7-Eleven stores throughout the country to help prevent retailers from selling alcohol to minors. Anheuser-Busch provides 7-Eleven managers and clerks with a set of tools that helps them more effectively check and verify IDs. It also

gives them a toll-free number from which customers can order free copies of the brewer's "Family Talk About Drinking." Anheuser-Busch's "ServSafe" program has trained over 115,000 bartenders and store clerks to serve and sell alcohol safely, avoid abuse situations, prevent drunk driving, and spot fake IDs.

To amplify these and other programs, and to get their messages across to millions of Americans, Anheuser-Busch advertises through print, billboards, and national television and radio. Its television commercials feature celebrities and run during some of America's most-watched programs. During a recent Super Bowl, the brewer aired a spot with the tag line "Know When to Say When" featuring world welterweight boxing champion and Olympic gold medalist Oscar de la Hoya. Through advertising, the company has brought its message about the potential dangers of alcohol abuse to 75 percent of America's beer drinkers.

Anheuser-Busch isn't alone among alcoholic beverage companies in its efforts. *Beer Marketer's Insights,* an industry trade publication, reports that brewers' promotional activities have changed. Most brewers no longer hire student representatives to promote beer brands on campuses, a common practice until recently. In addition, alcohol marketers are increasingly aiming ads that say "we don't want your business" at underage consumers. The Century Council, an industry-supported group, engages in such community-oriented alcohol awareness projects as the "Sober Graduation and Prom," which reaches about 8,000 U.S. high schools. The Distilled Spirits Council has revised its code of good marketing and advertising practices to discourage alcohol ads in college newspapers and to bar contests that invite drinking.

Anheuser-Busch believes that its work, along with that of other companies and organizations, has led to some encouraging changes. The U.S. Department of Transportation recently reported that over the last fifteen years, deaths due to teenage drunk driving fell 64 percent, and studies at the University of Michigan indicate that the level of drinking by high school seniors is at its lowest in twenty years.[19]

Questions for Discussion

1. Why is Anheuser-Busch engaging in promotional efforts to reduce underage drinking and alcohol abuse?

2. What are the major components of the promotion mix being used by Anheuser-Busch in its campaign to reduce alcohol abuse?

3. Evaluate the effectiveness of Anheuser-Busch and other organizations in tackling alcohol-related issues.

Advertising and Public Relations

OBJECTIVES

- To become aware of the nature and types of advertising
- To explore the major steps involved in developing an advertising campaign
- To find out who is responsible for developing advertising campaigns
- To gain an understanding of public relations
- To analyze how public relations is used and evaluated

The Horn Group: "The Magic of PR"

Founded in 1991, the Horn Group is a $6 million public relations firm representing software makers and service providers from two locations—its headquarters in San Francisco and its offices in Boston. The firm is divided into four technology segments: Customer Relationship Management, Commerce Chain Management, Enterprise Information Solution, and Business and Online Services. Its clients currently include such companies as BroadQuest, Commerce One, Send.com, Patricia Seybold Group, U.S. Interactive, Norwest Venture Capital, and Actuate Software. The firm's mission is to "elevate its clients to market leadership positions through exceptional public relations counsel and results."

To accomplish its mission, the Horn Group offers strategic counsel, presentation development and training, product and company launch support, online media relations, analyst relations, corporate communications, investor relations, and measurement of results. Horn's clients receive strategic advice on a variety of elements, ranging from product planning and positioning to crisis management. Every week, account teams meet to brainstorm about and discuss clients' public relations opportunities. They also meet face-to-face or by phone with clients to provide advice, to report on current programs, and to suggest changes. When public relations crises like product flaws or controversial issues arise, the Horn Group helps clients manage them to minimize losses and maintain credibility.

Referring to press relations as "the magic of PR," the firm maintains extensive contacts with trade magazines, such as *Computerworld* and *PC Week;* national business publications, such as *Forbes, Fortune, Business Week* and *The Wall Street Journal;* and broadcast media, including "Good Morning America" and "CNN News." Getting the news out fast regarding awards, product enhancements, mergers, earnings, and personnel is paramount for Horn Group PR teams. A typical press kit includes an overhead slide presentation, a printed press release, a fact sheet, information on corporate and product backgrounds, sample customer testimonials and references, photos of executives and products, brochures, and article reprints. Each month, Horn provides clients with press clippings and reports covering publicity highlights, quantative and qualitative results, and reprint recommendations.

In 1998, the Horn Group reported its seventh consecutive year of sales growth and is currently an *Inc.* 500 company. The company's CEO attributes her company's success to three factors. First, it is highly selective about accepting clients. For example, in one year the PR firm selected only twelve clients from among four hundred sales leads resulting from referrals it received. Second, although many PR firms shy away from offering clients measurable results, Horn prides itself in its ability to do so and motivates employees to perform to the highest standards of service and quality. Finally, the company, which won the award for Best Employer in 1999 from *Working Woman* magazine, credits much of its success to its fifty enthusiastic and talented employees. Assert's Horn's CEO, "When our clients go to sleep at night, the one thing they don't have to worry about is public relations, because we're taking care of that."[1]

THE HORN GROUP
San Francisco   Boston

Organizations like BroadQuest, Norwest Venture Capital, and Actuate Software sometimes use public relations, along with other promotional efforts, such as advertising, to change the corporate image, launch new products, or promote current brands. This chapter explores many dimensions of advertising and public relations. Initially, we focus on the nature and types of advertising. Next, we examine the major steps in developing an advertising campaign and describe who is responsible for developing such campaigns. We then discuss the nature of public relations and how public relations is used. We examine various public relations tools and ways to evaluate the effectiveness of public relations. Finally, we focus on how companies deal with unfavorable public relations.

The Nature and Types of Advertising

advertising Paid nonpersonal communication about an organization and its products transmitted to a target audience through mass media

Advertising permeates our daily lives. At times, we may view it positively; at other times, we tune it out or avoid it by taping television programs and then zipping over commercials with the VCR fast-forward button. Some advertising informs, persuades, or entertains us; some bores and even offends us.

As mentioned in Chapter 17, **advertising** is a paid form of nonpersonal communication transmitted through mass media, such as television, radio, the Internet, newspapers, magazines, direct mail, outdoor displays, and signs on mass transit vehicles. Organizations use advertising to reach a variety of audiences, ranging from small, specific groups, such as stamp collectors in Idaho, to extremely large groups, such as all athletic shoe purchasers in the United States.

When people are asked to name major advertisers, most immediately mention business organizations. However, many types of organizations—including governments, churches, universities, and charitable organizations—take advantage of advertising. In 1997, the U.S. government was the twenty-seventh largest advertiser in the country, spending $622 million on advertising.[2] Even though we analyze advertising in the context of business organizations here, much of what we say applies to all types of organizations.

Advertising is used to promote goods, services, ideas, images, issues, people, and anything that advertisers want to publicize or foster. Depending on what is being promoted, advertising can be classified as institutional or product advertising. **Institutional advertising** promotes organizational images, ideas, and political issues. It can be used to create or maintain an organizational image. For example, Pioneer Electronics, through a $100 million global image campaign that initially featured Pioneer's new red logo and new packaging, is trying to position itself as an aggressive leader in developing key consumer electronics products and technologies.[3] Institutional advertisements may deal with broad image issues, such as organizational strength or the friendliness of employees. They may also be aimed at creating a more favorable view of the organization in the eyes of noncustomer groups, such as shareholders, consumer advocacy groups, potential stockholders, or the general public. When a company promotes its position on a public issue—for instance, a tax increase, abortion, welfare, or international trade coalitions—institutional advertising is referred to as **advocacy advertising.** Institutional advertising may be used to promote socially approved behavior like recycling and moderation in consuming alcoholic beverages. This type of advertising not only has societal benefits, but also helps build an organization's image.

Product advertising promotes the uses, features, and benefits of products. There are two types of product advertising: pioneer and competitive. **Pioneer advertising** focuses on stimulating demand for a product category (rather than a specific brand) by informing potential customers about the product's features, uses, and benefits. This type of advertising is employed when the product is in the introductory stage of the product life cycle.

The second type of product advertising, **competitive advertising,** attempts to stimulate demand for a specific brand by promoting a brand's features, uses, and

institutional advertising Promotes organizational images, ideas, and political issues

advocacy advertising Promotes a company's position on a public issue

product advertising Promotes products' uses, features, and benefits

pioneer advertising Tries to stimulate demand for a product category rather than a specific brand by informing potential buyers about the product

competitive advertising Points out a brand's special features, uses, and advantages relative to competing brands

Figure 18.1
Comparative Advertising
This Toaster Strudel ad is an example of a comparative advertisement, which sites a competing brand and makes comparisons based on one or more product characteristics.

comparative advertising
Compares two or more brands on the basis of one or more product characteristics

reminder advertising
Reminds consumers about an established brand's uses, characteristics, and benefits

reinforcement advertising Assures users they chose the right brand and tells them how to get the most satisfaction from it

advantages sometimes through indirect or direct comparisons with competing brands. To make direct product comparisons, marketers use a form of competitive advertising called **comparative advertising,** in which two or more brands are compared on the basis of one or more product characteristics. Often, the brands promoted through comparative advertisements have low market shares and are compared with competitors that have the highest market shares in a product category. The Toaster Strudel ad in Figure 18.1 is a comparative advertisement. Product categories in which comparative advertising is common include soft drinks, toothpaste, pain relievers, foods, tires, automobiles, and detergents. Under the provisions of the 1988 Trademark Law Revision Act, marketers using comparative advertisements must not misrepresent the qualities or characteristics of competing products. Other forms of competitive advertising include reminder and reinforcement advertising. **Reminder advertising** tells customers an established brand is still around and that it has certain characteristics, uses, and advantages, as shown in the Sara Lee and Kitchen Aid ads in Figure 18.2. **Reinforcement advertising** assures current users they have made the right brand choice and tells them how to get the most satisfaction from that brand.

Developing an Advertising Campaign

advertising campaign
The creation and execution of a series of advertisements to communicate with a particular target audience

An **advertising campaign** involves designing a series of advertisements and placing them in various advertising media to reach a particular target market. As Figure 18.3 indicates, the major steps in creating an advertising campaign are (1) identifying and analyzing the target audience, (2) defining the advertising objectives, (3) creating the advertising platform, (4) determining the advertising appropriation, (5) developing the media plan, (6) creating the advertising message, (7) executing the campaign, and (8) evaluating advertising effectiveness. The number of steps and the exact order in which they are carried out may vary according to an organization's resources, the nature of its product, and the type of target audience to be reached. These general guidelines for developing an advertising campaign are appropriate for all types of organizations.

Figure 18.2
Reminder Advertising
These advertisements remind customers about established brands and their characteristics.

Identifying and Analyzing the Target Audience

target audience The group of people at which advertisements are aimed

1 Identify and analyze target audience

2 Define advertising objectives

3 Create advertising platform

4 Determine advertising appropriation

5 Develop media plan

6 Create advertising message

7 Execute campaign

8 Evaluate advertising effectiveness

The **target audience** is the group of people at which advertisements are aimed. Advertisements for Barbie cereal are targeted toward young girls who play with Barbie dolls, whereas those for Special K cereal are directed at health-conscious adults. Identifying and analyzing the target audience are critical processes; the information yielded helps determine other steps in developing the campaign. The target audience may include everyone in a firm's target market. Marketers may, however, direct a campaign at only a portion of the target market. For example, while Fossil's watches are aimed at people aged 14 to 44, a recent advertising campaign for the product was aimed at young females, with ads appearing in *Jane* and *Seventeen*.[4]

Advertisers research and analyze advertising targets to establish an information base for a campaign. Information commonly needed includes location and geographic distribution of the target group; the distribution of demographic factors, such as age, income, race, sex, and education; lifestyle information; and consumer attitudes regarding purchase and use of both the advertiser's products and competing products. The exact kinds of information an organization finds useful depend on the type of product being advertised, the characteristics of the target audience, and the type and amount of competition. Generally, the more an advertiser knows about the target audience, the more likely the firm is to

Figure 18.3
General Steps for Developing and Implementing an Advertising Campaign

develop an effective advertising campaign. When the advertising target is not precisely identified and properly analyzed, the campaign may not succeed. Targeting vulnerable groups can be ethically questionable, as discussed in Marketing Citizenship.

Defining the Advertising Objectives

The advertiser's next step is determining what the firm hopes to accomplish with the campaign. Because advertising objectives guide campaign development, advertisers should define objectives carefully. Advertising objectives should be stated clearly, precisely, and in measurable terms. Precision and measurability allow advertisers to evaluate advertising success at the end of the campaign, assessing whether or not objectives have been met. To provide precision and measurability, advertising objectives

MARKETING CITIZENSHIP

Is It Fair to Advertise to Vulnerable Groups?

Targeting precise markets with certain products and promotions is not inherently unethical. When a pharmaceutical company advertises its newest blood pressure medication in a medical journal or a golf equipment manufacturer advertises in the latest issue of a golfing magazine, no one finds these actions unprincipled. However, what if relatively uneducated, poor consumers are the target market for a state lottery, or teenagers are the target of tobacco advertising? When marketers target vulnerable groups, such as young children, teens, the elderly, disabled, or disadvantaged racial and ethnic minorities, the ethics of their practices can become questionable.

Vulnerable can be interpreted to mean any group that can too easily be taken advantage of because its members lack experience or information and thus have little chance of making informed choices. According to a recent Roper study, 80 percent of adults believe that advertising exploits children by persuading them to buy things that are bad for them. New studies by the Center for Science in the Public Interest reveal that online alcohol ads target young people with the message that drinking is glamorous and essential to a fun and friend-filled life and that television commercials teach adolescents it is safe to drink relatively large amounts of beer. An investigation by the Center for Media Education found that twenty-four out of the thirty-five Internet sites promoting major liquor or beer brands are youth-oriented, using cartoon-style characters in interactive games (such as "Berserk in Banff" and "J.C. Roadhog's Adventure") that appeal to those under the age of 21. As a result of its study, the CMC has asked the Federal Trade Commission and the U.S. Congress to conduct an investigation. Recently

released tobacco industry documents reveal that since 1960, cigarette manufacturers have persistently and purposefully targeted potential smokers as young as 16.

Because of their lack of experience and insight, children and young people clearly fit the definition of vulnerable. But are certain adult markets also vulnerable? Some state lotteries heavily target people in poor neighborhoods with the message that buying a lottery ticket will free them from their financial burdens. Is it ethical to persuade people to gamble their grocery money on a lottery ticket? Liquor manufacturers target their promotion of malt liquor, a beverage with a much higher alcohol content than regular beer, at African-Americans. Health care maintenance organizations (HMOs) often fail to communicate the restrictions of managed care to the elderly.

Defenses of segmented promotion practices include the constitutional guarantee of free speech, the claim that there is nothing wrong in promoting legal products, and the insistence that people don't have to buy anything they don't want to. Spokespersons for the Distilled Spirits Council and the Beer Institute assert that it is unfortunate that material of interest to 23-year-old legal drinkers and late teenagers is so similar, but that they do not intentionally target underage drinkers. Finally, businesses ask whether it is ethical to contend that certain groups aren't intelligent enough to make their own rational decisions.

Critics of the practice of targeting vulnerable groups assert that just because something is legal doesn't necessarily mean it's ethical. They maintain that various types of promotional efforts associated with targeting certain groups can shape beliefs and that industries should therefore make every effort to refrain from actions that have the potential to do harm.

should contain benchmarks and indicate how far the advertiser wishes to move from these benchmarks. If the goal is to increase sales, the advertiser should state the current sales level (the benchmark) and the amount of sales increase that is sought through advertising. An advertising objective should also specify a time frame, so that advertisers know exactly how long they have to accomplish the objective. An advertiser with average monthly sales of $450,000 (the benchmark) might set the following objective: "Our primary advertising objective is to increase average monthly sales from $450,000 to $540,000 within twelve months."

If an advertiser defines objectives on the basis of sales, the objectives focus on raising absolute dollar sales, increasing sales by a certain percentage, or increasing the firm's market share. Even though an advertiser's long-run goal is to increase sales, not all campaigns are designed to produce immediate sales. Some campaigns are designed to increase product or brand awareness, make consumers' attitudes more favorable, or increase consumers' knowledge of product features. If the goal is to increase product awareness, the objectives are stated in terms of communication. A specific communication objective might be to increase product feature awareness from 0 to 40 percent in the target audience by the end of six months.

Creating the Advertising Platform

advertising platform
Basic issues or selling points to be included in the advertising campaign

Before launching a political campaign, party leaders develop a political platform, stating major issues that are the basis of the campaign. Like a political platform, an **advertising platform** consists of the basic issues or selling points that an advertiser wishes to include in the advertising campaign. A single advertisement in an advertising campaign may contain one or several issues from the platform. Although the platform sets forth the basic issues, it does not indicate how to present them.

An advertising platform should consist of issues important to customers. One of the best ways to determine those issues is to survey customers about what they consider most important in the selection and use of the product involved. Selling features must not only be important to customers; they should also be strongly competitive features of the advertised brand.

Although research is the most effective method for determining what issues to include in an advertising platform, it is expensive. Therefore, an advertising platform is most commonly based on opinions of personnel within the firm and of individuals in the advertising agency, if an agency is used. This trial-and-error approach generally leads to some successes and some failures.

Because the advertising platform is a base on which to build the advertising message, marketers should analyze this stage carefully. A campaign can be perfect in terms of the selection and analysis of its target audience, statement of its objectives, its media strategy, and the form of its message. But the campaign will still fail if the advertisements communicate information that consumers do not deem important when selecting and using the product.

Determining the Advertising Appropriation

advertising appropriation   Advertising budget for a specified period

The **advertising appropriation** is the total amount of money a marketer allocates for advertising for a specific time period. It is hard to decide how much to spend on advertising for a specific period because the potential effects of advertising are so difficult to measure precisely.

Many factors affect a firm's decision about how much to appropriate for advertising. Geographic size of the market and the distribution of buyers within the market have a great bearing on this decision. As Table 18.1 shows, both the type of product advertised and a firm's sales volume relative to competitors' sales volumes also play a part in determining what proportion of a firm's revenue is spent on advertising. Advertising appropriations for business products are usually quite small relative to product sales, whereas consumer convenience items, such as soft drinks, soaps, and cosmetics, generally have large appropriations.

Table 18.1   Twenty Leading National Advertisers

	Advertising Expenditures ($ millions)	Sales ($ millions)	Advertising Expenditures as Percentage of Sales
1 General Motors	3,087.4	127,128.0	2.4
2 Procter & Gamble	2,743.2	18,460.0	14.9
3 Philip Morris Companies	2,137.8	33,208.0	6.4
4 Chrysler	1,532.4	52,006.0	2.9
5 Ford	1,281.8	120,474.0	1.1
6 Sears, Roebuck	1,262.0	37,808.0	3.3
7 Walt Disney	1,249.7	19,255.0	6.5
8 PepsiCo	1,244.7	13,878.0	9.0
9 Diageo	1,206.6	9,236.5	13.1
10 McDonald's	1,041.7	4,602.7	22.6
11 Time Warner	1,013.2	19,255.0	5.3
12 IBM	924.9	32,663.0	2.8
13 Johnson & Johnson	920.2	11,757.0	7.8
14 Unilever	908.9	9,321.1	9.8
15 J.C. Penney	906.2	37,808.0	2.4
16 Bristol-Meyers Squibb	885.2	11,014.0	8.0
17 Toyota	851.9	31,551.9*	2.7*
18 Tricon Global Restaurants	851.2	13,500.0	6.3
19 AT&T	781.1	51,319.0	1.5
20 Sony	777.5	15,923.5	4.9

* Estimate

Source: Reprinted with permission from the September 28, 1998, issue of *Advertising Age*. Copyright, Crain Communications Inc., 1998.

objective-and-task approach Budgeting for an advertising campaign by first determining its objectives and then the cost of all the tasks needed to attain them

Of the many techniques used to determine the advertising appropriation, one of the most logical is the **objective-and-task approach.** Using this approach, marketers determine the objectives that a campaign is to achieve and then attempt to list the tasks required to accomplish them. The costs of the tasks are calculated and added to arrive at the total appropriation. This approach has one main problem; marketers sometimes have trouble accurately estimating the level of effort needed to attain certain objectives. A coffee marketer, for example, might find it extremely difficult to determine how much of an increase in national television advertising is needed to raise a brand's market share from 8 to 10 percent.

percent-of-sales approach Budgeting for an advertising campaign by multiplying the firm's past and expected sales by a standard percentage

In the more widely used **percent-of-sales approach,** marketers simply multiply a firm's past sales, plus a factor for planned sales growth or decline, by a standard percentage based on both what the firm traditionally spends on advertising and the industry average. This approach, too, has a major flaw; it is based on the incorrect assumption that sales create advertising rather than the reverse. A marketer using this approach during declining sales will reduce the amount spent on advertising, but such a reduction may further diminish sales. Though illogical, this technique has been favored because it is easy to use.

competition-matching approach Determining an advertising budget by trying to match competitors' ad outlays

Another way to determine advertising appropriation is the **competition-matching approach.** Marketers following this approach try to match their major competitors' appropriations in absolute dollars or to allocate the same percentage of sales for advertising as their competitors do. Although a marketer should be aware of what competitors spend on advertising, this technique should not be used alone because a firm's competitors probably have different advertising objectives and different resources

Table 18.2	Total Advertising Expenditures (in millions of dollars)			
	1980	**1985**	**1990**	**1997**
Newspapers	$14,794	$25,170	$ 32,281	$41,670
Magazines	3,279	5,341	6,803	9,821
Television	11,366	20,738	28,405	45,519
Radio	3,777	6,490	8,726	13,491
Outdoor	600	945	1,084	1,455
Direct mail	7,596	15,500	23,370	36,890
Business press	1,674	2,375	2,875	4,109
Internet	NA	NA	NA	545
Miscellaneous	10,767	18,159	25,096	34,029
Total	$53,853	$94,718	$128,640	$187,529

Source: DDB Needham, *Worldwide Media Trends,* 1987 Edition; Robert J. Coen, "Coen: Little Ad Growth," *Advertising Age,* May 6, 1991, pp. 1, 16; and Robert J. Coen, "Advertising Spending" McCann Erickson, www.mccann.com/res/detail.shtml.

available for advertising. Many companies and advertising agencies review competitive spending on a quarterly basis, comparing competitors' dollar expenditures on print, radio, and television with their own spending levels. Competitive tracking of this nature occurs at both the national and regional levels.

arbitrary approach
Budgeting for an advertising campaign as specified by a high-level executive in the firm

At times, marketers use the **arbitrary approach,** which usually means that a high-level executive in the firm states how much to spend on advertising for a certain period. The arbitrary approach often leads to underspending or overspending. Although hardly a scientific budgeting technique, it is expedient.

Deciding how large the advertising appropriation should be is critical. If the appropriation is set too low, the campaign cannot achieve its full potential. When too much money is appropriated, overspending results and financial resources are wasted.

Developing the Media Plan

media plan   Specifies media vehicles and schedule for running the advertisements

As Table 18.2 shows, advertisers spend tremendous amounts of money on advertising media. These amounts have grown rapidly during the past two decades. To derive maximum results from media expenditures, marketers must develop effective media plans. A **media plan** sets forth the exact media vehicles to be used (specific magazines, television stations, newspapers, and so forth) and the dates and times the advertisements will appear. The plan determines how many people in the target audience will be exposed to the message. It also determines, to some degree, the effects of the message on those individuals. Media planning is a complex task requiring thorough analysis of the target audience. Sophisticated computer models have been developed in an attempt to maximize the effectiveness of media plans.

To formulate a media plan, the planners select the media for a campaign and prepare a time schedule for each medium. The media planner's primary goal is to reach the largest number of persons in the advertising target that the budget will allow. A secondary goal is to achieve the appropriate message "reach" and "frequency" for the target audience while staying within budget. *Reach* refers to the percentage of consumers in the target audience actually exposed to a particular advertisement in a stated

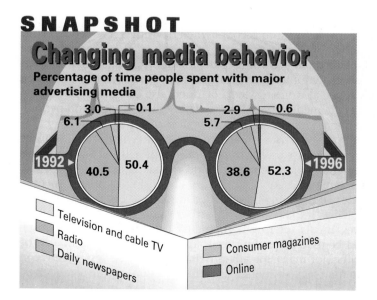

SNAPSHOT

Changing media behavior

Percentage of time people spent with major advertising media

1992 ▶   3.0   0.1   6.1   40.5   50.4

2.9   0.6   5.7   38.6   52.3   ◀1996

Television and cable TV
Radio
Daily newspapers
Consumer magazines
Online

Figure 18.4
Promotion by Media Organizations
Organizations such as the U.S. Postal Service and STAR TV promote their media capabilities to media planners.

period. *Frequency* is the number of times these targeted consumers are exposed to the advertisement.

Media planners begin with broad decisions but eventually make very specific ones. They first decide which kinds of media to use: radio, television, the Internet, newspapers, magazines, direct mail, outdoor displays, or signs on mass transit vehicles. As shown in Figure 18.4, media organizations such as the U.S. Postal Service (direct mail) and STAR TV (TV that can reach 300 million Asians) promote their capabilities to media planners. They assess different formats and approaches to determine which are the most effective. Some media plans are quite focused and use just one medium. For example, when Kodak introduced its DC-210 Plus digital camera, it ran a $5 million ad campaign using only magazines, including *Time, Newsweek, Sports Illustrated, Entertainment Weekly, Wired,* and inflight publications.[5] The media plans of manufacturers of consumer packaged goods can be quite complex and dynamic. Currently, some of these companies, like Kraft and Procter & Gamble, are changing their media plans to include considerably larger expenditures on direct mail.[6]

Media planners take many factors into account when devising a media plan. They analyze location and demographic characteristics of people in the target audience because people's taste in media differ according to demographic groups and locations. There are radio stations especially for teenagers, magazines for men aged 18 to 34, and television cable channels aimed at women. Media planners also consider the sizes and types of audiences that specific media reach. Several data services collect and periodically provide information about circulations and audiences of various media.

The content of the message sometimes affects media choice. Print media can be used more effectively than broadcast media to present complex issues or numerous details in single advertisements. For example, to build market share by more effectively reaching postcollege females, Nike launched an advertising campaign focused on being a woman and not just on being an athlete. Due to the complexity of these issues, Nike used just magazines initially.[7] If an advertiser wants to promote beautiful colors, patterns, or textures, media offering high-quality color reproduction—magazines or television—should be used instead of newspapers. For example, food can be effectively promoted in full-color magazine advertisements but is far less effective in black and white. Compare the black-and-white and color versions of the same advertisement in Figure 18.5.

Figure 18.5
Black-and-White versus Color Advertisements
This example highlights the importance of using color in advertisements for various types of products such as foods.

cost comparison indicator   A means of comparing the cost of vehicles in a specific medium in relation to the number of people reached

The cost of media is an important but troublesome consideration. Planners try to obtain the best coverage possible for each dollar spent. Yet there is no accurate way of comparing the cost and impact of a television commercial with the cost and impact of a newspaper advertisement. A **cost comparison indicator** lets an advertiser compare the costs of several vehicles within a specific medium (such as two magazines) in relation to the number of persons reached by each vehicle. The "cost per thousand" (CPM) is the cost comparison indicator for magazines; it shows the cost of exposing a thousand persons to a one-page advertisement.

Table 18.2 shows that the extent to which each medium is used varies quite a bit and that the pattern of use has changed over the years. For example, the proportion of total media dollars spent on television has risen since 1980 and now surpasses that spent on newspapers. The proportion of total advertising dollars spent on direct mail has also risen considerably since 1980. Media are selected by weighing the various characteristics, advantages, and disadvantages of each (see Table 18.3). Tech*know on page 468 discusses advertising on the Internet, one of the fastest-growing media available to advertisers.

Creating the Advertising Message

The basic content and form of an advertising message are a function of several factors. A product's features, uses, and benefits affect the content of the message. Characteristics of the people in the target audience—their gender, age, education, race, income, occupation, lifestyle, and other attributes—influence both content and form. When Procter & Gamble promotes its Crest toothpaste to children, the company emphasizes daily brushing and cavity control. When Crest is marketed to adults, tartar and plaque are discussed. To communicate effectively, advertisers use words, symbols, and illustrations that are meaningful, familiar, and attractive to people in the target audience.

An advertising campaign's objectives and platform also affect the content and form of its messages. If a firm's advertising objectives involve large sales increases, the message may include hard-hitting, high-impact language and symbols. When campaign objectives aim at increasing brand awareness, the message may use much repetition of the brand name and words and illustrations associated with it. Thus, the advertising platform is the foundation on which campaign messages are built.

Table 18.3	Characteristics, Advantages, and Disadvantages of Major Advertising Media		
Medium	**Types**	**Unit of Sale**	**Factors Affecting Rates**
Newspaper	Morning Evening Sunday Sunday supplement Weekly Special	Agate lines Column inches Counted words Printed lines	Volume and frequency discounts Number of colors Position charges for preferred and guaranteed positions Circulation level Ad size
Magazine	Consumer Farm Business	Pages Partial pages Column inches	Circulation level Cost of publishing Type of audience Volume discounts Frequency discounts Size of advertisement Position of advertisement (covers) Number of colors Regional issues
Direct mail	Letters Catalogs Price lists Calendars Brochures Coupons Circulars Newsletters Postcards Booklets Broadsides Samplers	Not applicable	Cost of mailing lists Postage Production costs
Radio	AM FM	Programs: sole sponsor, co- sponsor, participative sponsor Spots: 5, 10, 20, 30, 60 seconds	Time of day Audience size Length of spot or program Volume and frequency discounts
Television	Network Local CATV	Programs: sole sponsor, co- sponsor, participative sponsor Spots: 5, 10, 15, 30, 60 seconds	Time of day Length of program Length of spot Volume and frequency discounts Audience size
Internet	Web sites Banners Buttons Sponsorships Interstitials Classified ads	Not applicable	Length of time Complexity Type of audience Keywords Continuity
Inside transit	Buses Subways	Full, half, and quarter showings sold on monthly basis	Number of riders Multiple-month discounts Production costs Position
Outside transit	Buses Taxicabs	Full, half, and quarter showings; space also rented on per-unit basis	Number of advertisements Position Size
Outdoor	Papered posters Painted displays Spectaculars	Papered posters; sold on monthly basis in multiples called "showings" Painted displays and spectaculars: sold on per-unit basis	Length of time purchased Land rental Cost of production Intensity of traffic Frequency and continuity discounts Location

Cost Comparison Indicator	Advantages	Disadvantages
Milline rate = cost per agate line × 1,000,000 divided by circulation	Reaches large audience; purchased to be read; national geographic flexibility; short lead time; frequent publication; favorable for cooperative advertising; merchandising services	Not selective for socioeconomic groups; short life; limited reproduction capabilities; large advertising volume limits exposure to any one advertisement
Cost per thousand (CPM) = cost per page × 1,000 divided by circulation	Demographic selectivity; good reproduction; long life; prestige; geographic selectivity when regional issues are available; read in leisurely manner	High absolute dollar cost; long lead time
Cost per contact	Little wasted circulation; highly selective; circulation controlled by advertiser; few distractions; personal; stimulates actions; use of novelty; relatively easy to measure performance; hidden from competitors	Expensive; no editorial matter to attract readers; considered junk mail by many; criticized as invasion of privacy
Cost per thousand (CPM) = cost per minute × 1,000 divided by audience size	Highly mobile; low-cost broadcast medium; message can be quickly changed; reaches large audience; geographic selectivity; demographic selectivity	Provides only audio message; has lost prestige; short life of message; listeners' attention limited because of other activities while listening
Cost per thousand (CPM) = cost per minute × 1,000 divided by audience size	Reaches large audience; low cost per exposure; uses audio and video; highly visible; high prestige; geographic and demographic selectivity	High dollar costs; highly perishable message; size of audience not guaranteed; amount of prime time limited
Cost per thousand or by the number of click-throughs	Immediate response; potential to reach a precisely targeted audience; ability to track customers and build databases; very interactive medium	Costs of precise targeting are expensive; inappropriate ad placement; effects difficult to measure; concerns about security and privacy
Cost per thousand riders	Low cost; "captive" audience; geographic selectivity	Does not reach many professional persons; does not secure quick results
Cost per thousand exposures	Low cost; geographic selectivity; reaches broad, diverse audience	Lacks demographic selectivity; does not have high impact on readers
No standard indicator	Allows for repetition; low cost; message can be placed close to point of sale; geographic selectivity; operable 24 hours a day	Message must be short and simple; no demographic selectivity; seldom attracts readers' full attention; criticized as traffic hazard and blight on countryside

Sources: Information from William F. Arens, *Contemporary Advertising* (Burr Ridge, Ill.: Irwin/McGraw-Hill, 1999); and George E. Belch and Michael Belch, *Advertising and Promotion* (Burr Ridge, Ill.: Irwin/McGraw-Hill, 1998).

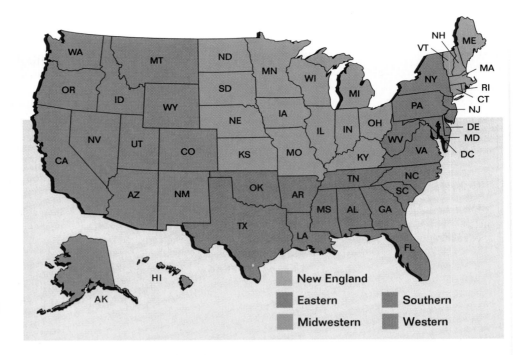

Figure 18.6
Geographic Divisions for
Sports Illustrated **Regional**
Issues
Source: *Sports Illustrated.*

New England

Eastern   Southern

Midwestern   Western

Choice of media obviously influences the content and form of the message. Effective outdoor displays and short broadcast spot announcements require concise, simple messages. Magazine and newspaper advertisements can include considerable detail and long explanations. Because several kinds of media offer geographic selectivity, a precise message can be tailored to a particular geographic section of the target audience. Some magazine publishers produce **regional issues,** in which advertisements and editorial content of copies appearing in one geographic area differ from those appearing in other areas. As Figure 18.6 shows, *Sports Illustrated* publishes five regional issues. A clothing manufacturer advertising in *Sports Illustrated* might decide

regional issues Versions of a magazine that differ across geographic regions

Tech•know

Netting Out Net Ads

Internet advertising is coming of age as companies learn to use the medium to communicate effectively with targeted customer segments and to build strong customer relationships. Company Web sites function as advertising vehicles, as do sponsored sites and advertising banners, buttons, links, and interstitials placed on other Web sites. Marketers of all sizes, from tiny start-ups to gigantic multinationals, are experimenting with advertising on this fast-growing medium. One highly visible example is Procter & Gamble, which recently budgeted $3 million for just three months of Internet advertising. As a P&G official explained, "Any medium that can help us deepen our bonds with [customers] is, by definition, of tremendous interest to us."

The $2 billion that marketers spend each year on Internet advertising is expected to skyrocket to $15 billion or more within a few years, paralleling the spectacular growth of Internet users. As the medium matures, the average cost-per-thousand for ad banners and buttons is dropping in many product categories.

Unfortunately, click-through rates are also going down. At present, fewer than 1 percent of the people exposed to an ad banner or button will click on it. This low response rate raises concerns about the effectiveness of Internet ads.

How can companies encourage higher click-through on banners, buttons, and links? The first step is to go where the target audience goes. This means putting computer-related ads on computer-related sites, food-related ads on food-related sites, and so on. Next, experts say offering a chance to win something valuable will increase click-through rates. Giving consumers something for nothing is also an effective way to boost click-through, as is inviting participation in an activity (search a site, play a game). Because the Web excels at one-to-one communication, it has great potential for marketing. Advertisers should take the time to understand what customers want and where they surf and then use that knowledge to design ads that will involve the audience in a meaningful way.

to use one message in the western region and another in the rest of the nation. A company may also choose to advertise in only one region. Such geographic selectivity lets a firm use the same message in different regions at different times.

All the basic components of a print advertisement are shown in Figure 18.7. Messages for most advertisements depend on the use of copy and artwork. Let us examine these two elements in more detail.

copy The verbal portion of advertisements

Copy Copy is the verbal portion of an advertisement and may include headlines, subheadlines, body copy, and signature. Not all advertising contains all of these copy elements. The headline is critical because often it is the only part of the copy that people read. It should attract readers' attention and create enough interest to make them want to read the body copy. The subheadline, if there is one, links the headline to the body copy and sometimes is used to explain the headline.

Body copy for most advertisements consists of an introductory statement or paragraph, several explanatory paragraphs, and a closing paragraph. Some copywriters have adopted guidelines for developing body copy systematically: (1) identify a specific desire or problem, (2) recommend the product as the best way to satisfy that desire or solve that problem, (3) state product advantages and benefits and indicate why the product is best for the buyer's particular situation, (4) substantiate advertising claims, and (5) ask the buyer for action. When substantiating claims, it is important to present the substantiation in a credible manner. The proof of claims should help strengthen the image of the product and company integrity.

The signature identifies the advertisement's sponsor. It may contain several elements, including the firm's trademark, logo, name, and address. The signature should be attractive, legible, distinctive, and easy to identify in a variety of sizes.

Figure 18.7
Components of a Print Advertisement
This advertisement includes all the major components of a print advertisement.

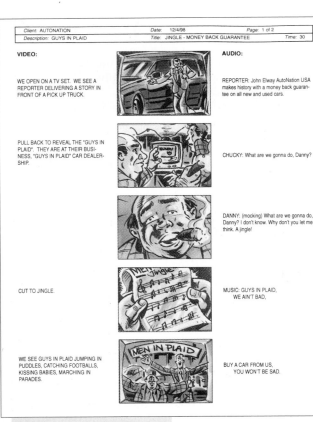
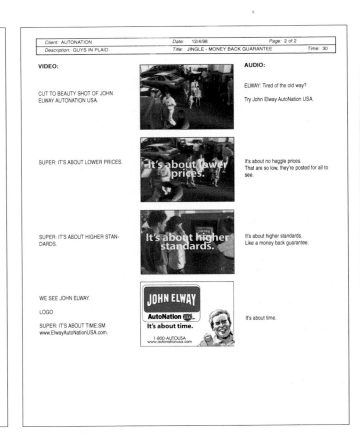

Figure 18.8
Planning a Television Message
This combined parallel script and storyboard was used to create a television advertisement for AutoNation USA.

storyboard A mockup combining copy and visual material to show the sequence of major scenes in a commercial

artwork An ad's illustration and layout

illustrations Photos, drawings, graphs, charts, and tables used to spark audience interest

layout The physical arrangement of an ad's illustration and copy

Because radio listeners often are not fully "tuned in" mentally, radio copy should be informal and conversational to attract listeners' attention, resulting in greater impact. Radio messages are highly perishable and should consist of short, familiar terms. The length should not require a rate of speech exceeding approximately two and one-half words per second.

In television copy, the audio material must not overpower the visual material and vice versa. However, a television message should make optimal use of its visual portion, which can be very effective for product demonstrations. Copy for a television commercial is sometimes initially written in parallel script form. Video is described in the left column and audio in the right. When the parallel script is approved, the copywriter and artist combine copy with visual material by using a **storyboard,** which depicts a series of miniature television screens showing the sequence of major scenes in the commercial. Beneath each screen is a description of the audio portion to be used with that video segment. Figure 18.8 shows a combined parallel script and storyboard. Technical personnel use the storyboard as a blueprint when producing the commercial.

Artwork **Artwork** consists of an advertisement's illustrations and layout. Although **illustrations** are often photographs, they can also be drawings, graphs, charts, and tables. Illustrations are used to attract attention, to encourage audiences to read or listen to the copy, to communicate an idea quickly, or to communicate ideas that are difficult to put into words.[8] They are especially important because consumers tend to recall the visual portion of advertisements better than verbal portions. Advertisers use a variety of illustration techniques. They may show the product alone, in a setting, in use, or the results of its use. Illustrations can also be in the form of comparisons, contrasts, diagrams, and testimonials.

The **layout** of an advertisement is the physical arrangement of the illustration and the copy—headline, subheadline, body copy, and signature. These elements can be arranged in many ways. The final layout is the result of several stages of layout preparation. As it moves through these stages, the layout promotes an exchange of ideas among people developing the advertising campaign and provides instructions for production personnel.

Executing the Campaign

Execution of an advertising campaign requires extensive planning and coordination because many tasks must be completed on time and many people and firms are involved. Production companies, research organizations, media firms, printers, photoengravers, and commercial artists are just a few of the people and firms contributing to a campaign.

Implementation requires detailed schedules to ensure that various phases of the work are done on time. Advertising management personnel must evaluate the quality of the work and take corrective action when necessary. In some instances, changes are made during the campaign so that it meets objectives more effectively. Sometimes, one firm develops a campaign, but another executes it.

Evaluating Advertising Effectiveness

There are a variety of ways to test the effectiveness of advertising. They include measuring achievement of advertising objectives; assessing effectiveness of copy, illustrations, or layouts; and evaluating certain media.

pretest   Evaluation of ads performed before a campaign begins

consumer jury   A panel of a product's actual or potential buyers who pretest ads

Advertising can be evaluated before, during, and after the campaign. An evaluation performed before the campaign begins is called a **pretest.** A pretest usually attempts to evaluate the effectiveness of one or more elements of the message. To pretest advertisements, marketers sometimes use a **consumer jury,** a panel of actual or potential buyers of the advertised product. Jurors judge one or several dimensions of two or more advertisements. Such tests are based on the belief that consumers are more likely than advertising experts to know what influences them.

To measure advertising effectiveness during a campaign, marketers usually rely on "inquiries." In a campaign's initial stages, an advertiser may use several advertisements simultaneously, each containing a coupon, form, or toll-free phone number through which potential customers can request information. The advertiser records the number of inquiries returned from each type of advertisement. If an advertiser receives 78,528 inquiries from advertisement A, 37,072 inquiries from advertisement B, and 47,932 inquiries from advertisement C, advertisement A is judged superior to advertisements B and C.

posttest   Evaluation of advertising effectiveness after the campaign

Evaluation of advertising effectiveness after the campaign is called a **posttest.** Advertising objectives often determine what kind of posttest is appropriate. If the objectives focus on communication—to increase awareness of product features or brands or to create more favorable customer attitudes—then the posttest should measure changes in these dimensions. Advertisers sometimes use consumer surveys or experiments to evaluate a campaign based on communication objectives. These methods are costly, however.

For campaign objectives stated in terms of sales, advertisers should determine the change in sales or market share attributable to the campaign. However, changes in sales or market share brought about by advertising cannot be measured precisely; many factors independent of advertisements affect a firm's sales and market share. Competitors' actions, government actions, and changes in economic conditions, consumer preferences, and weather are only a few factors that might enhance or diminish a company's sales or market share. By using data about past and current sales and advertising expenditures, advertisers can make gross estimates of the effects of a campaign on sales or market share.

recognition test
A posttest in which individuals are shown the actual ad and asked if they recognize it

Because it is difficult to determine the direct effects of advertising on sales, many advertisers evaluate print advertisements according to how well consumers can remember them. Posttest methods based on memory include recognition and recall tests. Such tests are usually performed by research organizations through surveys. If a **recognition test** is used, respondents are shown the actual advertisement and asked whether they recognize it. If they do, the interviewer asks additional questions to determine how much of the advertisement each respondent read. When recall is evaluated, the respondents are not shown the actual advertisement but instead are asked about what they have seen or heard recently.

unaided recall test
A posttest in which subjects identify ads they have recently seen but are given no recall clues

aided recall test
A posttest that asks subjects to identify recent ads and provides clues to jog their memories

Recall can be measured through either unaided or aided recall methods. In an **unaided recall test,** subjects identify advertisements that they have seen recently but are not shown any clues to help them remember. A similar procedure is used with an **aided recall test,** but subjects are shown a list of products, brands, company names, or trademarks to jog their memories. Several research organizations, such as Daniel Starch, provide research services that test recognition and recall of advertisements.

The major justification for using recognition and recall methods is that people are more likely to buy a product if they can remember an advertisement about it than if they cannot. However, recalling an advertisement does not necessarily lead to buying the product or brand advertised. Researchers also use a sophisticated technique called single-source data to help evaluate advertisements. With this technique, individuals' behaviors are tracked from television sets to checkout counters. Monitors are placed in preselected homes, and microcomputers record when the television set is on and which station is being viewed. At the supermarket checkout, the individual in the sample household presents an identification card. Checkers then record the purchases by scanner, and data are sent to the research facility. Some single-source data companies provide sample households with scanning equipment for use at home to record purchases after returning from shopping trips. Single source data provides information that links exposure to advertisements with purchase behavior.

Who Develops the Advertising Campaign?

An advertising campaign may be handled by an individual or a few persons within a firm, by a firm's own advertising department, or by an advertising agency.

In very small firms, one or two individuals are responsible for advertising (and for many other activities as well). Usually, these individuals depend heavily on personnel at local newspapers and broadcast stations for copywriting, artwork, and advice about scheduling media.

In certain large businesses—especially large retail organizations—advertising departments create and implement advertising campaigns. Depending on the size of the advertising program, an advertising department may consist of a few multiskilled persons or a sizable number of specialists, such as copywriters, artists, media buyers, and technical production coordinators. Advertising departments sometimes obtain the services of independent research organizations and hire freelance specialists when a particular project requires it.

When an organization uses an advertising agency, the firm and the agency usually develop the advertising campaign jointly. How much each participates in the campaign's total development depends on the working relationship between the firm and the agency. Ordinarily, a firm relies on the agency for copywriting, artwork, technical production, and formulation of the media plan. Consumer product companies rely the most on advertising agencies for the development and implementation of advertising campaigns; wholesalers and some manufacturers of business products rely on them less.[9]

Advertising agencies assist businesses in several ways. An agency, especially a large one, can supply the services of highly skilled specialists—not only copywriters, artists, and production coordinators, but also media experts, researchers, and legal advisers. Agency personnel often have broad advertising experience and are usually more objective than a firm's employees about the organization's products.

Because an agency traditionally receives most of its compensation from a 15 percent commission paid by the media from which it makes purchases, firms can obtain some agency services at low or moderate costs. If an agency contracts for $400,000 of television time for a firm, it receives a commission of $60,000 from the television station. Although the traditional compensation method for agencies is changing and now includes other factors, media commissions still offset some costs of using an agency.

Like advertising, public relations can be a vital element in a promotion mix. We turn to it next.

Public Relations

public relations
Communications efforts used to create and maintain favorable relations between an organization and its publics

Public relations is a broad set of communication efforts used to create and maintain favorable relationships between an organization and its publics. An organization communicates with various publics, both internal and external. Public relations efforts can be directed toward any and all of these. A firm's publics can include customers, suppliers, employees, stockholders, the media, educators, potential investors, government officials, and society in general.

Public relations can be used to promote people, places, ideas, activities, and even countries. It focuses on enhancing the image of the total organization. Assessing public attitudes and creating a favorable image are no less important than direct promotion of an organization's products. Because the public's attitudes toward a firm are likely to affect the sales of its products, it is very important for firms to maintain positive public perceptions. In addition, employee morale is strengthened if the firm is perceived positively by the public.[10] Although public relations can make people aware of a company's products, brands, or activities, it can also create specific company images, such as innovativeness or dependability. Ben & Jerry's has a reputation for being socially responsible not only because this organization engages in socially responsive behavior, but because this behavior is reported through news stories and other public relations efforts. By getting the media to report on a firm's accomplishments, public relations helps a company maintain positive public visibility. Some firms use public relations for a single purpose; others use it for several purposes.

Public Relations Tools

Figure 18.9
Annual Reports Used as Communication Tools
These annual reports, created by Cahan & Associates, generated considerable public relations value for Adaptec.

Companies use a variety of public relations tools to convey messages and to create images. Public relations professionals prepare written materials, such as brochures, newsletters, company magazines, news releases, and annual reports, that reach and influence their various publics. As shown in Figure 18.9, Adaptec, marketer of computer hardware and software solutions, uses highly creative annual reports (produced by Cahan & Associates) to communicate with stockholders, potential stockholders,

from
Houghton Mifflin Company 222 Berkeley Street, Boston, Massachusetts 02116-3764

For immediate release
November 12, 1998

Media Contact:
    Margaret Sherry
    Director, Media Relations
    (617) 351-5113
    margaret_sherry@hmco.com

Investor Contact:
    Susan E. Hardy
    Vice President, Investor Relations
    (617) 351-5114
    susan_hardy@hmco.com

HOUGHTON MIFFLIN INVESTS IN ONLINELEARNING.NET

BOSTON, MA, November 12, 1998 – Houghton Mifflin Company (NYSE:HTN) has reached an agreement with OnlineLearning.net, the leading distributor of continuing higher education online and the exclusive provider of UCLA Extension online courses, that will enable Houghton Mifflin to extend its presence in the emerging lifelong learning market.

Through a minority investment in OnlineLearning.net, Houghton Mifflin will market and sell distance learning courses to its existing customers, and develop new online courses using OnlineLearning.net's successful online education model expertise.

"We are delighted to partner with OnlineLearning.net, a leader in online continuing education committed to providing customers with first-class content and customer service." said Nader F. Darehshori, Chairman, President and Chief Executive Officer of Houghton Mifflin. "The distance learning market is experiencing solid growth, and this is the right time to forge this relationship. As a company in the business of ideas, we aim to meet the learning needs of students everywhere, at any age. This move will enable us to offer our customers world-class continuing education courses via a convenient and interactive medium."

OnlineLearning.net offers courses and certificated programs in Education, Business and Management, Computers and Information Systems, and Writing. "This venture is also very attractive to Houghton Mifflin because over 50 percent of the students enrolled are teachers. For over a century, Houghton Mifflin has been fostering relationships with teachers -- we know teachers well, we are sensitive to their needs, we are committed to

their professional development, and we think that OnlineLearning.net is an excellent vehicle through which to deliver continuing higher education. We are eager to serve education professionals wherever learning takes place," continued Mr. Darehshori.

"We are excited to be Houghton Mifflin's partner in online education. OnlineLearning.net is dedicated to providing today's educators with the tools needed to [meet] learning objectives—anytime, anywhere, and at any stage in life. [partne]rship between the nation's leading textbook and curriculum materials [and the l]eading provider of online continuing higher education greatly enhances [our mark]et to busy teachers and business professionals around the world," said [Onli]neLearning.net President and CEO.

[...]t has exclusive rights to more than 4,500 courses offered through [...] the nation's largest single-campus continuing higher education [...com]pany has developed and distributed more than 400 online courses to [student]s in all 50 states and in 30 foreign countries. Courses are [...inte]ractive, and are limited to 25 students per class. The company boasts [...] course completion percentage of nearly 90 percent. Enrollments are [...] in 1999.

[...]OnlineLearning.net is a privately held company whose investors and [...i]nclude: Sylvan Learning Systems, Inc., the leading provider of [...s] to families, schools, and industry; the Times Mirror Company, [...larg]est training companies in the world; and St. Paul Venture Capital, one [...pre]miere venture capital firms. The Company's Internet site can be found [...lear]ning.net

[...] is a leading publisher of textbooks, instructional technology, [...o]ther educational materials for the elementary and secondary school and [...] The Company also publishes an extensive line of reference works, [...fic]tion for adults and young readers, and multimedia entertainment [...com]pany's Internet site can be found at www.hmco.com.

-30-

Figure 18.10
Example of a News Release
Houghton Mifflin Company issued this information release to publicize its new relationship with OnlineLearning.net, which will result in distance learning courses for its existing customers.

and other publics about the company's products, image, and software solutions. Having received coverage in *USA Today* and numerous other newspapers around the country, as well as on CNBC, these annual reports have had considerable public relations value for Adaptec.

Public relations personnel also create corporate identity materials, such as logos, business cards, stationery, and signs, that make firms immediately recognizable. Speeches are another public relations tool. Because what a company executive says publicly at meetings or to the media can affect the organization's image, his or her speech must convey the desired message clearly.

Event sponsorship, in which a company pays for part or all of a special event, such as a benefit concert or a tennis tournament is another public relations tool. Examples are Home Depot's sponsorship of NASCAR and the U.S. Olympic team and Evian's sponsorship of the *Food and Wine* Classic, a convention for gourmet food lovers and chefs.[11] Sponsoring special events can be an effective means of increasing company or brand recognition with relatively minimal investment. A company doesn't have to be a big spender to participate in event sponsorship. For example, Moishe's Moving and Storage, a local company, helps sponsor the annual New York City Marathon by providing muscle power and several trucks at the race that attracts 30,000 runners and 2 million spectators.[12]

Event sponsorship can provide companies with considerable amounts of free media coverage. Organizations try to make sure that their product and the sponsored event target a consistent audience. Associating a 10K race with a sports drink like Gatorade is more consistent than associating it with a brand of baby food. Public relations personnel also organize unique events to "create news" about the company. These may include grand openings with celebrities, prizes, hot-air balloon rides, and other attractions that appeal to a firm's publics.

As noted in Chapter 17, publicity is a part of public relations. **Publicity** is communication in news story form about an organization, its products, or both, transmitted through a mass medium at no charge. Although public relations has a larger, more comprehensive communication function than publicity, publicity is a very important aspect of public relations. Publicity can be used to provide information about goods or services; to announce expansions, acquisitions, research, or new-product launches; or to enhance a company's image.

The most common publicity-based public relations tool is the **news release,** sometimes called a press release, which is usually a single page of typewritten copy containing fewer than 300 words and describing a company event or product. A news release gives the firm's or agency's name, address, phone number, and contact person, as shown in Figure 18.10. Automakers, as well as other manufacturers, sometimes use news releases when introducing new products. When Wal-Mart made a special effort to carry environmentally safe products and packaging, its public relations department sent out news releases to newspapers, magazines, television contacts, and suppliers, resulting in public relations in the form of magazine articles, newspaper acknowledgements, and television coverage. As Table 18.4 shows, news releases tackle a multitude of specific issues. A **feature article** is a manuscript of up to 3,000 words prepared for a specific publication. A **captioned photograph** is a photograph with a brief description explaining the picture's content. Captioned photographs are effective for illustrating new or improved products with highly visible features.

There are several other kinds of publicity-based public relations tools. A **press conference** is a meeting called to announce major news events. Media personnel are invited to a press conference and are usually supplied with written materials and photographs. Letters to the editor and editorials are sometimes prepared and sent to newspapers and magazines. Videos and audiotapes may be distributed to broadcast stations in the hope that they will be aired.

The use of publicity-based public relations tools has several advantages, including credibility, news value, significant word-of-mouth communications, and a perception of being endorsed by the media. The public may consider news coverage more truthful and credible than an advertisement because the media are not paid to provide the

publicity   A news story type of communication transmitted through a mass medium at no charge

news release   A short piece of copy publicizing an event or a product

feature article   A manuscript of up to 3,000 words prepared for a specific publication

captioned photograph   A photo with a brief description of its contents

press conference   A meeting used to announce major news events

Table 18.4 Possible Issues for Publicity Releases	
Changes in marketing personnel	Packaging changes
Support of a social cause	New products
Improved warranties	New slogan
Reports on industry conditions	Research developments
New uses for established products	Company's history and development
Product endorsements	Employment, production, and sales records
Quality awards	Award of contracts
Company name changes	Opening of new markets
Interviews with company officials	Improvements in financial position
Improved distribution policies	Opening of an exhibit
International business efforts	History of a brand
Athletic event sponsorship	Winners of company contests
Visits by celebrities	Logo changes
Reports on new discoveries	Speeches of top management
Innovative marketing activities	Merit awards
Economic forecasts	Anniversary of inventions

information. In addition, stories regarding a new-product introduction or a new environmentally responsible company policy, for example, are handled as news items and are likely to receive notice. Finally, the cost of publicity is low compared with the cost of advertising.[13]

Publicity-based public relations tools do have some limitations. Media personnel must judge company messages to be newsworthy if they are to be published or broadcast at all. Consequently, messages must be timely, interesting, accurate, and in the public interest. Many communications do not qualify. It may take a great deal of time and effort to convince media personnel of the news value of publicity releases. Although public relations personnel usually encourage the media to air publicity releases at certain times, they control neither the content nor the timing of the communication. Media personnel alter length and content of publicity releases to fit publishers' or broadcasters' requirements and may even delete the parts of messages that company personnel view as most important. Furthermore, media personnel use publicity releases in time slots or positions most convenient for them. Thus, messages sometimes appear in locations or at times that may not reach the firm's target audiences. Although these limitations can be frustrating, properly managed publicity-based public relations tools offer an organization substantial benefits.

Evaluating Public Relations Effectiveness

Because of the potential benefits of good public relations, it is essential that organizations evaluate the effectiveness of their public relations campaigns. Research can be conducted to determine how well a firm is communicating its messages or image to its publics. *Environmental monitoring* identifies changes in public opinion affecting an organization. A *public relations audit* is used to assess an organization's image among its publics or to evaluate the effect of a specific public relations program. A *communications audit* may include a content analysis of messages, a readability study, or a readership survey. If an organization wants to measure the extent to which publics view it as being socially responsible, it can conduct a *social audit.*

One approach to measuring the effectiveness of publicity-based public relations is to count the number of exposures in the media. To determine which releases are published in print media and how often, an organization can hire a clipping service, a firm that clips and sends news releases to client companies. To measure the effectiveness of television coverage, a firm can enclose a card with its publicity releases, requesting that the television station record its name and the dates when the news item is broadcast, although station personnel do not always comply. Though some television and radio tracking services exist, they are extremely costly.

Counting the number of media exposures does not reveal how many people have actually read or heard a company's message, or what they thought about the message afterward. However, measuring changes in product awareness, knowledge, and attitudes resulting from the publicity campaign does. To assess these changes, companies must measure these levels before and after public relations campaigns. Although precise measures are difficult to obtain, a firm's marketers should attempt to assess the impact of its public relations efforts on the organization's sales.

Dealing with Unfavorable Public Relations

We have thus far discussed public relations as a planned element of the promotion mix. However, companies may have to deal with unexpected and unfavorable public relations resulting from an unsafe product, an accident, controversial actions of employees, or some other negative event or situation. For example, an airline that experiences a plane crash is faced with a very tragic, and distressing situation. Charges of anti-competitive behavior against Microsoft have raised public concern and generated unfavorable public relations for that organization. The public's image of The Body Shop as a socially responsible company diminished considerably when it was reported that the company's actions were not as socially responsible as its promotion promised. Unfavorable coverage can have quick and dramatic effects. A single negative event that produces unfavorable public relations can wipe out a company's favorable image and destroy positive customer attitudes established through years of expensive advertising campaigns and other types of promotional efforts. Moreover, today's mass media, including online services and the Internet, disseminate information faster than ever before, and bad news generally receives considerable media attention.

To protect an organization's image, it is important to avoid unfavorable public relations or at least to lessen its effects. First and foremost, organizations should try to prevent negative incidents and events through safety programs, inspections, and effective quality control procedures. However, because negative events can happen to even the most cautious of firms, organizations should have predetermined plans in place to handle them when they do occur. Firms need to establish policies and procedures for news coverage of a crisis or controversy. These policies should aim at reducing the adverse impact. In most cases, organizations should expedite news coverage of negative events rather than trying to discourage or block them. If news coverage is squelched, rumors and misinformation may replace facts and be passed along anyway. An unfavorable event can easily balloon into ugly problems or public issues and become quite damaging. By being forthright with the press and public and taking prompt action, firms may be able to convince the public of their honest attempts to deal with the situation, and news personnel may be more willing to help explain complex issues to the public. Dealing effectively with a negative event allows an organization to lessen, if not eliminate, the impact on the organization's image.

Summary

Advertising is a paid form of nonpersonal communication transmitted to consumers through mass media, such as television, radio, the Internet, newspapers, magazines, direct mail, outdoor displays, and signs on mass transit vehicles. Both nonbusiness and business organizations use advertising. Institutional advertising promotes organizational images, ideas, and political issues. When a company promotes its position on a public issue like taxation, institutional advertising is referred to as advocacy advertising. Product advertising promotes uses, features, and benefits of products. The two types of product advertising are pioneer advertising, which focuses on stimulating demand for a product category rather than a specific brand, and competitive advertising, which attempts to stimulate demand for a specific brand by indicating a brand's features, uses, and advantages. To make direct product comparisons, marketers use comparative advertising, in which two or more brands are compared. Two other forms of competitive advertising are reminder advertising, which tells customers that an established brand is still around, and reinforcement advertising, which assures current users they have made the right brand choice.

Although marketers may vary in how they develop advertising campaigns, they should follow a general pattern. First, they must identify and analyze the target audience—the group of people at which advertisements are aimed. Second, they should establish what they want the campaign to accomplish by defining advertising objectives. Objectives should be clear, precise, and presented in terms that can be measured. The third step is creating the advertising platform, which contains basic issues to be presented in the campaign. Advertising platforms should consist of issues important to consumers. Fourth, advertisers must decide how much money to spend on the campaign; they arrive at this decision through the objective-and-task approach, percent-of-sales approach, competition-matching approach, or arbitrary approach.

Advertisers must then develop a media plan by selecting and scheduling media to use in the campaign. Some of the factors affecting the media plan are location and demographic characteristics of the target audience, content of the message, and cost of the various media. The basic content and form of the advertising message are affected by product features, uses, and benefits; characteristics of the people in the target audience; the campaign's objectives and platform; and the choice of media. Advertisers use copy and artwork to create the message. The execution of an advertising campaign requires extensive planning and coordination. Finally, advertisers must devise one or more methods for evaluating advertisement effectiveness. Evaluations performed before the campaign begins are called pretests; those after the campaign are called posttests. Two types of posttests are a recognition test, in which respondents are shown the actual advertisement and asked whether they recognize it, and a recall test. In aided recall tests, subjects are shown a list of products, brands, company names, or trademarks to jog their memories. In unaided tests, no clues are given.

Advertising campaigns can be developed by personnel within the firm or in conjunction with advertising agencies. When a campaign is created by the firm's personnel, it may be developed by an individual or a few people, or it may be the product of an advertising department within the firm. Use of an advertising agency may be advantageous to a firm because an agency provides highly skilled, objective specialists with broad experience in advertising at low to moderate costs to the firm.

Public relations is a broad set of communication efforts used to create and maintain favorable relationships between an organization and its publics. Public relations can be used to promote people, places, ideas, activities, and countries and to create and maintain a positive company image. Some firms use public relations for a single purpose; others use it for several purposes. Public relations tools include written materials, such as brochures, newsletters, and annual reports; corporate identity materials, such as business cards and signs; speeches; event sponsorships; and special events. Publicity is communication in news story form about an organization, its products, or both, transmitted through

a mass medium at no charge. Publicity-based public relations tools include news releases, feature articles, captioned photographs, and press conferences. Problems that organizations confront in using publicity-based public relations include reluctance of media personnel to print or air releases and lack of control over timing and content of messages.

To evaluate the effectiveness of their public relations programs, companies conduct research to determine how well their messages are reaching their publics. Environmental monitoring, public relations audits, and counting the number of media exposures are all means of evaluating public relations effectiveness. Organizations should avoid negative public relations by taking steps to prevent negative events that result in unfavorable publicity. To diminish the impact of unfavorable public relations, organizations should institute policies and procedures for dealing with news personnel and the public when negative events occur.

Important Terms

Advertising	Target audience	Cost comparison indicator	Recognition test
Institutional advertising	Advertising platform	Regional issues	Unaided recall test
Advocacy advertising	Advertising appropriation	Copy	Aided recall test
Product advertising	Objective-and-task	Storyboard	Public relations
Pioneer advertising	approach	Artwork	Publicity
Competitive advertising	Percent-of-sales approach	Illustrations	News release
Comparative advertising	Competition-matching	Layout	Feature article
Reminder advertising	approach	Pretest	Captioned photograph
Reinforcement advertising	Arbitrary approach	Consumer jury	Press conference
Advertising campaign	Media plan	Posttest	

Discussion and Review Questions

1. What is the difference between institutional and product advertising?

2. What is the difference between competitive advertising and comparative advertising?

3. What are the major steps in creating an advertising campaign?

4. What is a target audience? How does a marketer analyze the target audience after it has been identified?

5. Why is it necessary to define advertising objectives?

6. What is an advertising platform, and how is it used?

7. What factors affect the size of an advertising budget? What techniques are used to determine an advertising budget?

8. Describe the steps required in developing a media plan.

9. What is the function of copy in an advertising message?

10. Discuss several ways to posttest the effectiveness of advertising.

11. What role does an advertising agency play in developing an advertising campaign?

12. What is public relations? Whom can an organization reach through public relations?

13. How do organizations use public relations tools? Give several examples that you have observed recently.

14. Explain the problems and limitations associated with publicity-based public relations.

15. In what ways is the effectiveness of public relations evaluated?

16. What are some of the sources of negative public relations? How should an organization deal with negative public relations?

Application Questions

1. An organization must define its objectives carefully when developing an advertising campaign. Which of the following advertising objectives would be most useful for a company and why?

   a. The organization will spend $1 million in order to move from second in market share to market leader.

   b. The organization wants to increase sales from $1.2 million to $1.5 million this year, which will give them the lead in market share.

   c. The advertising objective is to gain as much market share as possible within the next twelve months.

   d. The advertising objective is to increase sales by 15 percent.

2. Copy is the verbal portion of advertising and is used to move readers through a persuasive sequence called AIDA: attention, interest, desire, and action. To achieve this, some copywriters have adopted guidelines for developing advertising copy. Select a print ad and identify how it (1) identifies a specific problem, (2) recommends the product as the best solution to the problem, (3) states the product's advantages and benefits, (4) substantiates the ad's claims, and (5) asks the reader to take action.

3. Advertisers use several types of publicity mechanisms. Look through several recent newspapers and magazines, and identify a news release, a feature article, and a captioned photograph used to publicize a product. Describe the type of product.

4. Negative public relations, if not dealt with properly, can be harmful to an organization's marketing efforts. Identify a company that recently has been the target of negative public relations. Describe the situation and discuss the company's response. What did marketers at this company do well? What would you recommend that they change about their response?

Internet Exercise & Resources

L'Eggs Web Site Wins Ad Agency Prestigious Clio Gold Award

For its development of the L'Eggs Web site, the Proxima Advertising Agency received the first Clio Gold to be awarded in the field of Internet advertising. See why by visiting this site at

www.leggs.com

1. What form of advertising discussed in the chapter best exemplifies the L'Eggs Web site?

2. What advertising objectives are L'Eggs attempting to achieve through its Web site?

3. Who is the primary target audience for the Internet advertisement? How might this differ from other product advertisements in other media?

E-Center Resources

Visit http://www.prideferrell.com to find several resources to help you succeed in mastering the material in this chapter, plus additional materials that will help you expand your marketing knowledge. The Web site includes

 Internet exercise updates plus additional exercises

 ACE self-tests

abc Chapter summary with hotlinked glossary

 Hotlinks to companies featured in this chapter

 Resource Center

 Career Center

 Marketing plan worksheets

VIDEO CASE 18.1

Winkler Advertising: Racing to Reach Consumers of High-Tech Products

In today's high-tech markets, where products come and go quickly, the compressed product life cycle allows advertisers only a short but precious window of opportunity in which to stimulate sales by reaching out to consumers. Winkler Advertising, based in San Francisco, is an advertising agency experienced at handling just this type of challenge. Winkler's planning, creative, and media specialists routinely pour on the speed when analyzing high-tech market opportunities and developing print, television, radio, and Web ads to encourage consumers in targeted segments to try and buy.

The agency's growing client list covers a spectrum of cutting-edge firms and products. Eidos Interactive makes Tomb Raider, Fighting Force, and other action-packed computer games; Sony Information Technologies of America markets sophisticated computer systems; Autodesk is known for its computer-aided design software; Ascend is a telecommunications company; and Hewlett-Packard has earned a reputation for quality printers. For all these high-tech marketers, advertising plays a critical role in strengthening brands over the long run while motivating consumers to buy right now.

Given the rapid pace of change in high-tech markets, Winkler's founder and CEO, Agnieszka Winkler, emphasizes that long-term brand-building must be a primary goal of advertising in this category. "In technology, the brand strategy you develop must be sustainable because the products change so rapidly," she says. "Companies that brand individual products at the expense of branding the company or a platform or a family are wasting their money."

Before Winkler's creative experts start working on a campaign—even before they develop the advertising platform—the agency's researchers conduct in-depth studies of brand attitudes and buying behavior. They go out and talk with customers and noncustomers, managers at the client company, wholesalers and retailers that handle the product, stockholders (if the company is publicly held), and securities analysts. For particularly complex markets or products, the agency may hold as many as a hundred or more individual interviews, probing attitudes and unearthing the rational and emotional drivers of consumer behavior.

Then the account planners analyze the results, examining customer perceptions of the product and its competition and identifying criteria used by consumers in the purchasing decision. They also sift through the data searching for early signs of attitude shifts that might affect the product or brand in the future. All this information helps the creative and media personnel decide on an appropriate advertising

platform to drive the individual messages and delivery methods for each client's campaign.

Knowing that speed is critical in high-tech markets, Winkler is a power user of sophisticated computer tools designed to expedite the advertising process, start to finish. Clients like Hewlett-Packard can click into the agency's online system to attend group discussions of strategy. They can also participate in online brainstorming sessions with agency staffers. After the ads have been designed, clients can go back to the online system to look at, comment on, and sign off on the finished ads. This approach shaves days off the entire advertising process and gets approved ads on the air or into print even faster.

Many high-tech clients, such as Hewlett-Packard, hire different agencies to create advertising for different parts of their product lines. Although this practice allows each agency to become thoroughly familiar with the market and the opportunities for a few assigned products, it complicates the integration of the company's marketing communications materials. Winkler, as one of twelve Hewlett-Packard agencies, solved this potential problem by putting together a special computer network to coordinate the work of all the agencies.

CEO Winkler also makes the point that building strong brands and long-lasting relationships with customers requires marketers to look beyond advertising to coordinate all their marketing communications and customer contacts. "You've got service and support, how your company responds when a customer calls with a complaint, how the customer gets upgrades," she explains. "You've also got your Web site, which connects your customer directly to you. If you don't do one of them right, the customer will know right away. You can't say one thing in your advertising and behave another way over the phone or the Internet. You've got to keep your brand promise in every aspect of your communications and your corporate behavior."

Questions for Discussion

1. In what ways can makers of high-tech products benefit from the use of an advertising agency like Winkler?
2. If Hewlett-Packard were introducing a new high-speed color printer, what kinds of objectives should it set for advertising created by Winkler?
3. In the course of developing an ad campaign for a new Eidos computer game, how might Winkler use a consumer jury?
4. In formulating a media plan for this Eidos campaign, why would the agency have to consider both reach and frequency?

CASE 18.2

Microsoft: Crafting Image through Public Relations

A monopoly and a bully, or a champion of free enterprise and high-tech innovation? Different people have different images of Microsoft, the largest and most successful software company in the world, and of Bill Gates, its founder and chairman. And image is important to Microsoft, which operates in a highly competitive, high-stakes industry. That's why the company has a team of 150 managers and outside experts dedicated to public relations. Their role is to shape and protect the image of Microsoft and its products, including the Windows operating system, the Internet Explorer Web browser, and a cornucopia of software programs for business and personal use.

Microsoft applies well-honed public relations skills to maintaining favorable relationships with its publics and to supporting new-product introductions. For example, in the weeks leading up to the launch of every major update of Windows, computer users are bombarded by media coverage in newspapers, magazines, television, and radio; many also receive newsletters and brochures in the mail or pick these up at local computer stores. These carefully timed, well-orchestrated public relations campaigns are designed to generate excitement in advance of the actual product launch. By the time the new product finally arrives on store shelves—accompanied by special launch-day events—the enormous anticipatory buzz has created pent-up demand that boosts early sales and generates considerable word-of-mouth communication.

Giving Microsoft a good-guy image is another key public relations objective. Targeting students, the company has stepped up giveaways to get its products into grade schools, high schools, and colleges throughout the United States and around the globe. For example, Microsoft is providing free software for Indiana University's 91,000 students and free software training for its instructors, a deal worth $6 million. In addition, the chairman's charitable foundation is donating millions of dollars worth of Microsoft software to U.S. public libraries. Such arrangements allow Microsoft to display its strong support for education publicly while simultaneously building brand equity. As the general manager of Microsoft's education consumer unit has observed, "Today's fifth-grader is tomorrow's business leader. The sooner we have them using our software, the more they carry that brand name forward."

Over time, Microsoft has developed a reputation for extremely aggressive competitive tactics. This combative behavior has long been under regulatory scrutiny, culminating in a recent lawsuit brought against the company by the Department of Justice and investigations by state attorneys general into violations of antitrust law, which Microsoft vigorously denies. Well before the Department of Justice trial began, Microsoft had its public relations experts thinking about how to

present the company's side most effectively and contain the damage to its image. In addition to increasing its use of lobbyists in Washington, D.C., the company explored ways of countering public perception of Microsoft and its chairman as tough and arrogant.

To begin with, top Microsoft executives traveled around the United States making personal appearances and meeting with reporters. Taking a "kinder, gentler" approach, they downplayed the company's competitive strengths and stressed the message that Microsoft favored technological innovation and wanted consumers to have more software choices. Brandishing the results of opinion polls, they also announced that U.S. consumers and computer users were giving Microsoft its highest ratings ever. "We have the support of the American people," said the chief operating officer.

As the richest man on the planet, Bill Gates is a natural magnet for media attention, and the company started using this celebrity to its advantage. In the past, Gates had courted publicity about company matters but insisted on keeping his private life out of the media spotlight. Now, however, the chairman agreed to talk more about his family life during interviews with Barbara Walters and with reporters for *Time* and other publications. He scheduled visits to schools and made other public appearances, where he talked about Microsoft products and mingled a bit with audiences. This higher visibility gave Microsoft a chance to show Gates's human side and allowed the chairman to air his forward-looking views on computer technology and other topics.

In addition, Microsoft conducted research to determine its standing with business decision makers and information technology professionals, two important publics that influence Microsoft purchases. Then, through informational ads in major newspapers, including the *Washington Post* and the *New York Times,* the company communicated its message that the antitrust case against Microsoft would only stifle innovation and dampen free choice in the marketplace. "At Microsoft, the freedom to innovate for our customers is more than a goal, it is a principle worth standing up for," stated the ads.

Even as these activities gained momentum, however, Microsoft came under fire after word leaked out about a proposed multimillion-dollar public relations plan targeting twelve states, including those where the company was under investigation. The proposal called for compiling statewide media lists, identifying potential supporters in the academic world, and having people write opinion pieces and letters for placement in local newspapers. A Microsoft spokesperson said the company would probably implement some but not all of the tactics. "I wouldn't be doing my job if I weren't looking for ways to make Microsoft more visible with the local press," he said. "We are particularly interested in telling our story in states where there have been questions about Microsoft."

As Microsoft continues to introduce new products and pursue its marketing goals, its executives remain well aware of the power of public relations. They are committed to using that power to polish the company's image among its publics—keeping the Microsoft brand one of the best known in the computer industry.

Questions for Discussion

1. What major public relations tools does Microsoft use?
2. Who are the publics that Microsoft wants to reach with its public relations efforts?
3. How should Microsoft evaluate the results of its public relations programs?
4. How do you think Microsoft should have used public relations to communicate its views during the antitrust trial? Explain your answer.

19

Personal Selling and Sales Promotion

OBJECTIVES

- To understand the major purposes of personal selling

- To learn the basic steps in the personal selling process

- To be able to identify the types of sales force personnel

- To learn about sales management decisions and activities

- To become aware of what sales promotion activities are and how they can be used

- To become familiar with specific consumer and trade sales promotion methods

McDonald's—Turning Success Into an Annual Event

In 1997, McDonald's conducted a promotion that succeeded beyond the fast-food franchiser's wildest expectations. With the purchase of a "Happy Meal," customers received one of ten "Teenie Beanie Babies," miniature cousins of the extremely popular "Beanie Babies" made by Ty Inc. At McDonald's all over the United States, lines for the drive-through windows wound around buildings and out into the street, and the waiting time in lines inside many restaurants was an hour long. Customers sometimes returned several times a day, not for food, but for a chance to get another Teenie Beanie Baby. At some restaurants, police had to be called in to control crowds. Having anticipated that 100 million toys would last for the month-long promotion, McDonald's gave them all away in ten days. Less than a year later, McDonald's launched a second Teenie Beanie Baby promotion that was a hit almost before it even started.

To avoid the pandemonium and customer frustration accompanying its first promotion, McDonald's doubled its order of Teenie Beanies for the second one. The new menagerie included "Inch the Worm," "Happy the Hippo," "Scoop the Pelican," "Twigs the Giraffe," and eight other brand new creatures created by Ty specifically for the promotion. This time around, customers could get free Teenie Beanies with the purchase of Happy Meals, but they could also buy them for $1.59 with the purchase of other food or drink items. During the promotion, three different toys were offered at one time, and customers could identify which one they wanted while supplies lasted. To no one's surprise, McDonald's second promotion was as successful as the first. Despite a stock of 240 million of the miniature critters, many of the company's 2,772 franchises ran out of them well before the event was scheduled to end. One franchise reported going through more than 1,500 toys a day.

During typical promotions, McDonald's sells about 40 million Happy Meals. When its promotion of Disney's *101 Dalmatians* sold 86 million Happy Meals, company executives were astonished. The Teenie Beanie Baby promotion, however, generated sales considerably higher than that. Hoping to turn this success into an annual event, McDonald's recently scheduled a third promotion linked to the Teenie Beanie Baby national phenomenon.[1]

At McDonald's, sales promotion efforts, such as giving away Teenie Beanie Babies, play a major role in maintaining long-term, satisfying customer relationships, which, in turn, contribute to the company's success. As indicated in Chapter 17, personal selling and sales promotion are two possible elements in a promotion mix. Sales promotion sometimes is a company's sole promotional tool, although it is generally used in conjunction with other promotion mix elements. It plays an increasingly important role in marketing strategies. Personal selling is becoming more professional and sophisticated, with sales personnel acting more as consultants and advisers.

This chapter focuses on personal selling and sales promotion. We consider the purposes of personal selling, its basic steps, and types of salespersons and how they are selected. We also discuss major sales force management decisions, including setting objectives for the sales force and determining its size; recruiting, selecting, training, compensating, and motivating salespeople; managing sales territories; and controlling and evaluating sales force performance. We then examine several characteristics of sales promotion, reasons for using sales promotion, and sales promotion methods available for use in a promotion mix.

The Nature of Personal Selling

personal selling   Paid personal communication that informs customers and persuades them to buy products

Personal selling is paid personal communication that attempts to inform customers and to persuade them to purchase products in an exchange situation. A salesperson describing the benefits of a Kenmore dryer to a customer in a Sears store engages in personal selling. Personal selling gives marketers the greatest freedom to adjust a message to satisfy customers' information needs. Compared with other promotion methods, personal selling is the most precise, enabling marketers to focus on the most promising sales prospects. Other promotion mix elements are aimed at groups of people, some of whom may not be prospective customers. However, a major disadvantage of personal selling is cost. Generally, it is the most expensive element in the promotion mix. The average cost of a sales call is $157.[2]

Millions of people, including increasing numbers of women, earn their living through personal selling. Mary Kay Cosmetics, for example, has a sales force of several hundred thousand individuals, most of whom are women. Sales careers can offer high income, a great deal of freedom, a high level of training, and a high level of job satisfaction. Although personal selling is sometimes viewed negatively, major corporations, professional sales associations, and academic institutions are changing negative stereotypes of salespeople.

Personal selling goals vary from one firm to another. However, they usually involve finding prospects, persuading prospects to buy, and keeping customers satisfied. Identifying potential buyers interested in an organization's products is critical. Because most potential buyers seek information before making purchases, salespersons can ascertain prospects' informational needs and then provide relevant information. To do so, sales personnel must be well trained regarding both their products and the selling process in general.

Salespeople must be aware of their competitors. They must monitor the development of new products and know about competitors' sales efforts in their sales territories—how often and when the competition calls on their accounts and what the competition is saying about their product in relation to its own. Salespeople must emphasize the benefits that their products provide, especially when competitors' products do not offer those specific benefits.

Few businesses survive solely on profits from one-time customers. For long-run survival, most marketers depend on repeat sales and thus need to keep their customers satisfied. Besides, satisfied customers provide favorable word-of-mouth communications, attracting new customers. Even though the whole organization is responsible for providing customer satisfaction, much of the burden falls on salespeople since they are almost always closer to customers than anyone else in the company and often

provide buyers with information and service after the sale. Such contact gives salespeople an opportunity to generate additional sales and offers them a good vantage point for evaluating the strengths and weaknesses of the company's products and other marketing mix components. Their observations help develop and maintain a marketing mix that better satisfies both customers and the firm.

Elements of the Personal Selling Process

The specific activities involved in the selling process vary among salespersons and selling situations. No two salespersons use exactly the same selling methods. Nonetheless, many salespersons move through a general selling process as they sell products. This process consists of seven elements, or steps, outlined in Figure 19.1: prospecting, preapproach, approach, making the presentation, overcoming objections, closing the sale, and following up.

Prospecting

prospecting Developing a list of potential customers

Developing a list of potential customers is called **prospecting.** Salespeople seek names of prospects from company sales records, trade shows, commercial databases (Figure 19.2), newspaper announcements (of marriages, births, deaths, and so on), public records, telephone directories, trade association directories, and many other sources. Sales personnel also use responses to advertisements that encourage interested persons to send in information request forms. Seminars and meetings targeted at particular types of clients, such as attorneys or accountants, may also produce leads.

A number of salespeople prefer to use referrals—that is, recommendations from current customers—to find prospects. Obtaining referrals requires that the salesperson have a good relationship with the current customer and so must have performed well before asking the customer for help. Research shows that one referral is as valuable as twelve cold calls. Also, 80 percent of clients are willing to give referrals but only 20 percent are ever asked. Sales experts indicate that the advantages of using referrals are that the sales leads that result are highly qualified, the sales rates are higher, initial transactions are larger, and the sales cycle is shorter.[3]

Some organizations use their own databases to identify prospects. John Deere has used its database of 750,000 farm equipment owners to find prospects for its retail dealers' parts and service businesses. By researching owners of older equipment, John Deere identified prospects and, through special offers, enticed them to go to John Deere dealers for parts and service.[4]

Consistent activity is critical to successful prospecting. Salespersons must actively search the customer base for qualified prospects that fit the target market profile. After developing the prospect list, a salesperson evaluates whether each prospect is able, willing, and authorized to buy the product. Based on this evaluation, prospects are ranked according to desirability or potential.

Figure 19.1
General Steps in the Personal Selling Process

1. Prospecting
2. Preapproach
3. Approach
4. Making the presentation
5. Overcoming objections
6. Closing the sale
7. Following up

Preapproach

Before contacting acceptable prospects, a salesperson finds and analyzes information about each prospect's specific product needs, current use of brands, feelings about available brands, and personal characteristics. The most successful salespeople are thorough in their preapproach, which involves identifying key decision makers, reviewing account histories and problems, contacting other clients for information, assessing credit histories and problems, preparing sales presentations, identifying product needs, and obtaining relevant literature. A salesperson with a lot of information about a prospect is better equipped to develop a presentation that precisely communicates with the prospect.

Figure 19.2
Sources of Prospects
Marketers employ commercial databases to identify prospects.

Approach

approach   The way a salesperson contacts a potential customer

The **approach**—the manner in which a salesperson contacts a potential customer—is a critical step in the sales process. In more than 80 percent of initial sales calls, the purpose is to gather information about the buyer's needs and objectives. Creating a favorable impression and building rapport with prospective clients are important tasks in the approach because the prospect's first impressions of the salesperson are usually lasting ones. During the initial visit, the salesperson strives to develop a relationship rather than just to push a product. The salesperson may have to call on a prospect several times before the product is considered. The approach must be designed to deliver value to targeted customers. If the sales approach is inappropriate, the salesperson's efforts are likely to have poor results.

One type of approach is based on referrals; the salesperson approaches the prospect and explains that an acquaintance, associate, or relative suggested the call. The salesperson who uses the "cold canvass" approach calls on potential customers without prior consent. Repeat contact is another common approach; when making the contact, the salesperson mentions a previous meeting. The exact type of approach depends on the salesperson's preferences, the product being sold, the firm's resources, and the prospect's characteristics.

Making the Presentation

During the sales presentation, the salesperson must attract and hold the prospect's attention, stimulating interest and sparking a desire for the product. The salesperson should have the prospect touch, hold, or use the product. If possible, the salesperson

Figure 19.3
Enhancing Sales Presentations
Audiovisual equipment assists salespeople in sales presentations.

should demonstrate the product. Audiovisual equipment and software may also enhance the presentation, as shown in Figure 19.3.

During the presentation, the salesperson must not only talk, but also listen. The sales presentation gives the salesperson the greatest opportunity to determine the prospect's specific needs by listening to questions and comments and observing responses. Even though the salesperson plans the presentation in advance, she or he must be able to adjust the message to meet the prospect's informational needs.

Overcoming Objections

An effective salesperson usually seeks out a prospect's objections in order to address them. If they are not apparent, the salesperson cannot deal with them, and the prospect may not buy. One of the best ways to overcome objections is to anticipate and counter them before the prospect raises them. However, this approach can be risky because the salesperson may mention objections that the prospect would not have raised. If possible, the salesperson should handle objections as they arise. They also can be addressed at the end of the presentation.

Closing the Sale

closing The stage in the selling process when the salesperson asks the prospect to buy the product

Closing is the stage of the selling process when the salesperson asks the prospect to buy the product. During the presentation, the salesperson may use a "trial close" by asking questions that assume the prospect will buy the product. The salesperson might ask the potential customer about financial terms, desired colors or sizes, or delivery arrangements. Reactions to such questions usually indicate how close the prospect is to buying. Properly asked, questions may allow prospects to uncover their own problems and to identify solutions themselves. One questioning approach uses broad questions (what, how, why) to probe or gather information and focused questions (who, when, where) to clarify and close the sale. A trial close allows prospects to indicate indirectly that they will buy the product without having to say those sometimes difficult words, "I'll take it."

A salesperson should try to close at several points during the presentation because the prospect may be ready to buy. One closing strategy involves asking the potential customer to place a low-risk tryout order. An attempt to close the sale may result in objections. Thus, closing can uncover hidden objections, which the salesperson can then address.

Following Up

After a successful closing, the salesperson must follow up the sale. In the follow-up stage, the salesperson determines whether the order was delivered on time and installed properly, if installation was required. He or she should contact the customer to learn if any problems or questions regarding the product have arisen. The follow-up stage is also used to determine customers' future product needs. See Building Customer Relationships for a discussion of how salespeople can work on customer satisfaction at every stage of the selling process.

Types of Salespersons

To develop a sales force, a marketing manager decides what kind of salesperson will sell the firm's products most effectively. Most business organizations use several different kinds of sales personnel. Based on the functions performed, salespersons can be classified into three groups: order getters, order takers, and support personnel. One salesperson can, and often does, perform all three functions.

Order Getters

order getter   The salesperson who sells to new customers and increases sales to current ones

To obtain orders, a salesperson informs prospects and persuades them to buy the product. The **order getter**'s job is to increase sales by selling to new customers and by increasing sales to present customers. This task sometimes is called creative selling. It requires that salespeople recognize potential buyers' needs and give them necessary information. Order getting is sometimes divided into two categories: current-customer sales and new-business sales.

BUILDING customer relationships

Selling Customer Satisfaction throughout the Selling Process

"No matter what you sell, you've got to sell satisfaction," says Stanley Marcus, chairman emeritus of Neiman Marcus. Although there are as many variations on personal selling as there are products in the marketplace, experts like Marcus know that to forge a lasting customer relationship, the salesperson has to work on customer satisfaction at every stage of the selling process.

First, salespeople should adjust the personal selling process to fit the customer's buying process. This is especially important in organizational markets, where purchases take more time and involve numerous members of the buying center. Organizations generally need a great deal of information at different points in the buying process, so salespeople must be prepared to get the right data to the right people at the right time.

Second, the sale is all about what the customer wants to buy, not what the salesperson has to sell. This means the salesperson has to ask tactful questions to learn as much as possible about the customer's needs and then show how the product meets those needs. "By asking very specific questions, salespeople can give the customer a deeper understanding of what he or she truly wants," says the founder of Domain Home Fashions.

Third, there is no such thing as a one-time sale. "Anyone who views a sale as [just] a [single] transaction is going to be toast down the line," comments Marilyn Carlson Nelson, president of Carlson Companies, which owns Radisson Hotels and other service companies. Rather, a sale is one event in a string of events that create and sustain trust, strengthening the relationship between buyer and seller.

Follow-up after the sale is particularly important to customer satisfaction. Experts say that salespeople can establish trust and build satisfaction by obeying the following "dos and don'ts":

• Do not merely recite the sales presentation; do keep the presentation short and simple while probing for the customer's real problem or need.

• Do not stress ambiguous or overinflated claims; do explain how specific features deliver benefits that the customer values.

• Do not listen passively to a customer's objections; do request specifics to clarify the customer's expectations and prepare an appropriate response.

Current-Customer Sales   Sales personnel who concentrate on current customers call on people and organizations that have purchased products from the firm before. These salespeople seek more sales from existing customers by following up previous sales. Current customers can also be sources of leads for new prospects.

New-Business Sales   Business organizations depend to some degree on sales to new customers. New-business sales personnel locate prospects and convert them into buyers. Salespersons in many organizations help generate new business, but organizations that sell real estate, insurance, appliances, heavy industrial machinery, and automobiles depend in large part on new-customer sales.

Order Takers

order taker The salesperson who primarily seeks repeat sales

Taking orders is a repetitive task salespersons perform to perpetuate long-lasting, satisfying customer relationships. **Order takers** seek repeat sales. One major objective is to be certain that customers have sufficient product quantities where and when needed. Most order takers handle orders for standardized products purchased routinely and not requiring extensive sales efforts. The role of order takers is changing, however. In the future, they will probably serve more as identifiers and problem solvers to better meet the needs of their customers. There are two groups of order takers: inside order takers and field order takers.

Inside Order Takers   In many businesses, inside order takers, who work in sales offices, receive orders by mail, telephone, and the Internet. Certain producers, wholesalers, and retailers have sales personnel who sell from within the firm rather than in the field. That does not mean that inside order takers never communicate with customers face to face. For example, retail salespersons are classified as inside order takers. As more orders are placed through the Internet, the role of the inside order taker will continue to change, as discussed in Tech*know.

Field Order Takers   Salespersons who travel to customers are outside, or field, order takers. Often, customers and field order takers develop interdependent relationships. The buyer relies on the salesperson to take orders periodically (and sometimes to deliver them), and the salesperson counts on the buyer to purchase a certain quantity of products periodically. Use of small computers has improved the field order taker's inventory and order tracking capabilities.

   Field and inside order takers are not passive functionaries who simply record orders in a machinelike manner. Order takers generate the bulk of many organizations' total sales.

Support Personnel

support personnel Sales staff members who facilitate selling but usually are not involved solely with making sales

Support personnel facilitate selling but usually are not involved solely with making sales. They are engaged primarily in marketing industrial products, locating prospects, educating customers, building goodwill, and providing service after the sale. Although there are many kinds of sales support personnel, the three most common are missionary, trade, and technical salespersons.

missionary salespersons Support salespeople who assist the producer's customers in selling to their own customers

Missionary Salespersons   **Missionary salespersons,** usually employed by manufacturers, assist the producer's customers in selling to their own customers. Missionary salespersons may call on retailers to inform and persuade them to buy the manufacturer's products. When they succeed, retailers purchase products from wholesalers, who are the producer's customers. Manufacturers of medical supplies and pharmaceuticals often use missionary salespersons, called detail reps, to promote their products to physicians, hospitals, and retail druggists.

trade salespersons
Salespeople mainly involved in helping a producer's customers promote a product

Trade Salespersons **Trade salespersons** are not strictly support personnel because they usually take orders as well. However, they direct much effort toward helping customers, especially retail stores, promote the product. They are likely to restock shelves, obtain more shelf space, set up displays, provide in-store demonstrations, and distribute samples to store customers. Food producers and processors commonly employ trade salespersons.

technical salespersons
Support salespeople who give technical assistance to a firm's current customers

Technical Salespersons **Technical salespersons** give technical assistance to the organization's current customers, advising them on product characteristics and applications, system designs, and installation procedures. Because this job is often highly technical, the salesperson usually has formal training in one of the physical sciences or in engineering. Technical sales personnel often sell technical industrial products, such as computers, heavy equipment, and steel.

When hiring sales personnel, marketers seldom restrict themselves to a single category because most firms require different types of salespersons. Several factors dictate

Tech•know

Personal Selling Confronts Cyber-Selling

Hoping to travel to San Francisco on the day before Christmas, a consumer logs onto an Internet travel service to find the best deal, books a flight, reserves a rental car and a hotel room, and pays for everything with a credit card. When an engineer at a chemical plant needs a specific type of valve in a hurry, she logs onto an Internet marketplace that handles industrial parts, holds a real-time auction, finds a supplier with the best price and quickest delivery, places an order, and receives the valve the next day. In these scenarios, both the traveler and the engineer made purchases without the help of a sales representative. Internet business transactions like these are known as E-commerce. Studies predict that by the year 2000, E-commerce revenues will exceed $200 billion. Although industry experts praise E-commerce as a way to save organizations time and money, they assert that it will require dramatic changes in the nature of personal selling.

Traditionally, personal selling entailed explaining product features and benefits and processing orders. On the Internet, however, buyers can often easily handle these transactions themselves. The job of the salesperson will thus be more about service, advice, and building strong relationships with customers and less about taking orders. For example, at NECX, provider of computer network equipment, no human beings take sales orders. Twenty salespeople, however, concentrate on acquiring customers and fostering relationships. Experts agree that when first-time Internet purchases are complex, they will probably continue to require personal sales assistance and that the more complex a purchase, the more that a salesperson's input will be needed.

When customers know what they want, they can easily make purchases through E-commerce, especially if a company's Web site provides all the information necessary for an informed decision. Cisco Systems sells millions of dollars worth of networking equipment from its Web site, and Priceline.com offers airline tickets, new cars, and other products through its Internet system. With five times the revenues of Amazon.com, Dell Computer is the undisputed king of E-commerce. One year after its launch in July 1996, Dell Online was recording sales of $3 million a day. By the end of 2000, the company expects half of its sales to take place on the Internet. Customers at Dell Online can shop at their leisure, configure their own systems, save that information for up to two weeks, shop around at other companies, purchase what they want, and check on the status of the order as often as they like, all without benefit of a human sales representative.

Recently, *Business Week* reported that the cost of generating a paper purchase order is about $150, whereas the same order can be handled electronically for about $25. If E-commerce is so efficient, economical, and customer-pleasing, what will happen to the salesperson? Many analysts agree that although customers like the ease of buying via E-commerce, many want the reassurance they get from face-to-face transactions. After all, humans can offer buyers wisdom, expertise, and courtesy—things a computer cannot provide.

how many of each type a particular company should have. Product use, characteristics, complexity, and price influence the kind of sales personnel used, as do the number of customers and their characteristics. The types of marketing channels and the intensity and type of advertising also affect the composition of a sales force.

Management of the Sales Force

The sales force is directly responsible for generating one of an organization's primary inputs: sales revenue. Without adequate sales revenue, businesses cannot survive. In addition, a firm's reputation is often determined by the ethical conduct of its sales force. The morale and ultimately the success of a firm's sales force depend in large part on adequate compensation, room for advancement, adequate training, and management support—all key areas of sales management. When these elements do not satisfy salespeople, they may leave. Evaluating the input of salespeople is an important part of sales force management because of its strong bearing on a firm's success.

We explore eight general areas of sales management: establishing sales force objectives, determining sales force size, recruiting and selecting salespeople, training sales personnel, compensating salespeople, motivating salespeople, managing sales territories, and controlling and evaluating sales force performance.

Establishing Sales Force Objectives

To manage a sales force effectively, sales managers must develop sales objectives. Sales objectives tell salespersons what they are expected to accomplish during a specified time period. They give the sales force direction and purpose and serve as standards for evaluating and controlling the performance of sales personnel. Sales objectives should be stated in precise, measurable terms and should specify the time period and geographic areas involved.

Sales objectives are usually developed for both the total sales force and each salesperson. Objectives for the entire force are normally stated in terms of sales volume, market share, or profit. Volume objectives refer to dollar or unit sales. For example, the objective for an electric drill producer's sales force might be to sell $18 million worth of drills or 600,000 drills annually. When sales goals are stated in terms of market share, they usually call for an increase in the proportion of the firm's sales relative to the total number of products sold by all businesses in that industry. When sales objectives are based on profit, they are generally stated in terms of dollar amounts or return on investment.

Sales objectives, or quotas, for individual salespersons are commonly stated in terms of dollar or unit sales volume. Other bases used for individual sales objectives include average order size, average number of calls per time period, and ratio of orders to calls.

Determining Sales Force Size

The size of the average sales force is declining; between 1996 and 1998, it fell by about 25 percent.[5] Sales force size is important because it influences the company's ability to generate sales and profits. Moreover, size of the sales force affects the compensation methods used, salespersons' morale, and overall sales force management. Sales force size must be adjusted periodically because a firm's marketing plans change, as do markets and forces in the marketing environment. One danger in cutting back the size of the sales force to increase profits is that the sales organization may lose strength and resiliency, preventing it from rebounding when growth occurs or better market conditions prevail.

There are several analytical methods for determining optimal sales force size. One method involves determining how many sales calls per year are necessary for an organization to serve customers effectively and then dividing this total by the average number of sales calls a salesperson makes annually. A second method is based on marginal analysis, whereby additional salespeople are added to the sales force until the cost of an additional salesperson equals the additional sales generated by that person. Although marketing managers may use one or several analytical methods, they normally temper decisions with subjective judgment.

Recruiting and Selecting Salespeople

recruiting   Developing a list of qualified applicants for sales positions

To create and maintain an effective sales force, sales managers must recruit the right type of salespeople. **Recruiting** is a process by which the sales manager develops a list of qualified applicants for sales positions. Costs of hiring and training a salesperson are soaring—they are reaching over $60,000 in some industries. Yet the average sales force turnover rate is about 10 percent.[6] Thus, recruiting errors are expensive.

To ensure that the recruiting process results in a pool of qualified salespersons from which to hire, a sales manager establishes a set of qualifications before beginning to recruit. Although for years marketers have tried to identify a set of traits characterizing effective salespeople, there is still no set of generally accepted characteristics. Sales managers must determine what set of traits best fits their companies' particular sales tasks. Two activities help establish this set of required attributes. The sales manager should prepare a job description listing specific tasks salespersons are to perform. The manager also should analyze characteristics of the firm's successful salespersons, as well as those of ineffective sales personnel. From the job description and analysis of traits, the sales manager should be able to develop a set of specific requirements and be aware of potential weaknesses that could lead to failure.

Figure 19.4
Recruiting and Selecting Salespeople
Sales managers sometimes uses the specialized services provided by other companies to help them in recruiting and hiring salespeople.

A sales manager generally recruits applicants from several sources: departments within the firm, other firms, employment agencies, educational institutions, respondents to advertisements, and individuals recommended by current employees. The specific sources depend on the type of salesperson required and the manager's experiences with particular sources.

The process of recruiting and selecting salespersons varies considerably from one company to another. Companies intent on reducing sales force turnover are likely to have strict recruiting and selection procedures. State Farm Life Insurance, for example, strives to retain customers by having low sales force turnover. Applicants for the job of State Farm Insurance agents must endure a yearlong series of interviews, tests, and visits with agents before finding out if they have been hired. Approximately 80 percent of State Farm agents are still employed four years after being hired, compared with an industry average of only 30 percent.

Sales management should design a selection procedure that satisfies the company's specific needs. Some organizations use the specialized services of other companies to hire sales personnel (see Figure 19.4). The process should include steps that yield the information required for making accurate selection decisions. However, because each step incurs a certain amount of expense, there should be no more steps than necessary. Stages of the selection process should be sequenced so that the more expensive steps, such as a physical examination, are near the end. Fewer people will then move through higher-cost stages.

Recruitment should not be sporadic; it should be a continuous activity aimed at reaching the best applicants. The selection process should systematically and effectively match applicants' characteristics and needs with the requirements of specific selling tasks. Finally, the selection process should ensure that new sales personnel are available where and when needed.

Training Sales Personnel

Many organizations have formal training programs; others depend on informal on-the-job training. Some systematic training programs are quite extensive, whereas others are rather short and rudimentary. Whether the training program is complex or simple, developers must consider what to teach, whom to train, and how to train them.

A sales training program can concentrate on the company, its products, or on selling methods. Training programs often cover all three. Such programs can be aimed at newly hired salespeople, experienced salespersons, or both. Training for experienced company salespersons usually emphasizes product information, although salespeople must also be informed about new selling techniques and changes in company plans, policies, and procedures. Ordinarily, new sales personnel require comprehensive training, whereas experienced personnel need both refresher courses about established products and training regarding new-product information. Training programs can be directed at the entire sales force or at a segment of it.

Sales training may be done in the field, at educational institutions, in company facilities, or in several of these locations. Some firms train new employees before assigning them to a specific sales position. Others, however, put them into the field immediately, providing formal training only after they have gained a little experience. Training programs for new personnel can be as short as several days or as long as three years; some are even longer. Sales training for experienced personnel is often scheduled when sales activities are not too demanding. Because training of experienced salespeople usually recurs, a firm's sales management must determine the frequency, sequencing, and duration of these efforts.

Sales managers, as well as other salespeople, often engage in sales training—whether daily on the job or periodically during sales meetings. Salespeople sometimes receive training from technical specialists within their own organizations. In addition, a number of outside companies specialize in providing sales training programs. Materials for sales training programs range from videos, texts, manuals, and cases to programmed learning devices and audio- and videocassettes. Lectures, demonstrations, simulation exercises, and on-the-job training can all be effective teaching methods. Choice of methods and materials for a particular sales training program depends on type and number of trainees, program content and complexity, length and location, size of the training budget, number of teachers, and teacher preferences.

Compensating Salespeople

To develop and maintain a highly productive sales force, a business must formulate and administer a compensation plan that attracts, motivates, and retains the most effective individuals. The plan should give sales management the desired level of control and provide sales personnel with acceptable levels of freedom, income, and incentive. It should be flexible, equitable, easy to administer, and easy to understand. Good compensation programs facilitate and encourage proper treatment of customers. Obviously, it is quite difficult to incorporate all of these requirements into a single program.

Developers of compensation programs must determine the general level of compensation required and the most desirable method of calculating it. In analyzing the required compensation level, sales management must ascertain a salesperson's value to the company on the basis of the tasks and responsibilities associated with the sales position. Sales managers may consider a number of factors, including salaries of other

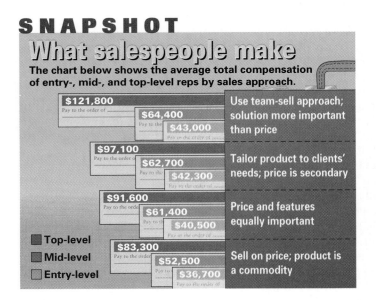

SNAPSHOT

What salespeople make

The chart below shows the average total compensation of entry-, mid-, and top-level reps by sales approach.

$121,800		Use team-sell approach; solution more important than price
	$64,400	
		$43,000
$97,100		Tailor product to clients' needs; price is secondary
	$62,700	
		$42,300
$91,600		Price and features equally important
	$61,400	
		$40,500
$83,300		Sell on price; product is a commodity
	$52,500	
		$36,700

■ Top-level
■ Mid-level
□ Entry-level

types of personnel in the firm, competitors' compensation plans, costs of sales force turnover, and nonsalary selling expenses. The average entry-level salesperson earns about $40,000 annually, while the average experienced salesperson makes about $125,000 yearly.[7]

Sales compensation programs usually reimburse salespersons for selling expenses, provide some fringe benefits, and deliver the required compensation level. To do that, a firm may use one or more of three basic compensation methods: straight salary, straight commission, or a combination of salary and commission. In a **straight salary compensation plan,** salespeople are paid a specified amount per time period. This sum remains the same until they receive a pay increase or decrease. In a **straight commission compensation plan,** salespeople's compensation is determined solely by sales for a given period. A commission may be based on a single percentage of sales or on a sliding scale involving several sales levels and percentage rates. In a **combination compensation plan,** salespeople receive a fixed salary plus a commission based on sales volume. Some combination programs require that a salesperson exceed a certain sales level before earning a commission; others offer commissions for any level of sales. Table 19.1 lists major characteristics of each sales force compensation method. Notice that the combination method is most popular. When selecting a compensation method, sales management weighs the advantages and disadvantages listed in the table.

straight salary compensation plan Paying salespeople a specific amount per time period

straight commission compensation plan Paying salespeople according to the amount of their sales in a given time period

combination compensation plan Paying salespeople a fixed salary plus a commission based on sales volume

Table 19.1 Characteristics of Sales Force Compensation Methods

Compensation Method	Frequency of Use (%)*	When Especially Useful	Advantages	Disadvantages
Straight salary	17.5	Compensating new salespersons; firm moves into new sales territories that require developmental work; sales requiring lengthy presale and postsale services	Gives salesperson security; gives sales manager control over salespersons; easy to administer; yields more predictable selling expenses	Provides no incentive; necessitates closer supervision of salespersons; during sales declines, selling expenses remain constant
Straight commission	14.0	Highly aggressive selling is required; nonselling tasks are minimized; company uses contractors and part-timers	Provides maximum amount of incentive; by increasing commission rate, sales managers can encourage salespersons to sell certain items; selling expenses relate directly to sales resources	Salespersons have little financial security; sales manager has minimum control over sales force; may cause salespeople to give inadequate service to smaller accounts; selling costs less predictable
Combination	68.5	Sales territories have relatively similar sales potentials; firm wishes to provide incentive but still control sales force activities	Provides certain level of financial security; provides some incentive; can move sales force efforts in profitable direction	Selling expenses less predictable; may be difficult to administer

*The figures are computed from *Dartnell's 30th Sales Force Compensation Survey*, Dartnell Corporation, Chicago, 1999.

Source: Charles Futrell, *Sales Management* (Ft. Worth, Tex.: Dryden Press, 1998, pp. 507–518.

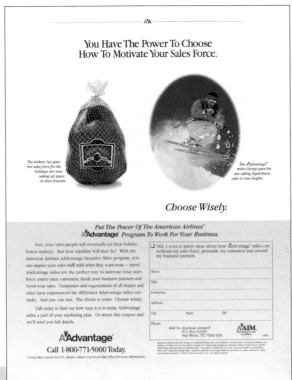

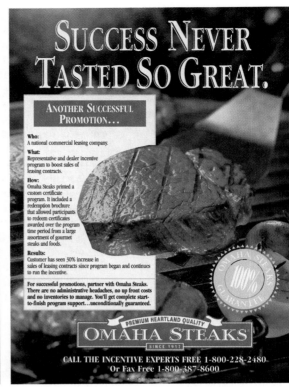

Figure 19.5
Incentive Programs
Companies have access to a variety of incentive progams aimed at motivating salespeople.

Motivating Salespeople

A sales manager should develop a systematic approach for motivating salespersons to be productive. Motivating should not be reserved for periods of sales decline. Effective sales force motivation is achieved through an organized set of activities performed continuously by the company's sales management.

Although financial compensation is an important incentive, motivational programs are needed to satisfy nonfinancial needs. Sales personnel, like other people, join organizations to satisfy personal needs and to achieve personal goals. Sales managers must recognize their personnel's motives and goals and attempt to create an organizational climate that lets them satisfy personal needs. Recognition of individual goals is becoming more challenging as cultural diversity increases.

A sales manager can use a variety of motivational incentives other than financial compensation. Enjoyable working conditions, power and authority, job security, and opportunity to excel are effective motivators, as are company efforts to make sales jobs more productive and efficient.

Sales contests and other incentive programs can also be effective motivators. Sales contests can motivate salespersons to increase sales or add new accounts, promote special items, achieve greater volume per sales call, cover territories better, and increase activity in new geographic areas.[8] Some companies find such incentive programs powerful motivating tools that marketing managers can use to achieve company goals. The advertisements in Figure 19.5 show examples of the incentive programs.

Properly designed, incentive programs pay for themselves many times over. In fact, sales managers are relying on incentives more than ever. Recognition programs that acknowledge outstanding performance with symbolic awards, such as plaques can be very effective when done in a peer setting. Other common awards include travel, merchandise, and cash. The advantages of a travel award are that it is a high-profile honor, it can provide a unique experience that makes recipients feel very special, and it can build camaraderie among award-winning salespeople. The drawbacks to using travel are that the recipient may already travel too much, many factors are not controllable, and the travel experience may not live up to expectations. The benefits of providing a cash award are that it is easy to administer, almost always appreciated by recipients, and crosses all demographic barriers. The problems with giving cash are that it has no visible trophy value and few bragging rights since most people don't brag about money, and the awardee may feel dissatisfied at receiving only a check. The benefits of awarding merchandise are that it has visible trophy value, recipients who are allowed to select the merchandise feel more control, and it can help build momentum for the sales force. The disadvantages of using merchandise include administrative complications and problems with perceived value on the part of recipients; moreover, it is simply not as exciting as travel.[9]

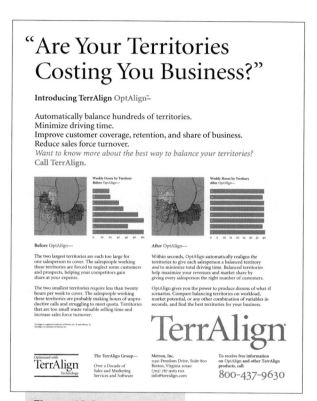

**Figure 19.6
Balancing Sales
Territories**
Sales managers some-
times use commercial
sources to assist them
in balancing sales
territories.

Managing Sales Territories

Effectiveness of a sales force that must travel to customers is somewhat influenced by management's decisions regarding sales territories. Sales managers deciding on territories must consider size, shape, routing, and scheduling.

Creating Sales Territories   Several factors enter into the design of a sales territory's size and shape. First, sales managers must construct territories so that sales potentials can be measured. Sales territories often consist of several geographic units, such as census tracts, cities, counties, or states, for which market data are obtainable. Sales managers usually try to create territories with similar sales potentials or requiring about the same amount of work. If territories have equal sales potentials, they will almost always be unequal in geographic size. Salespersons with larger territories have to work longer and harder to generate a certain sales volume. Conversely, if sales territories requiring equal amounts of work are created, sales potentials for those territories will often vary. If sales personnel are partially or fully compensated through commissions, they will have unequal income potentials. Many sales managers try to balance territorial workloads and earning potentials by using differential commission rates. At times, sales managers use commercial programs (see Figure 19.6) to help them balance sales territories. Although a sales manager seeks equity when developing and maintaining sales territories, some inequities always prevail.

A territory's size and shape should also help the sales force provide the best possible customer coverage and should minimize selling costs. Territory size and shape should take into account customer density and distribution.

Routing and Scheduling Salespeople   The geographic size and shape of a sales territory are the most important factors affecting the routing and scheduling of sales calls. Next in importance are the number and distribution of customers within the territory, followed by sales call frequency and duration. Those in charge of routing and scheduling must consider the sequence in which customers are called on, specific roads or transportation schedules to be used, number of calls to be made in a given period, and the time of day the calls will occur. In some firms, salespeople plan their own routes and schedules with little or no assistance from the sales manager; in other organizations, the sales manager draws up the routes and schedules. No matter who plans the routing and scheduling, the major goals should be minimizing salespersons' nonselling time (time spent traveling and waiting) and maximizing selling time (which is only about 47 percent of the average salesperson's time).[10] Planners should try to achieve these goals so that a salesperson's travel and lodging costs are held to a minimum.

Controlling and Evaluating Sales Force Performance

To control and evaluate sales force performance properly, sales management needs information. A sales manager cannot observe the field sales force daily and so relies on salespersons' call reports, customer feedback, and invoices. Call reports identify the customers called on and present detailed information about interaction with those clients. Traveling sales personnel often must file work schedules indicating where they plan to be during specific time periods.

Dimensions used to measure a salesperson's performance are determined largely by sales objectives, normally set by the sales manager. If an individual's sales objective is stated in terms of sales volume, then that person should be evaluated on the basis of sales volume generated. Even though a salesperson may be assigned a major objective, he or she is ordinarily expected to achieve several related objectives as well. Thus, salespeople are often judged along several dimensions. Sales managers evaluate many performance indicators, including average number of calls per day, average sales per customer, actual sales relative to sales potential, number of new-customer orders, average cost per call, and average gross profit per customer.

To evaluate a salesperson, a sales manager may compare one or more of these dimensions with predetermined performance standards. However, sales managers commonly compare a salesperson's performance with that of other employees operating under similar selling conditions or the salesperson's current performance with past performance. Sometimes management judges factors that have less direct bearing on sales performance, such as personal appearance, and product knowledge.

After evaluating salespeople, sales managers take any needed corrective action to improve sales force performance. They may adjust performance standards, provide additional training, or try other motivational methods. Corrective action may demand comprehensive changes in the sales force.

The Nature of Sales Promotion

sales promotion An activity and/or material meant to induce resellers or salespersons to sell a product or consumers to buy it

As defined in Chapter 17, **sales promotion** is an activity or material (or both) that acts as a direct inducement, offering added value or incentive for the product, to resellers, salespersons, or consumers. It encompasses all promotional activities and materials other than personal selling, advertising, and public relations. In competitive markets, where products are very similar, sales promotion provides additional inducements that encourage product trial and purchase.

The use of sales promotion has risen dramatically over the last fifteen years, primarily at the expense of advertising. Figure 19.7 shows the proportion of total promotional dollars spent on sales promotion and advertising. Notice that the proportion spent on sales promotion generally has increased, whereas the percentage spent on advertising has declined. This shift in how promotional dollars are used has occurred for several reasons. Heightened concerns about value have made customers more responsive to promotional offers, especially price promotions, coupons, and point-of-purchase displays. Because of their sheer size and access to scanner data, retailers have become much more powerful than manufacturers and are placing greater demands on them for sales promotion efforts that generate retail profits. Declines in brand loyalty have produced an environment in which sales promotions aimed at persuading customers to switch brands are more effective. Finally, the stronger emphasis placed on improving short-term performance results calls for greater use of sales promotion methods that yield quick (although perhaps short-lived) sales increases.[11]

An organization often uses sales promotion to facilitate personal selling, advertising, or both. Companies also use advertising and personal selling to support sales promotion activities. For example, marketers frequently use advertising to promote contests, free samples, and premiums. The most effective sales promotion efforts are highly interrelated with other promotional activities. Decisions regarding sales promotion often affect advertising and personal selling decisions, and vice versa.

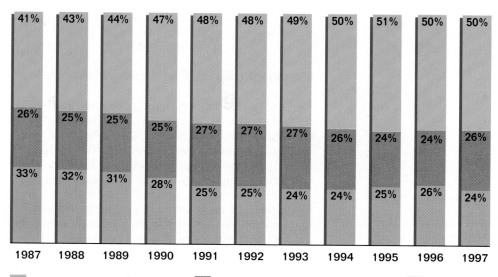

Figure 19.7
Proportion of Promotional Expenditures Allocated to Advertising, Consumer Sales Promotion, and Trade Sales Promotion

Source: From the *20th Annual Survey of Promotional Practices.* Copyright © 1998. Reprinted by permission of Cox Direct.

Sales Promotion Opportunities and Limitations

Sales promotion can increase sales by providing extra purchasing incentives. There are many opportunities to motivate consumers, resellers, and salespeople to take desired actions. Some kinds of sales promotion are designed specifically to stimulate resellers' demand and effectiveness; some are directed at increasing consumer demand; and others focus on both resellers and consumers. Regardless of the purpose, marketers must ensure that sales promotion objectives are consistent with the organization's overall objectives, as well as with its marketing and promotion objectives.

Although sales promotion can support brand image, excessive sales promotion efforts at price reduction, through coupons, for example, can negatively affect brand image. Indeed, in the future, brand advertising may become more important than sales promotion. Some firms that have shifted from brand advertising to sales promotion have lost market share. For instance, Minute Maid orange juice (owned by Coca-Cola Foods) experienced its most dramatic sales declines after shifting the majority of promotional spending to sales promotion while one of its major competitors, Tropicana, continued to focus on brand advertising. Tradeoffs exist between these two forms of promotion, and marketing managers must determine the right balance to achieve maximum promotional effectiveness.

Sales Promotion Methods

consumer sales promotion methods Ways of encouraging consumers to patronize specific stores or to try particular products

trade sales promotion methods Ways of persuading wholesalers and retailers to carry a producer's products and to market them aggressively

Most sales promotion methods can be grouped into consumer sales promotion and trade sales promotion. **Consumer sales promotion methods** encourage or stimulate consumers to patronize specific retail stores or to try particular products. **Trade sales promotion methods** stimulate wholesalers and retailers to carry a producer's products and to market these products more aggressively.

In deciding which sales promotion methods to use, marketers must take several factors into account. They must consider both product characteristics (size, weight, costs, durability, uses, features, and hazards) and target market characteristics (age, sex, income, location, density, usage rate, and shopping patterns). How products are distributed and the number and types of resellers may determine the type of method used. The competitive and legal environment may also influence the choice.

We examine several consumer and trade sales promotion methods to learn what they entail and what goals they can help marketers achieve.

Consumer Sales Promotion Methods

Consumer sales promotion methods initiated by retailers are often aimed at attracting customers to specific locations, whereas those used by manufacturers are generally directed at introducing new products or promoting established brands. In this section, we discuss coupons, demonstrations, frequent-user incentives, point-of-purchase displays, free samples, money refunds and rebates, premiums, cents-off offers, consumer contests and games, and consumer sweepstakes.

coupons A written price reduction used to encourage consumers to buy a specific product

Coupons   **Coupons** reduce a product's price and are used to prompt customers to try new or established products, to increase sales volume quickly, to attract repeat purchasers, or to introduce new package sizes or features. Savings may be deducted from the purchase price or offered as cash. For best results, the coupons should be easy to recognize and state the offer clearly, like the coupon in Figure 19.8. The nature of the product (seasonal demand for it, life cycle stage, frequency of purchase) is the prime consideration in setting up a coupon promotion. A recent coupon promotion occurred when the maker of Oral-B Cross-Action toothbrushes circulated 50 million $1 coupons during the product's introduction. This introduction was also backed by a $30 million advertising campaign.[12]

Coupons are the most widely used consumer sales promotion technique. In 1994, manufacturers distributed over 327 billion coupons. About 85 percent of all consumers use them, and their 1997 savings from coupons amounted to $3.5 billion. When selecting a grocery item brand, 35 percent of respondents in one survey said that a coupon is very important and 50 percent agreed it is somewhat important.[13]

Coupons are distributed on and in packages, through free-standing inserts (FSIs), print advertising, direct mail, and, in stores, through shelf dispensers, electronic

**Figure 19.8
Coupons**
Coupons should be easily recognized and should state the offer clearly.

dispensers, and at checkout counters. According to a recent survey, consumers' preferred methods of receiving coupons are through color leaflets in Sunday newspapers (86 percent) and by mail (67 percent).[14]

When deciding on the proper vehicle for coupons, marketers should consider strategies and objectives, redemption rates, availability, circulation, and exclusivity. The coupon distribution and redemption arena has become very competitive. To draw customers to their stores, grocers double and sometimes even triple the value of customers' coupons.

There are several advantages to using coupons. Print advertisements with coupons are often more effective at generating brand awareness than are print ads without coupons. Generally, the larger the coupon's cash offer, the better the recognition generated. Another advantage is that coupons reward present product users, win back former users, and encourage purchases in larger quantities. Because they are returned, coupons also let a manufacturer determine whether it reached the intended target market.

Drawbacks of coupon use include fraud and misredemption, which can be expensive for manufacturers. Another disadvantage, according to some experts, is that coupons are losing their value; because so many manufacturers offer them, consumers have learned not to buy without some incentive, whether it be a coupon, rebate, or refund. Furthermore, brand loyalty among heavy coupon users has diminished, and many consumers redeem coupons only for products they normally buy. It is believed that about three-fourths of coupons are redeemed by people already using the brand on the coupon. Thus, coupons have questionable success as an incentive for consumers to try a new brand or product. An additional problem with coupons is that stores often do not have enough of the coupon item in stock. This situation generates ill will toward both the store and the product.

demonstrations   A sales promotion method manufacturers use temporarily to encourage trial use and purchase of a product or to show how a product works

Demonstrations   **Demonstrations** are excellent attention getters. Manufacturers offer them temporarily to encourage trial use and purchase of a product or to show how a product works. Because labor costs can be extremely high, demonstrations are not used widely. They can be highly effective for promoting certain types of products, such as appliances, cosmetics, and cleaning supplies. Cosmetics marketers, such as Merle Norman and Clinique, sometimes offer potential customers "makeovers" to demonstrate product benefits and proper application.

Frequent-User Incentives   Many firms develop incentive programs to reward customers who engage in repeat (frequent) purchases. For example, most major airlines offer frequent-flyer programs through which customers who have flown a specified number of miles are rewarded with free tickets for additional travel. Frequent-user incentives foster customer loyalty to a specific company or group of cooperating companies. They are favored by service businesses, such as auto rental agencies, hotels, and credit card companies, as well as by marketers of consumer goods. An example of a successful frequent-user program is Subway's "Sub Club Cards"; customers earn card stamps with each purchase and redeem completed cards for free sandwiches.

point-of-purchase (P-O-P) materials   Signs, window displays, display racks, and similar means used to attract customers

Point-of-Purchase Displays   **Point-of-purchase (P-O-P) materials** include outdoor signs, window displays, counter pieces, display racks, and self-service cartons. Innovations in P-O-P displays include sniff-teasers, which give off a product's aroma in the store as consumers walk within a radius of four feet, and computerized interactive displays. These items, often supplied by producers, attract attention, inform customers, and encourage retailers to carry particular products. A retailer is likely to use point-of-purchase materials if they are attractive, informative, well-constructed, and in harmony with the store.

free samples   Samples of a product given out to encourage trial and purchase

Free Samples   Marketers use **free samples** for several reasons: to stimulate trial of a product, to increase sales volume in the early stages of a product's life cycle, and to obtain desirable distribution. Sampling is the most expensive of all sales promotion methods because production and distribution—at local events, by mail or door-to-door delivery, in stores, and on packages—entail very high costs. Most consumers (70%) prefer to get their samples by mail.[15] In designing a free sample, marketers should consider certain factors, such as seasonal demand for the product, market characteristics, and prior advertising. Free samples usually are not appropriate for slow-turnover products. Despite high costs, use of sampling is increasing. In a given year, it is not unusual for three-fourths of all consumer product companies to use sampling.

rebates A sales promotion technique whereby a customer is sent a specific amount of money for purchasing a single product

money refunds A sales promotion technique offering consumers money when they mail in a proof of purchase, usually for multiple product purchases

Money Refunds and Rebates   With **money refunds,** consumers submit proof of purchase and are mailed a specific amount of money. Usually, manufacturers demand multiple product purchases before consumers qualify for refunds. With **rebates,** the customer is sent a specified amount of money for making a single purchase. For a limited time, IBM offered rebates on its educational software titles, including $10 off Crayola titles of $14.95 and higher, $20 off Edmark purchases of $24.99 and higher, and $30 off World Book title purchases of $24.95 and higher.[16] Money refunds, used primarily to promote trial use of a product, are relatively low in cost, but because they sometimes generate a low response rate, they have limited impact on sales.

One of the problems with money refunds and rebates is that many people perceive the redemption process as too complicated. Consumers also have negative perceptions of manufacturers' reasons for offering rebates. They may believe that these are new, untested products or products that haven't sold well. If these perceptions are not changed, rebate offers may degrade the image and desirability of the products being promoted.

premiums Items offered free or at a minimum cost as a bonus for purchasing a product

Premiums   **Premiums** are items offered free or at minimum cost as a bonus for purchasing a product. They are used to attract competitors' customers, to introduce different sizes of established products, to add variety to other promotional efforts, and to stimulate consumer loyalty. Inventiveness is necessary, however; if an offer is to stand out and achieve a significant number of redemptions, the premium must match both the target audience and the brand's image. For example, Lee Jeans gave purchasers of original Straight Leg jeans and khakis free Motorola Pronto FLX pagers. The pager, as a premium, is a good fit with Lee's target market since 19- to 24-year-olds, the prime jeans target market, represent 31 percent of pager buyers.[17] To be effective, premiums must be easily recognizable and desirable. Premiums are placed on or in packages and can also be distributed by retailers or through the mail. Examples include a service station's giving a free carwash with a fill-up, a free toothbrush available with a tube of toothpaste, and a free plastic storage box given with the purchase of Kraft Cheese Singles.

cents-off offers Letting buyers pay less than the regular price to encourage purchase

Cents-Off Offers   When a **cents-off offer** is used, buyers pay a certain amount less than the regular price shown on the label or package. Similar to coupons, this method can be a strong incentive for trying products. It can stimulate product sales, yield short-lived sales increases, and promote products in off-seasons. It is an easy method to control and is often used for specific purposes. However, if used on an ongoing basis, cents-off offers reduce the price for customers who would buy at the regular price and may also cheapen a product's image. In addition, the method often requires special handling by retailers.

consumer contests and games Competitions for prizes used to generate retail traffic and to increase exposure to promotional messages

Consumer Contests and Games   In **consumer contests and games,** individuals compete for prizes based on analytical or creative skills. This method can be used to generate retail traffic and frequency of exposure to promotional messages. Marketers should exercise care in setting up a contest or game. Problems or errors may anger customers or result in lawsuits. Contestants are usually more involved in consumer contests and games than in sweepstakes, even though total participation may be lower. Contests and games may be used in conjunction with other sales promotion methods, such as coupons. To increase frequency of exposure of its promotional messages to its core teen market, Cherry Coke used a Web-linked adventure that included sampling and a direct mailing of a CD-ROM game to 500,000 teens.[18]

consumer sweepstakes
A sales promotion in which entrants submit their names for inclusion in a drawing for prizes

Consumer Sweepstakes   Entrants in **consumer sweepstakes** submit their names for inclusion in a drawing for prizes. For example, *Jump* magazine, a publication targeted at teenagers, sponsored a sweepstakes in which girls could win a cellular phone and $100 worth of phone service per month until age 20.[19] Sweepstakes are used to stimulate sales and are sometimes teamed with other sales promotion methods. Sweepstakes are used more often than consumer contests and tend to attract a greater number of participants. Successful sweepstakes can generate widespread interest and short-term increases in sales or market share.

Trade Sales Promotion Methods

To encourage resellers, especially retailers, to carry their products and to promote them effectively, producers use sales promotion methods. These include buy-back allowances, buying allowances, scan-back allowances, count-and-recount, free merchandise, merchandise allowances, cooperative advertising, dealer listings, premium or push money, sales contests, and dealer loaders.

buy-back allowance
Money given to a reseller for each unit bought after an initial deal is over

Buy-Back Allowances   A **buy-back allowance** is a sum of money a producer gives to a reseller for each unit the reseller buys after an initial deal is over. This method is a secondary incentive in which the total amount of money that resellers receive is proportional to their purchases during an initial consumer promotional offer, such as a coupon offer. Buy-back allowances foster cooperation during an initial sales promotion effort and stimulate repurchase afterward. The main drawback of this method is expense.

buying allowance
A temporary price reduction to resellers for purchasing specified quantities of a product

Buying Allowances   A **buying allowance** is a temporary price reduction to resellers for purchasing specified quantities of a product. A soap producer, for example, might give retailers $1 for each case of soap purchased. Such offers may be an incentive to handle new products, to achieve temporary price reductions, or to stimulate purchase of items in larger than normal quantities. The buying allowance, which takes the form of money, yields profits to resellers and is simple and straightforward. There are no restrictions on how resellers use the money, which increases the method's effectiveness. One hazard of buying allowances is that customers will buy "forward," meaning that they buy large amounts that keep them supplied for many months. Another problem is that competition can match (or beat) the reduced price, which can lower profits for all sellers.

scan-back allowance
A manufacturer's reward to retailers based on the number of pieces scanned

Scan-Back Allowances   A **scan-back allowance** is a manufacturer's reward to retailers based on the number of pieces moved through their scanners during a specific time period. To participate in scan-back programs, retailers usually are expected to pass along savings to consumers through special pricing. Scan-backs are becoming widely used by manufacturers because they link trade spending directly to product movement at the retail level.

count-and-recount
A producer's payment of a specific amount of money for each product unit moved from a reseller's warehouse in a given period

Count-and-Recount   The **count-and-recount** method is based on a producer's payment of a specific amount of money for each product unit moved from a reseller's warehouse in a given time period. Units of a product are counted at the start of the promotion and again at the end to determine how many units have moved out of the warehouse. This method can reduce retail stockouts by moving inventory out of warehouses and can also clear distribution channels of obsolete products or packages and reduce warehouse inventories. The count-and-recount method may benefit a producer by decreasing resellers' inventories, making resellers more likely to place new orders. However, this method is often difficult to administer and may not appeal to resellers with small warehouses.

free merchandise   A manufacturer's reward given to resellers for purchasing a stated quantity of products

Free Merchandise   Manufacturers sometimes offer **free merchandise** to resellers who purchase a stated quantity of products. Occasionally, free merchandise is used as payment for allowances provided through other sales promotion methods. To avoid handling and bookkeeping problems, the giving of free merchandise is usually accomplished by reducing the invoice.

merchandise allowance
A manufacturer's agreement to help resellers pay for special promotional efforts

Merchandise Allowances A **merchandise allowance** is a manufacturer's agreement to pay resellers certain amounts of money for providing promotional efforts, such as advertising or displays. This method is best suited to high-volume, high-profit, easily handled products. Its major drawback is that some retailers perform activities at a minimally acceptable level simply to obtain allowances. Before paying retailers, manufacturers usually verify their performance. Manufacturers hope that retailers' additional promotional efforts will yield substantial sales increases.

cooperative advertising
Sharing of media costs by manufacturer and retailer for advertising the manufacturer's products

Cooperative Advertising **Cooperative advertising** is an arrangement whereby a manufacturer agrees to pay a certain amount of a retailer's media costs for advertising the manufacturer's products. The amount allowed is usually based on the quantities purchased. Before payment is made, a retailer must show proof that advertisements did appear. These payments give retailers additional funds for advertising. Some retailers exploit cooperative advertising agreements by crowding too many products into one advertisement. Surprisingly, not all available cooperative advertising dollars are used. Some retailers cannot afford to advertise; others can afford it but do not want to advertise. A large proportion of all cooperative advertising dollars are spent on newspaper advertisements.

dealer listings Ads promoting a product and identifying retailers that sell it

Dealer Listings **Dealer listings** are advertisements promoting a product and identifying participating retailers that sell the product. Dealer listings can influence retailers to carry the product, build traffic at the retail level, and encourage consumers to buy the product at participating dealers.

premium, or push, money Extra compensation to salespeople for pushing a line of goods

Premium, or Push, Money **Premium**, or **push, money** is additional compensation provided to salespeople by the manufacturer in order to push a line of goods. This method is appropriate when personal selling is an important part of the marketing effort; it is not effective for promoting products sold through self-service. The method often helps manufacturers obtain a commitment from the sales force, but it can be very expensive.

sales contest A means of motivating distributors, retailers, and salespeople by recognizing outstanding achievements

Sales Contests A **sales contest** is designed to motivate distributors, retailers, and sales personnel by recognizing outstanding achievements. To be effective, this method must be equitable for all persons involved. One advantage of the method is that it can achieve participation at all distribution levels. However, positive effects may be temporary, and prizes are usually expensive.

dealer loader A gift, often part of a display, offered to a retailer who purchases a specified quantity of merchandise

Dealer Loaders A **dealer loader** is a gift to a retailer who purchases a specified quantity of merchandise. Often, dealer loaders are used to obtain special display efforts from retailers by offering essential display parts as premiums. For example, a manufacturer might design a display that includes a sterling silver tray as a major component and give the tray to the retailer. Marketers use dealer loaders to obtain new distributors and to push larger quantities of goods.

Summary

Personal selling is the process of informing customers and persuading them to purchase products through paid personal communication in an exchange situation. The three general purposes of personal selling are finding prospects, persuading them to buy, and keeping customers satisfied.

Many salespersons—either consciously or unconsciously—move through a general selling process as they sell products. In prospecting, the salesperson develops a list of potential customers. Before contacting prospects, the salesperson conducts a preapproach that involves finding and analyzing information about prospects and their needs. Approach is the way in which a salesperson contacts potential customers. During the sales presentation, the salesperson must attract and hold the prospect's attention to stimulate interest and desire for the product. If possible, the salesperson should handle objections as they arise. Closing is the stage in the selling process when the salesperson asks the prospect to buy the product or products. After a successful closing, the salesperson must follow up the sale.

In developing a sales force, marketing managers must consider which types of salespersons will sell the firm's products most effectively. The three classifications of salespersons are order getters, order takers, and support personnel. Order getters inform both current customers and new prospects and persuade them to buy. Order takers seek repeat sales and fall into two categories: inside order takers and field order takers. Sales support personnel facilitate selling, but their duties usually extend beyond making sales. The three types of support personnel are missionary, trade, and technical salespersons.

Sales force management is an important determinant of a firm's success because the sales force is directly responsible for generating an organization's sales revenue. Major decision areas and activities on which sales managers must focus are establishing sales force objectives, determining sales force size, recruiting, selecting, training, compensating, and motivating salespeople, managing sales territories, and controlling and evaluating sales force performance.

Sales objectives should be stated in precise, measurable terms and specify the time period and geographic areas involved. The size of the sales force must be adjusted occasionally because a firm's marketing plans change, as do markets and forces in the marketing environment.

Recruiting and selecting salespeople involves attracting and choosing the right type of salesperson to maintain an effective sales force. When developing a training program, managers must consider a variety of dimensions, such as who should be trained, what should be taught, and how training should occur. Compensation of salespeople involves formulating and administrating a compensation plan that attracts, motivates, and retains the right types of salespeople for the firm. Motivation of salespeople should allow the firm to attain high productivity. Managing sales territories, another aspect of sales force management, focuses on such factors as size, shape, routing, and scheduling. To control and evaluate sales force performance, sales managers must use information obtained through salespersons' call reports, customer feedback, and invoices.

Sales promotion is an activity or a material (or both) that acts as a direct inducement, offering added value or incentive for the product, to resellers, salespersons, or consumers. Marketers use sales promotion to identify and attract new customers, to introduce new products, and to increase reseller inventories. Sales promotion techniques fall into two general categories: consumer and trade. Consumer sales promotion methods encourage consumers to trade at specific stores or to try a specific product. These sales promotion methods include coupons, demonstrations, frequent-user incentives, point-of-purchase displays, free samples, money refunds and rebates, premiums, cents-off offers, consumer contests and games, and consumer sweepstakes. Trade sales promotion techniques can stimulate resellers to handle a manufacturer's products and to market those products aggressively. These sales promotion techniques include buy-back allowances, buying allowances, scan-back allowances, count-and-recount, free merchandise, merchandise allowances, cooperative advertising, dealer listings, premium (or push) money, sales contests, and dealer loaders.

Important Terms

Personal selling	Straight commission compensation plan	Point-of-purchase (P-O-P) materials	Buying allowance
Prospecting	Combination compensation plan	Free samples	Scan-back allowance
Approach		Money refunds	Count-and-recount
Closing	Sales promotion	Rebates	Free merchandise
Order getter	Consumer sales promotion methods	Premiums	Merchandise allowance
Order taker		Cents-off offers	Cooperative advertising
Support personnel	Trade sales promotion methods	Consumer contests and games	Dealer listings
Missionary salespersons		Consumer sweepstakes	Premium, or push, money
Trade salespersons	Coupons	Buy-back allowance	Sales contest
Technical salespersons	Demonstrations		Dealer loader
Recruiting			
Straight salary compensation plan			

Discussion and Review Questions

1. What is personal selling? How does personal selling differ from other types of promotional activities?

2. What are the primary purposes of personal selling?

3. Identify the elements of the personal selling process. Must a salesperson include all these elements when selling a product to a customer? Why or why not?

4. How does a salesperson find and evaluate prospects? Do you consider any of these methods questionable ethically? Explain.

5. Are order getters more aggressive or creative than order takers? Why or why not?

6. Identify several characteristics of effective sales objectives.

7. How should a sales manager establish criteria for selecting sales personnel? What do you think are the general characteristics of a good salesperson?

8. What major issues or questions should management consider when developing a training program for the sales force?

9. Explain the major advantages and disadvantages of the three basic methods of compensating sales-

persons. In general, which method would you prefer? Why?

10. What major factors should be taken into account when designing the size and shape of a sales territory?

11. How does a sales manager—who cannot be with each salesperson in the field on a daily basis—control the performance of sales personnel?

12. What is sales promotion? Why is it used?

13. For each of the following, identify and describe three techniques, and give several examples: (a) consumer sales promotion methods and (b) trade sales promotion methods.

14. What types of sales promotion methods have you observed recently? Comment on their effectiveness.

Application Questions

1. Briefly describe an experience you have had with a salesperson at a clothing store or when buying an automobile. Identify the steps used by the salesperson and describe them. Did the salesperson skip any steps? What did the salesperson do well? Not so well?

2. Refer to your answer to question 1. Would you describe the salesperson as an order getter, an order taker, or a support salesperson? Why? Did the salesperson perform more than one of these functions?

3. Leap Athletic Shoe, Inc., a newly formed company, is in the process of developing a sales strategy. Market research indicates sales management should segment the market into five regional territories. The sales potential for the North region is $1.2 million, $1 million for the West region, $1.3 million for the Central region, $1.1 million for the South Central region, and $1 million for the Southeast region. The firm wishes to maintain some control over the training and sales processes because of the unique features of its new product line, but Leap marketers realize that the salespeople need to be fairly aggressive in their efforts to break into these markets. They would like to provide the incentive needed for the extra selling effort that will be required. What type of sales force compensation method would you recommend to Leap? Why?

4. Consumer sales promotions are aimed at increasing the sales of a particular retail store or product. Identify a familiar type of retail store or product. Recommend at least three sales promotion methods that should be used to promote the store or product. Explain why you would use these methods.

5. Trade sales promotions are used by producers to encourage resellers to promote their products more effectively. Identify which method or methods of sales promotion a producer might use in the following situations, and explain why the method would be appropriate.

    a. A golf ball manufacturer wants to encourage retailers to add a new type of golf ball to current product offerings.

    b. A life insurance company wants to increase sales of its universal life products, which have been lagging in sales recently (the company has little control over sales activities).

    c. A light bulb manufacturer with an overproduction of 100-watt bulbs wants to encourage its grocery store chain resellers to increase their bulb inventories.

Internet Exercise & Resources

Val-Pak Coupons Online

Val-Pak Direct Marketing Systems has been mailing coupons to consumers' homes for twenty-five years. Recently, the firm mailed out over 10 billion coupons to 50 million U.S. and Canadian consumers and businesses. The company is expanding the reach of its coupons via its Web site. Find out whether you can save money by visiting this site at

www.valpak.com

1. How do Val-Pak online coupons work?
2. How might Val-Pak's online coupons change the way coupons have been traditionally distributed?
3. How will online coupons affect traditional redemption rates, coupon circulation, and consumer attitudes toward coupon use?

E-Center Resources

Visit http://www.prideferrell.com to find several resources to help you succeed in mastering the material in this chapter, plus additional materials that will help you expand your marketing knowledge. The Web site includes

 Internet exercise updates plus additional exercises

✔ ACE self-tests

abc Chapter summary with hotlinked glossary

 Hotlinks to companies featured in this chapter

✪ Resource Center

▢ Career Center

▤ Marketing plan worksheets

VIDEO CASE 19.1

Sales Compensation: All for One, One for All at Marshall Industries

Managing 600 salespeople who sell 250,000 different items from 150 suppliers to 50,000 customers can be quite a challenge for any company. A few years ago, California-based Marshall Industries added yet another level of complexity to this already daunting challenge when it made a major change in the way its salespeople were being compensated.

Marshall Industries, an electronics distributor, sells computer chips and related products to industrial customers all over the world. In addition to distributing ready-made electronic products and supplies from a global network of suppliers, the company offers engineering design services, component testing, inventory management, and many other services requested by its organizational customers.

Personal selling has always been a critical component in the company's marketing mix, but top management became concerned that its commission-based sales compensation plan was hurting, not helping, the sales effort. One concern was that salespeople were timing product shipments to meet their quotas and earn commissions, rather than scheduling shipments according to customers' needs. Another concern was that commission-driven compensation caused salespeople to shift costs to stay within budget and to ignore potential sales opportunities outside their assigned territories. Moreover, the commission structure encouraged salespeople to compete with one another rather than cooperate to satisfy customers.

For CEO Robert Rodin, a major concern was that the sales compensation plan seemed to be hurting the bottom line. Initially, he was unsure of exactly how to fix the compensation system. "How do you design an incentive system robust enough to accommodate every change in every customer and every product and every market every day?" he wondered. The more he thought about the problem, the more he became convinced that paying for individual achievement was not appropriate for the way Marshall Industries wanted to do business with its customers.

So Rodin took the admittedly radical step of doing away with all types of individual financial incentives for the firm's salespeople. "We've eliminated commissions for our sales staff. We've eliminated bonuses based on [profit and loss] in our business units," he noted. He also stopped awarding trips, appliances, and other incentives. In their place, he established an entirely new compensation plan in which salespeople are paid on straight salary. They also receive a profit-sharing payment based on a set percentage of the company's yearly profits, rather than on the profits of the divisions in which they work.

This change in sales compensation shifted the attention of the sales force away from quotas and commissions toward customer needs and satisfaction. It also encouraged salespeople to work more closely with every department and division in the company, instead of feeling tied to the successes or failures of one particular division. Soon after instituting these compensation changes, the company began equipping all salespeople with laptop computers and a connection to the company's computer system. In short order, the company noticed that communication had improved and that sales productivity was on the rise, too.

In addition to servicing its customers through personal selling, Marshall Industries has invested heavily in an elaborate Web site, which now brings in more than 20 percent of the firm's revenues. Designed specifically for global electronic commerce, the site provides detailed product information day and night in twenty-four languages, with live customer support available to customers who log on at any hour. Customers can use the site to compare product specifications, locate products for specific situations, and request samples. They can also order new products and reorder others using credit cards or purchase orders. The site even invites customers to participate in online industry chats and interactive training seminars. Whenever customers want to check the status of their orders, they can simply go to the site, type in their order numbers, and find out whether their shipments are being packed or are already on UPS trucks.

Despite these handy online tools, person-to-person contact may still be needed to close the sale and provide follow-up service. "One fallacy in the Internet world is the Internet customer is otherwise calling inside sales," says CEO Rodin. "A customer may use the Internet for convenience, then they may want to negotiate with a person, go back through an intranet for customer service, then go back to people. You're never all one or the other." This is why the company relies on the personal contact of its 600 salespeople, as well as backup support from thousands of knowledgeable representatives in its technical service center, who can answer questions and help customers around the clock.

Down the road, Rodin sees great potential in electronic commerce. "The Internet is a gateway into new opportunities," he observes. "Everything we're doing on it has a payoff in higher customer satisfaction, in billing, bookings, and shipping the right product at the right time."

Marshall Industries' changes in sales compensation and its investments in technology have paid off handsomely. Within five years of moving to straight salary plus profitsharing, the firm had increased annual revenues from $400 million to $700 million; revenues then exploded beyond $1.5 billion. Employee productivity has nearly tripled, turnover has dropped by half, and employees feel more motivated to cooperate in meeting customers' needs. Marshall Industries has moved from the sixth-largest to the fourth-largest electronics distributor in the world. Just as important, the company has become the distributor of choice for many suppliers.[20]

Questions for Discussion

1. What types of problems did Marshall Industries' commission-driven sales compensation plan create?

2. What type of sales compensation plan is Marshall Industries currently using?

3. What effect do you think Marshall Industries' profit-sharing plan has had on the motivation of its salespeople?

4. How would you classify the employees who staff Marshall Industries' Web site and its technical service center?

CASE 19.2

Sales Promotion Puts the Fizz into Dr Pepper

How can a soft drink company get its message across when its advertising budget is much smaller than the budgets of its deep-pocketed competitors? For Dr Pepper, pitted against Mountain Dew and Sprite in the noncola soft drink category, the way to put the fizz into sales is through sales promotion. Dr Pepper has scored solid market share increases for more than a decade with creative sales promotions targeted at light and occasional consumers; the company's focus is on encouraging these consumers to make more purchases, rather than trying to get non-Dr Pepper drinkers to switch. The company also uses trade sales promotion methods to support its bottlers and the retail chains that carry its products.

Sports play a critical role in Dr Pepper's sales promotions. The company sponsors the Washington-Erving Motorsport's Ford Taurus race car on the NASCAR circuit. Owned by former NFL great Joe Washington and former NBA star Julius "Dr. J" Erving, the car sports a bold Dr Pepper logo on its hood, visible to spectators and television viewers throughout each race. For a small fee, local bottlers can have the race car parked at key retail sites to generate excitement for the brand. For example, when the car was in Daytona Beach for a race, local bottlers arranged for it to be shown at Wal-Mart, Albertson's, Publix, and other nearby stores.

In addition, Dr Pepper mounts special sales promotions during the annual Southeast Conference championship football game, putting its logo on everything from T-shirts and cups to coolers and banners. In one recent year, consumers were invited to win free game tickets by checking under the caps of specially marked Dr Pepper bottles. Ticket winners were then entered into a drawing for the "$1 Million Pepper Pass Challenge," which invited a consumer to try throwing a 40-yard pass during halftime (the consolation prize was a check for $10,000). During the championship weekend, the company handed out 100,000 product samples at a special open house. On the trade side, Dr Pepper prepared a variety of items for in-store support of this promotion, including shelf labels, refrigerator case decorations, and display signs. Among the other sporting events around which Dr Pepper builds sales promotions are college golf tournaments and Big 12 Conference football games. Retailers get involved by creating point-of-purchase displays touting the Dr Pepper promotion; the best displays earn store employees free tickets to the events or free merchandise.

College students are a particular target for Dr Pepper. As the purveyor of the official soft drink of the Collegiate Players Tour, Dr Pepper can park its colorful van in a prominent place during the sixteen golf tournaments played at U.S. colleges and country clubs during the summer months, a peak period for soft drink consumption. In this way, the company reinforces brand awareness and encourages more purchases by thirsty college students.

The "Dr Pepper Ph.D. Final Exam Sweepstakes," another recent promotion targeting college students, invited visitors to the company's Web site to answer five trivia questions. Winners received a personalized "diploma" printed directly from the Web site. In addition, all contestants were entered in a sweepstakes to win a year's supply of Dr Pepper soft drinks. Students also looked for phone-card prizes placed on some Dr Pepper cans sold in vending machines on U.S. campuses. After using their free phone cards, students were instructed to go to the company's Web site, type in the special ID number found on the phone cards, and thus enter into a drawing for such prizes as backpacks, bicycles, and a personal computer. The phone card prizes doubled as 30-cent coupons for the next purchase of a Dr Pepper.

Although soft drink companies have long targeted students, promotions geared toward children below college age have drawn fire in some areas. Critics worry that such promotions encourage youngsters to drink too much soda—an average of three cans daily, according to some studies. Not long ago, Dr Pepper was criticized for paying the Grapevine-Colleyville school district, near Dallas, a fee to have its logo painted on two school rooftops that airplane passengers could see when passing overhead. The school district also received more than $3 million in exchange for making only Dr Pepper drinks available in its seventeen schools for the next decade. Questioned about the deal, a spokesperson for the school district explained that such agreements were not new. "We've had exclusive bottling agreements for about twenty-five years in the state," she said. "The thing that is new is that instead of having each campus determine what bottler it wants to stock its soda machine, districts are saying, 'We'll make you a deal for all of our campuses, and in return we get some extra funding.'"

Despite this controversy, Dr Pepper and its bottlers aim to be good corporate citizens, donating free products, logo merchandise, and money for many community events and fundraisers. As an example, a Dr Pepper bottler recently teamed up with Wal-Mart to raise money for the Red Cross by sponsoring a country music charity concert in Nashville. As another example, the company and its bottlers raised more than $35,000 for the central Mississippi March of Dimes by sponsoring a golf tournament fundraiser.

Because retailers account for a good chunk of Dr Pepper's sales, the company supports its consumer promotions with a constant stream of trade promotions that boost its products' point-of-purchase visibility. For example, a North Carolina store displayed 400 cases of Dr Pepper products as part of its Santa's Workshop exhibit. Thanks in part to this promotion, holiday sales of Dr Pepper rose 24 percent in that outlet.

Dr Pepper's Web site plays an integral role in its sales promotions. In addition to inviting online entries to games and sweepstakes, the Web site allows visitors to download a variety of personal computer screensavers, each emblazoned with the Dr Pepper name and logo. This brings sales promotion directly into the customer's home or office, where Dr Pepper fans can chug their favorite brand of soda while sitting in front of their computer screens. As Dr Pepper's sales increases attest, properly targeted and well-designed sales promotions can help any company compete against a rival's gigantic advertising budget.[21]

Questions for Discussion
1. Identify the major sales promotion methods used by Dr Pepper.
2. Why does Dr Pepper use both trade and consumer sales promotion methods?
3. How would you recommend that Dr Pepper respond to those who believe sales promotions should not target students younger than college age?
4. Which trade sales promotion methods do you think are most suitable for Dr Pepper? Explain your answer.

STRATEGIC CASE 5

The American Dairy Industry: Got Promotion?

A television commercial begins by panning a room full of papers and artifacts relating to the notorious duel between Aaron Burr and Alexander Hamilton. At a table sits a man spreading peanut butter on a slice of bread. As he takes a big bite, the radio announces the day's random telephone trivia question worth $10,000 to the person answering correctly. The question is, "Who shot Alexander Hamilton in that famous duel?" The phone rings and, of course, the man knows the answer. However, thanks to his mouthful of peanut butter, the words come out sounding like "Awuh Bwuh." Frantically, he tries to pour a glass of milk to wash down his sticky sandwich, but the carton is empty. The radio announcer hangs up. As a dial tone sounds and the scene fades, on the screen appears this phrase: "Got Milk?" In magazine advertisements and on billboards from New York to Hollywood, celebrities like Kate Moss and Pete Sampras proudly wear something mothers have been wiping off children's faces for centuries—milk mustaches. These examples of creative advertising for milk illustrate only a small portion of the American dairy industry's aggressive promotional program designed to increase milk consumption.

Dairy Promoters Struggle to Make Milk Popular

For generations, milk was synonymous with health and nutrition in the minds of Americans. What conveyed the all-American image more than the milkman delivering bottles of fresh milk at dawn or Mom pouring tall, cold glasses of milk to go with her children's after-school snack? Although this image might endure, U.S. milk consumption has been in a steady decline since the 1960s, largely the result of increasing concerns for more healthy eating and the perception that milk contains large amounts of fat.

During the 1980s, national milk promoters tried to counter those perceptions with advertising that touted milk's healthy attributes. Fresh faces and wholesome beauties drank frothy glasses of milk and assured consumers, "Milk. It Does a Body Good." Research revealed that the ads successfully heightened awareness of milk's healthy qualities and convinced many Americans that they should be drinking milk. Despite the dairy industry's investment of millions of dollars to promote its product, however, milk consumption continued to decline. Americans agreed milk did a body good, but each of them continued to drink about sixteen fewer gallons of it every year. Concerned about the failure of past efforts, various organizations within the dairy industry—including the National Dairy Board, the American Dairy Association, the National Dairy Promotion and Research Board, the United Dairy Industry Association, the National Fluid Milk Processors' Association, and various state and local organizations—have banded together in an all-

out effort to promote milk as the perfect drink for people of all ages.

Advertising Efforts

Because milk is not a cool or trendy drink, competing with soft drinks is bound to be a losing battle. Therefore, advertising agencies for the dairy industry decided to position milk as an accompaniment to foods that just aren't the same without it. The Got Milk? campaign was born because milk, not Diet Coke or Snapple, is the drink people want with brownies or breakfast cereal. A number of television spots kicked off the $72 million campaign, each one depicting the predicaments of people who need milk but don't have it. A man with a mouthful of chocolate cake pounds on a vending machine that won't release a container of milk. A man who believes he has gone to heaven realizes that he has really gone the other direction when he discovers that all the milk cartons in a giant refrigerator are empty. Although the campaign relies predominantly on television, there are also billboards showing brownies, cookies, and peanut butter sandwiches missing big bites, and the simple tag line, "Got Milk?" Television spots and billboards never mention calcium, strong bones, or healthy skin.

The Got Milk? campaign has won many awards, including an Obie for excellence in outdoor advertising. Follow-up studies show that three months after the premiere of the Got Milk? campaign, consumption of milk in one twenty-four-hour period rose 2 percent. Now planning tie-in spots with Nestlé, General Mills, Nabisco, and Kraft, new ads will center around foods people wouldn't think of eating without milk. For example, the long-suffering Trix Rabbit, who has tried all his animated life to steal Trix cereal, finally succeeds. The victory is hollow, however, because when he gets home, he finds he is out of milk.

Unlike the Got Milk? campaign, the dairy industry's $52 million milk mustache advertising campaign *does* focus on the health advantages of drinking skim and low-fat milk. Ads that run in major monthly magazines feature sports figures, musicians, movie stars, and television personalities wearing very noticeable milk mustaches. In slightly humorous ways, each ad highlights a particular health feature that milk provides and includes the tag line, "Milk. What a surprise!" Ice skater Kristi Yamaguchi advocates milk for its potassium and vitamin content. Billy Ray Cyrus promotes milk as a way to reduce dietary fat. Vanna White credits milk's calcium with giving her the perfect white teeth in her famous smile. Model Christie Brinkley reminds pregnant women and nursing mothers that they need extra calcium, and milk is the best way to get it.

Follow-up research reveals that the milk mustache campaign is having an impact on how people perceive milk. In an independent nationwide survey, *USA Today*

discovered that of the 523 women polled, 60 percent had seen the ads and 69 percent considered them effective. In addition, the number of respondents who believe milk is good after exercising rose 22 percent, and the number who believe milk is an adult drink rose 22 percent. Encouraged by the campaign's success, the dairy industry plans to expand the program's target audience to include teenage girls and younger women and men. Ads in teen and men's magazines will focus on getting people to substitute milk for water in preparing foods like soups and hot chocolate. Mustaches in those ads will be colored instead of white—red for tomato soup or brown for chocolate milk, for example. Although the campaign will be primarily print-based, marketers plan to increase the number of billboards and bus-stop signage.

Sales Promotion Efforts

To stimulate milk sales and reinforce its advertising message, the dairy industry developed several sales promotions, including contests, sweepstakes, premiums, and rebates. The Milk Mustache Contest asked people to submit photos of themselves wearing milk mustaches. Prizes included cameras and film, with the winner's picture appearing in *Life* magazine. By sending in their answers to three "Test Your Milk Mustache IQ" questions, consumers entered a sweepstakes for a $500 health club membership. Chocolate milk drinkers could receive a premium of fifteen free removable tatoos by sending in proofs of purchase from two gallons of chocolate milk, or a self-liquidating premium of a cow puppet with proofs of purchase and $4.50. To receive a $13 rebate off the price of Reebok sports and fitness videos, milk drinkers could submit proof-of-purchase seals from milk cartons.

Public Relations Efforts

In addition to the extremely visible advertising campaigns and very successful sales promotions, the dairy industry conducts lower-profile but equally important public relations efforts. These keep milk in the spotlight and make it easier for people to learn about milk's positive health attributes. The milk mustache campaign generated a great deal of publicity, showing up on David Letterman's Top 10 List, as an answer on *Jeopardy,* in Jay Leno's *Tonight Show* monologue, and as a story on the *Saturday Night Live* "Weekend Update." When one of the characters in an episode of

Fox Broadcasting's popular family program *Party of Five* looked in the refrigerator and asked, "Got milk?" the resulting publicity augmented the national launch of the Got Milk? print and television campaign.

The dairy industry's public relations efforts also include organized events to generate news about milk and an extensive public education program. National Milk Mustache Week, officially proclaimed in major U.S. cities including New York, Chicago, San Francisco, St. Louis, and Seattle, is a week-long celebration of milk's contribution to women's health. About eighty media markets cover events like the Milk Mustache March in New York City. The industry's toll-free hotline, 1-800-WHY-MILK, provides information about milk ranging from nutritional data to recipes. Consumers who call in can listen to recorded messages on milk-related topics, get answers to specific questions from registered dieticians and nurses, and order free informative brochures such as "Trim with Skim," "Milk. What a Surprise," and "Milk Matters to Mothers-To-Be." In its first year of operation, the toll-free milk line received 72,000 calls, and to date, over 7 million brochures have been distributed.

For years, Americans harbored a number of negative attitudes toward milk: milk is fatty; milk is a kid's drink; milk doesn't taste good; milk causes heart disease. Thanks to the American dairy industry's promotional efforts, these misperceptions are finally fading. For example, more young women believe milk is good for their health, and more people identify milk as a thirst-quenching drink after a workout. Whether positive attitudes toward milk will translate into long-term increased milk consumption is not yet clear.[22]

Questions for Discussion

1. What types of promotional objectives is the American dairy industry attempting to achieve?
2. Assess the dairy industry's approach of advertising milk as an indispensable accompaniment to foods that traditionally go with a glassful, such as brownies and cereal.
3. Why have the milk mustache and Got Milk? campaigns generated significant publicity?
4. Do you believe that the American dairy industry's current promotional efforts will increase long-term milk consumption? Explain your answer.

Part Six

Pricing Decisions

I f an organization is to provide a satisfying marketing mix, the price must be acceptable to target market members. Pricing decisions can have numerous effects on other parts of the marketing mix. For example, a product's price can influence how customers perceive it, what types of marketing institutions are used in distributing the product, and how the product is promoted. In Chapter 20, we discuss the importance of price and look at some of the characteristics of price and nonprice competition. We then examine the major factors that affect marketers' pricing decisions. Eight major stages in the process used by marketers to establish prices are discussed in Chapter 21.

20

Pricing Concepts

OBJECTIVES

- **To understand the nature and importance of price**

- **To become aware of the characteristics of price and nonprice competition**

- **To become familiar with various pricing objectives**

- **To explore key factors that may influence marketers' pricing decisions**

- **To consider issues affecting the pricing of products for organizational markets**

The Price is Right on the Buy.com Site

Many marketers guarantee that their prices are the lowest customers will find. Very few, however, back up their claims by helping customers compare their prices with those of competitors. One company that does do this is Buy.com, a fast-growing Internet retailer founded by Scott A. Blum in 1996. At the company's Web site, customers can, with the click of a mouse, take a look at the prices offered by Buy.com's competitors.

The company initially focused on selling computer hardware and software, guaranteeing that its prices were the best anywhere on the Web. Delivering on this promise meant unleashing a secret weapon: sophisticated software that checks prices on competitors' Web sites from one to seven times a day. After the software identifies the lowest competing price for a product that Buy.com sells, the company sets its price lower. It then registers this price with the many price-comparison search engines used by shoppers who chase bargains on the Internet.

Buy.com rang up approximately $125 million in its first twelve months of Internet retailing. Then, as sales momentum approached $1 million a day, CEO Blum boldly expanded beyond computer retailing into books, videos, electronic games,

and music. Blum has had to sharpen his company's pricing even more to go head-to-head with the Internet's two top booksellers, Amazon.com and Barnes & Noble. Again, technology is the key. Instead of simply quoting book prices to customers, the Buy.com site invites them to compare prices with those at Amazon.com and Barnes & Noble by clicking on a special button. Thanks to the company's never-ending price comparisons, it can safely guarantee the lowest prices anywhere on the Web—and back up that promise by showing competing prices on demand.

Buy.com's best-price policy translates into low profit margins. But the company, like OnSale and other low-margin Internet retailers, generates additional revenue by selling advertising banners and buttons to companies that want to reach its growing customer base. In effect, Buy.com's pricing is designed to attract more shoppers, which in turn attracts more advertisers. The company provides additional value through convenience, quality, and a commitment to excellence. Blum is already thinking about BuyCars.com, BuyInsurance.com, and even BuyCheeseburgers.com, all with one common denominator: the guaranteed best price in cyberspace.[1]

BUY.COM
The Internet Superstore

Buy.com uses pricing as a tool to compete effectively against numerous competitors, both in and out of cyberspace. It's fast, convenient, and efficient for customers who have decided on a specific product and are simply searching for the very best price. For products purchased as commodities in which price is the main criterion for purchase, the approach Buy.com uses is attractive to customers. In this chapter, we focus first on the nature of price and its importance to marketers. We then consider some characteristics of price and nonprice competition. Next, we explore the various types of pricing objectives that marketers may establish, and we examine in some detail the numerous factors that can influence pricing decisions. Finally, we discuss selected issues related to the pricing of products for organizational markets.

The Nature of Price

price   Value exchanged for products in a marketing exchange

barter
The trading of products

The purpose of marketing is to facilitate satisfying exchange relationships between buyer and seller. **Price** is the value exchanged for products in a marketing exchange. In most marketing situations, the price is very evident, and buyers and sellers are aware of the amount of value each must give up to complete the exchange.[2] However, it is a mistake to believe that price is always money paid. In fact, trading of products—**barter**—is the oldest form of exchange. Money may or may not be involved.

Buyers' interest in price stems from their expectations about the usefulness of a product or the satisfaction they may derive from it. Because buyers have limited resources, they must allocate these resources so that they can obtain the most desired products. Buyers must decide whether the utility gained in an exchange is worth the buying power sacrificed. Almost anything of value—ideas, services, rights, and goods—can be assessed by a price. In our society, financial price is the measurement of value commonly used in exchanges.

Terms Used to Describe Price

Value can be expressed in different terms for different marketing situations. For instance, students pay *tuition* for a college education. Automobile insurance companies charge a *premium* for protection from the cost of injuries or repairs stemming from an automobile accident. An officer who stops you for speeding writes a ticket that requires you to pay a *fine*. If a lawyer defends you, a *fee* is charged, and if you use a railway or taxi, a *fare* is charged. A *toll* is charged for the use of bridges or toll roads. *Rent* is paid for the use of equipment or an apartment. A *commission* is remitted to a broker for the sale of real estate. *Dues* are paid for membership in a club or group. A *deposit* is made to hold or lay away merchandise. A *tip* helps pay waitpersons for their services. *Interest* is charged for a loan, and *taxes* are paid for government services. Although price may be expressed in a variety of ways, the purpose of price is to quantify and express the value of the items in a marketing exchange.

The Importance of Price to Marketers

As pointed out in Chapter 11, developing a product may be a lengthy process. It takes time to plan promotion and to communicate benefits. Distribution usually requires a long-term commitment to dealers that will handle the product. Often, price is the only thing a marketer can change quickly to respond to changes in demand or to the actions of competitors. Under certain circumstances, however, the price variable may be relatively inflexible.

Price is a key element in the marketing mix because it relates directly to the generation of total revenue. The following equation is an important one for the entire organization.

$$\text{Profit} = \text{Total Revenue} - \text{Total Costs}$$
$$\text{or}$$
$$\text{Profits} = (\text{Price} \times \text{Quantity Sold}) - \text{Total Costs}$$

Prices affect an organization's profits in several ways since price is a major component of the profit equation and can be a major determinant of the quantities sold. Furthermore, total costs are influenced by quantities sold.

Because price has a psychological impact on customers, marketers can use it symbolically. By pricing high, they can emphasize the quality of a product and try to increase the prestige associated with its ownership. By lowering a price, marketers can emphasize a bargain and attract customers who go out of their way to save a small amount of money. Thus, as this chapter details, price can have a strong effect on a firm's sales and profitability.

Price and Nonprice Competition

The competitive environment strongly influences the marketing mix decisions associated with a product. Pricing decisions are often made according to the price or nonprice competitive situation in a particular market. Price competition exists when consumers have difficulty distinguishing competitive offerings and marketers emphasize low prices. Nonprice competition involves a focus on marketing mix elements other than price.

Price Competition

price competition
Emphasizing price and matching or beating competitors' prices

When engaging in **price competition,** a marketer emphasizes price as an issue and matches or beats the prices of competitors. To compete effectively on a price basis, a firm should be the low-cost seller of the product. If all firms producing the same product charge the same price for it, the firm with the lowest costs is the most profitable. Firms that stress low price as a key marketing mix element tend to market standardized products. A seller competing on price may change prices frequently or at least must be willing and able to do so. Whenever competitors change their prices, the seller usually responds quickly and aggressively.

Price competition gives a marketer flexibility. Prices can be altered to account for changes in the firm's costs or in demand for the product. If competitors try to gain market share by cutting prices, an organization competing on a price basis can react quickly to such efforts. However, a major drawback of price competition is that competitors, too, have the flexibility to adjust their prices. If they quickly match or beat a company's price cuts, a price war may ensue. Chronic price wars, such as those in the airline industry, can substantially weaken organizations.

Nonprice Competition

nonprice competition
Emphasizing factors other than price to distinguish a product from competing brands

Nonprice competition occurs when a seller decides not to focus on price and instead emphasizes distinctive product features, service, product quality, promotion, packaging, or other factors to distinguish its product from competing brands. Thus, nonprice competition allows a company to increase its brand's unit sales through means other than changing the brand's price. A major advantage of nonprice competition is that a firm can build customer loyalty toward its brand. If customers prefer a brand because of nonprice factors, they may not be easily lured away by competing firms and brands. In contrast, when price is the primary reason customers buy a particular brand, a competitor is able to attract these customers through price cuts. However, one study indicates that price is the primary consideration for only 15 to 35 percent of buyers in most product categories.[3]

Nonprice competition is workable under the right conditions. A company must be able to distinguish its brand through unique product features, higher product quality, promotion, packaging, or excellent customer service. For example, through research that included a survey of 2,000 motorists, Mobil determined that only about 20 percent of gasoline purchasers are highly price-sensitive. Based on this research, Mobil introduced its "friendly serve" concept, which includes free full service, immaculate restrooms, occasional free coffee or newspapers, and calling regular customers by name.[4] Buyers not only must be able to perceive these distinguishing characteristics; they must also view them as important. The distinguishing features that set a particular brand apart from its competitors should be difficult, if not impossible, for competitors to imitate. Finally, the organization must extensively promote the distinguishing characteristics of the brand to establish its superiority and to set it apart from competitors in the minds of buyers.

Still, a marketer trying to compete on a nonprice basis cannot simply ignore competitors' prices. It must be aware of them and will probably price its brand near or slightly above competing brands. Therefore, price remains a crucial marketing mix component even in environments that call for nonprice competition.

Pricing Objectives

pricing objectives
Overall goals that describe what a firm wants to achieve through pricing

Pricing objectives are overall goals that describe what a firm wants to achieve through pricing. Because pricing objectives influence decisions in many functional areas, including finance, accounting, and production, the objectives must be consistent with the organization's overall mission and goals. A marketer can use both short- and long-term pricing objectives, and can employ one or multiple pricing objectives. For instance, a firm may wish to increase market share by 18 percent over the next three years, achieve a 15 percent return on investment, and promote an image of quality in the marketplace. In this section, we examine a few of the pricing objectives that companies might set for themselves. The major pricing objectives and typical actions associated with them are shown in Table 20.1.

Survival

A fundamental pricing objective is survival. Most organizations will tolerate difficulties, such as short-run losses and internal upheaval, if they are necessary for survival. Because price is a flexible variable, it is sometimes used to keep a company afloat by

Table 20.1	Pricing Objectives and Typical Actions Taken to Achieve Them
Objective	**Possible Action**
Survival	Adjust price levels so that firm can increase sales volume to match organizational expenses
Profit	Identify price and cost levels that allow firm to maximize profit
Return on investment	Identify price levels that enable firm to yield targeted ROI
Market share	Adjust price levels so that firm can maintain or increase sales relative to competitors' sales
Cash flow	Set price levels to encourage rapid sales
Status quo	Identify price levels that help stabilize demand and sales
Product quality	Set prices to recover research and development expenditures and establish high-quality image

Figure 20.1
Profit as a Pricing Objective
By advocating the use of tiered pricing, the Washington Apple Commission urges grocers to set profit-oriented pricing objectives for apples.

increasing sales volume to levels that match expenses. For example, a women's apparel retailer may run a three-day, 60 percent-off sale to generate enough cash to pay creditors, employees, and the rent.

Profit

Although businesses may claim that their objective is to maximize profits for their owners, the objective of profit maximization is rarely operational because its achievement is difficult to measure. Because of this difficulty, profit objectives tend to be set at levels that the owners and top-level decision makers view as satisfactory. Specific profit objectives may be stated in terms of actual dollar amounts or in terms of percentage change relative to profits of a previous period. As shown in Figure 20.1, the Washington Apple Commission encourages grocers to set profit-related pricing objectives for apples and to employ tiered pricing.

Return on Investment

Pricing to attain a specified rate of return on a company's investment is a profit-related pricing objective. Most pricing objectives based on return on investment (ROI) are achieved by trial and error because not all cost and revenue data needed to project the return on investment are available when prices are set. General Motors uses ROI pricing objectives.

Market Share

Many firms establish pricing objectives to maintain or increase market share, which is a product's sales in relation to total industry sales. For example, both Quaker Oats and Malt-O-Meal have set a market share pricing objective for their ready-to-eat cereals. By packaging cereal in bags instead of boxes, these companies have been able to price cereal at about $1 less than competitors' prices. In an industry with declining sales, Malt-O-Meal's market share has risen from 2 percent to 4 percent, and Quaker's share has increased from 8 percent to over 10 percent.[5] Many firms recognize that high relative market shares often translate into higher profits. The Profit Impact of Market Strategies (PIMS) study conducted over the last twenty-five years has shown that both market share and product quality heavily influence profitability. Thus, marketers often use an increase in market share as a primary pricing objective.

Maintaining or increasing market share need not depend on growth in industry sales. Remember that an organization can increase its market share even though sales for the total industry are decreasing. On the other hand, an organization's sales volume may increase while its market share decreases if the overall market is growing.

Cash Flow

Some organizations set prices so they can recover cash as fast as possible. Financial managers are understandably interested in quickly recovering capital spent to develop products. This objective may have the support of a marketing manager who anticipates a short product life cycle.

Although it may be acceptable in some situations, the use of cash flow and recovery as an objective oversimplifies the value of price in contributing to profits. If this pricing objective results in high prices, competitors with lower prices may gain a large share of the market.

Status Quo

In some cases, an organization may be in a favorable position and, desiring nothing more, may set an objective of status quo. Status quo objectives can focus on several dimensions: maintaining a certain market share, meeting (but not beating) competitors' prices, achieving price stability, and maintaining a favorable public image. A status quo pricing objective can reduce a firm's risks by helping stabilize demand for its products. The use of status quo pricing objectives sometimes minimizes pricing as a competitive tool, leading to a climate of nonprice competition in an industry.

Product Quality

A company may have the objective of leading its industry in product quality. This goal normally dictates a high price to cover the high product quality and, in some instances, the high cost of research and development. For example, Moen faucets and Mercedes-Benz cars are priced to reflect and emphasize high product quality (see Figure 20.2). As previously mentioned, the PIMS study has shown that both product quality and market share are good indicators of profitability. The products and brands that customers perceive to be of high quality are more likely to survive in a competi-

Figure 20.2
Using Product Quality as a Pricing Objective
Moen faucets and Mercedes-Benz automobiles are high-quality products that are priced to reflect this level of quality.

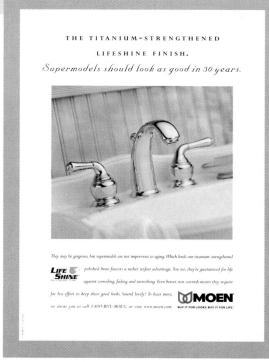

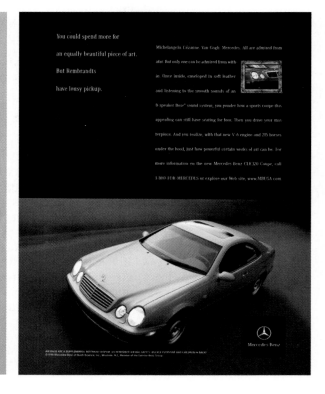

tive marketplace. High quality usually enables a marketer to charge higher prices for the product. For example, by setting the price of the MACH3 razor at approximately 35 percent above the Sensor price, Gillette clearly communicates that the MACH3 is a high-quality product. The premium prices on Pampers Premium and Huggies Supreme diapers signal high product quality to customers.[6]

Factors Affecting Pricing Decisions

Pricing decisions can be complex because of the number of factors that must be considered. Frequently, there is considerable uncertainty about the reactions to price on the part of buyers, channel members, and competitors. Price is also an important consideration in marketing planning, market analysis, and sales forecasting. It is a major issue when assessing a brand's position relative to the position of competing brands. Most factors that affect pricing decisions can be grouped into one of the eight categories shown in Figure 20.3. In this section, we explore how each of these eight groups of factors enters into price decision making.

Organizational and Marketing Objectives

Marketers should set prices that are consistent with the organization's goals and mission. For example, a retailer trying to position itself as value-oriented may wish to set prices that are quite reasonable relative to product quality. In this case, a marketer would not want to set premium prices on products but would strive to price products in line with this overall organizational goal.

Pricing decisions should also be compatible with the organization's marketing objectives. Say, for instance, that one of a producer's marketing objectives is a 12 percent increase in unit sales by the end of the next year. Assuming that buyers are price-sensitive, increasing the price or setting a price above the average market price would not be in line with this objective.

Types of Pricing Objectives

The type of pricing objectives a marketer uses obviously has considerable bearing on the determination of prices. An objective of a certain return on investment requires that prices be set at a level that will generate a sales volume high enough to yield the specified return. A market share pricing objective usually causes a firm to price a

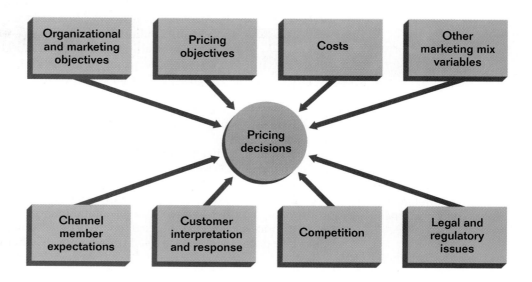

Figure 20.3
Factors That Affect Pricing Decisions

product below competing brands of similar quality to attract competitors' customers to the company's brand. A marketer sometimes uses temporary price reductions in the hope of gaining market share. A cash flow pricing objective may cause an organization to set a relatively high price, which can place the product at a competitive disadvantage. However, this type of objective is more likely to be addressed by using temporary price reductions, such as sales, rebates, and special discounts.

Costs

Clearly, costs must be an issue when establishing price. A firm may temporarily sell products below cost to match competition, to generate cash flow, or even to increase market share, but in the long run it cannot survive by selling its products below cost. Even when a firm has a high-volume business, it cannot survive if each item is sold slightly below what it costs. A marketer should be careful to analyze all costs so that they can be included in the total cost associated with a product.

To maintain market share and revenue in an increasingly price-sensitive market, many marketers have concentrated on reducing costs. As shown in Figure 20.4, Grainger Integrated Supply Operations helps its customers control their costs, which in turn affects Grainger's customers' prices. Labor-saving technologies, a focus on quality, and efficient manufacturing processes have brought productivity gains that translate into reduced costs and lower prices for customers. In an industry ravaged by labor concerns and monetary losses, Southwest Airlines has managed to stay one step ahead of its larger rivals. Southwest is the low-fare leader on more of the top one hundred routes in the United States than the three largest airlines, American, Delta, and United. One reason for the Texas-based airline's success is its ability to control costs. Southwest's per-seat mile costs are considerably less than those of American, United, and Delta.

Besides considering the costs associated with a particular product, marketers must also take into account the costs that the product shares with others in the product line. Products often share some costs, particularly the costs of research and development, production, and distribution. Most marketers view a product's cost as a minimum, or floor, below which the product cannot be priced. We discuss cost analysis in more detail in Chapter 21.

Other Marketing Mix Variables

All marketing mix variables are highly interrelated. Pricing decisions can influence decisions and activities associated with product, distribution, and promotion variables. A product's price frequently affects the demand for the item. A high price, for instance, may result in low unit sales, which in turn may lead to higher production costs per unit. Conversely, lower per-unit production costs may result from a low price. For many products, buyers associate better product quality with a high price and poorer product quality with a low price. This perceived price/quality relationship influences customers' overall image of products or brands. Sony, for example, prices its television sets higher than average to help communicate that Sony television sets are high-quality electronic products. Consumers recognize the Sony brand name, its reputation for quality, and the prestige associated with buying the product. Individuals who associate quality with a high price are likely to purchase products with well-established and recognizable brand names.[7]

The price of a product is linked to several dimensions of its distribution. Premium-priced products are often marketed through selective or exclusive distribution; lower-

Figure 20.4
Cost as a Major Pricing Consideration
Grainger Integrated Supply Operations assists its customers in controlling their costs, which in turn affects Grainger's customers' prices.

priced products in the same product category may be sold through intensive distribution. For example, Cross pens are distributed through selective distribution, and Bic pens through intensive distribution. When setting a price, the profit margins of marketing channel members, such as wholesalers and retailers, must be considered. Channel members must be adequately compensated for the functions they perform.

Price may determine how a product is promoted. Bargain prices are often included in advertisements. Premium prices are less likely to be advertised, though they are sometimes included in advertisements for upscale items, such as luxury cars or fine jewelry. Higher-priced products are more likely than lower-priced ones to require personal selling. Furthermore, the price structure can affect a salesperson's relationship with customers. A complex pricing structure takes longer to explain to customers, is more likely to confuse the potential buyer, and may cause misunderstandings that result in long-term customer dissatisfaction. For example, the pricing structures of many airlines are complex and frequently confuse ticket sales agents and travelers alike.

Channel Member Expectations

When making price decisions, a producer must consider what members of the distribution channel expect. A channel member certainly expects to receive a profit for the functions it performs. The amount of profit expected depends on what the intermediary could make if it were handling a competing product instead. Also, the amount of time and the resources required to carry the product influence intermediaries' expectations.

Channel members often expect producers to give discounts for large orders and prompt payment. At times, resellers expect producers to provide several support activities, such as sales training, service training, repair advisory service, cooperative advertising, sales promotions, and perhaps a program for returning unsold merchandise to the producer. These support activities clearly have costs associated with them, and a producer must consider these costs when determining prices.

Customers' Interpretation and Response

When making pricing decisions, marketers should be concerned with a vital question: How will our customers interpret our prices and respond to them? *Interpretation* in this context refers to what the price means or what it communicates to customers. Does the price mean "high quality" or "low quality," "great deal," "fair price," or "rip off"? Customer *response* refers to whether the price will move customers closer to the purchase of the product and the degree to which the price enhances their satisfaction with the purchase experience and with the product after purchase.

Customers' interpretation of a price and response to it are to some degree determined by their assessment of what they receive compared with what they give up in order to make the purchase. In evaluating what is received, customers will consider product attributes, benefits, advantages, disadvantages, the probability of using the product, and possibly status associated with the product. In assessing the cost of the product, customers likely will consider the product's price, the amount of time and effort required to obtain the product, and perhaps the resources required to maintain it after purchase.

At times, customers interpret a higher price as higher product quality. They are especially likely to make this price-quality association when they cannot judge the quality of the product themselves. This is not always the case, however; whether price is viewed as a surrogate for quality depends on the types of customers and products involved. Obviously, marketers that rely on customers' making a price-quality association and that provide moderate- or low-quality products at high prices will be unable to build long-term customer relationships.

When interpreting and responding to prices, how do customers determine if the price is too high, too low, or about right? In general, they compare prices with

Figure 20.5
Value-Conscious
Customers
Many of Biscuitville's customers are very likely to be value-conscious.

internal reference price
Price developed in the buyer's mind through experience with the product

external reference price
Comparison price provided by others

internal or external reference prices. An **internal reference price** is a price developed in the buyer's mind through experience with the product. It is a belief that a product should cost approximately a certain amount. As consumers, our experiences have given each of us internal reference prices for a number of products. For example, most of us have a reasonable idea of how much to pay for a six-pack of soft drinks, a loaf of bread, or a gallon of milk. For the product categories in which we are less experienced, we rely more heavily on external reference prices. An **external reference price** is a comparison price provided by others, such as retailers or manufacturers. For example, a retailer in an advertisement might state "while this product is sold for $100 elsewhere, our price is only $39.95." Customers' perceptions of prices are also influenced by their expectations about future price increases, by what they paid for the product recently, and by what they would like to pay for the product. Other factors affecting customers' perception of whether the price is right include time or financial constraints, the costs associated with searching for lower-priced products, and expectations that products will go on sale.

Buyers' perceptions of a product relative to competing products may allow a firm to set a price that differs significantly from the prices of competing products. If the product is deemed superior to most of the competition, a premium price may be feasible. However, even products with superior quality can be overpriced. Columbia Sportswear had to discontinue its upscale youth sportswear line because it was priced too high.[8] Strong brand loyalty sometimes provides the opportunity to charge a premium price. On the other hand, if buyers view a product unfavorably (though not extremely negatively), a lower price may generate sales.

Buyers can be characterized according to their degree of value consciousness, price consciousness, and prestige sensitivity. Marketers who understand these characteristics are better able to set pricing objectives and policies. **Value-conscious** consumers are concerned about both price and quality of a product. Customers who eat at Biscuitville (see Figure 20.5) are very likely to be value-conscious consumers. **Price-conscious** individuals strive to pay low prices. Individuals who are **prestige-sensitive** focus on purchasing products that signify prominence and status.[9]

value-conscious
Concerned about price and quality of a product

price-conscious
Striving to pay low prices

prestige-sensitive
Drawn to products that signify prominence and status

Competition

A marketer needs to know competitors' prices so that the firm can adjust its own prices accordingly. This does not mean that a company will necessarily match competitors' prices; it may set its price above or below theirs. However, for some organizations (such as airlines), matching competitors' prices is an important strategy for survival.

When adjusting prices, a marketer must assess how competitors will respond. Will competitors change their prices and, if so, will they raise or lower them? In Chapter 3, we described several types of competitive market structures. The structure that characterizes the industry to which a firm belongs affects the flexibility of price setting. For example, because of reduced pricing regulation, firms in the telecommunications industry have moved from a monopolistic market structure to an oligopolistic one, which has resulted in significant price flexibility and price competition. See Marketing Citizenship for a discussion of win-win approaches to price negotiations.

When an organization operates as a monopoly and is unregulated, it can set whatever prices the market will bear. However, the company may not price the product at the highest possible level to avoid government regulation or to penetrate a market by using a lower price. If the monopoly is regulated, it normally has less pricing flexibility; the regulatory body lets it set prices that generate a reasonable, but not excessive, return. A government-owned monopoly may price products below cost to make them accessible to people who otherwise could not afford them. Transit systems, for example, sometimes operate this way. However, government-owned monopolies sometimes charge higher prices to control demand. In some states with state-owned liquor stores, the price of liquor is higher than in states where liquor stores are not owned by a government body.

The automotive, mainframe-computer, and steel industries exemplify oligopolies, in which there are only a few sellers and the barriers to competitive entry are high. A company in such industries can raise its price, hoping that its competitors will do the same. When an organization cuts its price to gain a competitive edge, other companies

MARKETING CITIZENSHIP

Making Price Negotiation a Win-Win Proposition

The often unpleasant process of negotiating the price of a car or truck makes many consumers and organizational customers want to avoid price negotiations altogether. By the time marketers and customers finish negotiating price, one side may feel taken advantage of, while the other wonders just how good the deal really is. Neither reaction leads to a positive long-term relationship. But experts say both sides can feel like winners if they understand how negotiation works and do their homework in advance.

First, the participants should establish their own priorities. What do they want from this price negotiation, and what are they willing to give up? Is just-in-time delivery or customization ultimately more important than price? If a mutually acceptable price cannot be negotiated, what other alternatives are available?

Next, each participant must learn as much as possible about the other side's circumstances and viewpoint. What is the other participant seeking from this negotiation, and why? How does the other side tend to negotiate? Taking time to understand the other party's situation shows respect—and it puts participants in a better position to come to a win-win agreement. "The goal is not to destroy the other side," stresses a lawyer who negotiates contracts for sports stars. "The goal is to find the most profitable way to complete a deal that works for *both* sides."

Once negotiations start, both sides should remember that price is purely a business issue. Any successful outcome will be undermined by judgmental comments and personal attacks. In productive negotiations, participants focus on the points that best meet the needs of both sides. If neither party wants to budge on a particular point, taking a break, offering a more creative option, or simply discussing another point can keep negotiations moving toward a win-win outcome. In the end, says the sports lawyer, "It's *never* acceptable if you lie to or mislead someone—that's the one thing that can destroy what we do."

are likely to follow suit. Thus, very little advantage is gained through price cuts in an oligopolistic market structure.

A market structure characterized by monopolistic competition has numerous sellers with differentiated product offerings. The products are differentiated by physical characteristics, features, quality, and brand images. The distinguishing characteristics of its product may allow a company to set a different price than its competitors. However, firms in a monopolistic competitive market structure are likely to practice nonprice competition, discussed earlier in this chapter.

Under conditions of perfect competition, there are many sellers. Buyers view all sellers' products as the same. All firms sell their products at the going market price, and buyers will not pay more than that. This type of market structure, then, gives a marketer no flexibility in setting prices. Farming as an industry has some of the characteristics of perfect competition. Farmers sell their products at the going market price. Recently, corn, soybean, and wheat growers have had bumper crops and have been forced to sell them at depressed market prices.[10] See Tech*know for a discussion of the pressures that are pushing prices ever lower in the high-tech wireless communications markets.

Legal and Regulatory Issues

As discussed in Chapter 3, legal and regulatory issues influence pricing decisions. To curb inflation, the federal government can invoke price controls, freeze prices at certain levels, or determine the rates at which prices may be increased. In some states, regulatory agencies set prices on such products as insurance, dairy products, and liquor.

Many regulations and laws affect pricing decisions and activities. The Sherman Antitrust Act prohibits conspiracies to control prices, and in interpreting the act, courts have ruled that price fixing among firms in an industry is illegal. Marketers must refrain from fixing prices by developing independent pricing policies and setting prices in ways that do not even suggest collusion. Both the Federal Trade Commission Act and

Tech*know

Price Cuts in Cutting-Edge Communications

Pricing of high-tech products tends to follow a particular pattern, starting out on the high end for new products and then dropping quickly as competitors enter the market and cut prices to fuel faster adoption. So it goes in the fast-changing world of wireless communications, where the price of cellular phone service is dropping precipitously as rivals aggressively court customers who want to stay in touch anytime and anywhere. Already, 66.5 million U.S. customers have gone wireless, and that number is expected to balloon to 110 million by 2002. With a growing number of businesses and consumers cutting the cord and using cellular phones, telecommunications companies are using pricing to increase their share of this burgeoning market.

Customers are the big winners as wireless communications companies jockey for position and aggressively promote lower prices. In just one year, the price of cellular phone service fell 11 percent, with customers hopping from company to company in search of ever-lower cellular phone bills. Although the average price for cellular phone usage is 44 cents per minute, some companies are offering an all-inclusive rate of 10 cents per minute. How low can companies go? There may be even more dramatic price cuts, up to 20 percent per year. "Price will hemorrhage over the next two years," predicts one competitor. "We think you'll see 3 cents a minute in the near future."

Competing in the wireless world means major investments. Telecommunications giants like AT&T and Sprint have spent heavily to put up wireless towers so that their U.S. customers can use wireless service in virtually any corner of the country. Now, with downward pressure on pricing, "roaming charges" (levied when customers leave designated service regions) and long-distance charges are starting to disappear in favor of single, all-inclusive rates, some, as we've noted, as low as 10 cents a minute. These pricing changes are not only bringing competition to a rapid boil; they also are making bills for cellular service much simpler to decipher—and much easier on the customer's wallet.

Table 20.2	Discounts Used for Organizational Markets	
Type	**Reasons for Use**	**Examples**
Trade (Functional)	To attract and keep effective resellers by compensating them for performing certain functions, such as transportation, warehousing, selling, and providing credit	A college bookstore pays about one-third less for a new textbook than the retail price paid by a student who purchases the book.
Quantity	To encourage customers to buy large quantities when making purchases, and in the case of cumulative discounts, to encourage customer loyalty	Large department store chains purchase some women's apparel at lower prices than do individually owned specialty stores.
Cash	To reduce expenses associated with accounts receivable and collection by encouraging prompt payment of accounts	Numerous companies serving organizational markets allow a 2% discount if an account is paid within 10 days.
Seasonal	To allow a marketer to use resources more efficiently by stimulating sales during off-peak periods	Florida hotels provide companies holding national and regional sales meetings with deeply discounted accommodations during the summer months.
Allowance	In the case of a trade-in allowance, to assist the buyer in making the purchase and also because the resale of used equipment may be profitable; in the case of a promotional allowance, to ensure that dealers participate in advertising and sales support programs	A farm equipment dealer takes a farmer's used tractor as a trade-in on a new one. Nabisco pays a promotional allowance to a supermarket for setting up and maintaining a large, end-of-aisle display for a two-week period.

the Wheeler-Lea Act prohibit deceptive pricing. In establishing prices, marketers must guard against deceiving customers.

The Robinson-Patman Act has had a strong impact on pricing decisions. For various reasons, marketers may wish to sell the same type of product at different prices. Provisions in the Robinson-Patman Act, as well as those in the Clayton Act, limit the use of such price differentials. The practice of providing price differentials that tend to injure competition by giving one or more buyers a competitive advantage over other buyers is called **price discrimination;** it is prohibited by law. However, not all price differentials are discriminatory. Marketers can use price differentials if they do not hinder competition, if they result from differences in the costs of selling or transportation to various customers, or if they arise because the firm has had to cut its price to a particular buyer to meet competitors' prices.

price discrimination
Providing price differentials that injure competition by giving one or more buyers a competitive advantage

Pricing for Organizational Markets

Organizational markets consist of individuals and organizations that purchase products for resale, for use in their own operations, or for producing other products. Establishing prices for this category of buyers is sometimes different from setting prices for consumers. Differences in the size of purchases, geographic factors, and transportation considerations require sellers to adjust prices. In this section, we discuss several issues unique to the pricing of organizational products: discounts, geographic pricing, and transfer pricing.

Price Discounting

Producers commonly provide intermediaries with discounts, or reductions, from list prices. Although there are many types of discounts, they usually fall into one of five categories: trade, quantity, cash, seasonal, and allowance. Table 20.2 summarizes some reasons to use each type of discount and provides examples.

trade, or functional, discount A reduction off the list price given by a producer to an intermediary for performing certain functions

quantity discounts Deductions from list price for purchasing large quantities

cumulative discounts Quantity discounts aggregated over a stated period

noncumulative discounts One-time reductions in price based on specific factors

cash discount A price reduction given to buyers for prompt payment or cash payment

Trade Discounts   A reduction off the list price given by a producer to an intermediary for performing certain functions is called a **trade,** or **functional, discount.** A trade discount is usually stated in terms of a percentage or series of percentages off the list price. Intermediaries are given trade discounts as compensation for performing various functions, such as selling, transporting, storing, final processing, and perhaps providing credit services. Although certain trade discounts are often a standard practice within an industry, discounts do vary considerably among industries. It is important that a manufacturer provide a trade discount large enough to offset the intermediary's costs, plus a reasonable profit, to entice the reseller to carry the product.

Quantity Discounts   Deductions from list price that reflect the economies of purchasing in large quantities are called **quantity discounts.** Quantity discounts are used to pass to the buyer cost savings gained through economies of scale.

Quantity discounts can be either cumulative or noncumulative. **Cumulative discounts** are quantity discounts aggregated over a stated time period. Purchases totaling $10,000 in a three-month period, for example, might entitle the buyer to a 5 percent, or $500, rebate. Such discounts are supposed to reflect economies in selling and to encourage the buyer to purchase from one seller. **Noncumulative discounts** are one-time reductions in prices based on the number of units purchased, the dollar value of the order, or the product mix purchased. Like cumulative discounts, these discounts should reflect some economies in selling or trade functions.

Cash Discounts   A **cash discount,** or price reduction, is given to a buyer for prompt payment or cash payment. Accounts receivable are an expense and a collection problem for many organizations. A policy to encourage prompt payment is a popular practice and sometimes a major concern in setting prices.

Discounts are based on cash payments or cash paid within a stated time. For example, "2/10 net 30" means that a 2 percent discount will be allowed if the account is paid within ten days. If the buyer does not make payment within the ten-day period, the entire balance is due within thirty days without a discount. If the account is not paid within thirty days, interest may be charged.

SNAPSHOT

Discounts for organizational markets

Where small businesses find discounts

Telephone rates	67%
Office supplies	42%
Overnight delivery	37%
Health insurance	33%

seasonal discount A price reduction given to buyers for purchasing goods or services out of season

allowance A concession in price to achieve a desired goal

Seasonal Discounts   A price reduction to buyers who purchase goods or services out of season is a **seasonal discount.** These discounts let the seller maintain steadier production during the year. For example, automobile rental agencies offer seasonal discounts in winter and early spring to encourage firms to use automobiles during the slow months of the automobile rental business.

Allowances   Another type of reduction from the list price is an **allowance,** or concession in price to achieve a desired goal. Trade-in allowances, for example, are price reductions granted for turning in a used item when purchasing a new one. Allowances help give the buyer the ability to make the new purchase. This type of discount is popular in the aircraft industry. Another example is a promotional allowance, which is a price reduction granted to dealers for participating in advertising and sales support programs intended to increase sales of a particular item.

geographic pricing Reductions for transportation and other costs related to the physical distance between buyer and seller

f.o.b. factory The price of the merchandise at the factory, before shipment

Geographic Pricing

Geographic pricing involves reductions for transportation costs or other costs associated with the physical distance between the buyer and the seller. Prices may be quoted as being F.O.B. (free-on-board) factory or destination. An **F.O.B. factory** price

f.o.b. destination A price indicating that the producer is absorbing shipping costs

indicates the price of the merchandise at the factory, before it is loaded onto the carrier, and thus excludes transportation costs. The buyer must pay for shipping. An **F.O.B. destination** price means that the producer absorbs the costs of shipping the merchandise to the customer. This policy may be used to attract distant customers. Although F.O.B. pricing is an easy way to price products, it is sometimes difficult for marketers to administer, especially when a firm has a wide product mix or when customers are dispersed widely. Because customers will want to know about the most economical method of shipping, the seller must be informed about shipping rates.

uniform geographic pricing Charging all customers the same price, regardless of geographic location

To avoid the problems involved in charging different prices to each customer, **uniform geographic pricing,** sometimes called postage-stamp pricing, may be used. The same price is charged to all customers regardless of geographic location, and the price is based on average shipping costs for all customers. Gasoline, paper products, and office equipment are often priced on a uniform basis (see Figure 20.6).

zone pricing Pricing based on transportation costs within major geographic zones

Zone pricing sets uniform prices for each of several major geographic zones; as the transportation costs across zones increase, so do the prices. For example, a Florida manufacturer's prices may be higher for buyers on the Pacific Coast and in Canada than for buyers in Georgia.

base-point pricing Geographic pricing combining factory price and freight charges from the base point nearest the buyer

Base-point pricing is a geographic pricing policy that includes the price at the factory, plus freight charges from the base point nearest the buyer. This approach to pricing has virtually been abandoned because its legal status has been questioned. The policy resulted in all buyers paying freight charges from one location, such as Detroit or Pittsburgh, regardless of where the product was manufactured.

freight absorption pricing Absorption of all or part of the actual freight costs by the seller

When the seller absorbs all or part of the actual freight costs, **freight absorption pricing** is being used. The seller might choose this method because it wishes to do business with a particular customer or to get more business; more business will cause the average cost to fall and counterbalance the extra freight cost. This strategy is used to improve market penetration and to retain a hold in an increasingly competitive market.

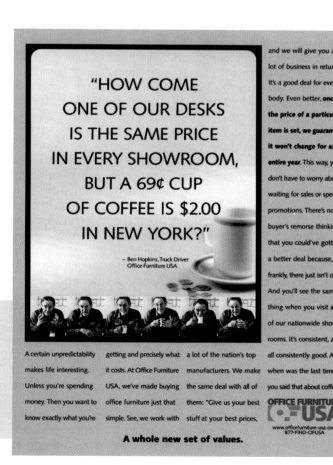

Figure 20.6
Uniform Geographic Pricing
Office Furniture U.S.A. uses uniform geographic pricing, meaning that all its customers pay exactly the same price for the same product items.

Transfer Pricing

When one unit in an organization sells a product to another unit, **transfer pricing** occurs. The price is determined by one of the following methods:

Actual full cost: calculated by dividing all fixed and variable expenses for a period into the number of units produced

Standard full cost: calculated on what it would cost to produce the goods at full plant capacity

Cost plus investment: calculated as full cost, plus the cost of a portion of the selling unit's assets used for internal needs

Market-based cost: calculated at the market price less a small discount to reflect the lack of sales effort and other expenses

The choice of a method of transfer pricing depends on the company's management strategy and the nature of the units' interaction. An organization must also ensure that transfer pricing is fair to all units involved in the purchases.

Summary

Price is the value exchanged for products in marketing transactions. Price is not always money paid; barter, the trading of products, is the oldest form of exchange. Price is a key element in the marketing mix because it relates directly to the generation of total revenue. The profit factor can be determined mathematically by multiplying price by quantity sold to get total revenue, and then subtracting total costs. Price is the only variable in the marketing mix that can be adjusted quickly and easily to respond to changes in the external environment.

A product offering can compete on either a price or a nonprice basis. Price competition emphasizes price as the product differential. Prices fluctuate frequently, and price competition among sellers is aggressive. Nonprice competition emphasizes product differentiation through distinctive features, service, product quality, or other factors. Establishing brand loyalty by using nonprice competition works best when the product can be physically differentiated and the customer can recognize these differences.

Pricing objectives are overall goals that describe the role of price in a firm's long-range plans. The most fundamental pricing objective is the organization's survival. Price usually can be easily adjusted to increase sales volume or to combat competition so that the organization can stay alive. Profit objectives, which are usually stated in terms of sales dollar volume or percentage change, are normally set at a satisfactory level rather than at a level designed for profit maximization. A sales growth objective focuses on increasing the profit base by increasing sales volume. Pricing for return on investment (ROI) has a specified profit as its objective. A pricing objective to maintain or increase market share implies that market position is linked to success. Other types of pricing objectives include cash flow, status quo, and product quality.

Eight factors enter into price decision making: organizational and marketing objectives, pricing objectives, costs, other marketing mix variables, channel member expectations, customer interpretation and response, competition, and legal and regulatory issues. When setting prices, marketers should make decisions consistent with the organization's goals and mission. Pricing objectives heavily influence price-setting decisions. Most marketers view a product's cost as the floor below which a product cannot be priced. Because of the interrelation of the marketing mix variables, price can affect product, promotion, and distribution decisions. The revenue that channel members expect for their functions must also be considered when making price decisions.

Buyers' perceptions of price vary. Some consumer segments are sensitive to price, but others may not be; thus, before determining price, a marketer needs to be aware of its importance to the target market. Knowledge of the prices charged for competing brands is essential so that the firm can adjust its prices relative to those of competitors. Government regulations and legislation influence pricing decisions. Congress has enacted several laws to enhance competition in the marketplace by outlawing price fixing and deceptive pricing. Legislation also restricts price differentials that injure competition. Moreover, the government can invoke price controls to curb inflation.

Unlike consumers, organizational buyers purchase products for resale, for use in their own operations, or for producing other products. When adjusting prices, organizational sellers take into consideration the size of the purchase, geographic factors, and transportation requirements. Producers commonly provide discounts off list prices to intermediaries. The categories of discounts include trade, quantity, cash, seasonal, and allowance. A trade discount is a price reduction for performing such functions as storing, transporting, final processing, or providing credit services. If an intermediary purchases in large enough quantities, the producer gives a quantity discount, which can be either cumulative or noncumulative. A cash discount is a price reduction for prompt payment or payment in cash. Buyers who purchase goods or services out of season may be granted a seasonal discount. A final type of reduction from the list price is an allowance, such as a trade-in allowance.

Geographic pricing involves reductions for transportation costs or other costs associated with the physical distance between the buyer and the seller. A price

quoted as F.O.B. factory means that the buyer pays for shipping from the factory. An F.O.B. destination price means that the producer pays for shipping; this is the easiest way to price products, but it is difficult for marketers to administer. When the seller charges a fixed average cost for transportation, the practice is known as uniform geographic pricing. Zone prices are uniform within major geographic zones; they increase by zone as the transportation costs increase. Basepoint pricing resembles zone pricing; prices are adjusted for shipping expenses incurred by the seller from the base point nearest the buyer. A seller who absorbs all or part of the freight costs is using freight absorption pricing.

Important Terms

Price
Barter
Price competition
Nonprice competition
Pricing objectives
Internal reference price
External reference price

Value-conscious
Price-conscious
Prestige-sensitive
Price discrimination
Trade, or functional, discount
Quantity discounts

Cumulative discounts
Noncumulative discounts
Cash discount
Seasonal discount
Allowance
Geographic pricing
F.O.B. factory

F.O.B. destination
Uniform geographic pricing
Zone pricing
Base-point pricing
Freight absorption pricing
Transfer pricing

Discussion and Review Questions

1. Why are pricing decisions so important to an organization?
2. Compare and contrast price and nonprice competition. Describe the conditions under which each form works best.
3. How does a return on investment pricing objective differ from an objective to increase market share?
4. Why must marketing objectives and pricing objectives be considered when making pricing decisions?
5. In what ways do other marketing mix variables affect pricing decisions?
6. What types of expectations may channel members have about producers' prices, and how do these expectations affect pricing decisions?
7. How do legal and regulatory forces influence pricing decisions?
8. Compare and contrast a trade discount and a quantity discount.
9. What is the reason for using the term *F.O.B.?*
10. What are the major methods used for transfer pricing?

Application Questions

1. Price competition is evident in the fast-food, air travel, and personal computer industries. Discuss a recent situation in which companies had to meet or beat a competitor's price in a price competitive industry. Did you benefit from this situation? Did it change your perception of the companies and/or their products?
2. Customers' interpretation and response regarding a product and its price are an important influence on marketers' pricing decisions. Perceptions of price are affected by the degree to which a customer is value-conscious, price-conscious, or prestige-sensitive. Discuss how value consciousness, price conscious-

ness, and prestige sensitivity influence the buying decision process for the following products:
   a. a new house
   b. weekly groceries for a family of five
   c. an airline ticket
   d. a soft drink from a vending machine
3. Organizations often use multiple pricing objectives. Locate an organization that uses several pricing objectives, and discuss how this approach influences marketing mix decisions. Are some objectives oriented toward the short term and others toward the long term? How does the marketing environment influence these objectives?

Internet Exercise & Resources

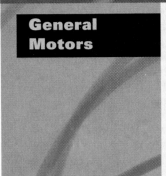

| **General Motors** | GM has developed a comprehensive Web site displaying all its products and providing information about dealers, prices, monthly payments, and the cost of leasing. It is possible to look at a specific model and configure the exact automobile you desire. Go to the GM Web site at |

www.gm.com/

1. Find the lowest-priced Saturn available today and examine its features. What Saturn dealership is closest to you?

2. If you wanted to purchase this Saturn, what are the lowest monthly payments you could make over the longest time period?

3. If you wanted to lease the Saturn, what would the monthly lease cost be?

E-Center Resources

Visit http://www.prideferrell.com to find several resources to help you succeed in mastering the material in this chapter, plus additional materials that will help you expand your marketing knowledge. The Web site includes

 Internet exercise updates plus additional exercises

 ACE self-tests

 abc Chapter summary with hotlinked glossary

 Hotlinks to companies featured in this chapter

 Resource Center

 Career Center

 Marketing plan worksheets

VIDEO CASE 20.1

Low Prices and Fun: The Winning Combination at Southwest Airlines

Southwest Airlines has a simple but profitable formula for success: low prices and lots of fun. The airline industry has long been plagued by fierce price wars, in which one carrier announces drastic price cuts only to have them matched or undercut by rivals. This downward pricing spiral has taken its toll on profits, throwing many airlines into a financial crisis. Between 1990 and 1992, airlines representing roughly 40 percent of the total capacity of the airline industry either ceased operations or filed for Chapter 11 bankruptcy protection. Most of the companies that managed to survive this brutally competitive period lost enormous sums of money. And the struggle goes on, with periodic price wars and new low-price carriers bringing turbulence to the industry.

Southwest Airlines, however, has managed to remain consistently profitable. Established as Air Southwest Company by Herb Kelleher and Rollin King in 1967, the airline originally planned to fly only within Texas, linking Dallas, San Antonio, and Houston with low-priced, frequent flights. Almost immediately, other airlines in the Texas market filed suit against the upstart, claiming that the market was already sufficiently served. After several years of legal maneuvering, the Texas Supreme Court ruled in favor of the newly renamed Southwest Airlines, and the company made its initial flight between Dallas and San Antonio. At the time, the fledgling carrier's fleet consisted of just three Boeing 737s.

Playing on the name of its home airport—Dallas's Love Field—Southwest weaves a "love" theme into its promotions and operations, even using "LUV" as the airline's stockmarket symbol. The love theme extends to close teamwork among employees, who speak of the Southwest "family" and pull together to keep flights running smoothly and on time. Never taking itself seriously, the airline is known for its quirky sense of humor; it may be the only U.S. company that actually requires its employees to laugh. This work-hard–play-hard corporate culture is fostered by CEO Herb Kelleher, who often stars in Southwest's humorous commercials.

For their part, frequent flyers and new customers alike love the airline because of its uncommonly low ticket prices. Studies by the U.S. Department of Transportation show that Southwest almost always offers the lowest fare between two cities; on the rare occasion that another airline undercuts Southwest, the price difference is only a few dollars. When Southwest experimented with a nonstop transcontinental flight between Baltimore and Oakland, California, priced at $99 for a one-way ticket, the plane quickly filled to capacity—and nearly half the passengers were taking their first Southwest flight. In recent years, Southwest has expanded its low-price offerings to serve Rhode Island, New York, and other East Coast destinations.

Low operating costs and no frills keep Southwest's ticket prices well below those of competing airlines. By flying just one type of plane (the Boeing 737), Southwest reduces its maintenance costs. The airline wrings the most productivity from its 261 planes by minimizing the turnaround time between flights. Flying to and from smaller airports means the planes waste less time waiting to take off or land, it also means the airline pays lower ground costs than it would at larger, more popular airports. On board, passengers get no meals (just peanuts), no movies, no seat assignments, and no first class. Instead, they get a seat, a smile, and an excellent chance of arriving on time.

An efficient fleet, low airport fees, and no-frills service give Southwest a major cost advantage over its competitors. On a 500-mile flight, Southwest's costs are well under 9 cents per passenger mile, whereas rivals spend close to 12 cents per passenger mile. Even on flights of 1,500 miles, Southwest maintains a cost advantage over other airlines. Lower costs help Southwest keep prices low, which in turn keeps its market share high.

Cost containment is part of the culture at Southwest. In fact, the CEO says he might never have become interested in expanding service to more distant locales had it not been for a recent change in federal taxes on airline tickets. Instead of a percentage tax, airlines now pay a flat fee per flight segment, which has the effect of taking a proportionately larger chunk out of lower fares. For this reason, Southwest has been increasing its number of flight segments that exceed 1,000 miles, thereby boosting its annual revenues beyond $4.2 billion and spreading its wings over several new markets.

When Southwest enters a new market, it uses a high-frequency schedule, which means that competitors brace for lower ticket prices—and the airports involved prepare for higher travel volume. Southwest's well-known low-fare policy brings in more passengers and cuts the average one-way fare in its new markets. For example, after the airline started flying out of Providence, Rhode Island—joined by Delta Express, a low-fare affiliate of Delta Airlines—the average one-way fare at that airport dropped by 70 percent—and passenger volume increased nearly tenfold. After entering a new market with especially low introductory fares, Southwest may raise its prices, while competitors may lower their fares to compete.

USAirways, United, Delta, Continental, and other airlines are now following Southwest's lead by offering low fares, on-time flights, and no-frills service. The entire industry is also enjoying lower fuel costs, which helps the bottom line all around. But only Southwest is zany enough to give away peanuts labeled "A complete airline meal in a nutshell." Winning awards for on-time performance, customer satisfaction, and efficient baggage handling keeps the airline's reputation flying high. And its emphasis on giving customers what they want and no more—low prices and basic but personal service with a smile—has made Southwest the industry's benchmark for thrifty operating costs and enviable profitability.[11]

Questions for Discussion

1. In an industry in which pricing has driven many companies out of business or into bankruptcy protection, why has Southwest Airlines been so successful in competing on the basis of price?
2. What are Southwest's primary pricing objectives?
3. What effects are Southwest's prices likely to have on internal reference prices for flights to and from the cities Southwest serves?
4. Discuss any possible negative aspects of Southwest's strategy of entering new markets with low prices.

CASE 20.2

Priceline.com Lets Customers Set Prices

One of Priceline.com's customers reports that he has used the company's "Leisure Airline Ticket" service five times. On two occasions, he offered to pay $225 for a roundtrip ticket from Washington state to Detroit, about $175 less than the lowest published advanced fare, and his bids were accepted. Priceline.com is the only service on the Internet that allows customers to name the price they are willing to pay for a ticket on a major airline, a hotel room, or a new car or truck. The company's system for buying and selling on the Internet is so original that the U.S. Patent and Trademark Office recently issued Priceline.com a patent. In its first four months of operation, the company sold 40,000 airline tickets and continues to attract over a million visitors a week. At peak times, it sells a ticket every seventy seconds.

Unsold airline seats and hotel rooms are wasted; they cannot be stored in warehouses for later sale. Although airlines and hotels would like to be able to lower prices when demand is low, these organizations would create problems for themselves if they were to sell their products for less than published rates. Enter Priceline.com, which provides an anonymous link between buyers and sellers. Priceline.com gives buyers an opportunity to obtain a price they can afford and sellers the chance to reduce waste if they accept a buyer's offer. Since planes fly with over 500,000 empty seats a day, waste and lost revenues are a major problem for airlines, and many have seen fit to take advantage of Priceline.com's service.

How does Priceline.com's airline ticket service work? Using the lowest available advance purchase fares as a guideline, customers go to Priceline's homepage, enter their itineraries and travel dates, and offer a price for a ticket. (They can also call the company's toll-free phone number. Travel must begin in the United States, and customers must be flexible in the time of day they are willing to travel, but destinations can be worldwide, and there are no blackout dates or advance purchase requirements. After receiving an offer, Priceline searches seat availability on the fifteen major domestic and international carriers participating in the service. Within one hour (one day for international flights), Priceline informs customers whether an airline is willing to release a seat for the offered fare. When travelers are unsuccessful, they can try again immediately by changing departing or arrival airports or travel dates. Whether a deal is struck or not, Priceline's service is free to the customer.

Shopping at Priceline.com sounds easy and economical, and most of its customers agree. Critics, however, point out that Priceline's airline ticket service has some drawbacks. In addition to committing themselves to fly at hours that will not be specified until after their offers are accepted, customers must be willing to take flights that may include up to one stop or connection and possibly a long layover. Tickets are nonrefundable, cannot be changed, and do not earn passengers any frequent-flyer miles. To test Priceline's service, reporters from *U.S. News and World Report* recently submitted bids for several itineraries starting from Washington, D.C. All were unsuccessful, including bids for $90 for a weekend flight to Chicago, $170 for a round-trip ticket to Buffalo, and $550 for a trip to Paris in July. The bottom line, assert these reporters, is that Priceline works best for people who must fly on short notice. Unable to meet advance purchase requirements, they can avoid paying top fares by securing a ticket through Priceline.com.

Customers can use Priceline.com's services to book hotel rooms in twelve major cities around the United States, including New York, Los Angeles, and Chicago. Customers tell Priceline the destination, dates, number of rooms, the desired quality level of the hotel (two, three, four, or five stars), and how much they are willing to pay a night. The customer must provide a credit card number that locks in the reservation if Priceline finds accommodations that meet the customer's criteria. Priceline then searches its database of participating hotels for one with an unadvertised rate at or below the customer's request, books the room, buys it from the hotel, and charges the customer $5 more than the price it paid. Because major cities have dozens of competitive hotels that routinely have unsold rooms, industry analysts predict that Priceline's hotel service will generate more seller interest than its other services do.

About ninety days after launching its airline ticket service, Priceline launched its "New-Car Buying Service." Going to the company's Web site, customers fill out an online "Priceline Vehicle Request," naming the exact vehicle they want, price they are willing to pay, date the car must be available, and how far they are willing to travel to pick it up. To help buyers submit reasonable requests, Priceline's Web site displays manufacturer's suggested retail prices and dealer invoices. Priceline contacts every authorized dealer in the customer's specified area, and the dealer can either accept the offer or submit a nonbinding counteroffer. Within one business day, Priceline E-mails the dealer's response to the customer. Once a dealer agrees to a price, the buyer receives an E-mail purchase agreement confirming the price, make, model, and options. When the sale is complete, the customer pays Priceline a $25 fee, and the dealer pays a $75 fee.

Priceline.com's popularity continues to soar. RelevantKnowledge, Inc., a leading provider of information about the Internet, recently named Priceline.com as one of the world's top ten commerce Web sites. Yahoo!Internet Life, recognized as the top guide to the best sites on the Web, gave Priceline.com its highest rating, calling it "the most creative way to get a good deal on leisure airline tickets." Priceline's founder and CEO believes his E-commerce system benefits consumers and plans to continue introducing name-your-own-price services. The newest addition is a home-mortgage service. Asserts the company's CEO, "Consumers will recognize Priceline.com as the Internet brand that means name your price."[12]

Questions for Discussion

1. When an organization like an airline is deciding whether to accept a customer's bid, which factors in Figure 20.3 is it most likely to consider?
2. Does the pricing facilitated by Priceline.com result in price or nonprice competition?
3. What are the advantages and disadvantages of Priceline.com's pricing approach for buyers and for sellers?

Setting
Prices

OBJECTIVES

- **To understand eight major stages of the process used to establish prices**
- **To explore issues connected with developing pricing objectives**
- **To grasp the importance of identifying the target market's evaluation of price**
- **To learn about demand curves and the price elasticity of demand**
- **To examine the relationships among demand, costs, and profits**
- **To learn about analyzing competitive prices**
- **To become familiar with the bases used for setting prices**
- **To understand the different types of pricing strategies**

In the Long-Distance Race, Sprint Sets the Pace

Pricing of long-distance phone service has never been the same since the breakup of AT&T in 1984. Sprint, the third-largest U.S. long-distance telephone company, has been leading the way with highly competitive pricing strategies. For a decade after AT&T's breakup, cost-conscious consumers still had to keep one eye on the clock any time they dialed long distance, especially during weekdays, when rates were generally highest. Occasional price breaks would make calling cheaper at certain times, but lengthy long-distance calls remained a luxury for most consumers in this $80 billion-a-year market.

In the mid-1990s, Sprint broke with its main competitors, AT&T and MCI, by dramatically slashing long-distance prices. Its unprecedented 10-cents per minute calling plan was the first shot in what has become an all-out price war in long-distance telephone service. Not long after Sprint's dime-a-minute move, MCI retaliated by launching another novel pricing scheme: nickel-a-minute long-distance rates on Sundays only. Soon, AT&T not only matched MCI's Sunday rate; it extended the 5-cent offer to all day Saturday as well.

Sprint again redefined the competitive landscape by introducing another innovation: unlimited long-distance phone calls on weekends for a flat rate of $25 per month. Called "Sprint Unlimited," this program allows callers to stop worrying about the minutes ticking by whenever they phone someone in another county or another state. Weekday calls are still priced at 10 cents per minute, but consumers willing to wait until the weekend to place long-distance calls can talk for hours without any extra charge.

To make Sprint Unlimited profitable, the company decided to limit usage to voice calls, disallowing Internet connections, which can tie up telephone lines for hours on end. Despite this limitation, Sprint's flat-rate pricing is so attractive that analysts expect it to give a sharp boost to Sprint's long-distance revenues, which account for more than half the company's overall revenues. Even if competitors later match Sprint's pricing, being the first to announce this type of pricing plan has given the company a head start and reaffirmed its position as a pricing innovator.[1]

1   Development of pricing objectives

2   Assessment of target market's evaluation of price

3   Determination of demand

4   Analysis of demand, cost, and profit relationships

5   Evaluation of competitors' prices

6   Selection of a basis for pricing

7   Selection of a pricing strategy

8   Determination of a specific price

Figure 21.1
Stages for Establishing Prices

Sprint is the first company to use flat pricing for residential long-distance telephone service. This type of pricing is a distinguishing component of Sprint's marketing mix for residential long-distance. Setting prices of products requires careful analysis of numerous issues. In this chapter we examine eight stages of a process that marketers can use when setting prices. Figure 21.1 illustrates these eight stages. Stage 1 is the development of a pricing objective that is congruent with the organization's overall objectives and its marketing objectives. In stage 2, the target market's evaluation of price must be assessed. Then, in stage 3, marketers should examine the nature and price of elasticity of demand. Stage 4, which consists of analyzing demand, cost, and profit relationships, is necessary for estimating the economic feasibility of alternative prices. Evaluation of competitors' prices, which constitutes stage 5, helps determine the role of price in the marketing strategy. Stage 6 involves choosing a basis for setting prices. Stage 7 is the selection of a pricing strategy, or the guidelines for using price in the marketing mix. Stage 8, determining the final price, depends on environmental forces and marketers' understanding and use of a systematic approach to establishing prices. These stages are not rigid steps that all marketers must follow but rather guidelines that provide a logical sequence for establishing prices.

Development of Pricing Objectives

In Chapter 20 we discussed the various types of pricing objectives. Developing pricing objectives is an important task because pricing objectives form the basis for decisions about other stages of pricing. Thus pricing objectives must be stated explicitly, and the statement should include the time frame for accomplishing them.

Marketers must make sure that the pricing objectives they set fit in with the organization's overall objectives and marketing objectives. Inconsistent objectives cause internal conflicts and confusion and can prevent the organization from achieving its overall goals. Normally, organizations have multiple pricing objectives, some short-term and others long-term. In response to changing market conditions, a marketer typically alters pricing objectives over time.

Figure 21.2
Target Markets' Evaluation of Price
Customers may expect prices of certain products to be lower for children than for adults, as is the case with Jesse James Historic Sites.

SO PAINSTAKINGLY AUTHENTIC WE EVEN TAKE YOUR MONEY.

Admission: Adults $4.00/Children $1.75

JESSE JAMES HISTORIC SITES
COURTHOUSE SQUARE, LIBERTY, MO 64068 FARM HOME: (816) 635-6065 BANK MUSEUM: (816) 781-4458

Assessment of the Target Market's Evaluation of Price

Despite the general assumption that price is a major issue for buyers, the importance of price depends on the type of product, the type of target market, and the purchase situation. For example, buyers are probably more sensitive to gasoline prices than to luggage prices. With respect to the type of target market, adults may have to pay more than children for certain products (See Figure 21.2). The purchase situation also affects the buyer's view of price. Most moviegoers would never pay in other situations the prices charged for soft drinks, popcorn, and candy at movie concession stands. By assessing the target market's evaluation of price, a marketer is in a better position to know how much emphasis to put on price. Information about the target market's price evaluation may also help a marketer determine how far above the competition a firm can set its prices.

Because some consumers are seeking less expensive products and shopping more selectively, some manufacturers and retailers are focusing on the value of their products. Value combines a product's price and quality attributes, which customers use to differentiate among competing brands. Consumers are looking for good deals on products that provide better value for their money. Understanding the importance of a product to customers, as well as their expectations about quality and value, helps marketers correctly assess the target market's evaluation of price.

SNAPSHOT

How much would you pay for a textbook?

Depending on a person's evaluation of price, he or she may be willing to spend across a broad range of prices.

Used book purchased from another student	$42.00
Used book from bookstore	$63.40
New book purchased online	$73.06
New book purchased from bookstore	$84.50

Determination of Demand

Determining the demand for a product is the responsibility of marketing managers, who are aided in this task by marketing researchers and forecasters. Marketing research and forecasting techniques yield estimates of sales potential, or the quantity of a product that could be sold during a specific period. These estimates are helpful in establishing the relationship between a product's price and the quantity demanded.

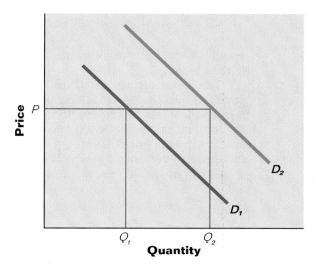

Figure 21.3
Demand Curve Illustrating the Price/Quantity Relationship and Increase in Demand

The Demand Curve

For most products, the quantity demanded goes up as the price goes down, and as the price goes up, the quantity demanded goes down. Thus there is an inverse relationship between price and quantity demanded. As long as the marketing environment and buyers' needs, ability (purchasing power), willingness, and authority to buy remain stable, this fundamental inverse relationship will continue.

Figure 21.3 illustrates the effect of one variable—price—on the quantity demanded. The classic **demand curve** (D_1) is a graph of the quantity of products expected to be sold at various prices, if other factors remain constant.[2] It illustrates that as price falls, the quantity demanded usually rises. Demand depends on other factors in the marketing mix, including product quality, promotion, and distribution. An improvement in any of these factors may cause a shift to, say, demand curve D_2. In such a case, an increased quantity (Q_2) will be sold at the same price (P).

There are many types of demand and not all conform to the classic demand curve shown in Figure 21.3. Prestige products, such as selected perfumes and jewelry, seem to sell better at high prices than at low ones. These products are desirable partly because their expense makes buyers feel elite. For example, in Figure 21.4, the Steuben crystal and the Gregg Ruth jewelry are examples of prestige products. If the price fell

demand curve A graph of the quantity of products expected to be sold at various prices, if other factors remain constant

Figure 21.4
Prestige Products
Handcrafted-glass artwork and fine jewelry are examples of prestige products.

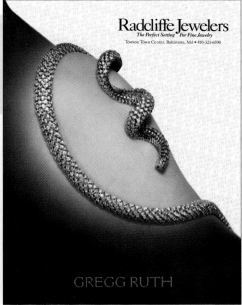

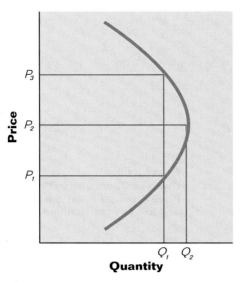

Figure 21.5
Demand Curve Illustrating the Relationship Between Price and Quantity for Prestige Products

drastically and many people owned these products, they would lose some of their appeal.

The demand curve in Figure 21.5 shows the relationship between price and quantity demanded for prestige products. Quantity demanded is greater, not less, at higher prices. For a certain price range—from P_1 to P_2—the quantity demanded (Q_1) goes up to Q_2. After a certain point, however, raising the price backfires. If the price of a product goes too high, the quantity demanded goes down. The figure shows that if the price is raised from P_2 to P_3, the quantity demanded goes back down from Q_2 to Q_1.

Demand Fluctuations

Changes in buyers' needs, variations in the effectiveness of other marketing mix variables, the presence of substitutes, and dynamic environmental factors can influence demand. Restaurants and utility companies experience large fluctuations in demand daily. Toy manufacturers, fireworks suppliers, and air-conditioning and heating contractors also face demand fluctuations because of the seasonal nature of their products. The demand for online services, milk, and fur coats has changed over the last few years. In some cases, demand fluctuations are predictable. It is no surprise to restaurants and utility company managers that demand fluctuates. However, changes in demand for other products may be less predictable, and this leads to problems for some companies. Other organizations anticipate demand fluctuations and develop new products and prices to meet consumers' needs.

Assessing Price Elasticity of Demand

price elasticity of demand A measure of the sensitivity of demand to changes in price

Up to this point, we have been discussing how marketers identify the target market's evaluation of price and its ability to purchase and how they examine demand to learn whether price is related inversely or directly to quantity. The next step is to assess price elasticity of demand. **Price elasticity of demand** provides a measure of the sensitivity of demand to changes in price. It is formally defined as the percentage change in quantity demanded relative to a given percentage change in price (see Figure 21.6)[3]. The percentage change in quantity demanded caused by a percentage change in price is much greater for elastic demand than for inelastic demand. For a product such as electricity, demand is relatively inelastic. When its price is increased, say, from P_1 to P_2, quantity demanded goes down only a little, from Q_1 to Q_2. For products such as recreational vehicles, demand is relatively elastic. When price rises sharply, from P_1 to P_2, quantity demanded goes down a great deal, from Q_1 to Q_2.

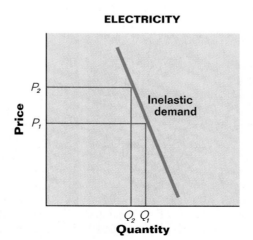

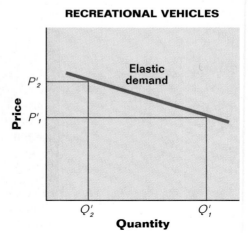

Figure 21.6
Elasticity of Demand

If marketers can determine the price elasticity of demand, then setting a price is much easier. By analyzing total revenues as prices change, marketers can determine whether a product is price-elastic. Total revenue is price times quantity; thus 10,000 rolls of wallpaper sold in one year at a price of $10 per roll equals $100,000 of total revenue. If demand is *elastic,* a change in price causes an opposite change in total revenue: an increase in price will decrease total revenue, and a decrease in price will increase total revenue. *Inelastic* demand results in a change in the same direction in total revenue: an increase in price will increase total revenue, and a decrease in price will decrease total revenue. The following formula determines the price elasticity of demand:

$$\text{Price Elasticity of Demand} = \frac{\%\ \text{Change in Quantity Demanded}}{\%\ \text{Change in Price}}$$

For example, if demand falls by 8 percent when a seller raises the price by 2 percent, the price elasticity of demand is −4 (the negative sign indicating the inverse relationship between price and demand). If demand falls by 2 percent when price is increased by 4 percent, then elasticity is −1/2. The less elastic the demand, the more beneficial it is for the seller to raise the price. Products without readily available substitutes and for which consumers have strong needs (for example, electricity or appendectomies) usually have inelastic demand.

Marketers cannot base prices solely on elasticity considerations. They must also examine the costs associated with different volumes and see what happens to profits.

Analysis of Demand, Cost, and Profit Relationships

The analysis of demand, cost, and profit is important because customers are becoming less tolerant of price increases and thus forcing manufacturers to find new ways to control costs. In the past, many customers desired premium brands and were willing to pay extra for these products. Today, customers pass up certain brand names if they can pay less without sacrificing quality. To stay in business, a company has to set prices that not only cover its costs, but also meet customers' expectations. This section explores two approaches to understanding demand, cost, and profit relationships: marginal analysis and breakeven analysis.

fixed costs   Costs that do not vary with changes in the number of units produced or sold

average fixed cost   The fixed cost per unit produced

variable costs   Costs that vary directly with changes in the number of units produced or sold

average variable cost   The variable cost per unit produced

total cost   The sum of average fixed and average variable costs times the quantity produced

average total cost   The sum of the average fixed cost and the average variable cost

marginal cost (MC)   The extra cost a firm incurs by producing one more unit of a product

Marginal Analysis

Marginal analysis is the examination of what happens to a firm's costs and revenues when production (or sales volume) is changed by one unit. Both production costs and revenues must be evaluated. To determine the costs of production, it is necessary to distinguish among several types of costs. **Fixed costs** do not vary with changes in the number of units produced or sold. For example, a wallpaper manufacturer's cost of renting a factory does not change because production increases from one shift to two shifts a day or because twice as much wallpaper is sold. Rent may go up, but not because the factory has doubled production or revenue. **Average fixed cost** is the fixed cost per unit produced and is calculated by dividing fixed costs by the number of units produced.

Variable costs vary directly with changes in the number of units produced or sold. The wages for a second shift and the cost of twice as much paper are extra costs that occur when production is doubled. Variable costs are usually constant per unit; that is, twice as many workers and twice as much material produce twice as many rolls of wallpaper. **Average variable cost,** the variable cost per unit produced, is calculated by dividing the variable costs by the number of units produced.

Total cost is the sum of average fixed costs and average variable costs times the quantity produced. The **average total cost** is the sum of the average fixed cost and the average variable cost. **Marginal cost (MC)** is the extra cost a firm incurs when it produces one more unit of a product. Table 21.1 illustrates various costs and their relationships. Notice that the average fixed cost declines as the output increases. The

Table 21.1   Costs and Their Relationships

1 Quantity	2 Fixed Cost	3 Average Fixed Cost (2) ÷ (1)	4 Average Variable Cost	5 Average Total Cost (3) + (4)	6 Total Cost (5) × (1)	Marginal Cost
1	$40	$40.00	$20.00	$60.00	$60	
						$10
2	40	20.00	15.00	35.00	70	
						5
3	40	13.33	11.67	25.00	75	
						15
4	40	10.00	12.50	22.50	90	
						20
5	40	8.00	14.00	22.00	110	
						30
6	40	6.67	16.67	23.33	140	
						40
7	40	5.71	20.00	25.71	180	

average variable cost follows a U shape, as does the average total cost. Because the average total cost continues to fall after the average variable cost begins to rise, its lowest point is at a higher level of output than that of the average variable cost. The average total cost is lowest at 5 units at a cost of $22.00, whereas the average variable cost is lowest at 3 units at a cost of $11.67. As shown in Figure 21.7, marginal cost equals average total cost at the latter's lowest level. In Table 21.1 this occurs between 5 and 6 units of production. Average total cost decreases as long as the marginal cost is less than the average total cost, and it increases when marginal cost rises above average total cost.

marginal revenue (MR)
The change in total revenue made by the sale of an additional unit of a product

Marginal revenue (MR) is the change in total revenue that occurs when a firm sells an additional unit of a product. Figure 21.8 depicts marginal revenue and a demand curve. Most firms in the United States face downward-sloping demand curves for their products. In other words, they must lower their prices to sell additional units. This situation means that each additional product sold provides the firm with less revenue than the previous unit sold. MR then becomes less than average revenue, as Figure 21.8 shows. Eventually, MR reaches zero, and the sale of additional units actually hurts the firm.

However, before the firm can determine whether a unit makes a profit, it must know its cost, as well as its revenue, because profit equals revenue minus cost. If MR is a unit's addition to revenue and MC is a unit's addition to cost, then MR minus MC tells us whether the unit is profitable or not. Table 21.2 illustrates the relationships among price, quantity sold, total revenue, marginal revenue, marginal cost, and total cost. It indicates where maximum profits are possible at various combinations of price and cost.

Profit is maximized where MC = MR (see Table 21.2). In this table MC = MR at four units. The best price is $33.75 and the profit is $45.00. Up to this point, the addi-

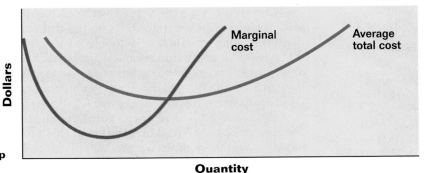

Figure 21.7
Typical Marginal Cost and Average Total Cost Relationship

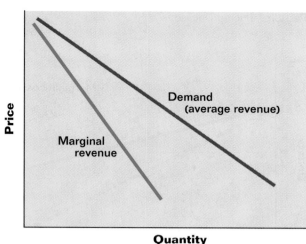

Figure 21.8
Typical Marginal
Revenue and Average
Revenue Relationship

Price

Demand
(average revenue)

Marginal
revenue

Quantity

tional revenue generated from an extra unit sold exceeds the additional total cost. Beyond this point, the additional cost of another unit sold exceeds the additional revenue generated, and profits decrease. If the price was based on minimum average total cost—$22.00 (Table 21.1)—it would result in less profit: only $40.00 (Table 21.2) for five units at a price of $30.00 versus $45.00 for four units at a price of $33.75.

Graphically combining Figures 21.7 and 21.8 into Figure 21.9 on page 544 shows that any unit for which MR exceeds MC adds to a firm's profits, and any unit for which MC exceeds MR subtracts from a firm's profits. The firm should produce at the point where MR equals MC because this is the most profitable level of production.

This discussion of marginal analysis may give the false impression that pricing can be highly precise. If revenue (demand) and cost (supply) remained constant, then prices could be set for maximum profits. In practice, however, cost and revenue change frequently. The competitive tactics of other firms or government action can quickly undermine a company's expectations of revenue. Thus marginal analysis is only a model from which to work. It offers little help in pricing new products before costs and revenues are established. On the other hand, in setting prices of existing products, especially in competitive situations, most marketers can benefit by understanding the relationship between marginal cost and marginal revenue.

Breakeven Analysis

breakeven point Point at which the costs of producing a product equal the revenue made from selling the product

The point at which the costs of producing a product equal the revenue made from selling the product is the **breakeven point.** If a wallpaper manufacturer has total annual costs of $100,000 and the same year it sells $100,000 worth of wallpaper, then the company has broken even.

Table 21.2   Marginal Analysis: Method of Obtaining Maximum Profit-Producing Price

1	2	3	4	5	6	7
Price	Quantity Sold	Total Revenue (1) × (2)	Marginal Revenue	Marginal Cost	Total Cost	Profit (3) − (6)
$57.00	1	$ 57	$57	$—	$ 60	−$ 3
55.00	2	110	53	10	70	40
39.00	3	117	7	5	75	42
33.75*	**4**	**135**	**15**	**15**	**90**	**45**
30.00	5	150	15	20	110	40
27.00	6	162	12	30	140	22
25.00	7	175	13	40	180	−5

*Boldface indicates best price-profit combination

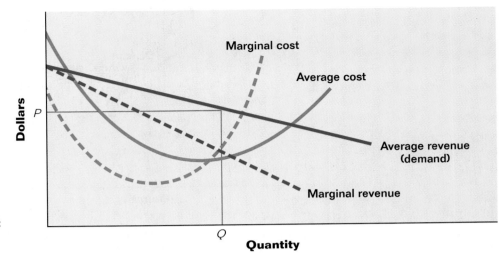

Figure 21.9
Combining the Marginal
Cost and Marginal Revenue
Concepts for Optimal Profit

Figure 21.10 illustrates the relationships of costs, revenue, profits, and losses involved in determining the breakeven point. Knowing the number of units necessary to break even is important in setting the price. If a product priced at $100 per unit has an average variable cost of $60 per unit, then the contribution to fixed costs is $40. If total fixed costs are $120,000, here is the way to determine the breakeven point in units:

$$\text{Breakeven Point} = \frac{\text{Fixed Costs}}{\text{Per Unit Contribution to Fixed Costs}}$$

$$= \frac{\text{Fixed Costs}}{\text{Price} - \text{Variable Costs}}$$

$$= \frac{\$120,000}{\$40}$$

$$= 3,000 \text{ Units}$$

To calculate the breakeven point in terms of dollar sales volume, multiply the breakeven point in units by the price per unit. In the preceding example, the breakeven point in terms of dollar sales volume is 3,000 (units) times $100, or $300,000.

To use breakeven analysis effectively, a marketer should determine the breakeven point for each of several alternative prices. This determination allows the marketer to

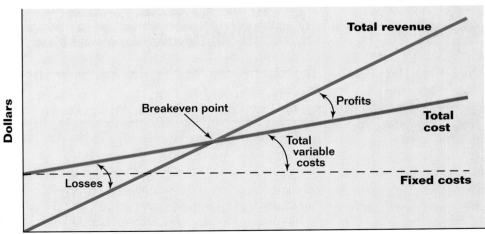

Figure 21.10
Determining the Breakeven
Point

compare the effects on total revenue, total costs, and the breakeven point for each price under consideration. Although this comparative analysis may not tell the marketer exactly what price to charge, it will identify highly undesirable price alternatives that should definitely be avoided.

Breakeven analysis is simple and straightforward. It does assume, however, that the quantity demanded is basically fixed (inelastic) and that the major task in setting prices is to recover costs. It focuses more on how to break even than on how to achieve a pricing objective, such as percentage of market share or return on investment. Nonetheless, marketing managers can use this concept to determine whether a product will achieve at least a breakeven volume.

Evaluation of Competitors' Prices

In most cases, marketers are in a better position to establish prices when they know the prices charged for competing brands. Learning competitors' prices may be a regular function of marketing research. Some grocery and department stores, for example, have full-time comparative shoppers who systematically collect data on prices. Companies may also purchase price lists, sometimes weekly, from syndicated marketing research services.

Finding out what prices competitors are charging is not always easy, especially in producer and reseller markets. Competitors' price lists are often closely guarded. Even if a marketer has access to competitors' price lists, these lists may not reflect the actual prices at which competitive products are sold because those prices may be established through negotiation.

Knowing the prices of competing brands can be very important for a marketer. Competitors' prices and the marketing mix variables that they emphasize partly determine how important price will be to customers. A marketer in an industry in which price competition prevails needs competitive price information to ensure that its prices are the same as, or lower than, its competitors' prices.

In some instances, an organization's prices are designed to be slightly above competitors' prices to give its products an exclusive image. Alternately, another company may use price as a competitive tool and price its products below those of competitors. Category killers like Toys "R" Us and Home Depot have acquired large market shares through highly competitive pricing.

Selection of a Basis for Pricing

The three major dimensions on which prices can be based are cost, demand, and competition. The selection of the basis to be used is affected by the type of product, the market structure of the industry, the brand's market-share position relative to competing brands, and customer characteristics. In this section, we discuss each basis separately. However, when setting prices, an organization generally considers two or all three of these dimensions, even though one may be the primary dimension on which it bases its prices. For example, if an organization is using cost as a basis for setting prices, marketers in that organization are also aware and concerned about competitors' prices. If a company is using demand as a basis for pricing, those making pricing decisions don't ignore costs and competitors' prices.

Cost-Based Pricing

cost-based pricing
Adding a dollar amount or percentage to the cost of the product

When using **cost-based pricing,** a dollar amount or percentage is added to the cost of a product. This approach thus involves calculations of desired profit margins. Cost-based pricing does not necessarily take into account the economic aspects of supply and demand, nor does it necessarily relate to just one pricing strategy or pricing objective. Cost-based pricing is straightforward and easy to implement. Two common forms of cost-based pricing are cost-plus and markup pricing.

cost-plus pricing Adding a specified dollar amount or percentage to the seller's cost

Cost-Plus Pricing   In **cost-plus pricing,** the seller's costs are determined (usually during a project or after a project is completed), and then a specified dollar amount or percentage of the cost is added to the seller's cost to establish the price. When production costs are difficult to predict, cost-plus pricing is appropriate. Projects involving custom-made equipment and commercial construction are often priced by this technique. The government frequently uses such cost-based pricing in granting defense contracts. One pitfall for the buyer is that the seller may increase costs to establish a larger profit base. Furthermore, some costs, such as overhead, may be difficult to determine. In periods of rapid inflation, cost-plus pricing is popular, especially when the producer must use raw materials that are fluctuating in price. In industries in which cost-plus pricing is common and sellers have similar costs, price competition may not be especially intense.

markup pricing Adding to the cost of the product a predetermined percentage of that cost

Markup Pricing   A common pricing approach among retailers is **markup pricing.** In markup pricing, a product's price is derived by adding a predetermined percentage of the cost, called *markup,* to the cost of the product. Although the percentage markup in a retail store varies from one category of goods to another—35 percent of cost for hardware items and 100 percent of cost for greeting cards, for example—the same percentage often is used to determine the price on items within a single product category, and the percentage markup may be largely standardized across an industry at the retail level. Using a rigid percentage markup for a specific product category reduces pricing to a routine task that can be performed quickly.

Markup can be stated as a percentage of the cost or as a percentage of the selling price. The following example illustrates how percentage markups are determined and points out the differences in the two methods. Assume that a retailer purchases a can of tuna at 45 cents, adds 15 cents to the cost, and then prices the tuna at 60 cents. Here are the figures:

$$\text{Markup as a Percentage of Cost} = \frac{\text{Markup}}{\text{Cost}}$$

$$= \frac{15}{45}$$

$$= 33.3\%$$

$$\text{Markup as a Percentage of Selling Price} = \frac{\text{Markup}}{\text{Selling Price}}$$

$$= \frac{15}{60}$$

$$= 25.0\%$$

Obviously, when discussing a percentage markup, it is important to know whether the markup is based on cost or selling price.

Markups normally reflect expectations about operating costs, risks, and stock turnovers. Wholesalers and manufacturers often suggest standard retail markups that are considered profitable. To the extent that retailers use similar markups for the same product category, price competition is reduced. In addition, using rigid markups is convenient and is the major reason that retailers, who face numerous pricing decisions, favor this method.

Demand-Based Pricing

demand-based pricing Pricing based on the level of demand for the product

Marketers sometimes base prices on the level of demand for the product. When **demand-based pricing** is used, customers pay a higher price when demand for the product is strong and a lower price when demand is weak. For example, hotels that otherwise attract numerous travelers often offer reduced rates during lower-demand

Figure 21.11
Demand-Based Pricing
Many hotels employ demand-based pricing. Westin Hotels and Resorts offers value stays during selected periods when demand for accommodations is lower.

periods (see Figure 21.11). Some long-distance telephone companies, such as MCI, Sprint, and AT&T, also use demand-based pricing. To use this pricing basis, a marketer must be able to estimate the amounts of a product that consumers will demand at different prices. The marketer then chooses the price that generates the highest total revenue. Obviously, the effectiveness of demand-based pricing depends on the marketer's ability to estimate demand accurately.

Compared with cost-based pricing, demand-based pricing places a firm in a better position to reach higher profit levels, assuming that buyers value the product at levels sufficiently above the product's cost. See Tech*know for a discussion of how demand-based pricing works in the high-tech world of auction Web sites.

Competition-Based Pricing

competition-based pricing Pricing influenced primarily by competitors' prices

In using **competition-based pricing,** an organization considers costs as secondary to competitors' prices. The importance of this method increases when competing products are relatively homogeneous and the organization is serving markets in which price is a key purchase consideration. A firm that uses competition-based pricing may

Tech*know

Going, Going, Gone: Differential Pricing at Online Auctions

Differential pricing has taken on a new dimension in the high-tech world of online auctions. At eBay, OnSale, and other Web sites, buyers electronically bid against each other for all kinds of products, from Beanie Babies to laptop computers. Some of the items are new; some are refurbished (overhauled to "good as new" condition); and some—in true "tag sale" spirit—are used. Bidders in search of a bargain read the merchandise descriptions and then type in their bids, hoping to top competing bidders and still pay low prices.

Some auctions go on for days, while other go on for just a few minutes. The Dutch-style auctions at Klik-klok (www.klik-klok.com), for example, last a mere two minutes. These auctions work differently than traditional American auctions in that prices go down as the auction progresses. At the start of a Klik-klok auction, a limited quantity of the product for sale is available at a set price. During the next two minutes, the price drops steadily every few seconds; bidders can buy the item at the current price by clicking on their screens. Bidders who hold out until the end will pay the lowest price—if any products are still available.

Most online auctions, however, start at the low end of the price continuum and then invite competing bidders to enter ever-higher bids until time runs out. Bidders who get caught up in the excitement of winning can easily overpay, which is why one auction site (www.ubid.com) displays a "maximum bid price" next to each item being auctioned. People can choose to go over that maximum, which often represents an item's undiscounted retail price, but knowing the maximum gives them a reference point to consider as they bid.

Before placing any bids, first-time participants should carefully read each auction site's instructions and requirements. The Auction Insider Web site (www.auctioninsider.com) offers tips for smart online bidding and also ranks the top auction sites for popular items like collectibles and computers. Because of the potential for fraud, bidders may also want to visit the National Consumer League's Internet Fraud Watch site (www.fraud.org/ifw.htm) to check out possible problems in advance.

choose to price below competitors' prices, above competitors' prices, or at the same level. Airlines use competition-based pricing, often charging identical fares on the same routes.

Although not all introductory marketing texts have exactly the same price, they do have similar prices. The price that the bookstore paid to the publishing company for this textbook was determined on the basis of competitors' prices. Competition-based pricing can help a firm achieve the pricing objective of increasing sales or market share. Competition-based pricing may necessitate frequent price adjustments. For example, for many competitive airline routes, fares are adjusted often.

Selection of a Pricing Strategy

A pricing strategy is an approach or a course of action designed to achieve pricing and marketing objectives. Generally, pricing strategies help marketers solve the practical problems of establishing prices. Table 21.3 lists the most common pricing strategies, which we discuss in the rest of this section.

Differential Pricing

An important issue in pricing decisions is whether to use a single price or different prices for the same product. Using a single price has several benefits. A primary one is its simplicity. A single price is easily understood by both employees and customers, and since many salespeople and customers do not like having to negotiate a price, it reduces the chance of a marketer's developing an adversarial relationship with a customer. The use of a single price does create some challenges, however. If the single price is too high, a number of potential customers may not be able to afford the product. If it is too low, the organization loses revenue from those customers who would have paid more if the price had been higher.

differential pricing
Charging different prices to different buyers for the same quality and quantity of product

Differential pricing means charging different prices to different buyers for the same quality and quantity of product. For differential pricing to be effective, the market must consist of multiple segments with different price sensitivities, and the method should be used in a way that avoids confusing or antagonizing customers. Customers paying the lower prices should not be able to resell the product to the individuals and organizations paying higher prices, unless that is the intention of the seller. Differential pricing can occur in several ways, including negotiated pricing, secondary market discounting, periodic discounting, and random discounting.

negotiated pricing
Establishing a final price through bargaining

Negotiated Pricing **Negotiated pricing** occurs when the final price is established through bargaining between the seller and the customer. Negotiated pricing

Table 21.3 **Common Pricing Strategies**	
Differential Pricing	**Psychological Pricing**
Negotiated Pricing	Reference Pricing
Secondary-Market Pricing	Bundle Pricing
Periodic Discounting	Multiple-Unit Pricing
Random Discounting	Everyday Low Prices
New-Product Pricing	Odd-Even Pricing
Price Skimming	Customary Pricing
Penetration Pricing	Prestige Pricing
Product-Line Pricing	**Professional Pricing**
Captive Pricing	**Promotional Pricing**
Premium Pricing	Price Leaders
Bait Pricing	Special-Event Pricing
Price Lining	Comparison Discounting

occurs in a number of industries and at all levels of distribution. Even when there is a predetermined stated price or a price list, manufacturers, wholesalers, and retailers may still negotiate to establish the final sales price. Consumers commonly negotiate prices for houses, cars, and used equipment.

secondary-market pricing Setting one price for the primary target market and a different price for another market

Secondary-Market Pricing   **Secondary-market pricing** means setting one price for the primary target market and a different price for another market. Often, the price charged in the secondary market is lower. However, when the costs of serving a secondary market are higher than normal, secondary-market customers may have to pay a higher price. Examples of secondary markets include a geographically isolated domestic market, a market in a foreign country, and a segment willing to purchase a product during off-peak times. For example, during the early evening hours, some restaurants offer special "early-bird" prices; some cellular phone users are offered off-peak discounted prices; and some textbooks and pharmaceutical products are sold for considerably less in certain foreign countries than in the United States. Secondary markets provide an organization with an opportunity to use excess capacity and to stabilize the allocation of resources.

periodic discounting Temporary reduction of prices on a patterned or systematic basis

Periodic Discounting   **Periodic discounting** is the temporary reduction of prices on a patterned or systematic basis. For example, many retailers have annual holiday sales, and some women's apparel stores have two seasonal sales each year: a winter sale in the last two weeks of January, and a summer sale in the first two weeks in July. Automobile dealers regularly discount prices on current models when the next year's models are introduced. From the marketer's point of view, a major problem with periodic discounting is that because the discounts follow a pattern, customers can predict when the reductions will occur and may delay their purchases until they can take advantage of the lower prices.

random discounting Temporary reduction of prices on an unsystematic basis

Random Discounting   To alleviate the problem of customers' knowing when discounting will occur, some organizations such as Pier 1 Imports in Figure 21.12 employ **random discounting,**—that is, they temporarily reduce their prices on an unsystematic basis. When price reductions of a product occur randomly, current users of that brand are not likely to be able to predict when the reductions will occur and so will not delay their purchases in anticipation of buying the product at a lower price. Marketers also use random discounting to attract new customers. For example, Lever Brothers may temporarily reduce the price of one of its bar soaps in the hope of attracting new customers.

New-Product Pricing

Setting the base price for a new product is a necessary part of formulating a marketing strategy. The base price is easily adjusted (in the absence of government price controls), and its establishment is one of the most fundamental decisions in the marketing mix. The base price can be set high to recover development costs quickly or to provide a reference point for

Figure 21.12
Random Discounting
To provide special values to its customers, Pier 1 Imports employs random discounting.

developing discount prices to different market segments. When marketers set base prices, they also consider how quickly competitors will enter the market, whether they will mount a strong campaign on entry, and what effect their entry will have on the development of primary demand. Two strategies used in new-product pricing are price skimming and penetration pricing.

price skimming Charging the highest possible price that buyers who most desire the product will pay

Price Skimming   **Price skimming** is charging the highest possible price that buyers who most desire the product will pay. This approach provides the most flexible introductory base price. Demand tends to be inelastic in the introductory stage of the product life cycle.

Price skimming can provide several benefits, especially when a product is in the introductory stage of its life cycle. A skimming policy can generate much-needed initial cash flows to help offset sizable developmental costs. When introducing a new model of camera, Polaroid initially uses a skimming price to defray large research and development costs. Price skimming protects the marketer from problems that arise when the price is set too low to cover costs. When a firm introduces a product, its production capacity may be limited. A skimming price can help keep demand consistent with a firm's production capabilities. The use of a skimming price may attract competition into an industry because the high price makes that type of business appear to be quite lucrative.

penetration pricing Setting prices below those of competing brands to penetrate a market and gain a significant market share quickly

Penetration Pricing   To penetrate a market and gain a large market share quickly, **penetration pricing** sets prices below those of competing brands. For example, Qwest Communications Corporation, trying to gain market share quickly, introduced its Internet long-distance calling plan for 7.5 cents a minute.[4] This approach is less flexible for a marketer than price skimming because it is more difficult to raise a penetration price than to lower or discount a skimming price. It is not unusual for a firm to use a penetration price after having skimmed the market with a higher price.

Penetration pricing can be especially beneficial when marketers suspect that competitors could enter the market easily. If penetration pricing allows the marketer to gain a large market share quickly, competitors may be discouraged from entering the market. In addition, entering a market may be less attractive to competitors when penetration pricing is used because the lower per-unit price results in lower per-unit profit; this may cause competitors to view the market as not being especially lucrative.

Product-Line Pricing

product-line pricing Establishing and adjusting prices of multiple products within a product line

Rather than considering products on an item-by-item basis when determining pricing strategies, some marketers employ product-line pricing. **Product-line pricing** means establishing and adjusting the prices of multiple products within a product line. When marketers use product-line pricing, their goal is to maximize profits for an entire product line rather than focusing on the profitability of an individual product. Product-line pricing can provide marketers with flexibility in price setting. For example, marketers can set prices so that one product is quite profitable while another increases market share by virtue of having a lower price than competing products.

Before setting prices for a product line, marketers evaluate the relationship among the products in the line. When products in a line are complementary, sales increases in one item increase demand for other items. For instance, desk-top printers and toner cartridges are complementary products. When products in a line function as substitutes for one another, buyers of one product in the line are unlikely to purchase one of the other products in the same line. In this case, marketers must be sensitive to how a price change for one of the brands may affect the demand not only for that brand, but also for the substitute brands. For example, if decision makers at Procter & Gamble were considering a price change for Tide detergent, they would be concerned about how the price change might influence the sales of Cheer, Bold, and Gain.

When marketers employ product-line pricing, they have several strategies from which to choose. These include captive pricing, premium pricing, bait pricing, and price lining.

captive pricing Pricing the basic product in a product line low, but pricing related items at a higher level

Captive Pricing   When **captive pricing** is used, the basic product in a product line is priced low, but the price on the items required to operate or enhance it can be at a higher level. For example, a manufacturer of cameras and film may set the price of the cameras at a level low enough to attract customers, but the film can have a relatively high price because to use the cameras, customers must continue to purchase film.

premium pricing Pricing the highest-quality or most versatile products higher than other models in the product line

Premium Pricing   **Premium pricing** is often used when a product line contains several versions of the same product; the highest-quality products or those with the most versatility are given the highest prices. Other products in the line are priced to appeal to price-sensitive shoppers or to those who seek product-specific features. Marketers that use premium strategy often realize a significant portion of their profits from premium-priced products. Examples of product categories in which premium pricing is common are small kitchen appliances, beer, ice cream, and television cable service.

bait pricing Pricing an item in the product line low with the intention of selling a higher-priced item in the line

Bait pricing   To attract customers, marketers may put a low price on one item in the product line with the intention of selling a higher-priced item in the line; this strategy is known as **bait pricing.** For example, a computer retailer might advertise its lowest-priced computer model, hoping that when customers come to the store, they will purchase a higher-priced one. This strategy can facilitate sales of a line's higher-priced products. As long as a retailer has sufficient quantities of the advertised low-priced model available for sale, this strategy is considered acceptable. However, *bait and switch* is an activity in which retailers have no intention of selling the bait product; they use the low price merely to entice customers into the store to sell them higher priced products. Bait and switch is considered unethical, and in some states it is illegal as well.

price lining Setting a limited number of prices for selected groups or lines of merchandise

Price Lining   When an organization sets a limited number of prices for selected groups or lines of merchandise, it is using **price lining.** A retailer may have various styles and brands of similar quality men's shirts that sell for $15. Another line of higher quality shirts may sell for $22. Price lining simplifies customers' decision making by holding constant one key variable in the final selection of style and brand within a line.

The basic assumption in price lining is that the demand is inelastic for various groups or sets of products. If the prices are attractive, customers will concentrate their purchases without responding to slight changes in price. Thus a women's dress shop that carries dresses priced at $85, $55, and $35 might not attract many more sales with a drop to, say, $83, $53, and $33. The "space" between the price of $85 and $55, however, can stir changes in consumer response. With price lining, the demand curve looks like a series of steps, as shown in Figure 21.13.

**Figure 21.13
Price Lining**

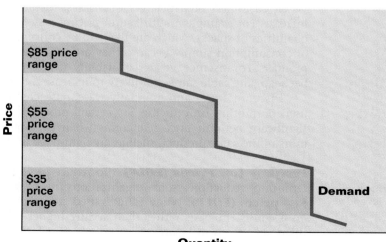

Psychological Pricing

psychological pricing
Pricing that attempts to influence a customer's perception of price to make a product's price more attractive

Learning the price of a product is not always a pleasant experience for customers. It can sometimes be surprising (as at a movie concession stand) and sometimes downright horrifying; most of us have been afflicted with "sticker shock." **Psychological pricing** attempts to influence a customer's perception of price to make a product's price more attractive. In this section, we consider several forms of psychological pricing: reference pricing, bundle pricing, multiple-unit pricing, everyday low prices (EDLP), odd-even pricing, customary pricing, and prestige pricing.

reference pricing   Pricing a product at a moderate level and positioning it next to a more expensive model or brand

Reference Pricing   **Reference pricing** means pricing a product at a moderate level and positioning it next to a more expensive model or brand in the hope that the customer will use the higher price as an external reference price (i.e., a comparison price). Because of the comparison, the customer is expected to view the moderate price favorably. Reference pricing is based on the "isolation effect," meaning an alternative is less attractive when viewed by itself than when compared with other alternatives. When you go to Sears to buy a VCR, a moderately priced VCR may appear especially attractive because it offers most of the important attributes of the more expensive alternatives on display and at a lower price. It is not unusual for an organization's moderately priced private brands to be positioned alongside more expensive, well-known manufacturer brands.

bundle pricing   Packaging together two or more complementary products and selling them for a single price

Bundle Pricing   **Bundle pricing** is the packaging together of two or more products, usually of a complementary nature, to be sold for a single price. To be attractive to customers, the single price is usually considerably less than the sum of the prices of the individual products. Being able to buy the bundled combination of products in a single transaction may be of value to the customer as well. For example, Gateway Computers bundles a computer, software, and Internet service and makes the entire package available for a single monthly charge. Bundle pricing not only helps increase customer satisfaction; by bundling slow-moving products with ones with higher turnover, an organization can stimulate sales and increase its revenues. Selling products as a package rather than individually may also result in cost savings. Bundle pricing is commonly used for banking and travel services, computers, and automobiles with option packages.

multiple-unit pricing
Packaging together two or more identical products and selling them for a single price

Multiple-Unit Pricing   **Multiple-unit pricing** occurs when two or more identical products are packaged together and sold for a single price. This normally results in a lower per-unit price than the one regularly charged. Multiple-unit pricing is commonly used for twin packs of potato chips, four-packs of light bulbs, and six- and twelve-packs of soft drinks. Customers benefit from the cost saving and convenience this pricing strategy affords. A company may use multiple-unit pricing to attract new customers to its brand and in some instances to increase consumption of its brands. When customers buy in larger quantities, their consumption of the product may increase. For example, multiple-unit pricing may encourage a customer to buy larger quantities of snacks, which are likely to be consumed in higher volume at the point of consumption simply because they are available. However, this is not true for all products. For instance, greater availability at the point of consumption of light bulbs, bar soap, and table salt is not likely to increase usage.

Discount stores and especially warehouse clubs, such as Sam's Club, are major users of multiple-unit pricing. For certain products in these stores, customers receive significant per-unit price reductions when they buy packages containing multiple units of the same product, such as an eight-pack of canned tuna fish.

everyday low prices (EDLP)   Setting a low price for products on a consistent basis

Everyday Low Prices (EDLP)   To reduce or eliminate the use of frequent short-term price reductions, some organizations use an approach referred to as **everyday low prices (EDLP).** When EDLP is used, a marketer sets a low price for its products on a consistent basis rather than setting higher prices and frequently discounting them. As shown in Figure 21.14, Onsale uses EDLP to market computer equipment online. Everyday low prices, though not deeply discounted, are set far enough below

Figure 21.14
Everyday Low Prices
As an online marketer of computer equipment, Onsale employs EDLP.

competitors' prices to make customers feel confident they are receiving a fair price. EDLP is employed by retailers like Wal-Mart and manufacturers like Procter & Gamble. A company that uses EDLP benefits from reduced promotional costs, reduced losses from frequent markdowns, and more stability in its sales. A major problem with this approach is that customers have mixed responses to it. Over the last decade, many marketers have trained customers to seek and to expect deeply discounted prices. In some product categories, such as apparel, finding the deepest discount has become almost a national consumer sport. Thus, failure to provide deep discounts can be a problem for certain marketers. In some instances, customers simply don't believe that everyday low prices are what they say they are but are instead a marketing gimmick.

Odd-Even Pricing   Through **odd-even pricing**—ending the price with certain numbers—marketers try to influence buyers' perceptions of the price or the product.[5] Odd pricing assumes that more of a product will be sold at $99.95 than at $100. Supposedly, customers will think, or at least tell friends, that the product is a bargain—not $100, but $99 and change. Also, customers are supposed to think that the store could have charged $100 but instead cut the price to the last cent, to $99.95. Some claim, too, that certain types of customers are more attracted by odd prices than by even ones. However, no substantial research findings support the notion that odd prices produce greater sales. Nonetheless, odd prices are far more common today than even prices.

Even prices are often used to give a product an exclusive or upscale image. An even price supposedly will influence a customer to view the product as being a high-quality, premium brand. A shirt maker, for example, may print on a premium shirt package a suggested retail price of $32.00 instead of $31.95; the even price of the shirt is used to enhance its upscale image.

odd-even pricing Ending the price with certain numbers to influence buyers' perceptions of price

customary pricing
Pricing on the basis of tradition

Customary Pricing   In **customary pricing,** certain goods are priced primarily on the basis of tradition. Recent economic uncertainties have made most prices fluctuate fairly widely, but the classic example of the customary, or traditional, price is the price of the candy bar. For years, a candy bar cost 5 cents. A new candy bar would have had to be something very special to sell for more than a nickel. This price was so sacred that rather than change it, manufacturers increased or decreased the size of the candy bar itself as chocolate prices fluctuated. Now, of course, the nickel candy bar has disappeared. Yet most candy bars still sell at a consistent, but obviously higher, price. Thus, customary pricing remains the standard for this market.

prestige pricing Prices set at an artificially high level to provide prestige or a quality image

Prestige Pricing   In **prestige pricing,** prices are set at an artificially high level to provide prestige or a quality image. Prestige pricing is used especially when buyers associate a higher price with higher quality.[6] Pharmacists report that some consumers complain when a prescription does not cost enough. Apparently, some consumers associate a drug's price with its potency. Typical product categories in which selected products are prestige-priced include perfumes, automobiles, liquor, and jewelry. If producers that use prestige pricing lowered their prices dramatically, it would be inconsistent with the perceived high-quality images of their products.

Professional Pricing

professional pricing
Fees set by persons with great skill or experience in a particular field

Professional pricing is used by persons who have great skill or experience in a particular field. Professionals often feel that their fees (prices) should not relate directly to the time and involvement in specific cases; rather, a standard fee is charged regardless of the problems involved in performing the job. Some doctors' and lawyers' fees are prime examples: $55 for a checkup, $1,500 for an appendectomy, and $399 for a divorce. Other professionals set prices in other ways.

The concept of professional pricing carries with it the idea that professionals have an ethical responsibility not to overcharge customers. In some situations, a seller can charge customers a high price and continue to sell many units of the product. Medicine offers several examples. If a diabetic requires one insulin treatment per day to survive, the individual will buy that treatment whether its price is $1 or $10. In fact, the patient surely would purchase the treatment even if the price went higher. In these situations, sellers could charge exorbitant fees. Drug companies claim that despite their positions of strength in this regard, they charge ethical prices rather than what the market will bear. See Building Customer Relationships for a discussion of how health care professionals are using discounts to forge better relationships with patients and insurers.

Promotional Pricing

Price, as an ingredient in the marketing mix, is often coordinated with promotion. The two variables sometimes are so interrelated that the pricing policy is promotion-oriented. Examples of promotional pricing include price leaders, special-event pricing, and comparison discounting.

price leaders Products priced below the usual markup, near cost, or below cost

Price Leaders   Sometimes a firm prices a few products below the usual markup, near cost, or below cost, which results in prices known as **price leaders.** This type of pricing is used most often in supermarkets and restaurants to attract customers by giving them especially low prices on a few items. Management hopes that sales of regularly priced products will more than offset the reduced revenues from the price leaders.

BUILDING
customer relationships

Satisfying Customers with Healthy Discounts on Medical Fees

In this era of rising medical costs, some health care professionals are building relationships with patients—their customers—by offering them discounts on fees for services and hospitalization. Such discounts are sometimes obtained on behalf of patients by health care insurance companies, which use their considerable buying power to bring down the fees charged by doctors and hospitals that participate in their plans. In other cases, the discounts are arranged by companies that act as intermediaries between patients and health care providers or by professional fee negotiators. In exchange for these discounts, doctors receive immediate cash payments and avoid the frustrating, time-consuming hassle of filing paperwork and waiting for reimbursement from insurers. "It's like Wal-Mart. You get your service; you pay your money," is the way one family physician describes the arrangement. "It's the fastest growing part of our practice."

Major insurers pay the health care bills for thousands and thousands of patients. Therefore, they are often able to negotiate significant volume discounts from the "usual and customary" fees that apply to particular medical procedures. Patients as well as insurers get a break in such instances, since patients are generally expected to pay a set percentage of what they are billed for certain medical services.

For consumers who are not covered by medical insurance or who have very high deductibles, companies like North American Care (NAC) can step in to negotiate lower health care prices. NAC has successfully negotiated medical fees as much as 70 percent lower than the "usual and customary" fees for common procedures; it gets paid a commission of up to 30 percent.

Some insurers are now hiring professional fee negotiators to try for lower fees from hospitals and doctors. In preparation for talking about pricing with health care providers, these negotiators first analyze the volume and type of medical procedures typically reimbursed by the insurers. On average, insurers using professional negotiators may be able to shave as much as 15 percent from the prices charged by medical providers. In turn, those savings help keep costs and insurance premiums under control—and strengthen the provider's bond with insurers and health care consumers.

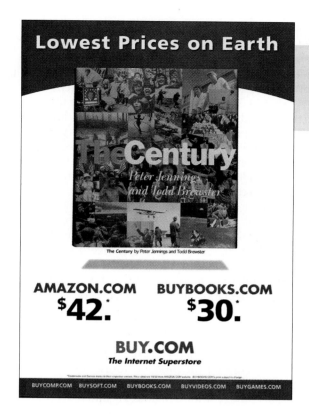

Figure 21.15
Comparison Discounting
Buy.com uses comparison discounting to demonstrate the difference in its price of a specific product relative to the price of the same product marketed by Amazon.com.

special-event pricing
Advertised sales or price cutting linked to a holiday, season, or event

comparison discounting
Setting a price at a specific level and comparing it with a higher price

Special-Event Pricing   To increase sales volume, many organizations coordinate price with advertising or sales promotions for seasonal or special situations. **Special-event pricing** involves advertised sales or price cutting linked to a holiday, season, or event. If the pricing objective is survival, then special sales events may be designed to generate the necessary operating capital. Special-event pricing entails coordination of production, scheduling, storage, and physical distribution. Whenever there is a sales lag, special-event pricing is an alternative that marketers should consider.

Comparison Discounting   **Comparison discounting** sets the price of a product at a specific level and simultaneously compares it with a higher price. The higher price may be the product's previous price, the price of a competing brand, the product's price at another retail outlet (as shown in Figure 21.15), or a manufacturer's suggested retail price. Customers may find comparative discounting informative, and it can have a significant impact on them. However, because this pricing strategy has on occasion led to deceptive pricing practices, the Federal Trade Commission has established guidelines for comparison discounting. If the higher price against which the comparison is made is the price formerly charged for the product, sellers must have made the previous price available to customers for a reasonable period of time. If sellers present the higher price as the one charged by other retailers in the same trade area, they must be able to demonstrate that this claim is true. When they present the higher price as the manufacturer's suggested retail price, then the higher price must be similar to the price at which a reasonable proportion of the product was sold. Some manufacturers' suggested retail prices are so high that very few products are actually sold at those prices; in such cases, it would be deceptive to use comparison discounting. An example of deceptive comparison discounting occurred when a major retailer was found to have sold 93 percent of its power tools on sale, with discounts ranging from 10 to 40 percent. The retailer's frequent price reductions meant that the tools were sold at sale prices most of the year. Thus, comparisons with regular prices were deemed to be deceptive.

Determination of a Specific Price

A pricing strategy will yield a certain price. However, this price may need refinement to make it consistent with pricing practices in a particular market or industry.

Pricing strategies should help in setting a final price. If they are to do so, it is important for marketers to establish pricing objectives, to have considerable knowledge about target market customers, and to determine demand, price elasticity, costs, and competitive factors. Also, the way that pricing is used in the marketing mix will affect the final price.

In the absence of government price controls, pricing remains a flexible and convenient way to adjust the marketing mix. In most situations, prices can be adjusted quickly—in a matter of minutes or over a few days. This flexibility and freedom do not characterize the other components of the marketing mix.

Summary

The eight stages in the process of setting prices are (1) selecting pricing objectives; (2) assessing the target market's evaluation of price; (3) determining demand; (4) analyzing demand, cost, and profit relationships; (5) evaluating competitors' prices; (6) choosing a basis for pricing; (7) selecting a pricing strategy; and (8) determining a specific price.

The first stage, setting pricing objectives, is critical because pricing objectives form a foundation on which the decisions of subsequent stages are based. Organizations may use numerous pricing objectives: short-term and long-term ones, and different ones for different products and market segments.

The second stage in establishing prices, assessing the target market's evaluation of price, tells a marketer how much emphasis to place on price and may help determine how far above the competition the firm can set its prices. Understanding how important a product is to customers in comparison with other products, as well as customers' expectations of quality, helps marketers correctly assess the target market's evaluation of price.

In the third stage, the organization must determine the demand for its product. The classic demand curve is a graph of the quantity of products expected to be sold at various prices, if other factors hold constant. It illustrates that, as price falls, the quantity demanded usually increases. However, for prestige products, there is a direct positive relationship between price and quantity demanded: demand increases as price increases. Next, price elasticity of demand—the percentage change in quantity demanded relative to a given percentage change in price—must be determined. If demand is elastic, a change in price causes an opposite change in total revenue. Inelastic demand results in a parallel change in total revenue when a product's price is changed.

Analysis of demand, cost, and profit relationships—the fourth stage of the process—can be accomplished through marginal analysis or breakeven analysis. Marginal analysis is the examination of what happens to a firm's costs and revenues when production (or sales volume) is changed by one unit. Marginal analysis combines the demand curve with a firm's costs to develop an optimum price for maximum profit. Fixed costs do not vary with changes in the number of units produced or sold; average fixed cost is the fixed cost per unit produced. Variable costs vary directly with changes in the number of units produced or sold. Average variable cost is the variable cost per unit produced. Total cost is the sum of average fixed cost and average variable cost times the quantity produced. The optimum price is the point at which marginal cost (the cost associated with producing one more unit of the product) equals marginal revenue (the change in total revenue that occurs when one additional unit of the product is sold). Marginal analysis is only a model; it offers little help in pricing new products before costs and revenues are established.

Breakeven analysis (determining the number of units that must be sold to break even) is important in setting the price. The point at which the costs of production equal the revenue from selling the product is the breakeven point. To use breakeven analysis effectively, a marketer should determine the breakeven point for each of several alternative prices. This determination makes it possible to compare the effects on total revenue, total costs, and the breakeven point for each price under consideration. However, this approach assumes that the quantity demanded is basically fixed and that the major task is to set prices to recover costs.

A marketer needs to be aware of the prices charged for competing brands. This allows a firm to keep its prices the same as a competitor's prices when nonprice competition is used. If a company uses price as a competitive tool, it can price its brand below competing brands.

The three major dimensions on which prices can be based are cost, demand, and competition. When using cost-based pricing, a firm determines price by adding a dollar amount or percentage to the cost of the product. Two common cost-based pricing methods are cost-plus and markup pricing. Demand-based pricing is based on the level of demand for the product. To use this method, a marketer must be able to estimate the amounts of a product that buyers will demand at different prices. Demand-based pricing results in a high price when demand for a product is strong and a low price when demand is weak. In the case of competition-based pricing, costs and revenues are secondary to competitors' prices.

A pricing strategy is an approach or a course of action designed to achieve pricing and marketing objectives. Pricing strategies help marketers solve the practical problems of establishing prices. The most common pricing strategies are differential pricing, new-product pricing, product-line pricing, psychological pricing, professional pricing, and promotional pricing.

When marketers employ differential pricing, they charge different buyers different prices for the same quality and quantity of products. Negotiated pricing, secondary-market discounting, periodic discounting, and random discounting are all ways in which differential pricing can occur. Establishing the final price through bargaining between the seller and customer is called negotiated pricing. The strategy of secondary-market pricing involves setting one price for the primary target market and a different price for another market; often, the price charged in the secondary market is lower. Marketers employ a strategy of periodic discounting when they temporarily lower their prices on a patterned or systematic basis; the reason for the reduction may be a seasonal change, a model-year change, or a holiday. Random discounting occurs on an unsystematic basis.

Two strategies used in new-product pricing are price skimming and penetration pricing. With price skimming, an organization charges the highest price that buyers who most desire the product will pay. A penetration price is a low price designed to penetrate a market and gain a significant market share quickly.

Product-line pricing establishes and adjusts the prices of multiple products within a product line. This strategy includes captive pricing, in which marketers price the basic product in a product line low, but price related items at a higher level; premium pricing, in which prices on higher-quality or more versatile products are set higher than those on other models in the product line; bait pricing, in which marketers try to attract customers by pricing an item in the product line low with the intention of selling a higher-priced item in the line; and price lining, in which an organization sets a limited number of prices for selected groups or lines of merchandise. Organizations that employ price lining assume that the demand for various groups of products is inelastic.

Psychological pricing attempts to influence customers' perceptions of price to make a product's price more attractive. Reference pricing is a strategy in which marketers price a product at a moderate level and position it next to a more expensive model or brand. Another strategy, bundle pricing, is the packaging together of two or more complementary products that are sold for a single price. In multiple-unit pricing, two or more identical products are packaged together and sold for a single price. To reduce or eliminate use of frequent short-term price reductions, some organizations employ everyday low pricing, a strategy of setting a low price for products on a consistent basis. When employing odd-even pricing, marketers try to influence buyers' perceptions of the price or the product by ending the price with certain numbers. Customary pricing is pricing based on tradition. With prestige pricing, prices are set at an artificially high level to provide prestige or a quality image.

Professional pricing is used by people who have great skill or experience in a particular field, therefore allowing them to set the price. This concept carries with it the idea that professionals have an ethical responsibility not to overcharge customers. Price, as an ingredient in the marketing mix, is often coordinated with promotion. The two variables are sometimes so interrelated that the pricing policy is promotion-oriented. Promotional pricing includes price leaders, special-event pricing, and comparison discounting.

Special-event pricing involves advertised sales or price cutting linked to a holiday, season, or event. Marketers who use a comparison discounting strategy price a product at a specific level and compare it with a higher price.

Once a price is determined by using one or more pricing strategies, it will need to be refined to a final price consistent with the pricing practices in a particular market or industry.

Important Terms

Demand curve	Breakeven point	Random discounting	Bundle pricing
Price elasticity of demand	Cost-based pricing	Price skimming	Multiple-unit pricing
Fixed costs	Cost-plus pricing	Penetration pricing	Everyday low prices (EDLP)
Average fixed cost	Markup pricing	Product-line pricing	Odd-even pricing
Variable costs	Demand-based pricing	Captive pricing	Customary pricing
Average variable cost	Competition-based pricing	Premium pricing	Prestige pricing
Total cost	Differential pricing	Bait pricing	Professional pricing
Average total cost	Negotiated pricing	Price lining	Price leaders
Marginal cost (MC)	Secondary-market pricing	Psychological pricing	Special-event pricing
Marginal revenue (MR)	Periodic discounting	Reference pricing	Comparison discounting

Discussion and Review Questions

1. Identify the eight stages involved in the process of establishing prices.

2. Why do most demand curves demonstrate an inverse relationship between price and quantity?

3. List the characteristics of products that have inelastic demand. Give several examples of such products.

4. Explain why optimum profits should occur when marginal cost equals marginal revenue.

5. The Chambers Company has just gathered estimates for doing a breakeven analysis for a new product. Variable costs are $7 a unit. The additional plant will cost $48,000. The new product will be charged $18,000 a year for its share of general overhead. Advertising expenditures will be $80,000, and $55,000 will be spent on distribution. If the product sells for $12, what is the breakeven point in units? What is the breakeven point in dollar sales volume?

6. Why should a marketer be aware of competitors' prices?

7. What are the benefits of cost-based pricing?

8. Under what conditions is cost-plus pricing most appropriate?

9. A retailer purchases a can of soup for 24 cents and sells it for 36 cents. Calculate the markup as percentage of cost and as percentage of selling price.

10. What is differential pricing? In what ways can it be achieved?

11. For what type of products would price skimming be most appropriate? For what type of products would penetration pricing be more effective?

12. Describe bundle pricing and give three examples using different industries.

13. What are the advantages and disadvantages of using "everyday low prices"?

14. Why do customers associate price with quality? When should prestige pricing be used?

15. Are price leaders a realistic approach to pricing?

Application Questions

1. Price skimming and penetration pricing are strategies commonly used to set the base price of a new product. Which strategy is most appropriate for the following products? Explain.
   a. short airline flights between cities in Florida
   b. DVD player
   c. backpack or book bag with a lifetime warranty
   d. season tickets for a newly franchised NBA basketball team

2. Price lining is used to set a limited number of prices for selected lines of merchandise. Visit local retail stores to find examples of price lining. For what types of products and stores is this most common? For what products and stores is price lining not typical or usable?

3. Professional pricing is used by persons who have great skill in a particular field, such as doctors, lawyers, and business consultants. Find examples (advertisements, personal contacts) that reflect a professional pricing policy. How is the price established? Are there any restrictions on the services performed at that price?

Internet Exercise & Resources

Southwest Airlines

For years, Southwest Airlines has successfully taken a low-cost, on-time, no-frills, no-reserved-seats, and no-meals approach to air travel. Southwest launched a "ticketless" electronic travel system to trim travel agent commissions, and it also uses an advanced computer reservation system for automated booking of passengers. Visit the Southwest Airlines Web site at

   http://iflyswa.com

1. Determine the various promotional prices available for a flight from Little Rock, Arkansas, to Dallas, Texas.
2. How many different fares are available from Little Rock to Dallas?
3. What type of pricing policy is Southwest using on its Little Rock–Dallas route?

E-Center Resources

Visit http://www.prideferrell.com to find several resources to help you succeed in mastering the material in this chapter, plus additional materials that will help you expand your marketing knowledge. The Web site includes

 Internet exercise updates plus additional exercises

 ACE self-tests

abc Chapter summary with hotlinked glossary

 Hotlinks to companies featured in this chapter

 Resource Center

 Career Center

 Marketing plan worksheets

VIDEO CASE 21.1

Vector Aeromotive: Pricing Luxury Sports Cars

How does a company set the right price for one of the fastest sports cars in the world? Vector Aeromotive, based in Green Cove Springs, Florida, is facing that challenge with its line of limited-edition M12 automobiles. Crafted by hand, each M12 contains an extremely powerful 500-horsepower V-12 motor in a sleek, exotic chassis. The company's president identifies the target segment for Vector cars as people with significant disposable income. This segment includes sports car collectors and successful businesspeople who want to treat themselves after completing a major deal.

Pricing a product like the M12 is far from simple. Vector Aeromotive must think carefully about how much its customers are willing to pay. It also must consider how much revenue it needs to cover its costs and to provide an appropriate return on investment for its investors. On the basis of the company's costs, the prices of competing luxury sports cars, and the price elasticity of demand for such cars, Vector set the price of the M12 at $207,000.

The largest items in Vector's yearly budget relate to the research, development, and engineering activities needed to support the car's leading-edge automotive design and technology. Although these vary annually, they totaled over $4 million in one recent year. Included in the development budget is the cost of complying with government regulations that require automakers to build and crash-test their models to determine the probable damage in the event of an accident.

Giant automakers like General Motors lose relatively little when they pluck a few of their millions of mass-produced vehicles off the assembly lines for mandated crash testing. However, Vector's manufacturing process is entirely different from GM's; the company painstakingly builds every car by hand, including any models that will be used for crash-testing. Vector's cost of compliance is very high, adding up to as much as 15 to 20 percent of its development costs. This cost must ultimately be passed along to customers as part of the price of the M12.

By looking closely at how competitors price their high-end sports cars and tracking how many cars each competitor sells, Vector's management is able to estimate the general level of demand and the price elasticity for luxury models like the M12. For example, Vector sees the Diablo, made by Italy's Lamborghini, as a close rival of the M12 in the global market. By studying the Diablo's historical sales volume and price points, Vector can get a sense of the M12's sales potential and the reference prices its customers have in mind when shopping for this kind of high-performance car.

Part of Vector's competitive pricing strategy is to position the M12 as a luxury sports car with a bit of American value. The car's six-figure price places it in the prestige pricing category, well above what buyers might pay for any mainstream sports car. But at the same time, the company keeps a close eye on world prices for sports cars to be sure that the price of the M12 never gets too far out of line.

To compete more effectively against well-known global brands like Lamborghini, Vector is building the reputation of its brand by entering a track version of its M12 in high-profile racing events, such as the Nevada Grand Prix. Entering the car in races that receive extensive public exposure through television coverage and sports press, allows the company to showcase the M12's speed and handling.

Building good relationships with the world press, especially with influential sportswriters, helps the company garner more publicity and generate a word-of-mouth buzz to spread the brand's fame beyond the racing world. For example, Vector recently invited an automotive writer for the London *Sunday Times* to drive the M12. After spending some time behind the wheel, the writer glowingly described the experience in a newspaper article, concluding, "This is what supercars are all about."

Selling high-end sports cars in the $200,000+ category is not an easy marketing task, as Vector has learned. In some years, the company has managed to sell just a handful of its M12 models. Because quality is an important ingredient in a luxury sports car, the company is moving slowly to increase production. Vector has been able to offset part of the high cost of development by selling some of its proprietary chassis technology to Lamborghini. Whether the company will gain an edge in the race for market share among high-end sports cars remains to be seen. But with proper pricing in its marketing mix, Vector is in a good position to compete with other makers of luxury sports cars in the United States and abroad.[7]

Questions for Discussion

1. How does building its cars by hand affect Vector's variable costs? How does it affect Vector's fixed costs?
2. Is Vector using cost-based, demand-based, or competition-based pricing? Explain you answer.
3. Does Vector appear to be using price or nonprice competition?
4. What would be the likely effect on potential customers if Vector dramatically lowered its price? Why?

The Apple iMac: Byting into Pricing

One product brought Apple Computer back to profitability: the colorful and stylish iMac. Apple scored big in the 1980s with its Macintosh line of personal computers, which were hailed for their compact size and easy operating system. Then the company lost significant market share in the 1990s as competitors launched new Windows-based personal computers priced lower than the Macintosh. In a three-year period, Apple's share of the education market plummeted from 47 percent to just 27 percent. Its share of the consumer market for PCs also dropped during that period, falling from nearly 15 percent to a mere 5 percent.

By the time Apple was getting set to launch the iMac, it was playing catch-up in highly competitive markets that were growing by as much as 15 percent every year. As market share slipped, so did the retail space devoted to software titles for Apple computers, and the ranks of developers writing new programs for Apple products got considerably thinner, too. Worse, the company was having profitability problems and posted hefty losses for six consecutive quarters.

Then came the sleek iMac, a computer designed to be plugged in and turned on right out of the box. The iMac has an integrated monitor unlike desktop Windows-based PCs, which have separate monitors that must be connected by cable to the main processing unit. The iMac also sports a CD-ROM and a built-in modem for convenient access to the Internet. The product's simplicity appeals to first-time buyers who were often intimidated by the complexity of Windows-based PCs. However, some experts have been bothered by the lack of a floppy-disk drive; some have also expressed concern that the factory-installed modem on the iMac runs at slower speeds than those available on competing PCs.

With the iMac, Apple also launched a new pricing strategy, putting a $1,299 price tag on the first models. "People are seeing the value at these prices, and our goal is to continue to lower prices on products like iMac," CEO Steven Jobs explained. "An iMac costs about as much as heating a New England home in the winter, a lot less than the cost of an automobile. We're not in the sweet spot totally, but we're getting there. For Apple, this is a pretty big step. Apple hasn't had a compelling product under $2,000 for the last several years."

The "sweet spot" of the PC market has been drifting downward to the under-$1,000 category. Major competitors such IBM, Compaq, and Hewlett-Packard have been using basic models, low prices, and heavy advertising to attract customers who want to buy PCs for family or home-office use. Just weeks after Compaq went below a $1,000 price tag by offering a $699 Windows-based PC, IBM responded with a $599 PC. These low-priced products were sold without monitors, and they lacked the features prized by power users, like the fastest chips and the largest hard-disk capacity.

Apple fought back with a $100 million multimedia campaign to boost consumer demand for the iMac and its other products, including PowerBook laptops. With the theme "Think Different," the television and print ads did not rely on head-to-head comparisons of technical specifications, the way ads for many competing products did, nor did they mention anything about price. Instead, Apple's ads re-emphasize that Apple computers are different from and, by implication, better than other computers.

The company took a number of other steps to focus on profitability. In addition to slashing operating expenses by 32 percent, Apple changed the depth of its product mix. Reducing the number of different models in each product line allowed the company to lower production and distribution costs. Apple changed its distribution strategy as well by concentrating on only two wholesale distributors and two main retail chains. Finally, following the popular (and profitable) lead of Dell Computer, Apple began offering build-to-order computers sold directly to customers.

Combined with the new lower-pricing strategy, all these marketing mix changes gave Apple the leverage it needed to regain ground in the marketplace and reverse the downward trend in profitability. Before the computer even hit store shelves, the company had 150,000 orders. More than 500,000 iMacs were sold in the United States during the year-end holiday shopping season following the product's introduction. Interest also ran high outside the United States. When the iMac was exhibited at the Apple Expo in Paris, it drew crowds of consumers, educators, and business customers clamoring to try out the colorful new product.

Supported by the iMac, Apple's sales and profit margins improved dramatically. Its fourth-quarter profits were 223 percent higher than the same period one year earlier, and its fourth-quarter profit margins were nearly three times higher than in the previous year. In all, Apple sold more than $6 billion worth of computers and accessories the year it introduced the iMac.

Using aggressive pricing and other marketing efforts, Apple not only boosted its financial performance, it convinced more software developers to work on programs for its products. For example, Intuit, which makes Quicken personal-finance software, had not planned to update its Macintosh version of the program. However, after Apple showed the iMac to company executives, Intuit had a change of heart and started planning a Quicken upgrade for the Macintosh. And more software means customers have more reason to consider iMac computers—and buy one, if the price is right.[8]

Questions for Discussion

1. What type or types of pricing objectives did Apple set for its iMac computer?
2. Which new-product pricing approach did Apple use for the iMac? Explain your answer.
3. When the iMac's price was set at $1,299, was Apple using cost-based, demand-based, or competition-based pricing? Explain.
4. Should Apple use pricing to more effectively compete with Windows-based PCs priced under $1,000? Why or why not?

STRATEGIC CASE 6

United States Postal Service Competes through Pricing

The American mail delivery system, established two decades before the country's independence, was changed forever in 1970 when the United States Post Office was transformed into a government-owned corporation called the United States Postal Service (U.S.P.S.). In creating the U.S.P.S., the government retained the power to approve or veto postal rates, but not to set them. The U.S.P.S.'s 775,000 employees now handle nearly 200 billion letters and packages going to more than 130 million addresses every year. Pricing is a key marketing weapon in the organization's battle with FedEx and United Parcel Service, its two most formidable rivals in the hotly competitive delivery business.

A Profusion of Services at Different Prices

Originally, the U.S.P.S. was directed to provide universal service for every class of mail and to price letter mail uniformly. The growing number and types of mail service, however, have led to much variety in pricing. First-class mail, which generates more than half of the U.S.P.S.'s revenue, presently starts at 33 cents for a one-ounce letter and 20 cents for a postcard. Other rates apply to parcel post delivery and various classifications of periodicals, printed matter, standard mail, and library mail.

Two other U.S.P.S. services, Priority Mail and Express Mail, compete head-on with services offered by FedEx and United Parcel Service. Priority Mail, priced at $3.20 for up to two pounds, offers expedited delivery of first-class mail in just two to three days. For an extra fee, customers can order delivery confirmation to find out exactly when their Priority Mail item was received. Priority Mail is significantly less expensive than two-day and three-day delivery by FedEx and United Parcel Service—which is why it is producing nearly three times the annual revenue contributed by Express Mail. Express Mail guarantees overnight delivery of domestic letters and packages, even on weekends and holidays, at a price of $11.75 for a half-pound package or $15.75 for up to two pounds.

Coping with a Slow Pricing Process

Postal price increases take time because the U.S.P.S. must go through the lengthy process of appealing to the Postal Rate Commission for official approval to change its rates. The U.S.P.S. must also cope with personnel costs that take up 77 percent of its budget, compared with just 60 percent at United Parcel Service. But other than offering a minimal price break for presorted packages, the U.S.P.S. is not allowed to discount its prices, even for high-volume customers, which means it has less flexibility than competitors when it comes to pricing strategies. Not long after a recent U.S.P.S. rate increase, FedEx and United Parcel Service announced rate hikes as well, raising their delivery rates an average of less than 3 percent, still well above what the U.S.P.S. charges for Priority Mail.

Delivering Packages and Information

The number of domestic and international delivery options offered by FedEx and United Parcel Service dwarfs the U.S.P.S.'s offerings. Their prices are higher, but customers can choose exactly when they want their shipments delivered. Customers can also track every item through every stage in the delivery process, from the initial pick-up to the point at which the recipient signs for the package. In this way, they can quickly verify that their packages have been safely delivered to the right recipient at the right time.

The U.S.P.S. cannot match its rivals' elaborate tracking mechanisms, but its ability to confirm package delivery is a big step forward. "Delivery confirmation enhances the U.S.P.S. to the point where it might be the future of the catalog industry," says a catalog retailer that shifted half its shipments to Priority Mail once the confirmation option became available. Internet retailers like Amazon.com offer Priority Mail delivery because of its cost efficiency. Yet because Priority Mail does not guarantee delivery on a particular day, it does not meet the expectations of all Internet and catalog shoppers. "A lot of customers want to know exactly when their packages are going to arrive," notes another catalog retailer.

Promoting Priority Mail

Advertising campaigns by FedEx and United Parcel Service keep those brands in the public eye throughout the year. Fighting back, the U.S.P.S. has used various promotional techniques to position Priority Mail as the low-priced alternative to its rivals, second-day services. It has also drawn attention to the fact that, unlike its competitors, it delivers on Saturdays at no extra charge. "There were several reasons for focusing on Priority Mail—including the legal constraints of not being able to aggressively sell Express Mail at a discount—that also precluded us from pushing Parcel Post," explains David Shinnebarger, the U.S.P.S.'s manager of expedited and package services, "but I knew we could build a program around Priority Mail to grow revenue for the package businesses."

The U.S.P.S. has used print ads, television and radio commercials, outdoor ads, direct mail, and sponsorship deals to convey its low-price message to businesses as well as consumers. For example, one direct mail campaign targeted 300,000 businesses that annually spend more than $100,000 on shipping—a segment that accounts for 70 percent of all domestic shipping. CEOs and CFOs, key members of a business's buying center, received three different postcards every few days, each with a message about Priority Mail's low price, convenient drop-off and pick-up locations, and Saturday delivery. Of the targeted businesses, 10 percent responded to the campaign, and telemarketing raised that response rate to 27 percent. Priority Mail revenues jumped following this campaign; the full-year increase was $535 million more than the service had rung up during the previous year. The U.S.P.S. also has run an aggressive price-oriented television campaign, comparing its Priority Mail rates with the rates charged by FedEx and UPS.

As part of a brand-building campaign, the U.S.P.S. recently agreed to become the official delivery service of the Heisman Trophy, a college football award. "We're looking to elevate the Priority Mail brand as a top performer by associating it with the Heisman," says Shinnebarger. Such sponsorships let the organization put the spotlight on the quality of Priority Mail service, not just on the lower price. At the same time, the U.S.P.S. is continuing to ask Congress for more freedom to compete with rivals that are agitating for a bigger slice of the package delivery pie.[9]

Questions for Discussion
1. What might customers use as reference prices when evaluating the pricing of Priority Mail service?
2. Do the U.S.P.S. and FedEx have similar pricing objectives when pricing their similar services? Explain.
3. What pricing strategy is the U.S.P.S. using?
4. What issues must U.S.P.S. officials confront when making pricing decisions that affect competition with FedEx and United Parcel Service?

Part Seven

Implementation and Electronic Marketing

We have divided marketing into several sets of variables and have discussed the decisions and activities associated with each variable. By now you should understand how to analyze marketing opportunities and how to identify the components of the marketing mix. It is time to focus on how these components are implemented in a dynamic environment. In Chapter 22 we explore approaches to organizing a marketing unit, issues regarding strategy implementation, and techniques for controlling marketing strategies. Chapters 23 provides a framework for understanding the use of the Internet in marketing strategy. It offers insights about characteristics of the Internet and how marketing strategy can be implemented. Online Chapter 24 is an extension of Chapter 23 with the most up-to-date information and examples about "electronic marketing."

22

Marketing Implementation and Control

OBJECTIVES

- To describe the marketing implementation process and the major approaches to marketing implementation

- To understand the components of the marketing process

- To learn about the role of the marketing unit in a firm's organizational structure

- To identify the alternatives for organizing a marketing unit

- To understand the control processes used in managing marketing strategies

- To learn how cost and sales analyses are used to evaluate the performance of marketing strategies

- To learn about the major components of a marketing audit

564

Amtrak Rides into the Twenty-First Century

In 1971, the federal government created the National Railroad Passenger Corporation, better know as Amtrak, to manage the nation's intercity passenger rail service. Like the U.S. Postal Service, Amtrak operates as a quasi-public corporation. The agency serves five hundred communities in forty-four states, and in 1998 it earned more than $1 billion in passenger revenue by carrying more than 21 million passengers a total of 5 billion miles. Despite its effective monopoly, Amtrak has yet to turn a profit. Facing a Congressional mandate to become self-sufficient by 2002, Amtrak is implementing a challenging new four-year business plan to ride into the twenty-first century.

Amtrak's strategic plan to become a self-sufficient modern rail service includes the development and implementation of five key strategies. The first of these strategies entails building a marketing-oriented network. To implement it, the agency has begun extensive marketing research aimed at defining consumer demand, identifying growth opportunities, and increasing its share of travel business inside the United States. Amtrak's second strategy involves working with states and other partners to develop new rail corridors in the West Midwest, Southeast, along the Gulf Coast, and in New York State; this strategy includes the launching a high-speed rail program in 1999. To implement Amtrak's third strategy of delivering a consistently high level of service, the agency is developing a service standards program, which ultimately will boost customer loyalty and ridership. To implement the fourth strategy—revitalizing the Amtrak brand—the firm has taken a commercial approach to defining Amtrak's product and positioning it competitively among other transportation carriers. Finally, Amtrak is working to identify commercial and investment partners to generate additional revenues to support basic rail services and to maximize Amtrak's own investments.

To implement these strategies, Amtrak has established a number of performance goals. These include increasing revenues by $789 million by offering new and more frequent passenger services, expanding mail and express businesses, and exploiting new commercial opportunities; increasing ridership by 21 percent over the four-year business plan; producing net incremental revenues of $10 million a year by launching high-speed rail service; and improving annual operating performance by $426 million in 2002.

To respond to customer complaints about service, Amtrak is revamping its onboard services with new menus, more legroom, and tougher standards for employee conduct. It is also sprucing up train stations, restoring trains, and adding new trains—including the nation's first high-speed train, which can travel up to 150 miles per hour between Boston and Washington—to provide better, faster service. According to Amtrak's new chief executive George Warrington, "The key to Amtrak's long-term success depends on transforming the national passenger rail system into a more market-based system that delivers services that customers want and takes them to and from destinations of their choice."[1]

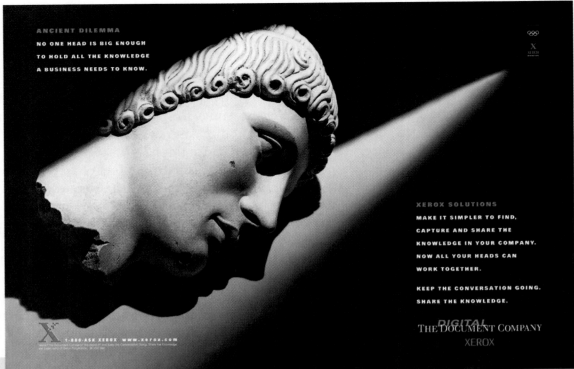

ANCIENT DILEMMA

NO ONE HEAD IS BIG ENOUGH
TO HOLD ALL THE KNOWLEDGE
A BUSINESS NEEDS TO KNOW.

XEROX SOLUTIONS

MAKE IT SIMPLER TO FIND,
CAPTURE AND SHARE THE
KNOWLEDGE IN YOUR COMPANY.
NOW ALL YOUR HEADS CAN
WORK TOGETHER.

KEEP THE CONVERSATION GOING.
SHARE THE KNOWLEDGE.

THE *DIGITAL* DOCUMENT COMPANY
XEROX

Figure 22.1
Marketing
Implementation
Xerox links strategic
implementation to
employee productivity
and business success.

To achieve its objective of becoming self-sufficient, Amtrak must carefully implement its strategic plan. Even the best strategic plan will fail if it is poorly implemented. This chapter therefore concentrates on how marketing strategies should be implemented and controlled. First, we explore several issues regarding implementation. We then focus on the marketing unit's position in the organization and the ways the unit itself can be organized. Next, we consider the basic components of the process of control and discuss the use of cost and sales analyses to evaluate the effectiveness of marketing strategies and measure the firm's performance. Finally, we describe a marketing audit.

The Marketing Implementation Process

marketing implementation   The process of putting marketing strategies into action

Marketing implementation is the process of putting marketing strategies into action. It is the "how?" of marketing strategy. Although implementation is often neglected in favor of strategic planning, the implementation process itself can determine whether a marketing strategy is successful. In short, good marketing strategy combined with bad marketing implementation is a guaranteed recipe for failure. In Figure 22.1, Xerox provides data management solutions to assist customers in implementing their marketing strategies.

An important aspect of the implementation process is understanding that marketing strategies almost always turn out differently than expected. In essence, all organizations have two types of strategy: intended strategy and realized strategy.[2] **Intended strategy** is the strategy the organization decided on during the planning phase and wants to use, whereas **realized strategy** is the strategy that actually takes place. The difference between the two is often the result of how the intended strategy is implemented. The realized strategy, though not necessarily any better or worse than the intended strategy, often does not live up to planners' expectations.

intended strategy
Strategy the company decides on during the planning phase

realized strategy
Strategy that actually takes place

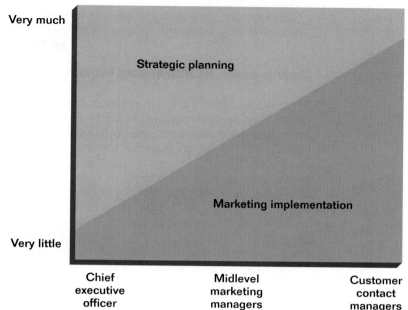

Time spent on

Figure 22.2
The Separation of Strategic Planning and Marketing Implementation
Source: Adapted from O. C. Ferrell, Michael D. Hartline, George H. Lucas, Jr., and David Luck, *Marketing Strategy.* Copyright © 1999

Problems in Implementing Marketing Activities

Why do marketing strategies sometimes turn out differently than expected? The most common reason is that managers fail to realize that marketing implementation is just as important as marketing strategy. The relationship between strategic planning and implementation creates a number of problems for managers when they plan implementation activities. Three of the most important problems are as follows:[3]

- *Marketing strategy and implementation are related.* Companies often assume that strategic planning always comes first, followed by implementation. In reality, marketing strategies and implementation should be planned simultaneously. The content of the marketing strategy determines how it will be implemented. Likewise, implementation activities may require changes in the marketing strategy. Thus, it is important for marketing managers to understand that strategy and implementation are really two sides of the same coin.

- *Marketing strategy and implementation are constantly evolving.* Strategy and implementation are both affected by the marketing environment. Since the environment is constantly changing, both marketing strategy and implementation must remain flexible enough to adapt. The relationship between strategy and implementation is never fixed; it is always evolving to accommodate changes in customer needs, government regulation, or competition. For example, when Western Pacific Airlines began service from Colorado Springs, competitors like American and United moved to match Western Pacific's discount fares to the same destination cities. When Western Pacific went out of business, the competitors responded by raising their fares, although they remain lower than before Western Pacific entered the picture.[4]

- *The responsibility for marketing strategy and implementation is separated.* This problem is often the biggest obstacle in implementing marketing strategies. Typically, marketing strategies are developed by the top managers in an organization. However, the responsibility for implementing those strategies rests at the frontline, or customer-contact point, of the organization. This separation, shown in Figure 22.2, can impair implementation in two ways. First, because top managers are separated from the frontline, where the company interacts daily with customers, they may not grasp the unique problems associated with implementing marketing activities.

Second, customer-contact managers and employees are often responsible for implementing strategies, even though they had no voice in developing them. Consequently, some customer-contact employees may lack motivation and commitment. We will discuss the importance of employee motivation later in this chapter.

Components of Marketing Implementation

As shown in Figure 22.3, the implementation process has several components, all of which must mesh if implementation is to succeed. At the center of marketing implementation are shared goals and objectives. They occupy the central position because they draw the entire organization together into a single, functioning unit, holding all components together to ensure successful marketing implementation. Goals may be simple statements of the company's objectives. Northwest Airlines, for example, has communicated to all levels of the organization its goal of on-time arrivals. On the other hand, the goals may be derived from mission statements that outline the organization's philosophy and direction. Without shared goals or objectives to hold the organization together, different parts of the firm may work at cross-purposes and limit the success of the entire organization.

The employee component of marketing implementation includes the functional area of human resources and such factors as the quality, skill, and diversity of the firm's work force. In Figure 22.4, GTE and Nordstrom discuss the relevance of valuing diversity in the workplace. Issues like employee recruitment, selection, and training have great bearing on the implementation of marketing activities.[5] Organizations must design programs to recruit and select the right employees for the job. Through training and socialization programs, employees learn what is expected of them in implementing a marketing strategy.[6]

Closely linked to the employee component is leadership, the art of managing people. The leadership provided by an organization's managers and the performance of employees go hand in hand in the implementation process. How managers communicate with employees and how they motivate them to implement a marketing strategy are important facets of leadership. Research suggests that marketing implementation may be more successful when leaders create an organizational culture characterized by open communication between employees and managers. This type of leadership creates a climate in which employees feel free to discuss their opinions and

Figure 22.3
Marketing Implementation

"The **more diverse** we are inside, the better able we are to **help** our **customers** on the outside."

Cassandra Henderson,
Human Resources Manager

AT NORDSTROM, WE UNDERSTAND THAT SUCCESS TAKES MANY CONTRIBUTORS. THAT'S WHY WE STRIVE TO MAINTAIN A WORK FORCE THAT REPRESENTS PEOPLE OF ALL RACES, CULTURES, AGES AND ABILITIES. IT'S PART OF OUR COMMITMENT TO SUPPORT THE COMMUNITIES IN WHICH WE DO BUSINESS. IF YOU'D LIKE INFORMATION ABOUT CAREER OPPORTUNITIES AT NORDSTROM, CONTACT HUMAN RESOURCES AT THE STORE NEAREST YOU. OR, IF YOU'RE INTERESTED IN OUR SUPPLIER DIVERSITY PROGRAM, CALL (206) 373-4368.

NORDSTROM

Figure 22.4
Components of Marketing Implementation
GTE and Nordstrom value diversity. GTE encourages its partners and clients to share its philosophy. Nordstrom explains that a diverse work force can better serve a variety of customers and support their local communities.

external customers
Individuals who patronize a business

internal customers
A company's employees

internal marketing
Coordinating internal exchanges between the firm and its employees to achieve successful external exchanges between the firm and its customers

ideas about implementation tasks, and managers and employees trust each other.[7] We examine additional components of marketing implementation—internal marketing, total quality management, marketing structure, and marketing control—as well as employee motivation and communication, later in this chapter.

Approaches to Marketing Implementation

Once they grasp the problems and recognize the components of marketing implementation, marketing managers can decide on an approach for implementing marketing activities. Just as organizations can achieve their goals by using different marketing strategies, they can implement their marketing strategies by using different approaches. In this section, we discuss two general approaches to marketing implementation: internal marketing and total quality management. Both approaches represent mindsets that marketing managers may adopt when organizing and planning marketing activities. These approaches are not mutually exclusive; indeed, many companies adopt both when designing marketing activities.

Internal Marketing   **External customers** are the individuals who patronize a business—the familiar definition of customers—whereas **internal customers** are the employees who work for a company. For implementation to be successful, the needs of both groups of customers must be met. If the internal customers are not satisfied, then it is likely that the external customers will not be, either. Thus, in addition to targeting marketing activities at external customers, firms use internal marketing to attract, motivate, and retain qualified internal customers by designing internal products (jobs) that satisfy their wants and needs. **Internal marketing** is a management philosophy that coordinates internal exchanges between the organization and its employees to achieve successful external exchanges between the organization and its customers.[8]

Generally speaking, internal marketing refers to the managerial actions necessary to make all members of the marketing organization understand and accept their respective roles in implementing the marketing strategy. This means that everyone, from the president of the company down to the hourly workers on the shop floor, must understand the role they play in carrying out their jobs and implementing the marketing strategy. Consider Planet Hollywood, a chain of Hollywood-theme restaurants whose owners include such celebrities as Bruce Willis, Whoopi Goldberg, and Arnold Schwarzenegger. The restaurants touted their link with the firm's famous investors, but the movie stars were seldom seen after opening-day festivities at each restaurant. Unable to rub shoulders with the heavily promoted celebrities, customers focused instead on the food, which many judged a poor value. Consequently, many never went back a second time, and the company was forced to close several restaurants and to revise its strategy.[9] On the other hand, at Southwest Airlines, flight attendants are encouraged to deliver safety instructions to passengers in song or comedy routines worthy of a celebrity. Southwest's organizational culture of fun encourages employees to interact positively with customers to keep them smiling and provide a satisfying experience.[10] In short, anyone invested in the firm, both marketers and those who perform other functions, must recognize the tenet of customer orientation and service that underlies the marketing concept. Internal customers may also include a firm's franchisees. Building Customer Relationships describes one firm's efforts to help its franchisees succeed and satisfy customers.

Customer orientation is fostered by training and education and by keeping the lines of communication open throughout the firm. Southwest Airlines, for example, sends new employees to its "University for People" training program, where they learn about the airline's playful culture and history, its demanding standards for customer service, and how these standards can be achieved. According to Libby Sartain, Southwest's vice president for people, "We always tell our people to do what it takes to get the job done, and we always give them the tools."[11] Southwest's strong training program helps employees understand their role in satisfying the airline's customers and ensures they have the tools to do so.

Like external marketing activities, internal marketing may involve market segmentation, product development, research, distribution, and even public relations and sales promotion.[12] The internal marketing framework is shown in Figure 22.5. As

Figure 22.5
The Internal Marketing Framework

Source: Adapted from Nigel F. Piercy, *Market-Led Strategic Change,* Copyright © 1992, Butterworth-Heinemann Ltd., p. 371. Used with permission.

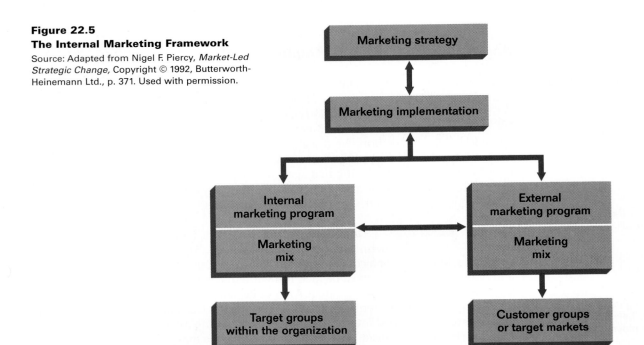

in external marketing, the marketing mix in internal marketing is designed to satisfy the needs of customers—in this case, both internal and external customers. For example, an organization may sponsor sales contests to inspire sales personnel to boost their selling efforts. This helps employees (and ultimately the company) to understand customers' needs and problems, teaches them valuable new skills, and heightens their enthusiasm for their regular jobs. In addition, many companies use planning sessions, workshops, letters, formal reports, and personal conversations to ensure that employees comprehend the corporate mission, the organization's goals, and the marketing strategy. The ultimate results are more satisfied employees and improved customer relations.

Total Quality Management   Quality has become a major concern in many organizations, particularly in light of intense foreign competition, more demanding customers, and poorer profit performance owing to reduced market shares and higher costs. Over the last few years, several U.S. firms have lost the dominant, competitive positions they had held for decades. To regain a competitive edge, a number of firms

BUILDING
customer relationships

Great Harvest Bread Company Grows through Learning Relationships

Like a number of successful startups, the Great Harvest Bread Company began in a garage. In this particular garage, located in Durham, Connecticut, Pete and Laura Wakeman baked bread and sold it at a roadside stand to put themselves through college. After college, the Wakemans moved to Great Falls, Montana, where in 1976 they opened a bakery called Great Harvest Bread. The venture proved so successful that friends and customers regularly inquired about how they might open stores based on the Great Harvest Bread concept. So, in 1982, the Wakemans sold their Great Falls store to Pete Rysted, the company's first franchisee. Today, the Great Harvest Bread Company, based in Dillon, Montana, oversees 130 franchised bakeries in thirty-four states. The bakeries generate annual revenues of more than $60 million. The franchiser is committed to "baking the best bread and providing the best customer service around" and to fostering productive relationships with and among its franchisees.

Unlike most franchise operations, Great Harvest doesn't impose standardized procedures on its franchisees but instead encourages innovation and fast learning. The company attributes its growth to its belief that "expansion comes from experimentation." So, new Great Harvest franchisees operate their bakeries as they see fit, although they may consult an operating manual that describes the best practices of established stores. One of the few conditions Great Harvest imposes on its franchisees is that they share what they learn with other franchisees.

In fact, Great Harvest believes that "owners make the best teachers." When Great Harvest grants a new franchise, the new owners attend a week-long training session on baking bread and running a small business. During training, which takes place at company headquarters, an experienced franchise owner serves as a role model and offers examples to help the new owner get started. After this week of training, new franchise owners are expected to visit two established franchises in different parts of the country to observe how their peers operate.

To help its new franchisees learn the trade, Great Harvest has an experienced franchise owners pay their stores a checkup visit within six months of their opening. The company pays for the visitor's travel expenses; it also covers half the expenses whenever one established owner visits another. In addition, Great Harvest maintains a companywide intranet that serves as a storehouse for recipes and ideas about managing, marketing, promotions, and decorating. Eighty percent of Great Harvest's franchisees communicate regularly with one another through E-mail. The interaction between franchiser and franchisee, and among franchises, helps keep the company growing and responding to its external customers' needs. As one franchisee says, "We stay in touch with the owners we met in Dillon and with the people we've visited. They're our best source for ideas."

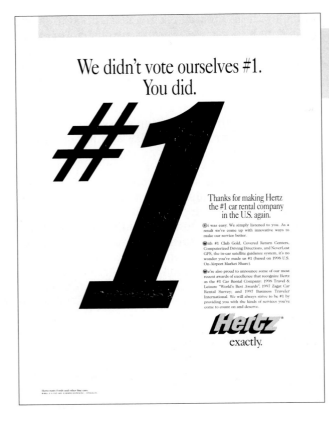

Figure 22.6
Total Quality Management
Hertz provides a service that is perceived
as high quality and a market leader.

have adopted a total quality management philosophy. **Total quality management (TQM)** is a philosophy that uniform commitment to quality in all areas of the organization will promote a culture that meets customers' perceptions of quality. It involves coordinating efforts at improving customer satisfaction, increasing employee participation and empowerment, forming and strengthening supplier partnerships, and facilitating an organizational culture of continuous quality improvement. Customers evaluate quality and support businesses that excel, such as Hertz (see Figure 22.6). Customer satisfaction can be improved through higher-quality products and better customer service, such as reduced delivery times, faster responses to customer inquiries, and treatment of customers that shows caring on the company's part.

As a management philosophy, TQM relies heavily on the talents of employees to continually improve the quality of the organization's goods and services. TQM is founded on three basic principles:[13]

total quality management (TQM)   A philosophy that uniform commitment to quality in all areas of an organization will promote a culture that meets customers' perceptions of quality

- *Continuous quality improvement.* Continuous improvement of an organization's goods and services is built around the notion that quality is free; by contrast, *not* having high quality goods and services can be very expensive, especially in terms of dissatisfied customers.[14] Continuous quality improvement requires more than simple quality control, or the screening out of bad products during production. Rather, continuous improvement means building quality from the very beginning—totally redesigning the product if necessary. It is a slow, long-term process of creating small improvements in quality. Companies that adopt TQM realize that the major advancements in quality occur because of an accumulation of these small improvements over time.

benchmarking   Comparing the quality of a firm's goods, services, or processes with that of the best-performing competitors

A primary tool of the continuous improvement process is **benchmarking,** the measuring and evaluating of the quality of an organization's goods, services, or processes as compared with the quality produced by the best-performing companies in the industry.[15] Benchmarking lets an organization know where it stands competitively in its industry, thus giving the company a goal to aim for over time. The design of the Ford Taurus attests to the value of benchmarking. By asking customers what they wanted in a car, Ford compiled a list of over four hundred desired features. Ford engineers then examined the best-selling cars in the industry, primarily foreign makes like the Honda Accord and Toyota Camry, to determine how the competition delivered each of these features. The result was an improved Taurus, which at one time was the best-selling car in America.

empowerment   Giving customer-contact employees authority and responsibility to make marketing decisions on their own

- *Empowered employees.* Ultimately, TQM succeeds or fails because of the efforts of the organization's employees. Thus, employee recruitment, selection, and training are critical to the success of marketing implementation. **Empowerment** gives customer-contact employees the authority and responsibility to make marketing decisions without seeking the approval of their supervisors.[16] Although employees at any level in an organization can be empowered to make decisions, empowerment is used most often at the front line, where employees interact daily with customers. Southwest Airlines, for example, gives its customer-contact employees permission to break the rules if that will help a customer.[17]

One of the characteristics of empowerment is that employees can perform their jobs the way they see fit, as long as their methods and outcomes are consistent with the mission of the organization. However, empowering employees is successful only if the organization is guided by an overall corporate vision, shared goals, and a culture that supports the TQM effort.[18] A great deal of time, effort, and patience is needed to develop and sustain a quality-oriented culture in an organization.

• *Quality-improvement teams.* The idea behind the team approach is to get the best and brightest people with a wide variety of perspectives working together on a quality-improvement issue. Team members are usually selected from a cross-section of jobs within the organization, as well as from among suppliers and customers. As we discussed in Chapter 15, suppliers can have a tremendous impact on the ability of a company to deliver quality products and services to its customers. Customers are included in quality-improvement teams because they are in the best position to know what they and other customers want from the company.

Total quality management can provide several benefits. Overall financial benefits include lower operating costs, higher returns on sales and investment, and an improved ability to use premium pricing rather than competitive pricing. For example, after Union Pacific upgraded the railroad's scheduling, maintenance, and customer service, it eliminated more than $700 million a year in lost revenue.[19] Additional benefits include faster development of innovations, improved access to global markets, higher levels of customer retention, and an enhanced reputation.[20]

Putting the TQM philosophy into practice requires a substantial investment of time, effort, money, and patience on the part of the organization. However, companies that have the resources needed to implement TQM and the commitment of top management gain an effective means of achieving major competitive advantages within their industries.

Organizing Marketing Activities

The structure and relationships of a marketing unit, including lines of authority and responsibility that connect and coordinate individuals, strongly affect marketing activities. This section looks at the role of marketing within an organization and examines the major alternatives available for organizing a marketing unit.

The Role of Marketing in an Organization's Structure

As industries become more competitive, both domestically and globally, marketing activities gain in importance. Firms that truly adopt the marketing concept develop a distinct organizational culture—a culture based on a shared set of beliefs that makes the customer's needs the pivotal point of a firm's decisions about strategy and operations.[21] Instead of developing products in a vacuum and then trying to persuade customers to make purchases, companies using the marketing concept begin with an orientation toward their customers' needs and desires. Recreational Equipment, Inc. (REI), for example, gives customers a chance to try out sporting goods in conditions that approximate how the products will actually be used. Customers can try out hiking boots on a simulated hiking path with a variety of trail surfaces and inclines, or test climbing gear on an indoor climbing wall. One store has an outdoor trail for testing cross-country skis, while a store planned for Denver will allow customers to try out kayaks and canoes on the South Platte River. Giving customers the opportunity to "test-drive" equipment in more realistic conditions enhances satisfaction by helping them get the right product for their needs and preferences. They're also less likely to return products.[22]

As we discussed in Chapter 1, a marketing-oriented organization concentrates on discovering what buyers want and on providing it in such a way that it achieves its objectives. Such a company has an organizational culture that effectively and efficiently produces a sustainable competitive advantage. It focuses on customer analysis, competitor analysis, and the integration of the firm's resources to provide customer value and satisfaction, as well as long-term profits.[23] At Chili's restaurants, for example, well-trained, competent, friendly staff provide customers with the best service in the restaurant industry. To ensure customer satisfaction, Chili's created "sizzle service," an approach in which servers are trained to acknowledge customers quickly. Chili's also recognizes the importance of the leadership provided by managers in fostering a marketing-oriented culture. Managers' attitudes regarding service and employee training are important ingredients in Chili's success.[24]

If the marketing concept serves as a guiding philosophy, the marketing unit will be closely coordinated with other functional areas, such as production, finance, and human resources. Marketing must interact with other departments in a number of key areas. It needs to work with manufacturing in determining the volume and variety of the company's products. Those in charge of production rely on marketers for accurate sales forecasts. Research and development departments depend heavily on information gathered by marketers about product features and benefits desired by consumers. Decisions made by the physical distribution department hinge on information about the urgency of delivery schedules and cost/service tradeoffs.

Alternatives for Organizing the Marketing Unit

How effectively a firm's marketing management can plan and implement marketing strategies also depends on how the marketing unit is organized. Effective organizational planning can give the firm a competitive advantage. The organizational structure of a marketing department establishes the authority relationships among marketing personnel and specifies who is responsible for making certain decisions and performing particular activities. This internal structure helps direct marketing activities.

centralized organization
A structure in which top management delegates little authority to levels below it

decentralized organization A structure in which decision-making authority is delegated as far down the chain of command as possible

One of the crucial decisions regarding structural authority is that of centralization versus decentralization. A **centralized organization** is one in which the top-level managers delegate very little authority to lower levels of the organization. In a **decentralized organization,** decision-making authority is delegated as far down the chain of command as possible. The decision to centralize or decentralize the organization directly affects marketing. Most traditional organizations are highly centralized. In these organizations, most, if not all, marketing decisions are made at the top levels of the organization. However, as organizations become more marketing-oriented, centralized decision making proves to be somewhat ineffective. In these organizations, decentralized authority allows the organization to respond faster to customer needs.

In organizing a marketing unit, managers divide the work into specific activities and delegate responsibility and authority for those activities to persons in various positions within the unit. These positions include, for example, the sales manager, the research manager, and the advertising manager.

No single approach to organizing a marketing unit works equally well in all businesses. The best approach or approaches depend on the number and diversity of the firm's products, the characteristics and needs of the people in the target market, and many other factors. A marketing unit can be organized according to (1) functions, (2) products, (3) regions, or (4) types of customers. Firms often use some combination of these organizational approaches. Product features may dictate that the marketing unit be structured by products, whereas customers' characteristics require that it be organized by geographic region or by types of customers. By using more than one type of organization, a flexible marketing unit can develop and implement marketing plans to match customers' needs precisely.

Organizing by Functions   Some marketing departments are organized by general marketing functions, such as marketing research, product development, distribution, sales, advertising, and customer relations. The personnel who direct these functions report directly to the top-level marketing executive. This structure is fairly common because it works well for some businesses with centralized marketing operations, such as Ford and General Motors. In more decentralized firms, such as grocery store chains, functional organization can cause serious coordination problems. But the functional approach may suit a large centralized company whose products and customers are neither numerous nor diverse.

Organizing by Products An organization that produces and markets diverse products may find the functional approach inadequate. The decisions and problems related to a single marketing function for one product may be quite different from those related to the same marketing function for another product. As a result, businesses that produce diverse products sometimes organize their marketing units according to product groups. Organizing by product groups gives a firm the flexibility to develop special marketing mixes for different products. Procter & Gamble, like many firms in the consumer packaged goods industry, is organized by product group. One product manager oversees paper products, another oversees soap and cleaning products, and so on. Each group develops its own product plans, implements them, monitors the results, and takes corrective action as necessary. The product group manager may also draw on the resources of specialized staff in the company, such as the advertising, research, or distribution manager. Although organizing by products allows a company to remain flexible, this approach can be rather expensive unless efficient categories of products are grouped together to reduce duplication and improve coordination of product management.

Organizing by Regions A large company that markets products nationally (or internationally) may organize its marketing activities by geographic regions. Managers of marketing functions for each region report to their regional marketing manager; all the regional marketing managers report directly to the executive marketing manager. Frito-Lay, for example, is organized into four regional divisions, allowing the company to get closer to its customers and to respond more quickly and efficiently to regional competitors. This form of organization is especially effective for a firm whose customers' characteristics and needs vary greatly from one region to another. Firms that try to penetrate the national market intensively may divide regions into subregions.

Organizing by Types of Customers Sometimes a company's marketing unit is organized according to types of customers. This form of internal organization works well for a firm that has several groups of customers whose needs and problems differ significantly. For example, Bic may sell pens to large retail stores, wholesalers, and institutions. Retailers may want more rapid delivery of small shipments and more personal selling by the producer than do either wholesalers or institutional buyers. Because the marketing decisions and activities required for these two groups of customers differ considerably, the company may find it efficient to organize its marketing unit by types of customers.

In a marketing department organized by customer group, the marketing manager for each group directs all activities needed to market products to that specific customer group. The marketing managers report to the top-level marketing executive.

Implementing Marketing Activities

Through planning and organizing, marketing managers provide purpose, direction, and structure for marketing activities. Likewise, understanding the problems and elements of marketing implementation, as well as selecting an overall approach, sets the stage for the implementation of specific marketing activities. As we have stated before, people are ultimately responsible for implementing marketing strategy. Therefore, the effective implementation of any and all marketing activities depends on motivating marketing personnel, effectively communicating within the marketing unit, coordinating all marketing activities, and establishing a timetable for the completion of each marketing activity.

Motivating Marketing Personnel

People work to satisfy physical, psychological, and social needs. To motivate marketing personnel, managers must discover their employees' needs and then develop motivational methods that help employees satisfy those needs. It is crucial that the plan to motivate employees be fair, ethical, and well understood by employees. Additionally, rewards to employees should be tied to organizational goals. In general, to improve employee motivation, companies need to find out what workers think, how they feel, and what they want. Some of this information can be obtained from an employee attitude survey. A firm can motivate its workers by directly linking pay with performance, informing workers how their performance affects department and corporate results, following through with appropriate compensation, implementing a flexible benefits program, and adopting a participative management approach.[25] Motivation is also facilitated by keeping employees apprised of how their performance affects their own compensation. Some companies are using their corporate intranets to help employees know where they stand. At IBM, for example, sales representatives can log onto the company's intranet to obtain an estimate of their compensation based on their projections of their performance.[26]

Besides tying rewards to organizational goals, managers should use a variety of other tools to motivate individuals. Selecting effective motivational tools has become more complex because of greater differences among workers in terms of race, ethnicity, gender, and age. Indeed, one of the most common forms of diversity in today's organizations is the diversity in generations of employees. Such differences broaden the range of individual value systems within an organization, which in turn calls for a more diverse set of motivational tools. For example, an employee might value autonomy or recognition more than a slight pay increase. Managers can reward employees not just with money and additional fringe benefits, but also with such nonfinancial rewards as prestige or recognition, job autonomy, skill variety, task significance, increased feedback, or even a more relaxed dress code (see Figure 22.7). It is crucial for management to show that it takes pride in its work force and to motivate employees to take pride in their company. At Tricon Global Restaurants, owner of fast-

Figure 22.7
Motivating Employees
The Sharper Image and Windstar Cruises provide corporate incentive programs to help companies motivate their employees.

food chains Taco Bell, Pizza Hut, and Kentucky Fried Chicken, a "Roving Recognition Band" holds impromptu parties to honor employees for good performance. Executives at KFC may hand out rubber chickens to top performers, while employees at Taco Bell may get giant chili peppers.[27] Although such efforts may seem frivolous, they acknowledge employees' efforts and thereby boost morale and motivation. Tech*know describes another firm's efforts to communicate with and motivate employees in today's fast-paced environment.

Communicating within the Marketing Unit

With good communication, marketing managers can motivate personnel and coordinate their efforts. Poor communication can harm morale and reduce productivity. According to a survey by Office Team, executives believe that 14 percent of each work week is squandered because of poor communication between managers and employees. Poor communication can be especially damaging in emotionally charged situations, and it can affect how employees feel about their company.[28]

Marketing managers must be able to communicate with the firm's top management to ensure that marketing activities are consistent with the company's overall goals. Communication with top-level executives keeps marketing managers aware of the company's overall plans and achievements. It also guides the marketing unit's activities and indicates how they are to be integrated with those of other departments, such as finance, production, or human resources, with whose management the marketing manager must also communicate to coordinate marketing efforts. For example,

BSG Creates an Organizational Culture to Reduce Cycle Time

BSG Corporation, a computer services company based in Austin, Texas, believes the only way to compete against larger and better-funded rivals like Andersen Consulting and EDS is through an organizational culture "that accelerates time." *Organizational culture* refers to the set of values, beliefs, goals, norms, and rituals that members or employees of an organization share. Organizational culture and effective communication within a firm can enhance productivity by reducing cycle time—the time it takes to complete a process. Firms like BSG are using improved information to reduce cycle times, thus reducing costs and improving employee performance and customer service. While faster access to information enables employees to make faster decisions, it also contributes to a corporate culture that focuses on speed and efficiency.

Speed and change are at the core of everything BSG does. The company holds "annual" meetings every quarter because of its belief that it experiences a year's worth of change every three months. These meetings not only address current issues, but also reinforce the firm's culture and values. In addition to the quarterly meetings, the firm recently began holding monthly meetings over its high-speed, wide-area network. These online meetings function much like an Internet chatroom; they are interactive electronic forums in which people exchange ideas and information in real time.

A firm's culture may be expressed formally through codes of conduct, memos, manuals, and ceremonies, but it is also expressed informally through work habits, dress codes, extracurricular activities, and anecdotes. BSG's culture includes Monday dress that bars white shirts and blue skirts. To foster a sense of community and an awareness of cycle time, BSG divides its regional locations into "neighborhoods" and installs street signs and mileage markers in the offices to indicate the distance to other BSG locations.

Like many companies, BSG believes effective communication can motivate employees by increasing their sense of autonomy and giving them useful feedback, which can also lead to improved customer satisfaction. To ensure that marketing activities are consistent with the company's overall goals, marketing managers must be able to communicate with the firm's top management. Communication with top-level executives keeps managers and employees aware of the company's overall plans and achievements. It also guides the marketing unit's activities and indicates how they are to be integrated with those other departments, such as finance, production, or human resources, with whose management the marketing manager must also communicate to coordinate marketing efforts.

BSG recognizes that cycle-time reduction begins with employees. It has therefore created a corporate culture that promotes a sharing of values and ideas, team work, and a sense community among employees.

marketing personnel must work with the production staff to help design products that customers want. To direct marketing activities, marketing managers must communicate with marketing personnel at the operations level, such as sales and advertising personnel, researchers, wholesalers, retailers, and package designers.

One of the most important types of communication in marketing is communication that flows upward from the frontline of the marketing unit to higher-level marketing managers. Customer-contact employees are in a unique position to understand customers' wants and needs. By taking steps to encourage upward communication, marketing managers can gain access to a rich source of information about what customers require, how well products are selling, whether marketing activities are working, and what problems are occurring in marketing implementation.[29] Upward communication also allows the marketing manager to understand the problems and needs of employees. As we noted earlier, such communication is an important aspect of the internal marketing approach.

To facilitate communication, marketing managers should establish an information system within the marketing unit. The marketing information system (discussed in Chapter 6) should make it easy for marketing managers, sales managers, and sales personnel to communicate with one another. Marketers need an information system to support a variety of activities, such as planning, budgeting, sales analyses, performance evaluations, and the preparation of reports. An information system should also expedite communications with other departments in the organization and minimize destructive interdepartmental competition for organizational resources.

SNAPSHOT

Dressing down at the office

Fridays 24%

Every day 66%

Other 10%

66% of office workers ages 25–49 say they can dress casually every day, all year; 24% on Fridays, all year; 1% on Fridays, summer only; 1% every day, summer only.

Copyright © 1999 *USA Today*, a division of Gannett Co., Inc.

Coordinating Marketing Activities

Because of job specialization and differences among marketing activities, marketing managers must synchronize individuals' actions to achieve marketing objectives. They must work closely with managers in research and development, production, finance, accounting, and human resources to see that marketing activities mesh with other functions of the firm. They must coordinate the activities of marketing staff within the firm and integrate those activities with the marketing efforts of external organizations—advertising agencies, resellers (wholesalers and retailers), researchers, and shippers, among others. Marketing managers can improve coordination by making each employee aware of how his or her job relates to others and how his or her actions contribute to the achievement of marketing objectives.

Establishing a Timetable for Implementation

Successful marketing implementation requires that employees know the specific activities for which they are responsible and the timetable for completing each activity. One company that is very good at establishing implementation timetables is Domino's Pizza. Every activity in creating and delivering a pizza, from taking the phone order to handing the pizza to the customer, has an employee who is responsible for its implementation. In addition, all employees know the specified time frame for the completion of their activities.

Establishing an implementation timetable involves several steps: (1) identifying the activities to be performed, (2) determining the time required to complete each

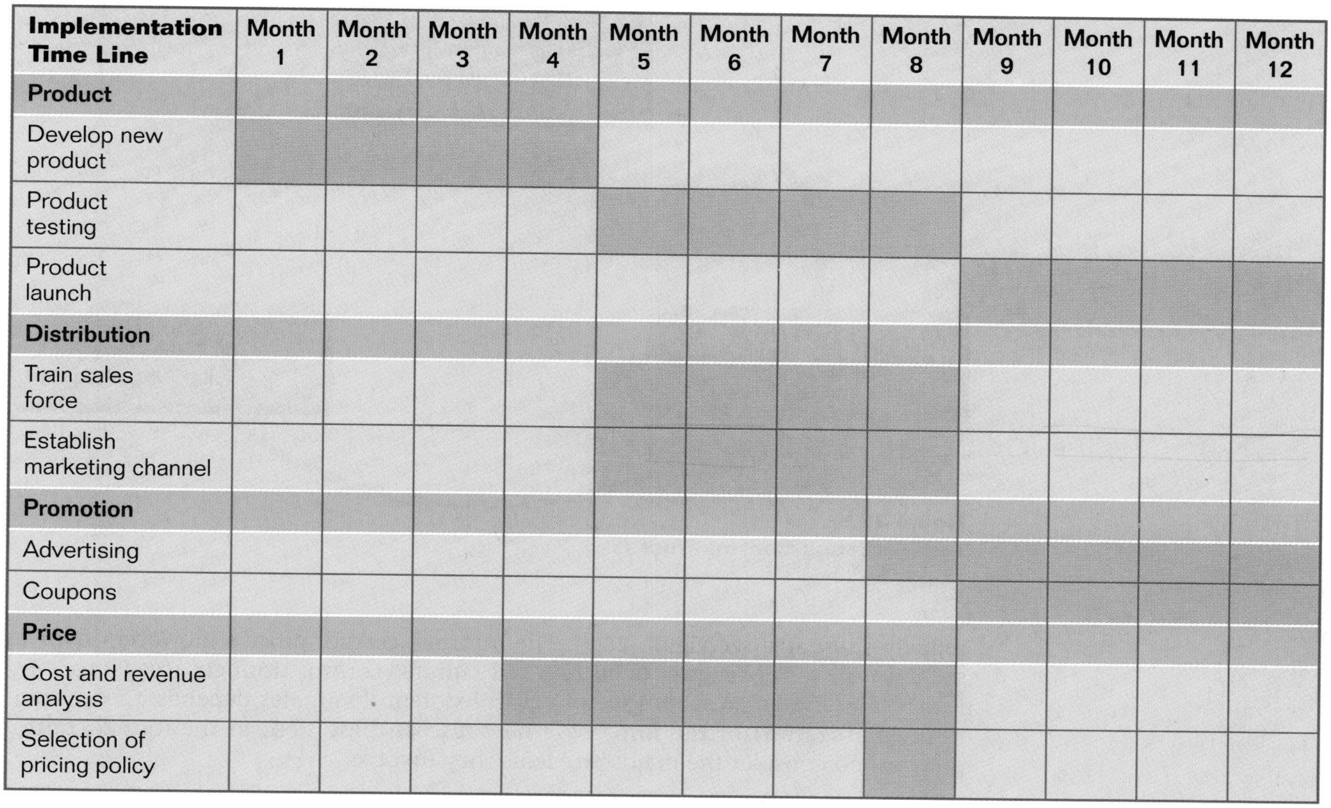

Implementation Time Line	Month 1	Month 2	Month 3	Month 4	Month 5	Month 6	Month 7	Month 8	Month 9	Month 10	Month 11	Month 12
Product												
Develop new product												
Product testing												
Product launch												
Distribution												
Train sales force												
Establish marketing channel												
Promotion												
Advertising												
Coupons												
Price												
Cost and revenue analysis												
Selection of pricing policy												

Figure 22.8
An Example of an Implementation Timetable

activity, (3) separating the activities that must be performed in sequence from those that can be performed simultaneously, (4) organizing the activities in the proper order, and (5) assigning the responsibility for completing each activity to one or more employees, teams, or managers. Some activities must be performed before others, whereas others can be performed at the same time or later in the implementation process. Completing all implementation activities on schedule requires tight coordination between departments—marketing, production, advertising, sales, and so on. Pinpointing those implementation activities that can be performed simultaneously will greatly reduce the total amount of time needed to put a given marketing strategy into practice. Since scheduling is a complicated task, most organizations use sophisticated computer programs to plan the timing of marketing activities. Figure 22.8 is an example of an implementation timetable for a new product.

Controlling Marketing Activities

marketing control process Establishing performance standards and trying to match actual performance to those standards

To achieve both marketing and general organizational objectives, marketing managers must effectively control marketing efforts. The **marketing control process** consists of establishing performance standards, evaluating actual performance by comparing it with established standards, and reducing the differences between desired and actual performance.

Although the control function is a fundamental management activity, it has received little attention in marketing. Organizations have both formal and informal control systems. The formal marketing control process, as mentioned before, involves performance standards, evaluation of actual performance, and corrective action to

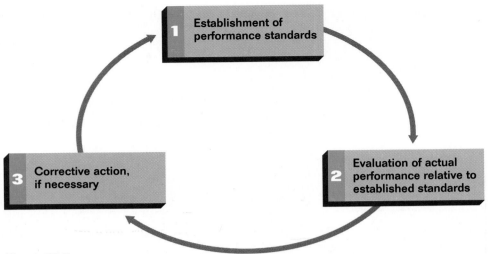

Figure 22.9
The Marketing Control Process

remedy shortfalls (see Figure 22.9). The informal control process, however, involves self-control, social or group control, and cultural control through acceptance of a firm's value system. Which type of control system dominates depends on the environmental context of the firm.[30] We now discuss these steps in the formal control process and consider the major problems they involve.

Establishing Performance Standards

performance standard
Expected level of performance

Planning and controlling are closely linked because plans include statements about what is to be accomplished. For purposes of control, these statements function as performance standards. A **performance standard** is an expected level of performance against which actual performance can be compared. A performance standard might be the reduction of customers' complaints by 20 percent, a monthly sales quota of $150,000, or a 10 percent increase per month in new customer accounts. Performance standards are also given in the form of budget accounts; that is, marketers are expected to achieve a certain objective without spending more than a given amount of resources. As stated earlier, performance standards should be tied to organizational goals. McDonald's, for example, has a goal of increasing the percentage of children age 8 and under who eat at McDonald's at least once a month from 89 percent to 100 percent.[31] Performance standards can also relate to products or service quality. Achieving performance standards is becoming increasingly difficult as a shortage of high-quality service employees grows more severe.[32]

Evaluating Actual Performance

To compare actual performance with performance standards, marketing managers must know what employees within the company are doing and have information about the activities of external organizations that provide the firm with marketing assistance. Saturn, for example, evaluates its product and service level by how well it ranks on the J.D. Power & Associates Sales Satisfaction Survey; Saturn ranked number one among domestic automakers.[33] (We discuss specific methods for assessing actual performance later in this chapter.) Information is required about the activities of marketing personnel at the operations level and at various marketing management levels. Most businesses obtain marketing assistance from one or more external individuals or organizations, such as advertising agencies, intermediaries, marketing research firms, and consultants. To maximize benefits from external sources, a firm's marketing control process must monitor their activities. Although it may be difficult to obtain the necessary information, it is impossible to measure actual performance without it.

Records of actual performance are compared with performance standards to determine whether and how much of a discrepancy exists. For example, if McDonald's determines that 95 percent of children age 8 and under have eaten at McDonald's at least once a month, then a discrepancy exists because its goal was 100 percent.

Taking Corrective Action

Marketing managers have several options for reducing a discrepancy between established performance standards and actual performance. They can take steps to improve actual performance, reduce or totally change the performance standard, or do both.

In Figure 22.10, iMarket promotes its database management tools to improve sales force productivity. To improve actual performance, the marketing manager may have to use better methods of motivating marketing personnel or find more effective techniques for coordinating marketing efforts.

Performance standards are sometimes unrealistic when they are written, and sometimes changes in the marketing environment make them unrealistic. For example, a company's annual sales goal may become unrealistic if several aggressive competitors enter the firm's market. In fact, changes in the marketing environment may dictate radical revisions in marketing strategy. Consider AutoNation, a chain of twenty-nine used-car superstores. The company's original strategy was to offer a vast selection of used late-model vehicles in good condition with set prices (no negotiating). However, at the time the company introduced its used-car superstore concept, the economy was booming, and low unemployment and interest rates were making new cars and trucks more affordable for more people. In addition, prices of new vehicles were very competitive, especially when consumers factored in rebates and other incentives offered by dealers and manufacturers. Consequently, sales of used cars were flat. Moreover, research suggested that although customers liked the kind of customer service and showrooms AutoNation offered, they still preferred to haggle over the price of a used car. In response to these conditions, AutoNation has modified its marketing strategy, offering more accessory packages (e.g., car alarms and CD players), opening a store in Houston for the sale of used trucks only, operating seventeen John Elway AutoNation dealerships in Denver, and selling older, less expensive vehicles in some stores. It has even considered creating its own line of new cars, possibly to be manufactured by a Korean firm.[34] Whether these adjustments will improve AutoNation's performance will depend on economic conditions, as well as on AutoNation's implementation of its new strategy.

Figure 22.10

Improving Sales Force Productivity
iMarket provides database management services to enhance sales force productivity.

Problems in Controlling Marketing Activities

In their efforts to control marketing activities, marketing managers frequently run into several problems. Often the information required to control marketing activities is unavailable or is available only at a high cost. Even though marketing controls should be flexible enough to allow for environmental changes, the frequency, intensity, and unpredictability of such changes may hamper control. In addition, the time lag between marketing activities and their results limits a marketing manager's ability to measure the effectiveness of specific marketing activities. This is especially true for all advertising activities.

Because marketing and other business activities overlap, marketing managers cannot determine the precise cost of marketing activities. Without an accurate measure of marketing costs, it is difficult to know if the outcome of marketing activities is worth the expense. Finally, marketing control may be difficult because it is very hard to develop exact performance standards for marketing personnel.

Methods of Evaluating Performance

There are specific methods for assessing and improving the effectiveness of a marketing strategy. A marketer should state in the marketing plan what a marketing strategy is supposed to accomplish. These statements should set forth performance standards—usually in terms of profits, sales, costs, or communication standards—relating to such matters as brand recall. Actual performance should be measured in similar terms so that comparisons are possible. In this section, we consider three general ways of evaluating the actual performance of marketing strategies: sales analysis, marketing cost analysis, and the marketing audit.

Sales Analysis

sales analysis Use of sales figures to evaluate a firm's current performance

Sales analysis uses sales figures to evaluate a firm's current performance. It is probably the most common method of evaluation because sales data partially reflect the target market's reactions to a marketing mix and often are readily available, at least in aggregate form.

Marketers use current sales data to monitor the impact of current marketing efforts. However, that information alone is not enough. To provide useful analyses, current sales data must be compared with forecasted sales, industry sales, specific competitors' sales, or the costs incurred to achieve the sales volume. For example, knowing that a specialty store attained a $600,000 sales volume this year does not tell management whether its marketing strategy has been successful. However, if managers know that expected sales were $550,000, then they are in a better position to determine the effectiveness of the firm's marketing efforts. In addition, if they know that the marketing costs needed to achieve the $600,000 volume were 12 percent less than budgeted, they are in an even better position to analyze their marketing strategy precisely.

Although sales may be measured in several ways, the basic unit of measurement is the sales transaction. A sales transaction results in an order for a specified quantity of an organization's product sold under specified terms by a particular salesperson or sales group on a certain date. Many organizations record these bits of information about their transactions. With such a record, a company can analyze sales in terms of dollar volume or market share.

Firms frequently use dollar volume in their sales analyses because the dollar is a common denominator of sales, costs, and profits. However, price increases and decreases affect total sales figures. This is especially true in the auto industry, where profit margins are being squeezed. Even though prices are increasing, customers are demanding rock bottom prices and low lease rates on everything but the hottest selling trucks.[35] If a company increased its prices by 10 percent this year and its sales volume is 10 percent greater than last year, it has not experienced any increase in unit sales. A marketing manager who uses dollar volume analysis should factor out the effects of price changes.

A firm's market share is the firm's sales of a product stated as a percentage of industry sales of that product. Market-share analysis lets a company compare its marketing strategy with competitors' strategies. The primary reason for using market-share analysis is to estimate whether sales changes have resulted from the firm's marketing strategy or from uncontrollable environmental forces. When a company's sales volume declines but its share of the market stays the same, the marketer can assume that industry sales declined (because of some uncontrollable factors) and that this decline was reflected in the firm's sales. However, if a company experiences a decline in both sales and market share, it should consider the possibility that its marketing strategy is not effective or was improperly implemented.

Even though market-share analysis can be helpful in evaluating the performance of a marketing strategy, the user must interpret results cautiously. When attributing a sales decline to uncontrollable factors, a marketer must keep in mind that such factors do not affect all firms in the industry equally. Not all firms in an industry have the same objectives and strategies and some change strategies from one year to the next. Changes in the strategies of one company can affect the market shares of one or all companies in that industry. For instance, when UPS introduced same-day long-distance package delivery at a minimum price of $159, FedEx had to match the service and price to avoid losing market share. Within an industry, the entrance of new firms, the launch of new products by competing firms, or the demise of established ones also affects a specific firm's market share, and market-share analysts should attempt to account for these effects. KFC, for example, had to reevaluate its marketing strategies when McDonald's introduced its own fried chicken product.

Marketing Cost Analysis

marketing cost analysis Breaking down and classifying costs to determine those that stem from specific marketing activities

fixed costs Costs based on how money was actually spent

Although sales analysis is critical for evaluating the effectiveness of a marketing strategy, it gives only part of the picture. A marketing strategy that successfully generates sales may also be extremely costly. To get a complete picture, a firm must know the marketing costs associated with using a given strategy to achieve a certain sales level. **Marketing cost analysis** breaks down and classifies costs to determine which are associated with specific marketing activities. By comparing costs of previous marketing activities with results generated, a marketer can better allocate the firm's marketing resources in the future. Marketing cost analysis lets a company evaluate the effectiveness of marketing strategy by comparing sales achieved and costs incurred. By pinpointing exactly where a company is experiencing high costs, this form of analysis can help isolate profitable or unprofitable customer segments, products, and geographic areas.

The task of determining marketing costs is often complex and difficult. Simply ascertaining the costs associated with marketing a product is rarely adequate. Marketers must usually determine the marketing costs of serving specific geographic areas, market segments, or even specific customers.

Four broad categories are used in marketing cost analysis: fixed costs, variable costs, traceable common costs, and nontraceable common costs. **Fixed costs**—such as rent, salaries, office supplies, and utilities—are based on how the money was actually spent. In Figure 22.11, Aquila Energy helps customers manage risk and energy costs with its financial products. However, fixed

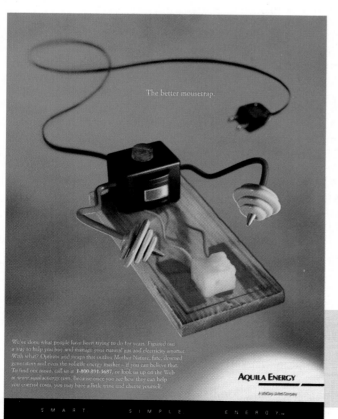

The better mousetrap.

We've done what people have been trying to do for years. Figured out a way to help you buy and manage your natural gas and electricity smarter. With what? Options and swaps that outfox Mother Nature, fate, downed generators and even the volatile energy market—if you can believe that. To find out more, call us at 1-800-891-5687, or look us up on the Web at www.aquilaenergy.com. Because once you see how they can help your control costs, you may have a little wine and cheese yourself.

AQUILA ENERGY

SMART. SIMPLE. ENERGY.™

Figure 22.11
Marketing Cost Analysis
Aquila Energy works with wholesale customers of natural gas and electricity (such as utilities) by developing financial products aimed to manage risk and control energy costs.

variable costs Costs directly attributable to production and selling volume

traceable common costs Costs allocated indirectly to the functions they support

nontraceable common costs Costs assignable only on an arbitrary basis

full-cost approach Including direct costs and both traceable and nontraceable common costs in the cost analysis

direct-cost approach Including only direct costs and traceable common costs in the cost analysis

costs often do not explain what marketing functions were performed through the expenditure of those funds. It does little good, for example, to know that $80,000 is spent for rent each year. The analyst has no way of knowing whether the money is spent for the rental of production, storage, or sales facilities. **Variable costs** are directly attributable to production and selling volume. For example, sales force salaries might be allocated to the cost of selling a specific product, selling in a specific geographic area, or selling to a particular customer. **Traceable common costs** can be allocated indirectly, using one or several criteria, to the functions they support. For example, if the firm spends $80,000 annually to rent space for production, storage, and selling, the rental costs of storage could be determined on the basis of cost per square foot used for storage. **Nontraceable common costs** cannot be assigned according to any logical criteria; they are assignable only on an arbitrary basis. Interest, taxes, and the salaries of top management are nontraceable common costs.

How costs are dealt with depends on whether the analyst uses a full-cost or a direct-cost approach. When a **full-cost approach** is used, cost analysis includes variable costs, traceable common costs, and nontraceable common costs. Proponents of this approach claim that if an accurate profit picture is desired, all costs must be included in the analysis. However, opponents point out that full costing does not yield actual costs because nontraceable common costs are determined by arbitrary criteria. With different criteria, the full-costing approach yields different results. A cost-conscious operating unit can be discouraged if numerous costs are assigned to it arbitrarily. To eliminate such problems, the **direct-cost approach,** which includes variable costs and traceable common costs but not nontraceable common costs, is used. However, critics of this approach say it is not accurate because it omits one cost category.

The Marketing Audit

marketing audit A systematic examination of the marketing group's objectives, strategies, organization, and performance

A **marketing audit** is a systematic examination of the marketing group's objectives, strategies, organization, and performance. Its primary purpose is to identify weaknesses in ongoing marketing operations and to plan improvements to correct these weaknesses. In Figure 22.12, Dun & Bradstreet assists companies in evaluating their performance. Like an accounting or financial audit, a marketing audit should be conducted regularly instead of just when performance evaluation mechanisms show that the system is out of control. The marketing audit is not a control process to be used only during a crisis, though, of course, it can help a business in trouble isolate problems and generate solutions. Marketing audits have become more difficult as organizations have merged and acquired other firms, thus gaining technology, world market share, new products, and distribution systems. Citicorp, for example, having merged with Travelers Group, is now Citigroup with $700 billion in assets to serve customers' total financial needs, from banking to stock brokerage to insurance.[36]

A marketing audit may be specific and focus on one or a few marketing activities, or it may be comprehensive and encompass all of a company's marketing activities. Table 22.1 on pages 586 and 587 lists many possible dimensions of a marketing audit.

customer-service audit A comparison of the performance of specific customer-service activities with service goals and standards

One specialized type of audit is the **customer-service audit,** in which specific customer-service activities are analyzed and service goals and standards are compared with actual performance.[37] Table 22.2 on page 588 provides a typical outline for a customer-service audit. Another type is the social audit, which helps a firm evaluate its social responsibility efforts (refer back to Table 4.7). Specialized audits can also be performed for product development, pricing, sales, advertising, and other promotional activities. The scope of any audit depends on the costs involved, the target markets served, the structure of the marketing mix, and environmental conditions. The results of the audit can be used to reallocate marketing efforts and to reexamine marketing opportunities.

The marketing audit should aid evaluation by doing the following:

1. Describing current activities and results related to sales, costs, prices, profits, and other performance feedback

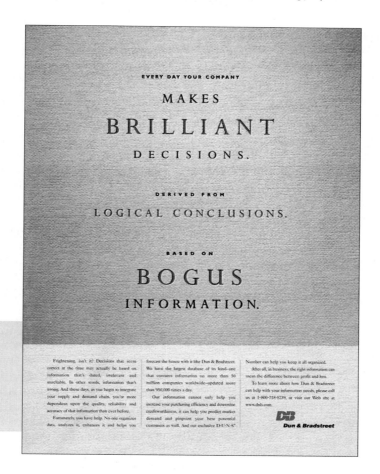

Figure 22.12
The Marketing Audit
Consulting groups such as Dun & Bradstreet assist their corporate customers in assessing their performance.

2. Gathering information about customers, competition, and environmental developments that may affect the marketing strategy

3. Identifying opportunities and alternatives for improving the marketing strategy

4. Providing an overall database to be used in evaluating the attainment of organizational goals and marketing objectives

Marketing audits can be performed internally or externally. An internal auditor may be a top-level marketing executive, a companywide auditing committee, or a manager from another office or functional area. Although it is more expensive, an audit by outside consultants is usually more effective because external auditors bring to the task more objectivity, more time for the audit, and greater experience.

There is no single set of procedures for all marketing audits. However, firms should adhere to several general guidelines. Audits are often based on a series of questionnaires administered to the firm's personnel; these questionnaires should be developed carefully to ensure that the audit focuses on the right issues. Auditors should develop and follow a step-by-step plan to guarantee that the audit is systematic. When interviewing personnel, the auditors should strive to talk with a diverse group of people from many parts of the company.

Although the concept of auditing implies an official examination of marketing activities, many organizations audit their marketing activities informally. Any attempt to verify operating results and to compare them with standards can be considered an auditing activity. Many smaller firms probably would not use the word *audit,* but they do perform auditing activities.

Marketing audits can present several problems. They can be expensive and time-consuming, and selecting the auditors may be difficult if objective, qualified personnel are not available. Employees sometimes fear comprehensive evaluations, especially by outsiders, and in such cases, marketing audits can be extremely disruptive.

Table 22.1 Dimensions of a Marketing Audit

Part I. Marketing Environment Audit

Macroenvironment

A. Demographic	What major demographic developments and trends pose opportunities or threats to this company? What actions has the company taken in response to these developments and trends?
B. Economic	What major developments in income, prices, savings, and credit will affect the company? What actions has the company been taking in response to these developments and trends?
C. Environmental	What is the outlook for the cost and availability of natural resources and energy needed by the company? What concerns have been expressed about the company's role in pollution and conservation, and what steps has the company taken?
D. Technological	What major changes are occurring in product and process technology? What is the company's position in these technologies? What major generic substitutes might replace the company's products?
E. Political	What changes in laws and regulations might affect marketing strategy and tactics? What is happening in the areas of pollution control, equal employment opportunity, product safety, advertising, price control, and so forth, that affects marketing strategy?
F. Cultural	What is the public's attitude toward business and toward the company's products? What changes in customer lifestyles and values might affect the company?

Task Environment

A. Markets	What is happening to market size, growth, geographical distribution, and profits? What are the major market segments?
B. Customers	What are the customers' needs and buying processes? How do customers and prospects rate the company and its competitors on reputation, product quality, service, sales force, and price? How do different market segments make their buying decisions?
C. Competitors	Who are the major competitors? What are their objectives, strategies, strengths, weaknesses, sizes, and market shares? What trends will affect future competition and substitutes for the company's products?
D. Distribution dealers	What are the main channels for bringing products to customers? What are the efficiency levels and growth potentials of the different channels?
E. Suppliers	What is the outlook for the availability of key resources used in production? What trends are occurring among suppliers?
F. Facilitators and marketing firms	What is the cost and availability outlook for transportation services, warehousing facilities, and financial resources? How effective are the company's advertising agencies and marketing research firms?
G. Publics	Which publics represent particular opportunities or problems for the company? What steps has the company taken to deal effectively with each public?

Part II. Marketing Strategy Audit

A. Organizational mission	Is the organization's mission clearly stated in market-oriented terms? Is it feasible?
B. Marketing objectives and goals	Are the company and marketing objectives and goals stated clearly enough to guide marketing planning and performance measurement? Are the marketing objectives appropriate, given the company's competitive position, resources, and opportunities?
C. Strategy	Has the management articulated a clear marketing strategy for achieving its marketing objectives? Is the strategy convincing? Is it appropriate to the stage of the product life cycle, competitors' strategies, and the state of the economy? Is the company using the best basis for market segmentation? Does it have clear criteria for rating the segments and choosing the best ones? Has it developed accurate profiles of each target segment? Has the company developed an effective positioning and marketing mix for each target segment? Are marketing resources allocated optimally to the major elements of the marketing mix? Are enough resources or too many resources budgeted to accomplish the marketing objectives?

Part III. Marketing Organization Audit

A. Formal structure	Does marketing management have adequate authority and responsibility for company activities that affect customer satisfaction? Are the marketing activities optimally structured along functional, product, segment, end-user, and geographical lines?

| B. Functional efficiency | Are there good communication and working relations between marketing and sales? Is the product management system working effectively? Are product managers able to plan profits or only sales volume? Are there any groups in marketing that need more training, motivation, supervision, or evaluation? |
| C. Interface efficiency | Are there problems between marketing, manufacturing, R&D, purchasing, finance, accounting, and legal? |

Part IV. Marketing Systems Audit

A. Marketing information system	Is the marketing information system producing accurate, sufficient, and timely information about marketplace developments with respect to customers, prospects, distributors and dealers, competitors, suppliers, and various publics? Are company decision makers asking for enough marketing research, and are they using the results? Is the company employing the best methods for market measurement and sales forecasting?
B. Marketing planning systems	Is the marketing planning system well conceived and effectively used? Do marketers have decision support systems available? Does the planning system result in acceptable sales targets and quotas?
C. Marketing control system	Are the control procedures adequate to ensure that objectives are being achieved? Does management periodically analyze the profitability of products, markets, territories, and channels of distribution? Are marketing costs and productivity periodically examined?
D. New-product development system	Is the company well organized to gather, generate, and screen new-product ideas? Does the company do adequate concept research and business analysis before investing in new ideas? Does the company carry out adequate product and market testing before launching new products?

Part V. Marketing Productivity Audit

| A. Profitability analysis | What is the profitability of the company's different products, markets, territories, and channels of distribution? Should the company enter, expand, contract, or withdraw from any business segments? |
| B. Cost-effectiveness analysis | Do any marketing activities seem to have excessive costs? Can cost-reducing steps be taken? |

Part VI. Marketing Function Audits

A. Products	What are the company's product-line objectives? Are they sound? Is the current product line meeting the objectives? Should the product line be stretched or contracted upward, downward, or both ways? Which products should be phased out? Which products should be added? What are the buyers' knowledge of and attitudes toward the company's and competitors' product quality, features, styling, brand names, and so on? What areas of product and brand strategy need improvement?
B. Price	What are the company's pricing objectives, policies, strategies, and procedures? To what extent are prices set on cost, demand, and competitive criteria? Do the customers see the company's prices as being in line with the value of the products? What does management know about the price elasticity of demand, experience-curve effects, and competitors' prices and pricing policies? Are price policies compatible with the needs of distributors, dealers, and suppliers, and with government regulations?
C. Distribution	What are the company's distribution objectives and strategies? Is there adequate market coverage and service? How effective are distributors, dealers, manufacturers' representatives, brokers, agents, and others? Should the company consider changing its distribution channels?
D. Advertising, sales promotion, publicity, and direct marketing	What are the organization's advertising objectives? Are they sound? Is the right amount being spent on advertising? Are the ad themes and copy effective? What do customers and the public think about the advertising? Are the advertising media well chosen? Is the internal advertising staff adequate? Is the sales promotion budget adequate? Is there effective and sufficient use of sales promotion tools, such as samples, coupons, displays, and sales contests? Is the public relations staff competent and creative? Is the company making enough use of direct, online, and database marketing?
E. Sales force	What are the sales force's objectives? Is the sales force large enough to accomplish the company's objectives? Is the sales force organized along the proper principles of specialization (territory, market, product)? Are there enough (or too many) sales managers to guide the field sales representatives? Do the compensation level and structure provide adequate incentive and reward? Does the sales force show high morale, ability, and effort? Are the procedures adequate for setting quotas and evaluating performance? How does the company's sales force compare with competitors' sales forces?

Source: Philip Kotler, *Marketing Management: Analysis, Planning, Implementation, and Control*, 9th ed. Copyright © 1997 Prentice-Hall, a division of Simon & Schuster, Inc. Used with permission.

Table 22.2   Dimensions of a Customer-Service Audit

A. Identify Activities

1. What specific customer-service activities does the company currently provide?
   Product-related activities: repairs, maintenance, technical assistance
   Pricing-related activities: credit, financing, billing
   Distribution-related activities: delivery, installation, locations
   Promotion-related activities: customer-service phone lines, complaint handling
2. Are these customer services provided by our company or by outside contractors? If outside contractors provide these services, how are they performing?
3. What customer-service activities do customers want or need?

B. Review Standard Procedures for Each Activity

1. Do written procedures (manuals) exist for each activity? If so, are these procedures (manuals) up-to-date?
2. What oral or unwritten procedures exist for each activity? Should these procedures be included in the written procedures, or should they be eliminated?
3. Do customer-service personnel regularly interact with other functions to establish standard procedures for each activity?

C. Identify Performance Goals by Customer-Service Activity

1. What specific, quantitative goals exist for each activity?
2. What qualitative goals exist for each activity?
3. How does each activity contribute to customer satisfaction with each marketing element (i.e., product, pricing, distribution, promotion)?
4. How does each activity contribute to the long-term success of the company?

D. Specify Performance Measures by Customer-Service Activity

1. What are the internal, profit-based measures for each activity?
2. What are the internal, time-based measures for each activity?
3. How is performance monitored and evaluated internally by management?
4. How is performance monitored and evaluated externally by customers?

E. Review and Evaluate Customer-Service Personnel

1. Are the company's current recruiting, selection, and retention efforts consistent with the customer-service requirements established by customers?
2. What is the nature and content of our employee-training activities? Are these activities consistent with the customer-service requirements established by customers?
3. How are customer-service personnel supervised, evaluated, and rewarded? Are these procedures consistent with customer requirements?
4. What effect do employee evaluation and reward policies have on employee attitudes, satisfaction, and motivation?

F. Identify and Evaluate Customer-Service Support Systems

1. Are the quality and accuracy of our customer-service materials consistent with the image of our company and its products? (Examples: instruction manuals, brochures, form letters, etc.)
2. Are the quality and appearance of our physical facilities consistent with the image of our company and its products? (Examples: offices, furnishings, layout, etc.)
3. Are the quality and appearance of our customer-service equipment consistent with the image of our company and its products? (Examples: repair tools, telephones, computers, delivery vehicles, etc.)
4. Are our record-keeping systems accurate? Is the information always readily available when it is needed? What technology could be acquired to enhance our record-keeping abilities (i.e., bar code scanners, portable computers)?

Source: Reprinted from Christopher H. Lovelock, *Services Marketing*, Second Edition. Copyright © 1991 Prentice-Hall, a division of Simon & Schuster, Inc. Used with permission.

Summary

Marketing implementation, the process of putting marketing strategies into action, is an important part of the marketing management process. To help ensure effective implementation, marketing managers must consider why the intended marketing strategies do not always turn out as expected. Realized marketing strategies often differ from the intended strategies because of three implementation problems: marketing strategy and implementation are related, they are constantly evolving, and the responsibility for them is separated. Marketing managers must also consider other vital components of implementation —shared goals and objectives, employees, and leadership —to ensure the proper implementation of marketing strategies.

Organizations often follow two major approaches to marketing implementation: internal marketing and total quality management (TQM). Internal marketing is a management philosophy that coordinates internal exchanges between the organization and its employees to achieve successful external exchanges between the organization and its customers. In this approach, all employees are considered internal customers. For implementation to be successful, the needs of both internal and external customers must be met. The TQM approach relies heavily on the talents of employees to continually improve the quality of the organization's goods and services. The three essentials of the TQM philosophy are continuous quality improvement, empowered employees, and the use of quality improvement teams. One of TQM's primary tools is benchmarking, or measuring and evaluating the quality of an organization's goods, services, or processes in relation to the quality produced by the best-performing companies in the industry.

The organization of marketing activities involves the development of an internal structure for the marketing unit. The internal structure is the key to directing marketing activities. In a marketing-oriented organization, the focus is on finding out what buyers want and providing it in a way that lets the organization achieve its objectives. A centralized organization is one in which the top-level managers delegate very little authority to lower levels of the firm. In a decentralized organization, decision-making authority is delegated as far down the chain of command as possible. The marketing unit can be organized by functions, products, regions, or types of customers. An organization may use only one approach or a combination.

Proper implementation of a marketing plan depends on the motivation of personnel who perform marketing activities, effective communication within the marketing unit, the coordination of marketing activities, and the establishment of a timetable for implementation. To motivate marketing personnel, managers must discover their employees' needs and then develop motivational methods that help employees satisfy those needs. A company's communication system must allow the marketing manager to communicate with high-level management, with managers of other functional areas in the firm, and with personnel involved in marketing activities both inside and outside the organization. Marketing managers must coordinate the activities of marketing personnel and integrate these activities with those in other areas of the company and with the marketing efforts of personnel in external organizations. Finally, successful marketing implementation requires that employees know the specific activities for which they are responsible and the timetable for completing each activity.

The marketing control process consists of establishing performance standards, evaluating actual performance by comparing it with established standards, and reducing the difference between desired and actual performance. Performance standards, which are established in the planning process, are expected levels of performance with which actual performance can be compared. To evaluate actual performance, marketing managers must know what employees within the firm are doing and have information about the activities of external organizations that provide the firm with marketing assistance. When actual performance is compared with performance standards, marketers must determine whether a discrepancy exists and, if so, whether it requires corrective action, such as changing the performance standards or improving actual performance.

The control of marketing activities is not a simple task. Problems encountered include environmental changes, time lags between marketing activities and their effects, and difficulty in determining the costs of marketing activities. In addition, it may be hard to develop performance standards.

Control of marketing strategy can be facilitated through sales and cost analyses. For the purpose of analysis, sales are usually measured in terms of either dollar volume or market share. For a sales analysis to be effective, it must compare current sales performance with forecasted company sales, industry sales, specific competitors' sales, or the costs incurred to generate the current sales volume.

Marketing cost analysis involves an examination of accounting records and fixed costs, variable costs, and traceable and nontraceable common costs. Such an analysis is often difficult because there may be no logical, clear-cut way to allocate fixed costs into functional accounts. The analyst may choose either direct costing or full costing.

A marketing audit is a systematic examination of the marketing group's objectives, strategies, organization, and performance. A marketing audit attempts to identify what a marketing unit is doing, to evaluate the effectiveness of these activities, and to recommend future marketing activities. The scope of a marketing audit can be very broad or very narrow. Some companies use specialized audits, such as a customer-service audit, to address problems within specific marketing functions.

Important Terms

Marketing implementation
Intended strategy
Realized strategy
External customers
Internal customers
Internal marketing
Total quality management
(TQM)

Benchmarking
Empowerment
Centralized organization
Decentralized
organization
Marketing control process

Performance standard
Sales analysis
Marketing cost analysis
Fixed costs
Variable costs
Traceable common costs

Nontraceable common
costs
Full-cost approach
Direct-cost approach
Marketing audit
Customer-service audit

Discussion and Review Questions

1. Why does an organization's intended strategy often differ from its realized strategy?

2. Discuss the three problems associated with implementing marketing activities. How are these problems related to the differences between intended and realized marketing strategies?

3. What is internal marketing? Why is it important in implementing marketing strategies?

4. How does the total quality management approach relate to marketing implementation? For what types of marketing strategies might TQM be best suited?

5. What factors can be used to organize the decision-making authority of a marketing unit? Discuss the benefits of each type of organization.

6. Why might an organization use multiple bases for organizing its marketing unit?

7. Why is the motivation of marketing personnel important in implementing marketing plans?

8. How does communication help in implementing marketing plans?

9. What are the major steps of the marketing control process?

10. Discuss the major problems in controlling marketing activities.

11. What is a sales analysis? What makes it an effective control tool?

12. Identify and contrast two cost analysis methods.

13. How is the marketing audit used to control marketing program performance?

Application Questions

1. IBM has decentralized its product development and marketing operations in order to be more responsive to its customers. Explain to what degree and how you would decentralize the following types of businesses. Would you empower the customer-contact employees?
   a. full-service restaurant
   b. prestigious clothing store
   c. automobile dealership

2. Marketing units may be organized according to functions, products, regions, or types of customers. Describe how you would organize the marketing units for the following:
   a. toothpaste with whitener; toothpaste with extra-strong nicotine cleaners; and toothpaste with bubble-gum flavor
   b. national line offering all types of winter and summer sports clothing for men and women
   c. life insurance company that provides life, health, and disability insurance

3. Why would it be important to implement both an internal and external marketing strategy for the following companies?
   a. McDonald's
   b. Ford Motor Company
   c. Hoover Vacuum

4. Assume that you are the marketing manager for a small printing company in your city. Convince the owner of the company of the need for a customer-service audit, and explain briefly what will be involved in conducting the audit. What benefits would you expect? How often would you suggest conducting the audit?

Internet Exercise & Resources

Lower Colorado River Authority

The Lower Colorado River Authority (LCRA) is a conservation and reclamation district created in 1934 by the Texas Legislature to improve the quality of life in central Texas. The organization supplies electricity to many central Texans and water to numerous customers, including cities, municipal utility districts, and agricultural users. In addition to working to control floods in central Texas, the LCRA protects the quality of the lower Colorado River and its tributaries, provides parks and recreation facilities, helps water and waste-water utilities, and provides soil, energy, and water conservation programs. The organization's revenues come from its provision of services, not from taxes. Learn more about this organization by exploring its Web site at

www.lcra.org

1. Find the LCRA's mission statement. Judging from the activities that its site describes, do you think the LCRA is fulfilling its mission?

2. How is the LCRA organized? Does this structure foster effective marketing implementation?

3. What plans does the LCRA have for implementing its marketing strategies in the future?

E-Center Resources

Visit http://www.prideferrell.com to find several resources to help you succeed in mastering the material in this chapter, plus additional materials that will help you expand your marketing knowledge. The Web site includes

  Internet exercise updates plus additional exercises

✔ ACE self-tests

abc Chapter summary with hotlinked glossary

  Hotlinks to companies featured in this chapter

✪ Resource Center

▢ Career Center

▤ Marketing plan worksheets

VIDEO CASE 22.1

Kitchen Etc.: Combining the Right Ingredients in the Recipe for Success

Allan Coviello had a dream of developing a kitchen store to supply people who love to cook with cookware, cutlery, kitchen gadgets, china, silver, crystal, everyday glassware, and the like. Because baby boomers were buying an increasing number of culinary items, Coviello's vision was well timed. Since entering the marketplace in 1987 as Kitchen Etc., the company has catered to both the gourmet and the harried family cook. Kitchen Etc. sells dinnerware from

Noritake, Royal Doulton, Mikasa, Wedgewood, Lenox, and Pfatlzgraff; cookware from All-Clad, Calphalon, and Revere; and cutlery from Chicago Cutlery, Henckels, Hoffritz, and Wustof-Trident through nine New England retail stores. The company also offers a bridal gift registry, which accounts for 40 percent of store revenues, and builds a database of customers. It differentiates itself in the marketplace by offering what it believes are the right products at the right prices, which can be up to 40 percent below the prices of other specialty stores and of department stores. Customers who don't live in New England can shop at Kitchen Etc. at its Web site (www.kitchenetc.com).

Building on its twelve years of experience, Kitchen Etc. plans to double its number of stores and roll out the concept nationally. To support its growth and expansion plans, the company recognized that it needed some outside retailing expertise to develop and implement a new strategy. It hired George Scala from Dayton Hudson. Scala, who had specific expertise in retailing in the New England area, helped Kitchen Etc. find additional experts and professionals to collaborate on the development of a successful new retailing concept.

With Scala's support, marketing research was conducted to determine customers' likes and dislikes when buying upscale culinary items for their kitchens. A recent study found customers perceive Kitchen Etc.'s everyday low prices and brand name products as very attractive. However, the company learned it was not communicating frequently enough with consumers. In response, Kitchen Etc. has increased its advertising and used newspaper supplements to inform current and potential customers about its diverse products and discount prices. Research also revealed that consumers were not totally comfortable with the stores layout or "shopability." Kitchen Etc. has therefore designed its new stores to allow for "ease of shopping," making products easier to find, reach, and evaluate. Kitchen Etc. has thus focused on discovering what buyers want and providing it in a way that supports the company's growth and expansion plans. Through this process, its customer database has served as the foundation for continuous improvement of its marketing strategy.

Kitchen Etc. has used some of the basic elements of marketing implementation to reach its objectives. Its managers have implemented the company's new marketing strategy from both an internal and external marketing perspective. Motivating employees and informing them about how communication with customers affects the company's performance has been very effective in improving the company's image. Coordinating programs to communicate with target markets about the firm's product mix has increased sales. Redesigning stores to be customer-friendly has improved the company's competitive position. Its Web site has expanded distribution and promotion beyond New England. Finally, through performance standards, evaluation, and corrective action, Kitchen Etc. has made available the quality of culinary items that its customers demand for their kitchens. All these activities were executed in an environment in which marketing strategy and implementation were constantly evolving in response to changes in customer needs and the dynamics of competition.

Given customers' heightened awareness of retail options and price sensitivity, Kitchen Etc. is well positioned to take advantage of a definite market opportunity. Although consumers can buy kitchen items in department and discount stores, these places offer less convenient shopping than specialty stores like Kitchen Etc. By offering a diversity of high-quality items at reduced prices, Kitchen Etc. has clearly differentiated itself from full-price kitchen stores, such as William-Sonoma. Moreover, the company's Web site is making Kitchen Etc. available on a global basis.[38]

Questions for Discussion

1. Why did Kitchen Etc. hire a retail consultant to evaluate its operations? How did this decision benefit the company?
2. What elements of the marketing implementation process helped Kitchen Etc. the most?
3. How has Kitchen Etc. synchronized marketing strategy and implementation?

CASE 22.2

Implementing a New Culture at Denny's

Based in Spartanburg, South Carolina, Flagstar operates one of the largest food-service businesses in the United States. Its restaurants include Denny's, Canteen, El Pollo Loco, Hardee's, and Quincy's Family Steakhouse. Since 1993, several racial discrimination lawsuits have forced Flagstar to develop and implement new plans to salvage its reputation.

The problems surfaced on March 24, 1993, in San Jose, California, when thirty-two African-Americans filed suit against Denny's—a nationwide chain of 1,460 restaurants known for around-the-clock service and reasonably priced meals—alleging a pattern of racial discrimination in Denny's 330 California restaurants. They cited such practices as black customers' being required to pay a cover charge to enter Denny's restaurants, having to pay for meals in advance, and being charged for services and items usually given free to white customers, such as dinner rolls. Additionally, the suit alleged that Denny's managers had made derogatory, sometimes threatening, racial remarks to black patrons, had forcibly removed some blacks from the restaurants, and had used "racial coding" to indicate situations in which too large a proportion of customers in a given restaurant were black. (This alleged racial coding resembled charges brought against Shoney's—Denny's chief competitor—in 1992, when it was accused of engaging in discriminatory hiring practices. The Shoney's case resulted in a $105 million settlement.)

In response to a Justice Department investigation that substantiated the allegation of bias against blacks cited in the San Jose suit, Denny's agreed to take measures to ensure the fair treatment of all customers, regardless of their race. Spokespersons for the company denied a pattern of discrimination in California, but admitted that the company had identified isolated areas of concern. They stated that these situations had developed from late-night security measures enacted because of customers' leaving without paying for their meals. Denny' assured all parties involved in the dispute that any time racially motivated discriminatory activity was brought to the attention of management, it was dealt with harshly.

A day after the California suit was filed, Denny's signed a consent decree with the Justice Department in an effort to settle the dispute. Among the corrective actions Denny's agreed to take on were providing diversity training to restaurant employees, inserting nondiscrimination statements in all newspaper and television advertisements, and hiring a "civil rights monitor" to oversee operations and guard against racial discrimination for a four-year period—during which time "spot testing" of Denny's restaurants would occur. Denny's management pointed out that in 1992, a year before the California lawsuit was filed, the firm had implemented a program with goals of improving minority hiring and employee promotions, as well as increasing the number of black franchisees in the Denny's system.

Little more than a month later, in May 1993, Denny's fired a manager in Annapolis, Maryland, for failing to report complaints lodged against the restaurant by a group of six black Secret Service agents. Just hours before the firing, the group had filed a racial discrimination suit in the U.S. District Court in Baltimore. The new charges alleged that the group had entered the restaurant with a group of white Secret Service agents for breakfast, and that although the white agents were served within ten minutes of ordering, the black agents had to wait some forty-five minutes before their food arrived. Ironically, this incident took place on the very day—April 1—that Denny's settled the original suit brought against it in California.

In June, after civil rights leader Jesse Jackson and the National Association for the Advancement of Colored People (NAACP) became involved in negotiations with Denny's, Flagstar Companies hired Norman J. Hill to head human resource operations. Hill, an African-American and the former vice president of human resources for a competitor (Perkins Family Restaurants), vowed to bring a different perspective and greater sensitivity to the situation.

In addition, Denny's announced a new advertising campaign addressing its racial problems. A sixty-second commercial featured its chairman and employees of various races assuring viewers that although mistakes were made, they were isolated and not indicative of the Denny's chain as whole. The ad pledged that Denny's would provide fair and equal treatment to all customers. However, even before Denny's executives got a chance to view the finished commercial, the company landed in court again. Five current and former black employees in Cleveland, Ohio, filed a lawsuit charging the restaurant chain with racial bias and harassment. In 1994, Flagstar paid $54 million to settle these civil rights actions.

Apparently, the charges had not gone far enough. In 1995, to combat the allegations of racial discrimination and to bring boycotting customers back into Denny's restaurants, Flagstar launched a sweeping reformation, starting with the hiring of James B. Adamson, former CEO of Burger King, as chairman and CEO. Recognizing that change begins at the top, Adamson carefully set a new tone for Flagstar and its restaurants.

Adamson implemented sweeping changes from the boardroom to the kitchen. He centralized authority for restaurant operations to bring consistency to restaurant management, set strict rules, and warned employees and franchisees alike: "If you discriminate, you're history." Eight of Flagstar's twelve top executives—all white males—left the company, and the management committee now includes a Hispanic male, two white women, and a black woman in a newly created position responsible for diversity initiatives. Regional and district managers have been replaced with one layer of three hundred managing partners, who oversee company-owned restaurants, and twenty-two franchise managers. A percentage of store managers' pay is now linked to diversity goals in hiring and promotion. At the store level, kitchens and dining rooms have been reengineered. Any evidence of bigotry results in termination. A monitor continues to oversee operations to guard against racial discrimination. All restaurants have a complaint number posted for customers.

The results of these changes are beginning to show. Blacks now constitute 17 percent of Flagstar's management, and twenty-seven of the six hundred franchised restaurants are black-owned (three years ago, there was just one minority Denny's franchisee). However, these figures are much higher at McDonald's and Burger King. Flagstar's purchasing contracts with minorities have surpassed $50 million, four years ahead of the NAACP goal.

Whether the sweeping changes Adamson has implemented will bring back the customers that

Denny's has lost remains to be seen. Proactive leadership has set a positive tone for the whole organization to follow. Flagstar only recently began tracking demographic trends, but already Denny's same-store sales are up 0.9 percent during a period in which its rivals struggled. Reforming an entire organizational culture cannot be accomplished overnight, but Flagstar's James B. Adamson has developed and implemented a plan to transform Denny's into a marketer that focuses on satisfying customers, whatever their race.[39]

Questions for Discussion

1. How did Denny's realized marketing strategy differ from its intended marketing strategy in serving racially diverse customers?
2. What problems might have occurred in implementing the marketing strategy of separating top-level and mid-level managers and front-line managers? Explain.
3. Explain how Denny's could use total quality management and internal marketing to improve its service to all customers.

Marketing on the Internet

OBJECTIVES

- To define *electronic marketing* and *electronic commerce* and recognize their increasing importance in strategic planning

- To understand the characteristics of electronic marketing—addressability, interactivity, memory, control, accessibility, and digitalization—and how they differentiate electronic marketing from the traditional marketing environment

- To examine how the characteristics of electronic marketing affect marketing strategy

- To become aware of the legal and ethical considerations associated with electronic marketing

Dell Reshapes PC Industry

ell Computer is truly the stuff of entrepreneurial legend. The company traces its origins to a dorm room at the University of Texas where in 1984 Michael Dell was busy assembling and selling personal computers. When the business took off, Dell dropped out of school to sell PCs full-time. His company has since grown into one of the world's leading computer makers, having now achieved sales of $18 billion. Based in Round Rock, Texas, Dell Computer manufactures and sells computer hardware (notebooks, PCs, and network servers) and markets third-party software and peripherals. More than 90 percent of these products are sold to business and government customers. Michael Dell still runs the company, making him the longest-tenured chief executive of a major computer company.

Dell focuses on providing competitively priced, high-quality computers and fast delivery. Direct sales via the Internet or telephone are one way Dell keeps prices down. The company's customers often depend on rapid delivery to keep their operations running smoothly. In one instance, Dell was able to ship 2,000 PCs and 4,000 servers, with proprietary and multimedia software already installed, to 2,000 Wal-Mart stores in just six weeks. It also delivered eight customized network servers to NASDAQ in thirty-six hours, allowing the stock exchange to handle high trading volumes resulting from an Asian economic crisis. To ensure that customers get their orders quickly, the company is constantly looking for ways to improve and shorten manufacturing and distribution cycle times. One way it does so is by having PCs and monitors shipped separately to customers from their respective factories.

Dell Computer has a strong presence outside the United States. About 31 percent of its sales come from overseas, and its European sales are increasing by 50 percent a year. To market to overseas customers, Dell maintains six toll-free call centers in Europe and Asia. In Asia, where social and legal factors make direct sales more difficult, it also employs some resellers. To supply its overseas customers, Dell operates factories in Limerick, Ireland, and Penang, Malaysia.

Remaining true to its dorm-room origins by bypassing middlemen and marketing custom-built computers directly to buyers, Dell has reshaped the computer industry. The company sells $12 million worth of computers a day through its Web site and expects that half its sales will be Web-based by 2000. The company's Web site allows customers to configure and order the ideal machine for their needs. Dell's Web site was one of the first online retailing operations to be profitable. Michael Dell, however, views the Internet not just as a retail venue but as an opportunity to build strong relationships with customers.[1]

Having reached 50 million users in just four years, the Internet represents the fastest growing medium to date. (It took radio thirty-eight years to reach 50 million listeners, and television did not achieve this milestone until thirteen years after its introduction.) In fact, experts say traffic on the Internet is doubling approximately every hundred days.[2] The phenomenal growth of this medium presents exciting opportunities for marketers like Dell to forge relationships with consumers and business customers on an interactive basis. The interactive nature of the Internet, and particularly of the World Wide Web, has made it possible to target markets more precisely and even to reach markets that previously were inaccessible. It also facilitates supply chain management, allowing companies to network with manufacturers, wholesalers, retailers, suppliers, and outsource firms to serve customers more efficiently. Because of its ability to enhance the exchange of information between customer and marketer, the Internet has become an important component of many firms' marketing strategies— so important that many consider it marketing's new frontier.

We devote this chapter to exploring this new frontier. We begin by defining electronic marketing and examining the characteristics that differentiate it from traditional marketing activities. Next, we explore how marketers are using the Internet to build competitive advantage. Finally, we consider some of the ethical and legal issues that affect Internet marketing.

What Is Electronic Marketing?

electronic commerce (E-commerce) Sharing business information, maintaining business relationships, and conducting business transactions by means of telecommunications networks

A number of terms have been used to describe marketing activities and transactions on the Internet. One of the most popular is **electronic commerce** (or **E-commerce**), which has been defined as "the sharing of business information, maintaining business relationships, and conducting business transactions by means of telecommunications networks."[3] The mass media have used the term *E-commerce* to describe the technology infrastructure for targeting customers, conducting customer transactions, and maintaining online relationships with all members of the marketing channel. In this chapter, however, we focus on how the Internet and especially the World Wide Web relate to all aspects of marketing, including strategic planning. Thus, we use the term **electronic marketing** (or **E-marketing**) to refer to the strategic process of creating, distributing, promoting, and pricing products for targeted customers in the virtual environment of the Internet.

electronic marketing (E-marketing) The strategic process of creating, distributing, promoting, and pricing products for targeted customers in the virtual environment of the Internet

There are a variety of ways to look at E-marketing. Buying collectibles through online auctions, such as eBay, is a consumer-based aspect of E-marketing. E-marketing also includes automation of a retailer's inventory orders from a supplier via computer—an electronic data interchange (EDI) activity that was available long before the World Wide Web came into widespread use. Thus, E-marketing involves both business-to-consumer and business-to-business dimensions. Business-to-business marketing accounts for approximately 90 to 95 percent of all E-commerce profits. Table 23.1 compares business-to-business E-commerce revenues with total business-to-business revenues; Table 23.2 displays amounts of online sales for various product categories. While the business-to-consumer dimension of E-commerce is relatively small in terms of profitability, it has the greatest potential, given the growing number of consumers with Internet access.[4]

Another important aspect of E-marketing involves the ability of marketers and customers to share information. The Internet has changed the way marketers communicate and develop relationships not only with their customers, but also with their employees and suppliers. Price Waterhouse Cooper is one of many companies that use E-mail, groupware (software that allows people in different locations to access and work on the same file or document over the Internet), and video conferencing to coordinate activities and communicate with employees. Internet technology has made it possible for the accounting firm to eliminate permanent office space for its account consultants. Instead of permanent offices, the consultants arrange to "rent" an office space, complete with desk, Internet connection, and the employee's name on the cubicle, at various branch offices as needed.

Table 23.1   Business-to-Business E-Commerce Revenues Compared with Total Business-to-Business Revenues, by Industry Sector

Industry Sector	Year	Total revenue (in billions)	Internet revenue (in billions)	Internet % of total
Computing, electronics	1997	$ 477.8	$ 8.7	1.8%
	2003, projected	1,005.4	395.3	39.3
Utilities	1997	490.2	3.2	0.7
	2003, projected	656.9	169.5	25.8
Shipping/warehousing	1997	312.6	0.5	0.2
	2003, projected	358.3	61.6	17.2
Motor vehicles	1997	915.9	1.5	0.2
	2003, projected	1,445.3	212.9	14.7
Petrochemicals	1997	987.3	2.1	0.2
	2003, projected	1,323.0	178.3	13.5
Paper/office products	1997	826.7	0.6	0.1
	2003, projected	1,166.0	65.2	5.6
Food/agriculture	1997	1,489.6	0.1	0.0
	2003, projected	1,778.6	53.6	3.0
Other	1997	4,411.9	2.0	0.0
	2003, projected	6,412.9	194.4	3.0
Total	1997	9,911.9	18.6	0.2
	2003, projected	14,146.5	1,330.9	9.4

Source: George Anders, "Click and Buy: Why—and Where—Internet Commerce Is Succeeding," *Wall Street Journal,* Interactive Edition, http://interactive.wsj.com/archive, Dec. 7, 1998.

Yet another important aspect of E-marketing relates to the transaction of business (business-to-business or business-to-customer) through telecommunications networks. Telecommunications technology offers a number of potential advantages to marketers, including rapid response, expanded customer service capability (e.g., twenty-four hours a day, seven days a week, or "24 x 7"), reduced costs of operation, and reduced geographic barriers. In today's fast-paced world, the ability to shop for books, clothes, and other merchandise at midnight, when traditional stores are closed, is a

Table 23.2   Online Sales, by Product Category

Product Category	1997 (in millions)	2002, Projected (in millions)
Travel	$911	$11,699
PC hardware	986	6,434
Books	152	3,661
Grocery	63	3,529
Apparel and accessories	103	2,884
Software	85	2,379
Ticketing	52	1,810
Specialty gifts	100	1,357
Music	37	1,591
Health and beauty	2	1,183
Consumer electronics	15	792
Videos	15	575
Toys	2	555
Other	485	2,689

Source: George Anders, "Click and Buy: Why—and Where—Internet Commerce Is Succeeding," *Wall Street Journal,* Interactive Edition, http://interactive.wsj.com/archive, Dec. 7, 1998.

Figure 23.1
E-Business Depends on Communication Infrastructure and Software
GTE assists companies with E-business by offering Web-hosting services and software solutions.

benefit for both buyers and sellers. The Internet allows even small firms to reduce the impact of geography on their operations. E-marketing activities are certainly increasing outside the United States. For example, Coastal Tool & Supply, a small power tool and supply store in Connecticut, has generated sales from around the world through its Web site. In one instance, a Saudi Arabian citizen, who worked for Saudi Airlines, E-mailed an order for $8,000 worth of Bosch power tools to Coastal's Web site. He flew to New York, rented a car, drove two and a half hours to the firm's Hartford store, picked up his order, paid cash, drove back to the airport, and flew home.[5] (Globalmarketing on page 601 looks at barriers to E-marketing in Asia.)

Electronic marketing activity depends on three elements: communications infrastructure, software, and products and markets. The communications infrastructure, which consists of Internet service providers (ISPs) like America Online and Netcom, telecommunications services like MCI and AT&T, and corporate and government computer networks, tends to change at the slowest pace. Innovations in software (e.g., Web browsers and plug-ins), products (e.g., electronic catalogs, digital currency, online banking services, online brokerage services, electronic benefit systems), and markets (e.g., E-auctions, direct-search markets, interorganizational supply-chain management structures) are emerging at an astounding rate. In Figure 23.1, GTE promotes its assistance to businesses in building Web sites or other Web-based application software for E-marketing. Often, the time available to exploit an opportunity presented by a new type of software or market is measured in weeks and months, not years. Thus, keeping up with new developments and identifying new opportunities are major research tasks in E-marketing.

Basic Characteristics of Electronic Marketing

Before discussing marketing strategy in an E-marketing environment, it is helpful to understand the basic characteristics that distinguish this environment from the traditional marketing environment. These characteristics are addressability, interactivity, memory, control, accessibility, and digitalization.

Addressability

addressability
A marketer's ability to identify customers before they make a purchase

The technology of the Internet makes it possible for visitors to a Web site to identify themselves and to provide information about their product needs and wants before making purchases. The ability of a marketer to identify customers before they make a purchase is called **addressability.** Many Web sites encourage visitors to register in order to maximize their use of the site or to gain access to premium areas; some even require it. Registration forms typically ask for basic information, such as name, E-mail address, age, and occupation, from which marketers can build user profiles to enhance their marketing efforts. CDNow, for example, asks music lovers to supply information about their listening tastes so that the company can recommend new releases (Figure 23.2). Some Web sites even offer contests and prizes to encourage users to register. Marketers can also conduct surveys to learn more about the people who access their Web sites, offering prizes as motivation for participation.

Marketers have always had the ability to identify potential customers. Long before the advent of the World Wide Web, they were able to purchase databases or use sales personnel to develop lists of potential customers. However, these methods are not the most efficient way to target customers. They often limit marketers to targeting groups of homogeneous individuals or organizations, and because they are relatively expensive, they are used only for higher-priced products. It was not until the introduction of the Internet that mass marketers could duplicate the capabilities of a sales force on a large scale at relatively low cost.

Addressability represents the ultimate expression of the marketing concept. With the knowledge they garner about individual customers through their Web sites, marketers can tailor marketing mixes more precisely to target customers with narrow interests, such as recorded blues music or golf. Table 23.3 lists the elements required to build E-marketing relationships. Addressability also facilitates tracking Web site visits and online buying activity, which makes it easier for marketers to accumulate data about individual customers to enhance future marketing efforts. Amazon.com, for example, stores data about customers' purchases and uses that information to make recommendations the next time they visit the site.

Exploiting addressability to access customer information is somewhat controversial, however. Some Web site software can store a **cookie,** or identifying string of text, on a visitor's computer. Marketers use cookies to track how often a particular user visits the Web site, what he or she may look at while there, and in what sequence.

cookie An identifying string of text stored on a Web site visitor's computer

Figure 23.2
CDNow
CDNow asks music lovers to supply information about their listening tastes so that the company can recommend new releases.

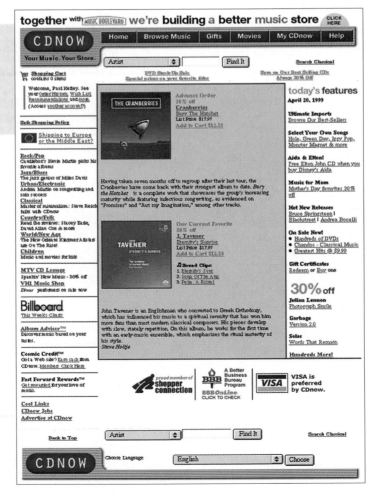

Table 23.3	**Developing E-marketing Relationships**

- Create a learning relationship with the customer
- Develop a relationship database to track customers who grant the company permission to do so
- Develop a marketing strategy that customers can understand so they can provide the company with continuous information about their needs and preferences
- Work to deepen the commitment of a customer who has developed loyalty to the company

Source: William C. Taylor, "Permission Marketing," *Fast Company*, Apr./May 1998, p. 206.

 Cookies also permit Web site visitors to customize services, such as virtual shopping carts, as well as the particular content they see when they log onto a Web page. CNN, for example, allows visitors to its Web site to create a custom news page tailored to their particular interests. The use of cookies can be an ethical issue, however, depending on how cookie data are used. If a Web site owner can use cookies to link a visitor's interests to a name and address, that information could be sold to advertisers and other parties without the visitor's consent or knowledge. The potential for misuse has left many consumers nervous about cookie technology. Because technology allows access to large quantities of data about individual customers' use of Web sites, companies must carefully consider how the use of such information affects individuals' privacy, as we discuss in more detail later in this chapter.

Globalmarketing

Barriers to E-Commerce in Asia

Although the Internet seems to have taken the world by storm, electronic marketing does not yet have the same presence overseas that it does in the United States. E-marketing is catching on in Europe, where revenues reached $165 million in 1998, up from $68 million the year before; experts predict sales there will double every year through 2002. The picture in Asia, however, is quite different. In 1998, online spending for goods and services in the United States was almost forty times that in Asia, excluding Japan.

Asia presents many barriers to E-marketing. One of the most obvious is the relatively small number of Internet users. Asians account for just 12 percent of the Internet users worldwide; in comparison, the United States and Canada comprise 62 percent of the Internet community. The fact that most Web sites are currently in English also inhibits online transactions by Asian customers. Asian shopping patterns that are at odds with American-style online retailing are a very significant barrier. In Asia, where consumers tend to haggle and pay cash and where shopping is often a family affair, the notion of impersonal shopping on a Web site that requires a credit card to complete a transaction is truly foreign. Lack of familiarity with credit cards and the absence of laws that encourage secure online credit card transactions give many Asians a reason not to shop online. Most Hong Kong banks don't even permit online baking. Moreover, establishing an online presence can be quite expensive for Asian compa-

nies, and many are reluctant to put their businesses online for fear that they will fail.

Despite these barriers, some E-marketing is occurring in Asia, and experts believe it will continue to grow. Chinese and Hong Kong companies in particular are beginning to establish Web sites to reach customers abroad. An online presence has helped Shenzhen Power, a battery manufacturer in China, secure contracts with business customers in Israel, India, and Russia. By marketing through an online shopping mall, another Chinese manufacturer—DB Products, which makes buzzers used in a variety of other products—was able to reduce the time it takes to get orders to customers. DB now gets 10 percent of its orders through the Net. Online consumer marketing has been slower to take hold, but U.S.-based Charles Schwab reports that 80 percent of its Asian trades are accomplished online, compared with 50 percent in the United States. And two of Hong Kong's largest supermarket chains have recently begun encouraging customers to order groceries via a digital TV set top box.

The fact that six out of every seven dollars spent online in Asia go to non-Asian companies may motivate more Asian companies to join the electronic revolution; if they don't, they risk losing more sales to foreign companies. As these firms and their foreign competitors learn to modify their online marketing strategies to address Asian customers' concerns, the Internet will increasingly make the world one global marketplace.

Interactivity

interactivity   The ability to allow customers to express their needs and wants directly to the firm in response to the firm's marketing communications

Another distinguishing characteristic of E-marketing is **interactivity,** which allows customers to express their needs and wants directly to the firm in response to the firm's marketing communications. This means that marketers can interact with prospective customers in real time (or a close approximation of it). Of course, salespeople have always been able to do this, but at much greater cost. The Web provides the advantages of a sales representative's presence, but with broader market coverage and at lower cost.

One implication of interactivity is that a firm's customers can also communicate with other customers (and noncustomers). For this reason, differences in the amount and type of information possessed by marketers and their customers are not as pronounced as in the past. One result is that the new- and used-car business has become considerably more competitive because buyers are coming into the dealerships armed with more complete product and cost information obtained through comparison shopping on the Net. By providing information, ideas, and a context for interacting with other customers, E-marketers can enhance an individual's interest and involvement with their products.

community   A sense of group membership or feeling of belonging

Interactivity enables marketers to capitalize on the concept of community to help customers derive value from the firm's products and Web site. **Community** refers to a sense of group membership or feeling of belonging by individual members of a group.[6] One such community is Tripod, a Web site where Generation Xers can create their own Web pages and chat or exchange messages on bulletin boards about topics ranging from cars and computers to health and careers. Much of the site's content has been developed by members of the Tripod community. Tripod, like many online communities, is free, but it requires members to register to access the site.[7] The success of Web sites like Tripod, Women's Wire, and Parents' Soup corroborates analysis by *Business Week* that suggests the most successful online marketers do not just duplicate existing businesses online, but fully exploit the interactivity of the Web for the benefit of their customers. The most successful Web sites become "virtual communities" where "like-minded cybernauts congregate, swap information, buy something, and come back week after week."[8] They encourage visitors to "hang out" and contribute to the community (and see the Web site's advertising) instead of clicking elsewhere. Because such communities have well-defined demographics and common interests, they represent a valuable audience for advertisers, which typically generate the funds needed to maintain such sites.[9]

In the business-to-business environment, many firms are utilizing telecommunications technology, such as video conferencing, to bring together representatives of the firm and their customers over the Internet. This reduces travel costs, saves time, and allows more frequent contact with a firm's customer base. Firms are also using Web technology to bring sales personnel in widely dispersed offices together with the home office for conferences, group discussions, and training sessions. Intranets, as we discussed in Chapter 6, allow employees in widespread locations to access internal marketing data, such as customer profiles and product inventory, to enhance the firm's marketing efforts. For example, Weyerhaeuser's intranet includes software that can track inventory and compare prices, which has helped the company reduce the costs and time required to manufacture doors.[10]

Memory

memory   The ability to access databases or data warehouses containing individual customer profiles and past purchase histories and to use these data in real time to customize a marketing offer

Memory refers to a firm's ability to access databases or data warehouses containing individual customer profiles and past purchase histories and to use these data in real time to customize its marketing offer to a specific customer. Although companies have had database systems for many years, the information they contain did not become available to the marketer on a real-time basis until fairly recently. Current software technology allows marketers to identify a visitor to a Web site instantaneously, locate that customer's profile in their database, and then display the customer's past purchases or suggest new products based on past purchases while the customer is still visiting the site. For example, Bluefly, an online clothing retailer, asks visitors to provide their E-mail address, clothing preferences, brand preferences, and sizes so it can create a customized online catalog ("My Catalog") of clothing matching the customer's specified preferences. The firm uses customer purchase profiles to manage its merchandise buying. Whenever it adds new clothing items to its inventory, it checks them against its database of customer preferences and, if a match is found, it alerts the individual in an E-mail message. E-marketers' ability to identify and store specific customer information to customize their offerings increases the value provided to each customer. Applying memory to large numbers of customers represents a profound advantage when a firm uses it to learn more about individual customers each time they visit the firm's Web site.

Control

control   Customers' ability to regulate the information they view, as well as the rate and sequence of their exposure to that information

In the context of E-marketing, the term **control** refers to customers' ability to regulate the information they view, as well as the rate and sequence of their exposure to that information. The Web is sometimes referred to as a *pull* medium because users determine what they view at Web sites; Web site operators' ability to control the content users look at and in what sequence is limited. In contrast, television can be characterized as a *push* medium because the broadcaster determines what the viewer sees once he or she has selected a particular channel. Both television and radio provide "limited exposure control" (you see or hear whatever is broadcast until you change the station). With the World Wide Web, customers have a greater degree of control because they can simply click to another site or log off the system.

hypertext   Highlighted text that permits visitors to jump from one point in a Web site to other points or even to other Web sites

Most Web sites employ **hypertext,** which has been defined as "text that branches and allows choices to the reader, best read at an interactive screen. As popularly conceived, this is a series of text chunks connected by links which offer the reader different pathways."[11] It is hypertext that permits visitors to jump from one point in a Web site to other points or even to other Web sites. Different viewers may experience the same Web site in different ways, depending on the path of their progress through the content. Firms using hypertext in their marketing content cannot control the sequence in which the viewer looks at the content.

For E-marketers, the primary implication of control is that attracting, and retaining, customers' attention is more difficult. Marketers have to work harder and more creatively to communicate the value of their Web site clearly and quickly, or the viewer will lose interest and click to another site. With literally hundreds of millions of unique pages of content available to any Web surfer, simply putting a Web site on the Internet does not guarantee anyone will visit it or make a purchase. Innovative promotional activities may be required to publicize the Web site. For example, three online brokerage houses—DLJDirect, E*Trade Securities, and Waterhouse Securities—agreed to pay America Online $75 million to carry advertisements for their Websites in the finance area of the online giant's Web site.[12] Because of AOL's growing status as a **portal** (a multiservice Web site that serves as a gateway to other Web sites), firms are eager to link to it and other such sites to help draw attention to their own sites.

portal   A multiservice Web site that serves as a gateway to other Web sites

Accessibility

accessibility   The ability to obtain the information available on the Internet

An extraordinary amount of information is available on the Internet. The ability to obtain it is referred to as **accessibility.** Because customers can access in-depth information about competing products, they are much better informed about a firm's products and their relative value than ever before. Someone looking to buy a new truck, for example, can go to the Web sites of Ford, General Motors, and Dodge to compare the features of the Ford F-150, the GMC Sierra, and the Dodge Ram. The truck buyer can also visit online magazines and pricing guides, as well as dealers' Web sites to get more specific information about product features, performance, and prices.

Accessibility also dramatically increases the competition for the Internet user's attention. Without significant promotion—such as advertising on portals like Yahoo! and Netscape or other frequently visited sites—it is becoming increasingly difficult to attract a visitor's attention to a particular Web site. Consequently, E-marketers are having to become more creative and innovative to attract visitors to their sites. We look closer at promotion on the Web later in this chapter.

Another implication of accessibility is that recognizable brand names may become a more important competitive weapon for E-marketers. Consumers have no real way to assess the benefits or quality of the escalating number of unknown brands they may encounter on the Web. Consequently, they may prefer to stick with familiar or recognizable brands to ensure quality. More firms are therefore attempting to build brand recognition among online consumers. For its online marketing strategy, MasterCard International, for example, has shifted its focus from simply touting its credit card to providing online shoppers with security and service. It even grants a sort of MasterCard "seal of approval"—the Shop Smart seal—to E-commerce sites that use advanced security systems for credit card purchases. This tactic allows MasterCard International to post its well-known logo on the most popular online shopping sites, thus promoting its Internet image.[13]

uniform resource locator (URL) A Web site address

A related consideration is the recognition value of a firm's **Uniform Resource Locator (URL),** or Web site address. The first firm to register a particular URL with the Inter-Networking Information Center (Inter Nic) gains the exclusive right to use that as its Web site address. Imagine the difficulty of maintaining a Web site for Coca-Cola and not being to use www.coke.com as a URL. As the number of Web sites proliferates, Web surfers will have increasing difficulty learning or remembering the Web site addresses for various firms and products. A URL that doesn't match the brand or company name can represent a serious obstacle to new or first-time visitors looking for a particular product on the Web. For example, eToys was the first toy seller to register the URL "eToys.com." When Toys "R" Us set up a Web site sometime later, it was thus unable to use that URL for its cyberstore. Other URLs that gave companies instantaneous advantage include cooking.com (cookware and specialty foods), iPrint.com (business cards and letterheads), and Sportscape.com (sporting goods).[14]

Digitalization

digitalization The ability to represent a product, or at least some of its benefits, as digital bits of information

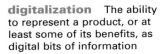

Digitalization refers to the ability to represent a product, or at least some of its benefits, as digital bits of information. Digitalization means the Internet can be used to distribute, promote, and sell those features apart from the physical item itself. Streamline, for example, is a Boston-based company that takes orders for a variety of goods and services and delivers them to the consumer's home. The digitalization component of Streamline's product comes from the practice of inputting an inventory of each consumer's pantry into a computer database. Each week or month, customers fax or E-mail a checklist of the items they want to order and have delivered directly to their pantries. Streamline stores the purchase history in its computers to learn more about each customer, so it can continually suggest new goods or services to order.[15] FedEx has developed Web-based software that allows consumers and organizational customers to track their own packages from their starting point to their destination. FedEx's Web site receives 1.7 million tracking requests a month, up to 40 percent of which would otherwise have gone through the company's toll-free telephone number for tracking information. This has saved FedEx up to $8 million a year in customer-support costs.[16] Distributed over the Web at very low cost, the online tracking system adds value to FedEx's delivery services.

In addition to creating distribution efficiencies, digitizing part of a product's features allows new combinations of features and services to be created quickly and inexpensively. For example, a service station that keeps a customer's history of automotive oil changes in a database can E-mail that customer about the need for an oil change and at the same time suggest other types of preventive maintenance, such as tire rotations or a tune-up. Digital features are easy to mix and match to meet the demands of individual customers.

E-Marketing Strategy

Now that we have looked at the distinguishing characteristics of doing business on the Internet, it is time to consider how these characteristics affect marketing strategy. Marketing strategy involves identifying and analyzing a target market and creating a marketing mix to satisfy individuals in that market, regardless of whether those individuals are accessible online or through more traditional avenues. However, there are significant differences in how marketing mix components are developed and combined into a marketing strategy in the electronic environment of the Web. As we continue this discussion, keep in mind that the Internet is a very dynamic environment, which means that E-marketing strategies may need to be modified frequently to keep pace.

Target Markets

E-marketing permits companies to target customers more precisely and accurately than ever before. The addressability, interactivity, and memory characteristics of E-marketing enable marketers to identify specific customers to establish interactive dialogues with them to learn their needs, and to combine this information with their purchase histories to customize products to meet their needs. The ability to identify individual customers allows marketers to shift their focus from targeting groups of similar customers to increasing their share of an individual customer's purchases. Thus, the emphasis shifts from "share of market" to "share of customer." For example, Virtual Vineyards, an online wine merchant, can track the content visitors look at on its Web site, as well as customers' purchases. This makes it possible for the vintner to notify a customer of the arrival of an interesting new vintage from a winery in which he or she has previously shown an interest.[17] Being able to learn more about each customer's tastes and preferences helps Virtual Vineyards improve its ability to satisfy individual customers and thereby increase sales to each customer.

One caveat accompanying the shift in perspective from "share of market" to "share of customer" is that a firm should ensure that individual target customers have the potential to do enough business with the firm to justify such specialized efforts. Indeed, one of the benefits arising from the addressability characteristic of E-marketing is that firms can track and analyze an individual customer's purchases and identify the most profitable and loyal customers. Given the increased availability of such individualized customer data, many firms are looking to see who their most valuable customers are.

One of the characteristics of firms engaged in E-marketing is a renewed focus on building customer loyalty and retaining customers—in other words, on relationship marketing. As we noted in Chapter 1, relationship marketing continually deepens a buyer's dependence on the company, and as the customer's confidence grows, this in turn increases the firm's understanding of the customer's needs. Eventually, this interaction becomes a solid relationship that allows for cooperation and mutual dependency. Studies have shown that retaining current customers is as much as five times more profitable than spending company resources to attract new customers.[18] A focus on retaining customers is possible in E-marketing because of marketers' ability to target individual customers. This effort is enhanced over time as the customer invests more time and effort in "teaching" the firm what he or she wants. Commitment to the firm increases the costs the customer would incur by switching to another company. Once a customer has learned how to trade stocks online through eSchwab, for example, there is

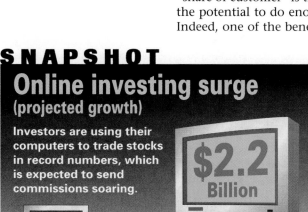

SNAPSHOT

Online investing surge
(projected growth)

Investors are using their computers to trade stocks in record numbers, which is expected to send commissions soaring.

$2.2 Billion

$300 Million

1997   2002

a cost of leaving to find a new brokerage firm; not only may another firm offer less service, but it also takes time to find a new firm and to learn a new system. Anytime a firm can learn more about its customers to improve the match between its marketing mix and the target customer's desires, it increases the perceived costs of switching to another firm. E-marketing enhances this effort for the benefit of both marketer and customer.

Product Considerations

The exponential growth of the Internet and the World Wide Web presents exciting opportunities for marketing products to both consumers and organizations. Computer giant IBM, for example, purchases $4 billion worth of goods and services a year over the Internet; 3Com, a communications equipment firm, orders 50 percent of its supplies through the Web and believes that figure will rise to 100 percent in five years. Internet purchases are helping reduce these firms' costs and are improving their customer service and communications with both customers and suppliers.[19] Computers and computer peripherals, industrial supplies, and packaged software are the leading organizational purchases online. Consumer products account for a small but growing percentage of Internet transactions, with securities trading, travel/tourism, and books among the largest consumer purchases.[20] Through E-marketing, companies can provide products, including goods, services, and ideas, that offer distinct benefits and improve customer satisfaction.

The online marketing of such goods as computer hardware and software, books, videos, CDs, toys, automobiles, and even groceries is accelerating rapidly. Dell Computer, for example, sells $12 *million* worth of computers online every day to consumers and businesses[21] (see Figure 23.3). Autobytel has established an effective model for online auto sales by helping consumers find the best price on their preferred model and then arranging for local delivery. Streamline and Peapod offer busy consumers the opportunity to shop online for groceries at their convenience and to have the goods delivered to their door or, in the case of Streamline, stocked directly in their pantries.

Figure 23.3
Dell Computer
Dell Computer sells $12 million worth of computers online every-day to consumers and businesses.

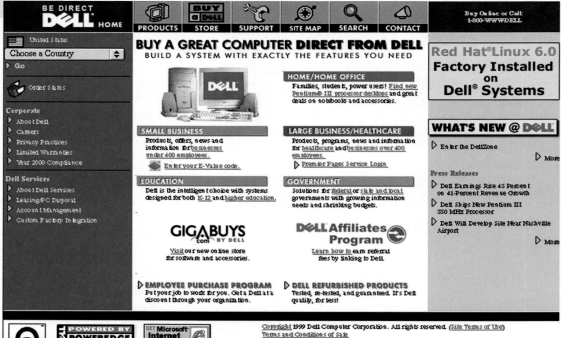

eBay˜ **connects**

buyers and sellers.

On the Internet.

On Oracle.

Companies who know the Internet best use Oracle˚ for e-business. Do you?

For more information, visit *www.oracle.com/info/ebusiness.*

©1999 Oracle Corporation. All rights reserved. Oracle is a registered trademark of Oracle Corporation.
All other names are trademarks of their respective owners.

ORACLE®
the e-business engine

Figure 23.4
Product Considerations in E-Marketing Strategy
eBay makes available a diverse assortment of products to link buyers with sellers.

In Figure 23.4, eBay serves as an online auction connecting sellers of diverse products with buyers. However, the ability of firms to deliver tangible goods has been challenged by low profit margins due to customized delivery.

Some other services can also be marketed online, perhaps even more successfully than goods. At Century 21's Web site, for example, you can search for the home of your dreams anywhere in the United States, get information about mortgages and credit and tips on buying real estate, and learn about the company's relocation services. Charles Schwab is one of several online brokerage firms that offer online trading of stocks and bonds and that provide quotes, news, research, planning, and other specialized services. Airlines are increasingly booking flights via their Web sites. American Airlines, for example, sold more than $100 million worth of airplane tickets online in a recent year.[22]

Brand recognition is likely to become increasingly important in the marketing of services online. Remember from Chapter 13 that goods have search qualities (tangible attributes, such as engine size for cars or hard-drive size for computers) that customers can evaluate before making a purchase. Services, however, tend to have experience qualities, which buyers can assess only if they buy and use the product. Because it is difficult for customers to judge the quality of services before they purchase and use them, they often look for recognizable brand names as a means to ensure quality. Well-known brand names are even more likely to give a firm a competitive advantage online, given the huge number of Web sites and products available. Edmund's, for example, has established a reputation for providing accurate auto price, product feature, and road test information in its thirty years of publishing *Edmund's New Car Prices and Reviews* and other publications. Customers' trust in the accuracy of the information found on Edmund's Web site is a function of their past experience with the firm or their recognition of the brand. Using "Bob's" car prices as a source of product and price information might not inspire the same level of trust.

The proliferation of information on the World Wide Web has itself spawned new services. Web search engines and directories like Yahoo!, Excite, HotBot, Alta Vista, and Infoseek are among the most heavily accessed sites on the Internet. Without these services, which track and index the vast quantity of information available on the Web, the task of finding something of interest would be tantamount to searching for that proverbial needle in a haystack. Many of these services, most notably Yahoo!, have evolved into portals by offering additional services, including news, weather, chat rooms, free E-mail accounts, and shopping.

Marketers have also created Web-based services to target specific markets. GolfWeb, for example, provides links to 35,000 golf-related Web pages, a virtual ProShop, and the opportunity to subscribe to special services, such as handicapping and online games. Advertising, which accounts for 35 percent of GolfWeb's revenues, can therefore be targeted precisely at this market niche.[23] Online city guides like Sidewalk, Digital City, Yahoo! Local, and CitySearch are another popular new product. At CitySearch Nashville, for example, residents can find out about local sporting events and recreational opportunities, movie listings and reviews, restaurants and businesses, museums, news, and weather, and exchange views on local issues. Most major cities now have one or more such guides.

Even ideas have the potential to be successfully marketed on the Internet. Web-based distance learning and educational programs are becoming increasingly popular. Corporate employee training is a $55 billion industry, and online training modules are growing rapidly. Additional ideas that are being marketed online include marriage and personal counseling; medical, tax, and legal advice; and even psychic services.

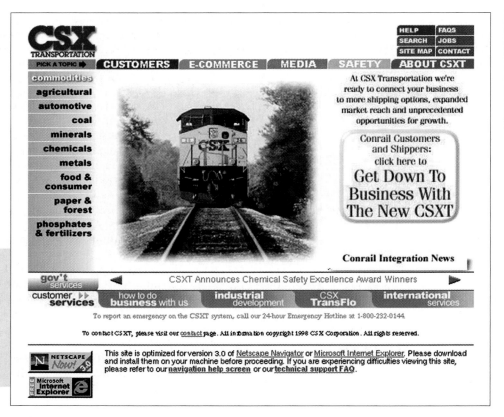

**Figure 23.5
CSX Corporation**
The Web site for CSX, one of the nation's largest shipping companies, permits customers to get price quotes, book shipments, and track the exact location of their shipments.

Distribution Considerations

The role of distribution is to make products available at the right time at the right place in the right quantities. Physical distribution is especially compatible with E-marketing. The ability to process orders electronically and to increase the speed of communications via the Internet reduces inefficiencies, costs, and redundancies throughout the marketing channel. It also speeds delivery times and improves customer service. The interactive nature of the Internet allows firms to develop close working relationships with members of their supply chain. For example, the Web site for CSX, one of the nation's largest shipping companies, permits General Motors, Home Depot, PepsiCo, and other customers to get price quotes, book shipments, and track the exact location of their shipments (see Figure 23.5).[24]

More firms are exploiting advances in information technology to synchronize the relationships between their manufacturing or product assembly and their customer contact operations. This increase in information sharing among various operations of the firm makes product customization easier to accomplish. Marketers can use their Web sites to query customers about their needs and then manufacture products that exactly fit those needs. Gateway and Dell, for example, help their customers build their own computers by asking them to specify what components to include; these firms then assemble and ship the customized product directly to the customer within a few days.

Granting suppliers access to customer transaction databases fosters better coordination within the marketing channel. By observing electronically what a firm's customers are ordering, a supplier knows exactly when to ship the materials needed to meet demand, and the firm can keep less inventory on hand. This lowers distribution costs for the firm, allowing it to become more competitive. Wal-Mart, for example, exchanges data about inventory levels and product availability with Procter & Gamble and other manufacturers, thus creating partnerships that maximize opportunities for profits and competitive advantage for all members of its supply chain.[25] Supply chain management is enhanced because the Internet provides the network necessary to optimize cooperation and communication.

Business-to-business transactions, in particular, have been enhanced by the creation of technologically advanced networks among manufacturers and other members of the supply chain. The use of *extranets* (secure Web-based networks that connect companies with their customers and suppliers) has facilitated the coordination of physical distribution of products, order processing, and inventory management. For example, Weyerhaeuser's DoorBuilder intranet was so successful that the manufacturer expanded it into an extranet to improve communications with its suppliers and customers. Through Weyerhaeuser's extranet, builders, architects, and other customers can order a complete package of doors, frames, hardware, and stains from Weyerhaeuser's product list and vendors of related products.[26] The extranet also enhances long-term relationships with suppliers. The development of business-to-business E-marketing infrastructures makes product distribution more efficient, flexible, and less costly, thereby increasing customer satisfaction.

One of the most visible members of any marketing channel is the retailer, and the Internet is increasingly becoming a retail venue. The Internet provides an opportunity for marketers of everything from computers to travel reservations to encourage exchanges. According to Jupiter Communications, an Internet research firm, online shopping now stands at $2.6 billion, and Jupiter projects that figure will rise to $37.5 billion over the next five years. If that forecast proves accurate, online retailing will begin to catch up with mail-order transactions, which now amount to $46 billion.[27] Amazon.com of Seattle sells $610 million of products a year directly from its Web site, and more than 80 percent of its customers complete the transaction online.[28] Indeed, Amazon.com's success at marketing books online has been so phenomenal that a host of imitators have adopted its retailing model for everything from CDs to toys. Another retailing adventure is supplied by online auctioneers, such as First Auction, Haggle Online, and Onsale Inc., which auction everything from fine wines and golf clubs to computer goods and electronics.[29] Even small firms are distributing their products through the Internet. Consider the Great Southern Sauce Company, a store in Little Rock, Arkansas, whose Web site has sold hot sauce, BBQ sauce, and other Southern condiments to customers as far away as London and Saudi Arabia.[30]

Promotion Considerations

The Internet is an interactive medium that can be used to inform, entertain, and persuade target markets to accept an organization's products. The accessibility of the Internet presents marketers with an exciting opportunity to expand and complement their traditional promotional efforts or to operate in the Internet exclusively. For example, Monster.com uses the Internet exclusively to promote its services (see Figure 23.6). Many companies augment their TV and print advertising campaigns with Web-based promotions. Kraft and

With access to millions of candidates, who you don't see is as important as who you do.

The fact is, you hire better people when you have more people to choose from. And now finding the right person among the millions is easier with Monster.com. Prospects who apply to your posted jobs fill out a skill screen you create for each position – a sorted, prioritized list of the best résumés is sent to you as candidates respond. You see the best people faster and never have to see the unqualified applicants. You can also search a million résumés without looking at a million – your personal agent can search our database and return only those that meet your hiring criteria. So while we attract millions to our site, you only see the ones you want. Call us. We'll explain how becoming a Monster.com member can help you hire smart people more intelligently. **1-800-MONSTER.**

monster.com

Figure 23.6
Promotion Considerations
Monster.com operates an Internet-based business to assist companies in hiring the right employees.

Ragú have both created Web sites with recipes and tips on entertaining to help consumers get the most out of their products (see Figure 23.7). Numerous movie studios have set up Web sites at which visitors can view clips of their latest movie releases, and television commercials for new movies often encourage viewers to visit these sites. Additionally, some television networks have developed Web sites that offer viewing guides and additional content to enhance viewers' enjoyment. The Web site for the Discovery Channel, for example, offers schedules for that network and for the Animal Planet and Learning Channel networks, as well as feature articles and online shopping opportunities. Some television shows even have their own Web sites. HGTV's "Your New House," for instance, has a Web site that provides building and remodeling tips, a mortgage calculator, floor plans, and links to hundreds of Web sites operated by manufacturers of building products, appliances, and fixtures.

The characteristics of E-marketing make promotional efforts on the Internet significantly different from those that use more traditional media. First, because Internet users can control what they see, customers who visit a firm's Web site are there because they choose to be, which implies they are interested in the firm's products and therefore may be more involved in the message and dialogue provided by the firm. Second, the interactive nature of the Internet allows marketers to enter into dialogues with customers to learn more about their interests and needs. This information can then be used to tailor promotional messages to the individual customer. Amazon.com, for example, recognizes visitors by name if they have purchased books from the site before and then offers suggestions about titles they might be interested in based on their previous purchases. Finally, addressability means that marketing efforts directed at specific customers can be more effective. Indeed, direct marketing combined with effective analysis of customer databases may become one of E-marketing's most valuable promotional tools.

Ironically, however, the control and accessibility that characterize the E-marketing environment combine to make it harder to attract the attention of potential customers. Consequently, Web sites that have clearly demonstrated their ability to generate traffic, such as portal sites like Yahoo!, America Online, and Netscape, have become more valuable and expensive for firms to become associated with. Accessibility means that as the number of pages available to Web users increases, each individual Web site has to work harder to attract viewers.

Figure 23.7
Ragú
Ragú's Web site offers recipes and tips to help consumers get the most out of its products.

Advertising and Publicity.   Advertising and publicity are probably the most visible of the promotion mix elements on the World Wide Web. Thousands of well-known firms, from Adidas to Wal-Mart, have set up Web sites to tout their products, circulate company information, post press releases, list job opportunities, and entertain, inform, and interact with customers. More and more companies are using the Web to present "infotainment," thereby fostering brand identity and loyalty and long-term customer relationships.[31]

> **banner ads**   Small, rectangular ads, static or animated, that typically appear at the top of a Web page

Marketers can also advertise their products on the Web sites of other organizations. You are most likely to encounter these in the form of **banner ads**—small, rectangular ads, static or animated, that typically appear at the top of a Web page. Clicking on a banner takes the visitor to the advertiser's site for more information.[32] Many Web sites, including GolfWeb, Tripod, Women's Wire, ESPNet SportZone, and the Internet Movie Database, fund their sites through banners that advertise other firms' goods and services. Using Web search engines or indexes, you are likely to encounter **keyword ads,** which relate to text or subject matter specified in a Web search. For example, if you search for the term *laptop* on Yahoo!, a banner ad for an IBM product pops up because the company has purchased the rights to that and some two hundred other terms on Yahoo![33]

> **keyword ads**   Ads that relate to text or subject matter specified in a Web search

> **button ads**   Small ads, square or rectangular in shape, bearing a corporate or brand name or logo and usually appearing at the bottom of a Web page

Button ads are small ads, square or rectangular in shape, bearing a corporate or brand name or logo; they usually appear at the bottom of a Web page. Like banner ads, clicking on the button takes the user directly to the advertiser's Web site.[34] By clicking on button ads for Netscape Navigator or Internet Explorer, which appear at the bottom of many Web pages, you go directly to the site, where you can download the latest browser software. **Interstitials,** or "in-your-face" ads, are more like traditional television commercials with video and sound.[35] For example, when browsers visit the work area at Tripod, an animated ad for a Procter & Gamble product pops up in a separate window. Interstitials are controversial, however, because some Web users consider them intrusive.[36]

> **interstitials**   "In-your-face" ads similar to traditional television commercials with video and sound

> **sponsorship ads**   Ads that integrate companies' brands and products with the editorial content of Web sites

Finally, **sponsorship ads,** also called "advertorials," integrate companies' brands and products with the editorial content of Web sites. More subtle than other Web advertisements, sponsorship ads are intended to link the advertiser with the Web site's mission in the visitor's mind.[37] For instance, Johnson & Johnson, a sponsor of iVillage.com, has an advertorial on skin care on that site.[38] Parent Soup, an online community of more than 200,000 parents, recruits corporate sponsors and even helps them create companion Web sites closely linked to Parent Soup. The makers of Triaminic children's cough syrup sponsor an ad on the Parent Soup site that not only promotes the product, but also offers child safety tips and other parenting information. These sponsorships have been so beneficial for Parent Soup and its sponsors that the site retains 80 percent of its advertisers.[39]

The actual dollar amount spent on Web advertising is the subject of some debate, but no one doubts that Web advertising generates millions of dollars in revenues for companies that choose to employ such advertising. Jupiter Communications forecasts that advertising on the World Wide Web and commercial online services will generate $8 billion in revenues by the year 2002, about 4.1 percent of total advertising dollars. The bulk of Web advertising has been for high-tech products, but consumer goods companies, recognizing the opportunity to reach specific target markets, are now increasing their online advertising budgets. As Andrew S. Grove, CEO of computer chip giant Intel, says, "Net advertising is becoming a big deal."[40]

Personal Selling and Sales Promotion.   Companies are also using the Internet to facilitate personal selling and sales promotion. The Internet can help salespeople do their jobs more effectively and efficiently, particularly in the prospecting and preapproach phases of the personal selling process. In fact, the Internet, E-mail, and notebook computers are among the high-tech tools most commonly used by salespeople. Of companies that have more than a hundred salespersons, 80 percent are using notebook computers and the Internet to link their organization with customers.[41] Heidelberg USA, which manufactures offset presses, uses a customer relationship management system, which allows its global sales force to access critical customer and product information quickly. By linking customers, suppliers, and employees, this system has allowed Heidelberg to forge optimal customer relationships.[42]

Many marketers are promoting sales by offering buying incentives or adding value to their products online. For example, Carter-Wallace, a consumer products company, created an online game to complement its "Get a Little Closer" promotion campaign for Arrid XX deodorant. Players who read promotional information throughout the game were given the chance to win a free trip to the Caribbean.[43] Many firms, including Johnson & Johnson and EyeMasters, have offered coupons through their Web sites or the sites they sponsor. Additionally, many Internet sites, such as Val-Pak's, make coupons available online.

Pricing Considerations

The Internet gives consumers access to more information about the cost and price of products than has ever been available to them before. For example, car shoppers can access many automakers' Web pages, configure an ideal vehicle, and get instant feedback on its cost. They can also visit Edmund's and other Web sites to obtain pricing information on both new and used cars. They can then go to a car dealer armed with significantly more price-related information than in the past. The Internet not only helps customers with comparison shopping, but also gives manufacturers that want to make price a key element in their marketing mix another opportunity to get pricing information to customers. Marketers can use the Internet to facilitate both price and nonprice competition.

Some organizations are implementing low-price policies through the Internet. Autobytel.com is a service company that helps customers find an attractive deal or a low price on new and previously owned cars and trucks (see Figure 23.8). Consumers

Figure 23.8
Autobytel
Autobytel helps customers find a good deal on new and previously owned cars.

who visit www.autobytel.com can extensively research vehicles and pricing. When they are ready to purchase a vehicle, they submit a purchase request, which is sent to an Autobytel.com Accredited Dealer who pays a fee to belong to the program. The dealer calls the consumer with a no-haggle, no-hassle price within twenty-four hours and arranges a convenient delivery of the vehicle. Most major airlines have Web sites that publicize their fares and, in some cases, offer lower prices to customers who are willing to wait to book their flights at the last moment. Northwest Airlines, for example, makes seats available over the Internet and gives customers a chance to save money by making travel arrangements online. Lower promotion costs on the Web may result in lower product prices. Mailing catalogs, for example, is very expensive, but if companies can replace paper catalogs with interactive ones on the Web, they may be able to pass the cost savings onto consumers in the form of lower prices and thereby gain a competitive advantage.

digital currency A system of exchange in which consumers set up accounts at Web sites and place credits (based on a monetary amount) in those accounts

One development in the price-related aspects of E-marketing that is currently in the embryonic stage is **digital currency**—a system of exchange in which consumers set up accounts at Web sites and place credits (based on a monetary amount) in those accounts. Such a system functions much like today's debit cards. What differentiates it is that the credits are entirely digital. They can be transferred electronically and are infinitely divisible. Visitors to a sports site, for instance, might be charged one-eighth of a penny (0.125 cents) to get the latest scores. Several firms, including Cybercash and Digicash, are presently developing digital currency systems. These developments raise the possibility of "brands" of digital cash (e.g., Visa, American Express, or Microsoft digital cash).

However, it may be some time before digital currency systems are in widespread use. Given the open architecture and uncontrolled development of the Internet, many long-time users are accustomed to free and open access to most content posted on the Web, and they may resist the idea of pay-per-use content. To implement a pay-per-use model, marketers will have to persuade users that the content offered on their Web sites is sufficiently valuable to warrant payment. In the meantime, consumers are becoming accustomed to using credit cards to make online purchases. If enough consumers get used to using credit cards online, a digital currency system may have a hard time succeeding without an innovative marketing strategy.

Legal and Ethical Issues Associated with E-Marketing

The Internet has evolved so rapidly that numerous new legal and ethical concerns have emerged, and these are being hotly debated both online and off. Among these concerns are invasions of personal privacy, unsolicited E-mail, and the misappropriation of registered trademarks.

One of the most controversial privacy issues has to do with the personal information that companies collect from Web site visitors. A Federal Trade Commission investigation found that 92 percent of the 674 commercial Web sites it surveyed compile personal information about visitors.[44] Cookies are the most common means of obtaining such information. Some people fear that collecting personal information from Web site users may violate their privacy, especially if it is done without their knowledge. In fact, in a *Business Week*/Harris Poll survey, 65 percent of respondents indicated they are not willing to share personal and financial information about themselves online so that ads can be targeted to their tastes and interests.[45] Others, however, consider this practice just as acceptable as the traditional retailing practice of copying information from checks or asking customers for their name, address, and phone number before processing their transactions.

In response to privacy concerns, the FTC has investigated how personal information is gathered and used by Web site operators. It found that just 14 percent of the sites surveyed reveal what they do with the personal information they collect.[46] Many in the industry are urging self-policing on this issue to head off potential regulation. One effort toward self-policing is the online privacy program developed by the

**Figure 23.9
The BBB*Online* Privacy Program**
The BBB*Online* Privacy Program awards a privacy seal to companies that abide by its privacy policies.

BBB*OnLine* subsidiary of the Council of Better Business Bureaus (see Figure 23.9). The program awards a privacy seal to companies that clearly disclose to their Web site visitors what information they are collecting and how they are using it. A Web site that violates the principles of the program can lose its seal or have the violation referred to a government enforcement agency.[47] Marketing Citizenship examines another online privacy program that is gaining in popularity.

Few laws specifically address personal privacy in the context of E-marketing, but the standards for acceptable marketing conduct implicit in other laws and regulations can generally be applied to E-marketing. Personal privacy is protected by the U.S. Constitution, various Supreme Court rulings, and laws like the 1971 Fair Credit Reporting Act, the 1978 Right to Financial Privacy Act, and the 1974 Privacy Act, which deals with the release of government records. However, with few regulations on how businesses use information, companies can legally buy and sell information about customers to gain competitive advantage. Some have suggested that if personal data were treated as property, it would give customers greater control over the use of their personal data.

E-marketing, as we have pointed out, differs from traditional marketing in that information about customers is far more accessible. Of particular concern is the collection of data from children. Of 212 children's Web sites studied by the FTC, 89 percent collected personally identifiable information directly from children, but fewer than 10 percent directed children to obtain parental consent before providing this information. Because of the concern for children's privacy, Congress enacted the Children's Online Privacy Protection Act of 1998. The act mandates that the FTC establish rules and enforcement strategies requiring online researchers to obtain parental permission before collecting personal information from minors, including name, address, E-mail address, and phone number.[48] At present, a federal judge has blocked implementation of the act on the grounds that it may violate the First Amendment. The future of the law will be determined by the U.S. Supreme Court.

The first real strides toward regulating privacy issues associated with E-marketing are emerging in Europe. The European Union Directive on Data Protection, which went into effect in 1998, regulates the use of data pertaining to European citizens. It specifically requires companies that want personal information to explain what the information will be used for and to get the individual's permission. Companies must make customer data files available upon request, much as U.S. companies must grant customers access to their personal credit histories. Web site operators may not use cookies to track visitor's movements and preferences or sell E-mail addresses without first obtaining permission. As a result of this directive, no company may deliver personal information about European Union (EU) citizens to countries whose privacy laws do not meet the EU standards.[49] The directive may ultimately establish a precedent for Internet privacy that other nations will emulate.

spam Unsolicited commercial E-mail

Spam, or unsolicited commercial E-mail (UCE), is likely to be the next target of government regulation in the United States. Many Internet users feel that spam violates their privacy, steals their resources, and is rather like receiving a direct-mail promotional piece with postage due. Some angry recipients of spam have even organized boycotts against companies that advertise in this manner. Other recipients, however, appreciate the opportunity to learn about new products. Most Internet service providers and commercial online services (America Online and CompuServe, among others) offer their subscribers the option of filtering out E-mail from Internet addresses that generate a large volume of spam. Nonetheless, the debate over spam is far from over, and legislation to regulate it is being considered on both the federal and state level. Whatever the outcome, it will certainly affect the ability to use E-mail for marketing purposes.

The Internet has also created issues associated with registered trademarks. In some cases, for example, companies have discovered that another firm has registered a URL that duplicates or is very similar to their own trademarks. The "cybersquatter" then attempts to sell the right to use the URL to the legal trademark owner. Taco Bell, MTC, and KFC have paid thousands of dollars to gain control of domain names that match

MARKETING CITIZENSHIP

TRUSTe: "Building a Web You Can Believe In"

TRUSTe is a nonprofit organization devoted to building global trust in the Internet by providing a standardized, third-party oversight program that addresses the privacy concerns of consumers, Web site operators, and government officials. A cornerstone of the program is the "trustmark," a seal that TRUSTe awards only to Web sites that adhere to its privacy principles and that agree to comply with its oversight and resolution process. Web sites that display the trustmark must disclose their policies regarding the collection and use of personal information in a straightforward "privacy" statement, generally done via a link from their home pages. TRUSTe is supported by a network of corporate, industry, and nonprofit sponsors, including the Electronic Frontier Foundation, CommerceNet, America Online, Compaq Computer, CyberCash, Ernst and Young, Excite, IBM, MatchLogic, Microsoft, Netcom, and Netscape.

Internet users have a right to expect online privacy and a responsibility to exercise choice over how personal information is collected, used, and shared by Web sites. The TRUSTe program was designed expressly to ensure that users' privacy is protected by fostering open disclosure and empowering users to make informed choices. Its privacy principles embody fair information practices developed by the U.S. Department of Commerce, the Federal Trade Commission, and prominent industry organizations and associations.

To obtain a trustmark to display on its Web site, an organization submits a copy of its privacy statement to TRUSTe,

along with two signed copies of TRUSTe's license agreement. It must also pay an annual license fee; the amount is based on its annual revenues. TRUSTe then reviews the application and, if it approves it, signs both license agreements and returns one to the submitting organization, thereby granting it permission to display the trustmark on its Web site.

TRUSTe recognizes that when it comes to privacy, children under the age of 13 have special needs. Young children often do not comprehend the consequences of giving out personally identifiable information. TRUSTe has therefore instituted a "Children's Privacy Seal Program." A Web site displaying the Children's Seal is committed to obtaining parental consent before collecting information from children under age 13, as well as giving parents notice of how that information will be used.

Organizations that join the TRUSTe online seal program are leading the way in "building a Web you can believe in," one in which consumers can feel secure in exchanging information and making purchases and Web sites can thrive and profit. The program's members believe that creating an environment of mutual trust and openness will help keep the Internet a free, comfortable, and safe community for everyone. TRUSTe's goal is to give online consumers control over their personal information; to provide Web site operators with a standardized, cost-effective solution for addressing consumer anxiety about privacy issues while achieving their own business objectives; and to demonstrate to government regulators that the industry can successfully regulate itself.

or parallel their company trademarks.[50] To help companies address this conflict, Congress passed the Federal Trademark Dilution Act of 1995. This legislation gives trademark owners the right to protect their trademarks, prevents the use of trademark-protected entities, and requires the relinquishment of names that duplicate or closely parallel registered trademarks.

As the Internet continues to evolve, more legal and ethical issues will certainly arise. Recognizing this, the American Marketing Association has developed a Code of Ethics for Marketing on the Internet (see Table 23.4). Such self-regulatory policies may help head off government regulation of electronic marketing. Marketers and all other users of the Internet, should make an effort to learn and abide by basic "netiquette" (Internet etiquette) to ensure they get the most out of the resources available on this growing medium. Fortunately, most marketers recognize the need for mutual respect and trust when communicating through the Internet, or any other public medium. They know that doing so will allow them to maximize the tremendous opportunities the Internet offers to foster long-term relationships with customers.

Table 23.4   **American Marketing Association's Code of Ethics for Marketing on the Internet**
Preamble
The Internet, including online computer communications, has become increasingly important to marketers' activities, as they provide exchanges and access to markets worldwide. The ability to interact with stakeholders has created new marketing opportunities and risks that are not currently specifically addressed in the American Marketing Association Code of Ethics. The American Marketing Association Code of Ethics for Internet marketing provides additional guidance and direction for ethical responsibility in this dynamic area of marketing. The American Marketing Association is committed to ethical professional conduct and has adopted these principles for using the Internet, including on-line marketing activities utilizing network computers.
General Responsibilities
Internet marketers must assess the risks and take responsibility for the consequences of their activities. Internet marketers' professional conduct must be guided by:
1. Support of professional ethics to avoid harm by protecting the rights of privacy, ownership and access.
2. Adherence to all applicable laws and regulations with no use of Internet marketing that would be illegal, if conducted by mail, telephone, fax or other media.
3. Awareness of changes in regulations related to Internet marketing.
4. Effective communication to organizational members on risks and policies related to Internet marketing, when appropriate.
5. Organizational commitment to ethical Internet practices communicated to employees, customers and relevant stakeholders.
Privacy
Information collected from customers should be confidential and used only for expressed purposes. All data, especially confidential customer data, should be safeguarded against unauthorized access. The expressed wishes of others should be respected with regard to the receipt of unsolicited e-mail messages.
Ownership
Information obtained from the Internet sources should be properly authorized and documented. Information ownership should be safeguarded and respected. Marketers should respect the integrity and ownership of computer and network systems.
Access
Marketers should treat access to accounts, passwords, and other information as confidential, and only examine or disclose content when authorized by a responsible party. The integrity of others' information systems should be respected with regard to placement of information, advertising or messages.
Source: American Marketing Association, www.ama.org/about/ama/ethcode.asp, Dec. 15, 1998.

Summary

Electronic commerce (E-commerce) refers to sharing business information, maintaining business relationships, and conducting business transactions by means of telecommunications networks. Electronic marketing (E-marketing) is the strategic process of creating, distributing, promoting, and pricing products for targeted customers in the virtual environment of the Internet. E-marketing involves both business-to-consumer and business-to-business dimensions. The Internet has changed the way marketers communicate and develop relationships with their customers, employees, and suppliers. Telecommunications technology offers marketers potential advantages, including rapid response, expanded customer service capability, reduced costs of operation, and reduced geographic barriers. Electronic commerce depends on three elements: communications infrastructure, software, and products and markets.

The basic characteristics that distinguish the E-marketing environment from the traditional marketing environment are addressability, interactivity, memory, control, accessibility, and digitalization. A marketer's ability to identify customers before they make a purchase is called addressability. One way Web sites achieve addressability is through the use of cookies, identifying strings of text placed on a visitor's computer. Interactivity allows customers to express their needs and wants directly to the firm in response to the firm's marketing communications. It also enables marketers to capitalize on the concept of community to help customers derive value from the firm's products and Web site. Memory refers to a firm's ability to access databases or data warehouses containing individual customer profiles and past purchase histories and to use these data in real time to customize its marketing offer to a specific customer. Control refers to customers' ability to regulate the information they view, as well as the rate and sequence of their exposure to that information. Accessibility refers to customers' ability to obtain the astonishing amount of information available on the Internet. Digitalization is the representation of a product, or at least some of its benefits, as digital bits of information.

There are significant differences between how marketing mix components are developed and combined into a marketing strategy in the traditional marketing environment and in the electronic environment of the Web. The addressability, interactivity, and memory characteristics of E-marketing enable marketers to identify specific customers, to establish interactive dialogues with them to learn their needs, and to combine this information with their purchase histories to customize products to meet their needs. E-marketers can thus focus on building customer loyalty and retaining customers—in other words, on relationship marketing.

The growth of the Internet and the World Wide Web presents opportunities for marketing products (goods, services, and ideas) to both consumers and organizations.

Brand recognition is likely to become increasingly important in the marketing of services online.

The ability to process orders electronically and to increase the speed of communications via the Internet reduces inefficiencies, costs, and redundancies throughout the marketing channel. It also speeds delivery time and improves customer service. More firms are exploiting advances in information technology to synchronize the relationships between their manufacturing or product assembly and their customer contact operations. This increase in information sharing among various operations of the firm makes product customization easier to accomplish. The use of extranets has facilitated the coordination of physical distribution of products, order processing, and inventory management. The Internet is increasingly becoming a retail venue.

The Internet is an interactive medium that can be used to inform, entertain, and persuade target markets to accept an organization's products. The accessibility of the Internet presents marketers with an opportunity to expand and complement their traditional promotional efforts. The characteristics of E-marketing make promotional efforts on the Internet significantly different from those that use more traditional media. Advertising and publicity are probably the most visible of the promotion mix elements on the World Wide Web. Advertising often occurs in the form of banner ads, keyword ads, button ads, interstitials, and sponsorship ads. Companies are also using the Internet to facilitate personal selling and sales promotion.

The Internet gives consumers access to more information about the cost and price of products than has ever been available to them before. Marketers can use the Internet to facilitate both price and nonprice competition. Some organizations are implementing low-price policies through the Internet. Several firms are presently developing digital currency—systems of exchange in which consumers set up accounts at Web sites and place credits (based on a monetary amount) in those accounts.

The Internet has evolved so rapidly that numerous new legal and ethical concerns have emerged. One of the most controversial issues has to do with personal privacy, especially the personal information that companies collect from Web site visitors, often through the use of cookies. Few laws in the United States specifically address personal privacy in the context of E-marketing. The European Union Directive on Data Protection regulates the collection and use of data pertaining to European citizens. Additional issues relate to spam, or unsolicited commercial E-mail (UCE), and the misappropriation of registered trademarks. More issues are likely to emerge as the Internet and E-marketing continue to evolve.

Important Terms

Electronic commerce (E-commerce)
Electronic marketing (E-marketing)
Addressability
Cookie
Interactivity

Community
Memory
Control
Hypertext
Portal

Accessibility
Uniform Resource Locator (URL)
Digitalization
Banner ads
Keyword ads

Button ads
Interstitials
Sponsorship ads
Digital currency
Spam

Discussion and Review Questions

1. What is electronic marketing? Explain the advantages telecommunications technology offers to marketers?

2. How does addressability differentiate E-marketing from the traditional marketing environment? How do marketers use cookies to achieve addressability?

3. Define interactivity and explain its significance. How can marketers exploit this characteristic to improve relations with customers?

4. How can marketing managers use the concept of community to add value to their products?

5. Memory gives marketers quick access to customers' purchase histories. How can a firm use this capability to customize its product offerings?

6. Explain the distinction between "push" and "pull" media. What is the significance of control in terms of using Web sites to market products?

7. Vast numbers of goods and services from many different countries are available on the Web. Do you think brand name recognition is more important in electronic marketing than it is in more traditional marketing environments? Why?

8. What is the significance of digitalization?

9. How can E-marketers use relationship marketing to increase their customers' loyalty and perceived costs of switching to another firm?

10. How can marketers exploit the characteristics of the Internet to improve the product element of the marketing mix?

11. How is the Internet changing relationships among supply chain members?

12. How do the characteristics of E-marketing affect the promotion element of the marketing mix?

13. A number of different types of advertisements have evolved on the Internet. List and define each of these types of advertisements, and provide an example of each.

14. One potential model that may be applied to marketing on the Internet is the pay-per-use approach. Do you think the Web is better suited to this approach or to the current model, in which viewers have free and open access to most Web content? Why?

15. E-marketing has raised a number of ethical questions related to consumer privacy. How can cookies be misused? Should the use of cookies by marketers be regulated by the government?

Application Questions

1. Amazon.com is one of the Web's most recognizable marketers. Visit the company's site (www.amazon.com) and identify how the company adds value to its customers' book-buying experiences.

2. Some products are better suited to electronic marketing than others. For example, Art.com is a firm that sells art prints through its online store. It displays a variety of prints in many different categories, thus providing customers with a convenient and efficient way to search for art. On the other hand, Nike's Web site displays the company's products, but customers must visit a retailer to actually purchase shoes. Visit www.art.com and www.nike.com and compare how each firm uses the electronic environment of the Internet to help its marketing efforts.

3. ClosetMaid is a manufacturer of wire shelving, hardware, and storage products, which it markets under the brand names ClosetMaid and Clairson International. Visit ClosetMaid's Web site at www.closetmaid.com and explore the content found there. Based on the Web site's content, speculate about the firm's target market(s). How does ClosetMaid's Web site add value to its products?

Internet Exercise & Resources

iVillage.com

iVillage.com is an example of an online community. Explore the content of this Web site at

www.ivillage.com

1. What target market can marketers access through this community?

2. How can marketers target this community to market their goods and services?

3. Based on your understanding of the characteristics of E-marketing, analyze the advertisements you observe on this site.

E-Center Resources

Visit http://www.prideferrell.com to find several resources to help you succeed in mastering the material in this chapter, plus additional materials that will help you expand your marketing knowledge. The Web site includes

 Internet exercise updates plus additional exercises

 ACE self-tests

 Chapter summary with hotlinked glossary

 Hotlinks to companies featured in this chapter

 Resource Center

 Career Center

 Marketing plan worksheets

VIDEO CASE 23.1

Extricity Software Links Supply Chain Partners

More firms are using advances in information technology to synchronize their operations, from production to customer contact, which for E-marketers means their Web sites. Such sharing of information is crucial to marketing orientation. One firm that has benefited from the increasing demand for tools for managing information and relationships within supply chains is Extricity Software, Inc. (formerly known as CrossRoute, Inc.) Founded in 1996 and based in Redwood Shores, California, the company markets software for online use in business-to-business integration. Extricity's flagship product, Alliance software, automates business interactions among all members of supply chains—manufacturers, suppliers, resellers, distributors, contract manufacturers, third-party providers, and customers. Alliance can be used to develop and manage such processes as vendor-managed inventory and collaborative planning and engineering.

The increasing use of electronic data interchange (EDI) has created numerous problems, including keeping up with supply chain partners' demands for information, information distortion, and incompatible systems. When supply chain members use incompatible software, they may be unable to access the right information when needed, and the result may be lost sales. Extricity's Alliance software addresses such problems by integrating partners' diverse applications, including programs from Oracle, PeopleSoft, and Microsoft, so that information systems become compatible even though each company continues to use its existing software. Alliance thus facilitates information transfer by enabling supply chain members to converse in a common language.

With Alliance software, supply chain partners can exchange catalog content and transaction information securely over the Internet. Being able to grant suppliers fast and secure access to customer transaction databases fosters better coordination. By observing electronically what a firm's customers are ordering, a supplier can quickly respond by shipping the necessary materials to meet demand, and the firm can keep less inventory on hand. Alliance also improves marketers' ability to query customers about their needs and to adjust their manufacturing processes to supply products that precisely match those needs.

Alliance software costs about $300,000, but by ensuring compatibility within a supply chain and fostering better coordination, it can significantly reduce a firm's inventory costs and shorten its cycle time by up to one-third. One company saved $10 million in inventory costs after it began using Alliance. Monty Botkin, general manager of North American operations for the Taiwan Semiconductor Manufacturing Corporation, says Extricity's Alliance product allowed his firm "to integrate and automate ordering, forecasting, design, and manufacturing processes with . . . customers and partners—enhancing customer service and retention and reducing product lead times by up to 40 percent." According to Botkin, to compete in today's business environment requires the ability to assemble communities of customers and suppliers of diverse sizes rapidly so that they can function and

compete as a single world-class corporation. Nina Lytton, President of Open Systems Advisors, says, "In a world where new business partnerships form opportunistically and evolve continuously, companies' interconnected business processes are stretched to the breaking point. Extricity enables independent organizations to work together with the speed and agility of a single entity."[51]

Questions for Discussion

1. Extricity (formerly CrossRoute) is one of many new companies that have emerged to serve the E-marketing industry. Evaluate Extricity's ability to sell its product over the Internet.
2. How does Extricity's Alliance software facilitate supply chain management?
3. What does Extricity need to know about the marketing environment to ensure its continuing success?

CASE 23.2

Amazon.com

Self-billed as the "Earth's biggest bookstore," Amazon.com pioneered—and some say, even perfected—the art of marketing products on the Internet. Founded in 1994 by Jeffrey P. Bezos (where else but in a garage?), the company has grown briskly. Its 1998 revenues were $610 million, up from $148 million the year before. Early on, Bezos recognized the Internet's potential to link just about anyone to almost any product without the costly overhead of building and operating multiple stores and employing legions of clerks. Through its Web site, Amazon.com offers a selection of 3.1 million books, fifteen times more than any other bookstore, and many are sold at discounts of up to 40 percent. The Seattle-based online retailer has also branched out into sales of music, CDs, videos, and selected toys and electronics, as well as some Web-based services.

Amazon.com's Web site provides customers with a powerful search engine to find in-print and out-of-print books. Customers can also read extensive reviews, and place an order with a few clicks of a mouse. To make purchases easy, Amazon.com securely stores customer's shipping and credit-card information so that the next time they order, they can do so with a single mouse click. Amazon.com E-mails customers notices about new books and makes recommendations for subjects in which they have shown interest. Its GiftClick service allows customers to choose a gift and specify the recipient's E-mail address; Amazon.com takes care of the rest. With such customer service, it's no wonder that 64 percent of

Amazon.com's orders come from repeat customers. To enhance the shopping experience, Bezos has encouraged customers to post their own reviews and allowed them to interact with authors in online chats, thus building Amazon.com into an online community. When the company invited author John Updike to start a short story online, some 400,000 people sent in contributions to complete it. This environment makes shopping online at Amazon.com a relaxed, effortless, and entertaining experience. For many customers, it is an experience that takes less time than finding a parking place at a nearby shopping mall.

In many ways, Amazon.com is as much a software developer as it is a retailer. To build its online superstore, the company had to develop technology that could securely handle online orders and coordinate distribution of millions of different products. It also developed "collaborative-filtering" technology, which enables it to analyze customers' purchase histories to predict what other books they might like to buy and to make recommendations based on what other customers with similar purchase histories have bought. This technology permits Amazon.com to offer a huge selection and personalized service—to its 4.5 million customers.

Amazon.com fills customers's orders directly through distributors or publishers, and most orders are delivered in two to three days. Traditional "brick-and-mortar" bookstores stock five to six months' worth of inventory to be sure they can provide the selection buyers want. These booksellers must pay distributors or publishers forty-five to ninety days after they order books, meaning that, on average, they carry the costs of those books for as long as four months. Amazon.com, however, carries just fifteen days' worth of inventory and, moreover, it gets paid immediately by credit card when a customer orders. The difference gives Amazon.com about a month's use of interest-free money, which generates a large percentage of the funds it needs to cover operating expenses.

Amazon's practice of recommending books and encouraging customers to post reviews helps promote individual books. Through the company's Associates Program, other Web sites can offer books related to their visitors' interests via a link to Amazon; for this, they pay 15 percent of sales. There are now 140,000 such associated sites. Amazon also offers publishers cooperative advertising packages that result in prominent displays and recommendations of their books on its Web site. The company has been criticized for not informing customers that some of its recommendations are, in effect, sponsored by the books' publishers, but CEO Bezos contends that Amazon does not recommend any book unless it meets the company's standards. Nonetheless, Amazon.com annnounced in 1999 that it would offer a refund for any book it has recommended and also promised to inform customers whenever a publisher pays for a prominent display on its Web site.

Amazon.com originated many of the techniques used to market products online. Not surprisingly, some competitors have launched their own online book superstores, using tactics that mimic Amazon's. Chief among these rivals are Barnes & Noble and Borders Books. Barnes & Noble, with 11 percent of the U.S. book market, still has less than a quarter of Amazon's online customer base. Although Barnes & Noble and Borders have a strong presence with hundreds of bookstores across the country, these chains entered E-commerce relatively late and have had to spend time learning the ropes and making substantial investments—time during which Amazon has contin-

ued to gain customers and improve its offerings. However, many book lovers still prefer to patronize local independent bookstores, which often specialize in particular genres and offer strong customer service. And, as Amazon enters new industries, such as music and videos, it will face even tougher competition. In the online music market, for example, CDNow has emerged with rival N2K and formed a venture with Reel.com, Cyberian Outpost, eToys, and other experienced online marketers to launch ShopperConnection, a virtual mall.

Having entered online markets for CDs, videos, and toys, CEO Bezos is now exploring further avenues for growth, including consumer electronics, games, software, clothing, and travel. The company made several strategic acquisitions in the late 1990s, including Junglee Corporation (a developer of comparison-shopping software), PlanetAll (service that helps people stay in touch with friends online by organizing their address books and coordinating their appointment calendars), and Drugstore.com (a start-up retailer of pharmaceuticals and personal care products). With these acquisitions, Bezos is working to establish Amazon.com as an online Wal-Mart or E-commerce hub like Yahoo! and other Web portals. "Our goals is to be an E-commerce destination," says CEO Bezos. These forays into new markets will pit Amazon.com against Internet-savvy competitors like Microsoft and Yahoo! How the company will perform against increasing competition remains to be seen, but for many companies looking to establish online stores, Amazon.com remains the model for successful marketing.[52]

Questions for Discussion

1. What characteristics of E-marketing is Amazon.com using to create value for its customers?
2. Describe Amazon.com's marketing mix. How does this mix compare with the mix offered by traditional "brick-and-mortar" booksellers?
3. Assess Amazon.com's strategy for growth.

STRATEGIC CASE 7

Apple Computers

Apple Computer is the original stuff of entrepreneurial legend in the personal computer world. Founded in a garage in 1976 by two college dropouts, Steven Jobs and Stephen Wozniak, the company has since experienced numerous highs and lows. An exceedingly low point occurred in 1996 when Apple reported a loss of $1 billion and laid off 1,300 employees. At that time, its future as an independent company looked rather doubtful, but new leadership and a strategic focus have helped the company rebound. To understand how the company found itself in such dire straits and how it managed to survive them, we need to consider the firm's history, culture, and changes in marketing strategy.

Birth of an Icon

Stephen Wozniak developed Apple's first product, the Apple I computer, which he and Steven Jobs built in Jobs's garage and sold without a monitor, keyboard, or casing. The Apple I's success indicated to Jobs a demand for small, "user-friendly" computers. Wozniak therefore added a keyboard, color monitor, and eight slots for peripheral devices, giving the firm's next product, the Apple II, greater versatility and encouraging other firms to develop add-on devices and software. It worked: by 1980, Jobs and Wozniak had sold more than 13,000 Apple IIs, and revenues had climbed from $7.8 million in 1978 to $117 million. The next ventures, the Apple III and Lisa computers, flopped, but Apple scored a huge success with the Macintosh, introduced in 1984. The Mac, which incorporated an easy-to-use graphical interface, was billed as the computer "For the Rest of Us." The Mac's rapid popularity soon established Apple as a leader in the expanding computer industry. Apple moved into the office market in 1986 with the Mac Plus and the LaserWriter printer. Wozniak left the company in 1983, and Jobs brought in John Sculley, a former PepsiCo executive, to manage the growing firm.

Jobs and Wozniak, both iconoclasts, so engraved their personalities on Apple Computer's culture that the culture survived long after both men had left the company. Their do-your-own-thing, ignore-the-Establishment philosophy gave Apple a unique culture of rebels, right down to the pirate flag flying over headquarters. Scorning dress codes, formal meetings, and other traditional business trappings, Apple's creative, defiant culture nurtured the development of the groundbreaking Macintosh computer and operating system, as well as numerous other successful products, and propelled Apple to the top of the computer industry.

Cultural Conflict

The do-it-your-way culture also created strife within the company, pitting the inventive "gearheads" and "wizards"—the engineers and programmers who developed products—against the managers Jobs imported to bring order and good business practices to the firm. Jobs, in fact, left the firm in 1985 because of a power struggle with Sculley, largely over the future of the Macintosh platform. When Sculley took over the reins, he realized that Apple's employees would resent the big-business systems he wanted to implement. He also recognized that he had to retain Apple's technical wizards if the firm was to succeed. He therefore decided not to tinker with Apple's unique culture. However, glorifying Apple's technical personnel made them very tough to supervise. Combined with Sculley's feel-good approach to management, the result was a company run largely by consensus, and decisions were rarely final. One joke on the Apple grapevine was that "a vote can be 15,000 to 1 and still be a tie."

The Revolving Door

Apple's culture contributed to frequent power struggles and a seemingly revolving door on management offices. In 1995 alone, fourteen out of forty-five vice presidents left or were dismissed. Major management upheavals occurred in 1981, 1985, 1990, 1993, 1996, and 1997, with numerous minor ones in between. Several of these disturbances led to the removal of chief executives. Sculley, for example, was dethroned in 1993 after an 84 percent drop in earnings. His replacement, Michael "Diesel" Spindler, brought a focus on business basics to the firm and quickly worked to address Apple's problems: overpriced products, inflated costs, and sluggish product development. He laid off 2,500 workers, cut R&D costs by more than $100 million a year, and launched a new product line based on the PowerPC microprocessor (which Apple developed with IBM and Motorola). Spindler's back-to-the-basics approach helped Apple rebound, but Spindler soon stumbled under Apple's consensus culture. An insider close to Spindler says, "It was fine for a while. But the system converts people. People don't convert the system." Spindler was ousted in 1996 and replaced by Gilbert F. Amerlio as president and CEO. Amerlio was gone by July 1997, when founder Steven Jobs returned to stem the tide of red ink. Each of these management upheavals brought restructurings and changes in strategy.

Frequent Strategy Changes

These frequent strategy changes may be the biggest source of Apple's disappointing performance in recent years. Over the years, Jobs, Sculley, Spindler, Amerlio, then Jobs again reversed, delayed, or evaded outright key decisions while trying to push their own agendas. For example, in April 1995, Spindler implemented a major reorganization but was forced to recant that decision six months later under fiscal pressures. A late 1995 decision to launch an all-out bid for market share failed because executives had misread the market. The result was a storehouse of low-end computers, at a time when consumers wanted expensive powerhouse machines, and an $80 million inventory write-off. Meanwhile, savvy rivals IBM, Hewlett-Packard, and Compaq made further inroads into Apple's market share.

It could be argued that Apple has been consistent only in its inconsistency over the years. For example, Apple has traditionally relied on high-priced products to fund development and marketing of new technology. However, in a desperate bid to boost market share and improve efficiency, the firm has occasionally deviated from this strategy by introducing lower-priced Apple machines. But management has never given the latter strategy time to work, and it failed to implement other tactics that might have generated the desired results.

One of the most significant examples of this inconsistency and wavering was the issue of whether to license the Mac operating system to other computer makers in order to create a "clone" industry that would increase market share for the Mac platform, much as IBM had done with its personal computer. The clone decision was debated as early as 1985, but until 1994, every time top management came close to making the licensing decision, it was stymied by lack of consensus. As one former Apple executive says, "I've never understood why somebody didn't just say: 'I'm the leader. This is the way it's going to be. Thanks for the discussion, but if you don't want to do it, leave.' "

When Spindler finally made the decision to license the technology in 1994, the popularity of Microsoft's Windows operating environment for the IBM-PC platform made the clone decision too late. Apple executives asserted that they could raise the Mac's share of the global market to 20 percent in five years, with Apple adding 1 percent each year and the clones bringing in the rest. However, even though Apple executives said they would "aggressively" pursue licensees, Apple licensed the Mac design only to Pioneer, Power Computing, Unmax, and Daystar. Together, these firms sold about 200,000 Mac clones in 1995, a drop in the bucket compared with the 4.5 million shipped by Apple. In 1996, in a last-ditch attempt to revive Mac software's faltering market share, Apple gave Motorola the rights to use its current and future operating systems, as well as the right to sublicense the operating system to other computer makers likely to produce Apple clones. Motorola soon tired of Apple's tough antilicensing stance and ceased development of Mac clones in late 1997.

When Steve Jobs returned to the fold as "interim" CEO in 1997, one of his first moves was to acquire Power Computing, the largest cloner of Macs, effectively signaling yet another about-face on the licensing issue. Jobs also worked quickly to reduce Apple's large number of new-product ideas and to focus the company on a small number of key new products. Among the products Jobs scrapped was the Newton Message Pad, a handheld computer, that Apple had spent more than a decade developing.

A major issue for Apple has been the thorn of Microsoft's Windows. Windows, with its graphical interface, makes PCs work much like the Macintosh. When the first successful version of Windows appeared in 1990, Apple executives dismissed the threat, although they filed a lawsuit against Microsoft and Hewlett-Packard, claiming copyright protection for the "look and feel" of the Macintosh user interface. Apple lost the suit in 1992. Macintosh users continue to be passionate in their insistence that the Macintosh is a better machine than a Windows-based PC, but Apple has failed to capitalize on their fervor. At the same time, Microsoft has been very aggressive in upgrading Windows to the point where buyers just entering the market fail to see significant differences between a PC and a Mac beyond the fact that the Mac costs more.

Current Marketing Strategies

Under Jobs, Apple has narrowed its focus to market segments in which it already has a solid presence, a strategy that may mean forever abandoning the possibility of regaining the position of industry leader. And, apparently like everyone else inside and outside the computer industry, Apple is turning to the Internet. "Any project that doesn't have the word Internet in it doesn't get approved anymore," says one Apple manager. Apple already has an edge in the Internet arena: its Web servers sell for $2,000 to $3,000 less than the cheapest models from Sun. The firm's expertise in media and entertainment, where many content providers are moving to the Web, may enhance its edge. Says one industry executive, "This whole Internet explosion is a real opportunity for Apple. It's not so much an advantage for them, but it takes away some of their disadvantages."

In 1997, to exploit this opportunity, Apple acquired NeXT, a company that Steve Jobs had founded to develop and market software that allows customers to implement business applications on the Internet. Apple plans to extend its Internet emphasis with the MacMC, a network computer designed primarily for Internet and intranet applications. The company also launched the iMac—which retails for $1299, including monitor—to compete with PC makers like Compaq and Packard Bell. Apple positioned the iMac, which sports curvy lines in a translucent case available in five colors, as a simple way to access the Internet. The iMac proved to be a resounding success; 278,000 units sold during the first six weeks the product was on the market. Strong sales of Apple's Power Book line of notebook computers have also contributed to the company's improving financial picture. The company launched a new operating system, the Mac OS 8, in July 1997 and is planning major upgrades to it, including one that integrates the best of Mac's OS with functional advances developed by NeXT. In 1998, thanks to these new products and Jobs's strong focus on innovation, Apple racked up its first profitable fiscal year in four years.

To sustain this momentum and continue its turn-around, Apple will have to market its new products astutely and consistently. Shareholders and staunch Apple customers believe Jobs will bring to Apple much-needed focus, consistency, and the strength to make sound decisions in the face of the firm's long tradition of consensual decision making. Whether Jobs will continue to drive Apple toward profitable innovations in a dynamic industry dominated by Windows-based PCs remains to be seen. When he took over in 1997, he insisted his return was temporary. However, in 1998, Apple's board suggested that Jobs could remain CEO for as long as he wanted, and he has given no indication that he is ready to give up the challenge.[53]

Questions for Discussion

1. Describe how Apple's unique culture contributed to its problems in the 1990s. If you were Apple's new chief executive, how would you deal with this culture?
2. How have Apple's frequent strategy changes brought it to where it is today? What do you see as the single most costly error made by executives?
3. Describe Apple's current strategy.
4. Propose a new strategy for Apple Computer, keeping in mind such factors as Microsoft Windows and the Internet. Describe how you would implement your strategy.

E-Marketing

The Internet is changing design and implementation of marketing strategies. This dynamic technology provides marketers with efficient, powerful methods of designing, promoting, and distributing products, conducting research, and gathering market information. Chapter 24 has been developed to complement Chapter 23 by providing the most current statistics about usage patterns and emerging trends in E-marketing. In addition, up-to-date strategies are provided to illustrate the best practices in E-marketing.

Chapter 24 is updated on a regular basis to stay current with this dynamic are of marketing

Chapter 24 is located on the Pride/Ferrell Marketing Learning Center at http://www.prideferrell.com. This unique site serves as a forum for students to explore how the Internet is changing marketing. In addition to Chapter 24, the Marketing Learning Center contains **Internet Exercises** and **Summaries** for Chapters 1 through 23; a **Resource Center,** with links to marketing organizations, publications, and other information sources; **Self-Tests;** a **Glossary** of key terms; **Marketing Plan Worksheets;** and the **Idea Exchange,** which invites you to share your perspectives on marketing and the Internet.

By using the dialogue created through the Marketing Learning Center, we hope to help track the evolution of online marketing and practice *as it is happening.*

Appendix A
Careers in Marketing

Changes in the Workplace

Between one-fourth and one-third of the civilian work force in the United States is employed in marketing-related jobs. Although the field offers a multitude of diverse career opportunities, the number of positions in each area varies. For example, millions of workers are employed in many facets of sales, but relatively few people work in public relations and marketing research.

Many nonbusiness organizations now recognize that they perform marketing activities. For that reason, the number of marketing positions in government agencies, hospitals, charitable and religious groups, educational institutions, and similar organizations is increasing. In fact, during the 1990s, nonprofit organizations became more competitive and better managed, with job-growth rates often matching those of private-sector firms. Another area ripe with opportunities is the Internet's World Wide Web. With so many businesses setting up Web pages, demand will rise for people who have the skills to develop and design marketing-related materials for the Web.

When searching for a job, you might want to consider the many alternatives outside the traditional large corporation. Within the last five years, companies with more than five hundred employees have shed over 5 million jobs through downsizing, reorganizations, and mergers. However, the job losses in larger companies have been more than offset by gains in smaller businesses employing fewer than five hundred employees. In recent years, two-thirds of new jobs were created by new companies with fewer than twenty-five workers, and most were in firms employing fewer than ten.[1]

Many of the workers outplaced from large corporations are choosing an entrepreneurial path, creating even more new opportunities for first-time job seekers. Even some of those who have secure managerial positions are leaving corporations and heading to smaller companies, toward greater responsibility and autonomy. The traditional career path used to be graduation from college, then a job with a large corporation, and a climb up the ladder to management. This pattern has changed, however. People today are more likely to experience a career path of sideways "gigs" rather than sequential steps up a corporate ladder.

Career Choices Are Major Life Choices

Many people think career planning begins with an up-to-date résumé and a job interview.[2] In reality, it begins long before you prepare your résumé. It starts with *you* and what you want to become. In some ways, you have been preparing for a career ever since you started school. Everything you have experienced during your lifetime you can use as resources to help define your career goals. Since it's likely you will spend more time at work than at any other single place during your lifetime, it makes sense to spend that time doing something you enjoy. Unfortunately, some people just work at a *job* because they need money to survive. Other people choose a *career* because of their interests and talents or commitment to a particular profession. Whether you are looking for a job or a career, you should examine your priorities.

Personal Factors Influencing Career Choices

Before choosing a career, you need to consider what motivates you and what skills you can offer an employer. The following questions may help you define what you consider important in life.

1. *What types of activities do you enjoy?* Although most people know what they enjoy in a general way, a number of interest inventories exist. By helping you determine specific interests and activities, these inventories can help you land a job that will lead to a satisfying career. In some cases, it may be sufficient just to list the activities you enjoy, along with those you dislike. Watch for patterns that may influence your career choices.

2. *What do you do best?* All jobs and all careers require employees to be able to "do something." It is extremely important to assess what you do best. Be honest with yourself about your ability to succeed in a specific job. It may help to make a list of your strongest job-related skills. Also try looking at your skills from an employer's perspective. What can you do that an employer would be willing to pay for?

3. *What kind of education will you need?* The amount of education you need is determined by the type of career you choose. In some careers, it is impossible to get an entry-level position without at least a college degree. In other careers, technical or hands-on skills may also be important. Generally, more education increases your potential earning power, as illustrated in Figure A.1.

4. *Where do you want to live?* When you enter the job market, you may want to move to a different part of the country. According to the Bureau of Labor Statistics, the western and southern sections of the United States will experience the greatest population increase between now and 2005; the population in the Midwest will stay about the same, whereas the Northeast's population will decrease slightly. These population changes will affect job prospects in each region. Before entering the job market, some people think they will be free to move any place they want, while others want to reside in only one specific area. In reality, successful job applicants must be willing to go where the jobs are.

Figure A.1
Education and Income
The income of most Americans is tied to the number of years of education they have obtained.
Source: Bureau of the Census, *Statistical Abstract of the United States* (Washington, D.C.: Government Printing Office, 1997).

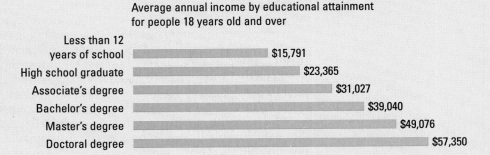

Average annual income by educational attainment for people 18 years old and over

Less than 12 years of school	$15,791
High school graduate	$23,365
Associate's degree	$31,027
Bachelor's degree	$39,040
Master's degree	$49,076
Doctoral degree	$57,350

Job Search Activities

When people begin to search for a job, they often turn first to the classified ads in their local newspaper. Those ads are an important source of information about jobs in a particular area, but they are only one source. Many other sources can lead to employment and a satisfying career. Because there is a wealth of information about career planning, you should be selective in both the type and the amount of information you use to guide your job search.

The library, a traditional job-hunting tool, has been joined in recent years by the Internet. Both the library and the Internet are sources of everything from classified newspaper ads and government job listings to detailed information on individual companies and industries. You can use either of them to research an area of employment that interests you or a particular company. In addition, the Internet allows you to check electronic bulletin boards for current job information, exchange ideas with other job seekers through online discussion groups or E-mail, and get career advice from professional counselors. You can also create your own Web page to inform prospective employers of your qualifications. And you may even have a job interview online. Many companies use their Web sites to post job openings, accept applications, and interview candidates.

As you start a job search, you may find the following Web sites helpful. (Addresses of additional career-related Web sites appear in the Pride/Ferrell Learning Center.)

America's Job Bank: www.ajb.dni.us
This massive site contains information on nearly 250,000 jobs. Listings come from 1,800 state employment offices around the country and represent every line of work, from professional and technical to blue-collar, and from entry-level on up.

CareerPath.com:www.careerpath.com
This site features classified employment ads from twenty-one major newspapers, including the *New York Times,* the *Washington Post,* the *Chicago Tribune,* the *Los Angeles Times,* and the *Boston Globe,* as well as from some smaller newspapers.

Hoover's Online: www.hoovers.com
Hoover's offers a variety of job-search tools, including information on potential employers and links to sites that post job openings.

The Monster Board: www.monster.com
The Monster Board carries hundreds of job listings and offers links to related sites, such as company home pages and sites with information about job fairs.

Federal jobs: www.fedworld.gov/jobs/jobsearch.html
For those interested in working for a government agency, this site lists positions all across the country. You can limit your search to specific states or do a general cross-country search for job openings.

Other Web addresses for job seekers include www.starthere.com/jobs; www.career-mag.com; www.careermosaic.com; www.espan.com; www.occ.com; and www.bold-facejobs.com.

In addition to the library and the Internet, the following sources can be of great help when you are trying to find the "perfect job":

1. *Campus placement offices.* Colleges and universities have placement offices staffed by trained personnel specialists. In most cases, these offices serve as clearing-houses for career information. The staff may also be able to give you guidance on how to create your résumé and prepare for a job interview.

2. *Professional sources and networks.* A network is a group of people—friends, relatives, and professionals—who are in a position to exchange information, including information about job openings. According to many job applicants, networking is one of the best sources of career information and job leads. Start with as many people as you can think of to establish your network. (The Internet can be very useful in this regard.) Contact these people and ask specific questions about job opportunities that they may be aware of. Also, ask each of these individuals to introduce or refer you to someone else who may be able to help you continue your job search.

3. *Private employment agencies.* Private employment agencies charge a fee for helping people find jobs. Typical fees can be as high as 15 to 20 percent of an employee's first-year salary. The fee may be paid by the employer or the employee. Like campus placement offices, private employment agencies provide career counseling, help create résumés, and provide preparation for job interviews. Before you use a private employment agency, be sure you understand the terms of any contract or agreement you sign. Above all, make sure you know who is responsible for paying the agency's fee.

4. *State employment agencies.* The local office of your state employment agency is a source of information about job openings in your immediate area. Some job applicants are reluctant to use state agencies because most jobs available through these agencies are for semiskilled or unskilled workers. From a practical standpoint, it can't hurt to consult state employment agencies. They will have information about some professional and managerial positions available in your area, and you will not be charged a fee if you obtain a job through a state employment agency.

Many people want a job immediately and are discouraged at the thought that an occupational search could take months. But people seeking entry-level jobs should expect that their job search may take considerable time. Of course, the state of the economy and whether employers are hiring or not can shorten or extend a job search for anyone.

During a job search, you should use the same work habits that effective employees use on the job. When searching for a job, resist the temptation to "take the day off." Instead, make a master list of the activities you want to accomplish each day. If necessary, force yourself to make contacts, do job research, or schedule interviews that might lead to job opportunities. (Actually, many job applicants look at the job hunt as their job and work eight hours a day, five days a week, until they find the job they want.) Above all, realize that an occupational search requires patience and perseverance. According to many successful job-hunters, perseverance may be the job-hunter's most valuable trait.

Planning and Preparation

The key to landing the job you want is planning and preparation—and planning begins with goals. In particular, it is important to determine your *personal* goals, to decide on the role your career will play in reaching those goals, and then to develop your career goals. Once you know where you are going, you can devise a reasonable plan for getting there.

The time to begin planning is as early as possible. You must, of course, satisfy the educational requirements for the occupational area you wish to enter. Early planning will give you the opportunity to do so. But some of the people with whom you will be competing for the better jobs will also be fully prepared. Can you do more? Company recruiters say the following factors give job candidates a definite advantage:

- *Work experience*—You can get valuable work experience in cooperative work/school programs, during summer vacations, or in part-time jobs during the school year. Experience in your chosen occupational area carries the most weight, but even unrelated work experience is useful.

- *The ability to communicate well*—Verbal and written communication skills are increasingly important in all aspects of business. Yours will be tested in your letters to recruiters, in your résumé, and in interviews. You will use these same communication skills throughout your career.

- *Clear and realistic job and career goals*—Recruiters feel most comfortable with candidates who know where they are headed and why they are applying for a specific job.

Again, starting early will give you the opportunity to establish well-defined goals, to sharpen your communication skills (through elective courses, if necessary), and to obtain solid work experience.

The Résumé

An effective résumé is one of the keys to being considered for a good job. Because your résumé states your qualifications, experiences, education, and career goals, a potential employer can use it to assess your compatibility with the job requirements. For both the employer's and the individual's benefit, the résumé should be accurate and current.

In preparing a résumé, it helps to think of it as an advertisement. Envision yourself as a product and the company you are interested in working for, particularly the person or persons doing the hiring, as your target market. To interest the customer in buying the product—hiring you—your résumé must communicate information about your qualities and indicate how you can satisfy the customer's needs—that is, how you can help the company achieve its objectives. The information in the résumé should persuade the organization to take a closer look at you by calling you in for an interview.

To be effective, the résumé should be targeted at a specific position, as Figure A.2 shows. This document is only one example of an acceptable résumé. The job target section is specific and leads directly to the applicant's qualifications for the job. The qualifications section details capabilities—what the applicant can do—and also shows that the person has an understanding of the job's requirements. Skills and strengths that relate to the specific job should be emphasized. The achievement section ("Experiences" in Figure A.2) indicates success at accomplishing tasks or goals on the job and at school. The work experience section in Figure A.2 includes an unusual listing, which might pique the interest of an interviewer: "helped operate relative's blueberry farm in Michigan for three summers." That is something that could help launch an interview discussion. It tends to incite rather than satisfy curiosity, thus inviting further inquiry.

Figure A.2
A Résumé Targeted at a Specific Position

LORRAINE MILLER
2212 WEST WILLOW
PHOENIX, AZ 12345
(416) 862-9169

EDUCATION: B.A. Arizona State University, 2000, Marketing, achieved a 3.4 on a 4.0 scale throughout college

POSITION DESIRED: Product manager with an international firm providing future career development at the executive level

QUALIFICATIONS:

- Communicates well with individuals to achieve a common goal
- Handles tasks efficiently and in a timely manner
- Understands advertising, sales management, marketing research, packaging, pricing, distribution, and warehousing
- Coordinates many activities at one time
- Carries out assigned tasks or directives
- Writes complete status or research reports

EXPERIENCES:

- Assistant Editor of college newspaper
- Treasurer of the American Marketing Association (student chapter)
- Internship with 3-Cs Advertising, Berkeley, CA
- Student Assistantship with Dr. Steve Green, Professor of Marketing, Arizona State University
- Solo cross-Canada canoe trek, summer 1996

WORK RECORD:

1998–Present	Blythe and Co., Inc. —Junior Advertising Account Executive
1997–1998	Assistantship with Dr. Steve Green —Research Assistant
1995–1996	The Men —Retail sales and consumer relations
1993–1995	Farmer —Helped operate relative's blueberry farm in Michigan for three summers

---

Another type of résumé is the chronological résumé, which lists work experience and educational history in order by date. This type of résumé is good for those just entering the job market because it helps to highlight education and work experience.

In some cases, education is more important than unrelated work experience because it indicates the career direction you desire, despite the work experience you have thus far.

Common suggestions for improving résumés include deleting useless information, improving organization, using professional printing and typing, listing duties (not accomplishments), maintaining grammatical perfection, and avoiding an overly elaborate or fancy format.[3] Keep in mind that the person who will be looking at your résumé may have to look through hundreds in the course of his or her day, in addition to handling other duties. Consequently, it is important to keep your résumé short (one page is best, never more than two), concise, and neat. Moreover, you want your résumé to be distinctive so that it will stand out from all the others.

In addition to having the proper format and content, a résumé should be easy to read. It is best to use only one or two kinds of type and plain, white paper. When a résumé is sent to a large company, several copies are made and distributed. Textured, gray, or colored paper may make a good impression on the first person who sees the résumé, but it will not reproduce well for the others, who will see only a poor copy. You should also proofread your résumé with care. Typos and misspellings will grab attention—the wrong kind.

Along with the résumé itself, always be sure to submit a cover letter. In the letter, you can convey a bit more than is included in your résumé and send a message that expresses your interest and enthusiam about the organization and the job.

The Job Interview

Your résumé and cover letter are, in essence, an introduction. The deciding factor in the hiring process is the interview (or several interviews) with representatives of the firm. It is through the interview that the firm gets to know you and your qualifications. At the same time, the interview provides a chance for you to learn about the firm.

Here, again, preparation is the key to success. Research the firm before your first interview. Learn all you can about its products, its subsidiaries, the markets it operates in, its history, the locations of its facilities, and so on. If possible, obtain and read the firm's most recent annual report. Be prepared to ask questions about the firm and the opportunities it offers. Interviewers welcome such questions. They expect you to be interested enough to spend some time thinking about your potential relationship with their firm.

Prepare also to respond to questions the interviewer may ask. Table A.1 is a list of typical interview questions that job applicants often find difficult to answer. But don't expect interviewers to stick to the list given in the table or to the items appearing in your résumé. They will be interested in anything that helps them decide what kind of person and worker you are.

Make sure you are on time for your interview and are dressed and groomed in a businesslike manner. Interviewers take note of punctuality and appearance, just as they do of other personal qualities. Have a copy of your résumé with you, even if you have already sent one to the firm. You may also want to bring a copy of your course transcript and letters of recommendation. If you plan to furnish interviewers with the names and addresses of references rather than with letters of recommendation, make sure you have your references' permission to do so.

Consider the interview itself as a two-way conversation, rather than as a question-and-answer session. Volunteer any information that is relevant to the interviewer's questions. If an important point is skipped in the discussion, don't hesitate to bring it up. Be yourself, but emphasize your strengths. Good eye contact and posture are important, too. They should come naturally if you take an active part in the interview. At the conclusion of the interview, thank the recruiter for taking the time to see you.

In most cases, the first interview is used to *screen* applicants, or choose those who are best qualified. These applicants are then given a second interview, and perhaps a

Table A.1   Interview Questions Job Applicants Often Find Difficult to Answer

1. Tell me about yourself.
2. What do you know about our organization?
3. What can you do for us? Why should we hire you?
4. What qualifications do you have that make you feel you will be successful in your field?
5. What have you learned from the jobs you've held?
6. If you could write your own ticket, what would be your ideal job?
7. What are your special skills, and where did you acquire them?
8. Have you had any special accomplishments in your lifetime that you are particularly proud of?
9. Why did you leave your most recent job?
10. How do you spend your spare time? What are your hobbies?
11. What are your strengths and weaknesses?
12. Discuss five major accomplishments.
13. What kind of boss would you like? Why?
14. If you could spend a day with someone you've known or known of, who would it be?
15. What personality characteristics seem to rub you the wrong way?
16. How do you show your anger? What type of things make you angry?
17. With what type of person do you spend the majority of your time?

Source: The *Ultimate Job Hunter's Guidebook,* 2nd ed. by Susan D. Greene and Melanie C. L. Martel. Copyright © 1998 by Houghton Mifflin Company. Reprinted with permission.

third—usually with one or more department heads. If the job requires relocation to a different area, applicants may be invited there for these later interviews. After the interviewing process is complete, applicants are told when to expect a hiring decision.

After the Interview

Attention to common courtesy is important as a follow-up to your interview. A brief note of thanks should be sent to the interviewer, and it should receive as much care as the résumé. A short, typewritten letter is preferred to a handwritten note or card. Avoid not only typos, but also arrogant and overconfident statements, such as "I look forward to helping you make Universal Industries successful over the next decade." Even in the thank-you letter, it is important to show team spirit and professionalism, as well as to convey proper enthusiasm. Everything that is said and done reflects the candidate.

After the Hire

Clearly, performing well in a job has always been a crucial factor in keeping a position. In a tight economy and job market, however, a person's attitude, as well as his or her performance, counts greatly. People in their first jobs can commit costly political blunders and mistakes by being insensitive to their environments. Politics in the business world includes how you react to your boss, how you react to your coworkers, and your general demeanor. Here are a few of the rules to live by:

1. *Don't bypass your boss.* One of the major blunders an employee can make is to go over the boss's head to resolve a problem. This is especially hazardous in a bureaucratic organization. Employees should become aware of the generally accepted chain of command, and when problems occur, follow that protocol, beginning with their immediate superior. No boss likes to look incompetent, and making

him or her appear so is sure to crush or hamper a budding career. However, there may be exceptions to this rule in emergency situations. It would be advantageous for an employee to discuss with his or her supervisor what to do in an emergency, before an emergency occurs.[4]

2. *Don't criticize your boss.* Adhering to the old adage "praise in public and criticize in private" will keep you out of the line of retaliatory fire. A more sensible and productive alternative is to present the critical commentary to your boss in a diplomatic way during a private session.

3. *Don't show disloyalty.* If dissatisfied with the position, a new employee may start a fresh job search, within or outside the organization. However, it is not advisable to begin a publicized search within the company for another position unless you have held your current job for some time. Careful attention to the political climate in the organization should help you determine how soon to start a new job campaign and how public it may be. In any case, it is not a good idea to publicize that you are looking outside the company for a new position.

4. *Don't be a naysayer.* Employees are expected to become part of the organizational team and to work together with others. Behaviors to avoid—especially if you are a new employee—include being critical of others, refusing to support others' projects, always playing devil's advocate, refusing to help others when a crisis occurs, and complaining all the time, even about such matters as the poor quality of the food in the cafeteria, the crowded parking lot, or the temperature in the office.

5. *Learn to correct mistakes appropriately.* No one likes to admit having made a mistake, but one of the most important political skills you can acquire is how to minimize the impact of a blunder. It is usually advantageous to correct the damage as soon as possible to avoid further problems. Some suggestions: be the first to break the bad news to your boss; avoid being defensive; stay poised and don't panic; and have solutions ready for fixing the blunder.[5]

Types of Marketing Careers

In considering marketing as a career, the first step is to evaluate broad categories of career opportunities in the areas of marketing research, sales, industrial buying, public relations, distribution management, product management, advertising, retail management, and direct marketing. Keep in mind that the categories described here are not all-inclusive and that each encompasses hundreds of marketing jobs.

Marketing Research

Clearly, marketing research and information systems are vital aspects of marketing decision making. Marketing researchers survey customers to determine their habits, preferences, and aspirations. The information about buyers and environmental forces that research and information systems provide improves a marketer's ability to understand the dynamics of the marketplace and make effective decisions.

Marketing research firms are usually employed by a client organization, such as a provider of goods or services, a nonbusiness organization, a research consulting firm, or an advertising agency. The activities performed include concept testing, product testing, package testing, advertising testing, test-market research, and new-product research.

Marketing researchers gather and analyze data relating to specific problems. A researcher may be involved in one or several stages of research, depending on the size of the project, the organization of the research unit, and the researcher's experience. Marketing research trainees in large organizations usually perform a considerable amount of clerical work, such as compiling secondary data from a firm's accounting and sales records and from periodicals, government publications, syndicated data services, and unpublished sources. A junior analyst may edit and code questionnaires or tabulate survey results. Trainees also may participate in gathering primary data through mail and telephone surveys, personal interviews, and observation. As a marketing researcher gains experience, he or she may become involved in defining problems and developing research questions; designing research procedures; and analyzing, interpreting, and reporting findings. Exceptional personnel may assume responsibility for entire research projects.

Although most employers consider a bachelor's degree sufficient qualification for a marketing research trainee, many specialized positions require a graduate degree in business administration, statistics, or other related fields. Today, trainees are more likely to have a marketing or statistics degree than a liberal arts degree. Courses in statistics, information technology, psychology, sociology, communications, economics, and technical writing are valuable preparation for a career in marketing research.

The Bureau of Labor Statistics indicates that marketing research provides abundant employment opportunity, especially for applicants with graduate training in marketing research, statistics, economics, and the social sciences. Generally, the value of information gathered by marketing information and research systems becomes more important as competition increases, thus expanding the opportunities for prospective marketing research personnel.

The major career paths in marketing research are with independent marketing research agencies/data suppliers and marketing research departments in advertising agencies and other businesses. In a company in which marketing research plays a key role, the researcher is often a member of the marketing strategy team. Surveying or interviewing customers is the heart of the marketing research firm's activities. A statistician selects the sample to be surveyed, analysts design the questionnaire and synthesize the gathered data into a final report, data processors tabulate the data, and the research director controls and coordinates all these activities so that each project is completed to the client's satisfaction.

Salaries in marketing research depend on the type, size, and location of the firm, as well as the nature of the position. Overall, the salaries of marketing researchers have increased slightly during the last few years. However, the specific position within the marketing research field determines the percentage of fluctuation.[6] Generally, starting salaries are somewhat higher and promotions somewhat slower than in other occupations requiring similar training.

Sales

Millions of people earn a living through personal selling. Chapter 19 defined personal selling as paid personal communication that attempts to inform customers and persuade them to purchase products in an exchange situation. Although this definition describes the general nature of sales positions, individual selling jobs vary enormously with respect to the type of businesses and products involved, the educational background and skills required, and the specific activities sales personnel perform. Because the work is so varied, it offers numerous career opportunities for people with a wide range of qualifications, interests, and goals. The two types of career opportunities we discuss next relate to business-to-business sales.

Sales Positions in Wholesaling   Wholesalers buy products intended for resale, for use in making other products, and for general business operations and sell them directly to organizational markets. Wholesalers thus provide services to both retailers and producers. They can help match producers' products to retailers' needs and provide services that save producers time, money, and resources. Some activities a sales representative for a wholesaling firm is likely to engage in include planning and negotiating transactions; assisting customers with sales, advertising, sales promotion, and publicity; facilitating transportation and storage; providing customers with inventory control and data processing assistance; establishing prices; and giving customers technical, managerial, and merchandising assistance.

The background needed by wholesale personnel depends on the nature of the product handled. A sales representative for a drug wholesaler, for example, needs extensive technical training and product knowledge and may have a degree in chemistry, biology, or pharmacology. A wholesaler of standard office supplies, on the other hand, may find it more important for its sales staff to be familiar with various brands, suppliers, and prices than to have technical knowledge about the products. A person just entering the wholesaling field may begin as a sales trainee or hold a nonselling job that provides experience with inventory, prices, discounts, and the firm's customers. A college graduate usually enters a wholesaler's sales force directly. Competent salespersons also transfer from manufacturer and retail sales positions.

The number of sales positions in wholesaling is expected to grow about as fast as the average for all occupations. Earnings for wholesale personnel vary widely because commissions often make up a large proportion of their incomes.

Sales Positions in Manufacturing   A manufacturer's sales personnel sell the firm's products to wholesalers, retailers, and industrial buyers; they thus perform many of the same activities as a wholesaler's representatives. As in wholesaling, educational requirements for a sales position depend largely on the type and complexity of the products and markets. Manufacturers of nontechnical products usually hire college graduates who have a liberal arts or business degree and train them so that they become knowledgeable about the firm's products, prices, and customers. Manufacturers of highly technical products generally prefer applicants who have degrees in fields associated with the particular industry and market.

Sales positions in manufacturing are expected to increase at an average rate. Manufacturers' sales personnel are well compensated and earn above-average salaries; most are paid a combination of salaries and commissions. Commissions vary according to the salesperson's efforts, abilities, and sales territory, as well as the type of products sold.

Industrial Buying

Industrial buyers, or purchasing agents, are responsible for maintaining an adequate supply of the goods and services that an organization requires for its operations. In general, industrial buyers purchase all items needed for direct use in producing other products and for use in day-to-day operations. Industrial buyers in large firms often specialize in purchasing a single, specific class of products—for example, all petroleum-based lubricants. In smaller organizations, buyers may be responsible for many different categories of purchases, including raw materials, component parts, office supplies, and operating services.

An industrial buyer's main job is selecting suppliers that offer the best quality, service, and price. When the products to be purchased are standardized, buyers may base their purchasing decisions on suppliers' descriptions of their offerings in catalogs and trade journals. Buyers who purchase highly homogeneous products often meet with salespeople to examine samples and observe demonstrations. Sometimes, buyers must inspect the actual product before purchasing it; in other cases, they invite suppliers to bid on large orders. Buyers who purchase equipment made to specifications often deal directly with manufacturers. After choosing a supplier and placing an order, an industrial buyer usually must trace the shipment to ensure on-time delivery. Sometimes the buyer is also responsible for receiving and inspecting an order and authorizing payment to the shipper.

Training requirements for a career in industrial buying relate to the needs of the firm and the types of products purchased. A manufacturer of heavy machinery may prefer an applicant who has a background in engineering. A service company, on the other hand, may recruit liberal arts majors. Although it is not generally required, a college degree is becoming increasingly important for industrial buyers who wish to advance to management positions.

Employment prospects for industrial buyers are expected to increase faster than average. Opportunities will be excellent for individuals with a master's degree in business administration or a bachelor's degree in engineering, science, or business administration. Companies that manufacture heavy equipment, computer equipment, and communications equipment will need buyers with technical backgrounds.

Public Relations

Public relations encompasses a broad set of communication activities designed to create and maintain favorable relations between an organization and its publics—customers, employees, stockholders, government officials, and society in general. Public relations specialists help clients create the image, issue, or message they wish to present and communicate it to the appropriate audience. According to the Public Relations Society of America, 120,000 persons work in public relations in the United States. Half the billings of the nation's 4,000 public relations agencies and firms come from Chicago and New York. The highest starting salaries can also be found there. Communication is basic to all public relations programs. To communicate effectively, public relations practitioners first must gather data about the firm's client publics to assess their needs, identify problems, formulate recommendations, implement new plans, and evaluate current activities.

Public relations personnel disseminate large amounts of information to the organization's client publics. Written communication is the most versatile tool of public relations, thus making good writing skills essential. Public relations practitioners must be adept at writing for a variety of media and audiences. It is not unusual for a person in public relations to prepare reports, news releases, speeches, broadcast scripts, technical manuals, employee publications, shareholder reports, and other communications aimed at both organizational personnel and external groups. In addition, a public relations practitioner needs a thorough knowledge of the production techniques used in preparing various communications. Public relations personnel also establish distribution channels for the organization's publicity. They must have a thorough understanding of the various media, their areas of specialization, the characteristics of their target audiences, and their policies regarding publicity. Anyone who hopes to succeed in public relations must develop close working relationships with numerous media personnel to enlist their interest in disseminating an organization's communications.

A college education combined with writing or media-related experience is the best preparation for a career in public relations. Most beginners have a college degree in journalism, communications, or public relations, but some employers prefer a business background. Courses in journalism, business administration, marketing, creative writing, psychology, sociology, political science, economics, advertising, English, and public speaking are recommended. Some employers ask applicants to present a portfolio of published articles, scripts written for television or radio programs, slide presentations, and other work samples. Other agencies require written tests that include such tasks as writing sample press releases. Manufacturing firms, public utilities, transportation and insurance companies, and trade and professional associations are the largest employers of public relations personnel. In addition, sizable numbers of public relations personnel work for health-related organizations, government agencies, educational institutions, museums, and religious and service groups.

Although some larger companies provide extensive formal training for new personnel, most new public relations employees learn on the job. Beginners usually perform routine tasks, such as maintaining files about company activities and searching secondary data sources for information that can be used in publicity materials. More experienced employees write press releases, speeches, and articles and help plan public relations campaigns.

Employment opportunities in public relations are expected to increase faster than the average for all occupations. One caveat is in order, however. Competition for beginning jobs is keen. The prospects are best for applicants who have solid academic preparation and some media experience. Abilities that differentiate candidates, such as an understanding of information technology, are becoming increasingly important.

Distribution Management

A distribution manager arranges for the transportation of goods within firms and through marketing channels. Transportation is an essential distribution activity that permits a firm to create time and place utility for its products. It is the distribution manager's job to analyze various transportation modes and to select the combination that minimizes cost and transit time while providing acceptable levels of reliability, capability, accessibility, and security.

To accomplish this task, a distribution manager performs many activities. First, the individual must choose one or a combination of transportation modes from the five major modes available: railroads, trucks, waterways, airways, and pipelines. The distribution manager must then select the specific routes that the goods will travel and the particular carriers to be used, weighing such factors as freight classifications and regulations, freight charges, time schedules, shipment sizes, and loss and damage ratios. In addition, this person may be responsible for preparing shipping documents, tracing shipments, handling loss and damage claims, keeping records of freight rates, and monitoring changes in government regulations and transportation technology.

Distribution management employs relatively few people and is expected to grow about as fast as the average for all occupations in the near future. Manufacturing firms are the largest employers of distribution managers, although some distribution managers work for wholesalers, retail stores, and consulting firms. Salaries of experienced distribution managers vary but generally are much higher than the average for all nonsupervisory personnel. Entry-level positions are diverse, ranging from inventory control and traffic scheduling to operations or distribution management. Inventory management is an area of great opportunity because of increasing global competition.

Most employers of distribution managers prefer to hire graduates of technical programs or people who have completed courses in transportation, logistics, distribution management, economics, statistics, computer science, management, marketing, and commercial law. A successful distribution manager must be adept at handling technical data and be able to interpret and communicate highly technical information.

Product Management

The product manager occupies a staff position and is responsible for the success or failure of a product line. Product managers coordinate most of the activities required to market a product. However, because they hold a staff position, they have relatively little actual authority over marketing personnel. Even so, they take on a large amount of responsibility and typically are paid quite well relative to other marketing employees. Being a product manager can be rewarding both financially and psychologically, but it can also be frustrating because of the disparity between responsibility and authority.

A product manager should have a general knowledge of advertising, transportation modes, inventory control, selling and sales management, sales promotion, marketing research, packaging, pricing, and warehousing. The individual must be knowledgeable enough to communicate effectively with personnel in these functional areas and to make suggestions and help assess alternatives when major decisions are being made.

Product managers usually need college training in an area of business administration. A master's degree is helpful, although a person usually does not become a product manager directly out of school. Frequently, several years of selling and sales management experience are prerequisites for a product management position, which often is a major step in the career path of top-level marketing executives.

Advertising

Advertising pervades our daily lives. Business and nonbusiness organizations use advertising in many ways and for many reasons. Advertising clearly needs individuals with diverse skills to fill a variety of jobs. Creativity, imagination, artistic talent, and expertise in expression and persuasion are important for copywriters, artists, and account executives. Sales and managerial abilities are vital to the success of advertising managers, media buyers, and production managers. Research directors must have a solid understanding of research techniques and human behavior. A related occupation is an advertising salesperson—one who sells newspaper, television, radio, or magazine advertising to advertisers.

Advertising professionals disagree on the most beneficial educational background for a career in advertising. Most employers prefer college graduates. Some employers seek individuals with degrees in advertising, journalism, or business; others prefer graduates with broad liberal arts backgrounds. Still other employers rank relevant work experience above educational background.

"Advertisers look for generalists," says a staff executive of the American Association of Advertising Agencies, "thus there are just as many economics or general liberal arts majors as M.B.A.s." Common entry-level positions in an advertising agency are found in the traffic department, account service (account coordinator), or in the media department (media assistant). Starting salaries in these positions are often quite low, but to gain experience in the advertising industry, employees must work their way up in the system.

A variety of organizations employ advertising personnel. Although advertising agencies are perhaps the most visible and glamorous of employers, many manufacturing firms, retail stores, banks, utility companies, and professional and trade associations maintain advertising departments. Advertising jobs can also be found with television and radio stations, newspapers, and magazines. Other businesses that employ advertising personnel include printers, art studios, letter shops, and package-design firms. Specific advertising jobs include advertising manager, account executive, research director, copywriter, media specialist, and production manager.

Retail Management

Although a career in retailing may begin in sales, there is more to retailing than simply selling. Many retail personnel occupy management positions. Besides managing the sales force, they focus on selecting and ordering merchandise, promotional activities, inventory control, customer credit operations, accounting, personnel, and store security.

How retail stores are organized varies. In many large department stores, retail management personnel rarely engage in the actual selling to customers; these duties are performed by retail salespeople. However, other types of retail organizations may require management personnel to perform selling activities from time to time.

Large retail stores offer a variety of management positions, including assistant buyers, buyers, department managers, section managers, store managers, division managers, regional managers, and vice president of merchandising. The following list describes the general duties of four of these positions; the precise nature of these duties may vary from one retail organization to another.

A section manager coordinates inventory and promotions and interacts with buyers, salespeople, and ultimate consumers. The manager performs merchandising, labor relations, and managerial activities and can usually expect to work more than a forty-hour workweek.

The buyer's task is more focused. In this fast-paced occupation, there is much travel and pressure and the need to be open-minded with respect to new and potentially successful items.

The regional manager coordinates the activities of several stores within a given area, usually monitoring and supporting sales, promotions, and general procedures.

The vice president of merchandising has a broad scope of managerial responsibility and reports to the organization's president.

Most retail organizations hire college-educated people, put them through management training programs, and then place them directly in management positions. They frequently hire candidates with backgrounds in liberal arts or business administration. Sales positions and retail management positions offer the greatest employment opportunities for marketing students.

Retail management positions can be exciting and challenging. Competent, ambitious individuals often assume a great deal of responsibility very quickly and advance rapidly. However, a retail manager's job is physically demanding and sometimes entails long working hours. In addition, managers employed by large chain stores may be required to move frequently during their early years with the company. Nonetheless, positions in retail management often offer the chance to excel and gain promotion. Growth in retailing, which is expected to accompany the growth in population, is likely to create substantial opportunities during the next ten years.

Direct Marketing

One of the most dynamic areas in marketing is direct marketing, in which the seller uses one or more direct media (telephone, mail, print, or television) to solicit a response. The telephone is a major vehicle for selling many consumer products. Telemarketing is direct selling to customers using a variety of technological improvements in telecommunications. Direct mail catalogs appeal to such market segments as working women or people who find going to retail stores difficult or inconvenient. Newspapers and magazines offer great opportunity, particularly in special market segments. *Golf Digest,* for example is obviously a good medium for selling golfing equipment. Cable television provides many new opportunities for selling directly to consumers. Home shopping channels, for instance, have been very successful. The Internet offers numerous direct marketing opportunities to consumers.

The most important asset in direct marketing is experience. Employers often look to other industries to locate experienced professionals. This preference means that if you can get an entry-level position in direct marketing, you will have an advantage in developing a career.

Jobs in direct marketing include buyers, such as department store buyers, who select goods for catalog, telephone, or direct mail sales. Catalog managers develop marketing strategies for each new catalog that goes into the mail. Research/mail-list management involves developing lists of products that will sell in direct marketing and lists of names of consumers who are likely to respond to a direct mail effort. Order fulfillment managers direct the shipment of products once they are sold. Direct marketing's effectiveness is enhanced by periodic analysis of advertising and communications at all phases of contact with the consumer. Direct marketing involves all aspects of marketing decision making.

Appendix B
Financial Analysis in Marketing*

Our discussion in this book focuses more on fundamental concepts and decisions in marketing than on financial details. However, marketers must understand the basic components of financial analyses if they are to explain and defend their decisions. In fact, they must be familiar with certain financial analyses if they are to reach good decisions in the first place. To control and evaluate marketing activities, they must understand the income statement and what it says about the operations of their organization. They also need to be acquainted with performance ratios, which compare current operating results with past results and with results in the industry at large. We examine the income statement and some performance ratios in the first part of this appendix. In the last part, we discuss price calculations as the basis of price adjustments. Marketers are likely to use all these areas of financial analysis at various times to support their decisions and to make necessary adjustments in their operations.

The Income Statement

The income, or operating, statement presents the financial results of an organization's operations over a certain period. The statement summarizes revenues earned and expenses incurred by a profit center, whether it is a department, brand, product line, division, or entire firm. The income statement presents the firm's net profit or net loss for a month, quarter, or year.

Table B.1 is a simplified income statement for Stoneham Auto Supplies, a fictitious retail store. The owners of the store, Rose Costa and Nick Schultz, see that net sales of $250,000 are decreased by the cost of goods sold and by other business expenses to yield a net income of $83,000. Of course, these figures are only highlights of the complete income statement, which appears in Table B.2.

The income statement can be used in several ways to improve the management of a business. First, it enables an owner or manager to compare actual results with budgets for various parts of the statement. For example, Rose and Nick see that the total amount of merchandise sold (gross sales) is $260,000. Customers returned merchandise or received allowances (price reductions) totaling $10,000. Suppose that the budgeted amount was only $9,000. By checking the tickets for sales returns and allowances, the owners can determine why these events occurred and whether the $10,000 figure could be lowered by adjusting the marketing mix.

After subtracting returns and allowances from gross sales, Rose and Nick can determine net sales. They are pleased with this figure because it is higher than their sales target of $240,000. Net sales is the amount the firm has available to pay its expenses.

Table B.1	Simplified Income Statement for a Retailer
Stoneham Auto Supplies	
Income Statement for the Year Ended December 31, 1999	
Net Sales	$250,000
Cost of Goods Sold	45,000
Gross Margin	$205,000
Expenses	122,000
Net Income	$ 83,000

*We gratefully acknowledge the assistance of Jim L. Grimm, Professor of Marketing, Illinois State University, in writing this appendix.

Table B.2   Income Statement for a Retailer

Stoneham Auto Supplies
Income Statement for the Year Ended December 31, 1999

Gross Sales			**$260,000**
Less: Sales returns and allowances			10,000
Net Sales			**$250,000**
Cost of Goods Sold			
Inventory, January 1, 1999 (at cost)		$48,000	
Purchases	$51,000		
Less: Purchase discounts	4,000		
Net purchases	$47,000		
Plus: Freight-in	2,000		
Net cost of delivered purchases		$49,000	
Cost of goods available for sale		$97,000	
Less: Inventory, December 31, 1999			
(at cost)		52,000	
Cost of goods sold			$ 45,000
Gross Margin			**$205,000**
Expenses			
Selling expenses			
Sales salaries and commissions	$32,000		
Advertising	16,000		
Sales promotions	3,000		
Delivery	2,000		
Total selling expenses		$53,000	
Administrative expenses			
Administrative salaries	$20,000		
Office salaries	20,000		
Office supplies	2,000		
Miscellaneous	1,000		
Total administrative expenses		$43,000	
General expenses			
Rent	$14,000		
Utilities	7,000		
Bad debts	1,000		
Miscellaneous (local taxes, insurance, interest, depreciation)	4,000		
Total general expenses		$26,000	
Total expenses			$122,000
Net Income			**$ 83,000**

A major expense for most companies that sell goods (as opposed to services) is the cost of goods sold. For Stoneham Auto Supplies, it amounts to 18 percent of net sales. Other expenses are treated in various ways by different companies. In our example, they are broken down into standard categories of selling expenses, administrative expenses, and general expenses.

The income statement shows that for Stoneham Auto Supplies, the cost of goods sold was $45,000. This figure was derived in the following way. First, the statement shows that merchandise in the amount of $51,000 was purchased during the year. In paying the invoices associated with these inventory additions, purchase (cash) discounts of $4,000 were earned, resulting in net purchases of $47,000. Special requests for selected merchandise throughout the year resulted in $2,000 in freight charges, which increased the net cost of delivered purchases to $49,000. When this amount is added to the beginning inventory of $48,000, the cost of goods available for sale during 1999 totals $97,000. However, the records indicate that the value of inventory at the end of the year was $52,000. Because this amount was not sold, the cost of goods that were sold during the year was $45,000.

Rose and Nick observe that the total value of their inventory increased by 8.3 percent during the year:

$$\frac{\$52,000 - \$48,000}{\$48,000} = \frac{\$4,000}{\$48,000} = \frac{1}{12} = .0825, \text{ or } 8.3\%$$

Further analysis is needed to determine whether this increase is desirable or undesirable. (Note that the income statement provides no details concerning the composition of the inventory held on December 31; other records supply this information.) If Nick and Rose determine that inventory on December 31 is excessive, they can implement appropriate marketing action.

Gross margin is the difference between net sales and cost of goods sold. Gross margin reflects the markup on products and is the amount available to pay all other expenses and provide a return to the owners. Stoneham Auto Supplies had a gross margin of $205,000:

Net Sales	$250,000
Cost of Goods Sold	− 45,000
Gross Margin	$205,000

Stoneham's expenses (other than cost of goods sold) during 1999 totaled $122,000. Observe that $53,000, or slightly more than 43 percent of the total, constituted direct selling expenses:

$$\frac{\$53,000 \text{ selling expenses}}{\$122,000 \text{ total expenses}} = .434, \text{ or } 43\%$$

The business employs three salespersons (one full-time) and pays competitive wages. The selling expenses are similar to those in the previous year, but Nick and Rose wonder whether more advertising is necessary because the value of inventory increased by more than 8 percent during the year.

The administrative and general expenses are essential for operating the business. A comparison of these expenses with trade statistics for similar businesses indicates that the figures are in line with industry amounts.

Net income, or net profit, is the amount of gross margin remaining after deducting expenses. Stoneham Auto Supplies earned a net profit of $83,000 for the fiscal year ending December 31, 1999. Note that net income on this statement is figured before payment of state and federal income taxes.

Income statements for intermediaries and for businesses that provide services follow the same general format as that shown for Stoneham Auto Supplies in Table B.2. The income statement for a manufacturer, however, is somewhat different in that the "purchases" portion is replaced by "cost of goods manufactured." Table B.3 shows the entire Cost of Goods Sold section for a manufacturer, including cost of goods manufactured. In other respects, income statements for retailers and manufacturers are similar.

Performance Ratios

Rose and Nick's assessment of how well their business did during fiscal year 1999 can be improved through use of analytical ratios. Such ratios enable a manager to compare the results for the current year with data from previous years and industry statistics. However, comparisons of the current income statement with income statements and industry statistics from other years are not very meaningful because factors like inflation are not accounted for when comparing dollar amounts. More meaningful comparisons can be made by converting these figures to a percentage of net sales, as this section shows.

Table B.3	Cost of Goods Sold for a Manufacturer			

ABC Manufacturing
Income Statement for the Year Ended December 31, 1999

Cost of Goods Sold				$ 50,000
Finished goods inventory January 1, 1999				
Cost of goods manufactured				
Work-in-process inventory, January 1, 1999			$ 20,000	
Raw materials inventory, January 1, 1999	$ 40,000			
Net cost of delivered purchases	240,000			
Cost of goods available for use	$280,000			
Less: Raw materials inventory, December 31, 1999	42,000			
Cost of goods placed in production		$238,000		
Direct labor		32,000		
Manufacturing overhead				
Indirect labor	$ 12,000			
Supervisory salaries	10,000			
Operating supplies	6,000			
Depreciation	12,000			
Utilities	10,000			
Total manufacturing overhead		$ 50,000		
Total manufacturing costs			$320,000	
Total work-in-process			$340,000	
Less: Work-in-process inventory, December 31, 1999			22,000	
Cost of Goods Manufactured				$318,000
				$368,000
Cost of Goods Available for Sale				
Less: Finished goods inventory, December 31, 1999				48,000
Cost of Goods Sold				**$320,000**

The first analytical ratios we discuss, the operating ratios, are based on the net sales figure from the income statement.

Operating Ratios

Operating ratios express items on the income, or operating, statement as percentages of net sales. The first step is to convert the income statement into percentages of net sales, as illustrated in Table B.4.

After making this conversion, the manager looks at several key operating ratios: two profitability ratios (the gross margin ratio and the net income ratio) and the operating expense ratio.

Table B.4   Income Statement Components as Percentages of Net Sales

Stoneham Auto Supplies
Income Statement as a Percentage of Net Sales for the Year Ended December 31, 1999

			Percentage of net sales
Gross Sales			103.8%
Less: Sales returns and allowances			3.8
Net Sales			100.0%
Cost of Goods Sold			
Inventory, January 1, 1999 (at cost)		19.2%	
Purchases	20.4%		
Less: Purchase discounts	1.6		
Net purchases	18.8%		
Plus: Freight-in	0.8		
Net cost of delivered purchases		19.6	
Cost of goods available for sale		38.8%	
Less: Inventory, December 31, 1999 (at cost)		20.8	
Cost of goods sold			18.0
Gross Margin			82.0%
Expenses			
Selling expenses			
Sales salaries and commissions	12.8%		
Advertising	6.4		
Sales promotions	1.2		
Delivery	0.8		
Total selling expenses		21.2%	
Administrative expenses			
Administrative salaries	8.0%		
Office salaries	8.0		
Office supplies	0.8		
Miscellaneous	0.4		
Total administrative expenses		17.2%	
General expenses			
Rent	5.6%		
Utilities	2.8		
Bad debts	0.4		
Miscellaneous	1.6		
Total general expenses		10.4%	
Total expenses			48.8
Net Income			33.2%

For Stoneham Auto Supplies, these ratios are determined as follows (see Tables B.2 and B.4 for supporting data):

$$\text{Gross margin ratio} = \frac{\text{gross margin}}{\text{net sales}} = \frac{\$205{,}000}{\$250{,}000} = 82\%$$

$$\text{Net income ratio} = \frac{\text{net income}}{\text{net sales}} = \frac{\$83{,}000}{\$250{,}000} = 33.2\%$$

$$\text{Operating expenses ratio} = \frac{\text{total expense}}{\text{net sales}} = \frac{\$122,000}{\$250,000} = 48.8\%$$

The gross margin ratio indicates the percentage of each sales dollar available to cover operating expenses and achieve profit objectives. The net income ratio indicates the percentage of each sales dollar that is classified as earnings (profit) before payment of income taxes. The operating expense ratio indicates the percentage of each dollar needed to cover operating expenses.

If Nick and Rose feel that the operating expense ratio is higher than historical data and industry standards, they can analyze each operating expense ratio in Table B.4 to determine which expenses are too high and then take corrective action.

After reviewing several key operating ratios, Nick and Rose, like many managers, will probably want to analyze all the items on the income statement. By doing so, they can determine whether the 8 percent increase in the value of their inventory was necessary.

Inventory Turnover Rate

The inventory turnover rate, or stockturn rate, is an analytical ratio that can be used to answer the question, "Is the inventory level appropriate for this business?" The inventory turnover rate indicates the number of times an inventory is sold (turns over) during one year. To be useful, this figure must be compared with historical turnover rates and industry rates.

The inventory turnover rate is computed (based on cost) as follows:

$$\text{Inventory turnover} = \frac{\text{cost of goods sold}}{\text{average inventory at cost}}$$

Rose and Nick would calculate the turnover rate from Table B.2 as follows:

$$\frac{\text{Cost of goods sold}}{\text{Average inventory at cost}} = \frac{\$45,000}{\$50,000} = 0.9 \text{ time}$$

Their inventory turnover is less than once per year (0.9 time). Industry averages for competitive firms are 2.8 times. This figure convinces Rose and Nick that their investment in inventory is too large and that they need to reduce their inventory.

Return on Investment

Return on investment (ROI) is a ratio that indicates management's efficiency in generating sales and profits from the total amount invested in the firm. For Stoneham Auto Supplies, the ROI is 41.5 percent, which compares well with competing businesses.

We use figures from two different financial statements to arrive at ROI. The income statement, already discussed, gives us net income. The balance sheet, which states the firm's assets and liabilities at a given point in time, provides the figure for total assets (or investment) in the firm.

The basic formula for ROI is

$$\text{ROI} = \frac{\text{net income}}{\text{total investment}}$$

For Stoneham Auto Supplies, net income is $83,000 (see Table B.2). If total investment (taken from the balance sheet for December 31, 1999) is $200,000, then

$$\text{ROI} = \frac{\$83,000}{\$200,000} = 0.415, \text{ or } 41.5\%$$

The ROI formula can be expanded to isolate the impact of capital turnover and the operating income ratio separately. Capital turnover is a measure of net sales per dollar of investment; the ratio is figured by dividing net sales by total investment. For Stoneham Auto Supplies,

$$\text{Capital turnover} = \frac{\text{net sales}}{\text{total investment}} = \frac{\$250,000}{\$200,000} = 1.25$$

ROI is equal to capital turnover times the net income ratio. The expanded formula for Stoneham Auto Supplies is

$$\text{ROI} = \frac{\text{net sales}}{\text{total investment}} \times \frac{\text{net income}}{\text{net sales}}$$

$$= \frac{\$250,000}{\$200,000} \times \frac{\$83,000}{\$250,000}$$

$$= (1.25)(33.2\%) = 41.5\%$$

Price Calculations

An important step in setting prices is selecting a basis for pricing, as discussed in Chapter 21. The systematic use of markups, markdowns, and various conversion formulas helps in calculating the selling price and evaluating the effects of various prices.

Markups

As indicated in the text, markup is the difference between the selling price and the cost of the item. That is, selling price equals cost plus markup. The markup must cover cost and contribute to profit; thus, markup is similar to gross margin on the income statement.

Markup can be calculated on either cost or selling price as follows:

$$\text{Markup as percentage of cost} = \frac{\text{amount added to cost}}{\text{cost}} = \frac{\text{dollar markup}}{\text{cost}}$$

$$\text{Markup as percentage of selling price} = \frac{\text{amount added to cost}}{\text{selling price}} = \frac{\text{dollar markup}}{\text{selling price}}$$

Retailers tend to calculate the markup percentage on selling price.

To review the use of these markup formulas, assume that an item costs $10 and the markup is $5.

$$\text{Selling price} = \text{cost} + \text{markup}$$
$$\$15 = \$10 + \$5$$

Thus,

$$\text{Markup percentage on cost} = \frac{\$5}{\$10} = 50\%$$

$$\text{Markup percentage on selling price} = \frac{\$5}{\$15} = 33\frac{1}{3}\%$$

It is necessary to know the base (cost or selling price) to use markup pricing effectively. Markup percentage on cost will always exceed markup percentage on price, given the same dollar markup, so long as selling price exceeds cost.

On occasion, we may need to convert markup on cost to markup on selling price, or vice versa. The conversion formulas are

$$\text{Markup percentage on selling price} = \frac{\text{markup percentage on cost}}{100\% + \text{markup percentage on cost}}$$

$$\text{Markup percentage} \atop \text{on cost} = \frac{\text{markup percentage on selling price}}{100\% - \text{markup percentage on selling price}}$$

For example, if the markup percentage on cost is 33⅓ percent, then the markup percentage on selling price is

$$\frac{33\frac{1}{3}\%}{100\% + 33\frac{1}{3}\%} = \frac{33\frac{1}{3}\%}{133\frac{1}{3}\%} = 25\%$$

If the markup percentage on selling price is 40 percent, then the corresponding percentage on cost would be as follows:

$$\frac{40\%}{100\% - 40\%} = \frac{40\%}{60\%} = 66\frac{2}{3}\%$$

Finally, we can show how to determine selling price if we know the cost of the item and the markup percentage on selling price. Assume that an item costs $36 and the usual markup percentage on selling price is 40 percent. Remember that selling price equals markup plus cost. Thus, if

$$100\% = 40\% \text{ of selling price} + \text{cost}$$

then,

$$60\% \text{ of selling price} = \text{cost}$$

In our example, cost equals $36. Then,

$$0.6X = \$36$$

$$X = \frac{\$36}{0.6}$$

$$\text{Selling price} = \$60$$

Alternatively, the markup percentage could be converted to a cost basis as follows:

$$\frac{40\%}{100\% - 40\%} = 66\frac{2}{3}\%$$

The computed selling price would then be as follows:

$$\begin{aligned} \text{Selling price} &= 66\frac{2}{3}\%(\text{cost}) + \text{cost} \\ &= 66\frac{2}{3}\%(\$36) + \$36 \\ &= \$24 + \$36 = \$60 \end{aligned}$$

By remembering the basic formula—selling price equals cost plus markup—you will find these calculations straightforward.

Markdowns

Markdowns are price reductions a retailer makes on merchandise. Markdowns may be useful on items that are damaged, priced too high, or selected for a special sales event. The income statement does not express markdowns directly because the change in price is made before the sale takes place. Therefore, separate records of markdowns would be needed to evaluate the performance of various buyers and departments.

The markdown ratio (percentage) is calculated as follows:

$$\text{Markdown percentage} = \frac{\text{dollar markdowns}}{\text{net sales in dollars}}$$

In analyzing their inventory, Nick and Rose discover three special automobile jacks that have gone unsold for several months. They decide to reduce the price of each item from $25 to $20. Subsequently, these items are sold. The markdown percentage for these three items is

$$\text{Markdown percentage} = \frac{3(\$5)}{3(\$20)} = \frac{\$15}{\$60} = 25\%$$

Net sales, however, include all units of this product sold during the period, not just those marked down. If ten of these items have already been sold at $25 each, in addition to the three items sold at $20, then the overall markdown percentage would be

$$\text{Markdown percentage} = \frac{3(\$5)}{10(\$25) + 3(\$20)}$$

$$= \frac{\$15}{\$250 + \$60} = \frac{\$15}{\$310} = 4.8\%$$

Sales allowances are also a reduction in price. Thus, the markdown percentage should include any sales allowances. It would be computed as follows:

$$\text{Markdown percentage} = \frac{\text{dollar markdowns} + \text{dollar allowances}}{\text{net sales in dollars}}$$

Discussion and Review Questions

1. How does a manufacturer's income statement differ from a retailer's income statement?

2. Use the following information to answer questions a through c:

   TEA Company
   Fiscal year ended June 30, 1999

Net sales	$500,000
Cost of goods sold	300,000
Net income	50,000
Average inventory at cost	100,000
Total assets (total investment)	200,000

   a. What is the inventory turnover rate for TEA Company? From what sources will the marketing manager determine the significance of the inventory turnover rate?

   b. What is the capital turnover ratio? What is the net income ratio? What is the return on investment (ROI)?

   c. How many dollars of sales did each dollar of investment produce for TEA Company?

3. Product A has a markup percentage on cost of 40 percent. What is the markup percentage on selling price?

4. Product B has a markup percentage on selling price of 30 percent. What is the markup percentage on cost?

5. Product C has a cost of $60 and a usual markup percentage of 25 percent on selling price. What price should be placed on this item?

6. Apex Appliance Company sells twenty units of product Q for $100 each and ten units for $80 each. What is the markdown percentage for product Q?

Appendix C
Sample Marketing Plan

NOTE: *This is a sample marketing plan for a hypothetical company that illustrates the marketing planning process described in Chapter 2. This plan lets you see how the planning concepts might be implemented. If you are asked to create a marketing plan, you may find it helpful to use this model for guidance, along with the concepts presented in Chapter 2.*

Star Software, Inc.: Marketing Plan

I. Executive Summary

Star Software, Inc., is a small, family-owned corporation in the first year of a transition from first-generation to second-generation leadership. Star Software sells custom-made calendar programs and related items to about four hundred businesses, which use the software mainly for promotion. Star's eighteen employees face scheduling challenges, as Star's business is highly seasonal, with its greatest demand during October, November, and December. In other months, the equipment and staff are sometimes idle. A major challenge facing Star Software is how to increase profits and make better use of its resources during the off-season.

An evaluation of the company's internal strengths and weaknesses and external opportunities and threats served as the foundation for this strategic analysis and marketing plan. The plan focuses on the company's growth strategy, suggesting ways in which it can build on existing customer relationships and on the development of new products and/or services targeted to specific customer niches. Since Star Software markets a product used primarily as a promotional tool by its clients, it currently is considered a business-to-business marketer.

II. Environmental Analysis

Founded as a commercial printing company, Star Software, Inc., has evolved into a marketer of high-quality, custom-made calendar software and related business-to-business specialty items. In the mid-1960s, Bob McLemore purchased the company and, through his full-time commitment, turned it into a very successful family-run operation. In the near future, McLemore's 37-year-old son, Jonathan, will take over as Star Software's president and allow the elder McLemore to scale back his involvement.

A. The Marketing Environment

1. *Competitive forces.* The competition in the specialty advertising industry is very strong on a local and regional basis but somewhat weak nationally. Sales figures for the industry as a whole are difficult to obtain since very little business is conducted on a national scale.

   The competition within the calendar industry is strong in the paper segment and weak in the software-based segment. Currently, paper calendars hold a dominant market share of approximately 90 percent; however, the software-based segment is growing rapidly. The 10 percent market share held by software-based calendars is divided among many different firms. Star Software, which holds 30 percent of the software-based calendar market, is the only company that markets a software-based calendar on a national basis. As software-based calendars become more popular, additional competition is expected to enter the market.

2. *Economic forces.* Nationwide, many companies have reduced their overall promotion budgets as they are faced with the need to cut expenses. However, most of these reductions have occurred in the budgets for mass media advertising (television, magazines, newspapers). While overall promotion budgets are shrinking, many companies are diverting a larger percentage of their budgets to sales pro-

motion and specialty advertising. This trend is expected to continue as a weak, slow-growth economy forces most companies to become more interested in the "value" they receive from their promotion dollar. Specialty advertising, such as can be done with a software-based calendar, provides this value.

3. *Political forces.* There are no expected political influences or events that could affect the operations of Star Software.

4. *Legal and regulatory forces.* In recent years, more attention has been paid to "junk mail." A large percentage of specialty advertising products are distributed by mail, and some of these products are considered "junk." While this label is attached to the type of products Star Software makes, the problem of junk mail falls on the clients of Star Software and not on the company itself. While legislation may be introduced to curb the tide of advertising delivered through the mail, the fact that more companies are diverting their promotion dollars to specialty advertising indicates that most companies do not fear the potential for increased legislation.

5. *Technological forces.* A major emerging technological trend involves personal information managers (PIMs), or personal digital assistants (PDAs). A PDA is a hand-held device, similar in size to a large calculator, that can store a wide variety of information, including personal notes, addresses, and a calendar. Some PDAs even have the ability to fax letters via microwave communication. As this trend continues, current software-based calendar products may have to be adapted to match the new technology.

6. *Sociocultural forces.* In today's society, consumers have less time for work or leisure. The hallmarks of today's successful products are convenience and ease-of-use. In short, if the product does not save time and is not easy to use, consumers will simply ignore it. Software-based calendars fit this consumer need quite well. A software-based calendar also fits in with other societal trends—a move to a paperless society, the need to automate repetitive tasks, and the growing dependence on computers, for example.

B. Target Market(s)

By focusing on commitment to service and quality, Star Software has effectively implemented a niche differentiation strategy in a somewhat diverse marketplace. Its ability to differentiate its product has contributed to superior annual returns. Its target market consists of manufacturers or manufacturing divisions of large corporations that move their products through dealers, distributors, or brokers. Its most profitable product is a software program for a PC-based calendar, which can be tailored to meet client specifications by means of artwork, logos, and text. Clients use this calendar software as a promotional tool, providing a disk to their customers as an advertising premium. The calendar software is not produced for resale.

The calendar software began as an ancillary product to Star's commercial printing business. However, due to the proliferation of PCs and the growth in technology, the computer calendar soon became more profitable for Star than its wall and desktop paper calendars. This led to the sale of the commercial printing plant and equipment to employees. Star Software has maintained a long-term relationship with these former employees, who have added capabilities to reproduce computer disks and whose company serves as Star's primary supplier of finished goods. Star's staff focuses on the further development and marketing of the software.

C. Current Marketing Objectives and Performance

Star Software's sales representatives call on potential clients and, using a template demonstration disk, help them create a calendar concept. Once the sale has been finalized, Star completes the concept, including design, copywriting, and customization of the demonstration disk. Specifications are then sent to the supplier, located about a thousand miles away, where the disks are produced. Perhaps what most differentiates Star from its competitors is its high level of service. Disks can be shipped to any location specified by the buyer. Since product development and customization of this type can require significant amounts of time and effort, particularly during the product's first year, Star deliberately pursues a strategy of steady, managed growth.

Star Software markets its products on a company-specific basis. It has an approximate 90 percent annual reorder rate and an average customer-reorder relationship of about eight years. The first year in dealing with a new customer is the most stressful and time-consuming for Star's salespeople and product developers. The subsequent years are faster and significantly more profitable.

The company is currently debt-free except for the mortgage on its facility. However, about 80 percent of its accounts receivable are billed during the last three months of the calendar year. Seasonal account billings, along with the added travel of its sales staff during the peak season, provide a special challenge to the company. The need for cash to fund operations in the meantime causes the company to borrow significant amounts of money to cover the period until customer billing occurs.

As the current fiscal year comes to an end, Star Software expects to see the best year in its history, with increases in both revenues and profits of approximately 10 percent over the previous year. Revenues are expected to exceed $4 million, and profits are expected to reach $1.3 million.

III. SWOT Analysis

A. Strengths

1. Star Software's product differentiation strategy is the result of a strong marketing orientation, commitment to high quality, and customization of products and support services.

2. There is little turnover among well-compensated employees who are liked by customers. The relatively small size of the staff promotes camaraderie with fellow employees and clients and fosters communication and quick response to clients' needs.

3. A long-term relationship with the primary supplier results in shared knowledge of the product's requirements, adherence to quality standards, and a common vision throughout the development and production process.

4. The high percentage of reorder business suggests a satisfied customer base, as well as positive word-of-mouth communication, which generates some 30 percent of new business each year.

B. Weaknesses

1. The highly centralized management hierarchy (the McLemores) and lack of managerial backup may impede creativity and growth. Too much knowledge is held by too few people.

2. Despite the successful, long-term relationship with the supplier, single-sourcing could make Star Software vulnerable in the event of a natural disaster, strike, or dissolution of the current supplier. Contingency plans for suppliers should be considered.

3. The seasonal nature of the product line creates bottlenecks in productivity and cash flow, places excessive stress on personnel, and strains the facilities.

4. Both the product line and the client base lack diversification. Dependence on current reorder rates could breed complacency, invite competition, or create a false sense of customer satisfaction. The development of a product that would make the software calendar obsolete would probably put Star out of business.

5. While the small size of the staff fosters camaraderie, it also impedes growth and new business development.

6. Star Software is reactive rather than assertive in its marketing efforts because of its heavy reliance on positive word-of-mouth communication for obtaining new business.

7. Star's current facilities are crowded. There is little room for additional employees or new equipment.

C. Opportunities

1. Advertising expenditures in the United States exceed $132 billion annually. More than $25 billion of this is spent on direct mail advertising, and another $20 billion is spent on specialty advertising. The potential for Star Software's growth is significant in this market.

2. Technological advances have not only freed up time for Americans and brought greater efficiency but also have increased the amount of stress in their fast-paced lives. Personal computers have become commonplace and personal information managers have gained popularity.

3. As American companies look for ways to develop customer relationships rather than just close sales, reminders of this relationship could come in the form of acceptable premiums or gifts that are useful to the customer.

4. Computer-based calendars are easily distributed nationally and globally. The globalization of business creates an opportunity to establish new client relationships in foreign markets.

D. Threats

1. Reengineering, right-sizing, and outsourcing trends in management may alter traditional channel relationships with brokers, dealers, and distributors or eliminate them altogether.

2. Calendars are basically a generic product. The technology, knowledge, and equipment required to produce such an item, even a computer-based one, are minimal. The possible entry of new competitors is a significant threat.

3. Theft of trade secrets and software piracy through unauthorized copying are difficult to control.

4. Specialty advertising through promotional items relies on gadgetry and ideas that are new and different. As a result, product life cycles may be quite short.

5. Single-sourcing can be detrimental or even fatal to a company if the buyer-supplier relationship is damaged or if the supplying company has financial difficulty.

6. Competition from traditional paper calendars and other promotional items is strong.

E. Matching Strengths to Opportunities/Converting Weaknesses and Threats

1. The acceptance of technological advances and the desire to control time create a potential need for a computer-based calendar.

2. Star Software has more opportunity for business growth during its peak season than it can presently handle because of resource (human and capital) constraints.

3. Star Software must modify its management hierarchy, empowering its employees through a more decentralized marketing organization.

4. Star Software should discuss future growth strategies with its supplier and develop contingency plans to deal with unforeseen events. Possible satellite facilities in other geographic locations should be explored.

5. Star Software should consider diversifying its product line to satisfy new market niches and develop nonseasonal products.

6. Star Software should consider surveying its current customers and its customers' clients to gain a better understanding of their needs and changing desires.

IV. Marketing Objectives

Star Software, Inc., is in the business of helping other companies market their products and/or services. Besides formulating a marketing-oriented and customer-focused mission statement, Star Software should establish an objective to achieve cumulative growth in net profit of at least 50 percent over the next five years. At least half of this 50 percent growth should come from new, nonmanufacturing customers and from products that are nonseasonal or that are generally delivered in the off-peak period of the calendar cycle.

To accomplish its marketing objectives, Star Software should develop benchmarks to measure progress. Regular reviews of these objectives will provide feedback and possible corrective actions on a timely basis. The major marketing objective is to gain a better understanding of the needs and satisfaction of current customers. Since Star Software is benefitting from a 90 percent reorder rate, it must be satisfying its current customers. Star could use the knowledge of its successes with current clients to market to new customers. To capitalize on its success with current clients, benchmarks should be established to learn how Star can improve the products it now offers through knowledge of its clients' needs and specific opportunities for new product offerings. These benchmarks should be determined through marketing research and Star's marketing information system.

Another objective should be to analyze the billing cycle Star now uses to determine if there are ways to bill accounts receivable in a more evenly distributed manner throughout the year. Alternatively, repeat customers might be willing to place orders at off-peak cycles in return for discounts or added customer services.

Star Software also should create new products that can utilize its current equipment, technology, and knowledge base. It should conduct simple research and analyses of similar products or product lines with an eye toward developing specialty advertising products that are software-based, but not necessarily calendar-related.

V. Marketing Strategies

A. Target Market(s)

Target market 1: Large manufacturers or stand-alone manufacturing divisions of large corporations with extensive broker, dealer, or distributor networks

For example, an agricultural chemical producer, such as Dow Chemical, distributes its products to numerous rural "feed and seed" dealers. Customizing calendars with Chicago Board of Trade futures or USDA agricultural report dates would be beneficial to these potential clients.

Target market 2: Nonmanufacturing, nonindustrial segments of the business-to-business market with extensive customer networks, such as banks, medical services, or financial planners

For example, various sporting good manufacturers distribute to specialty shop dealers. Calendars could be customized to the particular sport, such as golf (with PGA, Virginia Slims, or other tour dates), running (with various national marathon dates), or bowling (with national tour dates).

Target market 3: Direct consumer markets for brands with successful licensing arrangements for consumer products, such as Coca-Cola

For example, products with major brand recognition and fan club membership, such as Harley-Davidson motorcycles or the Bloomington Gold Corvette Association, could provide additional markets for customized computer calendars. Brands with licensing

agreements for consumer products could provide a market for consumer computer calendars, in addition to the specialty advertising product, which would be marketed to
the manufacturer/dealer.

Target market 4: Industry associations that regularly hold or sponsor trade shows,
meetings, conferences, or conventions

For example, national associations, such as the National Dairy Association or the
American Marketing Association, frequently host meetings or annual conventions.
Customized calendars could be developed for any of these groups.

B.   Marketing Mix

1. *Products.* Star Software markets not only calendar software, but also the service of
   specialty advertising to its clients. Star's intangible attributes are its ability to meet
   or exceed customer expectations consistently, its speed in response to customers'
   demands, and its anticipation of new customer needs. Intangible attributes are
   difficult for competitors to copy, thereby giving Star Software a competitive
   advantage.
2. *Price.* Star Software provides a high-quality specialty advertising product customized to its clients' needs. The value of this product and service is reflected in
   its premium price. Star should be sensitive to the price elasticity of its product and
   overall consumer demand.
3. *Distribution.* Star Software uses direct marketing. Since its product is compact,
   lightweight, and nonperishable, it can be shipped from a central location direct
   to the client via United Parcel Service, Federal Express, or the U.S. Postal Service.
   The fact that Star can ship to multiple locations for each customer is an asset in
   selling its products.
4. *Promotion.* Since 90 percent of Star's customers reorder each year, the bulk of promotional expenditures should focus on new product offerings through direct-mail
   advertising and trade journals or specialty publications. Any remaining promotional dollars could be directed to personal selling (in the form of sales performance bonuses) of current and new products.

VI. Marketing Implementation

A.   Marketing Organization

Because Star's current and future products require extensive customization to match
clients' needs, it is necessary to organize the marketing function by customer groups.
This will allow Star to focus its marketing efforts exclusively on the needs and specifications of each target customer segment. Star's marketing efforts will be organized
around the following customer groups: (1) manufacturing group, (2) nonmanufacturing, business-to-business group, (3) consumer product licensing group, and (4) industry associations group. Each group will be headed by a sales manager who will report
to the marketing director (these positions must be created). Each group is responsible
for the marketing of Star's products within that customer segment. In addition, each
group will have full decision-making authority. This represents a shift from the current highly centralized management hierarchy. Frontline salespeople will be empowered to make decisions that will better satisfy Star's clients.

These changes in marketing organization will enable Star Software to be more creative and flexible in meeting customers' needs. Likewise, these changes will overcome
the current lack of diversification in Star's product lines and client base. Finally, this
new marketing organization will give Star a better opportunity to monitor the activities of competitors.

B.   Activities, Responsibility, and Timetables for Completion

All implementation activities are to begin at the start of the next fiscal year on April 1. Unless specified, all activities are the responsibility of Star Software's next president, Jonathan McLemore.

- On April 1, create four sales manager positions and the position of marketing director. The marketing director will serve as project leader of a new business analysis team, to be composed of nine employees from a variety of positions within the company.

- By April 15, assign three members of the analysis team to each of the following projects: (1) research potential new product offerings and clients, (2) analyze the current billing cycle and billing practices, and (3) design a customer survey project. The marketing director is responsible.

- By June 30, the three project groups will report the results of their analyses. The full business analysis team will review all recommendations.

- By July 31, develop a marketing information system to monitor client reorder patterns and customer satisfaction.

- By July 31, implement any changes in billing practices as recommended by the business analysis team.

- By July 31, make initial contact with new potential clients for the current product line. Each sales manager is responsible.

- By August 31, develop a plan for one new product offering along with an analysis of its potential customers. The business analysis team is responsible.

- By August 31, finalize a customer satisfaction survey for current clients. In addition, the company will contact those customers who did not reorder for the 1998 product year to discuss their concerns. The marketing director is responsible.

- By January, implement the customer satisfaction survey with a random sample of 20 percent of current clients who reordered for the 1998 product year. The marketing director is responsible.

- By February, implement a new product offering, advertising to current customers and to a sample of potential clients. The business analysis team is responsible.

- By March, analyze and report the results of all customer satisfaction surveys and evaluate the new product offering. The marketing director is responsible.

- Reestablish the objectives of the business analysis team for the next fiscal year. The marketing director is responsible.

VII. Evaluation and Control

A.   Performance Standards and Financial Controls

A comparison of the financial expenditures with the plan goals will be included in the project report. The following performance standards and financial controls are suggested:

- The total budget for the billing analysis, new product research, and the customer survey will be equal to 60 percent of the annual promotional budget for the coming year.

- The breakdown of the budget within the project will be a 20 percent allocation to the billing cycle study, a 30 percent allocation to the customer survey and marketing information system development, and a 50 percent allocation to new business development and new product implementation.

- Each project team is responsible for reporting all financial expenditures, including personnel salaries and direct expenses, for their segment of the project. A standardized reporting form will be developed and provided by the marketing director.

- The marketing director is responsible for adherence to the project budget and will report overages to the company president on a weekly basis. The marketing director also is responsible for any redirection of budget dollars, as required for each project of the business analysis team.
- Any new product offering will be evaluated on a quarterly basis to determine its profitability. Product development expenses will be distributed over a two-year period, by calendar quarters, and will be compared with gross income generated during the same period.

B.   Monitoring Procedures

To analyze the effectiveness of Star Software's marketing plan, it is necessary to compare its actual performance with plan objectives. To facilitate this analysis, monitoring procedures should be developed for the various activities required to bring the marketing plan to fruition. These procedures include, but are not limited to, the following:

- A project management concept will be used to evaluate the implementation of the marketing plan by establishing time requirements, human resource needs, and financial or budgetary expenditures.

- A perpetual comparison of actual and planned activities will be conducted on a monthly basis for the first year and on a quarterly basis after the initial implementation phase. The business analysis team, including the marketing director, will report their comparison of actual and planned outcomes directly to the company president.

- Each project team is responsible for determining what changes must be made in procedures, product focus, or operations as a result of the studies conducted in its area.

Glossary

Accessibility The ability to obtain the information available on the Internet. (23)

Accessory equipment Equipment used in production or office activities; does not become a part of the final physical product. (10)

Addressability A marketer's ability to identify customers before they make a purchase. Visitors to a Web site may enhance addressability by providing information about their product needs or wants before making purchases. (23)

Advertising A paid form of nonpersonal communication about an organization and/or its products that is transmitted to a target audience through a mass medium. (18)

Advertising appropriation The total amount of money that a marketer allocates for advertising for a specific time period. (18)

Advertising campaign The creation and execution of a series of advertisements to communicate with a particular target audience. (18)

Advertising platform The basic issues or selling points that an advertiser wishes to include in the advertising campaign. (18)

Advocacy advertising A form of advertising promoting a company's position on a public issue. (18)

Aesthetic modification Modification directed at changing the sensory appeal of a product by altering its taste, texture, sound, smell, or visual characteristics. (11)

Agents Functional middlemen representing buyers or sellers on a permanent basis. (15)

Aided recall test A posttest method of evaluating the effectiveness of advertising in which subjects are asked to identify advertisements they have seen recently; they are shown a list of products, brands, company names, or trademarks to jog their memory. (18)

Allowance Concession in price to achieve a desired goal; for example, industrial equipment manufacturers give trade-in allowances on used industrial equipment to enable customers to purchase new equipment. (20)

Approach The manner in which a salesperson contacts a potential customer. (19)

Arbitrary approach A method for determining the advertising appropriation in which a high-level executive in the firm states how much to spend on advertising for a certain time period. (18)

Artwork The illustration in an advertisement and the layout of the components of an advertisement. (18)

Atmospherics The physical elements in a store's design that appeal to consumers' emotions and that encourage buying. (16)

Attitude An individual's enduring evaluation, feelings, and behavioral tendencies toward an object or idea. (8)

Attitude scale An instrument that can be used to measure consumer attitudes. It usually consists of a series of adjectives, phrases, or sentences about an object; subjects are asked to indicate the intensity of their feelings toward the object by reacting to the statements in a certain way. (8)

Automatic vending The use of machines to dispense products selected by customers when money is inserted. (16)

Average fixed cost The fixed cost per unit produced; it is calculated by dividing the fixed costs by the number of units produced. (21)

Average total cost The sum of the average fixed cost and the average variable cost. (21)

Average variable cost The variable cost per unit produced; it is calculated by dividing the variable cost by the number of units produced. (21)

Bait pricing The pricing of an item in the product line low with the intention of selling a higher-priced item in the line. (21)

Balance of trade The difference in value between a nation's exports and imports. (5)

Banner ads Small, rectangular ads, static or animated, that typically appear at the top of a web page. (23)

Barter The trading of products. (20)

Base-point pricing A geographic pricing policy that includes the price at the factory, plus freight charges from the base point nearest the buyer. (20)

Benchmarking The measurement and evaluation of the quality of an organization's goods, services, or processes as compared with the best-performing companies in the industry. (22)

Benefit segmentation The division of a market according to benefits that customers want from the product. (7)

Better Business Bureau A local, nongovernmental regulatory agency, supported by local businesses, that aids in settling problems between specific business firms and customers. (3)

Bonded storage A storage service provided by many public warehouses, whereby the goods are not released until U.S. customs duties, federal or state taxes, or other fees are paid. (15)

Brand A name, term, symbol, design, or combination of these that identifies a seller's products and differentiates them from competitors' products. (12)

Brand competitors Firms that market products with similar features, benefits, and prices to the same customers. (3)

Brand equity The marketing and financial value associated with a brand's strength in the market, including actual proprietary brand assets, brand name awareness, brand loyalty, perceived brand quality, and brand associations. (12)

Brand-extension branding A type of branding in which a firm uses one of its existing brand names as part of a brand for an improved or new product that is usually in the same product category as the existing brand. (12)

Brand insistence The strongest degree of brand loyalty in which a customer prefers a specific brand so strongly that he or she will accept no substitute. (12)

Brand licensing An agreement by which a company permits another organization to use its brand on products for a licensing fee. (12)

Brand loyalty A customer's favorable attitude toward a brand and likelihood of consistent purchase. (12)

Brand manager A type of product manager responsible for a single brand. (9) (11)

Brand mark The element of a brand, such as a symbol or design, that cannot be spoken. (12)

Brand name The part of a brand that can be spoken—including letters, words, and numbers. (12)

Brand preference A degree of customer loyalty in which a customer prefers one brand to competitive offerings and will purchase the brand if it is available but will accept substitutes if it is not. (12)

Brand recognition A customer's awareness that a brand exists and view that it is a purchase alternative. (12)

Breakdown approach A general approach for measuring company sales potential based on a general economic forecast and the market sales potential derived from it; the company sales potential is based on the general economic forecast and the estimated market sales potential. (7)

Breakeven point The point at which the costs of producing a product equal the revenue made from selling the product. (21)

Brokers Functional middlemen that bring buyers and sellers together temporarily and help negotiate exchanges. (15)

Buildup approach A general approach to measuring company sales potential in which the analyst initially estimates how much the average purchaser of a product will buy in a specified time period and then multiplies that amount by the number of potential buyers; estimates are calculated by individual geographic areas. (7)

Bundle pricing Packaging two or more usually complementary products together for a single price. (21)

Business analysis An analysis providing a tentative sketch of a product's compatibility in the marketplace, including its probable profitability. (11)

Business cycle Fluctuations in the economy following a general pattern: prosperity, recession, depression, and recovery. (3)

Business products Products bought to use in a firm's operations, to sell, or to make other products. (10)

Business services Intangible products an organization uses in its operations, such as financial products or legal services. (10)

Business-to-business buying behavior *See* Organizational buying behavior.

Business-to-business markets Markets consisting of individuals, groups, or organizations that purchase specific kinds of products for resale, for direct use in producing other products, or for use in day-to-day operations; also called organizational market. (7) (9) (20)

Button ads Small ads, square or rectangular in shape, bearing a corporate or brand name or logo and usually appearing at the bottom of a Web page. (23)

Buy-back allowance A sum of money given to a reseller for each unit bought after an initial deal is over. (19)

Buying allowance A temporary price reduction to resellers for purchasing specified quantities of a product. (19)

Buying behavior The decision processes and acts of people involved in buying and using products. (8)

Buying center The group of people within an organization who make organizational purchase decisions; these peo-ple take part in the purchase decision process as users, influencers, buyers, deciders, and gatekeepers. (9)

Buying power Resources such as money, goods, and services that can be traded in an exchange situation. (3)

Captioned photograph A photograph with a brief description that explains the picture's content. (18)

Captive pricing Pricing the basic product in a product line low, but pricing related items at a higher level. (21)

Cash-and-carry wholesalers Limited-service wholesalers whose customers pay cash and furnish transportation. (15)

Cash discount A price reduction to the buyer for prompt payment or cash payment. (20)

Catalog marketing A type of marketing in which an organization provides a catalog from which customers make selections and place orders by mail or telephone. (16)

Catalog showrooms A form of warehouse showroom in which consumers shop from a catalog and buy at a warehouse where all products are stored out of buyers' reach. (16)

Category killer A large specialty store that concentrates on a major product category and competes on the basis of low prices and product availability. (16)

Causal research Research in which it is assumed that a particular variable X causes a variable Y. (6)

Causal studies Studies in which it is assumed that a particular variable X causes a variable Y.

Cause-related marketing Linking a firm's products to a particular social cause on an ongoing or short-term basis. (4)

Centralized organization An organization in which the top-level managers delegate very little authority to lower levels of the organization. (22)

Cents-off offer Sales promotion device for established products whereby buyers receive a certain amount off the regular price shown on the label or package. (19)

Chain store A retail outlet that is part of a multiple outlet organization.

Channel capacity The limit on the volume of information that a communication channel can handle effectively. (17)

Channel captain The dominant member of a marketing channel or supply chain. (14)

Channel conflict Friction between marketing channel members, often resulting from role deviance or malfunction. (14)

Channel cooperation A helping relationship among channel members that enhances the welfare and survival of all necessary channel members. (14)

Channel leadership The guidance that a channel member with one or more sources of power gives to other channel members to help achieve channel objectives. (14)

Channel of distribution *See* Marketing channel.

Channel power The ability of one channel member to influence another channel member's goal achievement. (14)

Clayton Act A law passed in 1914 that prohibits specific practices, such as price discrimination, exclusive dealer arrangements, and stock acquisitions, that may decrease competition and tend to create a monopoly. (3)

Client-based relationships Satisfied customers who repeatedly use a service over time. (13)

Client publics The direct consumers of the product of a nonbusiness organization; for example, the client public of a university is its student body. (13)

Closing The part of the selling process in which the salesperson asks the prospect to buy the product. (19)

Co-branding The use of two or more brands on one product. (12)

Codes of conduct Formalized rules and standards that describe what a company expects of its employees. (4)

Coding process The process by which a meaning is placed into a series of signs that represents ideas; also called encoding. (17)

Cognitive dissonance Doubts that may occur shortly after the purchase of a product when the buyer questions whether or not he or she made the right decision in purchasing the product. (8)

Combination compensation plan A plan by which salespeople are paid a fixed salary and a commission based on sales volume. (19)

Commercialization A phase of new-product development in which plans for full-scale manufacturing and marketing must be refined and settled and budgets for the product must be prepared. (11)

Commission merchants Agents that receive goods on consignment and negotiate sales in large markets. (15)

Communication A sharing of meaning through the transmission of information. (17)

Community A sense of group membership or feeling of belonging by individual members of a group. (23)

Community shopping centers Shopping centers that include one or two department stores and some specialty stores, as well as convenience stores, which serve several neighborhoods and draw consumers who are not able to find desired products in neighborhood shopping centers. (16)

Company sales forecast The amount of a product that a firm actually expects to sell during a specific period at a specified level of company marketing activities. (8)

Company sales potential The maximum percentage of market potential that an individual firm within an industry can expect to obtain for a specific product. (7)

Comparative advertising Advertising that compares two or more identified brands in the same general product class; the comparison is made in terms of one or more specific product characteristics. (18)

Comparison discounting Pricing a product at a specific level and comparing it to a higher price. (21)

Competition Organizations marketing products that are similar to or that can be substituted for a marketer's products in the same geographic area. (3)

Competition-based pricing A pricing method in which an organization considers costs and revenues secondary to competitors' prices. (21)

Competition-matching approach A method of ascertaining the advertising appropriation in which an advertiser tries to match a major competitor's appropriations in absolute dollars or in using the same percentage of sales for advertising. (18)

Competitive advantage The result of a company's matching a core competency to the opportunities it has discovered in the marketplace. (2)

Competitive advertising Advertising that points out a brand's uses, features, and advantages that benefit consumers but may not be available in competing brands. (18)

Component parts Finished items ready for assembly or products that need little processing before assembly and that become a part of the physical product. (10)

Concentrated targeting strategy A market segmentation strategy in which an organization directs its marketing efforts toward a single market segment through one marketing mix. (7)

Concept testing The stage in the product development process in which initial buying intentions and attitudes regarding a product are determined by presenting a written or oral description of the product to a sample of potential buyers and obtaining their responses. (11)

Consideration set A group of brands in a product category that a buyer views as alternatives for possible purchase. (8)

Consistency of quality The ability of a product to provide the same level of quality over time. (11)

Consumer buying behavior Buying behavior of those persons who purchase products for personal or household use, not for business purposes. (8)

Consumer buying decision process A five-stage purchase decision process that includes problem recognition, information search, evaluation of alternatives, purchase, and postpurchase evaluation. (8)

Consumer contests Sales promotion devices for established products based on the analytical or creative skill of contestants. (19)

Consumerism Organized efforts by individuals, groups, and organizations seeking to protect consumers' rights. (3)

Consumer jury A panel used to pretest advertisements; it consists of a number of actual or potential buyers of the product to be advertised. (18)

Consumer market Purchasers and/or household members who intend to consume or benefit from the purchased products and who do not buy products for the main purpose of making profits. (7)

Consumer movement Organized efforts by individuals, groups, and organizations seeking to protect consumers' rights. (2)

Consumer products Products purchased for the ultimate satisfaction of personal and family needs. (10)

Consumer protection legislation Laws enacted to protect consumers' safety, to enhance the amount of information available, and to warn of deceptive marketing techniques. (3)

Consumer sales promotion methods A category of sales promotion techniques that encourages or stimulates customers to patronize a specific retail store or to try and/or purchase a particular product. (19)

Consumer socialization The process through which a person acquires the knowledge and skills to function as a consumer. (8)

Consumer sweepstakes A sales promotion device for established products in which entrants submit their names for inclusion in a drawing for prizes. (19)

Containerization The consolidation of many items into a single container that is sealed at the point of origin and opened at the destination. (15)

Control   Customers' ability to regulate the information they view, as well as the rate and sequence of their exposure to that information. (23)

Contract manufacturing   The practice of hiring a foreign firm to produce a designated volume of a firm's product to specification and the final product carries the domestic firm's name. (5)

Convenience products   Relatively inexpensive, frequently purchased items for which buyers want to exert only minimal effort to obtain. (10)

Cookie   An identifying string of text stored on a Web site visitor's computer that allows the sender to track Web site usage. (23)

Cooperative advertising   An arrangement in which a manufacturer agrees to pay a certain amount of a retailer's media costs for advertising the manufacturer's products. (19)

Copy   The verbal portion of advertisements; includes headlines, subheadlines, body copy, and signature. (18)

Core competencies   Things a firm does extremely well—sometimes giving the firm a competitive advantage. (2)

Corporate culture   *See* Organizational culture.

Corporate strategy   The strategy that determines the means for utilizing resources in the areas of production, finance, research and development, human resources, and marketing to reach the organization's goals. (2)

Cost-based pricing   A pricing policy in which a firm determines price by adding a dollar amount or percentage to the cost of a product. (21)

Cost comparison indicator   Allows an advertiser to compare the costs of several vehicles within a specific medium relative to the number of persons reached by each vehicle. (18)

Cost-plus pricing   A form of cost-based pricing in which first the seller's costs are determined and then a specified dollar amount or percentage of the cost is added to the seller's cost to set the price. (21)

Count-and-recount   A sales promotion method based on the payment of a specific amount of money for each product unit moved from a reseller's warehouse in a given period of time. (19)

Coupons   New-product sales promotion technique used to reduce a product's price and prompt trial of a new or improved product, to increase sales volume quickly, to attract repeat purchasers, or to introduce new package sizes or features. (19)

Credence qualities   Qualities of services that cannot be assessed even after purchase and consumption; for example, few customers are knowledgeable enough to assess the quality of an appendix operation, even after it has been performed. (13)

Culture   The accumulation of values, knowledge, beliefs, customs, objects, and concepts that a society uses to cope with its environment and that it passes on to future generations. (8)

Cumulative discount   A quantity discount that is aggregated over a stated period of time. (20)

Customary pricing   A type of psychological pricing in which certain goods are priced primarily on the basis of tradition. (21)

Customer(s)   The purchaser(s) of the products that organizations develop, promote, distribute, and price. (1)

Customer contact   The necessary interaction between service provider and customer in order for the service to be delivered. (13)

Customer forecasting survey   The technique of asking customers what types and quantities of products they intend to buy during a specific period in order to predict the sales level for that period. (7)

Customer service audit   A specialized audit in which specific consumer service activities are analyzed and service goals and standards are compared to actual performance. (22)

Customer services   Anything a company provides in addition to the product that adds value and builds relationships with customers. (9)

Customer service standards   The level and quality of service a firm's management aims to provide for its customers. (16)

Cycle analysis   A method of predicting sales by analyzing sales figures for a period of three to five years to ascertain whether sales fluctuate in a consistent, periodic manner. (7)

Cycle time   The time it takes to complete a process. (15)

Database   A collection of information arranged for easy access and retrieval. (6)

Dealer brand   *See* Private distributor brand.

Dealer listing   An advertisement that promotes a product and identifies the names of participating retailers that sell the product. (19)

Dealer loader   A gift, often part of a display, that is given to a retailer for the purchase of a specified quantity of merchandise. (19)

Decentralized organization   An organization in which decision-making authority is delegated as far down the chain of command as possible. (22)

Decline stage   The stage in a product's life cycle in which sales fall rapidly. (10)

Decoding process   The stage in the communication process in which signs are converted into concepts and ideas. (17)

Delphi technique   A procedure in which experts create initial forecasts, submit them to the company for averaging, and have the results returned to them so that they can make individual refined forecasts. (7)

Demand-based pricing   A pricing policy based on the level of demand for the product—resulting in a higher price for the product when demand is strong and a lower price when demand is weak. (21)

Demand curve   A graph showing the relationship between price and quantity demanded. (21)

Demographic factors   Individual characteristics such as age, sex, race, ethnicity, nationality, income, family, life cycle stage, and occupation. (7)

Demonstrations   Sales promotion method manufacturers use temporarily to encourage trial use and purchase of the product or to show how the product works. (19)

Department stores   Large retail organizations characterized by wide product mixes and organized into separate departments to facilitate marketing efforts and internal management. (16)

Depression   A stage of the business cycle during which unemployment is extremely high, wages are very low, total disposable income is at a minimum, and consumers lack confidence in the economy. (3)

Depth of product mix The average number of different products offered to buyers in a firm's product lines. (10)

Derived demand A characteristic of business demand that arises because industrial demand stems from the demand for consumer products. (9)

Descriptive research Research conducted to clarify the characteristics of certain phenomena to solve a particular problem. (6)

Descriptive studies Research undertaken when marketers need to understand the characteristics of certain phenomena to solve a particular problem.

Differential pricing Charging different prices to different buyers for the same quantity of product. (21)

Differentiated targeting strategy A targeting strategy in which an organization directs its marketing efforts at two or more segments by developing a marketing mix for each segment. (7)

Digital currency A system of exchange in which consumers set up accounts at Web sites and place credits (based on a monetary amount) in those accounts. (23)

Digitalization The representation of a product, or at least some of its benefits, as digital bits of information, or using the Internet to distribute, promote, and sell product features apart from the physical item itself. (23)

Direct cost approach An approach to determine marketing costs in which cost analysis includes variable costs and traceable common costs but not nontraceable common costs. (22)

Direct marketing The use of the telephone and non-personal media to introduce products to consumers, who can then purchase them by mail, telephone, or Internet. (15)

Direct ownership A situation in which a company owns subsidiaries or other facilities overseas. (5)

Direct-response marketing A type of marketing that occurs when a retailer advertises a product and makes it available through mail or telephone orders. (16)

Direct selling The marketing of products to ultimate consumers through face-to-face sales presentations at home or in the workplace. (16)

Discount stores Self-service, general merchandise stores offering brand name and private brand products at low prices. (16)

Discretionary income Disposable income that is available for spending and saving after an individual has purchased the basic necessities of food, clothing, and shelter. (3)

Disposable income The amount of money left after payment of taxes. (3)

Distinctive competency Something that an organization does extremely well, sometimes so well that it gives the company an advantage over its competition.

Distribution The activities that make products available to customers when and where they want to purchase them. (14)

Distribution centers Large, centralized warehouses that receive goods from factories and suppliers, regroup the goods into orders, and ship the orders to customers quickly, with the focus on movement of goods rather than storage. (15)

Distribution variable The marketing mix variable in which marketing management attempts to make products available in the quantities desired, with adequate service, to a target market and to keep the total inventory, transportation, and storage costs as low as possible. (1)

Diversified growth Growth that occurs when new products are developed to be sold in new markets. (2)

Drop shippers Limited-service wholesalers that take title to products and negotiate sales but never actually take possession of products; also known as desk jobbers. (15)

Dual distribution The use of two or more channels to distribute the same product to the same target market. (14)

Dumping Selling products at unfairly low prices. (5)

Early adopters Individuals who choose new products carefully and are viewed by persons in the early majority, late majority, and laggard categories as being "the people to check with." (10)

Early majority Individuals who adopt a new product just prior to the average person; they are deliberate and cautious in trying new products. (10)

Economic forces Forces that determine the strength of a firm's competitive atmosphere and affect the impact of marketing activities because they determine the size and strength of demand for products. (3)

Economic order quantity (EOQ) The order size that minimizes the total cost of ordering and carrying inventory.

Effective buying income (EBI) Income similar to disposable income consisting of salaries, wages, dividends, interest, profits, and rents, less federal, state, and local taxes.

Electronic data interchange (EDI) A means of integrating order processing with production, inventory, accounting, and transportation. (15)

Electronic marketing (E-marketing) The strategic process of creating, distributing, promoting, and pricing products for targeted customers in the virtual environment of the Internet. (23)

Electronic commerce (E-commerce) The sharing of business information, maintenance of business relationships, and conduct of business transactions by means of telecommunications networks. (23)

Embargoes Suspensions, by a government, of trade of a particular product or within a given country. (5)

Empowerment Giving front-line employees the authority and responsibility to make marketing decisions without seeking the approval of their supervisors. (22)

Encoding *See* Coding process.

Environmental analysis The process of assessing and interpreting the information gathered through environmental scanning. (3)

Environmental scanning The process of collecting information about the forces in the marketing environment. (3)

Ethical issue An identifiable problem, situation, or opportunity requiring an individual or organization to choose from among several actions that must be evaluated as right or wrong, ethical or unethical. (4)

Evaluative criteria Objective and subjective characteristics that are important to a buyer and used to evaluate a consideration set. (8)

Every-day-low-prices (EDLP)   Pricing products low on a consistent basis. (21)

Exchange   The provision or transfer of goods, services, or ideas in return for something of value. (1)

Exchange controls   Restrictions on the amount of a particular currency that can be bought or sold. (5)

Exclusive dealing   A situation in which a manufacturer forbids an intermediary to carry products of competing manufacturers. (14)

Exclusive distribution   Using a single outlet in a fairly large geographic area to distribute a product. (14)

Executive judgment   A sales forecasting method based on the intuition of one or more executives. (7)

Experience qualities   Qualities of services that can be assessed only after purchase and consumption (taste, satisfaction, courtesy, and the like). (13)

Experiment   A research method that attempts to maintain certain variables while measuring the effects of experimental variables. (6)

Expert forecasting survey   Preparation of the sales forecast by experts, such as economists, management consultants, advertising executives, college professors, or other persons outside the firm. (7)

Exploratory research   Research conducted to gather more information about a problem or to make a tentative hypothesis more specific. (6)

Exploratory studies   Research conducted when more information is needed about a problem and the tentative hypothesis needs to be made more specific.

Exporting   The sale of products to foreign markets. (5)

Extended problem solving   A type of consumer problem solving process used when unfamiliar, expensive, or infrequently bought products are purchased. (8)

External customers   The individuals who patronize a business. (22)

External reference price   A comparison price provided by others. (20)

External search   The process of seeking information from sources other than one's memory. (8)

Facilitating agencies   Organizations engaging in activities that support channel functions, such as transportation companies and financial institutions.

Family branding   A policy of branding all of a firm's products with the same name or at least part of the name. (12)

Family packaging   A policy in an organization that all packages are to be similar or are to include one common element of the design. (12)

Feature article   A form of publicity, up to three thousand words long, that is usually prepared for a specific publication. (18)

Federal Trade Commission (FTC)   A government agency that regulates a variety of business practices and that curbs false advertising, misleading pricing, and deceptive packaging and labeling. (3)

Federal Trade Commission Act   A 1914 law that established the Federal Trade Commission, which currently regulates the greatest number of marketing practices. (3)

Feedback   The receiver's response to a decoded message. (17)

Field public warehouses   Warehouses established by a public warehouse at the owner's inventory location. (15)

Fixed costs   Costs that do not vary with changes in the number of units produced or sold; costs allocated on the basis of how money was actually spent, such as rent, salaries, office supplies, and utilities. (21) (22)

Fixed-order interval system   An approach to inventory control in which products are ordered at predetermined intervals.

F.O.B. (free-on-board) destination   Part of a price quotation used to indicate who must pay shipping charges. F.O.B. destination price means that the producer absorbs the costs of shipping the merchandise to the customer. (20)

F.O.B. (free-on-board) factory   Part of a price quotation used to indicate who must pay shipping charges. F.O.B. factory price indicates the price of the merchandise at the factory, before it is loaded onto the carrier vehicle; the buyer must pay for shipping. (20)

Focus-group interview   A research method involving observation of group interaction when members are exposed to an idea or concept. (6)

Food brokers   Intermediaries selling food and some general merchandise to merchant wholesalers, grocery chains, industrial buyers, and food processors.

Franchise store   A store owned by a franchisee who has contracted with the parent company to market specific products under conditions specified by the franchiser.

Franchising   An arrangement in which a supplier (franchiser) grants a dealer (franchisee) the right to sell products in exchange for some type of consideration. (5) (16)

Free merchandise   A sales promotion method aimed at retailers whereby free merchandise is offered to resellers that purchase a stated quantity of product. (19)

Free samples   A new-product sales promotion technique that marketers use to stimulate trial of a product, to increase sales volume in early stages of the product's life cycle, or to obtain desirable distribution. (19)

Freight absorption pricing   Pricing for a particular customer or geographical area whereby the seller absorbs all or part of the actual freight costs. (20)

Freight forwarders   Businesses that consolidate shipments from several organizations into efficient lot sizes. (15)

Full-cost approach   An approach to determining marketing costs in which cost analysis includes variable, traceable common costs, and nontraceable common costs. (22)

Full-service wholesalers   Marketing intermediaries providing the widest range of wholesaling functions. (15)

Functional discount   *See* Trade, or function, discount.

Functional middlemen   Intermediaries that negotiate purchases and expedite sales for a fee but do not take title to products. (15)

Functional modification   A change that affects a product's versatility, effectiveness, convenience, or safety, usually requiring the redesign of one or more parts of the product. (11)

GATT   *See* General Agreement on Tariffs and Trade.

General Agreement on Tariffs and Trade (GATT)   International marketing negotiations to reduce worldwide tariffs and increase trade. (5)

General-merchandise retailer A retail establishment that offers a variety of product lines that are stocked in depth. (16)

General-merchandise wholesalers Full-service wholesalers with a wide product mix but limited depth within product lines. (15)

General publics The indirect consumers of the product of a nonbusiness organization; for instance, the general public of a university includes alumni, trustees, parents of students, and other groups. (13)

Generic brands Brands that indicate only the product category (such as *aluminum foil*), not the company name and other identifying terms. (12)

Generic competitors Firms that provide very different products that solve the same problem or satisfy the same basic customer need. (3)

Geodemographic segmentation A method of market segmentation that divides people into Zip Code areas and smaller neighborhood units based on lifestyle information. (7)

Geographic pricing A form of pricing that involves reductions for transportation costs or other costs associated with the physical distance between the buyer and the seller. (20)

Globalization The development of marketing strategies as though the entire world (or regions of it) were a single entity. (5)

Good A tangible item. (10)

Government markets Markets made up of federal, state, county, and local governments, spending billions of dollars annually for goods and services to support their internal operations and to provide such products as defense, energy, and education. (9)

Green marketing Development, pricing, promotion, and distribution of products that do not harm the natural environment. (4)

Gross domestic product (GDP) Overall measure of a nation's economic standing in terms of the market value of the total output of goods and services produced in that nation for a given period of time. (5)

Growth stage The product life cycle stage in which sales rise rapidly; profits reach a peak and then start to decline. (10)

Heterogeneity A condition resulting from the fact that services are typically performed by people; there may be variation from one service to another or variation in the service provided by a single individual from day to day and from customer to customer. (13)

Heterogeneous market A market made up of individuals with diverse needs for products in a specific product class. (7)

Homogeneous market A type of market in which a large proportion of customers have similar needs for a product. (7)

Horizontal channel integration Combining institutions at the same level of operation under one management. (14)

Hypermarkets Stores that combine supermarket and discount store shopping in one location. (16)

Hypertext Highlighted text that permits visitors to a Web site to jump from one point in a Web site to other points or even to other Web sites. (23)

Hypothesis An informed guess or assumption about a certain problem or set of circumstances. (6)

Idea generation The search by businesses and other organizations for product ideas that help them achieve their objectives. (11)

Ideas Concepts, philosophies, images, or issues. (10)

Illustrations Photographs, drawings, graphs, charts, and tables used to encourage an audience to read or watch an advertisement. (18)

Importing The purchase of products from a foreign source. (5)

Import tariff Any duty levied by a nation on goods bought outside its borders and brought in. (5)

Impulse buying An unplanned buying behavior that involves a powerful, persistent urge to buy something immediately. (8)

Income The amount of money received through wages, rents, investments, pensions, and subsidy payments for a given period. (3)

Independent store A single retail outlet owned by an individual, partnership, or corporation.

Individual branding A branding policy in which each product is named differently. (12)

Industrial distributor An independent business organization that takes title to industrial products and carries inventories. (14)

Inelastic demand A type of demand in which a price increase or decrease will not significantly affect the quantity demanded. (9)

Information inputs Sensations received through sense organs. (8)

In-home (door-to-door) interview A personal interview that takes place in the respondent's home. (6)

Innovators The first consumers to adopt a new product; they enjoy trying new products and tend to be venturesome. (10)

Input-output data A type of information, sometimes used in conjunction with the Standard Industrial Classification system, that is based on the assumption that the output or sales of one industry are the input or purchases of other industries. (9)

Inseparability A condition in which the consumer frequently is directly involved in the production process because services normally are produced at the same time that they are consumed. (13)

Installations Facilities and nonportable major equipment. (10)

Institutional advertising A form of advertising promoting organizational images, ideas, and political issues. (18)

Institutional markets Markets that consist of organizations with charitable, educational, community, or other nonbusiness goals. (9)

Intangibility A characteristic of services; because services are performances, they cannot be seen, touched, tasted, or smelled, nor can they be possessed. (13)

Integrated marketing communication The coordination of promotional elements and other marketing efforts. (17)

Intended strategy   In implementing marketing strategies, the strategy that the organization decided on during the planning phase and wants to use. (22)

Intensive distribution   Using all available outlets to distribute a product. (14)

Intensive growth   The type of growth that can occur when current products and current markets have the potential for increasing sales. (2)

Interactivity   The ability to allow customers to express their needs and wants directly to the firm in response to the firm's marketing communications; marketers and customers can interact in close to or real time. (23)

Intermodal transportation   Combining and coordinating two or more modes of transportation. (15)

Internal customers   The employees who work for a company. (22)

Internal marketing   A management philosophy that coordinates internal exchanges between the organization and its employees to better achieve successful external exchanges between the organization and its customers. (22)

Internal reference price   The price in the buyer's mind that has been developed through experience with the product. (20)

Internal search   An aspect of an information search in which buyers first search their memory for information about products that might solve their problem. (8)

International marketing   Developing and performing marketing activities across national boundaries. (5)

Interstitials   "In-your-face" ads similar to traditional television commercials with video and sound. (23)

Introduction stage   The stage in a product's life cycle beginning at a product's first appearance in the marketplace, when sales are zero and profits are negative. (10)

Inventory management   Developing and maintaining adequate assortments of products to meet customers' needs. (15)

Joint demand   A characteristic of industrial demand that occurs when two or more items are used in combination to produce a product. (9)

Joint venture   A partnership between a domestic firm and a foreign firm and/or government. (5)

Just-in-time (JIT)   Making products and materials arrive just as they are needed for use in production or for resale. (15)

Keyword ads   Ads that relate to text or subject matter specified in a web search. (23)

Kinesic communication   Commonly known as body language, this type of interpersonal communication occurs in face-to-face selling situations when the salesperson and customers move their heads, eyes, arms, hands, legs, and torsos. (17)

Labeling   Providing identifying, promotional, or other information on package labels. (12)

Laggards   The last consumers to adopt a new product; they are oriented toward the past and suspicious of new products. (10)

Late majority   People who are quite skeptical of new products; they eventually adopt new products because of economic necessity or social pressure. (10)

Layout   The physical arrangement of the illustration, headline, subheadline, body copy, and signature of an advertisement. (18)

Learning   A change in an individual's behavior caused by information and experience. (8)

Legal forces   Forces that arise from the legislation and interpretation of laws; these laws, enacted by government units, restrain and control marketing decisions and activities. (3)

Level of involvement   The intensity of interest and importance placed on a product by an individual. (8)

Level of quality   The amount of quality a product possesses. (9) (11)

Licensing   An alternative to direct investment that requires a licensee to pay commissions or royalties on sales or supplies used in manufacturing. (5)

Lifestyle   An individual's pattern of living expressed through activities, interests, and opinions. (7)

Limited-line wholesalers   Full-service wholesalers that carry only a few product lines but offer an extensive assortment of products within those lines. (15)

Limited problem solving   A type of consumer problem-solving process employed when buying products occasionally and when information about an unfamiliar brand in a familiar product category is needed. (8)

Limited-service wholesalers   Intermediaries that provide some services and specialize in a few functions. (15)

Line extension   A product that is closely related to existing products in the line but meets different customer needs. (11)

Long-range plans   Plans that cover more than five years. (2)

Mail-order wholesalers   Limited-service wholesalers that sell products through catalogs. (15)

Mail surveys   Questionnaires sent to respondents who are encouraged to complete and return them. (6)

Manufacturer brands   Brands initiated by a producer; make it possible for a producer to be identified with its product at the point of purchase. (12)

Manufacturers' agents   Independent middlemen who represent more than one seller and offer complete product lines. (15)

Marginal cost (MC)   The cost associated with producing one more unit of a product. (21)

Marginal revenue (MR)   The change in total revenue that occurs after an additional unit of a product is sold. (21)

Market   A group of individuals and/or organizations that have needs for products in a product class and have the ability, willingness, and authority to purchase such products. (2) (6) (7)

Market density   The number of potential customers within a unit of land area, such as a square mile. (7)

Marketing   The process of creating, distributing, promoting, and pricing goods, services, and ideas to facilitate satisfying exchange relationships with customers in a dynamic environment. (1)

Marketing audit A systematic examination of the marketing group's objectives, strategies, organization, and performance. (22)

Marketing channel A group of individuals and organizations that directs the flow of products to customers; also called channel of distribution or distribution channel. (14)

Marketing citizenship The incorporation of economic, legal, ethical, and philanthropic concerns into marketing strategies. (4)

Marketing concept A managerial philosophy that an organization should try to satisfy customers' needs through a coordinated set of activities that also allows the organization to achieve its goals. (1)

Marketing control process A process that consists of establishing performance standards, evaluating actual performance by comparing it with established standards, and reducing the differences between desired and actual performance. (22)

Marketing cost analysis Breaking down and classifying costs to determine which are associated with specific marketing activities. (22)

Marketing decision support system (MDSS) Customized computer software that aids marketing managers in decision making. (6)

Marketing environment The competitive, economic, political, legal and regulatory, technological, and sociocultural forces that surround the customer and affect the marketing mix. (1)

Marketing ethics Principles and standards that define acceptable conduct in marketing as determined by various stakeholders. (4)

Market-growth/market-share matrix A strategy planning tool based on the philosophy that a product's market growth rate and its market share are important considerations in determining its marketing strategy. (2)

Marketing implementation The process of putting marketing strategies into action. (22)

Marketing information system (MIS) A framework for the management and structuring of information gathered regularly from sources inside and outside an organization. (6)

Marketing intermediary A middleman linking producers to other middlemen or ultimate consumers through contractual arrangements or through the purchase and resale of products. (14)

Marketing management The process of planning, organizing, implementing, and controlling marketing activities to facilitate exchanges effectively and efficiently. (1)

Marketing mix Four marketing activities—product, distribution, promotion, and pricing—that a firm can control to meet the needs of customers within its target market. (1)

Marketing objective A statement of what is to be accomplished through marketing activities. (2)

Marketing plan A written document that specifies an organization's resources, objectives, marketing strategy, and implementation and control efforts planned for use in marketing a specific product or product group. (2)

Marketing planning A systematic process of assessing marketing opportunities and resources, determining marketing objectives, defining marketing strategies, and establishing guidelines for implementation and control of the marketing program. (2)

Marketing planning cycle A circular process using feedback to coordinate and synchronize all stages of the marketing planning process. (2)

Marketing program A set of marketing strategies that are implemented and used at the same time.

Marketing research The systematic design, collection, interpretation, and reporting of information to help marketers solve specific marketing problems or take advantage of market opportunities. (6)

Marketing strategy A plan of action for analyzing a target market and developing a marketing mix to meet the needs of that market. (2)

Market manager A person responsible for the marketing activities that are necessary to serve a particular group or class of customers. (11)

Market opportunity A combination of circumstances and timing that permits an organization to take action to reach a particular target market. (2)

Marketing orientation The organizationwide generation of market intelligence pertaining to current and future customer needs, dissemination of the intelligence across departments, and organizationwide responsiveness to it. (1)

Market potential The total amount of a product for all firms in an industry that customers will purchase within a specified period at a specific level of industry-wide marketing activity. (7)

Market requirements Relate to customers' needs or desired benefits.

Market segment A group of individuals, groups, or organizations sharing one or more similar characteristics that make them have relatively similar product needs. (7)

Market segmentation The process of dividing a total market into groups of people or organizations with relatively similar product needs, to enable marketers to design a marketing mix that more precisely matches the needs of consumers in a selected segment. (7)

Market share The percentage of a market that buys a specific product from a specific comapny. (2)

Market test A stage of new-product development that involves making a product available to buyers in one or more test areas and measuring purchases and consumer responses to promotion, price, and distribution efforts. (7)

Markup pricing A pricing method where the price is derived by adding a predetermined percentage of the cost to the cost of the product. (21)

Maslow's hierarchy of needs The five levels of needs that humans seek to satisfy, from the most to least important. (8)

Materials handling Physical handling of products. (15)

Maturity stage A stage in the product life cycle in which the sales curve peaks and starts to decline as profits continue to decline. (10)

Media plan A plan that sets forth the exact media vehicles to be used for advertisements and the dates and times that the advertisements are to appear. (18)

Medium of transmission That which carries the coded message from the source to the receiver or audience; examples include ink on paper and air wave vibrations produced by vocal cords. (17)

Medium-range plans   Plans that encompass two to five years. (2)

Megacarriers   Freight transportation companies providing several methods of shipment. (15)

Memory   The ability to access databases containing individual customer profiles and past purchase histories and to use these data in real time to customize a marketing offer. (23)

Merchandise allowance   A sales promotion method aimed at retailers; it consists of a manufacturer's agreement to pay resellers certain amounts of money for providing special promotional efforts, such as setting up and maintaining a display. (19)

Merchant wholesalers   Independently owned businesses that take title to goods, assume ownership risks, and buy and resell products to organizational or retail customers. (15)

Micromarketing   An approach to market segmentation in which organizations focus precise marketing efforts on very small geographic markets. (7)

Missionary salesperson   A support salesperson, usually employed by a manufacturer, who assists the producer's customers in selling to their own customers. (19)

Mission statement   A long-term view, or vision, of what the organization wants to become. (2)

Modified rebuy purchase   A type of organizational purchase in which a new-task purchase is changed the second or third time, or the requirements associated with a straight-rebuy purchase are modified. (9)

Money refunds   Sales promotion techniques in which the producer mails a consumer a specific amount of money when proof of purchase is established. (19)

Monopolistic competition   A competitive structure in which a firm with many potential competitors attempts to develop a marketing strategy to differentiate its product. (3)

Monopoly   A competitive structure in which a firm offers a product that has no close substitutes, making the organization the sole source of supply. (3)

Motive   An internal energizing force that directs a person's behavior toward satisfying needs or achieving goals. (8)

MRO supplies   An alternative term for supplies; supplies can be divided into Maintenance, Repair, and Operating (or overhaul) items. (9)

Multinational enterprise   A firm with operations or subsidiaries in many countries. (5)

Multiple sourcing   An organization's decision to use several suppliers. (9)

Multiple-unit pricing   Packaging two or more of the same products together and for sale at a single price. (21)

NAFTA   *See* North American Free Trade Agreement.

NAICS   *See* North American Industrial Classification System.

National Advertising Review Board (NARB)   A self-regulatory unit that considers cases in which an advertiser challenges issues raised by the National Advertising Division (an arm of the Council of Better Business Bureaus) about an advertisement. (3)

Negotiated pricing   Establishing a final price through bargaining between the seller and the customer. (21)

Neighborhood shopping centers   Shopping centers that usually consist of several small convenience and specialty stores and serve consumers living within ten minutes' driving time from the center. (16)

New product   Any product that a given firm has not marketed previously. (11)

New-product development process   A process consisting of seven phases: idea generation, screening, concept testing, business analysis, product development, test-marketing, and commercialization. (11)

News release   A form of publicity that is usually a single page of typewritten copy containing fewer than three hundred words. (18)

New-task purchase   A type of orgainzational purchase in which an organization is making an initial purchase of an item to be used to perform a new job or to solve a new problem. (9)

Noise   Anything that reduces the clarity and accuracy of communication. (17)

Noncumulative discount   A one-time price reduction based on the number of units purchased, the size of the order, or the product combination purchased. (20)

Nonprice competition   A policy in which a seller elects not to focus on price and instead emphasizes distinctive product features, service, product quality, promotion, packaging, or other factors to distinguish its product from competing brands. (20)

Nonprobability sampling   A sampling technique in which there is no way to calculate the likelihood that a specific element of the population being studied will be chosen. (6)

Nonprofit marketing   Marketing activities conducted by individuals and organizations to achieve some goal other than ordinary business goals such as profit, market share, or return on investment. (13)

Nonstore retailing   The selling of products outside the confines of a retail facility. (16)

Nontraceable common costs   Costs that cannot be assigned to any specific function according to any logical criteria and thus are assignable only on an arbitrary basis. (22)

North American Free Trade Agreement (NAFTA)   An alliance that merges Canada, the United States, and Mexico into a single market. (5)

North American Industrial Classification System (NAICS)   A system for classifying industries that will generate comparable statistics among the United States, Canada, and Mexico. (9)

Objective-and-task approach   An approach to determining the advertising appropriation: marketers determine the objectives a campaign is to achieve and then ascertain the tasks required to accomplish those objectives; the costs of all tasks are added to ascertain the total appropriation. (18)

Observation methods   Research methods in which researchers record respondents' overt behavior, taking note of physical conditions and events. (6)

Odd-even pricing   A type of psychological pricing that assumes that more of a product will be sold at $99.99 than at $100.00, indicating that an odd price is more appealing than an even price to customers. (21)

Off-peak demand   The time when consumers do not want to use the service. (13)

Off-price retailers   Stores that buy manufacturers' seconds, overruns, returns, and off-season merchandise for resale to consumers at deep discounts. (16)

Oligopoly A competitive structure in which a few sellers control the supply of a large proportion of a product. (3)

Online retailing Makes products available between buyers and sellers through computer connections. (16)

Online survey A research method in which respondents answer a questionnaire via E-mail or on a Web site. (6)

On-site computer interview A variation of the shopping mall intercept interview in which respondents complete a self-administered questionnaire displayed on a computer monitor. (6)

Opinion leader The member of a reference group who provides information about a specific sphere of interest to reference group participants seeking information. (8)

Opportunities Favorable conditions in the environment that could produce rewards for the organization if acted upon properly. (2)

Opportunity cost The value of the benefit that is given up by selecting one alternative rather than another. (13)

Order getter A type of salesperson who increases the firm's sales by selling to new customers and by increasing sales to present customers. (19)

Order lead time The average time lapse between placing an order and receiving it. (15)

Order processing The receipt and transmission of sales order information in the physical distribution process. (15)

Order taker A type of salesperson who primarily seeks repeat sales. (19)

Organizational buying behavior The purchase behavior of producers, government units, institutions, and resellers; also called industrial buying behavior. (9)

Organizational, or **corporate, culture** A set of values, beliefs, goals, norms, and rituals that members of an organization share. (4)

Organizational, or **industrial, market** Individuals or groups that purchase a specific kind of product for one of three purposes: resale, direct use in producing other products, or use in general daily operations. (7) (9)

Outsourcing The contracting of physical distribution tasks to third parties who do not have managerial authority within the marketing channel. (15)

Patronage motives Motives that influence where a person purchases products on a regular basis. (8)

Peak demand A point in time when consumers want to maximize the use of service activities. (13)

Penetration pricing Pricing below the prices of competing brands; designed to penetrate a market and gain a significant market share quickly. (21)

Percent-of-sales approach A method for establishing the advertising appropriation whereby marketers simply multiply a firm's past sales, forecasted sales, or a combination of the two by a standard percentage based on both what the firm traditionally has spent on advertising and what the industry average is. (18)

Perception The process by which an individual selects, organizes, and interprets information inputs to create a meaningful picture of the world. (8)

Performance standard An expected level of performance against which actual performance can be compared. (22)

Periodic discounting The temporary lowering of prices on a patterned or systematic basis. (21)

Perishability A condition where, because of simultaneous production and consumption, unused capacity to produce services in one time period cannot be stockpiled or inventoried for future time periods. (13)

Personal interview survey A face-to-face interview that allows in-depth interviewing, probing, follow-up questions, or psychological tests. (6)

Personality A set of internal traits and distinctive behavioral tendencies that result in consistent patterns of behavior in certain situations. (8)

Personal selling Personal, paid communication that attempts to inform customers and persuade them to purchase products in an exchange situation. (19)

Physical distribution The activities used to move products from producers to consumers and other end users. (15)

Pioneer advertising A type of advertising that stimulates demand for a product by informing people about the product's features, uses, and benefits. (18)

Pioneer promotion A type of promotion that informs potential customers about a product, what it is, what it does, how it can be used, and where it can be purchased. (17)

Point-of-purchase (P-O-P) materials A sales promotion method that uses such items as outside signs, window displays, and display racks to attract attention, to inform customers, and to encourage retailers to carry particular products. (19)

Political forces Forces that strongly influence the economic and political stability of a country not only through decisions that affect domestic matters but through their authority to negotiate trade agreements and to determine foreign policy. (3)

Population All elements, units, or individuals that are of interest to researchers for a specific study. (6)

Portal A multiservice Web site that serves as a gateway to other web sites. (23)

Portfolio retailing A situation in which one company operates multiple chains of stores.

Posttest An evaluation of advertising effectiveness after the campaign. (18)

Premium, or **push, money** Extra compensation to salespeople for pushing a line of goods. (19)

Premium pricing Pricing higher-quality or more versatile products higher than other models in the product line. (21)

Premiums Items that are offered free or at a minimum cost as a bonus for purchasing a product. (19)

Press conference A meeting used to announce major news events. (18)

Prestige pricing Setting prices at a high level to facilitate a prestige or quality image. (21)

Prestige-sensitive A characteristic of buyers who purchase products that signify prominence and status. (20)

Pretest Evaluation of an advertisement before it is actually used. (18)

Price The value that is exchanged for products in a marketing transaction. (20)

Price competition A policy whereby a marketer emphasizes price as an issue and matches or beats the prices of competitors. (20)

Price-conscious   A characteristic of buyers who strive to pay low prices. (20)

Price differentiation   A demand-based pricing method whereby a firm uses more than one price in the marketing of a specific product; differentiation of prices can be based on several dimensions, such as type of customers, type of distribution used, or the time of the purchase. (21)

Price discrimination   A policy of charging some buyers lower prices than other buyers, which gives those paying less a competitive advantage. (20)

Price elasticity of demand   A measure of the sensitivity of demand to changes in price. (21)

Price leaders   Products sold at less than cost to increase sales of regular merchandise. (21)

Price lining   A form of psychological pricing in which an organization sets a limited number of prices for selected lines of products. (21)

Price skimming   Charging the highest possible price that buyers who most desire the product will pay. (21)

Price variable   A marketing mix variable that relates to decisions and actions associated with establishing pricing objectives and policies and determining product prices. (1)

Pricing objectives   Overall goals that describe the role of price in an organization's long-range plans. (20)

Primary data   Data observed and recorded or collected directly from respondents. (6)

Primary demand   Demand for a product category rather than for a specific brand of product. (17)

Private brand   *See* Private distributor brand.

Private distributor brand   A brand that is initiated and owned by a reseller; also called private brand, store brand, or dealer brand. (12)

Private warehouses   Facilities operated by companies for storing and shipping their own products. (16)

Probability sampling   A sampling technique in which every element in the population being studied has a known chance of being selected for study. (6)

Problem definition   The first step in the research process toward finding a solution or launching a research study; the researcher thinks about the best ways to discover the nature and boundaries of a problem or opportunity. (6)

Process materials   Materials used directly in the production of other products; unlike component parts, they are not readily identifiable. (10)

Procompetitive legislation   Laws enacted to preserve competition. (3)

Producer markets   Markets consisting of individuals and business organizations that purchase products for the purpose of making a profit by using them in their operations. (9)

Product   A good, service, and/or idea received in an exchange. It is a complexity of tangible and intangible attributes, including functional, social, and psychological utilities or benefits. (1) (10)

Product adoption process   The five-stage process of buyer acceptance of a product: awareness, interest, evaluation, trial, and adoption. (10)

Product advertising   Advertising that promotes the uses, features, and benefits of products. (18)

Product competitors   Firms that compete in the same product class but their products have different features, benefits, and prices. (3)

Product deletion   The process of eliminating a product from the product mix when it no longer satisfies a sufficient number of customers. (11)

Product design   How a product is conceived, planned, and produced. (11)

Product development   The phase in which the firm finds out if producing the product is feasible and cost-effective. (11)

Product differentiation   The process of creating and designing products so that consumers perceive them as different from competing products. (11)

Product features   Specific design characteristics allowing a product to perform certain tasks. (11)

Product item   A specific version of a product that can be designated as a distinct offering among an organization's products. (10)

Product life cycle   The course of product development, consisting of four major stages: introduction, growth, maturity, and decline. As a product moves through these stages, the strategies relating to competition, pricing, promotion, distribution, and market information must be evaluated and possibly changed. (10)

Product line   A group of closely related products that are considered a unit because of marketing, technical, or end-use considerations. (10)

Product-line pricing   The establishing and adjusting prices of multiple products within a product line. (21)

Product manager   A person who holds a staff position in a multiproduct company and is responsible for a product, a product line, or several distinct products that are considered an interrelated group. (11)

Product mix   The composite of products that an organization makes available to customers. (10)

Product mix depth   *See* Depth (of product mix).

Product mix width   *See* Width (of product mix).

Product modification   The changing of one or more of a product's characteristics. (11)

Product-portfolio analysis   A strategic planning approach based on the philosophy that a product's market growth rate and its relative market share are important considerations in determining its marketing strategy.

Product positioning   The decisions and activities that are directed toward trying to create and maintain the firm's intended product concept in customers' minds. (11)

Product variable   That aspect of the marketing mix dealing with researching customers' product wants and planning the product to achieve the desired product characteristics. (1)

Professional pricing   Pricing used by persons who have great skills or experience in a particular field or activity, indicating that a price should not relate directly to the time and involvement in a specific case; rather, a standard fee is charged regardless of the problems involved in performing the job. (21)

Promotion   The communication with individuals, groups, or organizations to directly or indirectly facilitate exchanges by influencing audience members to accept an organization's products. (17)

Promotion mix   The specific combination of promotional methods that an organization uses for a particular product. (17)

Promotion variable   A marketing mix variable used to inform individuals or groups about an organization and its products. (1)

Prospecting   Developing a list of potential customers for personal selling purposes. (19)

Prosperity   A stage of the business cycle characterized by low unemployment and relatively high total income, which together cause buying power to be high (provided the inflation rate stays low). (3)

Proxemic communication   A subtle form of interpersonal communication used in face-to-face interactions when either party varies the physical distance that separates them. (17)

Psychological influences   Factors that operate within individuals to partially determine their general behavior and thus influence their behavior as consumers. (8)

Psychological pricing   Pricing that attempts to influence a customer's perception of price to make a product's price more attractive. (21)

Publicity   Nonpersonal communication in news story form, regarding an organization and/or its products, that is transmitted through a mass medium at no charge. (18)

Public relations   A broad set of communication activities used to create and maintain favorable relations between the organization and its publics, such as customers, employees, stockholders, government officials, and society in general. (18)

Public warehouses   Organizations that rent storage and related physical distribution facilities. (16)

Pull policy   Promotion of a product directly to consumers with the intention of developing strong consumer demand. (17)

Purchasing power   *See* Buying power.

Pure competition   A competitive structure in which there is a large number of sellers, not one of which could significantly influence price or supply. (3)

Push policy   The promotion of a product only to the next institution down the marketing channel. (17)

Quality   The overall characteristics of a product that allow it to perform as expected in satisfying customer needs. (11)

Quality modification   A change that relates to a product's dependability and durability and is generally executed by alterations in the materials or production process used. (11)

Quantity discount   Deductions from list price that reflect the economies of purchasing in large quantities. (20)

Quota   A limit set on the amount of goods an importing company will accept for certain product categories in a specific period of time. (5)

Quota sampling   Nonprobability sampling in which the final choice of respondents is left to the interviewers. (6)

Rack jobbers   Full service specialty-line wholesalers that own and maintain display racks in stores. (15)

Random discounting   Temporarily reducing a regular-priced product using an unsystematic time schedule. (21)

Random factor analysis   A method of predicting sales whereby an attempt is made to attribute erratic sales variations to random, nonrecurrent events, such as a regional power failure or a natural disaster. (7)

Random sampling   A type of sampling in which all the units in a population have an equal chance of appearing in the sample. (6)

Raw materials   Basic materials that become part of a physical product; obtained from mines, farms, forests, oceans, and recycled solid wastes. (10)

Realized strategy   In implementing marketing strategies, the strategy that actually takes place. (22)

Rebates   Sales promotion techniques in which the producer mails a consumer a specified amount of money for making a single purchase. (19)

Receiver   The individual, group, or organization that decodes a coded message. (17)

Recession   A stage of the business cycle during which unemployment rises and total buying power declines, stifling both consumer and business spending. (3)

Reciprocity   A practice unique to organizational sales in which two organizations agree to buy from each other. (9)

Recognition test   A posttest method of evaluating the effectiveness of advertising; individual respondents are shown the actual advertisement and asked whether they recognize it. (18)

Recovery   A stage of the business cycle during which the economy moves from depression or recession toward prosperity. (3)

Recruiting   A process by which the sales manager develops a list of applicants for sales positions. (19)

Reference group   Any group that positively or negatively affects a person's values, attitudes, or behavior. (8)

Reference pricing   The pricing of a product at a moderate level and positioning it next to a more expensive model or brand. (21)

Regional issues   Versions of a magazine that differ across geographic regions and in which a publisher can vary the advertisements and editorial content. (18)

Regional shopping centers   A type of shopping center that usually has the largest department stores, the widest product mix, and the deepest product lines of all shopping centers in an area. (16)

Regression analysis   A method of predicting sales whereby a forecaster attempts to find a relationship between past sales and one or more independent variables, such as population or income. (7)

Regulatory forces   Forces arising from regulatory units at all levels of government; these units create and enforce numerous regulations that affect marketing decisions. (3)

Reinforcement advertising   An advertisement attempting to assure current users that they have made the right choice and telling them how to get the most satisfaction from the product. (18)

Relationship marketing   Establishing long-term, mutually satisfying buyer–seller relationships. (1)

Reliability   A condition existing when use of a research technique produces almost identical results in successive repeated trials. (6)

Reminder advertising Advertising used to remind consumers that an established brand is still around and that it has certain uses, characteristics, and benefits. (18)

Reorder point The inventory level that signals the need to place a new order. (15)

Research design An overall plan for obtaining the information needed to address a research problem or issue. (6)

Reseller markets Markets consisting of intermediaries, such as wholesalers and retailers, that buy finished goods for profit. (9)

Retailer An organization that purchases products for the purpose of reselling them to ultimate consumers. (16)

Retailing Transactions in which the buyer intends to consume the product through personal, family, or household use. (16)

Retail positioning Identifying an unserved or underserved market niche, or segment, and serving it through a strategy that distinguishes the retailer from others in the minds of persons in that segment. (16)

Robinson-Patman Act A 1936 law prohibiting price discrimination that decreases competition and also prohibiting provision of services or facilities to purchasers on terms not offered equally to all purchasers. (3)

Role A set of actions and activities that a person in a particular position is supposed to perform, based on the expectations of both the individual and the persons surrounding the individual. (8)

Routinized response behavior A type of consumer problem solving process used when buying frequently purchased, low-cost items that require very little search and decision effort. (8)

Safety stock The amount of extra stock a firm keeps to guard against stockouts. (15)

Sales analysis The use of sales figures to evaluate a firm's current performance. (22)

Sales branches Manufacturer-owned middlemen selling products and providing support services to the manufacturer's sales force. (15)

Sales contest A sales promotion method used to motivate distributors, retailers, and sales personnel through the recognition of outstanding achievements. (19)

Sales-force forecasting survey Estimation by members of a firm's sales force of the anticipated sales in their territories for a specified period. (7)

Sales forecast The amount of a product a company expects to sell during a specific period at a specified level of marketing activities. (7)

Sales offices Manufacturer-owned operations that provide services normally associated with agents. (15)

Sales promotion An activity and/or material that acts as a direct inducement to resellers, salespersons, or consumers; it offers added value or incentive to buy or sell the product. (19)

Sample A limited number of units choosen to represent the characteristics of a total population. (6)

Sampling The process of selecting representative units from a total population. (6)

Scan-back allowance Reward given by manufacturers to retailers based on the number of pieces scanned. (19)

Scrambled merchandising The addition of unrelated products and product lines to an existing product mix, particularly fast-moving items that can be sold in large volume. (16)

Screening A stage in the product development process in which the ideas that do not match organizational objectives are rejected and those with the greatest potential are selected for further development. (11)

Search qualities Tangible attributes that can be viewed prior to purchase. (13)

Seasonal analysis A method of predicting sales whereby an analyst studies daily, weekly, or monthly sales figures to evaluate the degree to which seasonal factors, such as climate and holiday activities, influence sales. (7)

Seasonal discount A price reduction that sellers give buyers who purchase goods or services out of season; these discounts allow the seller to maintain steadier production during the year. (20)

Secondary data Data compiled inside or outside the organization for some purpose other than the current investigation. (6)

Secondary-market pricing Setting a price, for use in another market, that is different from the price charged in the primary market. (21)

Segmentation variables Dimensions or characteristics of individuals, groups, or organizations that are used to divide a market into segments. (7)

Selective demand Demand for a specific brand. (17)

Selective distortion The changing or twisting of currently received information that occurs when a person receives information inconsistent with his or her feelings or beliefs. (8)

Selective distribution Using only some available outlets to distribute a product. (14)

Selective exposure The process of selecting some inputs to be exposed to our awareness while ignoring many others. (8)

Selective retention Remembering information inputs that support personal feelings and beliefs and forgetting inputs that do not. (8)

Self-concept One's own perception or view of oneself. (8)

Selling agents Middlemen marketing a whole product line or a manufacturer's entire output. (15)

Service An intangible result of the application of human and mechanical efforts to people or objects. (10) (13)

Service heterogeneity *See* Heterogeneity.

Service inseparability *See* Inseparability.

Service intangibility *See* Intangibility.

Service perishability *See* Perishability.

Service quality Customers' perceptions of how well a service meets or exceeds their expectations. (13)

Sherman Antitrust Act Legislation passed in 1890 to prevent businesses from restraining trade and monopolizing markets. (3)

Shopping mall intercept interviews A research method that involves interviewing a percentage of persons passing by "intercept" points in a mall. (6)

Shopping products Items for which buyers are willing to put forth considerable effort in planning and making the purchase. (10)

Short-range plans Plans that cover a period of one year or less. (2)

Significant others Superiors, peers, and subordinates in an organization who influence the ethical decision-making process.

Single-source data Information provided by a single firm on household demographics, purchases, television viewing behavior, and responses to promotions like coupons and free samples. (6)

Situational influences Influences resulting from circumstances, time, and location that affect the consumer buying decision process. (8)

Social class An open aggregate of people with similar social ranking. (8)

Social influences The forces that other people exert on one's buying behavior. (8)

Social responsibility An organization's obligation to maximize its positive impact and minimize its negative impact on society. (4)

Sociocultural forces The influences in a society and its culture(s) that change people's attitudes, beliefs, norms, customs, and lifestyles. (3)

Socioeconomic factors *See* Demographic factors.

Sole sourcing An organization's decision to use only one supplier. (9)

Source A person, group, or organization with a meaning that it intends and attempts to share with a receiver or an audience. (17)

Spam Unsolicited commercial E-mail. (23)

Special-event pricing Advertised sales or price cutting to increase revenue or lower costs. (21)

Specialty-line wholesalers Full-service wholesalers that carry only a single product line or a few items within a product line. (15)

Specialty products Items that possess one or more unique characteristics that a significant group of buyers is willing to expend considerable purchasing efforts to obtain. (10)

Sponsorship ads Ads that integrate companies' brands and products with the editorial content of Web sites. (23)

Standard Industrial Classification (SIC) System A system developed by the federal government for classifying business organizations, based on what the firm primarily produces; also classifies selected economic characteristics of commercial, financial, and service organizations; uses code numbers to classify firms in different industries. (9)

Statistical interpretation An interpretation that focuses on what is typical or what deviates from the average, and so indicates how widely respondents vary and how they are distributed in relation to the variable being measured. (6)

Stockout A shortage of a product resulting from carrying too few products in inventory. (15)

Store brand *See* Private distributor brand.

Storyboard A blueprint used by technical personnel to produce a television commercial; combines the copy with the visual material to show the sequence of major scenes in the commercial. (18)

Straight commission compensation plan A plan according to which a salesperson's compensation is determined solely by the amount of his or her sales for a given time period. (19)

Straight rebuy purchase A type of organizational purchase in which a buyer purchases the same products routinely under approximately the same terms of sale. (9)

Straight salary compensation plan A plan according to which salespeople are paid a specified amount per time period. (19)

Strategic alliances Partnerships formed to create competitive advantage on a worldwide basis. (5)

Strategic business unit (SBU) A division, product line, or other profit center within a parent company that sells a distinct set of products and/or services to an identifiable group of customers and competes against a well-defined set of competitors. (2)

Strategic channel alliance A marketing channel that distributes the products of one organization through the marketing channels of another organization. (14)

Strategic market plan An outline of the methods and resources required to achieve an organization's goals within a specific target market.

Strategic market planning A process that yields a marketing strategy that is the framework for a marketing plan.

Strategic planning The process of establishing an organizational mission and goals, corporate strategy, marketing objectives, marketing strategy, and a marketing plan. (2)

Strategic window(s) Temporary period of optimum fit between the key requirements of a market and the particular capabilities of a firm competing in that market. (2)

Stratified sampling A type of sampling in which the population of interest is divided into groups according to a common characteristic or attribute; then a probability sample is conducted within each group. (6)

Strengths Competitive advantages or core competencies that give the firm an advantage in meeting the needs of its target markets. (2)

Styling The physical appearance of the product. (11)

Subculture A group of individuals who have similar values and behavior patterns within the group and differ from people in other groups; usually based on geographic regions or human characteristics, such as age or ethnic background. (8)

Suboptimization A situation in which managers or individual distribution functions take cost-reducing actions that increase the costs of other distribution functions.

Supermarkets Large, self-service stores that carry complete lines of food products, and some nonfood products. (16)

Superstores Giant retail outlets that carry food and nonfood products found in supermarkets, as well as most routinely purchased consumer products. (16)

Supply chain management Long-term partnerships among marketing channel members working together to reduce inefficiencies, costs, and redundancies in order to satisfy customers. (14)

Support personnel Members of the sales staff who facilitate selling but usually are not involved only with making sales. (19)

Survey methods Data-gathering methods that include interviews by mail, telephone, E-mail, and personal interviews. (6)

Sustainable competitive advantage An advantage that cannot be copied by the competition. (2)

SWOT analysis An assessment of an organization's strengths, weaknesses, opportunities, and threats. (2)

Tactile communication   Interpersonal communication through touching. (17)

Target audience   The group of people at which advertisements are aimed. (18)

Target market   A specific group of customers on whose needs and wants a company focuses its marketing efforts. (1)

Target public   A group of people who have an interest in or a concern about an organization, a product, or a social cause. (13)

Technical salespersons   Support salespersons who direct efforts toward the organization's current customers by providing technical assistance in system design, product application, product characteristics, or installation. (19)

Technology   The application of knowledge and tools to solve problems and perform tasks more efficiently. (3)

Technology assessment   A procedure for anticipating the effects of new products and processes on a firm's operation, other business organizations, and society. (3)

Telemarketing   The performance of marketing-related activities by telephone. (16)

Telephone surveys   The soliciting of respondents' answers to a questionnaire over the telephone, with the answers being written down by the interviewer. (6)

Television home shopping   A form of selling in which products are presented to television viewers who buy products by calling a toll-free number and pay with credit cards. (16)

Test marketing   A limited introduction of a product in areas chosen to represent the intended market to determine probable buyers' reactions to various parts of a marketing mix. (11)

Threats   Conditions or barriers that may prevent the firm from reaching its objectives. (2)

Time series analysis   A forecasting method that uses the firm's historical sales data to discover patterns in the firm's sales volume over time. (7)

Total budget competitors   Firms that compete for the limited financial resources of the same customers. (3)

Total cost   The sum of average fixed and average variable costs times the quantity produced. (21)

Total quality management (TQM)   A philosophy that uniform commitment to quality in all areas of the organization will promote a culture that meets customers' perceptions of quality. (22)

Traceable common costs   Costs that can be allocated indirectly, using one or several criteria, to the functions that they support. (22)

Trade, or **functional, discount**   A reduction off the list price a producer gives to an intermediary for performing certain functions. (20)

Trademark   A legal designation indicating that the owner has exclusive use of a brand or part of a brand and that others are prohibited by law from using it. (12)

Trade marts   Facilities that firms rent to exhibit products year-round.

Trade name   The legal name of an organization rather than the name of a specific product. (12)

Trade salesperson   A type of salesperson not strictly classified as support personnel because he or she takes orders as well. (19)

Trade sales promotion methods   A category of sales promotion techniques that stimulate wholesalers and retailers to carry a producer's products and to market these products more aggressively. (19)

Trade shows   Industry exhibitions offering both selling and nonselling benefits.

Trading company   A company that links buyers and sellers in different countries but is not involved in manufacturing or owning assets related to manufacturing. (5)

Traditional specialty retailers   Stores that carry a narrow product mix with deep product lines. (16)

Transfer pricing   The type of pricing used when one unit in a company sells a product to another unit; the price is determined by one of the following methods: actual full cost, standard full cost, cost plus investment, or market-based cost. (20)

Transportation   Moving a product from where it is made to where it is purchased and used, thus adding time and place utility to the product. (15)

Transportation modes   The means of moving goods from one location to another. (15)

Trend analysis   An analysis that focuses on aggregate sales data, such as the company's annual sales figures, over a period of many years to determine whether annual sales are generally rising, falling, or staying about the same. (7)

Truck wholesalers   Limited-service wholesalers that transport products directly to customers for inspection and selection; also known as truck jobbers or wagon jobbers. (15)

Tying agreement   A practice requiring a channel member to buy other products from a supplier besides the one it wants. (14)

Unaided recall test   A posttest method of evaluating the effectiveness of advertising; subjects are asked to identify advertisements that they have seen recently but are not shown any clues to help them remember. (18)

Undifferentiated targeting strategy   A targeting strategy in which an organization defines an entire market for a particular product as its target market and designs a single marketing mix and directs it at that market. (7)

Uniform geographic pricing   A type of pricing, sometimes called "postage-stamp price," that results in fixed average transportation; used to avoid the problems involved in charging different prices to each customer. (20)

Uniform Resource Locator (URL)   A Web site address. (23)

Unit loading   Grouping one or more boxes on a pallet or skid. (15)

Universal product code (UPC)   A series of thick and thin lines that can be read by an electronic scanner to identify the product and provide inventory and pricing information. (12)

Unsought products   Products purchased because of a sudden need that must be solved (e.g., emergency automobile repairs), products of which customers are unaware, and products that people do not necessarily think of purchasing. (10)

Usage rate   The rate at which a product's inventory is used or sold during a specific time period. (16)

Validity   A condition existing when a research method measures what it is supposed to measure, not something else. (6)

Value   The customer's subjective assessment of benefits relative to costs in determining the worth of a product. (1)

Value analysis   An evaluation of each component of a potential purchase, including quality, design, or materials, to acquire the most cost-effective product. (9)

Value conscious   Concern about price and quality aspects of a product. (20)

Variable costs   Costs directly attributable to production and selling volume; costs that vary directly with changes in the number of units produced or sold. (21) (22)

Vending   *See* Automatic vending.

Vendor analysis   A formal, systematic evaluation of current and potential vendors. (9)

Venture team   An organizational unit established to create entirely new products that may be aimed at new markets. (11)

Vertical channel integration   Combining two or more stages of the marketing channel under one management. (14)

Vertical marketing system (VMS)   A marketing channel in which channel activities are coordinated or managed by a single channel member to achieve efficient, low-cost distribution aimed at satisfying target market customers. (14)

Warehouse clubs   Large-scale, members-only establishments that combine features of cash-and-carry wholesaling with discount retailing. (16)

Warehouse showrooms   Retail facilities in large, low-cost buildings with large on-premises inventories and minimal services. (16)

Warehousing   Designing and operating facilities for storing and moving goods. (15)

Warranty   Document that specifies what the producer will do if the product malfunctions. (10)

Weaknesses   Any limitations that a company might face in developing or implementing a marketing strategy. (2)

Wealth   The accumulation of past income, natural resources, and financial resources. (3)

Wheeler-Lea Act   Legislation enacted in 1938 to outlaw unfair and deceptive acts or practices, regardless of whether they injure competition. (3)

Wheel of retailing   A hypothesis that holds that new types of retailers usually enter the market as low-status, low-margin, low-price operators but eventually evolve into high-cost, high-price merchants. (16)

Wholesaler   An individual or organization that facilitates and expedites wholesale transactions. (15)

Wholesaling   All transactions in which products are bought for resale, for making other products, or for general business use. (15)

Width of product mix   The number of product lines a company offers. (10)

Willingness to spend   An inclination to buy because of expected satisfaction from a product as well as the ability to buy. (3)

World Trade Organization (WTO)   An entity that promotes free trade among member nations by eliminating trade barriers and educating individuals, companies, and governments about trade rules around the world. (5)

Zone pricing   Regional prices that vary for major geographic zones, as the transportation costs increase. (20)

Box Sources

Page 14: William C. Symonds, "Duracell's Bunny Buster?" *Business Week,* Mar. 2, 1998, p. 42; "Why Use Duracell Ultra in High-tech Devices," Duracell Web site, www.duracell.com/ultra/why.html, accessed on Dec. 7, 1998. *Page 17:* "About the Museum," Florida International Museum Web site, www.floridamuseum.org/abou-tus.html, accessed on Dec. 7, 1998; "Exhibition Design," Florida International Museum Web site, www.floridamuseum.org/exhibi-tion_design.html, accessed on Dec. 7, 1998; and Brent Swager, "Raising the Titanic," *Marketing Tools,* Apr. 1998, www.demograph-ics.com/publications/mt98_mt/9804_mt/mt980419.htm. *Page 36:* Michelle Wirth Fellman, "Ky.-Based Public Radio Network to Target High-Income Listeners," *Marketing News,* Apr. 13, 1998, p. 9; and "What on Earth Is World Radio?" www.worldradio.org/home.html, Jan. 7, 1999. *Page 39:* "About Gibson," www.gibsongreetings.com-stage/about.cfm, Jan. 6, 1998; Maricris G. Briones, "Gibson Goes from Greeting Cards to Gabbing Beanbags," *Marketing News,* Mar. 2, 1998, p. 10; "Corporate America Gets Silly," press release, Nov. 1998; www.gibsongreetings.com/1998/wirthlin.html. "Gibson Greetings, Inc.," Company Briefing Book, *Wall Street Journal,* Interactive Edition, http://interactive.wsj.com, Jan. 5, 1999; and "Gibson Greetings Launches *Star Trek*™ Even Further into Cyberpace via E-Greetings Network," press release, www.gib-songreetings.com/1998/kingofhill.html, Dec. 1998. *Page 59:* Heidi Dawley, with William Echikson, "Cracks in the Diamond Trade," *Business Week,* Mar. 2, 1998, p. 106; and "Welcome to the De Beers Canada Corporation Web Site," www.debeers.ca, Jan. 12, 1999. *Page 70:* Company Briefing Book, *Wall Street Journal,* Interactive Edition, http://interactive.wsj.com, Jan. 11, 1999; "Company Profile and History," www.andreaelectronics.com/corp.htm, Jan. 11, 1999; and Nikhil Hutheesing, "The Little Company That Wouldn't Die," *Forbes,* Apr. 20, 1998, pp. 226, 228. *Page 83:* Adapted from a case prepared by Carol A. Rustad-LaCasse and Linda E. Rustad with materials from Alexander Law Firm, www.defrauded.com/sunbeam.shtml, Sep. 13, 1998; Martha Brannigan and Ellen Joan Pollock, "Dunlap Offers Tears and a Defense," *Wall Street Journal,* July 9, 1998, p. B1; John A. Byrne, "How Al Dunlap Self-Destructed," *Business Week,* July 6, 1998, pp. 58–65; "Dunlap and Kersh Resign from Sunbeam Board of Directors," Company News On-Call, www.prnewswire.com, Sep. 13, 1998; "Sunbeam to Restate Financial Results," Company News On-Call, www.prnewswire.com, Sep. 13, 1998; "Sunbeam Outlines New Strategy, Organizational Structure, Senior Management Team," Company News On-Call, www.prnewswire.com, Sep. 13, 1998; Albert J. Dunlap and Bob Aldeman, "How I Save Bad Companies and Make Good Companies Great," in *Mean Business,* rev. ed. (New York: Simon and Schuster, 1997); Daniel Kadlec, "Chainsaw Al Gets the Chop," *Time* (June 29, 1998), http://cgi.pathfinder.com/time/magazine/1998/dom/980629/busi-ness.chainsaw-al-get15.html; Matthew Schifrin, "Chainsaw Al Dunlap to the Rescue," *Forbes* (Aug. 26, 1996), www.forbes.com/forbes/082696/5805042a.html; Matthew Schifrin, "The Sunbeam Soap Opera: Chapter 6," *Forbes,* July 6, 1998, pp. 44–45; Matthew Schifrin, "The Unkindest Cuts," *Forbes* (May 4, 1998), www.forbes.com/forbes/98/0504/6109044a.html; Patricia Sellers, "First: Sunbeam's Investors Draw Their Knives—Exit for Chainsaw?" *Fortune,* June 8, 1998, pp. 30–31; and "Sunbeam Corporation," Company Capsules, www.hoovers.com/cap-sules/11414.html, Sep. 19, 1998. *Page 90:* Richard Behar, "Why Subway Is The Biggest Problem in Franchising," *Fortune,* March 16, 1998 (via www.pathfinder.com/fortune/1998/9803/sub.html); and "Subway Sandwich Shops, Inc." Hoover's Company Profiles (www.hoover.com), April 23, 1998. *Page 114:* Peter Elstrom, with Catherine Yang, "Now, That's Long Distance," *Business Week,* Dec. 14, 1998, pp. 132–134; Jonathan Friedlan, "U.S. Phone Giants Find Telmex Can Be a Bruising Competitor," *Wall Street Journal,* Interactive Edition, http://interactive.wsj.com, Oct. 23, 1998; and Elisabeth Malkin, "Mexico: Why AT&T and MCI Are Up in Arms," *Business Week,* Feb. 23, 1998, p. 56. *Page 124:* Terril Yue Jones, "Musical Chairs," *Forbes,* Jan. 12, 1998, pp. 60, 63; "Airlines Create 'oneworld'," http://cnnfn.com/fntraveler/9809/21/airlines, Sep. 21, 1998; Lorraine Woellert, "U.S. Airlines: Make Sure Your Partners Are Safe," *Business Week,* Oct. 19, 1998, p. 132; and Wendy Zellner, with Nicole Harris, "Where Are All Those Airline Tie-Ups Headed?" *Business Week,* May 11, 1998, pp. 32–33. *Page 147:* Michael J. McCarthy, "Teenage Research Unlimited Stalks the Elusive Trendsetter," *Wall Street Journal,* Interactive Edition, http://interac-tive.wsj.com, Nov. 19, 1998; Nina Munk, "Girl Power!" *Fortune,* www.pathfinder.com/fortune/1997/97/1208/gen.html, Dec. 8, 1997; and Chris Woodyard, "Generation Y," *USA Today,* Oct. 6, 1998, pp. A1, A2. *Page 152:* Dawn Barrs, "Tailor Made," *Profit Magazine,* Nov. 1998, p. 108; Peter R. Peacock, "Data Mining in Marketing: Part I," *Marketing Management,* Winter 1998, pp. 9–18; Peter R. Peacock, "Data Mining in Marketing: Part II," *Marketing Management,* Spring 1998, pp. 15–24; and Srikumar S. Rao, "Diaper-Beer Syndrome," *Forbes,* Apr. 6, 1998, pp. 128–130. *Page 172:* Loretta Grantham, "Baby Boomers Now Have 'More,' *The Kansas City Star,* Sept. 17, 1998, p. E3; Paul D. Colford, "One for the Ages/More is Not Less," *Newsday,* Sept. 1, 998, p. BO3; Lambath Hochwald, "Booming Business," *American Demographics,* Dec. 1998, pp. 32–35; Karen Hudes, "More and Less int eh Women's 35+ Category," *Folio,* July 15, 1998, p. 12; Meredith Corp. Home Page, www.meredith.com, Dec. 9, 1998. *Page 188:* "Technographics Segments Consumers by Technology Behavior," *Research Alert,* Apr. 18, 1997; Paul C. Judge, "Are Tech Buyers Different?" *Business Week,* Jan. 26, 1998, pp. 64–65, 68; "The NPD Group to Incorporate Forrester's Technographics into the NPD Online Panel and SiteSelect," www.businesswire.com/5141052, May 14, 1998; and David Tebbutt, "Can You Sell to a Mouse Potato?" *Director,* May 1997, p. 87. *Page 200:* Based on information from Stephanie Gruner, "Can We Reduce the Cost of Handling Customers' Complaints?" *Inc.,* Dec. 1997, p. 148; Sarah Kennedy, "Waking Up to the Realities of Customer Satisfaction," *CMA Magazine,* Feb. 1997, p. 28; "Turn Customer Complaints into Profits," *Selling Success,* May 1997, p. 27; Oren Harari, "Thank Heavens for Complainers," *Management Review,* March 1997, pp. 25–29; Robert D. Ramsey, "How to Handle Customer Complaints," *Supervision,* Jan. 1998, pp. 16–19; and Allan J. Magrath, "Mining for New Product Successes," *Business Quarterly,* Winter 1997, pp. 64–68. *Page 213:* Mel Mandell, "Asia: Converting Crisis to Opportunity," *World Trade,* Apr. 1998, p. 36–39; Melinda Ligos, "Direct Sales Dies in China," *Sales & Marketing Management,* Aug. 1998, p. 14; "Avon Puts on New Face with Marketing Reposition," *Frohlinger's Marketing Report,* (Aug. 31, 1998), www.web1.iac-insite.com, Nov. 13, 1998; "Avon: The Power of Direct Selling," www.avon.com/about/financial/company/power.html, Nov. 13, 1998; "Avon: Backgrounder," www.avon.com/about financial/company/background.html, Nov. 13, 1998; Joanna Slater, "Cosmetic Surgery," *Far Eastern Economic Review,* Oct. 22, 1998, www.feer.com/Restricted/98oct_22/companies.html, Dec. 30, 1998; Leslie Kaufman, "Avon's New Face," *Newsweek,* Nov. 16, 1998, pp. 59–60. *Page 228:* Mike Azure, "Victory State Bank Exceeding Expectations," *Staten Island Advance,* Apr. 23, 1998; Chris Astuter, "Bank Opens Doors in Closed Culture," *Crain's New York Business,* Feb. 16, 1998, p. 12; Matt Murray, "Bank with a Giant, or Bank with Menton Corn," *Wall Street Journal,* Aug. 28, 1998, p. Be, Be; and Victory State Bank, *Annual Report,* 1997. *Page 236:* Eric Matson, "Two Billion Reasons Cisco's Sold on the Net," *Fast Company,* Feb./Mar. 1997, pp. 34, 36; "The Information Technology 100," *Business Week,* Nov. 2, 1998, p. 116; Mary Beth Grover, "Wired," *Forbes* (Dec. 28, 1998), www.forbes.com/forbes/98/1228/6214122a.html, Jan. 6, 1999; and "Cisco's Live Wire," *Business Week,* Jan. 11, 1999, p. 75. *Page 254:* "Science and Technology: The Sweet Smell of Success," *Economist,* Sep. 5, 1998, pp. 75–78; Marcia Mogelon-sky, "Dollars and Scents," *American Demographics,* June 1997, p. 32;

Calice Becker, "A Fragrant Future," *Drug & Cosmetic Industry,"* June 1998, p. 42; and Cathy Newman, "Perfume: The Essence of Illusion," *National Geographic,* Oct. 1998, pp. 94–119. *Page 262:* Duke Ratliff, "DVD: Talk of the Town," *Discount Merchandiser,* Jan. 1998, pp. 57–60; Cornelius Armentrout, "DVD Looms as Newest Format," *Dealerscope Consumer Electronics Marketplace,* Sep. 1998, p. 22; "What's in a Name?" *Discount Merchandiser,* Sep. 1998, pp. 71–74; David Coursey, "Harbingers of DVD," *Upside,* Oct. 1998, p. 46; and "Two Thumbs Up: DVD Dealer Does the Right Thing," *Direct,* Jan. 1999, p. 54. *Page 276:* Robert G. Cooper, "Fixing the Fuzzy Front End of the New Product Process: Building the Business Case," *Cost & Management,* Oct. 1997, pp. 21–23; Garrett De Young, "Listen, Then Design," *IW,* Feb. 17, 1997, pp. 76, 78, 80; Geoffrey Brewer, "The Customer Stops Here," *Sales & Marketing Management,* March 1998, pp. 34–35; "The Voice of the Consumer," *Progressive Grocer,* July 1997, pp. 26, 28, 30; and Ian P. Murphy, "Amtrak Enlists Customers' Help to Bring Service Up to Speed," *Marketing News,* Oct. 27, 1997, pp. 14, 47. *Page 280:* "Big Tobacco Targets Russia," CNNfn (Mar. 16, 1998), http://207.25.71.65/hotstories/companies/9803/16/rir/ index.htm, Jan. 25, 1999; "Russia: R.J. Reynolds Plans to Open a New Production Facility in St. Petersburg," *Inzhenernaya Gazeta,* June 17, 1998; Herb Rotfeld, "Marketing Is Target When Product 'Undesirable,'" *Marketing News,* Aug. 31, 1998, p. 8; "Hand Rolling along the Global Path," *World Tobacco,* Sep. 1998, pp. 101–104; Audrey Woods, "World's No. 2 and 4 Cigarette Firms Rothmans, BAT Announce Merger," *Boston Globe* (Jan. 11, 1999), www.boston. com/dailynews/wirehtml/011/World s No 2 and 4 cigarette firms.shtml, January 25, 1999. *Page 296:* James Bell, "Brand Management for the Next Millennium," *Journal of Business Strategy,* Mar./Apr. 1998, pp. 7–10; Lisa Campbell, "Global Branding Ads for Compaq," *Marketing,* June 18, 1998, p. 7; Tobi Elkin, "Dell Delivers," *Brandweek,* June 8, 1998, p. 3; Anne M. Loomis, "The Hidden Power of Global Branding," *Pharmaceutical Executive,* May 1998, pp. 82–93; Tobi Elkin, "Acer Trims Brands, Plots New Beginning," *Brandweek,* May 4, 1998, p. 15; "Schweppes Pumps Agencies for Global Branding Strategy," *Marketing Week,* April 23, 1998, p. 13; and "Staples Want to Be a Global Brand," *Discount Store News,* April 6, 1998, p. 10. *Page 311:* Jeffrey Edelstein, "Private Labels under New Pressure," *Brandweek,* Mar. 30, 1998, p. 18; Michael Harvey, James T. Rothe, and Laurie A. Lucas, "The 'Trade Dress' Controversy: A Case of Strategic Cross-Brand Cannibalization," *Journal of Marketing Theory and Practice,* Spring 1998, pp. 1–15; and Vicki M. Young, "Copycat Suits Increase with Competition," *Women's Wear Daily,* Sep. 14, 1998, p. 20. *Page 329:* "Rebates for Gamblers with First USA Card," *American Banker,* Sept. 24, 1998, p. 14; "Save the Children Teams Up with First USA to Help Children," First USA news release, www.businesswire.com, Oct. 19, 1998; and "First USA Offers Great Consumer Holiday Tips," First USA news release, www.prnewswire.com, Nov. 23, 1998. *Page 333:* Simon Reeve, "End Checkout Queues with Shopping That Pays for Itself," *European,* March 16, 1998, p. S11; Cathy Stapells, "Fed Up with the Waiting Game: Nothing Takes As Long as It Seems," *Toronto Sun,* Aug. 22, 1998, p. 4; Mark Houston, Lance Bettencourt, and Sutha Shanmuganathan, "Over the Line?" *Bank Marketing,* Nov. 1997, pp. 44–46; Richard Gibson, "Merchants Mull the Long and the Short of Lines," *Wall Street Journal,* Sept. 3, 1998, p. B1; and Ron Ruggless, "Put an End to Waiting in Line for Movies," *Nation's Restaurant News,* Dec. 8, 1997, p. 30. *Page 354:* Laurie Joan Aron, "Can Logistics Cure Health Care?" *Inbound Logistics,* Oct. 1997, pp. 30–38; "Comfort in JIT," *Inbound Logistics,* Oct. 1997, p. 38; and "Stockless Success," *Inbound Logistics,* Oct. 1997, p. 34. *Page 360:* Christopher Palmeri, "Radio Shack Redux," *Forbes,* Mar. 23, 1998, pp. 54–56; "Radio Shack History," www.radioshack.com/information/body_radioshack_history.asp, accessed Feb. 16, 1999. *Page 383:* Leslie Hansen Harps, "Partnering for Performance," *Inbound Logistics,* July 1998, pp. 26–40. *Page 394:* Peter Buxbaum, "Fancy Footwork: Timberland Boots Rivals," *Inbound Logistics,* Mar. 1998, pp. 36–41; Company Briefing Books, *The Wall Street Journal* Interactive Edition, interactive.wsj.com, accessed Feb. 17, 1999; "History," www.timberland.com/boot/ history/history_body.html, accessed Feb. 22, 1999. *Page 412:* George Anders, "How eBay Will Try to Battle Sham Bids and Mislabeling," *The Wall Street Journal* Interactive edition, Jan. 15,

1999, interactive.wsj.com; "Benchmarks," www.ebay.com/ aboutebay/overview/ benchmarks.html, accessed Feb. 24, 1999; Company Briefing Books, *The Wall Street Journal* Interactive Edition, interactive.wsj. com, accessed Feb. 24, 1999; and "eBay Probed for Fraud," CNNFN, Jan. 26, 1999, www.cnnfn.com. *Page 419:* Company Briefing Books, *The Wall Street Journal* Interactive Edition, interactive.wsj.com, accessed Feb. 23, 1999; "Current Strategy," www.jcpenneyinc.com/news/jcpinfo/jcpup006.htm, accessed Feb. 23, 1999; Stephanie Anderson Forest, "One More Face-Lift for Penney," *Business Week,* Mar. 23, 1998, pp. 86–88; and "Today's Retail Marketplace," www.jcpenneyinc.com/news/jcpinfo/ jcpup005.htm, accessed Feb. 23, 1999. *Page 441:* Columbia Sportswear Company, corporate information packet, 1998; Stephanie Gruner, "Our Company, Ourselves," *Inc.,* Apr. 1998, pp. 127–128; Thomas J. Ryan, "Columbia Trims IPO," *WWD,* Mar. 12, 1998, p. 10; "Columbia Sportswear's Japanese Subsidiary Officially Open for Business," www.businesswire.com/09290187, Sep. 29, 1997; "Hot Numbers," *Footwear News,* May 4, 1998, p. 22; Michael Rose, "Columbia Sportswear Ramps Up Foreign Sales Push," *Business Journal - Portland,* Sep. 19, 1997, p. 7; "Nagoya Becomes Home to Columbia Sportswear's First Retail Store in Japan," www.businesswire.com/p. 5080068, May 8, 1998; Janet Bamford, "The Working Woman 50: America's Top Women Business Owners," *Working Women,* May 1995, pp. 43–44; Emily Mitchell, "Do What Mother Says," *Time,* Feb. 6, 1995; "The Best of 1994," *Business Week,* Jan. 9, 1995, pp. 101–107; Mike Sheridan, "Mother's Nature," *Sky,* Jan. 1995, pp. 54–58; Jamie Goldman, "Columbia Sportswear," *Advertising Age,* June 26, 1995, p. S32; Beth Berselli, "One Tough Mother," *Oregonian,* Sept. 1, 1996, p. L1; Bill MacKenzie, "Two Portland Women Make Top 50 Listing," *Oregonian,* April 24, 1996, p. D1; Anita Marks, "Columbia Sportswear Booting Up for Market," *Business Journal - Portland,* March 8, 1996, p. 1; Anita Marks, "Columbia Hopes Korean Climate Spells Hot Sales," *Business Journal - Portland,* May 31, 1996, pp. 1–2; and Columbia Sportswear, www.columbia.com. *Page 443:* Richard Halverson, "Retailers Try On-Line Coupons," *Discount Store News,* Nov. 1997, p. 4; Elizabeth Hilts, "Online Coupon Strategies for Small Newspapers," *Editor & Publisher,* Dec. 6, 1997, pp. 30–31; Paulette Thomas, " 'Clicking' Coupons On-Line Has a Cost: Privacy," *Wall Street Journal,* June 18, 1998, pp. B1, B8; J. D. Mosley-Matchett, "Banner Ads Not the Only Way to Make Money," *Marketing News,* July 7, 1997, p. 18; Deena Amoto-McCoy, "Big Retailers Join Program Using Internet for Coupons," *Supermarket News,* Dec. 2, 1997, p. 15; Isabelle Sender, "Internet Coupons Driving Store Traffic," *Chain Store Age Executive,* Sep. 1997, pp. 127–128; "Consumer Access," *Progressive Grocer,"* Feb. 1997, p. 68; Elain Pofeldt, "Commando Marketing on the Internet," *Success,* Sep. 1997, pp. 84–88; and ValuPage, http://www. valupage.com. *Page 460:* Mark Curtis, "New Media," *Marketing Week,* Apr. 10, 1997, p. 25; Kevin Heubusch, "Is It OK to Sell to Kids?" *American Demographics,* Jan. 1997, pp. 55; Michael Kavanagh, "Tobacco and Alcohol Websites Face Crackdown," *Marketing Week,* Mar. 28, 1997, p. 28; Dan Trigoboff, " 'Net Alcohol, Tobacco Marketing Targets, Youth,' Group Says," *Broadcasting & Cable,* March 10, 1997, p. 74; Richard W. Pollay, "Targeting Tactics in Selling Smoke," *Journal of Marketing Theory and Practice,* Winter 1995, pp. 1–22; Kirk Davidson, "Targeting Is Innocent Until It Exploits the Vulnerable," *Marketing News,* Sep. 11, 1995, pp. 4, 10; Naresh K. Malhotra and Gina L. Miller, "Ethical Issues in Marketing Managed Care," *Journal of Health Care Marketing,* Spring 1996, pp. 60–65; "Alcohol Marketers Snare Kids on the World Wide Web," statement by George Hacker, director, Alcohol Policies Project, Center for Science in the Public Interest, Mar. 6, 1997; and Center for Science in the Public Interest, "Beer Ads on TV Beguile Adolescents, Study Finds," press release, July 24, 1996. *Page 468:* Bob Woods, "AdTech: Procter & Gamble Encourages Interactive Ads," Newsbytes, (May 7, 1998), www.news-bytes.com, Sep. 8, 1998; Melinda Gipson, "Advertisers Want Ready-to-Buy Customers," *Advertising Age,* July 17, 1998, p. S10; Annette Hamilton, "Secrets of Super-High Web Ad Click-Through," ZDNet (Aug. 19, 1998), www.zdnet.com/anchordesk/story/ story_2439.html, Jan. 28, 1999; Michael Moon, "Why Banner Ads on the Web Stink," *Emediaweekly,* Sep. 7, 1998, p. 3; Dylan Tweney, "Market Pressures Will Change the Shape of Online Advertising:

Only the Clever Will Survive," *Infoworld,* Sep. 7, 1998, p. 49; Adrienne Mand, "Acting Up," *Mediaweek,* Sep. 14, 1998, p. S32; "Report: E-Commerce Sparking Web Ad Growth," Internet News, Advertising Report (Jan. 26, 1999), www.internetnews.com/IAR/ 1999/01/2601-report.html, Jan. 28, 1999. *Page 489:* "Selling: Two Tools for Probing Customer Satisfaction," *Institutional Investor,* Jan. 1, 1997; Jerry Vass, "Ten Expensive Selling Errors," *Agency Sales Magazine,* July 1998, pp. 38–39; "Unit of One; Sales School," *Fast Company,* Nov. 1998, pp. 105+; and Jim Dickie, "Staple Yourself to a Prospect," *Sales and Field Force Automation,* Feb. 1999, pp. 22–26. *Page 491:* David Sumner Smith, "Net's Scope," *Marketing,* July 10, 1997, p. 25; David Plunkert, "How Dell Sells on the Web," *Fast Company,* Sep. 1998, pp. 58, 60; James Champy, "The Cyber-Future Is Now," *Sales & Marketing Management,* Sep. 1997, pp. 28–29; Erika Rasmusson, "Purchasing Goes to the Net," *Sales & Marketing Management,* , p. 16; "Home Mortgage Buyers Can Name Their Price," http://my.excite.com/news, Sep. 2, 1998; and Kevin Davis, "Increasing Profits in a Wired World," *Agency Sales Magazine,* Jan. 1997, pp. 32–35. *Page 525:* Patrick Doland, "Negotiating Price: Improving Your Bargaining Power," *TMA Journal,* May/June 1998, pp. 58–61; and Alan M. Webber, "How to Get Them to Show You the Money," *Fast Company,* Nov. 1998, pp. 198–208. *Page 526:* Peter Elstrom, "A Cell Phone in Every Pocket?" *Business Week,* Jan. 18, 1999, pp. 38–39; Daniel Roth, "The Tech Boom Will Keep On Rocking: Supersmart Cellular," *Fortune,* (Feb. 15, 1999), www.pathfinder.com/fortune, Feb. 10, 1999; and Jared Sandberg,

"She's Baaack!" *Newsweek,* Feb. 15, 1999, pp. 44–46. *Page 547:* Howard Millman, "Online Auctions Are Changing the Face of Retail Landscape: In These Global Flea Markets, Almost Anything Is for Sale," *InfoWorld,* Mar. 9, 1998, p. 77; Katherine Mieszkowski, "What Am I Bid?" *Fast Company,* Nov. 1998, pp. 288–290, 296–298, 300; and Pam Black, "All the World's an Auction," *Business Week,* Feb. 8, 1999, pp. 120–121. *Page 554:* Judy Feldman, "Avoid Getting Overcharged on Health-Care Costs," *Money,* June 1997, pp. 26+; Ron Gray, "Health Care Payer Savings Strategies," *Business Insurance,* Aug. 31, 1998, p. 37; and Anita Sharpe, "Discounted Fees Cure Headaches, Some Doctors Find," *Wall Street Journal,* Sep. 15, 1998, p. B1. *Page 571:* "History," www.greatharvest.com/history.htm, Mar. 2, 1999; Heath Row, "Great Harvest's Recipe for Growth," *Fast Company,* Dec. 1998, pp. 46–48; and "Great Harvest Bread Co.," www.greatharvest.com, Mar. 2, 1999. *Page 577:* Robert Bryce, "At BSG, There's Only One Speed—Faster," *Fast Company,* www.fastcompany.com/online/02/bsgsec.html, Sep. 18, 1998; and James Wetherbe, *The World on Time* (Santa Monica, Cal.: Knowledge Exchange, 1996), pp. 20–21, 133–135. *Page 601:* Julie Schmit, "Asia's Culture Hampers Internet Commerce," *USA Today,* Feb. 16, 1999, p. 6B; and Kimberley A. Strassel, "E-commerce Finally Blooms as Europe Takes to the Net," *Wall Street Journal,* Interactive Edition, http://interactive.wsj.com, Dec. 7, 1998. *Page 615:* "Building a Web You Can Believe In," www.truste.org, Feb. 26, 1999.

Notes

Chapter 1

1. Brandon Mitchener and Greg Steinmetz, "After Prolonged Skid, Mercedes Is Regaining Much of Its Prestige," *Wall Street Journal,* July 6, 1998, pp. A1, A8; Bill Vlasic, "Germans in the Fast Lane," *Business Week,* Apr. 13, 1998, pp. 78, 80, 82; and David Woodruff, "The Race Moves to the Champagne Circuit," *Business Week,* Apr. 13, 1998, p. 82.

2. Darryl Estrine, "The Jordan Effect," *Fortune,* June 22, 1998, pp. 124–138.

3. David Fischer, "The New Meal Deals," *U.S. News & World Report,* Oct. 30, 1995, p. 66.

4. Leslie Goff, "Mom-and-Pop Businesses Go Boom on the Web," CNN Interactive, www.cnn.com, Aug. 27, 1998.

5. Gail DeGeorge, "Dilbert to the Rescue," *Business Week,* May 4, 1998, p. 166.

6. William C. Symonds, "Would You Spend $1.50 for a Razor Blade?" *Business Week,* Apr. 27, 1998, p. 46.

7. Jagdish N. Sheth and Rajendras Sisodia, "More than Ever Before, Marketing Is under Fire to Account for What It Spends," *Marketing Management,* Fall 1995, pp. 13–14.

8. Betsy Morris, "Doug Is It," *Fortune,* May 25, 1998, pp. 70–84.

9. "Coffee, Tea, or Another Airline?" *Business Week,* Apr. 6, 1998, p. 6.

10. Ajay K. Kohli and Bernard J. Jaworski, "Market Orientation: The Construct, Research Propositions, and Managerial Implications," *Journal of Marketing,* Apr. 1990, pp. 1–18.

11. Ibid.

12. Bethany McLean, "What's Really Going on with Amazon?" *Fortune,* Aug. 3, 1998, pp. 265–266.

13. Dottie Enrico, "M&M's Candies Singing the Blues," *USA Today,* Sept. 5, 1995, p. B1.

14. Alan Grant and Leonard Schlesinger, "Realize Your Customers' Full Profit Potential," *Harvard Business Review,* Sept./Oct. 1995, p. 59.

15. O. C. Ferrell, Michael D. Hartline, George H. Lucas, Jr., and David Luck, *Marketing Strategy* (Ft. Worth, Tex.: Dryden, 1999), p. 121.

16. Sources: O. C. Ferrell, "Saturn," in O. C. Ferrell, Michael D. Hartline, George H. Lucas, Jr., and David Luck, *Marketing Strategy* (Ft. Worth, Tex.: Dryden Press, 1999), pp. 187–193; "A Different Kind of Company," www.saturn.com/index.html, Jan. 28, 1999; Keith Bradsher, "GM Announces Two Steps to Streamline Its Operations," *New York Times,* Mar. 11, 1997, p. D4; "FAQ," www.saturn.com/communications/index3.html, Jan. 28, 1999; Randolph Heaster, "Cooperation Pays Off, Saturn Executive Says," *Kansas City Star,* July 17, 1997, p. B1; "Interactive Pricing Center," www.saturn.com/car/ipc, Jan. 28, 1999; Susan Karlin, "Musing for Fun and Profit," *Working Woman,* Feb. 1997, p. 45; Michelle Maynard, "Saturn Gets Its Star Back," *USA Today,* Nov. 9, 1998, p. 9B; "Road Hazard," *Advertising Age,* May 5, 1997, p. 30; and David Rouse, "O'Toole, Jack," *Booklist,* Sep. 1, 1996, pp. 45–46.

17. Sources: "AutoZone Removes Confusion 'WITT' Technology," *Discount Store News,* May 15, 1995, p. 77; AutoZone, *The AutoZone Success Story,* corporate video; Jerry Minkoff, "AutoZone on the Move," *Discount Merchandiser,* Jan. 1995, pp. 74–76; Shelley Neumeierm, "Companies to Watch," *Fortune,* Dec. 2, 1991, p. 110; Patrick Spain, Altra Campbell, and Alan Chai, eds., *Hoover's Handbook of Emerging Companies,* 1993-1994 (Austin, Tex.: Reference Press, 1993); and "To Our Customers, AutoZoners, and Stockholders," AutoZone, "Ten-Year Review" *Annual Report,* 1998, www.autozone.com/investor/annualreport, Jan. 27, 1999; Rebecca Walters, "Nationwide Automotive Crafts Turn Around Plan," *Business First-Columbus,* June 5, 1995, p. 1; and AutoZone, "Widening the Gap," *Annual Report,* 1995.

Chapter 2

1. Based on information from Linda Himelstein, et al. "Yahoo! The Company, the Strategy, the Stock," *Business Week,* Sep. 7, 1998, pp. 66–76; Yahoo!, "Company History," www.yahoo.com/info/misc/history.html, Jan. 5, 1999; and "Yahoo Inc.," Company Briefing Book, *Wall Street Journal,* Interactive Edition, http://interactive.wsj.com, Jan. 5, 1999.

2. O. C. Ferrell, Michael D. Hartline, George H. Lucas, Jr., and David J. Luck, *Marketing Strategy* (Ft. Worth, Tex.: Dryden, 1999), pp. 1–2.

3. Ibid.

4. Roger O. Crockett, "Gateway Loses the Folksy Shtick," *Business Week,* July 6, 1998, pp. 80, 84.

5. Robert F. Hartley, *Marketing Mistakes and Successes* (New York: Wiley, 1998), pp. 250–267.

6. Ferrell et al., *Marketing Strategy,* p. 46.

7. Emily Harrison, "Home Sweet Home," *Smart Money,* Sept. 1998, pp. 138–139.

8. Derek F. Abell, "Strategic Windows," *Journal of Marketing,* July 1978, p. 21.

9. "Is Your Company's Bottom Line Taking a Hit?" www.prnewswire.com, May 29, 1998.

10. From "Values and Views," www.intel.com/intel/oppty/why/values.htm., Oct. 18, 1998.

11. Charles Ornstein, "Columbia/HCA Prescribes Ethics Program," *Tampa Tribune,* Feb. 20, 1998, p. 4.

12. Michelle Wirth Fellmon, "Just the Name, Thanks—Why Beamer Bought Rolls," *Marketing News,* Sept. 14, 1998, p. 6.

13. Andrew Campbell, Michael Goold, and Marcus Alexander, "Corporate Strategy: The Quest for Parenting Advantage," *Harvard Business Review,* Mar./Apr. 1995, pp. 120–132.

14. Larry Light and David Greising, "Litigation: The Choice of a New Generation," *Business Week,* May 25, 1998, p. 42.

15. Joseph P. Guiltinan and Gordon W. Paul, *Marketing Management: Strategies and Programs* (New York: McGraw-Hill, 1991), p. 43.

16. George S. Day, "Diagnosing the Product Portfolio," *Journal of Marketing,* Apr. 1977, pp. 30–31.

17. William C. Symonds, "Would You Spend $1.50 for a Razor Blade?" *Business Week,* Apr. 27, 1998, p. 46.

18. Stephanie Anderson Forest, "Drugs to the Rescue," *Business Week,* Mar. 23, 1998, p. 88.

19. Roger A. Kerin, Vijay Majahan, and P. Rajan Varadarajan, *Contemporary Perspectives on Strategic Marketing Planning* (Boston: Allyn & Bacon, 1990).

20. Stephanie Anderson with Heidi Dawley, "Pulp Fiction at Kimberly-Clark," *Business Week,* Feb. 23, 1998, pp. 90–91.

21. Martha Brannigan, "Rocky Road: Alamo Maps a Turnaround," *Wall Street Journal,* Aug. 14, 1995, pp. B1, B4.

22. Crockett, "Gateway Loses the Folksy Shtick."

23. Cyndee Miller, "X Marks the Lucrative Spot, but Some Advertisers Can't Hit Target," *Marketing News,* Aug. 2, 1993, pp. 1, 14.

24. "On-line Music," *USA Today,* June 12, 1998, p. B1.

25. Lauren Young, "Are You Being Served?" *Smart Money,* Sept. 1998, p. 134.

26. "The Turnaround Champ of Haute Couture," *Fortune,* Nov. 27, 1997, p. 306.

27. "Cheerios Adds X's to O's," *Marketing News,* July 19, 1993, p. 1.

28. "Busch Taps Japanese Beer Market," *Marketing News,* Oct. 11, 1993, p. 1.

29. Kathleen Kerwin, "Carmakers May Be Flooding the Engine," *Business Week,* May 18, 1998, p. 43.

30. Robert J. Dolan, "How Do You Know When the Price Is Right?" *Harvard Business Review,* Sept./Oct. 1995, pp. 174–183.

31. Ronald D. Michman, "Linking Futuristics with Marketing Planning, Forecasting, and Strategy," *Journal of Consumer Marketing,* Summer 1984, pp. 17, 23.

32. Ferrell et al., *Marketing Strategy,* p. 18.

33. James U. McNeal, "Kids' Markets," *American Demographics,* Apr. 1998, p. 39.

34. Light and Greising, "Litigation."

35. Ferrell et al., *Marketing Strategy,* p. 61.

36. Douglas Bowman and Hubert Gatignon, "Determinants of Competitor Response Time to a New Product Introduction," *Journal of Marketing Research,* Feb. 1995, pp. 42–53.

37. Martha Brannigan and Eleena de Lisser, "A Slimmer Delta Still Loves to Fly, but Does It Show?" *Wall Street Journal,* Jan. 26, 1996, p. B3.

38. Kevin T. Higgins, "Never Ending Journey," *Marketing Management,* Spring 1997, p. 6.

39. Michael Levy and Barton A. Weitz, *Retailing Management* (Homewood, Ill.: Irwin, 1992), p. 208.

40. Kathleen Morris, "The Rise of Jill Barad," *Business Week,* May 25, 1998, p. 118.

41. Sources: Christie Brown, "Pooper-Scooper Dooper," *Forbes,* Feb. 13, 1995, pp. 78–81; "Business Units and Subsidiaries," www.petsmart.com/business.html, Jan. 29, 1999; "PETsMART, Inc.," Company Briefing Book, *Wall Street Journal,* Interactive Edition, http://interactive.wsj.com, Jan. 29, 1999; Julie Liesse, "Superstores Add Bite to Pet Market's Bark," *Advertising Age,* Apr. 25, 1994, p. 42; Ryan Mathews, "Pet Projects," *Progressive Grocer,* July 1995, pp. 69–70; Jerry Minkoff, "Perking Up Pet Supplies," *Discount Merchandiser,* July 1995, pp. 30–32; Marcia Mogelonsky, "Reigning Cats and Dogs," *American Demographics,* Apr. 1995, pp. 30–32; "Pet Consolidation in Offing," *Discount Store News,* Mar. 21, 1994, pp. 3, 46; "PETsMART Concept," www.petsmart.com/html/mission.html, Jan. 29, 1999; PETsMART, company video; Marguerite Smith, "The New World of Health Care for Your Pet," *Money,* Apr. 1994, pp. 144–158; R. Lee Sullivan, "Puppy Love," *Forbes,* Dec. 20, 1993, pp. 138–142; and Tim Triplett, "Superstores Tap into Bond between Owners and Pets," *Marketing News,* Apr. 25, 1994, pp. 1–2.

42. Based on information from Stephanie Armour, "IBM, Lotus Transcend Often-Fatal Culture Clash," *USA Today,* Mar. 26, 1998, pp B1, B2; Company Briefing Book, *Wall Street Journal* Interactive Edition, http://interactive.wsj.com, Jan. 26, 1999; O. C. Ferrell, "IBM," in O. C. Ferrell, Michael D. Hartline, George H. Lucas, Jr., and David Luck, *Marketing Strategy* (Ft. Worth, Tex.: Dryden Press, 1999), pp. 231–236; Saul Hansell, "Big Blue Rediscovers Its Soul—Bringing Aid to Baffled Firms," *Commercial Appeal,* Jan. 18, 1998, pp. C1, C4; "History," www.ibm.com/ibm/history/story/text.html, Jan. 26, 1999; and "Who We Are," www.ibm.com/ibm/aboutibm.html, Jan. 26, 1999.

Chapter 3

1. Based on information from Hoover's Online, Company Capsules, www.hoovers.com, Sep. 15, 1998; "Our History," www.celestialseasonings.com/whoweare/corporatehistory/history.html, Jan. 15, 1999; and Alison Stein Wellner, "Eat Drink and Be Healed," *American Demographics* (Mar. 1998), www.marketingtools.com/publications.

2. Constance L. Hays, "Fickle Finger of Fat," *Continental,* Aug. 1998, pp. 61–63.

3. P. Varadarajan, Terry Clark, and William M. Pride, "Controlling the Uncontrollable: Managing Your Market Environment," *Sloan Management Review,* Winter 1992, pp. 39–47.

4. O. C. Ferrell, Michael D. Hartline, George H. Lucas, Jr., and David J. Luck, *Marketing Strategy* (Ft. Worth, Tex.: Dryden, 1999), p. 33.

5. Ibid., pp. 33–35.

6. George S. Day, "The Capabilities of Market-Driven Organizations," *Journal of Marketing,* Oct. 1994, pp. 37–52.

7. Jacob M. Schlesinger, "Finally, U.S. Median Income Approaches Its Old Heights," *Wall Street Journal,* Interactive Edition, http://interactive.wsj.com, Sept. 25, 1998.

8. Todd Lewon, "One Company's Efforts to Pack a Punch," *(Fort Collins) Coloradoan,* Sept. 13, 1998, p. E1.

9. Mary Lou Steptoe, "Sherman Tank," *Journal of Business Strategy,* Jan./Feb. 1994, p. 12.

10. Linda Himelstein and Ronald Grover, "Will Ticketmaster Get Scalped?" *Business Week,* June 26, 1995, pp. 64–70.

11. Anne G. Perkins, "Advertising: The Costs of Deception," *Harvard Business Review,* May/June 1994, pp. 10–11.

12. Michelle Wirth Fellman, "Preventing Viagra's Fall," *Marketing News,* Aug. 31, 1998, p. 8.

13. "NAD Asks Spalding to Modify Advertising for 'Top-Flite Ball/Clubs System T.' Spalding Appeals to NARB," National Advertising Division Press Release, Better Business Bureau, www.bbb.org/advertising/NADrelease. html, Sept. 25, 1998.

14. Ibid.

15. "1997 AT&T Survey of Teleworker Attitudes and Work Styles," *(Fort Collins) Coloradoan,* Sept. 21, 1998.

16. G. Pascal Zachary, "Restaurant Computers Speed Up Soup to Nuts," *Wall Street Journal,* Oct. 25, 1995, p. B1.

17. Mary George Beggs, "Seniors at Work," *Commercial Appeal,* Oct. 17, 1995, p. C1.

18. Bureau of the Census, *Statistical Abstract of the United States, 1997* (Washington, D.C.: Government Printing Office, 1997), pp. 63, 68.

19. Ibid., p. 15.

20. Ibid., pp. 25–26.

21. Leah Rickard and Jeanne Whalen, "Retail Trails Ethnic Changes," *Advertising Age,* May 1, 1995, pp. 1, 41.

22. Marcia Mogelonsky, "Watching in Tongues," *American Demographics,* April 1998, www.marketingtools.com/ publicationsad/index.html.

23. Reon Carter, "Khakis Rock: Versatile Fabric Scores Huge Hit," *(Fort Collins) Coloradoan,* Sept. 13, 1998, p. C7.

24. Alison Stein Wellner, "Eat Drink, and Be Healed," *American Demographics,* March 1998, www.marketingtools. com/publicationsad/index.html.

25. Norvel D. Glenn, "What Does Family Mean?" *American Demographics,* June 1992, pp. 30–37.

26. Marcia Mogelonsky, "Food on Demand," *American Demographics,* Jan. 1998, www.marketingtools.com/ publicationsad/index.html.

27. "Better Child-Resistant Packages on the Way," *Consumer Reports,* June 1992, p. 567.

28. Sources: "PC Card Version of RadioLAN's 10-Mbps Wireless LAN Gives Users Mobility without Sacrificing Speed," www.radiolan.com/prpcmcia.html, Jan. 25, 1999; Edward C. Prem, "Wireless Local Area Networks," www.netlab.ohiostate.edu/~jain/cis788-97/wireless_lans/ index.html; "RadioLAN Introduces First FCC-Approved High-Speed Wireless Network for National Information Infrastructure Band," www.radiolan.com/uniify.html, Jan. 25, 1999; "RadioLAN Overview," www.radiolan.com/ overview.html, Feb. 4, 1999; and "RadioLAN Unveils First Wireless Campus Network Solution Operating at Full 10-Mbps," www.radiolan.com/campuslink.html, Jan. 25, 1999.

29. Sources: Matt Kelley, "ADM Top Executives Told of Possible Indictments, Company Admits," (Sept. 26, 1996), www.sddt.com/files/librarywire/96wireheadlines/09_96/DN 96_09_26/DN96_09_26_fk.html, Mar. 5, 1998; Matt Kelley, "Archer Daniels Midland Sues FBI Mole for $30 Million," (Sept. 20, 1996), www.sddt.com/files/librarywire/ 96wireheadlines/09_96/DN96_09_20/DN96_09_20_far. html Mar. 5, 1998; "Former ADM Executive Gets Probation" (Mar. 1, 1998), www.grainnet.com/ ArticleLibrary/articles.html?ID=1567, Feb. 22, 1999; "Mentoring: A Double-Edged Sword (Cont.)," *Maxima's Inside Fraud-Bulletin,* www.maximag.co.uk/bull0025.htm, Feb. 28, 1999; "Former ADM Official Mark E. Whitacre Indicated on Criminal Charges," Department of Justice press release, (Jan. 15, 1997), www.usdoj.gov/opa/pr/1997/ January97/019crm.htm, February 28, 1999; "Dutch Company Charged with Price Fixing on Citric Acid: Agrees to Pay $400,000 Criminal Fine," Department of Justice press release (June 23, 1998), www.usdoj.gov/opa/pr/1998/ June/298.html, Oct. 12, 1998; "Japanese Subsidiary Charged with International Conspiracy to Fix Prices for Graphite Electrodes in U.S.," Department of Justice press release (Feb. 23, 1998), www.usdoj.gov/opa/pr/1998/ February/078.htm.html, Oct. 12, 1998; John Bovard, "Corporate Welfare Fueled by Political Contributions: Archer Daniels Midland's Ethanol Program," *Business and Society Review,* June 22, 1995, p. 22; Greg Burns and Richard A. Melcher, "A Grain of Activism at Archer Daniels Midland," *Business Week,* Nov. 6, 1995, p. 44; Dan Carney, "Dwayne's World: Archer Daniels Midland CEO Dwayne Orville Andreas," *Mother Jones,* July 1995, p. 44; Major Garrett, "The Supermarket to the World Pols: Clinton, Dole Helped Campaign Contributor ADM, Now Probed for Price Fixing," *Washington Times,* Sep. 5, 1995, p. A1; Ronald Henkoff, "So Who Is This Mark Whitacre, and Why Is He Saying These Things about ADM?" *Fortune,* Sep. 4, 1995, pp. 64–68; Hoover's Handbook Database (Austin, Tex.: Reference Press, 1995), via America Online; David C. Korten, *When Corporations Rule the World* (West Hartford, Conn.: Kumarian Press, 1995), pp. 75, 224; Joann S. Lublin, "Is ADM's Board Too Big, Cozy, and Well-Paid?" *Wall Street Journal,* Oct. 17, 1995, p. B1; Richard A. Melcher and Greg Burns, "Archer Daniels' Cleanup: Don't Stop Now," *Business Week,* Jan. 29, 1996, p. 37; Robyn Meredith, "Archer Daniels Investors Launch Revolt," Oct. 20, 1995, pp. B1, B2; "10 Little Piggies: Corporations That Receive Government Benefits," *Mother Jones,* July 1995, p. 48; Mark Whitacre and Ronald Henkoff, "My Life as a Corporate Mole for the FBI," *Fortune,* Sep. 4, 1995, pp. 52–62; Laurie P. Cohen, "Tough Battle Looms as ADM Lawyers Plot Price-Fixing Defenses, *Wall Street Journal,* Mar. 27, 1996, p. A1; and James Bovard, "Archer Daniels Midland: A Case Study in Corporate Welfare," http://livelinks.com/sumeria/politics/adm.html, Cato Institute, Policy Analysis No. 241, Sep. 26, 1995.

Chapter 4

1. Based on information from Starbucks, "About Starbucks," www.occ.com/starbucks/about, Apr. 23, 1998; Hoover's Online, Company Capsules, "Starbucks Corporation," www.hoovers.com, accessed on Apr. 23, 1998; Howard Schultz and Dori Jones Yang, *Pour Your Heart into It,* as excerpted in "Starbucks: Making Values Pay," *Fortune,* Sept. 29, 1997, pp. 261–272; and "Starbucks Pays Premium Price to Benefit Workers," *Business Ethics,* Mar./Apr. 1998, p. 9.

2. Dale Kurschner, "5 Ways Ethical Busine$$ Creates Fatter Profit$," *Business Ethics,* Mar./Apr. 1996, p. 21; and Avon, www.avon.com, Oct. 27, 1998.

3. Archie Carroll, "The Pyramid of Corporate Social Responsibility: Toward the Moral Management of Organizational Stakeholders," *Business Horizons,* July/Aug. 1991, p. 42.

4. "Europe's New 35-Hour Week," *Business Ethics,* Mar./Apr. 1998, p. 9.

5. Department of Labor, Corporate Citizenship Resource Center, Company Profiles, www.ttrc.doleta.gov/citizen, Nov. 6, 1998.

6. Debbie Thorne LeClair, O. C. Ferrell, and John P. Fraedrich, *Integrity Management: A Guide to Legal and Ethical Issues in the Workplace* (Tampa, Fla.: University of Tampa Press, 1998), pp. 139–140.

7. Lorrie Grant, "Originals Increasingly Taking Knockoffs to Court," *USA Today,* Oct. 26, 1998, p. 6B.

8. Elizabeth Weise, "First Federal Net Privacy Law Approved," *USA Today,* Oct. 22, 1998, p. D1.

9. Stan Crock, "When Charity Doesn't Begin at Home," *Business Week,* Nov. 27, 1995, p. 34.

10. "Worth Noting," *Business Ethics,* July/Aug. 1998, p. 9.

11. "The Only Way to 'Tie One On' before Driving," *Business Ethics,* Nov./Dec. 1997, p. 18.

12. Catherine Arnst, with Stanley Reed, Gary McWilliams, and De'Ann Weimer, "When Green Begets Green," *Business Week,* Nov. 10, 1997, pp. 98–106.

13. Liz Butler and Dave Wise, "Home Depot Day of Action—Wednesday, October 14," press release, Oct. 12, 1998.

14. Paul Hawken and William McDonough, "Seven Steps to Doing Good Business," *Inc.,* Nov. 1993, pp. 79–90.

15. John Carey, "'A Society That Reuses Almost Everything,'" *Business Week,* Nov. 10, 1997, p. 106.

16. "Diversity Takes Hold," *Business Ethics,* Mar./Apr. 1998, p. 9.

17. Home Depot, "Did You Know?" www.HomeDepot.com/dykfacts/dykful.htm, Apr. 23, 1998.

18. "NLC Names Corporate Names in Sweatshop Report," *Business Ethics,* Jan./Feb. 1998, p. 9.

19. "Company Watch," *Business Ethics,* Jan./Feb. 1998, p. 6.

20. Dana Milbank, "Real Work: Hiring Welfare People, Hotel Chain Finds, Is Tough but Rewarding," *Wall Street Journal,* Oct. 31, 1996, pp. A1, A10.

21. *Business Ethics,* Jan./Feb. 1995, p. 13.

22. Susan Headen, with Stephen J. Hedges and Gary Cohen, "Code Blue at Columbia/HCA," *U.S. News & World Report,* Aug. 11, 1997, pp. 20–22.

23. Louis M. Brown and Anne O. Kandel, *The Legal Audit: Corporate Internal Investigation* (Deerfield, Ill.: Clark, Boardman, Callaghan, 1995), pp. 1–2.

24. "Honda's Bribery Suit Settlement Gets Final Approval," www.Bloomberg.com, Oct. 9, 1998.

25. "Chrysler, Agencies Settle U.S. Deceptive Ad Charges," www.Bloomberg.com, Oct. 15, 1998.

26. "U.S. Lawsuit Says Tobacco Firms Target Blacks, Enquirer Reports," *Philadelphia Enquirer,* www.phillynews.com, Oct. 22, 1998, p. A1.

27. Saul Hansell, "By Moving into Online Sales, Ingram Puts Relationships at Risk," *Newsweek,* May 18, 1998.

28. Karen Thomas, "Teen Ethics: More Cheating and Lying," *USA Today,* Oct. 19, 1998, p. D1.

29. Peggy H. Cunningham and O. C. Ferrell, "The Influence of Role Stress on Unethical Behavior by Personnel Involved in the Marketing Research Process" (working paper, Queens University, Ont., 1998), p. 35.

30. Joseph W. Weiss, *Business Ethics: A Managerial, Stakeholder Approach* (Belmont, Calif.: Wadsworth, 1994), p. 13.

31. O. C. Ferrell, Larry G. Gresham, and John Fraedrich, "A Synthesis of Ethical Decision Models for Marketing," *Journal of Macromarketing,* Fall 1989, pp. 58–59.

32. "Survey Links Workplace Pressure to Unethical Behavior," *Federal Ethics Report,* July 1997, p. 7.

33. "Company Watch," *Business Ethics,* Mar./Apr. 1998, p. 7.

34. Ferrell, Gresham, and Fraedrich, "A Synthesis of Ethical Decision Models."

35. "Hercules Settles Suit by Whistle-Blower," AP News, May 18, 1998.

36. Linda K. Trevino and Stuart Youngblood, "Bad Apples in Bad Barrels: A Causal Analysis of Ethical Decision Making Behavior," *Journal of Applied Psychology* 75, no. 4, 1990, pp. 378–385.

37. Gene R. Laczniak and Patrick E. Murphy, *Ethical Marketing Decisions: The Higher Road* (Boston: Allyn & Bacon, 1993), p. 14.

38. Win Swenson, "The Organizational Guidelines Carrot and Stick Philosophy and Their Focus on Effective Compliance," in *Corporate Crime in America: Strengthening the "Good Citizen" Corporation* (Washington, D.C.: U.S. Sentencing Commission, 1993), p. 17.

39. Aaron Bernstein, "A Floor under Foreign Factories?" *Business Week,* Nov. 2, 1998, pp. 126–129.

40. *Ethics Today,* Winter 1998, p. 1; and Society for Human Resources Management, Ethics Resource Survey, 1997.

41. Susan Gaines, "Handing Out Halos," *Business Ethics,* Mar./Apr. 1994, p. 21.

42. "Call the Ethics Hotline, Get Fired," *Business Ethics,* Mar./Apr. 1998, p. 10.

43. Edward Petry, "Six Myths about the Corporate Ethics Office," *Ethikos,* Mar./Apr. 1998, p. 4.

44. Sir Adrian Cadbury, "Ethical Managers Make Their Own Rules," *Harvard Business Review,* Sept./Oct. 1987, p. 33.

45. O. C. Ferrell, Michael D. Hartline, George H. Lucas, Jr., and David J. Luck, *Marketing Strategy* (Ft. Worth, Tex.: Dryden, 1999), p. 169.

46. Isabelle Maignan, "Antecedents and Benefits of Corporate Citizenship: A Comparison of U.S. and French Businesses" (Ph.D. dissertation, University of Memphis, 1997).

47. Kurschner, "5 Ways Ethical Busine$$ Creates Fatter Profit$," pp. 20–23.

48. Margaret A. Stroup, Ralph L. Newbert, and Jerry W. Anderson, Jr., "Doing Good, Doing Better: Two Views of Social Responsibility," *Business Horizons,* Mar./Apr. 1987, p. 23.

49. "The Sky Is Not Falling, Costs of Environmental Regs Are," *Business Ethics,* Jan./Feb. 1998, p. 11.

50. Arnst, Reed, McWilliams, and Weimer, "When Green Begets Green."

51. Ferrell et al., *Marketing Strategy,* p. 170.

52. Sources: "Did You Know?" www.homedepot.com/dykfacts.dykful.htm, Jan. 26, 1999; "Environmental Information," www.homedepot.com/cominfo/enviro/enviro3.htm, Jan. 26, 1999; Kirstin Downey Grimsley, "Home Depot Settles Gender Bias Lawsuit," *Washington Post,* Sep. 20, 1997, p. D1; Susan Jackson and Tim Smart, "Mom and Pop Fight Back," *Business Week,* Apr. 14, 1997, p. 46; and "Kmart Completes Builders Square Sale," www.foxnews.com/business, Sep. 26, 1997.

53. Sources: Anthony Bianco, "Is Rick Scott on the Critical List?" *Business Week,* Aug. 4, 1997, pp. 65–68; Columbia/HCA Healthcare Corporation, *Annual Report,* 1996; "Columbia/HCA Launches Ethics and Compliance Training Program," www.aol.com/news, Feb. 12, 1998; "Columbia/HCA to Sell Part of Business," *Commercial Appeal,* June 3, 1998, p. B8; Kurt Eichenwald, "Reshaping the Culture at Columbia/HCA," *New York Times,* Nov. 4, 1997, p. C2; Kurt Eichenwald and N.R. Kleinfield, "At Columbia/HCA, Scandal Hurts," *Commercial Appeal,* Dec. 21, 1997, pp. C1, C3; Lucette Lagnado, "Columbia Taps Lawyer for Ethics Post: Yuspeh Led Defense Initiative of 1980s," *Wall Street Journal,* Oct. 14, 1997, p. B6; Tom Lowry, "Columbia/HCA Hires Ethics Expert," *USA Today,* Oct. 14, 1997, p. 4B; Tom Lowry, "Loss Warning Hits Columbia/HCA Stock," *USA Today,* Feb. 9, 1998, p. 2B; Charles Ornstein, "Columbia/HCA Prescribes Employee Ethics Program," *Tampa Tribune,* Feb. 20, 1998, p. 4; Eva M. Rodriguez, "Columbia/HCA Probe Turns to Marketing Billing," *Wall Street Journal,* Aug. 21, 1997, p. A2; and Chris Woodyard, "FBI Alleges Systemic Fraud at Columbia," *USA Today,* Oct. 7, 1997, p. 1B.

Chapter 5

1. Based on information from Cindy Kano and Alex Taylor III, "The Cult of the Astra Van," www.pathfinder.com/fortune/1997/970818/fir6.html; Aug. 18, 1997; and Lisa Shuchman, "How Does GM's Saturn Division Sell Cars in Japan? Very Slowly," *Wall Street Journal,* Interactive Edition, Aug. 25, 1998, http://interactive.wsj.com.

2. Karen Pennar, "Two Steps Forward, One Step Back," *Business Week,* Aug. 31, 1998, p. 116.

3. Wal-Mart, *Annual Report,* 1997; and Coca-Cola Company, *Annual Report,* 1997.

4. David Leonhardt, "It Was a Hit in Buenos Aires—so Why Not Boise?" *Business Week,* Sep. 7, 1998, pp. 56–58.

5. O. C. Ferrell, Michael D. Hartline, George H. Lucas, Jr., and David J. Luck, *Marketing Strategy* (Ft. Worth, Tex.: Dryden, 1999), p. 176.

6. Pennar, "Two Steps Forward, One Step Back."

7. General Motors, *Annual Report,* 1997.

8. Louise Lee, "Ad Agencies in Asia Hit a Nerve, Showing Men Doing Housework," *Wall Street Journal,* Interactive Edition, http://interactive.wsj.com, Aug. 14, 1998.

9. "Etiquette: When in Japan Don't Cross Your Legs," *Business Ethics,* Mar./Apr. 1996, p. 50.

10. Nigel G.G. Campbell, John L. Graham, Alain Jolibert, and Hans Gunther Messner, "Marketing Negotiations in France, Germany, the United Kingdom, and the United States," *Journal of Marketing,* Apr. 1988, pp. 49–62.

11. Brian Mark Hawrysh and Judith Lynne Zaichkowsky, "Cultural Approaches to Negotiations: Understanding the Japanese," *International Marketing Review* 7, no. 2, 1990, pp. 28–42.

12. Joseph Albright and Marcia Kunstel, "Schlotzsky's First China Opening Less than Red-Hot," *Austin American-Statesman,* www.austin360.com, May 27, 1998.

13. Dave Izraeli and Mark S. Schwartz, "What We Can Learn from the Federal Sentencing Guidelines for Organizational Ethics," *Journal of Business Ethics,* July 1998, pp. 9–10.

14. Stan Crock, "Sanctions against Cuba: The Beginning of the End?" *Business Week,* Aug. 3, 1998, p. 45.

15. Robert Kuttner, "Globalization's Dirty Little Secret," *Business Week,* Sep. 7, 1998, p. 20.

16. James C. Cooper and Kathleen Madigan, "U.S.: Return of the Monster Trade Deficit," *Business Week,* Dec. 8, 1997.

17. Elia Kacapyr, "Trade Deficits and Well-Being," *American Demographics,* May 1998, www.marketingtools.com/publications/ad/index.html.

18. Bureau of the Census, *Statistical Abstract of the United States,* (Washington, D.C.: Government Printing Office, 1997), pp. 829–831, 839, 845.

19. Earl Naumann and Douglas J. Lincoln, "Non-Tariff Barriers and Entry Strategy Alternatives: Strategic Marketing Implications," *Journal of Small Business Management,* Apr. 1991, pp. 60–70.

20. Thane Peterson and Stephen Baker, "A High-Tech Europe Is Finally in Sight," *Business Week,* Aug. 31, 1998, pp. 120, 122.

21. "China: Soon the Largest Mobile Telephone Market?" CNN Interactive, www.cnn.com/TECH/science/, Aug. 16, 1998.

22. Bureau of the Census, *Statistical Abstract,* pp. 829, 839.

23. William C. Symonds, "Meanwhile, to the North, NAFTA Is a Smash," *Business Week,* Feb. 27, 1995, p. 66.

24. Bureau of the Census, *Statistical Abstract,* pp. 803, 829–831, 839; and "Mexico Becomes Number-Two Export Market," *Inbound Logistics,* Apr. 1998, p. 16.

25. Elisabeth Malkin, "Holding Off Asia's Assault," *Business Week,* Apr. 13, 1998, pp. 44–45.

26. Geri Smith and Elisabeth Malkin, "Why Mexico Scares the UAW," *Business Week,* Aug. 3, 1998, pp. 37–38.

27. "Six Candidate Nations Begin EU Membership Talks," CNN Interactive, www.cnn.com, March 31, 1998.

28. Maricris G. Briones, "The Euro Starts Here," *Marketing News,* July 20, 1998, pp. 1, 39.

29. Eric G. Fribert, "1992: Moves Europeans Are Making," *Harvard Business Review,* May/June 1989, p. 89.

30. Mark Memmott, "U.S.: Japan Must Ease Import Rules," *USA Today,* Feb. 20, 1995, p. B1.

31. Martha T. Moore, "Latest Japan-U.S. Rift," *USA Today,* Nov. 6, 1995, p. B1.

32. James Aley, "New Lift for the U.S. Export Boom," *Fortune,* Nov. 13, 1995, p. 74.

33. Brian Bremner, with Edith Hill Updike, " 'Made in America' Isn't the Kiss of Death Anymore," *Business Week,* Nov. 13, 1995, p. 62.

34. Dexter Roberts, with Joyce Barnathan and Robert J. Dowling, "Now, It's Reform or Bust," *Business Week,* Apr. 6, 1998, p. 54.

35. Louis Kraar, "The Risks Are Rising in China," *Fortune,* Mar. 6, 1995, p. 179.

36. "U.S.-China July Trade Deficit Widens to $5.420 Bln," www.bloomberg.com, Sep. 17, 1998.

37. Bureau of the Census, *Statistical Abstract,* p. 803.

38. Louis Kraar, "Asia's Rising Export Powers," *Fortune,* Special Pacific Rim Issue, 1989 pp. 43–50.

39. World Trade Organization, "About the WTO," www.wto.org, accessed on March 26, 1998.

40. Dom Del Prete, "Winning Strategies Lead to Global Marketing Success," *Marketing News,* Aug. 18, 1997, pp. 1, 2.

41. John Benjamin Harris, "Export Strategies for the 1990s: A Strategic Plan for Minority Firms' Participation in Global Markets" (Virginia State University, Aug. 31, 1991), pp. 40–42.

42. Farok J. Contractor and Sumit K. Kundu, "Franchising versus Company-Run Operations: Model Choice in the Global Hotel Sector," *Journal of International Marketing,* Nov. 1997, pp. 28–53.

43. Andrew Kupfer, "How to Be a Global Manager," *Fortune,* Mar. 14, 1988, pp. 52–58.

44. Kathryn Rudie Harrigan, "Joint Ventures and Competitive Advantage," *Strategic Management Journal,* May 1988, pp. 141–158.

45. Margaret H. Cunningham, "Marketing's New Frontier: International Strategic Alliances" (working paper, Queens University, Ont., 1998).

46. Nitin Pangarkar and Saul Klein, "Bandwagon Pressures and Interfirm Alliances in the Global Pharmaceutical Industry," *Journal of International Marketing,* Nov. 1997, pp. 54+.

47. Thomas Gross and John Neuman, "Strategic Alliances Vital in Global Marketing," *Marketing News,* June 1989, pp. 1–2.

48. "Airlines Create 'Oneworld'," CNNFN, www.cnnfn.com, Sep. 21, 1998.

49. Larry Armstrong, "Daewoo: Big Car on Campus?" *Business Week,* Aug. 31, 1998, p. 32.

50. Ford Motor Company, *Annual Report,* 1997, pp. 5, 10, 18.

51. Theodore Levitt, "The Globalization of Markets," *Harvard Business Review,* May/June 1983, p. 92.

52. Keith Naughton and Emily Thornton, with Kathleen Kerwin and Heidi Dawley, "Can Honda Build a World Car?" *Business Week,* Sep. 8, 1997, 100–108.

53. Sources: Susanna P. Barton, "Chip Selling Tough, and That's No Bull," *Jacksonville Business Journal,* Sep. 27, 1996, p. 1; "Datil Pepper History & Other Interesting Stuff," www.datldoit.com/history.htm, Jan. 28, 1999; "Dat'l Do-it Products Online," www.datldoit.com/products.htm, Jan. 28, 1999; "Florida Company Cashing In on Hot Pepper Craze," *Chattanooga Free Press,* June 18, 1995; Jan Norris, "The Pepper Cult," *Palm Beach Post,* July 28, 1994; and

Steven Wolcott, "Hotter Is Better at Dat'l Do-It in St. Augustine," *Jacksonville Business Journal,* Jan. 21, 1994, p. 1–1.

54. This case was prepared by Dr. Neil Herndon, City University of Hong Kong, based on information from Joan Bergmann, "China Reassessed," *Discount Merchandiser,* May 1995, pp. 94, 96, 97, 105; Christine Chan, "Pokphand and Wal-Mart Split," *South China Morning Post,* June 27, 1996, Business section, p. 2; "The Global 500," *Fortune,* Aug. 3, 1998, p. F-1; Alkman Granitsas, "(Un)Real Estate," *Far Eastern Economic Review,* Dec. 10, 1998, p. 12; Bob Hagerty and Peter Wonacott, "Wal-Mart Expands Cautiously in Asia," *Asian Wall Street Journal,* Aug. 12, 1996, p. 28; Neil Herndon, "HK Shoppers Tell Value Club: Wrong Place, Wrong Product," *Asian Retailer,* May 1996, pp. 30, 32; Neil Herndon, "Hong Kong Shoppers Cool to Wal-Mart's Value Club," *Marketing News,* Nov. 20, 1995, p. 11; Neil Herndon, "Wal-Mart Goes to Hong Kong, Looks at China," *Marketing News,* Nov. 21, 1994, p. 2; Neil Herndon and Cecilia Chi-Yin Yu, "A New Retail Technology in Asia: Warehouse Clubs," *Management Research News,* 19, no. 9, 1996, pp. 5–27; Bob Howlett, ed., *Hong Kong 1997,* (Hong Kong: Information Services Department, Hong Kong Government, 1997), p. 117; Louise Lee, Nopporn Wong-Anan, and Bob Hagerty, "Wal-Mart Ends China Venture with CP Group," *Asian Wall Street Journal,* Jan. 11, 1996, p. 1; Jo Pegg, "New York Shop Rents Beat SAR," *South China Morning Post,* Nov. 14, 1998, p. 4; and Simon Ng, "New York Takes Causeway Bay Title," *Hong Kong Standard,* Nov. 14, 1998, p. 2.

55. Sources: This case was prepared by Jeffrey A. Krug, University of Illinois at Urbana-Champaign. Research assistance was provided by Phylis Mansfield, The University of Memphis. All rights reserved by Jeffrey A. Krug. Based on information from personal contacts at PepsiCo, Inc., Purchase, NY and Dallas, TX, Tricon Global Restaurants, Louisville, KY, and Arby's International, Fort Lauderdale, TX; Standard & Poor's Industry Surveys, "Restaurants," April 10, 1997; *Nation's Restaurant News,* "NRN Top 100," annual August editions; International Monetary Fund, *International Financial Statistics,* Department of Commerce, Washington, DC; International Monetary Fund, *Direction of Trade Statistics,* Department of Commerce, Washington, DC; Annual and 10-K reports from PepsiCo, Inc. (www.pepsico.com), KFC (www.triconglobal.com), McDonald's (www.mcdonalds.com), Wendy's (www.wendys.com), Boston Market (www.bostonchicken.com), and Nation's Restaurant News (www.nrn.com);

Chapter 6

1. Sources: "Breakplace," www.conoco.com/brandedsupport/breakplace/index.html, Jan. 19, 1998; Gail Gaboda, "Filling Up a Niche," *Marketing News,* Oct. 27, 1997, p. 2; and "Quick Facts," www.conoco.com/about/glance/quick.html, Jan. 19, 1998.

2. "Cats Favored by a Hair," *Marketing News,* Aug. 3, 1998, p. 2.

3. Robert M. McNath, "Flaunt What You've Got," *American Demographics,* July 1998, p. 64.

4. Marcia Mogelonsky, "Home Meal Replacement," *American Demographics,* July 1998, p. 38.

5. "Marketing Briefs," *Marketing News,* Sep. 28, 1998, p. 2.

6. "Shoppers' Bizarre," *Marketing News,* Aug. 3, 1998, p. 2.

7. "Lean, Teen Eating Machines," *Marketing News,* Aug. 3, 1998, p. 2.

8. "The Big Picture: Workstyles of the Rich and Famous," *Business Week,* July 27, 1998, p. 6.

9. Martha Farnsworth Riche, "Who Says Yes?" *American Demographics,* Feb. 1987, p. 8.

10. Peter S. Tuckel and Harry W. O'Neill, "Call Waiting," *Marketing Research,* Spring 1995, p. 8.

11. Martin Opperman, "E-mail Surveys—Potentials and Pitfalls," *Marketing Research,* Summer 1995, pp. 29, 32.

12. Cynthia Webster, "Consumers' Attitudes toward Data Collection Methods, in *Marketing: Toward the 21st Century,* ed. Robert L. King (Atlanta: Proceedings of the Southern Marketing Association, Nov. 1991), p. 221.

13. Jagdip Singh, Roy D. Howell, and Gary K. Rhoads, "Adaptive Designs for Likert-Type Data: An Approach for Implementing Marketing Surveys," *Journal of Marketing Research,* Aug. 1990, pp. 304–321.

14. Michael J. Olivette, "Marketing Research in the Electric Utility Industry," *Marketing News,* Jan. 2, 1987, p. 13.

15. Cynthia Crossen, "Margin of Error," *Wall Street Journal,* Nov. 14, 1991, p. A7.

16. Keith L. Alexander, "For Fliers, First Class No Longer Means Prestige," *USA Today,* Nov. 24, 1995, p. 1B.

17. Emily Nelson, "Why Wal-Mart Sings, 'Yes, We Have Bananas!' " *Wall Street Journal,* Interactive Edition, http://www.interactive.wsj.com, Oct. 6, 1998.

18. Richard S. Teitelbaum, "*Reader's Digest:* Are Times Tough? Here's an Answer," *Fortune,* Dec. 2, 1991, pp. 101–102.

19. Laurence N. Goal, "High Technology Data Collection for Measurement and Testing," *Marketing Research,* Mar. 1992, pp. 29–38.

20. Alison L. Sprout, "The Internet inside Your Company," *Fortune,* Nov. 27, 1995, pp. 161–168.

21. Christine Mormon, Gerald Zaltman, and Rohit Deshpande, "Relationships between Providers and Users of Market Research: The Dynamics of Trust within and between Organizations," *Journal of Marketing Research,* Aug. 1992, pp. 314–328.

22. O. C. Ferrell, Michael D. Hartline, and Stephen W. McDaniel, "Codes of Ethics among Corporate Research Departments, Marketing Research Firms, and Data Subcontractors: An Examination of a Three-Communities Metaphor," *Journal of Business Ethics,* Apr. 1998, p. 60.

23. O. C. Ferrell and Steven J. Skinner, "Ethical Behavior and Bureaucratic Structure in Marketing Research Organizations," *Journal of Marketing Research,* Feb. 1988, pp. 103–104.

24. Jerry Stafford and Neil Ubmeyer, "Product Shortages Hamper Research in the Soviet Union," *Marketing News,* Sep. 3, 1990, p. 6.

25. Lambeth Hochwald, "Are You Smart Enough to Sell Globally?" *Sales & Marketing Management,* July 1998, pp. 52–56.

26. Ibid.

27. Source: "Good-bye Guesswork: How Research Guides Today's Advertising," *Advertising Education Foundation.*

28. Based on information from Company Briefing Book, *Wall Street Journal,* Interactive Edition, http://interactive.wsj.com, Jan. 26, 1999; O.C. Ferrell, "Eagle Hardware and Garden, Inc.," in O.C. Ferrell, Michael D. Hartline, George H. Lucas, Jr., and David Luck, *Marketing Strategy* (Ft. Worth, Tex.: Dryden Press, 1999), pp. 219–224; "A Little about Lowe's," www.lowes.com/frames/inslowes/company.htm, Feb. 11, 1999; and "Lowe's Acquires Eagle in Move That Strengthens West Coast Market Entry," Lowe's press release, www.shareholder.com/lowes/News/19981127-5450.htm, Feb. 11, 1999.

Chapter 7

1. Based on information from "Streamline Delivers," *Fast Company,* Aug. 8, 1998, pp. 154–156; "Streamline," www.streamline.com, Sep. 15, 1998; "Benes Communications, Inc. Announces the Launch of New Web Site Design for Streamline, Inc.," Streamline press release, May 27, 1998; "Streamline Selects 1-800-DATA-BASE to Develop Database of Product Images, Information for Online Shopping Solution," Streamline press release, May 12, 1998; Shelly Reese, "Streamline Looks beyond Groceries to Broader Home Market," *Stores,* Jan. 1998, pp. 94–96; and Kevin T. Higgins, "Delivering the Goods," *Marketing Management,* Winter 1998, pp. 4–7.

2. Service Corporation International Web site, www.sci-corp.com.

3. Bureau of the Census, *Statistical Abstract of the United States* (Washington, D.C.: Government Printing Office, 1997), p. 14.

4. Michael Warshaw, "Nick Tunes into Kids," *Fast Company,* Mar. 1998, pp. 120–129.

5. Bureau of the Census, *Statistical Abstract.*

6. J. D. Mosley-Matchett, "Marketers: There's a Feminine Side to the Web," *Marketing News,* Feb. 16, 1998, p. 6.

7. Yuri Radzievsky, "Untapped Markets: Ethnics in the U.S.," *Advertising Age,* June 21, 1993.

8. Bureau of the Census, *Current Population Survey* (Washington, D.C.: Government Printing Office, 1970, 1990).

9. Gregory A. Patterson, "Different Strokes: Target 'Micromarkets' Its Way to Success," *Wall Street Journal,* May 31, 1995, p. A1.

10. Joseph T. Plummer, "The Concept and Application of Life Style Segmentation," *Journal of Marketing,* Jan. 1974, p. 33.

11. Rebecca Piirto Heath, "You Can Buy a Thrill: Chasing the Ultimate Rush," *American Demographics,* June 1997, pp. 47–51.

12. Dan Fost, "The Fun Factor: Marketing Recreation to the Disabled," *American Demographics,* Feb. 1998, pp. 54–58.

13. Philip Kotler, *Marketing Management: Analysis, Planning, Implementation, and Control,* 6th ed. (Englewood Cliffs, N.J.: Prentice Hall, 1997), p. 131.

14. Charles W. Chase, Jr., "Selecting the Appropriate Forecasting Method," *Journal of Business Forecasting,* Fall 1997, pp. 2, 23, 28–29.

15. Sources: Ryka administrative assistant, telephone interview by author, Oct. 18, 1995; Mark Tedeschi, "Ryka Sizes Up Sizing with University Study," *Sporting Goods Business,* July 24, 1998, p. 23; Kristina Grish, "Ryka's New Apparel Line Tells Market to Shape-Up," *Sporting Goods Business,* June 10, 1998, p. 28; Maggie Spilner, "Find the Perfect Pair," *Prevention,* June 1998, p. 126; "Correction: For the Record," *Boston Globe,* Feb. 16, 1998, p. A2; "Global Sports Reports Record Third Quarter Results," www.businesswire.com,/1068, Nov. 3, 1998; Claude Solnik, "Magazine's Rating a Silent Victory—Cashing In on *Consumer Reports* a No-No," *Athletic Footwear News,* Aug. 24, 1998, p. 4; Maryann LoRusso, "Women from Mars," *Footwear News,* Feb. 16, 1998, p. 30; Deni Kasrel, "Footwear Pair Steps into Deal," *Philadelphia Business Journal,* Jan. 9, 1998, pp. 1–2; Greg Melville, "Second Tier's Turn as Women Consumer's Demand for Athletic Shoes Increases," *Footwear News,* July 7, 1997, pp. 26–27; and Ryka Shoes, Inc., sales training video.

16. Sources: Jake Holden, "High-Tech Take-Out," *American Demographics,* Oct. 1998, pp. 16, 18; Kitty Kevin, "A Golden Age for Meal Solutions: LifeSource Nutrition Solutions' Line of Nutritionally-Balanced Meals," *Food Processing,* Oct. 1998, pp. 37+; "New Ventures," www.agewave.com/agewave/lifesource.html, Nov. 30, 1998; and John Hale, LifeSource COO, personal communication with author, Dec. 4, 1998.

Chapter 8

1. Sources: eatZi, "The Market Tour" and "Meals for the Taking," www.eatzis.com; Stacy Perman, "The Joy of Not Cooking," *Time,* June 1, 1998, pp. 66–68; Christopher Palmeri, "The Wow! Factor," *Forbes,* May 18, 1998; and Greg Hassell, "The Whole Romano Empire," *Houston Chronicle,* Sep. 14, 1997, p. B1.

2. Paul M. Herr, Frank R. Kardes, and John Kim, "Effects of Word-of-Mouth and Product-Attribute Information on Persuasion: An Accessibility-Diagnosticity Perspective," *Journal of Consumer Research,* Mar. 1991, pp. 454–462.

3. Michael J. Houston, Terry L. Childers, and Susan E. Heckler, "Picture-Word Consistency and the Elaborative Processing of Advertisements," *Journal of Marketing Research,* Nov. 1987, pp. 359–369.

4. Russell W. Belk, "Situational Variables and Consumer Behavior," *Journal of Consumer Research,* Dec. 1975, pp. 157–164.

5. Akshay R. Rao and Kent B. Monroe, "The Moderating Effect of Prior Knowledge on Cue Utilization in Product Evaluations," *Journal of Consumer Research,* Sep. 1988, pp. 253–264.

6. Marchi Mogelonsy, "Snap, Crackle, Profits," *American Demographics,* Jan. 1995, p. 10.

7. Jane Irene Kelly, "Prunes Go for Laughs," *Adweek Western Advertising,* July 14, 1997, p. 7.

8. Shannon Dortch, "New Hues," *American Demographics,* Jan. 1997, p. 24.

9. Chip Walker, "Meet the New Vegetarian," *American Demographics,* Jan. 1995, pp. 9–11.

10. Valerie Lynn Gray, "Going After Our Dollars," *Black Enterprise,* July 1997, p. 68.

11. David Kiley, "Black Surfing," *Brandweek,* Nov. 17, 1997, p. 36.

12. Gray, "Going After Our Dollars," p. 74.

13. Carol Radice, "Hispanic Consumers: Understanding a Changing Market," *Progressive Grocer,* Feb. 1997, p. 109.

14. Shannon Dortch, ed., "New People," *American Demographics,* Feb. 1997, p. 22.

15. Radice, "Hispanic Customers," p. 114.

16. Jack Neff, "Elusive Ad Effectiveness Frustrates Top Marketer P&G," *Advertising Age,* Nov. 17, 1997, p. S16.

17. "Marketing to Asians," *Progressive Grocer,* June 1996, p. 116.

18. Saul Gitlin, "Cars: Dealing with Asians," *Brandweek,* Jan. 5, 1998, pp. 15–16.

19. Sources: "AC Nielsen, IRI to Track HMR," *Food Institute Report,* Mar. 2, 1998, p. 3; Maryellen Lo Bosco, "IRI Calls Frozen Items 'Pacesetters,'" *Supermarket News,* June 1, 1998, p. 64; "New Solutions Address Top Industry Issues," *Progressive Grocer,* July 1998, p. 10; "Information Resources Builds Largest, Most Accurate In-Home Consumer Scanner Panel in U.S.," IRI news release (July 23, 1998), web3.iac-insite.com, Nov. 16, 1998; "Halloween Is a Real Treat for Candy Manufacturers, Retailers," IRI news release (Oct. 26, 1998), www.infores.com/public/marketing/press/new/hween.html, Dec. 31, 1998; and Jon Bigness, "Cereal Giants Feeling Crunch," *Chicago Tribune,* Nov. 1, 1998, p. C1+.

20. Sources: "Around Town: The Susan G. Komen Breast Cancer Foundation," www2ford.com/display.asp?story=133, Jan. 5, 1999; Bob Black, "No Letup in Demand for Trucks," *Chicago Sun-Times,* Feb. 7, 1997, p. 45; Daniel Howes, "GM: Automaker with a Cause," *Detroit News,* June 22, 1997, p. D3; Patrick Barrett, "Who's in the Driver's Seat?" *Marketing* (Aug. 14, 1997), www.dbu.texshare.edu/ovidweb/ovidwebb . . . &ST=6&R=8&totalCIT=12&D=infoz&S=15 84003, Dec. 1, 1998; "Ford Focuses on Women, Minorities," *Orlando Sentinel,* Aug. 28, 1997, p. F13; Elena Scotti, "Born to Be Mild, or Wild?" *BrandWeek,* Mar. 16, 1998, pp. 22–23; "Automotive Overview," *Women Consumers, '98 Highlights,* About Women, Inc., 1998, p. 4; Katherine Yung, "Hot Lexus Sport-Ute Wins Over Drivers," *Detroit News,* Aug. 4, 1998, p. B1; "Women Cyclists Convene in North Carolina," Subaru press release (Sept. 25, 1998), www.subaru.com/corporate_newsroom/press_release/pr_98/09_25_women_cyclists.html, Jan. 6, 1999,; Keith Bradsher, "Light Trucks Exceed Cars in U.S. Sales," *New York Times,* Dec. 4, 1998, p. C4; "Acura Presents Local Events," www.acura.com/presents/ap-local.html, Jan. 5, 1999; "The 'Masters' of Women's Professional Golf," www.toyota.com/events/dinashore_golf.html, Jan. 5, 1999; "General Motors Presents More than Half a Million Dollars to the National Alliance of Breast Cancer Organizations," General Motors press release (Oct. 21, 1997), www.gm.com/about/community/pink/pressrelease.html, Jan. 5, 1999; "Women's Day Planned at Auto Show," DaimlerChrysler News Release (Jan. 5, 1999), www1.daimlerchrysler.com/news/daily/index_e.html; "1999 Sneak Preview," General Motors press release, www.gm.com/about/community/cure/99sneakpreview.html, Jan. 5, 1999; and Susan

Whitall, "What Women Want . . . in Their Dream Cars," *Detroit News* (Jan. 11, 1999), http://detnews. com/1999/features/9901/11/01110011.html (Jan. 13, 1999).

Chapter 9

1. Based on information from Chuck Salter, "Roberts Rules the Road," *Fast Company,* Sep. 1998, pp. 114–128; and Roberts Express Web site, www.roberts.com.

2. Bureau of the Census, *Statistical Abstract of the United States* (Washington, D.C.: Government Printing Office, 1997), p. 332.

3. Ibid., pp. 537, 544.

4. Ibid., p. 332.

5. Ibid., p. 297.

6. Brook Southall, "Maple Donuts Ad Gimmicks Fatten Sales," *Central Penn Business Journal,* Apr. 14, 1995, p. 1.

7. J. Carlos Jarillo and Howard H. Stevenson, "Cooperative Strategies: The Payoffs and the Pitfalls," *Long Range Planning,* Feb. 1991, pp. 64–70.

8. Geoffrey Brewer, "The Customer Stops Here," *Sales & Marketing Management,* Mar. 1998, pp. 30–36.

9. Weld F. Royal, "Cashing In on Companies," *Sales & Marketing Management,* May 1995, pp. 88–89.

10. Frederick E. Webster Jr. and Yoram Wind, "A General Model for Understanding Organizational Buyer Behavior," *Marketing Management,* Winter/Spring 1996, pp. 52–57.

11. Robert D. McWilliams, Earl Naumann, and Stan Scott, "Determining Buying Center Size," *Industrial Marketing Management* 21, 1992, pp. 43–49.

12. Charles Waltner, "Marketers Rev Up Campaigns," *Business Marketing,* May 1998, pp. 3, 45.

13. Robert W. Haas and Thomas R. Wotruba, "From SIC to NAICS—What Does It Mean for Business Marketers?" *Agency Sales Magazine,* Jan. 1998, pp. 29–33.

14. Sources: Anthony Bianco, "It's Not Wretched Excess–It's a Necessity," *Business Week* (Apr. 14, 1997), www.businessweek.com, Dec. 31, 1998; Anthony Bianco, "Iguana Upholstery? It's the Only Way to Fly," *Business Week* (Apr. 14, 1997), www.businessweek.com, Dec. 31, 1998; Anthony Bianco, "Gulfstream's Pilot," *Business Week* (Apr. 14, 1997), www.businessweek.com, Dec. 31, 1998; Hoover's Online, Company Capsules, "Gulfstream Aerospace Corporation," www.hoovers.com/capsules/ 40194.html, Jan. 15, 1999; "Gulfstream Celebrates Sale of 100th Gulfstream V Aircraft by Awarding 100 Stock Options to All Employees," Gulfstream news release (July 8, 1998), www.web3.iac-insite.com, Nov. 16, 1998; Mark Human, "From Tears to Cheers in Cleveland," *Business Week,* Nov. 16, 1998, p. 108; Martha Brannigan, "Not Just for Highfliers, Corporate Planes Take off," *Wall Street Journal,* Jan. 8, 1999, pp. B1, B4.

15. Sources: Alessandra Bianchi, "Without You, I'm Nothing," *Inc.,* Nov. 1998, pp. 50–58; "About Jo's Candies," www.joscandies.com/about.html, Nov. 23, 1998; and Tom King, Jo's Candies CEO, personal communication with author, Dec. 1998.

16. Sources: Anthony Lazarus, "USR Wants to Be Your Co-Pilot," CNet News.com (Mar. 10, 1997), www.news.com/ News/Item/0,4,8665,00.html?st.cn.nws.rl.ne, Jan. 13, 1999; Suruchi Mohan, "PalmPilot Leads the Pack,"

Computerworld (Nov. 27, 1997), www.computerworld.com/ home/print9497.nsf/all/SL47ROBOT16FB2, Jan. 13, 1999; Stephanie Miles, "PalmPilot In, Newton Out," CNet News.com (Feb. 27, 1998), www.news.com/News/ Item/0,4,19551,00.html?st.cn.nws.rl.ne, Jan. 13, 1999; Deborah Radcliff, "The Undesktop," *Computerworld* (May 4, 1998), www.computerworld.com/home/print.nsf/ all/9805447B2, Jan. 13, 1999; Pat Dillon, "The Next Small Thing," *Fast Company,* June/July 1998, pp. 97–110; Melanie Warner, "A Much Anticipated Sequel: Silicon Valley Awaits Palm Creators' New Project," *Fortune* (Jan. 11, 1999), www.pathfinder.com/fortune, Jan. 18, 1999; "Reading the Palm Market Right," *Business Week,* Jan. 11, 1999, p. 95; and "Palm Future," ZDNet Products (Jan. 13, 1999), www.zdnet.com/products/stories/reviews/ 0,4161,2186825,00.html, Jan. 19, 1999.

Chapter 10

1. Based on information from Bill Vlasic, "Still Groovy after All These Years," *Business Week,* Mar. 2, 1998, p. 145; David Kiley, "Steve Wilhite: Finding the Soul of a Brand," *Brandweek,* Oct. 12, 1998, pp. 8–16; Jean Halliday, "Marketer of the Year: Volkswagen of America," *Advertising Age,* Dec. 14, 1998, pp. 1, 20, 22; and Dr. Jens Neumann (Chairman, North American Region, Volkswagen AG), speech at press conference, North American International Auto Show, Detroit (Jan. 4, 1999), www.autoshow.vw.com/ speech_text.htm, Jan. 22, 1999.

2. Theodore Levitt, "Marketing Intangible Products and Product Intangibles," *Harvard Business Review,* May–June 1981, pp. 94–102.

3. Adapted from Everett M. Rogers, *Diffusion of Innovations* (New York: Macmillan, 1962), pp. 81–86.

4. Ibid., pp. 247–250.

5. Paul Lukas, "The Ghastliest Product Launches," *Fortune,* Mar. 16, 1998, p. 44.

6. Gerald Tellis and Peter Golder, "First to Market, First to Fail? Real Causes of Enduring Market Leadership," *Sloan Management Review,* Winter 1996, pp. 65–75.

7. Lukas, "The Ghastliest Product Launches," p. 44.

8. Based on information from T. L. Stanley, "Toymakers Grab Post Position for the Holidays," *Brandweek,* Oct. 20, 1997, p. 8; Sloane Lucas, Rob Lenihan, and Hank Kim, "New Campaigns," *Adweek,* Feb. 2, 1998, p. 42; Joseph Pereira, "Slighted in the U.S., Whimsical Toy Is a Wow in Europe," *Wall Street Journal,* May 21, 1998, pp. B1–B2; Lisa Friedman Miner, "They're All K'nected," *Chicago Daily Herald,* Jan. 23, 1997, pp. 4-1, 4-3; Jane M. Von Bergen, "Success Is Nothing to Play At," *Philadelphia Inquirer,* Aug. 25, 1997, pp. F1, F12; John T. George, "Joel Glickman: Hatfield Toymaker Connects with K'NEX," *Business Ledger,* April 1997, p. 8; and K'NEX Industries, Inc., press kits, 1997, 1998.

9. Based on information from Judith Crown, "Zell & Co. Peddling Schwinn," *Crain's Chicago Business,* May 12, 1997, p. 1; Andy Pargh, "Pedal Back in Time with New Retro-Bikes," *Design News,* May 19, 1997, p. 134; Roy Furchgott, "Retro Bikes with '90s Pizzazz,'" *Business Week,* May 19, 1997, p. 143; Jerd Smith, "Acquisition Gives Schwinn Muscle," *Rocky Mountain News,* Aug. 14, 1997, pp. 1B, 20B; Elana Ashanti Jefferson, "Michigan Firm Buys Schwinn," *Denver Post*, Aug. 14, 1997, p. B1; "Questor Buys Schwinn, Hopes for Revival of Brand," *USA Today*, Aug. 14, 1997; Patrick McGeehan, "Biking Icon Wants to Lose Training Wheels," *USA Today*, Aug. 8, 1995, pp. 1B, 2B; Jan Larson, "The Bicycle Market," *American Demographics*, Mar. 1995, pp. 42–43, 46–48, 50; Laura Loro, "Schwinn Aims to Be a Big Wheel Again," *Advertising Age*, Jan. 2, 1995, p. 4; and John Beauge, "New Process Used to Make Bicycles," *Evening News (Harrisburg, Penn.)*, June 5, 1995, p. 3.

Chapter 11

1. Sources: "Best-Managed Companies: Emphasis on Business Travel Drives Midwest Express Service," *Aviation Week and Space Technology*, Aug. 10, 1998, p. 64; "Travel & Leisure Readers Again Name Midwest Express 'Best Domestic Airline,' " Midwest Express news release, www.prnewswire.com, Aug. 26, 1998; Ellen Jovin, "Buckling Up the Business Traveler," *American Demographics*, Dec. 1998, pp. 48–52; "Midwest Express Holdings Reports Record Fourth Quarter and Year-to-Date Earnings," Midwest Express news release, www.prnewswire.com, Jan. 25, 1999; David Leonhardt, "Revolt of the Executive Class," *Business Week*, Feb. 1, 1999, pp. 68, 70–71.

2. Tobi Elkin, "Brand Builders," *Brandweek*, Sept. 7, 1998, pp. 29–31.

3. Kim B. Clark and Takahiro Fujimoto, "The Power of Product Integrity," *Harvard Business Review*, Nov./Dec. 1990, pp. 108–118.

4. Robert M. McMath, "When Cold Coffee Gets Iced," *American Demographics*, Mar. 1997, p. 60.

5. Peter F. Drucker, "The Discipline of Innovation," *Harvard Business Review*, May/June 1985, pp. 67–68.

6. "The Top 50 U.S. Research Organizations," *Marketing News*, June 8, 1998, p. H4.

7. Mike Beime, "Comin' at Chew," *Brandweek*, July 20, 1998, p. 3.

8. Robert M. McMath, "Why Detergent Sheets Are Washed Up," *American Demographics*, June 1997, p. 64.

9. Faye Rice, "How to Deal with Tougher Customers," *Fortune*, Dec. 3, 1990, pp. 39–48.

10. Sal Marino, "Is 'Good Enough' Good Enough?" *IW*, Feb. 3, 1997, p. 22.

11. Shelly M. Reese, "Suitcase Savy," *American Demographics*, June 1995, p. 58.

12. Adapted from Michael Levy and Barton A. Weitz, *Retailing Management* (Homewood, Ill.: Irwin/McGraw Hill, 1998), p. 570.

13. Steve Gelsi, "Nike Plans to Export 800 Telephone Service," *Brandweek*, Sep. 25, 1995, p. 8.

14. Norton Paley, "Back from the Dead," *Sales & Marketing Management*, July 1995, pp. 30–31.

15. Terry Lefton, "Widening the Expressway," *Brandweek*, Sep. 7, 1998, pp. 33–35, 38.

16. Sources: "Gillette Introduces Proprietary Clear Stick Technology into Gillette Series and Right Guard Anti-Perspirants and Deodorants," www.businesswire.com/ 7101069, July 10, 1996; Chris Reidy and Alex Pham, "Gillette Makes $7.8b Deal for Battery King Duracell,"

Boston Globe, Sept. 13, 1996, p. A1; "Gillette Plans Spate of Introductions," *Chain Drug Review*, Feb. 3, 1997, pp. 53–54; Chatal Tode, "Gillette Cleans Up Men's Grooming," *WWD*, Apr. 4, 1997, p. 10; Linda Grant, "Gillette Knows Shaving—and How to Turn Out Hot New Products," *Fortune*, Oct. 14, 1996, pp. 207–209; Mark Maremont, "How Gillette Brought Its MACH3 to Market," *Wall Street Journal*, Apr. 15, 1998, pp. B1, B5; William C. Symonds, "Would You Spend $1.50 for a Razor Blade?" *Business Week*, Apr. 27, 1998, p. 46; and William C. Symonds and Carol Matlack, "Gillette's Edge: The Secret of a Great Innovation Machine?" *Business Week*, Jan. 19, 1998, pp. 70–77.

17. Sources: Nikhil Deogun, "Beverages: New Sweetener—Pepsi Pounces, Coke Ponders," *Wall Street Journal*, July 1, 1998, p. B1; Nikhil Deogun, "Marketing: Pepsico Draws New Battle Plan to Fight Coke,' *Wall Street Journal*, Jan. 27, 1998, p. B1; Pepsi press release, "Pepsi Launches Breakthrough Product: Pepsi One," June 30, 1998; "Cuba Gooding, Jr. Stars in New Pepsi ONE Commercials," www.prnewswire.com/2214, Oct. 15, 1998; Lucas Sloane, "Pepsi One," *Mediaweek*, July 6, 1998, p. 36; Denise Gellene, "Advertising and Marketing: Ad Reviews—Pepsi Hopes Ads Help Show Them the Money," *Los Angeles Times*, Oct. 22, 1998, p. C6; Bruce Horovitz, "One-calorie Product May Spell Sweet Success," *USA Today*, Oct. 6, 1998, pp. 1A–1B; Louise Kramer, "Pepsi-Cola Puts Hopes, Dreams, $$ into Pepsi One," *Advertising Age*, Oct. 5, 1998, p. 16; and Nikhil Deogun, "Pepsi Takes Aim at Coke with New One-Calorie Drink," *Wall Street Journal*, Oct. 5, 1998, p. B4.

Chapter 12

1. Based on information from David Leonhardt, "The Hip New Drink: Milk," *Business Week*, Feb. 16, 1998, p. 44; Greg Erickson, "Dress for Success: Single-Serve Is Gaining Momentum, but Even Gabletops and Jugs Can Improve Their Images," *Dairy Foods*, July 1997, p. 14; "Dean Foods to Revolutionize Milk Consumption with Milk Chugs Introduction," prnewswire.com/1104CGTU034, Nov. 4, 1997; Judann Pollack, "Milk Marches into New Era with Branded Product Push," *Advertising Age*, Jan. 26, 1998, p. 14; Rekha Balu, "Dean Foods Attempts to Reintroduce Milk to Consumers," *Wall Street Journal*, Mar. 26, 1998, p. B4; and Sue Markgraf, "Milk Moves to the Front Seat," *Dairy Foods*, Sep. 1997, pp. 30–32.

2. Peter D. Bennett, ed., *Dictionary of Marketing Terms* (Chicago: American Marketing Association, 1995), p. 27.

3. U.S. Patent and Trademark Office, "Patent and Trademark Office Review," 1998.

4. Matthew Klein, "Brand X (and Sometimes Y)," *American Demographics*, Aug. 1997.

5. David A. Aaker, *Managing Brand Equity: Capitalizing on the Value of a Brand Name* (New York: Free Press, 1991), pp. 16–17.

6. Jonathan Asher, "For Marketing Icons, Character Counts," *Brandweek*, July 13, 1998, p. 20.

7. Kurt Badenhausen, "Most Valuable Brands," *Financial World*, Sep./Oct. 1997, pp. 62–70.

8. Private Label Manufacturer's Association, *PLMA's 1998 Private Label Yearbook*, p. 15.

9. Jeffrey Edelstein, "Private Labels under New Pressure," *Brandweek*, Mar. 30, 1998, p. 18.

10. Private Label Manufacturer's Association, *1998 Yearbook*, p. 15.

11. Patent and Trademark Office, "Office Review."

12. Gerry Khermouch, "Triarc's Smooth Move," *Brandweek*, June 22, 1998, pp. 26–31.

13. Leonard Berry, Edwin E. Leikowith, and Terry Clark, "In Services, What's in a Name?" *Harvard Business Review*, Sep./Oct. 1988, pp. 2–4.

14. Dorothy Cohen, "Trademark Strategy," *Journal of Marketing*, Jan. 1986, p. 63.

15. U.S. Trademark Association, "Trademark Stylesheet," no. 1A.

16. Dorothy Cohen, "Trademark Strategy Revisited," *Journal of Marketing*, July 1991, pp. 46–59.

17. Sandra Smith, "Brand-Name Pirates Plunder Open Borders," *European*, June 19, 1997, p. 4.

18. Robert M. McMath, "Sinking the Flagship," *American Demographics*, May 1997, p. 60.

19. Stephanie Thompson, "Brand Buddies," *Brandweek*, Feb. 23, 1998, pp. 22–30.

20. Bart A. Lazar, "Licensing Gives Known Brands New Life," *Marketing News*, Feb. 16, 1998, p. 8.

21. Miles Socha, "Brand Extension Catapults Awareness," *Women's Wear Daily*, Nov. 19, 1997, p. S30.

22. James U. McNeal, *Consumer Behavior: An Integrative Approach* (Boston: Little, Brown, 1982), pp. 221–222.

23. Stephanie Thompson, "New Post," *Brandweek*, Sep. 7, 1998, p. 3.

24. Lauren Swann, "Are Food Product Labels Effective?" *Food Processing*, June 1997, pp. 62–63.

25. John Carey, "Fresh Canned Veggies?" *Business Week*, Oct. 10, 1997, p. 6.

26. Kathleen DesMarteau, "No Change for 'Made in USA' Standards," *Bobbin*, Feb. 1998, p. 18.

27. Mark Tedeschi, "New Balance to Continue FTC Fight," *Sporting Goods Business*, Jan. 6, 1998, p. 16.

28. Kristin Carpenter, "Jan Sport/Eastpak Caught in a Homespun Web," *Sporting Goods Business*, Feb. 25, 1998, p. 16.

29. Sources: "New Technologies in Meat Processing and Packing," American Meat Institute (n.d.), *http://www.meatami.org/indupg04.htm* (April 12, 1999); "AMI Says Country-of-Origin Labeling Will Cost More Than $1 Billion Per Year With No Benefits to Consumers, Industry," American Meat Institute, March 22, 1999, *http://www.meatami.org* (April 12, 1999); "Beef's Market Share Will Drop with Import Labeling," American Meat Institute, August 27, 1998, *http://www.meatami.org* (April 12, 1999); "AMI Releases Meat and Poultry Facts 1998," September 17, 1998, *http://www.meatami.org* (April 12, 1999).

30. Sources: Rodney Ho, "Brand-Name Diamonds: A Cut Above?" *Wall Street Journal*, June 1, 1998, pp. B1–B2; Samantha T. Smith, "A Cut above the Rest," *Boston Business Journal*, Jan. 16, 1998, p. 1; "Brand Slam," *Modern Jeweler*, May 1998, pp. 51–52, 54, 56, 58; and Di-Star Ltd. press kit.

Chapter 13

1. Based on information from Susana Schwartz, "Technology plus Customer Loyalty Equals Higher Profits," *Insurance & Technology*, Sep. 1997, p. 76; Geoffrey Brewer, "The Customer Stops Here," *Sales & Marketing Management*, Mar. 1998, pp. 32–33; Bill Rossello, "Customer Service Superstars," *ABA Banking Journal*, Oct. 1997, pp. 96–104; USAA, "Fact Sheet," Aug. 20, 1998; Carol Hildebrand, "C10 100 - Best Practices: Satisfaction Guaranteed," *CIO*, Aug. 1995, pp. 98–100; Vanessa O'Connell, "The Best Bank in America," *Money*, June 1995, pp. 126–133; and David Gertz, "Beating the Odds," *Journal of Business Strategy*, July/Aug. 1995, pp. 20–24.

2. Leonard L. Berry and A. Parasuraman, *Marketing Services: Competing through Quality* (New York: Free Press, 1991), p. 5.

3. Michael Levy and Barton A. Weitz, *Retailing Management* (Homewood, Ill.: McGraw-Hill/Irwin, 1998), p. 570.

4. Megan Rowe, "The Promus Premise," *Lodging Hospitality*, June 1997, pp. 20–22.

5. Kevin Heubusch, "Enlightened and Still Working," *American Demographics*, June 1997, pp. 31–32.

6. The material in this section has been adapted from Christopher H. Lovellock, *Services Marketing*, 3rd ed. (Englewood Cliffs, N.J.: Prentice-Hall, 1996), pp. 15–19; K. Douglas Hoffman and John E. G. Bateson, *Essentials of Services Marketing* (Ft. Worth, Tex.: Dryden Press, 1997), pp. 25–38; and Valarie A. Zeithaml, A. Parasuraman, and Leonard L. Berry, *Delivering Quality Service: Balancing Customer Perceptions and Expectations* (New York: Free Press, 1990).

7. Leonard L. Berry, *On Great Service: A Framework for Action* (New York: Free Press, 1995), pp. 53–54.

8. Paul Peter and James H. Donnelly, *A Preface to Marketing Management* (Homewood, Ill.: McGraw-Hill/Irwin, 1997), p. 225.

9. Michael D. Hartline and O. C. Ferrell, "Service Quality Implementation: The Effects of Organizational Socialization and Managerial Actions of Customer-Contact Employee Behavior," *Marketing Science Institute Working Paper Series*, no. 93-122 (Cambridge, Mass.: Marketing Science Institute, 1993).

10. Zeithaml, Parasuraman, and Berry, *Delivering Quality Service*.

11. Valarie A. Zeithaml, "How Consumer Evaluation Processes Differ between Goods and Services," in *Marketing of Services*, ed. James H. Donnelly and William R. George (Chicago: American Marketing Association, 1981), pp. 186–190.

12. A. Parasuraman, Leonard L. Berry, and Valarie A. Zeithaml, "An Empirical Examination of Relationships in an Extended Service Quality Model," *Marketing Science Institute Working Paper Series*, no. 90-112 (Cambridge, Mass.: Marketing Science Institute, 1990), p. 29.

13. Valarie A. Zeithaml, Leonard L. Berry, and A. Parasuraman, "Communication and Control Processes in the Delivery of Service Quality," *Journal of Marketing*, Apr. 1988, pp. 35–48.

14. Chuck Salter, "Progressive Makes Big Claims," *Fast Company,* Nov. 1988, pp. 176–194.

15. Valarie A. Zeithaml, Leonard L. Berry, and A. Parasuraman, "The Nature and Determinants of Customer Expectations of Service," *Journal of the Academy of Marketing Science,* Winter 1993, pp. 1–12.

16. Hartline and Ferrell, "Service Quality Implementation," p. 36.

17. Mary Jo Bitner, "Evaluating Service Encounters: The Effects of Physical Surroundings and Employee Responses," *Journal of Marketing,* Apr. 1990, p. 70.

18. Hartline and Ferrell, "Service Quality Implementation," pp. 17–19.

19. Elliot Markowitz and Joe Wilcox, "Compaq to Pay ASPs Based on Performance," *Computer Retailer News,* Dec. 22, 1997, p. 5.

20. Deborah Grandinetti, "Quality: Your New Pay Yardstick," June 23, 1997, pp. 73–77.

21. Philip Kotler, *Marketing for Nonprofit Organizations,* 2nd ed. (Englewood Cliffs, N.J.: Prentice-Hall, 1982, p. 37.

22. Ibid.

23. Sources: www.grucci.com, Sep. 11, 1998; Laurie Niles, "Fireworks Sky Dance Is No Hurry-Up Job," *Omaha World-Herald,* June 30, 1995, p. B13; Glen Jochum, "Sky's No Limit for Felix Grucci," *LI Business News,* Mar. 20, 1995, p. 23; and Fireworks by Grucci, press kit and company video.

24. Sources: David Greising, "Harrah's Goes for Broke," *Business Week,* Jan. 27, 1997, pp. 78–79; Peter Elkind, "The Big Easy's Bad Bet," *Fortune,* Dec. 8, 1997, pp. 162–167, 170, 172, 174, 176; Seth Lubove, "Where Are All the Slots?" *Forbes,* Feb. 24, 1997, pp. 42–43; Rita Rousseau, "Upping the Ante," *Restaurants and Institutions,* May 15, 1997, pp. 74–77, 79, 81, 83–84, 86; Takia Mahmood and Stephen P. Bradley, "The Promus Companies," *Harvard Business School Publishing,* Feb. 28, 1995, pp. 34–36; Pauline Yoshihashi, "Promus to Split into Casino, Hotel Firms," *Wall Street Journal,* Jan. 31, 1995, p. A3; Martha Brannigan, "Promus Casino in New Orleans Begins Poorly," *Wall Street Journal,* June 12, 1995, p. A4; Harrah's, "Survey of Casino Entertainment," 1995; Harrah's Entertainment Co., *Annual Report,* 1994; Promus Companies, "Corporate Fact Sheet"; Harrah's, "Casino's Fact Sheet"; and Elaine Underwood, "Casino Gambling's New Deal," *Brandweek,* Apr. 10, 1995, pp. 21–25.

25. Sources: "Barbie Site a Hit with Consumers, Marketers," *Youth Markets Alert,* Dec. 7, 1997; "Margin Magic: Collectibles," *Discount Store News,* Feb. 9, 1998, p. 63; "Mattel Celebrates the Birthday of the Barbie Doll with the Launch of Barbie.com for Girls," Mattel news release, www.prnewswire.com, Mar. 9, 1998; Lisa Bannon, " 'Hi, Barbie! I'm Samantha. Can I Boost Your Sales?' " *Wall Street Journal,* June 16, 1998, pp. B1, B3; "Mattel to Consider Book Publishing after Purchase of Pleasant Company," *BP Report,* June 22, 1998; Karen Springen, "Hi There, Dollface. You Look Like Someone We Know," *Newsweek,* Nov. 16, 1998, p. 14; "Mattel Buys Software Giant The Learning Company," *New York Times* (Dec. 14, 1998) www.nytimes.com/library/tech/98/12/biztech/articles/14mattel.html, Jan. 26, 1999; Sue Zeidler, "Mattel Finds Famous Friends for Barbie," Reuters, Jan. 20, 1999; Larry Carlat, "Queen of the Aisles," *Brandweek,* Feb. 12, 1996, pp. 20–22, 24, 26; Gary Hoover, Alta Campbell, and Patrick J. Spains, eds., *Hoover's Handbook of American Business* (Austin, Tex.: Reference Press, 1995), pp. 732–734; Karen Benezra, "Toymakers & Animated Friends Take Heroic Steps toward Girls," *Brandweek,* Feb. 20, 1995, p. 9; Elizabeth Stephenson, "Mattel Dolls Up Barbie for Adult Collectors," *Advertising Age,* Oct. 9, 1995, p. 44.

Chapter 14

1. "Barnes & Noble, Inc.," www.shareholder.com/bks/, accessed Feb. 17, 1999; Company Briefing Books, *The Wall Street Journal* Interactive Edition, interactive.wsj.com, accessed Feb. 17, 1999; and Connie Gentry, "Logistics by the book," *Inbound Logistics,* June 1998, p. 26.

2. Lisa Harrington, "How to Join the Supply Chain Revolution," *Inbound Logistics,* Nov. 1995, p. 21.

3. Roberta J. Duffy and Julie Murphree, "The Power of Purchasing and Supply Chain Management," *Fortune,* Oct. 26, 1998, p. 52.

4. Laurie Joan Aron, "Home Depot Finds Logistic Strength in Numbers," *Inbound Logistics,* Nov. 1994, p. 29.

5. James D. Martin, "Intermodal Needs Supply Chain Partnerships," *Inbound Logistics,* Apr. 1995, p. 16.

6. Phillip W. Seely, "Using Technology to Meet Customer Needs," *Inbound Logistics,* July 1995, p. 46.

7. Shane McLaughlin, "Using Supply-Chain Technology to Create Competitive Advantage," *Inc.,* www.inc.com, Mar. 17, 1998.

8. Harrington, "How to Join the Supply Chain Revolution," p. 20.

9. Linda Himelstein, with Heather Green, Richard Siklos, and Catherine Yang, "Yahoo! The Company, the Strategy, the Stock," *Business Week,* Sep. 7, 1998, pp. 66–76.

10. Sumit K. Majumdar and Venkatram Ramaswamy, "Going Direct to Market: The Influence of Exchange Conditions," *Strategic Management Journal,* June 1995, pp. 353–372.

11. Steven Burke, "Intel Seeks Closer Ties to Channel Elite," *Computer Reseller News,* May 15, 1995, p. 1.

12. James D. Hlavacek and Tommy J. McCuistion, "Industrial Distributors: When, Who, and How?" *Harvard Business Review,* Mar./Apr. 1983, p. 97.

13. Roger O. Crockett, "Gateway Loses the Folksy Schtick," *Business Week,* July 6, 1998, pp. 80, 84.

14. Rajiv Dant, Patrick Kaufmann, and Audesh Paswan, "Ownership Redirection in Franchised Channels," *Journal of Public Policy and Marketing,* Spring 1992, pp. 33–34.

15. Leo Aspinwall, "The Marketing Characteristics of Goods," in *Four Marketing Theories* (Boulder: University of Colorado Press, 1961), pp. 27–32.

16. Allan J. Magrath, "Differentiating Yourself via Distribution," *Sales & Marketing Management,* Mar. 1991, pp. 50–57.

17. Robert D. Buzzell and Gwen Ortmeyer, "Channel Partnerships Streamline Distribution," *Sloan Management Review,* Spring 1995, p. 85.

18. Tony Siedeman, "Get with the Program," *Inbound Logistics,* Sep. 1998, p. 29.

19. Janet E. Keith, Donald W. Jackson, and Lawrence A. Crosby, "Effect of Alternative Types of Influence Strategies under Different Dependence Structures," *Journal of Marketing,* July 1990, pp. 30–41.

20. Zachary Schiller, David Woodruff, Kevin Kelly, and Michael Schroeder, "GM Tightens the Screws," *Business Week,* June 22, 1992, pp. 30–31.

21. Kenneth G. Hardy and Allan J. Magrath, "Ten Ways for Manufacturers to Improve Distribution Management," *Business Horizons,* Nov./Dec. 1988, p. 68.

22. Sandra Skrovan, "Partnering with Vendors: The Ties That Bind," *Chain Store Age Executive,* Jan. 1994, p. 6MH.

23. Wroe Alderson, *Dynamic Marketing Behavior* (Homewood, Ill.: Irwin, 1965), p. 239.

24. James C. Anderson and James A. Narus, "A Model of Distributor Firm and Manufacturer Firm Working Partnerships," *Journal of Marketing,* Jan. 1990, pp. 42–58.

25. Steven J. Skinner, Julie B. Gassenheimer, and Scott W. Kelley, "Cooperation in Supplier-Dealer Relations," *Journal of Retailing,* Summer 1992, pp. 174–193.

26. Seideman, "Get with the Program," p. 31.

27. Erle Norton, "Last of the U.S. Tire Makers Ride Out Foreign Invasion," *Wall Street Journal,* Feb. 4, 1993, p. 86.

28. Adel I. El-Ansary, "Perspectives on Channel System Performance," in *Contemporary Issues in Marketing Channels,* ed. Robert F. Lusch and Paul H. Zinszer (Norman: University of Oklahoma Press, 1979), p. 50.

29. Hardy and Magrath, "Ten Ways."

30. Elizabeth Jensen, " 'What's Up Doc?' Vertical Integration," *Wall Street Journal,* Oct. 16, 1995, p. B1.

31. Jordan D. Lewis, "Using Alliances to Build Market Power," *Planning Review,* Sep./Oct. 1990, pp. 1–9, 48.

32. Buzzell and Ortmeyer, "Channel Partnerships Streamline Distribution."

33. Bert Rosenbloom, *Marketing Channels: A Management View* (Hinsdale, Ill.: Dryden, 1991), p. 103.

34. Ibid., p. 104.

35. Ibid., pp. 108–109.

36. Sources: Keith Anderson, "Reader Can Replace Her CUTCO Knives: Firm Still Guarantees Product," *Denver Post,* Jun. 17, 1995, p. E4; Susan Burns, "The Amway Army," *Sarasota Magazine,* Jan. 1996, p. 48; Pamela Davis-Diaz, "No More Waiting for the Avon Lady," *St. Petersburg Times,* Mar. 13, 1995, p. 8; David W. Cravens, "The Changing Role of the Sales Force: Now It's Urgent," *Marketing Management,* Fall 1995, p. 49; Direct Selling Organization, "Industry Facts," www.dsa.org/factsht.stm, accessed Feb. 12, 1999; Paul Johnson, "Vector Suspends Recruiting," *Wisconsin State Journal,* Apr. 21, 1994, p. 1F; Stratford Sherman, "Will the Information Superhighway Be the Death of Retailing?" *Fortune,* Apr. 18, 1994, p. 98; Debby Garbato Stankevich, "Henckels Sets Biggest Ad Push for Twinstar," *HFN: The Weekly Newspaper for the Home Furniture Network,* Sep. 11, 1995, p. 33; Debby Garbato Stankevich, "Pitching Upscale Cutlery: Vendors Boost Instore Support," *HFN: The Weekly Newspaper for the Home Furniture Network,* Dec. 25, 1995, p. 33; Laurel Touby, "Direct Selling: Behind the Hype," *Executive Female,* Mar. 1994, p. 19; and "Vector Marketing," www.cutco.com/vector1.html, accessed Feb. 12, 1999.

37. Based on information from Larry Armstrong, "Downloading Their Dream Cars," *Business Week,* Mar. 9, 1998, pp. 93–94; Company Briefing Book, *Wall Street Journal,* Interactive Edition, http://interactive.wsj.com, Feb. 24, 1999; Gail DeGeorge, with Bill Vlasic, "Republic Learns Cars Ain't Videos," *Business Week,* Feb. 9, 1998, pp. 82–84; "DealerNet Links Auto Buyers, Sellers Nationwide," *Marketing News,* July 31, 1995, p. 30; Mike McKesson, " '96 Promises to Transform Car Industry," *Marketing News,* Feb. 12, 1996, p. 7; and Keith Naughton, with Kathleen Kerwin, Bill Vlasic, Lori Bongiorno, and David Leonhardt, "Revolution in the Showroom," *Business Week,* Feb. 19, 1996, pp. 70–76.

Chapter 15

1. J. Taylor Buckley, "World's Top Air Freight Center Is Put to the Test This Week," *USA Today,* Dec. 16, 1997; Company Briefing Books, *The Wall Street Jounral* Interactive Edition, interactive.wsj.com, accessed Feb. 17, 1999; "Who Is FedEx?" www.fedex.com/us/about/facts.html, accessed Feb. 22, 1999.

2. Bureau of the Census, *Statistical Abstract of the United States* (Washington, D.C.: Government Printing Office, 1997), p. 544.

3. Hoover's Handbook Database, via America Online.

4. Bert Rosenbloom, *Marketing Channels: A Management View* (Hinsdale, Ill.: Dryden, 1991), p. 450.

5. Donald J. Bowersox and M. Bixby Cooper, *Strategic Marketing Channel Management* (New York: McGraw-Hill, 1992), pp. 41–42.

6. Hoover's Handbook Database, via America Online.

7. Tony Seideman, "Get with the Program," *Inbound Logistics,* Sep. 1998, pp. 28–34.

8. Anne G. Perkins, "Manufacturing: Maximizing Service, Minimizing Inventory," *Harvard Business Review,* Mar./Apr. 1994, pp. 13–14.

9. Tom Richman, "How 20 Best-Practice Companies Do It," *Harvard Business Review,* Sep./Oct. 1995, pp. 11–12.

10. Leslie Hanson Harps, "Partnering for Performance," *Inbound Logistics,* July 1998, pp. 26–27.

11. Laurie Joan Aron, "Speeding the Plow," *Inbound Logistics,* Dec. 1995, p. 28.

12. James Wetherbe, "Principles of Cycle Time Reduction," *Cycle Time Research* 1, no.1, 1995, p. iv.

13. Connie Gentry, "Logistics IT," *Inbound Logistics,* Apr. 1998, p. 21.

14. Getahn M. Ward, "Firms Tell Suppliers to Trash Paper, Take Orders by Computer," *Commercial Appeal,* July 16, 1995, p. C1.

15. Jeffrey H. Dyer, "Dedicated Assets: Japan's Manufacturing Edge," *Harvard Business Review,* Nov./Dec. 1994, pp. 174–178.

16. Douglas M. Lambert and James R. Stock, *Strategic Logistics Management* (Homewood, Ill.: Irwin, 1993), p. 265.

17. Carl M. Guelzo, *Introduction to Logistics Management* (Englewood Cliffs, N.J.: Prentice-Hall, 1986), p. 102.

18. "Plant Site Logistics: Beyond Location, Location, Location," *Inbound Logistics,* Aug. 1997, pp. 34–39.

19. Ibid.

20. "Satisfying Customers Worldwide," *Inbound Logistics,* Nov. 1994, pp. 32–35.

21. Based on information from Company Briefing Books, *The Wall Street Journal* Interactive Edition, interactive.wsj.com, accessed Feb. 17, 1999; Bob Krummert, "The Corporate Giants: Does Bigger Mean Better?" *ID: The Voice of Foodservice Distribution,* Nov. 1, 1996, pp. 44–60; SYSCO Corporation, www.sysco.com; SYSCO Corporation 1997 Annual Report; and SYSCO Corporation Fiscal 1997 Fact Book.

22. Based on information from "About the Company," www.mwh.com/about.html, accessed Feb. 18, 1999; "Did You Know?" www.homedepot.com/dykfacts.dykful.htm, accessed Jan. 26, 1999; and Laurie Joan Aron, "Home Depot Finds Logistics Strength in Numbers," *Inbound Logistics,* Nov. 1995, pp. 28–31.

Chapter 16

1. Based on information from Donald Blount, "Canada's Circus of Commerce," *Denver Post,* Nov. 29, 1998, pp. 1J, 10J; Donald Blount, "World's Largest Mall Is Quite a (Day) Trip," *Denver Post,* Nov. 29, 1998, p. 10J; "West Edmonton Mall Attractions," www.westedmall/attractions/html/index.htm, accessed Feb. 23, 1999.

2. Bureau of the Census, *Statistical Abstract of the United States* (Washington, D.C.: Government Printing Office, 1997), p. 544.

3. *Chain Store Age Executive,* May 1995, pp. 78–80.

4. *Chain Store Age Executive,* Feb. 1995, p. 102.

5. Emily DeNitto, "Hypermarkets Seem to Be Big Flop in U.S.," *Advertising Age,* Oct. 4, 1993, p. 20.

6. J. Barry Mason, Morris L. Mayer, and Hazel F. Ezell, *Retailing* (Homewood, Ill.: Irwin, 1994), pp. 3–4.

7. Chuck Bartels, "Sam's Aims to Add New Products to 200 Stores," *Commercial Appeal,* June 7, 1998, p. C1.

8. Julie Liesse, "Welcome to the Club," *Advertising Age,* Feb. 1, 1993, p. 3.

9. "Ikea Finds New Living Rooms to Conquer," *International Herald Tribune,* July 30, 1998, p. 13.

10. Barry Berman and Joel Evans, *Retail Management: A Strategic Approach* (New York: Macmillan, 1992), pp. 104–105.

11. Ann Marsh, "Not Your Dad's Hardware Store," *Forbes,* Jan. 26, 1998, p. 45.

12. Kelly Shermach, "Retail Catalogs Designed to Boost In-store Sales," *Marketing News,* July 3, 1995, p. 1.

13. Laurel Campbell, "Fewer Catalogs in the Mail This Year," *Commercial Appeal,* Oct. 19, 1995, pp. B4, B7.

14. Ibid.

15. Elaine Underwood, "Why I'm a Home Shopper," *Brandweek,* Apr. 19, 1993, pp. 23–28.

16. Faith Bremner, "Quirky Little Business Makes eBay a Big Buy," *USA Today,* Oct. 28, 1998, p. 3B.

17. Linda Himelstein, with Heather Green, Richard Siklos, and Catherine Yang, "Yahoo!" *Business Week,* Sep. 7, 1998, pp. 66–76.

18. Daisy Whitney, "Merchants Tighten 'Net,' " *Denver Post,* Oct. 26, 1998, p. 10E.

19. "Franchising Fellowship," *Marketing Management,* Fall 1995, pp. 4, 5.

20. Bruce Horovitz, "Taco Bell Finds a Dog's Life Quite Fetching," *USA Today,* Oct. 22, 1998, pp. 1B, 2B; "Lean, Teen Eating Machines," *Marketing News,* Aug. 3, 1998, p. 2.

21. *Chain Store Age Executive,* Dec. 1994, pp. 114–115.

22. George H. Lucas, Jr., and Larry G. Gresham, "How to Position for Retail Success," *Business,* Apr./June 1988, pp. 3–13.

23. Kelly Barron, "Cool It," *Forbes,* Nov. 2, 1998, p. 218.

24. Daniel Roth, "This Ain't No Pizza Party," *Fortune,* Nov. 9, 1998, p. 164.

25. Julie Baker, Dhruv Grewal, and A. Parasuraman, "The Influence of Store Environment on Quality Inferences and Store Image," *Journal of the Academy of Marketing Science,* Fall 1994, p. 328.

26. Becky Ebenkamp, "The Show Must Go On . . . the Shelves," *Brandweek,* March 16, 1998, p. 32.

27. Wendy Zellner, "Look Out, Supermarkets—Wal-Mart Is Hungry," *Business Week,* Sep. 14, 1998, pp. 98–99.

28. Ibid.

29. Stephen Brown, "The Wheel of Retailing: Past and Future," *Journal of Retailing,* Summer 1990, pp. 143–149.

30. James R. Hagerty, "U.S. Stores Offer Status among Drill Bits," *International Herald Tribune,* July 30, 1998, p. 13.

31. Laurel Campbell, "Retail Forecast for First Half of '96: Slow," *Commercial Appeal,* Jan. 6, 1996, p. B8.

32. Ibid.

33. "All American Food Group, Inc.," www.thebagelpage.com, accessed Feb. 22, 1999; "A Hole In One," *Restaurant Business,* May 15, 1997; Bruce Horovitz, "Need for Speed Drives Cereal Killer," *USA Today,* Jan. 22, 1999, p. B1; George W. Kromer, Jr, "Building on Quality," *Today's Investor,* Dec. 15, 1997, p 1; "Hot Brands . . . Hot Concepts . . . Hot Profits," All American Food Group company brochure, 1999

34. Sources: R. Michelle Breyer, "All-Natural Capitalist," *Austin American-Statesman,* May 10, 1998, pp. A1, A8; "Children of the Earth Go Corporate," *Austin American-Statesman,* May 10, 1998, p. A10; and "Labor Practices Draw Praise and Pickets," *Austin American Statesman,* May 10, 1998, p. A10.

35. This case was prepared by Neil Herndon, City University of Hong Kong, based on information from Andrew Backover, "Bass Pro Shops Signs Grapevine Superstore Deal," *Fort Worth Star-Telegram,* Oct. 7, 1997, p. 1; Eddie Bass, "Renovations Add More Retail Space," *Springfield News-Leader,* Dec. 1, 1997, p. 11; Bass Pro Shops, "Outdoor World," promotional pamphlet CL-670, n.d.; Bass Pro Shops, "The Outdoor World Showroom," *Springfield News-Leader,* Special Advertising Supplement, Aug. 20, 1989, p. 1; Bass Pro Shops, "Welcome to Outdoor World," promotional pamphlet, CL-902, n.d.; "Bass Pro Shops: An RV/Fishing Venue," *RV Business,* July 1996, pp. 34, 41–42; Robert E. Carr, "Bass Pro Challenges Vendor Price Policies," *Sporting Goods Business,* Feb. 1994, p. 8; Paul Flemming, "Civic Park Tops List of Tax Beneficiaries," *Springfield Business Journal,* Jan. 26, 1998, p. 1; Michael Grunwald, "Megamall Sells Stimulation," *Boston Globe,*

Dec. 9, 1997, p. 1A; Matt Hiebert, "Restaurant Offers More than Delicious Food," *Springfield News-Leader,* Special Advertising Supplement, Aug. 20, 1989, p. 6; Steve Koehler, "A New Zenith for Bass Pro," *Springfield News-Leader,* Jan. 16, 1997, p. 1A; Jeff Kurowski, "Bass Pro Shops Goes to Illinois, Texas," *Boating Industry,* Sep. 1996, p. 16; Kate Marymount, "Hemingway's Makes Debut with Flavor," *Springfield News-Leader,* Apr. 24, 1987, p. 1C; Kathleen O'Dell, "Bass Pro Plans Big Renovation," *Springfield News-Leader,* Jan. 6, 1988, pp. 1A, 10A; Kathleen O'Dell, "Old Sea Tales: Bass Pro Barbershop Cuts Hairs with Nautical Flair," *Springfield News-Leader,* Oct. 1, 1987, pp. 6B, 8B; John Rogers, "State Conservation Department Pledges $2.5 Million toward Wildlife Museum," *St. Louis Post-Dispatch,* Dec. 19, 1997, p. 6C; Dan Sewell, "After the Strike: UPS Tries to Recoup Losses," *Commercial Appeal,* Aug. 21, 1997, p. B8; and "Wildlife Museum Backers Seek Millions from Public," *St. Louis Post-Dispatch,* May 3, 1997, p. 18.

Chapter 17

1. Based on information from Saint Paul Saints, www.spsaints.com; St. Paul Saints, press notes; St. Paul Saints, *Yearbook,* 1998; Kevin Reichard, "Living the Dream," *Corporate Report,* Sep. 1998, pp. 37–49; Russell Scott Smith, "Rock and Roll Baseball," *Minnesota Monthly,* June 1997, pp. 22–23; and "William Souder, "The Joys of Summer," *Washington Post,* July 2, 1997, pp. A1, A12.

2. Terence A. Shimp, *Advertising, Promotion, and Supplemented Aspects of Integrated Marketing Communications* (Fort Worth, Tex.: Dryden Press, 1997), p. 15

3. In case you do not read Chinese, the message, prepared by Chih Kang Wang, says, "In the factory we make cosmetics, and in the store we sell hope."

4. Shimp, *Advertising,* p. 105.

5. John S. McClenahen, "How Can You Possibly Say That?" *Industry Week,* July 17, 1995, pp. 17–19.

6. "VW Drives Pitch for New Beetle with Print, TV Spread," *Brandweek,* Mar. 16, 1998, p. 5.

7. Angela Dawson and Sloane Lucas, "Ski Group Loads $20M," *Brandweek,* Sept. 28, 1998, p. 15.

8. "Sara Lee Bids for More Frequent Consumer Use," *Brandweek,* Oct. 19, 1998, p. 16.

9. Mark Lacek, "Loyalty Marketing No Ad Budget Threat," *Advertising Age,* Oct. 23, 1995, p. 20.

10. John J. Burnett, *Promotion Management* (Boston: Houghton Mifflin, 1993), p. 7.

11. Christine Bittar. "J&J Plots Supreme Command," *Brandweek,* Nov. 16, 1998, pp. 1, 8.

12. Chip Walker, "Word of Mouth," *American Demographics,* July 1995, pp. 38–40.

13. James M. Stearns and Shaheen Borna, "The Ethics of Lottery Advertising: Issues and Evidence," *Journal of Business Ethics,* Jan. 1995, pp. 43–51.

14. Weld F. Royal, "Scapegoat or Scoundrel?" *Sales & Marketing Management,* Jan. 1995, pp. 62–69.

15. Susan Edelman, "Sweepstakes Lawsuit Goes to Trial," *Record,* Mar. 12, 1995, p. A3.

16. A.H. Maslow, *Motivation and Personality* (New York: Harper and Row, 1954).

17. Ira Teinowitz and Keith J. Kelly, "PM Fires Up Warning over Tobacco Ad Limits," *Advertising Age,* Nov. 20, 1995, pp. 3, 23.

18. Sources: Ben Van Houten, "Learning Latin," *Restaurant Business,* Apr. 15, 1997, pp. 58–68; Christine Foster, "Down-Home Girl Makes Good," *Forbes,* Nov. 17, 1997, pp. 73–78; Bill Carlino, "Churchs Has Faith That New Ad Agency Will Strengthen Image," *Nation's Restaurant News,* Jan. 19, 1998, p. 22; Katy Eckmann, "Austin Kelley Recalls Former Icon in Initial Commercials for Churchs," *Adweek Southeast,* Apr. 20, 1998, p. 5; Jack Hayes, "Churchs Aims for Broader Reach with New Venues, Products," *Nation's Restaurant News,* Apr. 20, 1998, p. 3; Valerie Fields, "Franklin Invests in Churchs; Gospel Singer to Own 15 Restaurants," *Arlington Morning News,* June 18, 1998, p. 1A; "AFC Enterprises Keeps Promise to Habitat for Humanity International; Dedicates 200th Home Worldwide in Atlanta, GA," Churchs news release, (Nov. 6, 1998), www.afc-online.com/Media/200.html, Jan. 26, 1999; Candace Talmadge, "Using Cows to Build Chicken Brand," Reuters, January 26, 1999; and "Churchs at A Glance," www.churchs.com/Glance/index.html, Jan. 26, 1999.

19. Sources: "New National Effort Announced to Help Prevent Underage Alcohol Beverage Purchases," www.prnewswire.com/513NYTU112, May 13, 1997; Francine Katz, "One Giant Step for Prevention; One Giant Slurpee for Teens," *Prevention Pipeline,* www.beeresponsible.com, May 13, 1998; "Anheuser-Busch College Marketing Code," *Prevention Pipeline,* www.beeresponsible.com, May 13, 1998; "Oscar de la Hoya Fights Alcohol Abuse during Super Bowl," Anheuser-Busch press release, Jan. 22, 1998; Robert Emproto and Greg Prince, "College Binge Drinking Data Shows Anti-Abuse Effort Has Miles to Go," *Beverage World,* Jan. 31, 1995, pp. 1, 3; Chris Reidy, "Questions Arise on Liquor Marketing," *Boston Globe,* Apr. 6, 1995, p. 69; Fara Warner, "Liquor Industry Tackles Teenage Drinking," *Wall Street Journal,* June 30, 1995, p. B4; and Anheuser-Busch Company, press kit, 1995.

Chapter 18

1. Based on information from "The Horn Group Opens Public Relations Office in Boston Area to Serve East Coast Market," www.businesswire.com/3101184 Mar. 10, 1997; Geoffrey Brewer, "Selling an Intangible," *Sales & Marketing Management,* Jan. 1998, pp. 52–56, 58; and Horn Group, www.horngroup.com, May 15, 1998.

2. "100 Leaders by U.S. Advertising Spending," *Advertising Age,* Sep. 28, 1998, p. 54.

3. Tobi Elkin, "Pioneer Sets Table for Makeover in New Print Push," *Brandweek,* Sep. 28, 1998, p. 13.

4. Becky Ebenkamp, "Fossil Test Could Spur Regular Media Sked," *Brandweek,* Nov. 2, 1998, p. 6.

5. Tobi Elkin, "Kodak Bets $5M to Grow Digital Cam," *Brandweek,* Sep. 28, 1998, p. 4.

6. Diane Cyr, "Getting More Direct," *Brandweek,* Oct. 9, 1995, pp. 29–36.

7. Terry Lefton, "Nike Looks to Reconnect with Women in Issue-based Campaign," *Brandweek,* Nov. 9, 1998, p. 4.

8. William F. Arens, *Contemporary Advertising* (Burr Ridge, Ill.: Irwin/McGraw-Hill, 1999), p. 378.

9. M. Louise Ripley, "What Kind of Companies Take Their Advertising In-House?" *Journal of Advertising Research,* Oct./Nov. 1991, pp. 73–77.

10. George E. Belch and Michael A. Belch, *Advertising and Promotion* (Burr Ridge, Ill.: Irwin/McGraw-Hill, 1998), p. 519.

11. Terry Lefton, "Nascar Inks Home Depot," *Brandweek,* Nov. 2, 1998, p. 4.

12. Liza Rodriguez, "Will Work for Sponsorship," *Sales & Marketing Management,* Nov. 1998, p. 15.

13. Belch and Belch, *Advertising and Promotion,* p. 525.

14. Sources: Winkler McManus video, BATV show #713, air date February 9, 1997; "Branding, New and Improved," Winkler Advertising, *http://www.winklerad.com* (April 5, 1999).

15. Sources: Rick Tetzeli and David Kirkpatrick, "America Loves Microsoft," *Fortune,* Feb. 2, 1998, pp. 80+; Steve Hamm, " 'I'm Humble, I'm Respectful,' " *Business Week,* Feb. 9, 1998, pp. 40–42; Greg Miller and Leslie Helm, "Microsoft Plans Stealth Media Blitz," *Los Angeles Times,* Apr. 10, 1998, p. A1; Thomas W. Haines, "Lesson Plan: Microsoft Hits the Hallways, because Today's Fifth-Grader Is Tomorrow's Software Buyer," *Seattle Times,* Apr. 12, 1998, p. F1; Bradley Johnson, "Microsoft Eyes Ads in Antitrust Struggle with Justice Dept.," *Advertising Age,* Apr. 13, 1998, p. 39; David Bank and John Simons, "Microsoft Is on Defensive over Media Strategy," *Wall Street Journal,* Apr. 13, 1998, p. B8; Amy Cortese, "Emperor of High Tech, Sultan of Spin," *Business Week,* May 18, 1998, p. 37; Geoffrey James, "Image Making at Mighty Microsoft," *Upside,* June 1998, pp. 81–86; Susan B. Garland, "A Tough Sell, but Not Impossible," *Business Week,* Jan. 18, 1999, p. 44; and Mike France and Susan B. Garland, "Microsoft: The View at Halftime," *Business Week,* Jan. 25, 1999, pp. 78–82.

Chapter 19

1. Based on information from Kathleen Mulvihill, "Oh, Baby," *New Orleans CityBusiness,* Apr. 27, 1998, p. 1; Louise Kramar, "MCD's Promo Plan for 1999 Includes Beanie Babies III," *Advertising Age,* June 8, 1998, p. 4; Richard Gibson, "At McDonald's, a Case of Mass Beaniemania," *Wall Street Journal,* June 5, 1998, pp. B1, B5; and "Ty(R) Teenie Beanie Babies (TM) Return to McDonald's (R)," www.prnewswire.com/0518CGM023 May 18, 1998.

2. "What a Sales Call Costs," *Sales & Marketing Management,* Dec. 1998, p. 4.

3. Sarah Lorge, "The Best way to Prospect," *Sales & Marketing Management,* Jan. 1998, p. 80.

4. Allison Lucas, "The Thrill of Victory," *Sales & Marketing Management,* Nov. 1995, p. 92.

5. Melinda Ligos, "The Incredible Shrinking Sales Force," *Sales & Marketing Management,* Dec. 1998, p. 15.

6. Michele Marchetti, "Hiring," *Sales & Marketing Management,* Dec. 1998, p. 32.

7. Michele Marchetti, "Compensation," *Sales & Marketing Management,* Dec. 1998, p. 34.

8. Sandra Hile Hart, William C. Moncrief, and A. Parasuraman, "An Empirical Investigation of Salespeople's Performance, Effort and Selling Method during a Sales Contest," *Journal of the Academy of Marketing Science,* Winter 1989, pp. 29–39.

9. Nora Wood. "What Motivates Best?" *Sales & Marketing Management,* Sep. 1998, pp. 71–78.

10. Andy Cohen, "Process," *Sales & Marketing Management,* Dec. 1998, p. 36.

11. George E. Belch and Michael A. Belch, *Advertising and Promotion,* (Burr Ridge, Ill.: Irwin/McGraw-Hill, 1998), pp. 472–475.

12. "Oral-B Readies $30M in U.S. Ads for Cross-Action Intro," *Brandweek,* Nov. 2, 1998, p. 9.

13. Cox Direct, "The 20th Annual Survey of Promotional Practices," 1998, pp. 22–23.

14. Ibid., p. 26.

15. Ibid., p. 27.

16. Tobi Elkin, "IBM Taps Crayola License to Score Software Distribution at Walgreens," *Brandweek,* Sep. 28, 1998, p. 9.

17. Becky Ebenkamp, "Less Is Latest with Pager Premium Lure," *Brandweek,* Oct. 12, 1998, p. 12.

18. Karen Benezra, "Cherry Coke Looks to Enhance Edge with $3–5M Web Mystery," *Brandweek,* Mar. 16, 1998, p. 15.

19. "Promo Has Teenage Girls *Jump*-ing for Free Phone Use," *Brandweek,* July 13, 1998, p. 8.

20. Sources: Ann Steffora, "Rodin's Goal: 'A Happy Customer,' " *Electronic News,* Feb. 16, 1998, p. 50; Tim Wilson, "Wholesale Shift to the Web," *InternetWeek,* July 20, 1998, p. 1; Geoffrey Colvin, "What Money Makes You Do," *Fortune,* Aug. 17, 1998, p. 213; Dana Blankenhorn, "Marshall Still the Best," *Business Marketing,* Aug. 1998, p. 25; Clint Willis, "How Winners Do It," *Forbes,* Aug. 24, 1998, pp. 88–92; and John H. Mayer, "Online @Distribution.com," *Electronic Buyers News* (Jan. 23, 1999), www.cmp.com, Feb. 2, 1999.

21. Sources: "Pepper Progress," *Dr Pepper Clockdial,* May 1998, pp. 9–14; "Corporate News," *Dr Pepper Clockdial,* May 1998, pp. 16–17; "Dr Pepper Congratulates the Collegiate Players Tour," www.drpepper.com/files/college-golf/golf.html, Feb. 1, 1999; "Now Is the Time . . . to Pepperize!!" www.drpepper.com/files/pepper/savers.html, Feb. 1, 1999; "Theresa Howard, "Brand Builders: Strategy: The Pepper Paradigm," *Brandweek,* Nov. 2, 1998, pp. 24, 28; Jordan Mackay, "The Fight over Soft Drinks in the Public Schools Fizzes Up in Texas," *Texas Monthly,* Dec. 1998, p. 30; and "Third Quarter Ad Spending Up 8.8%," www.cmr.com, Feb. 1, 1999.

22. Sources: Jeff Manning, "How the Udder Beverage Aims to Steal Share," *Beverage World,* Jan. 15, 1998, pp. 115–116; Jeff Wilson, "Hollywood's Cool Fashion Statement: A Milk Mustache," *San Diego Daily Times* (Apr. 23, 1998), http://sddt.com/files/librarywire/98/04/23/lc.html, Feb. 2, 1999; "Milk—Better Bones Tour," National Fluid Milk Processor Promotion Board, www.whymilk.com/bones/mobile.html, Feb. 2, 1999; "Elway Goes for Superbowl Repeat: Consecutive Milk Mustache Ads," www.businesswire.com/photowire/pw.012799.975409.htm, January 27, 1999 (February 2, 1999); National Fluid Milk Processor Promotion Board, press kit, 1995; Wisconsin Milk Marketing Board, press kit; Anthony Vagnoni, "The 1995 Obie Awards," *Advertising Age,* May 8, 1995, p. 66.

Chapter 20

1. Sources: "Buycomp.com Launches New Internet Superstore; Becomes Buy.com," Buy.com news release (Nov. 16, 1998), www.buy.com/bc/noframes/companyinfo/981116b.asp, Feb. 9, 1999, "Online Buy.com Adds Books, Takes on Amazon.com," Internetnews.com, (Nov. 17, 1998), www.internetnews.com/Reuters/1998/11/, Feb. 9, 1999; "Company Background," www2.buy.com/book/dyn/info/company.html, Feb. 9, 1999; Larry Armstrong, "Anything You Sell, I Can Sell Cheaper," *Business Week,* Dec. 14, 1998, pp. 130–132; and "OnSale Set to Wholesale PCs; Margins Narrow," Internetnews.com, (Jan. 19, 1999), www.internetnews.com/Reuters/1999/01, Feb. 9, 1999.

2. Donald Lichtenstein, Nancy M. Ridgway, and Richard G. Netemeyer, "Price Perceptions and Consumer Shopping Behavior: A Field Study," *Journal of Marketing Research,* May 1993, pp. 234–245.

3. Kevin J. Clancy, "At What Profit Price?" *Brandweek,* June 23, 1997, pp. 24–28.

4. "A New Vision at Mobile," *National Petroleum News,* June 1995, p. 62.

5. David Leonhardt, "Cereal-Box Killers Are on the Loose," *Business Week,* Oct. 12, 1998, pp. 72–77.

6. Jack Neff, "Small Luxuries Move Sales in Package Goods," *Advertising Age,* May 11, 1998, p. 26.

7. Lichtenstein, Ridgway, and Netemeyer, "Price Perceptions."

8. Hollee Actman, "Little Editions," *Sporting Goods Business,* May 5, 1995, pp. 48–50.

9. Lichtenstein, Ridgway, and Netemeyer, "Price Perceptions."

10. Gary Strauss, "Many Farms Could Be in Final Season," *USA Today,* Oct. 13, 1998, pp. B1–B2.

11. Sources: Jennifer Michaels, "DOT Report Adds to the Debate over Low Fares," *Travel Agent,* Jan. 19, 1998, p. 67; Liz Fisher, "Success in a Nutshell," *Accountancy,* July 1998, pp. 28–29; Laura Goldberg, "Southwest Airlines to Test Coast-to-Coast Flights," *Houston Chronicle,* (Nov. 25, 1998), www.houstonchronicle.com, Dec. 4, 1998; Wendy Zellner, "Southwest's New Direction," *Business Week,* Feb. 8, 1999, pp. 58–59. "Southwest Airlines' Herb Kelleher: Unorthodoxy at Work," *Management Review,* Jan. 1995, pp. 9–12; Bridget O'Brian, "Southwest Air Says First-Half Results Are Likely to be Hurt by Competition," *Wall Street Journal,* Feb. 13, 1995, p. A2;

12. Sources: "Priceline.com Keeps Affordable Leisure Airline Tickets within Reach of Nation's Budget-Conscious Travelers," www.businesswire.com/8191346, Aug. 19, 1998; "Priceline.com Debuts in the Top-10 Most-Visited Commerce Web Sites," www.businesswire.com/05191358, May 19, 1998; Paul Davidson, "Web Site Lets You Decide How Much to Pay," *USA Today,* Sep. 16, 1998, p. 12B; "Priceline.com Expands 'Name Your Own Price' Service with an Entirely New Way to Buy a Car or Truck," www.businesswire.com/7061006, July 6, 1998; Katherine T. Beddingfield, "Airfare Roulette," *U.S. News & World Report,* Apr. 27, 1998, p. 75; Katherine Mieszkowski, "Name Your Price!" *Fast Company,* Nov. 1998, p. 292; and Priceline.com, www.priceline.com, Oct. 26, 1998.

Chapter 21

1. Sources: Steve Rosenbush and Melanie Wells, "Sprint Dials Up Nontraditional Calling Plan," *USA Today,* November 5, 1998, p. 1B; Rebecca Blumenstein, "Sprint Ups the Ante in Long-Distance Price War," *Wall Street Journal,* November 6, 1998, p. B10; Seth Schiesel, "Sprint Offers Monthly Plan for Unlimited Long-Distance Calls," *New York Times,* November 6, 1998, p. C20; "Sprint's Bottom Line Improved, But Results Didn't Meet Targets," Dow Jones on SmartMoney Today, February 2, 1999, http://www.smartmoney.com/smt/news/on/index.cfm?story=on-19990202-000246-0823 (February 11, 1999).

2. Peter D. Bennett, *Dictionary of Marketing Terms* (American Marketing Association, 1995), p. 79.

3. Ibid., p. 215.

4. Steven V. Brull, "At 7 ½ Cents a Minute, Who Cares if You Can't Hear a Pin Drop?" *Business Week,* Dec. 29, 1997, p. 46.

5. Robert M. Schindler and Alan R. Wiman, "Effects of Odd Pricing on Price Recall," *Journal of Business Research,* Nov. 1989, pp. 165–177.

6. John C. Groth and Stephen W. McDaniel, "The Exclusive Value Principle: The Basis for Prestige Pricing," *Journal of Consumer Marketing* 10, no. 1, 1993, pp. 10–16.

7. Sources: "Vector Files Reports Showing Strong Turnaround; 2nd Half of Year Profitable," Vector Aeromotive news release, www.prnewswire.com, Mar. 31, 1998; "Vector Aeromotive Corp (VCAR) Annual Report (SEC Form 10-K)" (Mar. 31, 1998), http://sec.yahoo.com/e/980331/vcar.html, Nov. 23, 1998; Mark Basch, "Vector Climbs Back into the Driver's Seat," *Jacksonville Times-Union* (Apr. 1, 1998), www.jacksonville.com/tu-online/stories/040198/bus_1b4vecto.html, Nov. 23, 1998; "Vector M12 Sports Car Competes at Nevada Grand Prix," Vector Aeromotive news release, www.businesswire.com, (SEC Form 10-Q)" Apr. 29, 1998; and "Vector Aeromotive Corp (VCAR) Quarterly Report (Sep. 30, 1998), http://sec.yahoo.com/e/980923/vcar.html, Nov. 23, 1998.

8. Sources: Ira Sager and Peter Burrows, "Back to the Future at Apple," *Business Week,* May 25, 1998, http://www.businessweek.com (February 19, 1999); Ira Sager and Peter Burrows, "Steve Jobs: 'There's Sanity Returning,' " *Business Week,* May 25, 1998, http://www.businessweek.com (February 19, 1999); Stephen H. Wildstrom, "Is Apple's iMac for You?" *Business Week,* September 7, 1998, p. 18; Stephen H. Wildstrom, "Where Wintel Fears to Tread," *Business Week,* September 14, 1998, p. 19; Kristi Essick, "Europeans Hungry for Apple's iMac," *Computerworld,* September 16, 1998, http://www.computerworld.com/home/news.nsf/all/9809163apple (February 19, 1999); Ira Sager, "Dream Days for Desktops," *Business Week,* November 16, 1998, pp. 148, 150, 152; Penelope Patsuris, "Apple Is More Than the iMac," *Forbes,* January 13, 1999, http://www.forbes.com/tool/html/99/jan/0113/mu5.htm (February 19, 1999); "Corporate Scoreboard," *Business Week,* March 1, 1999, p. 86.

9. Sources: Mary Beth Regan, "The Post Office Delivers a Banner Year," *Business Week* (Jan. 19, 1998), www.businessweek.com, Feb. 11, 1999; "Brand Builders: The Post Office's Priority," *Brandweek,* Feb. 23, 1998, pp. 18–19;

"USPS Postal Exec Points to PR as Key to 'Priority Mail' Campaign," *PR Newswire*, (Mar. 9, 1998), through IAC Insite, Oct. 27, 1998; Paul Miller, "USPS Readies Confirmation System," *Catalog Age*, Apr. 15, 1998, p. 5; Paul Miller, "Focus Group Scolds USPS," *Catalog Age*, July 7, 1998, p. 7; Terry Lefton, "Postal Service Scores Heisman; Merrill Lynch aboard Road Show," *Brandweek*, Aug. 24, 1998, p. 14; "New Rates," U.S.P.S. news release (Jan. 10, 1999), www.usps.gov/history/rates/test2.htm, Feb. 11, 1999; "New Postal Service Annual Report: A Tradition of Delivering Value," U.S.P.S. news release (Feb. 2, 1999), www.usps.gov/news/press/99/99010/new.htm, Feb. 11, 1999; Bill McAllister, "Postal Service to Make 2-Day Parcels a Priority," *Washington Post*, Jan. 22, 1996, p. A17; Ho Rodney, "UPS Raising Rates, but Customer Impact Varies," *Atlanta Constitution*, Jan. 4, 1996, p. F1; Mario C. Aguilera, "Post Office Tries New Services to Get an Edge," *San Diego Daily Transcript*, Oct. 18, 1995, p. A1; Dorothy Gjiobbe, "Postal Service Plans Unaddressed Saturation Program," *Editor & Publisher*, Sept. 9, 1996, p. 24; Jim McTeague, "D.C. Current: Runyonesque Approach Would Let the Post Office Borrow in the Credit Markets, Expand into Other Services," *Barron's*, Nov. 27, 1996, p. 35.

Chapter 22

1. Based on information from "Amtrak Board Approves Landmark Business Plan to Revitalize National Passenger Rail for the 21st Century," Amtrak press release, www.amtrak.com/news/pr/atk98184.html, Oct. 19, 1998; "Amtrak Fact Sheet," www.amtrak.com/news/pr/factsheet.html, Feb. 24, 1999; "Highlights of Amtrak's FY 1999–02 Strategic Business Plan," www.amtrak.com/news/pr/hilites.html, Feb. 24, 1999; and Daniel Marchalaba, "Fast Trains, Local Beer Mark Makeover Effort at Amtrak," *Wall Street Journal*, Interactive Edition, http://interactive.wsj.com, Jan. 27, 1999.

2. Based on Orville C. Walker, Jr., and Robert W. Ruekert, "Marketing's Role in the Implementation of Business Strategies: A Critical Review and Conceptual Framework," *Journal of Marketing*, July 1987, pp. 15–33.

3. Robert Howard, "Values Make the Company: An Interview with Robert Haas," *Harvard Business Review*, Sep./Oct. 1990, pp. 132–144.

4. David Field, "New Airlines' Cut Rates Could Be Too Good to Keep Flying," *USA Today*, Oct. 27, 1998, p. 3B.

5. Myron Glassman and Bruce McAfee, "Integrating the Personnel and Marketing Functions: The Challenge of the 1990s," *Business Horizons*, May/June 1992, pp. 52–59.

6. Michael D. Hartline and O.C. Ferrell, "Service Quality Implementation: The Effects of Organizational Socialization and Managerial Actions on the Behaviors of Customer-Contact Employees," *Marketing Science Institute Working Paper Series*, no. 93-122 (Cambridge, Mass.: Marketing Science Institute, 1993), pp. 36–40.

7. O. C. Ferrell, Michael D. Hartline, George H. Lucas, Jr., and David Luck, *Marketing Strategy* (Ft. Worth, Tex.: Dryden, 1999), pp. 135–136.

8. Adapted from Nigel F. Piercy, *Market-Led Strategic Change* (Newton, Mass.: Butterworth-Heinemann, 1992), pp. 374–385.

9. Richard Gibson, "Planet Hollywood's Star Dims," *Denver Post*, Oct. 12, 1998, p. E2.

10. Chris Woodyard, "Southwest Airlines Makes Flying Fun," *USA Today*, Sep. 22, 1998, p. 4E.

11. Chad Kaydo, "Riding High," *Sales & Marketing Management*, July 1998, p. 64.

12. Sybil F. Stershic, "Internal Marketing Campaign Reinforces Service Goals," *Marketing News*, July 31, 1998, p. 11.

13. Adapted from Joseph R. Jablonski, *Implementing Total Quality Management* (Albuquerque, N.M.: Technical Management Consortium, 1990).

14. Philip B. Crosby, *Quality is Free: The Art of Making Quality Certain* (New York: McGraw-Hill, 1979), pp. 9–10.

15. Piercy, *Market-Led Strategic Change*.

16. Kenneth W. Thomas and Betty A. Velthouse, "Cognitive Elements of Empowerment: An 'Interpretive' Model of Intrinsic Task Motivation," *Academy of Management Review*, Oct. 1990, pp. 666–681.

17. Kaydo, "Riding High," p. 67.

18. Hartline and Ferrell, "Service Quality Implementation."

19. "Consultants Never Mind the Buzzwords: Roll up Your Sleeves," *Business Week*, Jan. 26, 1996, via America Online.

20. Fred Steingraber, "Total Quality Management: A New Look at a Basic Issue," *Vital Speeches of the Day*, May 1990, pp. 415–416.

21. Rohit Deshpande and Frederick E. Webster, Jr., "Organizational Culture and Marketing: Defining the Research Agenda," *Journal of Marketing*, Jan. 1989, pp. 3–15.

22. Kerry A. Dolan, "Backpackers Meet Bottom Line," *Forbes*, Nov. 16, 1998, p. 161.

23. Ajay K. Kohli and Bernard J. Jaworski, "Marketing Orientation: The Construct, Research Propositions, and Managerial Implications," *Journal of Marketing*, Apr. 1990, pp. 1–18.

24. Brinker International, Inc., "Chili's Grill & Bar Suggestion Selling Training Guide," and "Creating the Sizzle Experience."

25. David C. Jones, "Motivation the Catalyst in Profit Formula," *National Underwriter*, July 13, 1987, pp. 10, 13.

26. Michele Marchetti, "Helping Reps Count Every Penny," *Sales & Marketing Management*, July 1998, p. 77.

27. Peter Galuszka, with Kathleen Morris, "With All This Fizz, Who Needs Pepsi?" *Business Week*, Oct. 19, 1998, p. 72.

28. Stephanie Armour, "Failure to Communicate Costly for Companies," *USA Today*, Sep. 30, 1998, p. B1.

29. Hartline and Ferrell, "Service Quality Implementation," pp. 36–48.

30. Bernard J. Jaworski, "Toward a Theory of Marketing Control: Environmental Context, Control Types, and Consequences," *Journal of Marketing*, July 1988, pp. 23–39.

31. Bruce Horovitz, "McDonald's Going after the Small Fry," *USA Today*, Oct. 8, 1998, p. B3.

32. Richard A. Melcher, "Industry Outlook 1996: Business Services," *Business Week*, Jan. 8, 1996, p. 107.

33. J.D. Power and Associates, "1998 Sales Satisfaction Study," and "Awards, Automotive Industry," www.jdpower.com/award-au.html, Nov. 11, 1998.

34. Kerry Pipes, "Used-Car 'Superstores' Fail to Dominate Market," *Car and Driver,* Nov. 1998, p. 36.

35. Kathleen Kerwin and Keith Naughton, "Cruise Control?" *Business Week,* Jan. 8, 1996, pp. 82–83.

36. William Glasgall, with John Rossant and Thane Peterson, "Citigroup: Just the Start?" *Business Week,* Apr. 20, 1998, pp. 34–37.

37. Christopher H. Lovelock, *Services Marketing,* 2nd ed. (Englewood Cliffs, N.J.: Prentice-Hall, 1991), p. 270.

38. Source: Kitchen Etc. Web site, www.kitchenetc.com, Feb. 25, 1999.

39. Sources: Laura Bird, "Denny's TV Ad Seeks to Mend Bias Image," *Wall Street Journal,* June 21, 1993, p. B4; Laurie Campbell, "New Denny's Exec Relishes Challenge: Facing Firestorm," *Commercial Appeal,* June 20, 1993, p. C1; "Denny's to Settle Federal Bias Charge," *Commercial Appeal,* Mar. 27, 1993, p. B2; "Denny's Fires Annapolis Manager," *Commercial Appeal,* May 15, 1993, p. B1; James Harney, Civil Rights Leaders Divided over Denny's," *USA Today,* June 4, 1993, p. 2A; Nicole Harris, "A New Denny's Diner by Diner," *Business Week,* Mar. 25, 1996, pp. 166, 168; Benjamin A. Holden, "TW Holdings' Denny's Restaurants Unit Signs Consent Decree in U.S. Bias Case," *Wall Street Journal,* Mar. 26, 1993, p. A6; Julia Lawlor, "Denny's Vows to Fix Unequal Treatment," *USA Today,* Mar. 26, 1993, p. 2B; Andrew E. Serwer, "What to Do When Race Charges Fly," *Fortune,* July 12, 1993, pp. 95–96; and Amy Stevens, "Denny's Agrees to Alter Practices in Bias Settlement," *Wall Street Journal,* Mar. 30, 1993, p. B9.

Chapter 23

1. Company Briefing Book, *Wall Street Journal,* Interactive Edition, http://interactive.wsj.com, Mar. 2, 1999; Ira Sager, "Don't Look for Dell's Secrets Here," *Business Week,* Mar. 8, 1999, p. 20; Andy Serwer, "Dell International: It Works," *Fortune* (May 11, 1998), www.pathfinder.com/fortune/1998/980511/del3.html; Andy Serwer, "Michael Dell Rocks," *Fortune* (May 11, 1998), www.pathfinder.com/fortune/1998/980511/del.html; and Andy Serwer, "Winning the PC Wars," *Fortune* (May 11, 1998), www.pathfinder.com/fortune/1998/980511/del1.html.

2. "Government Study Finds Blazing Growth on Web," CNN Interactive, www.cnn.com, Apr. 15, 1998.

3. Vladimir Zwass, "Electronic Commerce: Structures and Issues," *International Journal of Electronic Commerce,* Fall 1996, pp. 3–23.

4. Thomas P. Novak and Donna L. Hoffman, "Bridging the Racial Divide on the Internet," *Science,* Apr. 17 1998, p. 390.

5. Jaclyn Easton, "Cybertales," *Internet Business,* Dec. 1998, p. 122.

6. Jon Mark Giese, "Place without Space, Identity without Body: The Role of Cooperative Narrative in Community and Identity Formation in a Text-Based Electronic Community" (Ph.D. diss., Pennsylvania State University, 1996).

7. Robert D. Hof, with Seanna Browder and Peter Elstrom,

"Internet Communities," *Business Week,* May 5, 1997, pp. 64–80.

8. Kathy Rebello, with Larry Armstrong and Amy Cortese, "Making Money on the Net," *Business Week,* Sep. 23, 1996, pp. 104–118.

9. Hof, "Internet Communities."

10. Bill Richards, "A Total Overhaul," *Wall Street Journal,* Interactive Edition, http://interactive.wsj.com, Dec. 7, 1998.

11. George P. Landow, *Hypertext 2.0: The Convergence of Contemporary Critical Theory and Technology* (Baltimore: John Hopkins University Press, 1997).

12. J. William, Gurley, "Above the Crowd: The New World of Virtual Distribution," www.news.com/Perspectives/Column/0.176.221.00.html, July 13, 1998.

13. Ellen Neuborne, with Robert D. Hof, "Branding on the Net," *Business Week,* Nov. 9, 1998, pp. 76–86.

14. Joshua Macht, "Upstarts: Toy Seller Plays Internet Hard Ball," *Inc.,* Oct. 1998, p. 18.

15. Eric Ransdell, "How Do You Win on the Web?" *Fast Company,* Aug. 1998, pp. 152–165.

16. Jared Sandberg, "Users Are Choosing Information over Entertainment on the Web," *Wall Street Journal,* Interactive Edition, http://interactive.wsj.com, July 20, 1998.

17. Nick Wingfield, "A Marketer's Dream: The Internet Promises to Give Companies a Wealth of Invaluable Data about Their Customers. So Why Hasn't It?" *Wall Street Journal,* Interactive Edition, http://interactive.wsj.com, Dec. 7, 1998.

18. Frederick Reichheld, *The Loyalty Effect* (Cambridge, Mass.: Harvard Business School Press, 1997).

19. George Anders, "Click and Buy: Why—and Where—Internet Commerce Is Succeeding," *Wall Street Journal,* Interactive Edition, http://interactive.wsj.com/archive, Dec. 7, 1998.

20. John W. Munsell, "How to Increase Sales and Develop Customer Relationships on the Web" (paper presented to American Marketing Association, Tampa, Nov. 20, 1998).

21. Gary Hamel and Jeff Sampler, "The E-Corporation," *Fortune,* Dec. 7, 1998, p. 86.

22. Maricris G. Briones, "Interactivity," *Marketing News,* Dec. 7, 1998, p. 17.

23. Rebello, "Making Money on the Net."

24. Anders, "Click and Buy."

25. Tony Seideman, "Get with the Program," *Inbound Logistics,* Sep. 1998, pp. 28–34.

26. Richards, "A Total Overhaul."

27. Warren Cohen, "Online Malls Move Closer to Home," *U.S. News & World Report,* Dec. 1, 1997, p. 86.

28. Anthony Bianco, "Virtual Bookstores Start to Get Real," *Business Week,* Oct. 27, 1997, pp. 146–148; and Evan Ramstad, "Buying on the Internet Rises as Fear of Credit Card Fraud Falls," *Commercial Appeal,* May 25, 1996, p. B3.

29. Edward C. Baig, "Going Once, Going Twice, Cybersold!" *Business Week,* Aug. 11, 1997, pp. 98–99.

30. Leslie Goff, "Mom-and-Pop Businesses Go Boom on the Web," CNN Interactive, www.cnn.com, Aug. 26, 1998.

31. Gary Welz, "The Ad Game," *Internet World,* July 1996, p. 50–57.

32. Linda Himelstein, with Ellen Neuborne and Paul M. Eng, "Web Ads Start to Click," *Business Week,* Oct. 6, 1997, pp. 128–138.

33. Himelstein, "Web Ads Start to Click."

34. Ibid.

35. Ibid.

36. Ibid.

37. Ibid.

38. Vanessa O'Connell, "Soap and Diaper Makers Pitch to Masses of Internet Women," *Wall Street Journal,* Interactive edition, http://interactive.wsj.com, July 20, 1998.

39. Hof, "Internet Communities."

40. Himelstein, "Web Ads Start to Click."

41. Ginger Conlon, "Plug and Play," *Sales & Marketing Management,* Dec. 1998, p. 65.

42. Conlon, "Plug and Play."

43. William C. Taylor, "Permission Marketing," *Fast Company,* Apr./May 1998, p. 208.

44. Wingfield, "A Marketer's Dream."

45. Keith H. Hammonds, "*Business Week*/Harris Poll: A Lot of Looking, Not Much Buying—Yet," *Business Week,* Oct. 6, 1997, p. 140.

46. Wingfield, "A Marketer's Dream."

47. Michelle Baun, "BBB*OnLine* Sets Standards for Internet Business Practices, Privacy Policies," *Ft. Collins Coloradoan,* Dec. 7, 1998, p. B2.

48. James Heckman, "A Look at What the Year Ahead Will Bring," *Marketing News,* Dec. 7, 1998, p. 1, 16.

49. Stephen Baker, with Marsha Johnston and William Echikson, "Europe's Privacy Cops," *Business Week,* Nov. 2, 1998, pp. 49–51.

50. William T. Neese and Charles R. McManis, "Summary Brief: Law Ethics and the Internet: How Recent Federal Trademark Law Prohibits a Remedy against Cyber-squatters," (Proceedings of the Society of Marketing Advances, Nov. 1998).

51. Sources: David Cope, "Extricity Software Product Alliance Receives Prestigious Crossroads A-List Award Based on Customer Input and Benefits," Extricity Software press release, www.extricity.com/press_releases/award.html, Jan. 4, 1999; and David Cope, "Extricity Software Announces Support for Commerce XML (cXML)

Standard for Business-to-Business E-Commerce," Extricity Software press release, www.extricity.com/press_releases/press020899.html, Feb. 8, 1999.

52. Sources: George Anders, "Online: Amazon Buys Stake in Upstart Drugstore.com," *Wall Street Journal,* Interactive Edition, http://interactive.wsj.com, Feb. 25, 1999; Company Briefing Book, *Wall Street Journal,* Interactive Edition, http://interactive.wsj.com, Mar. 1, 1999; Robert D. Hof, "A New Chapter for Amazon.com," *Business Week,* Aug. 17, 1998, p. 39; Robert D. Hof, " 'Technology, Technology, Technology," *Business Week,* Dec. 14, 1998, p. 112; Robert D. Hof, with Ellen Neuborne and Heather Green, "Amazon.com: The Wild World of E-commerce," *Business Week,* Dec. 14, 1998, pp. 106–119; and "Online Bookseller Offers Refunds for Recommended Books," CNN Interactive, www.cnn.com/books/news/9902/10/amazon.com.ap, Feb. 10, 1999.

53. Sources: Peter Burrows, "An Insanely Great Paycheck," *Business Week,* Feb. 26, 1996, p. 42; Company Briefing Book, *Wall Street Journal,* Interactive Edition, http://interactive.wsj.com, Mar. 1, 1999; O.C. Ferrell, "Apple Computer, Inc.," in O.C. Ferrell, Michael D. Hartline, George H. Lucas, Jr., and David Luck, *Marketing Strategy* (Ft. Worth, Tex.: Dryden Press, 1999), pp. 225–230; *Hoover's Company Profile* database (Austin, Tex.: Reference Press, 1996), via America Online; Martha Mendoza, "Apple Has a Profitable Year," *Coloradoan,* Oct. 15, 1998, p. B1; Kathy Rebello and Peter Burrows, "The Fall of an American Icon," *Business Week,* Feb. 5, 1996, pp. 34–42; and Ira Sager and Peter Burrows, with Andy Reinhardt, "Back to the Future at Apple," *Business Week,* May 25, 1998, pp. 56–60.

Appendix A Notes

1. Jean Koretz, "Where the New Jobs Are," *Business Week,* Mar. 20, 1995, p. 24.

2. This section and the three that follow are adapted from William M. Pride, Robert J. Hughes and Jack R. Kapoor, *Business* (Boston: Houghton Mifflin, 1999), pp. A1–A11.

3. Sal Divita, "Resume Writing Requires Proper Strategy," *Marketing News,* July 3, 1995, p. 6.

4. Andrew J. DuBrin, "Deadly Political Sins," *Wall Street Journal's Managing Your Career,* Fall 1993, pp. 11–13.

5. Ibid.

6. Cyndee Miller, "Marketing Research Salaries Up a Bit, but Layoffs Take Toll," *Marketing News,* June 19, 1995, p. 1.

Name Index

Subject Index

CHAPTER 2 Opening vignette: Reprinted with permission of Yahoo!®, Inc. Fig. 2.2: © American Plastics Council Fig. 2.3: Used with permission of Ben & Jerry's Homemade Holdingas, Inc. 2000 Fig. 2.5(left): (Albert Einstein: Think Different ad) Courtesy of Apple Computer, Inc. Used with trademarks of Apple Computer, Inc. registered in the U.S. and other countries. Albert Einstein TM represented by The Roger Richman Agency, Inc. Beverly Hills, CA 90212. www.hollywoodlegends.com. /Archive Photos/StockSource. Fig. 2.5(right): Jim Henson ad Courtesy of Apple Computer, Inc. Used with permission. All rights reserved. Apple, the Apple logo, Macintosh, Powerbook and Think different are trademarks of Apple Computer, Inc. registered in the U.S. and other countries. Photo of Jim Henson and Kermit the Frog © The Jim Henson Company/Corbis Meida/ StockSource. Fig: 2.8: KELLOGG'S® logo; KELLOGG'S FROSTED FLAKES® and TONY THE TIGER® are trademarks of Kellogg Company. All rights reserved. Used with permission. Fig. 2.9: © Carol Lundeen Fig. 2.11: Courtesy of United States Postal Service Fig. 2.13 (left): © Motorola, Inc. 1998 Fig. 2.13 (right): Ad created by Hanna & Associates, Coeur D'alene, ID. Courtesy of The Big Mountain. Box: Image Copyright © 99 PhotoDisk, Inc.

CHAPTER 3: Opening vignette: © 1998 Celestial Seasonings, Inc. Fig. 3.1: Courtesy of FORD MOTOR COMPANY Fig. 3.2: Courtesy of FORD MOTOR COMPANY. Reproduced with permission of J. Walter Thompson USA, Inc. Fig. 3.3: California Department of Health Services Fig. 3.4: Reprinted with permission of Toyota Fig. 3.5: Thomas and Perkins Advertising. Courtesy of Pentax. Fig. 3.6 (left): Courtesy of IBM Fig. 3.6 (right): Used by permission of Fleet Bank/Courtesy of Arnold Communications Fig. 3.7 (left): Fourth Districk American Advertising Federation/Courtesy of Peter James Design, Plantation FL. Creative Director: Jim Spangler; Art Director: Keith Campbell; Copywriters: Jim Spangler, Wes Jones; Photographer: Ron Chapple; Project Supervisor: Bill Gregory. Fig. 3.7 (right): Used with permission of Phillips Petroleum Company. Box: Image Copyright © 99 PhotoDisk, Inc.

CHAPTER 4 Opening vignette: © Carol Lundeen Fig. 4.1: Winston Marketing & Communications Fig. 4.2: Forest Stewardship Council U.S. Fig. 4.3: UPS and UPS shield design are registered trademarks of United Parcel Service of America, Inc. Used by permission. Fig. 4.4: Reprinted with permission of Sears Office of Ethics and Business Practices. Fig. 4.5: © 1998 Watson Wyatt Worldwide. Fig. 4.6: Reprinted with permission of Kelley Swofford Roy. Fig. 4.7: Courtesy of BMW Box: Image Copyright © 99 PhotoDisk, Inc.

CHAPTER 5 Opening vignette: Donald Dietz/Stock, Boston, Inc. Fig. 5.1: Courtesy of Apple Computer, Inc. Used with permission. All rights reserved. Shark image © Carl Roesler/Pacific Stock. Apple, the Apple logo, Macintosh, Powerbook and Think different are trademarks of Apple Computer, Inc. registered in the U.S. and other countries. Fig. 5.2: © 1998 Watson Wyatt Worldwide. Fig. 5.3: Courtesy of SPSS MR Fig. 5.4 (left): Reprinted with permission of AeroMexico® Fig. 5.4 (right): Used by permission of Continental Airlines Fig. 5.5: Reproduced with permission of Saatchi & Saatchi. Photographer: Lucas Dostal; Creative Director: Falko Maetzler; Concept: Falko Maetzler; Copy: Thomas Fiehn; Account Director: Walter Vielkind. Fig. 5.6: Courtesy of Horn International Packaging, Inc. Fig. 5.7: Courtesy of Marriott International Fig. 5.8: Bob Daemmrich/The Image Works, Inc. Box: Image Copyright © 99 PhotoDisk, Inc.

CHAPTER 6 Opening vignette: Courtesy of Conoco, Inc. Fig. 6.1: Advertisement used with permission of Harris Black International, LTD. And Robbett, Rosenthal & Jennings Advertising/Debra Greene Barer, Senior

Copywriter. Fig. 6.3: Reprinted with permission by Sales & Marketing Management Magazine Fig. 6.4: Ad reprinted by permission of QCS Fig. 6.5 (left): Courtesy of iMarket inc. Fig. 6.5 (right): Courtesy Acxiom Corporation Fig. 6.6 (left & right): Reprinted by permission of ETAK® The Digital Map Company Fig. 6.7 (left & right): Courtesy Hispanic & Asian Marketing Communication Research, Inc. Box: Image Copyright © 99 PhotoDisk, Inc.

CHAPTER 7 Opening vignette: Reprinted with permission of Streamline, Inc. Fig. 7.1 (left): Courtesy of Neutrogena Corp. Fig. 7.1 (right): Courtesy of 3M Fig. 7.4 (left & right): Reprinted with permission by Volkswagen of America, Inc. and Arnold Communications, Inc. Fig. 7.7: The Campbell Group, Baltimore, MD Fig. 7.9: Bates Reklamebyra,Oslo, Norway. Creative Director/Copywriter; Aris Theophilakis; Art Director: Thorbjorn Naug. Reprinted with permission of Audi of Norway. Fig. 7.10: Geoscape International, Inc. http:www.geoscape.com. Fig. 7.121: Courtesy of Experian Fig. 7.13: Riddell Advertising & Design, Jackson Hole, WY Fig. 7.14: Courtesy of Apian Software Box: Image Copyright © 99 PhotoDisk, Inc.

CHAPTER 8 Opening vignette: Image Copyright © 99 PhotoDisk, Inc. Fig. 8.1 (left): Courtesy of Emory Healthcare. Fig. 8.1 (right): Ad reproduced by permission of H.J. Heinz Company. All rights reserved. Fig. 8.3: Produced by D'Arcy Masius Benton & Bowelss, Inc. ç Procter & Gamble Productions, Inc. 1998. Fig. 8.4: The Dodge advertisements are used with permission from DaimlerChrysler Corporation. Fig. 8.5: M.C. Escher's "Sky and Water I" © 1999 Cordon Art B.V. - Baarn - Holland. All rights reserved. Fig. 8.7: Courtesy of Hi-Tec Sports USA, Inc. Fig. 8.8: © Carol Lundeen Fig. 8.9: Courtesy of The New England Life Insurance Company Fig. 8.10: Reprinted with permission of Pittsburgh Water Cooler Company Box: Image Copyright © 99 PhotoDisk, Inc.

CHAPTER 9 Opening vignette: Reprinted with permission by Roberts Express, Inc. Fig. 9.1: Courtesy of Komatsu Fig. 9.2 (left): Courtesy of MasterCard Internationl Fig. 9.2 (right): Courtesy of Maximus Fig. 9.3: Copyright the Fidelity & Deposit Company of Maryland. All rights reserved. DROPPED Fig. 9.4: The Dodge advertisements are used with permission from DaimlerChrysler Corporation. Fig. 9.5: Reprinted with permission of Teligent Fig. 9.7: © 1998 HotOffice Technologies, Inc. All rights reserved. HotOffice and the HotOffice logo are trademarks of HotOffice Technologies, Inc. Fig. 9.8: Reprinted with permission of Wal*Mart, Inc./ Courtesy of E. Morris Communicatios, Inc. Box: Image Copyright © 99 PhotoDisk, Inc.

CHAPTER 10 Opening vignette: © Carol Lundeen Fig. 10.1 (left): Reprinted with permission by Kim's Martial Arts Schools, Inc. Fig. 10.1 (right): Courtesy of MADD. Agency: Clarity Coverdale Fury Fig. 10.2: Reprinted with permission of McCann-Erickson, N.Y. Fig. 10.3 (left): Courtesy of Steve Madden Shoes. Agency-Hampel Stefanides. Fig. 10.3 (right): Courtesy of Nikon, Inc. Fig. 10.4 (left): Courtesy of The American Express Company Fig. 10.4 (right): Reprinted with permission of Arthur Andersen Fig. 10.7: © Unilever Home & Personal Care-USA. Reprinted with permission. All right reserved. Fig. 10.8 (left): Reprinted with permission by W. L. Gore & Associates Fig. 10.8 (right): © Nestle USA-Beverage Division Box: Image Copyright © 99 PhotoDisk, Inc.

CHAPTER 11: Opening vignette: © Midwest Express Airlines Fig. 11.1: Clorox and Floral Fresh are registered trademarks of The Clorox Company. Fig. 11.2: Energizer is a registered trademark of Eveready Battery Company, Inc. Fig. 11.3: Crayola and chevron design are registered trademarks, rainbow/swash is a trademark of Binney & Smith, used with permission. Fig. 11.7: Reproduced with permission of Andersen Windows Fig. 11.8: © 1996, AutoNation, Inc. Fig. 11.9: Courtesy of Northland Cranberries, Inc. Box: Image Copyright © 99 PhotoDisk, Inc.

CHAPTER 12 Opening vignette: Reprinted by permission of Dean Foods Company Fig. 12.1 (left): Printed with permission of Swiss Army Brands, Inc. Fig. 12.1 (right): Courtesy of Quaker Oats Company Fig. 12.2: Reprinted with permission by Del Monte Fresh Produce N.A., Inc. Illustration by Steve Snodgrass. Fig. 12.3: Courtesy of Levi Strauss, Australia Fig. 12.5: Tony Freeman/PhotoEdit Fig. 12.7: © 1998 Nestle. Used with permission. Fig. 12.8: KELLOGG'S® SMART START® is a registered trademark of Kellogg Company. All rights reserved. Used with permission. Fig. 12.9: Compaq Computer Corporation © 1999 Fig. 12.10 (left): © American Plastics Council Fig. 12.10 (right): The Etch A Sketch® product name and the configuration of the Etch A Sketch® product are registered trademarks owned by The Ohio Art Company. Fig. 12.11: Reprinted with permission by Good Housekeeping Box: © Carol Lundeen

CHAPTER 13 Opening vignette: Myrleen Ferguson/ PhotoEdit Fig. 13.2: Courtesy of U.S. Airways, Inc. Fig. 13.3: Courtesy of Deaconess Hospital. Reprinted with permission of Creative Alliance. Fig. 13.4: Courtesy of MCS advertising Ltd. Fig. 13.5: Courtesy of Southwestern Bell Tel. Fig. 13.6: Courtesy of Pacific Bell Fig. 13.8 (left): © 1998 Alamo Rent-A-Car, Inc. Fig. 13.8 (right): Courtesy of GM Goodwrench Service Plus Fig. 13.9 (left): Courtesy of The Negro Leagues Baseball Museum. Reprinted with permission of The Martin Agency. Fig. 13.9 (right): Courtesy of Utah's Hogle Zoo. Designed by FJC and N advertising. Fig. 13.10 (left): Compliments of the National Multiple Sclerosis Society Fig. 13.10 (right): Courtesy of The Bottomless Closet. Reprinted with permission of Fire Escap Advertising. Box: © Carol Lundeen

CHAPTER 14 Opening vignette: Courtesy of Barnes & Noble, Inc. Fig. 14.1: Courtesy of PeopleSoft, Inc. Reprinted with permission of Kirshenbaum, Bond and Partners. Photo by Norbert Schafer/The Stock Market. Fig. 14.3: Courtesy of J. D. Edwards Fig. 14.6: Reprinted with permission of Dor-O-Matic (???????) Fig. 14.7: © Carol Lundeen Fig. 14.8 (left): Crayola is a registered trademark of Binney & Smith, used with permission. Fig. 14.8 (right): Courtesy of Jaquar Cars (???????) Fig. 14.9: Courtesy FORD Motor Company Box: Image Copyright © 99 PhotoDisk, Inc.

CHAPTER 15 Opening vignette: © 1994-1998 Federal Express Corporation. All Rights Reserved. Fig. 15.1: Courtesy of E3 Corporation. Reprinted with permission of Whistle LLC (Marketing and Communications) Fig. 15.3: Reprinted with permission of Land O'Lakes, Inc. Fig. 15.6: © 1994-1998 Federal Express Corporation. All Rights Reserved Fig. 15.7: Reprinted with permission of The Dannon Company, Inc. © 1998 The Dannon Company, Inc. Fig. 15.9: Courtesy of Canadian National Rail Fig. 15.10: Reprinted with permission by Schneider Logistics Box: Image Copyright © 99 PhotoDisk, Inc.

CHAPTER 16 Opening vignette: Courtesy of West Edmonton Mall, Alberta, Canada Fig. 16.1: Reprinted with permission of Crate and Barrel Fig. 16.2: Courtesy of Macy's Fig. 16.3: Spencer Grant/PhotoEdit Fig. 16.4: Courtesy of IKEA, North America. Reprinted with permission of Roche MaCauley & Partners. Fig. 16.5: T.J. Maxx Fig. 16.6: DROPPED Fig. 16.7 Courtesy of Faneuil Hall Marketplace. Design by LittleBridge Design. Fig. 16.8: Target and the Bull's Eye Design are registered service marks of Dayton Hudson Brands, Inc. Used with permission. Box: Image Copyright © 99 PhotoDisk, Inc.

CHAPTER 17 Opening vignette: Reprinted with permission of the St. Paul Saints. Fig. 17.1: Courtesy of Alachua General Hospital Fig. 17.4: © 1999 Tyson Foods, Inc. Photography by Zanetti Productions, Inc. Fig. 17.5 (left): Reproduced with permission of The Newspaper Association of America. Photo courtesy of Gregory Heisler. Fig. 17.5 (right): Reprinted with permission by the Washington State Potato Commission. Fig. 17.6: © 1998 Elizabeth Arden Co. Photography by Jonathan Kantor. Fig. 17.7: Courtesy of Continental Airlines, Inc. Fig. 17.9 (left): © 1999 Yahoo!, Inc. Fig. 17.9 (right): Reprinted with permission of 24/7 Media. Fig. 17.11: California Department of Health Services. Box: Image Copyright © 99 PhotoDisk, Inc.

CHAPTER 18: Opening vignette: Courtesy of The Horn Group, Inc. Fig. 18.1: © 1998 The Pillsbury Company. Fig. 18.2 (left): Photo provided by Sara Lee Corproation and Beth Galton Fig. 18.2 (right): © 1998 KitchenAid Fig. 18.4 (left): © 1998 The United States Postal Service Fig. 18.4 (right): Reprinted with permission of Star TV Fig. 18.5 (left & right): © Nestle USA - Food Group, Inc., Frozen Food Division. Fig. 18.7: Reprinted with permission of the National Soft Drink Association Fig. 18.8: Courtesy of Hill, Holiday, Connors, Cosmopilos Fig. 18.9 (left & right): © Copyright Cahan & Associates Fig. 18.10: Copyright © 1999 Houghton Mifflin Company. All Rights Reserved Box: Image Copyright © 99 PhotoDisk, Inc.

CHAPTER 19 Opening vignette: © Carol Lundeen Fig. 19.2: Reprinted with permission by Harris InfoSource Fig. 19.3: © 1999 Pioneer New Media Technologies, Inc. Fig. 19.4: This ad is part of a series designed for the Objective Management Group, Inc.by Penta Communications, Inc. Agency of Record. Penta Communications, Inc., is a full service integrated marketing firm servicing growing companies worldwide. Penta Communications is located in Westboro, MA Fig. 19.5 (left): Courtesy pf American Airlines Fig. 19.5 (right): © Omaha Creative Group, affliated with Omaha Steaks. Fig. 19.6: Courtesy of the TerrAlign Group, Metron, Inc., Reston, VA 800-437-9603. Fig. 19.8: WhiteHall-Robbins Healthcare, Division of American Home Products Corporation Box: Image Copyright © 99 PhotoDisk, Inc.

CHAPTER 20 Opening vignette: Courtesy of Buy.Com Fig. 20.2: © Washington Apple Commission Fig. 20.3 (left): © 1998 Moen, Inc. Fig. 20.3 (right): Courtesy of Mercedes-Benz, USA, Inc. Fig. 20.4: © 1999 W.W. Grainger, Inc. Reprinted with permission. All rights reserved. Fig. 20.5: Reprinted with permission by Biscuitville Restaurant, Burlinton, N.C. Fig. 20.6: Courtesy of Office Furniture U.S.A. Reprinted with permission of Cadmus Com Marketing, Richmond, Virginia. Box: Image Copyright © 99 PhotoDisk, Inc.

CHAPTER 21 Opening vignette: Reprinted with permission by Sprint Communications Company L.P. All rights reserved. Fig. 21.2: Courtesy of Jesse James Farm and Museum/ Clay County, Missouri Visitors Bureau. Fig. 21.4 (left): Courtesy of Steuben Fig. 21.4 (right): Reprinted with permission by Gregg Ruth Jewelers Fig. 21.11: Courtesy of Westin Hotels & Resorts Fig. 21.12: © 1999 Pier 1 Imports Fig. 21.14: Created for Onsale, Inc. by USWeb/CKS. Reprinted with permission. Fig. 21.15: Courtesy of Buy.com Box: Image Copyright © 99 PhotoDisk, Inc.

CHAPTER 22 Opening vignette: Photo courtesy of Amtrak. Fig. 22.1: Copyright © 1999 Xerox Corporation. All Rights Reserved. Fig. 22.4 (left): Courtesy of GTE Service Corporation Fig. 22.4 (right): Reprinted with permission of Nordstrom. Fig. 22.6: © 1999 Hertz System, Inc. Hertz is a registered service mark and trademark of Hertz System, Inc. Dropped Fig. 22.7 (left): Reprinted with permission of The Sharper Image Fig. 22.7 (right): Courtesy of Windstar

Cruises Fig. 22.10: Courtesy of iMarket Incorporated. Fig. 22.11: Reprinted by permission of Aquila Energy Fig. 22.12: Courtesy of Dun & Bradstreet. Box: Image Copyright © 99 PhotoDisk, Inc.

CHAPTER 23 Opening vignette: Zigy Kaluzny/Gamma Liaison p 23.1: Reprinted with permission by GTE Internetworking p 23.4: © 1999 Oracle Corporation. All rights reserved. Oracle is a registered trademark of Oracle Corporation. All other names are trademarks of their respective owners. p 23.6: Courtesy of Monster.com Box: Image Copyright © 99 PhotoDisk, Inc.

SNAPSHOTS Chapter 7: Opinion Research for Motion Picture Association of America. Chapter 8: Compiled and analyzed by Graham Gregory Bozell, Market Segment Research and DemoGraph Corp.; American Demographics, Dec. 1998. Chapter 9: The H. R. Chally Group; Sales & Marketing Management, Aug. 1998, p. 78. Chapter 11: Kuczmarski & Associates Inc., Chicago; Marketing Management, Spring 1998, p.7. Chapter 12: PLMA's 1998 Private Label Yearbook, p.15. Chapter 13: Market Facts, Inc. Arlington Heights, IL; American Demographics, Feb. 1997, p. 53. Chapter 14: "Buyers Set high Standards for Suppliers," Weekly Survey, Purchasing, www.manufacturing.net/magazine/purchasing/pointpgs/survey56.html, accessed Feb. 7, 1999. Chapter 15: "Buyers Make Net Part of Sourcing Toolkit," Weekly Survey, Purchasing, www.manufacturing.net/magazine/purchasing/pointpgs/survey40.html, accessed Feb. 7, 1999. Chapter 18: Agency, Winter 1998, p.43. Chapter 19: Sales & Marketing Management's 1998 Productivity Study, Sales & Marketing Management, Dec. 1998, p.34. Chapter 20: Copyright 1997 USA Today, a division of Gannett Co., Inc. Chapter 23: Copyright 1997 USA Today, a division of Gannett Co., Inc.

Table 22.1 from Philip Kotler, Marketing Management: Analysis, Planning, Implementation, and Control, Ninth Edition, (c) 1997 Prentice Hall, pp. 780-781. Reprinted by permission of the author.